Anonymus

Market rights and tolls

Volume X

Anonymus

Market rights and tolls
Volume X

ISBN/EAN: 9783742801388

Manufactured in Europe, USA, Canada, Australia, Japa

Cover: Foto ©Lupo / pixelio.de

Manufactured and distributed by brebook publishing software
(www.brebook.com)

Anonymus

Market rights and tolls

ROYAL COMMISSION ON MARKET RIGHTS AND TOLLS.

MINUTES OF EVIDENCE

TAKEN BEFORE

The Assistant Commissioners

CHARLES W. BLACK, ESQUIRE,

AND

JOHN J. O'MEARA, ESQUIRE,

AT INQUIRIES HELD BY THEM IN THE

PROVINCES OF ULSTER, LEINSTER, AND MUNSTER,

TOGETHER WITH THEIR

REPORTS ON THE MARKETS,

From November 1st, 1888, to January 7th, 1889.

Vol. X.

Presented to both Houses of Parliament by Command of Her Majesty.

LONDON:
PRINTED FOR HER MAJESTY'S STATIONERY OFFICE,
BY EYRE AND SPOTTISWOODE,
PRINTERS TO THE QUEEN'S MOST EXCELLENT MAJESTY.

And to be purchased, either directly or through any Bookseller, from
EYRE AND SPOTTISWOODE, EAST HARDING STREET, FLEET STREET, E.C., and
32, ABINGDON STREET, WESTMINSTER, S.W.; or
JOHN MENZIES & Co., 12, HANOVER STREET, EDINBURGH, and
31, DRURY STREET, GLASGOW; or
HODGES, FIGGIS, & Co., 104, GRAFTON STREET, DUBLIN.

TABLE OF CONTENTS.

ROYAL COMMISSION ON MARKET RIGHTS AND TOLLS.

SCHEDULE of INQUIRIES held after the 31st October 1888 by Mr. CHARLES W. BLACK, Assistant Commissioner, arranged in alphabetical order.

No.	Where held.	Date.	Page.
1	Armagh (supplemental)	13th and 14th May 1889	9
2	Poyntzpass	29th November 1888	5
3	Saintfield	19th November "	1

SCHEDULE of INQUIRIES held after the 31st October 1888 by Mr. JOHN J. O'MEARA, Assistant Commissioner, arranged in alphabetical order.

No.	Where held.	Date.	Page.
1	Arklow	1st December 1888	431
2	Bagenalstown	7th December "	[illegible]
3	Balbriggan	6th December "	270
4	Baltinglass	13th December "	284
5	Bray	29th November "	311
6	Bruff	15th November "	119
7	Cahir	2nd November "	59
8	Callan	17th December "	314
9	Cappoquin	14th November "	181
10	Carlow	14th December "	[illegible]
11	Carrick-on-Suir	5th November "	76
12	Cashel	31st December "	[illegible]
13	Castlecomer	15th December "	307
14	Charleville	17th November "	143
15	Clonmel	3rd November "	67
16	Cloyne	23rd November "	[illegible]
17	Dungarvan	12th December "	231
18	Enniscorthy	4th December "	245
19	Fermoy	2nd January 1889	246
20	Gorey	3rd December 1888	[illegible]
21	Kilkenny	7th November "	[illegible]
22	Kilmallock	16th November "	134
23	Kinsale	21st November "	175
24	Lismore	20th December "	[illegible]
25	Macroom	26th November "	145
26	Midleton	22nd November "	162
27	New Ross	6th December "	[illegible]
28	New Castle West	7th January 1889	272
29	Queenstown	24th November 1888	[illegible]
30	Rathkeale	8th January 1889	[illegible]
31	Tipperary	1st November 1888	44
32	Waterford	6th November "	[illegible]
33	Wexford	5th December "	253
34	Wicklow	30th November "	[illegible]
35	Youghal	3rd January 1889	257

ALPHABETICAL LIST OF WITNESSES.

Witness.		Inquiry.	
Name.	Occupation.	Place.	Page.
Adams, William Sawyers	Executor of David Creent, former Lessee and Weighmaster.	Portglenone	5
Addy, William Henry	Farmer	Armagh	9
Ahern, James	Town Clerk	Queenstown	[illegible]
Ahern, William	-	Carrick-on-Suir	[illegible]
Aiken, James	Trader	Armagh	9
Ambrose, Charles	Secretary to Bridge Commissioners.	Waterford	[illegible]
Archer, Forster	-	Waterford	[illegible]
Armstrong, Captain A. M.	Agent to the Hamilton-Jones Estate.	Portglenone	4
Ashe, Richard	Solicitor; representing the joint Owners and the Lessee.	Macroom	145
Bagenal, B. F.	Owner	Bagenalstown	[illegible]
Baily, Alfred	Weighmaster	Bray	[illegible]
Barrett, Thomas	Owner of Beam and Scales	Kilmallock	[illegible]
Barry, Edmund	Secretary to Trustees of Fair Green.	Midleton	[illegible]
Baxter, Robert	Tinsmith	Armagh	9
Beary, Michael	Acting Town Clerk	Dungarvan	[illegible]
Behan, Patrick	Weighmaster	Queenstown	[illegible]
Best, Edwin	Solicitor, representing Tolls Committee.	Armagh	9
Best, William J.	Magistrate; member of James Best & Co., Merchants.	Armagh	9
Blackwell, James	Town Commissioner	Rathkeale	[illegible]
Boyd, William	Resident	Portglenone	5
Boyd, William	Owner of Butter Market	Carrick-on-Suir	76
Brawley, William	Cutler	Armagh	9
Breen, Michael	Town Commissioner	Tipperary	[illegible]
Brennan	Farmer	Arklow	[illegible]
Brien, Robert	Lessee of Markets	Fermoy	[illegible]
Brooks, John	Employed by Town Commissioners in obtaining signatures to the memorial.	Armagh	9
Brown, Thompson	Farmer	Armagh	9
Browne, William A.	Town Clerk	Wexford	[illegible]
Burke, Edward	Farmer	Carrick-on-Suir	[illegible]
Burke, Michael	Representing Owner	Fermoy	[illegible]
Byrne, John	Lessee of the Roundwood Fairs	Wicklow	[illegible]
Byrne, John	Weighmaster	Carlow	[illegible]
Byrne, Matthew	Farmer and Trader	Baltinglass	[illegible]
Byrne, Patrick	Chairman of Town Commissioners	Gorey	[illegible]
Byrne, Patrick	Cattle and Horse Dealer	Baltinglass	[illegible]
Cahill, George D.	Draper	Kilmallock	[illegible]
Caldwell, George	Representing Owner	Tipperary	[illegible]
Callaghan, Martin	Resident	Bagenalstown	[illegible]
Callaghan, Owen	Resident	Carrick-on-Suir	[illegible]
Carroll, John	Lessee of Markets and Fairs	Bruff	[illegible]
Casey, Stephen	Town Clerk	Rathkeale	[illegible]
Casey, William M.	Secretary to Butter Market Committee.	Clonmel	67
Chapman, John	Manager of the Fairs	Wicklow	[illegible]
Cleary, David J.	Town Clerk	Clonmel	67

Witness.		Inquiry.	
Name.	Occupation.	Name.	Page.
Clery, Patrick	Hon. Treasurer of Fair Committee	Kilmallock	184
Coady, Patrick	Chairman of Town Commissioners	Callan	314
Coffey, James	Poultry Dealer	Bray	311
Collins, Peter	Town Commissioner	Clonmel	67
Collins, Thomas	Superintendent of Markets	Carlow	297
Condon, Daniel	Chairman of Town Commissioners	Arklow	231
Condon, Thomas J.	Member of Parliament	Clonmel	67
Connolly, Jeremiah	Dealer	Cashel	343
Conway, James	Butter Dealer	Castlecomer	307
Corby, John	Town Clerk	Cashel	343
Corcoran, Patrick	-	Cashel	343
Cosgrove, Thomas	Town Commissioner	Youghal	357
Cotter, John	Town Commissioner	Fermoy	348
Coursey, Thomas	Toll Collector	Kinsale	173
Creede, Cornelius	Farmer	Macroom	165
Cregan, James	Trader	Newcastle West	378
Cronin, Daniel	Former Toll Collector	Cloyne	195
Crowe, Timothy	Owner	Cappawhite	131
Crowe, Thomas	Former Toll Collector	Cappawhite	131
Curling, Charles	C.E.; Receiver	Newcastle West	373
Curry, Francis E.	Former Agent to Owner	Lismore	[illegible]
Davey, John	-	Saintfield	1
Dawson, Jeremiah	Town Clerk	Tipperary	44
Deane, Colonel	-	Fermoy	348
Delahunt, Thomas	Chairman of Town Commissioners	Wicklow	223
Desmond, Michael T.	Butcher	Macroom	165
Dillon, Edward	Butter Weighmaster	Carlow	297
Dillon, Patrick J.	Borough Treasurer	Kilkenny	96
Dolan, Thomas	Resident	Armagh	9
Donnelly, John	Representing Lessee	Arklow	231
Doran, C. O.	Architect and former Chairman of Town Commissioners.	Queenstown	203
Douglas, Peter	-	Baltinglass	264
Dowling, Thomas	Former Agent to Owner	Cappawhite	131
Doyle, James	Weighmaster	Castlecomer	307
Doyle, Michael	Lessee of Fairs	Bray	311
Doyle, Michael	Representing Owner of Weighbridge.	Baltinglass	264
Duffy, Charles	Representing the Lessee of Fair green.	Bagenalstown	[illegible]
Duggan, Patrick	Weighmaster	Cashel	343
Egan, P. M.	Mayor	Kilkenny	96
Erskine, Robert	Flax Mill Owner	Armagh	9
Evans, John	Resident	Arklow	231
Fahy, Thomas	Resident	Armagh	9
Fisher, Patrick	Cattle Dealer	Charleville	148
Fitzgerald, J. Penrose	Agent to Owner	Midleton	183
Fitzgerald, M.	Representing Lessee	Charleville	148
Flannery, Charles J.	Town Clerk	Arklow	231
Fleming, William	Owner of Weighing Scale	Baltinglass	264
Flood, Bernard	Butcher	Gorey	[illegible]
Foster, Thomas	Merchant	Armagh	9
Fox, Samuel	Farmer	Armagh	9
Fraser, John	Pork Dealer	Armagh	9
Fulton, Thomas	Medical Practitioner	Saintfield	1
Gallagher, William	Solicitor, representing Town Commissioners.	Armagh	9
Gardiner, James	Secretary to Toll Committee	Armagh	9

Witness.		Inquiry.	
Name.	Occupation.	Name.	Page.
Gardner, Samuel	Assistant Secretary to Toll Committee.	Armagh	9
Garvey, J. H. Moore	Agent to Owner	Saintfield	1
Geakin, Joseph	-	Armagh	9
Gillespie, Robert	Merchant and Member of Toll Committee.	Armagh	9
Gorman, John	Dealer	Carlow	[illegible]
Grady, Maurice	Butcher	Kilmallock	184
Graham, M. J.	Resident	Gorey	239
Graham, William	Town Commissioner	Gorey	239
Gubbins, Michael	Resident	Kilmallock	134
Guise, Major-General	-	Gorey	239
Hallinan, Patrick	Magistrate	Midleton	[illegible]
Halloran, Michael	-	Tipperary	44
Halpin, Ven. Archdeacon	Joint Owner of Tolls	Rathkeale	[illegible]
Hammond, John	Chairman of Town Commissioners	Carlow	[illegible]
Hampson, Christopher	Farmer	Armagh	9
Healy, Edward	Superintendent of Markets	Midleton	183
Hanaigan, John	Trader	Arklow	221
Harding, Charles	Magistrate	Charleville	143
Harley, William	Butter Buyer	Tipperary	44
Harper, Alden	-	Enniscorthy	346
Harris	Butter Dealer	Kilmallock	184
Harris, William	Farmer	Tipperary	44
Hart	Resident	Charleville	143
Harrigan, Thomas	Weighmaster	Youghal	457
Hayden, John	Town Clerk	Wicklow	[illegible]
Healy, Maurice	Town Clerk	Lismore	335
Healy, Timothy	Weighmaster	Macroom	155
Hegarty, Michael	Town Clerk	Kinsale	173
Henley, Arthur	-	Bagenalstown	[illegible]
Heron, John	Weighmaster	Wexford	[illegible]
Hickey, John	Town Commissioner	Lismore	335
Hogan, Thomas	Chairman of Town Commissioners	Kinsale	173
Houston, Rev. John	Presbyterian Minister	Portglenone	5
Howard, Joseph	Town Clerk	Waterford	63
Hughes, John	Farmer Hotel Proprietor	Armagh	9
Hunt, Vere	Magistrate	Cappawhite	157
Hutchinson, Matthew	Chairman of Town Commissioners	New Ross	[illegible]
Hynes, Richard	Farmer Corn Merchant	Arklow	221
Jack, Alexander	Merchant	Portglenone	5
Jeffries, William	Dealer	Fermoy	348
Johnson, Stanley	Resident	Carlow	[illegible]
Jones, John	Farmer	Baltinglass	[illegible]
Kearney, Bernard	Town Commissioner	Arklow	231
Keatinge, Michael	Lessee of Markets	Cahir	59
Kehoe, P. J.	Town Commissioner	Bagenalstown	[illegible]
Kelleher, Andrew	Toll Collector	Macroom	155
Kelleher, Cornelius	-	Charleville	143
Kelleher, Daniel	Market Assistant	Macroom	155
Kelleher, Michael	Manager of Markets and Fairs	Fermoy	348
Kelleher, S.	Corn Merchant and Spirit Dealer	Macroom	155
Kelly, James	Town Clerk	Carlow	[illegible]
Kelly, Thomas	Weighmaster	Callan	[illegible]
Kennedy, J. R.	Town Clerk	Kilkenny	314
Kennedy, David	Member of Markets Committee	Newcastle West	93
Kennedy, Patrick	Town Commissioner	Rathkeale	373
Kenny, Martin P.	Member of Markets Committee	Castlecomer	[illegible]
Keogh	-	Dungarvan	307
Keogh, Henry	Weighmaster	New Ross	[illegible]
Kerwick, Michael	Town Clerk	Callan	[illegible]
King, Edward	Farmer	Balbriggan	614
Knipe, Thomas	Farmer and Mill Owner	Armagh	9
Knox, R. D., Rev.	Church of Ireland	Saintfield	1

Witness.		Inquiry.	
Name.	Occupation.	Place.	Page.
Laffan, Thomas	Chairman of Town Commissioners	Cashel	343
Landy, Richard	Town Clerk	Carrick-on-Suir	74
Langton, Stephen	Chairman of Town Commissioners	Bray	311
Lenox, George H.	Farmer	Armagh	9
Loftie, William	Sergeant R.I.C.	Saintfield	1
Loughlin, Michael	Town Commissioner	Youghal	257
Loughran, George	Farmer	Armagh	9
Lynch, Daniel	Draper	Macroom	165
Lyons, Roger	Lessee of Fish Market	Dungarvan	231
McCarthy	Solicitor	Newcastle West	373
McCarthy, Denis	Town Commissioner	Midleton	183
McCarthy, John	Draper	Midleton	183
McCarthy, John	Checker of Accounts	Macroom	165
McCarthy, Thomas	Former Town Commissioner	Dungarvan	231
McCloskey, Patrick		Balbriggan	279
McCloskey, William	Chairman of Town Commissioners	Balbriggan	279
MacCrumb, John	Residence	Armagh	9
McCullagh, Samuel	Town Clerk	Midleton	183
McDonagh, Patrick	Town Clerk	Bray	311
McDonnell, John	Boot Factor	Newcastle West	373
McKee, Samuel	Draper	Saintfield	1
McLaughlin, James	Residence	Armagh	9
McLaughlin, John	Secretary to Fair and Markets Committee.	Portglenone	5
McNeice	Farmer	Armagh	9
M'Crumb, Thomas	Pawnbroker	Armagh	9
M'Donald, Thomas	Superintendent of Markets	Armagh	9
Mahony, James	High Constable	Waterford	83
Mahony, Thomas	Clerk to Poor Law Union	Castlecomer	307
Mahony	Head Constable	Bagenalstown	289
Mulqueen	Trader	Clonmel	67
Mannix, John J.	Chairman of Town Commissioners	Fermoy	349
Massey, Francis A.	Meal and Flour Merchant	Armagh	9
Miller, Michael	Auctioneer	Charleville	143
Mooney, Rev. M.	Parish Priest	Cahir	49
Moore, Samuel	Sergeant R.I.C.	Baltinglass	294
Moran, Thomas	Lessee of Markets	Enniscorthy	345
Morris, Peter	Corn Merchant	Baltinglass	294
Morrell, Philip	Grain Dealer	Charleville	143
Moylan, John	Weighmaster	Newcastle West	373
Mullins, Captain	Receiver	Macroom	165
Mulqueen, J.	Weighmaster	Tipperary	44
Murphy, Daniel		Macroom	165
Murphy, Edward	Mayor	Clonmel	67
Murphy, John	Farmer	Macroom	165
Murphy, Patrick	Farmer	Kinsale	173
Murphy, Peter	Farmer	Gorey	290
Murray	Farmer	Arklow	231
Murray, G.		Wicklow	225
Murray, John	Postmaster; Lessee of Tolls	Bagenalstown	289
Noonan, John	Town Commissioners	Lismore	334
O'Brien, James	Chairman of Town Commissioners	Lismore	334
O'Brien, Peter	Trader	Wicklow	225
O'Brien, Thomas		Enniscorthy	345
O'Byrne, Matthew	Town Commissioner	Bray	311
O'Connor, John	Cattle Dealer	Charleville	143
O'Connor, Timothy	Trader	Newcastle West	373
O'Donnell, Patrick	Farmer	Cahir	49
O'Gorman, James	Chairman of Town Commissioners	Enniscorthy	346

Witness.		Inquiry.	
Name.	Occupation.	Name.	Page.
O'Kearney, P. R.	Agent to Owner	Charleville	143
O'Kelly, E. P.	Owner of Stalls	Baltinglass	294
O'Loughnane, William	Trader	Galway	59
O'Meara, Francis	Auctioneer	Bruff	129
O'Meara, J. F.	Solicitor	Waterford	53
O'Neill	Resident	Balbriggan	278
O'Neill, Rev.	Parish Priest	Bagenalstown	299
O'Neill, Thomas	Town Clerk	Gorey	239
O'Shea, James J.	Town Clerk	Youghal	357
O'Sullivan	Solicitor	Carrick-on-Suir	75
O'Sullivan, J. J.	Merchant	Kilmallock	134
O'Sullivan, Richard, Captain	Former Town Commissioner	Queenstown	313
Orrell, Charles	Pork Buyer	Armagh	9
Peel, Thomas O.	Town Clerk	Armagh	9
Perrse, Captain	Magistrate	Bagenalstown	299
Perry, Nathaniel	Draper	Saintfield	1
Phelan, William	Hon. Secretary to Markets and Fairs Committee	Newcastle West	373
Philpott, Robert	Resident	Arklow	271
Power, Michael	Chairman of Town Commissioners	Carrick-on-Suir	75
Price, J. N. Blackwood, Major	Representing Owner	Saintfield	1
Quin, Tobias	Trader	Cloyne	185
Quinn, Thomas	Farmer	Armagh	9
Quirke, Patrick	Solicitor, representing Town Commissioners	Carrick-on-Suir	75
Rea, James	Farmer	Saintfield	1
Redmond, Patrick	Borough Inspector	Kilkenny	98
Redmond, Patrick	Inspector of Markets	New Ross	222
Redmond, Peter	Grocer	Gorey	239
Rice	-	Fermoy	348
Richardson, Nicholas G.	Agent to Owner	Castlecomer	307
Riordan, Timothy	Market Assistant	Macroom	164
Roberts, George C.	Agent to Owner	[illegible]	345
Roche, William	Clerk to Poor Law Union	Midleton	153
Rochford, William	Representing Owner	Cahir	59
Rooney, Michael	Farmer	Wicklow	253
Ryan, Michael	Representing Weighmaster	Tipperary	44
Ryan, P.	Solicitor; representing Lessee	Charleville	148
Ryan, Thomas	Resident	Cappawhite	131
Saunders, Thomas	Magistrate	Charleville	143
Scott, Henry	Farmer	Armagh	9
Scott, J. A.	Town Councillor	Gorey	239
Seaver, J.	Town Commissioner	Balbriggan	278
Serjeant, The Town	-	Cashel	348
Shackleton, P. D.	Owner of Flour Mill	Carlow	297
Sheedy, John	Town Clerk	Fermoy	348
Sheehan, David, jun.	Owner	Cloyne	185
Sheehy, George L.	Farmer	Newcastle West	373
Sheehy, Joseph	Shopkeeper	Rathkeale	383
Shelley, Thomas	-	Callan	314
Sherry, George	Cattle Dealer	Armagh	9
Sherry, John	Cattle Dealer	Armagh	9
Sherwell, Michael	Farmer	Castlecomer	307
Simpson, William	Mill Owner	Armagh	9
Sinnott, Daniel	Town Clerk	Balbriggan	278
Smith, Joseph	-	Wicklow	253

Witness.		Inquiry.	
Name.	Occupation.	Name.	Page.
Stairs, Joseph	Farmer	Armagh	9
Storey, John	Farmer	Arklow	331
Sub-Sanitary Officer, The	-	Midleton	188
Sullivan, Denis	Market Superintendent	Kilkenny	96
Sullivan, John	Trader	Bruff	128
Summers, James	Merchant	Armagh	9
Switzer, John	Town Commissioner	Rathkeale	269
Thompson, William	Alderman	Wexford	246
Tobin, John	Town Clerk	New Ross	262
Tower, Francis	Farmer	Armagh	[illegible]
Townsend, H. H.	Agent to Owner	Tipperary	44
Townsend, H. B.	Agent to Owner	Queenstown	203
Tumby, John	Toll Collector	Wexford	253
Usher, Richard	Magistrate and Butter Weighmaster.	Dungarvan	331
Vale, John	Manager of Butter Market	Waterford	[illegible]
Vigors, Colonel	Magistrate	Bagenalstown	269
Wall	Poor Law Guardian	Carrick-on-Suir	74
Wall, John	Deputy Butter Taster	Dungarvan	321
Wallace, William	Farmer	Portglenone	5
Walsh, Maurice	Lessee of Tolls	Dungarvan	331
Walsh, Robert	Trader	Cloyne	183
Walsh, Thomas	Weighmaster	Lismore	326
Walsh, Thomas	Dealer	Callan	314
Ward, William	Chairman of Town Commissioners.	Bagenalstown	269
Warren, John B.	Town Clerk	Bagenalstown	269
Whelan, Thomas	Farmer	Fermoy	243
White	Resident	Cashel	248
Wilkinson, Thomas	Town Clerk	Enniscorthy	248
Willoughby, William H.	Weighmaster	Saintfield	1
Wood, Thomas	Town Commissioner	Cashel	248

Memorandum as to the Duties to be assigned to the Assistant Commissioner.

1. To visit any place which may be selected by the Commissioners, and if so directed, to hold an inquiry there, such inquiry to be open to the public.

2. To arrange with the Local Authorities and Market Owners the time and place of such inquiry.

3. To give sufficient notice of such inquiry by advertisement in some local newspaper.

4. To inspect the markets and report generally thereon.

Where a market is held wholly or partially in the open air, to report whether the market is held in a street or in an open space.

5. To inquire as to—

(a.) Tolls alleged to be due by prescriptive right where the market was originated by Charter.

(b.) The income derived severally from tolls, stallages, and rents of market standings, rents of shops, dwelling-houses, taverns, and other descriptions of property connected with the market.

(c.) Expenditure on the market and cost of management.

(d.) The application of surplus revenue.

(e.) The provision for reducing debt, if any.

6. To investigate complaints received by the Commissioners or Assistant Commissioner respecting—

(a.) The management of the market.

(b.) Insufficiency of accommodation.

(c.) Rate of tolls and other charges.

(d.) Inequality of tolls, &c.—

i. as between persons;

ii. as between commodities.

(e.) Tolls taken more than once on the same article.

(f.) Tolls taken on days not authorised.

(g.) Tolls taken on goods not brought into the market.

(h.) Restrictions on trade—

i. within the market.

ii. without the market.

7. To inquire as to the possibility of obtaining returns of prices of commodities sold in the market.

To report from time to time to the Commission the result of such inquiries, together with any special circumstances which the Sub-Commissioner may think deserving of notice.

Saintfield, [illegible] November [illegible].

Major J. N. Blackwood Price examined.

14,221. (*Mr. Commissioner Bland.*) Who is the owner of the market rights of Saintfield?—My father, James Charles Price, is the owner of the rights.

14,222. Can you give me particulars of the patent under which these rights were granted?—No, I am afraid I cannot give you all the particulars. All I know about it is that it was granted in the twenty-ninth of the reign of William the Third.

14,223. What is the market day here?—Monday.

14,224. There are no tolls, I understand, levied here?—None whatever.

14,225. What is the fair day in Saintfield?—The last Wednesday of each month.

14,226. There is a fair held every month?—There is.

14,227. You have no market accommodation except that provided by the market house?—That is all.

14,228. All the other business of the markets, except the weighing, is conducted on the streets?—It is.

14,229. You say there are no tolls whatever levied?—None, except for the weighbridge. The people using it pay so much for the weighing of their goods, but I consider it is not exactly in connexion with the markets.

14,230. Can you give us particulars of the charges for weighing?—No, I cannot, but you can get them from the weighmaster.

14,231. The weighmaster is employed by your father?—He is, and is paid [illegible] per month.

14,232. The people here, I understand, complain of the want of regulation in the markets?—They do.

14,233. What time does the market open in the morning?—Sometimes about half-past two o'clock.

14,234. Is that the regular hour for commencing business?—Yes, about that hour.

14,235. What is principally sold in this early market?—Eggs and fowl.

14,236. No corn or anything of that kind is sold at that hour?—No, nothing of that kind is sold here at any time.

14,237. Where is corn sold in the neighbourhood?—It goes chiefly to Ballynahinch or Downpatrick.

14,238. The general complaint about the markets of Saintfield is simply the want of regulation?—Yes; the hour at which business is commenced is the principal objection.

14,239. Market rights are really not enforced here?—There is nothing paid by anyone except for weighing. Mr. Price receives nothing out of the markets, but instead he has to pay a quit-rent of something like 12s. a year for the patent.

14,240. And, besides, he has to pay the weighmaster?—Yes, [illegible] a month.

14,241. I suppose there is no such thing here as factors or brokers through which market business is carried on?—No.

14,242. This is simply an open market, conducted by the people themselves?—Yes, without any restriction whatever. The people do pretty much as they please, and can hold the market in any part of the town, or at any hour they choose. The lower portion of the town is the most convenient place, as it is near the railway, and the people hold it chiefly there. Besides it is near the leading road from Belfast to Downpatrick, and that is another consideration. These are the only reasons that I know for holding the market in the lower end of the town.

14,243. Is it your idea that the local magistrates should fix the hour for holding the markets?—I think they should, as they understand the wants of the people. It would be much better, in my opinion, if they took the matter into their management.

14,244-5. There are no town commissioners here, or any local authority except the poor law guardians?—No local authority. The streets of the town are kept up by the county.

(*Mr. J. M. [illegible] Garrett, J.P., agent of the Price Estate.*) I wish to state that the quit-rent of the patent to which reference has been made amounts to 12s. [illegible] per annum.

14,246. (*Mr. Commissioner Bland to witness.*) Do you think it would be desirable that sales of fat cattle should be conducted by weight, and should be rendered [illegible] by [illegible] in that way?—There is nothing of the kind [illegible] selling fat cattle by weight, but I approve of it, and I think it would be beneficial to the farmer.

14,247. You say that selling cattle by weight is not known here?—No, not in the market.

14,248. What are sold chiefly in the fairs of Saintfield?—Fat cattle, springing cattle, horses, calves, sheep, and an occasional goat or two. There are also churns, wooden utensils, and that sort of ware. I forgot to mention that large numbers of pigs are also sold in our fairs.

14,249. There are no tolls or stallages collected at the fairs?—None.

14,250. And, of course, you have no rules made for the regulation of either markets or fairs?—No.

14,251. Do you keep a record of the prices of articles sold in Saintfield markets or fairs?—We do not, so far as I know.

Wm. Henry Williamson examined.

14,252. (*Mr. Commissioner Bland.*) You are the weighmaster here?—I am.

14,253. What are the charges levied by you?—Fivepence for each head of cattle (fat or otherwise) weighed; 2d. for each live or dead pig weighed; 1d. for each bag of oats, potatoes, or any other commodity weighed; and 2d. for each cartload weighed.

14,254. That is 2d. for every load of produce or other material whatever it may be?—Yes, for any description of cart.

14,255. The 5d. you refer to as the charge on black cattle is imposed only when the animals are weighed?—Quite so. It is a charge for weighing the cattle.

14,256. You also charge 1d. per bag for weighing articles that might be brought to market in that way?—Yes, 1d. a bag for wheat, or oats, or potatoes, or anything of the kind.

14,257. Do you ever weigh any black cattle here?—No; there have been none weighed that I remember.

14,258. And for how long have you been weighmaster?—For about 10 years.

14,259. You have never heard anyone asking to have an animal weighed when alive?—Very seldom. I have weighed a beast now and again, just to give the owner an idea of its weight, as sometimes such animals are sold on sight at so much per pound, and at other times just by the look of the eye.

14,260. Do many articles come here to be weighed?—I have told you the articles that come, but they certainly do not come in large quantities.

14,361. How many carts would you weigh in the year?—I could not give you an idea, as I keep no record. Perhaps at times there might be three in the week, sometimes six or seven, or it may be only one.

14,362. But whatever the number is you get 3d. for weighing each cart?—Yes, I do.

14,363. And those receipts go into your own pocket?—They do, in addition to the 5s. a month I get from Mr. Price.

14,364. What amount of potatoes are weighed?—There are not many potatoes weighed, except in the spring season, and up till the 1st of May. There might then be forty loads in a day weighed, but that would only be once a week, on a Monday, the market day.

14,365. Does any butter come here to be weighed?—None. The persons who buy butter provide the weighing accommodation themselves.

14,366. They bring their own beam, scales, and weights?—They do. They have each a house, which they rent by the week for the purpose of carrying on their business.

14,367. What other accommodation have you for public weighing besides the weighbridge?—There is a pair of large scales on which pigs are weighed when brought to market.

14,368. Do the parties who buy butter make a charge for weighing it with their own beams and scales?—They do not. They buy it at so much per pound, and pay for it fully.

14,369. Does any pork come to this market?—None. A shopkeeper may now and again buy a few dead pigs and weigh them here, and in that case 3d. is charged for each carcase.

14,370. Are you aware of any deductions being made by buyers from the prices they propose to give to the sellers or from the weight of the articles?—No; they pay fully for whatever they buy.

14,371. They do not deduct anything for porterage or anything of this kind?—Nothing whatever, but I suppose if there was a market fixed like other towns they would.

Dr. Thomas Fulton examined.

14,372. (Mr. Commissioner Bland.) I understand you wish to submit some evidence with regard to the fairs and markets of Saintfield?—Yes. I have been asked to make a statement with regard to the fairs and markets of this town, dealing with the circumstances under which they are held. I have been a resident of Saintfield for upwards of [illegible] years, and I believe I have a thorough knowledge of what the town requires, and the objections which the people for miles round have to the present system. The fairs are held in a very irregular manner, as far as arrangements for selling the different products brought there are concerned, whether live stock or goods. The horse fair is held upon the main street, and the animals are shown up and down the street, so that there is no room for pedestrians to pass with safety, nor is there room for goods to pass from the upper end of the town to the railway station. In consequence of this a great many injuries have been received; in fact, there is scarcely a fair day upon which there are not some accidents treated by myself, and other medical men, I presume, are called upon to perform similar duties. Indeed, in one instance death resulted from an accident received owing to a horse being shown on the public street. I think also that some better arrangement should be made for the sale of young pigs, or small pigs as they are called. I have seen as many as 150 carts of these pigs lining the street on both sides from the square down as far as the bank; and when the length of two carts is taken off the width of the street it leaves but a small space between for the passage of animals or individuals. The place in which the pigs called "shots" are sold is not a very convenient one, and as for the goods exposed for sale they are shown on the footpaths or next to the railings of the Presbyterian Church. I do not think there can be any objection raised to the accommodation provided for cattle, as the space is large; in fact, it is an open common.

14,373. What size is it?—I should say about two statute acres. The surface of the fair green is rocky, and affords a capital foundation. With regard to the markets, they commence at an early hour; sometimes, I think, they encroach upon the Sabbath day. I know, at any rate, the people must begin to prepare for them on the Sabbath, and this interferes with their enjoyment of the day set apart for rest. For miles round, those intending to be at the market on Monday morning must begin to prepare on Sunday afternoon and evening, which I look upon as a great hardship. I have travelled round the country a good deal during the night, and the people, I know, sit up on Sunday night to be in readiness to start for the early market. Owing to the early hour at which the market is held, the fowl dealers, in order to be the early bird for the early worm, go out on the Sabbath afternoon and scour the country, looking out to secure the best fowl. This is a thing I know myself is repeatedly done, and that being so, it is the general feeling of the community round about Saintfield for miles that the market is badly arranged, and that the hour should be changed.

14,374. But who should make the change you desire; should it be Major Price, or should it be entrusted to the magistrates?—I do not believe it should be entrusted to the magistrates. I think, where there is no corporate body, a matter of this kind should be entrusted to the men of business. I have no doubt they would be the best class to which the arrangement of a thing like this could be entrusted. The landlord of the district, or his agent, might, of course, be an ex-officio member of such a committee, but to trust it to the magistrates of the petty sessions district would be out of place. The majority of the magistrates who attend the court at Saintfield do not belong to the town, and have comparatively little interest in it.

14,375. Your idea is, then, to form a market committee?—Yes, of the business men of the town; but, as I have already said, there might be one or two ex-officio members in the persons of the landlord or his agent, or Major Price, to whom no one would object. As a magistrate, I would have no desire to act on such a committee. My great desire is to see prosperity returning to Saintfield, and as a professional man, I would not care to interfere; I would rather leave it to the business men, who are the proper parties to deal with it.

14,376. Would you give this committee power to levy tolls?—I think they should have such power. If the markets were enlarged and had proper accommodation provided for farm produce, then I think a toll sufficient to cover the expense of working the markets should be provided.

14,377. You do not think the levying of a small toll would interfere with the progress of the markets?—I do not think it would, and besides it would give some one an interest in looking after them.

14,378. But you think the toll should be limited?—It should in a place like this be very small, and by no means of a prohibitory character.

14,379. Would you fix that toll so as to permit of any profit being made off the markets?—That would be a question for after consideration. They would have it an open question what they would do with the surplus or profit, if such should arise.

14,380. Is there anything else, Dr. Fulton, to which you wish to refer?—You asked a question, Mr. Commissioner, of one of the witnesses with reference to the weighing of fat cattle and their sale by weight. There are a great many fat cattle brought to Saintfield and sold, and so far as their sale by weight is concerned, I believe some farmers would take advantage of it, although it has not hitherto been done here.

14,381. The question is whether it would be desirable that sales should be made by weight, and that the system should be rendered compulsory?—Well, I do not think it should be compulsory by any means. I am of opinion it should be left optional to sell by weight or otherwise, as the owner might feel inclined.

14,382. The way the law stands at present is this, that wherever a toll is levied on cattle the owner of the market must provide a weighbridge capable of weighing such cattle, if it is deemed necessary by either buyer or seller?—The weighbridge is already provided.

14,383. The question then is whether Parliament should go further and say that all fat cattle should be weighed and sold by weight. I may tell you that the cattle dealers are opposed to it?—Well, I think if they are opposed, the farmers should be in favour of it.

14,384. Is there anything else to which you wish to refer?—Nothing that I know of.

14,385. What time is the market usually over; I mean the market which begins so early in the morning?—In summer the fowl market commences about two o'clock in the morning; in winter it does not begin so early, but it is generally over at five o'clock. The owners of fowl, after bringing them to the market and selling them, have to go home again, often a distance of some miles, so that they may return again with their eggs and butter. The people are thus required to make two journeys where one might do. Another thing, owing to the early hour, there is every facility given to poachers to sell their produce. There are two extensive [illegible] close to Saintfield, and I know they are well [illegible], and the game brought to the early market and sold. It is, of course, sold secretly, but this could not take place if the market was held at any reasonable hour. Bad money is also passed in the darkness of the morning. I have heard that a farthing has often been given for half a sovereign.

14,386. Have the people no lights by means of which to continue the sales?—They have no lights except that of the moon, and when she is full, as she is now, it does pretty well. Sometimes they strike a match on the street, and try to work by its aid. Perhaps one or two of the publicans might be averse to the hours of the market being changed, as it is an advantage to them to keep their houses open. My opinion is the hour should be changed, and this would do away with the necessity of having these houses open.

14,387. (Rev. R. D. Kerr, Church of Ireland.) I wish to add, Mr. Commissioner, that holding the market so early gives facilities to poachers and fowl stealers to get rid of their game by selling them to the dealers who come here.

(*Dr. Fulton.*) I have just told that fact to the court. I have just been told by a gentleman who knows well what the market is, that a barrowful of fowl was brought into Saintfield at 11 o'clock last night to be in time for the market. I am often myself, in driving round Saintfield, that this early market interferes with the sanctity of the Lord's Day.

Mr. Samuel McKee examined.

14,388. (*Mr. Commissioner Black.*) You are a draper, residing in the town of Saintfield?—Yes, I carry on the drapery business here.

14,389. You have heard the evidence of Dr. Fulton and of Major Price; do you agree with it generally?—I do. I think that the fowl market should be kept back till eight o'clock. If this were done it would be better for both buyer and seller, and all parties would be satisfied with it.

14,390. Do you think this extraordinary early market is the fault of the buyers or the sellers?—I think it is the fault of the sellers, and for this reason: I had a conversation with Mr. Gilmore, of Belfast, a large buyer of fowl here, and he told me there had been an arrangement entered into some time ago not to commence the market till eight o'clock or so, and for two or three days he did not come before that hour. He, however, was obliged to give that up, as other buyers wanting to get the pick of the fowl forced the sellers to come as early as they chose, and when he came he had to buy at a [illegible], or buy none at all. It was this fact which obliged him to change to the old hour. I had also a correspondence with Mr. Mason, of Comber, another large buyer of fowl, and he states: "I am sorry I cannot attend the meeting to-day. I will "give my vote with the greatest of pleasure. I have not "been in the market but once these last five weeks, and "if they do not see their way to get it stopped I will "stop going to it. It is impossible for anyone to lay out "money so early in the morning. I hope you will succeed "to-day."

14,391. Is Mr. Mason an extensive buyer?—Yes, very extensive.

14,392. Have you any idea of the number of fowl brought to Saintfield [illegible]?—Not exactly, but I know the number is large; and I might say further, that the quality of fowl, and also of butter and eggs, brought here is considered to be very good. The buyers say they cannot get better anywhere, and that being so, it is a pity that the market is not better regulated, so that all might get the advantage.

14,393. What is your opinion with reference to the conduct of the market; would you prefer the matter being left to a market committee?—Yes, I think the matter should be left to such a committee, who should have the power of appeal to the magistrates to carry out their decisions.

14,396. Do you agree with Dr. Fulton as to the confusion existing at the fairs?—I do. I have always held that the course adopted at the horse fair is dangerous to the public. It is supposed to be held in Comber Street, but instead of that it is held on the main thoroughfare of the town, and there is scarcely a fair day on which there is not some one hurt.

14,397. I suppose, if we except the general absence of regulation and order, you do not hear of many complaints?—I think the markets and fairs would go well if a proper regulation were enforced, so that every one attending would be confined to his proper place, and business commenced at a proper hour. This is the only grievance I know that is complained of. Dr. Fulton has stated that the darkness allows poachers and fowl stealers to bring in their booty and dispose of it, which is true, and the police cannot detect them under the circumstances.

14,398. It is very hard, no doubt, to detect crimes of this character if there is no light?—Well, there is absolutely no light.

Mr. J. H. Moore Garrett, J.P., examined.

14,399. (*Mr. Commissioner Black.*) What is your opinion with regard to the conduct of the markets of Saintfield?—I have been agent for the Price Estate for the past 11 years. I have made several efforts to get the markets properly arranged. I went up to Dublin and saw Sir William Kaye on the subject, and we had a long interview, and afterwards some correspondence on the subject. I was informed by him that we had not sufficient population to come under the Town Improvement Act, and that, therefore, the magistrates had no power to arrange the markets and fairs.

14,400. What is the population of *Saintfield*?—About 670 at present.

14,401. You agree in the main with the other witnesses as to the want of regulation?—Yes; but there is an objection to Dr. Fulton's plan of placing the management in the hands of a market committee, as it is very doubtful whether such a committee would agree as to the way in which the markets should be held. Some years ago Mr. Price, the landlord, had some fowl sheds built for the accommodation of the people, and as these were adjacent to the court-house the traders of the lower portion of the town objected to the buyers coming up here, and the whole thing fell through. What I want to convey is this, that there might again be something of the kind done if matters were in the hands of a local committee, and the upper and lower ends of the town would be found pulling against each other. It is very natural that traders would not like the market changed if it took the trade away from their doors to another part of the town.

14,402. That is something similar to the state of affairs existing in Castlewellan?—Just the same, and you have already had some evidence regarding that. There is one place here suitable for holding the horse fair, and that is the old Comber Road. That thoroughfare could be used for the purpose, as there is another road along which the traffic could be conducted and would not interfere with anyone. Showing horses on the main street should be prevented, as I myself have seen a woman knocked down, and it is known to all that is very dangerous.

14,403. In the event of the markets being handed over to a committee, who would have power to levy toll?—I think it would only be fair that such a committee should pay the quit rent, which Mr. Price has been paying for years without getting any return.

14,404. Is not the quit-rent a very small thing?—It is very small, no doubt, but there is no reason why Mr. Price should pay it if he gets no advantage. The market house in which we are now assembled was built by Mr. Price's predecessor, and the weighbridge was also put up by the landlord; and if the committee referred to were established, they would, of course, be prepared to pay for them.

14,405. (*Mr. McKee.*) Does not the county pay for the courthouse?—It pays for the use of it as a petty sessions court, but Mr. Price is paying the balance of it. Within the

Mr. Nathaniel Perry examined.

14,406. (*Mr. Commissioner Bland.*) What is your calling?—I am a draper, carrying on business in Saintfield.

14,407. Have you anything to add with reference to the conduct of the markets?—I do not know that I can add much to the evidence already given. My opinion, however, is that the magistrates are the best parties to regulate the markets. The shopkeepers, as a rule, would rather the magistrates took it into their hands as anyone else.

14,408. You think, then, the magistrates should have the power?—I do. All the shopkeepers of Saintfield are represented here, and it is the prevailing opinion that the magistrates are an organised body, and would not be afraid to do their duty as business men might be.

14,409. (*Mr. Garrett.*) Do you not think that the rule of such a committee would tend to disagree?—I do. It would be far better; we shopkeepers would not act at all; we are so bashful. We have been complaining for years with regard to the time of commencing the markets and their regulation. No man here wishes the place altered, as the present accommodation is all right if the people were kept in their proper place.

14,410. Is the fair green much used?—It is very largely used, and it is an excellent green.

14,411. (*Mr. Garrett.*) You have observed that all the cattle brought on that green have to be driven down the main street where the horses are being shown, which causes very considerable trouble and annoyance?—I have. Very often the cattle in the confusion are driven into the shop windows, and all this arises for want of proper regulations, as there is a place for everything if it were availed of.

Mr. Jas. Rea examined.

14,412. (*Mr. Commissioner Bland.*) You are a farmer?—I am residing in the townland of Lisdalgan.

14,413. What is your opinion with regard to the early market for fowl?—I find it very inconvenient to come out and exhibit fowl in the middle of the night, as very often we lose some of them. We have been trying often to put an end to this early market, but I do not see how it is to be done, except we get a market to enter which we will have to pay toll.

14,414. You would not object to pay toll?—Certainly not. I, of course, object to the horses being shown on the public street, as it is dangerous. Comber Street is the best place for the showing of horses, as there is no danger out there, and it is out of the road.

(*Mr. Garrett.*) The thoroughfare to which I referred is the old road, not the main road. It is known as the old Comber Road, and is very little used.

14,415. (*Mr. Commissioner Bland.*) What is your opinion of the egg and butter market?—I have no complaint to make with regard to these markets. They are not held till half-past eight or so, when the buyers come from Belfast.

14,416. How is butter sold here?—In prints and lump, but mostly prints. When farmers wish to sell fowl they have to leave home in the middle of the night, and after having sold they are obliged to go home again and bring their other produce, and do whatever shopping they have to do.

14,417. What district of country does Saintfield serve in the way of markets?—I should say for three or four miles round, as far as Killinchy. I may tell you that I have spoken to the principal fowl dealers attending here, and all were anxious to come and do their business by daylight. There is, however, a class of hawkers going about who buy fowl as cheaply as possible at all hours of the night, and then sell them over again to such wholesale dealers as Gilmore and Magee.

14,418. Gilmore and Magee are large buyers?—They are the principal buyers; but all these men prefer meeting at eight o'clock, or so, if it could be arranged.

Sergeant Wm. Loftus, R.I.C., examined.

14,419. (*Mr. Commissioner Bland.*) Do you find much difficulty in regulating the markets of Saintfield?—Yes, I do, and I have also great difficulty in regulating the fairs. The horse fairs are held on the principal street, and it is at times almost impossible to pass up and down.

14,420. Accidents occasionally occur?—They do. There is scarcely a fair day on which some one is not knocked down and injured by the horses.

14,421. Do you find much difficulty in regulating this fowl market at the unearthly hour of two o'clock in the morning?—I do. I find it is an encouragement to fowl stealers and poachers, who pick up fowl along the roads and bring them in and sell them. Of course in the dark it is almost impossible to detect them.

14,422. Would you like to see some competent authority in charge of the markets so that their regulations might be attended to?—Of course I would. In the mornings shortly before Christmas there are as many as 150 carts of fowl coming to this market, and I find the greatest difficulty in regulating the traffic. There is no light; the people are going wherever they like in the dark, and I can scarcely work with them at all.

14,423. Have you ever known bad money to be passed in the darkness?—I have not. The fowl dealers from Belfast generally bring the change with them, I think.

Mr. John Davey examined.

14,424. (*Mr. Commissioner Bland.*) What is your opinion of the markets here?—I agree with Mr. Garrett as to the want of regulation.

14,425. And do you fall in with the idea that the magistrates should regulate the markets?—Yes, I fall in with all he proposed.

Rev. R. D. Knox examined.

14,426. (*Mr. Commissioner Bland.*) You are vicar of Saintfield?—I am.

14,427-8. What would you recommend to improve the regulation of the markets here?—I would say that whatever is done should be done stringently. I do not know whether it has been mentioned here in evidence or not, but an attempt was made by the magistrates some years ago to stop the showing of horses on the leading street of the town, which street communicates with all the principal roads, and is the direct way to the railway station from the upper end. Several parties were brought before the court on different occasions for showing their horses up and down the street at a rapid rate, accidents having occurred. Notices were also put up at the end of the town, and at different other places about,—I mean boards with printed notices upon them,—stating that the magistrates would fine any party who would infringe the rule. That was carried out for a length of time, but afterwards it was gradually broken through. It, however, had the effect of reducing the excess of speed at which the horses were driven, to the danger of the passers-by. I know myself there was an accident not very long ago, when a young [illegible] was kicked and hurt.

(*Sergeant Loftus.*) An accident occurred last fair day.

(*Witness.*) My object in coming forward to give evidence is to explain that whatever is done should be done in a stringent manner. I am perfectly satisfied, having experience of Saintfield for many years, that an attempt will be made to evade the law, and I am also sure that those who are in the habit of using this main street will not be satisfied to go to the road beyond Mr. Price's entrance gate to show their horses.

(*Mr. Garrett.*) The only thing the magistrates could do was to fine the parties who were brought before them for furious showing of their horses. They had no other power in the world.

(*Witness.*) Some time ago an attempt was made to prevent young cattle being shown on the footpaths, and Mr. Crawford and Mr. Price got a wall built in order to keep them on the fair green. The fair green, however, is a thing which we must take for granted, as it is all right. The arrangement worked well enough for some time, but in a few years the cattle were back again on the footpaths.

(*Major Price.*) This is certainly a great nuisance, for on fair days no one can get along the footpaths.

(*Witness.*) It is impossible for anyone to get to the railway station on a fair day. The present arrangements put such a thing out of the question.

This concluded the inquiry.

Portglenone, November 20th, 1889.

Capt. Alexander Moore Armstrong [illegible].

14,430. (*Mr. Commissioner Bland.*) You are trustee for the Hamilton-Jones estate?—I am agent for the trustees of the late Kenrick Hamilton-Jones. It is the Moneyglass estate. And the last Mr. Jones was tenant for life.

14,431. The trustees are the owners of the market rights of Portglenone?—They are.

14,432. Can you give me any particulars of the charter giving these rights?—No, I cannot.

14,433. Is there a market place in Portglenone?—There is not to my knowledge. There is a market house, or what is called by that name, but it is now in a very dilapidated condition. The street is the only market place at the present time.

(*Mr John McLaughlin.*) That is quite right.

(*Witness.*) I understand there is no market accommodation whatever at present.

14,434. (*Mr. Commissioner Bland.*) How often is a market held here?—There is no market here so far as I am aware. The market was got up by some of the merchants here, including Mr. McLaughlin and Mr. Jack, but there is no regular established market so far as I know.

(*Mr. McLaughlin.*) You are referring to the fairs, and not to the markets. I have something to do with reviving the fairs of this town.

(*Rev. John Heaston.*) The regular day upon which the market was held formerly was Tuesday in each week, but this is now only the nominal market day. There is no market in Portglenone, or no business done except what is done in the shops.

14,435. (*Mr. Commissioner Bland.*) The desire of the people is to get the market re-established, and if this is the wish of the trustees, I suppose, Captain Armstrong, you will not throw any obstacle in the way?

(*Witness.*) Certainly not.

14,436. Is there any weighbridge for weighing commodities in Portglenone?—I believe there is an old beam and scales, but they are worthless for weighing purposes at present.

14,437. You have not appointed a weighmaster?—I have not.

Mr. William Stewart Adams examined.

14,438. (*Mr. Commissioner Bland.*) You are an executor of the late lessee, David Crossett?—Yes. He had the market house at a time, and it was bought from us by the late Mr. Kenrick Hamilton-Jones.

14,439. How did David Crossett go into possession?—He got a lease of the place and built the house, or rather rebuilt it, and was then appointed weighmaster.

14,440. From whom did he receive that appointment?—From Thomas Hamilton-Jones, deceased.

14,441. You have not made the lease over to the Jones family; he built the market house, or rebuilt it, I refer to Mr. Crossett, and was then appointed deputy weighmaster of the town of Portglenone?—Quite so.

14,442. And Mr. Crossett died?—Yes, about three or two years ago.

14,443. In David Crossett's time was there a regular market at Portglenone?—There was.

14,444. How often was it held?—Every Thursday there was a grain market, and every Tuesday there was a general market for all classes of produce. The fairs were held on the first Tuesday of each month.

14,445. You say the first Tuesday of each month was the fair day?—It was.

14,446. When Crossett was in possession, did he do all the weighing of the stuff that came into the town for sale?—He did, except on the flax, of which there was a very large market here. It was taken to some other house and weighed.

14,447. Did he make a charge for weighing?—He did. I think it was 1½d. a bag for corn, 3d. for the dead carcase of a pig, and 2s. 6d. a ton for flax.

14,448. Are these all the charges made by him?—I think so.

14,449. Did he charge anything at the fairs?—Not that I remember. To the best of my knowledge there was no charge or toll at the fairs, as they were held on the open street.

14,450. Then there were no other charges but what you have given us; there was no charge on these stalls?—None.

14,451. The charges, I presume, were made merely for the weighing?—That is so.

14,452. He acted as weighmaster up till the time of his death?—He did.

14,453. And the house was sold to Mr. Kenrick Hamilton-Jones?—It was.

14,454. After he bought from you, did he carry on the business of the market?—There was a man appointed named Thomas Norris, who had been selected by a committee which had been previously appointed, and this was done with Mr. Jones' consent.

14,455. How long did Norris remain in office?—Two or three years, but the market commenced to dwindle away gradually.

14,456. Has Norris anything to do with the market now?—He is dead.

14,457. You say the markets fell away?—They did, gradually. Mr. Jones bought the market house and all connected with it from us for the sum of 180*l*., and he died shortly afterwards. We got no money for our property. The estate held the keys, and we gave the lease to Mr. Jones' agent, who held on and never gave us either keys, or money, or anything. The matter was then left to arbitration. Mr. Hugh MacNeile McCormick, the Clerk of the Crown for Antrim, being the arbitrator. He arranged that we should get a sum of 50*l*. for the damage done, that the market house should be put in proper order, as it had been previously, and that it should be given over to us. Nothing, however, has been done; the matter remains as it was, but I suppose Captain Armstrong will be able to explain all this.

(*Capt. Armstrong.*) Before the award was delivered, Mr. Jones died. The award took effect from the 1st February, and Mr. Jones died on the 15th January.

14,458. (*Mr. Commissioner Bland.*) Did you ever see the lease yourself?

(*Witness.*) I did.

14,459. Was it a lease of the market rights of Portglenone, or merely of the market house? It was of the market house, and then a party got control over the markets and tolls. Formerly there was a good market here. It was held on the open street. The business was carried on after David Crossett got possession. Mr. Jones got the consent of the whole, ejected the man who had it previously, and gave David Crossett the right and title to it.

14,460. I suppose the estate you represent would have no hesitation in parting with the interest it has in this market house?—We have no interest in it. They bought it, and we gave up everything. If we had an interest we would be willing to give it over to any person who would arrange with you.

(*Mr. McLaughlin.*) There must be an interest in it as you were never paid the award.

14,461. (*Mr. Commissioner Bland.*) Then was there anything like a fair green in this town?

(*Witness.*) Never.

Mr. John McLaughlin examined.

14,462. (*Mr. Commissioner Bland.*) You are the secretary of the existing fair and market committee of Portglenone?—I am.

14,463. That committee is a voluntary committee supported by voluntary subscriptions?—Yes. It is a committee got up by the townspeople, just among ourselves, to try and carry on the sale of cattle in an open market where no tolls would be charged. Of course we have no weighbridge here to weigh cattle.

14,464. Your great anxiety is to encourage the sale of produce in the town?—That is the anxiety of the townspeople, expressed through me to-day. Our great desire is to develop and revive the markets of Portglenone, which, I may say, have fallen entirely into disuse.

14,465. In the memorial you sent forward to Mr. Burke, the secretary of the Commission, you state that the landlord leased the market rights and premises to a private party, who exercised absolute control and did whatever he pleased with the public, and that the persons coming to the market to do business suffered thereby; what is the exact date of the granting of that lease?—I came here in the year 1861, and I am convinced of the truth of what I am going to tell you, although I have had no observation of it myself. I understand, previous to 1853, the markets of Portglenone had got a bit down, and a committee of the townspeople appointed Mr. John M'Aleny weighmaster. They erected on the public street, in the wide part of the town, a shed or market place for weighing, and empowered M'Aleny to take tolls and make charges. The then owner was the late Mr. Alexander, the present Mr. Alexander's father, Nathaniel Alexander, and from some cause the estate was sold by the Encumbered Estates Court to the late Mr. Hamilton-Jones, who became the owner of Portglenone. I understand among the things Mr. Jones purchased were the patent rights of this market—if such a thing exists—and that subsequent to 1853, finding he had these rights, he arranged with the late David Crossett to lease these rights and certain premises therewith. He then undertook to dispossess, or eject, or put away John M'Aleny, who had been exercising his right under the previous—a right he got from the inhabitants.

14,466. (*Capt. Armstrong.*) Was this man, however, exercising the right he got from the inhabitants, or that reserved from Bishop Alexander?

(*Witness.*) The right given him by a committee of the inhabitants, with the consent of the owner. I understand one of the Alexanders, one of the late sons of that family, or the bishop, erected sheds on the public street without any cost. This, I might say, is a matter of tradition, but I know it to be a fact. I believe it was the late Nathaniel Alexander from whom Mr. Jones bought the property who erected the sheds. The town voluntarily collected the money, and the timber was given by the landlord. I understand the rent of the present market-house was [illegible] a year, and the premises were held as a [illegible] for the [illegible], and by an arrangement entered into David Crossett took the premises on lease at 7*l.* a year, bound himself to rebuild the weigh-house, and Mr. Jones consented to lease all the rights and privileges of the markets. The market flourished, and was very large in the years 1853, 1854, and 1855, and that portion of it which flourished best was the flax market. It was so large, indeed, that the market accommodation was quite inadequate, particularly as regards the weighing and the storage, which may be set down at nil. In the year 1863 or 1864 the leading inhabitants of the town came to the rescue of David Crossett, and voluntarily offered to weigh flax free of charge, and also store it free of charge. I myself weighed for the Messrs. Gelloy, of Moneymore, on different occasions. The result of this was that the principal merchants went to those private parties, and got their flax weighed, and it was the habit of both the merchants and the public to go to the free resort, and, in addition, secure good storage. In fact, the storage was the thing looked for, and the flax, as a rule, was taken to the places where this could be insured. David Crossett, seeing himself lose so much money, I understand, threatened those parties who had, in the first instance, come to his rescue, and tried to keep the market in the town. He went and served them with legal notices, and sought damages, and, on the whole, his manner so annoyed the buyers that they stopped coming to Portglenone, although they considered that the best hand-scutched flax in Ireland was to be found in this neighbourhood. Things went on in this way, the market getting worse and worse, and at his death, owing to the complications with his successors, the market house became closed entirely against the public, and this is the second year in which not a single bag of corn has been weighed in the registered patent weigh-house of Portglenone, which, I believe, is one of six in all Ireland holding the same privileges. A committee was then formed to try and revive these markets. The first thing set about was to revive the flax, and this met with encouraging success. We then approached the owners as to what could be done regarding the markets, and their representative, Captain Armstrong, would do and did do all he could, but from some cause or other nothing has been done. The grievance of the people of the town is this, that through the actions of others, not through their own doings, that is to say, the landlord in the first instance, and the lessee in the second, the markets have been fairly driven out of the place, out of a town which used to be prosperous, and our position now is that we are 10 miles off a market on the one hand, and seven on the other. Another grievance we have is that no machine was ever provided for weighing produce by the landlord, and that the town had to depend on the enterprise of private individuals, such, for instance, as the late William Smyth and Mr. Jack, with whom the people were fairly satisfied, and have paid them toll for so doing. A good many, however, who cannot do so are [illegible] friends.

14,467. What does Mr. Jack charge for weighing a cart?—Threepence for the cart or for the load.

14,468. What is your idea about the markets; is it that the town has lost through the absence of the money the people used to bring into it?—The town has lost its revenue through the money having gone to neighbouring markets.

14,469. The produce is being taken to other markets?—It is. It is being taken from Portglenone, and from four or five miles beyond it to Ballymena.

14,470. Your idea is that it should be sold here, and the people of the town get the benefit?—Quite so.

14,471. Do you find any difficulty in getting produce to buy?—Decidedly. I would go to Ballymena for many things I want, and, again, if I am desirous of selling, I must, for instance, take my pork to Ballymena or sell it myself, which, I suppose, would be a trouble thing to do. We live here, as it were, at crossroads in the country seven or ten miles from a market town.

14,472. Is it your opinion that such a small town as Portglenone should have market rights vested in a small committee?—I have an objection to a small committee. Anybody who would manage the markets should be stronger than a committee. I would go in for a market company, and that that company should receive, as a gift from the owners, all the rights and privileges, as they would be increasing the value of the estate, or let the owners go in and take share and share alike for the benefit of the town.

14,473. What would such a company do when established?—When they got all the rights they would be able to find money to build storage, just the same as they have done in Antrim, where the market company pays 5 per cent.

14,474. And whatever revenue would be derived from the markets would go into the company's pocket?—Just so.

14,475. Would you give this company supreme control of the markets, or would you have any authority placed over it?—I thought the Lord Lieutenant had authority over all market bodies in Ireland.

14,476. You would not suggest any authority more local than the Lord Lieutenant?—No.

14,477. Would not some jealousy, in your opinion, arise as to the position of the markets, about having them in particular ends of the town?—I think a public company would work with a common aim and not with jealousies. I suggested before to build a market in the centre of the street and let the business houses be right round it, the same as in Coleraine.

14,478. And the revenue, supposing there was a profit or surplus should, in your opinion, go into the pockets of the shareholders?—Yes.

14,479. That means, I suppose, would be that these men spend the money first and take their chance?—They run the risk, of course. I think the landlords, for their own sakes, should give up the rights and privileges of the markets, and if a company run the risk they were entitled to the profit, as, in the case of Belfast, they would have to bear the loss.

14,480. (*Capt. Armstrong.*) Suppose the landlord gave you a long lease, would it not satisfy you?—The company might, of course, come to grief, but a lease for 999 years at a shilling a year could not be opposed by anyone, and this would provide a right of preemption.

14,481. Supposing the company came to grief, the landlord would require to have some hold so that his rights might be protected?—I suppose he should get this as a member of the suggested company.

14,482. My remark, of course, is merely a suggestion?—Just so. We have been putting our hands into our pockets this many a day, and we would rather have to pay a company, for if we never saw the money again we would, at least, see some work done for it.

14,653. (*Mr. Commissioner Black.*) Would you recommend this suggested company to charge tolls at the fairs? —I think not; it would be better to have a few free here. I am told that at some of the fairs in Ireland the Government is forcing them to put up weighbridges for the purpose of weighing fat cattle.

14,654. Do you think the selling of cattle by live weight is a desirable practice?—Well, I would think that is a matter for the butchers.

14,655. It is a custom the breeders oppose very strongly, even [illegible], indeed, a very few of them?—I think it is a matter of [illegible] dealing, and my idea is that the farmer should not be taken in in any way. On second consideration, I would go in for the sale of cattle by live weight.

14,656. Do you think the fairs should be held on the square as they are at present, or should a green be provided?—Except Portglenone exceeds my expectation, the square will accommodate our fairs for many a long day.

Mr. William Wallace examined.

14,657. (*Mr. Commissioner Black.*) You are a merchant, I understand, carrying on business in Portglenone?—I was, but I am not now.

14,658. What do you know, Mr. Wallace, about the markets of this town?—Before Mr. Crommie got the market house from Mr. Jones I was in the grain trade. I was buying oats, and was paying at that time something like [illegible] a week when the old market house was in the middle of the street. We had a good market that time every Thursday, for about eight or nine months of the year, and then when Mr. Jones got the property he took the notion of letting the markets to Crommie. He was making money out of the affair. For the old court-house he got [illegible] a year, and for the markets [illegible] a year; but he had trouble in putting M'Aleery off the streets, and had to invest Crommie with more public rights than most public weighmasters in large towns before he could put him off. When Crommie got possession there was not accommodation for nearly all the produce coming in at that time. We had then a better flax market than Ballymena, Kilrea, or Maghera. I have seen Portglenone full of loads of flax. I have seen Mr. Gailey's people of Coleraine weighing flax until nearly midnight on the Tuesday night, and coming back on Wednesday and finishing it out. At that time I gave storage to different parties and weighed for them. I weighed then about 10 tons of flax every market day. This David Crommie served me with a notice, along with others, that he would take an action against us for weighing the flax to accommodate the people, and charging nothing for doing so. Different other parties in Portglenone weighed the flax free as well as I, and it was all with the object of helping the town, so far as the markets were concerned. As long as David Crommie lived we had a grain market here. After he died his family weighed for a year or two, and then this man Nevin came in and weighed again, and afterwards William M'Caw, who, I think was appointed by Mr. Jones, held the office. I do not know who appointed Nevin, but he weighed for a year or two, and M'Caw succeeded him. Subsequently the market house was closed by Mr. Jones and his agent, and the market fell off from year to year. At present if we wanted to buy a ton of corn, we would have to go to Ballymena, as we could not get it here in Portglenone. This is the biggest part of what I know about it. You cannot sell anything here, not even a load of potatoes. What has been done has put the market out of the town entirely.

14,659. When you speak of a large flax market being held in Portglenone at a particular time, I suppose you are aware that there was more of the article grown in the country then?—I do not know about that. Some years now there is as large an acreage of flax sown as ever there has been.

14,660. Is it the practice here to go round the mills and buy flax?—Some is bought in that way still, but so long as I mind, even when was bought in that way came into the market and was weighed. We have only one spinning mill in Ballymena, and some of it goes there direct, but the greater portion of it is taken to the market on market days.

14,661. You are a farmer yourself?—I am.

(*Capt. Armstrong.*) What is really wanted in this town is weighing accommodation.

Mr. William Boyd examined.

14,662. (*Mr. Commissioner Black.*) Have you anything to say with reference to the revival of the markets of Portglenone?—Yes. I think there is another grievance from which we labour. We have no [illegible] against Ballymena as well as against Kilrea, both of which places have a means of taking away produce when bought. We have nothing of the kind here; we have no railway, and if it were within the scope of the Commission, I would like that in its report it would advise the construction of light railways, the want of which militates very considerably against us here. The merchants very naturally say to themselves, why go to Portglenone to buy stuff, as we can get it in Ballymena, where we have not to pay cartage.

Rev. John Hamilton examined.

14,663. (*Mr. Commissioner Black.*) You are a Presbyterian minister in Portglenone?—I am, and have been for some years.

14,664. Have you anything to add to the evidence already given?—Well, I think the testimony so far has been more prospective than anything else. If we had restored to us the accommodation that we had in David Crommie's time we would not be satisfied by any means, because it did not suit the town, and did not give us all the facilities we wanted. I cannot speak from experience of what was the state of matters here when Mr. M'Aleery had the scales on the street, but about 24 or 25 years ago, when I came here, there was no market, I may say, owing to the contention between Mr. Jones and the gentleman I have referred to. I wished to have a market established in the town, and I consulted with some of the older and most respectable merchants, the late Mr. M'Caw, the late Mr. Smyth, who did an extensive trade, and the late Mr. Agnew, and we formed a market committee, of which I was chairman for some years. Through that committee, but not without very great exertion, we sustained the markets, especially that for flax. I wrote circulars and got them sent off to the various flax dealers, and for three or four years the market was very successful. I remember going round one day and counting no less than 400 carts of flax in Portglenone market. I tried as far as I could to keep Mr. Crommie in good humour, in order to encourage the market, but it was no easy matter. The late Mr. Gailey was the largest buyer in this country, and he came and bought largely at our market. We had, with some difficulty, to get help to weigh and provide proper storage, but Crommie objected when he found so much money being taken out of his own pocket. Then he gave offence to Gailey and others, and they did not continue to buy. We also tried to revive the grain and pork markets, but there was no weighing or storage accommodation, for even had the present, or what was then the present, scale accommodation been satisfactory, it was placed at the wrong part of the town. It was situated at a narrow part of the street, so that the carts got jammed and the people came into collision, and I had often to mediate between them and the police. All this was the result of the want of accommodation. In our meetings of committee I urged the people to give proper accommodation by weighing on their own account, and let Mr. Crommie take whatever course he pleased, as the bugbear was thrown before us of a patent or charter that I never saw. I deny there was any such patent or charter, or if there was such a patent or charter there must have been conditions attached to it, and these must have been of a poor description, if they were fulfilled by the weighmaster appointed by the late proprietor of the town. I held then and still hold—and it is with my own that I would follow it up—that this charter has lapsed through non-fulfilment of conditions. I went to Mr. Jones, and I met him often in Mr. Orr's office, Ballymena, and spoke to him about the lease he had given to Crommie, and he pointed out that his hands were tied, owing to the right of weighing he had given this gentleman. I questioned then, and question still, the right of Mr. Jones, or anyone in his position, to give the right to any man of weighing in this town. He is not, or was not, the sole proprietor of the town, and if there is a charter, which he never produced, it must be so long out of date as to have no binding power at all.

14,665. I think, Mr. Hamilton, you do not seem to understand the power conferred by a charter. A charter was granted by the Crown to some person here 200 or 300 years ago, granting some land and the right of holding markets in certain places. The landlord holds his land still under this charter, and has his rights legally with reference to the holding of the markets. The charter recites the holding of markets, and the landlord has the rights and tolls to some person, or it may be he exercises the power himself, but, in the process of time, if he did not collect those tolls, the right to collect them would no doubt lapse?—That is what I mean. It is said the right to collect these tolls was given through the late Miss McNeill, to whom this property belonged. I deny, however, that the granting of a charter for the benefit of a property, with the right of collecting tolls, should hinder others of good market accommodation. That is the thing I question on the part of any proprietor. That is the thing that has hindered us all along, and I maintain, if a landlord has a charter for holding markets and collecting tolls, he is bound to provide proper market accommodation, and if his power has ceased, the townspeople should provide themselves with such accommodation.

14,496. At all events, whatever you recommend here will affect a number of towns of like size as Portglenone, and probably with like conditions. Is it your opinion that a market company should be established in each town?—That is a matter of opinion. I would, I think, go in with what Mr. McLaughlin has stated, and from what I have heard of Antrim, I would be disposed to put this town under similar conditions.

14,497. (*Capt. Armstrong.*) Would you wish such a company to have exclusive rights so that no other market in the way of opposition could be started?—Certainly; the company should have the rights of the landlord, whatever they are.

14,498. Would it not be rather bad if other parties could start an opposition to such a company?—It would.

14,499. (*Mr. Commissioner Black.*) I know the affairs of the Antrim company pretty well; they have 1,300*l.* capital.

(*Mr. McLaughlin.*) If the landlord gives 1,000*l.*, we will find the other 300*l.*

Mr. Alexander Jack examined.

15,000. (*Mr. Commissioner Black.*) Have you anything to add, Mr. Jack?—I am not the oldest man in Portglenone, but I am one of the oldest in business here, and my impression about the whole thing is this: our "great decrease" here, as has been already remarked, is want of proper market accommodation. To my mind that accommodation must be supplied either by the landlord or his representatives, and, failing to do so, he must withdraw entirely from the field, claiming no rights except those to which he is entitled as a landlord—a thing which I would not object to. He must either do the work or withdraw, as the work cannot be done with both in the field. As far as I am concerned, I would have nothing to do with a company, except it was a free and *fair* field and no favour, so that we might not be receiving continual annoyance by attorney's letters, and such like. We have all the resources here for creating a good market and working it, if we only had the accommodation. That has been the great want of Portglenone, for when good markets were gathered there was no place to which the stuff could be taken, and the merchants would not put it at the back of a ditch until they arranged to have it taken away, probably next week. This accommodation must be provided either by the landlord or by a company, and I would prefer the landlord doing the work, expending the money, and so playing into his own hands, instead of allowing us to do all we can while he reaps all the benefits.

15,001. If any change is made you may rely upon it that it will be of a comprehensive character?—I suppose it will, but these are my opinions on the subject.

(*Mr. M'Laughlin.*) Our case, I am sure, is that of many small towns in Ireland.

(*Rev. John Houston.*) I wish to say, Mr. Commissioner, that Portglenone and district have not failed in the matter of produce. This should be distinctly understood and reported. We have no market now, but we have not changed our locality. We have still need of market accommodation—a place where we might sell our produce.

(*Mr. Boyd.*) The farmers have to cart it away to these strange markets instead of delivering it here.

(*Rev. John Houston.*) The farmers want to sell here and leave the expense of taking it away to the buyer.

(*Mr. Commissioner Black.*) If the purchaser of produce here has to send it to Ballymena, probably by cart, the seller cannot expect to get as good a price.

(*Mr. M'Laughlin.*) The want of business in a market is not due to the absence of a railway, but the reverse.

(*Mr. Jack.*) A market here would soon bring the railway to our door.

(*Mr. M'Laughlin.*) In the matter of a railway we are fixed between the broad and narrow gauges. The broad gauge is in use at present, but before the Ballymena and Portglenone Company was formed it was said there was traffic for both.

(*Rev. John Houston.*) Unfortunately, we are between two stools.

(*Capt. Armstrong.*) I wish to say a word, as my name is connected with the market question. I became connected with the property in August 1884, and at that time I found no market here; the market place was closed up. One individual was weighing on his own authority, but he was not recognised in any way by me. When I discovered the state of affairs existing, some time after, I made an arrangement to have an arbitration with the executors of the late Mr. [illegible] who had the market. This arbitration was carried on in Belfast before Mr. Hugh M'Neill M'Cormick, the Clerk of the Crown and Peace, but he made no order in the case just then, which I think Mr. Adams explained. His award, unfortunately, was not made until after the death of young Mr. Jones, and matters remained unsettled ever since. Some of the leading inhabitants of the town came to me some time ago to see what assistance could be rendered if they started a fair or market, and I told them, so far as I was concerned, I would render them every assistance in my power. They started the fair, and it has been successful so far. They came again to me and asked for the use of the old market house for weighing purposes temporarily, so that the success of the present arrangement might be seen. I called on the solicitor to the estate about the 8th October, and he said there was no difficulty in having the temporary use of it, and it was handed over to them to use during the winter months. They, however, never removed the key or had anything to do with it. I wish to say, Mr. Commissioner, that I did not neglect the matter, which I considered was for the good of the people.

15,002–3. (*Mr. Commissioner Black.*) So far as you are concerned, you would advise the people to look after their own interests?

(*Witness.*) I would when no one will do anything for their benefit.

(*Capt. Armstrong.*) I have told you the facts, so far as I know. There must have been some legal difficulties afterwards, of which I did not hear.

This concluded the inquiry.

Mr. Charles W. Black, Assistant Commissioner, sat in the rooms of the tolls committee on Monday, the 13th May 1889, to hear supplemental evidence with regard to the markets and fairs of Armagh.

Mr. Edwin Best, solicitor, represented the tolls committee, and Mr. William Gallagher, solicitor, the town commissioners. Mr. Isaac Gardner, secretary to the tolls committee, and Mr. Thomas G. Peel, town clerk, were present.

15,004. Mr. Best, in opening the proceedings, said: Mr. Commissioner, I wish to place before you briefly the course I wish to adopt on the present occasion on behalf of tolls committee. I was not present at the inquiry held here on the 11th June last; but I see from the printed evidence that everything was pretty well gone into, and I do not think you would have been troubled to-day had it not been that the clerk to the town commissioners went to Belfast, and appeared before the Royal Commission, and gave some evidence there. The tolls committee had no notice of this, and consequently Mr. Peel had an opportunity of making statements in evidence with no person to cross-examine him, or have them contradicted. In the evidence he gave before the Royal Commission he made some statements—I do not say he made those statements knowing them to be untrue, but they were not correct—as affecting the tolls charged in Armagh. These statements were made notwithstanding the evidence given before you on a former occasion, when there was a full opportunity of cross-examining any of our witnesses, either Mr. Gardner or any member of the tolls committee. On the occasion of Mr. Peel appearing before the Royal Commission, he took the opportunity of presenting a petition or memorial purporting to be signed by the people of Armagh; but I intend to produce before you a dozen people who never saw the memorial, and although their names are to it, they are not their names at all, or at least they are not there by their consent. I will produce a number of persons who will tell you they did not know what the purport of the memorial was, and Mr. Gardner will go into general evidence with regard to what was done before the Commission. On the last occasion we were twitted that we had not produced any farmers to express an opinion as to the management of the markets; but you will have an opportunity this time of hearing a number of such witnesses—at least a dozen—who will prove that they believe Armagh markets are all the best managed markets in the country. Mr. Peel also complained bitterly about there being no weighbridge in the cattle market for the weighing of live cattle. He said that it would be for the benefit of the farmers if such were provided, and that it was badly wanted. I will produce three of the largest victuallers in Armagh to show that such a weighbridge is not wanted in Armagh, and also some of the largest farmers of the district who will express a similar opinion. If you visit the cattle market, sir, you will see that there is a weighbridge existing there, and that cattle can be weighed upon it if the victuallers or farmers desire. We will show, in the first place, that the bridge is not required for weighing cattle, and, in the second, that a bridge is there, and can be so used if anyone requires it. I will also produce some of the largest pork-buyers to show you how the pork market is managed, and a number of merchants in the butter trade whom I will produce will show you how business is conducted in that department in Armagh markets. I intend also to examine Mr. Gillespie, and he will give evidence with regard to the grass seed and grain trades, and he will be able to show you that the markets here for such produce have improved very much. When this is done, I think the other side will find they would have been as well to have done nothing behind our backs in Belfast.

William B[illegible] examined.

15,005. (Mr. Best.) You are living in Armagh?—I am.

15,006. You live in Lower English Street?—I do.

15,007. Is there any other Brewing there besides yourself, I mean of your name?—None.

15,008. Is that your signature (pointing to his name to a memorial)?—It is not.

15,009. Did you authorise any person to sign your name to that memorial?—No one.

15,010. Whose signature is this?—As far as I can understand it was my son who signed it. It was represented to him, I understand, that the memorial was for the good of the town and he signed it. I did not know a single thing about it until I saw the affair with Mr. Gardner, some day last week.

Cross-examined by Mr. Gallagher.

15,010a. Where were you when this was signed?—I could not say.

15,011. What age is your son?—Fourteen years of age.

15,012. Have you a wife living?—I have.

15,013. When did you ascertain your name was in this memorial?—I tell you I never saw it until it was with Mr. Gardner.

15,014. When did you first ascertain your name was to the memorial?—It was, at any rate, a good many days after.

15,015. How many?—I could not say.

15,016. Was it the same day?—It was not.

15,017. Was it the next day?—It might be two or three days afterwards.

15,018. From whom did you ascertain?—From my wife. All she could tell me was that it was represented it was for the good of the town.

15,019. Did she say it was about the transfer of the tolls from the toll committee?—She did not.

15,020. Did she say whose name was put to it?—I think so.

15,021. Did she tell you the name of the person who brought it to your house?—It was my son who told me.

15,022. Well, according to him, who brought it to your house?—He said it was Mr. Brooks.

15,023. Did you go to see Mr. Brooks about it?—I did not. I never made an inquiry about it. I do not understand it yet.

15,024. Do you understand what we are here about?—I cannot say I do. I know it is something about the town commissioners. That is all I understand about it. (Laughter.)

15,025. Do you object to your name being put to this memorial?—I certainly do when I did not authorise it to be done.

15,026. Does your son or your wife transact business for you?—They may to a certain extent.

15,027. Was your wife present when your name was put down?—I understand she was.

15,028. Do you do any business in the markets yourself?—I do not.

15,029. You have no interest in the tolls?—I do not understand anything about that.

15,029a. What is your occupation?—I am minding the "Plough Hotel" yard. I am an ostler.

Thomas M'C[illegible] examined.

15,030. (Mr. Best.) Where do you live?—I live in English Street; I mean Lower English Street, Armagh.

15,031. Can you write?—No, sir.

15,032. You did not sign your name to this memorial?—No, Mr. Brooks wrote it himself. I did not understand anything about it, but he said it was for the good of the town.

15,033. Did you authorise him to write your name, or did you not?—Partly, but he did not explain it to me further than to say it was for the good of the town.

15,034. Have you any idea who put your name to it, I mean the memorial?—Brooks said it was for the good of the town, and that he was getting names to it. I got my name put to it, not knowing what it was for.

15,035. If you had known that it was to take the tolls from the toll committee and give them to the commissioners, would you have put your name to it?—I would not. I would not give my name against Mr. Gardner.

Cross-examined by Mr. Gallagher.

15,036. Against whom did you say you would not sign your name?—Mr. Gardner; and you will please withdraw my name from the memorial.

15,037. When were you asked to withdraw your name from the memorial?—Would you kindly speak a little louder, as I am hard of hearing?

15,038. When were you asked to withdraw your name from this memorial?—I was never asked to do so.

15,039. Were you waited upon by any person?—No.

15,040. How did they know to bring you here?—I heard it myself.

15,041. From whom?—There were parties speaking about it.

15,042. Who was the party?—Mr. Biggs asked me, did I give my name against him, and I said not to my knowledge.

15,043. Did Mr. Gardner speak to you?—He asked me, did I give my vote.

15,044. Were they both together?—They were not.

15,044a. Where did you see him?—I saw him in my own house.

15,045. Were you not aware whether you had authorised your name to go to the memorial?—I was not, at least not for that purpose.

15,046. Have you forgotten about it?—I have not. I did not understand really what it was for.

15,047. What did you think you were signing?—Mr. Brooks said it was for the good of the town.

15,048. Is it not for the good of the town?—I do not think it is. There is no better gentleman than some who have their names attached to the memorial.

15,049. You actually signed the memorial when you did not know what you were signing?—I never wrote it.

15,050. Did you authorise your name to go to the memorial?—I made my mark, not knowing what it was about. You will withdraw it now, please.

15,051. Since we have ascertained how honest a man you are, you wish your name withdrawn?—I am as honest as you are, and I am as long in Armagh.

15,052. Did you say, to put your name to this memorial?—He said it was for the good of the town, but he did not explain it to me. If it was against Mr. Gardner and Mr. Biggs, I would not sign it.

15,053. Will you tell me when you saw Mr. Gardner?—I saw him this morning at the markets.

15,054. Did you see him before with reference to this memorial?—Several times during this week.

15,055. Where did you see him with reference to it?—In Lower English Street.

15,056. Did he go to your house?—Honestly, he did. (*Laughter.*)

15,057. Did he ask you to come here and withdraw your name?—He did not.

15,058. Did any person?—No person.

15,059. What did Mr. Gardner say?—He asked me, did I sign against him, and I said not to my knowledge.

15,060. What is your occupation?—I am a pensioner.

George Sherry examined.

15,061. (Mr. Best.) You are largely in the cattle trade?—I am.

15,062. You are a large farmer as well?—I am.

15,063. What land do you hold?—Up to 200 acres.

15,064. You say you are extensively in the cattle trade?—I am, both in live cattle and also in the victualling trade.

15,065. How long have you been in the victualling trade in Armagh?—All my life.

15,066. (*Producing a memorial.*) Is that your writing, Mr. Sherry; is that your signature to that memorial?—It is not.

15,067. You live in English Street, that is your residence?—Yes, but that is not my signature.

15,068. Have you made inquiries as to who signed your name to this memorial?—I knew nothing at all about it until this morning. Mr. Gardner and your brother came into the shop and asked me to appear here to-day, and I said I would. They asked me if that was my signature, and I said it was not.

15,069. You know the memorial is about the transfer of the markets from under the control of the toll committee to the town commissioners. Would you, as a matter of fact, Mr. Sherry, sign a memorial to take the markets from the toll committee and hand over the management of them to the town commissioners?—I would not.

15,070. You have been attending the markets here for a good many years?—I have.

15,071. Can you give us an idea; just let us have your opinion how they are conducted?—I believe they are fairly conducted. I have no fault to find with them except the laying down of the carts on the streets on market days, to which I object. The carts are laid down opposite the shop doors, and they are an inconvenience.

15,072. But how long does this take place—I mean the laying down of the carts on the streets; does it not take place merely about six weeks in the year?—About that, when the potato markets are heavy.

15,073. You attend the Armagh markets regularly?—I do.

15,074. You buy cattle through the country?—I do at other fairs.

15,075. Have you any toll to pay in Armagh market?—None.

15,076. Is there toll paid in any of the adjacent towns?—No.

15,077. None in Portadown?—I do not attend Portadown market.

15,078. Is it the custom of yourself and other victuallers to buy cattle by weight?—It is not.

15,079. Have you, as a farmer, been asked to sell here by weight?—No.

15,080. And you never buy by weight?—Never, I might say.

15,081. Do you attend other markets?—I do. I attend markets in Clonbrough, Monaghan, Moy, and other towns.

15,082. Is there any provision made in those fairs for the weighing of live cattle?—None at all.

15,083. Is there a weighbridge in Armagh capable of weighing cattle, if such were desired?—There is.

15,084. Have you at any time been asked to buy cattle by weight?—Never.

Cross-examined by Mr. Gallagher.

15,085. Look at this signature again; whose writing is it, upon your oath?—It is my son's. I would not sign any such memorial.

15,086. I am not saying you would, Mr. Sherry; I am only wishing to glean the facts of the case. Your son, I suppose, assists you in the business?—He does.

15,087. Do you know by whose authority he signed that memorial, or had he any authority for so doing? —He had no authority from me at all. I was called upon by Mr. Gray to speak about the carts at the door, and I said I would certainly give my name to assist in having this grievance remedied.

15,088. Come round here, Mr. Sherry; is that your signature (*pointing to a name on the memorial*)?—It is not.

15,089. Whose signature is that?—It is my father's.

15,090. Your son, you have told me, assists you in the business?—He does.

15,091. With regard to the weighing of live cattle, do you not think it would be a proper thing to have a weighbridge in the market for this purpose?—It is never done. I do not think cattle will ever be sold in this country by weight.

15,092. Are they not sold in England by weight?—They are not that I know of.

15,093. Do you know of any markets in England where they are sold by weight?—No, I do not. I was in Manchester last Tuesday, and we sold 120 beasts there just by the hand. No one asks us there to sell by weight.

15,094. But all people are not as good judges as you are; do you not think it would be a good thing to sell by weight?—It is, I know, according to law, but it is never carried out.

15,095. (*Mr. Best.*) There is a weighbridge in the market if it is wanted for the weighing of live cattle? —There is.

15,096. You did not authorise your son to sign your name to this memorial?—I did not.

15,097. (*Mr. Commissioner Black.*) Have you ever attended Dublin markets?—I have often, but not lately.

15,098. Have you not seen them often weighing live cattle there?—People may do it, if they like, but it is not asked for.

15,099. (*Mr. Best.*) How many cattle do you dispose of in a year?—We dispose of well up to 100 a week.

15,100. (*Mr. Commissioner Black.*) Principally in the English markets?—Yes, chiefly there.

15,101. And you are never asked to weigh fat cattle? —Never.

15,102. Is it fat cattle you deal in?—Both kinds.

JAMES GARDNER examined.

15,103. (*Mr. Best.*) You were examined on the inquiry on the last occasion?—I was.

15,104. I believe you then handed in several documents relating to the arrangement and management of the markets in Armagh, and as to their condition and such like?—Yes, I may say I gave voluminous evidence then.

15,105. After that you read Mr. Peel's evidence before the Chief Royal Commissioners when sitting in Belfast? —I have seen it.

15,106. Had you notice of his going up to give evidence before that Commission; had you notice as secretary to the toll committee?—No.

(*Mr. Gallagher.*) The sitting of the Commission was convened by public notice.

(*Mr. Commissioner Black.*) The Royal Commissioners at the time were holding an inquiry into the condition of the Belfast markets, and Mr. Peel came up from Armagh, and gave some evidence placing before them, as he said, some facts that had not been previously communicated at Armagh. Mr. Peel wrote to Mr. Neale, the secretary to the Commission, and he and a deputation from Armagh attended.

(*Mr. T. G. Peel.*) The advertisement, sir, was a general advertisement, and did not confine the giving of evidence to Belfast at all. You will find you are in error regarding that, as it was a general invitation to those who had complaints to make, and as we heard the toll committee were going to avail themselves of the opportunity we went ourselves.

(*Mr. Commissioner Black.*) At all events you were justified in attending.

(*Mr. Gallagher.*) Thank you, sir. It is alleged we went surreptitiously.

(*Witness.*) So you did.

(*Mr. Best.*) You had an opportunity of giving evidence on the 11th June last, the same as we had. You were not, however, content with this, but went to Belfast, without giving us notice, and began this inquiry.

(*Mr. Peel.*) Yes, when the toll committee threatened to go we were obliged to do so. One of the committee, at all events, threatened to go and give evidence before the Royal Commissioners, and we have men here who can prove it. You threatened, and we availed ourselves of the conditions of the inquiry in Belfast, and went down and gave evidence. The toll committee have no right to say we went behind their backs.

15,107. (*Mr. Best to witness.*) In reading over Mr. Peel's evidence before the Chief Royal Commissioners, he stated, it appears, that some years you have taken off 6d. to carry out the terms of your trust. Have you at any time reduced the amount of the debentures?—As I said at the last inquiry, originally the debentures were 2*l.* Irish; but they were reduced by two separate payments to 1*l.* sterling.

15,108. On these old debentures six per cent. was paid?—Yes; they were issued at six per cent., and, so far as I know, they have always paid six per cent. However, at the Royal Commission held some time ago, I think in 1852, and of which I have no record, it would appear that it transpired in the evidence of the then treasurer, my predecessor, that five per cent. had been paid for some time. As I said before, I have no record of this, but I got it from the evidence placed before the 1852 Commission, of which Mr. Black has a copy.

15,109. How many old debentures were there?—Fifty-eight.

15,110. How many do the members of the toll committee hold themselves?—Some 16 or 17.

15,111. Of the eight members of the toll committee, how many are town commissioners?—Four or five.

15,112. And the remainder, have they ever been members of the town commissioners?—Most of them at one time or another.

15,113. Was the chairman of your board the chairman of the town commissioners?—He had been.

15,114. How many poor law guardians sit for this electoral division?—Four.

15,115. And of these four, how many belong to the toll committee?—I am not sure; but I should say about three.

15,116. These three are returned by the votes of the people?—I believe so.

15,117. One of these three is deputy vice-chairman of the board of guardians?—He is.

15,118. Who nominated these guardians?—I have no personal recollection.

15,119. Mr. Peel, in the evidence he gave before the Royal Commission in Belfast, was asked if it were the wish of the inhabitants of Armagh that weighbridges for weighing live cattle should be constructed, and he said there was no doubt about that. Has there been a request made to you, as secretary of the toll committee, that such should be done?—There has never been an inquiry for such a bridge so far as I know. There was an intimation from the constabulary when the Act came into operation, that we should comply with the Statute; but seeing there was no toll charged on cattle in any markets and fairs, they did not see that they came within the meaning of the terms of the Act. There is a weighbridge available; it is well constructed, and quite capable of weighing any fat beasts that may be put upon it. It is all nonsense that there is a refusal to comply with the wish of the people in this respect.

15,120. Have you ever received a requisition or memorial from the town commissioners, or from the people generally of Armagh, on the subject?—No, never to erect a weighing machine.

15,121. And you have never received such a memorial from buyers or dealers?—Never.

15,122. Some objection has been raised to your spending money upon the Infirmary and the Mall and other places; do you remember when the money was spent on the Mall?—The expenditure upon the Mall took place from 18[illegible] till 18[illegible].

15,123. There was no obligation with the Primate that this was to be done?—None that I know of; but it was an understood matter——

(*Mr. Gallagher.*) I must object to understood matters.

(*Witness.*) Please do not interrupt me.

(*Mr. Gallagher.*) I am interrupting not you, but anything going forth as an understood matter, or anything that is understood we should have some evidence, either a written document or evidence of a conversation with the Primate, that this money was to be expended, or that the toll committee were under an obligation to expend it.

(*Mr. Commissioner Black.*) Let Mr. Gardner proceed first of all.

(*Witness.*) That expenditure took place before I had any recollection——

(*Mr. Gallagher.*) Therefore you can give no evidence about it.

(*Mr. Best.*) He can from his books.

(*Mr. Gallagher.*) Produce the books.

15,124. (*Mr. Best.*) Show me the minute of the 18th April 18[illegible], just read it, and see if it will refresh your memory as to how the money was spent?—Yes, there is a minute about the Tontine Room passed on the 4th March 18[illegible].

15,125. (*Mr. Gallagher.*) Are these the treasurer's books you are producing?—It is the minute book.

15,126. Have you a treasurer's book?—I have not; perhaps Mr. Peel can tell you.

(*Mr. Peel.*) I think that very improper; unless I saw the book I could not have it.

15,127. (*Mr. Gallagher.*) Have you a treasurer's book?—I have not. There was no book handed me belonging to my predecessor as treasurer.

15,128. Was there any such book kept?—How could I tell you? I never saw it.

15,129. (*Mr. Best.*) With reference to the money expended on the Tontine Rooms, at whose request was it expended?—At the suggestion of the Primate.

15,130. At that time did the Primate offer to give you a new lease without any fine if this and other work were done?—Yes; the resolution went on to say that in consideration of the Lord Primate having agreed to renew the lease of the tolls for 21 years free of charge, his Grace having expressed a wish that larger accommodation should be provided for the [illegible] society and for other public matters than the present room could afford, and it having been suggested that the room should be enlarged to give the necessary accommodation, it was agreed to have the Tontine Rooms examined by an architect and have his opinion.

15,131. Have you any recollection, in reading over the minutes, of where the Primate requested or recommended that money should be expended on the Mall?—I have not; but it came through his agent, the sovereign of the town.

(*Mr. Gallagher.*) This is giving evidence of what happened before you were connected with the town at all.

(*Mr. Best.*) It extends simply to what he knows over and above the minutes.

15,132. (*To witness.*) You have not stated that of which you have no knowledge. What do you know about the Mall?—I remember the boundary wall being built, and I remember the men who built it; a [illegible] money there was also covered over, and these were paid for by the toll committee.

15,133. Have you any resolution on the books with reference to the money expended on the Infirmary?—I find an order for 100*l.* to be paid to the treasurer of the county Infirmary for improvements. Captain Pelton having intimated to the committee that the Lord Primate intended to renew the lease free of rent or fine, as had been done by his Grace's predecessors, so long as the funds were applied to local useful purposes.

15,134. With reference to the live pig market, is there any charge upon pigs on foot coming from Armagh?—None.

15,135. Is there any charge upon any class of live pig?—There is no charge except upon those coming in in carts—[illegible], as they are called.

15,136. And what do the toll committee charge for a crate or cart of suckers?—Twopence.

15,137. It is not 6*d.* per pig?—Not at all.

15,138. Mr. Peel, in his evidence before the Chief Commissioners, stated that 6*d.* was collected for every live pig sold in the market; is that so?—No, it is not.

(*Mr. Peel.*) I did not say so.

(*Mr. Best.*) If you look at page 15 of the evidence then given you will see that Mr. Peel pointed out there that the toll committee collected 6*d.* on every live pig sold in the market on Tuesdays, and that because they did so they were bound to provide scales, but failed to do so.

15,139. (*To witness.*) Are there any live pigs sold by weight?—No, I never heard of it.

15,140. And you have known the market for a long time?—Yes.

15,141. What is the charge made on pigs sold by dead weight?—Fourpence a pig.

15,142. Does that cover all the charges of the toll committee?—Everything that the toll committee derive from the market.

15,143. Is it not, as stated, that 6*d.* is charged on every dead pig in Armagh?—No, not, at all events, by the toll committee.

15,144. Do you ever remember a charge of 6*d.* being made on dead pigs in Armagh?—No.

15,145. Since you became treasurer it is only 4*d.*?—Yes, since I remember.

15,146. Within the last eight or nine years has the toll been taken off any produce coming to Armagh market?—Yes, it has been entirely removed from oats.

15,147. When was the toll taken off the oats?—In November of 18[illegible].

15,148. Do you remember what amount was allowed the man who had the tolls then rented on account of the toll on oats being removed?—The contract had been entered into at the 1st November before the committee had agreed to remove the toll referred to. Subsequently the change was made, and we had to modify the terms of the contractor's bargain by taking off 1[illegible]. In other words, there was an allowance of 1[illegible] off the price at which he contracted for the tolls in order to meet the remission on oats.

15,149. That brought the contract in that year up to [illegible]?—I suppose it did.

15,150. What was the return of tolls for 18[illegible]?—For the year ending November 18[illegible] the return was [illegible] 14*s.* 8*d.*

15,151. Since 18[illegible] there has been no toll charged on oats?—None.

15,152. The markets have increased in the meantime, and instead of their bringing in [illegible] odd when the toll was taken off oats in 18[illegible], the return was [illegible] 14*s.* [illegible]

15,153. Have you a return of the average tolls received for the past 11 years?—Yes. This was prepared for the last inquiry. The average for the 11 years up till 18[illegible] was [illegible]. I also prepared a three years' average, and for 18[illegible], 18[illegible], and 18[illegible] it amounted to [illegible].

15,154. The highest year was 18[illegible]?—Yes.

15,155. It was, I believe, [illegible] more than 18[illegible]?—It was. The three years I have given applied altogether to our own management and collection.

15,156. (*Mr. Gallagher.*) And the higher price refers to the time they were formed out?—Partly, and partly to ourselves.

15,157. (*Mr. Best.*) You know the flax market?—I do.

15,158. You know it is not rated now?—It has been struck off the rate.

15,159. Is there any toll on wheat coming into Armagh?—No, nor never was.

15,160. Was there a toll at that time on grass seed?—At one time there was, but it has been abandoned.

15,161. Is there any toll on flax?—No.

15,162. Who provided the flax market?—The toll committee.

15,163. At what expense?—Over 600*l*.

15,164. Was there any toll collected on flax?—Never to my knowledge. The flax market, to my mind, has been an incubus upon the committee. They have never received anything from it.

15,165. Was that the reason you asked it was to be rated?—Partly. The rating went on for a good while, but it was a trifling thing so long as we were subject to a moderate and equitable borough rate. When the rating was altered, and we were brought under the operation of Sanitary Acts, we were taxed for water in this market, and there was no water in it. We were taxed also for water in other places, even for those rooms out in the yard attached to this building. We were also taxed for it in the pork market, and in the hay and straw market, where we never used it. In fact, in some places the water is not even introduced, although it is charged for, and that being so I thought it a great hardship. I thought we ought to endeavour to modify the valuation so as to meet what I believed was altogether objectionable, and I submitted to the valuator some remarks about this modification. He believed the valuation of the flax market should be included in the valuation of 1884, as we derive no benefit whatever from it. It was merely an adjunct to a large valuation. That was my argument before the valuator.

15,166. Is the flax market still held where it was last year?—Yes.

15,167. The place is not made in the ordinary sense of the word?—It is not rated this year.

15,168. Do you know the price of ground taken by the toll committee for the purpose of enlarging the gardens?—Yes.

15,169. How long had the town commissioners had it in their hands?—It was lying, and no offer could be got for it.

15,170. Did you offer the place to be let?—We did.

15,171. Did you get a single offer for it?—No, not one.

15,172. How long did it lie useless to the toll committee?—Oh, for some years.

15,173. It was afterwards taken by the Messrs. McCrum and Best?—It was. We were in a difficulty for money, and had this piece of surplus land on our hands. We felt that we would either have to issue fresh debentures to carry out the improvements we had commenced, or let the land if possible.

15,174. Is it true, as stated by Mr. Peel, that the toll committee made 600*l*. out of this ground, and did not devote it to the proper purpose?

(*Mr. Peel.*) I did not say that.

(*Witness.*) They never made one halfpenny out of it.

15,175. (*Mr. Best.*) Was it an advantage to the toll committee for these people to take the land?—It was decidedly an advantage. They were the only public-spirited people who came forward to do good for the town.

15,176. This place is all built upon now?—It is.

15,177. And bringing in a considerable revenue?—It ought to be bringing in a large revenue now.

15,178. Mr. Peel says that while they lost money upon the past affair, they sold what we have been referring to and made 600*l*., and did not place anything of this to the credit of the Trust. What is your opinion of the matter?—They never made anything by it. I was struck by the implication of this evidence, and the gross calumny it was upon the toll committee.

15,179. Is it a fact that formerly you were not rated?—Long ago we were allowed to go free, but at that time the toll committee were giving money as free, as they could afford it, to the town commissioners.

15,180. At the present time, in taxes alone, how much do you pay?—The gross amount in 1883 was 64*l*. 7*s*.

15,181. How much of this went to the town commissioners?—That might be rather misleading, as I think there would be 20*l*. of the first item of 53*l*. that belonged to the previous year.

15,182. How much would the town commissioners be getting from you in this year?—It would be something like 62*l*. for borough and water rates.

15,183. You had the county cess to pay?—Yes, and income tax and poor rates.

15,184. And taking off the 20*l*. from the 64*l*. would leave 73*l*.?—Yes.

15,185. In 1887 how much did you pay in taxes?—The borough, sanitary, and water rates in 1887 amounted to 9*l*. 2*s*. 1*d*., but then there is what I took off for the succeeding year, and that would bring it up to over 40*l*.

15,186. The town commissioners therefore in 1887 got 40*l*. from the toll committee?—They did.

15,187. What did they receive in 1880?—They received 32*l*. 2*s*. 6*d*.

15,188. And in 1883?—63*l*. 4*s*. 6*d*.; the two years were identical.

15,189. What was it in 1884?—It was 27*l*. 5*s*. 5*d*.

15,190. In 1885?—62*l*. 8*s*. 4*d*.

15,191. As a matter of fact, you have been paying more and more gradually to the town commissioners?—Yes. In 1882, I might add, we paid 62*l*. 14*s*. 8*d*.

15,192. What taxes have you to pay in addition to the taxes?—With regard to the borough rate, if you go back to 1858, you will find that all we had to pay was 13*l*. 8*s*. 3*d*., but it has been increasing gradually ever since.

15,193. Of the moneys collected by the toll committee you have certain amounts to pay in the shape of rents?—Yes, we have to pay the Crown quitrent of 4*s*. 8*d*., and other items, amounting in all last year to 84*l*. 4*s*. 5*d*.

15,194. Of all the money that is collected by the toll committee, how much is paid away to the shareholders or debenture holders?—There was six per cent. paid on the old debentures of 10*l*. each.

15,195. How much is paid on the old and new?—There is 43*l*. 4*s*. on the old and 82*l*. on the new.

15,196. The new are at five per cent.?—Yes.

15,197. That is 127*l*. 4*s*. for interest?—Just so.

15,198. And the rest is devoted to the purposes of rates and taxes?—Yes, and the balance is laid out on the maintenance of the markets, such as necessary repairs.

15,199. Mr. Biggs is your chairman?—He is.

15,200. Does he go round the markets every Tuesday?—He and I have gone every Tuesday together for many years. Sometimes Mr. Ferris or Mr. McClelland goes round. Ever since the improvements began in the markets we have gone round, and a year or two before that we endeavoured to see that the collector was doing his duty in providing proper carriers and attending to the other business of the market.

15,201. How much does this terribly interested party—this chairman of yours—get for the interest of his money?—All he gets is about 13*s*. per annum.

15,202. (*Mr. Gallagher.*) Is Mr. William John Best a member of the toll committee?—He is.

15,203. Is *Mr.* McCrum a debenture holder?—He is.

15,204. Was there a lease of the ground you have spoken of to Messrs. McCrum and Best?—I believe so.

15,205. Are you aware of it as treasurer and secretary to the toll committee?—I am aware there were two leases made of surplus ground.

15,206. Did they pay anything for it?—No, no purchase money.

15,207. Were you here upon the last occasion when this inquiry was proceeding?—I was.

15,208. Did you hear Mr. William John Paul examined?—I think I did.

15,209. Did you hear him state that he made [illegible] out of these grounds?—I did not hear him state that, but I saw it reported.

15,210. That is in accurate what Mr. Paul stated, only that [illegible] was the sum spoken of instead of [illegible]?—I do not admit the accuracy of anything Mr. Paul states.

15,211. Is it because Mr. Paul says it, it must be necessarily inaccurate?—As a general rule his statements are so misleading that it is very hard to understand them. That is one of the misleading statements I refer to.

15,212. Do you think your board was acting within the terms of the trust in demising portions of the trust premises to their debenture holders?—If it is a question of law; I am no lawyer.

15,213. It was done, however?—I believe what they did was justified by the terms of the deed.

15,214. Did you state at the last inquiry that the case of a man called McGlinchy was withdrawn by him, and that he paid the costs?—So he did.

15,215. Will you look at that notice (produced); is that not from your own solicitor, Mr. Bell?—I do not know anything about it.

15,216. Well, it runs to the effect that notice is hereby given that the notice of appeal in this case—meaning the case of McGlinchy—is withdrawn, and that he would not be further prosecuted, and that the appellants were prepared to pay any costs incurred by the respondents up till the date of the notice. Are you aware, sir, that John McGlinchy got a dismiss, and that the notice of appeal was withdrawn, and the costs paid?—We were put out of court by a preliminary objection raised by Mr. Paul.

15,217. But I should know all about it, as I happened to be the solicitor acting?—Well, it must be another case.

15,218. So much for your own accuracy, Mr. Gardiner?—I do not set myself up as infallible.

15,219. But you should not make charges against others?—We are all liable to commit errors.

15,220. With regard to the debentures, are you aware of the terms of your trust deed?—Yes; at least I have read the trust deed.

15,221. You are aware it provides for the establishment of a sinking fund?—Yes.

15,222. Since the year [illegible] has any money been put to the credit of this sinking fund?—Yes, two sums of [illegible] each.

15,223. Were these sums at one payment, or were they contributed from time to time?—They were two payments; two instalments of [illegible] each.

15,224. Can you say at the time that these sums were so placed to the credit of the sinking fund, was there on each occasion a balance to the credit of the toll committee?—I could not say just at once, but I know the balance must have been small, with the prospect of its immediate ending to a considerable extent. As a matter of fact, since the last reduction of the value of the old debentures there has been a continuous outlay, and we have been constantly wanting. If we have a respectable balance at the close of one year, it is immediately taken away by the payments that become due.

15,225. Your present position is this, you have, on the one hand, paid off 13 old debentures?—I do not know that they are paid off. There were only [illegible] in existence when I came into office.

15,226. You have reduced their value from [illegible] to [illegible]?—Yes.

15,227. You have added [illegible] new debentures?—Yes; we have issued these at [illegible] each, bearing interest at five per cent.

15,228. You have increased your indebtedness by over [illegible]?—We have increased it by [illegible].

15,229. But I mean your indebtedness from the trust deed in [illegible], when there was a sum of [illegible] Irish?—That was the purchase money. There was also an expenditure amounting to a couple of hundred pounds.

15,230. Can you say what was the amount of your debentures in cash in the year [illegible], when the trust deed was executed?—I suppose it was [illegible]; that is what is in the deed.

15,231. I make it up as [illegible]; is that correct?—It may be.

15,232. What is your present indebtedness?—It is [illegible].

15,233. Then have you not, since the year [illegible], increased your indebtedness by over [illegible]?—Well, perhaps it may be. I never looked into it in that way.

15,234. Is that your idea of establishing a sinking fund?—We have made the purchase of the——

15,235. I say, sir, is that your idea of establishing a sinking fund?—It is not.

15,236. Is there any present idea amongst the members of your board of establishing a sinking fund or paying off the debentures?—There is the nucleus of a sinking fund.

15,237. What does it amount to?—To [illegible] or [illegible].

15,238. Was there a meeting of your committee held on the 1st November last?—We always hold a meeting on the 1st day of November.

15,239. Was there any motion proposed then by Mr. McCrum to establish a sinking fund?—There was, I think. There were both a resolution and an amendment, but I do not think either found a seconder.

15,240. Was the resolution to the effect that a substantial addition should be made to the sinking fund, and that the matter should be considered at an early date?—That may be right, but as it found no seconder, it is questionable whether I took any record of it.

15,241. You have nothing on the books to that effect?—No.

15,242. Do you remember a resolution to that effect being proposed?—I think I do.

15,243. But it was not seconded?—No.

15,244. And still you say that there is, amongst the members of your committee, the intention to establish a sinking fund?—I believe so.

15,245. Is that evidence of it, the want of a seconder for the resolution?—I do not say it is. That took place at the annual meeting of the proprietors. It was not at a meeting of committee.

15,246. Do not you believe, Mr. Gardiner, it is altogether illusory, I mean this sinking fund?—I do not believe anything of the kind.

15,247. The putting past of a sum of [illegible] since [illegible] is, I suppose, sufficient evidence of it?—It is an evidence either substantial or the reverse.

15,248. I suppose you believe you are keeping within the terms of your trust by so doing?—We are not stepping outside of it, at all events.

15,249. Is that your object in putting aside the [illegible]?—I cannot say.

15,250. You are the secretary, and should know the object of putting aside this sum?—I think it is very likely.

15,251. And not pay it off?—How could we pay it off with such a constant drain upon our resources, such a continual expenditure for public purposes. The committee has never, for the last [illegible] years, allowed themselves such a substantial sum as would pay off even the instalments of the debentures.

15,252. Do you think if some of these so-called improvements had not been carried out, there would have been ample means available to pay off some of your indebtedness?—If we had done so, what would have become of the town. The improvements were a legitimate object of the committee, the carrying of them out was a legitimate expenditure.

15,253. Do you think it was legitimate to expend the sum of [illegible] on the Hall instead of spending it for the benefit of the markets?—The markets were improved considerably.

15,254. You think it was more important, more beneficial to the town, that the sum of 950l. should be spent on the Mall than getting rid of your indebtedness?—I must explain, with regard to this sum of [illegible], that it was spread over a great number of years, and it was very important that that part of the town should be improved.

15,255. Has not your trust extended over a great number of years?—It has.

15,256. And is it not also desirable that your indebtedness should be extinguished and the money at your disposal legitimately applied?—I believe the terms of the deed have been properly complied with, so far as the expenditure of the profits derivable from the markets are concerned.

15,257. And the sinking fund is a myth, and should be so treated?—It is not a myth.

15,258. You have, on the one hand, reduced your debentures, and, on the other, increased them?—Yes, and got 950l. worth of value.

15,259. Have you any power under your trust deed to issue new debentures at all?—I believe we have.

15,260. Did you take the advice of counsel on the subject?—I do not know; but the issue of the debentures was made, I think, under legal advice.

15,261. Although you have undertaken this large outlay or liability, you do not know whether counsel has advised whether you have such power or not?—I believe the proprietors of the tolls have the power of empowering the trustees to issue new debentures for the purposes described in the deed.

15,262. I may tell you, Mr. Gardner, you are entirely in error?—Very well, I may, but I do not want to get into law.

15,263. Do you think an expenditure of 400l. on the market house clock a legitimate expenditure?—I do.

15,264. Although the committee are indebted to this large amount?—Yes; a clock was very much wanted here, and we provided an admirable one and a good bell, which I consider excellent value for the money.

15,265. Have you or your board considered whether these tolls should or should not be managed by a board elected by the people, or, in other words, an elective board?—The toll committee are an elective board, and I believe——

15,266. Never mind your belief. Is not the constituency very small?—It is not large, no doubt; but the toll committee comprise merchants of the town, who are most competent to discharge the functions of such a body.

15,267. You would not like to extend the franchise?

(*Mr. Best.*) If we proposed that you would tell us we had no power under our trust deed.

15,268. (*Mr. Gallagher to witness.*) Would you or your board be satisfied to see the tolls administered by a board elected by the people—thoroughly representative of the public?—Certainly, if they were properly elected. If we had a properly constituted board of town commissioners, who would be men of independence, and not under the control of any one individual. (Hear, hear.)

15,269. You would be satisfied with that?—Well, I do not know whether I would be quite satisfied or not.

15,270. Do you think the tolls should be managed as they have been for the past three years?—I think they have been very well managed.

15,271. Do you not think they should be managed by a popular body elected by the people?—If we were placed under a board in this town, that would give all the people proper representation, I would be quite satisfied. But, this does not exist; it is not so.

15,272. Do you know that the board represent every person in the city rated at 4l. and upwards; is not that the franchise?—Yes, it is; but if we had the clauses of the Towns Improvement Act in operation it would give a fairer representation to the different classes of the people.

15,273. What clauses would you like to see in operation?—Well, if I answered your question, I would be wandering into [illegible], and I do not want to do so.

15,274. Not at all, Mr. Gardner. What particular clauses of the Act of Parliament you refer to would you like to see introduced in reference to Armagh?—I will not go into them.

15,275. You object to the constitution of the board of town commissioners?—I do.

15,276. On the principle of Dr. Fell, I suppose. You have the rate book there; do you see the name of the flax market?—I have seen it; it is marked "waste."

15,277. Is that a fair and honest representation?—It is.

15,277a. It is a fair and honest representation and description of property that the flax market of Armagh is waste?—If we consider as waste what yields nothing, that is my definition.

15,278. Do you think that a trader in Armagh, who is making no profit out of his trade, would be justified in putting his house upon the rate-book as waste?—The cases are by no means parallel.

15,279. You told us a moment ago that because it was yielding no profit, it was represented to the revising valuer as waste?—I told the revising valuer that I believed it to be a hardship to be charged for borough, sanitary, and water rates, in addition to poor rate and income tax, on a property such as it was.

15,280. And it was owing to the account you gave him that he described it as waste?—I did not get it described as waste.

15,281. What description did you ask him to put upon it?—I did not ask him to put any description upon it.

15,282. Did you ask to get it so described as to enable you to get it marked waste?—I did not ask him for that description. I did not define the description in any way.

15,283. Well, what did you do?—I told him the flax market was a place that cost the toll committee a large sum of money, and that there was no toll or charge in any way for the goods the people brought to it. I also said that it is put upon the rate book, and this makes us liable for not only the town rates, but also the whole of the other rates.

15,284. The flax market is a very important market in Armagh, although not yielding any revenue?—It used to be a good market when flax was grown largely in the country.

15,285. Was it not owing to the exertions of the town commissioners that the flax market was revived in Armagh?—We had that referred to at the last inquiry. The town commissioners and the members of the toll committee also subscribed and got up premiums or prizes for the best qualities of flax in order to resuscitate the market.

15,286. Had that the effect of reviving it?—I believe it had to some extent, but I look upon such performances always to bring more or less [illegible] to their efforts.

15,287. Is this a true description of it, given by one of your members, Mr. Wm. John Best, that the town commissioners had made a great effort to restore the flax market, and their efforts were crowned with success, so that Armagh flax market became one of the best markets in Ireland?—It may be true, and I must say that Mr. Best would not have said it if it were not true.

15,288. And that is the board you would not entrust with the management of the tolls?—Yes.

15,289. (*Mr. Best.*) What is the date to which you refer?

15,290. (*Mr. Gallagher.*) It is 18[illegible]. (*To witness.*) Was there any arrangement come to under resolution of your board to sell the tolls?—No, never that I know of.

15,291. I ask you again, was there any arrangement?—There was no arrangement nor proposition before the toll committee to sell the tolls that ever I heard of.

15,292. Did no deputation on the subject ever wait upon your board from the town commissioners?—That I cannot tell; but there was a letter at one time from the town commissioners, suggesting the purchase by them from the toll committee when wishing to sell. We, however, made no effort to sell.

15,292. Did any person else make an effort to buy?—They wanted to know if we would sell, and our answer was we do not want to sell. In fact we had no power to sell.

15,293. I will give you the minute taken from the books. Here it is:—"Armagh, Oct. 27, 1879. A special meeting of commissioners was held this evening in the Tontine Room, a regular requisition, signed by seven commissioners, having been presented for the purpose, the only business being to consider, and, if necessary, to take steps regarding the purchase of the tolls. A deputation consisting of Messrs. Matthew Bell, W. J. Best, W. B. Jarvis, and Joseph Gillespie waited on the commissioners. They represented that the farmers attending Armagh Market felt that the toll on oats was a great hardship, and the commissioners, as representing the ratepayers of the town, should take steps to remove the burden. The several members of the deputation were heard, and on their retiring the following resolution was moved by Mr. James Best, seconded by Mr. Robert Gillespie, and it was resolved, 'That our town clerk write the toll committee in order to ascertain from them what sum they will accept from the commissioners for their and the other shareholders' interests in the tolls, or else lease the tolls in perpetuity, as the 41 & 42 Vict. c. 52 empowered the commissioners to take the same, giving the present interest to the toll debenture holders, which they receive, providing in the lease for the payment of debentures yearly as the commissioners may be able, with a view of extinguishing the levying of the tolls and attracting farmers to our markets, and that an answer be requested, if possible, for next board day.' The commissioners present at this meeting were—Mr. William Best in the chair; Messrs. James Best, Robert Gillespie, Thomas Marshall, R. Williamson, R. Walker, W. B. Jarvis, Edward B. Taylor, Henry Hillock, Joseph Anderson, Benjamin Robinson, all of whom concurred with the resolution. J. G. Winder, chairman."

(O'Fees.) Very good. Here is the letter I was instructed to write to the commissioners.

15,294. (Mr Gallagher.) Have you any minute asking you to write that letter?—This is the reply:—"Armagh, 1st Nov. 1879. Dear Sir,—I duly received your favour of the 27th ultimo, with its enclosure, namely, the resolution passed at a meeting of the town commissioners, held on that day, and addressed to the Armagh Toll Committee, which I brought before the committee at their meeting this day. In reply, I am directed to say that whilst the toll committee are anxious to adopt any suggestion tending to improve the public markets, yet, as guardians of an important trust, they feel the necessity of acting with care, to avoid a breach of it, and that as the town commissioners are anxious to acquire their rights they will, if they are indemnified for the expense, submit a case to counsel, setting forth all matters connected with the toll trusts as well as the object of the commissioners in acquiring their acquisition, namely, the abolition of the tolls. Should counsel's advice be given in accordance with the wishes of the commissioners, the toll committee will, with pleasure, entertain their proposal of leasing or selling.—I am, dear Sir, your obedient servant, JAMES GARDNER, Secretary, Armagh Toll Committee. To T. G. Peel, Esq., Town Clerk." I may add that the abolition of the tolls was the object at that time.

15,295. You are aware that in compliance with that resolution a case was stated to counsel, to the present Master of the Rolls?—Not by the toll committee. We do not know what was stated on the other side. We got no copy of what passed between the town commissioners, their solicitor, and counsel.

15,296. Your solicitor would not inform us of the case submitted to counsel?—I do not recollect very much about it. I know this, that he was asked to give copies of whatever deeds were required for the purpose, and he had a great number of these prepared, and at very considerable expense, but many of them were never either taken or paid for.

15,297. There was a special meeting of the commissioners held on the 27th October 1879, and the resolution passed that I have read to you?—Yes, and what I have read is a reply to that communication. No deputation, however, went from the toll committee to the town commissioners. Mr. Bell was never a member of the committee, and several others mentioned never were. You are in error about these men.

15,298. Are your accounts ever officially audited?—They are audited by the committee before the 1st November, when the meeting of the proprietors is held, and then they are presented at that meeting; I may say at every meeting which is a finance one, at every quarterly meeting, the accounts are thoroughly investigated. In fact they get a double audit.

15,299. Have you considered the item of 202*l.* 11*s.* 6*d.* for law costs; is it not a large item?—It is a large item, but there were several leases to be made out.

15,300. What leases?—Two leases for surplus land at the Shambles.

15,301. Did the lessees not pay for these leases?—Of course they did; but there were costs between attorney and client, and costs also after with reference to the acquisition of the property.

15,302. But did the lessees not pay?—Yes, I am sure they paid whatever they were obliged to pay.

15,303. For what were these costs then incurred?—If you require the items you can get them.

15,304. There is one other matter with reference to these law costs. There is in 1885 an item of 142*l.*, and it is entered Mr. Vogan, for cost of ejectment, 40*l.* What about that?—You ought to know about that, Mr. Gallagher.

15,305. I know a great deal, but I want this to go down on the notes of the evidence. What is that item of 40*l.* as costs of the ejectment proceedings in the name of Mr. Vogan?—That was for a virtual ejectment proceeding which Mr. Vogan was obliged to initiate with regard to overholding of one of the markets by Messrs. Carberry and Ballantine.

15,306. On the last occasion these people who were proceeded against were described as squatters?—I know; this is one of the comments our friend has attached, but they were not the squatters referred to. The squatters referred to were——.

15,307. Was not Mr. Sherry, who has just been examined, one of the squatters?—No.

15,308. Do you solemnly say Mr. Sherry was not one of the defendants to the ejectment appeal?—He was but he is not one of the persons referred to as squatters. The tender was so long holding over, and notwithstanding the attempt to keep the place closed, there were other persons who had not access to the consignments getting in one way or other and sending themselves down.

15,309. Whether he was a squatter or not, was he one of the defendants in the ejectment proceedings?—No.

15,310. I would ask you to think for a moment, and tell me seriously whether he was or not?—I know he was one of the defendants to the ejectment proceedings, but you are describing him as a squatter.

15,311. And so with Mr. Ballantine?—Yes.

15,312. And Mr. Carberry?—Yes.

15,313. And all of them are substantial men residing in Armagh?—I believe so.

15,314. And respectable men?—I believe so.

15,315. And men of wealth?—Mr. Sherry is a wealthy man, I believe.

15,316. Were the costs you paid for Vogan for the use of his name?—No.

15,317. Who was your solicitor?—Mr. Bell.

15,318. And for what did you pay costs for Mr. Vogan, except for the use of his name?—I cannot explain it quite to you, but it was in reference to the position of matters, that it became necessary for Mr. Vogan to take the initiative in these proceedings of ejectment.

15,319. Do not you know that the proceedings were initiated in the name of Mr. Vogan, and not in the name of the toll committee?—Yes, it was.

15,320. And was not the 40*l.* paid for Vogan allowing his name to be used?—I cannot say what it was for.

15,321. Was not the reason for using Vogan's name because the title of the toll committee was so bad that they had no hope of recovery?—I cannot tell that.

15,322. And even with the assistance of Vogan they did not recover?—We were advised it was better to compromise the matter.

15,223. Discretion was the better part of valour, and you bought them out?—Yes.

15,224. For the sake of accuracy, was it not yourself who used the word squatter on the last occasion, I mean at the last inquiry?—I think I did.

15,225. Was it not suggested by you?—It was adopted and repeated by Mr. Peel.

15,226. Were you not at the time referring to those particular persons named already?—I was not applying it to them.

15,227. In one of the questions put the last time you were asked to take one case, that of Carberry; how much did you pay altogether connected with that person? You had to take legal proceedings against him, and after several failures, but you say they were not all failures, was not the money paid on the ground that you had allowed him to enter in and remain there; in other words, it was paid for the recovery of your own property? That answer to that is, exactly, they had become squatters; what do you say to that, Mr. Gardner?—The report is incorrect; it sets forth what was not in my mind. The squatters were people who had got in surreptitiously, and were making themselves at home.

[*Mr. Gallagher.*] Mr. Gardner, put me, at all events, that all the [illegible] are not with us.

15,228. (*Mr. Kent.*) As to this terrible bugbear, the Mall and the expenditure upon it, did not that take place half a century ago?—It was coincident with the beginning of the trust.

15,229. What is the date?—From [illegible] till 1844. We spent then 970*l.*

15,230. Is not the Mall about the highest rated portion of the city?—I believe it is.

15,231. And yields a large income to the town commissioners?—The best houses in the town are there.

15,232. Mr. Gallagher spoke to you about increasing the liabilities of the commission; did you increase your assets at the time you increased your debentures?—We spent 1,463*l.* on the markets at the time we issued our new debentures; we expended this on improvements in the markets, and about the same time the purchase fee of the tolls involved an outlay of 1,463*l.*

15,233. That was about 2,900*l.* expended in three years?—About that.

15,234. What did you realise by the issue of the new debentures?—1,500*l.* and we expended 2,463*l.*, so that I think we were not insolvent.

15,235. Would the market square have been of sufficient size for the markets if you had not increased it?—Oh, no; the hay and straw market were much too circumscribed, and I should also say the pork market, and great inconvenience resulted from it. There were also a great many complaints about the blocking of the streets on market days, and those were the chief incentives for the outlay of money. We would not have laid out so much if we could have purchased a small quantity of land, but they were obliged to take the surplus land to get what they wanted.

15,236. What rent did you get out of it before Messrs. M'Crum and Best got it?—[illegible] a year.

15,237. What rent did they pay?—[illegible]; they gave a good ground rent.

15,238. It was unoccupied?—It had been so for several years, and they paid rent when getting nothing from it.

15,239. (*Mr. Commissioner Black.*) As I understand from one of your prepared statements, you farmed out the tolls down to 18[illegible]?—Yes.

15,240. You returned your receipts less wages?—Yes; what you see in that statement is the receipts less wages.

15,241. The wages are not included in the payments on the other side of the account?—No.

15,242. I see here you have an average for 11 years, and another for three years?—Yes. I did not know at first what you wanted, and I prepared it for 11 years; but as soon as I knew it was for three years I also made that out, so that you have them both.

15,243. This item of 18[illegible]*l.* [illegible]*s.* [illegible]*d.* is an average of wages?—Yes.

15,244. There are the rents running from [illegible]*l.* in 1876 to [illegible]*l.* in 18[illegible]?—In 18[illegible] the rents were [illegible]*l.* [illegible]*s.* [illegible]*d.* There was the quit-rent or Crown rent, the rent to Lord Dartrey, of [illegible]*l.* [illegible]*s.* [illegible]*d.* on the pork, hay, and straw market; then to the representatives of William Boyd, for the fowl and egg market, the sum of [illegible]*l.* [illegible]*s.* [illegible]*d.*; to Mr. Jenkinson, for weighbridge house in [illegible] Square, [illegible]; and to John Vogan, shambles and pork market, [illegible].

15,245. It was Mr. Vogan's name as landlord, I observe, you wished to see in these agreements proceedings?—Quite so.

15,246. How often do the toll committee meet?—Their stated meetings are quarterly now. There are, of course, special meetings called for any particular purpose, and as for the annual meeting it must be held, according to the terms of the deed, on the 1st day of November, unless this falls on a Sunday.

15,247. (*Mr. Gallagher.*) Mr. Jenkinson is landlord of a portion of the premises?—He is the agent.

15,248. Has he the house adjoining the flax market?—He has several houses. Part of the flax market was his property or that of some of his clients, and the transfer of it was arranged through his father.

15,249. He is one of the debenture holders of the toll commission?—He is. He is also a town commissioner and a poor law guardian. He is not on the bench yet, but I hope he soon will.

15,250. He has a house there?—He has, as I have said before, several houses.

15,251. With reference to the one nearest his own house, has it a door opening from his own house to the flax market?—It has, under the agreement, access to the flax market by the yard of the house adjoining it.

15,252. When did he get that permission?—About a year or two ago.

15,253. What is the object of this?—It was for the convenience of the house.

15,254. Does he pay the toll committee anything for this privilege?—Yes, 1*d.* per week.

15,255. I would not like to say it has been regularly collected?—It has been paid.

15,256. It is like a sinking fund?—No. Mr. Jenkinson is very good pay; he pays everything he has to pay.

John [illegible] examined.

15,257. (*Mr. Kent.*) You are extensively in the pork trade?—I do a little.

15,258. How long are you in the trade?—I am 47 years a buyer in Armagh.

15,259. Have you during that period observed the changes in the market here?—I have observed very great changes in the markets.

15,260. Have the changes been for the benefit of the markets?—Decidedly. Armagh used to be a very irregular market, but now it is a model.

15,261. What other markets do you attend?—Monaghan, Clones, Dungannon, and formerly Aughnacloy.

15,262. Is there different markets in the accommodation so good as in Armagh?—Not at present. The accommodation in Armagh long ago was worse than other places, but since the toll commission took it into their own hands it is a model market.

15,263. Is it a large market at present?—It is one of the largest markets in Ulster except Ballymena. Taking it all the year round, it is one of the largest, and I speak only of what I know.

15,264. Does it continue all the year round?—It does. Since the merchants have begun to cure with ice it is all the year round, although formerly pork was sold only seven months in the year.

15,265. Is there ample accommodation for buyers?—Yes, ample. Since the toll committee got it into their own hands it is well conducted and well managed.

15,266. You are a farmer?—I am, but not on a large scale. I have, however, attended the markets regularly, and I do not think for 47 years I have missed 20 markets in Armagh.

15,267. What is your opinion of the management of the general markets?—I do not know anything about it.

Cross-examined by Mr. Gallagher.

15,268. What do you mean by the toll committee getting the markets?—What I mean is simply this:—some time ago the toll committee set the markets to contractors, and they did not pay the same attention to it as has been paid since the toll committee ceased letting them and took the management in their own hands.

15,269. The toll committee were, however, the owners at that time also?—Yes, but they farmed out the markets by tender. A great deal of it is due to Mr. Biggs, who goes to the markets in all weathers, and sees how things are going on.

15,270. How long has that continued?—Oh, several years.

15,271. Since the agitation got up?—I am not an agitator. I am a peaceable man.

15,272. (Mr. Commissioner Bland.) You would rather see the markets in the hands of the toll committee?—It is immaterial to me, so long as they are well conducted or conducted in a proper manner.

15,273. (Mr. Best.) But could they be better conducted?—I do not think they could; in fact I defy them to have them better conducted.

John Sherry examined.

15,274. (Mr. Best.) You are a victualler and an extensive dealer in cattle?—Yes, I am.

15,275. How long have you been in Armagh?—I was born in it.

15,276. And have been carrying on business all the time?—All the time.

15,277. You are a large farmer as well?—I own a good deal of land.

15,278. You can write, I need scarcely ask?—I can.

15,279. Look at this signature, John Sherry, as attached to this memorial, presented by the town commissioners to the Royal Commission in Belfast, and tell us if that is your handwriting?—I did not sign that.

15,280. Did you authorise any person to sign it for you?—No, sir.

15,281. The memorial is as follows:—

"To the Royal Commission on Market Rights and Tolls.

"Memorial of the professional men, merchants, tradesmen, and other ratepayers in the city of Armagh.

"Humbly showeth—That your memorialists have seen statements given in evidence before Mr. Assistant Commissioner Bland when in Armagh, and in order to inform the Royal Commission beg to state—1. That we are in favour of the markets being placed under the control of the town commissioners, who elected by the ratepayers represent them at the municipal board. 2. That, without unduly reflecting upon anybody in person, your memorialists are of opinion that the irresponsible body called the toll committee, has not looked after the interests of the farmers, townsfolk, and others having business in the markets, and there is a strong conviction that so long as they control the tolls, customs, and markets, a serious injustice will continue to be done to the general public of Armagh and neighbourhood. 3. That your memorialists have observed that one of the objects of the inquiry is to ascertain what accommodation has been given in return for the toll collected. In former years the tolls were farmed out, and the markets were, as many others now are, held upon the streets; and it was the business of the lessee to make as much out of the tolls during the year he held them as he could, and that not unfrequently injustice was done to sellers of farm produce who were not protected or properly accommodated. 4. That memorialists respectfully but earnestly press the importance of having the markets placed under the control of an elected popular body, such as the town commissioners, who are responsible to the ratepayers."

Would you sign that memorial?—I would not.

15,282. Do you know how the markets are conducted?—I do.

15,283. And with reference to the cattle market especially?—I live convenient to the pork market, and I see a great improvement there. The farmers are well satisfied with the treatment they get in Armagh.

15,284. Do you hear any complaints about the management of the markets?—No; we buy a great deal of cattle; we have therefore a good knowledge of the people, and they all speak highly of Armagh. They prefer also to come to Armagh to sell pork.

15,285. You deal largely in fat cattle?—We do, very largely.

15,286. You know the market here, I suppose, very well?—I do.

15,287. Has any farmer ever asked you to buy cattle by weight?—Never.

15,288. Do you attend Portadown market?—I do occasionally. On one occasion I bought cattle by weight in Portadown.

15,289. Going through the country, do you buy by the head or by weight?—We never buy by weight, just as they stand.

15,290. Is it the desire of the victuallers that a weighbridge should be erected for weighing fat cattle?—I have never heard of it.

15,291. Do you, as a matter of fact, think it necessary?—I see weighbridges for the purpose in Enniskillen and Clones. I have been speaking to the parties there, and they say they get no cattle to weigh. There is one at Enniskillen in the cattle market, and they get so little to do there that four beasts would not be put on it during the whole day.

15,292. Would the bridge in the market in Armagh be suitable?—If a rail were put round it, it would be very suitable.

15,293. You say if a rail were put round it, it would be suitable?—I do.

15,294. What is your opinion with reference to the conduct of the markets; are they well or ill managed?—They are very well conducted. The farmers in the country, in Monaghan and Tyrone, are well pleased with the pork market in Armagh.

15,295. Do you think it would be for the benefit of the town if the markets were taken from the toll committee?—I think no one could manage them better than they are managed at present.

15,296. The people whom you know are well satisfied, and not anxious that the markets should be taken from the toll committee?—Yes. I believe, and so do the public, so far as I know them, that the markets could not be in the hands of better men than those who have the present management.

Cross-examined by Mr. Gallagher.

15,297. Whose writing is that in the memorial, if it is not yours?—I believe it is my wife's.

15,298. Do you not know for a certainty if it is your wife's?—I believe it is.

15,299. Did you ask her if she signed the memorial?—I never asked her, and she never mentioned anything about it.

15,400. You do not find any fault with her signing your name to the document?—I told her it was wrong to sign anything without my consent and approval.

15,401. Did you hear the memorial?—I did not hear it read.

15,402. Do you, as a matter of fact, think it would be for the good of the town—for the benefit of the people—if the tolls were placed under the management of persons elected by the people, either for the purpose of having the tolls altogether extinguished, or having the amount accruing from them expended on town improvements?—I could not say with regard to that, but I know from what I see that a great improvement has been effected.

15,403. Before anything was done, I suppose an improvement was required?—It was very much required, so far as I know about the markets.

15,404. But up till five years ago, when the town commissioners began to stimulate the toll committee, the markets were badly managed?—Ten or fifteen years ago the markets were not well managed. I speak more especially with regard to the pork market.

15,405. But I am speaking of the markets generally, and you knew them for a long time. Up till six or seven years ago were not the markets indifferently managed?—I believe the pork market—the market near where I live—was not well managed. The farmers were kept late at night, and they objected to this. They were sometimes kept till nine o'clock at night over the weighing of their pork.

15,406. Do not you know the toll committee allowed the flax market to be extinguished in Armagh?—With regard to the flax market I can say nothing, as it is not near where I live.

15,407. Do you know anything else about the markets?—No, nothing but about the pork and the hay and straw markets.

15,408. Where is the hay and straw market held?—In the pork market.

15,409. Is there accommodation for it there?—There is.

15,410. You know the fairs better?—Yes, but I know the markets too.

15,411. You have more to do in the fair?—I have.

15,412. Have the fairs been reviving within recent times?—I believe there has been no improvement since they first started.

15,413. When did the fairs first start?—I mean to say that I do not see any improvement in the cattle fair since it first started.

15,414. Is it more than 20 years since it started?—It may be, but I cannot say how long. I remember, however, when it was established.

15,415. Mr. Gardner says it is 60 years; is it so long?—It is not 60 years, but I cannot say how long. I cannot guess.

(Mr. Gardner.) There was a cattle fair in existence in Armagh at the time the toll committee was created.

(Mr. Gallagher.) Yes, on paper, but not in reality.

(Mr. Gardner.) As a matter of fact, it was in reality, and there is besides a record showing that it was the subject of occasional rehabilitation.

(Mr. Gallagher.) It was dead and buried.

(Mr. Gardner.) And there were premiums given sometimes for the best classes of cattle.

(Mr. Gallagher.) Who started it?

(Mr. Gardner.) I do not know.

(Mr. Gallagher.) Was it started by the toll committee?

(Mr. Gardner.) It was.

(Mr. Gallagher.) Have you a minute of the affair?

(Mr. Gardner.) Is it the restoration of the fairs of which you are speaking?

(Mr. Gallagher.) Yes, the recent restoration, owing to the action of the toll committee.

(Mr. Gardner.) Partly; they subscribed to it.

(Mr. Gallagher.) Did they subscribe as a board?

(Mr. Gardner.) They gave £15.

(Mr. Gallagher.) Have you a minute of it?—I have.

15,416. (Mr. Best.) Mr. Gallagher asked you if you thought the tolls would be better in the hands of the people; do you consider that the town commissioners represent the people of Armagh?—(Witness.) I believe there is a large section of them not represented.

15,417. I believe one section of the people is looked upon as a political body?—I do not take an active part in anything of the kind.

15,418. You mentioned that long ago some of the farmers were kept late at night on account of not being able to get their pork weighed in time; but the market increased since then?—It is greatly increased and improved.

15,419. And notwithstanding the great increase the people get away earlier now?—They do.

15,420. You remember a large sum of money being laid out on the markets?—I do.

15,421. And the accommodation then provided and the additions made to the markets was the cause of the farmers getting away earlier?—The farmers now all appear to me to be satisfied with the treatment they receive. They bring pork here from a mile of the town of Monaghan, and also from the County Tyrone.

15,422. If this sum of £1,442 had not been laid out on the markets, these farmers would not come here?—Probably not. No doubt a great improvement has been effected.

15,423. In Portadown is a toll charged on cattle?—Yes. I think it is 2d. on every animal coming into the fair.

15,424. Is there anything charged here in the cattle market?—Nothing.

SAMUEL FOX examined.

15,425. (Mr. Best.) Where do you reside?—In Killylea, about two miles from Armagh.

15,426. How long have you been living there?—I was born there. I am a farmer.

15,427. How much land do you hold?—About 120 acres.

15,428. What is your principal market town?—Armagh.

15,429. Have you been attending the markets there for a long time?—I have.

15,430. You know the markets well?—I do.

15,431. How long have you known the pork market?—For 30 years.

15,432. Is the market accommodation sufficient?—It is a great deal better than what it was formerly.

15,433. It is now a good market and largely increased?—There is beyond doubt a great improvement visible.

15,434. You know the hay and straw market?—I do.

15,435. It is also a good market?—Very good.

15,436. You know the flax market?—Yes.

15,437. Is there sufficient accommodation there?—There is, but the growing has dropped away in the country.

15,438. Can you give me an idea of how much the flax crop has dropped away within these 15 or 18 years?—I can form no idea, but, as a matter of fact, it has largely decreased. The flax mills are idle, and have been idle for a year or two; there is so little flax sown.

15,439. Do you know anything about the corn market?—I cannot say I do.

15,440. What about the butter market?—Well, I do not know very much about it.

15,441. You know something, I understand, about the corn market?—I do.

15,442. You fatten cattle yourself?—I do.

15,443. Have you ever been asked to sell any by weight?—I never sold any by weight.

15,444. Are the people about you in the country satisfied with the way the markets are managed in Armagh?—They are pretty well satisfied. Those attending the markets think they are well managed. These gentlemen here, members of the toll committee, go through the markets and see that all is right.

15,445. Yes, for which one gentleman gets the large sum of 15s. per session; are you aware of that?—I heard it to-day.

Cross-examined by Mr. GALLAGHER.

15,446. There is no charge whatever against individuals; we bring the charges against the toll committee, as a public body, in Armagh. We bring a charge against them of not acting within the terms of their Trust. Do you remember the Armagh markets prior to 1880?—I do.

15,447. Do you remember the toll on oats?—I do.

15,448. Was that a municipal toll?—It was.

15,449. Do you remember it being removed?—I do.

15,450. Do you know by what means it was removed?—I do not.

15,451. The pork market is the one regarding which you chiefly gave your evidence?—Principally.

15,452. You have been in the flax market?—I have sold flax often in it.

15,453. What is your idea with reference to the market?—I think it is well managed.

15,454. Since when?—It is well managed now. There are no tolls to be paid going into it.

15,455. Do you remember before the year [illegible] the flax market had gone down?—I believe it had.

15,456. Do you know, as a matter of fact, that it was almost extinguished?—Not altogether. Portadown got up an opposition market, and it took a great many of the Armagh people away.

15,457. A great number?—Well, I would not say a great number, but a good many went to it.

15,458. The markets here of flax became very small?—They did.

15,459. Was the flax market then revived?—Yes, there was an effort to revive it; but owing to the fact that not one-third of the quantity is grown in the country, it has dropped away very much.

15,460. Were the markets afterwards revived?—They were a good deal.

15,461. Have you been in the flax market lately?—Not very lately. I sold some flax in it last season.

15,462. How many carts have been in that market in one day this season?—I could not form an idea; there is very little flax going to the mills now, and very little grown.

15,463. Were you in the flax market the Tuesday before last?—I was not. It was in November I was there.

15,464. How long before that was it since you were in the flax market?—I might be once or twice in it during the year. I do not go there except I have flax to sell. I am generally more through the other markets, as they are in my way.

15,465. The potato market is held on the street?—Yes.

15,466. Any other market held on the street?—That is the only one.

15,467. (Mr. Best.) Is not the potato market held on the street only when the square is not able to hold them?—Quite so.

15,468. And only when the square is not sufficient to accommodate them?—Only then.

15,469. The markets are generally held in the square?—They are.

15,469a. You spoke of Portadown Market drawing the people away from Armagh. As a matter of fact, new markets do draw?—They do.

15,470. But afterwards they came back, and Armagh resumed its normal condition?—I believe Portadown is done with altogether now.

WILLIAM H. ABBEY examined.

15,471. (Mr. Best.) You have been attending Armagh markets for some time?—Yes, for 30 years.

15,472. You know the working of them?—I do, very well, indeed.

15,473. You know the accommodation that is provided in the hay and straw and pork market?—Yes, I do.

15,474. Is there in your opinion sufficient accommodation in that market?—I think there is at present.

15,475. Was the accommodation in that market sufficient previous to the enlargement in [illegible]?—Certainly [illegible].

15,476. The enlargement of this market was for the benefit of both country and town?—Yes.

15,477. You know the grain market?—I do.

15,478. And the grass-seed market?—Yes.

15,479. Is the Armagh grain market a large one?—I cannot say now; but when I bought in it, six or eight years ago, it was very large. I see it occasionally now, but I am not buying.

15,480. You have occasion to attend it?—Well, no. I cannot say I have, except I go to buy a load of oats for my horses.

15,481. You know the grass-seed market?—Yes; it is very large.

15,482. How do you think are the Armagh markets conducted?—I do not know any markets as well conducted.

15,483. Are the farmers satisfied?—They have every reason to be satisfied.

15,484. You have heard no complaints about the management of the markets?—None for the last five or six years.

15,485. Do you think they would be improved if they were taken from the toll committee?—I do not think I could express an opinion on that. I know when the Portadown Market was opened the flax men came from Belfast, and gave a higher price for it there than in Armagh, and that had the effect of taking the market from us to a certain extent. Portadown Market is now going down, because they could not continue to give these high prices.

Cross-examined by Mr. GALLAGHER.

15,486. Is the flax market of Armagh a large one?—It is.

15,487. Do you remember the toll committee of Armagh endeavouring to levy a toll on grass seed?—I did not hear of it.

15,488. Do you know anything about the grass-seed market?—I see it frequently, but that is all I know about it. It is, however, a large market.

15,489. Is not that all you know about the markets?—I have been both a buyer and a seller, and I should know something about them generally.

15,489a. Has the toll on oats been removed?—Yes, it has. Oats are sold on one day in the week, on the Saturday.

15,490. Since when has the toll been removed?—I think before I stopped buying myself.

15,491. There used to be a toll on oats, that is well known?—Yes; I tried myself all along to get it abolished.

15,492. And it was abolished?—It was, but I do not know by what means. I remember that when I, along with others, tried to get the markets removed from this to the shambles, the people were going to destroy us.

15,493. Who was trying to get them removed?—Several of the corn buyers, Mr. Riddall, Mr. Best, and several others.

15,494. Was Mr. Ferris not favourable to that?—I cannot say whether or not, but he is here and can speak for himself. I have nothing to do with the toll committee or the town commissioners. I am merely expressing my opinion as an outsider.

15,495. You do not know anything of the relative merits of the cases of the two bodies?—No, nor do I want to know.

WILLIAM SIMPSON examined.

15,496. (Mr. Best.) You are a large farmer and mill-owner residing in the neighbourhood of Armagh?—Yes, about a mile and a half from Armagh.

15,497. What is your valuation?—[illegible].

15,498. You are a millowner besides being a farmer?—I am.

15,499. Is Armagh your market town?—Yes.

15,500. How long have you known the markets of Armagh?—As long as I remember.

15,500a. You have been attending the grain market in Armagh for some time?—[illegible].

15,501. As a farmer, are you satisfied that it is properly conducted?—It is, as far as I know.

15,502. As to the grass-seed market, is it properly managed?—It is, as far as I know.

15,503. What about the pork market?—I do not think it could be better managed than it is at present.

15,504. You were in it recently?—I sold pork in it a week or a fortnight ago.

15,505. Is there sufficient accommodation in the flax market for all the flax coming in?—There is, indeed.

15,506. Are the most of the mills closed for want of flax?—The greater part of them is closed for want of something to do; I know myself of several that are closed for this reason. There might be 150 hands altogether stopped for want of flax, although I have not totted them up exactly.

15,507. You remember the time Portadown was started?—I do.

15,508. You remember the Belfast men gave a large price for the flax there, and this had the effect of drawing it away from Armagh?—I cannot say that, as a number of parties took flax to Portadown that I know, and not being satisfied with the price it was sold in Armagh afterwards.

15,509. You say the accommodation in Armagh is quite sufficient?—It is.

15,510. But Portadown injured this market for some time?—It did.

15,511. Has Armagh Market come back again to its normal condition?—It has, to some extent. I will tell you the reason why the flax market is not very large here. It is owing to the fact that most of the buying is done at the mills through the country. That is the chief cause, but besides that, the quantity is not grown at present in the country.

15,512. How long has the buying at the mills been going on?—As long as I remember.

15,513. Has it been increasing latterly?—It has. The greater portion of the output is bought at the mills, and is not allowed to come into the market at all.

Cross-examined by Mr. Gallagher.

15,514. Was not that resorted to owing to the imperfect management of the markets?—Nothing of the kind.

15,515. Well, to what do you attribute it?—They simply go round to the mills and buy the flax, that is all. I saw 80 carts laden with flax often leave my mills on a Monday. That does not take place now.

15,516. You remember the year [illegible], and the state of the market then?—I do.

15,517. There was a considerable impetus given to it at that time?—Yes, prizes were given for the best flax then.

15,518. Where do the farmers prefer selling, at the mills or in the market?—When they sell at the mills it shows that they prefer selling there.

15,519. Even if the markets were well managed, do you think they would continue to sell there?—The markets could not be better managed.

15,520. Do you know anything about the grass-seed market?—Not very much, except selling there once a year or so.

15,521. Do you remember that it was threatened with a toll?—I have not heard of it.

15,522. What would your opinion be with regard to the markets and their management if they were under the control of a body elected by the people?—I will not express an opinion on that.

15,523. You are not a townsman, and have not the same interest in Armagh as a townsman would have?—Even if I were in the town I would express no opinion on that subject.

Henry Scott examined.

15,524. (Mr. *Best*.) You are a large farmer, residing near Armagh?—Pretty large.

15,525. What is your valuation?—[illegible].

15,526. You have been attending the Armagh markets for a considerable time?—I have. I have been doing business all my life here; in fact since I was able to do business.

15,527. Do you know all the markets here?—I have done business in them all.

15,528. Do you know the pork market?—I do. I have been frequently in it.

15,529. Is the accommodation sufficient?—I would say so.

15,530. Is the attendance of the servants of the toll committee sufficient?—It is.

15,531. Could anything be done to improve the pork market at present?—There have been improvements made, and great improvements, especially in the matter of carrying.

15,532. You do all the carrying for the Great Northern Railway Company?—I do.

15,533. Is there sufficient accommodation for you as a carrier in the pork market?—There is.

15,534. It has been much improved within the last 10 years?—It has, very much.

15,535. Do you know the hay and straw market?—I do; it is a first-class market.

15,536. Do you know the butter market?—I do. I have known it all my life.

15,537. You have taken a great interest in the making of butter?—Yes, for a considerable time.

15,538. You have won several prizes at Belfast and other shows?—I have.

15,539. Is there sufficient accommodation in the butter market here for all the butter brought in?—There is ample accommodation. There is, however, one thing I would suggest with regard to the retail department of the market, that is where the farmers sell to the townspeople and householders, and that is that this portion should be covered as a protection from the weather.

15,540. The accommodation for dealers is sufficient?—It is.

15,541. The accommodation you suggest is covering a portion over for people who are buying small quantities through the town?—Yes, for household purposes.

15,542. What is your opinion with regard to the general management of the markets?—In my opinion they would not be better managed.

15,543. You know the grass seed and other markets?—I do. They are large markets, and well attended to by the toll committee.

15,544. You are intimate with a great number of farmers in the country?—I am.

15,545. What is their opinion of the markets?—They are well satisfied with the management of the toll committee. For some years past I have not heard of any dissatisfaction.

Cross-examined by Mr. Gallagher.

15,546. Were you always of opinion that the markets were well managed?—I was not.

15,547. When did you change your opinion?—Since the improvements were effected. I do not know how many years ago.

15,548. You remember going to London in company with Mr. Peel, the town clerk?—Very well; but I do not remember the year now.

15,549. Was it not in the year [illegible]?—I cannot say.

15,550. Did you go over there on account of some complaint about the Armagh markets?—I was deputed by the toll committee, and, in company with Mr. Peel, went over to see what could be done to meet the demand of the English public in the way of improving our butter.

15,551. Did you say you were deputed by the toll committee?—I understood so.

15,552. Who paid your expenses?—I do not know by whom they were paid, but I know it was Mr. Robert Gillespie who paid me. I think the toll committee paid a portion of the expenses; but, at all events, Mr. Robert Gillespie paid me.

15,553. You had to complain then as to the state of the markets?—It was the state of the butter brought into the market I complained of.

15,554. Had you anything else to complain of in the markets then?—Nothing else that I know of.

15,555. Did you consider them well managed before that?—Generally speaking, they were fairly managed. We went with a view to improve the make and quality of the butter coming into Armagh.

15,556. What was your complaint about the markets before [illegible]?—The first complaint was regarding the tolls charged in the fruit market.

15,557. Did you consider them excessive?—At that time apples were sold in small crauls representing about one-eighth of a hundredweight, and 1*d*. per craul was charged, which was looked upon as a grievance.

15,558. You considered that a grievance?—I did.

15,559. Are you aware it exists at the present day?—Certainly not. It has not existed for the last 10 years.

15,560. Do you state that positively?—Yes, the charge of ½d. a creel is not now existing.

15,561. It is 1d. now instead of the ½d.?—It is 1d. a hamper, bag, or package. The creels are abolished.

15,562. If the creels came to market, are they admitted free of charge?—I understand so.

15,563. And there is a charge upon every other package of apples?—They are charged in large baskets or packages.

15,564. Supposing the hamper is twice the size of a creel, and you charge 1d. instead of ½d., would it not amount to the same thing?—It would, no doubt; but a barrel basket would hold four creels and a bag would hold eight.

15,565. On the poor man there is therefore an exaction still when he brings in small quantities of fruit?—No, there is no exaction at present. It does not exist.

15,566. By whose action was the toll on oats removed?—I do not know.

15,567. Do you know that there was an agitation about it?—I do remember something about that.

15,568. Do you know that the town commissioners of Armagh were the parties at the head of this agitation?—I cannot say of my own knowledge.

15,569. (Mr. Best.) At the time you speak of the fruit were brought in in these small creels?—Generally speaking, they were.

15,570. Did ever you know a poor man to come to the market with only one creel?—No; the fruit market is abolished, and they are now sold to English and Scotch dealers in quantity, generally in the orchards.

15,571. There is very little fruit sold in the market now?—Not one-tenth of what used to be.

George Loughran examined.

15,572. (Mr. Best.) You are a farmer?—I am.

15,573. You are a dealer in meal?—Yes.

15,574. How long are you in the neighbourhood of Armagh?—Half a century.

15,575. You know the markets very well?—I do.

15,576. Do you know the oats market?—I do. I attend it regularly.

15,577. Is it a large and prosperous market in Armagh?—It is.

15,578. Do you know many farmers who attend the Armagh markets?—I do, a great many who attend the markets generally.

15,579. Have you heard any expression of opinion as to how they are managed?

(Mr. Gallagher.) I object to this, Mr. Commissioner. What is it really worth?

(Mr. Best.) Never mind. (To witness.) Have the farmers expressed any opinion on the subject?

(Mr. Gallagher.) I must object again to this.

15,580. (Mr. Best to witness.) What is the general opinion of the farmers with regard to the management of the markets?—I have heard no complaints. I have never heard them say anything about them.

15,581. But you have heard them saying they were satisfied?—I have heard them state that they had every accommodation.

15,582. Has the oat market of Armagh increased?—Well, it has held its ground.

15,583. Do you know the pork market?—I do. I know where it is held.

15,584. Is there plenty of accommodation there?—Yes, a great improvement has taken place.

15,585. You know the hay and straw market?—Yes, I do. It is also improved.

15,586. You know the butter market?—I do, but I know nothing about the management of it.

15,587. Would you be satisfied with the taking of the tolls from the toll committee and giving them to the town commissioners?—I hope that will not take place.

15,588. Why do you hope so?—I would rather see the markets in the hands of the toll committee than in those of the town commissioners, because I think they would not manage them so well.

15,589. What ground have you for saying so?—I judge them by their former works.

15,590. How is this?—I judge from the way they manage their own affairs.

15,591. You fatten cattle?—Yes.

15,592. You do not know of any person selling cattle by weight?—No.

15,593. Is there any use for a weighbridge to weigh fat cattle?—None.

15,594. Flax has decreased in the country?—It has greatly.

15,595. Is there ample accommodation in Armagh in the flax market?—There is.

15,596. Do you, as a farmer and dealer, think the markets well or ill managed?—I believe they are well managed.

15,597. Is there anybody in existence to which you would wish to transfer the management of the markets?—Not at present.

Cross-examined by Mr. Gallagher.

15,598. Who are the farmers who have expressed to you their admiration of the markets?—I could not name them, but they are all very well satisfied.

15,599. This is very general evidence. You are giving evidence as to the opinion of the farmers; can you not name a few of them whom you have heard express that opinion?—I could not name them.

15,600. I suppose they are myths?—No, they are not. They are all well satisfied.

15,601. Did you ever in your life hear a man make a remark about the markets?—No, sir; but they are all well satisfied.

15,602. You saw people coming from the counties of Tyrone and Monaghan, and they said nothing to you?—Yes, one man did. Patrick Mullan said he came here to sell his oats because he was well accommodated. That is the only man I had any deal with.

15,603. And upon Patrick Mullan's evidence you are called upon to give testimony with regard to the opinion of the farmers of and around Armagh?—There were different parties, but I do not remember their names.

15,604. Have the markets been improved recently?—The market places have.

15,605. At whose instance?—I do not know.

15,606. Do you know the flax market?—Yes.

15,607. Do you know that it was owing to the action of the town commissioners that it was improved?—I do not.

15,608. You are not aware of that?—No.

15,609. Are you aware that they gave prizes for the best flax coming to the market?—I heard so.

15,610. Is that one of the works for which you are condemning them?—No.

15,611. Are you aware that it was through the action of the town commissioners that the toll on oats was abolished?—I do not know through whose action it took place.

15,612. You believe that that improved the market?—It was to the benefit of the market certainly.

15,613. And it was for the benefit of the district?—Certainly.

15,614. And for the benefit of the town?—I do not know about the town, but it was a benefit to the country farmers.

15,615. Is not the bringing in of the country farmers to the town a great benefit to the town?—That may be.

15,616. Do you not think it is the object of the traders to bring them in to sell their produce?—Of course it is.

15,617. And has it not done that?—It has.

15,618. Do not you know this was brought about by the action of the town commissioners of Armagh?—I do not know by whose action it was brought about, but I know it has improved the market.

15,619. Are you in favour of popular representation?—What do you mean? I know I go in for each householder being represented at the board of town commissioners.

15,620. Do you think a narrow corporation, such as the toll committee, should have control of the Armagh markets?—I do believe they should.

15,621. That they may apply a portion of the profits for their own benefit?—I do not know what they do with them.

15,622. Should the tolls derivable go to the benefit of the town or the benefit of the farmers?—The town and farmers both.

15,623. And not to the benefit of individuals who are debenture holders?—Certainly not.

15,624. Would you be in favour of entrusting the tolls of the town, I mean of the markets, to a body of men elected by the people?—Certainly, a body elected by the householders.

15,625. Would not such a board be more likely to take an interest in the markets?—Of course they should take an interest in them.

15,626. Then your only objection is to the composition of the present board of commissioners?—Yes, that is it.

15,627. You would not have the same objection to another board?—Not if it were truly representative.

15,628. It is only individuals and not the system you object to?—I object to the system at present in operation of nomination by individuals.

15,629. What do you object to?—I object to parties nominating each other. I would like to see a thoroughly representative body.

15,630. Then if the town commissioners were nominated by the popular suffrage of the people of the town, you would be satisfied to transfer them the tolls?—Not at present, because I would like to see some Act of Parliament passed to give the people proper representation.

15,631. If the people are allowed to vote, are they not represented?—Yes, if each householder had a vote.

15,632. That is, you go in for an extended franchise?—Yes, either an extended or amended franchise.

15,633. (*Mr. Best.*) Is the present board of town commissioners a representative body?—No; nearly two-fifths of the people are unrepresented, and no one could call that body representative.

15,634. Is the board of town commissioners satisfactory to two-fifths of the people?—I think not even that.

15,634a. (*Mr. Gallagher.*) Do the members of the toll committee represent the views of the people?—They do well. The farmers are well satisfied, and so are the labourers and mechanics also.

15,635. You are satisfied to leave things just as they are?—At present I am.

15,636. (*Mr. Best.*) You do not like one-man nominees?—Not by any means.

CHRISTOPHER HAMPTON examined.

15,637. (*Mr. Best.*) You are a farmer?—Yes, and I reside about 1½ mile from Armagh.

15,638. What is your valuation?—About 100*l.*

15,639. How long have you been attending the markets of Armagh?—All my life.

15,640. Do you know the pork market?—I do.

15,641. What is your opinion of its management?—I think it is well managed. There is sufficient accommodation and sufficient attendance.

15,642. Is not Armagh pork market uncommonly well managed?—I think so at the present time.

15,643. Are you satisfied with the hay and straw market?—Properly satisfied.

15,644. Are you satisfied with the grass-seed market?—Quite.

15,645. What about the corn market; is it well managed?—It is.

15,646. Is the grass-seed a large market; is there good competition there?—There is. I always take anything to it which I have to sell.

15,647. You live between Armagh and Portadown?—I do. I have been in Portadown Market before now, but I prefer this.

15,648. You know the cattle market here?—I do.

15,649. Did you ever know of the farmers selling cattle by weight in it?—I never saw it; I never thought about it. I have read about it, but I never knew a farmer here wishing to sell by weight.

15,650. Is the weighbridge for weighing live cattle in the market of any use?—It may be; I cannot say.

15,651. You know the butter market?—I do.

15,652. What do you think about the accommodation there?—There is sufficient accommodation for the farmers. The attendance also is sufficient, and good buyers come to it.

15,653. Have you any objection to any of the rates levied by the board?—Not a bit; they are reasonable when compared with other towns.

Cross-examined by Mr. GALLAGHER.

15,654. Do you remember the markets here before 1851?—I do.

15,655. Were they in any way objectionable before that date?—They may have been. I think, however, they are better now than long ago.

15,656. Do you remember the rate being levied on oats?—I do.

15,657. Has not that been abolished?—It has.

15,658. Do you know at whose instance?—I could not say, but I know it has been abolished.

15,659. You do not live in the town, and of course do not care who has the management?—I am interested no way at all.

15,660. It is the same to you whether the toll committee get the benefit of the money, or apply it for the good of the town?—It is all the same.

15,661. (*Mr. Best.*) You think the markets are well managed?—Yes. I would not care for a change except it were for the better.

15,662. (*Mr. Commissioner Bland.*) If there was a change, would you like to see the farmers represented at the board?—I have not heard it suggested. I am not thinking about that.

15,663. (*Mr. Best.*) Would you think that the farmers were represented at the board if a change were made; would you give all the power to the men of the town, or would you have farmers on the board as well?—Oh, I would, no doubt, like to see the farmers represented.

JOHN HUGHES examined.

15,664. (*Mr. Best.*) As we all know, Mr. Hughes, you have been a long time in Armagh?—Yes, more than half a century.

15,665. You were formerly proprietor of the "Charlemont Arms" Hotel?—Yes.

15,666. And a large farmer as well?—Yes.

15,667. You were for some time a member of the town commissioners?—Yes, off and on, since 1848, but I cannot fix the dates. I was on for a period of three years, about 1860.

15,668. You have not been on since that?—Not since then.

15,669. You are well acquainted with the markets of Armagh?—Yes, in a general way.

15,670. You know the pork market. It is opposite some of your property?—It is.

15,671. You see what is going on?—I see it very often.

15,672. Is the pork market well managed?—I consider it very well managed now; it is wonderfully improved.

15,673. Would the same remark apply to the hay and straw market?—It would, more especially.

15,674. You remember the time the markets were improved?—I do.

15,675. You consider the toll committee laid out their money well at that time?—Yes. The new markets are wonderfully improved, and are rendered of more benefit to both town and country.

15,676. Do you know anything about the butter market?—I cannot judge as to its working.

15,677. You know the flax market?—I do.

15,678. Is the accommodation there sufficient?—More than sufficient now. I recollect when the market would not hold nearly the quantity coming to the market, but now there is quite accommodation for all the material coming to it.

15,679. Is that on account of the same amount of flax not being grown in the country?—Yes, it is in consequence of the decrease in production.

15,680. You know that many flax markets are closed?—I am not much through the country. The flax market here was one of the best in the north of Ireland, but the quantity of flax growing in the country is nothing like what it used to be.

15,681. You attribute the falling off to the decrease in the sowing?—Quite so. It is, in fact, due to two causes, one of which is the fact that much of the flax is sold at the mills where it is prepared; the other is the gradual decrease in acreage.

15,682. What is bought in the mills of course is not brought to market?—No. As one of those who took an active part in trying to divert the system, I know it; but the main cause of the falling off is that the flax is not produced in the country.

15,683. You know the grass-seed market?—I do; but I am not now taking an active part in it.

15,684. But you have taken an active part in growing flax and oats?—I had on my own occupancy 20 acres of flax in one year. In fact I had that much often, but within the last 15 or 20 years it has fallen off gradually, until it is much decreased at present.

15,685. You know the oat market in Armagh?—I do. It is held here at the market house, and extends along the streets if the market is large. As a rule, I hear no complaints about it.

15,686. There was an objection got up by the town commissioners, I presume, and they asked that the tolls should be taken from the toll committee and given to them; do you think such a step would be for the benefit of the town?—My own opinion is that I do not think we would change for the better. It is a very small matter what body manages the fairs, but I think the toll committee are managing them well. I see some good business men taking an active part in them, and they are, I believe, giving satisfaction.

15,687. Do you know the members of the toll committee?—I do some of them.

15,688. Do you know the members of the board of town commissioners?—Not all by name.

15,689. You know the majority of them?—I do.

15,690. Whether have the town commissioners or the toll committee done most to encourage the farmers to come in?—As individuals, the town commissioners are respectable men, but as a corporation I consider they are quite as exclusive as the toll committee. Of course I know it is invidious to draw comparisons. I do not think the town commissioners represent the bulk of the people of Armagh. It is a delicate question, no doubt, to answer, as they are worthy men; but, as at present constituted, I do not think they are more representative than the toll committee.

15,691. Do you, or do you not, consider that there is a large section of the people of Armagh not represented by the individuals on the town commissioners' board?—It is my opinion, from my knowledge of Armagh, that a large section of the people are not represented by either board—the town commissioners or the toll committee. The one is an elected board, but the members are so elected—it is so constituted—that a great portion of the people whose feelings, I understand, in the matter are not represented in any shape.

15,692. I believe at one time they were represented?—They were.

15,693. But not for the last six or seven years?—No. There was an interval when there were a few of those whom I allude to on the board; but I would like to see a representation according to the numbers.

15,694. Was that the time when there was an effort made to revive the flax market?—It was.

15,695. Was that the time the toll was taken off the oats?—I remember the board at the time an effort was made to revive the flax market, but my memory does not bring me back to the action with regard to the oats.

15,696. You know how the town commissioners are elected?—I know it is a £4 franchise.

15,697. It is by vote?—It is.

15,698. The toll committee are elected by the debenture holders?—The toll committee is not even nominally a representative board.

15,699. You know they are elected by themselves, and have not an interest in the tolls?—I do not know the system of election.

15,700. Do you consider that the charges levied by the toll committee on the several articles are fair and moderate?—I have not heard anyone complain. I did not make any inquiries, but from my own observations I think there is a great improvement in the system. I have formed this idea because the tolls were let some years ago to contractors, and I think satisfaction was not given; but since the committee have taken it into their own personal management, I see a great improvement, both in the order and system of things.

15,701. You are so well satisfied with the way things are managed at the present time by the committee, that you would not like to see them given over to the town commissioners unless some change were made in the constitution of that body?—I would not. I think a public board should be an elected body, but in the present instance I do not think it would be an advantage to change.

Cross-examined by Mr. Gallagher.

15,702. You were a town commissioner in or about the year 1880?—Yes, I was, some time about that.

15,703. Were you a member of the market committee?—I could not say. I know I took an active part in it.

15,704. Do you remember a committee being appointed at the time to look after the markets?—I do.

15,705. Was there a considerable impetus given to the markets because of that?—There was. Allow me to explain my recollection of this. I think it was not exclusively who brought that about. I think it was mutually supported by the committee referred to, by the town commissioners, and by the toll committee.

15,706. As a matter of fact, was not the idea originated at a meeting of the town commissioners?—If you go to the origin of the movement, I rather think it was not. I think it was originated by a man here who was subsequently a town commissioner, and he was elected into the body for the action he took with reference to the flax market. He was the only Roman Catholic in that body.

15,707. At all events, whether I am correct, otherwise or not, did the town commissioners take a great interest in it?—They took a laudable interest in it, and the townspeople, commissioners, and non-commissioners worked hard, called upon everybody, and raised a fund to provide premiums.

15,708. Was it afterwards that a stimulus was given to the Armagh markets?—There was a stimulus, but I think it was very temporary. The produce of flax had fallen off, the system of buying at the mills had gone on, and it was not so successful as we expected.

15,709. Do you know anything of the flax market at all?—No, not latterly; not anything special.

15,710. Would you be surprised to know there were 95 carts of flax in the Armagh market on Tuesday fortnight?—It is a larger quantity than I expected to hear of being in the market; I am speaking from general reports.

15,711. Taking the entire of your evidence, as a matter of opinion it comes to this, that the toll committee and the town commissioners, in your opinion, represent only a certain section of the townspeople?—That is my impression.

15,712. Would you be in favour of giving the tolls into the hands of a body of town commissioners more representative than the present body?—To answer that question as I feel, I do not conceive that until there would be a reform in the Corporation Act in the system of electing commissioners that it would have any effect at all.

15,713. No one would do more than enlarge the franchise?—They would do more. If we were under the Town Improvement Act, and the town was divided into wards, the different sections of the people would be represented, and until that is done I have no faith in an elective franchise.

15,714. Does your opinion come to this, that with a Town Improvement Act the town commissioners would be a more representative body than the present toll committee?—It is possible they would. The people would be represented. I need not say that the people would then fairly be represented, the dissension and difficulties would be removed, because then it would be in the hands of the poor people to elect their representative.

15,715. Are not the toll committee politically and religiously pretty much the same as the town commissioners?—Very much the same in that way, but I do not think they have an opportunity of putting themselves so unfairly before the public as an exclusive body as the other has.

15,716. They have not the command of such large sums of money as the town commissioners?—Not so large. I hold on that point that public money should not be applied for the benefit of any person privately.

15,717. Are you aware that a sum of 177*l.* is gone into the pockets of the debenture holders every year?—I do not know how much, but this I will say, that if I were individually interested I would not feel that it would be an improvement to change the system.

15,718. And you think the money is better employed going into the private purses of these gentlemen than if it were employed beneficially for the town?—I think you are putting a question to me rather difficult to answer. If I answered that question I might then ask myself what my opinion would be of the way other funds of the town were administered, and I would not like to answer it as I am not well enough conversant with one or the other to show whether there is any money unlawfully appropriated or not. But I speak of the system from the knowledge I have of the gentlemen who are administering it, and I think it is as safe in the hands of these as with those to whom you would transfer the tolls until you have properly elected bodies.

15,719. (*Mr. Reed.*) With regard to this sum of 177*l.* 6*s.* referred to by Mr. Gallagher, did you hear that they had to issue more debentures to enlarge the markets?—I heard this being referred to when I came into the room.

15,720. Do you think this was right?—I should say so. To do what has been done in providing new markets and improving others is not badly laid out money. The new markets are a vast improvement, and a credit to the town.

15,721. Do you know of any body which could be raised that would manage the tolls more satisfactorily than the toll committee?—I have not gone into the matter minutely, but, as far as I can see, I am satisfied with the present management.

Patrick McK[illegible] examined.

15,722. (*Mr. Reed.*) You live in Armagh?—Yes, I have lived here for some years.

15,723. How long have you been attending the markets here?—All that time. I know the city of Armagh for 25 years and more, and I know the markets for the same time.

15,724. Do you live close to the pork market?—Yes, close beside it.

15,725. You know the hay and straw market?—I do.

15,726. In your avocation you come frequently across people attending the markets?—Yes, I know a great many attending the Armagh markets. I know people coming here from Castleblayney and [illegible], the former of which is 10 Irish miles distant, and the latter 13. People come from those districts to the markets here.

15,727. Did you ever hear them express any opinion with regard to the management of the markets?—They say they are pleased to come all the way as they are well accommodated.

15,728. You know the sheds at the markets?—I do.

15,729. Is there sufficient accommodation there for all the material coming in?—There is.

15,730. Is there sufficient accommodation for people taking hay and weighing it off?—There is.

15,731. If the markets had not been enlarged that accommodation could not have been given?—No. With regard to the sheds, I saw a man from the county Antrim through them recently, and he said they were the best sheds he had seen anywhere.

15,732. Did you sign the memorial asking that the tolls should be taken from the toll committee and given over to the management of the town commissioners?—No.

15,733. Would you sign such a memorial?—I would not.

15,734. Did you authorise any person to sign it for you?—I did not, I never heard of it.

15,735. Is that your handwriting (pointing to a name on the memorial referred to)?—No.

15,736. You say you did not authorise any person to sign it for you?—I did not.

15,737. In your contact with the farmers round about, have you heard any suggestions made as to the improvement of the markets?—I never heard any suggestions made as to the improvement of the markets. The people are well pleased with the treatment they receive in Armagh.

Cross-examined by Mr. Gallagher.

15,738. Who signed this memorial for you?—I believe it was my wife, I heard from her it was. She did not know what it meant, it was only within the last few days I heard it was she.

15,739. You do not approve of this?—If you mean the memorial, I do not. I am satisfied with the way the markets are going on. I have no right to complain.

15,740. Do you do much business there?—I do a good deal in selling pork and turnips.

15,741. You have often business in the pork market?—I have seen business transacted in the pork market. I might be once or twice during the year in the pork market on my own business.

15,742. Had you business once there last year?—I had. I might be twice a year there.

15,743. Would that be the oftenest you had business in this market?—I had business in the market more than once or twice during the year, but I was there twice on my own business. I am often in the hay and straw market on my own business. I have bought 100 tons of hay there in a year.

15,744. Are you a farmer?—I am.

15,745. How much land do you hold?—About 20 or 25 acres. I occupy this land, I hold it from year to year. I hold it for the owner.

15,746. Do you, sir, hold an acre of land as a farmer?—I have no land of my own. I do not hold it from year to year, I occupy it from year to year.

15,747. Do you drive a car?—I do not drive a car.

15,748. Have you a car?—I have, but my men drive them.

15,749. You have cars, and you buy hay to feed your horses?—Yes, and I feed cows also.

15,750. (*Mr. Reed.*) The 100 tons of hay you bought was not to feed your cows?—No, it was as a dealer.

15,751. You see the markets of Armagh often?—I do.

15,752. You keep a yard for horses, I suppose you hear the opinion of the farmers as they come into your place?—Yes, and they say they are very well pleased. The presence of Mr. Biggs and Mr. Gardner in the markets is a guarantee that the people will be well treated. These gentlemen are there constantly, almost every market day.

THOMAS DOLAN examined.

15,753. (Mr. Reid.) You signed the petition?—I did.

15,754. Who brought it to you?—Mr. Thomas Brooks.

15,755. What did he tell you?—He said it was for the general good of the town.

15,756. It was on his recommendation you signed it?—It was.

CROSS-EXAMINED by Mr. GILLESPIE.

15,757. You can read?—I can.

15,758. Did you read the memorial?—I may have read some of it, but not all.

15,759. Do you mean to say you signed a memorial which you had never read, and of the contents of which you were ignorant?—I signed it on Mr. Brook's word.

15,760. What did Brook's tell you?—I cannot say, exactly.

15,761. Do not you know it was to take the markets from the toll committee and give them to the town commissioners?—I do not like any one to put words in my mouth. I never thought anything about the memorial he asked me to sign it as it was for the good of the town, and that being so, I signed it at once, as I would sign anything with that object.

15,762. Are you of opinion it would improve the trade of the town if the management of the markets were handed over to the town commissioners?—I do not know, but according to general report it would not.

15,763. Have you yourself formed any opinion?—None whatever.

15,764. Your mind is a complete blank as to that, I suppose?—Very well, you may say so.

15,765. Have you formed any opinion on the subject at all?—I cannot say I have; I cannot say I have formed a strong opinion. You asked me one question, if the markets were handed over to the town commissioners would that be for the benefit of the town, well, I think it would not.

15,766. The toll debenture holders being a permanent body, do you think it is for the benefit of the town that they should hold the markets?—I cannot say.

15,767. Are you in favour of elective representation for the distribution of the tolls of the town?—If I thought it was for the benefit of the town in general, I would.

15,768. But do you think it would be for the benefit of the town to hand over the tolls to the town commissioners?—Well, to hand them over to the town commissioners, I do not think it would be for the benefit of the town.

15,769. If we had an elective body representative of the views of the entire citizens, would that be a proper body to hand over the tolls to?—It might, if the body were elected by the householders. It might, or it might not.

15,770. Then it comes to this, you have no opinion on the subject?—Very likely.

ROBERT GILLESPIE examined.

15,771. (Mr. Reid.) You are a merchant residing in this town?—Yes.

15,772. And a member of the toll committee?—Yes, and a member of the toll committee.

15,773. Were you formerly a member of the board of town commissioners?—I was.

15,774. How long is it since you resigned your seat at the board?—I cannot exactly say; it might be seven years.

15,775. You are an extensive buyer in the grass-seed market?—Yes.

15,776. Have you been so for many years?—Since its commencement.

15,777. The Armagh grass-seed market is improving?—It is.

15,778. At the present stage, do you consider it is a first class market?—I do. I consider it one of the best in Ireland, if not the best.

15,779. Who are the principal buyers in the market?—From Belfast, we have Mr. Cleeland, Lytle, and others; from Banbridge, we have the Martin's, and other men ranged along the country, in addition to our local buyers.

15,780. What quantity of grass seed did you buy during last season?—About 7,000l. worth this last season, or a quantity about 700 tons.

15,781. What quantity is brought annually to the market?—About 1,000 tons every season.

15,782. You remember when this grass seed market was not the market it is now?—I do.

15,783. And what did you do to get it improved?—I bought seed in Newry then and some in Portadown, which at that time was flourishing. The bulk of the seed growing here went to Portadown, and I went there also and saw how things were being managed. I gave the Armagh men 6d. per cwt. more for their seed for the purpose of making them draw it back to Armagh.

15,784. Had that a tendency to make the people go to Armagh market?—Well, I think it had, as they got 6d. per cwt. more.

15,785. That improved the Armagh market?—Of course it did.

15,786. Is Armagh better now than Portadown?—It is much larger. There is more seed offered here in the season than in Portadown. They have but a one day market, but we have two.

15,787. There is no toll on grass seed in Armagh?—None. They may weigh where they like.

15,788. It is not compulsory on the farmers to weigh in the market?—It is not.

15,789. Do you find it compulsory on the farmers to weigh in the market in some other towns?—It is not compulsory in Portadown, but it is in Newry and Belfast. In this district Armagh, Portadown, and Newry compete for the produce. There is the Market Hill district between Newry and Armagh, and the Rich Hill district between Portadown and Armagh.

15,790. The toll committee offer greater advantages to the farmers with reference to the grass-seed market than are offered in other places?—They do, and besides if it is sold in Newry by sample, it is bound to be weighed in their market and paid for. It is the same in many other places.

15,791. In Belfast market is it a fact that any person bringing in a load at all is obliged to pay the toll?—They must.

15,792. The merchant may buy by sample, but when it is delivered toll must be paid?—The merchant must get permission from the town council to take seed without going to the market, and they must refund to the town council the toll chargeable thereon the same as if it had been in the market.

15,793. Your evidence generally is that there is more encouragement here in Armagh for the farmers than any market you go to?—There is.

15,794. You go about the pork market in Armagh?—I do.

15,795. It is a large and flourishing market?—It is.

15,796. You live close to it?—I do.

15,797. On the same day as it is held there is also a hay and straw market?—Yes.

15,798. I suppose you come in contact more with the farmers than most men?—I know I come very largely in contact with them.

15,799. Have you heard any of the farmers expressing their dissatisfaction with the grass seed, hay, or straw or pork markets?—No. On the other hand, it is no uncommon thing to hear at our stores, some days during the season, 20 or 30 cars from Monaghan, and the district. It speaks well for our markets when it pays men to come to them all the way from Monaghan.

15,800. With reference to the pork market, how is it managed?—It is managed very well. There does not seem to be any complaint, for the inspector seems to be an active man, and he reports and sets the farmers right at once.

15,801. You formerly bought a good deal of corn?—Yes.

15,802. There is no toll on it at present?—None.

15,803. You were one of those who tried to get the toll taken off?—I was.

15,804. Is the corn market prosperous?—It is; but it has not been so large this year as the quantity of oats sown would lead one to expect. This arises from the farmers, owing to the low prices offered, using a large quantity for their own use. The country mills have been deluged with oats this year, sent there to be crushed up for the farmers.

15,805. Is there any toll on oats in Newry?—Yes, all the oats coming into Newry market must be weighed there.

15,806. Is that the case in Armagh?—No.

15,807. What have they to pay for the weighing of oats in Newry?—I have got the list of charges from under the hand of the town clerk of Newry. I wrote to Mr. Dodd, who is a member of the corporation there, and I told him we had a little agitation about the market charges in Armagh, the charges on farm produce coming in, and he forwarded me a list of what is paid there. Oats are charged 2d. per bag, and if over 2 cwt. 7 lbs., 3d.; grass seed, 1½d. per bag; wheat, 2d. per bag; if over 2 cwt. 7 lbs., 3d.; pork, 4d. per pig; live pigs, 1d.; suckers, ½d. each; lump butter, 1½d. per piece; print, 1d. per 4 lbs.; eggs, 1d. per 120; potatoes, 4d. per load, 1d. per bag, and 1½d. if over 2 cwt.; fowl, 2d. per dozen; plums, 4d. and 6d. per load; hay and straw, oats, turnips, mangold, and carrots, 4d. per load; turf, large load, 2d.; ass load, 1d.; milk, per churn, 1d. These tolls include weighing, where it is required, except in the case of butter, where an additional charge is made for weighing.

15,808. Have you gone over the list of charges in Newry, and compared it with those of Armagh?—I have, and they are much lower here.

15,809. Have you compared the Newry and other lists with the list made out by the toll committee?—I have, and Armagh is more advantageous to the farmer than any other market about.

15,810. You remember the toll committee enlarging the markets?—I do.

15,811. Was it necessary that they should then issue new debentures to enable them to do so?—It was necessary, at all events, that the market should be enlarged to accommodate the stuff coming in, or if not the market would have gone down.

15,812. If the new debentures were issued for this purpose, do you think it was a proper course to adopt?—Certainly.

15,813. Are all the markets in Armagh popular with the farmers?—They are.

15,814. You know the cow fair?—I am not much in the fair, but I have a large connexion of friends who feed cattle very largely.

15,815. Do you think it would be for the benefit of the town if the tolls were transferred to the town commissioners?—I do not know they would be so well managed.

Cross-examined by Mr. Gallagher.

15,816. You are a member of the government now?—Yes, and you are in the opposition.

15,817. Have your views changed since you were in the opposition?—Not one bit.

15,818. You are in favour of having the tolls as low as possible?—Certainly.

15,819. I suppose, any profits made from the tolls you would like to see go to the benefit of the town?—I would.

15,820. Having regard to that, and considering that the toll committee was in debt to the extent of 1,700l., would you consider the expenditure of 800l. on the Mall a prudent, or proper expenditure?—I do not know in what state the Mall was when the expenditure was made.

15,821. No matter what state it was in, would you consider it a prudent expenditure?—I look upon it as an ornament to the Mall or to the town.

15,822. I know, but do you think the object of the toll committee is to ornament the town?—It ought to improve it.

15,823. It ought to improve the markets chiefly?—Yes, the markets first.

15,824. Was it prudent to expend 800l. in ornamenting the town?—I would have liked to have seen what state the Mall was in. The Mall is an ornament to the town, and it is worthy of support from the town.

15,825. Should a man in debt begin to ornament his premises before he clears off that debt?—I believe in every person paying off his debt.

15,826. You have heard the toll committee were in debt to the extent of 1,700l., and having regard to that, do you think it prudent to expend 800l. in ornamenting the town?—Yes, if they derived a revenue from the town. What was done was not a cause of injury to the markets, it was an improvement.

15,827. Does the same remark apply to what was done for the Tontine Rooms?—I know nothing about them. The Tontine Rooms are a public accommodation, and we have no public hall in Armagh suitable for public meetings and such like.

15,828. Is not this room we are in a better room?—It is not.

15,829. Is not this room itself a larger and better room?—No, it is not. No doubt every person forms his own idea about things, but the Tontine is a better room than this in every way.

15,830. We had this room in the town at all events and notwithstanding this a sum of 800l. was spent on the Tontine?—I do not know anything about that expenditure.

15,831. Was it a legitimate expenditure, considering the committee were so much in debt?—I would go in for building a good public room for Armagh.

15,832. And float new debentures for it?—Well, I do not know about that.

15,833. You were a town commissioner at one time?—I was.

15,834. The grass-seed market, has that been a success owing to the action of the toll committee, or despite the action of the toll committee?—Despite the action.

15,835. Did not the toll committee endeavour to levy a toll on grass seed?—They did, or at least the then contractor, for the markets were then farmed out, did. Mr. Calvert was the contractor at that time.

15,836. And he endeavoured to levy a toll on grass seed?—I am aware of what occurred, I went down to the gates where the carts were stopped, and I said to them, to go on, and I would be responsible for the action taken against them, if any.

15,837. Was any action taken against them?—I am not quite clear as to that.

15,838. Did the toll committee support Calvert?—I do not know, but I know the whole thing was ultimately abandoned.

15,839. I think Mr. Best supported him?—He did.

15,840. Was it through your action or that of Mr. Best, that the idea of imposing a toll on grass seed was abandoned?—I do not think it was ever established. It was abandoned to my cost. I took decided action in the matter, and I would do the same to-morrow.

15,841. You believed, I suppose, they had no power?—I believed they had no power, because it was a new thing.

15,842. And that view of the matter was supported by the present Master of the Rolls? Look at this memorial, Mr. Gillespie, is that your signature?—It is my brother's.

15,843. Were you aware he signed this memorial?—I do not know yet what the memorial is.

15,844. It is your brother's signature you say; is he not in partnership with you?—Yes.

15,845. I will read you a memorial received in 1881 by the town commissioners (having read the memorial). Do you recollect that?—No, but I am quite sure it is quite correct, you were one of the commissioners to whom it was addressed.

15,846. We were both commissioners?—We were.

15,847. Are you aware of elective representation for the management of the tolls?—You would have to define what you mean by this. I have heard a great many questions asked about this to-day, and I have heard a great many answers given, but to my mind it would be necessary for the governing body of the markets to have an interest in them so as to bring them in contact with the people coming to the markets.

15,848. Would not a body like the town commissioners have such an interest?—There is no one would have such an interest except one who came directly in contact with the farmer himself in the way of purchasing from him.

15,849. Are not the town commissioners of the same class of the population as the toll committee?—They are not.

15,850. What is the difference?—The difference is members of the toll committee buy the produce coming into the markets; but, as far as I know, there is no member of the board of town commissioners, or very few, who do so. Some may buy from the farmer directly in the market, but it will be only a load of hay or oats for his own horses.

15,851. You would then be in favour of no board except one composed of members who bought in the markets themselves?—I will give you the grass seed question as an illustration. If I had not had that interest in the grass-seed market, the Armagh people would probably not have had it yet. I do not care for such a matter, but I took such an interest in it that I was bound to make the remark.

15,852. Is it not a mere accident that you were buying grass seed, and at the same time that you were a member of the toll committee?—I was buying grass seed 20 years before I was a member of the committee. It is a mere accident, I am a member of the toll committee at all.

15,853. Well, I suppose a board may be so composed that its members will be brought into contact with the farmers and the markets?—In that case the market would be a success.

15,854. Having regard to the toll committee's position, is it a desirable body to have control of the markets?—Yes; until you provide a better.

15,855. You are not in favour, are you—or are you not in favour of elective representation?—I have always been in favour of it.

15,856. Would you be in favour of elective representation with a more extended franchise?—I believe we will have household suffrage by and by. Whether we are in favour of it or not, it will come at any rate. I mean the municipal franchise will be reduced to the parliamentary.

15,857. With a more extended franchise, would you be in favour of handing over the markets to the management of the town commissioners?—You could not have a more extended franchise with the present rating, you would require to have it reduced.

15,858. But on a more extended franchise, would you be in favour of the town commissioners having control of the markets?—As a truth, large bodies very seldom work very well, when I want to get anything well done, I like to have very few about it.

15,859. There are a large number of debenture holders?—But they are not all members of the toll committee.

15,860. But they have a right to elect?—They have. If you take the cases of Newry and Portadown, where the markets are in the hands of corporations, the tolls are in excess of what they are here.

15,861. They had, however, to begin and make new markets?—They had the same thing to do here. In my memory besides they have made great improvements here.

15,862. Is it idle to compare what has been done in Newry with what has been done in Armagh?—I know there are old markets in Newry 150 years old.

15,863. Four times as much have been expended in Newry as in Armagh?—You are speaking now of the markets near the railway station, but they have old markets also in which the toll is the same as the new.

15,864. Of course they must complain?—You observed to several witnesses, and asked them did they object to the toll committee putting a large sum of money into their own pockets. Well, I am one of the debenture holders, 15*l.* worth, and I get 15*s.* per annum for one year. That is the interest I have in the toll committee and their workings.

15,865. (*Mr. Best.*) Do you know that a main sewer runs by the side of the Mall. I know a dirty river runs there.

15,866. Would you think that the covering of this river was a laudable object?—I would.

15,867. There are some members of the toll committee who are large buyers in the markets?—Mr. Ferris, Mr. Best, and Mr. McClelland attend the markets, and they are large buyers.

15,868. Are there any members of the town commissioners who buy so largely in the markets, except Mr. M'Clelland and Mr. Ferris, who are not members of the toll committee?—Only two members of the town commissioners.

15,869. (*Mr. Commissioner Meek.*) Is there any charge in connexion with the weighing of oats?—No toll whatever.

15,870. No deduction for porterage?—None whatever.

THOMAS FOSTER examined.

15,871. (*Mr. Best.*) You are a merchant?—Yes, I am. I reside in Dobbin Street.

15,872. Was the memorial presented to you to sign?—It was.

15,873. By whom?—I do not remember.

15,874. Were you aware it was for the purpose of taking the markets from under the control of the toll committee and putting them under the town commissioners?—I do not know.

15,875. If you had known such to be the case, would you have signed it?—I might not have signed it.

15,876. Would you say that the town commissioners would manage the markets better than the toll committee?—I do not think they would.

15,877. (*Mr. Gallagher.*) Are you in favour of the toll committee having charge of the markets?—Yes.

15,878. Were you always so?—I may not have been.

15,879. You signed the memorial?—I did.

15,880. Did you sign the other memorial in 1868?—I did.

15,881. Do you remember signing this memorial?—I do not, but I believe it is my signature.

15,882. Do you sign everything that is put before you, good, bad, and indifferent?—Not everything.

15,883. Do not you know that the memorial was in favour of handing over the markets to the town commissioners?—I did not know at the time; I saw a lot of names before me; I was asked to sign it, and I did so.

15,884. Do you, as a merchant, sign anything that comes in your way?—A memorial does not do much harm.

15,885. Are you really serious that you sign memorials on all occasions of which you do not know the object?—I did not take time to read it. I do not read them on every occasion. I saw a few names that I thought were right before me, and I signed it in a hurry.

JAMES McLAUGHLIN examined.

15,886. (*Mr. Best.*) You signed the memorial?—I did.

15,887. Who presented it to you?—Mr. Thomas Brooks.

15,888. What did he say to you?—He said, would you be in favour of doing away with the tolls? But I had no idea it was to do away with the tolls committee. I did not ask to see the memorial, and it was not read.

15,889. Were you prepared to see the markets transferred to the town commissioners?—If there was proper representation, but we need a sweeping change before that.

15,890. But as matters stand you prefer the toll committee?—Certainly.

Cross-examined by Mr. Gallagher.

15,891. You have no political objection to the board?—I might have, but I am not arguing on that ground. Their election is a farce.

15,892. Is it not held in pursuance of the provisions of the Act of Parliament?—It is; but there is no representation on this board at all. I urge my case on their general incompetency for the discharge of public business.

15,893. It is not on political or religious grounds you urge it?—It is not.

15,894. Have you any objection to them on this ground?—These people represent themselves, but nobody else.

15,895. Is it a political or religious difference?—Well, I might urge this. I am not in favour of the toll committee, or their system of levying tolls. I am in favour of the change. Mr. Sexton got for the Orangemen of Belfast (Ulster), the assimilation of the Municipal and Parliamentary franchise.

15,896. In other words, you are in favour of the existence of the town commissioners on a more extended franchise?—I am not in favour of the town commissioners elected under the present system, or anything approaching to it. If we had such a change as Mr. Sexton got for the Orangemen of Belfast in the shape of household franchise, I would approve of it. I think any man who has a house should have a vote.

15,897. (Mr. Best.) They do not represent the feelings of the people of Belfast, I mean the town commissioners?—Not of any section of the people. I do not think they even represent themselves.

(The inquiry was resumed on the morning of the 15th of May 1888.)

Robert Baxter examined.

15,898. You live in Armagh?—Yes.

15,899. Where?—In Castle Street.

15,900. Was a memorial presented to you for signature by Mr. Brooks?—Yes.

15,901. Is that your signature which appears upon it?—Yes.

15,902. Did he tell you what the memorial was about? He did.

15,903. What did he say? Did he say that the object of the memorial was to prevent the town commissioners from getting the tolls?—He did.

15,904. And was it that representation that induced you to sign the memorial?—Yes.

15,905. You then object to the town commissioners getting charge of the tolls?—Certainly.

15,906. And you signed the memorial because you were told that its object was to prevent the town commissioners from getting it?—Yes; I would rather put my hand into the fire than sign any document in favour of the town commissioners getting charge of the tolls.

Cross-examined by Mr. Gallagher.

15,907. Do you attend the Armagh Market?—Yes.

15,908. How often?—Every Tuesday.

15,909. What business do you follow?—I am a blacksmith.

15,910. Do you pay tolls?—Yes; every Tuesday I come into the market I have to pay tolls.

15,911. Do you know who collects the tolls?—Yes, Thomas McCartan.

15,912. Do you know Mr. McDonald or Mr. Gardner?—Yes, by seeing them.

15,913. Do you know that Mr. Gardner has anything to do with the market?—I see him there.

15,914. Do you know that he is secretary to the toll committee?—I am not aware of it.

15,915. Do you know that the toll committee receive the tolls?—Yes, I pay these tolls myself.

15,916. What did you mean when you said that you signed this memorial to keep the town commissioners out of the tolls?—I meant that I would keep the town commissioners from having anything to do with the tolls if I could.

15,917. What is your reason for that?—Because I have no confidence in them.

15,918. Are they not all respectable men?—Yes, they are respectable enough.

15,919. And are they not all townspeople?—Yes.

15,920. Well, I want you to tell me why you would object to the town commissioners, whom you admit are respectable townspeople, from having the administration of these tolls?—I have already told you that it is because I have no confidence in them.

15,921. But what is your reason for having no confidence in them?—My reason is that I have no confidence in them at all.

15,922. Do not you think that they have the interest and welfare of the town at heart?—No; they have the interests of the shops more at heart than the welfare of the town.

15,923. Why do you think that?—I know that they want to have the market in their own shops.

15,924. Surely you do not want to make out that they want to have the market for hay and straw and flour in their shops?—They want to have everything in their shops.

15,925. Now, do not you know very well that they could not have the market for farm produce in their shops?—I do not know anything of the kind.

15,926. Mention any articles of farm produce that they would have in their shops?—They sell butter and eggs and meal, and everything like that.

15,927. And is that your only objection to the Commissioners have charge of the tolls?—Yes.

15,928. Do you not think that the Commissioners would manage the tolls right?—I do not.

15,929. And have you any other reasons for your objections?—None.

15,930. And why do you support the toll committee?—Because they have had charge of the tolls for a very long time, about 50 years, I think, and have always acted fairly by us.

15,931. Do you know anything about the flax market?—Yes.

15,932. Do you remember it previous to the year 1880?—Yes.

15,933. Now, was there a flax market there at all?—There was.

15,934. Was it not overgrown with grass?—I do not know, because I was never on it, but for that matter the grass was growing on the streets as well as in the flax market.

15,935. Do you not know that it is better than it was?—No.

15,936. Do you know anything about the pork market?—Yes, I was in it many a time.

15,937. Do you know what the charges are for selling a pig?—I do not.

15,938. Are you able to read and write?—I can write my name, that is all.

15,939. Can you read?—I could read a printed paper, but I could not read writing.

15,940. Can you read this memorial?—No, I can only read my own name.

15,941. Did you try to read the memorial?—I did not.

15,942. Did you look at it at all?—Yes, I looked at it, but I could not read it.

Charles Crowe examined by Mr. Best.

15,943. What business do you follow?—I am a pork buyer for Mr. Morton, of Banbridge.

15,944. How long have you been a pork buyer?—About 11 years.

15,945. You attend Armagh market in the capacity of a buyer of pork?—Yes.

15,946. And you are acquainted with the tolls charged in the market?—Yes.

15,947. Was a petition or memorial presented to you by Mr. Brooks for the purpose of obtaining your signature to it?—Yes.

15,948. And did you sign it?—I did.

15,949. What did he tell you was the object of the memorial?—He said it was to look after the money of the tolls.

15,950. Did he say anything else?—Yes, he said it was for the good of the town.

15,951. I suppose you have considerable experience of the Armagh markets?—Yes.

15,952. And from that experience would you be in favour of the transfer of the market rights from the toll committee to the town commissioners?—I would not.

15,953. Are you in the habit of attending other markets besides those of Armagh?—Yes.

15,954. Name some of them?—Well, I attend Lisnaskea, Clones, Dundalk, and Portadown.

15,955. Do you attend others?—I went to Newry sometimes.

15,956. Did you ever attend Dungannon?—Yes, about three years.

15,957. Well, now after your experience of all these towns, what is your opinion of the accommodation and facilities afforded in Armagh as compared with the other places you have mentioned?—Well, here we have an inspector for looking after the pork, but there is nothing of that kind in Lisnaskea, Dundalk, or Clones. In Newry and Portadown there is an official of that kind.

15,958. In your opinion is the accommodation in Armagh market of a superior character?—Yes, it is superior to that of any other market I ever attended.

15,959. In Lisnaskea, Clones, and other places is there a market all the year round?—No.

15,960. During what portion of the year then is the market held?—From 1st October to 1st May.

15,961. And am I right in saying that in Armagh there is a market all the year round?—Yes.

15,962. Do you consider that the tolls charged in Armagh are of a reasonable character?—They are the same as other places.

15,963. In your opinion is the toll charged upon pigs in Armagh too high?—No.

15,964. And is the accommodation in the pig market sufficient in your opinion to meet all the demands made upon it?—Yes.

15,965. And you say that they have in Armagh what you say they have not in other places which you attend, namely, a man to look after the pigs?—That is so.

Cross-examined by Mr. Gallagher.

15,966. I presume you live at Banbridge?—No, I do not. I only buy pork for a merchant in Banbridge.

15,967. And I suppose you know the Banbridge market?—No, I do not attend it.

15,968. Do you know what are the charges in Banbridge?—No.

15,969. What are the charges here?—Fourpence for weighing, 2d. for signing, and 6d. for house money.

15,970. That is 1s. altogether?—Yes.

15,971. You know what the charges are at Newry?—Yes.

15,972. Do they amount to 1s. also?—No, I think it is only 10d. in Newry.

15,973. Can not you tell us exactly what you have paid yourself?—I am not altogether sure, but I think it is only 10d.

15,974. Do you know what the charges are in Portadown?—I think about 10d.

15,975. Now, do you know or do you not? We do not want to know what you think?—I do not know what the charge for weighing is exactly.

15,976. When Mr. Brooks brought you this memorial, you signed it?—Yes.

15,977. Did you read it?—I did not.

15,978. And are we to understand that you are in the habit of signing documents without reading them and ascertaining what they are about?—No.

15,979. Then, why did you sign this memorial without reading it?—Because Mr. McLaughlin said it was for the good of the town.

15,980. Did Mr. McLaughlin sign it?—I do not know whether he did or not.

15,981. Would you be in favour of transferring the care and management of the tolls from the toll committee to the town commissioners?—I would not.

15,982. What is your reason for that?—Well, I do not see any cause why there should be a change. If the town commissioners had had the tolls for the last 80 years, as the toll committee have had, I would be equally opposed to any change. I have no objection to either body, but after the toll committee have had the tolls for such a long time, I do not see any necessity whatever to take their powers from them and hand them over to the town commissioners.

15,983. All you want, I suppose, is that the market should be properly conducted?—That is so.

15,984. (Mr. Commissioner Black.) Do you live in Armagh?—Yes.

15,985. And you are opposed to the transference of the market rights to the town commissioners from the present toll committee?—Yes.

Re-examined by Mr. Best.

15,986. On each pig that is brought into the market, how much does the toll committee get?—Fourpence.

15,987. That is for weighing?—Yes.

15,988. The toll committee have nothing whatever to say to the 6d. which is charged?—That is so.

15,989. That 6d. is what is called house money?—Yes.

Joseph Gaskin examined by Mr. Best.

15,990. Was a petition presented to you by Mr. Brooks to sign?—Yes.

15,991. And did you sign it?—Yes.

15,992. Why did you do so?—On the condition that they were to remove the market from the present position.

15,993. Would you have signed that memorial if you had known that its object was to hand the tolls over to the town commissioners?—No, I would not.

Cross-examined by Mr. Gallagher.

15,994. What employment do you follow?—Different things.

15,995. What are you doing at present?—I am in the employment of Mr. Ferris.

15,996. Mr. Ferris, I believe, is a member of the toll committee?—I believe so.

15,997. Do you know whether he is or not?—I believe he is.

15,998. Do not you know very well he is?—I am not certain.

15,999. Did you never hear before that Mr. Ferris was a member of the toll committee?—I heard that he was, but I do not know anything about it. He may be, but I cannot say positively.

16,000. Do you know any of the members of the toll committee?—I do.

16,001. Whom do you know?—I know Mr. Jenkinson.

16,002. Had you any conversation with any of the members of the toll committee about this memorial?—No.

16,003. With none of them?—That is so.

16,004. Did anyone of them speak to you about signing it?—No.

16,005. Are you sure, now, that you had no conversation with any member or members of the toll committee upon this matter?—I did not speak to anyone of them concerning it.

16,006. Well, now, if that is so, how did you know to come here and give evidence?—I was sent for.

16,007. By whom?—By someone here.

16,008. What did you come here to do?—I was sent for, and was told to come to the market-house.

16,009. And do you mean to say, that no one knew what you were coming here to say?—No.

14,010. Did nobody know that you were coming here to state that you signed the memorial without reading it?—No.

14,011. Did you never have a word with Mr. Parvis as to the character of the evidence you were about to give to the Commissioner?—No.

14,012. Or with any other member of the toll committee?—No.

14,013. And did not one of them know what you were going to say?—That is so.

14,014. Did any member of the toll committee know that you had not read this memorial before signing it?—No.

14,015. Then how did they know to send for you to give evidence?—I do not know.

14,016. Come sir, I want you to tell me how the members of the toll committee became aware that you would come here, that you had signed this memorial without having read it?—I told several parties.

14,017. Whom did you tell?—Mr. Baxter.

14,018. Did you tell anyone else?—Yes.

14,019. Whom?—Mr. M'Creech.

14,020. Anyone else?—Mr. Boyd.

14,021. Come, now, had you no word of conversation with Mr. Parvis about this matter?—No.

14,022. This morning?—No.

14,023. I think you knew he was a member of the toll committee?—I am not positive as to whether he is or not.

14,024. And you still adhere to the statement that you had no conversation with him about this matter?—Yes.

14,025. Nor with any other member of the toll committee?—No.

Thomas Fahy examined by Mr. Bury.

14,026. Where have you been living for sometime?—I have been in America.

14,027. For how long?—17 months.

14,028. When did you come home?—I arrived in Armagh at half past two o'clock on last Monday morning.

14,029. Was there a petition presented to you within the last twelve months?—No.

14,030. Where do you live?—I used to live in Mill Street before I went to America.

14,031. Is that your signature, "Thomas Fahy, Mill Street, Armagh"?—That is my name, but I did not write it.

14,032. Did you authorise anyone to attach your signature to that document?—No.

14,033. Is there any other man of that name that you know of?—No. There is a Patrick Fahy, but there is no other Thomas Fahy, beside myself, that I am aware of.

Cross-examined by Mr. Gallagher.

14,034. Do you know who signed your name to that memorial?—I do not.

14,035. Are you sure?—I do not recognise the writing.

14,036. Are you a married man?—I am.

14,037. And do you mean to say that you do not recognise the handwriting of your own wife?—That is not my wife's handwriting at all.

14,038. Now are you positive about that?—Yes.

14,039. And you say that you do not know whose writing it is?—Yes.

14,040. Your wife has been in Armagh, I believe, while you were away in America?—Yes.

14,041. And how long were you away?—It is exactly 17 months to-day since I went away.

14,042. Are you not the tenant of the house in which you are living?—I suppose I am.

14,043. Do you not know that you are?—No, I do not know where my wife has been living since I went away.

14,044. Are you not the tenant of your house?—I do not know.

14,045. Is the tenancy not in your name?—I cannot tell.

14,046. Are you in any employment at the present time?—I am.

14,047. And is your wife in any employment?—Yes.

Re-examined by Mr. Bury.

14,048. Has your wife been out at service while you were away?—Yes.

Robert [illegible] examined by Mr. Bury.

14,049. Do you attend the Armagh Markets?—I do.

14,050. For how long?—Well, I should say I knew the Armagh Markets for about 50 years.

14,051. Do you know the pork market in Armagh?—Yes.

14,052. Have you any experience of the manner in which it is conducted?—Yes.

14,053. And also of the amount of the toll which is levied in the market?—I have.

14,054. Now as to the former matter, that is the manner in which the market is conducted, what is your opinion?—I have no fault to find with it in that respect.

14,055. But are you of opinion that it is well and effectually conducted?—I am.

14,056. Well, now to come to the question of the amount of the toll which is charged, do you consider it [illegible]?—I think it is very moderate.

14,057. Do you ever attend any other market?—Oh yes, I have gone to other markets.

14,058. Where?—Portadown, for instance.

14,059. For what purpose did you go to the market at Portadown?—Well, I went there because I was told it was a better market for pork.

14,060. Than Armagh?—Yes, so I was told.

14,061. And you went there?—Yes.

14,062. What had you to sell?—I killed six pigs to take to it.

14,063. And what was your experience? Was it favourable to Portadown or Armagh?—I prefer Armagh.

14,064. Was that your first visit to Portadown?—Yes.

14,065. And after the result of that visit did you ever go back to it again?—No.

14,066. You say you would rather have the market in Armagh?—Yes, I certainly would.

14,067. Do you attend the oat market here?—Yes.

14,068. I believe I am right in saying that there is no toll charged upon the oats in the Armagh Market?—Yes, that is so.

14,069. Now you have long experience of the Armagh Markets, and of the manner in which they have been conducted and managed by the toll committee, and I want you to give me your opinion upon the subject. Are you yourself satisfied with the markets?—I am.

14,070. And with the manner in which they have been conducted by the toll committee?—Yes.

14,071. Now I suppose you have some experience of what those who attend the markets think on the same subject?—Yes. Of course I hear them talking about it now and then.

14,072. Have you heard the farmers speak about the way in which the markets are conducted?—Yes.

14,073. And what is their opinion?—They seem to be satisfied with the markets.

14,074. And has that been the case for some time back?—Yes, as far as I know, it has.

Cross-examined by Mr. Gallagher.

14,075. Do you think that a charge of 1s. on every pig is a moderate toll?—I do.

16,076. Is it more or less than that charged in other market towns round about?—I think it is about the same.

16,077. Take Portadown for instance, is the charge per pig the same both in Armagh and Portadown?—I think it is, but in Portadown I had to deliver the pigs at the railway station.

16,078. Do you know anything of the management of the pork market in other towns with the exception of Portadown and Armagh?—No.

16,079. What is your reason for preferring Armagh to Portadown?—Well, in Portadown it is necessary to deliver the pigs at the railway station as I have already said, and that is both inconvenient and dangerous, as we have to run the risk of having our horses frightened by the trains. In Armagh there is nothing of that sort, as the pigs are taken from us at the shambles.

16,080. Can you remember the time when there was a toll charged upon oats in Armagh?—Yes.

16,081. I believe I am right in saying that that charge was abolished.

Re-examined by Mr. Rose.

16,082. There were then two market days in the week, were there not?—That is so.

16,083. And that charge, I believe, was only made upon one of the two days?—Yes.

16,084. What were the days?—Wednesday and Saturday.

16,085. And on which of the two days was the charge made on oats?—On Saturday.

16,086. Have you got a flax mill?—Yes.

16,087. I believe it is not working now?—That is so.

16,088. To what cause do you attribute the fact that your flax mill is not working now. Is it because of the want of flax?—Yes, that is the reason to a very great extent.

16,089. Did you ever go to the flax market in Portadown?—Yes.

16,090. What made you go there?—I heard that it was a better market for flax than Portadown.

16,091. And what was your experience of that visit?—Well, I would not go back again.

16,092. What is your reason for saying that? Did you not get a good price for your flax?—No, I did not.

16,093. In your opinion, could you have got a better price for your produce if you had disposed of it in Armagh?—Yes, I could have sold it in Armagh for 6d. more per load.

16,094. When did this occur, how long was it ago?—Well, I suppose it might be 10 years ago.

16,095. Was that about the time that the flax market was removed in Armagh?—I could not say.

16,096. In your opinion, is the accommodation in the Armagh Market sufficient to meet all the demands made up it?—Certainly, it is quite sufficient.

16,097. And do you think that the people are desirous of seeing a change in the management of the markets?—As far as I know they do not want any change whatever.

Thomas Knipe examined by Mr. Rose.

16,098. You are a large farmer, I believe, Mr. Knipe?—Yes.

16,099. And a mill owner as well?—Yes.

16,100. You live near the city of Armagh?—Yes.

16,101. What is the valuation of your property?—About 800l.

16,102. You were, I believe, a member of Lord Cowper's Commission which was appointed to inquire into the working of the Land Act?—I was.

16,103. How long have you attended the markets in Armagh?—Oh, for a long time.

16,104. About how long?—Forty years, or thereabouts.

16,105. You know the pork market?—Yes.

16,106. I suppose you have attended it regularly?—I have.

16,107. You know the accommodation it gives?—Yes.

16,108. Is it good?—Quite ample, in my opinion.

16,109. For all purposes?—Yes.

16,110. Are you also acquainted with the hay and straw market?—Yes.

16,111. Does it afford good accommodation?—I do not know any better accommodation in any market with which I am acquainted.

16,112. Do you know the flax market?—Yes.

16,113. In your opinion is it large enough?—Yes, I think it is quite sufficient for all requirements at present.

16,114. I believe it is not availed of so much as it ought to be, as large quantities of flax are sold at the mills?—That is so.

16,115. The buyers go to the mills?—They do.

16,116. You keep a very large number of cattle, do you not?—Yes.

16,117. About how many?—Well, I have about 200 head of cattle at the present moment.

16,118. Do you ever sell cattle by weight?—Never.

16,119. Have you ever known any dealers in cattle who asked you to sell by weight?—No, I never was asked to do so.

16,120. Do you think it is necessary to have a weighbridge for the weighing of cattle?—I have never been asked to weigh them. The question has never been put.

16,121. Now do you consider that the management of the Armagh markets is what it ought to be?—As far as I know, the management is exceedingly good at present.

16,122. Is the grass-seed market largely attended?—It is; in fact, it is one of the largest in the country.

16,123. And are you as a large farmer satisfied with the tolls which are charged in the markets?—They have been abolished to a very large extent. There used to be excessive tolls, but they have been abolished.

16,124. At the present time are they moderate?—The charges upon pork are moderate, and the same remark applies to grain. In the case of the latter, if it is sold at a merchant's in the town, there is no charge whatever.

16,125. Are you satisfied yourself?—They are better than in Portadown.

16,126. Speaking generally of the markets, are you satisfied with them?—There is no doubt that there is a great improvement in the shambles.

16,127. But speaking generally, what is your opinion?—Well, I have not much experience of the others.

16,128. With reference to the toll upon grass seed, when was that made?—Quite a number of years ago.

16,129. That was resisted by the people?—Yes, and I resisted it myself.

16,130. Was it levied for any length of time?—It was not.

16,131. It was resisted by the people of both the town and the country?—Yes, we were advised to resist it.

16,132. On what ground?—I do not know, but they were never able to collect it.

16,133. Do you remember the time when the toll upon oats was charged?—Yes.

16,134. When was it abolished?—A number of years since.

16,135. Was it, in your opinion, detrimental to the interests of the markets of Armagh?—I should say it was.

16,136. There were a number of markets held in the streets?—Yes, the flax market was principally held in the streets until the new place was made.

16,137. When was that?—I remember the time, but I am not prepared to say exactly when it occurred.

16,138. About how long ago was it?—About 15 years ago, perhaps.

16,139. Are there any other markets held in the streets?—Yes.

16,140. Which?—Well, the market for live pigs was held in the street, but it has been changed to where it is now, and I consider that a great improvement.

16,141. Where is it now?—In the square in front of the gaol.

16,142. And you consider that an improvement, you say?—Yes. When in the street the thoroughfare was much obstructed, and it was in other ways a source of great inconvenience. However, there is no reason for any complaint of that kind now that it is held in the square in front of the gaol.

16,143. Is not that a portion of the street too?—Yes, but it is an improvement to have it there, and I may add that the farmers are very much pleased with the change.

16,144. The potato market is held in the street, so is not?—The place where it is held is called Market Street, but there is a barrier between the ground upon which the market is held and the street.

16,145. But do not the potato carts sometimes extend into the street?—That is only when the market is an exceptionally large one.

Re-examined by Mr. Best.

16,146. Have you any complaint to make about the management of the markets?—No.

16,147. (*Mr. Commissioner Bleach.*) Do you think it is desirable that cattle should be sold by live weight?—I do not think it is either necessary or desirable that cattle should be sold by live weight in this part of the country.

16,148. (*Mr. Commissioner Bleach.*) Why are you of that opinion?—There are so few cattle.

(*Mr. Gardiner.*) And the grass does not fatten well.

16,149. (*Mr. Commissioner Bleach.*) Then am I to take it, Mr. Kelpe, that you think selling by live weight is desirable in the case of fat cattle?—Yes, if the dealers wished the cattle weighed, then, in my opinion, it would be desirable; but, as I have said before, I have sold a great many cattle, and I have never yet been asked to have them weighed.

Thomas Quinn examined by Mr. Best.

16,150. How long have you been attending the markets in Armagh?—For, I think, about 33 years.

16,151. Which of them have you been in the habit of attending?—Principally the oat market.

16,152. On what days is it held?—Wednesdays and Saturdays.

16,153. Do you attend the pork market at all?—Yes, a little.

16,154. Do you find the accommodation afforded by the markets ample for all purposes?—Yes, I think it is very good.

16,155. Are you satisfied with the toll upon pork?—Yes.

16,156. Now it has been alleged that it was impossible for farmers to get up their carts and have their produce weighed quickly unless they greased the hands of the carriers. In your long experience, did you ever find that or anything like it to be the case?—No. I never saw anything of the sort.

16,157. You never found it necessary to grease the hands of the carriers?—No.

16,158. Do you know anything about the other markets?—No, not much.

16,159. From your experience of the markets, are you satisfied with the manner in which they are conducted?—Yes.

16,160. At present?—Yes, more than ever I was before.

16,161. Do you think the tolls are excessive or moderate?—In my opinion they are moderate.

16,162. How often is the gooseneck market held?—Once a year.

16,163. And are you satisfied by the accommodation afforded by it?—It is very good.

Cross-examined by Mr. Gallagher.

16,164. What are the arrangements for the weighing of pork?—There are a number of scales.

16,165. And have the toll committee any man there?—Yes, there is a man to help you.

16,166. Are the pigs taken out of the carts for the purpose of being weighed?—Yes.

16,167. Do you take your pigs out of the cart yourself?—No; I have told you already there is a man there to help you.

16,168. Is that man in the employment of the toll committee?—I think so.

16,169. Now are there any runners on the pork market?—No, not to my knowledge.

16,170. Are you sure?—Well, I never saw any of them there.

16,171. Did you ever see a woman assisting there?—No; it was always a man I saw there.

16,172. Do you know a woman in town called Dawley?—I never had much acquaintance with the people there. It is not in my part of the town, and I might not be there for three months at a time.

Wm. John Best, J.P., examined by Mr. Best.

16,173. You are a member of the firm of James Best and Sons?—Yes.

16,174. What business does the firm follow?—They are corn and flour merchants and seed merchants.

16,175. How long have you done business in Armagh?—For the last thirty years.

16,176. During that time have you attended the markets in Armagh?—Yes, I knew them for thirty years.

16,177. I believe I am right in saying that you are a member of the toll committee?—Yes.

16,178. To what extent are you interested?—I am the proprietor of one share which produces for me the large income of 12s. a year.

16,179. Do you visit the markets in your capacity as a member of the toll committee to see that matters are properly arranged and carried out, and that the markets are properly conducted?—Yes.

16,180. Do you remember the shambles market before it was enlarged?—I do.

16,181. In consequence of its not being sufficient to accommodate the produce that was brought into it, it was enlarged by the toll committee?—Yes, we spent a large sum of 1,100l., I think, in improving it.

16,182. And in your opinion, does it now afford sufficient accommodation?—Except on the occasion of very large markets.

16,183. How often would that be?—It might occur three or four times in the year.

16,184. Then you believe that for the ordinary demands of the market the accommodation is large enough?—Yes, it is ample in every way.

16,185. How many weighbridges are there?—Two.

16,186. Are there stalls?—Yes, there were three new stalls erected.

16,187. Is there also good store accommodation?—Yes.

16,188. And is there also accommodation for paying farmers?—Yes, there are a number of offices in which payment takes place.

16,189. Now, before the market was enlarged did you take a portion of ground from the toll committee?—Yes; Mr. McCrum and I took a piece of ground from the toll committee which no one else would take, and many people came to the conclusion and expressed the opinion that we had made a bad bargain, but subsequent events have proved that that was not the case.

16,190. Now how long did that piece of ground be upon your hands?—For about three years.

16,191. Was no portion of it let?—No, and it looked very like a bad bargain, but it turned out very well.

16,192. Has it been built upon?—Yes, and it proves a source of revenue to the town commissioners. It is now a credit to the town.

14,193. Is it true that the toll committee made 60*l.* out of it?—The toll committee derive 30*l.* a year out of it; that is all they make out of it that I know of.

14,194. Is 30*l.* a year the amount of the rent which Mr. McCrum and yourself pay the toll committee for it?—Yes.

14,195. Then the toll committee did not make 60*l.* in ready money out of that piece of ground?—They got 30*l.* a year rent, that is all.

14,196. Does that 30*l.* a year go to the credit of the funds of the toll committee?—Yes. Mr. McCrum and I pay it to the treasurer of the toll committee.

14,197. Well, now to come to speak of the markets themselves, do you attend the grass-seed markets?—Yes.

14,198. You buy large quantities of grass seed, I suppose?—Yes, we do.

14,199. And you buy corn largely?—Yes.

14,200. To what extent?—From 1,500 to 2,000 tons every year.

14,201. How is the grass-seed market well attended?—Yes, it is one of the leading markets in the north of Ireland.

14,202. Is there good accommodation in connexion with it?—Yes, very good.

14,203. Is there any toll?—No, a farmer can have his produce weighed if he likes. It is a purely optional matter with them, but I should like to see everybody weighing.

14,204. You mean in the market?—Yes, I think everybody should weigh there.

14,205. Then I take it that farmers who sell to the merchants in their shops in town have nothing whatever to pay?—That is so, the produce is weighed in the merchant's shop and does not come to the market to be weighed so that there is no charge at all made upon it.

14,206. Now with reference to the oat market, is there any toll?—No, not now.

14,207. But there used to be a toll, I believe?—Yes, and it was a very objectionable one.

14,208. About how long is it since that toll was done away with?—About seven years ago.

14,209. Did you take an interest in the efforts that were made to get that toll abolished?—Yes; I was of opinion that the charging of such a toll was the cause of doing the market a great deal of harm, and therefore in the interests of both the town and the markets, I thought that it should be done away with.

14,210. You know something about the wheat market?—I do.

14,211. Does much wheat come into it?—Very little.

14,212. Not so much as formerly?—Not by any means.

14,213. How is that?—Well there is now only one flour mill where there used to be a dozen formerly.

14,214. Now with reference to the flax market, is there as much business done there as there used to be?—No. A number of the mills have been closed.

14,215. And have no mills been started since to take their place?—No. Of course I am only speaking now of the larger mills.

14,216. Is the accommodation in the flax market ample for the flax grown in the country?—Unfortunately it is. I remember the market from Primrose Hill to Poor School Lane being as full as possible.

14,217. I believe you are in the flax seed trade?—Yes.

14,218. The quantity sold is, I am told, very small?—That is so.

14,219. Now with reference to the cattle market, have you attended it?—Yes, sometimes.

14,220. Have you ever known live cattle to be sold by weight in the market?—I have not.

14,221. Was there ever any representation made with a view to having a weighbridge for the purpose of weighing live cattle?—No. There is a weighbridge in the market and there is no objection to fixing it so that it may be made suitable for weighing live cattle if such a course is considered necessary, anything of that kind we will be only happy to do.

14,222. Is it necessary?—Well, I have never seen it done before in the market.

14,223. But if it is necessary, you are prepared to do it at once?—Certainly.

14,224. I believe you have said that the toll committee never had any representation made to them to the effect that a weighbridge capable of weighing live cattle was required?—No; and if it is wanted, it can be carried out, and any other improvement that may be suggested as being necessary.

14,225. Do you know the live pig market?—Yes.

14,226. Did you take an interest in having it removed from its former position to where it is at present?—Yes, and it was a decided advantage to remove it from a position where it was a source of inconvenience and an obstruction to the traffic, to a position where there is ample room for it.

14,227. And what is the charge in this market?—Twopence per cart.

14,228. Is there any charge upon live pigs coming into the market?—No; Mr. Best said there was, but there is not.

(*Mr. Gardiner.*) Yes; he said that there was a charge of 2*d.*

(*Mr. Best.*) Upon every live pig coming into the market.

(*Mr. Gardiner.*) Yes.

(*Mr. Best.*) I did not. That is a total misrepresentation of my evidence.

14,229. (*Mr. Best to Witness.*) Did you ever know of 2*d.* a pig being charged?—No, it was 2*d.* a cart.

14,230. And how many might a cart contain?—Oh, it would hold a dozen.

14,231. And do you think that the farmers are satisfied with things as they are now?—Yes. I believe, if you took a poll of the country, 99 per cent. would say that they were perfectly satisfied. There was a time when there was great dissatisfaction amongst them, and I must admit that there was good cause for it, but I am glad to say there is nothing of that kind now.

14,232. Those things which were then complained of have been remedied?—Yes.

14,233. And do you know if the farmers are satisfied with the tolls as being moderate?—They are.

Cross-examined by Mr. Gallagher.

14,234. How long have you been a member of the toll committee?—I think for about seven or eight years.

14,235. Did you ever read this book containing the provisions of the constitution of the committee?—I cannot say that I did read it all through.

14,236. Do you know its provisions?—Not very well.

14,237. I believe you only possess one share?—That is all.

14,238. Do you attend the general meetings of the committee?—I do.

14,239. As a proprietor?—Yes.

14,240. And do you take part in the proceedings at those meetings?—Yes, I do.

14,241. And I believe you get 1*l.* a year?—Yes.

14,242. You are a large merchant in Armagh?—Yes.

14,243. And before you became a member of the toll committee, I believe you took an interest in the working of the markets?—Yes; I had every right to do so.

14,244. Your interests are bound up in the welfare and prosperity of the city of Armagh?—Certainly.

14,245. And I suppose it is the same with the other members of your family?—Quite so.

14,246. Did the fact of your becoming a member of the toll committee slacken in any way your exertions in this respect?—It did.

14,247. Were you a member of the market committee?—No, but my father was.

14,248. Your father is, I believe, one of the partners in the firm of which you are a member?—He is.

16,249. There was, I believe, a considerable amount of good done at the time?—Yes; and money was subscribed.

16,250. What was the principal object in view?—The removal of the flax market; and also we endeavoured to put a stop to the practice of buying and selling at the mills.

16,251. Do you consider that that practice was prejudicial to the market?—Certainly.

16,252. Explain what you mean by that?—Well, some buyers went to the mills and purchased whatever quantity they required, leaving the remainder to go to the markets. This acted most detrimentally upon other buyers who came to the market in the ordinary way. It was a great hardship upon them to find in the market only the produce which had not been bought at the mills, and, in my opinion, it had a very injurious effect upon the market.

16,253. You tried to put an end to the buying at the mills?—Yes, and to induce both buyers and sellers to come to the market to transact their business.

16,254. You consider that the practice of buying at the mills is injurious to the markets?—Yes.

16,255. Do not you know that the improvement which was carried out in the market was done by people outside the toll committee?—No, it was the result of argument and pressure from inside the toll committee.

16,256. From whom did the pressure arise?—It came from a few members of the toll committee.

16,257. You were interested in bringing about the improvement referred to?—Yes, I always took an interest in anything which had for its object the improvement of the markets generally. For instance, I subscribed towards the fund got up for removing the toll upon cars, and I also pushed them very hard with the object of having the market extended.

16,258. Did Mr. Gillespie become a member of the toll committee at the same time that you joined it?—No, he did not become a member for some time after I did.

16,259. About how long?—I think about two years.

16,260. Was he a supporter of yours in the endeavours you made to bring about reforms in the markets?—Yes, we always pulled together in any movement which had for its object the good of the markets.

16,261. You were in opposition to the toll committee, were you not?—As far as the toll upon cars was concerned I was.

16,262. And you considered that the removal of that toll was an improvement to the market?—Yes.

16,263. This place, which Mr. McCrum and you rented from the toll committee is beside the pork market, is it not?—Yes, at the back of it.

16,264. And around the side of it?—Yes.

16,265. Was that where the old depôt was?—Yes, and now there are a number of fine houses upon it.

16,266. Are you aware that the town commissioners paid a rent to the toll committee for it?—I do not know.

16,267. When was it that you took the land from the toll committee?—I cannot tell exactly.

16,268. About how long ago was it?—I think it was about seven years ago.

16,269. Were you at that time a member of the toll committee?—I was.

16,270. And was Mr. McCrum also a debenture holder?—I believe he was.

16,271. Was that just the time when there was a proposal for the construction of a light railway?—I think we had taken the land before the project for the railway was on the cards at all.

16,272. Was the light railway project not even talked about at that time?—It was not.

16,273. Now, was there a proposal also to make a new road there?—Yes, and it was passed by the Presentment Sessions, but it was afterwards thrown out by the grand jury.

16,274. If the grand jury had approved of the work and if that road had been made, would it not have run through your land?—It would have run through one corner of it.

16,275. Was the street there made before the new road was thought of?—Yes.

16,276. And if the proposed road had been made, would it not have been a great improvement to your street?—I do not know that it would be of any advantage to me, but it would certainly be a great advantage to farmers.

16,277. Now, would it not have been an advantage to you as well?—No.

16,278. Even indirectly?—I do not think so.

16,279. Then, again, was there not a proposal to make a new street through a little corner of your land; is not that so?—Yes.

16,280. The street you have now would have formed a part of it, would it not?—Yes.

16,281. Would not the proposed road connect your street with another street?—Yes, and it would be a great advantage.

16,282. Was it after that the proposal to make the light railway was started?—Yes.

16,283. And were you one of the promoters of the proposed railway?—Yes, and I hope it will soon be made.

16,284. Well, personally, I may say that I have not the slightest objection to your hopes in that respect being realised, were you present at the last meeting of the debenture holders?—I believe I was.

16,285. Were you present when a resolution was proposed having for its object the establishment of a sinking fund?—I think so.

16,286. For the purpose of carrying out their trusts?—Yes, and I think it would be a very desirable thing if they had the money necessary to do so.

16,287. Now what was the credit balance at that meeting?—I have no recollection as to the amount of the balance.

16,288. Was it not 350l. 10s.?—I do not remember what it was, but the documents will show it at once if referred to.

16,289. Well, you may take it that that is right that at the last meeting you had a balance of 350l. 10s.?—Yes, but we have to pay interest to the debenture holders.

16,290. Yes, I know that, but then you had the receipts from the tolls for that purpose. Now, is it not a fact that at the last meeting of your debenture holders, although you had a balance at your bankers of 350l. 10s., yet Mr. McCrum could not find a seconder for his motion to establish a sinking fund, is not that so?—I do not know.

16,291-2. Did he find a seconder?—I do not think he did.

(Mr. Best.) As a matter of fact, there is no doubt about it that Mr. McCrum's motion was not seconded.

16,293. Now, what is your opinion of this matter?—As I have already said you you cannot do what is impossible. It would be a very desirable thing to establish a sinking fund if the money was available, but you cannot lay out your money and have it as well.

16,294. But at your last meeting you had 350l. according to your own admission?—Yes, that is so.

16,295. And a motion for the establishment of a sinking fund fell through?—It was not seconded.

16,296. Well we have that fact, and it will speak for itself. Now, have you any objection to the management of the markets being vested in another board?—I have every objection to the markets being handed over to the town commissioners.

16,297. What is the ground of your objection to the town commissioners?—I will tell you. Some time ago a meeting of the town commissioners was called for the purpose of considering the very important subject of railway rates and charges, and out of a board consisting of 21 commissioners, only four considered it worth their while to put in an appearance, while the chairman of the board was amongst the absentees. He did not think it necessary to take any interest in a matter which vitally affects the prosperity of Armagh and of the whole of Ireland.

16,298. Have you any other objection?—Yes.

16,299. What is it?—I object to their getting charge of the markets because of the way in which they keep the streets of the town. They are clean to-day for a wonder, but they are generally kept in a very bad state.

(Mr. Gallagher.) Because they have not got the money to do things in the way they would wish.

16,300. (Mr. Best.) There is one question which I forgot to put to the witness, and which I want to ask him now, and that is, did the toll committee subscribe anything towards the fund which was raised for the removal of the flax market?—Yes, 10l.

(Mr. Gallagher.) Oh yes, they did give 10l., that appears in a statement of the different amounts subscribed.

Re-examination continued.

16,301. Were you present at the last inquiry here by the Assistant Commissioner?—I was.

16,302. Had you any witnesses here?—There were a good many examined here yesterday and to-day.

16,303. But I am referring to the former occasion when Mr. Commissioner Black sat here, were there any witnesses present upon that occasion?—No.

16,304. Now, with reference to the amount of 336l. which has been referred to, was that the amount in hands at the end of October?—Yes.

16,305. But had not all the debenture holders to be paid out of that?—Yes.

16,306. And how much would that take?—About 300l.

(Mr. Gallagher.) Yes, but that is going upon the supposition that nothing would be made in the meantime.

16,307. And I believe that the toll committee have also made an arrangement for putting up a new clock at the market house?—That is so.

16,308. And do they not also give 50l. towards certain flagging?—Yes.

16,309. Out of this 336l.?—Yes.

16,310. That flagging was at Mr. Edwards' property?—No, it was at the toll committee's property.

16,311. Close to it?—Mr. Edwards was getting flagging done separately.

16,312. Was it for the markets this flagging was done?—Yes.

16,313. Does it connect English Street with Edwards' property?—It does with this exception, that you have to cross the road.

16,314. (Mr. Commissioner Black.) You say there is no toll upon flax?—No, there never was.

16,315. And is there any other charge?—No, the flax market was always free.

16,316. Are there any deductions made by the buyers?—Yes, for storage.

Joseph [illegible], examined by Mr. Best.

16,317. What are you?—A farmer.

16,318. Where do you live?—Near Armagh.

16,319. About how far from the town?—Two miles.

16,320. How long have you been attending the markets in Armagh?—Oh for a very long time.

16,321. Give us an idea of how long?—About 40 years.

16,322. And, I suppose, after attending the markets for so long a time as that you are thoroughly acquainted with them, and the manner in which they are conducted?—Yes.

16,323. Do you know the pork market?—Yes, very well.

16,324. And what is your opinion of the accommodation afforded by it?—I think the accommodation is very fine indeed.

16,325. Do you think there is sufficient room for the produce brought into it?—All I can say is that I never saw any of it going away for want of room.

16,326. Do you think the arrangements for weighing are good?—I should think so.

16,327. You know that the toll is 4d.?—Yes, but there are other charges.

16,328. Are those made by the buyers?—Yes.

16,329. But the toll committee have nothing to do with those charges?—No.

16,330. Well now, confining your attention solely to the charge made by the toll committee which you say is 4d., do you think that that charge is a moderate one, considering the accommodation they afford?—I do not think the toll is unreasonable, but I think the other charges are.

16,331. You are now referring to the charges made by pork merchants?—Yes.

16,332. You think they charge too much?—Yes.

16,333. Have you ever experienced any difficulty in getting your pork weighed without, as has been alleged, greasing the hands of the man?—Well, of course, there is a lot of bother, but I do not think it could be avoided.

16,334. Now, with reference to the hay and straw market, is there good accommodation in it?—I think it is good.

16,335. Is the accommodation in the grass-seed market good?—Yes.

16,336. And is it a well-managed market?—I think it is.

16,337. Have you any complaint against the manner in which it is managed?—No.

16,338. You are satisfied with it?—Yes.

16,339. And with the pork market?—Yes; I am very well satisfied with it.

16,340. In your opinion are the markets generally well conducted?—Well, yes; the worst thing I see in connexion with the markets is the fruit market.

16,341. And what is your complaint about it?—I consider that the toll is too high.

16,342. What is the amount of the toll?—No matter whether you have much or little fruit, the toll is the same.

16,343. How much is that?—Fourpence.

16,344. You consider that too much?—I do; for a man might only have one creel with him in his cart.

16,345. I believe it is the custom for the fruit growers about Armagh to sell the produce of their orchards to English and Scotch buyers?—Yes.

16,346. Wholesale?—Yes.

16,347. And I suppose the result of that is that very little fruit is brought into the market for sale?—That is so.

16,348. Do you know anything about the butter market?—Yes.

16,349. Is the accommodation ample?—I think so.

16,350. And you are satisfied with the way in which it is conducted?—Yes, in fact, I may say that I am perfectly satisfied with the markets generally, my only exception to that being the toll in the fruit market.

16,351. You consider it too high?—Yes, and I wish also to say that the charges in the pork market are very high?—There is not a pig I bring into the market that does not cost me 1s.

16,352. But only 4d. of that is charged by the toll committee?—Yes.

16,353. The remaining 8d. being put on by the buyers?—That is so.

Thornton Brown examined by Mr. Best.

16,354. You are a large farmer, I believe?—I am.

16,355. And you are in the habit of attending the Armagh markets?—Yes.

16,356. Which of them are you best acquainted with?—I principally attend the grass-seed market and the pork market.

16,357. Is there good accommodation in the pork market, in your opinion?—Yes, ample.

16,358. Is it a good market?—Yes, it has been greatly improved.

16,359. And is it well attended by buyers?—Yes.

16,360. I ask you, as a farmer, in your opinion are the facilities and accommodation afforded to the farmers satisfactory?—Yes, it is very good.

16,361. Is it well looked after by the members of the toll committee?—It is.

16,362. And have you any complaint to make with regard to the management of the markets generally by the toll committee?—I have not.

16,363. Then you think the markets are well managed?—I do.

16,364. Do you think that the toll of 4d., which is charged in the park market, is excessive?—No.

16,365. You know the grass-seed market?—Yes.

16,366. And the oat market?—Yes.

16,367. Are they well attended?—Yes.

16,368. From what distance do the people come to Armagh?—They come from long distances; some from beside Keady(?).

16,369. That is a long distance?—Yes.

16,370. And you say that you are quite satisfied with the style in which the markets are managed by the toll committee?—Yes.

16,371. And have you heard any complaints amongst the farmers?—No, not for a long time.

16,372. Do you know anything about the other markets?—No, I do not know so much about the others.

16,373. You know something about the cattle fair, I suppose?—Yes.

16,374. In your opinion, is it necessary to have a weighbridge for weighing live cattle?—At some future date it may be necessary, but I do not think it is required at present.

16,375. Have you ever sold live cattle by weight?—No.

16,376. Have you ever heard a wish expressed by those attending the market that cattle should be sold by weight?—Never.

16,377. Well then, generally, you are satisfied with the markets?—Yes, but I do not think that the potato market should be held in the streets. Then there are two charges, and I think one would be enough. I think a man going into the market should pay one charge going in, and then that should cover weighing.

16,378. But if you do not weigh you are not charged for weighing?—That is so.

16,379. Then weighing is not compulsory?—No, it is not compulsory, but as a general rule you must weigh your produce if you sell it.

16,380. I believe you know nothing about the dispute between the town commissioners and the toll committee?—Nothing whatever.

16,381. You know nothing of it one way or other?—No.

Francis [illegible] examined by Mr. Best.

16,382. How long have you been in Armagh?—For about 11 years.

16,383. Do you know something about the markets?—Yes.

16,384. Do you know the park market?—Very well.

16,385. What is your opinion of the way in which it is managed by the toll committee?—I believe it is conducted very honestly, both for the buyers and for sellers.

16,386. Do you make it a habit of going into the market?—Yes, generally.

16,387. And do you generally see members of the toll committee there looking after the arrangements?—Yes.

16,388. Do you know anything about the hay and straw market?—Yes.

16,389. Is it well managed?—Yes.

16,390. Is the accommodation in it good?—Yes, I think so, except when there is a very large market.

16,391. Have you ever heard any complaint from those attending the markets as to the way in which they are managed by the toll committee?—No, as far as I can say, everyone appears to be very well satisfied.

16,392. Do you think it would be advisable to take the management of the markets from the present toll committee, and hand it over to the town commissioners?—No.

16,393. Do you think that the toll committee conduct the markets as well, or even better, than the town commissioners could?—I do not think the markets could be conducted in a better style than they are at present.

16,394. Then you would let things remain as they are?—Certainly.

Cross-examined by Mr. Gallagher.

16,395. Do you think it right or desirable that any portion of the money derivable from the markets should go for the use and benefit of any individuals?—I consider that the members of the toll committee having invested their money in this way have a right to some return. If the markets are handed over to the town commissioners they will be compelled to borrow money to discharge their duties, and the townspeople will have to pay for it.

16,396. But do you think it right that a number of private individuals should reap the benefit of any profit upon the working of the markets?—I have already said, and I repeat it, that having regard to the manner in which the markets are being conducted at present, the members of the toll committee have a right and are entitled to some return for the money they have invested.

John [illegible] examined by Mr. Best.

16,397. Do you reside in Armagh?—Yes.

16,398. What part of it?—Market Street.

16,399. I believe that is close by the building in which we are sitting?—Yes.

16,400. How long have you lived there?—Oh, for a very long time.

16,401. How many years?—About 50 years.

16,402. You are well acquainted, I suppose, with the markets?—I am, especially with the one right opposite my house.

16,403. Well, speaking of that, will you tell us how it is managed?—I have noticed a great improvement latterly. One very proper step was the taking away of the stands of the dealers who used to cause a great deal of confusion by obstructing the thoroughfare.

16,404. The result has been to leave more room for the general market?—Yes.

16,405. Do you also know the hay and straw market?—I do.

16,406. What is your opinion as to the sufficiency or otherwise of the accommodation?—At present it is ample, but that was not the case some years ago.

16,407. Do you think the markets are better in the hands of the toll committee than they would be if they were vested in the Town Commissioners?—I do not think they could be in better hands than in those of the toll committee.

Cross-examined by Mr. Gallagher.

16,408. Then I take it that you do not wish to see the management of the markets vested in an elective body?—I do not desire any change, because I am perfectly satisfied with things as they are at present.

16,409. You object to the markets being transferred to the Town Commissioners?—Yes.

16,410. Why do you object?—Because I do not see any necessity for a change.

16,411. But what is the ground of your objection to the Town Commissioners, is it a political one?—No.

16,412. Is it a personal ground?—No.

16,413. Now, sir, tell me what is the ground of your objection?—Well, I object, because I am of opinion that the men who have charge of the markets at present are doing their work very well.

16,414. They were not doing it some time ago?—That is so, but they have greatly improved since then.

16,415. Is it not a fact that some time ago the markets were looked upon as a disgrace to the town?—Well, I could not go the length of saying that.

16,416. Were they good?—They were not.

16,417. Then were they bad; they must have been either one or the other?—They were bad, but, as I have already said, a great improvement has taken place since that was the case.

THOMAS M'DOWELL examined by MR. BEST.

16,418. You are in the employment of the toll committee?—Yes.

16,419. In what capacity?—As superintendent of the markets.

16,420. How long have you occupied that position?—For the last six years.

16,421. Then you are intimately acquainted with the management of the markets?—Yes.

16,422. The markets are well attended, I believe?—Yes.

16,423. And the people come very long distances to attend them?—Yes.

16,424. Do the members of the toll committee give you any assistance in the regulation of the affairs of the markets?—Yes, they visit all the different markets during the day.

16,425. Is that for the purpose of seeing that everything is going on properly?—Yes.

16,426. Have you heard the farmers who attend the market expressing their satisfaction with the manner in which the markets are conducted?—Yes.

16,427. Frequently?—Yes.

16,428. And you have never heard any complaints against the toll committee with reference to the charges they make, or their manner of conducting the business of the market?—No. I have heard complaints about charges made by the buyers, such as a reduction for damaged pork.

16,429. But I take it that that is a matter with which the toll committee have nothing whatever to do?—That is so.

16,430. And you say you have never heard any complaint against the toll committee?—None whatever.

16,431. In cases of offence against the market regulations, what course do you generally take?—I generally bring the parties before a magistrate, sometimes Mr. Best and sometimes Mr. Gillespie.

16,432. Did you ever hear any complaint about the pork market?—No.

16,433. Or about the weighbridge being insufficient for the work it has to do?—No. We are always able to get through the stuff very quickly. We can weigh 500 pigs before two o'clock.

16,434. That is at the rate of 170 per hour?—Yes.

16,435. How many porters have you to assist?—Five.

16,436. Is it the case, as has been said, that it is almost impossible for a man to get his stuff weighed without greasing the hands of the porters?—I have never known anything about it. On one occasion one of the men wanted drink, and I told him that if anything of the kind occurred again he would be discharged. That case is the only one of the kind that has ever come under my attention.

16,437. Now with reference to the hay and straw market, what kind of accommodation is there in it?—Very good accommodation indeed.

16,438. And is there ample shedding?—Yes, and we let the offices to the buyers for the purpose of paying the farmers, and transacting their other business.

16,439. That is intended, I suppose, as an inducement to buyers to attend the market?—Yes.

16,440. You know the butter market?—Yes.

16,441. I believe there is also ample shed and other accommodation there?—Yes.

16,442. In fact, in your opinion, is the accommodation in the different markets sufficient for all the requirements of the case?—Quite.

Cross-examined by MR. GALLAGHER.

16,443. Did you ever hear any complaint about inaccuracy in weighing produce?—Yes.

16,444. Do you know whether there was anything of the kind?—No.

16,445. Do you know a man named *Lawther*?—Yes.

16,446. And do you remember being 1 cwt. 2 qrs. wrong in weighing a certain commodity for him on one occasion?—I do not.

16,447. You do not remember it?—No.

16,448. Might such a thing have occurred without your remembering it?—I do not believe it did.

16,449. How often are the weighbridges tested?—I test them very often.

16,450. But tell us how often?—Six times every year.

16,451. How is that testing done?—We get the weights tested twice a year, and then I test the bridge with them.

16,452. How much have you ever found them inaccurate?—Never, to any serious extent.

16,453. But how about this 1 cwt. 2 qrs.?—That must be an error. The bridge could not possibly be inaccurate to such an extent.

16,454. Who does the weighing?—It is a man who has charge in the hay market, and Mrs. Stevenson has charge in the goal square.

16,455. Who does the weighing for her?—It is her daughter-in-law, a very intelligent person.

16,456. The potato market, I believe, is held in the streets?—Yes.

16,457. Beside the Provincial Bank?—Yes.

Re-examined by MR. BEST.

16,458. You know the live pig market?—Yes.

16,459. Is there any necessity to have a weighbridge there?—Certainly not.

16,460. What is your reason for saying that?—Well, there are very few live pigs sold, and any that are sold are not weighed.

SAMUEL GALLAGHER examined by MR. BEST.

16,461. I believe you assist your father, who is secretary to the toll committee?—Yes.

16,462. In the management of the markets?—Yes.

16,463. You know the markets very well?—Yes, I have attended them regularly for several years.

16,464. I believe some members of the toll committee go round the market every day?—Yes, Mr. Biggs, Mr. Best, and Mr. M'Clelland.

16,465. And you go round with them?—That is so.

16,466. For the purpose of seeing that everything is properly arranged?—Yes.

16,467. In your opinion are the markets well conducted?—I believe they are.

16,468. Is there ample accommodation for every one attending the markets?—Certainly.

16,469. Have you ever heard the farmers make any complaints against the way in which the markets are conducted?—No, on the contrary, I have heard them express great satisfaction at the entire arrangement.

16,470. Now with reference to this memorial, have you taken the trouble to discover whether those who have signed it are ratepayers?—Yes.

16,471. And what is the result?—I find that a number of the people whose names are appended to it are not rated.

16,472. How many?—14 or 15.

Cross-examined by Mr. Gallagher.

16,473. Did you take the trouble to ascertain if these people are householders in Armagh?—No, I did not. I found that they do not appear in the rate book, which was all that I wanted.

(Mr. Best.) Now, Mr. Commissioner, that is all the evidence I have to produce, and I beg to close the case on behalf of the toll committee.

(Mr. Gallagher.) Mr. Commissioner, in opening the case on behalf of the town commissioners of the city of Armagh, I have very little indeed to add to what has already been so well said by our witnesses before you, and to what was so well said by our Town Clerk, Mr. Peel, before the Chief Commissioners at their sitting in Belfast. It appears to me that the grievance of the charge against the toll committee is that they have been guilty of a breach of trust, that they have not applied the moneys which they have received from the markets of Armagh to the only purposes to which they could rightly apply them. Therefore we contend that in the way I have mentioned the members of the toll committee have failed to carry out the trusts of their trust deed. When notice was given that this inquiry was about to be held, my clients naturally expected that the toll committee were about to give some explanation which they had not previously given to show you that they had done their duty, but now the inquiry has taken place—the evidence for the toll committee—and I confidently assert that no evidence has been given here by the toll committee to rebut the case which we have made against them, that they have failed to properly discharge their trust. What has been complained of by the town commissioners is that the toll committee have not discharged that trust which provided that the money received from the tolls shall be expended in certain ways, the first of those ways being the payment of the costs and expenses incidental to the collection of the tolls and their management. Other ways are also mentioned in which the money is to be expended, one of them being the establishment of a sinking fund, and then the trust deed provides that any moneys which the toll committee receive over and above what is necessary for the performance of the trusts I have mentioned shall be expended for the improvement of the city of Armagh and the market place thereof. Now the question which then arises, Mr. Commissioner, is, has that been done, and the evidence which has been placed before you will supply the answer. You have heard, sir, how they have carried out that portion of their trust with regard to the establishment of a sinking fund. You have heard of the way in which new debentures have been issued, and also of the way in which their original indebtedness has been increased. Their trust deed provides that any surplus shall be expended for the improvement and benefit of the city of Armagh and the fairs and market places thereof, but instead of that I contend that the committee have expended in a way entirely foreign to the intention of their trust deed a sum more than sufficient to wipe out their debt. A sum of 1,[illegible]l. has been expended by the committee, one-half being upon the Mall as a place of amusement and recreation, and the other half upon the Tontine Rooms as a place for public meetings. You therefore have it that the toll committee since the year 18[illegible], instead of discharging their trust, instead of establishing a sinking fund, and instead of endeavouring to decrease their indebtedness, have failed to establish a sinking fund, and have increased their indebtedness by a very substantial amount. And further, the town commissioners, who are the body elected by the ratepayers to take charge of the affairs of the city, wish to remind you that this large sum of 700l. a year, which has been at the disposal of the toll committee, would, if it had been in the hands of the town commissioners, have materially assisted them in the improvement of the city. The Town Commissioners are of opinion, sir, that they are the proper authority to have charge of the toll, but then we have received this extraordinary answer from the members of the toll committee, that they would be quite willing to hand over the tolls to a properly elected body of town commissioners. Now I must confess that we really do not know what the toll committee are pleased to mean when they talk about a properly elected body of town commissioners. My clients are the board of town commissioners for the city of Armagh, and they have been elected to that position strictly in accordance with the requirements of the Act of Parliament referring to such matters. Under that Act of Parliament the members of the board are elected for a period of three years, and at the end of that time they retire, when if they have not discharged the trusts attaching to the position to the satisfaction of the ratepayers, it is in the power of the latter to decline to elect them, to get rid of them, and to select other gentlemen to represent them, and to manage the affairs of the town. If, therefore, the town commissioners of Armagh do not constitute in the correct meaning of the term a properly elected body of town commissioners, I fail to appreciate the meaning of the words. Here is a sum of 700l., which the town commissioners contend should be within bounds for the benefit and improvement of the city, and in order to show the opinion of the inhabitants upon the subject, I will put in a memorial which was presented to the town commissioners in the year 18[illegible], praying that something should be done for the purpose of vesting the management of the tolls in the town commissioners with a view to securing that the profits arising from the working of the markets should be applied for the improvements and benefit of the city. That memorial is signed by the firm of Messrs. J. and R. Gillespie, and one of the firm is now a member of the toll committee, and was examined before you upon the last day. In the year 18[illegible], that memorial was signed on his behalf, and on behalf of his firm, and I also see the name of Mr. Wm. Bright, who upon the occasion of your former sitting in Armagh was examined against the desirability of the tolls being vested in the town commissioners. That memorial which I will put in is of an extensive character, being signed both numerously and influentially, expressing the opinions and feelings upon the subject of the inhabitants of the town. Then with regard to the subject of the establishment of a sinking fund, you have heard it stated in evidence that at the meeting of the debenture holders which has already been referred to, a motion was brought forward having for its object the establishment of such a fund, but the gentleman who proposed it could not find anyone willing to second his resolution, which will show you whether or not there is a desire to discharge the provision of the trust deed in this respect upon the part of the toll committee. It has been said by a member of the toll committee that he would consider it a very desirable thing to establish such a fund if they had the money to set apart for such a purpose, but you, sir, will remember that I elicited that at the meeting in question the toll committee had to their credit a balance of [illegible]l. [illegible]s. That proposal fell through for want of a seconder, and I repeat that from that fact you can judge by the intention or otherwise of the toll committee to discharge their trusts in this respect. In this matter, and also in the matter of the issue of new debentures, we contend that the toll committee have failed to discharge their trusts; and then there is another matter to which I wish to refer, and that is the fact that the toll committee have spent the very large sum of [illegible]l. upon law costs, but that matter has been dealt with far better than I could have hoped to have done it. Mr. Peel is solicitor to the town commissioners, and understood the question much better than I did. He is unfortunately absent to-day, and I have endeavoured to discharge my duty in this respect as well as I possibly could under the circumstances. There are, however, other matters which call for attention at my hands. We have heard a good deal about the improvement of the markets. Well, we admit that the markets have been very much improved, and I think that we had a good piece of evidence from one of the witnesses, I do not remember his name, who said that up to recently the markets were in such a bad state that they were really a disgrace to the city, but that they had been much improved of late. But it should not be forgotten that those improvements were the result of the action of gentlemen entirely unconnected with the toll committee, men who had a stake in the city, and whose interests were bound up with the welfare and prosperity of the city. Some of these improvements were carried to a successful issue entirely by voluntary effort and voluntary exertion, the toll committee giving no assistance whatever to bring about the result, the benefits of which are now so much felt and appreciated. The town commissioners felt very strongly that they, as the representatives of the ratepayers of the city, should have the management of the tolls in their hands. They had control of the affairs of the city, and they felt that it was their duty and their right also to have control of the markets. The town commissioners were the merchants and traders of the city, they were intimately acquainted with the wants and the feelings of the people, and they were of opinion that it would conduce to the best interest of the markets and of the whole city to have the management of the tolls of Armagh vested in their body. The feeling in Armagh, as well as in every other place, is that the control of the markets should be vested in the governing and representative body of the city. The intention, so far back as 1880, was that the markets should be managed for the benefit of the city, and I think you, Mr. Commissioner, will be convinced when this inquiry has concluded that that intention has not by any means been realised, and that the trusts contained in the trust deed of the toll committee have not been carried out. If the town commissioners had at their disposal the profits arising from the tolls, the result would be a great improvement not only in the markets but in the city generally. I do not think that I have any further remarks, and I will, therefore, conclude, and will call upon the town clerk to give evidence.

Thos. G. Peel examined by Mr. Gallagher.

16,474. You are clerk to the Town Commissioners of Armagh?—Yes.

16,475. And I believe you have been examined twice before?—Yes.

16,476. Once, I believe, in Armagh before Mr. Commissioner Black, and once before the Chief Commissioners at their sitting in Belfast?—Yes. And with regard to my appearance before the Chief Commissioners in Belfast I would like to make a few remarks by way of explanation. I wish to say that in going to Belfast I had not the slightest desire to go behind the back of the toll committee, but merely went there because I heard that the toll committee also intended to appear before the Royal Commissioners. I was desirous of making that explanation in order that my going to Belfast might not be misunderstood.

16,477. Well, now Mr. Peel, having made your explanation, I wish to know if you now approve every thing you said previously?—Certainly, every single word. I affirm everything I said, both here and in Belfast, which I believe to be strictly true.

16,478. How long have you occupied the position of town clerk?—About 10 years.

16,479. And how long were you a town commissioner previous to that?—For 15 years.

16,480. During that time you have taken an interest in the fairs and markets of Armagh?—Yes.

16,481. Do you remember the time that the cattle market became extinct?—Yes, and also the hiring fair.

16,482. You remember the re-establishment of the cattle fair?—Yes, it was re-opened and was held on the first Thursday of each month.

16,483. It was extinct previous to 1856, I believe?—Yes. I never remember it previous to that.

16,484. Was the initiative in the revival taken by persons not connected with the toll committee?—Yes, with the exception of Mr. Riggs, who held two debentures.

16,485. Then he and a number of other gentlemen voluntarily took up the work of reviving the fairs in Armagh?—Yes.

16,486. And those efforts were successful?—Yes, the fairs were re-established.

16,487. Speaking of the markets generally some time ago, what was their character?—They were not at all suited to the requirements of the place.

16,488. But I believe they have been improved lately?—Oh, yes, we do not dispute for a moment that the markets have been improved. We never disputed that there were excellent markets at the shambles.

16,489. Is the accommodation in the flax market sufficient?—Yes, the flax market is good enough, but there is this drawback, that on wet days the flax gets wet.

16,490. For want of proper shelter?—Yes.

16,491. Do you think that there is proper supervision over the markets?—I believe there is a want of supervision in the flax market.

16,492. Do you think it would improve matters if there was a proper officer appointed to have complete charge of and superintendence over the markets?—Yes. I think there should be a permanent official of that sort in each place, and not running about all over the markets like Mr. M'Donald, Mr. Gardiner, and Mr. Riggs. At the same time I wish to say that Mr. M'Donald is a very efficient man, but if there was a permanent official in each market a much more satisfactory state of things would be the result.

16,493. The potato market is held in the street, I believe?—Yes.

16,494. Are there any other markets held in the street?—Yes, the fowl market, a great deal of it is held in the street.

16,495. Am I right in saying that the toll committee have been endeavouring to assert a claim to a portion of the street which is under the care of the town commissioners, and to which they have no right whatever?—That is so. They have commenced to claim a certain portion with a view to asserting a right to it, but I have done little jobs in order to prevent these gentlemen getting possession of it by custom.

16,496. Now, with reference to the market which was established in 1880, how was that established?—It was inaugurated under the auspices of the town commissioners.

16,497. About that time was there a movement set upon foot with the object of having the markets improved?—Yes.

16,498. And was it taken up warmly?—Yes, a meeting was called, and the market committee was formed.

16,499. Was anything else done?—Yes, a resolution was adopted that certain members of the town commissioners should wait upon the toll committee with the object of having the markets improved.

16,500. Was that deputation appointed?—Yes.

16,501. Composed of members of the town commissioners?—Yes.

16,502. Did that deputation wait upon the members of the toll committee?—Yes.

16,503. They took no steps, I believe?—No, and there were no practical results except that they gave us a subscription of 10*l.*

16,504. The toll committee gave you that money?—Yes.

16,505. Towards the fund for the establishment of a flax market?—Yes.

16,506. What did that fund amount to?—300*l.*

16,507. But beyond giving you that sum of 10*l.*, they gave you no practical support, I believe?—No.

16,508. Then we may take it that anything that was accomplished was entirely the result of voluntary effort.

16,509. Did that stimulate the markets?—Yes, and I think it also stimulated the toll committee to a certain extent.

16,510. You think it gave them new life?—Yes, and one of the members of the market committee was absorbed by the toll committee.

16,511. Well, do you think that the result was to improve the markets generally?—Yes, the toll committee were to a certain extent wakened up, and the markets commenced to show some improvement.

16,512. Do you think it would be an advantage and a benefit to the markets if the tolls were vested in the town commissioners?—Most undoubtedly I do.

16,513. And the city as well?—Certainly.

16,514. You express that opinion entirely irrespective of politics?—In giving expression to that opinion I am going against my own politics.

16,515. Then you are not averse to a mixed board of commissioners being elected by the people?—No, I am not, and in fact I have from the very first been in favour of a mixed board. In the year [illegible], on the occasion of the dispute in the old board of town commissioners, I was of the same opinion.

16,516. You were in favour of the Town Improvement Act?—Yes, and am still; and I am in favour of lowering the franchise, but not bringing it down too low.

16,517. Are you in favour of a 4l. franchise?—Yes, and I would even go so far as to advocate a 3l one, but it should be irrespective of politics, because I believe that to be against the best interests of the town.

16,518. And you say that in your opinion the town commissioners are the proper parties to have charge of the tolls?—Yes.

16,519. What is the amount of the rate levied by the town commissioners—the borough rate?—It realises a sum of [illegible].

16,520. That is for borough purposes?—Yes, lighting, watching, and cleansing, and other purposes.

16,521. Is that amount sufficient for the purpose?—No, it is not near sufficient, for the town is a large one, and we could do a great deal more than we are able to do at present if we had the money. If we had charge of the markets, and had in our hands the profits arising from them, we would have command of a sum of money which would relieve the rates and enable the commissioners or the representatives of the town to carry out many improvements in the city.

16,522. Have the members of the toll committee ever assisted the town commissioners in any way in their efforts to improve the city?—Never. They never would help any movement which was not for their own exclusive benefit.

16,523. You are aware that efforts have been made to get the tolls transferred from the present toll committee to the town commissioners?—Yes, from time to time efforts were made to get the town commissioners to make a movement in that direction.

16,524. Is that the object of that memorial?—Yes.

16,525. Is it numerously signed?—Yes; and it is a memorial representative of all classes of society in the city.

16,526. I believe that memorial was presented to you for the purpose of having it laid before the town commissioners?—Yes.

16,527. That memorial asked that the town commissioners should take steps to have the tolls transferred from the toll committee to themselves?—Yes.

16,528. On the ground that the change would be for the benefit and advantage of the town?—Yes.

16,529. Does the holding of markets in streets increase the expenses of your board?—Yes. Where the markets are held in streets we have to clear them, and that entails an additional expense on the rates.

16,530. Do you think that means for weighing live cattle should be afforded in the market?—Yes.

16,531. And is there anything of that sort in it?—No; there is a weighbridge, but it is not suitable for the purpose.

16,532. (Mr. Rigg.) It wants very little to make it suitable. A couple of pounds would do all that is required.

16,533. You think a weighbridge for weighing live cattle is required?—Yes; and to show the importance of the matter I will read an extract from the "Irish "Farmers Gazette" upon the subject, which is as follows:—"An English farmer procured a weighbridge "of his own, and he challenged nine of his neighbours, "all experienced graziers (who had been assured time "after time by the butchers that they were excellent "judges of the value of fat bullocks) to estimate the "weight and value of four ripened beasts against "scale beam. The result was that the average guess "of the nine men fell nearly 3 cwt., or [illegible] lbs., "below the actual weight of the beasts as revealed by "the scales, which at the prevailing price would have "meant a loss to the seller of nearly 7l. a head on the "four head." Here is another extract dealing with the same subject. "Again, in an experiment made by "Mr. Wensley Richards, as shown in a paper read by "him before the London Farmers Club on the last "Monday in April 1869, it was shown that upon an "average for 27 head the scale showed 63 lbs. each "gain, which at 7d. per lb. would be 1l. 16s. each over "the estimated value." Now these two extracts go to show the great importance of weighing live cattle in order to ascertain their actual weight and value. I copied them from the papers, but as I thought there might be some question about their authenticity, I have copies of the papers with me, so that Mr. Ross can see them if he wishes to do so.

16,534. Now with reference to that meeting which was called by the chairman of the town commissioners with reference to the railway rates and charges, that meeting was called by the chairman, I believe, as a matter of courtesy?—Yes.

16,535. A requisition was presented to the chairman in the usual way?—Yes.

16,536. And the meeting was called in pursuance of that requisition?—Quite so.

16,537. Did you send out a circular to attend the meeting?—Yes, but not officially.

Cross-examined by Mr. Ross.

16,538. You say that you appeared before the Royal Commissioners in Belfast because you heard that the toll committee were going to do so?—Quite so.

16,539. Now who was it told you that were going to appear before the Royal Commissioners?—I do not think I am at liberty to tell you.

16,540. Oh, but you must tell me; who was it?—I will not tell you without his permission.

16,541. Well, upon behalf of the toll committee I deny it?—Very well, I knew you would.

16,542. Did you state before the Royal Commissioners that the toll committee could not get anyone to come forward to give evidence on their behalf?—Yes, except one gentleman.

16,543. Did you hear Mr. Gardiner say that we had witnesses in attendance ready to give evidence?—They must have been imaginary witnesses.

16,544. Now do you still stick to that statement?—I do. I say that there were no witnesses there, that is that there were no persons in the room as witnesses to give evidence.

16,545. You say again, that you knew that was true?—Yes. There was no appearance of any persons to give evidence.

16,546. Did you see John Hughes?—I do not remember if he was there.

16,547. Did you see Wm. Addey?—I do not remember.

16,548. And you adhere to the statement that we had no witnesses present?—Yes.

16,549. Now with regard to the hiring fair, where is it held?—At the [illegible].

16,550. On the public street?—Yes, because there is no other place provided by the toll committee for it.

16,551. Do you know any other town where the hiring fair is held anywhere else except on the street?—I do not know, I cannot speak of the rest of Ireland.

16,552. You say that you think that there ought to be a man like M'Donald in every market in town?—Yes.

16,553. But in order to get that you would have to increase the wages?—Not at all. You could get men for 8s. 6d.

16,554. Not men like M'Donald?—Quite as good.

16,555. With reference to this bridge for weighing live cattle, you think that is necessary?—Yes.

16,556. Have you heard the evidence of Mr. Sherry?—Yes.

16,557. And of Mr. Thos. Hodge?—Yes.

16,558. And of Mr. Wm. Simpson?—Yes.

16,559. Did you hear those experienced men say that a bridge was not necessary?—Yes.

16,560. And yet you now say it is?—Yes.

16,561. Do you know Portadown fair?—Yes.

16,562. You want cattle sold by weight?—Yes.

16,563. I believe you are not a very large farmer yourself?—No, not very large.

16,564. How much do you farm?—Twenty acres.

16,565. That is not much?—No, it is not; but I have a great deal of experience of farming matters.

16,566. You say you think the tolls should be transferred from the toll committee to the town commissioners?—Yes.

16,567. Why?—Because I think the toll committee are the proper persons to have charge of such matters.

16,568. Is not the toll committee composed of the same class of gentlemen as the town commissioners?—Yes.

16,569. And yet you think the tolls should be taken from the one body and handed over to the other?—Yes. I think the governing body is the proper one to have charge of such matters to manage them on behalf of the ratepayers whom they represent.

John Burns examined by Mr. Gallagher.

16,570. Did you go around the householders for the purpose of getting that memorial signed?—Yes. I went to a number of them.

16,571. What time did it take you to get the signatures that you obtained?—I did it all in the one day.

16,572. You were aware that it had to be done in a hurry?—Yes.

16,573. And you managed it all in one day?—Yes.

16,574. I suppose you were present here when a number of people were brought up to give evidence denying these signatures?—Yes.

16,575. Did you call upon Wm. Brearley?—Yes.

16,576. And did he sign it?—No, he did not, but he told his wife to sign it for him, and she did so.

16,577. Here is the name of Thomas M'Creesh, who signed in that case?—His wife.

16,578. George Sherry, did you go to his house?—Yes.

16,579. Who did you find there?—Mrs. Sherry and the son.

16,580. How was the memorial explained to the wife and son of this man?—Yes.

16,581. And they fully agreed with it?—Yes.

16,582. Who signed it?—The son.

16,583. Now, in the case of John Sherry, who signed it?—The wife.

16,584. Do you remember calling on Thomas Dolan?—I did not call on him.

16,585. Did you call on a man named Foster?—No.

16,586. Did you call on Charles O'Neill?—Yes.

16,587. Did he sign it?—Yes, in his own house.

16,588. Did he read the memorial?—No. I explained it to him, and he said it was just the thing we wanted.

16,589. Did you tell him that the object of the memorial was to get the tolls transferred from the toll committee to the town commissioners?—Yes.

16,590. And he approved of it?—Yes.

16,591. Were these all you called upon?—Yes.

16,592. You say that Mrs. Sherry signed it?—Yes.

16,593. Did you call upon Patrick Lavery?—Yes.

16,594. Did he sign it?—No, but the wife signed it.

16,595. Did you call upon a man named Clarke?—Yes.

16,596. Did he sign the memorial?—No.

16,597. Did you speak to him about it?—Yes.

16,598. Where?—I met him in the street.

16,599. How long is that ago?—Not long ago.

16,600. Was it you that saw Patrick Mallon?—Yes.

16,601. Who signed it?—Mallon's sister.

16,602. Did you call upon Thomas Fahy?—Yes, and I saw the wife, but she said he was not at home.

16,603. How long were you out altogether getting these signatures?—About four hours.

16,604. And you got all these names in that time?—Yes.

16,605. How often did you read it?—Not very often.

16,606. Did they ask you what it was about?—Yes.

16,607. Did you go to any who refused to sign it?—Not one.

George H. Lewis examined by Mr. Gallagher.

16,608. I believe you live about six miles from Armagh?

16,609. And you attend the markets in Armagh?—Yes, in fact, it is the only market which I attend.

16,610. Then you are well acquainted with the management of the markets?—Yes.

16,611. What is your opinion of it?—I think it is very badly managed.

16,612. Do you know the flax market?—Yes.

16,613. Have you any complaint to make with regard to it?—I have been boycotted in it.

16,614. Was that by the buyers?—Yes, at least I believe I was. However, I will tell you the circumstances under which the matter arose. Last October a buyer came to the mill where I was getting my flax scutched. He offered to buy it, but I said I would not sell until the flax had been scutched, and I told him that when it was scutched I would give him the preference. On the Tuesday week following I had the flax in the market at Armagh, and it was treated like rubbish, and I was treated like a dog.

16,615. Were you able to sell that flax in Armagh?—No.

16,616. Was there anyone in the market at the time on behalf of the toll committee?—I saw no one.

16,617. Where did you take the flax to?—I took it to the next market at Dungannon, which was about a fortnight afterwards.

16,618. And did you sell it there?—At once.

16,619. And that occurrence is your reason for stating that you were boycotted?—Yes.

16,620. Do you know the pork market?—Thoroughly.

16,621. There is a charge of 1*s.* exacted in it, I believe?—Yes.

16,622. On each pig?—Yes.

16,623. And as a farmer, are you of opinion that that charge is excessive?—Certainly.

16,624. (*Mr. Commissioner Bland.*) What is your opinion of the management?—I think the market is characterised by a want of management, and the result is that the buyers are able to rule it against the farmers.

(*Mr. Biggs.*) If the whole toll committee had been present upon the occasion you mention they could have done nothing.

Cross-examined by Mr. Rowe.

16,625. What you have described is the ground of your complaint against the markets?—That is my grievance.

16,626. Do not buyers usually try the flax before purchasing?—Of course.

16,627. Do you know a flax buyer named Maxwell?—No.

16,628. Were you offered a price by anyone?—Yes, but I would not take it.

16,629. What did you get for the flax at Dungannon?—I will not tell you.

16,630. Because you would not sell your flax at the mill the buyers formed a ring against you?—That is what occurred.

16,631. Have you ever attended any pork market except Armagh?—Yes, one or two.

16,632. And what charges did you pay?—I do not remember.

16,633. Did they not amount to the same as you pay in Armagh?—I have already told you that I do not remember.

16,634. Did you ever make a complaint with reference to the inaccuracy of a weighbridge in the market?—Yes, about two years ago I was having some hay weighed, and there was an inaccuracy in the weight to the extent of 1 cwt. 3 qrs.

JAMES AGNEW examined by Mr. GALLAGHER.

16,635. You live in Armagh?—Yes.

16,636. And you carry on business in the city?—Yes.

16,637. In Barrack Street?—Yes.

16,638. You have done so for several years?—Yes.

16,639. Do you attend the markets in Armagh?—Yes.

16,640. And you are acquainted with their management?—Yes.

16,641. And is it your opinion that the tolls should be vested in the town commissioners, to be managed by them and applied for the benefit of the city?—Yes, one body is quite sufficient for the city.

16,642. The town commissioners are only elected for a term of three years?—That is so.

16,643. And at the end of that time if the ratepayers are not satisfied with the manner in which they have performed their duties they can reject them and select others?—Certainly.

16,644. At present is the money derived from the markets applied for the benefit of the city?—No, it is applied to private purposes.

16,645. You know the markets?—Yes.

16,646. And in the pork market there is, I believe, a charge of 1d.?—Yes.

16,647. On each pig?—Yes.

16,648. Portion of that charge goes to the toll committee and portion is charged by the buyers?—That is so.

16,649. (Mr Commissioner Black.) Do you buy pork for curing purposes?—Yes.

16,650. I believe the charge for bonus money goes into the pockets of the buyers?—Yes.

16,651. And they give no value for it?—Not that I know of.

16,652. What is your opinion about the holding of markets in the streets?—Well, I would like to see the streets thronged if there was sufficient supervision and if they were properly kept.

16,653. Are they properly kept at present?—Nothing of the kind.

Cross-examined by Mr. BEST.

16,654. What part of the city do you live in?—Outside the pig market.

16,655. Do you approve of the change of the pig market to the goal square?—I do not. I think it was better where it was for 60 years.

16,656. Did the removal of the market mean a loss to you?—Yes.

16,657. Did you say that the change would mean a loss of 10,000*l.* a year?—Yes.

16,658. How many pigs do you buy in the year?—A good many.

JAMES SYMES examined by Mr. GALLAGHER.

16,659. You are a merchant in Armagh, I believe?—Yes.

16,660. You are not a town commissioner or a toll committee-man?—No.

16,661. What is your opinion about the proposed transfer of the tolls from the toll committee to the town commissioners, are you in favour it?—Yes, I am of opinion that the tolls of Armagh or a public trust should be in the hands of a public body, and that the profits arising from them should be applied to the reduction of the rates.

16,662. (Mr. Commissioner Black.) But why should there be any profit upon the management of the tolls?—Well, there appears that there is.

16,663. But that could be cured by reducing the tolls to such an amount as would be sufficient to maintain the markets?—Of course, that could be done, but I think that if there is to be a profit, it should be applied for the benefit of the city.

16,664. Why should the charges be more than is necessary to maintain the markets?—I would not have them so.

16,665. Why should farmers in the country have to pay for the maintenance of the streets of Armagh?—Well, they use them coming into the market.

Mr. GALLAGHER re-called.

16,666. (Mr. Commissioner Black.) Will you give me the names of the members of the toll committee?—They are Messrs. Gardiner, Boggs, Preston, Best, Gillespie, Robinson, M'Clelland, Ferris, and Jenkinson.

16,667. How often do they retire?—They retire annually.

16,668. Then they are only elected for one year?—That is so.

16,669. Is the annual meeting largely attended?—Yes.

16,670. And how are the members elected?—By ballot.

FRANCIS A. MASSEY examined by Mr. GALLAGHER.

16,671. You live in Armagh?—Yes.

16,672. And you are engaged in business?—The corn and flour business.

16,673. You know the markets very well, I suppose?—Yes.

16,674. Have you ever heard complaints about the way in which the markets are conducted?—Yes.

16,675. From whom?—The farmers.

16,676. What about?—I have heard them complain that they are not treated in Armagh as they are in Portadown and Newry.

16,677. Were these complaints grounded upon a want of supervision in the markets?—Yes.

16,678. Are you in favour of the transfer of the tolls from the toll committee to the town commissioners?—Yes.

16,679. What is reason for being of that opinion?—Well, I think the markets would be better looked after by the town commissioners.

16,680. You know the town commissioners?—Yes.

16,681. And, I believe, they are all business men?—Nearly all.

16,682. And they take an interest in the welfare of the city?—Yes.

16,683. Are you in favour of applying any profits that may arise from the tolls for the benefit of the city?—Yes.

(Mr. Gallagher.) Mr. Commissioner that closes the case for the town commissioners.

The inquiry then concluded.

TIPPERARY.

With reference to my inquiry in Tipperary on the 1st November 1888, I beg to report as follows :—

Tipperary is situated in the county of Tipperary, of which it is one of the chief towns. It is surrounded by a country rich and fertile, and the town has a good general trade. There are many fine buildings in the town, and the streets are many and of fair width, but, as in the case of Thurles, could be kept in a better state of cleanliness. The town is situated at the base of the Slievenamuck Hills and is a station on the Waterford and Limerick Railway Line. It is of some importance and possesses a butter trade perhaps second only to that of Cork. A board of town commissioners administer the local affairs. The population is 7,274.

The market days are Thursday and Saturday. A butter market is held daily. The fairs are held on the second Tuesday in January, second Tuesday in February, second Tuesday in March, 5th April, second Tuesday in May, 24th June, second Tuesday in July, second Tuesday in August, second Tuesday in September, 10th October, second Tuesday in November, and 10th December.

Tolls are levied at the market and at the fairs held on the 5th April, 24th June, 10th October, and 10th December, with the exception of horses, which are toll free at present, but the levying of a toll on them, it is stated, is in contemplation by the owner of the market rights. The fairs held on the second Tuesday in January, second Tuesday in February, second Tuesday in March, second Tuesday in May, second Tuesday in July, second Tuesday in August, second Tuesday in September, and second Tuesday in November, are toll free.

The market rights and tolls are the property of A. H. Smith Barry, Esq., M.P., of Queenstown, who is in the immediate receipt of the tolls through his agents and managers.

Mr. Richard Cooper Chadwick is the owner of the charges at the butter market, as he was appointed butter weigh-master in 1853 by the magistrates under the provisions of the 52 George III. c. 134. He rents a market building from Mr. Smith Barry at 52*l.* a year.

Two patents were granted for the town of Tipperary. The first is dated 18th July 1690, and granted to William Ryan a fair on Vigil Day and day following, and another on the Feast of Saint Andrew the Apostle. The second is dated 16th January 1858, and granted to James Hugh Smith Barry eight yearly fairs, "in addition to the four fairs "which the said J. H. S. Barry was then entitled to hold in the said town of Tip- "perary on the 5th April, 24th June, 10th October, and 10th December," viz. :— On the second Tuesday in each of the months of January, February, March, May, July, August, September, and November in each year subject to the yearly rent of 1*l.* 6*s.* 8*d.* No tolls are granted under this patent.

The following extracts from the abstract of Mr. Smith Barry's title will show the periods at which each of the fairs were established :—

"In 1735 one fair only held, and from 1738 four fairs were held in March, June, "September, and November until 1758, when four fairs were held, viz., March, June, "October, and December. From 1758 to 1858 four fairs were held, viz., April, July, "October, and December. From 1858 to present time 12 fairs, viz., one in each "month."

In accordance with my instructions I have inspected the fair green and market places.

The fairs are held in a large space on the road leading from the town to the railway station. It is some distance from the market place and is surrounded by a wall. Before the fairs were removed there the place was a partial commonage where a number of small cottages were built. There are now only a few of these cottages left. The fair green, as it is called, is enclosed by the wall built by Mr. Smith Barry, M.P.

The gates which were put there had to be removed owing to the right of way which was claimed across the green by those living in the cottages at the other side. There are eight pens erected, four on each of two sides of the enclosure, for the accommodation of buyers who wish to store pigs in them previous to their removal by train. A weigh-bridge for cattle has also been recently erected in compliance with the recent act. The general aspect of the green is on a par with that of other places in different towns, but at the entrance from the main road, owing to the softness of the soil, there is an accumulation of mud which a little filling up or paving would mitigate. In its state at the time of inspection it was most unpleasant to attempt to get beyond the entrance when endeavouring to enter the body of the field.

Cattle are occasionally sold out on the road facing the fair green.

The markets are held in an enclosed space situated a few yards off the main street. At the entrance there are on either side rows of stalls erected by Mr. Barry for huxters and retailers of every description of commodities. Passing beyond these stalls the market square opens into a large space surrounded by a high wall, against which some sheds are built. The town hall is also built here. This enclosure is called the market yard. On the left-hand side is a shed for weighing potatoes and storing them if required. Then there is a weigh-bridge for weighing the hay, with a small office close by, where the tickets are issued, and a small council for the use of the retailers. There are two entrances to this market yard.

The butter market is held daily. A large shed is rented by the weigh master from Mr. Smith Barry, and in this the butter is weighed, coopered, drained, and sold. The dimensions of the shed are about 150 feet by 50. It is evenly flagged, with a small channel made in the centre to convey the water from the firkins when drained, while the roof, which is lofty and well ventilated, is made of sheet iron. Around on the walls at small intervals are the names of the different buyers frequenting the market, and, according as a sale is effected, the butter is grouped under each name before being delivered. The house, it is stated, is capable of accommodating 1,000 firkins on one day. A large beam and scales is erected near the office where the butter is weighed and the ticket issued. A smaller scales is also provided for ascertaining the tare of the empty firkins.

All the butter brought into the town does not, however, pass through this market. The farmers take it direct to whichever merchant gives them the best price, and it is there weighed and coopered, if purchased, free of any charge. On an average 50 per cent. of the entire quantity brought to the town is disposed of in this manner.

This is one of the largest butter markets in the south of Ireland, as some 2,000 firkins are brought in weekly. The arrangements by Mr. Chadwick are good and considered satisfactorily carried out, and, on the whole, practically no complaints were made of the management or of accommodation, with the exception of a want of storage accommodation; but it is said that this is not so much needed, as some 95 per cent. of the firkins brought to the market place are sold.

A toll board is erected.

Complaints were made of the heavy charges on pigs. If pigs are brought into the fair in carts, each cart has to bear a charge of 6d., and if the pigs are subsequently sold, 2d. each additional has to be paid on their exit from the fair. In addition to these there is a storage charge of 1d. per pig if the accommodation is availed of. This is too much for the accommodation afforded. The seller has also to give the buyer the customary "luck penny" on each pig sold to him.

The inquiry was well attended, and great interest, indeed, was manifested in the proceedings.

Appended will be found a transcript of the evidence taken at the inquiry.

JOHN J. O'MEARA,
Assistant Commissioner.

45, Lower Mount Street, Dublin.

Mr. George Caldwell examined.

17,763. You represent here Mr. Smith Barry?—Well, I manage the office.

17,764. For the purpose of this inquiry you represent him?—Yes.

17,765. Is he the owner of the market rights in Tipperary?—He is.

17,766-7. What markets are here, and on what days are they held?—There are two markets in each week, Thursdays and Saturdays. These are the market days.

17,768. Are there any other market days here?—Well, any day is a market day for butter.

17,769. Every day?—Yes, but we have nothing to do with that.

17,770-2. Are tolls levied on these market days—Thursdays and Saturdays?—They are.

17,773. What market premises are owned here in Tipperary?—There are sheds, a market office, weighbridges, and stalls.

17,774. Are they all convenient to each other?—They are all in one square.

17,775. Is that square enclosed?—It is.

17,776. It does not form any portion of the public thoroughfare?—No; it does not.

17,777. Who was it erected those market sheds?—Mr. Smith Barry.

17,778. Do you know when?—Well, at different times within the last 20 or 30 years.

17,779. Have the markets been always held on that site, even previous to the erection of those sheds?—I believe not. I could not exactly say. I think the market was made newly; there was an old potato market at the back of the town hall.

17,780. Could you tell us what commodities are brought in on Thursdays?—There is hay, straw, potatoes, and vegetables.

17,781. Whether you obtain a toll or not?—We obtain a toll on hay and straw for weighing.

17,782. Is corn brought in here?—It is sold in the street generally, except it comes to us to be weighed, and then we charge for it.

17,783. Is turf brought in here?—It is not brought into the market. It is sold on the street. There is no toll charged.

17,784. The only commodities brought to the market proper are hay, straw, potatoes, and vegetables. Is that all?—That is all.

17,785. Are fowl brought in?—They are, and sold in the street.

17,786. Are cattle ever sold on market days?—Well sometimes there are auctions held in the market.

17,787. That is Mr. Smith Barry's?—Yes.

17,788. What are the auctions connected with?—Auctions of cattle by licensed auctioneers.

17,789. Would there be any toll on those cattle?—Yes, we charge 2d. a head.

17,790. Who is it pays that toll?—The auctioneer, just for liberty to sell.

17,791. It is only on each head sold you charge?—Yes.

17,792. Does the same description of commodities come in on Saturday?—Yes.

17,793-4. Have you got a schedule of your charges around?—Yes.

The witness then produced the schedule, of which the following is a copy:—

Schedule of Tolls at Tipperary Fairs.

Ox or cow	6d.
Two-year-old	4d.
One-year-old	3d.
Calf	1d.
Sheep, lamb, or goat	1d.
Pig, value 1l.	2d.
" under 1l.	1d.
Butter per cask	1d.
Standings	10d.
Carts with young pigs	6d.
Weighing a load on weighbridge	2d.
Weighing on small scale	1d.
	Per Cwt. or over.
Do. do.	1s. 6d.
	Under a Cwt.
Stalls, per week	6d.

17,795. Are these tolls what you call tolls proper, or are they weighing charges that you levy in the market?—Weighing charges you may say.

17,796. On hay, what is your charge?—2d. a load for every commodity weighed.

17,797. Whether hay or straw or a load of potatoes, if brought in a cart?—Yes.

17,798. Do you draw any distinction between a donkey's load and a horse's load?—No. We use one ticket, and it is for the ticket we get the 2d.

The following is a copy of the ticket handed in by the witness:—

No.

________ 18

Weighed for________

1 Load of________

	Cwts.	qrs.	lbs.
Gross,			
Cart,			
Nett,			

No. . . .

Tipperary Markets.

________ 18

Weighed for________

1 Load of________

				Cwts.	qrs.	lbs.
Gross,	...	...	...			
Cart,	...	...	...			
Nett Weight,	...	...				

____

Weighmaster.

17,799. You give a printed ticket?—Yes.

17,800. On this ticket do you put the gross weight and the tare?—The gross weight and net weight.

17,801. Do you always actually ascertain the tare of the cart?—Yes.

17,802. You never go by estimation?—Never by estimation except the parties agree. Sometimes, if parties wanted to take a load out in the country, I can leave, according to the weight of the cart.

17,803. The hay is always weighed?—Yes.

17,804. It is never bought by bulk?—It is sometimes bought by bulk.

17,805. Supposing a load of hay was brought into this market place of Mr. Barry's and sold, and the weight not ascertained at your weighbridge, would you ask for any charge?—I think the question has arisen once or twice. I think Mr. Mulqueen, who is in charge of the market, demanded payment.

17,806. Did he get it?—Yes.

17,807. Were there any legal proceedings over it?—No.

17,808. What is your charge on potatoes?—A halfpenny per hundredweight, and a penny for over that.

17,809. Is the smallest charge a halfpenny?—Yes.

17,810. And the highest a penny?—Yes.

17,811. You never charge higher than a penny, for instance, if it were three hundredweight?—I am not sure. I will ascertain that for you.

17,812. Is Mr. Mulqueen here?—He is at the market to-day.

17,813. That is the charge for weighing potatoes?—Yes.

17,814. But now, if a sack of potatoes is brought into the market place and exposed for sale and sold, but the weight of it was not ascertained, would the charge be levied, or have you ever known it to be done?—I have not known it to be done.

17,815. Are potatoes only sold at this market place?—That is what is called the potato market.

17,816. Does butter ever come to it at all?—No. Butter is sold in the street, and no toll charged. There could be tolls charged, but they are not.

17,817. Has Mr. Barry any connexion with the fairs here?—He has.

17,818. Where are the fairs held?—In the fair green.

17,819. Is that provided by him?—Yes.

17,820. Have the fairs always been held in that fair green?—Yes, within my memory.

17,821. How far does your memory extend?—13 or 14 years.

17,822. Do you know the dates on which every fair is held whether you receive any charges for them or not?—There are old fairs and new fairs. The old fairs are held on the 5th April, 24th June, 10th October, and 10th December. Those are the cattle fairs. Well, the pig fairs are held on the preceding Mondays or Thursdays, as the case may be.

17,823. Whichever is nearest to the date of the cattle fair?—Yes. If the cattle fair happened to fall on Thursday the pig fair would be held on the previous Monday.

17,824. What are the dates of the new fairs?—The new fairs are held on the second Tuesdays in the remaining months.

17,825. Are tolls levied at any of these fairs?—There are tolls levied at the four old fairs.

17,826. Are there any tolls at the new fairs?—No.

17,827. When were these old fairs established; do you know?—Under a patent of Charles the Second, dated the 22nd June 1663.

17,828-9. Have you got a copy of that here?—I have. (Witness then produced the patent.)

17,830. Do you know how Mr. Smith Barry obtained the right to these markets and fairs? Was it by purchase or did it descend to him?—It descended to him.

17,831. Is there any other market authority here in Tipperary besides Mr. Barry?—I believe Mr. Chadwick is the market authority for butter—that is, for butter specially.

17,832. How do you know what was the capital expenditure of Mr. Barry in the erection of this market place and sheds?—On the market yard it was 500*l*.

17,833. Was that the actual expenditure?—Yes.

17,834. In the erection of the sheds, I suppose?—Yes.

17,835. And on the market house?—No. The market house cost 300*l*.

17,836. Is the market house the town hall?—It is called the town hall.

17,837. Is what you call the market house utilised for market purposes?—Yes. It is a little off the weighbridges, and the sheds are around the enclosure.

17,838. What was the cost of this?—500*l*.; that is, of the whole place.

17,839. Is Mr. Barry at any expense for repairs?—You asked for the average expenditure for the past three years. I have taken two years in the books because the fairs have only been in our hands for the past two years. They were in the hands of a tenant before that.

17,840. Previous to the last two years the old fairs were sub-let?—Yes.

17,841. Who was the last tenant?—The representatives of Patrick Burke.

17,842. What rent were they paying?—100*l*. a year.

17,843. Subject to the ordinary deductions, I suppose?—Yes.

17,844. Would you kindly give me the average expenditure in repairs?—4*l*. 15*s*. 9*d*. I take as the average repairs in the market yard, and in the fair green 3*l*. 5*s*. 4*d*.

17,845. Are there any sheds erected in the fair green?—There are not.

17,846. Is the fair green enclosed?—Yes.

17,847. Is it convenient to the town?—It is just beside the railway. You passed it coming into the town.

17,848. Do you know the expenditure on that fair green?—I do not know, but I suppose it would be about 300*l*. I estimate it at about that.

17,849. That is for putting a wall around it?—For levelling and building the wall.

17,850. Is that in addition to the building of the site?—No. I do not include the value of the site at all. I do not take that as the value of the site. I could not find anything in the books. There were a lot of old houses there.

17,851. Supposing the fairs were not held there would the site be available for building purposes?—It would.

17,852. Would it answer the purposes of building ground at present?—Yes. There is a building plot at one corner of it.

17,853. Did you make up the average receipts for the past two years?—Yes. The gross receipts from the pig and cattle fairs were 171*l*. 9*s*. 9*d*. and the market yard 103*l*. 9*s*., that is for weighing all the hay and straw. The receipts from auctions were 4*l*. 15*s*. and from stalls 9*l*. 9*s*. That is all.

17,854. Is that the average for the two years or the total?—The average. The average expenditure was 68*l*. 9*s*. 7*d*. on the market yard.

17,855. How is that 68*l*. 9*s*. 7*d*. expended?—That is for salaries.

17,856. Could you segregate that amount so as to show the particulars of the expenditure?—It is for wages and so forth of the officers in the market yard.

17,857. You have not divided that in order to be able to tell me the individuals to whom you pay it?—There is the weighmaster and his assistant, and men occasionally employed as may be necessary.

17,858. For collecting the tolls?—Not for collecting the tolls but on days when there is a heavy market there must be men required to put a check under carts when they are being weighed, and to regulate and keep order in the market.

17,859. It is merely for the weighmaster and his assistants?—Yes, and occasional employés.

17,860. What would be the duties of the occasional employés?—To attend the weighmaster.

17,861. In repairs the average expenditure is 4l. 11s. 9d.?—Yes.

17,862. What is the expense for the removal of refuse and cleaning?—I do not expend anything on that.

17,863. For other purposes?—The market yard rates and taxes amount to 16l. 12s. 8d.; coals, gas, and stationery 4l. 2s. That is all.

17,864. What is the valuation of the market place?—62l. is the valuation of the market yard and 4l. the stalls.

17,865. What stalls have you erected in this market place?—There are 16 stalls.

17,866. What commodities are exposed in them?—Different things by hucksters, such as potatoes, vegetables, and apples.

17,867. How do you let them?—3d. a week for each stall.

17,868. What is the space for each stall?—About 10 feet by 8 feet.

17,869. You have 16 of them?—Yes.

17,870. Are they let throughout the year?—They are mostly. They are sometimes idle.

17,871. Are they utilized every day?—Yes.

17,872. But the charge is 3d. a week?—Yes.

17,873. What hour does the market usually begin in this market place?—I suppose about 10 o'clock.

17,874. What time does it terminate?—At 6 o'clock we shut the gates.

17,875. Have you any rules or regulations there?—No printed rules.

17,876. Do you restrain the sale or exposure for sale of any of these commodities, such as hay, straw, or potatoes in the town or in any place other than in your market place?—I suppose a restriction could be enforced if a necessity arose.

17,877. But I suppose no necessity arises?—No necessity arises. They all go to the market.

17,878. Have the Thursday and Saturday markets always been held here?—Yes.

17,879. When the potatoes are weighed, do you ever see them weighing yourself? What is the quantity that usually comes here in sacks?—It varies. I suppose about 12 or 14 or 16 tons.

17,880. It is 1d. per sack you charge?—Yes.

17,881. A halfpenny up to a hundredweight and 1d. afterwards?—Yes.

17,882. You have got a beam and scales there?—Yes.

17,883. Is there more than the one?—There is a beam and scales, a small crane, and a large weighbridge for carts.

17,884. But you have only one beam and scales?—Yes.

17,885. What is the smallest weight you have for measuring the weight of potatoes or any other commodities there?—A pound weight.

17,886. If a sack of potatoes is put into the scales,

17,897. It is not exposed in the street?—No.

17,898. Within your memory have proceedings ever been taken to restrain people from selling any commodities or exposing them elsewhere than in the market place or to recover the tolls?—No.

17,899. You have tolls levied at the fairs?—Yes.

17,900. At the four old fairs?—Yes.

17,901. Could you give me your receipts from these tolls?—I could.

17,902. You levy tolls on all the pig fairs previous to the old fairs?—Yes.

17,903. You do not levy tolls on the pig fairs held previous to the new fairs?—No, neither on the pigs nor cattle.

17,904. Would you kindly give me the receipts?—171l. 6s. 9d. is the gross.

17,905. That is from the pig and cattle fairs?—Yes. The cost of collection is 88l. 13s. 4d.; that includes 4l. a year for advertising; then there is 5l. 8s. 4d. for repairs.

17,906. How is that spent?—In cleaning and regulating the green.

17,907. What is the valuation of the fair green?—The poor law valuation is 70l.

17,908. What are the consolidated rates in Tipperary?—The poor rate is 2s. 10d., the county rate varies from 9d. to 10d. and 11d. in the £.

17,909. What number of men have you collecting tolls at these fairs?—We have about 24 or 30 men.

17,910. Are these men posted outside the walls of the fair green?—They are on each street which leads into the town; they are not at the fair green itself, but at the outlets of the town. The cattle fair is held on the fair green, but the pig fairs are held on the streets.

17,911. Do they ever sell cattle outside the fair green on the public thoroughfare?—They do.

17,912. If they do of course you collect a toll from them as they go out the gaps?—Yes; going out they declare whether they have sold or not, and then the toll is collected.

17,913. How many of these gaps are there?—I think there are seven or eight.

17,914. You have about four men at each on an average?—Yes; two at some gaps.

17,915. What is the average rate at which these men are paid?—They get 5s. 6d.—any strange men—and 1s. for dinner; that would be 6s. 6d. Our own farm men get 5s. and 1s. for their dinner. It varies from 5s. 6d. to 5s. 6d.

17,916. In that 171l. which you state is the gross amount received from the fairs, you could not give me the amount you receive on cattle and the amount you receive on pigs; you could not segregate the amounts?—I could, but I have not it here; I could make it up for you.

17,917-19. Is it only on the animals sold you levy this charge?—That is all.

17,928. The buyers always place a mark on the cattle?—Yes.

17,929. Have you ever heard any disputes arising at the toll gate?—Sometimes people have refused to pay, and they keep the cattle there. I think they canter them. There is a sort of declaration by placing their hand to the board.

17,930. They do not produce any book or paper?—No.

17,931. They ask them to touch the board to clear their conscience?—Yes.

17,932. Have you ever heard any complaints of the levying of this toll of 6d. on a head of cattle actually sold?—Nothing came to my knowledge officially.

17,933. Outside of that have you heard any complaints?—I suppose people would rather not pay if they could help it.

17,934. Have you heard complaints?—I have not.

17,935. Have you heard complaints that the facilities afforded for weighing in the market place have been insufficient?—I have not since the fair green came under my control.

17,936. I mean in the market place?—No.

17,937. Is yours the only public crane in the town?—Yes.

17,938. Are there not some private individuals in the town having cranes or weighbridges?—The railway company have a weighbridge.

17,939. They do not utilise for the public?—No. There is another at the gas house, but they do not utilise it either.

17,940. Have you consulted Mr. Barry as to the schedule of queries forwarded to him or have they been brought under his notice?—They were brought to Mr. Townsend's notice.

17,941. You say some cattle are sold on the streets of the town?—Yes; sometimes.

17,942. But the pig fairs are held on the streets?—Yes. The cattle are not, except going to and from the fair green they might be purchased. All cattle are carried to the fair green, and sometimes they are kept about the gates of the fair green.

17,943. When you weigh these different commodities mentioned you have got printed tickets to give denoting the weight?—Yes.

The following are copies of the tickets handed in by witness:—

TIPPERARY BUTTER MARKET.

No. ...... ______ - __________ 18[illegible].

Mr.___ ______________________

______ firkins of butter, at ______ per firkin.

TIPPERARY MARKET.

______________________ 188 .

Weighed for ______________________

________ bags of ______________________

at lbs.

J. MULQUEEN, Weighmaster.

17,944. You put the gross and net weight on them?—Yes.

17,945. When your men are doing that do they ever ascertain the contract price entered into between the buyer and seller?—Almost always.

17,946. Do they keep any record of that?—They do on the block.

17,947. Then you keep blocks to the tickets?—Yes.

17,948. If the ticket is lost you are always able to give a copy of it?—We are always able to give a copy of the weight, but not of the price.

17,949. Is it entered from the copy into the book?—It is not entered in total, but just for cash purposes.

17,950. If it was required to make up a periodical return of the average prices of the different commodities do you think it would be possible to keep it?—I think it would.

17,951. And such a return you think would be pretty accurate?—I think it would be fairly accurate.

17,952. Do you ever keep any record of the number of cattle brought to the fair green?—No.

17,953. But you tell me you could segregate the amounts received from each species, how much do you receive from cattle and pigs?—There is one thing I did not mention. There is 6d. charged for young pigs brought in a cart; a man selling young pigs.

17,954. That is irrespective of the number in the cart?—Yes.

17,955. If they are brought in a cart you charge 6d.?—Yes.

17,956. If a smaller number, say two or three, are brought in a cart?—It is all the same.

17,957. Are empty carts ever brought in?—I do not think they are.

17,958. Have you got such a thing as clothes dealers coming in on fair days?—They used to be here on market days.

17,959. Where used the carts to be placed?—In the market yard.

17,960. If on fair days such as I have mentioned, clothes dealers, carts, or anything like that were brought into the town, would you levy any charge?—No; that was given up about 1870.

17,961. Previous to that you did levy a charge?—Yes.

17,962. Is fish brought here at all?—Yes.

17,963. Is there any charge on it?—No charge so far as tolls are concerned. It is sold on the streets.

17,964. The pig fair being held on the streets of the town does not that occasion much filth and dirt about the streets?—Yes.

17,965. Have you ever heard complaints of the fact of these fairs being held on the streets?—Some people of the town are for the fair green and others for the streets.

17,966. Do you know of your own knowledge does Mr. Smith Barry contribute anything towards the additional expense occasioned by the cleaning of the streets?—I have heard there is a rush for the cleaning of the streets after these days between the road contractors and the town commissioners.

17,967. So that the manure acts as an equivalent for any expense they incur?—I have heard so.

17,968. Directly, Mr. Smith Barry does not contribute anything?—No, except when tax he bears.

17,969. Do you know the districts from which the marketable commodities are brought?—I suppose from within a radius of 10 or 12 miles.

17,970. From what districts are the cattle brought?—From the surrounding districts.

17,971. When were these new fairs established?—In 18[illegible].

17,972. You do not know under what authority. Were they established by Mr. Smith Barry?—Yes.

17,973. He does not levy any toll?—No.

17,974. Mr. Frewen, solicitor, said:—I appear for the town commissioners in this matter, and with your permission I will ask Mr. Caldwell a few questions.

17,975. The witness was then cross-examined as follows:—

17,976. You say that the market yard is principally supplied with hay, &c.?—Yes.

17,977. Have you room enough for all the hay that comes to the market in this yard?—In spring time there is not.

17,978. Have you had enough of room this year?—No, I think not.

17,979. Have you had during the season the streets—that is, this street, Nelson Street—crowded with hay?—Yes, but that is the case in every town just at the fall of the spring.

17,980. I understand that is the principal time of the year hay comes into the market?—No. It is all through the year around. For average accommodation I think it is fair enough.

17,981. At the principal time of the year for hay it is greatly insufficient?—There is a glut in the market for a few days.

17,982. When the season proper for selling hay comes in are the accommodation afforded altogether insufficient?—I do not understand what you mean by the season proper.

17,983. Say the months of February, March, and April?—In the spring of the year it is insufficient.

17,984. Have not the streets been blocked this year by hay brought in?—Yes.

17,985. Do you collect a toll out of the hay sold in the street?—When it is weighed, certainly.

17,986. You charge the same for that as if it were sold in the market?—Certainly, when it is weighed.

17,987. I did not catch whether you stated there was a patent for holding the market yard?—Yes, the old patent applies to that.

17,988. Is it a fact that carts are brought in on pig-market days with pigs in them, and even if the pigs are not sold they are charged 6d. each?—I do not think so.

17,989. You are not sure of that?—I think it is contrary to the instructions.

17,990. Now you have said that Mr. Smith Barry does not give anything to clean or repair the streets after the pig markets?—No.

17,991. The pig markets in the streets are very heavy?—They are.

17,992. It is very hard to get through the streets on pig-market days?—It is.

17,993. Are not the flags more or less injured and broken by the crowds and things which are put on the flags?—I suppose so.

17,994. And the commissioners have to pay for them?—I suppose so.

17,995. You do not remember when the cattle fairs were held in the town?—I do not.

17,996. You do not remember the railway being made here?—I do not.

17,997. You do not remember the present green where the fairs are now held being at one time a commonage?—No, but I heard there were houses on it.

17,998. That was before the fairs were removed to it?—Yes.

17,999. Now is not there another landlord holding houses in the fair green at present?—No.

18,000. Are not those houses there belonging to the trustees of Bowman Smith?—Not on the fair green. He has a little plot in the angle at the end of the fair green.

18,001. (To the Commissioner.) The instructions you give your toll-collectors are, not to levy any charge on pigs not sold, whether they are in carts or not?—Yes.

18,002. Up to the present you have not heard any complaints of their having disobeyed those instructions?—In fact, I have seen cases from which I could infer that they did not charge.

18,003. Cross-examination by Mr. Preston continued: Now you state that 67l. 7s. 7d. was the expenditure in the market. Then you give exact figures for taxes and tolls. Does that 67l. 7s. 7d. include the taxes and tolls, or does it mean the entire expenditure in the market?—No. Every item I gave was separate. There was a question I was not asked, and that is the excess in the receipts above the expenditure. In the case of the markets it was 20l. 2s.

18,004. That is the net profit?—Yes. In the case of the old fairs it was 104l.

18,005. (The Assistant Commissioner.) The reason I did not ask that was because I had the gross receipts and the expenditure, and I could easily deduct one from the other afterwards, and the difference would represent the net profit.

18,006. (Mr. Preston to Witness.) You have certain accommodation sold in the market yard that were removed there lately for sale, off the streets. What are they?—Standings they used to be called.

18,007. How many standings were there on the street, could you tell?—I could not tell you.

18,008. Were there 20?—I do not suppose there were.

18,009. There were about 10?—Yes.

18,010. They have been there for a number of years?—They were. There used to be a toll charged in the streets at one time.

18,011. But not lately?—No.

18,012. Not for some years before they were removed?—No.

18,013. (The Assistant Commissioner.) Was there any compulsory influence exercised to remove them off the street, or was the removal voluntary?—I think there was. The magistrates fined them.

18,014. (Mr. Preston.) They were summoned for obstruction and fined, and had to remove. Last year it occurred. The magistrates asked Mr. Townsend to procure a place for them, and he said he would.

18,015. (To Witness.) You gave the tax that you pay for the market yard. Do you include in that the amount of tax paid for the town hall itself?—No.

18,016. (The Assistant Commissioner.) Has Mr. Barry provided a town hall for the commissioners?—He has.

18,017. At his own expense?—Yes.

18,018. Is that solely within his control?—Yes.

H. H. Townsend, Esq., J.P., examined.

18,019. You are the agent to Mr. Barry?—I am.

18,020. Did you bring the schedule of queries I forwarded you before Mr. Barry?—No. Mr. Barry has gone to England.

18,021. I sent one to him. Has he had any communication with you?—The secretary sent it to me.

18,022. He did not give you any instructions to answer any of the questions?—None whatever.

18,023. From your knowledge of Mr. Barry and his affairs perhaps you could answer one query, and that is, whether Mr. Barry would approve, or would he have any objection to a body such as the town commissioners obtaining compulsory powers to acquire his rights?—Not the slightest. He would be perfectly ready to sell to the town commissioners his rights to the fairs; he would be perfectly willing to sell them.

18,024. Has he ever expressed such an opinion?—Yes. In fact he thought frequently that the town commissioners were empowered legally to purchase because he thought the control of fairs and markets should be in the hands of local bodies having control of the town.

18,025. Previous to the last two years he had the fairs and markets sub-let?—Yes.

18,026. Do you think they are managed better since you took them into your control?—I think so. I am not prepared to say. I could not say particularly well how it was managed before. We put up additional accommodation in some respects.

18,027. You have had some experience of these fairs?—Yes.

18,028. Do you think if the town commissioners or local authority acquired such rights that they should work them themselves and not sub-let them?—I think they should work them themselves, and not sub-let them.

18,029. Have you ever heard any complaints as to any insufficiency of accommodation?—I should very much like to extend the market yard if possible. I was trying a couple of years ago, but unfortunately there was no way to extend it. I was trying to negotiate with a gentleman having the adjoining place, but negotiations fell through, and he was not in a position to let me have it. It does not belong to Mr. Barry, and he would be very glad to make the yard larger.

18,030. You think the space insufficient at present?—I think in certain times of the year there is an overplus quantity of hay, and we cannot weigh it in the market.

18,031. Are the weighing appliances—the beam and scales, weighbridge and crane—ample for the trade of the town?—I think so.

18,032. You have never heard any complaints of undue delay in weighing the different commodities?—No. There were never any complaints made to me, and if there were I should at once attend to them. I may explain two things. First and foremost about the stands; it was the resident magistrate, Mr. Mahon, made the order that they be removed off the streets as they were obstructing the street, and then he asked me to put up sheds to convenience the people, and I put up shedding there and let them at a small rent.

18,033. Those are the stalls Mr. Caldwell says are let for 3d. a week?—Yes. In reference to the pig fairs held in the town, they are the greatest possible nuisance. I think they should be all carried down to the fair green, and then there would be no annoyance or injury to the dogs, but there is a strong feeling in the town against removing them off the streets. It would be far better for the town if they were removed.

18,034. Is it the trading element would object to their removal off the streets?—I think all the public-house keepers would object, they want to keep them on the streets to have the people near the shops.

18,035. I suppose for trade purposes they would put up with any inconvenience caused by the obstruction?—Yes. In fact the inconvenience is so great that the streets are completely blocked, and traffic blocked, and the town commissioners then arranged with the constabulary and some action was taken, and then it was a good deal better. If they kept clear of the footpaths it would not be so inconvenient.

18,036. Is this weighbridge erected capable of weighing cattle?—There is a cattle weighbridge specially erected in the fair green. There are two different weighing machines; there is one for weighing hay in the townhall yard, and the other one was put up according to the Act of Parliament in the fair green.

18,037. What was the amount expended in the erection of these?—I suppose about 70l.

18,038. How many head of cattle can you weigh at the same time on it?—Only one; and my private opinion is that it is never used.

18,039. Never used?—Never used, and, probably, never will.

18,040. Supposing a head of cattle was sold and weighed, you charge 2d. at the sale and the ordinary 2d. for weighing?—Whatever our legal rights would be.

18,041. Have you ever claimed any rights to this butter market that has, I believe, been established here?—We get the fixed rent for the building. We get nothing else.

18,042. From whom?—From Mr. Cooper Chadwick.

18,043. You leave the building let to him?—Yes, at 20l. a year.

18,044. Where is this butter market house. Is it convenient to the ordinary market yard?—No, it is separate. It is a detached large building, over near the church. Mr. Chadwick was appointed by the magistrates as butter weighmaster for the county.

18,045. Who was it built the house?—There was a house built by the original weighmaster here. Mr. Smith Barry and the weighmaster entered into a compact, and Mr. Barry built the house.

18,046. Have you suggestions or observations to offer on the subject of the inquiry?—Not the slightest.

18,047. Any suggestions to make as to what you think would be for the better working of them?—I think the town commissioners should put it up. They would not work it better than ours. At the same time, I think it is very much better for local bodies to have control in these things. When they have control of the town they should have control of the markets and fairs of the town, and they will have no one to blame but themselves if they do not work them properly.

18,048. Cross-examined by Mr. Fravan: What means have you of checking the tolls that are collected?—Practically, no means. We rely on the honesty of the collectors. We pick out the best men and put several of them together.

18,049. Do you keep some men as always?—A certain number of men are always in our own permanent employment, but according as we want men we send for help.

18,050. Some men from your own employment?—Certain men from our own employment.

18,051. These are your workmen?—Yes.

18,052. Do you employ any person to keep order at the fairs and markets held in the town?—There is a weighmaster there.

18,053. That is with reference to the general market. I am speaking with reference to the pig market held in the street, where you say there is a great deal of disorder. Do you appoint a man?—We have no control over it.

18,054. You never appoint men to keep order?—No. It would be useless.

18,055. Are you aware that the town commissioners have two of their town sergeants employed during this market to keep order?—I say it would be very much better for the town if the pig markets were removed out of the streets into the fair green.

18,056. Do you remember the fairs to be held in the streets of the town?—Not in my time.

18,057. Have you heard it?—I heard they were.

18,058. Can you give us any idea when they were removed to the green?—No. It was all before my time.

18,059. How long are you here?—About 10 years.

18,060. Can you tell us anything about what the fair green was before the fairs were removed there?—There were houses I know there.

18,061. Do you know that a large portion of it was a commonage?—I do not. I know the houses were on a lot of it. There were a lot of tumbledown cottages on it.

18,062. Were there gates erected some time ago leading into the green?—Yes. I think there were. I think Mr. Burke asked me to put them up.

18,063. Do you remember at that time some parties going and breaking down the gates and claiming a right through the place?—There is a right of passage across the fair green, and they disputed Burke's right to lock the gates.

18,064. Have the gates been sustained there since?—No.

18,065. Were the gates taken down after that?—I think so. I do not exactly remember the exact cause for taking down the gates. There is a commonage right—a right of way—to the houses at the other side.

18,066. Who owns the houses at the other side?—They belong to Emerson Smith.

18,067. They are at the other side of the fair green?—Yes.

18,068. (*The Assistant Commissioner.*) This right you refer to is it a private right to the individuals who inhabit the houses or a public right?—It is a right to the individuals at the other side. It would be an improvement to the fair green if it was made like the Middleton fair green, with pens.

18,069. Have you any pens there for the accommodation of the buyers?—I had to put up pens for holding pigs.

18,070. You have no pens for holding cattle?—No. That would be a very great advantage. If I was sure the people would appreciate it I would be very glad to put them up.

18,071. Mr. Fravan's cross-examination continued.—Is not there a great deal of mud and things like that remaining after the fairs, particularly in the winter time?—I suppose there is a great deal of mud.

18,072. Do you ever clear off that?—I always give directions to the clerk of works to have it cleared before the fairs.

18,073. I mean after the fairs do you clean the place?—I do not think I do.

18,074. The fair green adjoins the road leading from the railway to the town?—Yes. It used to be very bad and I got the green drained.

18,075. I believe there was a footpath put down at the expense of the county?—It has nothing to say to the fairs.

18,076. Is not it along the wall of the fair green. It is the approach to the railway and was not that put down by reason of the great dirt from the fairs being held on the green?—It was put there for the purpose of developing trade. It is the main approach to the railway.

18,077. Do not you think that most of the dirt and mud that accumulates is caused by the fairs being held in the fair green?—No. I do not think so. I do not think there is any mud in the fair green.

18,078. Do you think the fair causes any mud?—If the cattle stopped in the fair green there would be no mud on the road.

18,079. Do not many of the cattle lie on the road?—Very often.

18,080. And on fair days is not the road blocked with cattle?—Yes.

18,081. After all that do you say the holding of fairs does not cause any smell?—I do not say it does not cause smell, but if the cattle were forced to go into the fair green it would not.

18,082. But as it stands at present it causes smell?—Yes.

18,083. Do you know, as a matter of fact, that some of the coping-stones on the side-walls were broken by the cattle?—I never heard that.

18,084. Do you ever take any trouble to inquire?—Never.

18,085. Did you look at them to see if they were broken?—Never.

18,086. You do nothing except to collect the tolls?—No. I pass by every day and never look at it. It must be a very small damage, but the town commissioners can get rid of that if they insist on having the cattle go into the fair green.

18,087. Are you aware that carts with pigs are brought in there on fair days are charged a toll of 6d. coming in for the stand of the cart?—I never heard it.

18,088. Would you be surprised to hear it?—I do not know much about it.

18,089. It could occur without your knowledge?—Yes, without my personal knowledge.

18,090. (*By the Assistant Commissioner.*) You have storage for pigs in the fair green?—Yes; yards for them after they are bought.

18,091. Do you levy any additional charge for such storage?—We do.

18,092. What is it?—A penny each pig.

18,093. Is that in addition to the other charge?—It is in addition to the 2d. each charged. These places are used by the pig buyers to put their pigs in before they are sent by train.

18,094. For the period they occupy the place as storage for their pigs you charge a penny however long or short it might be?—Yes.

18,095. Have you any storage in the market yard for potatoes?—No.

18,096. Have you ever heard complaints of the want of storage?—I have not.

Mr. Michael Ryan examined.

18,097. You represent Mr. Chadwick?—Yes.

18,098. Is he butter master in Tipperary?—He is weigh-master.

18,099. Who appointed him?—The magistrates of the county under an Act of Parliament.

18,100. When?—About 25 or 30 years ago. I think in 1865 he was appointed.

18,101. Mr. Chadwick could not attend here?—He is in Dublin to-day.

18,102. Did he tell you to attend?—He did.

18,103–5. I suppose any answers you give to any questions I put he will agree to them?—Yes.

18,106. I believe he is paying for this butter house 20*l.* a year?—Yes.

18,107. Has he to pay rates and taxes?—All rates and taxes.

18,108. In addition to the rent?—Yes.

18,109. What do they amount to in the year on an average?—About six or eight pounds.

18,110. He has only the premises?—Only the weigh-house and yard adjoining.

18,111. Has he shelter accommodation there for the horses?—Yes.

18,112. Would you kindly mention to me who he has in his employment to manage this?—I manage it for him, and we have a man to weigh the butter.

18,113. What is his name?—Patrick Keane, and two coopers named Halloran and English.

18,114. Who else?—Four porters.

18,115. What are their duties?—To hand the butter up to the butter scales and about the house.

18,116. To assist the coopers and weighmaster?—Yes, and the sellers and to arrange the butter for the buyers.

18,117. Is there anybody else?—Mr. Chadwick delivers the butter to the merchants' stores.

18,118. That is when it is bought?—Yes.

18,119. Is it to the private merchants in town?—Yes.

18,120. To all buyers?—Yes.

18,121. Does he levy any charge for that delivery?—The legal charge is 2d. a firkin, and he puts on a penny for doing all the work I told you.

18,122. That is 3d. altogether on each firkin?—Yes.

18,123. Then it is coopered, weighed, and delivered for 3d.?—Yes.

18,124. Supposing merchants have their own carts, and wish to deliver themselves does he charge the 3d.?—The merchants have no carts, they only ask him as a favour to do it, and he does it. The sellers used to deliver it, and there was some confusion and then the merchants got Mr. Chadwick to agree to the delivery goods, and he does that.

18,125. When he did not deliver the butter to the merchants' stores did he still charge the 3d.?—I think since he was appointed he delivered the butter at least while I am with him, and that is for the last 20 years.

18,126. What scales has he erected there?—A beam and scales.

18,127. Only one?—Yes.

18,128. Is that sufficient for the trade?—Quite enough.

18,129. Do you ever keep any record of the number of firkins brought in here?—Always.

18,130. Have you got any particulars of them here?—I have.

18,131. Could you tell me the average number that comes in on market day or do they come every day in the week?—Yes.

18,132. So, practically, the butter market is every day?—It is a daily market.

18,133. What is the average number weekly?—About 2,000 firkins; sometimes more or less.

18,134. Are they always brought in firkins?—In firkins.

18,135. Lump butter is not brought in?—Lump butter is brought in, but sold in the street.

18,136. Is it exposed for sale in the street?—I have nothing to do with that.

18,137. You get no charge?—No.

18,138. Did Mr. Chadwick ever take any proceedings to compel the lump butter into his place?—Not the slightest. He never looked after it at all.

18,139. Is he of opinion he has any right to do so?—I think not.

18,140. Are these two coopers able to cooper all the firkins brought in?—They are.

18,141. How many would be brought in on an ordinary day?—Over 1,000 firkins the best day, but not very often.

18,142. Would these two coopers be able to cooper 1,000 firkins in sufficient time?—If the market was large we would employ one or two more if we wanted them.

18,143. Would the one weigh-master be able to weigh 1,000 firkins?—Yes.

18,144. Would not that cause undue delay?—We commence early and our system is very practical.

18,145. What time does the market commence?—We begin to weigh and cooper the butter about six o'clock. The butter is in at seven, or eight in the morning.

18,146. Is the butter sold, or a contract entered into between the buyer and seller previous to its being coopered and weighed?—As a rule most of it is coopered and weighed before it is bought, but anything that comes into the market after 10 o'clock is sold. At 10 the merchants commence to buy, and any that is not weighed before that is bought by the merchants before being weighed.

18,147. Have you any tasters employed?—No.

18,148. The buyers have to taste the butter themselves?—Yes.

18,149. Have you ever heard complaints by the public that no tasters were employed by Mr. Chadwick?—No, I have not. We had some tasters some time ago and they complained of them.

18,150. Do your coopers completely drain the firkins before weighing them?—As a rule they generally do.

18,151. Do they take the butter out of the firkin?—If they suspect any water in the firkin they take it out. All the firkins are turned up and the bungs loosened and after they do that if there be no water, they never strip the firkins, but they strip several of them to ascertain the tare.

18,152. Then, as to the quality of the butter, the buyer himself has to rely on his own knowledge?—He has; it is a very open market.

18,153. How do you pay the coopers?—One gets 1*l.* a week and the other 18*s.*

18,154. You have the two permanently employed?—All are permanently employed that I have mentioned.

18,155. Can you tell me what Mr. Chadwick's expenses are?—About 400*l.* he spends in the market.

18,156. Could you aggregate that amount in order to give each item?—I get 50*l.* a year; the two coopers 1*l.* a week and 18*s.*; four men 4*s.* each week.

18,157. What is Mr. Keane paid?—I think 80*l.* a year; it may be a little more. Then the rent is 50*l.*, and the rates or taxes 4*l.* or 5*l.* There is 70*l.* a year for the delivery of the butter.

18,158. These are not his own carts that are used?—No; it is a contract he has entered into.

18,159. Anything else?—No.

18,160. Have you got weigh tickets?—We have.

18,161. Printed forms?—Yes.

18,162. Have you any of them here?—No, but I can get them in a few minutes.

18,163. On that ticket do you put the gross weight of the firkin?—Yes, the gross weight and tare.

18,164. Do you estimate the tare of the firkin?—Yes.

18,165. You never actually weigh it?—We do very often.

18,166. I suppose that is in case of dispute?—When there is a doubt we weigh it.

18,167. Did you ever when you were estimating the tare of the firkins know of any frauds being committed in selling lighter firkins?—They very often would, and it is because we watch them closely they bring them right.

18,168. Supposing you do actually ascertain the tare, do you charge anything additional?—No; 3*d.* is the only charge.

18,169. And never less than 3*d.*?—Never less than 3*d.*

18,170. Whether you deliver it or not?—It is always delivered, as a rule.

18,171. But if such a case arose that a man took it himself?—Let him deliver it.

18,172. Still you would seek for your 3*d.*?—He would have the 3*d.* paid.

18,173. Is it in return for the ticket he pays the 3*d.*?—We deliver the butter then.

18,174. Have you ever heard any complaints of inaccuracy in the scales for weighing the butter?—Some people very often grumble a little; but, on the whole, it is very fair. Some merchants here can tell you.

18,175. Do you ever chalk the firkin?—Yes, I always mark it.

18,176. Is that the gross weight?—The gross weight and tare. When they strip it it is marked.

18,181. Do you keep a block of the ticket?—Yes.

18,182. Do you enter them in a book?—Yes.

18,183. When was this butter market established first?—It is a very old market.

18,184. It has always been independent of the other markets?—Always, as far as I could hear.

18,185. From what districts is the butter brought here?—Every district around here for 10 or 15 miles, and 20 miles in many cases, but, as a rule, 10 or 15.

18,186. Are there any extra facilities offered by the railway companies to the farmers in the surrounding country districts to bring the butter to Tipperary?—They give cheap rates on the Waterford and Limerick Railway.

18,187. Is that to bring the butter here?—To bring the butter and the seller.

18,188. Is it cheaper than the ordinary rate?—It is.

18,189-90. Do any Limerick producers send butter here?—A large number of them.

18,191. In preference to sending it to Limerick?—They bring it here from very near Limerick.

18,192. Does Cork butter ever come?—We get some, but not much though. A small quantity comes from that direction.

18,193. That is, I suppose, because it is a nearer market than the Cork market?—No; there are nearer markets, but this is a good butter market.

18,194. Do you ever ascertain what prices the buyers pay for the different classes of butter?—Always.

18,195. Do you keep any account of it?—I do. I send a report of the prices to the papers.

18,196. You do not keep any permanent form officially?—I do. I very often take a note of it and send it away. You get them daily in the *Freeman* or *Irish Times*.

18,197. And these prices are returned officially by you?—Yes, officially and as correctly as I can.

18,198. You think they are pretty accurate?—Yes, as near as I can go.

18,199. There is nothing put on in order to induce sellers to come?—I never put on a price that was not paid to my knowledge.

18,200. Then you mean that these returns made periodically by you are accurate returns of the prices obtained for butter in the Tipperary market?—They are.

18,201. Have you any storage accommodation?—We do not require any. The butter is sold daily. There may be a firkin or two unsold; that is removed by the seller, who takes it away again.

18,202. Supposing butter was brought in and coopered and weighed, but subsequently not sold, if you give a docket you must get your 3*d.*?—I must.

18,203. You never take into calculation whether it is sold or not?—Very often we would, but, as a rule, we do charge.

18,204. Has a case of that occurred?—It has, where I did not charge.

18,205. That is, I suppose, you returned the money previously obtained?—No, but I did not get the money; he did not come for his ticket.

18,206. When the weight is ascertained do not they take the ticket?—They take the ticket after the butter is weighed.

18,207. You will not give the ticket without the money?—No; but those people who do not sell would not have it weighed at all. Sometimes it might be weighed after the market is over, and then there would

18,211. Supposing that man does not sell his firkin during the day, will he come to you and demand a return of the 3d.?—He will not, and he never came.

18,212. In that case for weighing and coopering of the butter you get your charge although subsequently it is not sold?—It is a very trifling thing. If I got it I would give it to a man.

18,213. Would you say that 90 per cent. of the firkins brought here are sold?—I would, and 95 per cent. There might be two or three firkins left after a day. It is such a trifling thing it is not worth talking about.

18,214. Have you any accommodation there in the market?—We have a fine weigh-house.

18,215. Is that sufficient to accommodate all the firkins?—It is. Over a thousand firkins can be bought and sold there.

18,216. The firkins are never exposed for sale in the open yard?—Not at the butter market.

18,217. Of course the lumps are exposed elsewhere in the town?—They are sold on the streets.

18,218. Are they exposed standing in the street?—Standing in the street. If they wish to take it to the houses they can sell the butter, but, as a rule, they stand in the street, and the people go and buy them from them.

18,219. Mr. Townsend stated. I just wish to mention that Mr. Barry has spent 1,000l. in erecting this butter house.

18,220. I presume Mr. Barry is the owner in fee of the place we have mentioned?—Yes.

18,221. (To Witness.) Do you know what are Mr. Chadwick's gross receipts in the year?—I think about 470l. a year is the net profit. I made up a calculation for 10 years.

18,222. Could you give me that return?—Yes.

18,223. The witness then handed in the return, of which the following is a copy, but it is not to be taken as a statement of the quantity of butter brought to Tipperary but only of the quantity brought to Mr. Chadwick's market. There are private stores in the town, and the total quantity brought to them is estimated to equal the quantity as under:—

	No. of Firkins.	£	s.	d.
1877	73,420	946	18	3
1878	80,132	1,071	10	5
1879	76,273	933	8	8
1880	70,315	895	13	1
1881	73,928	940	0	0
1882	73,[illegible]	926	8	0
1883	71,759	935	19	9
1884	65,494	919	6	6
1885	65,304	914	0	0
1886	65,516	912	14	0
1887	63,132	833	10	0
	783,348			
Average	65,[illegible]	870	14	[illegible]
Average expenses		400	14	[illegible]
		470	0	0

Tipperary Butter Market.

18,223a. Cross-examined by Mr. Frewen.—Mr. Barry has no claim on the market except merely the rent of the house?—No.

18,224. Is not he the owner of the soil on which the market is built?—Yes.

18,225. Now Mr. Chadwick is the owner of the market?—Yes.

18,226. He is a private individual?—He is.

18,227. How far does he live from Tipperary?—Three or four miles.

18,228. And the net returns goes to his own use?—Yes.

18,229. He has been appointed by the magistrates of the district?—Of the county.

18,230-1. How long is Mr. Chadwick owner of the place?—In 1865 I think he was appointed.

18,232. He invested no capital?—No; he did not. At the time he was appointed there was a dispute. I think he had to purchase a weighmaster's right or interest, and did lose some money.

18,233. It was a very standard thing to get his goodwill?—I think so.

18,234. Mr. Chadwick has no property in this town?—No.

18,235. Or connected with it in any way?—He is a neighbouring gentleman.

18,236. The only connexion is that he lives within four or five miles of the town?—Yes, the same as any other gentleman.

18,237. You have never heard that Mr. Chadwick on any occasion expended any of the money he received for the benefit of the town?—I think he is very liberal.

18,238. You mean he gives a subscription to a collection the same as anybody else?—I find him a generous and liberal man.

18,239. You never knew he appropriated any part of the tolls he collected for the benefit of any works in the town, or anything of that kind?—I think he would contribute towards a collection about the town for charity or anything else.

18,240. Would you say he does not apply any portion of the profits he receives except to give a personal subscription to a collection?—Yes. I do not know any works he could give money to.

18,241-2. In the streets of the town where this butter is brought is not there a great thoroughfare during those, and is not the town sergeant required to keep order?—We keep order ourselves.

18,243. Have not the town commissioners to clean the streets?—Yes.

18,244. Mr. Chadwick does not contribute anything towards that?—He pays the rates.

18,245. You have a butter market every day?—Yes.

18,246. All the year round?—Yes.

18,247. It has always been held every day?—Yes.

18,248. No special days are allotted off?—On holidays or Sundays no business is done.

18,249. The witness then produced a notice, of which the following is a copy:—

TIPPERARY BUTTER MARKET.

Notice to Coopers.

After this date the names of the coopers whose firkins are found not made according to the printed directions, will be posted up in the market-house.

By Order.

(The following rules and regulations are posted up in the butter market-place, for the observance of those frequenting the market.)

TIPPERARY BUTTER MARKET.—Incorporated under 49 Geo. 3. c. 124.

Byelaws.

The market opens at 6 a.m., and the buying commences at 10 a.m.

Each lot of butter shall be examined and weighed according as it arrives to market.

All butter shall be bought and sold subject to the standard weight of 3 qrs. 14 lbs. tare, and every pound over or under the standard (as the case may be) shall be paid for, or deducted according to the published scale.

A toll of 3d. shall be paid for each and every firkin in market.

The weight and tare of each firkin shall be ascertained by the officers of the weigh-house, and a ticket of same given to the seller.

No person shall buy or sell butter before the appointed hour, 10 o'clock.

The weighmaster delivers the butter free at the merchants' stores, pays porterage and all other market expenses; it is therefore particularly requested that no money will be given to any of the employés of the market, as any of them discovered asking or receiving gratuities will be instantly dismissed.

Smoking strictly prohibited while the business of the market is being transacted.

Any person giving annoyance, interrupting business, or violating any of the byelaws or rules of the market will be removed therefrom.

By Order,
R. Cooper Chadwick,
Weighmaster.

TIPPERARY BUTTER MARKET.

The following Scale may be used in paying for over or deducting for under the Standard Weight of 2 qrs. 14 lbs. Tare:—

	s.	d.		s.	d.	
At	41	0	per firkin - -	0	7	per pound.
"	46	6	" - -	0	8	"
"	52	6	" - -	0	9	"
"	58	6	" - -	0	10	"
"	64	0	" - -	0	11	"
"	70	0	" - -	1	0	"
"	75	0	" - -	1	1	"
"	81	6	" - -	1	2	"
"	87	6	" - -	1	3	"
"	93	2	" - -	1	4	"
"	99	0	" - -	1	5	"
"	105	0	" - -	1	6	"
"	111	0	" - -	1	7	"

TIPPERARY BUTTER MARKET.

Scale showing the Price per Keg of 56 lbs. at any given price per 70 lbs. Firkin.

	s.	d.		s.	d.	
At	40	0	per firkin - -	32	0	per keg.
"	41	0	" - -	32	10	"
"	42	0	" - -	33	7	"
"	42	6	" - -	34	0	"
"	43	0	" - -	34	5	"
"	44	0	" - -	35	2	"
"	45	0	" - -	36	0	"
"	46	0	" - -	36	10	"
"	47	0	" - -	37	7	"
"	47	6	" - -	38	0	"
"	48	0	" - -	38	5	"
"	49	0	" - -	39	2	"
"	50	0	" - -	40	0	"
"	51	0	" - -	40	10	"
"	52	0	" - -	41	7	"
"	52	6	" - -	42	0	"
"	53	0	" - -	42	5	"
"	54	0	" - -	43	2	"
"	55	0	" - -	44	0	"
"	56	0	" - -	44	10	"
"	57	0	" - -	45	7	"
"	57	6	" - -	46	0	"
"	58	0	" - -	46	5	"
"	59	0	" - -	47	2	"
"	60	0	" - -	48	0	"
"	61	0	" - -	48	10	"
"	62	0	" - -	49	7	"
"	62	6	" - -	50	0	"
"	63	0	" - -	50	5	"
"	64	0	" - -	51	2	"
"	65	0	" - -	52	0	"
"	66	0	" - -	52	10	"
"	67	0	" - -	53	7	"
"	67	6	" - -	54	0	"
"	68	0	" - -	54	5	"
"	69	0	" - -	55	2	"
"	70	0	" - -	56	0	"
"	71	0	" - -	56	10	"
"	72	0	" - -	57	7	"
"	72	6	" - -	58	0	"
"	73	0	" - -	58	5	"
"	74	0	" - -	59	2	"
"	75	0	" - -	60	0	"
"	76	0	" - -	60	10	"
"	77	0	" - -	61	7	"
"	77	6	" - -	62	0	"
"	78	0	" - -	62	5	"
"	79	0	" - -	63	2	"
"	80	0	" - -	64	0	"
"	81	0	" - -	64	10	"
"	82	0	" - -	65	7	"
"	82	6	" - -	66	0	"
"	83	0	" - -	66	5	"
"	84	0	" - -	67	2	"
"	85	0	" - -	68	0	"
"	86	0	" - -	68	10	"
"	87	0	" - -	69	7	"
"	87	6	" - -	70	0	"
"	88	0	" - -	70	5	"
At	89	0	per firkin - -	71	2	per keg.
"	90	0	" - -	72	0	"
"	91	0	" - -	72	10	"
"	92	0	" - -	73	7	"
"	92	6	" - -	74	0	"
"	93	0	" - -	74	5	"
"	94	0	" - -	75	2	"
"	95	0	" - -	76	0	"
"	96	0	" - -	76	10	"
"	97	0	" - -	77	7	"
"	97	6	" - -	78	0	"
"	98	0	" - -	78	5	"
"	99	0	" - -	79	2	"
"	100	0	" - -	80	0	"

*** Note.—The keg should be sold as if it were a full-sized firkin, and the relative value afterwards made out as in the above Scale.

Mr. M[illegible] examined.

18,950. Do you know how long the markets have been held on Thursday?—Since I came to the place.

18,951. How long ago is that?—About 15 years only I am connected with the place.

18,952. Supposing a farmer brought in a load of potatoes and weighed them at your scales, he would have to pay 1d. per sack?—Yes.

18,953. Supposing he sold them to another man in the market place, who subsequently retailed them, and weighed them over again, would he have to pay a charge?—No.

18,954. You do not charge retailers?—No.

18,955. As a matter of fact, do people retail in the market place?—Certainly. We have 16 stalls let to women.

18,956. Have they only to pay 6d. a week?—Yes.

18,957. Do you supply scales in the stalls?—There is a small scales.

18,958. For them?—Yes.

18,959. One in each stall?—No.

18,960. How many have you altogether?—Only one.

18,961. They all have the use of this?—Yes.

18,962. During the season when the new potatoes come in do they sell them by measure?—They do not.

18,963. They have always to be weighed?—Yes.

18,964. At any portion of the year?—Yes.

18,965. Cross-examined by Mr. Preston.—Are potatoes sometimes carried to the market on which fees are collected, although not sold?—Many of them go out on the pretence that they have not sold for the purpose of weighing outside and saving the penny.

18,966. Although you do not weigh you charge?—I demand it. I say, if you wish to get them weighed, go over and get them weighed, and I will mark them for you. I have detected them going out on the pretence they had not sold in order to save the penny to go and sell outside.

18,967. Then they have no objection to pay the penny?—I do not know what is their objection, but I am giving you facts.

Mr. Jeremiah Da[illegible], Town Clerk, examined.

18,968. You are the town clerk of Tipperary?—Yes.

18,969. When were the commissioners established here?—Under the 9th of George the Fourth, a long time previous to 1814; but the Towns Improvement Act was introduced in December 1872, and it came into operation on the 1st January 1873.

18,970. What duties or powers have they taken upon themselves to exercise? Are they the sanitary authority?—No, not by law. When they commenced they used to do all the cleansing of the streets, but they found out it was too expensive, and latterly they require the grand jury to clean the central roadways, but they employ men and a cart to clean the channels and footways, and they cart the manure to a depôt they have at the end of the town.

18,971. Did you place the schedule of queries forwarded to you before the commissioners?—They were all considered at a special meeting of the commissioners specially called on last Monday.

18,272. As a body did they give you any instructions to answer the question as to whether they think it desirable to obtain compulsory powers to acquire the rights of Mr. Chadwick and Mr. Barry?—Yes; they consider the application of the present tolls is entirely opposed to the public good, a misappropriation, and detrimental to the public good. They would reasonably consider what would be just and equitable so far as Mr. Smith Barry would be concerned.

18,273. Supposing they obtained such compulsory powers, would they contemplate the continuance of a toll, or would they be inclined to abolish tolls altogether?—With regard to abolishing the tolls I do not think they would entertain that matter. There might be a reduction, certainly there would be no increase; but even if things remained as they are the revenue that would be derived from the profits of the tolls at the pig market, cattle fairs, and butter markets would be and away exceed the present revenue.

18,274. It is purely for the purpose of increasing their revenue they would wish to obtain these rights?—Purely for the purpose of reducing taxation and doing more good than at present is done.

18,275. Have they considered if they obtained such compulsory powers that it would be better to work them themselves by officers appointed by them than to sub-let them to an individual?—I do not think for a moment they considered sub-letting. They would work them energetically themselves.

18,276. And do they think their own united efforts would tend to better management and working of the markets and fairs than having them in the hands of an individual?—With regard to the present management the complaints are very small, but what we complain of most, as a great grievance, is the source to which the profits go.

18,277. Have they any complaints to make of the management of the markets and fairs?—We have no reason to complain but of the dirty state of the streets. We have to turn round and have to pay them down at the expense of the grand jury.

18,278. Have you ever received any contribution to that expense?—None in the way of cleansing, not a penny.

18,279. Have you any connexion with the markets or fairs as a buyer or seller?—Sometimes I go as a buyer and seller and regret it.

18,280. Have you any knowledge of the surrounding country and the farmers?—Yes.

18,281. Do you think the exaction of a toll acts as a deterrent on people bringing their cattle and commodities to the market and fairs?—If the town were properly managed it would only increase the importance of the fairs. For instance, as regards the establishment of a horse fair, if we had capital enough to contribute towards the promotion of that we could make it a success. Six pounds were given as a means of encouragement by the townspeople, who formed a committee, and if we had some five hundred pounds, or a thousand, and invite buyers to come, and give them a free hotel and encourage the fair, the place is sufficiently large, and one of the best towns in Ireland. It is one calculated to develop trade, that is, with regard to the fairs and markets. It is very central, so close to the Limerick Junction, and in the centre of a rich country—the golden vale.

18,282. Are the commissioners as a body in favour of the removal of the pig fair off the streets?—Under the present management they prefer having them as they are.

18,283. On the streets?—Yes.

18,284. Although an additional liability is incurred by them?—They are consulting the interests of the traders in the town.

18,285. I suppose the town commissioners themselves are, generally speaking, traders of the town?—They are all-important ones too.

18,286. Have you ever heard that any accidents have happened from the fact of some of the cattle being exposed for sale in the streets?—They are not exposed for sale. They would be on the roadway to the railway station. In fact that place is utilised for calves.

18,287. Is that fair-green in close proximity to the business portion of the town or have any complaints been made that it is out of the way or inconveniently situated?—So far as proximity to the town is concerned it is suitable. I think other places would be more suitable if we could find them, but taking into account the difficulty of finding any other place it is the best possible one that could be got. It might be kept cleaner in winter time.

18,288. Is it utilised at all in any way between fairs for grazing purposes or otherwise?—No. Sometimes bottles and stones used to be thrown there and broken glass.

18,289. No profit is derived from the use of it between fairs?—No.

18,290. It is a commonage?—It is styled a commonage in the rate books.

18,291. Have you any statement you wish to make?—With regard to the butter market in the town I might give an extract or copy of a letter from the minutes and it is very important.

18,292. Mr. Frewen, solicitor for the town commissioners said: Permit me to explain. It appears long before there was anything in connexion with this commission and as far back as 1864, the town commissioners thinking a grievance existed considered the matter with reference to the butter market and also with respect to the fairs in the town. They then had some communication with members of Parliament and the result of their action at that time appears on the minutes of the commissioners, which the clerk has before him and will read for you. The commissioners always considered that a private person like Mr. Chadwick living four or five miles off and having no interest in the town or any property in the town having got this grant so far back as 20 years ago from the magistrates in pursuance of the Act of Parliament, and that it was merely a private gift of that kind; they considered it was too bad that the town should be deprived of a profit arising from the market and that all should be centered in this individual. With a view of remedying that grievance they entered into negotiations with members of Parliament and parties, as on the minutes.

18,293. The town clerk then read as follows:—The butter market of Tipperary is, Cork excepted, the largest in Ireland. From it is exported from 140,000 to 160,000 firkins of butter, representing a money value of 600,000*l.* to 700,000*l.* Of this number 60,000 firkins are purchased by the merchants at their own private stores. The remaining 80,000 to 100,000 firkins pass through the public market and bring to the weighmaster a net income of 848*l.* per year or thereabouts, and had the entire quantity sold in the town passed through the market, as would be the case under the management of the town commissioners, the net profit would amount to 1,460*l.* per year or thereabouts. The weighmaster was appointed to this office by the county magistrates, scarcely one of whom has the slightest interest in the welfare of the town by virtue of the 32nd of George III. cap. 124, and as this Act, so far as the commissioners know, is still in force, the commissioners apprehend that in the event of the death of the present weighmaster the magistrates would elect another, or in case the commissioners purchased the weighmaster's interest in the market, their power over it would cease at his death. It may be proper also to state that should the Act referred to above be repealed a claim to the tolls of the butter market would probably be made by the local landlord, who is supposed to hold an appointment as general weighmaster under an Act passed in the reign of Queen Anne. These particulars are brought under your notice in the hope that during the discussion of the bill in committee (that was the Public Health Act of 1878) some lucky opportunity may offer by which you may be able to carry out the views of the commissioners and obtain for them control and secure for them the profits of their own markets. Should you succeed great and permanent benefit will be conferred on this town and its inhabitants, who must ever feel you are entitled to their lasting gratitude.

18,294. To whom was that addressed?—That is signed by me and addressed to Mr. Edward Dwyer Gray, county member. One of the commissioners, a most important butter merchant in Tipperary, and one of the most respectable inhabitants, gave it his undivided attention. So far as Mr. Chadwick himself is concerned he is a most estimable, nice gentleman, and nobody blames. He is appointed to take the tolls and he would be more than human to care if he did not do that, but we must complain of the state of the law.

18,295. Have you any other observations to make, Mr. Dawson?—No observations, but the law on the subjects is a great hardship. It would be a great source of profit if we had the tolls instead of a little rate of 1½d. in the £, which comes to 300l. a year, and we have to light and cleanse the town, and keep inspectors out of the miserable 300l. a year. We have to do more than we can do. If we had a 1,000l. a year between the butter weighhouse and the fairs and markets that would enable us to do three times as much as now, and we would have no taxation.

18,296. Examined by Mr. Fraser:—It was stated that Mr. Smith Barry is owner in fee of the place in which the markets are held. Do you know that Mr. Stafford O'Brien owns a portion of the town?—Certainly.

18,297. Do you know from the corner of Church Street to the top of Henry Street?—Yes.

18,298. It is a continuation of the main street?—Yes.

18,299. How much of the main street would that represent?—About a third.

18,300. The Assistant Commissioner said he need not labour the point, as it was quite sufficient to have it in evidence that there were other owners besides Mr. Smith Barry in the town.

18,301. Examination continued by Mr. Fraser:—What is the principal object of the Commissioners' men in cleaning the streets?—There are carters specially appointed.

18,302. When have they any heavy duty to perform?—After the pig market days, and after the cattle fairs too.

18,303. These men are appointed by the commissioners, and paid by them?—Yes.

18,304. What is the entire amount they pay for cleaning the street?—30l. a year.

18,305. Does it cost that exclusively for cleaning the streets after the fairs and markets, or does it include everything?—The men are allocated to other duties.

18,306. What other duties?—The street inspectorship.

18,307. But the men who clean the streets, is their particular duty to clean them after the markets and fairs?—Yes, the other cleaning because there is of a trifling character. They have to be attended to all the same, and we have to get additional men after the fairs and markets, and more if we could afford it. We should have 300l. a year for cleaning the town.

18,308. (By the Assistant Commissioner.) Does the manure obtained from cleaning the streets after the fairs act as an equivalent for any expense you are at?—It becomes reproductive to a certain extent.

18,309. Does it act as an equivalent—do you sell it?—We get about 50l. a year on an average for it, and have about close on 100l. a year.

18,310. Would you be able to tell me the actual additional expenditure occasioned by the fact of the pig fairs being held in the streets?—About 50l. I would say.

18,311. On ordinary occasions, what would they cost each week?—It would not be one-tenth part of that.

18,312. Then you say on an average 10s. a day would be the additional expenditure?—Yes, to do the thing properly.

18,313. Cross-examined by Mr. Townsend:—Supposing I wanted to clean the streets after the four pig fairs and four cattle fairs would the commissioners be satisfied to give me the manure?—You could not be expected to get the manure for those four fairs alone.

18,314. Would the commissioners wish instructions to be given to the constabulary not to allow any cattle on the road on fair days between the town and the railway station?—It is more than I can take upon myself to say.

18,315. The town commissioners objected before. They stated that they wished to get the control into their own hands, and an arrangement was come to that this would be done in reference to the town, and no exception was taken?—I know.

18,316. Do not you think that the pig fairs should be removed from the town to the fair green, and that that would get rid of the whole complaint about dirtying and injuring the streets by having the markets held there?—It might lead us to be poor and doomed. We prefer to be as we are, and let every trader have his chance. Besides, I wish to say that people who come in the morning early, after being up all night, would want a place to get a glass of whisky.

18,317. As I understand, you consider the convenience of a glass of whisky, and having the fairs and markets in the proper compensation for the dirt in the street?—What I say is that there is a better distribution of the trade generally.

18,318. (The Assistant Commissioner.) I have got that out that the traders would put up with any inconvenience caused by the fairs and markets being held on the streets for trade purposes?—Yes.

18,319. (To Witness.) Have the markets always been held on Thursdays and Saturdays?—Thursdays and Saturdays are the recognised market days.

18,320. Have they been always held within your knowledge?—Yes.

18,321. And the four old fairs have always been held?—Yes, as far as I remember.

18,322. You never remember any less number than four?—Four is the number for years past.

18,323. Did you ever hear that tolls were levied on any days other than those days, and at the pig fairs?—No. In 1853 the new fairs were established.

18,324. No tolls were levied at the new fairs?—No.

18,325. Did you ever hear complaints being made of the tolls?—No. People are so accustomed they do not know how to complain. They pay them away.

18,326. Are retailers ever charged in the market? Supposing potatoes were brought in by a producer and sold to a retailer, who subsequently retailed them, would he be also charged a toll?—I think so.

18,327. (By Mr. Fraser.) Is there an objection to the holding of the fairs on the days on which they are held?—A change would be desirable for the new fairs.

18,328. What would be the proposed change?—I do not exactly remember.

18,329. Is the reason of the proposed change here that the fairs clash with other fairs?—Certainly, that is the reason.

18,330. With what fairs?—With the monthly fairs.

18,331. Where are the fairs held?—In Limerick, Cork, Clonmel, Thurles, Charleville, and Kenmare. They think the new cattle fairs should be held on the third Friday in each month.

18,332. Is that purely because they clash with other fairs?—Yes.

18,333. You think if they were held on the dates suggested more buyers would attend?—Yes, and more cattle too.

18,334. There was a resolution passed by the commissioners on the 9th November 1887?—Yes.

18,335. Still it is required to be carried out?—Yes.

18,336. Did you ever make any representation to Mr. Smith Barry to assist you?—Yes. I think he is quite unfriendly to the change.

18,337. Do you remember when the fairs were held on the streets?—No. They were held there about 35 years ago.

18,338. They were then removed to the fair green?—Yes.

18,339. Was there a roadway leading through the fair green and going out at the other side?—By an old inhabitant, I am told, there was, and several roads in the fair green, and four squares of houses. The place was surrounded by houses. As a matter of fact, the road was there long after the railway was constructed.

18,340. (By the Assistant Commissioner.) Was there ever an application made to the Local Government Board to alter the fair?

18,341. (Mr. Fraser.) There were instructions given to me to take the necessary steps, and the first thing to consider was the expense. I believe the commissioners will not pass to undergo all the costs of an inquiry which will be held before the sheriff.

18,342. (The Assistant Commissioner.) It can be done by applying to the Local Government Board if you obtain the consent of the owner.

18,343. (Mr. Townsend.) We are quite inclined to join in any change.

Mr. William Hanly examined.

18,344. What evidence do you wish to give?—All the butter that is brought to Tipperary does not pass through Mr. Chadwick's market place, nor is it compulsory for any to pass through it.

18,345. Is some of it brought direct by the farmers to the private stores?—Yes, and sold and weighed there.

18,346. Do these private merchants levy any charge at all?—No charge.

18,347. But have these farmers their own particular customers or do they go round from one to another every morning?—They call at the different stores to get the best price.

18,348. Does any great number of them resort to that mode of disposing of their butter?—It is a system that is declining. It was done on a far larger scale some years ago.

18,349. Was it done with the object of evading the 3d. charge?—I do not think so. It is the principal way of disposing of the butter. The butter going to the weighhouse is the exception.

18,350. Is the butter the same quality as is sold in the market?—Yes. The same people will sell one day in the weigh-house and another day outside.

18,351. Are you a butter buyer?—Yes.

18,352. What is your own opinion of that practice and the opinion of the other buyers, or have you formed any opinion as to whether it is a practice that should be stopped?—I think freedom should exist between the buyer and seller.

18,353. Have you an ample opportunity of seeing the butter. Of course it would be necessary to store in your own private store and examine the butter?—Yes.

18,354. There are no facilities afforded for testing the butter?—No. There was a public taster, but his testing did not bind the buyer or seller. It was a mere matter of form.

18,355. Do the buyers think it is the best arrangement to leave it to themselves?—Yes. In fact, wherever tasting has been established it has given dissatisfaction. It has been abandoned everywhere except in Cork.

18,356. It is the seller always who pays the 3d.?—Yes. He has not always charged 3d. 2d. is the legal charge, but at the request of the buyers and sellers he agreed to the weighing, taring, and examining the butter, and delivering it, and then he charged an additional 1d.

18,357. Previous to that the butter was not examined?—No, except by the buyer. We found it did not work satisfactorily.

18,358. Is the tare of the firkin the only deduction from the gross weight?—The only deduction.

18,359. When you are paying the farmer, what deduction do you make or do you deduct any charge for brokerage or the bad scale of the butter?—Nothing whatever. We make no deduction. Everything is on the face of the ticket.

18,360. Do you deduct anything as a luck-penny?—No.

18,361. In some places they deduct 1s.?—I know, but it has not been the practice here. There are some gratuities to the coopers or men in our employment, but we have nothing to do with it, nor do we countenance it.

18,362. Would not the proportion of butter sold outside greatly depend on the demand?—Yes.

18,363. If there is a great demand for butter the buyers are anxious to meet the butter on the streets and buy it?—Yes.

Mr. Ryan re-examined.

18,364. This return of yours, Mr. Ryan, is not a return of the number of firkins that come into the town, but of the number that attend the butter market?—Yes.

18,365. Would you say it is a greater number by far than the number actually going to the private stores?—The number varies from year to year.

18,366. Is half the number brought to your market that goes to the private merchants?—About 50 per cent. goes to the merchants. I would say at present not 50 per cent., but if you take an average it is about that. It may increase or diminish.

Mr. Michael Barry, Town Commissioner, examined.

18,367. Examined by Mr. Brown, as follows:—What have you to say generally with reference to the tolls at the fairs and markets?—What I have to say has been already stated. It has been stated by one of Mr. Smith Barry's witnesses that he did not charge 6d. on a cart that conveys slips (bonhams) on fair and market days, although not sold. I saw two men going around every fair day and market day through the crowds and saw them charging the 6d., and if a man had not the 6d. he would have to get it.

18,368. The man would have left a part of what you say, and he would have to pay for the stand of the cart whether he sold or not?—Yes.

18,369. (*By the Commissioner.*) Is that as they enter the market place?—They might be there an hour or two.

18,370. Have you anything further to add?—If this was a pig market day, and if a load of slips were unsold and came the next day, they would have to pay 6d. more for the standing.

18,371. Are bonhams brought in on a cattle fair day as well as on the pig fair day?—They are, and if you sell these slips out of that cart, no matter what you get, there is 3d. each charged. Supposing there were 10 slips that would be 2s. 6d. in addition to the 6d. for the standing of the cart.

18,372. Do you know that of your own knowledge?—Of my own knowledge. I can swear I know it for last 50 years, although it was stated by Mr. Smith Barry's clerk it was not done to his knowledge.

18,373. Do you know that 6d. has been paid and subsequently a payment of 3d. for each pig in the cart?—Yes. I positively know it is quite true. I was present at the payment repeatedly. The men are placed at the custom gaps, and then they swear a mock sort of oath, and if they swear they did not buy they are let free. If they swear they have bought they have to pay 3d. a pig.

18,374. Is it not the seller who pays the 6d. charge?—It is.

18,375. Is it not the buyer who pays the 3d. charge?—Yes.

18,376. It is not the one individual who pays both of them?—No.

18,377. When the buyer is paying for these pigs does he deduct the 3d. he has to pay subsequently from the price?—That is an arrangement among themselves.

18,378. That is not the practice?—They generally give a small luck-penny.

18,379. Is there any rule regulating the value of the luck-penny or is it left to the disposition of the seller?—Yes. You need not give the buyer anything if you wish.

18,380. You are one of the town commissioners?—Yes.

18,381. Do you think it would be desirable that the days on which the new fairs are held ought to be changed?—I think it would be a greater advantage to the interest of the town if they were changed.

18,382. For the reasons already given that they clash with other fairs?—Yes.

Mr. Mulqueen re-examined.

18,383. Do you attend the fairs at all?—No, but I know the working of them.

18,384. Do you know is what Mr. Brown states correct?—I send out men, and my directions are to get 6d. for the car.

18,385. Nothing in addition for every individual pig in the car?—Certainly not.

18,386. Did you ever see 3d. charged?—Mr. Brown knows what I am saying. I send out two men, and my directions are to get the 6d.

18,387. Of your own knowledge you have not received subsequently 3d. for each pig?—No. The men return the money to me at night.

Mr. William Hanrin examined.

18,288. What do you wish to say?—I was charged 6d. each for two bonhams.

18,289. What was the value of each of them?—6s. a piece.

18,290. Were they in a cart?—Yes, in an ass's cart. They would not let the bonhams go unless I paid.

Michael Halloran examined.

18,291. What do you wish to state?—I remember when the fair green was a common.

18,292. How long ago is that?—About 46 years ago.

18,293. Do you remember what time were the fairs changed to the fair green?—I do not.

18,294. At the time it was a commonage there was liberty for everybody to go into the place?—Yes, every-one came in and out. There was nothing there but dung-pits and dung-holes.

18,295. [By Mr. Prosser.] Is this fair green a stoney kind of ground on which nothing grows?—Yes.

18,296. Previous to their removal to the fair green where were the fairs held?—In the streets of the town.

18,297. When were they removed?—I could not say.

18,298. Was it 25 or 30 years ago?—About that time.

E. Townsend, Esq., J.P., re-examined.

18,299. Is the site of the fair green on portion of Mr. Barry's property?—Yes.

18,400. On the property that descended to him?—Yes. Mr. Freeman Smith's immediately adjoins it.

18,401. Is there any other gentleman who has any observations to make?—(*No answer.*)

CAHIR—CO. TIPPERARY.

With reference to my inquiry in Cahir, on the 2nd November 1888, I beg to report as follows:—

Cahir is situated in the southern portion of the county of Tipperary. It is a station on the Waterford and Limerick Railway line, and has other local advantages for a fair trade in agricultural produce. The surrounding country is very fertile. The town has a few squares, or open spaces, around which houses are neatly and substantially built. It is clean and apparently well kept, notwithstanding the fact that there is no town commission established there. The population is 2,469.

The market day is Friday, but corn is sold every day in the week.

The fairs are held on the 8th February, 12th April, 26th May, 20th July, 18th September, 20th October, and 7th December. A pig fair is held on the last Thursday in each month.

Tolls are not levied at the pig fairs, or at the fairs held on the 8th February, 12th April, and 20th October.

Tolls are levied at the fairs held on the 26th May, 20th July, 18th September, and 7th December. No tolls are levied at the markets or pig fairs, unless they happen to fall upon the same ordinary fair day at which tolls are leviable, but at the former weighing charges are exacted if any of the marketable commodities are weighed at the public appliances.

The market rights and tolls are the property of Lady Margaret Charteris, of Cahir House, who is not, however, in the immediate receipt of the tolls, but has them sub-let to Mr. Michael Keating, of Cahir, at the yearly rent of 40*l*.

Two patents were granted for the town of Caher, as appears by the public records. The first is dated 24th November 1614 (12 James I.), which authorised the Earl of Cahir to hold a Thursday market and a fair on the 15th and 16th of May. This is the fair at present held on the 26th May. The other patent is dated the 7th June 1776 (16 George III.) and authorised Lord Cahir to hold two additional fairs on the 20th July and 7th December. The fairs at present held on the 8th February, 12th April, and 20th October were established about 30 years ago, as stated in evidence, but afterwards fell into abeyance and were subsequently re-established about twenty-two years ago. I have been unable to trace the establishment of the fair of the 18th September, at which tolls are levied, but it was held long anterior to the establishment of the toll free fairs.

The owner and tenant have a toll board erected for public inspection, and have likewise provided one of the finest weighbridges I have as yet seen at any of the fairs.

The fairs in Cahir are held on the square called "Grosvenor Square" and streets, with the exception of the pig fair, which is held in a second square off the public street called the "Potato Market." A shed is provided there with two beams and scales for the purpose of weighing the potatoes and other commodities required to be weighed. This space is not enclosed, but is situated at the rear of the houses in the street. As before mentioned a large weighing machine for cattle has been erected there since the passing of the recent Act. The accommodation afforded in the way of shedding is very small and scarcely adequate. In the general market held in Grosvenor Square—a portion of the public thoroughfare—there is no shelter accommodation whatever provided, and the necessity for such is acknowledged by the witnesses, though there would be a considerable difficulty in procuring a suitable site, and one that would give satisfaction both to the traders of the town and those frequenting the markets and fairs. Some private traders in the town have also beams and scales on which they weigh marketable commodities, and exact a charge for the services they perform.

The same practice exists here as in Tipperary in levying two charges off small pigs. If they are brought into the fair in a cart a standing charge of 3½d. has to be paid, and if they are subsequently sold each has to bear an additional charge of 1½d.

Appended will be found a transcript of the evidence taken at the inquiry.

John J. O'Meara,
Assistant Commissioner.

45, Lower Mount Street, Dublin.

Cahir, 2nd November 1888.

William [illegible], Esq., J.P., examined.

18,402. You represent the owner?—Yes.

18,403. Who is the owner?—Lady Margaret Charteris.

18,404. Where does she reside?—In Grosvenor Square, London. She has also a residence here, Cahir Lodge.

18,405. Does she own the markets and fairs in the town?—I think so. She does not levy any tolls. It is rather difficult to answer yes or no to that question, but there are certain fairs held by patents to levy tolls on.

18,406. What is the market day?—It is a weekly market day held every Friday, which is included in her patent.

18,407. Is that the only day on which marketable commodities are brought to the town and exposed for sale in the market square?—Corn comes daily to market.

18,408. The general market is every Friday?—Yes.

18,409. What are the fairs held in the town, whether Lady M. Charteris has anything to do with them or not?—There are seven fairs in the year. There is the 9th February, 17th April, 26th May, 20th July, 10th September, 22nd October, and 7th December.

18,410. These are the only fairs held in the town?—Yes.

18,411. Which of these is the owner connected with?—Four of the above are toll fairs.

18,412. Which are they?—The 26th May, 20th July, 10th September, and 7th December. In addition to these there is a monthly pig market the last Thursday in the month, which is toll free. As a matter of fact, we do not levy tolls, whether our patent would cover it or not.

18,413. At the pig fair?—Yes. There are no tolls sought to be raised.

18,414. Have you another pig fair on the day previous to the ordinary cattle fair?—No. That is the only pig fair.

18,415. Could you tell me under what authority the owner collects the tolls on these days mentioned?—The markets are held under a patent of the 12th year of James the First, granted to Thomas Baron Cahir to hold one fair and weekly markets with the tolls and customs thereof.

18,416. It does not specify the date of the fair?—No.

18,417. Was there another one granted?—Yes. By patent in the 16th year of George the Third there was granted to James, Baron Cahir, the right of holding two additional fairs on the 20th July and 7th December with the usual tolls.

18,418. How long have you been connected with this property?—About five years.

18,419. Then you cannot give any information as to what happened previous to that?—No.

18,420. I believe she has these tolls sub-let?—Yes.

18,421. To whom?—To Mr. Michael Hastings before you.

18,422. Is it let on lease?—Yes, but whether there is an actual lease or yearly agreement, I am not quite sure.

18,423. At what rent?—At a rent of 50l. a year.

18,424. I suppose the taxes as well?—We pay the taxes.

18,425. All the taxes?—Yes.

18,426. What is the valuation of the tolls?—I have not that before me.

18,427. There is a question in the query sheet as to what capital expenditure the owner has been at. Had you any means of ascertaining that?—Well, to some extent.

18,428. Will you kindly give it to me?—Well, to begin with, the fee-simple value of the site of the market.

18,429. Is that the market square?—No; what they call the potato market off Market Street, which belongs to Lady Margaret. If it was not occupied, the market would be available for building purposes.

18,430. It is a private site, and in no wise dedicated to the public?—No, that is our own.

18,431. Is it enclosed?—No.

18,432. It is off the public thoroughfare?—Yes.

18,433. It is in a way separated from it?—Yes. We can usually exercise the rights of ownership, and do constantly exercise them.

18,434. What did you put down as the fee-simple value of that?—I have not estimated that.

18,435. Have you any buildings in the market proper?—There is a shed which was erected in 1876 at a cost of 60l.

18,436. Where is that erected?—In the square; and a weighbridge was put up recently which cost 60l., including the cost of its erection.

18,437. Where is that erected?—In the same place; in the potato square. Previous to that there was a smaller weighbridge, but it was not deemed sufficient under the new Act for weighing cattle.

18,438. Have you that still there?—Both are still there.

18,439. Have you any beams and scales there?—There are two.

18,440. Provided by the owner?—Yes.

18,441. You did not put down the value of these?—No.

18,442. What would you estimate the value of it?—I suppose the value would be 5l.

18,443. Are these in the main square?—In the shed where the potatoes are weighed.

18,444. Does Mr. Keatinge do any repairs, if required, to the beams and scales, tackle, and shed?—As a matter of fact, Mr. Keatinge has kept them in repair.

18,445. The market has not been at any expense?—No, not recently.

18,446. Does she own in fee?—Yes.

18,447. Does she own the greater portion of the town? —The greater portion of the town, but she is not exclusively the owner.

18,448. I suppose you had not an opportunity of bringing these queries under her notice?—No, not yet.

18,449. I believe no local authority exists here?—Not at present.

18,450. If town commissioners were established, or a market committee, would she be in favour of those acquiring compulsory powers to obtain her rights?—As far as I am acquainted with her views, if she were compensated by what she would consider fair compensation, I do not say she would attach any particular importance to these rights.

18,451. From your own experience do you think it would be advisable here and elsewhere to have the markets and fairs under the control of a body like the town commissioners or a market committee, if such were established? Do you think the united efforts of a number of gentlemen would tend to promote the markets or fairs better than having them in the hands of individuals?—I think if the town commissioners really represent the intelligent portion of the mercantile community and attended to their business, I think they would be the proper parties.

18,452. That is general throughout the country?—Yes, if they represent the best mercantile intelligence of the town.

18,453. Is there any other market authority in this town?—Not what I should call a market authority.

18,454. Or anybody claiming market rights?—There are private individuals who have weigh-bridges, which have sprung up from time to time, and Lady Margaret has never taken steps to see how much they have infringed her rights.

18,455. These people weigh the different commodities and make charges?—I believe they do. I have every reason to know they do.

18,456. The other fairs are toll free?—Yes.

18,457. Are tolls levied at the Friday market?—I think not.

Mr. Michael Keaveney examined.

18,458. You are the lessee of the markets and tolls?—Yes.

18,459. And you pay a rent of 40*l.* a year for them?—Yes.

18,460–1. Do you levy tolls at the Friday market?—No.

18,462. Do you levy tolls at any market?—None, save when the pig market and cattle market fall on the same day. I have power then to tax the pigs as a commodity in the fair.

18,463. That is, if the pig *fair* falls on the cattle fair on which tolls are levied?—Yes. It has only occurred twice.

18,464. Have you got a schedule of the tolls at the fair?—I have.

18,465. Where are the markets held?—On the streets.

18,466. Has the square outside any particular name?—It is called the market square.

18,467. Then you have the potato square?—Yes.

18,468. Are these the only ones?—Yes.

18,469. There is a shed, I believe, erected in the potato square?—Yes.

18,470–1. And each of these form practically portion of the public thoroughfare, and carts indiscriminately go over them?—Quite so.

18,472. Will you give me the names of the different descriptions of marketable commodities brought into the market square?—Potatoes, corn, eggs, butter, fowl, fish, vegetables, wicker ware, and fruit.

18,473. Do they bring cattle at all to the market?—None.

18,474. The corn comes in every day?—Yes.

18,475. And is exposed for sale?—No. It generally goes to the mills.

18,476. Is corn ever exposed in the market square?—Never.

18,477. Do you levy any charges on these different commodities you have mentioned?—No.

18,478. When you weigh them do not you levy a charge?—Yes, when I weigh them on the weigh-bridge or at the potato scales.

18,479. You never weigh corn?—Very seldom. It is weighed in bulk.

18,480. Have you got a list of your charges created?—Yes. 3*d.* for a cart-load and 1*d.* per hundred for potatoes.

18,481. For a horse-load you charge 3*d.*?—Yes.

18,482. What would you charge for a donkey-load?—Half that, or 2*d.*

18,483. That is the regular charge?—Yes.

18,484. That is irrespective of what the commodity is in the cart?—Yes.

18,485. Have you any charge on butter?—No.

18,486. Do you weigh butter at all?—No.

18,487. This is not a butter market?—No. It is said to be so.

18,488. Have you any standing charges at all?—No, unless on the toll fair days.

18,489. When weighing potatoes, do you give any ticket denoting the weight?—Yes.

18,490. You have a printed ticket?—It is in manuscript form.

18,491. Are all the potatoes that are brought here weighed at your scales?—No. My scales are trespassed on by parties outside.

18,492. Is there any rule confining the sale of potatoes to this market—the potato square?—Yes.

18,493. Is it printed?—I have it under the direction of the patent. In fact, everything that comes to the market ought to be tolled under the patent, on Friday, as well as fair days.

18,494. Have you ever had occasion to use legal proceedings against these people?—I do frequently threaten, but I never carried them out. Mr. Rochford [illegible] the people weighing outside my scale that they would be prosecuted if they continued.

18,495. What percentage of the potatoes brought to the town goes to these people?—It is small.

18,496. Would you say 25 per cent.?—No.

18,497. Is it 20 per cent.?—It might be 15 or 20 per cent.

18,498. The greater portion goes to you?—Yes.

18,499. When weighing potatoes, are they all brought in sacks?—Yes. We sometimes weigh a horse-load of eight sacks on the cart.

18,500. Then your only charge 3*d.*?—Under the patent I charge 1*d.* per hundredweight to relieve them of the necessity of taking them into the scale.

18,501. When you weigh them in a cart, do you actually ascertain the weight of the cart?—I do.

18,502. Do you also estimate the tare, or do you actually ascertain the weight of the sacks?—The tare of the sacks is understood.

18,503. You always go by estimation for the tare of the sacks?—Quite so.

18,504. That is seven pounds?—Yes.

18,505. What quantity of potatoes is in the sack for which you allow the tare of seven pounds?—They weigh 20 and 21 stone, and sometimes 18. When it comes under 18, the allowance is five pounds.

18,506. Then you go by the appearance of the sack as to whether it is the small or large tare that will be allowed?—Yes. This allowance is principally owing to the fact that potatoes are not brought quite clean. They are full of earth and sand, and that is the reason there is an allowance of seven pounds.

18,507. Is that the only deduction from the weight of the bag?—Yes.

18,508. Would that be the same tare on a sack of potatoes brought in to-day, and one brought on a wet day, when the sack is completely saturated with wet?—It is always about the same.

18,509. You have no charge on fish?—No charge on any commodity coming into the market, only at the potatoe market.

18,510. If you weigh corn, what is your charge?—Very seldom I am troubled with corn. It is 1d. per hundred.

18,511. Were there ever any charges on the corn here?—No, save on the toll fair day.

18,512. You never remember any proceedings being taken to enforce any market rights for the collection of a toll on corn, or on any of the marketable commodities?—Yes. I prosecuted myself, frequently.

18,513. How long are you connected with the fairs and markets here?—Thirty-five years.

18,514. What was the result of the proceedings?—A conviction.

18,515. Did you follow it up?—The man was fined.

18,516. How did the collection of the toll fall into disuetude?—It never did; but this man forced his [illegible].

18,517. I mean as regards the marketable commodities. Did you ever take proceedings to recover the toll on potatoes, corn, butter, and eggs?—No, the Cahir family were always liberal in that way.

18,518. Do you remember, later, during your experience, tolls being collected at the market on market days?—Never.

18,519. Where is the butter sold?—In the streets.

18,520. Is it exposed for sale in the streets, or does it go around to the shops?—The people have customers, and they bring it to and bulk is sold on the streets.

18,521. Does it come in any quantity? I suppose in large lumps?—Yes.

18,522. Does it come in firkins?—No.

18,523. I suppose it is the shopkeepers principally who buy this?—Yes.

18,524. They have to test it, and ascertain the weight themselves?—Yes.

18,525. Do you know do they levy any charge on the seller for weighing it for him?—No. I believe there was one or two small houses that were in the habit of weighing heretofore, and they used to charge some small fee for doing so, but I do not know that that exists just now.

18,526. You have only an interest in four fairs?—Yes.

18,527. And also on a pig fair, if it falls before any of those fairs?—Quite so.

18,528. Where are the fairs held?—On the square, and the streets leading into it.

18,529. That is the potatoe square?—No. Young pigs go to the potatoe square exclusively.

18,530. Then it is on the square here, opposite the court house, they are held?—Yes.

18,531. Have you different portions of the square and the streets adjacent allotted for each description of cattle?—No.

18,532. They intermix?—Yes.

18,533. Does that cause confusion, or accidents to cattle?—No. The sheep are in two streets, and the cattle in the square.

18,534. Have they two portions?—Yes.

18,535. Cattle are separated from the sheep?—Yes.

18,536. Cattle and sheep are then brought here?—Yes.

18,537. Are any horses brought in?—No; a very odd horse.

18,538. But still some occasionally are brought in?—No.

18,539. Are pigs brought to the cattle fairs?—No, unless the pig fairs fall on the coincident day.

18,545. Witness then produced the toll board, of which the following is a copy:—

A SCHEDULE

Of the tolls and customs payable and to be levied at the fairs of Cahir, viz.:—

	s.	d.
For every horse, gelding, mare, or mule sold -	1	0
For every bullock, cow, bull, or heifer sold -	0	4½
For every yearling or calf sold -	0	2½
For every sheep, ram, lamb, or goat sold -	0	1
For every pig sold -	0	3½
For every suckling pig sold -	0	1½
For each upon every tent or booth in which goods, wares, merchandise, or refreshments are exposed for sale -	1	0
For every pedler's or dealer's high stand -	0	6½
For every car on which wool, coopers or turners' ware, timber, manufactured or unmanufactured, fruit, or goods whatsoever exposed for sale, same being deemed a standing -	0	4½
For every butcher's stall and pitt, and every upload of frieze or flannel -	0	4½
For every single piece of delf -	0	4
Every shoemaker's, brogue-maker's, glover's, hatter's, and breeches maker's stand -	0	6½
For every hawker exposing goods for sale -	0	3½
For and upon all goods, wares, or merchandise, not particularly stated herein, same being exposed for sale on a stand -	0	4½

The Hon. LADY MARGARET CHARTERIS,
Patroness.

MICHAEL KEATING,
Lessee.

18,546. These are the charges you levy at present?—Yes.

18,547. And have been in the habit of levying for a number of years?—Quite so.

18,548. Do you remember any period when these charges were greater or smaller?—No.

18,549. Have you made any alteration in them?—None whatever.

18,550. And these have always been the rates you charge?—Yes.

18,551. The charges are only on the animals actually sold?—Yes.

18,552. For every pig 3½d. Do you charge that?—Yes.

18,553. Has that charge ever been complained of?—Never.

18,554. Although the value of one pig, on which a charge might be levied, would be more than the other pigs?—Anybody who sells a pig does not object to the charge.

18,555. You never take any note of the value of the animal?—No.

18,556. On young pigs the charge is 1½d.?—Yes.

18,557. Have you ever heard complaints of that?—No.

18,558. Supposing they brought a cart of young pigs, what do you charge?—They are taken as a load.

18,559. What do you charge for a load?—5½d.

18,560. Would you levy that charge on the cart, whether the pigs were subsequently sold or not?—The charge is paid coming in.

18,561. Outside the town you have gaps?—Yes.

18,562. And men watching as they enter the town?—Yes.

18,563. Have they to pay the charges as they enter?—Yes.

18,564. Supposing they had eight or ten small pigs in the car, they pay 5½d. entering, but if they fail to sell any one of them during the day?—They go home free.

18,569. Accommodation afforded to the seller in the way of liberty to bring his cart on the public thoroughfare?—To the market square.

18,570. That is the public square?—Yes.

18,571. No shelter is given in the place?—No, except the present shed.

18,572. They do not go to the shed on fair days?—They do not go to the sheds. It is simply confined to the protection of the beam and scales.

18,573. Said there is not sufficient space to afford special accommodation for the people?—It is only intended for the beam and scales, and the clerks attending to give tickets.

18,574. The charge on cattle is 2½d. and on horses 1s.?—Yes.

18,575. Are these only where sold?—Yes.

18,576. If unsold there is no charge?—No charge.

18,577. For every yearling 2½d. Why did they put on the fractions of a penny?—I do not know.

18,578. Have they been always so?—Yes. I have the board 100 years old, and the same due as the one produced.

18,579. Do you ever collect the fractions of a penny, or do you ever get them?—No, we give and take.

18,580. For every yearling or calf 2½d., but if the animal passed a year would there be a jump from 2½d. to 5½d.?—After the May fair we charge them 5½d. Up to May they are charged as yearlings.

18,581. You have standings on fair days?—Yes, hawkers.

18,582. The charge is 3½d. for a cartload?—Yes, they may spread that cartload.

18,583. I suppose for every single piece of flannel you charge 4d.?—Yes.

18,584. What would be the quantity in that piece, or what would be the value of it?—I suppose they would have from 20 to 30 and 40 yards.

18,585. Was the quantity ever less?—Yes, 10 yards.

18,586. What would be the value of 10 yards of the cheapest flannel?—8s., 9s., or 10s.

18,587. On that 8s. or 9s. you charge 4d.?—Yes.

18,588. For every hawker exposing goods for sale on a fair day, what would you charge?—3½d. and 5½d. when a cart is brought in.

18,589. That 3½d. is for a small standing on the street?—Yes.

18,590. A couple of barrels with boards on them?—Yes.

18,591. Irrespective of what the commodity is which is placed on it, whether it is fish, ornaments, or anything else?—Yes.

18,592. How do you collect these? Have you men going about the town to collect them?—I collect them in the square.

18,593. Are these standings confined to the square?—Yes.

18,594. They do not go about the streets?—Yes. I collect them in the square and on the roads.

18,595. That charge is for taking up a position, and not for selling anything, because you do not take into consideration whether they are sold or not?—It is for the position they take up in the square.

18,596. Did they ever complain to you that they did not sell?—Nobody comes there who does not sell something.

18,597. Is it at the beginning of the fair you collect the charges?—At the commencement.

18,598. I mean the standing charges?—At the conclusion of the fair the men go around. I have two men for the collection in the square, and we collect about 3 o'clock.

18,599. What time does the fair begin?—About 10 o'clock. The cattle fair begins earlier and the standing fair at 11.

18,600. What time does it usually terminate?—The hours vary but the place is generally cleared out about 4 o'clock.

18,601. When your men go about collecting the standing charge from the hawkers and they had not the change to give you, did any of your men ever seize any of the commodities?—Yes.

18,602. When did that last occur?—Well, it has not occurred for the last three years.

18,603. What was the result of the seizure?—They redeemed them afterwards.

18,604. How long were they retained?—Until some time in the afternoon.

18,605. What was the commodity which was seized?—On one occasion a man had spades and handles, and we took them.

18,606. Did you ever take any perishable commodities such as fish?—No. In fact, I have very seldom recourse to such a proceeding.

18,607. Had the individual the charge at all when it was demanded?—Well, I suppose he had for he made his market.

18,608. Have you known instances where a seizure occurred, and the person had not the charge to pay?—I do remember some such case.

18,609. Have they complained when such a seizure is made that they have not been given an opportunity of effecting a sale of the commodity when it was in your man's possession?—I always took care that the opportunity was afforded.

18,610. Then no such complaints have been made?—No.

18,611. Will you kindly tell me what are the principal standings?—Old clothes, shoes and boots, fruit, confectionery, cakes, sweetstuffs and vegetables generally. Half the things mentioned on the toll board do not exist now.

18,612. When levying the charge of 3½d. do you take into consideration the extent of the ground they occupy?—Not at all.

18,613. You only draw a distinction between a cart and a standing that is not a cart?—Yes.

18,614. Although an ordinary standing would not occupy a greater extent of ground than a cart?—Quite so.

18,615. Do you know the value of the smallest quantity of vegetables brought in on the smallest standing?—There would be a place for a donkey and cart with fruit.

18,616. What would be the usual value?—We do not exact the full charge. I charge 2d.

18,617. Supposing there was a small standing of vegetables, what would be the value of the vegetables a person would come to have?—That would depend on the season they were brought in.

18,618. Did they ever bring in about 5s. worth?—Yes, and 10s. and 15s. worth.

18,619. Did they ever bring a small quantity that would make less than 5s.?—Well, no, indeed.

18,620. You say about 5s.?—Yes.

18,621. On that 5s. there would be 3½d. charge?—We generally run down the donkey load to 2d.

18,622. But as regards the ordinary standing, would that be the charge?—If a standing we would charge 3½d.

18,623. No matter what stock is on it?—Yes.

18,624. And no matter whether the value was 5s. or 2l.?—Yes.

18,625. Is furniture brought in?—Yes.

18,626. Is it brought in any quantity?—No. A country carpenter makes up a lot of small chairs, forms, and stools.

18,627. Is there a 5½d. charge on that?—Yes.

18,628. I suppose he brings in a cart?—Yes.

18,629. Have they brought them in an ordinary standing?—No.

18,630. Do they ever carry them themselves?—Yes, always in a cart. Then they lay them down and the ass is beside them.

18,631. What is the smallest number of the different articles of furniture they have brought in on such occasion?—They have brought half a dozen chairs, a small table, and some stools.

18,632. What would be the total value of such stock they bring in?—I can form no idea.

18,633. Your charges are stationary, although the value of the entire stock might vary?—Yes.

18,634. If these marketable commodities or these standings were in any portion of the town other than the

H 4

towns and districts adjacent, would you still levy your charge?—Yes.

18,635. Is that the only charge they have to pay?—Yes, anywhere within the circuit of my collection.

18,636. How far do you think your jurisdiction extends?—As far as the houses go.

18,637. Where do you place your custom gaps?—At the extreme end of every street—at the railway, for instance.

18,638. How many of these have you?—Seven.

18,639. How many men do you usually have at each?—It takes three-and-twenty men to do the work.

18,640. At what rate do you pay these men usually?—The collectors get half-a-crown, and the men 2s. for the day. Some of the collectors get 3s.

18,641. Would you say the average would be half-a-crown?—Yes.

18,642. You give some 2s. and others 3s.?—Yes.

18,643. Have you got a copy of this toll-board at each gap?—Yes.

18,644. So that when the farmers are coming out they have an opportunity of seeing what the charges are?—Yes, always.

18,645. Do your men inquire from them whether they have bought or sold?—The cattle are generally marked going out, and the principal buyers are all recognised, and they know the men who buy cattle there.

18,646. If they sold one farmer to another the farmer would not mark the head of cattle?—They sometimes go unmarked.

18,647. Do the collectors inquire whether they have bought or sold?—Yes.

18,648. Supposing the answer was that they had not bought nor sold, and your man doubted it, or had a suspicion the sale was effected, what course would they adopt?—They simply ask the man to lay his hand on the board, which is an affirmation.

18,649. They ask him to clear his conscience?—Yes.

18,650. Do they ever produce any book or paper?—No.

18,651. To swear them?—Never.

18,652. You never heard of such a thing being done?—No. They lay their hand on the board, and that is an affirmation of truth, which I am sorry to say very often is not the truth.

18,653. Is there a frequent necessity of appealing to the toll-board?—There is when the drovers are driving out cattle.

18,654. They are not the people of the neighbourhood or the farmers?—No, nor the owners.

18,655. They are only the men who travel from town to town?—Yes.

18,656. Now, supposing a farmer was bringing in his band of cattle into the fair, and outside the limits of your custom gap he met a buyer and a sale was effected on the road before he entered the fair, would you ask for your charge?—No, I could not.

18,657. You have never done so?—No.

18,658. Supposing they do not go to the square, but as they enter one of the streets a sale is effected, would you ask for your charge?—For anything done outside the toll board I do not charge.

18,659. Where you place your board is outside the last house?—It is outside the last house.

18,660. Supposing some farmer did not bring his cattle up where the crowd actually congregated, but brought them to another portion of the town and sold there?—I cannot approach him unless the cattle go through the fair.

18,661. Has a case arisen such as I state?—The cattle have been bought outside the [illegible], as you state, and driven into the market through the railway with the statement that they have not been sold or bought in the fair.

18,662. You never ask for your charge?—Oh, yes. I have sought for and got a charge on those days, though my act was frequently challenged.

18,663. Do they ever complain of the charges?—No, they are so long established.

18,664. Will you tell me what return is given for them by the owner, that is, Lady Margaret Charteris—practically she is owner and you are the lessee, in receipt of them—what return is given by her, or by you, for these charges, or is there any shelter accommodation afforded?—None beyond the private market.

18,665. So there are no duties performed other than the collection of these customs?—None.

18,666. And you do not know instances of where any of your collectors ever levied a toll on the animals when they were not sold other than on the pigs if they were brought in a cart?—They would be soon pulled up for that.

18,667. There is a toll on pigs in a cart, whether subsequently sold or not?—They pay for the cart coming in.

18,668. They pay for standing, and they pay for the pigs if they sell them afterwards?—It is the man who buys pays a second time.

18,669. Have they got the system of luck-penny here?—Yes, and a liberal one sometimes.

18,670. Is there any rule regulating the value of the luck-penny?—No.

18,671. It is always left to the disposition of the seller?—Yes, and if he is well-pleased with the buyer he treats him decently. I believe there is an established charge made on pigs. The buyer gets a big charge on pigs as a luck-penny.

18,672. Is it fixed?—Yes, 6d.

18,673. That is the buyer gets it from the seller?—Yes. I do not know what authority there is for it, but it is an excessive charge.

18,674. Have all these fairs at which you levy tolls been held in the town within your knowledge?—Yes, always.

18,675. The 6th February, 12th April, and 20th October, have they at any time within your knowledge been established?—I remember the establishment of them. It was a gift to the people by Lord Cahir.

18,676. Were these three fairs established at the same time?—Yes.

18,677. What time?—I have no idea of the period.

18,678. Could you not give an approximate idea?—They are 40 or 60 years old, but I think they were in abeyance for a time and re-established about 22 years ago.

18,679. Previous to the first establishment of these fairs the other four fairs were held and have always been held?—Yes.

18,680. Do you remember any period when there were less than four fairs held?—Never.

18,681. Do you remember a period when any of these four fairs were toll free?—Never.

18,682. Do you know, does Lady Charteris contribute anything directly to the cleansing of the town or square except by payment of rates and taxes?—No. She has no people engaged cleansing the square. The town is so constructed, and the sewerage so perfect, that a shower of rain washes it.

18,683. Is it the board of guardians and grand jury who look after the local affairs?—The sanitary authority is the board of guardians. At one period Lord Glengall gave these tolls for the purpose of cleansing the town. We were then under the town commission.

18,684. When did the commission cease to exist?—I suppose 30 years ago.

18,685. What was the cause of their disestablishment?—Mismanagement of the grossest kind.

18,686. Then did the tolls revert to the owner, who collected them?—Yes.

18,687–8. Since then the town has derived no benefit from them?—No. I may tell you the tolls passed through the Encumbered Estates Court and Landed Estates Court. They were sold twice.

18,689. You heard the question I asked Mr. [illegible] as to whether Lady Charteris would be disposed to sell to a local authority any legal interest vested in her. Would you be disposed to do likewise?—Unquestionably.

18,690. You would not resist?—No, provided I got compensation for any legal right vested in me.

18,691. From what districts are these cattle bought?—Distances of 10 or 16 miles around. We are very well circumstanced here.

18,692. From what districts do the marketable commodities come?—The neighbouring towns.

18,693. Within what limits?—Eight miles around from Dunleer and Clonmel.

18,694. Whom have you employed? You say you have [illegible] men for the collection of the toll. In the potato market, have you a clerk?—I have.

18,695. Is he a government official?—Yes.

18,696. What is his name?—Nicholas [illegible].

18,697. His duties are to make up the tickets, and weigh the commodities?—Yes.

18,698. Instead of giving a ticket, does he ever mark the weight on bag in chalk?—No, only in giving out the tickets he may put on the price.

18,699. The tickets are made up for the buyer and seller?—Yes.

18,700. Then you have an opportunity of knowing the contract price between the buyer and seller?—Always.

18,701. Of any of the commodities weighed, if it was required, you could make a return of the average price of them?—I could not.

18,702. Are not your clerks in the habit of making it up?—He keeps no record.

18,703. I am asking as to do it now, but would it be possible to do it in future?—It would not be possible, because he has no entry in the book.

18,704. Does not he put down the price?—Not in his book.

18,705. But he puts it on the ticket?—Of course he does.

18,706. But could not he put it into a book?—Yes.

18,707. It would then be possible to do it, and make such a return?—Under so.

18,708. You think if such a return was required to be made by you, it would be a pretty accurate one?—I would form a very good average of the fairs, and the price charged for potatoes.

18,709. Do you ever memorandum the number of cattle brought here, and the different description of animals?—No. We give an account of the pigs only. They go to the railway.

18,710. You do not know what were the actual receipts from each description of animals?—No. It all goes into a bulk sum.

18,711. How many men have you at each gap for the collection of the tolls?—Two at some, three at others, and four at others.

18,712. The rest of the men assist them?—Yes.

18,713. You have no particular check on those men to secure the toll or sum?—No, only their honour.

18,714. And one man a check on the other?—They simply take the money, and I trust them.

18,715. Would you have any objection to give me your receipts from the fairs, or have you made them up [illegible] here.

18,716. Do you keep any record?—I keep a yearly record.

18,717. There are several shops around this square?—Yes.

18,718. On a fair day, supposing these people put out standings on the roadside, outside their own doors, would they have to pay a standing charge?—Yes.

18,719. So that the shopkeepers and the people in the square have to pay a toll?—It never occurred. They do not put out anything.

18,720. Do they put them out on ordinary days?—No.

18,721. They never have any carts there?—No.

18,722. Is there a lot of milk brought here?—The milk goes to the creamery.

18,723. But if they brought it to the market, would you charge them for standing on the pathway or roadside?—They would not be on the pathway; and I do not know whether I would charge or not.

Mr. Wm. O'Loughlin's examined.

18,724. Your name was forwarded to me as a person who would give me some information, and accordingly I sent you a communication?—I have one.

18,725. You have heard Mr. [illegible]'s evidence. Do you agree with it?—I do.

18,726. Are you interested in the trade of the town?—I am.

18,727. Do you consider in any way objectionable the holding of these fairs and markets on the public thoroughfare, or do you think where tolls are collected by the owners and lessees, that a fair green properly enclosed with sufficient shelter accommodation should be provided, or have you formed any ideas on that at all?—I would rather have them on the streets as they are, as far as I am concerned.

18,728. Have the people of the town ever discussed that question to your knowledge?—Yes.

18,729. I suppose there is a division of opinion on that matter?—The opinion, as far as I am concerned, is that they should be held as they are.

18,730. The traders, I presume, are in favour of that, and against any alteration whatever?—They are, in that respect.

18,731. Are these traders belonging to any particular trade?—All traders.

18,732. Would those who have drapery establishments be opposed to a removal?—They would prefer to have them as they are, as far as I know.

18,733. Does not the fact of the fairs and markets being held on the public thoroughfare, occasion much filth and dirt about the streets?—They do.

18,734. Do not the people be put to much inconvenience by reason of that?—No.

18,735. Who cleans the dirt away?—All the shopkeepers have to clean their footpaths opposite their doors, and the road contractors have to clean the streets.

18,736. Does the road contractor perform his duty immediately after the fair, or does he neglect it for any length of time?—He cleans it the next day, or the day after.

18,737. Have complaints been made that he neglected his duty in that way?—A few complaints have been made.

18,738. I take it the traders generally would rather put up with any inconvenience caused by the fact of the markets and fairs being held on the public thoroughfare than have them removed?—Yes. They would prefer having them as they are, as far as the holding of the fairs in the streets is concerned.

18,739. Do you think a necessity exists in the square, or elsewhere, of any shelter accommodation for those perishable marketable commodities brought to the town?—I think not.

18,740. You do not think if any such were erected, it would tend to extend the trade of the town?—It is impossible to do it. They are held in the streets.

18,741. But if in the centre of the square there was a shed?—That might be a benefit.

18,742. You have formed no ideas on the subject?—No.

18,743. Have you ever heard complaints on a winter market day, that people, or their commodities have been injured by the inclemency of the weather?—The only people I see looking for shelter in that respect are those who push eggs, and then they do not care about the cold. What they object to is the rain, and they want some place or other to pack the eggs.

18,744. On a hot summer's morning, do not they bring butter in, and would not that butter be deteriorating by the heat of the sun?—I never heard a complaint.

18,745. There are no town commissioners established here?—No.

18,746. Are the people in favour of the re-establishment of such a body, or have they such an intention?—They have been speaking about it, but they never held any meetings about the matter.

18,747. Were you ever a town commissioner yourself?—Never. We never had any town commissioners in this town as far as I am aware. I believe I heard Mr. [illegible] state that they had them formerly.

18,748. Have you formed any ideas as to whether these markets and fairs should generally be under the control of a local authority like the town commissioners or market committee if established, and manage them for the improvement of the town?—What I heard all people and the farmers object to is the levying of tolls at all. We pay the county cess for the streets, the cattle are not on the property of Lady Charters, and the people think it is an injustice to be charged.

18,749. You refer to a portion of the square here?—This portion of the square opposite the court house does not belong to Lady Charters. It does not belong to any person in particular.

18,750. It is portion of the public thoroughfare?—It is the street belonging to the grand jury.

18,751. What about the potato market?—The people look upon that as the property of Lady Charters, and that only so far as the fairs and markets are concerned.

18,752. Do you think the levying of a toll acts as a deterrent upon the farmers bringing their goods?—I heard several farmers say so, and they said so[illegible].

18,753. Do you think if the toll was abolished altogether that that would tend to increase the trade here in this town?—I believe it would.

18,754. Would it induce farmers to bring their animals in greater numbers?—I believe firmly it would.

18,755. Have you any knowledge of the places where no toll is levied?—I have in Clonmel, but they never levy tolls at the fairs or markets except for weighing potatoes, turnips, and other things.

18,756. At the fairs no tolls are levied?—No tolls whatever. I remember one great grievance that happened. A man was driving the cattle home, not being sold, and he told Mr. Keatinge the animal was not sold or bought, and in driving back the animal rushed through a heap of stones and glass, and the animal was hurt. That was two or three years ago.

18,757. (Mr. Keatinge.)—I never heard it.

(The Assistant Commissioner.)—Have you ever heard of injury being caused to animals by the toll collectors?—That is the only time I heard that complaint.

18,758.

18,759. Have you ever heard complaints that they injured the cattle, or injured the owners of the cattle?—No. My men always try to keep the town, but the owners abuse them fearfully, trying to evade the toll, and they succeed very often.

18,760. Have you anything further to say?—Nothing, but the general complaint about the levying of tolls at all, simply because the market does not belong to Lady Charters, and for the privilege of standing on the street, the people should pay tolls to anybody. They consider it a grievance, because they consider it enough to pay county cess to improve and repair the streets.

18,761. Then you consider if individuals collect toll that they should give a return other than the liberty of selling cattle on the public thoroughfare?—I do not see how they could give any return to the farmers.

18,762. Not to the farmers, but to the inhabitants of the town by cleaning the street and taking the burden of that expense off them?—They could do that.

18,763. Do you think if tolls are levied that such a return should be given or duty performed by the owners of them?—I do think that such a thing should be done by the owners. Lady Charters does not own one-third of the property, and it is not right she should be paid anything.

Rev. M. Mockery, P.P., examined.

18,764. Do you think it would be advisable to remove the sale of these cattle from the public thoroughfare to a properly enclosed fair-green as in other towns, or do you think it works better at present?—I do not know.

18,765. Do you think it would work better than the present arrangement?—As far as my experience goes, I think the present condition of the markets are satisfactory.

18,766. You have never heard of any accidents having happened to any person by reason of their being held on the square?—I did not. With regard to the abolition of tolls, I remember 45 years ago there were eight or nine pike-gap tolls into Dungarvan.

18,767. They were distinct from the market tolls?—Yes.

Mr. Patrick O'Donnell examined.

18,768. What observations have you got to make?—I may state that I am a farmer living in the vicinity. There was an observation made by Mr. Keatinge and Mr. Keatinge with regard to the pig market which I think did not place the correct view before you. There is a market for young pigs held in this town on every cattle fair day. They are held on the potato market, and they have been charged tolls. With reference to changing the fairs, the pig fair off the street, the pig fairs were held formerly in the potato market. The shopkeepers of the town, considering it would be more to their interest to have the fairs held on the streets, they entered into an arrangement with Mr. Keatinge and Lady Margaret Charters's agent of that day to have the pig market changed from the potato market to the streets.

18,769. Was that change effected?—Yes. I think about 20 years ago; something less than 20 years ago.

18,770. Are you in trade in the town as well as a farmer?—No, I have no interest in the town.

18,771. Do you think yourself the present system of selling on the streets better than having them in an enclosed fair green?—There is no objection.

18,772. You never heard of any injury being done to the cattle?—No injury whatever. Formerly the battlements of the river here were very low, and I have seen some cattle jump into the river, but the battlements have been raised recently, and such occurrences will not happen in future.

18,773. You have heard the answer of Mr. O'Loughnane as to the abolition of the toll. Do you, as a farmer, think that the levying of a toll acts as a deterrent on you and your colleagues in bringing in your cattle and marketable commodities?—I am sure it gives the preference of the fair to Clonmel.

18,774. Is that because no tolls are levied there?—Yes.

18,775. So then the levying of a toll is a material consideration?—It is a grievance felt by the community.

18,776. Do you think if tolls were abolished, of course giving whatever compensation would be necessary for the legal rights vested in the owners and lessees, do you think that would tend to extend the trade generally of Cable?—I am certain it would be a great advantage to the town.

18,777. Tolls are here only levied on cattle actually sold. Supposing tolls were found to be necessary to levy, do you think it should be much smaller than the present one, and be levied on all cattle as they enter, irrespective of whether they are subsequently sold or not. Would that work better than the toll at present on cattle actually sold?—I never turned the matter over in my mind.

18,778. Are you aware that system exists elsewhere?—Yes. I believe in the cattle market in Dublin and Limerick.

18,779. Do you think that would work here?—I do not think it would be any mitigation of the present arrangement. It is not true that the buyers pay the custom. Farmers generally pay the custom. They are told by the men who buy at fairs to drive the cattle to the railway station, and the buyers, as a matter of course, are never there. The farmers have to pay the custom.

18,780. The individual who pays the custom is the person who has the animal in his possession at the time of passing the custom gap, whether buyer or seller?—Yes. I was present on some occasions and paid the custom on my own cattle. I am quite well aware that the buyers frequently ask the seller to drive for their own convenience the cattle to the railway station or yard.

18,781. Then the seller after the agreement for sale of the animals is still in possession while passing the custom gap, and he pays the toll if the animal is sold?—Certainly.

18,782. Have you any other observations to make?—I think if a shed were erected in the potato market it would be a matter of great convenience there. I think also there should be a shed in the square. It would be a matter of great convenience, because it is one of the largest egg and fowl markets in the South of Ireland, and here in the winter days people have to come and push eggs without any shed in the potato market, such a shed being absolutely necessary.

18,783. If such accommodation was given for the markets would these people have any objection to pay a small toll in order to cover the expenditure of such an erection?—I am sure they would not.

18,784. Do you think a necessity exists for the erection of such a shed as you suggest?—There is no question at all about it.

18,785. Have you ever heard complaints that any of the perishable commodities were materially injured by that exposure?—I do not think so, but at all events the people suffer very much from the severity of the weather.

18,786. Have you any other observations to make?—No.

Mr. M. Keating re-examined.

18,787. Have you formed any ideas about the tolls?—I find the fairs growing annually smaller owing to the monthly fairs in the surrounding towns. At Cashel, Fethard, and Clonmel there are monthly fairs. We did not establish monthly fairs here because they were first a success in other towns. I doubt if it would increase the cattle fairs at the least, for this reason, that the farmer has never anything to complain of. He is charged no tolls coming in. It is the man who comes from Waterford, Cork, and elsewhere. They are the men who pay the tolls, but the farmer has no grievance that way. He has never to pay the toll.

18,788. Do you think it would be better to have a smaller toll collected than a larger one on the cattle actually sold?—A smaller toll would yield nothing.

18,789. You do get it at present on the cattle actually sold?—Yes.

18,790. What percentage of them is sold?—Two-thirds at some fairs, and not so much at any of the other fairs.

18,791. Would you say that is the highest percentage sold?—Yes. At some of the earlier fairs the cattle went at intervals and were left unsold. The farmers never pay the toll, as stated by Mr. O'Donnell.

18,792. Is not it from the man in possession of the animal passing the gap you get the toll?—The principal buyers make an arrangement that all cattle go through, so that the farmer never pays.

18,793. When do you collect that toll then?—From these buyers on their going to the railway in the afternoon, but the general public are charged at the gap.

18,794. You never consider whether they are buyer or seller. If sold the charge must be paid?—Yes, and the seller is always there because he goes to the railway to be paid.

18,795. What are your receipts?—The receipts for the last four years from the potato market are as follows:—1884, 33l. 16s. 8d.; 1885, 48l. 13s.; 1886, 60l. 11s. 6d.; 1887, 34l. 15s. 1d. Then I make about 30l. or 35l. a year from the fairs. Out of the receipts I have to pay a weigh-master 20l., 40l. rent, and then [illegible] on an average 4s. a day, as well as my own time and labour expended and my name.

18,796. Is there any other gentleman who has any observations to make?—No answer.

The inquiry then concluded.

CLONMEL—CO. TIPPERARY.

With reference to my inquiry in Clonmel on the 3rd November 1888, I beg to report as follows:—

Clonmel is an inland town, situated chiefly in the county of Tipperary, but partly in the county of Waterford. It is built on both sides of the River Suir, and is a station on the Waterford and Limerick Railway line. It is the chief town of the county of Tipperary, and certainly deserves to be for its extent and trade. The streets are many—well paved, wide, and cleanly kept. The houses are well and symmetrically built, and the local industries consist in a tannery, brewery, millers, and an extensive general trade. The local affairs are administered by the mayor, aldermen, and councillors of the Corporation of Clonmel, and the population is 9,325.

The market day is Saturday; but the potato market is held on Tuesday and Saturday, and the milk market every day in the week.

The fairs are held on the first Wednesday of each month, with the exception of the months of May and November, when the fairs are held on the 5th of each respectively. A pig fair is held on the first Monday of each month.

All the markets and fairs are free from toll, except the butter and potato markets. In the former a charge of 3d. is levied if the butter is brought into the market before 10 o'clock a.m., and 6d. if brought in after that hour; in each case whether the butter is subsequently weighed or not. In the potato market a charge of 1d. per sack is levied for weighing that commodity.

The potato market is the property of Mr. Henry McCarthy. The butter market is the property of the Corporation of Clonmel. No rights are exercised by the Corporation or other authority over the general markets or fairs.

The public records show that three patents were granted for the borough of Clonmel. The first is dated 19th May, 6 James I., and granted to a Walter Lawless the lawful customs of said manor. The second is dated 5th July, 6 James I., and granted to the mayor, &c. of Clonmel the customs, tolls, &c. of the town, and a market on Tuesday and Saturday. The third patent is dated 22nd February, 54 George III., and granted to John Bagwell 10 fairs, viz., the first Wednesday in every month, except the months of May and November. It is stated that the fairs on the 5th of the months of May and November have been held from time immemorial.

The Corporation contemplate the establishment and erection of an enclosed market for fish, fowl, fruit, vegetables, and roll butter, and are about applying in this present Session to Parliament for a special Act.

In accordance with my instructions I have inspected the market place and fair places, &c.

The general market is held on the streets of the town, different portions of which are allotted by custom to the exposure and sale of the various commodities. Beyond whatever the streets and houses in them afford, there is no shelter or accommodation provided for those frequenting the markets.

The fairs are also held on the streets. As at the markets they have different streets for the sale of each species of animal.

The butter market is held in a large, well-ventilated house off the public street, and situated in a central and suitable position. There are two entrances to it. A scale is provided for the weighing of butter, and it is stated to be ample for the trade done there. The butter market is completely covered in, and all firkin butter brought to the town sold there. Each buyer has his name posted up around the wall, and according as the butter is bought it is arranged under the name of the buyer.

The potato market is held in an enclosed space of about one-quarter acre off the public street. A shed runs down one side of the market, and on the whole it seems to give satisfaction.

Hay and straw is weighed at two private crancils in the town, where a charge of 3d. per load is levied.

In 1872 the Corporation appointed a Mr. Bagwell the "butter weighmaster," who worked the market and applied the profits to the benefit of the town generally. In 1882 he gave over the entire control to the Corporation, who now work it and rent the building from Mr. Bagwell.

A rule exists in the butter market restraining the buying of butter until after 11 o'clock a.m., and a practice likewise prevails in allowing a deduction of 1 lb. for soakage, in addition to the actual tare of the empty firkin, from the gross weight.

Appended will be found a transcript of the evidence taken at the inquiry.

JOHN J. O'MEARA,
Assistant Commissioner.

45, Lower Mount Street, Dublin.

Clonmel, 3rd November 1888.

DAVID J. CLANCY, Esq., Solicitor, Town Clerk, examined.

18,797. You are the town clerk of Clonmel?—Yes.

18,798. A corporation is established here?—Yes.

18,799. When were they established?—Under a charter of Charles the Second.

18,800. Are they the market authority here in Clonmel?—The only market they have any control over is the butter market.

18,801. On what day is that held?—That is held on Saturday.

18,802. Is the sale of butter confined to that Saturday?—Well, practically it is. There are one or two private buyers who buy at their own establishments on other days.

18,803. Have you any restrictions on the sale of butter?—No.

18,804. I suppose it is customary to bring it in in quantities on Saturday?—Yes.

18,805. What other markets are there existing here in Clonmel?—There is the potato market, which belongs to a private owner.

18,806. What is his name?—Mr. Henry McCarthy, of Dublin. I do not know his address more particularly.

18,807. Has he got any superintendent or manager in that?—He has got an agent here, Mr. O'Donnell.

18,808. What is his address?—3, Queen's Street, Clonmel.

18,809. What day is that potato market held?—The potato market is held on Tuesday and Saturday, I think. He exacts a toll of 1d. per sack.

18,810. Is that for weighing the commodity, or is it a toll proper?—It is for the liberty of selling in the market.

18,811. Then he ascertains the weight of the sacks of potatoes?—I am not aware.

18,812. Is that potato market an enclosed space?—It is.

18,813-14. Walled in?—Yes.

18,815. Could you give me a description of it? Has it shelter accommodation, or is it a large building?—It is a yard—a bare yard—I suppose about a quarter of an English acre in extent, off New Street in this town.

18,816. Are there any sheds in it?—No. There is one shed, I think, at one side.

18,817. Is that a shed under which the beams and scales is, or has he any beams and scales there?—I do not know.

18,818. Is that penny per sack charged irrespective of the quantity in the sack?—As far as I am aware it is.

18,819. What other markets are there in Clonmel?—There is a market held indiscriminately on the street, over which we have no control. It is held just at the Main Guard, Clonmel, for lump butter, fowl, vegetables, eggs, fruit, and other matters sold there.

18,820. About the streets?—Yes.

18,821-2. Are these by hawkers or the producers bringing them in carts?—By the producers in carts and baskets.

18,823. Do they always stand in this particular street?—Yes, by custom.

18,824. That has created it practically into a market?—Yes.

18,825. You have no control over them?—No.

18,826. Has anybody control over them?—No.

18,827. No market rights are vested in anybody else?—No.

18,828. Nor have these people to pay any charge whatever?—No.

18,829. Do they cause much obstruction there?—They do a good deal.

18,830. Were proceedings ever taken for that obstruction?—No.

18,831. Was it ever contemplated by the corporation to establish a properly enclosed market place for the people, and confine the sale of all commodities to such premises?—Yes, it has been determined on lately, and the corporation have taken steps. They have appointed a committee to receive and report on the desirability of a site where a market might be established for the sale of those things now sold on the streets, and afford shelter to those people, because they suffer a good deal in winter from the inclemency of the weather.

18,832. Is that a committee of the corporation or of the inhabitants of the town?—Of the corporation.

18,833. Are they seeking for a provisional order?—They are, under the Public Health Act.

18,834. Have they taken the initial proceedings?—Not yet. I think the notice must be published in November, and we are going to do so at once.

18,835. Then do they contemplate making rules restraining these people from exposing their produce on the streets of the town?—Certainly.

18,836. Will that meet with the wishes of the inhabitants and traders of the district?—It will.

18,837. Have they offered any opposition?—No opposition. They are very anxious to get such a market provided.

18,838. Are potatoes sold anywhere in the town besides in the potato market?—They are sold generally through the town.

18,839. Are they exposed in the street along with the other commodities?—No, they are not.

18,840. You do not know under what authority Mr. McCarthy holds that market?—I do not know.

18,841. Has it always been held there?—It has. The corporation pay him a sum of 2l. 12s. a year to preserve the right to the public of entering it.

18,842. Was it originally belonging to the corporation?—I have been unable to trace that.

18,843. You do not know how he holds?—I do not.

18,844. Does he own the site?—He owns the site.

18,845. You do not know whether it is or not?—Yes, if it could be conveniently be used for but again.

18,846. Are there any other markets here?—There is a hay and straw market.

18,847. Where is that held?—That is held in a place called Barrack Street, the Mall and Barrack Street.

18,848. Is the other market for lump butter, eggs, fowl, and fruit held on Saturday?—Yes.

18,849. Is the hay and straw always allocated to Barrack Street?—Yes.

18,850. What other markets are there?—Then we have the cream and turnips on the same day. They are sold in the same place also—in Barrack Street and Richmond Street.

18,851. I suppose there are no rights claimed over them?—No.

18,852. Practically there are no rights whatsoever exercised over the people who hold their markets on the public thoroughfare?—No.

18,853. These are all the markets you have mentioned?—Then there are monthly fairs; the pig fair on the first Monday of each month. I am reminded of other markets held here. They are held on the streets. One is the milk market, which is held at the end of Mary Street.

18,854. On Saturday?—Every day; and the other is the cows milk market, which is held in Bland Street.

18,855. Every day?—Yes.

18,856. In this scheme prepared by the corporation do they contemplate exacting a toll from the people?—Certainly they do.

18,857. This butter market is, practically, the only one at present under the control of the corporation?—Yes.

18,858. Have you a committee of the corporation appointed to look after that?—We have. It yields a revenue to the corporation, averaging about 60l. a year net profit. However, the secretary will know more about that.

18,859. What is the name of that committee?—It is called the butter market committee.

18,860. Have you any bye-laws in the corporation regulating that butter market committee?—We have.

18,861. You have not got them with you?—No. I could send for them.

18,862. Who is the secretary?—Mr. William M. Casey.

18,863. That market is held on Saturday?—It is only held on Saturday.

18,864. Have you got scales and the ordinary appliances for ascertaining the weight of the butter?—Yes.

18,865. Do you restrain the sale of butter elsewhere than in the butter market?—No, we do not.

18,866. Except when it goes to the private consumers, does it go to your market?—There is a good deal sold to houses through the town.

18,867. Does any lump butter go into your market?—No.

18,868. Your market is an enclosed building?—It is.

18,869. Is there shelter accommodation there?—Yes. It is a very good market.

18,870. You have heard no complaints in that respect?—No. It is a very good building, in a very suitable and central position.

18,871. Does it afford ample space for the butter here?—Yes.

18,872. On the whole, would you say it is a good butter market in Clonmel?—I should say a very good one.

18,873. Does the opening of firkins come up to Tipperary?—It does not.

18,874. Where are the fairs held?—The pig fair on the first Monday in each month. The ordinary cattle and horse fair are held on the first Wednesday in each month, except May and November, when the fairs are on the 5th.

18,875. When was this monthly pig fair established?—Well, I have not been able to trace the commencement of it. It has been established for centuries.

18,876. On the first Monday in each month?—Yes.

18,877. Could you trace back the establishment of the cattle and horse fair?—No, I could not; that has been established for centuries, too.

18,878. Does the corporation exercise any rights over these fairs?—None whatever.

18,879. There is no toll levied at the fairs here?—No, there is not. There was up to 60 years ago by Mr. Bagwell. He exacted the toll, but after that time, for some reason or another, it ceased to be collected.

18,880. Where are the fairs held?—On the public streets throughout the town.

18,881. Are there different streets allocated for each description of animal; have you one street for cattle and another for horses?—The cattle are exposed in Gladstone Street, Parnell Street, and Main Street; the sheep in Mary Street, Peter Street, and Duncan Street; and the horses then on the Mall and the lower end of Parnell Street.

18,882. And the pigs?—On Fethard Road and Stephen's Street.

18,883. Are these the only animals brought in and exposed for sale at the fairs here?—These are the only ones. There is no ass market in the Mall.

18,884. Was the fact of the fairs being held on the streets ever complained of by the traders and private inhabitants of the town?—Not generally.

18,885. Were any representations ever made to the corporation to get them removed off the streets?—There were many years ago, but the project found very few supporters, and it fell through, and it has never been revived.

18,886. So that, although the corporation is going to establish a general market and confine the sale of all marketable commodities to it, you do not contemplate the removal of the fairs?—No.

18,887. If it was contemplated by the corporation, do you think it would receive opposition from the traders in the immediate neighbourhood of where the fairs are held?—Yes, considerable opposition.

18,888. The corporation cleans the streets?—Yes.

18,889. Does not the fact that the fairs are held on the public thoroughfare occasion considerable expense in cleaning the streets?—Yes, it does a good deal.

18,890. You could not give any approximate idea of the expense incurred?—No; but I could have the town inspector here, who would tell you.

18,891. Then, I presume, the traders in the immediate vicinity of these fairs would put up with any inconvenience caused to them, purely for trade purposes?—Yes. In their way they think the fairs ought to be held on the streets, the shops being opened and shelter given to those attending the fairs, while if they were exposed in a field, or anything that way, they would experience some discomfort. They very often stand in the doorway near where the cattle are, and they are able to keep themselves dry and warm there.

18,892. Do you think it would be better for the town of Clonmel, and for the proper management of the markets and fairs, if all were under the control of the corporation?—I am afraid I could not answer that.

18,893. You never considered it?—No.

18,894. Have you any ideas at all on that subject yourself, because from your position I would like an expression of opinion from you, if possible, as to whether you think throughout the country it would be advisable or desirable that the market authorities should be the local authority of the town, which would work the markets and fairs for the benefit of the town generally?—I should think so. I think it would be a great advantage.

18,895. Do you think the fact of the butter market being held and belonging to the corporation tends to the better management of it, and gives greater satisfaction to the producers and the buyers?—I am quite sure it does.

18,896. You would like to see the same thing existing all over the country?—I would.

18,897. Did you bring the queries I sent you before the corporation or any of the members?—No.

18,898. Was the corporation at any capital expenditure in the erection of this butter market?—I do not think they expended any money. They rent it from Mr. Bagwell.

18,899. I presume they pay the taxes?—Yes.

18,900. What is the consolidated rate here?—3s. 4d. in the pound.

18,901. Those are the municipal rates?—Yes.

18,902. The poor-rate is additional?—Yes.

18,903. What is that?—The poor-rate is 1s. 9d. in the pound, I think.

18,904. Then, I suppose, you get the ordinary deductions from Mr. Bagwell?—Yes.

18,905. They have got the place under lease?—Yes.

18,906. You do not know the particulars of that lease?—No.

18,907. Are there any special covenants in it by which they are bound to maintain the market place or market?—Mr. Carey will know that. My impression is we are bound to maintain it as a market.

18,908. Now, have you any suggestions yourself, Mr. Carey, to offer?—No, I have not.

Mr. MALCOMSON examined.

18,909. Is your establishment in the immediate vicinity of the fairs or any of them?—Yes, just at the horse market and the hay and straw market.

18,910. Does the fact of the fair being held opposite your door, or in the immediate vicinity, occasion you any inconvenience?—No, not the least. I think if they were removed it would be the greatest loss to the people in the locality. It is a very long and wide street; I believe 60 feet wide.

18,911. Within your recollection no accidents have happened there, by the fact of the horse fair being held on the street?—I have not known any accidents.

18,912. Would that be the opinion of all your neighbours, that they would be opposed to the removal of the fairs to a properly enclosed fair green?—Well, I think they would not be opposed to remove the fairs from that place. There are no horned cattle kept there.

18,913. Would they object to the removal of the fairs off the streets?—They would.

18,914. At all events you would do so?—I would object.

18,915. Have you any experience of other fairs besides those held in Clonmel, or did you ever buy and sell at other fairs?—Indeed I did.

18,916. In fairs where tolls are levied?—I have.

levied in other towns only as a detriment on people bringing their cattle or produce into the market or fair?—I think it does. Fethard is the nearest place where the people are obliged to pay tolls, and there are only a few fairs during the year.

18,918. But do you think where no tolls are levied that fact does not induce people to bring their animals to that particular fair, or their commodities to the market?—It might to parties who have a great deal of traffic in stock; it might prevent them from going to those fairs.

18,919. I gather from your answers that it is your opinion it is not the toll they look to but the market, and if a good market they go to it, whether a toll is levied or not?—Indeed I think they would. That is my opinion.

18,920. Here, in Clonmel, have they got the system of luck-penny?—That is a general thing in every place.

18,921. And it is here?—Yes, whatever a man wishes to give for luck.

18,922. Is there any fixed payment?—Not at all.

18,923. Is it always left to the disposition of the seller?—Yes.

18,924. Is anything fixed at the pig fair?—Yes, there is a fixed price there.

18,925. What is it?—You are obliged to pay 6d. to the buyer, to allow him 6d.

18,926. Although no toll is paid?—Yes.

18,927. Is there any fixed charge on any other animal?—Not that I know.

18,928. Have you any suggestions to offer about the fairs and markets in this town or elsewhere?—No.

Mr. PETER COLLINS, Town Commissioner, examined.

18,929. Have you anything to say on the subject of this inquiry?—Mr. Carey has given you all the information. The only thing I wish to say is that many shopkeepers, such as drapers and others who sell fancy goods, would do a great deal more business if the fairs were held outside the town, because scarcely any business in the fancy way is done in town on fair days. I know in my business, photography, I have done nothing on a fair day, and I am coming here over 20 years.

18,930. Is that on account of the filth occasioned?—It is owing to the throng of people and the cattle on the street.

18,931. Have you ever seen sheep on the pathways?—Sometimes I have, but they generally keep them on the road. Sheep are frequently on the pathway. I may mention that I have been resident in Tralee for many years, and there they hold the fairs in the vicinity of the town, and there is very much more business done than in Clonmel. The farmers' wives and daughters go into the town to do business while the men are in the fair green, and I have noticed that there is a great deal more business done than in any other town.

18,932. I take it you would approve of a system of confining the sale of these animals to a properly enclosed fair green just in the vicinity of the streets of the town?—Yes. The horse fair here is not much.

18,933. Is it objectionable?—No. It is partly out of the town.

18,934. But in any case you would not like the fair green to be any distance from the ends of the town?—No.

18,935. It should be convenient to all establishments?—Yes.

Mr. WILLIAM M. CAREY examined.

18,936. You are the secretary to the Butter Market Committee of the corporation?—Yes.

18,937. Is the sole duty of that committee the overseeing of the butter market?—Yes.

18,938. Have they any other duties to perform?—No.

18,939. How many members in it?—Five members, appointed by the corporation.

18,940. Have you got the rules regulating the working of this committee?—They are appointed under resolutions of the corporation, and under certain set regulations which were submitted to the Local Government Board in the year 188[illegible].

ration had the right of appointing a weighmaster, and they did appoint Mr. Richard Bagwell in the year 1872. Mr. Bagwell held the office in a nominal way, and he appointed deputies to manage the market, these deputies consisting of members of the corporation and one or two of the principal residents in the town.

18,942. Did he derive any profit from the place?—He gave them the entire control over the office, to work the market for the benefit of the town. The expense of the market was heavy owing to its being a weekly market, and required a staff to work it. The fact of it is, for a day's work a week's wages have to be paid, but the funds were allowed to accumulate, and in the end, whatever balance of the funds remained after the working of the market was handed over to the corporation; the corporation got from the butter market committee in 1882 a sum of 100*l.* In 1883, it being then in their own hands, they got 60*l.*

18,943. Was that the net profit?—The way in which it is managed is that at the end of every year the committee see what balance they have on hand. They keep a sum to work the market during the season, and the surplus is given over to the corporation.

18,944. This sum of 100*l.* in 1882 was an accumulation of previous years?—Yes.

18,945. What did they get in 1884?—They got 60*l.*; in 1885 [illegible]*l.*; in 1886 40*l.*; in 1887 [illegible]*l.*; and in 1888 [illegible].

18,946. These sums are over and above the actual expenses of management and the sum put to a reserve fund?—Yes.

18,947. Have you got the last balance sheet of the butter market committee?—I could let you have a copy of it. I should mention there are two balance sheets, one for the Local Government Board auditor, who audits the accounts as portion of the accounts of the corporate receipts. That account is made up to the 31st August in each year, that is the date the municipal accounts end; but the account that is handed to the committee is made up to 31st December in each year.

18,948. Does that go more fully into the particulars?—The corporation account would show what became of the balance every year. The account is made up to the 31st December, showing the balance then on hand, and when the committee have that balance before them they decide how much will go to the corporation and how much is necessary to be retained for the working of the market until the next season.

18,949. In the expenditure you have the salaries fully set out?—Yes, the books show the expenditure under the head of salaries, wages, rents, taxes, and all that.

18,950. You have not got the individuals names?—I am the secretary, and there is a weighmaster.

18,951–2. Have you got more than one weighmaster?—No, only one, and the superintendent of the market.

18,953–54. You have only one butter market each week?—Yes.

18,955. Have not this committee made some rules regulating the hours for the sale of butter in the market?—They have.

18,956. Are these rules printed?—They were printed up, but I am afraid they remained a good portion of the year. I think I could let you have copies of them.

18,957. I would like copies of any documents posted up regulating the working of the market?—Yes.

18,958. What hour does it usually begin?—During the season the market is open for the reception of butter at 8 o'clock, and it is covered up to half-past 10. Any butter coming to the market after half-past 10 is charged double toll.

18,959. What is the charge?—For earlier butter, that is, before half-past 10, the toll is 3*d.* per firkin, and after half-past 10, 6*d.*

18,960. Is that the butter market where I saw a lot of cars coming round the corner?—Yes, in Gladstone Street.

18,961. Can some come up when another is gone into the yard, they must go in singly?—Yes, but there is some official of the corporation in the street who marks it. If they are in the street or the neighbourhood of the market there is only a temporary charge.

18,962. Is that the only charge you levy on the butter, the 3*d.* and 6*d.*?—Yes.

18,963. It is only on the firkin of butter?—Yes.

18,964. Lump butter never comes into your market?—No.

18,965. Have you got coopers employed?—I will tell you the system shortly. When the butter is brought into the market it is [illegible], and the hoops removed, and then [illegible] by the two coopers. If there is any dispute about the tare, the owner claiming that the tare is less than that usually marked on the casks, the firkin is stripped and the tare obtained; but that does not occur in many instances, because the cooper mark on the firkin its weight as it leaves the block.

18,966. Do they burn it into the firkin?—Generally. Sometimes it is only pencilled, but the regulation is to allow 1 lb. in addition to what is marked for soakage. In weighing the butter they never take into account the [illegible] of 1 lb. If a firkin is marked 9 lbs. leaving the cooper's hands, it is marked 10 at the market, that is, allowing 1 lb. for the soakage of the water.

18,967. Do not the coopers completely drain it?—Yes, but still there is a certain soakage they must allow.

18,968. Is that allowance peculiar to Clonmel?—I think it is general. There have been instances in which, upon testing the weight of the firkin actually, it has been found to be considerably in excess of the pound.

18,969. Is that the cooper's fault?—In one case the committee had a prosecution for the purpose of punishing the cooper for marking the firkin 9 lbs. where it weighed 17 lbs. leaving the block. There have been a few instances of fraud in that way, and even the butter after being marked in that way had passed through the market, and [illegible] passed to the [illegible].

18,970. Have you printed tickets?—Yes, with blanks.

(*The following is a copy of the tickets in use, which the witness subsequently handed in.*)

CLONMEL BUTTER MARKET.

Mr. ______________________

Date__________ 188 .

Weight.	Tare.

CLONMEL BUTTER MARKET.

Mr. ______________________

Date__________ 188 .

Weight.	Tare.

18,971. Is it when you give this ticket to the seller he pays your charge?—He pays the charge in return for the ticket. Then I should explain, in regard to the ticket for double toll, that ticket is printed on double colour paper.

18,972. When you give this ticket and ascertain the weight of it, is the butter generally sold?—Oh, no. It is afterwards the sale takes place, when the farmer has the ticket in his possession, and he goes over with the ticket to the merchant he sells.

18,973. What hour do the buyers usually begin?—They generally commence about half-past 11.

18,974. When you suppose the butter brought in at 6 or 7 o'clock, and the buyers do not come for a couple of hours after, is the butter exposed to weather, or have you a shed for it?—It is in the market-house.

18,975. And that market-house affords sufficient shelter accommodation?—It is completely roofed in.

18,976. Do you keep any record of the number of firkins that come periodically to the market?—I can give you the numbers since the year 1881. From the 1st January to the 31st December 1881 the number of firkins brought in was 17,552; in 1882 the number went down to 13,820; in 1883 there were 16,862; in 1884, 16,807; in 1885, 17,584; in 1886, 18,[illegible]; in 1887, 13,737. I wish to mention, with regard to the falling off in the quantity coming to the market between 1886 and 1887, that at the end of 1886 there were creameries established in the neighbourhood and completely tapped the supply. There was one then but now two in Clonmel, and one or two at Fethard.

18,977. Are not the firkins occasionally brought to the private merchants' stores without passing through your market?—There is one merchant living outside the borough to whom the firkins are brought by the farmers, and they do not pass through the market.

18,978. Does he levy any charge?—I think not.

18,979. Is that the only merchant?—No. If it was in the borough we would be entitled to get the toll.

18,980. Did a case happen where the farmers go directly to the private merchants' stores?—Not that I am aware of.

18,981. If such an event happened you would take proceedings to recover the toll?—I would demand the toll.

18,982. Do you think the corporation rights extends to the municipal boundary?—Only to the municipal boundary.

18,983. Then is the butter always actually weighed before a sale is effected?—Yes. Sometimes there are exceptions. We get it by the train, and that comes in at half-past 11 or 12 o'clock, and in that case it is a little late. Then the butter is bought by lump, and if the farmers wish to have the butter weighed it is weighed for them.

18,984. Is the firkin itself bought by bulk?—Yes. The merchants come and offer so much for the firkin as it stands.

18,985. Do you receive a charge for that?—Certainly. Under the rules all butter brought into the market has to pay the toll, whether it is weighed or not.

18,986. Or whether you perform any duties or not?—Yes.

18,987. What appliances have you in the market for ascertaining the weight of the butter?—Only one scales.

18,988. Is that ample for the trade?—Yes, because we are able to weigh sometimes at the rate of 300 firkins an hour.

18,989. No undue delay is caused?—I believe, since the corporation got the management of the market, there has been a very great improvement, because, formerly, the system was to have the butter sold before being weighed, and then there were very often disputes as to the [illegible], and, occasionally, the butter was not weighed until 4 and 5 o'clock in the evening, and sometimes dark night. Now that is completely altered. They are able to buy at half-past 11 o'clock, and the whole market is clear and nearly all the butter paid for at 3 o'clock.

18,990. Down to what weight are you able to ascertain, or do you usually ascertain?—Down to a pound.

18,991. It must be a pound or nothing?—Yes.

18,992. Do you always give a cast of the beam, or do you weigh by standing beam?—Standing beam may mean a pound off.

18,993. Does the buyer usually obtain any charge from the seller of the firkin in clearance? In other places it is customary for the seller to give the buyer 1s. for each firkin. Does any such rule or practice exist here?—Not that I am aware of. The fact is the officials of the market interfere as little as possible between buyer and seller.

18,994. You have a clerk making up the tickets?—I issue the tickets and take the money. The tickets contain merely the weight and tare. They are not made up.

18,995. You never officially ask them the contract price paid for the firkin?—Sometimes I ask for curiosity.

18,996. Supposing it was required from the corporation to make a periodical return of the current price of the butter here in the market, could such a return be made, or is it possible to make it?—I keep no record of the prices.

18,997. If it was required in future, could you make such a return?—It would be possible from the newspapers.

18,998. Not from the newspapers, but from an official source directly from the buyers and sellers?—No, I could not do it.

18,999. Is it possible?—It is not possible. I have kept no record, for this reason, that the members of the corporation stated that they would interfere as little as possible between the buyer and seller, but provide the accommodation and see the weighing is properly done. If they do that to their satisfaction, but they do not want to interfere with the prices.

19,000. When you give the ticket your duties are performed so far as buyer and seller are concerned?—Yes.

19,001. With the exception of keeping order while the firkins are exposed for sale?—Yes.

19,002. How many firkins come there usually on a day?—It varies according to the season. For instance, to-day at the time I was leaving, there were more than 300, and last Saturday 400 or 600, and then in a heavy part of the season it went up to 700, but there used to be sometimes 900; that is, before the creameries were established.

19,003. Are there any of these in town?—There are two.

19,004. Did the corporation ever contemplate levying any charge off the establishments?—No. I do not see how they could.

19,005. From what districts is the butter brought here?—From a very wide district. From Ballyporeen and the borders of Kilkenny, and beyond Cahir, and then from the neighbourhood of Thurles, and the Dungarvan direction. The butter comes from distances 14 and 15 miles away.

19,006. Have you ever heard complaints of any inaccuracy in ascertaining the weights of a firkin of butter?—No. On the contrary, the sellers of butter are so confident that they are dealt fairly with that very often in a great many instances they do not see their butter weighed at all.

19,007. Do you ever mark the weight in chalk?—They always mark it in chalk.

19,008. And, in addition, you give the docket?—Yes.

19,009. The buyer would not complete his contract with the seller until he sees the docket?—He goes and examines the butter, and they agree to the price.

19,010. In order to see the weight, does he go by the chalk marks on the firkins?—He pays by the ticket, and has an opportunity of checking the marks afterwards.

19,011. Do you ever hear that the marks were altered on the firkin or your ticket?—No.

19,012. Have you ever had occasion to take any proceedings for fraud in the preparation of the butter?—I take it on myself to give directions and report the matter afterwards to the committee to get their approval of the action I took.

19,013. Does the committee of the corporation act on complaints?—It is generally the town inspector. If a clear case of fraud is reported to me either in the packing of butter by adding salt, or putting bad butter walls for harness [illegible] at the sides of the firkins, and that is discovered on the firkins being stripped for the purpose of tasting, I take out a summons in the name of the superintendent of the market, who is the town inspector. I have to do that, and I immediately report to the mayor or some other members of the committee, and if they [illegible] of the action the case goes at the borough petty sessions.

19,014. Do the fines go to the benefit of the corporation?—The fines in Clonmel go to the Fines and Penalties Fund.

19,015. Are these prosecutions of frequent occurrence?—They are very few. There were only three or four since 1882.

19,016. Then they are of rare occurrence?—Yes. I think the few prosecutions we have had had a very beneficial effect.

19,017. Do you know is there a weighbridge erected in the town by the corporation?—There is not.

19,018. Do they ever weigh hay and straw?—Hay and straw are weighed at a private [illegible].

19,019. Who is the owner of that?—Mr. Morgan James is the owner of the principal one, and there is also one at T. C. [illegible], Richmond Street.

19,020. Do they levy any charge for weighing the hay and straw?—Yes, 3d. a load. There is also another one, the mayor reminds me, in Fethard Road, belonging to Mr. Morrissey. A great many years ago, when there was a general weighmaster in Clonmel, he had a weighbridge outside the butter market, but it was taken up. It is not availed of much.

19,021. You say they charge 3d. a load?—So I understand.

19,022. Has the hay always to be weighed?—I believe so. I know very little about that. The oats and turnips and mangolds are also weighed, but this is at the private [illegible].

19,023. Mr. Clancy has stated that the corporation are moving for a provisional order to erect a general market place. Is that your committee?—No, it is the corporation; but it is only intended for fish, fowl, fruit, vegetables, and roll butter. It is not contemplated to have the hay and straw there.

19,024. The managing of such a market would be vested in your committee?—Yes.

19,025. However, no arrangements have been made?—No. The way in which the butter market is managed at present is subject to the sanction of the Local Government Board.

19,026. What is the number of the committee limited to?—Five. Perhaps I should mention, this year there has been a very considerable increase in the butter.

19,027. Do you think that the butter market is worked by the corporation to the satisfaction of the producers and buyers more than if it were an individual who was working it?—I am perfectly certain it is. I know there were many complaints before the present system was introduced, but everybody seems now to be pleased. The best test of the satisfaction given to the farmers is the fact that they do not even think it necessary to be present when the weight is ascertained.

19,028. The corporation never thought it necessary or desirable to lease the butter market to anybody?—Oh, no, not since 1882. The fact of it is no private person could work the butter market so economically as the corporation, because on Saturdays the labour that is necessary is supplied by men constantly in their employment, and paid for by the committee of the corporation. They have other duties to perform other days of the week.

19,029. If a firkin of butter was brought in any day of the week, could not they avail of your market?—Yes. The market is idle every day in the week.

19,030. Usually it is only opened on Saturday?—There was an attempt made 14 years ago, when the market was managed by Mr. [illegible]'s deputies, to establish a second market, but it was a failure.

19,031. You have not heard any complaints of the levying of this 3d. toll?—No; but they sometimes complain very much of having to pay 6d.

[*The following statement of accounts and byelaws were subsequently handed in by the foregoing witness.*]

CLONMEL BUTTER MARKET.

BALANCE SHEET FOR THE YEAR ENDING 31ST DECEMBER 1887.

	£	s.	d.		£	s.	d.
Balance from last statement - - -	[illegible]	15	5	Cr.—Paid to Clonmel Corporation out of proceeds of market for 1886 -	50	0	0
RECEIPTS.				EXPENDITURE.			
[illegible] firkins @ 3d. - - 157 [illegible] 0				Salaries - - - - 33 17 6			
161 firkins 6d. - - 4 0 6				Wages - - - - 20 11 1			
	161	[illegible]	6	Repairs - - - - 1 0 9			
12,757				Printing - - - - 4 13 1			
				Rent and taxes - - - 44 10 10			
				Sundries - - - - 4 5 3			
Interest from bank - - - -	0	6	0		[illegible]	19	0
Gleeson and White, for right of advertising - - - -	5	0	0	Balance to bank on 31st December 1887 -	[illegible]	16	11
	£[illegible]	16	11		£[illegible]	16	11

Date, 31st December 1887.

WM. M. CASEY, Secretary.

CLONMEL BUTTER MARKET.

This market has been established with the approval of the Local Government Board for Ireland, acting under the provisions of the Public Health (Ireland) Act, 1878, for the sale of butter in casks or firkins.

The provisions of the Markets and Fairs' Clauses Act, 1847 (10 Vict. cap. 14),

With respect to the holding of the market, and the protection thereof;

With respect to the weighing of goods and carts; and

With respect to stallages, rents, and tolls,

apply to this market.

The Local Government Board for Ireland has approved of there being charged in this market a toll of 3d. upon every cask or firkin of butter brought in before half-past 10 o'clock, a.m., and 6d. upon every cask or firkin of butter brought in between half-past 10 o'clock, a.m. and 12 o'clock noon, whether the same be weighed or qualified, or not weighed or qualified.

Under the provisions of the Act 10 Vict. c. 14 (Markets and Fairs' Clauses Act),

Every person who sells butter in firkins or casks in the borough of Clonmel, outside this market, in any place except in his own dwelling place or shop, shall, for every such offence, be liable to a penalty of 40s. (section 13).

Every person who exposes for sale in the market [illegible] provisions shall be liable to a penalty of 5l. (section 15).

Every person who assaults or obstructs the officials of the market will be liable to a penalty of 40s. (section 16).

EDWARD O. HACKETT,
Alderman,
Mayor of Clonmel.

JOHN THOMAS [illegible],
Town Clerk.

(Seal of Clonmel Corporation.)

CLONMEL BUTTER MARKET.

BYELAWS.

(41 & 42 Vict. c. 52.—10 Vict. c. 14.)

The town council hereby give notice that the business of this market will be conducted subject to the provisions of the above-mentioned Statutes and the following byelaws:—

1. The market will be held, until further notice, on Saturdays, and butter will be received from 7 o'clock, a.m., to 10.30 o'clock, a.m.; and between the latter hour and 12 o'clock, noon, upon payment of a double toll.
2. All butter will, according as it arrives in the house, be qualified, tared, drained, and then weighed. The taster employed by the committee will average the tares, and, when it is necessary to do so, will strip the butter, and weigh the casks or firkins in a scale provided for that purpose.
3. The standard tare of the market is 16 lbs. for ordinary firkins, subject to arrangement.
4. A bell will ring to signify when the weighing of butter is about to commence, and sellers are requested to be at the scales when their butter is being weighed, so as to prevent delay, otherwise they will be put to considerable inconvenience.
5. When butter is weighed, a ticket will be handed to the seller setting out the quality, weight, and tares, and the seller will pay a toll of 3d. upon every firkin brought by him to the market before half-past 10 o'clock, a.m., and 6d. upon every firkin admitted to the market after that hour.
6. Buying will commence at half-past 11 o'clock, a.m.
7. The managing committee will have in the market a sufficient staff of porters, who will carry the butter to the different parts of the market, as circumstances may require; but it is to be clearly understood that the committee incur no responsibility of any description with regard to the custody of the butter.
8. The seller is to be considered as having the custody of the butter until he shall have delivered it at a place in the market where the merchant purchasing shall appoint to have it delivered. The porters employed by the committee will give all possible assistance for this purpose.
9. Smoking in the market is strictly prohibited, and any person offending against this rule will be liable to expulsion.
10. No person in the employment of the committee is permitted, under any circumstances, to receive gratuities, and any of the officials offending against this rule will be instantly dismissed.

By Order.

EDWARD C. HACKETT,
Alderman,
Mayor of Clonmel.
JOHN THOMAS LATTNER,
Town Clerk.

(Seal of Clonmel Corporation.)

I hereby certify that the foregoing is a true copy of the byelaws for Clonmel Butter Market, adopted at a special meeting of the town council of Clonmel (of which 30 days' public notice was given) held on the 11th day of June 1883.

(Signed) JOHN THOMAS LATTNER,
Town Clerk.

These byelaws confirmed by the Local Government Board for Ireland, this 26th day of June 1883.

HENRY ROBINSON.
CHARLES CROFTON KING.
GERALD MORRIS.

(Local Government Board Seal. J. R.)

EDWARD MURPHY, Esq., Mayor of Clonmel, examined.

19,032. I believe the corporation deem it desirable to move for a provisional order to obtain power to erect a new market?—That is the intention just now.

19,033. Is that for the purpose of removing the people off the public thoroughfare?—That is the intention. It is complained by several respectable ratepayers that they are a cause of obstruction, and a disagreeable smell on every occasion continues from the fish, and it is the wish of the people that there should be a place provided for them.

19,034. Was it never thought desirable to remove the fairs off the public street to a properly enclosed fair green?—I really am not in a position to give an answer to that. I believe at one time there was some agitation, but it did not result in anything.

19,035. Would you have any objection to give your own opinion as to whether it would be desirable to remove them or allow them to remain where they are?—Well, I have a great objection.

19,036. Have you ever bought at any fairs where a toll was levied?—No, but I have some experience.

19,037. Do you think that the exaction of a toll acts as a deterrent on the producer in bringing in commodities or cattle to the markets and fairs?—I could not say that in the case of Kilkenny, because it is one of the largest monthly cattle fairs in the south of Ireland.

19,038. Have any complaints ever been made to the corporation of the filth and dirt created by these fairs in the streets?—There has never been a complaint made directly to the corporation since the corporation got control of the streets, but before that complaints were very often made that the dirt used to be left in the streets.

19,039. Have you formed any ideas on the question as to whether it would be desirable for local authorities, such as here in Clonmel, and where no town commissioners exist, market committees, having vested or obtaining compulsory powers to acquire the rights of the individual owners of the markets and fairs throughout the country? Do you think the corporation or a committee of gentlemen here in Clonmel would work the markets and fairs to the better satisfaction of the buyers and sellers?—I am quite certain they would. No private individual can give more satisfaction than a public body.

19,040. You would be in favour yourself of such compulsory powers to acquire these rights being given?—I certainly would.

THOMAS J. CONDON, Esq., M.P., examined.

19,041. Do you think that the levying of a toll at a fair acts in any way as a deterrent on the farmers bringing in their cattle or commodities, or do you think that the abolition or a radical reduction in the amount of the toll would act as an inducement to them to bring their animals in greater numbers?—I do not know whether it would be an inducement to bring the cattle to a fair or otherwise. I know from my own experience the exaction of a toll causes a good deal of friction between the buyers and sellers for a time.

19,042. Then you think it is not to the value of the toll they look, but to the position and state of the market?—I think both combined. It is a very disagreeable thing to have to pay tolls at one fair and not to have to pay them in another. I hold they are calculated to injure the market or fair where tolls are levied.

19,043. Have you any suggestions to offer?—None whatever.

19,044. Is there any other gentleman who has any observations to make or suggestions to offer?—No answer.

The inquiry then concluded.

CARRICK-ON-SUIR—CO. TIPPERARY.

With reference to my inquiry in Carrick-on-Suir held on the 5th November 1888, I beg to report as follows:—

Carrick-on-Suir is situated in the southern portion of the County of Tipperary. It is a station on the Waterford and Limerick Railway line. The River Suir runs along the side of Carrick-on-Suir, dividing it from Carrick-a-beg, a suburban district, which is situated in the County of Waterford. The two portions are, however, now united for the administration of their local affairs, and two Commissioners represent Carrick-a-beg on the Board of Town Commissioners.

The town, adjoining as it does, three counties, has a pretty good trade in agricultural produce. There are slate quarries in the neighbourhood, which afford additional employment. The streets are narrow, and the houses are fairly well-built. A fine and neat public park is situated between the railway station and the town. The population is 6,583.

The market day is Saturday. The butter market is held on Tuesday since 1869, previous to which it was held on Wednesday and Saturday.

The fairs are held on the last Thursday in each month, the 15th August, the 11th October, and Thursday afterwards, and Whitsun Thursday. A pig fair or market is held on the Monday previous to the ordinary fairs.

The markets and fairs are toll-free, but at the former weighing charges are levied.

No express grant was ever given of any markets or fairs in Carrick-on-Suir.

No rights are exercised over the markets or fairs with the exception of the butter market, which is belonging to a Mr. William Boyd. It appears some 25 years ago Mr. Boyd was appointed the butter weighmaster by the magistrates of the county, and since then he continues to levy a charge for weighing any firkins brought to his market, applying the profits derived therefrom to his own use. He holds the building and scales therein from a Major Bowen at 21*l.* a year, under a lease for 500 years. He also rents a beam and scales and crancil from the representatives of George Moore at 13*l.* a year.

All the butter is weighed before sold.

The weighing charge is levied when the butter is actually weighed, no matter whether it is subsequently sold or not; but if not sold storage accommodation is available, for which no extra charge is levied. The other commodities are sold before being weighed, and then the charge only becomes payable.

In accordance with my instructions I have inspected the market places and fair green, &c.

The markets are held in the main street on Saturday. In addition to the crancil provided by Mr. Boyd, there are two others provided for ascertaining the weight of loads by private individuals. A beam and scales for weighing potatoes and other commodities is also provided by Mr. Boyd, and erected in portion of the building used as a butter market, or, rather, in a place next to it.

The butter market is held in a large house in the main street. The market is flagged, and a lofty roof gives it the appearance of being well ventilated. It is considered quite large enough for the butter trade of the district.

The fairs are held in a commonage near the Court House. It is large, and affords ample space, but it is not enclosed in any way, and it is not provided with pens, sheds, or any other accommodation for the cattle brought there. It originally belonged to the Earl of Bessborough, and the only control exercised over it is when a booth or theatrical tent is erected therein, when the Town Commissioners receive a charge for the space occupied.

The establishment of the monthly fairs has been traced so far back as over 50 years, and the fair on Whitsun Thursday has been altered from Whitsun Tuesday within the past 30 years, as it was held on the latter date at the sitting of the Commission in 1852. The other fairs have also been held for a great length of time.

A practice, similar to that existing in Clonmel, exists here, in allowing a deduction from the gross weight of a firkin of butter, of a pound in addition to the actual or estimated tare of the empty firkin. This allowance is to be for cooperage.

Appended will be found a transcript of the evidence taken at the inquiry.

JOHN J. O'MEARA,
Assistant Commissioner.

45, Lower Mount Street, Dublin.

Carrick-on-Suir, 5th November 1888.

RICHARD LAHEY, Esq., Town Clerk, examined.

19,046. Are you the town clerk to the commissioners here?—Yes.

19,046-7. When were the commissioners established?—On the 1st January 1855, under the 17 and 18 Victoria. They were under the 9th George the Fourth previous to that.

19,048. Have the town commissioners any control over the markets and fairs in Carrick-on-Suir?—None whatever.

19,049. What is the market day?—The market day is Saturday; that is the ordinary market day, and, as I advised you, the butter market day is Tuesday.

19,050. Was the general market day always held on Saturday?—Yes.

19,051. You never remember its having been held on any other day?—I do not.

19,052. When was the butter market established on Tuesday?—In 1869. It was on Wednesday and Saturday previous to that, and now Tuesday has been substituted.

19,053. Where are the markets held?—The hay and straw market is held on the streets.

19,054. Are all the markets held on the streets?—Yes.

19,055. Have you different streets allotted for each description of commodity?—No; but, as a rule, the general market is held on the main street.

19,056. What commodities are usually brought in on Saturday?—Hay, straw, turnips, mangolds, cabbages, potatoes, and fowl. Milk is sold through the streets every day. We have lately come under the Contagious Diseases (Animals) Act, and appointed a man as clerk and inspector.

19,057. Do they ever bring cattle on market days?—No.

19,058. Or pigs?—Never on market day.

19,059. Are there any market buildings erected in Carrick-on-Suir?—No market buildings, except the butter market buildings, which belong to a private individual.

19,060. No charges whatever are levied on these marketable commodities?—None whatever.

19,061. Is there any means of ascertaining the weight of hay, straw, and turnips brought to the market?—There are two public cranes, which are private property.

19,062. Who has control over those cranes?—Mr. Boyd has control over one, I believe.

19,063. Who has the other?—Mr. David Byrne.

19,064. Are the two in use at present?—There is only one really in use, though there is a second.

19,065. The second is not utilised at all?—It is, but it is vacant at present.

19,066. Who had last control over it?—Mr. William Conway.

19,067. Was it Mr. Conway himself erected it?—He was only tenant in the house.

19,068. To whom?—To the representatives of Mr. Thomas Lynch, deceased.

19,069. Do you know his rate of charges?—I should say 3d. a load, but I am not so sure.

19,070. Irrespective of the commodity which was in the load?—Yes, irrespective of the commodity, whether straw, hay, straw, or turnips.

19,071. Did you ever see him weighing any load?—I did.

19,072. Did he ever weigh the cart?—Yes, the load was weighed first, and the cart afterwards.

19,073. Did he give tickets denoting the weight?—Yes, the gross weight and tare.

19,074. Is Mr. Thomas Lynch the owner?—The representatives of the late Thomas Lynch. I think it goes to a charitable institution now.

19,075. What fairs are held here?—The last Thursday in the month the ordinary cattle fairs are held. There are three old fairs besides them.

19,076. What are the dates of these?—The 15th August, 11th October, the Thursday after the 11th October, and Whitsun Thursday. Of these fairs held on Thursday, I may say the Monday previous is the pig market.

19,077. Where are these fairs held?—On the fair green.

19,078. Who was it provided the fair green?—I believe it is there from time immemorial. It belongs to the lord of the manor.

19,079. Have they been always held there?—Yes, always, from time immemorial.

19,080. The ground was never utilised for any other purpose within your memory?—None whatever. We make a charge for circuses, and those theatrical things that come.

19,081. In that way the commissioners have control?—Yes.

19,082. Supposing carts are brought in on fair day on the green, and there are goods exposed on them for sale, do you charge?—We never make any charge. It is only for a circus or photograph affair we would charge. Our charge for a circus is 1s. for the night.

19,083. What do you charge on other ordinary things?—About 2s. if it does not take up any space.

19,084. There are no charges whatever on cattle?—None whatever.

19,085. Or on pigs?—No.

19,086. Are the pigs sold in the fair green also?—Yes, young pigs are sold out of creels on fair days.

19,087. When was this monthly fair established, that is, the last Thursday in every month?—I recollect when Saturday was a market for pigs. Then the monthly fairs were established, and the market was done away with.

19,088. How far does your memory extend?—Fifty years of Carrick, and, so far as I think, we have the new fairs for that time.

19,089. Have you three old fairs, and monthly fairs in addition to them?—Yes.

19,090. So you have 16 altogether in the year?—Yes.

19,091. When was the Monday pig market established?—That must come with the establishment of the new fairs. It might be established after the fair in Carrick-beg.

19,092. Are there any fairs held in Carrick-beg at present?—Not now; but there was a patent for the fair in Carrick-beg, which was abolished. The only evidence I have is recorded in the list of fairs given from time to time.

19,093. Have the commissioners any right or control over the butter market here?—None whatsoever.

19,094. That solely is belonging to Mr. William Boyd?—Yes. We never complain, and I do not know of any authority that can be exercised, save it by the commissioners. Mr. Boyd is appointed by the grand jury.

19,095. Did the commissioners ever contemplate the removal of the markets off the public streets to an enclosed building?—Not that I am aware of. It never came under my notice that they contemplated any change.

19,096. Does the fact of the general market being held on the streets cause much filth and dirt?—Well, it does.

19,097. Who bears the expense—the expense of cleaning them?—We sweep the streets.

19,098. Have the people—the traders and private inhabitants of the town who live adjacent to the place—complained of the markets being held on the streets?—Yes. There is a general objection to the fish, but I never heard any general complaint.

19,099. You levy no standing charges for these at all?—None whatsoever.

19,100. Then you derive no revenue at all from either markets or fairs?—We get nothing whatever from the markets or fairs.

19,101. Were tolls ever levied in Carrick-on-Suir?—Not that I am aware of. There is some tradition that the tolls were charged.

19,102. To whom does this side of the town belong; who is lord of the manor?—Lord Bessborough.

19,103. Have you got any officials to regulate order in the markets?—No.

19,104. The people can go where they please to expose their commodities on the street?—They can.

19,105. You have no rules or regulations confining them to a particular district?—No. The police keep the streets clear.

19,106. Do you clean the fair green?—Well, I believe there is very little cleaning to be done there. The rubbish of the town goes into my own yards.

19,107. If there are any holes made during the fair you fill them in?—Yes, and we fill them in at our own expense.

19,108. Did you ever calculate the additional expense imposed on the commissioners in cleaning the streets after the markets, and repairing the fair green after the fairs?—No; for if the markets were not there at all we would have to sweep the streets.

19,109. But have you to sweep them oftener, and incur greater expense in doing so, by the fact of the markets being held there?—I do not know.

19,110. You never calculated it?—No.

19,111. What would you estimate the amount at?—We have a man weekly in winter, and an additional man one day, but he would clear his expenses.

19,112. What would be the expense?—About 1s. 6d. a day for one day in the week.

19,113. You say about 4l. in the year would cover your expenses?—Yes. Then there are some little matters in the way of manure that help to meet that.

19,114. Do you think, if the commissioners were disposed to erect shelter accommodation and confine all marketable commodities to an enclosed space, and animals to an enclosed fair green, where shelter accommodation would be provided—do you think that the farmers and those frequenting the fairs and markets would be disposed to pay a toll?—Really I would not wish to give an opinion.

19,115. Do you think the exaction of a toll rate in any way as a deterrent on people bringing their commodities?—I should say it would to some extent.

19,116. Have you any experience of other places where tolls are levied?—They are levied at Callan, a neighbouring place, but I am not aware it has any deterrent effect.

19,117. Had you ever any conversation with farmers on the subject?—No. I am well aware in many places, as a general rule, people will be opposed to tolls and charges.

19,118. Are there any means here of weighing a sack of potatoes?—Yes, the scales. Mr. Boyd has an ordinary scales and weights. They can weigh them anywhere they wish.

19,119. Did you bring the schedule of queries which I sent you before the commissioners?—We had no meeting since, but I advised all the commissioners.

19,120. Did they give you any instructions to answer any of the questions?—I advised the general public as far as I could.

19,121. Did you consult the commissioners?—The chairman, Mr. [illegible], is here, and Mr. [illegible], the ex-secretary officer. I notified the general public.

Mr. William Boyd examined.

19,122. You are the owner of the weighing crane?—Yes.

19,123. You have provided an crane and a beam and scales?—I did not provide the crane. I only rented that for [illegible]. I pay rent for it.

19,124. From whom do you rent the crane?—From the representatives of George [illegible].

19,125. Would you have any objection to tell me the rent?—13l. a year.

19,126. What do you charge per load for weighing on the crane?—Twopence for an unshod and 3d. for a horse's, and 2d. for a [illegible].

19,127. That is irrespective of the commodity?—It does not matter what the load may be.

19,128. Do you always ascertain the actual tare of the cart after weighing?—Yes.

19,129. You never go by estimates—you never estimate the tare?—No. If the parties are in for a long time on the street with a load of hay, such as on Saturday, a party would come and buy that, and they arrange the tare at five and a half hundredweight. It would be only five and a quarter on a dry day, and on a wet day a quarter of a hundred is allowed; but all carts are weighed. We generally take a list, and have it on parchment, and we can from time to time go over the blocks and see the tares.

19,130. Have you got printed tickets to give describing the weight?—Yes.

19,131. Do you keep a block of the tickets?—Yes.

19,132. So that during the course of the day, if a person loses his ticket, you can give him the weight again?—Yes. We keep the block for the last six or eight years.

The following is a copy of the ticket subsequently handed in by witness:—

ORIGINAL [illegible]'S PATENT WAGGON WEIGHING MACHINE.

Carrick-on-Suir ________________ 18__.

No. Load of

____

Gross Weight, . .

Deduct Cart, . .

____

Nett . .

19,133. Is the tare the only deduction from the gross weight?—That is all.

19,134. You never allow anything for the dampness of the weather or the dampness of the commodity?—Anybody who is weighing for the public has nothing to do with that. Let the buyer and seller agree to that. In the case of a load of hay or straw they allow half a hundredweight or a hundred on a wet day, and that is allowed when they are deducting the tare.

19,135. You only deduct it when the buyer and seller agree?—Yes.

19,136. You have a beam and scales provided, too?—Yes.

19,137. Did you provide that yourself?—No.

19,138. You also rent that?—Yes, for the same rent.

19,139. Have you the crane and beam and scales for 13l. a year?—Yes.

19,140. What commodities are usually weighed at the beam and scales?—Potatoes sometimes in bags, turnips, parsnips, and wool.

19,141. Do you ever weigh corn, or does corn come in here?—Yes; but very little.

19,142. What is your charge for weighing a bag of potatoes?—A penny per bag. If there is a large quantity, seven or eight bags, I allow a deduction, and weigh them for 6d.

19,143. Is that 1d. per bag for all description of commodities?—Yes; but if it is a small bag I only charge ½d.

19,144. What do you call a small bag?—Seven stone; and on that the charge is ½d.

19,145. Then you have no higher charge than 1d.?—No.

19,146. What is your charge for weighing wool?—Sometimes 2d. For a large pack, say 2 cwt., I would charge 1s. The profit goes away with the big sacks.

19,147. What is your ordinary charge?—For three or four packs I only charge 3d., and 6d. sometimes.

19,148. In weighing potatoes what is the smallest weight you use?—Four pounds.

19,149. It must be 4 lbs., or nothing?—Yes.

19,150. Do you give a turn of the beam when you are weighing?—Slightly. If it is marking beam with the 4 lbs. I throw that out.

19,151. Do you estimate always, or do you usually ascertain, the tare of the bag?—They allow 7 lbs. for the bag, but for some bags through the county Kilkenny they allow a stone, because they are homemade sacks, which weigh from 11 to 13 lbs. There might be 28 or 30 stone in these.

19,152. The customary allowance on such sacks is a stone, and on ordinary sacks 7 lbs.?—Yes.

19,153. Would that be the allowance on a sack of potatoes brought in on a fine day and on an inclement day when the bag is completely saturated with wet?—The same allowance.

19,154. Nothing additional is allowed?—If the sack weighed over 22 stone the buyer looks for a stone tare, and they arrange among themselves; and if the buyer and seller agree we have nothing to do with it.

19,155. What is the lowest weight used in weighing tare?—A pound.

19,156. Do you give a cast of the beam?—It is standing beam.

19,157. Always standing beam?—Yes. The bags must come back to be weighed.

19,158. What is the estimated weight?—They generally bring them back to be weighed.

19,159. Is that the only deduction for tare?—That is all.

19,160. Nothing is allowed for lowance?—Nothing.

19,161. Do you give a ticket for corn or potatoes?—Yes.

19,162. I suppose the same ticket is given for potatoes, corn, wool, and everything you weigh at the beam and scales?—It is only a slip of paper.

19,163. Is it a manuscript form?—Yes. We give a slip of paper, a copy of which we keep in the books. We take off the tare and make up the amount for them. If a man wants a copy of the ticket I must take a second copy for him.

19,164. Do you ever denote the weight in chalk on the sacks?—Sometimes.

19,165. But it is not the practice?—No. Perhaps a man may sell three sacks of potatoes—one to me, one to this man, and the other to a third person; then the weight is put on each sack, and I give a ticket for each.

19,166. You always give a ticket?—Yes, I give a ticket for everything.

19,167. Supposing they brought a cart-load of potatoes and weighed it at your scale?—They never do that.

19,168. Supposing it was done, would you charge 1d. per sack, or only 2d. for the load?—Twopence for the load.

19,169. No matter how many sacks are in the load?—Yes.

19,170. Then you only give the actual weight of the load?—I have often done it. We calculate 7 lbs. for every sack, and add that to the tare of the car, and deduct it from the gross weight.

19,171. When was this butter market established?—I really could not say.

19,172. How long have you been tenant of it?—About 24 years. The lease I hold was granted to my father-in-law, and is a 300 year lease.

19,173. Have you got the lease here?—No.

19,174. From whom do you rent it?—The owner now is Major Reeves.

19,175. What is the unexpired term at present?—I could not tell you.

19,176. You do not know the date?—I could get the date, but I gave all the documents up to the owner.

19,177. Is this the only lease of the butter market?—Of the beams and butter market altogether.

19,178. Is it a lease of the premises?—Of the premises.

19,179. Only?—Yes.

19,180. There is no lease or grant to you of any tolls or right to collect tolls?—No. The tolls formerly belonged to Lord Waterford in that side of the country.

19,181. Who incurred the expense of erecting this butter market?—Formerly the butter market used to be held on the street, but that is a great many years. The ground-rent is 5l. a year.

19,182. To whom is that 5l. a year payable?—It is the ground-rent.

19,183. Would you have any objection to tell the rent you are paying?—Twenty-one pounds.

19,184. Were you demised, or did you get the beams and scales with the lease and butter market premises?—Yes.

19,185. Did you provide any of these appliances yourself?—I did.

19,186. Have you effected any repairs in this butter market?—Indeed I did.

19,187. Did you make up any calculation of your estimated capital expenditure on the premises?—I did.

19,188. Could you give it to me?—In alterations from time to time I laid out over 800l.

19,189. In what way?—Alterations and building up the premises.

19,190. You could not give me the particulars of the expenditure?—Not at present.

19,191. Whom have you in your employment to manage this butter market?—I do the principal business myself with regard to the weighing and the issuing of tickets. I employ two boys at the gate, and every man's name is written on his firkin, and the number of firkins he has.

19,192. That is the name of the owner?—Yes. The marks are written on a wet day in white chalk, and on a dry day with [illegible].

19,193. Have you coopers employed?—Yes, one cooper.

19,194. Have you any tasters employed?—I used to taste it myself.

19,195. But do the buyers themselves taste it now?—Yes. If the butter is put up to the market I go and taste it, and tell them to the best of my ability the improvements required.

19,196. During the season, what is the average number of firkins brought? Every season, as I presume, the butter is brought in firkins?—All in firkins.

19,197. No lump butter is brought in?—No. You see on Saturdays the butter is sold in rolls, and there is a recommendation that in the inclement weather it would be more desirable for purchasers if a regulation was made that all butter sold in rolls be sold within the precincts of the market.

19,198. Could you give me the number of firkins brought in every year?—Yes.

19,199. Do you keep a record of the number?—I do. For the last three years it has been coming down very much. I should say the average is 6,500.

19,200. Is that the number each year?—Yes; that is the average for the last three years.

19,201. Have you anybody else employed besides the cooper and the two boys?—Yes, I have one man drawing nails or hoops, and two men draining.

19,202. These are assistants to the cooper?—Yes, to take the water off the firkins; one man putting the firkin into the scales, and two men taking it away, and myself weighing.

19,203. Is the firkin always bought before being weighed?—Always weighed now.

19,204. Before they are bought?—Yes.

19,205. What hour does your market usually begin?—As soon as the butter comes in.

19,206. What time is it brought in?—We open the market on market days about this time of the year at 7 o'clock, and in summer time at 6, but I commence to weigh about 8 o'clock.

19,207. What time does the buying usually commence?—We have only one local buyer, and he waits until 10 minutes to 11, and then he and the others buy from that to half-past 11.

19,208. Would all the butter be weighed then?—No, it would not be all in. In summer time it would be all in, but not at this time of the year.

19,209. What is the greatest number that has come in on one day?—A few years ago over 600.

19,210. How many beams and scales in use?—Only one.

19,211. Would that one scale here to do the weighing of the 600 firkins?—Yes, and it would do more if it came in earlier.

19,212. No undue delay is caused to the sellers?—Latterly they come from half-past 10 to 11, and then it is very crowded, indeed, by everyone rushing to get in, and for half an hour sometimes the place is blocked. All butter must be tilted; there is no butter allowed to be carried, and they must have all laid down neatly.

19,213. Do you completely strip each firkin?—No. We made arrangements that all the firkins should be branded with the initials of the coopers, and if there are wrong tares I get a list from the merchants, so that next day one or two firkins may be turned up to see are they right.

19,214. Then you drain them completely?—Yes.

19,215. What is the tare of the firkins?—Small firkins seven pounds, and others eight and nine, and in some country districts the tare is 10 and 11 pounds. If they have been keeping them over for a week they call one pound extra on the tare; that is, if a firkin is branded nine pounds they call it ten, and if branded seven they call it eight, with the exception of two or three men who come in here, and they get their firkins weighed, and they are correct.

19,216. What do you allow the additional pound for?—For soakage.

19,217. That is, whatever water remains in the firkin after the draining?—It is in the timber.

19,218. Supposing one of these firkins was actually weighed, would that be about the tare of it?—Yes, about a pound over.

19,219. Are the firkins now made stamped with the weight?—Yes. It is branded on them; some are burned.

19,220. Is that estimated tare and soakage allowance the only deductions from the gross weight of the firkin?—That is all. If any disputes arise they weigh the firkin.

19,221. Supposing they ask you to weigh a firkin itself, and you completely strip and weigh it, do you charge anything additional?—There was one time, and we stripped the firkins, but we did not charge. We used get the coopers into the market to strip the firkin and see what the tare was, and then the brokers brought them correct.

19,222. It is 2*d*. a firkin you charge?—Yes.

19,223. You have got printed tickets to give denoting the weight?—Yes.

The following is a copy of the ticket subsequently handed in by the witness:—

BUTTER MARKET.

CARRICK-ON-SUIR.

———————— 188 .

Buyer ————————————

Seller ————————————

19,224. In the course of the work of weighing these firkins and making up the tickets for them, did you ever hear the contract price for the different classes of butter between the buyer and seller?—No. There is a little secrecy between the buyer and seller.

19,225. Supposing it was required from you to make a periodical return of the current price of the different classes of butter, could you make an accurate return? I am not asking you to do it; but is it possible to make a return, or a pretty accurate return, of the average every week?—Yes, I take them down myself. I write it down.

19,226. It could be done?—I write it down in a book.

19,227. That is for your own information?—Yes.

19,228. So you actually do it?—Yes. We generally have eight or nine buyers, and I get a list from each buyer of how many he has bought for the day.

19,229. Is it of the number of firkins or of the price that you keep a record?—Of the firkins.

19,230. And the current price?—I keep that myself.

19,231. What would you say would be the average cost of the repairs to this place?—About 6*l*. a year.

19,232. What is the lowest weight you weigh butter with?—One pound.

19,233. Do you weigh by standing beam?—Yes.

19,234. Is the buyer always satisfied with standing beam?—He must be. If he is doubtful of a firkin, the firkin is weighed. Of course the firkins are not all perfection, and if a firkin goes to Waterford, and is not up to weight, the buyer sends it back to me.

19,235. From what districts is the butter brought here, or within what limits?—About 17 miles, but it is a greater distance, as they sometimes come 18 or 19 miles. Last year they came from within a mile of Kerry.

19,236. Would you say this butter market is a better market than the one in Tipperary?—I would not say that. I will not run down any market. Tipperary is also a large butter market. Here we are in the centre of eight or nine creameries. We have Clonmel, Waterford, and the County Waterford for nine miles, and not a single customer is coming in from those places.

19,237. It is in return for the docket denoting the weight you get your threepenny charge?—Yes.

19,238. You never consider whether the butter is subsequently sold or not?—If they do not sell they store it up until the next day, and I look after it.

19,239. Do you levy any storage charge?—No.

19,240. On the following market day do you levy any charge?—No.

19,241. Is it weighed again?—There may be some soakage, and I weigh it again.

19,242. Do you get a second threepence for that second weighing?—No.

19,243. What percentage of the supplies of firkins is sold?—They are mostly all sold. There has been only twice this year that they were left over.

19,244. Does the butter market afford sufficient space for the exposure of the butter and the accommodation of the buyers?—Yes, except on one or two days in the year, when there is an awful crowd there. Sometimes father and mother, son and brother, are all over one firkin of butter.

19,245. If these people did not come in, would you have ample room?—Yes, for 700 firkins. I have a place there for them to remain, so that they would not smoke in the market.

19,246. Do you levy any storage charge at all?—No. It is very seldom they store.

19,247. Have any brands within your memory been encouraged in the preparation of the butter?—Yes.

19,248. Have prosecutions resulted from them?—No. We had one this year, and there was a false name given in, and a different district, and we never got the party.

19,249. Who institutes these proceedings?—They are entitled.

19,250. Whose duty do you consider it is?—Mine.

19,251. Have you any rules or regulations in the market?—No.

19,252. You have no printed or written rules?—No.

19,253. The amount you have mentioned, is that your average receipts?—Yes.

19,254. Over and above the expenses?—I think the expenses are deducted. The net profit is 101*l.* 3*s.* 6*d.* Then the expenses are 40*l.* wages; 6*l.* repairs; for cleaning 4*l.*, and taxes 6*l.*

19,255. Is this only the profit derived from the butter market?—Yes.

19,256. You did not state the profit you derive from the beams and scales, and council?—The council forms no part of the butter market. That is the profit from the beam and scales in the butter house. The beam and scales are used for weighing wool, potatoes, parsnips, and everything that comes. [illegible]

19,257. Although you pay 15*l.*?—No. There was the council besides. I suppose, taking all together from first to last, it is 30*l.* or 35*l.* This was a good year, because a great deal of timber was weighed, but last year it was a good deal down. I would not be bothered with it. I have a boy there, and the man who lived there before me would not pay a man.

19,258. If a firkin of butter was brought into the town of Carrick-on-Suir, and was not taken to your market premises, but was sold in the town on a market day, would you seek for any charge?—No. I would not pay a man to look after it.

19,259. Do you think you would have a right to such a charge?—Yes.

19,260. You could not tell me the authority under which you would seek for the charge?—Under the reign of Queen Anne a special charter was given for the butter market.

19,261. Have you any suggestions to offer or any amendments in the law for the regulation of the butter market or other markets in the town?—I do not know of anything.

19,262. Are there any alterations you deem necessary for the better working of the butter market?—I do not know of any at present.

19,263. Have not you made a recommendation in the query sheet?—I do not know of anything I have said.

19,264. You have no suggestions to offer?—No. I know of nothing.

Mr. Owen Callaghan examined.

19,265. What observations do you wish to make?—At the date of Mr. Boyd's appointment he was appointed as butter taster. It is within the power of the magistrates to make the appointment. At that time the Town Commissioners made application to have their chairman appointed as butter taster with a view of depriving his authority to some one else to taste the butter, and after a great fight the magistrates appointed Mr. Boyd. Mr. Boyd was appointed merely as the butter taster and weighmaster for any butter brought into his place. He has given very great satisfaction. He merely rents the house he is living in, and uses it for the accommodation of persons bringing butter to be weighed at his place. You put a question as to what were the rights of persons at the weighing machine. The weighing machine is private property, one of them belonging to a man named Moore, who is a relation of Mr. Boyd's, and another to a man named Powell, who was succeeded by a reverend gentleman now dead. Then the place passed to a man named Crowley. This Crowley exercised a right over the renting of a house given him for the purpose of weighing anything brought to him up to a recent date, but it is not used at present. My object in giving you this information is to show that there is no private right in any market in Carrick, with the exception of the butter market.

19,266. Mr. O'Sullivan, solicitor, said: I appear for Mr. Boyd. My friend, Mr. Callaghan, is not conversant with the old charter of Anne.

19,267. (*The Assistant Commissioner.*) Mr. Boyd, I take it, claims the right to the butter market under the appointment mentioned by Mr. Callaghan?

19,268. (*Mr. O'Sullivan, solicitor.*) Apart from any controversy as to his appointment as butter taster and weighmaster we can give positive evidence, and it is not within the power of any person wishing to give information to the court to deny the existence of this charter. But, at all events, Mr. Boyd has them on good authority. He derived them from his father-in-law, and old documents which unfortunately were destroyed show that the charter is extant, but whether that creates a special [illegible] we do not know, and we, by virtue of devolution on marriage, are the direct representatives of the [illegible]. It will be easy to find if any such Act exists, and also the manner in which the [illegible] devolved.

19,269. (*The Assistant Commissioner.*) Apart altogether from any express appointment of Mr. Boyd, do you think the right is vested in him by prescription?—I should think so.

19,270. Was Mr. Boyd appointed for life?—Yes, by devolution on marriage.

19,271. Mr. Boyd produced notices posted up in the butter market, of which the following are copies:—

19,272. Meeting of Master Coopers of Waterford. The following resolution was passed:—"That no "firkin exceed 14 lbs., save with initials of the maker "branded on the side of the firkin."

"Notice.

"Owing to the crowded state of the market for the last few market days, no persons will be allowed into the market house but buyers and sellers only.

"All butter to be in early.

"Notice to Farmers.

"We, the undersigned merchants of the City of Limerick, will not, after Saturday, 17th September, purchase any butter packed in machine-made casks, as we find them to be most injurious to the keeping qualities of butter, and we strongly urge on the farmers of Limerick, Clare, and the surrounding counties the great necessity of packing butter in hand-made casks or firkins. (Here follows the names of the principal merchants.)

"Important Notice to Farmers and Coopers.

"In consequence of the necessity of the introduction of an improved style of butter firkin, and as the coopers and butter makers wish to ascertain the particular kind most suitable for the trade, the Waterford butter merchants met at the Market House on Monday, 14th December, 18[illegible], for the purpose of selecting some model firkins, and taking steps for the general adoption of the package decided on. At the meeting the following resolutions were unanimously passed:—

"We, the undersigned butter merchants of the City of Waterford, agree that the following be the approved sizes for casks for the coming season:—

"Casks to contain 56 lbs. and 84 lbs. nets of butter.

"Resolved—

"That the name of the cooper and the weight of the empty cask be branded on the side of each cask.

"That the farmers allow 3 lbs. on the large-sized cask, and 1 lb. on the small-sized cask, and the merchants hereby agree not to charge more, except in the case of any cask found to have been steeped, or weighing more than the branded weight on the cask; in such cases the excess tare will be charged double.

"That the casks be made air-tight, of well-seasoned timber, preference being given to oak, ash, and beech, and

"That the large-sized casks be full-hooped, and the small-sized quarter-hooped.

"That the casks be made with white hoops, and if possible with white twigs.

"That the following gentlemen act as a committee, to see that the foregoing rules are carried out, namely:—Harry Courtenay, James J. Phelan, R. Mahony, R. W. Pettigrew.

"Signed by Edward Courtenay, Chairman.

"P. A. Power & Co.	Joseph Clampett,
"Henry Ridgway & Son,	J. T. Fielding,
"R. W. Pettigrew.	J. Fawcett & Co.,
"R. Mahony & Co.	John Ryan.
"Nicholas Power,	

"Resolved also, that the committee take the necessary steps to have the foregoing resolutions printed and circulated amongst the coopers and farmers of the whole district.

"Patterns of the approved casks to be sent by the coopers to the following butter markets:—Waterford, Carrick-on-Suir, Clonmel, Fethard, Dungarvan, Kilkenny, New Ross, and Lismore, where they can be seen by farmers and coopers of these districts.

"It is recommended that the tare (leaving the block) of the large-sized cask be 10 to 12 lbs., and the tare of the small-sized cask be 6 or 7 lbs."

"Notice.

"Any firkins suspected to weigh more than the weight branded on them will be stripped and weighed by order of the merchants:

"Messrs. Egan, Courtenay, Ridgway, Pettigrew, Ryan, Fielding, P. A. Power, N. Power, Mahony & Co., John Ryan, Phelan & Co., Clonmel."

19,273. (Mr. P. Quirke, solicitor.) I appear for the town commissioners, who hold that Mr. Boyd's rights as weighmaster and butter taster cannot prevent the people from going elsewhere than to his place if they choose. He was appointed under the Act of Anne, amended by the eighth of George the First, which gives the grand jury and magistrates power to appoint a weighmaster in every town in Ireland.

19,274. (The Assistant Commissioner.) Do the commissioners claim any right to the butter market?

19,275. (Mr. Quirke.) No, they do not, but the commissioners think they should have control of the butter market.

19,276. (Mr. Sullivan.) The commissioners established a fish market, and it was discontinued.

19,277. (The Assistant Commissioner.) What was the cause of this?

19,278. (Mr. Gallaghan.) Complaints from time to time were made of the fish being too near the milk market. The commissioners were anxious to get them aside, and they secured a place for a small rent and obliged the fishmongers to go there, and they went there and kept off the streets. Subsequently this place was rented to a man named Venables, but why I could not give any opinion, because I ceased to be a commissioner. This Venables was ejected by the commissioners, and the place handed to Lord Bessborough. I do think, from observations, that the fishmongers defied the commissioners and refused to go there, but they did acquiesce in the arrangement for many years; but it was only extreme poverty and want of revenue that prevented the then commissioners from having a general market.

19,279. Were there any tolls levied on the fish then?—No tolls, only a small rent.

19,280. A stallage rent?—Yes.

Cross-examination continued.

19,284. Do not you think it would be more desirable if the town commissioners obtained an enclosed space, or would the cost be greater than the revenue derivable afterwards?—I think the cost would be too much for the ratepayers.

19,285. (Mr. Sullivan.) That question of enclosing a fair green arose a good many years since, when my father was a town commissioner, and the commissioners decided that it was better to leave it open as it is.

19,286. (By the Assistant Commissioner.) Have you experience of places where tolls are levied?—My opinion is that where the tolls are levied and accommodation is provided the people do not object to tolls, but the accommodation ought to be provided, because the tolls ought not be demanded without giving an equivalent.

19,287. Where such accommodation is provided you do not think that the levying of a toll acts as a deterrent?—I should think not.

19,288. It is your opinion that if a person is in receipt of the toll he should give a return in the way of accommodation?—I do, certainly, because I do not think they have a right to levy tolls without giving accommodation to those persons charged.

19,289. (Mr. Quirke.) As a matter of fact, the country people pay from 3d. to 6d. a-piece for stallage the night before the fair to the neighbouring farmers and townspeople.

19,290. For shelter accommodation for the animals?—Yes.

19,291. What is the stallage charge?—Threepence.

19,292. What is it for a pig?—From 2d. to 3d.

Patrick Quirke, Esq., Solicitor, examined.

19,293. Have you anything to state?—All I have to say is on behalf of the commissioners. They are desirous of getting control of the market, and after paying the expenses anything that came out of the markets should go to the benefit of the town. We will have a meeting of the commissioners this evening, and can send on afterwards any resolutions adopted on the subject.

Michael Power, Esq., Chairman of Town Commissioners, continued.

19,294. You are the chairman of the town commissioners?—Yes.

19,295. Did the commissioners, as a body, ever contemplate acquiring the rights to the markets and fairs in Carrick?—Well, not to my knowledge, while I am chairman of the commissioners.

19,296. Has it ever been discussed by the commissioners?—No.

19,297. Individually, are they desirous of obtaining the control of all markets?—Certainly.

19,298. Do you think that any steps will be taken in that direction by them?—If they have a legal right I would say that they would.

19,299. From your experience, you think a body like the commissioners are the proper persons to have control over the markets and fairs in this town and elsewhere?—I would say so.

19,300. Why did you form that opinion?—I think for the benefit of the people of the town the commissioners should have this right.

19,301. Over what?—Over the general market.

19,302. As well as over the fairs?—Yes.

and in 1858, by a motion of the town commissioners, it was enclosed, and, as far as I remember, his Lordship the Earl of Bessborough had to be consulted, notwithstanding that the grand jury proposed to exercise exclusive rights, although within their jurisdiction.

19,307. (Mr. Gallagher.) It was on a resolution proposed by me—I was then on the town commission—that the place was enclosed. The Earl of Bessborough gave a contribution, and, in addition to that, he verbally gave up his rights.

19,308. The public have acquired no rights over this portion?—No further than prescriptive right to hold the fairs.

Examination of Mr. Power continued.

19,309. Do you think the butter market would be worked better and to the greater satisfaction of those frequenting it if the commissioners were the controlling authority?—I think so.

19,310. Did you ever hear any complaints of the arrangement at present?—No, except that the receipts do not go to the benefit of the rates.

19,311. You would only seek control of it for the purpose of increasing your present revenue?—Yes; that is my view.

19,312. You never heard any complaints of inaccuracy in the weights or drainage in the butter market?—No. As far as the butter market is concerned, I never heard complaints, but there have been complaints of the weighing machine.

19,313. Have complaints been made of any inaccuracies?—I heard complaints made of shortcomings at the machine, and that it is not weighing properly.

19,314. Were these complaints mentioned to Mr. Boyd?—I do not know.

19,315. [Mr. Boyd has said: The weighing machine got out of order, and I had it repaired, and it cost me 3l. 10s.]

19,316. Have you (Mr. Powell) any experience of fairs where tolls are levied?—No.

Cross-examined by Mr. Sullivan.

19,317. You say it was not discussed, but the individual opinion of the town commissioners is that they should have control?—Yes.

19,318. Was there a special market for the sale of fish which was discontinued, and give the reason why the commissioners had it discontinued?—We tried to carry it out, and could not get fish enough to continue in the place we appointed.

19,319. Was not there a special fish market constituted at the end of the quay by the town commissioners, the town commissioners erecting it, and was not that discontinued?—I do not remember.

19,320. It was before your time?—Yes.

19,321. Were there any market buildings erected?—There were.

19,322. Were they erected by the town commissioners?—Not in my time.

19,323. Did the commissioners ever establish a fish market?—Not in my time.

19,324. Would you think it would conduce to the benefit of sellers of cattle and convenience the buyers if the green were enclosed and stalls put up?—Yes, if it could be done; but the rates of the town will not allow any such thing to be done.

19,325. In addition to the cattle sold on the green, if enclosed, do not you think the hay and other farm produce should be sold there and not on the street, as at present?—Yes.

19,326. (By the Assistant Commissioner.) Do you think if a toll was levied it would deter people from bringing their commodities into the market?—It would not, for the best of reasons possible, they cannot go anywhere else.

19,327. Have you got any town regulations?—No.

Mr. William Ahern examined.

19,328. Have you any remarks to make as to the better working, or what would tend to the better working, of the markets and fairs in Carrick-on-Suir?—I think you have all the information from Mr. Gallagher.

19,329. You have no suggestion to offer yourself?—No suggestion; but I would not like to have the green railed in and the markets taken off the street. The people would be against it. There would be some benefit got by the grocers and publicans where the markets are on the street.

19,330. You think the removal of the markets would be opposed by the traders?—Yes.

Cross-examined.

19,331. Could you give any good reasons why the grocers and publicans would object to a transfer from the main street to the green, or have you any tangible reason for the conclusion you arrive at?—The general public are in the habit of dealing with the people in the main street, and if the market was held in a different place they would go to new houses.

19,332. (By the Assistant Commissioner.) I take it, then, that the traders would put up with any inconvenience caused to them by the markets being held on the main street for trade purposes?—Yes.

19,333. Do they expose lump butter for sale in the streets here?—Yes.

19,334. Is it to the private individuals they sell or to the shopkeepers?—To private individuals.

19,335. Do they buy by bulk?—They buy on the streets, and go into one of the shops to weigh.

19,336. Do they levy any charge for weighing?—Not at all. It is to avoid the charge they go there.

Mr. Edward Burke examined.

19,337. What remarks do you wish to make?—I wish to state that I frequently had a conversation with many men who, from time to time, attend the markets and the greens where tollage is charged, and those men remind to me that the general public are getting totally opposed to it. There is a place not far distant, three or four miles below Piltown, and the people kicked against it, and they held the fairs on the roads instead of driving the cattle into the place where tollage was charged.

19,338. Was there any accommodation given in return for the toll there?—There was. A field was there where the fair was always held; and it seems since that ago—I do not know it of my own knowledge—that a man named Fahy took up the field. The field belonged to Lord Bessborough, and he rented it, but whether it was in his possession or not before that I could not say, and then he insisted on getting tollage, and a great many people bringing cattle and pigs there remained out on the road, and would not go into the field at all.

19,339. Could you tell me the reasons why you are opposed to the levying of a toll at fairs?—Only for the charges. I do not know any other reason.

19,340. Would you have any objection to pay a toll if an adequate return was given for it?—If a man had 20 head of cattle at 3d. each, would not that be 5s.?

19,341. If you brought 20 head of cattle and got an adequate return, would you object to pay the toll?—But I do not think there is any accommodation here in that way with regard to shelter.

19,342. I am only asking you, in a general sense, would you object to paying a toll for cattle brought in and exposed for sale in the fair green if you got an adequate return?—I would not if it was to pay the cost and expense of getting up the place.

19,343. Where tolls are levied, do you deem it right that the person in receipt of such tolls should give an adequate return?—Yes.

19,344. Otherwise you would be opposed to the payment of the tolls?—Yes.

19,345. Is that the general opinion of the drovers, farmers, and traders with whom you come in contact?—It is. Before this inquiry was to be held at all, I was often speaking to dealers and farmers coming to this place, and every one of them seems to have a decided objection to pay tolls—both dealers and farmers.

19,346. Would not you think, if the commissioners acquired the fair green, and the right to levy tollage, and had erected there stalls and pens for the cattle, that the farmers would not object to pay a toll of 3d. or 1s. instead of putting them on hand to graze the night before the fair?—It would be a very great convenience to farmers and dealers, but not in such a place as this.

19,347. As a matter of public convenience, if cattle pens were provided, do you think there ought to be rules by the commissioners fixing the hour for buying and for opening, and not have it struggling as it is?—My opinion is that if the commissioners went to the expense of walling in the fair green they would have to charge 2s. 6d. per head.

19,348. That is, if provided out of the rates; do not you think it more desirable that the place should be walled in and accommodation given?—I do not think it would be desirable, because the general public would not have it. They would not be pleased with it.

19,349. But you have got to consider the convenience to the town and the benefit to the revenue of the commissioners?—I think it would be a benefit, but not a benefit to the revenue of the commissioners; but if the commissioners got the sole supervision and control of the market, and have proper officers, I think the commissioners would be doing a good day's work. Let them take up the whole market, butter and everything else, and establish a market, because there is nobody in this town, but any control over the markets, and every person who comes into the town can go everywhere they like, or where they can get any convenience for their accommodation.

Mr. Wall, P.L.G., examined.

19,350. What observations do you wish to make?—I think the pigs should be kept in the yards of the town instead of at the railway.

19,351. What is your suggestion?—My suggestion is that when they are sold they should be put into the yards of the town.

19,352. (Mr. Harte.) You could not make that work. When a man buys a pig it is for him to drive the pig wherever he likes himself.

19,353. Would you suggest, Mr. Wall, that a properly enclosed pig market should be established, with pens for shelter?—There are plenty of yards idle in the town.

19,354. In return for the accommodation in those yards, would you and those who sell and buy pigs here be disposed to pay tollage?—Certainly. They get knocked about a good deal at the railway.

19,355. Do the pigs be deteriorated in value by this knocking about?—Certainly, and the people who buy them suffer, too. There are three or four principal buyers working here, and three or four yards would accommodate the whole of them.

19,356. Do pigs come in any great numbers?—Four hundred or five hundred every fair day.

19,357. Is there any other gentleman who has any observations to make?—No answer.

The inquiry then concluded.

WATERFORD.

With reference to my inquiry in Waterford on the 6th November 1882, I beg to

appointed by the old Corporation, in 1842, the public butter weighmaster, under the provisions of the Act of Parliament for his life. The profits derived from the market go to his own use. Acting upon the advice of his solicitor, his manager refused to attend the inquiry or assist the Commission, so that the necessary information had to be subsequently elicited from him at the market place.

It is the unanimous opinion of the members of the Corporation, that the profits of the butter market should go to augment the funds of the city treasury, and it is a customary practice at the election of a mayor each year to obtain from that municipal dignitary an undertaking that if during his term of office he should have occasion to exercise the privilege of appointing a butter weighmaster, he will do so for the public benefit, and not for his private use.

The charges received from the potato market, fish market, and roll butter and egg market, go to the Corporation.

The charges at the hay and straw market are payable, in the first instance, to the above named Mr. Charles Newport, but since 1874, the sum of 2d. per load is payable by Mr. Newport to the Corporation, in return, it is said, for regulating the market and keeping order.

There seems to have been four patents granted for Waterford. They are dated respectively 10th July 1609, 26th May 1626, 24th March, 4 James II., and 6th June 1706; and authorised markets to be held on Wednesday and Saturday, and a fair on 24th June to continue for five days, and another on 11th October to continue likewise for five days.

The site of the firkin butter market and the buildings thereon, are rented by Mr. Newport from the Corporation at 40l. a year.

It was stated that the monthly fair on the first Monday of each month was established without any express authority within the last 50 years.

In accordance with my instructions, I have inspected the fair green and market places, &c.

The fairs and pig fair, a market in Waterford, are held in a fair green on what is called the hill of Ballybricken, which is at the upper end of the city. It is a large open space, and between fairs used as a commonage. It affords sufficient space for the purposes for which it is availed of. It is not walled in, and there is no accommodation whatever provided there for those frequenting the fairs.

The only enclosed markets belonging to the Corporation, are the roll butter and egg market, and the fish market. These two markets adjoin each other, and are situate off the public street. They are fairly large, and provided with shedding accommodation for those transacting business there. There is a scale in the roll butter market, and seats around, and in the fish market also there is suitable accommodation. Both places are paved, and at the time of inspection presented a very clean and commendable appearance. These markets were only erected last year by the Corporation.

The large butter market belonging to Mr. Newport is held on the quay, where a spacious and lofty covered house is built. There are two entrances to it. A beam and scales are provided for weighing the butter. There is sufficient accommodation for a large supply of butter. An office, from which the weigh tickets are issued, is erected within the building. Coopers to drain the firkins, and assistant weighmaster are engaged by the owner.

In connexion with this last market there is a crane erected at which all commodities are weighed by the load. The hay and straw market is held on the public street in front of the large butter market, but there is no shelter or other accommodation.

All the other markets, the potato market, milk market, vegetable market, and fruit market, are held on portions of the different public thoroughfares in the city; and no immediate control is, it seems, exercised over them, except for the purpose of avoiding obstruction to the public.

In the potato market, when weighing a sack of potatoes, a deduction of one stone is made from the gross weight in order to cover the tare of the sack and dirt, &c. around the potatoes.

In the large butter market a deduction of 1 lb. on small firkins, and 2 lbs. on large firkins is made from the gross weight, in addition to the tare branded on the firkin. This additional allowance is said to be for soakage.

The firkins must be weighed before sale, and a charge per firkin is levied immediately after the weight being ascertained.

The charge for weighing a load of any commodity at the weighbridge, is fixed at the rate of 6d. per load, irrespective of the quantity contained in the load, or whether it is a horse or donkey load. A head of cattle was weighed thereon, and the same charge, 6d., levied.

During the inquiry I took an opportunity of asking some questions with reference to the bridge crossing the river Suir. There is only one bridge crossing the river, which practically divides the city into two parts. Every individual has to pay, and every animal, cart, or commodity has to bear a toll when crossing the bridge. This is complained of very much by the inhabitants and traders in the city, especially as the river separates the main business thoroughfare from the railway terminus.

The bridge is the property of the Waterford Bridge Commissioners.

Appended will be found a transcript of the evidence taken at the inquiry.

JOHN J. O'MEARA,
Assistant Commissioner.

45, Lower Mount Street,
Dublin.

Waterford, 6th November 1888.

Mr. James Mahony, High Constable, examined.

19,358. Are you the high-constable of Waterford?—Yes.

19,359. You were appointed by the Waterford Corporation?—Yes.

19,360. What are your particular duties, or have you any duties in connexion with the markets and fairs here?—As high-constable, I am superintendent of the markets.

19,361. What markets are there in Waterford?—The potato market, hay and straw market, fish market, High street butter and egg market; the square market for vegetables, and a fruit market for a couple of months in the year, at John street, and a new milk market, morning and evening, in Broad street, and Michael street.

19,362. Where is the potato market held?—On the quay.

19,363. Is it in the public thoroughfare?—Yes, I may mention that there are only two enclosed markets—the fish market, and the small butter and egg market.

19,364. Where is the fish market?—In Peter street.

19,365. Is it entirely enclosed?—Yes, shut out from the public.

19,366. Have they stalls in it?—They have, and slabs and all.

19,367. And sufficient shelter accommodation?—Certainly.

19,368. Do they sell underneath those stalls?—The carts are in the open yard.

19,369. Are there any sheds in the butter and egg market, in High street?—There are two.

19,370. Is this butter market entirely enclosed?—Yes, you can pass from the fish market to the butter and egg market. They adjoin each other.

19,371. Are all the other markets held on the public thoroughfare?—Yes.

19,372. Who are these markets belonging to?—The Corporation of Waterford.

19,373. When are they held?—The potato market is held daily, Sunday excepted; the hay and straw market on Wednesday, Thursday and Saturday; the fish market daily; the small butter and egg market in High street, on Wednesday and Saturday, but on Saturday principally.

19,374. When is the vegetable market held?—That is on Saturday.

19,375. And the fruit market?—That is only for a couple of months in the year, in the months of August and September, and finishes about Michaelmas. It is held on Wednesdays and Saturdays.

19,376. And the new milk market?—That is held twice a day, morning and evening.

19,377. Are charges levied in these markets?—I will name the charges.

19,378. Have you got a schedule?—I have no changes for the last three years.

19,379. That is of the accounts?—Yes.

19,380. But have you got a list of the charges on each commodity?—I will tell you them.

19,381. What is the charge at the potato market?—A penny a sack for weighing, and they get a ticket besides made up.

19,382. There is only one charge?—Yes, 1d. per sack.

19,383. Irrespective of the quantity in the sack?—It does not make a bit of difference. The average is over 10 stone.

19,384. You superintend these markets?—Yes, and I also did duty in them.

19,385. Do they always ascertain the actual tare of the sack?—They allow one stone, by a rule amongst themselves.

19,386. You always estimate the tare?—Yes, at one stone.

19,387. What would be the smallest quantity of potatoes in a sack, the tare of which would be one stone?—I do not know. Because dirt and clay, there is no loser or gainer on either side.

19,388. You would not say that the actual sack itself would weigh a stone?—No, I would not.

19,389. The difference between the weight of the sack and the stone weight would be an allowance for clay, or if the sack was saturated with wet?—Yes.

19,390. Do they ever mark the weight of the potatoes on the sack, with chalk?—No.

19,391. They always give the ticket?—Yes, a printed ticket. The duplicate of that is a book, which I examine once a week.

(*The following is a copy of the ticket in use.*)

397

WATERFORD POTATO MARKET.

day of 188

POTATOES.

Weighed for

Amount of Fees, s. d.

Purchased by

19,392. Is this a good potato market?—It is the only potato market in Waterford.

19,393. Is it well attended?—Very fairly.

19,394. Are there any rules restraining the sale of potatoes elsewhere, than in this market?—There are not.

19,395. Would the corporation prohibit people from selling potatoes elsewhere?—Not if they went into a private house, but they would not allow them to sell in any other part of the street.

19,396. Has a case of that kind ever happened?—There was once a case happened. During my time, I saw people to set up in the Quay weighing potatoes, and I put a stop to it.

19,397. Supposing they sold potatoes in the town, without weighing them at your scales, would you ask for any charge?—No, I would not look for a charge on anything but what is weighed there.

19,398. When you weigh a sack of potatoes, and the ticket denoting the weight is lost, you could give another ticket?—Yes. We can refer to the duplicate, and that is the reason it is kept.

19,399. What about the hay and straw market?—There is an agreement with the Newport family, since 1874, by which the corporation gets 3d. a load, by placing a man on duty. Mr. Vale pays that.

19,400. Mr. Vale, who represents the Newport family, pays this charge to the corporation?—Yes.

19,401. And have the corporation any duties, whatever to perform in return for this charge?—We place a man there to take charge on the public streets, and he makes ordinary arrangements with the people.

19,402. Where is the hay and straw market held?—On the public thoroughfare, beside the bridge, on the quay.

19,403. Mr. Newport levies a higher rate than this from the producers?—Yes.

19,404. In the potato market what facilities have you for ascertaining the weight of the potatoes. How many beams and scales have you?—Only one, and one officer attending. There is a constable in charge.

19,405. Is there only one officer in charge?—Yes. The market is right on the quay, and he has a box there, and the triangle is in front of that.

19,406. What is his salary?—He has other duties besides that. He has charge of a ward, looking after the obstruction, and other duties there.

19,407. What would you estimate his wages at, for performing this particular duty, in connection with the potato market?—52*l*. a year, is the entire salary.

19,408. Then would you say that 52*l*. a year, would cover his duties, so far as the potato market is concerned?—It is not earned in any way.

19,409. You have one man attending the hay and straw market?—Yes; he attends for three days, during the time of the market.

19,410. You do not know the terms of the arrangement between the corporation and the Newport family?—It is in 1874 the arrangement was made.

19,411. Previous to that the corporation derived no benefit from it?—No.

19,412. What are the charges in the fish market?—There are tolls for fish. The salmon trade is the greatest bulk in that.

19,413. Do you know the rate of charges?—A penny per salmon; 1*d*. for each salmon weighed, and for that they get a ticket, and a block is kept.

19,414. Is it only on the salmon you levy a charge?—There is 4*d*. a load for rough fish.

19,415. What sort of a load?—A horse's load.

19,416. Supposing a donkey load came, what would be the charge?—Two-pence. It is optional with the officer to levy only half on small loads.

19,417. He is left a discretionary power?—Yes.

19,418. Are those the only fixed rates, 1*d*. for each salmon, 4*d*. a horse load, and 2*d*. a donkey load? and weighing a sole fish, 1*d*. for 32lbs., or a penny a draft. The charge on rough fish is for the load.

19,419. You have a beam and scales there?—Yes.

19,420. Do you give a ticket denoting the weight?—Yes.

No. [illegible]

WATERFORD FISH MARKET.

day of 18

Salmon,

Weighed for

Amount of Fees, s. d.

Purchased by

19,421. Is it on entry to the market these charges are levied?—No. The rough fish pay on entry, but sometimes we cannot get it until they sell, but the charge on other fish is only when weighed.

19,422. Supposing they sell a salmon by bulk in the market?—They do not do that. It has all to be weighed.

19,423. Can the general public come in to buy in the market?—Yes.

19,424. Supposing they saw a salmon there, and estimated it themselves, and bought it by the bulk, would you charge?—They would not do that. It is the duty of the officer, not to leave it out of the market, until it is weighed.

19,425. Supposing it happened, would they have to pay the charge?—Undoubtedly, if they went away without being weighed, they would not pay, but I never knew a case of that kind.

19,426. The 4*d*. a load is paid on entry into the market?—Yes.

19,427. You do not consider whether the fish are subsequently sold or not?—When it returns they do not generally pay. As a rule, all the fish are sold, and during the day the tolls are levied.

19,428. Supposing they do not sell, but expose it for sale in the market, would the corporation be entitled to charge?—Yes, because the order is made.

19,429. Is the order, that the tolls be collected as they enter?—Not as they come. It is left to the discretionary power of the officer.

19,430. Is there any schedule covered?—It is not printed lately. They are after erecting a new market.

19,431. When was it erected?—Last year.

19,432. That is the fish market?—Yes. We had an old one adjoining, with the butter, and there were some complaints, and the corporation built a new one in Peter street.

19,433. Were tolls levied at the old one?—Yes.

19,434. At similar rates?—Not exactly. The loads of fish were not there regularly, and we got whatever we could out of them.

19,435. Were the charges they were entitled to levy similar to the present charges?—About the same thing.

19,436. Have they altered the rates?—There is some little change. There is a price laid on the table, but we cannot get it.

19,437. When the people bring in the fish, have they stalls they can occupy?—Yes, if they wish to use them.

19,438. Do you levy a charge for these stalls?—Yes, but they do not take them.

19,439. What is the charge?—Ninepence or 1*s*. for the week.

19,440. How many stalls have you?—Nine or ten or more, but as a rule they will not use them.

19,441. Is that in addition to the charge on fish, on salmon, and that class of fish?—Yes. The only people who occupy them are those dealing in them.

19,442. Supposing they sold a salmon by bulk, and did not weigh it, would the corporation, do you think, be entitled to their charge, or have they ever sought for it?—I never knew it. I will give you some idea of how the thing is done, and you can judge for yourself. All the fish come into the market, and at a certain hour the buyers come. Very little is bought by the general public. It is generally by the people in the trade and they come into

19,443. Is there any rule in the market that all fish coming in be weighed?—There is a rule. It is not printed, but they understand that rule amongst themselves.

19,444. You never heard of its being weighed at other scales than those belonging to the corporation?—None that comes into the market. There is a great deal that does not come into the market; more than four times the amount is sold in private houses.

19,445. Do they expose it elsewhere?—They bring it into the private houses.

19,446. Has the corporation any right to charge in that case?—No.

19,447. If the fish were exposed on the quay or public thoroughfare, would you charge?—Yes, on all public streets there would be a charge.

19,448. What would you charge?—Rough fish would pay the same as I have mentioned to you.

19,449. The butter and egg market is in High street?—Yes.

19,450. Belonging to the corporation?—Yes.

19,451. Are there two butter markets here?—There is one down in the quay. Mr. Newport, the weighmaster, holds it.

19,452. What is exposed in the one belonging to the corporation?—All small rolls.

19,453. Lump butter?—Yes.

19,454. Firkins are never brought there?—No. Nothing but rolls from 1 lb. up to 24 and 25 lbs.

19,455. What charges do the corporation levy?—A penny for each roll.

19,456. Do they take into consideration the quantity?—Up to 10 lbs. it is 1d., and then anything over that 1d. every 10 lbs.

19,457. It comes down to 1d.?—Yes.

19,458. Supposing the quantity was only 1 lb.?—They hardly ever bring such a quantity. They bring 10 lbs. or 20 lbs. in rolls, in a basket.

19,459. Is this charge for weighing?—If they do not weigh they are charged also.

(*The following is a copy of the ticket in use*).

339

WATERFORD BUTTER AND EGG MARKET,

day of 186

Butter and Eggs.

Weighed for

Amount of Fees, s. d.

Purchased by

19,460. If they effect a sale?—Yes.

19,461. If they brought in butter and did not effect a sale, and did not weigh, but exposed it for sale the whole day, would you charge?—Well, yes. When the officer goes his rounds at a certain portion of the day and sees a certain number of rolls in a woman's basket, he charges according to that.

19,462. He examines the quantity?—Yes.

19,463. Then they do not usually weigh them?—Not the small rolls, except there was a doubt, and then they are weighed for nothing.

19,464. How many collectors have you there?—One. The old sergeant we had assists the man who is there.

19,465. Does the collector of the tolls weigh also?—Yes.

19,466. Have you any small scales for the people themselves?—There are two persons who send butter and use the stalls, and they weigh out to the public after bringing a roll, generally 1 lb. or ½ lb. or so.

19,467. Is there any charge?—No charge. If you came into the market to buy, you could weigh it there and be satisfied before you left.

19,468. The charge you make is a standing charge for the use of the stall?—There is accommodation to vend their goods there, but beatters must weigh for themselves.

19,469. What is the quantity in the smallest roll brought in?—About 6 lbs.

19,470. Supposing they brought in ten 1 lb. rolls, what would you charge?—There would be 1d. charge.

19,471. Is there shelter accommodation in this place?—There are two sheds, one at each side of the market.

19,472. Does that afford sufficient shelter accommodation for the people and the butter?—At present it does. The fish was at one side until this year, but now we are pretty fairly off.

19,473. It affords sufficient accommodation?—It does.

19,474. No complaints are made of insufficiency?—Previous to this year there were.

19,475. No roll butter goes to Mr. Newport's market?—No.

19,476. All firkins?—Yes.

19,477. Supposing roll butter came there?—I never knew it in my experience.

19,478. When was the butter market established?—I am nearly 30 years an officer of the corporation, and it belongs to the corporation during that time.

19,479. Did Mr. Howard, the town clerk, give you an account of the receipts from the several markets?—Yes.

19,480. The vegetable market is on the public thoroughfare?—Yes.

19,481. Do you receive any tolls there?—No tolls at all of any description.

19,482. What is the charge in the fruit market in John Street?—We are not able to attend to that for the last few years as my staff got short. The charge was 2d. a load when they did business.

19,483. That was a standing charge?—Yes.

19,484. You do not collect it now?—No. We used to place an officer on Wednesdays and Saturdays to take care of them and look after them, but two men were put to sanitary duties, and I am short in my staff.

19,485. Have you any charges in the new milk market?—No.

19,486. Can you give me the receipts from each of these markets?—Yes. The receipts for one year ending the 31st August 1867 for the butter market were, [illegible]*l.* [illegible]*s.* [illegible]*d.*; for the potato market, [illegible]*l.* [illegible]*s.* [illegible]*d.*; fish market, [illegible]*l.* [illegible]*s.* [illegible]*d.*; hay and straw market, [illegible]*l.* [illegible]*s.* [illegible]*d.* [*The following is the statement subsequently handed in by witness*.]

Borough of Waterford.

An Abstract of the Account of the Borough Revenue, Receipts, and Expenditure, for one Year, from the 31st day of August 1866, to the 31st day of August 1867 (made out as required by the 139th section of the Municipal Act.

Patrick Kent, Borough Treasurer.

The Charge.

Rentals:

Arrears on 1st Sept. 1866 [illegible]

Rents paid within the period of this account [illegible]

Abatements allowed to tenants [illegible]

Arrears on 1st Sept. 1867 [illegible]

Tithe Rentcharges. [illegible]

Casual and Weekly Rents: [illegible]

Pecuniary Sources of Income: [illegible]

Casual Sources of Income: [illegible]

Balance:

Balance due by Corporation, 1st September 1867 [illegible]

Total charge [illegible]

The Discharge.

Balance:

Balance due to Corporation, 1st September 1866 [illegible]

Salaries:

Payments to general officers [illegible]

Law and Parliamentary Expenses:

Law expenses of every kind [illegible]

Municipal Expenses:

Expenses contingent on election of members of Corporation [illegible]

Head Rents and Taxes: [illegible]

Other Expenses: [illegible]

Payments of Borough Fund Debt: [illegible]

Application of Receipts: [illegible]

Public Health Act expenses [illegible]

Total Discharge [illegible]

19,447. The officials engaged in connection with the markets have other duties to perform?—They have. At present the three men who have charge of the potato market and fish market have all the city of Waterford to look after, and the public obstruction to look after, under the bye-laws of the corporation.

19,448. What is the total expense of looking after the markets?—The working expense is [illegible] a year. That might be repairs, &c., for the year.

19,449. Would they amount to so much as that?—They may that particular year.

19,450. I see in the statement of the accounts that the expenditure was only 6l. 12s. 1d. for repairs and outlay in 1866. What were the receipts that year?—The butter market, [illegible] 0s. 9d.; potato market, 40l. 17s. 7d.; fish market, 63l. 1s. 2d.; hay and straw market, 71l. 9s. 6d.; fruit market, [illegible] 6s. 7d.

19,451. What were the receipts in 1865?—From the butter market, [illegible] 10s. 2d.; potato market, [illegible] 1s. 4d.; fish market, 63l. 18s. 7d.; hay and straw market, 57l. 7s. 4d.; and fruit, on market days, 1l. 4s. 6d. They were coming on the new fish market then.

19,492. Did they purchase the site of that?—I am not able to say.

19,493. There is another market in Waterford besides that which belongs to the corporation?—Yes.

19,494. To whom does that belong?—At present it is in the hands of Mr. Newport.

19,495. Who is the owner?—The corporation is the lessee of the market, but he holds an appointment from the old corporation as weigh-master, and he holds during his life time.

19,496. Is that Mr. Charles Newport?—Yes. He is away in Belgium.

19,497. He was originally appointed?—Yes.

19,498. You do not remember the appointment?—No. I heard as long as I could remember that he was appointed by the old corporation.

19,499. Whatever benefits or profits are derived by the corporation go to their own use?—Yes.

19,500. Does Mr. Newport pay the corporation anything?—He pays some rent for the use of the market.

19,501. That is for the building?—As far as I remember it must be for that purpose. At his death it will fall into the corporation.

19,502. Did the corporation ever consider it advisable or desirable to purchase his right?—It has been talked of many a day. The merchants who come there are of opinion it should be in the hands of a public body.

19,503. Is there sufficient accommodation in that market for all the articles brought here?—Yes.

19,504. Are they ever exposed on the public thoroughfare?—I never saw them there.

19,505. On what days is this butter market held?—Wednesdays, Thursdays, and Saturday. They may be in any other day, but these are the principal days. In fact, Wednesdays and Saturdays are the principal days, although I gave three days.

19,506. What charge does he levy?—I could not exactly say. I have heard a [illegible], but I would rather have that come from Mr. Vale.

19,507. What fairs are held here?—There is one the first Monday of every month.

19,508. Where are they held?—On the hill of Ballybricken.

19,509. Is that on the other side of the river?—No, it is on the top of the city. Then there are three large fairs, the 4th May, 24th June, and 25th October.

19,510. Are these for any special animals?—They are for cattle, horses, and everything else, and pigs.

19,511. When were the monthly fairs established?—I think they are not long established. I remember a time when there were only three fairs—the three I have mentioned—and then, for the convenience of the farmers, they started the monthly fairs, but I could not exactly give the date.

19,512. How far does your memory extend?—It goes a long way back, nearly 50 years.

19,513. And these fairs have been established within that period?—They have been established within the 50 years.

19,514. Are tolls levied at the fairs?—They are not; they are free of tolls.

19,515. To whom does this hill of Ballybricken belong?—To the corporate body of Waterford.

19,516. Is that place convenient to the town?—There could not be a better place for a fair than what it is.

19,517. Does it afford sufficient space?—It is a tremendous large space, and there is easy access to it.

19,518. Is it walled in?—No.

19,519. How is it utilized before the fairs?—The Wednesday pig market is held there.

19,520. On every Wednesday?—Yes.

19,521. Are tolls levied at the pig market?—No; there are no tolls levied, only what I mentioned.

19,522. Between the pig markets and the ordinary monthly fairs, how is this utilized?—It is a waste there. It is a common open to the public like any other.

19,523. Are there any buildings on it?—No; it is a regular square.

19,524. Have the corporation any cranes or weighbridges?—They have not. The only weighbridge outside these own markets is the one weighing hay and straw, and that is in Mr. Newport's possession.

19,525. Does Mr. Newport pay any rent for that as well as the hay and straw market?—I could not tell you. I know he has the place itself, and that is appertaining to it.

19,526. The only two markets belonging to Mr. Newport are the butter market and the hay and straw market?—He has what is commonly called the butter market, and the weighbridge for commodities, such as hay, straw, and turnips.

19,527. Was that weighbridge erected by the corporation?—I could not tell you. It is there as long as I can tell you. I take it for granted it belonged to the old corporation, but I would not like to say it.

19,528. You do not know what the 2*d.* per load was given for by Mr. Newport to the corporation?—The country people in taking their places used to be wrangling and quarrelling on the public thoroughfare, and it was decided I should send a man, by permission of the mayor and corporation, during that time, and they were to get 2*d.* a load for that man's services.

19,529. Is it for keeping order?—Yes, and sending an official there.

19,530. Have you any charges at all in the pig market in Ballybricken?—None.

19,531. No pens?—None.

19,532. Is there any storage accommodation for cattle or pigs?—There may be some private places, yards, for which they charge, but we have nothing to do with it.

19,533. What descriptions of animals are brought to the fair green?—Horned cattle, pigs, horses, asses, and all sorts of animals; sheep, and everything in the way of cattle.

19,534. Are the fairs well attended?—They are fairly, and they have a horse fair.

19,535. Are different portions of this fair green allotted off for each different species of animals?—They are, by regular agreement amongst themselves; cattle go to one place, and pigs to another.

19,536. Is this fair green kept in repair by the corporation?—Yes, all streets are kept in repair.

19,537. You did not estimate the expense of repairing the fair green?—No. It is done by another gentleman, the borough surveyor.

19,538. Has this hay and straw market been always held here on the same site?—Yes. I give you 30 years' experience.

19,539. Previous to the erection of the fish market, the other fish market was always held?—Yes; it was at one time in Barr Street, and was then shifted to High Street, where it was found unpleasant to have the fish and butter together, and the new fish market was opened.

19,540. Was it ever represented to the corporation the necessity for getting proper market accommodation and sufficient buildings for the general market, and remove them from the streets?—It was, and they went to very heavy expense in having property valued, in order to purchase property and make the market.

19,541. What was the result of those inquiries?—The result was that the expense was high for making them. An architect came down from Dublin, and the project fell through. Whether they could get the money or not I do not know.

19,542. Do not some of the commodities depreciate in value by exposure on the streets?—There is no doubt they do. There is one unfortunate Square market—which is the principal vegetable market, and there is a good deal of offal meat for the poor, and I have it always in my mind whether I will have to cease it and have it destroyed from having it exposed.

19,543. You state, from your own experience, that a necessity exists for the erection of such a market?—Certainly.

19,544. Have the people frequently complained of it?—Certainly. It encourages the unfortunate people to go to drink. For the protection of the perishable commodities and the public health, if I had my way, I would concentrate all the markets in one place.

19,545. Is that the opinion of the corporation?—It is the feeling. It was often spoken of, and fell through. For mayors, Mr. Blake, in his time, and Alderman Keys, during his mayoralty, tried to have the markets erected.

19,546. Is the accommodation sufficient in the pig market?—It is; it is a very large place.

19,547. If the drovers or sellers bring their pigs and different animals overnight, must they seek for storage elsewhere at some neighbouring farmers?—Certainly.

19,548. Was the necessity for providing storage accommodation ever brought before the corporation?—To my knowledge, no.

19,549–50. In weighing potatoes, what is the lowest weight they weigh with?—A pound.

19,551. Do you always weigh down to a pound?—Yes.

19,552. When weighing, do you give a cast of the beam?—Certainly, a beam turn.

19,553. There is must be a pound or nothing?—Yes.

19,554. And that is in addition to the same turn?—Yes.

19,555. Does corn ever come in?—It does.

19,556. Where does it come to?—To the merchants' stores.

19,557. There is no market for that commodity?—No.

19,558. No tolls or charges are levied for weighing or otherwise?—No.

19,559. Do the private merchants levy any weighing charges?—No, I never heard it. They merely weigh for their own convenience and the public convenience.

19,560. You say there is no charge on eggs?—There is.

19,561. What is the charge?—A penny per basket. On a small one we would only charge a halfpenny.

19,562. But 1d. is the maximum?—It is for six or eight dozen of eggs.

19,563. If they brought them in a hamper, what would you charge?—Very seldom they bring them in that way. They are supplied to the market by farmers' wives, who bring four or five dozen of eggs and old shapes.

19,564. I take it, all the markets, with the the exception of the potato and fish market, are retail markets?—Yes; but the public buy large quantities of potatoes, and the dealers besides weigh sacks of potatoes. For instance, if I want a sack, or anybody else, we can go down and get it.

19,565. In the dockets you give denoting the weight of the butter, do you always put down the name of the seller?—Yes.

19,566. Do you take down the weight?—Yes.

19,567. You also put down the amount of your charge?—Yes.

19,568. Do you put down who bought the commodity?—Well, I believe sometimes they do.

19,569. Are potatoes sold before being actually weighed?—They are, as a rule. A man buys a lump of potatoes or four or five bags. Then the name of the seller is put down, and the amount and weight in the block. It is then made up in pounds, shillings, and pence. The people get that accommodation, although they are not bound exactly to do so, but for the public benefit the officers do so.

19,570. You put down the same things in the ticket for fish?—Yes.

19,571–2. And for butter the same?—Yes.

19,573. In weighing this lump butter and the other different commodities, do you ever, or do the men ever, ascertain what the actual contract price has been, that is, the contract price between the buyer and seller?—Certainly, as a rule.

19,574. If a return was required from the corporation of the current price of the different commodities on each market day, could a sufficiently accurate return be given?—Not in the blocks. The weighmaster is only bound to give the actual weight, a copy of which is in his block, but for the public benefit the price is entered. He marks it up, and gives a copy of the block made up with the full market price.

19,575. It is possible to keep it?—Certainly.

19,576. And a pretty accurate return could be given?—Yes, certainly; it could be done without the slightest trouble in the world.

JOSEPH HOWARD, Esq., Solicitor, Town Clerk, examined.

19,577. You are the town clerk of Waterford?—Yes.

19,578. Mr. Mahoney, your high constable, has mentioned the different markets immediately under the control of the corporation, with the exception of the second butter market on the quay, and the hay and straw market under the control at present of Mr. Newport?—Yes.

19,579. Was he appointed under the Act of George as butter weighmaster by the corporation?—As well as I understand, he holds these appointments. He was appointed by the then mayor; he was appointed by the mayor and aldermen, and by the mayor, aldermen, and council, because there was great doubt as to who had the appointment. It was supposed the mayor had it.

19,580. Does he pay anything to the corporation?—Yes, 60l. a year.

19,581. For the building alone?—Yes.

19,582. Does that include weighing appliances, or were they supplied by the corporation or himself?—I could not tell that.

19,583. It is the corporation erected the building?—It is corporate property.

19,584. You could not tell what capital was expended on the building?—No; it was built a hundred years ago.

19,585. Have you any means of finding it out?—There is no record of that.

19,586. What would be your approximate idea of the structural value of the building?—I suppose the erection of a building like that at present would cost from 1,000l. to 1,200l.

19,587. The hay and straw market is held on the public thoroughfare?—Yes.

19,588. Mr. Newport levies tolls from these; how is that?—He has a weighmaster as well as a butter taster.

19,589. Has he an overall there?—Yes.

19,590. Is that included in the rent of the building?—I could not tell whether that is our property or not.

19,591. Does he claim it?—I cannot say. The man has been out of the country for the last 20 years, in Belgium.

19,592. Is it 3d. a load he charges there?—I could not tell.

19,593. You receive 2d. per load?—We receive so much from each load.

19,594. Mr. Mahoney, the high constable, stated it was 2d. for every load?—I have no cognisance at all of these markets. They do not come into my department.

19,595. Have the corporation ever contemplated the erection of a general market in order to remove the markets off the streets?—They have.

19,596. Do they deem that a necessity exists for that?—Yes; and we had projects, and plans, and architects employed, and wasted a good deal of money in attempts to establish a market, but nothing came of them. The money could not be got.

19,597. Was it the expense prevented the building of them?—Yes.

19,598. On the decease of Mr. Newport, the butter market will revert to the corporation?—Yes.

19,599. As far as you know, in case of such a contingency, do the corporation intend to retain it themselves, and work it?—They intend to retain it themselves for a year or for a number of years. The mayor when elected used to be required to give a pledge, in case of a vacancy in the butter market, he would not appoint himself.

19,600. Have you got a committee of the corporation to look after the markets?—No; there is no actual committee for markets. If there is any report about the markets, it goes to the finance committee.

19,601. Still the corporation are of opinion that a necessity exists for the erection of another general market to remove the sale of commodities off the public thoroughfares?—Yes.

19,602. Have representations been made by those frequenting the markets and the public in general?—It is the public opinion that we have very bad market accommodation in Waterford.

19,603. Did the corporation ever consider the desirability of negotiating in any way for the bridge [illegible] the river?—It has been a constant subject of discussion at the corporation, and they actually had it before Parliament to try and obtain power to buy it, and the matter fell through. I was the solicitor concerned for the Bill in 1876.

19,604. What was the cause of its falling through?—We could not work it; we found we could not work it. It is a wooden bridge, and would have to be taken away, and a new bridge erected. The proprietors wanted 60,000*l.* for their interest in the bridge, and it would cost 40,000*l.* to build another bridge—a stone bridge.

19,605. They wanted 60,000*l.* for their rights alone?—Yes.

19,606. Do not the general public complain of that?—Yes.

19,607. I believe there are only three of those bridges in Ireland?—Yes. I believe this is one of the last of them.

19,608. Apart from the 40*l.* a year, the corporation do not derive any benefit from that butter market in Mr. Newport's possession?—No.

19,609. Has he to pay rates and taxes?—Yes.

19,610. Do you allow him the ordinary deductions?—I presume so, just like any ordinary tenant.

19,611. Whatever profits he derives from it goes to his own use?—Yes.

19,612. Although he derives a profit from the hay market, does he contribute anything towards the expense of cleaning the streets?—No, the corporation bears the entire cost of the borough fund.

19,613. Did the shopkeepers and inhabitants in the immediate vicinity of the markets ever make any representation to have them removed?—No.

19,614. The corporation thought themselves it would be for the public good to have them removed?—Yes. It was public opinion that they should have improved markets here in Waterford.

19,615. Do you think, from your experience, that the control of the markets generally should be vested in the local authorities, such as the corporation you have here?—Yes, decidedly.

19,616. You have formed that opinion yourself?—Yes. They are the proper parties, and not private individuals.

19,617. And if tolls are to be levied, that proper shelter accommodation, and facilities for weighing, should be given?—Certainly; and it is more likely to have proper accommodation provided by the corporation than by a private individual, who will try to have everything for his own pocket.

19,618. It was never considered desirable to levy any toll?—No. The matter has been mooted, but public opinion is too strong against it. We should have a toll levied on all cattle, but the project fell through.

19,619. Practically, the farmers who live at the other side of the river must pay a toll coming in, when crossing the bridge?—Yes; but they pay nothing for the use of the green, nor do they contribute anything towards the maintenance of the streets, which are very much injured by cattle, constantly, and the heavy traffic.

19,620. Do you think the fact of no toll being levied on that fair green induces people to attend it, or do you think the levying of a toll acts as a deterrent on farmers in bringing in their stock?—I do not think it would, if they have a good market. They would not mind paying 1*d.* for a pig if it is a good market, or 3*d.* or 4*d.* for a cow.

19,621. Do you know what are the consolidated town rates?—We have no such thing. We have only one water rate.

19,622. You have no improvement rate?—No. We have a large income from property.

19,623. What is the water rate?—Two shillings and sixpence in the pound. That is the only rate we have. We have no other taxes.

19,624. Your revenue from your property is able to meet all the expenses?—Yes.

[*The following witness was examined at his office in the butter market, as he was instructed not to attend the public inquiry.*]

Mr. JOHN VALE examined.

19,625. You are managing the butter market for Mr. Charles Newport, who is the weigh-master of the city since 1842, and appointed by the corporation?—Yes.

19,626. He is lessee of the building?—He pays 75*l.* a year rent.

19,627. It was mentioned to-day that he only pays 40*l.* Was that the total?—He pays 75*l.* a year to the corporation, and all taxes and wages.

19,628. He only pays that for the building?—Yes.

19,629. Is he allowed the ordinary deductions in the poor rate?—He is allowed half the poor rate. He pays income tax.

19,630. What is your charge on each firkin?—Threepence.

19,631. You have coopers employed?—We have; and 9 and 10 men in summer.

19,632. Are those coopers?—There are two men for opening the butter, and taking the milk out of it. There is another man to put the firkins into the scale, two for arranging it about the house, and three individuals and myself for weighing it.

19,633. Do they deal the butter?—They do, of course.

19,634. Do they strip the firkins?—No. There is a new rule, which was adopted in 1866, that all butters be weighed before being bought. The old system was to go and arrange it about the house, and then the merchants went about the house. That was not half as expeditious as the present system of weighing all the butter first. I commence weighing before nine, and I have that house half full at nine o'clock.

19,635. When you ascertain the weight, do you give a ticket denoting the weight?—Yes. This is the book.

19,636. Could you give me a blank one?—Yes. We keep a duplicate of that. Suppose I count when the weight is given outside, the ticket is taken across the desk, and handed out to the countryman. [*The following is a copy of the ticket in use.*]

WATERFORD BUTTER MARKET.

day of 18 .

19,637. On this ticket what do you put?—The name of the seller. The gross weight on this ticket (produced) is, say, 2 qrs. 14 lbs., the tare is 10 lbs., and what corresponds to that is put on the ticket. The seller then is paid for 2 qrs. 4 lbs.

19,638. The tare seems to vary?—Yes.

19,639. You do not strip the butter?—If I was called on I would, or if there was a doubtful firkin, I would have a man for the purpose of stripping it, so as to alter the tare.

19,640. How do you know whether the tare would be 9, 10, or 11 lbs.?—Since the rule made by the merchants in 1864, the firkins have to be branded by the cooper.

19,641. The cooper who makes the firkin brands the tare on it?—Yes. If that is found wrong, if I have a suspicion, or the merchant who buys has a suspicion, it has to stop there until I have time to get a man to strip that, and sometimes it may run two or three lbs. over the tare marked on the firkin.

19,642. Beyond the tare branded on the firkin?—Yes. In ordinary cases, supposing the firkin was branded nine, I call to the man 10, for soakage.

19,643. Do you always allow one lb.?—Yes. Then when I call out the weight, say, 2 qrs. 10 lbs., he puts that in the book, and gives a ticket accordingly.

19,644. In addition to the [illegible] weight branded on the firkin, a lb. is allowed for soakage?—That is the usual [illegible]. Supposing they come from 2 qrs. 12 lbs. t

8 qrs. or over, 7 lbs. are allowed on those heavy casks, along with the branded tare.

19,645. These are the only deductions from the firkin?—Yes, and they dare not alter them.

19,646. It is in return for the ticket they pay the 3d.?—Yes.

19,647. No matter whether they subsequently sell the firkin or not?—The butter is all sold. According as the butter is weighed, I tell my man to put the butter out of the scale. The taster is ready, and he has nothing to do but go to the window, and the ticket is handed out, and they sell their firkins. When they sell the firkin to the merchant, I take that ticket from him, and when they are ready to pay, I go to that man's office, and he pays me, because the ticket is in his office.

19,648. The weight is never denoted on the firkin in chalk?—It is on everyone I weigh.

19,649. So that they have the weight denoted on the firkin as well as the ticket?—Yes. The gross weight I put on the ticket and the tare.

19,650. On an average, what number of firkins come into the market in the year, or could you give me any approximate idea. Would you say it is a good butter market?—It is a good butter market. It is one of the principal butter markets.

19,651. It is better than Tipperary?—I think more butter comes here. There are three market days here.

19,652. You have Wednesday, Thursday, and Saturday?—Yes. We used to have a Monday's market, but the merchants did not think it worth while to be losing time, though they should come, even if they did not want any butter, for fear some man might get a cheaper market than others. They dispensed with that until the monthly fair day, who would have some stock to sell, or other business to do, the same day, and would have some butter to dispose of.

19,653. How many firkins, do you think, would come in a week during the season?—I know that; but a servant must be a servant, and if I had permission I would willingly tell you.

19,654. I only want to get the number so as to form an idea of the magnitude of the market?—Some thousands, I may tell you that.

19,655. They vary in different years?—Yes. In the summer of 1886 it was a good summer, but in 1887 the summer was very dry, and there was no grass, and of course there was a great falling off in the make of butter. We had some thousands short.

19,656. You say you begin to weigh butter at nine o'clock?—If I had butter at eight o'clock I would weigh it. I am there at half past eight o'clock myself.

19,657. What time do the buyers commence to buy?—There is no buying before 11 o'clock. I ring the bell then and say, "Eleven o'clock, gentlemen, buy away." I may wait for a few minutes, as a great deal of butter comes from the Tipperary and Carrick directions, and there may be three or four loads brought, and I do not ring the bell until a few minutes past 11, but generally at 11 I ring.

19,658. Do you weigh up to 11 o'clock?—Yes. There may be six or seven hundred firkins, and I would have them weighed at that hour.

19,659. Have the buyers different portions allotted off in the building?—They may buy in different portions, but the men put them altogether in one space in the house.

19,660. Is the space here sufficient to expose all the butter brought in?—Yes; and I could arrange 1,700 firkins, and have a space between them for men to walk and see butter and buy.

19,661. Have you any tasters?—No, because they have been dispensed with some years. The farmers objected, and one reason was that the weight and quality was called out publicly to the man taking the weight. The quality was entered and kept in the book, and when the people would go home they would say, so-and-so was cut to-day, and I was not cut at all; that is, if a man had three firkins, two being seconds, and one first quality. That was principally the reason the taster was dispensed with. Of course Mr. Newport was not going to pay for a taster when they did not want him; but he is ready and willing to have a taster.

19,662. The buyers now rely on their experience to judge the quality of the butter?—The buyers exercise their own judgment in buying.

19,663. On the whole do you think it works very well?—Yes. So far I have heard no complaints of the new rule. It has turned out most satisfactory for the farmers.

19,664. Would you say a great percentage of the butter brought in here is sold?—Every firkin is sold. I have often seen 600 brought in on a day, and they would not stand 15 minutes if the buyers wanted the butter badly.

19,665. Did it ever happen that some of the firkins were unsold?—That might happen if a person had bad butter, and was looking for an exorbitant price, or a farmer might be looking for too much, and of course a man is not going to pay 21s. for a £.

19,666. Have you storage accommodation if required?—Yes. They can leave it in the house at night at their own risk. The custom was to pay a man to watch it, because we close the place at five o'clock. The office hours, according to law, are from the 29th September to the 25th March, from eight o'clock in the morning until four in the afternoon; and from the 25th March to the 29th September, from six in the morning to six in the evening.

19,667. For that storage do you charge anything. Well, no. That used to be the thing long ago; but if a man had 20 firkins he could not sell, he would leave them there and pay a man belonging to the place for looking after them; but I charge nothing at all, I only oblige him.

19,668. Do frauds be committed in the preparation of the butter, or making it up, to any great extent?—Not to any extent; but it is sometimes found that firkins may be what are called "bosses;" that is, bad butter put by the side; that very seldom occurs.

19,669. Have you ever instituted prosecutions for that?—I have not.

19,670. Supposing prosecutions were deemed necessary, would it be in Mr. Newport's name a man would be prosecuted?—I am not aware of that; but I think if I bought it and found it wrong I would think it my duty to prosecute the man.

19,671. In your experience you have not prosecuted on behalf of Mr. Newport?—No.

19,672. I suppose instances of that kind are very rare in the market?—They are rare. I would not say there would be one in the year. I do not know when there was one like it. There may be some parties buying rolls and packing the butter like that, but I think it is not done at all now.

19,673. So far as your experience extends, you never heard any complaints that the market did not afford sufficient ventilation, or anything like that?—I never did, because, as I told you awhile ago, all parties are well satisfied with the mode they are dealt with now. Previous to this rule being made in 1886, they were at the mercy of the merchants in the town, and I often heard it said by the farmers they used to put on too much tare.

19,674. That is by the merchants?—Yes. I remember the time when it was 16 pounds the standard tare by the Act of Parliament. Well, the farmers themselves, in a great measure, are the cause of heavy tares being put on, because if 17 pounds was put on one day, they would give [illegible] to their company, and say, "Well, I lost a couple "of pounds of butter the other day. Have that much "timber in this firkin, and have the timber heavy." The buyer, on the next occasion, bought and paid according to the last day, and allowed the same tare; but, on stripping that butter shipping it to the other side, because they used to mark the tare, he found he did himself an injustice of two pounds. The next day again the buyer would put on that couple of pounds, and on that account excessive tares were put on. But all that unsatisfactory way of doing business is dispensed with under the new system, and merchants and farmers are well pleased, because the moment they sell their firkins they know what they are to get, and there are no deductions, or anything else.

19,675. All butter brought in must be weighed?—It must be weighed before being bought.

19,676. Is that one of the new rules?—That is one of the new rules, and it is carried out strictly.

19,677. Supposing firkins were brought into the town and sold to a [illegible] without going to the market, would you look for your charge?—I used to look after that, because Mr. Newport is entitled to it by Act of Parliament, if the butter comes into the town.

19,678. I suppose cases like that are very rare?—There might be an odd one come into the town, and be sold before going to the market, but we would know nothing about it.

19,679. If you knew it would you ask for your charge?—If I knew it I would look after it. Butter brought into the town after being brought in [illegible], we used to get [illegible], but do not get it at [illegible]. Mr. [illegible], a large butter merchant, took butter into his store, and there was some litigation between Mr. Newport and himself, and result was that every Saturday evening I took down the number of firkins for each day, and got 2d. a firkin for each.

19,680. Do you ever hear what is the current price between the buyers and sellers of the butter, and what they pay for the different class of butter?—I do.

19,681. Do you ever keep a record of it?—I do. I know the firkins each merchant buys from year to year, and I mark the prices. I have the number of firkins in a book, and the average price. The average price last Saturday was from 10[illegible]s. to 11[illegible]s. per hundredweight.

19,682. I suppose you supply the press with it?—Yes.

19,683. And these are, so far as you know, the accurate current prices, to the best of your knowledge?—I have no interest in them but to give them for the information of the public. I give also the price of hay and straw, and of those things that come to the market. Of course I have the satisfaction that I give the accurate prices for the information of the public.

19,684. Was it Mr. Newport erected the scale?—Yes.

19,685. On that you weigh loads of hay and straw?—Yes.

19,686. What is the charge for weighing a load?—Sixpence a load to Mr. Newport. There is 6d. a load charged since 1874. Twopence of that goes to the Corporation of Waterford for us to have one of their constables there to keep order, and to see that old women and boys are not going and pillaging from the load.

19,687. That 6d. is for weighing?—Yes; for weighing straw, hay, turnips, and mangolds.

19,688. Anything that comes in cartloads?—Yes.

(The following is a copy of the ticket in use at the weighbridge):—

WATERFORD WEIGHBRIDGE,

day of 188[illegible].

Gross Weight ... ...

Tare ... ...

19,689. Do parties ever buy hay and straw by the bulk?—That occurs very seldom.

19,690. Supposing a case like that took place, would you ask for your charge?—Yes. Whether a man sells by bulk or not he is supposed to pay after weighing the load.

19,691. Do you always ascertain the tare of the cart?—A man weighs the load gross in the first instance. Then he pulls out the cart, unyokes it in the street and sells to A, B, or C. Then he goes and delivers it and comes back again to tare the car and get his ticket.

19,692. Supposing they go and deliver it without weighing it?—They do not do that.

19,693. Supposing they did that, would you ask for your charge?—If I saw a man doing it, I would not allow him to go away without weighing it.

19,694. Supposing a donkey load of turnips were brought in, what would be the charge?—It is entered on the book, and counts as a load against me and I am accountable to Mr. Newport for that.

19,695. No matter what the load is?—Yes.

19,696. No matter what the load is or what commodity it is, the charge is 6d.?—Yes; no matter what commodity is weighed.

19,697. As regards what the corporation get, you make a return of the number of loads and give them 2d. each?—I settle with the borough treasurer every month.

19,698. I suppose you keep the current prices of the hay and straw?—Yes.

19,699. Did you ever hear of any frauds being committed in the weights of the cart after the load had been delivered?—Yes. I detected them weighing a heavier one and bringing in a light one first.

19,700. I suppose these are rare occurrences now?—It is over [illegible] years ago, and I did not know any case since and I did not remember one before. I am here [illegible] years the 1st last May, and during that time there was only one case.

19,701. Is the sale of hay confined to this place?—Yes.

19,702. Would they be permitted to sell in any other part of the town?—We have the only weighbridge in the town.

19,703. When was it erected?—It is a good many years ago.

19,704. Is there any weighbridge in the town capable of weighing cattle?—We weigh cattle on that.

19,705. You have got no railings around it?—No. Supposing there was a fat cow or bullock to be weighed, a man holds the animal by the head, and once on the weighbridge it does not take a second to ascertain the weight.

19,706. Do they weigh cattle here?—Very seldom. If a man wanted the weight for his own information, I would weigh a beast and take off, I believe, a third for parts; but that very seldom occurs.

19,707. What do you charge?—The charge is 6d.; but if there is a neighbour there, Mr. Newport will not charge. It is only for the sake of uniformity he struck the charge at 6d. per load. He is entitled by Act of Parliament to charge a halfpenny per hundredweight.

19,708. Practically for everything weighed on the weighbridge, whether for beast or load, you charge 6d.?—Yes. Twopence goes to the Corporation and 4d. to Mr. Newport. Fourpence was always charged by Mr. Newport until the arrangement was made with the mayor and Mr. William Cameron, town clerk. I made the arrangement on the part of Mr. Newport, and I knew he would be perfectly satisfied, for I remember his offering to pay half the constable's salary, and now we have had a constable for nothing by putting on 2d. extra on each load. I was told since Mr. Newport would be pleased, and he said I was perfectly right in what I did.

19,709. What would be the average cost of maintaining the butter market, including wages, and everything else?—Over 300l., including rent, wages, and taxes. Of course, there is no allowance for the [illegible] of what I tell you.

19,710. I would not like to ask the average profit?—That would be a breach of trust. As I said, I was prepared to answer the questions, but I was directed by what the solicitor would tell me, and that was to be silent.

19,711. Have you got copies of the rules and regulations?—Yes.

The witness produced a notice exposed in the butter market, of which the following is a copy:—

NOTICE TO FARMERS.

BUTTER MARKET REGULATIONS.

All butter coming to the Waterford market must be weighed before being bought.

The name of the cooper and the weight of the empty cask must be branded on the side of each cask.

Farmers to allow two pounds for large size casks and one pound for small size casks, and in case the cask is found weighing more than the branded weight the owner will be charged double.

M 3

The market officials must write the names of the owners on the side of each cask before weighing.

The tare to be allowed to the buyer must be marked on the firkins along with the weight.

All butter must be in the market early in order to be weighed before being bought.

Buying not to commence until 11 o'clock.

Farmers must take their firkins immediately on the butter being weighed.

By Order,
[illegible],
Deputy Weighmaster.

WATERFORD BRIDGE, on the river Suir.

CHARLES AW[illegible], Esq., LL.D., examined.

19,712. You are the secretary to the bridge commissioners?—Yes.

19,713–14. What is their distinctive title?—The Waterford Bridge Commissioners.

19,715. Have they all the rights to the bridge and the ferries attached to it?—Yes.

19,716. All communications from one side of Waterford to other?—Yes.

19,717. How did they acquire that right?—By grant from Charles the Second.

19,718. How do these commissioners hold. Are they a limited liability company?—A corporation under seal.

19,719. Have they any rules regulating the composition of the body?—The only rules they have are by our Act of Parliament.

19,720. What Act?—The [illegible] of George the Third. It is called the Waterford Bridge Commissioners Act. I can get it for you.

19,721. Supposing one of the commissioners does not desire to continue as such, or dies, I suppose there are the ordinary provisions in it for re-election?—The Act of Parliament arranges that the Bishop of Waterford and other dignitaries in Waterford shall become a corporation for the purpose of erecting a bridge over the river Suir and purchasing the river rights which belonged to an old family named [illegible], and they purchased these rights, and the mayor and several citizens became a corporation, and 21 or more of them do every act which is necessary to be done, for instance, in letting the tolls, or anything like that.

19,722. Is that 21 of the shareholders?—Twenty-one or more of the shareholders. Practically you can call them shareholders, but really there are no shares. The capital is divided into certain parts, and there are 21 votes.

19,723. What is the capital?—There are 300 shareholders.

19,724. What is the amount of each share?—It is sold for £70, but it is £10 now.

19,725. Is that at premium?—I cannot tell you that, because the thing was divided originally.

19,726. What was the original capital?—It was authorised to be issued at 50, and it is now the 50 as well as the £10, but I do not know it was sold at 50. I believe it was sold at 60.

19,727. What was the total capital expended in erecting the bridge?—I do not know that. I have no record of that, but I think it was something like 60,000l.

19,728. Have the corporation of Waterford any rights at all in that, or have they claimed any rights to the bridge as a corporation?—Never.

19,729. Did they ever contemplate, as far as your memory extends or experience go, purchasing from the the shareholders?—Under the grand jury laws, the grand juries of the adjoining counties have the power of purchasing if they joined together to purchase, and such a thing has been mooted. The grand of Kilkenny and of the city of Waterford are the two grand juries.

19,730. Is there a special provision in your Act?—No. There is no provision in our Act for purchasing it, but in the recent Grand Jury Act there are powers.

19,731. Are 21 shareholders the quorum?—Yes.

19,732. You have no special committee. Is each shareholder as much a member of the committee as another?—Yes, but for the purpose of carrying on the organisation they appoint, once a year, five of those members to act as a committee for the year, but they do no act.

19,733. But when sending out notices for any special act, such as to accept tenders, do they send them to every shareholder?—To every shareholder.

19,734. The commissioners are not in immediate receipt of the tolls of the bridge or ferries. Have they them sublet?—They can sublet them on a yearly tenancy or for a period not exceeding three years, by the special Act.

19,735. Is that by tender?—Yes, always by tender, but I should say they limit the contractor to half their legal toll. They do not allow him the full toll.

19,736. In the Act is there a schedule of the tolls to be levied mentioned?—There is a queer old section which enables certain tolls to be levied. It is not a schedule but sets them out in extenso.

19,737. The tolls mentioned in the Act are not the tolls actually levied?—No, only half.

19,738. When was the last letting made?—Three years ago in December last.

19,739. That will terminate in December next?—Yes.

19,740. Would you have any objection to tell me the amount of the tender?—I do not like to tell you that. We are just close to another one.

19,741. I wanted to see what would be the dividend derived by each shareholder, but you need not mention it if you think it would hurt against you?—I am afraid it would.

19,742. What would be the dividend you usually paid for the last three years?—Six pounds per share for the last five years.

19,743. Is the stock of the Waterford bridge commissioners sold in the exchange?—In one instance I knew a stockbroker in Dublin to have sold it.

19,744. Has every animal and foot-passenger, every horse and cart, to pay a toll passing the bridge?—Yes.

19,745. Are there any exemptions?—Yes, several exemptions by recent and former legislation. All post-office officials on duty, all officers of the army or navy on duty, and all telegraph messengers on duty are exempt.

19,746. Are not the private soldiers?—Yes, anyone on duty. Of course they pass out with a permit from the officer in charge.

19,747. What others besides those mentioned in the statute go free?—There are 13 persons who have to do with the railways on the side of the water, and when those railways came into existence there was an agreement between the railway company and the commissioners which enabled the directors of the railway company and certain of their officers to go free.

19,748. I suppose there was a consideration given for that?—There was a fixed yearly rent.

19,749. I suppose the mails go across, cart and all, free?—Yes.

19,750. Any other?—I know of no others.

19,751. Who are the present lessees?—The executors of Mr. Michael O'Meara.

19,752. Do you know the rates of charges?—I can give them to you.

19,753. Then you have got a copy of the actual charges at present levied?—I do not know what charges at present Mr. O'Meara or his representatives levy, but I know what we have authorised him to charge.

19,754. Could you give me a copy of it?—Yes.

19,755. The corporation, as a body, have never taken any steps to purchase themselves?—I do not know that they have.

19,756. There is no provision in your Act to sell?—No.

19,757. Have complaints been made of the tolls levied?—Yes; tremendous complaints constantly, but no remedy has been proposed by anyone.

19,758. Have you power to restrain the erection of another bridge, supposing the corporation were desirous of erecting one across the river?—Yes, undoubtedly.

19,759. You think you have a vested right in the crossing of the river?—There was a case called Lowry v. the Waterford and Limerick Company, which went to the Court of Appeal a very considerable time ago, but the question there discussed was whether anyone had any right to carry any boats or otherwise cross the river with merchandise, and it was decided that the Bridge Commissioners Act was sufficient to prevent any person doing so. There was a Bill called the Wexford Extension Bill, but the Commissioners contended that they had a right to prevent any bridge being built across the river, and a Select Committee of the House of Commons held that whilst they had a right to prevent any passenger bridge, they had no right to prevent a railway bridge, and directed that no foot passenger should cross the railway bridge which is authorised across the river within our limits.

19,760. In this case of Lowry v. the Waterford and Limerick Railway Company reported?—It is.

19,761. Are there any private boats on the river, or can private boats ply with the members of a family they belong to?—Yes; but no private boats can ply for hire.

19,762. Supposing people have a boat on the river, as I presume they have, cannot they go across to the other side, and remain a number of hours and return?—In Lowry's case, the Waterford and Limerick Company brought across the river certain passengers and goods, and it was held they had no right to do so, although it was not for profit at all. It was an evasion of the toll, and any evasion of the toll is illegal.

The witness then read out the charges exacted at the bridge as follows:—

	s.	d.
For every coach, berlin, chariot, chaise or chair drawn by six horses or other beasts of burden	6	6
For every calash, carriage, chaise or chair drawn by less than six horses	3	3
Drawn by four horses	3	0
For a carriage drawn by four horses or different description of berlin or chariot	2	0
For every carriage drawn by three horses	1	6
For every carriage drawn by two horses or other beasts of burden	0	10
Every waggon with four wheels	0	11
Every waggon with four wheels drawn by less than four horses	0	9
For every carriage with two wheels drawn by more than two horses	0	7½
For every cart drawn by two horses, including the driver	0	6
For every carriage drawn by one horse	0	4
For the like with four wheels, drawn as a cart	0	6
For every sedan chair	0	3½
Every cart with one horse, including the driver	0	2
Every carriage drawn by one horse or other beast of burden, and kishes except with bags (including driver)	0	2
Every sledge	0	1½
For other carriage drawn by any animal whatsoever	0	2
For every horse	0	1½
For every beast of burden	0	1
For every drove of cattle, each	0	1
For every drove of calves, hogs, sheep, or		

19,766. Is it only for the lifting of the span that the commissioners derive a benefit?—It is only by the lifting. They also have a ferry across the river.

19,767. That goes along with the bridge?—Yes.

19,768. How many of these ferry stages have they?—Two stages, one at each side.

19,769. Between the bridge and this ferry, is that the only means of getting across the river?—It is the only means.

19,770. Is not there a drawbridge in the centre of the bridge?—Yes.

19,771. Who derives the benefit from opening that?—No benefit is derived from it. It goes to the contractor.

19,772. Is he entitled to a charge for vessels that pass that way?—There is no toll charged, but there is a charge for opening the weighbridge—compensation for opening a weighbridge.

19,773. What is the amount of the charge?—One shilling per mast.

19,774. Is what you have stated the schedule in the Act?—It is the schedule in the Act reduced by one-half.

19,775. Is the charge on a cart of four wheels drawn by less than four horses 9d.?—That should be, less than four wheels 6d.

19,776. For every cart drawn by one horse, or kishes, except with bags?—That is 6d. It is the general cart, I take it.

19,777. That is a four wheeler?—No.

19,778. What is the charge for one of those large drays drawn by one horse?—I think the charge is 6d., but I am not sure.

19,779. Would the driver be included in that?—Yes; some of these drays are belonging to a gentleman named Murphy, and he contracts with the contractor for everything he brings across, and a great many of his bargains enter into a contract with the railway company, because they draw goods for the railway company.

19,780. There is a railway station at the other side of the river?—Yes.

19,781. What railway is that?—The Waterford and Limerick, and the Waterford and Central Ireland Railway.

19,782. All people who wish to go from the city to the railway have to go to the other side of the bridge?—Yes. There is also another railway—the Kilkenny Junction Railway.

19,783. There is one terminus?—Yes.

19,784. The people from the city must necessarily cross the bridge and pay the charge if they want to go to the railway?—Yes.

19,785. Does the bed of the river belong to the commissioners?—Yes; the bed and soil belongs to several people, to Her Majesty, and the Admiralty. The second mayor of Waterford was the old admiral of the port. It also belongs to the commissioners, and I am not sure but that it belongs to the owner in fee of the property adjoined.

19,786. To whom do the anchorage fees go?—To the Harbour Commissioners.

19,787. Are they a body separate and distinct from the corporation?—Yes, under a separate seal.

19,788. You derive no benefit whatever, or the contractor derives no benefit, from the vessels that come into the river?—No; that is altogether apart from the bridge. The contractor does not derive any benefit, because it costs a great deal more than 1s. a mast to open the drawbridge.

19,789. This bridge was at first erected by public subscription?—It was, and the rights of the Roche family were purchased out by subscription also.

Mr. FORSYTH ARNOTT examined.

19,794. What observations do you wish to make?—I met a man with cattle on the Ferrybank Road, at the other side of the bridge, and I asked him why he was returning from the fair so early in the day. He said he took his cattle as far as the bridge, and had not sufficient money to pay the tolls, and not being acquainted with the charges made, had to return his cattle without selling them.

19,795. Without reaching the fair?—Yes. It was impossible to get across the river except by that bridge.

19,796. How many head of cattle had he?—Between 40 and 50. He had to go from that to New Ross.

19,797. Mr. J. F. O'Meara, solicitor, said:—My mother has the contract for the collection of the tolls at the bridge, and if I knew a man had done that, I would not allow him remain there. Some people go over the bridge without paying every day, when they say they will pay coming back.

19,798. I take it you allow a discretion to the collector?—Certainly.

19,799. Is there any other gentleman who has any observations to make, or evidence to give, before the inquiry closes?—No answer.

The inquiry then concluded.

CITY OF KILKENNY.

WITH reference to my inquiry in Kilkenny on the 7th November 1888, I beg to report as follows:—

Kilkenny is a city and parliamentary borough, and the capital of the county. The

"And whereas the objects aforesaid cannot be effected without the authority of "Parliament. . . ."

The Markets and Fairs Clauses Act, 1847, is incorporated (section 5) with the special Act, in addition to the other Acts incorporated therewith.

Section 8 limits the Act to the municipal boundary of the borough of Kilkenny, and enacts that no other market (except the meat market, until it is purchased by the corporation) shall be held within the parliamentary boundary of the city: Provided that nothing should affect the market for cattle held in the fair green.

Section 14 gives the corporation power to take lands, and to construct and establish thereon a general market for all marketable commodities as aforesaid. Such lands cannot be outside the boundary of the borough (section 21), and they shall not exceed five acres (section 22).

Section 24 gives power to take existing meat market, making compensation for same.

Power is also given to remove the existing markets (section 27) and stalls, &c. from public places (section 28) to new general market when completed, and when opened, no person except a licensed hawker, &c. to sell articles in the streets within the limits of the Act.

Section 31 requires all articles sold or exposed for sale in the new general market to be weighed or measured at the public weighing places provided by the corporation, with a penalty on the seller for refusing to do so of forty shillings for the first offence, and five pounds for every subsequent offence. The weight is to be net after deducting the tare, and there is a penalty not exceeding ten pounds upon the buyer if he demands or takes any additional allowance or weight over and above the net, or any deduction from the true amount of the price according to such net weight.

Power is given to collect the tolls mentioned in Schedules C., D., E., and F. to the Act annexed (section 32–35).

Rents for the storage of articles remaining unsold to be reasonable (section 36). In the case of grain, corn, or butter, no additional storage charge is to be levied.

All butter brought for sale is to be inspected previous to sale subject to a penalty (section 37).

Section 39 provides that all moneys arising from tolls, &c. should be applied:—

First, in defraying the charges and expenses of the corporation preparatory and incident to the passing of the Act:

Secondly, in paying the interest of the moneys to be borrowed under the Act:

Thirdly, in paying the salaries and expenses of the officers appointed for carrying the Act into execution:

Fourthly, in making, providing, regulating, and maintaining the markets and market places belonging to the corporation, and carrying all the purposes of the Act into execution: and

Fifthly, in setting apart the sinking fund required by the Act, and in paying off the principal of the moneys so borrowed as aforesaid; and the residue (if any) should be applied towards the reduction of the tolls authorised to be taken under the Act.

The rents and tolls authorised to be taken by the Act it is enacted shall vest in the corporation as part of their corporate estate and borough fund.

The corporation, according to the provisions of the Act, have provided a general market place at the cost of over 5,000*l.*, which was borrowed in 1862, and paid off in 1882 from the receipts of the markets and some profit derived in the investments they had made of the sinking fund. The site was previously the property of the corporation, so that no actual expenditure was incurred in purchasing it.

The tolls and charges levied are somewhat smaller than those authorised by the Act, as a comparison will show.

In accordance with my instructions, I have inspected the market place and fair green.

The fairs in Kilkenny are held in walled-in enclosures beside the town. There are several spaces—one for each species of animals—horses, cattle, and sheep. Pens are erected in the portion used for the sheep fair, whilst adjacent to the space allotted for horses, a horse paddock is provided with leaps for the exhibition and exercise of the horses brought there to be sold.

The several enclosures seem adequate for the purposes for which they are utilised, and are the best and most suitable I have as yet inspected. A weighbridge capable of weighing cattle has been erected, as before mentioned, in the fair green by the corporation. There is, however, no shelter accommodation provided.

The markets are held in a spacious enclosure convenient to the principal street in the city. There are two iron gate entrances for the different commodities. In the enclosure various sheds are erected for potatoes, corn, vegetables, roll butter, eggs, fowl, &c. They apparently afford ample accommodation and shelter. There are five scales capable of being used if required.

The butter house is close to one of the entrances to the general market, and is within the enclosure. It was formerly used as a store, and is lofty and well ventilated. The house is by custom divided into two portions—there being no structural severance—one of which is set apart for the coopering, weighing, and draining the firkins, and the other for the sale subsequently. None but the officials are allowed within the former area. All the requirements of a comparatively well regulated and proper market are visible, not only in the place itself, but in its management by the corporation.

An "crane" is erected in the market place, and another on the Parade, where the hay, straw, and coal are sold. This "Parade" forms portion of the public thoroughfare, but is a wide space of ground, and the commodities are exposed under some trees which run along one side of the street.

At the fairs the charge is on each animal as they enter the fair green, and if the horse paddock, with the leaps, &c., is required, an additional charge of sixpence per animal is levied. A complaint was made of a system of forestalling the horse fair.

At the butter market on Friday the charge is twopence per firkin before 10 o'clock, and threepence afterwards.

A deduction of 1 lb. and 2 lb., according to the weight of the firkin of butter, is made from the gross weight in addition to the actual tare of the firkin. This is said to cover sinkage.

Appended will be found a transcript of the evidence taken at the inquiry.

John J. O'Meara,
Assistant Commissioner.

45, Lower Mount Street, Dublin.

Kilkenny, 7th November 1888.

P. M. Egan, Esq., Mayor of Kilkenny, examined.

19,800. The corporation, of which you are the head, are the owners of the markets and fairs in Kilkenny?—They are.

19,801. What markets are held here?—There is a general market held in Kilkenny for the sale of all agricultural produce on Saturday, and a market for butter on Friday, and this general market was held under the provisions of a special Act passed in the year 1861. There is a copy of the Act with which is incorporated the Land Clauses Consolidation Act of 1845, except certain sections, and the Markets and Fairs Clauses Act, 1847.

19,802. Is this general market confined to Saturday?—To Saturday and Friday. At the same time it is open on other days to certain portions of produce, such as vegetables and milk. The corn is weighed every day in the week; but two days are set apart specially for being the market days.

19,803. I presume the market premises are open each day in the week for any person who would wish to bring in produce?—Yes. The markets are open every day in the week at reasonable hours for the sale of any article which the Act first established.

19,804. Are these markets being held since 1861?—Since 1861.

19,805. Have you the particulars of the cost of the establishment of this market?—The markets and lands attached, and the appurtenances thereto, were established at a cost of about 5,000*l*.

19,806. You are not in a position at present to give me the particulars of the expenditure, the capital expenditure?—With regard to the items of expenditure, I have not them at present with me. That 5,000*l*. was to be paid off as a sinking fund, the money to be invested, and the whole 5,000*l*. was paid off in 1882. It was borrowed in 1862, and paid off in 1882.

19,807. From the profits derived exclusively from the market?—From the profits derived, and also the profits derived from the money invested, so that the 5,000*l*. was paid off by 3,000*l*. With regard to the payment of the 5,000*l*. witness read as follows from a statement made by the Borough Treasurer:—"As to Mr. Hewlett's mortgage "of 5,000*l*., which was borrowed in 1862, and paid off in "1882, each the corporation was enabled to do, not "wholly out of the profits, but in consequence of 1,822*l*. "of the principal sum borrowed having remained on hand "unexpended; 185*l*. profit realised on sale of the debenture stock, in which said sum was vested; 343*l*. like on "sale of the Three per cent., in which the sinking fund was "invested. The 3,000*l*. balance represented the profits of "the twenty years, being on an average of 150*l*. per "annum." That will show you, as I have just said, that the 5,000*l*. was paid off by 3,000*l*. arising from the market and the remaining 2,000*l*. by investments of portion of the capital originally borrowed.

19,808. What fairs are held here?—There is a monthly fair held the second Wednesday in every month. The pig fair is held the day before the monthly fair, being for cattle and horses.

19,809. When was this monthly fair established?—In 1859 the present fair green was established. There are annual fairs besides.

19,810. But previous to the establishment of the fair green were there monthly fairs held here?—There were no monthly fairs, but several fairs held on the streets.

19,811. Under what authority were they established?—There is a regular patent for the fair green.

19,812. Granted in 1859?—Yes.

19,813. You have not got a copy of it here?—I have not got a copy of the patent.

19,814. You say there is another annual fair?—There is a fair held on the 25th March.

19,815. In addition to the ordinary monthly fairs?—Yes, and one on the 1st May and 29th September. These are the old fairs.

19,816. These were the only fairs held in Kilkenny previous to 1859?—Yes.

19,817. Are tolls levied at all these fairs?—Yes.

19,818. The monthly fairs as well as the old fairs?—Yes.

19,819. Is there a schedule of the tolls exacted in the fair green on fair days?—There is.

19,820. Do you ever change or vary in any way the different rates of tolls?—Not in any perceptible way. The only change in the tolls occurred about two years ago in the butter market, when a penny was taken off the firkins.

19,821. Then you charge tolls also at the markets?—Yes.

19,822. Are they in the nature of tolls or weighing charges?—Some of them are in the nature of tolls and others in the nature of weighing charges. For instance, the corn is a weighing charge, but the charges on butter, fowl, and milk are in the nature of tolls.

19,823. Is that the schedule of charges I see there?—Yes.

19,824. Witness then produced the schedules at present levied at the fairs and markets, and of which the following are copies:—

KILKENNY FAIR GREEN.

List of Tariff.

	s.	d.
For every bull or cow aged one year and a half and upwards	0	2
Under that age	0	1
For every sheep or lamb	0	0½
" fat pig	0	1
" small pig	0	0½
" load of small pigs containing six and upwards	0	3
When less than six there is charged for each pig in car	0	0½
For every horse	0	4
" stallion	0	6
" ass	0	1
There is an extra charge made for horses admitted to paddock or jumping ground of	0	6

KILKENNY GENERAL MARKET.

List of Tariff.

	s.	d.
For weighing every cwt. of wheat	0	0½
" " oats	0	0½
" " bere or barley	0	0½
" " potatoes	0	0½
" " turnips, feathers, or any other miscellaneous article weighed in scales	0	0½
" every horse or ass load of coal, hay, straw, mangolds, turnips, &c., on ground	0	3
" every horse or ass load of coal, weighing under 10 cwt. are	0	1½
Wool.		
" under 14 lbs.	0	0½
" 14 lbs., and under 28 lbs.	0	1
" 28 lbs., and " 42 lbs.	0	1½
" 42 lbs., and up to 112 lbs.	0	2
Merchant's Wool. *Special Tariff.*		
" every cwt. of merchant's wool	0	1
Firkin Butter.		
For every firkin entering market after 10 o'clock a.m.	0	2
" " prior to that hour	0	1
Roll and Pan Butter.		
For weighing under 5 lbs.	0	0½
" 5 lbs., and under 14 lbs.	0	1
" 14 lbs., and " 28 lbs.	0	2
" 28 lbs., and " 56 lbs.	0	3

	s.	d.
For every horse load of plums	0	4
" ass "	0	3
" basket of "	0	2
" horse load of vegetables	0	3
" ass "	0	2
" basket of "	0	1
" horse load of fruit	0	3
For every ass load of fruit	0	2
" basket of "	0	1
" horse load of eggs	0	4
" ass "	0	2
" box of "	0	1
" basket of "	0	0½
" pair of small fowl	0	0½
" " turkeys	0	1
" " geese	0	1
" horse load of fish	0	6
" ass "	0	3
" hamper "	0	2
" barrel of herrings	0	2
" [illegible]	0	1
" churn of milk	0	1

The following are the tolls and charges which the corporation are empowered to levy under the provisions of the Kilkenny Markets Act, 1861:—

SCHEDULE C.

Rents and Tolls.

	s.	d.
For every barrel of 280 lbs. of wheat	0	2
" " 196 " oats	0	1
" " 224 " barley	0	1
" " 224 " bere	0	1
" " 280 lbs. of beans	0	1½
" " 280 " pease	0	1½
" " 280 " rye	0	1½
" " 224 " rape seed	0	1½
" " 224 " flax seed	0	1½
" " 280 " grain, corn or seeds not herein enumerated	0	1½
And rateably for any greater or lesser quantity.		
For every ton of flax, hemp, wool, and bark	0	6
Butter.		
For every firkin, tub, barrel or cask of butter not exceeding 112 lbs.	0	3
For every firkin, tub, barrel, or cask of butter exceeding 112 lbs.	0	4
For every basket, parcel, or quantity of butter not less than 14 lbs. weight	0	1
Other Articles.		
For every cartload of hay or straw drawn by one horse or other animal	0	4
If drawn by more than one horse or other animal, for every additional horse or other animal	0	2
For every cartload of clover, grass, rape, rye, vetches, or other green food for cattle, if drawn by one horse or other animal	0	3
If drawn by more than one horse or other animal, for each additional	0	1½
For every cartload of mangold wurzel, turnips, and all other agricultural produce whatever, save and except potatoes	0	4
" " fruit or potatoes or any other vegetables if drawn by one horse or other animal	0	3
If drawn by more than one horse or other animal, for each additional horse or other animal	0	1½
" " fish or eggs	0	6
" " native coal, or of iron, lead, copper or other mineral	0	2
" ton of hides of cows, salted or green	0	10
And rateably for a greater or lesser quantity not less than 56 lbs.		
" basket of live fowl containing not more than two pairs	0	1
" additional pair	0	0½
" load or kish of fowl containing not more than six pairs	0	3
" additional pair	0	0½
" two pairs of rabbits or wild fowl	0	0½

SCHEDULE D.

PROVISION AND VEGETABLE MARKET AND CABBAGE MARKET TOLLS.

SHOPS.

	s.	d.
For every occupier of every enclosed shop or stall, whether for sale of butchers' meat, [illegible], poultry, fish, vegetables, cheese, fruit, china, glass, earthenware, baskets, hardware, or other commodities, articles or things, according to the size and dimensions of such shop, namely, for each lineal foot of the frontage thereof, if let by the week, any weekly sum not exceeding -	2	0

BUTCHERS' STALLS.

	s.	d.
For every person occupying or using any butcher's stall or standing or any ground space for the sale of meat, according to the size and dimensions of same, namely, for each lineal foot of frontage of every such stall, standing, or ground space occupied or used by him, if let by the week, any weekly sum not exceeding - - -	1	6
If let by the day any daily sum not exceeding -	0	[illegible]

CARCASE AND SKIN TOLLS.

	s.	d.
For every carcase or part of a carcase of a bull, bullock, cow, steer, heifer, calf, sheep, or pig, brought into the market to be disposed of otherwise than by sale by retail, and whether sold or not, not exceeding - - - -	0	[illegible]
For every hide or skin, raw, undressed, or dressed, brought into the market for sale and whether sold or not, any sum not exceeding - -	0	[illegible]

PROVISION, VEGETABLE, AND OTHER STALLS, STANDS, AND GROUND SPACES.

	s.	d.
For every person occupying or using any stall, standing, cart, barrow, basket, pad, box, bench, or barrel for the sale of vegetables, provisions, fruit, fish, game, poultry, china, glass, earthenware, baskets, hardware, or other commodities, articles or things, according to the size and dimensions of the same, viz., for each superficial square foot and fractional part of a superficial square foot of the ground space covered or occupied by any such stall, standing, cart, barrow, basket, pad, box, bench, or barrel, any sum not exceeding for every day - - -	0	1

GROUND SPACE.

	s.	d.
For every person occupying or using any space on the surface of the ground, according to the size and dimensions of the same, viz., for each superficial square foot, and the fractional part of a superficial square foot of the ground space occupied or used by him, any daily sum not exceeding - - - - -	0	1

SCHEDULE E.

SLAUGHTER-HOUSE TOLLS.

	s.	d.
For every bull, bullock, cow, steer, or heifer, not exceeding - - - -	2	[illegible]
" calf, not exceeding - - -	1	[illegible]
" sheep, or lamb, not exceeding - -	0	[illegible]
" pig, not exceeding - - -	[illegible]	[illegible]
" other beast, not exceeding - -	[illegible]	0

SCHEDULE F.

WEIGHING AND MEASURING TOLLS.

	s.	d.
For weighing every piece of meat, or any article or thing, not being a cart or waggon, weighing not exceeding 20 lbs. avoirdupois - - -	0	0½
If weighing more than 20 lbs. and not exceeding 240 lbs. - - - - -	0	1
If exceeding 240 lbs. then for every additional 240 lbs., or fractional part of 240 lbs., not exceeding - - - - - -	0	1
For measuring every quantity of goods and things sold by measure, not exceeding one bushel -	0	0½
If exceeding one bushel and not exceeding two bushels - - - - -	0	1
And for every bushel and fractional part of a bushel beyond two bushels - - -	0	0½

19,825. Have you got the average receipts and expenditure?—Yes.

19,826. I presume the 5,000*l.* was expended in the erection of the market as well as in providing the fair green?—Yes, on both.

19,827. The market where all these marketable commodities are exposed for sale is an enclosed space?—Yes.

19,828. Is there shelter accommodation provided?—There is very ample shelter accommodation. There is a large corn shed under which there are five scales, and the number of scales varies with the corn in the market at any hour, so that at the largest market during the year the people would not have more than 15 or 20 minutes to wait except on very special occasions.

19,829. From your experience you deem the shelter accommodation afforded in the market sufficient for the trade of the town?—The shelter accommodation of the town, I believe to be quite ample. At the same time, in the present year, we are providing extended shelter accommodation. We are this year erecting a new row of sheds, not because we require so much shelter accommodation as we require to clear away one entrance which is obstructed by a shed quite close to the gate, and it is projected to remove that old shed, and give whatever accommodation there was there in the new sheds erected.

19,830. Is the fair green enclosed?—It is enclosed by a wall.

19,831. Are there any pens in it?—There are sheep pens in it.

19,832. Any sheds?—No.

19,833. Have you got a weighbridge capable of weighing cattle here?—We had erected last year a weighbridge capable of weighing cattle, and cattle and pigs are weighed very accurately.

19,834. Are the buyers and sellers who bring cattle to the fairs disposed to avail themselves of that weighbridge?—From what I have seen I do not think the buyers are disposed. I believe very many of the sellers would be anxious to sell by weight, but owing to the custom prevailing, and perhaps owing to the desire of the customers not to purchase by weight, the scales have not been availed of. As a matter of fact since the 1st January only 84 head of cattle have been weighed out of the thousands coming to the fairs.

19,835. Could you afterwards segregate the amount mentioned, 5,000*l.*, into the particulars of how it was expended?—I daresay we will be able to give the particulars by applying to the minute books. Some of it was spent on the fair green.

19,836. How was the fair green utilised previously?—It was private property, gardens, and the corporation bought it up.

19,837. Do you ever hear complaints of these tolls in any way here in Kilkenny?—I never did.

19,838. Have you much experience of other markets besides Kilkenny yourself?—I have.

19,839. From your experience do you think that the levying of a toll for bringing in commodities into the market of a town, or cattle into the fair, acts in any way as a deterrent on people bringing their cattle or produce?—I do not think it acts in the slightest degree as a deterrent. On the contrary, I think the levying of a toll is the greatest public benefit so long as the toll is moderate, for this reason, that the market has to be kept clean; it has to be kept in proper repair and a staff has to be paid, and I believe the small nominal tolls that are paid is a great public advantage by keeping the markets in a thorough state of organisation and repair.

19,840. I take it, then, you approve of the reduction of tolls to such an amount as would only meet the cost of management?—Yes; and also provide the necessary fund for improving the markets as they would require it.

19,841. Do you think the system at present here of having the market authority vested in the corporation works better than if it was in the hands of an individual in the town as elsewhere?—I think it works exceedingly better, and as a proof of that, I hear complaints of the great grievances existing in other towns where private individuals have control of the markets, and can levy tolls at their pleasure.

19,842. From your experience you would be in favour of town commissioners, board of guardians, or market trustees, if such were appointed, obtaining compulsory powers to acquire the rights of market authorities throughout the country?—Most decidedly. I think the markets in any town can never improve unless the local authority, such as the corporation or commissioners, have supreme control over the markets. I think the fact of a private individual having control over them is a positive bar to their progress.

19,843. Do you think they would be better managed by the corporation, or by an authority such as I suggest?—I think they would be better managed for this reason: that complaints could be made more easily to a corporate body, who are the principal representatives of the public, than to a private individual, because if the public complain to an individual of the body he immediately brings the grievance before the body, whereas if a complaint is made to a private individual, if it is not his wish to redress it, it remains there.

19,844. Do you think that the surplus funds, if any, derived from the markets and fairs should be applied in relief of the rates or the town expenditure, or in improving the market?—I do not think it should be applied in relief of the rates. I think it should be applied to the improvement of the market, or of the approaches to the market.

19,845. Any toll that would bring a larger revenue than necessary for the purpose should be abolished?—I do not think tolls should be levied for the purpose of decreasing the rates outside the market. They should be spent on the market alone, for providing the current expenses or developing the markets.

19,846. Do you consider, and I presume it is your opinion, that where tolls are levied, the persons in receipt of those charges should give some return—by return, of course, is meant a fair green and ordinary market buildings with appliances for weighing the various commodities. For instance, elsewhere throughout the country the fairs and markets are held on the public thoroughfare, and tolls levied for bringing in cattle and marketable commodities, and weighing them. Have you any experience of such places?—I have.

19,847. Is it your opinion that the owners who are in receipt of the charges should give some return other than that of allowing the people to expose their goods and commodities on the public thoroughfare?—I think the owners should not be allowed such a privilege at all, or if they have a claim by right or charter there should be compulsory powers vested in the local authority to purchase, after proper valuation, their rights in such a market.

19,848. With a view to providing sufficient accommodation?—With a view to providing adequate accommodation, and also with a view of preventing what I consider a great grievance—that is, any individual taking public money without giving a proper return for it.

19,849. Is there any other suggestion you would wish to make?—With regard to the butter market here, I may say that up to last year we had very frequent complaints in the butter market relative to tares and the regulation of tares. The buyers were allowed to put on tares simply at their will, and there was a constant struggle between the buyers and sellers, the buyers increasing the tares and the sellers endeavouring to decrease the tares beyond what the buyers would give them. Last year we finally checked such a proceeding. We have got the tares branded on the firkins by each cooper, and the buyers are not allowed to change those tares. They simply buy on the net amount put in the market, and the result is that it worked most satisfactorily last year.

19,850. By the net amount would you mean the difference between the gross and the tare marked on the firkin?—Yes.

19,851. Is anything additional allowed for soakage?—There is a pound allowed for soakage in certain weights, and two pounds in larger weights. That is put on by the market officials; the buyers are not allowed to touch it.

19,852. Is that one or two pound, as the case may be, added to the tare marked on the firkin?—Yes.

19,853. The tares are always branded on the firkin?—Yes.

19,854. Are those the only deductions from the gross weight?—The tare and soakage are the only deductions from the gross weight.

19,855. Is this a good butter market?—I consider that the rules at present regulating the Kilkenny butter market are the best I have known in the country. I have made special inquiries in other towns, and found complaints made in other cities, and it is by studying those complaints and applying them here we made the improvement in our market.

19,856. Have you got any rules restricting the sale of any commodities except through brokers and agents?—There are no rules regulating brokers. We have not very many of them; I do not think scarcely any.

19,857. Have you any suggestions to offer in the way of alterations to be made in the existing law?—I do not see there is any necessity for alterations. I think the best way is to leave the alterations to the market authority or corporation, and they can make any alterations that are necessary.

19,858. I mean alterations throughout the country and not in Kilkenny in particular?—The only alteration I would deem necessary to effect is that of giving compulsory powers to the local authorities. I would be very much in favour of that project, because I have heard in several towns the great grievances ventilated in consequence of private individuals having authority over the markets and fairs.

Patrick J. Dillon, Esq., Borough Treasurer, examined.

19,859. You are the Borough Treasurer of the city of Kilkenny?—Yes.

19,860. Did you make up the average receipts and expenditure?—I made up the average receipts of the market. The gross average receipts from the market were [illegible] [illegible]s. [illegible]d. for the past three years. That includes tolls, rents, and interest allowed by the bank.

19,861. Is that interest on the balance?—Yes, on the balance to our credit.

19,862. Did you make up your average expenditure?—I will show you that. The average profit for the three years on the market was [illegible]l. 13s. 4d. The average receipts from the fairs were [illegible]l. 11s. 1d.

19,863. You gave me the gross average profit for the fairs and markets. Could you give me the expenditure now?—The average profits for the fairs during the three years were [illegible]l. 1s. 4d.

19,864. The witness handed in the market and fair accounts for the three years, together with a summary thereof, and copies of which are as follows:—

Kilkenny Public Market Account for half year 1st September 188[illegible] to 1st March 188[illegible].

Dr.

£ s. d.	£ s. d.	£ s. d.

	£ s. d.	£ s. d.
Brought forward - -		
Miscellaneous Receipts:		
To R. Grady, seven months' rent to [illegible] February 18[illegible] - -	4 19 [illegible]	
" M. Kealy, five months' rent to 1st January 18[illegible] - -	5 0 0	
" P. Morrissey, six months' rent to 1st February 18[illegible] - -	5 0 0	
" Rep. M. Thomson, half-year's rent ending [illegible] September 18[illegible]	12 0 0	
" interest allowed during period of account - - -	0 [illegible] 0	
		27 1 9
		[illegible] 14 9

Cr.

Maintaining the Market and Market Places.

	£ s. d.	£ s. d.
Rents:		
By balance due by corporation last account, 1st September 18[illegible] -		[illegible]
" paid Abraham Alcock, half-year's rent of King Street Market, ending [illegible] September 18[illegible] - - - - -	[illegible] 0 0	
" Do. do., of Mr. Sullivan's part, ending do. - -	[illegible] 10 0	
	[illegible] 10 0	
Less income tax, at [illegible]d. - - - - - - -	1 1[illegible] 4	
		[illegible] 1[illegible] [illegible]
" Rev. G. [illegible] F. [illegible], half-year's rent out of public market, ended [illegible] September 18[illegible] - - - - - -	17 [illegible] 0	
Less income tax, at [illegible]d. - - - - - -	0 11 [illegible]	
		1[illegible] 14 [illegible]
Salaries and Wages:		
By paid Messrs. J. Dunne and J. Nolan, auditors for half-year ending [illegible] August 18[illegible] - - - - - -	[illegible] 10 0	
" Do. Denis O'Sullivan, six months' salary as butter [illegible] -	50 0 0	
" Do. P. J. Dillon, Esq., Borough Treasurer, balance of fees for half-year ending [illegible] August 18[illegible] - - -	[illegible] 10 [illegible]	
" Do. Staff expenses during period of account, including removing of [illegible], &c. - - - - -	[illegible] [illegible] 1	
		[illegible] [illegible] [illegible]
Printing, Advertising, and Stationery:		
By paid printing, advertising and stationery during period of account - - - - - - - -		[illegible] 1[illegible] [illegible]
Entrance Gateway:		
By paid cost of improving entrance to King Street Market -		[illegible] 7 [illegible]
Law Costs:		
By paid Lewis J. Watters, Esq., Sol., amount of his taxed costs in re [illegible] v. Borough Treasurer, and Borough Treasurer v. [illegible] - - - - - -		[illegible] 1[illegible] 0
Removing Obstruction in King Street:		
By paid John Morrissey, taking down, &c., the steps opposite Mr. J. Ayre's house, King Street, pursuant to contract -		[illegible] 0 0
Miscellaneous:		
By paid repairing at Michael Kealy's house, King Street - -	7 14 1	
" Do. timber, repairing sheds, [illegible] for porters, coal, telegrams re [illegible] Butter Market, and other miscellaneous expenses - - - - - - - -	[illegible] [illegible] 0	
		[illegible] 1[illegible] 1
Taxes:		
By paid taxes, grand jury cess, &c., on holdings of Messrs. Morrissey, Kealy, Redmond, and Grady - -		[illegible] 1[illegible] 4
Interest:		
By interest charged by bank on overdrawn account, ending [illegible] December 18[illegible] - - - - - - -		0 1[illegible] [illegible]
" balance to credit of corporation due 1st March 18[illegible] - -		7[illegible] 7 [illegible]
		[illegible] 14 9

We have examined the Treasurer's accounts of the Kilkenny public market from 1st September 18[illegible] to the 1st March 18[illegible], and find that the several payments have been supported by adequate vouchers, and find the foregoing to be a correct statement of the accounts respectively.

James Dunne, } Borough Auditors.
John Nolan }
John Coyne, Mayor's Auditor.
P. J. Dillon, Borough Treasurer.

Borough Treasurer's Office, April 7th, 18[illegible].

KILKENNY PUBLIC MARKET ACCOUNT, for half year 1st March [illegible] to 1st September [illegible].

Dr.

	£ s. d.	£ s. d.	£ s. d.
Receipts from Market Tolls:			
To balance on 1st March, [illegible]			73 7 0½
„ 805 cwts of wheat, weighed at ¼d. per cwt.	2 18 7		
„ 11,[illegible] cwts. of oats, weighed at [illegible]d. per cwt.	[illegible] 0 7½		
„ 3,[illegible] cwts. of barley, weighed at [illegible]d. per cwt.	10 6 2½		
15,761 cwts. *		[illegible] 1 [illegible]	
„ 4,716 firkins of butter, at 2d. and [illegible]d. each		78 [illegible] [illegible]	
„ 1,[illegible] cwts. of wool, at [illegible]d. per cwt.		14 8 11½	
„ [illegible] cwts. of wool, at 1d. per cwt.		3 19 6	
„ 10,[illegible] cwts. of potatoes, at ¼d. per cwt.		[illegible] 3 7	
„ amount received from roll and pan butter, eggs, fowl, vegetables, plants, rent of stands, fish, &c., &c.		127 8 [illegible]	
„ market [illegible]		15 14 [illegible]	
„ parade [illegible]		[illegible] 7 10	
„ churn milk		10 [illegible] 3	
„ miscellaneous articles weighed		0 12 [illegible]	
„ butter scrapings		8 [illegible] [illegible]	
Total receipts			[illegible] 16 7½
Miscellaneous Receipts:			
To E. Grady, six months' rent to 31st August [illegible]		4 [illegible] 0	
„ M. Kealy, seven months' rent to 1st August [illegible]		7 0 0	
„ P. Morrissey, six months' rent to 1st August [illegible]		[illegible] [illegible] 0	
„ Interest allowed during period of account		0 [illegible] 10	
			16 [illegible] 10
			[illegible] 13 6

* Calculations cannot be made of the receipts from above, as the full toll is charged for a part of a cwt. weight. This explanation I think is right to give, as I understand parties not so understanding have been erroneously trying to calculate.

P. J. D.

Cr.

Maintaining the Market and Market Places.

	£ s. d.	£ s. d.
Rents:		
By paid Abraham Alcock, half year's rent of King Street Market, ending 25th March [illegible]	[illegible] 0 0	
„ Do. do. of Mr. Sullivan's part, ending do.	[illegible] [illegible] 0	
	[illegible] [illegible] 0	
Less income tax, at [illegible]d.	1 14 [illegible]	
		[illegible] 13 [illegible]
„ Rev. G. B. P. Collins, half-year's rent out of public market, ended 25th March [illegible]	17 [illegible] [illegible]	
Less income tax, at [illegible]d.	0 11 [illegible]	
		16 16 [illegible]
„ Mrs. Brennan, one and a half-year's rent out of public market, ending 25th March [illegible]	4 4 [illegible]	
Less income tax at 5d. and [illegible]d.	0 3 [illegible]	
		4 1 0
Salaries and Wages:		
By paid Messrs. J. Dunne and J. Nolan, auditors for half year ending 28th February [illegible]	[illegible] [illegible] 0	
„ Do. Dennis O'Sullivan, six months' salary as butter inspector	[illegible] 0 [illegible]	
„ Do. P. J. Dillon, Esq., Borough Treasurer, fees for half-year ending 28 February [illegible]	[illegible] [illegible] [illegible]	
„ Do. staff expenses during period of account, including removing of manure, &c.	[illegible] 19 [illegible]	
		[illegible] 13 1
Printing, Advertising, and Stationery:		
By paid printing, advertising, and stationery during period of account		[illegible] 1 1
Miscellaneous:		
By paid timber, repairing sheds, &c., paint and hardware account and other miscellaneous expenses		14 19 3
Taxes:		
By paid rates, taxes, on holdings of Messrs. Morrissey, Kealy, Redmond, and Grady	[illegible] [illegible] [illegible]	
„ Do. Robert McCarthy, Esq., income tax assessment for year ending April [illegible]	[illegible] 13 [illegible]	
		11 [illegible] 11
Balance to credit of corporation the 1st September [illegible]		75 7 [illegible]
		[illegible] 13 6

We have examined the Treasurer's accounts of the Kilkenny public market from 1st March 1886 to the 1st September 1886, and find that the several payments have been supported by adequate vouchers, and find the foregoing to be a correct statement of the accounts respectively.

James Dunne, } Borough Auditors.
John Nolan, }
John Coyle, Mayor's Auditor.
P. J. Dillon, Borough Treasurer.

Borough Treasurer's Office, October 11th, 1886.

KILKENNY PUBLIC MARKET ACCOUNTS for half year from 1st September 1886 to 1st March 1887.

Dr.

	£ s. d.	£ s. d.	£ s. d.
Receipts from Market Tolls:			
To balance on 1st September 1886			78 7 0
" 6,827 cwts. of wheat, weighed at ½d. per cwt.	81 15 7½		
" 24,381 cwts. of oats, weighed at ½d. per cwt.	51 9 0½		
" 34,243 cwts. of barley, weighed at ½d. per cwt.	107 8 7	190 8 3	
65,451 cwts.*			
" 5,700 firkins of butter, at 2d. each		47 10 6	
" 174 cwts. of wool, at 2d. per cwt.		1 10 9	
" 100 cwts. of wool, at 1d. per cwt.		0 8 5	
" 16,454 cwts. of potatoes, at ½d. per cwt.		[illegible] 8 9½	
" amount received from roll and pot butter, eggs, fowl, vegetables, plants, rent of sheds, fish, &c., &c.		142 11 1	
" market cranell		98 11 10½	
" Parade cranell		73 10 3	
" churn mills		10 3 9	
" miscellaneous articles weighed		1 0 0	
" butter scrapings		8 13 9	
Total receipts			637 18 9
Miscellaneous Receipts:			
To representative Thomas, half-year's rent to 25th March 1886		19 0 0	
" M. Kealy, six months' rent, to 1st February 1887		6 0 0	
" P. Morrissey, six months' rent, to 1st February 1887		5 0 0	
" interest allowed during period of account		0 18 0	
			30 18 0
			838 18 9

* Calculations cannot be made of the receipts from above, as the full toll is charged for a part of a cwt. weight. This explanation I think is right to give, as I understand parties not so understanding have been erroneously trying to calculate.
P. J. D.

Cr.

Maintaining the Market and Market Places.

	£ s. d.	£ s. d.
Rents:		
By paid Abraham Aleock, half-year's rent of King Street Market, ending 29th September 1886	20 0 0	
" Do. do. of Mr. Sullivan's part, ending do.	31 10 0	
	51 10 0	
Less income tax, at 8d.	1 14 4	
		49 15 8
" Do. Rev. G. R. P. Collis, half-year's rent out of public market, ended 29th September 1886	17 6 0	
Less income tax, at 8d.	0 11 6	
		16 14 6
Salaries and Wages:		
By paid Messrs. J. Dunne and J. Nolan, auditors, for half year ending 31st August 1886	8 10 0	
" Do. Denis O'Sullivan, six months' salary as butter inspector	60 0 0	
" Do. P. J. Dillon, Esq., Borough Treasurer, balance of fees for half year ending 31st August 1886	81 15 8	
" Do. do. on account, half year, to 28th February 1887	50 0 0	
" Do. staff expenses during period of account, including removing of manure	227 10 10	
		336 15 1
Printing, Advertising, and Stationery:		
By paid printing, advertising, and stationery during period of account		21 19 4
Miscellaneous:		
By paid timber, repairing sheds, &c., paint and hardware accounts and other miscellaneous expenses		17 11 9
Carried forward		

	£ s. d.	£ s. d.
Brought forward - - -		
Taxes:		
By paid rates, taxes, on holdings of Messrs. Merriney, Kealy, Redmond, and Grady - - - - - - -		1 19
Boundary Wall:		
By paid John Ayres' contribution towards expense incurred by him in building boundary wall in market - - - - -		50 0 0
Porters' Jackets:		
By paid Messrs. R. Mahoney and Co. for four porters' jackets -		5 14 0
Maintaining Approaches to Market:		
By paid borough fund account for maintaining approaches to market - - - - - - - -		100 0 0
Balance to credit 1st March 1887 - - - -		71 [illegible] 1
		[illegible] 12 9

We have examined the Treasurer's accounts of the Kilkenny public market from 1st September 1886 to the 1st March 1887, and find that the several payments have been supported by adequate vouchers, and find the foregoing to be a correct statement of the accounts respectively.

James Dunne, } Borough Auditors.
Patrick Davis, }
Patrick Rowan, Mayor's Auditor.
P. J. Delany, Borough Treasurer.

Borough Treasurer's Office, May 18th, 1887.

Kilkenny Public Market Account for half year 1st March 1887 to 1st September 1887.

Dr.

	£ s. d.	£ s. d.	£ s. d.
Receipts from Market Tolls:			
To balance on 1st March 1887 - - -			71 [illegible] 1
" 1,[illegible] cwts. of wheat, weighed at ½d. per cwt. -	4 [illegible] [illegible]		
" 12,[illegible] cwts. of oats, weighed at ½d. per cwt. -	[illegible] [illegible] [illegible]		
" [illegible] cwts. of barley, weighed at ½d. per cwt. -	9 [illegible] [illegible]		
17,[illegible] cwts.*		[illegible] 16 [illegible]	
" [illegible] firkins of butter - - - - - -		41 [illegible] [illegible]	
" 1,[illegible] cwts. of wool, at 2d. per cwt. - - - -		14 [illegible] 7½	
" [illegible] cwts. of wool, at 1d. per cwt. - - - -		0 4 [illegible]	
" 1[illegible] cwts. of potatoes, at ½d. per cwt. - - - -		[illegible] [illegible] [illegible]	
" amount received from [illegible] and [illegible] butter, eggs, fowl, vegetables, plants, rent of sheds, fish, &c., &c. - -		1[illegible] [illegible] 10½	
" market [illegible] - - - - - - -		14 [illegible] [illegible]	
" Parade [illegible] - - - - - - -		7[illegible] 4 10½	
" [illegible] - - - - - - -		[illegible] 4 [illegible]	
" miscellaneous articles weighed - - - - -		0 1[illegible] [illegible]	
" [illegible] - - - - - - -		[illegible] 1[illegible] [illegible]	
Total receipts - - - - - - -			4[illegible] [illegible] [illegible]
Miscellaneous Receipts:			
To representative Thompson, one year's rent, to 25th March 1887 -		[illegible] [illegible] [illegible]	
" M. Kealy, six months' rent, to 1st August 1887 - - -		4 0 [illegible]	
" P. Merriney, six months' rent, to 1st August 1887 - -		[illegible] [illegible] [illegible]	
" R. O'Grady, six months' rent, to 28th February 1887 - -		4 [illegible] [illegible]	
" interest allowed during period of account - - -		0 [illegible] [illegible]	
			[illegible] 15 [illegible]
			51[illegible] 1 [illegible]

* Calculations cannot be made of the receipts from above, as the full toll is charged for a part of a cwt. weight. This explanation I think is right to give, as I understand parties not so understanding have been erroneously trying to calculate.

P. J. D.

	£ s. d.	£ s. d.
Brought forward - - -		
By paid Mrs. B. A. Brennan, one year's rent out of public market, to 25th March 1857 - - - - - -	4 [illegible] [illegible]	
Less income tax, at 9d. - - - - -	0 [illegible] 9	
		4 [illegible] [illegible]
Salaries and Wages:		
By paid Messrs. J. Dunne and J. Nolan, auditors, for half year ending 31st August 1857 - - - -	2 10 0	
" Do. Denis O'Sullivan, seven months' salary as butter inspector - - - - - - -	[illegible] [illegible] [illegible]	
" Do. P. J. Dillon, Esq., Borough Treasurer, balance of fees for half year ending 1st March 1857 - - -	3 [illegible] 4	
" Do. staff expenses during period of account, including removing of manure - - - - -	[illegible] 0 0	
		[illegible] 12 0
Printing, Advertising, and Stationery:		
By paid printing, advertising, and stationery during period of account - - - - - - - -		5 17 4
Miscellaneous:		
By paid timber, repairing sheds, &c., paint and hardware account and other miscellaneous expenses - - - -		6 7 [illegible]
Taxes:		
By paid rates, taxes, on holdings of Messrs. Morrissey, Kealy, Redmond and Grady - - - - - -		1 1 4
Income Tax:		
By paid income tax assessment - - - - -		7 19 0
Maintaining Approaches to Market:		
By paid Borough fund account for maintaining approaches to market - - - - - - - - -		100 0 0
Balance to credit 1st September 1857 - - -		[illegible] 7 7½
		[illegible] 1 6½

We have examined the Treasurer's accounts of the Kilkenny public market from 1st March 1857 to the 1st September 1857, and find that the several payments have been supported by adequate vouchers, and find the foregoing to be a correct statement of the accounts respectively.

James Dunne, } Borough Auditors.
Patrick Davis, }
Patrick Rowan, Mayor's Auditor.
P. J. Dillon, Borough Treasurer.

Borough Treasurer's Office, 4th November 1857.

Kilkenny Public Market Account for half year 1st September 1857 to 1st March 1858.

Dr.

	£ s. d.	£ s. d.	£ s. d.
Receipts from Market Tolls:			
To balance on 1st September 1857 - - -			[illegible] 7 7½
" [illegible] cwts.* of wheat, weighed at ½d. per cwt. -	[illegible] [illegible] [illegible]		
" [illegible] cwts. of oats, weighed at ½d. per cwt. -	[illegible] 17 [illegible]		
" [illegible] cwts. of barley, weighed at ½d. per cwt. -	[illegible] 9 [illegible]		
		[illegible] 4 [illegible]	
" [illegible] firkins of butter - - - - - -		[illegible] [illegible] [illegible]	
" [illegible] cwts. of wool, at [illegible]d. per cwt. - - -		1 1 [illegible]	
" [illegible] cwts. of wool, at 1d. per cwt. - - -		0 0 0	
" [illegible] cwts. of potatoes, at ½d. per cwt. - -		[illegible] [illegible] [illegible]	
" amount received from roll and pan butter, eggs, fowl, vegetables, plants, rent of stands, fish, &c., &c. - - -		[illegible] [illegible] [illegible]	
" market council - - - - - - - -		[illegible] 0 10½	
" Parade council - - - - - - - -		[illegible] [illegible] [illegible]	
" [illegible] - - - - - - - -		10 [illegible] [illegible]	
" miscellaneous articles weighed - - - - -		1 [illegible] 10	
" butter scrapings - - - - - - -		5 [illegible] 7	
			[illegible] 15 9½
Miscellaneous Receipts:			
To received from M. Kealy, six months' rent, to 1st February 1858		[illegible] 0 0	
" P. Morrissey, six months' rent, to 1st February 1858 - -		[illegible] 0 0	
" B. O'Grady, six months' rent, to 31st August 1857 - -		4 [illegible] 0	
" amount fine imposed on Patrick Money, porter - -		0 5 0	
" interest allowed during period of account - - -		[illegible] [illegible] [illegible]	
			[illegible] [illegible] [illegible]
			[illegible] [illegible] [illegible]

* Calculations cannot be made of the weights from above, as the full toll is charged for a part of a cwt. weight. This explanation I think it right to give, as I understand parties not so understanding have been erroneously trying to calculate.

P. J. D.

Cr.

Maintaining the Market and Market Places.

	£ s. d.	£ s. d.
Rent:		
By paid Abraham Alcock, half-year's rent of King Street Market, ending 29th September 1887	30 0 0	
" Do. do. of Mr. Sullivan's part, ending do.	21 10 0	
	51 10 0	
Less income tax, at 7d.	1 10 0	
		50 0 0
" Do. Rev. G. R. P. Colles, half-year's rent out of public [illegible], ending 29th September, 1887	17 6 0	
Less income tax, at 7d.	0 10 0	
		16 16 0
Salaries and Wages:		
By paid Messrs. J. Dunne and J. Nolan, auditors, for half year ending 31st August, 1887	2 10 0	
" Do. Dennis O'Sullivan, five months' salary as butter inspector	41 13 4	
" Do. P. J. Dillon, Esq., Borough Treasurer, fees for half year ending 31st August 1887	[illegible] 1 0	
" Do. staff expenses during period of account, including removing of manure	[illegible] 13 11	
		[illegible] 17 3
Printing, Advertising, and Stationery:		
By paid printing, advertising, and stationery during period of account		16 [illegible] 0
Miscellaneous:		
By paid timber, repairing stands, &c., paint and hardware accounts and other miscellaneous expenses		14 18 7
Taxes:		
By paid rates, taxes, on holdings of Messrs Morrissey, Healy, Redmond and Grady		1 13 4
Balance in credit 29th February 1888		[illegible] 15 [illegible]
		[illegible] 6 11

We have examined the Treasurer's accounts of the Kilkenny public market from 1st September 1887 to 29th February 1888, and find that the several payments have been supported by adequate vouchers, and the foregoing to be a correct statement of the accounts respectively.

Patrick Davis, } Borough Auditors.
Patrick [illegible], }
Patrick [illegible], Mayor's Auditor.
P. J. Dillon, Borough Treasurer.

Borough Treasurer's Office, 16th April 1888.

Kilkenny Public Market Account for half year 1st March 1888 to 1st September 1888.

Dr.

	£ s. d.	£ s. d.	£ s. d.
Receipts from Market Tolls:			
To balance on 1st March 1888			[illegible] 15 [illegible]
" [illegible] cwts. of wheat, weighed at ½d. per cwt.	0 10 4½		
" [illegible] cwts. of oats, weighed at ½d. per cwt.	18 15 5		
" 1,[illegible] cwts. of barley, weighed at ½d. per cwt.	4 19 [illegible]		
		24 5 5½	
" 4,[illegible] firkins of butter		[illegible] 17 5	
" 1,[illegible] cwts. of wool, at 2d. per cwt.		13 1 4½	
" [illegible] cwts. of wool, at 1d. per cwt.		1 1 1	
" [illegible] cwts. of potatoes, at ½d. per cwt.		40 10 1½	
" amount received from stall and pen hire, eggs, fowl, vegetables, plants, rent of stands, fish, &c., &c.		1[illegible] [illegible] 9½	
" market [illegible]		18 5 10½	
" Parade [illegible]		53 6 4½	
" [illegible]		[illegible] 19 5	
" miscellaneous articles weighed		0 [illegible] 7½	
" butter sweepings		7 13 10	
			[illegible] 8 4½
Miscellaneous Receipts:			
To received from M. Healy, six months' rent, to 1st August 1888		5 0 0	
" P. Morrissey, six months' rent, to 1st August 1888		5 0 0	
" R. O'Grady, six months' rent, to 1st March 1888		4 5 0	
" Mrs. [illegible], half-year's rent, ending 29th September 1887		12 0 0	
" interest allowed during period of account		0 13 9	
			27 10 9
			[illegible] 1 8½

CR.

Maintaining the Market and Market Places.

	£ s. d.	£ s. d.
Rents:		
By paid Abraham Alcock, half year's rent of King-Street Market, ending 25th March 18[illegible]	[illegible] 0 0	
" Do. do. of Mr. Sullivan's part, ending do.	[illegible] 10 0	
	[illegible] 10 0	
Less income tax	1 10 [illegible]	
		[illegible] 0 0
" Do. Rev. G. B. P. Collins, half year's rent on of public market, ended 25th March 18[illegible]	17 [illegible] 0	
Less income tax	0 10 0	
		16 1[illegible] 0
Salaries and Wages:		
By paid Messrs. J. Doone and P. Geary, auditors, for half-year ending 28th February 18[illegible]	[illegible] 10 0	
" Do. Denis O'Sullivan, seven months' salary as bailiff inspector	[illegible] 6 5	
" Do. P. J. Dillon, Esq., Borough Treasurer, fees for half-year ending 28th February 18[illegible]	[illegible] 14 4	
" Do. staff expenses during period of account, including removing of manure	11[illegible] 5 0	
		[illegible] 16 0
Printing, Advertising, and Stationery:		
By paid printing, advertising, and stationery during period of account	- -	10 10 7
Miscellaneous:		
By paid timber, repairing sheds, &c., paint, and other miscellaneous expenses	- -	10 16 4
Gravel and Hardware:		
By paid Power & Son, repairs to market and parade [illegible]	8 0 0	
" Do. do. miscellaneous hardware account	1 5 0	
		9 5 0
Jackets:		
By paid McStay & Co., three frieze jackets for porters	- -	1 10 [illegible]
By paid macadamizing approaches to public market	- -	75 0 0
Taxes:		
By paid income tax assessment for year	- -	[illegible] 15 8
" Do. rates, taxes, on holdings of Messrs. Morrissey, Healy, Redmond, and Grady	- -	[illegible] 12 1
Balance to credit, 31st August 18[illegible]	- -	[illegible] 1 4½
		[illegible] 1 9½

We have examined the Treasurer's accounts of the Kilkenny public market from 1st March 18[illegible] to 31st August 18[illegible], and find that the several payments have been supported by adequate vouchers, and the foregoing to be a correct statement of the accounts respectively.

PATRICK DAVIS } Borough Auditors.
PATRICK GEARY }
PATRICK ROWAN, Mayor's Auditor.
P. J. DILLON, Borough Treasurer.

Borough Treasurer's Office 2nd October 18[illegible].

KILKENNY FAIR GREEN. Abstract of Receipts and Disbursements from 1st September 18[illegible] to 1st September 18[illegible].

DR.

	£ s. d.
To received from tolls for year ending 31st August 18[illegible]	[illegible] [illegible] 4½
" balance due National Bank at close of this account	126 [illegible] [illegible]
	[illegible] 11 7

CR.

	£ s. d.	£ s. d.
Rents:		
By balance due National Bank and in Treasurer's hands 31st August 18[illegible]		311 7 3
" paid one year's rent due W. H. Flood, Esq., to 25th March 18[illegible]	41 15 0	
Less income tax, at 6d.	1 0 1	
		[illegible] 3 11
" Do. year's rent due rep. E. H. Robbins to 25th March 18[illegible]	16 18 [illegible]	
Less income tax, at 6d.	0 11 4	
		16 7 6
Carried forward		

	£ s. d.	£ s. d.
Brought forward		
By paid rep. F. Sullivan and Miss Mulhallen to do.	6 0 0	
Less income tax, at 6d.	0 6 0	
		5 16 0
Treasurer's Fees, Staff Expenses, &c.:		
By paid P. J. Dillon, Esq., Treasurer's fees for year ended 31st August 1886	22 11 6	
,, Do. Messrs. Dunne and Nolan for auditing accounts for year	5 0 0	
,, Do. staff expenses during period of account	44 7 0	
,, Do. caretakers' (Sunphy and Phelan) wages for year	44 18 6	
		116 12 4
Incidental Expenses:		
By paid carpenter work at sheep pens, paling, ticket boxes, &c.	4 3 8	
,, timber do.	4 10 8	
,, Do. removing manure from off green, repairing walls, &c., &c.	15 18 3	
,, Do. hardware accounts, oils, paint, &c., &c., &c.	5 17 0	
,, Do. income tax assessment for year	6 9 5	
,, Do. printing, advertising, and stationery	6 17 3	
		41 10 3
Macadamising:		
By paid stones for macadamising		30 5 6
Oil Lighting:		
By paid P. Casey, 750 gallons of oil per contract for lighting fair green	53 4 4	
,, Do. P. Casey, new lamps, &c.	9 17 9	
		63 1 1
Interest:		
By paid to National Bank, interest during period of account		8 1 0
		[illegible] 11 7

We have examined the Treasurer's accounts of the Kilkenny fair green from 1st September 1885 to the 1st September 1886, and find that the several payments have been supported by adequate vouchers, and find the foregoing to be a correct statement of the accounts respectively.

James Dunne } Borough Auditors.
John Nolan }
John Gerity, Mayor's Auditor.
P. J. Dillon, Borough Treasurer.

Borough Treasurer's Office, October 11th, 1886.

Kilkenny Fair Green. An abstract of Receipts and Disbursements from 1st September 1886 to 1st September 1887.

Dr.

	£ s. d.	£ s. d.
To received from tolls for year ending 31st August 1887		449 19 8
,, cheque received from ladies' account		20 0 0
,, balance due National Bank	246 16 0	
On Treasurer's hands	0 0 6¼	
		246 [illegible] 2¼
		736 0 0¼

Cr.

	£ s. d.	£ s. d.
Rents:		
By balance due National Bank and on Treasurer's hands 1st September 1886		128 8 3½
,, paid half year's rent due W. H. Flood, Esq., to 29th September 1886	21 16 8	
Less income tax, at 6d.	0 14 8	
		21 2 0
,, Do. year's rent due rep. R. H. Robbins to 25th March 1887	16 18 8	
Less income tax at 6d.	0 11 4	
		16 7 4
,, Do. rep. F. Sullivan and Miss Mulhallen do. to do.	6 0 0	
Less income tax, at 6d.	0 6 0	
		5 10 0
Treasurer's Fees, Staff Expenses, &c.:		
By paid P. J. Dillon, Esq., Treasurer's fees for year ended 1st September 1887	22 10 0	
,, Do. Messrs. Dunne and Nolan for auditing accounts for year	5 0 0	
,, Do staff expenses during period of account	43 [illegible] 6	
,, Do. caretaker (Phelan) wages for year	31 16 0	
		1[illegible] 15 6
Carried forward		

	£ s. d.	£ s. d.
Brought forward . . .		
Incidental Expenses:		
By paid carpenter work at sheep pens, pailing, ticket house, &c.	5 18 0	
" timber for ditto	0 7 6	
" Do. removing manure from off green	9 11 9	
" Do. hardware accounts, oils, paint, &c., &c., &c.	5 9 1	
" Do. income tax assessment for year	4 6 8	
" Do. printing, advertising, and stationery	1 9 0	
" Do. miscellaneous payments	1 18 10	
		[illegible] 17 9
Repairs to Baths:		
By paid cheques to baths' account, re recent repairs		230 0 0
Stephen Lalor's Malicious Injury Claim:		
By paid Thomas J. Bennett, Esq., solicitor, to pay costs awarded by the court against traverser		10 0 6
" Do. same, amount of his costs re same		17 8 10
Purcell's Orchard:		
By paid William Purcell, for surrender of his premises, known as "Purcell's Orchard"		160 0 0
Interest:		
By paid National Bank, interest during period of account		7 14 6
		£7[illegible] 9 0½

We have examined the Treasurer's accounts of the Kilkenny *fair* green from 1st September 1886 to the 1st September 1887, and find that the several payments have been supported by adequate vouchers, and the foregoing to be a correct statement of the accounts.

JAMES DUNNE, } Borough Auditors.
PATRICK DAVIS, }
PATRICK ROWAN, Mayor's Auditor.
P. J. DILLON, Borough Treasurer.

Borough Treasurer's Office, 4th November 1887.

KILKENNY FAIR GREEN. An abstract of Receipts and Disbursements from 1st September 1887 to 1st September 1888.

Dr.

	£ s. d.	£ s. d.	£ s. d.
To received from tolls for year ending 31st August 1888			472 10 9
" balance due National Bank		129 0 0	
" Cheque outstanding—rent, Purcell's orchard	0 0 0		
On Treasurer's hands	0 0 7½		
		0 9 1½	
			137 0 7½
			610 10 10½

Cr.

	£ s. d.	£ s. d.
Rents:		
By balance due National Bank and on Treasurer's hands 1st September 1887		344 0 8½
" paid one year's rent due W. H. Flood, Esq., to 29th September 1887	43 15 0	
Less income tax	1 7 2	
		42 5 10
" Do. one year's rent due Rep. R. H. Robbins to 25th March 1888	16 10 0	
Less income tax	0 10 0	
		16 0 0
" Do. rep. P. Sullivan and Miss Mulhallen do. to do.	6 0 0	
Less income tax	0 5 6	
		5 14 6
" Do. W. H. Flood, Esq., half-year's rent of Purcell's orchard, ending 29th September 1887	12 10 0	
Less deductions for grand jury cess, poor rate, &c.	4 0 8	
		8 9 4
Treasurer's Fees, Staff Expenses, &c.:		
By paid P. J. Dillon, Esq., Treasurer's fees for year ended 1st September 1888	52 18 8	
" Do. Messrs. Davis and Geary for auditing accounts for year	5 0 0	
" Do. staff expenses during period of account	41 8 8	
" Do. caretaker (Phelan) wages for year	21 4 0	
		121 6 3
Incidental Expenses:		
By paid carpenter work at sheep pens, pailing, ticket house, &c.	0 10 0	
" timber for ditto	9 14 11	
" Do. removing manure from off green	5 3 3	
" Do. hardware accounts, oils, paint, &c., &c., &c.	6 14 6	
" Do. income tax assessment for year	7 1 9	
" Do. printing, advertising, and stationery	3 7 6	
" Do. miscellaneous payments	2 13 1	
Carried forward . . .		43 6 4

	£ s. d.	£ s. d.
Brought forward		
Repairs to Baths:		
By paid cheque to baths' account		60 0 0
Jenkin's:		
By paid Mrs. Hoskins, [illegible] for caretaker and P. Walsh		9 7 6
Cattle Cranell and Sheep Pens:		
By paid Messrs. Power for erecting and repairing cranell for weighing of cattle	7 10 0	
„ Do. tradesmen and labourers at ditto	4 11 10	
„ Do. same for material and repairs to iron sheep pens	4 13 6	
		16 15 4
New Horse Fair:		
By paid [illegible], masons, macadamising, levelling, &c. new horse fair		30 15 8
„ Do. National Bank, interest during period of account		7 13 9
		610 19 10½

We have examined the Treasurer's accounts of the Kilkenny fair green from 1st September 1887 to 1st September 1888, and find that the several payments have been supported by adequate vouchers, and the foregoing to be a correct statement of the amounts respectively.

Patrick Davis }
Patrick Grace } Borough Auditors.
Patrick Rowan, Mayor's Auditor.
P. J. Dillon, Borough Treasurer.

Borough Treasurer's Office, 2nd October 1888.

Summary of Gross Receipts in respect of the Markets and Fair Green.

Receipts for the 3 years ending 31st August 1888.

	£ s. d.	Average gross receipts for three years ending 31st August 1888. £ s. d.
Fair Green:		
1886	459 8 4½	
1887	442 19 9	
1888	473 10 3	
	3)1,375 18 4½	458 11 1½

Total receipts for the 3 years.

	£ s. d.	£ s. d.
Markets:		
1886	1,030 0 6½	
1887	1,022 5 9½	
1888	885 5 5	
	3)2,939 10 10	[illegible] 16 11½

Summary.—Markets.

	£ s. d.	£ s. d.	£ s. d.
Tolls:			
1886	885 10 8½		
1887	835 12 0½		
1888	691 5 9		
	3)2,413 18 7	804 11 6½	
Rents:			
1886	48 4 9		
1887	48 3 0		
1888	48 14 5		
	3)145 4 2	48 8 0¾	
Interest:			
1886	0 5 10		
1887	1 8 0		
1888	1 5 8		

TRANSFERS FROM MARKETS AND FAIR GREEN ACCOUNTS DURING THREE YEARS ENDING 31ST AUGUST 1888.

		£	s.	d.
Fair Green:				
1886.	For Booth's account	230	0	0
1887.	For Powell's Orchard	150	0	0
1888.	Nil	—		
		3) 380	0	0
	Average for three years	126	13	4

		£	s.	d.
Markets:				
1886.	Nil	—		
1887.	For borough fund account	200	0	0
1888.	Ditto	75	0	0
		3) 275	0	0
	Average for three years	91	13	4

19,865. In connexion with your ordinary duties as borough treasurer I believe you are the superintendent of the markets?—No. Mr. [illegible] is the superintendent.

19,866. Have you any duties whatever in connexion with the markets and fairs?—I have the keeping of the books.

19,867. As borough treasurer?—Yes. For instance, each week there is a [illegible] book of the amounts received.

19,868. Have you got any particular committee of the corporation managing the markets?—Yes.

19,869. What committee is that called?—The market committee, and the fair green committee for the fair green. The mayor is ex-officio chairman of each.

19,870. You have two different committees?—Yes.

19,871. What is the constitution of each?—The mayor is ex-officio. Each committee consists of eight members.

19,872. And the officials connected with the markets and fairs are immediately under the control of the members of the corporation forming those committees?—Yes, and of the general body of the corporation.

19,873. I presume like elsewhere the committee have to report generally to the council?—Yes.

19,874. Have you stalls in the markets?—Yes.

19,875. Are any of them useless at present?—Only one. It is a trifling thing. They are let by the week.

19,876. Is your revenue at present at its highest?—No. There is a great decrease I should say.

19,877. Is that owing to the insufficiency of the produce brought into the market?—Yes. For instance, the largest corn market, and barley is the principal produce, for the largest week in this year was 3,033 barrels, which came in, and if you go back to 1878, ten years ago, we had 8,434 barrels coming to the market. That is a decrease in the present year of 4,401 barrels.

19,878. Have you got the particulars of the quantity that comes in every year?—Yes. There is a toll book kept of the receipts. That toll book is kept by the clerk in the office, and each Monday it is brought to my office and transferred to the weekly book, and that weekly book will show you the receipts from each commodity.

19,879. You give the weight and the tolls?—Yes, the tolls received.

19,880. You always keep a record of the quantities of wheat, oats, barley, potatoes, wool, and butter brought into the market, and also the amount you receive from weighing at the crane and from the King Street and Judge Street market for butter and fowl?—Yes.

19,881-2. Do you keep in any way an account of the average current prices of these different commodities?—Of butter only. It would be impossible to keep it of corn, because the custom is the merchants buy at their offices by sample and then it comes into the market to be weighed, but at the butter market we keep the prices for each week.

19,883. Who makes up the return of the current price?—The clerk makes it up and sends it to my clerk.

19,884. Is that a perfectly accurate return of the current price?—It is perfectly accurate. It is published in the newspaper each day following, and we are in the habit of sending a copy of it to the merchants who buy.

19,885. Within your experience you never heard of anything being added to the current price in order to induce producers to send to the market?—Not to my knowledge. I should mention that I also keep a fowl book.

19,886. In addition to the different quantities of the other commodities, you also keep a return of the quantity of fowl brought into the market?—Yes.

19,887. And of eggs?—Yes.

19,888. And the number of loads of fruit and vegetables brought in?—Yes.

19,889. Who is it prepares this document?—It is prepared in my office from the returns furnished by the [illegible].

19,890-1. When they weigh butter in the market they retain the block of the ticket?—We retain the block of the ticket and give the outer one to the purchaser.

19,892. So that if the producer loses his ticket you can give him a copy of it?—Yes, and sometimes there is a good deal of trouble, as it might be twelve months after they would look for it. I would wish to explain that the average profit for the three years is expended in pursuance of the [illegible] section of the Market Act.

19,893. This section provides how you are to expend the profit?—Yes, to transfer it to the borough fund committee for the purpose of maintaining and improving the approaches to the market, and that sum did not over-cover the expenses.

19,894. However, the surplus profits since the market was established has always been expended in accordance with the provisions of the Act?—Yes, and it does not go [illegible] maintaining the approaches to the market.

19,895. Have you anything else to say, Mr. Dillon?—No.

19,896. Do you think the present system of charging on animals as they enter the fair green is better than the other system?—I think so. I think it works better here than charging on each animal sold.

19,897. Have you had experience of it elsewhere?—No. There is a charge for removing the manure after the fair.

19,898. Do you dispose of this?—There is an auction.

19,899. Does it set as an equivalent for the cost of removing it?—It does not. We have [illegible] engaged them.

19,900. What would you say are the average repairs to the fair and market?—There are no accounts.

19,901. Have you any check on all the men who receive money in connexion with the markets and fairs?—Certainly. The books are brought up and checked at my office every evening. Each clerk has to lodge a docket for what he receives during the day.

F. M. EGAN, Esquire, the Mayor re-examined.

19,902. Do you wish to say anything further?—There is one thing arising out of Mr. Dillon's evidence I wish to refer to. These profits are used by the corporation for the public benefit, by developing the markets. For instance this year we opened a new fair called the horse fair, [illegible] and purchased a site and spent a good deal of money in the preparation of the site.

19,903. Will the horse fair be held on a different site from the ordinary fair?—A different site and different [illegible].

19,904. Have you completed the purchase?—We have recently held fairs at it for the last four months.

19,905. What is the amount of the purchase money?—We gave 150l. for the site, and there was expended in public money a fund of 20l. more, got up by the citizens and otherwise. There was erection made of the King Street market. That is portion of the general market, but there is a different gate through which certain produce goes in.

19,906. You regulate the market by having different portions allotted for each description of commodity?—Yes. It works well to have milk in one part, [illegible] in another, and potatoes in another.

19,907. None of the commodities are sold about the streets?—Occasionally vegetables are sold at the doors, and the corporation express a desire to prevent a recurrence of that, because the people having vegetable stores complain, and the corporation at the time the market was established had all the vegetables removed into the market. The people here have been paying a rent since that time, and it would be unfair to allow others vend vegetables before doors.

19,908. Have you a rule prohibiting the sale of marketable commodities elsewhere than in the market?—Yes. It has been in force, and we are empowered to fine, and a notice has been put up threatening a penalty of 40s. on people for purchasing fowl outside the market, and I recently attended the market at 7 o'clock and fined people for purchasing and selling fowl.

19,909. Have you ever heard complaints of forestalling, or has that been the cause of your interfering in the question of fowl?—I am sorry to say it is largely availed of in horse dealing. Horse dealers generally watch horses coming into the fair outside the fair if possible, believing that if they catch the proprietor and his horse outside they will knock a better bargain out of him than by purchasing in the open fair. We have been combating that by preventing the show of horses on the parade, and compelling them to go into the fair green.

Mr. Denis Sullivan, Market Superintendent, examined.

19,910. You are the superintendent of the market?—I am butter inspector and market superintendent.

19,911. Kindly mention to me the different marketable commodities that are brought in on Saturday — the general market day?—There is wheat, oats, and barley.

19,912. All descriptions of corn?—Yes, and fowl of every description. Vegetables, milk, hay, straw, turnips, and mangolds, and all farm produce. Coal, and butter in pails.

19,913. Anything else?—No.

19,914. Are cattle brought in or calves or pigs?—There are young calves brought into the market.

19,915. You have five scales in this market?—If required we can work five.

19,916. Have you any cranes in the market?—There is one crane in it and one on the Parade.

19,917. Is that on the public thoroughfare?—It is on the public thoroughfare, but it is not an inconvenience to the public.

19,918. How is the Parade crane utilised?—For weighing hay and straw and coal.

19,919. You have no hay and straw market proper?—No.

19,920. Where do they expose hay and straw for sale?—On the open street.

19,921. Therefore the hay and straw market are held on the public thoroughfare?—Yes.

19,922. What charges have you on it?—Threepence on the load of hay or straw.

19,923. For weighing?—Yes.

19,924. Supposing they exposed a load of hay or straw on the public thoroughfare and sold it by bulk and did not ascertain the weight, would the corporation seek for their charge?—I have not done so at any time, but I think it would be right to do so.

19,925. Has such an occasion ever happened, or have they ever sold hay in that way?—It has not come within my knowledge.

19,926. I presume the buyers will not buy straw by weight?—By weight.

19,927. Do you always ascertain at that crane the exact tare of the cart?—Yes.

19,928. You never go by estimation in any way?—Oh, certainly not.

19,929. You actually weigh it?—Yes. No such thing as a tare under any circumstances is given unless the cart is weighed.

19,930. Who have you in charge of the Parade crane?—A man named Crawford. Supposing the buyer and seller agree to take the cart at a fixed weight I give directions to the clerk in charge to write in the space where the weight of the cart is entered the words "Car not weighed."

19,931. Where the cart is not weighed, but the buyer and seller agree to the weight, you always take a note and put in "Car not weighed," and you only give the gross weight?—Yes.

19,932. In those tickets you give the gross weight, the tare, the net weight, description of the goods and the cart, the names of the buyer and seller, and the initials of the weighmaster?—Yes.

19,933. Has the one man, Crawford, to do the duty of weighing and filling up the tickets?—No. He is the clerk. He has two men to attend to the cars.

19,934. So that no undue delay is caused by the filling in the tickets?—No.

19,935. I suppose I have got the receipts from the crane at the amount given by Mr. Dillon?—Yes.

19,936. Is the hay the only commodity that is sold on the public thoroughfare?—Hay, straw, and coal.

19,937. Do they expose coal, too, for sale?—Yes.

19,938. In carts?—Yes.

19,939. Do you charge 3d. a load?—Yes.

19,940. Would you take into consideration whether it was a horse or a donkey load?—If it is a load of coal under 10 cwt. the charge is only 1½d.

19,941. Then you charge on the weight in coal?—Yes.

19,942. If a donkey load of hay came into the market would you charge 3d.?—Yes.

19,943. You do not care what quantity is on it?—No.

19,944. Is corn always brought into the market?—Yes.

19,945. The mayor just mentioned that a quantity of corn is purchased by the merchants of the town by sample, and when such a quantity is delivered does it go direct to the merchants or through your market?—It goes through our market to be weighed.

19,946. What is the charge for weighing corn?—It is according to the description of corn. There is ½d. a hundred for barley and wheat, and ¼d. a hundred for oats and potatoes.

19,947. You charge per hundred-weight?—Yes.

19,948. Supposing a merchant purchased by sample, and the corn was subsequently delivered to him without being weighed, would you charge?—He is liable to a penalty according to the Market Act. We would not permit it.

19,949. Has a case like that occurred?—No.

19,950. Within your memory?—No. It has not occurred.

19,951. All corn has to be weighed at your market?—Yes.

19,952. How many weighmasters have you in the market?—I have two permanent weighmasters.

19,953. You have a sufficient clerical staff?—Yes.

19,954. You give a ticket for the corn?—Yes, and keep a block.

19,955. They are printed forms you give?—Yes.

19,956. What is the charge on fowl?—A halfpenny a pair for small fowl, and a penny per pair for geese and turkeys.

19,957. Is that when they entered the market?—Yes.

19,958. Then you do not consider whether they are subsequently sold or not?—No.

19,959. It is for entry into the market?—Yes. They are not supposed to sell within the precincts unless they enter the market.

19,960. But supposing they brought in a pair of small fowl you charge a halfpenny, and a pair of turkeys a penny, and if they do not sell you still retain the charge?—Yes.

19,961. Then it is a charge for entering the market?—Yes.

19,961a. Do they take up possession of any stall?—No. They stand in the open market. There is a shed for shelter that they can avail themselves of.

19,962. On vegetables what is your charge?—A horse load of vegetables is 3d.

19,963. And a donkey load?—2d., and baskets 1d.

19,964. What would be the value of the smallest basket of vegetables you have known to be brought in. Would that ever be equivalent to 6d. only in value?—Certainly, and 1s.

19,965. Would they bring in as low as 6d. worth?—I could not say.

19,966. Did you ever know it?—Not to my knowledge.

19,967. Did they ever bring in 1s. worth or less?—I should think they would.

19,968. Did they ever bring in 6d. worth?—It has not come to my knowledge.

19,969. You would say 1s.?—I should say a basket of vegetables would be worth 1s. or more.

19,970. On that basket you would charge a twelfth of its entire value?—Yes.

19,971. No matter whether subsequently sold or not?—No.

19,972. It is for entry into the market?—Yes.

19,973. It is compulsory on them to enter the market, they cannot go elsewhere?—No.

19,974. You have a prohibitory regulation to that effect?—Yes.

19,975. On milk what is your charge?—A penny churn.

19,976. The same observations apply to the milk?—Yes. It is charged on entering the market.

19,977. The charge on turnips is for weighing?—Yes, 3d. a load.

19,978. Do they ever bring turnips and expose them for sale in the market?—Yes.

19,979. Have you then two charges—one for weighing and another for entry into the market?—No. For goods that are weighed there is no toll charged on entry.

19,980. Are the turnips weighed on the market scale?—They are weighed on the scale and sold in the market.

19,981. When do they pay the charge?—At the time of weighing.

19,982. Coal is sold in the Parade?—Yes.

19,983. Have you a charge on roll butter?—Yes.

19,984. What is it?—Fourteen pounds a 1d.; from 14 to 28, 2d.; from 28 to 56, 3d. There is a halfpenny for five pounds and under, and they get a ticket, of which we retain a blank also.

19,985. Do you always weigh the roll butter?—Certainly.

19,986. It is never sold by bulk?—No. It is not sold to our knowledge.

19,987. Are those people who sell it retailers?—No; they are the producers.

19,988. Do they retail to the public or to the merchants of the town?—They retail in the market, and the citizens purchase from them there.

19,989. The private consumers purchase?—Yes.

19,990. Have you a small scales to weigh this butter?—Yes.

19,991. Supposing a private consumer goes in and buys a roll of butter and says I will give you so much and buy it by bulk?—He would not be permitted.

19,992. Then you have a regulation in the market compelling all roll butter to be weighed before sold?—Yes. It may be sold and weighed afterwards, but it must not leave the market without being weighed.

19,993. When they are bringing the butter away do you ask them to show you any ticket to know whether the butter is weighed or not?—I often check them in that way.

19,994. How do you know it has been weighed and the charge paid?—There is a ticket for every roll weighed.

19,995. Do you go around and inspect them?—I go through the place. It passes in one gate to be weighed and back again, and a party checks each roll of butter and puts the tariff on it.

19,996. How can he check the ticket of those who have it severed or who may go out some other gate?—They cannot pass out without being checked.

19,997. What is the charge on young calves?—A penny.

19,998. Is that for entering the market place?—Yes.

19,999. Whether sold or not?—Yes.

20,000. I see wool comes into the market?—Yes.

20,001. You charge every merchant for wool a special tariff?—Yes.

20,002. Do you know the cause of that special tariff?—I do. For instance the merchants who buy wool, when shipping it off to the buyer in London or any port the tariff has been previously paid for, and they established a special tariff and did not consider it fair to charge them as much as the others.

20,003. What is the charge on roll butter over 28 lbs.?—From 28 to 62 three half-pence, and from 62 up to 112 lbs. twopence.

20,004. If it was over 112 lbs.?—It is the same ratio as before.

20,005. The butter market is held on Fridays?—Yes.

20,006. What is the charge on the butter?—2d. on each firkin before 10 o'clock, and 3d. after 10.

20,007. You have a regulation in the market increasing the toll on butter after 10 o'clock?—Yes.

20,008. What time have you the market open in the morning?—At 6 o'clock in the morning.

20,009. What number of firkins on an average come in during the season on market day?—Perhaps about 250.

20,010. What hour do the buyers commence to buy?—Half-past 11.

20,011. Have you a regulation to that effect?—Yes.

20,012. They cannot buy until half-past 11?—They can. The butter is generally qualified and weighed at that hour, and then the bell is rung notifying that the merchants are ready to buy.

20,013. But can the merchants buy until the bell rings?—They can to be sure.

20,014. You do not prohibit them?—No.

20,015. Is it you make the return of the number of firkins brought in?—One of the clerks makes the return, and I check it.

20,016. Have you tasters employed in the butter market?—No.

20,017. Is this charge on each firkin as they come in?—I qualify them and the salesman weighs them, and the clerk enters the weight on the ticket.

20,018. Do you taste the butter?—Yes.

20,019. Are the sellers and producers satisfied with your decision?—They seem to be.

20,020. You have heard no objection?—It is hard to please them.

20,021. When the buyers are purchasing, do they go by the quality you have decreed?—I should say so.

20,022. Do they taste it themselves?—They do, certainly.

20,023. You never heard them dispute the quality?—Yes. The buyer will know the value as much as he can.

20,024. Who have you engaged in the market beside yourself?—The market staff. I have men for weighing and keeping tickets.

20,025. When the butter comes in before 10 the charge is 2d.?—Yes.

20,026. Do you weigh the butter?—Yes, and qualify it for them.

20,027. Do you drain the butter at all?—Yes, when I suspect there is water.

20,028. Then you do not drain every firkin?—No.

20,029. You do not loosen them?—No.

20,030. You take them in the casks they come to the market?—Yes.

20,031. When weighing, do you leave the tops on?—Certainly not.

20,032. Do you loosen the hoops at all?—Yes.

20,033. You weigh no salt or water that is in them?—No.

20,034. Do you take off the hoops?—I clean away the dirt, and see by the lever if there is any water in the firkins, and then drain them if there is.

20,035. It rests with yourself whether they are drained or not?—No. The butter that requires to be drained I drain.

20,036. You do not make it a rule to turn up each firkin?—No, not if there is any necessity.

20,037. But are the buyers satisfied with your work?—Certainly.

20,038. All the firkins must be weighed?—All weighed.

20,039. Did they ever purchase the butter before it was weighed?—Certainly.

20,040. And they do so?—They do not at present.

20,041. Have you a regulation in the market, or have the butter buyers a regulation compelling each firkin to be weighed before it is sold?—Each firkin is supposed to be weighed and qualified before it is sold.

20,042. That is the practice?—Yes.

20,043. When you weigh do you ever put the weight in chalk on the firkin?—Yes.

20,044. As well as on the ticket?—Yes.

20,045. And in return for the ticket 2d. is paid?—Yes. I put the qualification on it with an iron mark. I describe the quality on the firkin, and that quality is written into the ticket. The weight of the firkin when weighed on the scales is written on the side with chalk.

20,046. Therefore they have the quality, the gross weight, and the net weight, and the tare as it is branded by the cooper?—Yes.

20,047. It is in return for this ticket the 2d. is paid?—On entering the market the 2d. is paid.

20,048. Before anything takes place at all?—Yes.

20,049. After 10 o'clock the charge is 3d.?—Yes.

20,050. Supposing a great number came up to the market, and they all could not get in before 10 o'clock, and they wait outside in the street awaiting their turn to come in, would you charge those people?—I do not know. I would take that advantage if they happened to be in a bulk outside. I do not think it would be fair to take that advantage.

20,051. When you say entering the market, do you mean entering the market premises?—Yes.

20,052. Not entering the street?—They must enter the market, and the tolls are collected on the butter when entering the market from the street. There is never a crush there at that place.

20,053. They all come in ample time?—Yes.

20,054. I see you have a column in this ticket for the price. Is that the contract price between the buyer and seller?—Yes.

20,055. Do you ever ascertain that?—I do.

20,056. You keep a return, as Mr. Dillon mentioned, of the current prices and the different qualities of butter?—Yes. We have the price set for the different class of

20,060. Always standing beam?—If a firkin is standing beam we look on it as weighed.

20,061. Are the buyers satisfied with that?—Certainly.

20,062. Is that the rule in the market?—It is.

20,063. Is that the rule to weigh down to standing beam and by down weight?—Yes.

20,064. How do you weigh wool?—The same way.

20,065. Down to a pound?—Half a pound for wool.

20,066. And corn?—Corn down to a pound weight.

20,067. Is it by standing beam?—We weigh it fine.

20,068. Are not the potatoes brought here?—Certainly.

20,069. What is the charge on potatoes?—A halfpenny per hundred.

20,070. Supposing a load of potatoes was brought in what would you charge on the load?—A halfpenny a hundred.

20,071. Then they would have to weigh each individual sack?—No. If there is a load of potatoes loosely in the cart, we weigh them on the crane and charge a halfpenny per hundred.

20,072. How would you ascertain the tare of the cart?—When the potatoes are emptied we weigh the car back again and take it from the gross.

20,073. Supposing they do not sell all the potatoes how is the empty car to be weighed?—What would remain of the potatoes and the weight of the cart would be taken from the gross total.

20,074. If they come in bags?—We weigh each sack separate.

20,075. When weighing a sack of potatoes what is the lowest weight you weigh with?—The same as corn.

20,076. Down to a pound?—Yes.

20,077. Is that the usual and customary way of weighing potatoes?—It is.

20,078. Do you give a cast of the beam?—Nothing but the same as corn.

20,079. Do you weigh the sack or estimate the tare of the sack?—Let the buyer arrange the weight of the sack.

20,080. You have nothing to do with the sack?—Nothing.

20,081. You only give the gross weight?—The gross weight for oats and potatoes.

20,082. Is it on the gross weight you charge on potatoes?—Yes.

20,083. On sacks of potatoes?—Yes.

20,084. You include the sack in your charge?—Yes.

20,085. Do you know the practice existing between the buyer and seller in ascertaining the tare of the bag?—For corn four pounds a sack and for potatoes seven pounds.

20,086. Is that allowance or deduction the same in different kinds of weather. Would the tare be seven pounds if the potatoes were brought in on a very fine day?—I should think it would with the clay.

20,087. If it was extremely wet and the sack became completely saturated with rain would it be the same?—The difference would be very little.

20,088. Would they allow anything extra?—They may, but it did not come within my knowledge.

20,089. But that seven pounds is supposed to include any sand around the potatoes as well as the tare of the sack.

20,090. And it is four pounds for corn?—Yes.

20,091. You give a ticket for this, I presume?—Yes.

20,092. Do you prohibit the sale of potatoes elsewhere than in this market place?—There are some potatoes sold through the town in the shops.

20,099. That is a small basket?—A good size basket.

20,100. These charges are as the parties enter the market?—Yes.

20,101. Supposing they had not the 2d., 3d., or 4d., as the case may be, what course do you adopt?—We often permit them to come in; in fact we always do where they have not it convenient.

20,102. Has a case occurred where the commodity was seized by the toll collector?—We do not go to that extremity.

20,103. A case of that kind has never occurred?—No.

20,104. You allow them in?—Yes.

20,105. And collect the charge during the day?—It is not customary to do it, but if there is a party during the week who would not leave the charge we permit them so.

20,106. You have stalls in the market place?—Yes.

20,107. How do you let them?—According to the size.

20,108. What is the rate?—About 10 feet square 6d. and 15 feet square 1s., and closed up stalls are 1s. 6d.

20,109. What sort of people rent them from you?—They are vegetable vendors and potato vendors.

20,110. Is there any dead meat sold in those stalls?—No.

20,111. Is that sold in the town about the butchers' shops?—Yes.

20,112. Do the people who bring in and sell butter on market days complain of the close proximity of the eggs, fowl, and vegetables?—No.

20,113. And that the butter becomes deteriorated?—No.

20,114. Are they sold in different portions of the market?—Yes, far apart.

20,115. From what districts do these commodities come?—From the country around the city for eight or ten miles or more. Firkins come from the County Carlow.

20,116. Have you any duties in connexion with the fair green?—No.

20,117. What time do you close the market?—On Saturday evenings we close at 9 o'clock. It is open from 6 in the morning until 9 during the summer six months.

20,118. Supposing potatoes are brought into the market, must they pay the charge?—No; only those weighed.

20,119. Supposing they are sold in the market in another town, and he retails them, have you a second charge?—No, only one charge. There is another matter I wish to mention. It is with reference to the tolls charged on certain commodities brought to the market. For instance, the value of a firkin of butter is 3l. 10s. or 4l., and it is weighed and qualified for 2d. In other markets they charge 6d., and in the Carrick market the charge is 6d. or 9d.

20,120. What suggestion have you to offer?—I think it is too low.

20,121. You want to suggest an increase in the charge?—I think so. It costs a good deal to work the market. The farmers would certainly fight against any increase.

20,122. You have heard no complaints from those frequenting the markets of any mismanagement there, or any inconvenience caused to them?—Not a particle.

20,123. Witness then produced a notice, of which the following is a copy:—

NOTICE.

All firkins are in future to be lined with muslin or parchment.

After the first Friday in September, buyers will be allowed to charge 6d. on each firkin not so lined.

By Order.

The witness also subsequently produced the several tickets in use in the markets and the rules in the butter market, and of which the following are copies:—

KILKENNY GENERAL MARKET ACT, 1861,
24 Vict. c. 49.

Roll and Pan Butter Market.

________ day of November 188[illegible]

________ lbs.

________ Clerk.

KILKENNY GENERAL MARKET ACT, 1861.
24 Vict. c. 49.

Roll and Pan Butter Market.

No.

________ day of November 188[illegible]

________ lbs.

________ Clerk.

KILKENNY GENERAL MARKET ACT, 1861.
24 Vic. cap. 49.

Potato Ticket.

No. 349.

Public Market ____ day of ______ 188_.

M ________

Stones lbs.

KILKENNY GENERAL MARKET ACT, 1861.
24 Vic. cap. 49.

Potato Ticket.

No. 349.

Public Market ____ day of ______ 188_.

M ________

Stones lbs.

N.B.—It is requested that no gratuity whatever will be given to any of the officials in connexion with these Markets.

KILKENNY GENERAL MARKET ACT, 1861.
24 Vict. c. 43.

WEIGHING MACHINE.

No. 207. ______________________ 186__

	Tons	Cwts.	Qrs.	Lbs.
Gross Weight,				
Car Weight,				
Nett Weight,				

Description of Goods ______________________

From ______________________

To ______________________

______________________ Weigh Master.

KILKENNY GENERAL MARKET ACT, 1861.
24 Vict. c. 43.

WEIGHING MACHINE.

No. 207. ______________________ 186__

	Tons	Cwts.	Qrs.	Lbs.
Gross Weight,				
Car Weight,				
Nett Weight,				

Description of Goods ______________________

From ______________________

To ______________________

______________________ Weigh Master.

KILKENNY GENERAL MARKET ACT, 1861.
24 Vict. c. 43.

BARLEY TICKET.

No. 203.

Corn Market, ______ day of ______ 186__.

Mr. ______________________

	Stones.	lbs.

N.B.—No deduction can be made from the above weight by the buyer, except the weight of the bag, tie, or fastening.

BOROUGH OF KILKENNY.

KILKENNY GENERAL MARKET ACT, 1861.
24 Vict. c. 43.

BARLEY TICKET.

No. 203.

Corn Market, ______ day of ______ 186__.

Mr. ______________________

	Stones.	lbs.

N.B.—No deduction can be made from the above weight by the buyer, except the weight of the bag, tie, or fastening.

☞ It is requested that no gratuity whatever will be given to any of the officials in connection with these Markets.

BOROUGH OF KILKENNY.

KILKENNY GENERAL MARKET ACT, 1861.
24 Vict. c. 43.

WHEAT TICKET.

No. 203.

Corn Market, ______ day of ______ 186__.

Mr. ______________________

	Stones.	lbs.

N.B.—No deduction can be made from the above weight by the buyer, except the weight of the bag, tie, or fastening.

BOROUGH OF KILKENNY.

KILKENNY GENERAL MARKET ACT, 1861.
24 Vict. c. 43.

WHEAT TICKET.

No. 203.

Corn Market ______ day of ______ 186__.

Mr. ______________________

	Stones.	lbs.

N.B.—No deduction can be made from the above weight by the buyer, except the weight of the bag, tie, or fastening.

☞ It is requested that no gratuity whatever will be given to any of the officials in connection with these Markets.

BOROUGH OF KILKENNY.

KILKENNY GENERAL MARKET ACT, 1861.
24 Vict. c. 49.

OATS TICKET.

No. 200.

Corn Market______ day of ______ 186_.

Mr. ____________________

	Stones.	lbs.

N.B.—No deduction can be made from the above weight by the buyer, except the weight of the bag, tie, or fastening.

BOROUGH OF KILKENNY.

KILKENNY GENERAL MARKET ACT, 1861.
24 Vict. c. 49.

OATS TICKET.

No. 200.

Corn Market______ day of ______ 186_.

Mr. ____________________

	Stones.	lbs.

N.B.—No deduction can be made from the above weight by the buyer, except the weight of the bag, tie, or fastening.

☞ It is requested that no gratuity whatever will be given to any of the officials in connection with these Markets.

BOROUGH OF KILKENNY.

KILKENNY GENERAL MARKET ACT, 1861.
24 Vict. c. 49.

BUTTER MARKET.

No. 200.

Public Market ______ day of ______ 186_.

Mr. ____________________

Residence ____________________

Qy.	Firm.	Gross Weight.			Tare.	Nett Weight.		
		Cwt.	Qrs.	Lbs.		Cwt.	Qrs.	Lbs.

N.B.—It is requested that no gratuity whatever will be given to any of the Officials in connection with these markets.

KILKENNY GENERAL MARKET ACT, 1861.
24 Vict. c. 49.

BUTTER MARKET.

No. 200.

Public Market ______ day of ______ 186_.

Mr. ____________________

Residence ____________________

Qy.	Firm.	Gross Weight.			Tare.	Nett Weight.		
		Cwt.	Qrs.	Lbs.		Cwt.	Qrs.	Lbs.

N.B.—It is requested that no gratuity whatever will be given to any of the Officials in connection with these markets.

KILKENNY GENERAL MARKET ACT, 1861.
24 Vict. c. 49.

WEIGHING MACHINE.

No. 160. ______ ______ 186_.

Description of Goods____________________

From____________________

To____________________

No.	Gross Weight.				Car Weight.		
	Tons.	Cwts.	Qrs.	Lbs.	Cwts.	Qrs.	Lbs.

____________ Weigh Master.

KILKENNY GENERAL MARKET ACT, 1861.
24 Vict. c. 49.

WEIGHING MACHINE.

No. 160. ______ ______ 186_.

Description of Goods____________________

From____________________

To____________________

No.	Gross Weight.				Car Weight.		
	Tons.	Cwts.	Qrs.	Lbs.	Cwts.	Qrs.	Lbs.

____________ Weigh Master.

KILKENNY GENERAL MARKET ACT, 1861.
24 Vict. c. 49.

WOOL MARKET.

No. 200.

King Street ______ day of ______ 186_.

Mr.____________________

	Cwts.	Qrs.	Lbs.

N.B.—No deduction can be made from the above weight by the buyer, except the weight of the bag, tie, or dressing.

BOROUGH OF KILKENNY.

KILKENNY GENERAL MARKET ACT, 1861.
24 Vict. c. 49.

WOOL MARKET.

No. 200.

King Street ______ day of ______ 186_.

Mr.____________________

	Cwts.	Qrs.	Lbs.

N.B.—No deduction can be made from the above weight by the buyer, except the weight of the bag, tie, or dressing.

☞ It is requested that no gratuity whatsoever will be given to any of the officials in connection with these Markets.

BOROUGH OF KILKENNY.

KILKENNY FIRKIN BUTTER MARKET.

The following rules have been adopted by the Kilkenny corporation:—

CUTS.

1st. That the cut in a firkin 56 lbs. gross or under, be 2s. 6d.

2nd. That the cut in a firkin 57 lbs. to 84 lbs. gross inclusive, be 3s. 9d.

3rd. That the cut in a firkin 85 lbs. to 112 lbs. gross inclusive, be 5s.

TARES.

4th. That tares disputed be settled by "proof tare" (stripping).

5th. That the tare from block be branded with Cooper's name on each firkin.

6th. That 1 lb. super-tare be allowed on each firkin 56 lbs. gross and under; and 2 lbs. on 56 lbs. and all above 56 lbs. gross.

The toll on firkins will be:—2d. before 10 o'clock; 3d. after 10 o'clock.

☞ Buying to commence every day at 11.30 o'clock, immediately at the ringing of the market bell.

P. M. EGAN,
Mayor.

July 1st, 1867.

Mr. Patrick [illegible], Borough Inspector, continued.

20,124. You are the borough inspector?—Yes.

20,125. You have duties to perform in connection with the fair green?—Yes.

20,126. What is the nature of the duties?—To provide a staff for working the green, and superintend the staff and open the gates in the morning.

20,127. What hour does the fair usually begin?—The gates are open. They vary in summer time. They are opened as early as half-past 4 o'clock, that is the cattle fair.

20,128. What description of animals are brought here to this fair green?—Sheep, cattle, and pigs.

20,129. Are pigs brought on cattle fair days?—Yes, small pigs in creels.

20,130. What else?—Horses.

20,131. Are horses brought on fair days?—Yes, to the special horse fair.

20,132. On the second Wednesday in each month?—Yes.

20,133. On the same fair green as the cattle are disposed of?—Yes; but it is a separate enclosure and a separate horse fair.

20,134. The one fair green is divided into two sections?—Yes.

20,135. And one portion is allotted for horses?—Yes, but one opens into the other by gateways.

20,136. A return is kept of the number of cows and calves, sheep, small pigs, &c., in fact every description of animal?—Yes.

20,137. Do you ever ascertain the current prices of these different animals?—No.

20,138. For curiosity even?—No.

20,139. These accounts produced are furnished to the borough treasurer, and he keeps them in his office?—Yes, and tolls are levied by ticket.

20,140. You say you have it open at 4 o'clock in the morning?—Yes.

20,141. And they commence to buy and sell at that hour?—They can.

20,142. There is no restriction?—No.

20,143. What is the toll on sheep?—Halfpenny for sheep.

20,144. Is that as they are entering the fair green or when they are going out?—Before they go into the fair green. They have to get a ticket at the box.

20,145. How many gates are there to the fair green?—There are four opened each morning.

20,146. You have men stationed at each?—A man with a haversack, and helpers to take the tickets.

20,147. Have you men stationed at each to take tickets?—No. The box is some distance from the gate at the entrance, and the man in the box issues the ticket.

20,148. Supposing there was a large number of sheep, would one ticket be necessary for the lot?—Yes.

20,149. Do the same observations apply to the horses and other descriptions of animals, cattle, bonhams, and pigs?—Yes. If a man had 12 pigs he would get a ticket for 10 and two.

20,150. The charge on cattle is 2d.?—Yes.

20,151. Yearlings?—A 1d.

20,152. Fat pigs a 1d.?—Yes.

20,152a. Bonhams are a ½d. each?—Yes.

20,153. A load of small pigs containing six or upwards?—3d.

20,154. Supposing there were five?—It would be 2½d.

20,155. For every horse 3d.?—Yes.

20,156. Standings 6d.?—Yes.

20,157. Asses?—A 1d. There is an extra charge for the horses that go into the paddock. That is a charge where loops are provided.

20,158. When the animal is sold in the market or fair do you collect these tickets coming out?—They must give them up going into the fair.

20,159. Then you have no duties whatever to perform in relation to these people, but keep order when they enter the fair green?—Yes.

20,160. There is no charge going out?—None.

20,161. Are they perfectly satisfied?—I have heard no complaint.

20,162. That charge must be paid whether they subsequently sell the animal or not?—Yes.

20,163. Do you think that system of paying on each animal as they enter the fair green is better than levying a larger toll on each animal when sold as they are brought away, as exists elsewhere?—I do not know how you could collect it at all.

20,164. Do not you know that practice prevails very much—in fact it is a surprise to find the other practice exists here. At present you have heard no objection to the existing system here?—None.

20,165. Would you say any great percentage of the animals brought to the fairs are sold?—I would say so.

20,166. Could you give me any idea of the percentage?—I could not.

20,167. You keep this return of the number coming in by ticket?—Yes.

20,168. Are there any salesmasters in the market or fair, or have you any rules regulating the sale through the salesmasters?—No.

20,169. The farmer can sell to whom he pleases?—Yes.

20,170. Do salesmasters attend?—No. There are what are called cattle dealers or jobbers.

20,171. Do they buy and sell themselves?—Yes.

20,172. They never sell as agents for others?—No, they do not.

20,173. Is this fair very well attended?—Yes; they are large fairs.

20,174. Where is the crane or weighbridge erected in the fair green?—It is on the cattle fair, about the centre of the fair green.

20,175. And if they wish to weigh, you have a man in charge of that?—Yes; there is a man there, a clerk and weighman, if necessary.

20,176. If they wish to ascertain the weight of an animal, you charge the additional sum fixed?—Yes.

20,177. Is it the stipulated charge?—Yes, by Act of Parliament. We have got a copy of it printed, and hung up at the crane.

20,178. I suppose the fair green is cleaned always after the fairs?—Yes.

20,179. Do you prohibit the sale of cattle on the roads outside the fair green?—Yes. We have the mayor's bailiff and another man employed solely to do that. He is paid at each fair for attending to that business.

20,180. Supposing a farmer was coming from one of the country districts with some animals to the fair, and he effected a sale on the road before reaching the fair green or the lane, would you seek for any charge on behalf of the corporation?—We would if we could find out that the sale was effected.

20,181. Has a case of that kind occurred?—Yes, in case of horses. We have detected that. We have a bailiff [illegible] outside the approaches. As the mayor mentioned they loiter outside for a considerable time before they go into the fair green.

20,182. Within what limits would the corporation be entitled to demand this charge?—Within the borough boundary.

20,183. You would not seek for it if a sale were effected without the borough boundary. I do not think we could. We would have no jurisdiction. The ownership outside [illegible] the fair green.

20,184. How is the fair green used between fairs?—It is [illegible] unemployed.

20,185. Does grass grow on any portion of it?—Only on the paddock of the horse fair.

20,186. Have you any suggestions to make?—None.

20,187. Have you ever heard any complaints in relation to the fairs?—None.

J. E. M[illegible], Esq., Town Clerk, examined.

[illegible]. You are the Town Clerk of Kilkenny?—Yes.

[illegible]. When was the corporation established?—It was established under the Municipal Reform Act.

[illegible]. Have you suggestions to offer, or any further information to give about the markets and fairs here?—No. You have got all the information that it was possible to get.

[illegible]. Is there any other gentleman who has any observations to make?—No answer.

The inquiry then closed.

CAPPAWHITE—COUNTY TIPPERARY.

With reference to my inquiry in Cappawhite on the 14th November 1888, I beg to report as follows:—

Cappawhite is an inland town, in the county of Tipperary. It is some five miles from the nearest railway station. It is a small town, and the trade is purely in agricultural produce. The houses are small and of a poor description. The local government is vested in the Board of Guardians and Grand Jury. The population is 629.

There is no special market day in Cappawhite, owing to its isolated position, but when any marketable commodities are brought into the town they are usually weighed on the weighbridge. No beam and scale is provided.

The fairs are held on the 10th January, 14th February, 10th March, 16th April, 9th May, 4th June, 27th July, 16th August, 29th September, 18th October, 16th November, and 21st December. A pig fair is held on the day previous to the ordinary fairs.

Tolls are levied at all the fairs.

A toll-board is erected for public inspection, and a weighbridge has been provided.

The tolls are the property of a Mr. Timothy Crowe, Cappawhite, who purchased on the 24th August 1872, from a Mr. Browne, for 1,000*l*.

The Public Records do not disclose any patent for Cappawhite, but one was granted for Cappagh, after which it is called. This is the patent referred to by Mr. Dowling in his evidence. It is dated 8th July 1729 (3 George II.), and authorised him to hold a Wednesday market and five fairs, viz.,—29th May, 26th July, 18th September, 5th November, and 21st December. The fairs on the 14th February, 9th May, 4th June, 27th July, 29th September, 16th November, and 21st December have been held for a great length of time. The fairs on the 10th January, 10th March, 16th April, and 16th August were established about 30 years ago, and the fair on the 18th October about 20 years ago.

No express authority seems, therefore, to have been granted for the fairs on the 10th January, 14th February, 10th March, 16th April, 9th May, 4th June, 27th July, 16th August, and 18th October.

In accordance with my instructions I have inspected the fair green, &c.

There is no weekly market in Cappawhite, nor any market at all except the days before the fairs. If commodities are to be disposed of during the ordinary days of the week, the people of the surrounding districts bring them to the shopkeepers and dispose of them by private contract. An attempt to establish a butter market was made by the townspeople, and a shed was erected in the centre of the square,—a large space in the middle of the principal street,—but the project resulted in failure, and the shedding is being allowed to fall into ruins.

The fairs are held in a green, and also on the streets. This green is about two acres in extent, and is partially enclosed, and approached by a narrow laneway which skirts the entire green on one side. There are no sheds or pens provided for the accommodation of those frequenting the fair.

If small pigs are brought to the fair in a cart a standing charge of tenpence is levied, whether the pigs are subsequently sold or not, but if they are subsequently sold they have to bear an additional charge of threepence each. In the first instance the seller has to pay the charge, and in the latter case the person in possession of the animal.

Appended will be found a transcript of the evidence taken at the inquiry.

John J. O'Meara,
Assistant Commissioner.

45, Lower Mount Street, Dublin.

Cappawhite, November 14th, 1888.

Mr. Timothy Crowe examined.

20,192. Are you the owner of the tolls and customs of Cappawhite?—Yes.

20,193. You produce this conveyance dated the 24th August 1872, as the deed conveying the property to you?—Yes.

20,194. Who was Mr. Brown, the grantor in this conveyance?—He was an Englishman.

20,195. Was he the previous beneficial owner?—Yes.

20,196. You do not know under what authority he conveyed this to you, or on what authority he held them?—I do not know. I was not the previous owner of the market at all.

20,197. He was the owner?—Yes. I was paying him rent.

20,198. Would you have any objection to mention the purchase money?—Not the least. It was 1,000*l*.

20,199. You paid 1,000*l*. for the tolls here?—Yes.

20,200. The witness then produced an indenture dated 24th August 1872, whereby Thomas Banks Brown assigned to Timothy Crowe all that and those the piece of ground commonly known as the fair field of Cappawhite, and also the market house or shed now standing in said village, together with the tolls and customs of Cappawhite, and all rents, issues, emoluments, and profits arising therefrom, and the right and power to sue for and recover and receive the tolls and customs of Cappa for ever. There are no special covenants.

20,201. (Assistant Commissioner.) Are these subject to any annual charge, Mr. Crowe?—No, only the quitrent.

20,202. What does that amount to in the year?—1*l*. 5*s*.

20,203. (The deed recites the conveyance dated the 20th February 1853, from the Judges of the Encumbered Estates Court, to Thomas Banks Brown of the customs as well as of the property.)

20,204. (Assistant Commissioner.) What is the market day here, or have you any market day at all, for the sale of marketable commodities?—No, only the day previous to the fair day.

20,205. Is there never a weekly market?—No weekly market.

20,206. What fairs are here?—There are 12 fairs.

20,207. When are they held?—On the 17th January, 14th February, 19th March, 16th April, 9th May, 4th June, 27th July, 15th August, 29th September, 19th October, 19th November, and 21st December.

20,208. Are tolls levied at all these fairs?—Yes.

20,209. Were any of these established since you obtained that conveyance in 1872?—No.

20,210. They were always held previous to that?—Yes.

20,211. You were the lessee previous to obtaining that purchase deed?—Well, I was collecting before I bought them.

20,212. How long are you connected with the fairs?—My father had them.

20,213. How far does your own recollection extend as to the management here? Were you managing in your father's time?—I was.

20,214. Do you remember having much to do in connexion with them for the last 30 years?—I do.

20,215. Then your recollection is that there were never a less number of fairs than 12?—Never. There was a new fair my father got, that was the 19th October.

20,216. When was that established?—I do not know.

20,217. Could you give me any date?—About 20 years ago or more.

20,218. Previous to that there were 11 fairs held?—Yes.

20,219. Do you remember when there were less than 11?—I never remember less than 11. When my father took

20,221. Do you know the year, or could you go as near as possible to the year, when your father obtained these other fairs?—I could not. I do not remember.

20,222. How long ago is it; is it 50 years ago?—It is, and longer.

20,223. At one time, then, there were only five fairs here?—I do not know. I could not tell you that. My brother states there were.

20,224. You do not recollect less than five?—I do not.

20,225. Were the other six fairs established by your father?—Yes.

20,226. Were they brought in from surrounding places when he obtained control here?—I think he brought them in from time to time. There were only five fairs established when my father took them.

20,227. The other six were not established at the same period?—They were not.

20,228. You could not give me any idea of when the last six were established?—No. They were established from year to year.

20,229. Have you got a toll-board erected?—Yes.

20,230. Have you got it here?—Yes.

20,231. Witness produced the toll-board, of which the following is a copy:—

Schedule of Tolls.

	£	s.	d.
Every cow - - - -	0	0	6
Every 2 year old - - - -	0	0	4
Every yearling - - -	0	0	4
Every weanling - - - -	0	0	2
Every mare gelding - - -	0	1	0
Every covered standing - - -	0	0	10
Every high standing - - -	0	0	10
Every flat standing - - -	0	0	4
Every pig basket - - -	0	0	3
Every car - - - -	0	0	10
Every tent - - - -	0	5	0
Every sheep, lamb, or goat - -	0	0	1
Every car-load of wool - -	0	1	0
Every sire - - - -	0	2	6

The above are the rates charged upon all animals sold.

Timothy Crowe,
Toll Collector.

20,232. Are these the tolls you levy at the 12 fairs?—Yes.

20,233. When these fairs were first established, these additional fairs, were they ever toll free, or when your father established them, did he afterwards levy a toll?—Yes, since I came over the place.

20,234. Are these the tolls you have been always in the habit of collecting at the fairs?—Yes.

20,235. You made no alteration?—No alteration; only I put on 2*s*. 6*d*. for entires, so that they would not be interfering with the horses.

20,236. Why did you put that half-crown on?—For the entire horses. They were interfering with the mares.

20,237. When did you put that half-crown on?—Two years ago.

20,238. It was with the intention of prohibiting the exposure of them in the fair?—Yes.

20,239. Does it act as a prohibitory charge? Are they brought here at all now?—They bring an odd one.

20,240. Do the people who own the animals consider the 2*s*. 6*d*. a charge that prohibits them from coming in here?—Some of them do not. They come in.

20,241. Previous to the levying of this charge, did they come in any great numbers?—They did not since that charge was levied. They consider that it was a little bit high, and they would rather stop outside. It was for that purpose I put it on.

20,242. Where are the fairs held?—They are held in the fair green here below and in the street.

20,243. Is this fair green you have enclosed?—It is not enclosed.

20,246. Does the house belong to you?—It does.

20,247. Do the public exercise any rights over that commonage between fairs?—It is partly enclosed. It is there for everybody.

20,248. Have you got a weighbridge erected?—Yes.

20,249. When did you erect the weighbridge?—On the 9th May.

20,250. What was the cost of it?—It cost me, I suppose, about 60l.

20,251. It is capable of weighing cattle?—Yes.

20,252. Have you weighed many?—I did not weigh any cattle.

20,253. What charge do you levy?—I do not charge anything.

20,254. Supposing they did come in, what charge do you levy?—I can give you the charge. It is fixed by the Act of Parliament.

20,255. You know the statutable charge?—Yes.

20,256. These charges you levy at the fairs are the charges only on the animals actually sold and as they are leaving the fair green?—On the animals sold. I do not get anything for the animals coming in.

20,257. What do you call the fair green? Is it on the animals brought to the fair green or to the town of Cappoquin you charge?—They stand on the streets and everywhere, and on every animal bought I charge.

20,258. The exposure of the animals is not confined to the fair green?—They have the accommodation of the town.

20,259. Have they always been held in that manner?—Yes, within my recollection.

20,260. And, to the best of your belief, you recollect for the last 30 years?—Yes.

20,261. They are held between this commons and the square?—Yes.

20,262. Have you any storage or shelter accommodation, or stalls or pens?—No.

20,263. Could you name the different description of animals brought here and exposed for sale?—Cattle, sheep, horses, pigs, goats, and donkeys.

20,264. Are there any standings at the fairs?—There are.

20,265. What description of standings?—Some of them covered and some of them not.

20,266. Do dealers erect standings here on fair days?—They do.

20,267. Could you describe the commodities exposed for sale on them?—Sweets and onions and apples.

20,268. Do not they expose furniture, wheels, or anything like that, or any wooden ware?—No. There is a charge for dressers.

20,269. On every cow you charge 6d.?—Yes.

20,270. That is only on the animal sold when leaving the fair?—Yes.

20,271. Within what limits do you think your jurisdiction extends for the collection of the toll?—I could not say. I suppose it extends about an English mile.

20,272. From where?—Here around the town.

20,273. Supposing a farmer was coming in from the country on the morning of a fair, and coming along the road he effected a sale of the animal, would you look for your charge?—I cannot be decided on that.

20,274. If it came to your knowledge, would you look for your charge?—I would.

20,275. No matter what distance away the sale was effected?—I could not say that.

20,276. Has a case of that kind ever occurred?—No, it has not.

20,277. You levy no charge on the animals as they are coming in?—No.

20,278. For a two-year-old you charge 6d. Is that the same as for an ordinary cow?—It is.

20,284. Has it come to your knowledge that complaints have been made?—No.

20,285. For every store you charge 1s.?—Yes.

20,286. These are the charges you levy?—Yes.

20,287. And you receive them?—Yes.

20,288. For every covered standing 10d.?—Yes.

20,289. Where would these standings be erected?—On the streets. They have a great these, but they do not stop in that place.

20,290. Every high standing is 6d. What would you call a high standing?—That is a high standing which is not covered.

20,291. Every flat standing is 4d. Would that mean a board stretched on a couple of barrels?—Yes.

20,292. What would they sell on that flat standing?—Cakes, and things like that.

20,293. Do they bring fish here?—Very seldom.

20,294. But if they do, do you ever collect a toll of 4d. if the fish were exposed on a flat standing?—I do not think I could.

20,295. They do not all bring cakes and sweetmeats, and things like that?—No; they bring onions.

20,296. What would be the value of the entire stock of a person having a flat standing of onions?—I could not say that.

20,297. Would the whole amount to half-a-crown?—Yes; they would bring in a cartload.

20,298. Supposing they brought in a cart, and they took the horse from underneath the cart, and left that be a standing, what would you charge for that, or would it come under the head of a high standing?—We generally charge for the space they take up.

20,299. What is the amount you levy on a cart if it stood in the street on a fair day?—I would put on 10d. on that.

20,300. You take that as a covered standing?—If a man brings in a cart-load of onions, I charge 10d. going out for the cart.

20,301. When do you collect that standing charge?—When they are going out. It is not easy to collect it.

20,302. Do you ever go around and collect it when they come in and take up their position?—I do not, because I consider the people would not have the money, and the whatever chance I would have of getting it is when they would be going home.

20,303. For every one pig you charge 3d.?—Yes.

20,304. And a heifer 3d.?—Yes.

20,305. For every car 10d.?—Yes.

20,306. For every tent 1s.—Yes.

20,307. Do they erect any tents?—They do not erect them now, but they used to erect them.

20,308. When they did erect them, used they be charged 1s.?—Yes.

20,309. For every sheep, lamb, or goat you charge 1d.?—Yes.

20,310. Is wool brought here?—It is not lately, but it used some time ago.

20,311. When you are collecting these standing charges at the fairs, if a person refused to pay you, would you seize the article they would have on the standing?—I suppose they would.

20,312. Have you ever done so?—I have not ever done so.

20,313. Have any of your men ever done so?—I do not believe they have.

20,314. Did you ever hear they did so?—I did not.

20,315. That is levied distress for the toll?—Well, I did not, but they may have done it.

20,316. Do you ever hear complaints made that they do so?—I did not.

20,319. If the bonhams were sold, would you levy 3d. on each going out?—Yes.

20,320. So that when they sell there are two charges payable, that is, 10d. for the standing of the cart, and 3d. each pig going out?—Yes.

20,321. In the first case the seller pays the charge?—Yes.

20,322. And the buyer pays the second charge?—Yes.

20,323. Did they ever complain of that?—They would be talking.

20,324. You have heard no complaints?—I did not; they generally got the charge for [illegible].

20,325. When the sale has been effected is it customary for the seller to give a luck-penny on the sale of pigs to the buyer?—Yes.

20,326. Is the amount fixed?—It is not fixed, but they generally keep 6d. a bonham. Then I saw a Lanarkshire man who would not take less than 6d. from any man.

20,327. Would you say the 6d. is fixed here?—Yes, 6d. for luck.

20,328. There is no fixed charge on the ordinary cattle, such as a horse or a cow, when sold?—No.

20,329. The luck-penny in that case is left to the disposition of the seller?—It is.

20,330. You have known cases where no such thing has been given?—There is no case but gives a luck-penny.

20,331. What would be the smallest number of bonhams they bring in a cart, or have you known them to bring in a cart?—They might bring three or two.

20,332. Supposing they bring three bonhams, what would be the value of each bonham?—That is according to the price. The prices might be high to-day and down to-morrow.

20,333. When they were down, what, within your recollection, was the smallest price for a bonham?—I often saw bonhams selling for 5s.

20,334. Supposing a cart with three bonhams was brought in, would it have to bear the standing charge of 10d., and if the bonhams were subsequently sold, would there be a further charge of 3d. on each bonham?—Yes.

20,335. That is, 1s. 1d. would go to you out of the 15s.?—Yes.

20,336. Have you any pig fair on the day previous to the ordinary cattle fair?—We have.

20,337. Then you have 12 pig fairs?—Yes.

20,338. When were these established?—They are going after the fairs always.

20,339. When the ordinary fairs were established the pig fairs were started at the same time?—Yes.

20,340. Do you ever keep any account of the number of cattle and different animals brought into these fairs?—I do not.

20,341. Where have you your custom gaps?—I just have them outside the fair.

20,342. On the outskirts of the town?—Yes.

20,343. How many of these custom gaps are there?—Four.

20,344. How many men do you have at each?—Three men at each.

20,345. Then you have about 12 men altogether employed in addition to your own labour?—Yes.

20,346. How do you pay these men on an average?—Sometimes 2s. 6d. a day and 3s.

20,347. Why do you alter the rate of payment? Is it

20,352. Do not you keep any account of what you receive?—I do not.

20,353. When you go home from the fair?—There are some fairs I would not receive 10d. and some fairs [illegible].

20,354. What is the most you have received?—I did not keep any entry of it.

20,355. Do not you enter it in a book?—No.

20,356. At all events, at a fair you have never received less than 10d.?—I have.

20,357. What was the lowest amount you received?—The 5th May I received 5d. or 6d., and at a good fair on the 4th June I received twice as much as that.

20,358. What is the biggest amount you have received at a fair?—I suppose about 40d.

20,359. What fair would that be at?—The 16th November.

20,360. You would say, then, you have received about 20d. on an average?—Yes.

20,361. Within the last number of years?—Yes.

20,362. You would not say you have received more than 20d. a year?—I would not say more.

20,363. That is profit over and above your expenses and the payment of 3s. to each of 12 men?—Yes. You know you will have one good fair and another bad fair.

20,364. Do the farmers ever bring their cattle here the night before the fair?—They do sometimes.

20,365. Where do they put them up?—They go round the village, or bring them to me, and I give them a yard for the cattle.

20,366. Where?—For any dealing man I would take them up to my own place.

20,367. You have a farm?—Yes.

20,368. What would you charge a man for that stand?—I may not charge anything.

20,369. Have not you got some fixed rate?—I would not charge a friend anything.

20,370. But supposing a stranger came, what would you charge him for the standing of his cattle until the following day—the fair day?—About 3d. or 6d. a head; 6d. a head the farmers round charge. The dealing men generally do not come to trouble me, because they know I would not take anything.

20,371. The custom of the neighbouring farmers is to charge 6d.?—Yes.

20,372. That is payable in addition to the tolls the following day if the cattle are sold?—Yes, if the cattle are sold I get my own charge.

20,373. Did they ever complain to you or make any complaints of the want of sallage in this fair green?—They did not.

20,374. You have heard no complaints yourself?—No.

20,375. When the fair is held have they different portions of this green, and the different streets allotted for each description of animal?—They have. They keep the [illegible] up in the green, and the cattle down in the village. The sheep stand generally outside the [illegible].

20,376. Where do the horses stand?—They go about the streets.

20,377. Any particular street?—No.

20,378. There is no stationary position for them?—They are on the square generally.

20,379. Is that the square with the shed in it?—Yes.

20,380. To whom does that shed belong?—It does not belong to me.

20,387. That is the pig market which is held on the day previous to the ordinary cattle fairs?—Yes.

20,388. Have you any fair near Copperhide where no tolls are levied?—There is a fair at Dundrum.

20,389. How far distant is that from Copperhide?—Four English miles.

20,390. Did you ever hear that farmers have preferred going to that fair where no tolls were levied than coming in here to Copperhide where tolls are levied?—I did not hear, but I know the fairs were interfered with on me by putting the market day before them.

20,391. Practically, they do go to this fair in preference to coming here?—I do not think so.

20,392. You say it interfered with you?—They have an important market before mine, and it keeps the people and pigs in Dundrum.

20,393. Are any of the fairs immediately following yours?—They are all before my fairs.

20,394. Do you know have animals been sent from the neighbourhood of Copperhide to those Dundrum fairs?—I do. I saw pigs going there. I saw cattle and pigs there, too, from here.

20,395. Now, have you heard at all any complaints of these tolls?—No, I have not.

20,396. No complaints have been made to you directly?—No complaints, so far as the dealing man are concerned. I do my best.

20,397. Does a great quantity of dairy cattle come here?—Yes.

20,398. From what direction?—From every district; from Thurles and around.

20,399. Within what limits do the animals come?—About five or six miles, and they come from Tipperary, 10 miles from here.

20,400. Would you say within a radius of 10 miles?—Yes, and I often saw them coming from the County Kilkenny here.

20,401. Do you have the toll-board erected on each fair day?—Yes.

20,402. Have you many copies of it?—I have four.

20,403. One at each gap?—Yes.

20,404. When the parties are bringing out the cattle, do your men require from them whether they have bought or sold?—Yes.

20,405. Do they always make that inquiry?—Yes.

20,406. Supposing a man in charge of an animal stated he did not buy or sell, and your man doubted the statement, what course would they adopt?—They would ask him to lay his hand on the board, and say whether he had sold or bought.

20,407. That is to clear his conscience?—Yes.

20,408. Do you know have they ever produced a book to swear them?—No.

20,409. Without your knowledge?—No.

20,410. Or any paper?—No.

20,411. They deem the fact of clearing their conscience sufficient?—Yes.

20,412. Do you give the people any receipt at all for this charge?—No.

20,413. I suppose the collectors know the cattle are marked when they are going out?—Yes.

20,414. Have your collectors ever seized the animals or detained them?—They would seize occasionally if they considered the animal would be bought.

20,415. How long do you know have they detained the animal?—Until they put their hand on the board.

20,416. So that if a man touched the board and said he did not buy they would let him go?—Yes.

20,417. Did you ever detain them after a man had done that?—No.

20,418. Did any of your collectors?—No, not that I know of.

20,419. What check have you on these men collecting the tolls?—No check at all.

20,421. Only one man receives the money?—Yes.

20,422. The other men go there to prevent the cattle going out?—Yes.

20,423. Did you ever hear that any undue delay was caused to men coming behind and crushing their cattle home by reason of any row or confusion?—I have to the high up great room.

20,424. Have they ever delayed others?—Never.

20,425. Have you ever heard complaints that any of the toll collectors injured the animals?—No.

20,426. Do they carry sticks?—They do. They must carry them.

20,427. They never injured any of the animals with them?—No, any way that I hear.

20,428. Were any representations ever made to you to provide a sufficiently large fair green for all the animals in order to take them off the streets of the town?—No.

20,429. Would the traders of the town rather have them on the streets than on a fair green?—I believe they would. The fair green is very near the place.

20,430. Is corn ever brought here?—Yes.

20,431. Are there any scales in the town?—No scales now, but the weighing-bridge.

20,432. There is no scales now, but was there ever one?—Yes.

20,433. Who owns it?—It belonged to my father. He gave it away.

20,434. There is no public scales in this town?—No, except the shopkeepers.

20,435. If farmers brought in their corn and potatoes some day in the week, unless they go to the shopkeepers they have no means of ascertaining the weight?—They can weigh them on the weighbridge.

20,436. Can they weigh small quantities?—I can weigh a pound weight.

20,437. Do they weigh?—They do.

20,438. What is the charge?—Generally, 1d. a bag. When there is a load of hay or potatoes I put on 4d.

20,439. You charge 4d. a load for weighing on the bridge?—Yes.

20,440. Irrespective of the commodity in the load, whether hay, straw, turnips, or potatoes?—Yes.

20,441. Supposing hay was brought in here, and was not weighed at your weighbridge and sold, would you levy any charge on it?—No.

20,442. You would not charge unless it was weighed?—No.

20,443. What commodities do you usually weigh on the bridge?—Hay and straw, turnips, potatoes. We would also weigh loads of stones and coal.

20,444. If a load you charge 4d.?—Yes.

20,445. You have one fixed charge?—Yes.

20,446. Is that irrespective of what the load would be, whether it would be a donkey or horse load?—I do not make any difference between a donkey load and horse load.

20,447. You charge 4d. for all?—Yes.

20,448. Is this weighbridge in use every day?—It is.

20,449. What would you strike as the average you received from the weighbridge alone?—I could not say.

20,450. Have you ever weighed potatoes at the bridge yourself?—I have not.

20,451. You say you weigh down to a pound?—Yes. The machine is guaranteed to do that.

20,452. When weighing a load do you always ascertain the tare of the cart?—Yes.

20,453. You always weigh the empty cart?—Always weigh the empty cart.

20,454. Do you ever estimate the tare of it?—Certainly.

20,455. The car you weighed before you would not weigh a second time if it came on a subsequent day?—Yes.

20,457. Do you give a ticket denoting the weight of these cars?—Yes.

20,458. Is it printed?—Yes.

20,459. You have a blank?—Yes.

20,460. Do you always keep these blanks up?—Yes.

20,461. Do you make an entry into any book?—I do not. I keep them in the blank.

20,462. Does all the hay, straw, and potatoes brought in here to Cappawhite be weighed at your crane?—I could not say that. They might get them weighed elsewhere.

20,463. They have no means of weighing a load elsewhere?—No. There is one at Captain Purefoy's.

20,464. Does he weigh for hire?—He does not.

20,465. There is no charge levied?—I think not.

20,466. Practically, whatever hay or straw comes to the town in a load must be weighed at your bridge?—It must, if they like.

20,467. That is if they want to weigh it?—Yes.

20,468. When you purchased the tolls were 12 fairs held?—They were.

20,469. And tolls were levied at them?—They were.

20,470. You were not aware that the patent establishing fairs in Cappawhite only gave a right to five fairs?—No.

20,471. Or you were not made aware of that when purchasing?—No.

20,472. Have you any other observations to make?—No.

Mr. Thomas Dowling examined.

20,473. I believe you have some suggestions to offer as to the fairs here?—Yes. I was agent on the property when Crowe became purchaser. His father was the previous lessee. At the time I sold to him there was a lease, and I may start by telling you there was a patent granted to a gentleman in Cork named Nettley, somewhere about 1753. The patent is in old Latin. I have read it in the Record Office. That provides for the establishing of five fairs in the town of Cappawhite on certain days named. I find the fairs through some changes the dates were altered subsequently. I do not know by whom. The tolls are provided for, and it is rendered imperative that the holder of the right to the tolls should hold weekly fairs every Wednesday in the town of Cappawhite.

20,474. Weekly markets?—Yes, every Wednesday throughout the year. The interest in that devolved on an ancestor of Mr. Hunt's. It was sold in 1853 to Mr. Beale Brown.

20,475. Do you know the purchase money to Mr. Brown?—I do. I received it.

20,476. Was there any fixed amount for the tolls and customs?—No.

20,477. He bought other property as well?—There was a fixed amount. What we sold him is contained in the original lease, which gave him two acres; that is what he calls the fair green, but it gave him no right to levy tolls on the streets. The lease is dated the 24th July 1849 for 31 years, to commence on the 1st May 1849. I sold to Crowe in 1872 or 1873. I was then aware of only selling him five fairs at which he could levy tolls legally, but, of course, that was a matter outside my province altogether; but I was to receive the most money I could.

20,478. At that time the five fairs were sold to Mr. Brown were the other fairs in existence and were tolls collected at them?—They were. I did not question what Mr. Crowe did, but all I know is that I was selling to him. I received 1,000*l.* from him, and he continued to receive the tolls from that time since. There was in addition to the Wednesday market, there was to be ample accommodation with sheds and other conveniences for the holding of these weekly markets. I had an interest in Cappawhite. Between Mr. Hunt and myself we own the village, and some years ago, when money was easier got than now, I was doing my best to improve the place. I thought it a very great improvement if tolls were not levied on the additional fairs. I went to prove the records to see his right and title to charge on the seven additional fairs. I went to the [illegible]

up until now. Of course it will now strike you as to what right Crowe has to levy the tolls, the amount of the tolls, and whether he discharged the duties incumbent on him in not endeavouring to establish the markets and in providing covered accommodation he is bound to have on the fair green. I am aware he levies a toll on the standings in the street. The question will arise as to what right has he to levy tolls on anything in the street.

20,479. Do you think a necessity exists here for a market?—It is rather a good sort of country, and I really think some of the fairs are the best in the whole country. There will be a fair to-morrow here, and it is most remarkable for its extent, and another in December. I have seen some of the finest fairs I remember seeing.

20,480. What is the reason that here, in Cappawhite, there are larger fairs than in Tipperary or Thurles?—It is a large centre. Nenagh on one side is 16 miles away, and Tipperary 13 or 14 miles, and then the fairs of Cashel are a long way off.

20,481. Do they come from Cashel here?—The buyers come from Meath and Dublin, and all parts of the country. What I would suggest, if possible, is that some encouragement be made for the poor people who come to sell in the markets on Wednesday and at the fair green.

20,482. Do they come in at all on Wednesday?—Certainly not. An odd load of turf comes in.

20,483. Do you think it would be advisable to foster a market or to establish one?—I would not like to be at much expense at the outset, until the thing paid for itself. That is the original property as well of Mr. Brown.

20,484. Have you formed any general ideas on the question of levying a toll?—I believe myself, and I have a very strong opinion, and an opinion I formed many years ago, that it would be good in Ireland if no tolls were charged anywhere, and that the present receivers of tolls ought to be compensated in some way. I think tolls are most injurious to the farmers, and that they are an embargo on business.

20,485. There is a general question I am in the habit of putting to men holding a position like yours, where I have held inquiries up to the present, and it is, do you think the levying of a toll acts as a deterrent on people bringing their commodities to the market or fair, and exposing them for sale?—There is a feeling that will always crop up. The toll is not much if the market is a good market. I would be for abolishing tolls *in toto*, and compensating the present holders. In the case of a man like Crowe, who has followed in the footsteps of his father, and not willing to do wrong, I think he should be compensated by whatever he would be legally entitled to.

20,486. At the time of the sale to Mr. Brown you represented the landlord?—Yes, I was agent for the estate.

20,487. You did not represent to Mr. Brown that tolls were levied at a greater number of fairs than was originally granted by the patent?—He was perfectly aware of it himself. He was an Englishman and rather exacting. He said, "Sell the best way we can, and if Crowe got a chance "of the other fairs keep the deed silent, and if I do not "mistake the deed is silent as to the number of fairs sold "to him" (Crowe).

20,488. At the time of the sale to Mr. Crowe, do you think Mr. Crowe was aware that the patent only gave him a right to collect on five fairs? Is it a question whether he had not a prescriptive right to collect at the other fairs?—I would not say for himself. He is a respectable man.

20,489. But when carrying on negotiations between him and Mr. Brown, you did not discuss the matter with Mr. Crowe?—I did with his attorney, because the attorney claimed a right to every something in the street, and then I put in the draft conveyance myself,—"We give you such right as we have, if we have any." He objected to that.

20,490. Was there any mention of the patent and the five fairs in the patent?—At this distance I do not recollect anything.

20,491. Previous to that it was leased out and he was paying 30*l.* a year for five fairs?—Yes, because Mr. Hunt originally could not let more than five fairs.

20,492. You have not got a copy of the lease, or could it be got?—It is mentioned in the rental. It is a deed for 31 years, and dated July 1849.

stipulated in the lease upon which the fairs were to be held? —I could not tell that, because I never saw the lease, but Mr. Crowe held a lease, and has it now.

20,495. It is your opinion that when a person is in receipt of tolls from markets or fairs, that he should give some return for them in the way of affording sufficient accommodation to those frequenting the markets?—I do, to be sure.

20,496. By accommodation I mean shelter accommodation for those frequenting the markets, and for the animals they bring in?—Certainly. I look on the thing in the street as just the thing the county surveyor may remove any day. We had no control, and could not control the streets, because they belong to the grand jury.

20,497. Have you any other suggestions to offer?—No, I have not.

20,498. Have you any general suggestions or remarks to make as to the fairs throughout the country? Have you had connexion with any here other than Copperwhite?—Very little. Tipperary fairs, where no tolls are charged, are very excellent fairs.

20,499. Have you ever purchased in those fairs?—Yes, and sold. The Copperwhite fair is no good coming on.

20,500. How do you account for that, the position of Copperwhite being so isolated from the railway?—That has something to do with it, because the real competitive fairs are at Thurles, and they do not affect this place. As a matter of fact, the buyers come from Meath and Dublin, and the cattle come from all directions.

VERE HUNT, Esq., J.P., examined.

20,501. You are a large grazier of cattle, and a large proprietor?—Yes.

20,502. Have you any suggestions to offer?—I have not, after all that has been said.

20,503. You have heard the evidence of Mr. Dowling?—I have.

20,504. Do you agree in the general remarks he has made as to the necessity of owners of tolls and markets providing accommodation in return for them?—I do not know; I do not see any great occasion for that. In the first place, it would be enormous expense to provide such accommodation, and they would never look for it, except on an inclement day, or something of the kind, and then only for a few hours.

20,505. Have you ever noticed the people on fair days at Copperwhite?—Yes.

20,506. Have you been here on a fair day?—Almost every fair.

20,507. Have you ever found people physically injured in the winter for want of shelter and in being exposed to the inclemency of the weather?—I know days are very hard, but the parties must stop with the cattle, and then if there was accommodation they should stay with the cattle to keep them together.

20,508. If good pens were erected in the fair green?—It is not usually done in the country. When the cattle are brought in they are turned into the yards of the town.

20,509. Have you formed any ideas of the fact of fairs being held on the public streets?—It is an old custom, and very hard to get rid of.

20,510. Apart altogether from the custom, do you think it would work better if the sale of animals at fairs, and of marketable commodities at the markets, was confined to a certain spot or fair green?—I think it would be better. Now, in Tipperary, you are not obliged to walk from one end of the town to another. It is quite too much to walk from one end of the fair to another, that is, when the fair is all over the town.

20,511. Is this fair green sufficiently large here?—Some fairs are very large.

20,512. Is that the reason some of the animals go about the streets?—No. In seven fairs out of the 12 there is scarcely a beast sent to the fair green at all.

20,513. I suppose, if they could effect a readier sale about the houses of the town, they would prefer to remain on the streets than to going into the fair green?—I cannot account for it. The fair green is generally selected for springers. A good many cattle for dairy purposes are sent to the green. They are easier kept there, and it is a nicer place for them to stand.

20,514. Is this green a commonage?—It is an open place. There is no fence between it and the public road. It is fenced on three sides, but the other side is quite open.

20,515. Do you say the public have a right over it?—The boys play there, and they make a commonage of it.

20,516. Have you formed any ideas as to the levying of a toll? Do you think it would tend the trade of the fairs and markets if no tolls at all were payable, only weighing charges or charges for accommodation and storage?—The tolls on cattle are generally not appreciated of by the buyers, but at the same time they will buy.

20,517. Both at fair or market, if the farmers can effect a ready sale, and if there is a good market or fair, the toll will not deter them from coming in?—Not at all. There is no fair better attended than Copperwhite. It is very well supplied with cattle.

20,518. Have you had experience in other places besides this?—Yes, I have.

20,519. Do you think in other towns where the markets and fairs are under the control of the corporation or town commissioners or market trustees—do you think they are worked better, and managed more to the satisfaction of those frequenting the market, than if they were subject to the control of an individual?—I have not seen the slightest improvement.

20,520. Do you think an individual would have a greater interest in working them up for his own pecuniary benefit than a corporation or town commissioners?—Where there is no custom paid of course the people find it very pleasant. They can drive their cattle in, and there is no question about them.

20,521. I will ask you a general question, and one that does not apply to Copperwhite. Do you think, if a toll must be levied, that the local authority, if any such exists, in a town should acquire compulsory rights to work and manage them themselves for the benefit of the town?—I could not give you any idea on that question.

20,522. You have formed no idea?—No.

20,523. Have you any other suggestions?—No. Mr. Dowling is right about the five original fairs. They belonged to an ancestor of mine. There were only five fairs, and Mr. Crowe's father, when he took the lease, increased the number of fairs, and a little time after the fairs were fixed, there was no change, but then the toll was changed.

20,524. That is as the additional fairs?—Yes.

20,525. Do you know when the first of the new fairs were established?—I could not say.

20,526. Have they been established within your recollection?—Everyone of them. I think the first of the new fairs must have been established in or about 60 years ago.

20,527. They have all been established within the last 60 years?—Yes.

20,528. And the last of them 30 years ago?—Yes. I have a recollection that the way they were got up was by a cattle fair, and the fair was established. There was no toll for a time, and then the toll began to be paid willingly.

20,529. The last additional fair would be 30 years ago?—Perhaps it is, or it may not be so long.

20,530. Do you remember were the five old fairs held on the dates mentioned?—Yes.

20,531. These dates have never been altered?—Never altered. They are the same as long as I recollect. Crowe spoke of the [illegible] fair. The [illegible] fair is quite a failure. They hold cattle fair and pig fair on the same day. The cattle fair is as much a failure as the pig fair.

20,532. Who is the owner?—I could not tell. Lord [illegible] is the landlord of any [illegible].

20,533. Have they been recently established?—Within seven or eight years.

Mr. THOMAS CROWE examined.

20,534. What do you wish to state?—With regard to the tolls, I was collecting them 30 years before this man (my brother) bought them, and there is no fair that was free.

20,535. You heard the remarks of Mr. Hunt, that when some of the additional fairs were first established they were toll free, but subsequently tolls were levied?—It was only for one fair. The first fair used to be generally free.

20,536. Have you anything else to say?—No.

Mr. Thomas Ryan examined.

20,537. What evidence do you wish to give?—As far as the traders are concerned they have nothing to complain of.

20,538. Do you think it would be better if the fairs were removed off the streets and confined to a sufficiently large fair green?—I think not. They are better as they are.

20,539. Would the traders of the town object to such a removal?—They would, every one of them.

20,540. Would those traders who would object be in any particular trade?—Oh, certainly they would.

20,541. Or would they all join?—I daresay all would join. They are nearly all publicans here.

20,542. Does not the fact of the fairs being held outside the shop doors occasion much filth and dirt?—Certainly.

20,543. Who removes that; is it the contractor?—Generally, but the shopkeepers sweep it passed the stone; and the road contractor cleans it away.

20,544. Would they put up with any inconvenience caused by the filth and dirt created for trade purposes?—Yes.

20,545. Solely for trade purposes?—Yes, and people would have no shelter in a fair green on a wet day, and they would not like to be away from the fair.

20,546–7. If in a fair green shelter accommodation was provided when the weather was inclement, do you think it would be the best place for them?—They can stand inside the doors here.

20,548. Mr. Dowling has mentioned a matter I would like your ideas on. Do you think a necessity exists for the creation of a market one day in the week?—I think there would be no market here. No marketable commodities come in.

20,549. The people have their own customers in town?—Yes.

20,550. They bring in their corn to them?—Yes.

20,551. Is there no mill in the neighbourhood?—It goes to Tipperary.

20,552. Then you think a market could not be fostered in Cappawhite?—Not at present, at any rate. There was a market some time ago, and it was a failure. They lost 250l. in a butter market, and it was a failure.

20,553. Does the fact of a market not being held enhance the price of commodities to any appreciable extent?—Not a bit.

20,554. You think the poorer members of the community get things as cheap from the traders of the town as they would in the market?—I think so.

20,555. You never heard complaints that the price of bread and potatoes was higher here than elsewhere or in an open market?—Not higher.

20,556. You heard no complaints?—No.

20,557. Is there any other gentleman who has any observations to make?—No answer.

The inquiry then concluded.

BRUFF—CO. LIMERICK.

With reference to my inquiry in Bruff on the 15th November 1888 I beg to report as follows:—

Bruff is an inland town, situated in the county of Limerick. It is some five miles from Kilmallock, the nearest railway station. The surrounding country is fertile, but much of it is in pasture. The trade of the town is principally in agricultural produce. The streets are of fair width, and houses apparently well built.

The local government is vested in the board of guardians and grand jury. The population is 1,600.

The market day is Friday. Butter market is on Monday.

The fairs are held on 25th January, 29th March, 16th May, 23rd July, 22nd August, 18th October, and 28th November.

The markets, which are very small, are toll free. Weighing charges are, however, levied if the commodity is weighed, but no rule exists making it compulsory to utilise the public scales.

Tolls are levied at the fairs held on the 16th May, 23rd July, 18th October, and 28th November. The fairs held on the 25th January, 29th March, and 22nd August are toll free.

The owner of the market rights and tolls is Lord Limerick, who has them, however, sublet to Mr. John Carroll, of Bruff, by lease, dated 13th October 1857, for the term of three lives, two of whom are still in being, at the yearly rent of 55l. 7s. The reduced rent of 35l. has been accepted by the owner for some time back.

The public records show that two patents were granted for the town of Bruff. The first is dated 28th January 1607, and granted to Sir James Fullerton a Wednesday market and fair on the feast of St. Matthew the Apostle (21st September) and Ascension Day and day following each. The Wednesday market does not seem to have been held, and likewise the fair on the feast of St. Matthew. The fair granted for Ascension Day was altered some 35 years ago to the 16th May without any express authority.

The second patent is dated 18th July 1764 (4 Geo. III.), and granted to Sir Henry Hartstonge two additional fairs on 23rd July and 18th October, and altered a fair held on the 21st November to the 28th November.

The fairs on the 25th January, 29th March, and 22nd August were established about 20 years ago by the townspeople and traders without any express authority.

A toll board has been erected for public inspection, and a weighbridge has been provided.

In accordance with my instructions I have inspected the market place and fair green.

The markets in Bruff are very small, and comparatively few commodities come now on Fridays. Corn and potatoes are brought in every day of the week, and are weighed on a beam and scales provided in what is called the weigh-house, a small shed in the public street. The potatoes are exposed for sale in the weigh-house and outside it, and the other commodities, including butter, are exposed on the public thoroughfare. Beyond the weigh-house and scales there are no market buildings or other accommodation provided.

The fairs are held in a fair green near the court house, and which is about four acres in extent. It is enclosed by a low wall. The fairs extend into the approaches to this fair green, and sometimes cattle are sold in the streets. There is no pen or shed accommodation provided in the fair green, either for the animals or those in charge of them.

The gross weight alone is ascertained at the beam and scales.

Appended will be found a transcript of the evidence taken at the inquiry.

JOHN J. O'MEARA,

45, Lower Mount Street, Dublin. Assistant Commissioner.

Bruff, 15th November 1888.

Mr. John Carroll examined.

20,558. You are the owner of the markets and fairs here in Bruff?—Yes.

20,559. Under what authority do you hold them?—I hold them by lease from Lord Limerick.

20,560-1. Is Lord Limerick the owner of the patent?—He is. (*The witness produced the lease.*)

20,562. You are not the John Carroll mentioned in this lease which was made on the 13th October 1857?—No.

20,563. Was the John Carroll mentioned there your father?—Yes.

20,564. The lease was made from the Right Hon. Edmund Henry, Earl of Limerick, to John Carroll. It demises to John Carroll and his heirs the tolls and customs due, receivable, and payable from the fairs in the town of Bruff, in the county of Limerick, at the yearly rent of £41, 7s.

20,565. I see there are no special covenants in this lease?—No.

20,566. The rent mentioned in this lease is not the actual rent payable at present?—No.

20,567. It has been reduced?—It has been reduced for 20 years.

20,568. What is the present rent?—32l. a year.

20,569. The lease is for the natural lives of Standish O'Grady, eldest son of the Honourable Standish O'Grady, and Joseph Barrington, eldest son of Mr. Barrington, city of Limerick, and William Carroll, eldest son of the lessee; or for the term of 31 years whichever was the longest to continue.

20,570. Are some of the lives in existence?—There are two, Mr. Barrington and Mr. Wm. Carroll.

20,571. Is there a covenant in that for perpetual renewal?—There is not.

20,572. The dues upon which tolls are collected at the markets and fairs are not mentioned in this lease?—No.

20,573. You are not aware under what authority the Earl of Limerick granted this lease?—There is a May fair—a very old fair—held here, and there is a patent since time in the reign of George the Third for the other three fairs.

20,574. Have you markets here?—Yes.

20,575. What market?—The pig markets.

20,576. Have you a general market?—Yes.

20,577. What day is set off for that?—You can sell potatoes any day, or corn if you bring it in.

20,578. Is there any particular day in the week allotted off for the exposure of the commodities for sale?—Friday is the nominal market day.

20,579. Do you collect any tolls at the market?—No.

20,580. What commodities generally come on Fridays?—Nothing now on Fridays but very little vegetables and poultry.

20,581. You say corn comes any day?—Corn does not come unless bought by myself, or anybody else. There is none comes to be weighed.

20,582. It is sold to private consumers?—Yes.

20,583. Are cattle ever brought on market day—on Friday?—No.

20,584. Or pigs?—No.

20,585. Is hay brought?—No, unless it is brought to be weighed.

20,586. It is never exposed for sale in any way?—Never exposed for sale. I never saw it.

20,587. Where are the potatoes exposed?—In the market.

20,588. Are there any market buildings here?—There is what is called the weigh-house.

20,589. Are the potatoes exposed on the public thoroughfare?—No, always inside. They bring them in sometimes 50 or 60 bags, and 100 sometimes, for sale, and if they do not sell I take charge of them, and I may buy them or sell them for them if they name a price, but I charge nothing until the weighing.

20,590. Do you compel them to weigh at your scales?—No.

20,591. They can weigh where they please?—Yes.

20,592. Do you charge them any storage?—No.

20,593. What is the rate of charge for weighing?—1d. per cwt.

20,594. What scales have you there?—Only the one scales in the market.

20,595. Are there any other private scales in the town?—There are not.

20,596. The only scale available for the farmers of the district for weighing any commodity, the weight of which they wish to ascertain, is yours?—Yes.

20,597. That is always available?—Day and night I would say.

20,598. What do you charge for weighing corn?—The same as potatoes, 1d. per cwt.

20,599. For weighing hay have you a bridge?—Yes. It is 6d. for hay, straw, or anything that comes in a load.

20,600. Are turnips brought?—They are never brought to be sold, but they come to be weighed.

20,601. You charge 6d. a load irrespective of the commodity on the load?—6d. a load, no matter what it is.

20,602. Would you charge 6d. for a donkey load?—I would not.

20,603. What do you charge?—Generally half price. I am never particular.

20,604. You never charge storage?—No; they might be there for a month and I would not charge.

20,605. Is butter ever brought in?—It is brought here on Mondays.

20,606. Is it brought in firkins?—All firkins.

20,607. Is that exposed for sale?—It is sold in the street, in what we call the market square.

20,608. That market square is portion of the public thoroughfare?—It is.

20,609. Are any tolls payable on the butter?—No toll.

20,610. Where do they weigh it?—They weigh with me.

20,611. What do you charge?—1d. per firkin; and I have two scales working for them on Monday.

20,612. Have you got any cooper employed?—No, I employ no cooper. The buyers employ coopers if they think it necessary.

20,613. Do you ever keep any record of the number of firkins that come in here?—No.

20,614. Is it always weighed at your scales before being actually sold?—After being sold.

20,615. That is practically different from other towns?—It is. In case the farmer does not sell he is at liberty to take it home again, and there is no charge.

20,616. The firkins are never drained?—When it is bought and taken into the store it is turned up there and left to drain, and when turned up it is marked on the bottom by me.

20,617. You drain it?—I merely turn it up.

20,618. Do you take off the head?—I leave the lid on and turn it on the head, and the man leaves it there until he has a lot bought. Some bring coopers, and others may not.

20,619. What fairs are held here?—Four fairs in the year; but the townspeople thought of starting new fairs.

20,620. Only four at present?—Yes.

20,621. Kindly mention to me the fairs annually held, whether tolls are levied at them or not?—The 25th January (no tolls); 25th March (no tolls); 16th May (tolls); 23rd July (tolls); 22nd August (no tolls); 10th October (tolls); 28th November (tolls).

20,622. So then there are four fairs at which tolls are levied, and three at which there are no tolls?—Yes.

20,623. How long are these four fairs at which you levy tolls established?—Well, from what I could learn there is a patent for the 16th May fair and the market. I suppose it is over 150 years or more. Then the other three fairs were held at the other side of the bridge. Sir Henry Hasson got a patent for three fairs, and he changed the 21st November to the 28th November.

20,624. When was that change made?—In the fourth year of George the Third.

20,625. As far as your memory goes back these four fairs were held on the dates mentioned?—Yes.

20,626. And held at the time of the date in the lease?—Yes.

20,627. Your memory does not go back as far as that?—No. One of them was altered before; that is the May fair.

20,628. When was it held?—It was held on the day before Ascension Thursday, and it is fixed for 40 years on the 16th May.

20,629. When were the fairs on which no tolls are levied established?—I think about 20 years ago.

20,630. By whom were they established?—The townspeople, and my father.

20,631. Tolls were never levied at these?—No.

20,632. Did you ever hear that at the other four fairs any one of them at all was toll free?—Never.

20,633. Tolls were always levied?—Yes.

20,634. You produce this as a copy of the schedule of the tolls?—Yes.

20,635. Are the same rates payable now as payable within your memory?—The same rates.

20,636. No change so far as you know has been made in the rate?—No change.

20,637. It was a combination of the townspeople who established the other fairs?—It was.

20,638. Are they held on the same site as the ordinary fairs on the fair green?—Yes.

20,639. You provide the fair green?—Yes.

20,640. What is the extent of it?—I suppose about four acres.

20,641. You hold that under this lease?—Yes.

20,642. Is that fair green enclosed?—It is.

20,643. All around?—Yes.

20,644. Is the sale or exposure of animals confined to that fair green?—No.

20,645. Do they go about the street?—No. It (the fair) is confined principally.

20,646. Does the fair green afford adequate space for the exposure of animals?—Yes, sufficient accommodation.

20,647. But still they do not avail themselves of it?—On a fair day they do.

20,648. Are animals sold elsewhere than this place on fair days?—They may chance to be sold.

20,649. Where?—On the street if they are driving out.

20,650. But the practice is to bring them to the fair green?—Yes.

20,651. You have no regulations at the fairs confining the exposure of the animals to that fair green?—No.

20,652. Have you any pens or sheds in this fair green?—No.

20,653. You have got a weighbridge?—I have.

20,654. Capable of weighing cattle?—Yes. It is a three ton lever.

20,655. Have you the ordinary railing around it?—I have one to put up in case it is required.

20,656. Was it yourself provided the house and scales for the butter, and also for the potatoes?—Yes. I provided weighbridge and all.

20,657. How much did you expend in providing these?—It was my father provided them.

20,658. And the weighbridge?—I bought that myself. It is second-hand. I paid 15l. for it and for putting it down.

20,659. What was the cost of the alteration last year in putting the railing around it?—That was not much.

20,660. After the fairs, do you clean the fair green?—I would if necessary.

20,661. Now you have in the schedule "for every horse a shilling"?—We have very few horses.

20,662. Are these charges on the animals actually sold?—Yes.

20,663. You never charge on the animal entering the fair?—No. There were only four or five horses sold the last day.

20,664. You only charge on all animals when they are sold?—When they are sold.

20,665. I see you have the same charge for a bonham as for an ordinary pig?—Yes.

20,666. Is that when they are sold?—Yes.

20,667. Supposing they brought in a number of bonhams in a cart, would you charge them one fixed sum for the cartload?—I would charge 2d. a bonham.

20,668. You charge on each individual pig?—Yes.

20,674. Do you levy a charge "for every car conveying stock to and from the fair"?—Mostly.

20,675. What description of stock?—Only pigs.

20,676. If a cart comes in with a number of pigs, would you charge 1s. a cart, and if the pigs were subsequently sold, would you charge 3d. on each pig?—Yes.

20,677. The seller pays the charge of 1s. in the first case and the buyer pays the other?—Yes.

20,678. If they brought three bonhams in a cart would you charge 1s.?—That is optional.

20,679. I suppose you allow your men to exercise a discretion?—They will not exercise a discretion unless they come to me, and I may leave them off altogether.

20,680. Have you ever levied the charge?—I have.

20,681. What is the smallest number of bonhams they would bring in a cart?—Well, perhaps they may bring in one or two and we might come to terms.

20,682. Have you ever levied the charge on two bonhams when brought in a cart?—I do not think I have.

20,683. On three?—I do not think I have.

20,684. On four?—I suppose I have.

20,685. Subsequently these four had to bear a charge of 3d. each when sold?—Yes.

20,686. In a bad fair what would be the value of each bonham? Would they be sold for 5s. each?—It is a long time ago since they were sold for that price.

20,687. What would be the ordinary current price?—About 1l. each.

20,688. You have not known them to be less?—I have seen them sold less.

20,689. What is the smallest sale you saw them sold this year or within the past two years?—I should think about 15s. That would be very few, and they would be very small. They go to 30s. and 2l., and they may have 10 or 12 in a cart.

20,690. Where would the cart be placed? Would it be on the street?—Outside the fair green; on the road near the fair green.

20,691. Is it only bonhams or small pigs they bring in carts?—That is all.

20,692. Do they bring sheep?—Some bring sheep and calves, but I do not charge.

20,693. Do they bring cattle in large floats?—Once in the way. I suppose I never saw six of them brought in.

20,694. "Every travelling hawker, 6d."; do you levy that charge?—No.

20,695. "Every tent, 6d."; do you charge that still?—There are no tents now. I used only to charge 2s. or 2s. 6d.

20,696. Every standing allowed for sale, that is, clothes dealers' standings, you demand 1s., and do not get it?—It is no use to demand it.

20,697. You have toll gates here?—Yes.

20,698. Where do you place them, outside the town or the fair green?—There is one outside the corner of the fair green and the outlet at the upper side at the barracks.

20,699. Is that at the other side of the fair green?—Yes; and there is one at the corner near the court house. 30 or 40 years ago, for the accommodation of the buyers, their cattle were allowed to pass down and then collect in lots. They were allowed to pass on condition that the cattle were to be marked. The toll is collected afterwards.

20,700. How many men do you have at each of these toll gates?—Well, I had at the last two fairs 20 and 25 men each day.

20,701. What rate of payment do you give them?—2s. 6d. or 3s. A good many of them charge me nothing.

20,702. These are friends of yours?—Yes.

20,703. What would you say is your average expense in collecting the tolls yearly?—Well, I never kept an account of it.

20,704. Would it be about 2l. 10s. each fair?—That would not be right. The sum would have to be divided and then.

20,705. Do you think 3l. would cover your expenses at a fair?—It would not, or 4l. a fair.

20,706. Would that be 16l. a year?—No, about 10l., because at some fairs I would not have as many men as at

20,707. Is that the only expense you are at in connexion with the fairs under the lease?—There is the poor rate, county cess, and rent besides.

20,708. I presume you are allowed the ordinary proportions of poor rate and income tax?—Yes.

20,709. Do you keep any account of your receipts?—No.

20,710. You never enter them at all?—No.

20,711. What do you say on an average you receive from each fair; we will take the first one, the 16th May?—I suppose about 10l.

20,712. What would you say you receive on the 23rd July?—12l.

20,713. Is that profit or the gross amount?—The gross.

20,714. What would you say you got on the 18th October?—It varies.

20,715. On an average what is it?—40l.

20,716. What would you say on the 29th November?—The same.

20,717. Then the gross receipts would be 102l. for the fairs?—Yes.

20,718. On an average?—Yes.

20,719. You never keep any account at all?—No. All I keep is an account of what is due to me.

20,720. What would you average your receipts at from this weighbridge and the scale for weighing butter?—The butter market is gone down terribly. It is not half what it was.

20,721. How many firkins do you say come in here during the season?—About 150 came in the last day. I suppose for six months I should think it did not average more than 240 firkins each day for the six months of the year, taking one week with the other.

20,722. What would you say would be the yearly average?—50l. for this year; other years it made a great deal more than that.

20,723. And at the weighbridge?—About 14l. or 15l.

20,724. Then your total gross receipts are 166l. or 170l. a year?—I suppose they would be.

20,725. Have you a weigh-master engaged?—No. An old man helps me now and again, and he takes charge in my absence.

20,726. You only have a weigh-master when you are absent yourself?—Yes.

20,727. You practically weigh yourself?—Yes, everything.

20,728. Does this town belong to the Earl of Limerick?—Yes, except the hotel.

20,729. The markets are held and the butter principally is exposed on the public thoroughfare?—It is.

20,730. Does he contribute anything directly towards the expense—outside, of course, his ordinary rates and taxes—to the cleansing of the streets of the town?—No.

20,731. Do you?—No.

20,732. Only through your rates and taxes?—Yes.

20,733. There is no shelter accommodation for the butter, to protect it in the summer from the heat of the sun or in winter from the inclemency of the weather?—The buyers and sellers would sooner have it as it is.

20,734. Do the traders of the town object to that?—The traders of the town would sooner have it as it is.

20,735. Do you think the market would improve if there was an enclosed market place with proper shelter accommodation provided?—No. It would be for worse.

20,736. It would not bring more buyers if they thought the butter was properly cared for?—No. The buyers would rather have it as they go through the streets themselves.

20,737. Have they ever complained that there is no cooper here to completely drain the firkins, and that they are put to any additional expense in providing coopers?—No; quite the contrary.

20,738. You have never levied any tolls other than the weighing charges at any of the markets?—Never.

20,739. When weighing any of these commodities, do you give a ticket denoting the weight?—Yes.

20,740. Is it a printed form?—I have an impressed

20,741. When you weigh the firkins do you mark the weight in chalk?—The buyers have tickets, and I put the weight at the back of them.

20,742. Have you got any of them?—No.

20,743. You mark with pen and ink the weight?—Yes.

20,744. You never strip the firkins?—No.

20,745. You never ascertain the tare?—No.

20,746. Do you put the estimated tare on the tickets as well?—I only weigh and put the weight on the ticket. I have no more to do with it.

20,747. What is the customary allowance as the tare of the firkin?—14 or 15 lbs.

20,748. Has the cooper always the weight branded on the firkin?—No.

20,749. Then you have not the same system here as in Tipperary and other places?—It is far broader than that, and there is more home trading.

20,750. Do you ever hear that coopers acted fraudulently in the preparation of the firkin?—Yes, very often.

20,751. Has not any prosecution been instituted?—No, except in the case of butter being packed fraudulently.

20,752. Who prosecuted?—The buyer.

20,753. You never prosecuted yourself?—No, except to assist the buyer in the prosecution.

20,754. You prove the case on account of exercising authority over the markets and fairs?—Yes. I put a particular mark on the firkin.

20,755. Do you ever mark with chalk on the firkin?—I do.

20,756. Is that the weight of the firkin?—No.

20,757. Do you ever keep an account of the weights in any book?—No.

20,758. You never keep a block of any ticket?—No, except at the weighbridge. Parties send in loads to be weighed, and of course they do not come prepared, and may be would weigh a load to-day and a load to-morrow if a man sold a rick of hay; so I keep an account of that, and no other accounts.

20,759. Only those you have dealings with?—Yes, for their accommodation.

20,760. If a strange farmer, whom you did not see before, brought a load of hay in to-morrow, would you give him a ticket denoting the weight?—Yes.

20,761. Do you give printed tickets?—They are not particular, and I am not either. They take anything I give them.

20,762. Do you ascertain the actual tare of the cart?—I weigh the cart always, except I weighed it before. I enter them on the book, and the charge is 6d. for weighing.

20,763. When you know the seller, and you have the weight of his cart before, you never weigh again, you leave it as the former tare?—Yes, if the buyer and seller are satisfied.

20,764. If not satisfied, you weigh?—Yes.

20,765. Do you know have frauds been committed by changing the wheels or changing the entire cart after the delivery of the hay?—A case of that kind never came under my notice.

20,766. The buyers have never complained?—Never.

20,767. In the case of hay or straw, or anything?—No.

20,768. Do the farmers ever bring their stock to the fairs the night before the fair?—They generally begin about 11 o'clock.

20,769. Where do they place them all night?—On the green.

20,770. They never ask for storage around the town?—They may or may not, but they are not charged on the green.

20,771. But have they been charged in other places?—Yes.

20,775. You always afford accommodation in the fair green if they wish to avail themselves of it, and you charge nothing additional?—No.

20,776. Except the charge the following day if the animal is sold?—Yes.

20,777. If the animal is not sold, for the exposure for sale and the use of the fair green as stallage the night before there is no charge?—No.

20,778. From what districts are these animals brought?—They vary some 20 miles, perhaps, to the two last fairs.

20,779. Would you say within a radius of 20 miles?—Yes.

20,780. Within what radius are the other commodities, such as potatoes and that, brought?—They might come in seven Irish miles.

20,781. Marketable commodities are brought within seven miles?—Yes.

20,782. Do the buyers require the seller to give a luck-penny on the sale of pigs?—Yes.

20,783. Is it a fixed rate?—It is partly a fixed rate.

20,784. What is it?—1s. on a cow.

20,785. I am dealing with the pigs?—6d.

20,786. Is that 6d. a fixed rate?—It is.

20,787. Does the luck-penny vary as regards the ordinary stock?—The general rule is they give 1s. for luck out of a cow. Some persons give more.

20,788. There is no rule regulating that?—There is nothing to bind anyone.

20,789. It is always left to the disposition of the seller?—Yes; but still it is insisted on, and is a common custom from time immemorial.

20,790. Have you any rules or regulations at all regulating the fairs?—No.

20,791. Have you got this toll board up in the fair green on fair days?—Of course.

20,792. At each gap?—At two gaps.

20,793. So that a stranger to the district can see the charges customary to be paid here?—He can.

20,794. When a man is driving some cattle from the fair, supposing he stated to your man he did not buy, and your man doubted the statement, what course would they adopt; would they detain the cattle?—They generally ask me what is to be done.

20,795. Are you always by?—I am at the outer gap. They would turn and ask me what was to be done, and I would go and ask and see, and if I could make no good of the man I would let him go.

20,796. Do your toll collectors swear them or produce any paper or book or ask them to clear their consciences on the toll board?—That practice has died 30 years ago. I never ask them now.

20,797. Supposing a farmer was driving his cattle into the fair, and on the road outside the town he met a buyer and effected a sale, would you ask for your charge, if in the town that is passed the first house, or are there any special limits to the town?—The town ends at a bridge coming across.

20,798. If a sale was effected at the other side?—I suppose I never got 1s. out of it.

20,799. Only when they come within what you call the limits of the town, that is, passed the first house?—Yes.

20,800. Have you sought for it and received it on such occasions?—I have sought for it, but never got it.

20,801. Still you are entitled to it?—Yes.

20,802. Have you ever heard complaints of this fair green?—No.

20,803. Is this it before the court house?—Yes.

20,804. In weighing potatoes what is the lowest weight you use?—4 lbs. weight, and 2 lbs., perhaps.

20,805. Is it usual to weigh down to 2 lbs.?—Not usual.

20,806. Do you give a cast of the beam when you are

20,910. Would that tare be the same in wet weather as on a fine day?—It would not.

20,911. When a bag is saturated with wet they actually weigh the bag?—They would.

20,912. Do the same observations apply to corn?—Invariably, I would not, because I am the principal buyer of corn, and I invariably weigh the bags.

20,913. Do you charge for weighing the bags when you buy yourself?—I make a bargain to charge nothing for weighing.

20,914. Are there other merchants in the town buying?—Yes.

20,915. Do they weigh themselves?—No; they come to me.

20,916. Do you charge a 1d. per cwt. for weighing?—Yes.

20,917. What is the lowest weight of the tare?—Four pounds; sometimes two.

20,918. What is the customary weight?—Four pounds.

20,919. Do you weigh their sacks?—I weigh what I buy myself. In case a person wanted to keep the corn in the bags he would empty the bag and place it outside the scale, and there get the net weight.

20,920. What was the weight of the bag?—Three pounds.

20,921. Now, to what weight do you weigh hay at the bridge?—To half a stone.

20,921a. The same applies to all particulars?—Yes.

20,922. Could you give me any approximate idea of the number of cattle brought to the fairs throughout the year?—I could not, indeed.

20,923. You never kept any record?—No. I calculated one year 4,000 calves brought in, and about 600 cows the same year; 100 horses, and 1,000 pigs.

20,924. Only 1,000?—At that one fair.

20,925. You say there were 4,000 calves?—Yes, at the October fair.

20,926. Did you make a calculation for the year?—No.

20,927. You perform no duties at the fairs that are toll free?—No.

20,928. Other than give the use of the fair green to them?—I give them the fair green.

20,929. Have these toll-free fairs always been held on the fair green?—Yes.

20,930. Was there any objection to their establishment by your father, or the Earl of Limerick, at the time?—I could not answer that.

20,931. Have you ever taken any proceedings to levy toll at them?—No.

20,932. Do you think yourself that they are fairly well attended for the time they are established as your ordinary fairs?—No, for two of them have gone down.

20,933. What do you assign as a reason for that?—The apathy of the farmers of the district. They would not send in their cattle.

20,934. Do they keep cattle only for the fairs late in the season?—They do. They do not send in cattle at the fairs in January and March, but the fairs in July and August are improving.

20,935. You never made any calculation of the number brought in at all the fairs throughout the year?—No.

20,936. It would be impossible to tell that?—It would be impossible to tell, except at my own fairs.

20,937. Could you at all approximate the number at the fairs that are toll free?—I suppose at the January and March fairs there are not 20 beasts sold there; then I should think there would be about 150 calves, about 50 cows, and 200 pigs at the August fair.

20,938. Are pigs sold the same day as cattle?—They are, and the day previous as well.

20,939. Where is the pig fair held?—In Connell Street.

20,940. You have no recollection of their being confined to the fair green, and the police putting them off the street?—I put them off the street myself, and put them on the fair green; but on a wet day they came back to the street again, and we left them there.

20,941. Did it afford sufficient space?—The green afforded sufficient, but they went on the street for shelter.

20,942. Would you say any great percentage of the cattle brought into the fairs is sold. What percentage was sold, we will say, on the 16th of May?—That is small. There is not much in that. You may count on the October and November fairs. At these, I should say, there are over 80 per cent. of the cattle.

20,943. At the other fairs?—The other fairs are not much. The July fair is the same thing.

20,944. And the August fair?—Half the calves were not sold the last time.

20,945. It is calves they bring principally?—Yes.

20,946. You charge the same for a yearling as a calf, 4d.?—Yes.

20,947. Do they ever bring them in when younger, when they are not yearlings?—Six months calf is a yearling.

20,948. What do you charge on a yearling?—The yearlings up to the 23rd July, 4d.; on the 16th October we charge them 6d.

20,949. Over a yearling you charge them the ordinary toll?—Yes.

20,950. That is on the October and November fairs?—Yes.

20,951. If they brought them in at the May fair?—I charge 6d., and at the July fair, 6d.

20,952. Is there a pig fair held the day previous to the fairs at which no tolls are levied?—Yes; but I only levy tolls on fours.

20,953. On the day previous to the days on which you levy tolls you charge tolls on pigs?—Yes, 2d. each. I do not charge for cows on market day.

20,954. What do you call market days?—The day previous to the ordinary cattle fair.

20,955. That is, the day before the cattle fair you do not charge the ordinary charge on the animal?—No.

Mr. John Sullivan examined.

20,956. You have here some fairs that are toll free, and others at which tolls are levied. Have you formed any ideas as to as to the levying of a toll?—No, I have not. I did not study the thing much.

20,957. Do you think the fairs at which tolls are not levied are better or equally as good as those at which tolls are levied?—The fairs on which the tolls are levied are old established fairs. Those at which no tolls are levied are new fairs which are struggling.

20,958. Do you think that the toll which is levied on animals actually sold in the fair acts in any way as a deterrent upon people bringing in animals and exposing them for sale?—I think it does.

20,959. Why do you form that opinion?—I have formed that opinion all my life.

20,960. Why?—Because the people look upon the custom as a thing they have no right to pay.

20,961. If a toll at all is to be levied would you approve, or would the farmers approve, of a toll considerably smaller than that at present allowed on all the animals as they enter the fair?—I do not think the smaller toll is required or would be required by the public.

20,962. Of course you should have any neighbourly feeling for Mr. Carroll out of consideration; but would you approve of a smaller toll on all animals as they enter the fair green than the larger one on the animals actually sold. Would it increase the fairs?—I do not think it would. My opinion is it would not increase them.

20,963. Then you say the farmers pay no consideration at all to the fact whether tolls are levied at a fair or not if the fair is a good one, and if they have an opportunity of effecting a sale?—Of course I believe the toll would have nothing to do with them if they thought they would have a good market to make good sales.

20,964. They would not mind paying the toll?—No.

20,965. Have you ever heard complaints of the tolls levied here?—I never heard a complaint.

20,966. Have you had experience of other fairs?—No.

20,967. Would you approve or do you think the markets here would be favoured and made better if a proper enclosed market space with sufficient and adequate accommodation was afforded the people?—I do not know. I know a good many people are better pleased to have the markets held on the streets, though I am not one myself.

20,668. Are you opposed to them?—I am opposed for a particular reason. It does not serve my business.

20,669. Would these people be in favour of it put up with any inconvenience caused to them by the markets being held on the streets for trade purposes?—That is my opinion.

20,670. For the same reason you object to them?—Yes.

20,671. Do not they occasion much filth and dirt about the place?—That is my objection.

20,672. Who removes it after the market?—The scavenger.

20,673. That is the road contractor?—We have a scavenger besides; we have a man for cleaning the towns and channels.

20,674. Who are his employers?—The sanitary authority.

20,675. The board of guardians?—Yes.

20,676. You have no local authority in Bruff?—No.

20,677. Do not the board of guardians and grand jury look after the local affairs?—Yes. Mr. Carroll is one of the guardians.

Mr. Francis O'Meara, Auctioneer, examined.

20,678. You have heard the remarks made by Mr. Sullivan; do you concur in them as to the fact that tolls in no way act as a deterrent on people bringing in their cattle or commodities?—It does not interfere one way or another with them. It has not the slightest effect on the fairs.

20,679. That is, if the tolls are levied only on the animal actually sold?—Just so.

20,680. Have you heard that the animals have been injured passing the toll gaps by the person collecting the toll there?—Never.

20,681-2. Or any undue delay caused to the farmers?—There must be a necessary delay when there is a large lot of cattle. I am often surprised at the quickness with which they let them through the gap, taking into account they have to take the number of them.

(Mr. Carroll.) I generally take their words for the number.

20,683. Why do you (Mr. O'Meara) form that opinion you have given about the tolls?—Well, the tolls generally go as luck, and buyers do not care three farthings if they can give satisfaction at the fairs. As a rule, buyers care very little for the toll.

20,684. Is this luck-penny they get from the seller an equivalent to the toll?—It is generally double the toll. In some cases, in consequence of that, they do not care about the toll.

20,685. Supposing a man bought 20 or 30 head of cattle would he get a luck-penny on each head?—Yes; and if a big price was paid to the seller it would encourage him to give a little more to the buyer as a luck-penny. They generally give much more than the toll.

20,686. You would be against the removal of the markets off the street?—I would. I would prefer to leave them on the street.

20,687. Have you ever heard of any of the perishable commodities brought in here being injured by the weather?—They are not long in it, and they are well protected when brought in.

20,688. How are they protected?—Protected by the grass and covering, and only exposed while the buyer is tasting.

20,689. That is the butter?—Yes.

20,690. Have you ever heard objections made by the buyers and yourself that the butter was not sufficiently exposed and completely drained before being weighed?—There might be an advantage in that.

20,691. Have you ever found you have been at a loss in buying butter that has not been drained?—Sometimes it does not stop the weight I put in, but that rarely occurs, and they would rather be at whatever little loss they are than be backing the butter and draining it.

20,692. Do you think it is sufficiently drained from the description Mr. Carroll gave of the practice of turning it up while the buyers are buying other firkins?—It does not sufficiently drain it, but the farmers are not in the habit of putting much pickle in it. They are getting better.

20,693. Would you approve of the system elsewhere established in the large markets of uncovering, draining, and boring?—I would approve of it.

20,694. Have you ever known from your own experience of firkins fraudulently made up?—I have to be sure. I found firkins here were 10 lbs. weight, and they should be only 1-4 lbs.

20,695. You would approve of the system adopted elsewhere?—I would approve of a check on the tares as much as possible.

20,696. Are they hand-made firkins brought here?—Yes, all hand-made. The buyers had a rule that every cooper should brand the tare on the firkins and his own name, and it was a capital arrangement if they kept up to it; but after a bit it fell through. It is a great check on fraudulent tares.

20,697. Have you heard any complaints, or have those who attended here any complaints, against the management; did you ever hear complaints that the animals are too long standing in the fair green, and no stalls or pens provided for them?—I never heard complaints.

20,698. Their value has not depreciated?—I never heard a complaint.

20,699. Would you approve of those stalls being erected?—No.

20,700. Do you think they are necessary?—I think the buyers would rather like being out in the open fair. They imagine they could not go through all the stalls and see the cattle properly.

20,701. Do you think for the town and the district around that the fairs are good?—Two fairs are very good; that is the October and November fairs.

20,702. You could not give any approximate idea of the number of cattle brought here to the fairs throughout the year?—I could not.

20,703. Is there any other gentleman who has any observations to make?—No answer.

The inquiry then ended.

KILMALLOCK—CO. LIMERICK.

With reference to my inquiry in Kilmallock on the 16th November 1888 I beg to

The market day is Friday. The fairs are held on the 4th January, 23rd February, 13th March, 8th April, 6th May, 20th June, 20th July, 4th August, 13th September, 14th October, 20th November, and 9th December.

No tolls are levied at the markets, but if any of the commodities are weighed a charge is payable to the private individual performing that duty.

Tolls are levied at the fairs held on the 4th January, 23rd February, 20th June, 4th August, 13th September, 20th November, and 9th December.

No charges are levied at the fairs held on the 13th March, 8th April, 6th May, 20th July, and 14th October.

No market or fair rights are exercised exclusively by any one individual, neither was any evidence forthcoming of any such rights being claimed.

A pig fair is held on the second day before the ordinary fair, except when the latter falls on a Tuesday when the pig fair or market is held on the previous Monday, and when the ordinary fair falls upon a Monday the pig fair is held on the previous Friday. No charges are levied at the pig fairs.

One patent was granted for the town of Kilmallock. It is dated 21st March, 2 George IV., and authorised the Provost, &c. of Kilmallock to hold six fairs, viz.:—21st February, 25th March, 23rd May, 6th July, 6th November, and 4th December.

The tolls at the fairs are payable to a committee of traders called "The Fair Committee." It appears the markets and fairs fell into abeyance until about 25 years ago, when the traders of the town voluntarily established the fairs on the 4th January, 23rd February, 8th April, 20th June, 4th August, 13th September, 20th November, and 9th December, and which were held in a field the property of a Mr. Kelly to whom a charge was payable on the entrance of each beast to the field. The fairs were subsequently removed to a field belonging to a Mr. Patrick Clery, then to one belonging to a Rev. Mr. Meldon, until about 10 years ago when the present "Fair Committee" was appointed. This committee was appointed to improve the fairs and markets and exercise control over them. Their first work was to purchase the tenants' interest for 120*l.* in the present field, which is used as a fair-green and is some four acres in extent. The rent is 27*l.* and it is held for 99 years. The committee then expended over 700*l.* in improvements on the green, and for the repayment of which each of the nine gentlemen forming the committee are jointly and severally liable.

The fairs on the 13th March, 8th May, 20th July, and 14th October were established in the year 1880 by the Fair Committee.

A schedule of charges is erected, and a weighbridge, belonging to one of the committee, is available if required by those frequenting the fairs.

The charges payable are on entrance to the fair-green, and if beasts are sold elsewhere none are claimed on them.

In accordance with my instructions I have inspected the fair-green and market places, &c.

The fairs are held in an enclosed fair-green situate off the main street and close to the railway station. There are three entrances, the principal one being by a large iron gate from the public street. The green is commodious and most suitable for fair purposes and, so far as space and convenience is concerned, afford every accommodation. There are, however, no pens or sheds erected for the shelter and accommodation of those frequenting the fair as buyers and sellers.

Horses, sheep, and pigs are sold on the public streets, and no fair rights are claimed over them when disposed of there.

The markets are not large, and though Friday is the day fixed upon for general purposes the commodities are sold every day during the week. Fowl and butter are generally brought to a private market square attached to the dwelling house of one of the Fair Committee. It is narrow, and at the time of inspection was not faultless as a market site. There is a large shed under which the butter is weighed after being previously sold in carts in the street outside this square. The fowl are exposed both inside and outside the square.

This square, it should be stated, is enclosed and forms portion of Mr. Sullivan's property. All the butter brought into town does not pass through the market nor is it sold on the public streets. The buyers buy two thirds of it on other days than Friday, and have it delivered at their stores where they ascertain the weight, &c. on their own private scales. A beam and scales and weighing machine for weighing loads of hay, straw, and other commodities are provided by Mr. Sullivan. The machine is capable of weighing cattle.

21,000. What percentage would you say, of the animals brought in are sold on a fair day?—That varies. If there was a good demand for cattle, most of those at the fair would be sold.

21,001. What would be the average for the year?—I think three-fourths would be too much to say would be sold, but I think there are more than half.

21,002. Are there fairs at which no tolls are levied as good as the fairs at which you levy tolls?—The fairs at which there are no tolls never amounted to much.

21,003. What was the reason for establishing these and not levying any tolls?—It was an inducement to the people to send in cattle so that they would be at no expense.

21,004. At the time of starting them did the committee contemplate the exaction of a toll at any future period?—I expect they did.

21,005. When the fairs were sufficiently established?—Yes.

21,006. And they have that opinion yet?—I think we have abandoned it now because the fairs have not amounted to anything.

21,007. Do you keep any record of the number of animals attending the fairs?—We do not, only the receipts.

21,008. Have you got here an account of the receipts?—I have got it here in the book as we received it.

21,009. You did not make any average for the couple of years previous?—I took the account for the last 12 months. I went back to the November fair, the 20th November last year, and we received that day 10*l.* 4*s.* 6*d.*, on the 9th December 3*l.* 16*s.* 3*d.*, the 4th January 5*s.*—that was a very stormy, wet morning, and nobody came to the fair.

21,010. Do you think if there was shelter accommodation provided in the fair-green that they would have brought their animals?—They would not, because the morning was so bad, stormy, and wet that the farmers could not drive in the cattle. They would not have thought of removing their cattle from the farms to bring them in.

21,011. Would they have removed them the night previous if there were any pens or stallage in the fair-green?—They would not except a very few who come a long distance.

21,012. Do they bring them in that way the night before?—Sometimes and at some seasons of the year.

21,013. Where do they place them?—They put them in fields around the town.

21,014. Do they pay stallage charges?—They pay for standing and for hay.

21,015. Is there any fixed amount?—No, but we would accommodate them in the fair field and charge nothing but what we charge the morning going in.

21,016. You are always quite willing to allow them the use of the fair-green for that purpose?—Yes, at any time.

21,017. Well, now, what did you receive on the 23rd February?—We received 14*l.* 7*s.* 1*d.*; on 8th April, 18*l.* 1*s.* 4*d.*; the 20th June, 11*l.* 17*s.* 7*d.*; the 6th August, 3*l.* 17*s.* 4*d.*; the 13th September, 3*l.* 11*s.* 10*d.*

21,018. What expense were you at last year or during that period?—The rent and taxes amounted to 30*l.* It may be a little over, and I think it would be a little; but it is 30*l.* in round numbers.

21,019. What other expense were you at?—For advertising and posting, 10*l.*

21,020. That was in order to push the fairs and give publicity to them?—Yes, and then for collecting 5*l.* That is what we paid a man to stand at the gate.

21,021. Is that the total expense?—There is then the interest which we pay, which is about 25*l.* a year.

21,022. What is the rate?—Five per cent.

21,023. From what bank?—From the Munster and Leinster Bank.

21,024. You would say about 500*l.* due to them at present?—There is not that amount due to the bank, but we owe about that.

21,025. That is the total liability of the members?—Yes.

21,026. Was the charge on entry of all the animals the only charge levied at all the fairs since they were established in the first instance?—That is the only charge. There has been no alteration in the charge.

21,027. Have you ever heard the farmers objecting to pay that charge when they might not subsequently sell the animal in the fair-green?—There is no doubt they have. They have complained about it; in fact, they have disliked to pay going in because in the other fairs around us, it is when the cattle are coming out there is a charge, and the farmers going to these fairs have looked upon what they pay as so much out of pocket, and if they want to, where else they would not have to pay it.

21,028. Did they ever state they were agreeable to pay in the other manner?—It is the buyers pay in the other instances.

21,029. Is it not customary for the seller to give the buyer a luck-penny?—It is.

21,030. Would that be equivalent to the toll payable by the buyer?—They give the luck-penny here all the same.

21,031. Although in the first instance they pay the charge on entering?—I think it makes no alteration in the luck-penny they give.

21,032. There is no rule regulating the value of the luck-penny?—No. It is a voluntary matter.

21,033. It is left to the disposition of the seller?—Yes.

21,034. Have they any fixed luck-penny on pigs?—They have about 6*d.* a pig.

21,035. Is that irrespective of the fact whether it is a fat pig or a bonham?—All the very same.

21,036. Now you have 6*d.* a cart on pigs brought into the fair-green?—Yes.

21,037. That is irrespective of the number of pigs in the cart?—It is.

21,038. What is the number that is usually brought in, or the smallest you recollect yourself they have brought in a cart?—I think I recollect seeing one, and the man objecting to pay 6*d.*, and the man at the gate let him in at half price.

21,039. Let him in for 3*d.*?—Yes, on account of his having only one. That may not occur for years. I never remember but once, but in another case it might be a dozen in the cart. I think the average number would be from six to twelve pigs.

21,040. That charge of 6*d.* is the only charge payable to the fair committee?—That is the only charge.

21,041. You charge nothing at all going out?—No.

21,042. Or for any standing in the fair-green?—Not on a fair day.

21,043. How is the fair-green utilised between fairs?—It is let for standings.

21,044. What benefit did you derive last year from that?—I suppose probably from all sources it amounted to about 10*l.*

21,045. In addition to the amount received from the fairs?—Yes.

21,046. What description of standings do you have there?—[illegible] cows coming here and going from one place to another, and they stop here for a night to rest.

21,047. What rate do you charge?—1*s.* a score—that is, for 20. Then there are dealing men from time to time between fairs.

21,048. But it is purely for standings?—Yes, and no charge for cows.

21,049. From what districts are the animals brought here and exposed for sale, or within what limits would you state?—They come from Charleville, Bruff, Hospital, Knocklong, and Kilmallock. Within a radius of seven or eight miles.

21,050. You say that they always bring the cattle into the fair-green. Do they ever sell about the fair-green, or avail themselves of the presence of the buyers?—Very seldom.

21,051. They always take them into the fair-green?—Yes, and, principally, dealing men bring cattle in calf to sell. They are brought from the King's County and Meath.

21,052. Purely dealers' cattle?—Yes, and sometimes from the Dublin Market they are brought here and sold.

21,053. Do you ever clean the fair-green after the fairs, or is it necessary?—No; it is not necessary to clean it. We only clean the approaches to it.

21,054. What expense is incurred in clearing the approaches? If you pay a man, what is the rate of payment, or would you say that is included in the 5*l.* for [illegible] collecting?—No. The cleaning would be outside that. It is not hard to clean.

21,055. But I want to get the total expense you are at?—I think you might say you have it.

21,056. You say it is included in the 1d. for collecting?—I should say it would.

21,057. Your right to collect this charge only extends to the limits of the fair-green?—That is all.

21,058. Do you ever take any steps to get them to expose their animals on the fair-green and not on the public thoroughfare?—We have asked the owners of the sheep to take them into the fair-field.

21,059. Did you ever induce the buyers only to buy when the sheep were exposed in the fair-green?—I do not think we did. I do not think we ever interfered with them in that way.

21,060. From what districts do the buyers come?—They come from Cork, Limerick, Dublin, and Waterford.

21,061. You could give no idea of the number of animals brought here and exposed for sale?—No.

Mr. J. J. O'Sullivan, merchant, examined.

21,062. What markets are held here?—There is only one market independent of the pig market.

21,063. When I say market I mean the general market for marketable commodities, not for any animals?—Friday—one day in the week.

21,064. Where are these markets held?—In the market square, quite convenient to our dwelling-house.

21,065. Does that market square form portion of the public thoroughfare?—No. It belongs to myself.

21,066. It is your own private property?—Yes.

21,067. What description of commodities is brought there on Friday?—Fowl and butter are the only two items I have.

21,068. Are potatoes brought there?—No.

21,069. Are not the potatoes exposed at all in the town?—They are.

21,070. I take it then that this is a private speculation of yours, and that there is another one in the town?—There is.

21,071. Only butter and fowl come to yours?—That is all.

21,072. This market square is entirely enclosed?—It is railed in.

21,073. Is it in firkins the butter is brought?—Yes; they are bought in the street, and brought in there to be weighed in the market.

21,074. Are all commodities exposed for sale in the public street?—Yes, except some fowl outside the railings, and some inside. I do not charge any tolls.

21,075. Do you charge any stallage?—No.

21,076. The sellers of the fowl have to pay no charge?—Nothing at all.

21,077. And they avail themselves of this market?—Yes; there is an arrangement put there for the accommodation of the market.

21,078. Have they shelter accommodation?—There is a shed.

21,079. They can go in there if the weather is in any way inclement?—Yes.

21,080. Is the butter brought in carts into the street?—Yes.

21,081. The butter is always sold here before it is weighed?—Yes; it is sold and then the weight is got.

21,082. The buyer will not pay for it or buy it—that is, conclude his contract—unless it is weighed?—I could not say that it is generally done.

21,083. Did they ever bring it away without ascertaining the weight?—I think it is generally brought before it is weighed.

21,084. Is it always weighed before being delivered?—It is.

21,085. What is your charge?—1d. a firkin for weighing.

21,086. What do you give in return for that?—I weigh it.

21,087. Have you a cooper employed?—No, only a man, and he gives the ticket.

21,088. He ascertains the gross weight of the firkin?—Yes.

21,089. He never denies it?—The cooper is in attendance.

21,090. Who is the cooper?—The buyer's cooper.

21,091. And he drains it?—Yes.

21,092. Are the firkins drained, as far as your knowledge extends, sufficiently, and to the satisfaction of the buyers?—I think so.

21,093. You never heard them complain?—Both parties interested are there, and it is to their satisfaction everything is done.

21,094. The firkins are not completely stripped?—They are sometimes.

21,095. That is when you are in doubt or when you think it has been fraudulently prepared and not correctly made up?—Yes.

21,096. You have a printed ticket?—Yes.

21,097. It is in return for this ticket you get the penny?—Yes.

21,098. Do you keep a block of that ticket?—Yes.

21,099. Do you ever enter it in any book?—It is a separate book in itself.

21,100. You always retain the books and keep them for a lengthened time, that if a person lost the ticket you could give another?—Yes.

21,101. In addition to giving the ticket, do you mark the gross weight in chalk on the outside of the firkin?—No.

21,102. Are the firkins branded with the tare by the coopers who make them?—Generally they are.

21,103. Is there any rule among the buyers here not to buy a firkin except the tare is branded on it?—I do not think so.

21,104. There is none here?—No.

21,105. But in the majority of cases the tare is branded?—Generally.

21,106. You never yourself ascertain the tare of the firkin?—No.

21,107. Do you put down the estimated tare on the ticket?—Always.

21,108. What is that estimated tare?—14 lbs.

21,109. Did you ever allow 15 lbs.?—If the cooper notices some timber about the firkin, he questions it, and another pound is put on for the tare.

21,110. Is all the butter brought here weighed at your scales?—Some of it is, I believe, weighed in the stores of the buyers, but very little.

21,111. That is for the private consumer?—In the stores of the local buyers.

21,112. They weigh at their own scales?—Yes, during the week.

21,113. But on Friday, do they?—On Fridays it is generally weighed in the market place.

21,114. That is at your scales on Friday?—Yes.

21,115. What is the lowest weight you weigh with or down to?—Down to a pound.

21,116. What is your system of weighing? Do you give a cast of the beam or do you weigh by counting beam?—I give a cast of the beam.

21,117. Would you say, then, the firkin must have a pound or nothing?—Yes.

21,118. If it were three-quarters of a pound over and above the ordinary pound the buyer would get the advantage?—Yes.

21,119. Is that tare and that pound and three-quarters of a pound the only deductions from the gross weight of the firkin, or is there any allowance for salt or anything?—No.

21,120. Or for pickle if there is any in it?—No.

21,121. Does the buyer rely on his own experience to taste the butter?—Yes.

21,122. There is no official taster employed?—No; the buyer does that himself.

21,123. What percentage would you say of the firkins brought in go to your scales? Would you say half as many again are not brought there?—There is three times more bought during the week than comes to my scales. The butter bought by the different buyers is brought into the town before it is shipped. One of the buyers may buy 100 firkins in Newcastle West, and another 100 firkins in Mitchelstown.

21,124. I mean the number of firkins brought in by the farmers to sell in the first instance here?—There is about one third weighed with me and two thirds go to the stores.

21,125. That is bought from the farmers and not at the adjoining markets?—They bring it into the stores during the night.

21,126. From what distance is the butter brought here?—Within a radius of four or five miles.

21,127. Have you any rules or regulations posted in the square for the observance of buyers and sellers?—No.

21,128. Have the buyers any rules?—There was a rule that they were not to buy at the stores on Fridays; they were to buy in the market.

21,129. Is that observed?—I think it is fairly.

21,130. Are the buyers who frequent the market square only local buyers?—They are buyers from Limerick, too, and Tipperary.

21,131. The rule was made by the local buyers that they should not buy at their own stores?—It was generally done for the benefit of the market.

21,132. That is the only commodity on which you receive any charge?—That is all.

21,133. You have receipts from no other source?—Except the weighing.

21,134. What scales have you for weighing the butter?—The ordinary beam and scales.

21,135. Is the one sufficient for the purpose?—We get two, if necessary.

21,136. You have got a crane?—Yes.

21,137. What commodities do you weigh on that crane?—Hay and straw principally; mangolds and turnips.

21,138. Is there another crane in the town?—I do not think there is.

21,139. Any load the weight of which it was desired to ascertain must come to your crane?—Yes. Mr. Walsh of the railway station has weighed; he weighs privately, but does not charge; he weighs hay and straw.

21,140. What is your charge for weighing a load?—4d. a load.

21,141. Irrespective of the commodity the load contains?—Yes.

21,142. Must the weight of hay and straw be always ascertained before it is delivered to the buyer?—It is generally bought by the ton.

21,143. Is it bought before it is weighed?—It is.

21,144. Where is the hay and straw exposed for sale?—It is bought generally at the farm. There is no market. The seller might come in from the country and sell it one day and then deliver it.

21,145. They never stand on the streets with hay?—No.

21,146. You weigh straw the same way?—Yes.

21,147. The same observations apply to that?—Yes.

21,148. And the turnips?—The same.

21,149. They never stand on the street and expose them?—No.

21,150. Neither the hay, straw, turnips, mangolds, nor carrots are exposed in loads?—No.

21,151. In weighing the load, do you always ascertain the tare of the cart?—Yes.

21,152. Supposing a farmer whom you have weighed his load to-day and came to-morrow with another load, would you ascertain the tare of the cart?—Yes.

21,153. You never go by estimation or recollection of the former weight of the cart?—No; it is always weighed.

21,154. You never heard any frauds committed by changing the wheels or substituting the other cart?—Never.

21,155. Or such complaints have never been made to you?—I never heard of any.

21,156. Would that 4d. be charged for a donkey load if it came in?—Yes.

21,157. What is the lowest weight you weigh down to in a load?—Any weight at all they wish to weigh.

21,158. I do not mean the smallest load, but the lowest weight you weigh down to?—Down to 7 lbs.

21,159. Do you weigh down to 7 lbs. in weighing a load of hay?—No.

21,160. What is the customary smallest weight you weigh down to?—7 cwt.

21,161. It must be 7 cwt. or nothing?—Yes.

Mr. Thomas Barrett examined.

21,162. You have another beam and scales?—Yes.

21,163. What commodities do you weigh on it?—Potatoes.

21,164. Do you weigh corn in addition to potatoes?—Yes.

21,165. Anything else?—Nothing else.

21,166. Are the potatoes always weighed at your beam and scales?—Yes.

21,167. What is your charge?—1d. per bag.

21,168. Is the bag of potatoes always sold before you weigh it?—Yes.

21,169. They never ascertain the weight of it before they sell it?—No.

21,170. Have you got any square similar to Mr. O. Sullivan's or any market place?—I have a little place that holds a few bags of potatoes.

21,171. Do they expose them there for sale?—They expose them in the street and sell them, and then I weigh them.

21,172. Do you always weigh the empty bag?—There is a general allowance for them.

21,173. What is it?—Four pounds and five pounds.

21,174. How would you know whether it would be four pounds or five pounds?—There might be an idle bag, and then they throw one into the scale and weigh it.

21,175. Would that estimated tare be the same on a wet day as on a dry day?—If the bag is wet they take that into consideration.

21,176. I take it if there was a dispute between the buyer and seller as to the weight of an empty bag they would weigh it?—They never dispute.

21,177. Supposing it was a very wet day and a bag was brought in, whether corn or potatoes, and it got completely saturated with wet, what would be the weight of the bag or what would be allowed for it?—It would be 10 pounds if the day was wet. I often saw a bag 10 pounds and often saw a bag one.

21,178. What is your charge for weighing the corn?—1d. a bag.

21,179. What is the estimated tare of a bag in that case?—Four pounds or five.

21,180. The same as potatoes?—Yes.

21,181. Could you give me your receipts from this?—Yes, perhaps.

21,182. What are they in the year?—I could not say.

21,183. Do you make 5l.?—Yes, that is the most, and I would not make that same, only I buy a handful of potatoes myself when they have no one to buy for them.

21,184. You deal in these commodities yourself?—Yes.

21,185. Do you use the pound weight when weighing?—I do sometimes.

21,186. What do you usually weigh down to?—Four pounds, and often two.

21,187. And in corn?—Down to a pound in corn.

Mr. George D. Cahill examined.

21,188. There is no other person or trader in the town having any beam and scales to weigh the different commodities than what has been mentioned?—No.

21,189. Have you heard from the people of the town that those are quite sufficient for the purpose?—One is quite sufficient. Mr O. Sullivan's one is quite sufficient; in fact, it does not get quarter enough to do.

21,190. Did you ever hear the people here in the town discussing the advisability of having a general market for all marketable commodities?—Certainly, I think it is very necessary.

21,191. Have they ever discussed that?—The fair committee have discussed it.

21,192. The establishment of a market as well as fairs?—Yes.

21,193. Did they ever take any steps to establish one?—No, because they could not; they have got no patent.

21,194. They took no steps, you say?—A gentleman reminds me that one year they paid a yearly sum to Mr. Sullivan for the market, and attempted to establish it, and it failed and did not pay.

21,195. Within your knowledge or within the knowledge of any gentleman here at present has at any time exercised any rights over the market?—Never.

21,196. Other than Mr. Sullivan or Mr. [illegible] for weighing purposes?—Yes.

21,197. Do you think a necessity exists for a general market?—I certainly say there is no town in the world wants it more.

21,198. What was the cause of the failure to establish a market?—It did not succeed. It was an oats market. The [illegible] market was the only thing that held on, and that is holding on still, but the butter market is a failure also.

21,199. Are you in trade in the town?—Yes, a draper.

21,200. Are there any objections to these fairs of sheep and pigs and horses being held on the street?—I certainly say I have an objection to the horses on the street, but would not object to the pigs or butter.

21,201. Why?—Because I think it is very well to have them there. Every thing is there about the [illegible].

21,202. Why do you object to the horses?—Because they are very dangerous.

21,203. Have accidents ever happened?—Certainly.

21,204. The fact of pigs being sold on the streets occasions such filth and dirt about the public thoroughfares?—The people put up with that. When the people scatter each person gets a share of trade, and if they collected at one end of the town one party would have a better centre than another.

21,205. Would you say that, although the holding of the fairs on the street occasions such filth and dirt, the traders would put up with that inconvenience for trade purposes?—They would. There is not so much filth and dirt caused, because the scavenger in the town comes and removes them away in a short time afterwards.

21,206. Is that scavenger in the payment of the road contractor?—He is in the employment of the board of guardians as the sanitary authority.

21,207. He performs the duty of cleaning after the fairs?—Yes.

21,208. You heard no complaints?—Not in that line, but there is against the road contractor, who leaves stuff there for a week.

21,209. Do you think the traders would be opposed to a removal of the fairs off the streets?—They would be opposed to the removal of the pig fair.

Mr. Maurice Grady examined.

21,210. You are in trade in the town?—Yes.

21,211. In what trade?—Butchering and public business.

21,212. Have you formed any ideas as to the establishment of a general market here in Kilmallock?—I declare there is not a man in town but would be proud if we could establish a general market.

21,213. You are a member of the fair committee?—Yes.

21,214. Do the fair committee contemplate a renewal of an application for a patent?—They had no idea of renewing it until notice of this inquiry was given.

21,215. What deters them from applying for it and endeavouring to form a market here. Is it the expense?—It is the expense.

Mr. Haggis examined.

21,216. Are you connected with the butter trade here?—Yes.

21,217. Did you ever hear that the butter was depreciated in quantity or value by its exposure to the elements on the public thoroughfares?—Certainly. I always have an objection to buy butter in carts on the public thoroughfare. There should always be a house provided to have the butter taped and examined as it is at Limerick where I frequently bought a lot of butter.

21,218. Supposing it was a very warm day and the [illegible] was exposed here in the public thoroughfares, would it not be depreciated in quantity?—Certainly.

21,219. And the value has been lowered to the producer than it otherwise would be if there was sufficient accommodation?—Yes, and when the buyers goes to buy, it is so soft that it cannot be handled, examined, or tested.

21,220. You think a necessity exists for a proper enclosed market?—Certainly. It would be the greatest possible improvement.

21,221. Would Mr. Sullivan's market square afford sufficient space if the butter were removed and exposed there?—The nicest place possible, and at the first meetings about the market it was agreed by the farmers and the buyers that all butter should be brought into the shed and exposed. It was carried out for several markets until [illegible] little split occurred, and it was broken up.

21,222. Was that the buyers fault?—It was more the sellers'. There were some people who did not bring the butter in as nice a condition as they should, and they did not like to have it exposed.

21,223. Have prosecutions taken place for fraud of that description?—I had one.

21,224. It is always the buyer who institutes proceedings?—I will tell you how it occurred. I bought a firkin from one man and found 14 pounds of pickle in it; I told the man to take away the firkin, that I did not want to prosecute, and he refused; and then I went to a constable and asked him to prosecute, and he instituted the proceedings.

21,225. You consider these fraudulent practices are owing to the want of proper facilities for inspecting and sheltering the butter?—I think so, and it would serve the farmer ultimately, because, if I was buying butter in Limerick, I would pay more for it in Limerick than in Kilmallock, because I could rely invariably on what I get in Limerick, the tares and everything else.

21,226. Do you consider from the practice and manner here that the price of good butter is lower than in other places?—It is certainly lower than in other towns because I paid 2s. more for butter in Limerick than in Kilmallock.

21,227. You state that the tares in weight is fraudulently prepared here?—Yes, because when I go into Limerick I can see a man's ticket, and I am prepared to get the contents of that ticket. Another thing exists to the farmers is this, if a firkin of butter is brought to the town and he gets 60s. for it, he gets nothing for the extra pounds. Some farmers ascertain the weight of their firkins at home. A firkin may weigh three quarters and three pounds, but the farmer gets nothing for the three pounds, because it is three quarters of butter that is bought, and the buyer gets the benefit of the three pounds over.

21,227a. Of course four pounds is the lowest weight?—A pound.

21,228. They would knock off three pounds?—Yes, six pounds, but I frequently saw two or three pounds. They would not get a penny for anything over three quarters of butter.

21,229. What remedy would you suggest? Is it that the farmers should provide themselves with scales?—What I told you put it into a house and then the farmer would get an equivalent for the quantity of butter he would bring it. In Limerick they pay so much a pound for every pound over. The ticket is shown, and if 60s. are given for the quarter calculating according to the ticket, if there were two pounds of butter over, the seller is paid for it.

21,230. Here the farmer would only be paid for three quarters?—Yes; and they are charged for anything they are short of the three quarters.

21,231. They are charged for anything under, and then they lose anything over it?—Yes. Another thing is because the tares are very objectionable and often a great loss to the buyer.

21,232. How is that?—There may be 16 pounds tare and you buy 14. The buyer is then out two pounds.

21,233. Are they hand-made firkins?—Yes.

21,234. Do you think when the firkins are not completely stripped that gives an opportunity to producers to [illegible] resort to the fraudulent practice of making heavier firkins than usual?—The farmers leave them a little heavy when there will not be a check.

21,235. Would not the buyers agree among themselves to buy only in a more?—I am sorry to say I think there is not a more disunited lot of people on earth than butter buyers. They make rules and break them.

21,236. Would it not be to their own advantage ultimately?—It would be, but I found the contrary. When buying butter I found a firkin that would be 16 pounds over, and another buyer would come up and say do not allow anything about that. We have no rules here about stripping butter. There is no organisation among the buyers in the local country markets. It would be the greatest boon if a patent could be obtained for the fairs, and the people would be fairly inclined to do so, but they are afraid that local influence would be used and put them to a great deal of cost.

21,237. To whom does the town belong?—It is divided. The right of tolls belongs to the Oliver family.

21,238. Who is the representative of this family at present?—Sir George Colthurst.

21,239. This Oliver family have never within your memory exercised any right they might have considered vested in them?—Not for 50 years, at all events.

21,240. Have you any other observations to make?—No. I know people who take their cattle from this side of the country to Charleville because they are charged [illegible] going in here.

21,241. Do you think the fact of a toll or charge being levied deters farmers from bringing their animals to the fair?—There is not the slightest doubt in the world about it. They take them to Charleville and Bruff in order not to come here, but I have been jawing with the farmers for penny, but they think it a great hardship to have to pay when they come to a fair and do not sell.

21,242. It is the charge on entry they object to, but they have no objection to pay on the animal if sold?—It is the buyer pays there.

21,243. Then the luck-penny is an equivalent?—It is all the very same.

21,244. And it is all the same amount?—Yes. There is no distinction for that. The buyers are very much pleased with the arrangement here and the sellers are not.

21,245. If the buyers are pleased with the arrangement, does not that tend to bring more buyers to the fair?—They do not get the quantity of cattle they like. Men from Dublin come here, and they are disappointed when they do not get a waggon of cattle and only want three or four.

21,246. Is there any greater demand for cattle with more buyers than in other towns?—There is no fair in Ireland where there are better cattle or better prices.

21,247. Why does not that induce the farmers to come, or do not consider they are mistaken in going to other towns for a matter of 2d.?—I have scolded them frequently for doing so. If you could get a patent or assist them for the tolls and markets here, this town would become one of the most prosperous towns in the South of Ireland.

21,248. Do you think you have exceptional facilities here by having a railway station?—There is no doubt of it. There are better facilities here than in the town of Charleville because the people take their cattle to the railway here and buy there, whereas in Charleville they put them into yards, but here they will not be paid until they put them into the box at the railway.

21,249. The farmer always delivers the animal at the railway station?—Yes.

21,250. If you were to levy a toll only on the animal sold, would not the seller have to pay it, because the animal would be in his possession passing the gate?—No, because the buyer's man would be with him and would tell how many head of cattle there were going out.

21,251. In the period that elapses between the contract and the delivery at the railway station is the seller responsible for the possession of the animal?—He is at the present time as the tolls are levied there.

21,252. Supposing an accident happened to the animal whilst being driven from the fair-green to the railway station, would the seller be responsible?—I think he would at present, but if the tolls were levied going out the man who paid the custom would have charge of the beast, and then the seller would not be responsible.

21,253. Have you anything else to suggest?—No.

Mr. Michael Gubbins examined.

21,254. Have you any remarks to make?—Before the late Mr. O'Sullivan died we went very near having a railway down to the fair-green, that is a siding. I believe the committee have some claim on the road from the fair-green to the station house. Again, I would like to remark that before this committee was formed the authorities ordered the buyers off the streets to the fair-green; but since the committee was formed, and since we got charge of the fair-green, the police took no steps to have them removed off the public thoroughfare.

21,255. Have they summoned them, or have those summonses had the effect of making them remove their beasts?—No. They got such trouble and opposition that they tired of it and gave it up.

21,256. (*Mr. Grady.*) We open the fair-green gratis, and do not actually want to charge, and they will not go in.

21,257. (*Mr. Harris.*) I think ultimately there will be a siding down to the fair-green that will afford additional facilities. There is a bye-road alongside the fair-green to the railway station, and it is not difficult. They then went so far as to buy a piece of the workhouse farm.

21,258. Was it on your representations the railway was going to put that down?—On the representation of the late committee. They made an application to put down the siding stating it would be for their benefit as well as ours, and would improve the fairs very much when the cattle could be bought, turned up there, and boxed immediately. There is another matter to which I wish to refer, about the shedding or pens. I think it most desirable that there should be shedding and pens for cattle and sheep, as in Fermoy particularly.

21,259. In Fermoy there is practically the same charge on cattle coming in as here, and it is said to work very well?—There is a great census about Fermoy. They have no fairs to avail of, but here we are surrounded by Bruff, Charleville, and other places, and it takes away from our fairs not to have tolls charged going out.

Mr. Patrick Cleary re-examined.

21,260. What further remarks have you to make?—There is a great mistake made by the farmers in not coming here, because undoubtedly they would get better prices at the fairs here than at the surrounding fairs. I often heard buyers say they never bought dearer cattle than at Kilmallock, and, strange to say, the farmers know this, and have an objection to pay 2d. coming in.

21,261. From the number of buyers attending here, making the demand so great, and where the supply is so small, how has such a small per-centage remained unsold?—That varies sometimes. If there was a great demand for cattle more would be bought, but if you have a [illegible] fair, the demand not being so much and the price down, then more cattle will remain unsold, because the sellers would not be prepared for the fall and the buyers would not advance.

21,262. You never heard of any combination among the buyers to give only a certain price for the cattle?—None whatever.

21,263. They all act independently of one another?—Indeed they do.

21,264. Have you had experience at any other fairs besides Kilmallock?—No, nothing more than that I attended other fairs.

21,265. Do you buy and sell at them?—Yes.

21,266. From your experience of this and these places, do you think, where fairs and markets arise, that they should be under the control of a local body, if any such exist; if not, under the authority of a fair or markets committee, and not have them in the hands and subject to the control of an individual?—I think it is better to have them in the hands of a committee.

21,267. Do you think the united efforts of the members of a committee or local authority, such as the town commissioners, would tend to work them to the better satisfaction of the farmers and those frequenting the market?—No doubt about it.

71,368. What is your reason for expressing that opinion? —Because they would take more trouble in working up the fairs and making them larger, and give more facilities to the buyer and seller. I think a committee would do that better than an individual. From a pecuniary point of view the entire fair committee do not want or care to derive any benefit. What they simply want is to improve the fairs for the benefit of the town. I do not think the committee are likely to derive any benefit for many years.

71,369. Messrs. Lewis and O'Sullivan agreed with the opinions expressed by Mr. Cary, and no other gentlemen coming forward to give evidence, the inquiry terminated.

CHARLEVILLE—CO. CORK.

With reference to my inquiry in Charleville on the 17th November 1888, I beg to report as follows:—

Charleville is an inland town situated in the county of Cork. It is a station on the Great Southern and Western Railway line, and on the Waterford and Limerick Railway line. The town is fairly well built, and the streets apparently looked after. The principal street is of a good width, and the others of moderate size. The trade is agricultural and the local government is vested in the board of guardians and grand jury. The population is 2,266.

The market days are Wednesday and Saturday. The fairs are held on the 10th January, 3rd February, 16th March, 14th April, 12th May, 9th June, 6th July, 15th August, 12th September, 10th October, 12th November, and 5th December. A pig fair is held on the day previous to the ordinary fairs.

Tolls are levied at the markets and also on the fairs held on the 10th January, 16th March, 12th May, 15th August, 10th October, and 12th November. The fairs held on the 3rd February, 14th April, 9th June, 6th July, 12th September, and 5th December are toll free, as are also the pig fairs. Previous to last year tolls were collected at the pig fairs held the day previous to the ordinary fairs at which tolls were levied, but in that year they ceased to be demanded, as the result of legal proceedings.

If, however, any of the pig fairs or any of the fairs held on the 3rd February, 14th April, 9th June, 6th July, 12th September, and 5th December fall on a market day, tolls are collected on each animal according to the rate mentioned in the scale of charges.

A toll board is erected, and beams and scales and a weighbridge have been provided.

The market rights and tolls are the property of the Earl of Cork. They are sublet, however, to a Mrs. M. Fitzgerald, of Charleville, under a lease for 16 years, of which eight years are unexpired, at the yearly rent of 144*l*.

Although in the evidence it has been mentioned that four patents were granted for Charleville, the public records only disclose two. The first is dated 7th June 1620, and was granted for Rathgogan *alias* Charleville, and authorised one Roger L. Brigshill to hold a Wednesday market and fairs on the 24th June and 29th September, and the day following each. The second patent is dated 13th September 1828 (9 Geo. IV.), and authorised the Earl of Cork and Orrery to hold fairs on 10th January, 16th March, 12th May, and 15th August. The markets and fairs held, therefore, under express authority are the Wednesday market and the fairs on the 10th January, 16th March, 12th May, 6th July, 15th August, and 10th October, and the markets and fairs not held under any express authority disclosed by the public records are the Saturday market and the fairs on the 3rd February, 14th April, 9th June, 12th September, 12th November, and 5th December, and the pig fairs.

The fairs on the 3rd February, 16th March, 14th April, 12th May, 9th June, 6th July, 12th September, and 5th December were established in 1864, and those on the 10th January and 15th August must have been first held a few years previously, as the fairs only held at the sitting of the Royal Commission in 1852 were those on the 10th October and 12th November. The latter two have been held for a considerable period.

In accordance with my instructions, I have inspected the market and fair places.

The markets are held in what is called the market yard. It is an enclosed space situate off the public street and near the courthouse. There are two beams and scales and a weighing machine erected. Sheds are built in a portion of the yard, where corn can be stored. The space is, however, not very large, but no complaints were made of its being insufficient to meet the requirements of the trade of the town. Several of the marketable commodities are exposed on the public street outside the market yard.

The fairs are held on the public streets. There is no shelter accommodation whatever, except that afforded by the houses, for those frequenting the fairs. There are no pens or stalls or other essentials provided for the cattle.

Neither the owner or tenant contribute anything towards the cleansing of the streets other than their ordinary rates and taxes.

An *ad valorem* toll is levied on corn to the amount of 6d. in the £, but this is said to be only half the charge to which the owners are entitled. It includes cranage. If the commodity is weighed on days other than market days, 1*d*. per bag is charged, and an additional penny for a ticket denoting the weight if it is required. The tare is not mentioned on the ticket so charged for, and similar charges are made in the case of potatoes.

Complaint was also made of the charges on fowl, which are for the standing on the public thoroughfare. An instance was cited where a woman brought some fowl to the market in a cart, and had to pay 4d. standing toll on the load for three consecutive market days, as she was unable to effect a sale the previous market days.

Strong opinions were expressed as to the inconvenience caused to the inhabitants of the town by the fact of the fairs being held on the public streets, but these statements were canvassed by other witnesses.

Appended will be found a transcript of the evidence taken at the inquiry.

JOHN J. O'MEARA,
Assistant Commissioner.

45, Lower Mount Street,
Dublin.

Charleville, November 17th, 1888.

Mr. M. Fitzgerald, examined.

21,270. Mrs. Fitzgerald is the immediate owner of the markets and fairs here?—Yes.

21,271. Whom does she hold under?—The Earl of Cork.

21,272. He is the owner of the patent granting any markets and fairs in this town?—Yes.

21,273. How does she (Mrs. Fitzgerald) hold?—By lease.

21,274. You have not got the particulars of the lease here?—No.

21,275. For what term is the lease?—Sixteen years.

21,276. Are the sixteen years unexpired?—No, there are eight unexpired.

21,277. What is the rent?—144*l*.

21,278. What market day have you here?—The days specially set apart for the disposal of the general commodities are Wednesdays and Saturdays, but there is no market on Wednesday. The entire market is held on Saturday.

21,279. Wednesdays and Saturdays are specially set apart?—Those are the patented ones.

21,280. Have they been always held on those days?—Yes.

21,281. Will you kindly mention what commodities are usually brought in on Wednesdays and Saturdays?—Corn and potatoes; in the spring season, plants; for the Christmas market, fowl.

21,282. Is hay or straw brought here?—No hay and straw market. It comes in to be weighed, but there is no regular market.

21,283. It is never exposed for sale in the town?—No.

21,284. Are cattle ever brought in on market day?—Very rarely. They sell Kerry cattle passing.

21,285. Are pigs ever brought in on market day?—No.

21,286. Do you collect tolls on Wednesday and Saturday?—Yes.

21,287. Have you got a schedule of them?—Yes.

21,288. You produce this as the schedule of the tolls you collect at the markets in Charleville?—I only collect half the toll for corn.

A Schedule of the Tolls and Customs payable in the Town and Manor of Charleville on Market and Fair days.
Christopher Townsend.
Charleville, June 29, 1812.

——	Market Days.	Fair Days.
	d.	d.
For every horse, cow, bull, or bullock sold	5	6
" yearling	4	4
" sheep	0½	1
" lamb	0½	0½
" pig	2	2
" slip	1	2
" goat	1	2
" calf	0½	1
" calf and goat skin	0½	1
" hide	1	2
" car-load of skins or hides	4	4½
" hamper of turnips or oranges	1	2
" car-load of apples	4	4½
" basket-load of ditto	2	4
" bag of feathers under 8 lbs.	1	2
" pack of wool	4	4½
" car-load of timberware	4	4½
" back-load of ditto	2	4
" car-load of spade handles	4	4½
" back-load of ditto under a dozen	2	4
" car-load of loose spades	4	4½
" load of cabbage	4	4½
" " onions	4	4½
" cwt of iron	2	10
" covered pedlar's standing	2	10
" small standing of any description	1	2
" table standing	2	4
" brogue-maker's standing	1	10
" car standing	6	8
" stand standing outside the shambles	6	4
For all butchers' standing	4	10
" broguemakers' ditto	4	10
For every hawker	1	2
" piece of flannel, 1s. in the pound	—	—
For pedlars, ditto	—	—
Weighing the [illegible].		
For every bag or sack, 1d. the 10 stone on week days	—	—
" bag or sack on market or fair days, 1½d. to the [illegible] of [illegible]	—	—
For weighing butter of all kinds	1	[illegible]
For every quarter of any grain	1	—
Every bale	1	—
For every load of coal under 10 cwt.	4	—
For leather, 1d. to the cwt.	—	—

The above tolls and customs, to be collected on Wednesdays, Saturdays, and fair days only, by Martin Finion, William Herne, and Julian Moriarty.

Fairs on 10th of October and 12th of November, except falling on Saturday.

*** All corn brought or delivered within the manor of Charleville on market or fair days is liable to due custom.

By Chr. Townsend.

21,289. Have you got a copy of this erected in the market place?—Yes, at the reduced rate, sixpence to the pound.

21,290. Mr. O'Shaughnessy, a solicitor, said:—I am going away. I appear here on behalf of some people who complain that they have been overcharged by this gentleman. A toll case was litigated, and we succeeded in establishing that he made overcharges, and that he charged tolls on days on which he was not entitled, and Mr. Sheehy, who represents the ratepayers, will attend here in a few minutes. He will produce an extract from the certified copy of the tolls lodged with the clerk of the peace, and these are the tolls entitled to be levied.

21,291. (*The Assistant Commissioner to Witness.*) Is the schedule produced a copy of what is erected in the market place?—It is a copy of the schedule with the exception of the charge for corn.

21,292. Is it a copy of the schedule you have always erected in the market place?—Yes.

21,293. (*Mr. O'Shaughnessy.*) Here is the certified extract and you can compare the two.

A Schedule of the Tolls and Customs payable in the Town and Manor of Charleville on Market Days to the Right Hon. Edmund Earl of Cork and Orrery Boyle. Late Irish currency.

—	Market Days.	Fair Days.
For every horse, cow, bull, or bullock sold	d. 6	d. 6
" springing	6	6
" sheep	½	1
" lamb	½	1
" pig	1	2
" slip	1	2
" goat	1	2
" calf	½	1
" " and goat skin	½	1
" hide	1	2
" car-load of skins or hides	4	6½
" hamper of lemons or oranges	1	2
" car-load of apples	4	6½
" back load of do.	2	4
" bag of feathers under 5 lbs.	1	2
" bunch of wool	4	6½
" cart-load of [illegible]	4	6½
" back-load of do.	2	4
" cart-load of spade handles	4	6½
" back-load of do. or dozen	2	4
" cart-load of iron spades	4	6½
" load of cabbage	4	6½
" " plants	4	6½
" set of [illegible]	8	10
" covered pedlar's standing	8	10
" small standing of any description	1	2
" table standing	2	4
" brogue-makers' standing	1	10
" car standing	4	6
" each standing outside the shambles	2	4
For all butchers' standing	4	10
" harness-makers' standing	4	10
For every basket	1	2
" piece of flannel, ½d. to the pound	—	—
[illegible] free.		
Weigh-house Fees.		
For every bag or sack, 1d. for 10 stone on week days.		
" bag or sack on market or fair days, 4d. to the pound of money.		
For weighing [illegible] of all kinds, 1d. per cwt.		
For every quarter of any wheat	1	—
" do.	1	—
" load of coal under 10 cwt.	4	—
For hauling, 1d. to the cwt.		

The above tolls and customs to be collected on Wednesdays, Saturdays, and fair days only by Thomas Cooke, Edmund Scanlan, M. B. Barrigand, Michael Barrett, and Michael Doyle.

William Townsend.

Fairs on the 10th January, 16th March, 12th May, 15th August, and also on the 10th October, and on the 12th November, except falling on Saturday, in which case the fair is to be held on the Monday following.

All corn brought or delivered within the manor of Charleville on market or fair days is liable to due custom.

21,294. (*The Assistant Commissioner.*) I see this schedule applies to fair days as well as market days?—Yes, there are two rates for the market and fair.

21,295. Do you ever collect tolls on any commodity that is brought in any day of the week other than Wednesday or Saturday?—We do not collect tolls now, but there is a pig market held previous to the fairs, and so long as I remember—and a great deal longer—tolls were always charged on those days up to about twelve months ago. A case was contested and parties refused to pay, and the magistrates decided that it was not legal to collect on that day.

21,296. Will you mention the days you hold the fairs on?—The 10th January, 16th March, 12th May, 15th August, 10th October, 12th November.

21,297. You collect tolls at all?—Yes.

21,298. Are there any fairs toll free?—There are. There are fairs held on the 3rd February, 14th April, 9th June, 9th July, 13th September, and 5th December.

21,299. These are toll free?—Yes, unless they happen to fall on a market day, when a market toll is taken.

21,300. What is the difference in the toll? Would you collect on those days the same toll as is collected on ordinary fair days?—No; only the market toll. The market toll is the same as the fair toll on a great many articles.

21,301. Are these toll-free fairs held on the same site as the ordinary fairs?—Yes.

21,302. Where are the fairs held?—On the public street.

21,303. You have no fair green provided?—No.

21,304. Have you got a weighbridge?—Yes.

21,304a. Erected last year?—Yes, in compliance with the late Act.

21,305. Who was it erected that weighbridge?—It was erected by my mother.

21,306. At her sole expense?—Yes.

21,307. What was the expense of erecting it?—About 40*l.*

21,308. It is capable of weighing cattle?—Yes.

21,309. Has it been availed of for that purpose?—To a very limited extent. During the time it is up five cattle only were weighed on it.

21,310. What charge do you levy for weighing cattle?—I think it is twopence.

21,311. Is that the charge you do levy?—It is whatever is stipulated in the Act. I think it is twopence, but I am not sure.

21,312. Will you kindly mention the different description of animals brought in on fair days?—Cattle, sheep, and pigs.

21,313. Are horses?—Very few.

21,314. Are pigs brought in on the ordinary fair days?—Yes.

21,315. Anything else?—That is all.

21,316. You have a pig fair the day previous to the ordinary fair?—Yes.

21,317. Is that held the day previous to all fairs, whether you collect tolls or not?—Yes.

21,318. You were always in the habit of collecting tolls at those pig fairs, that is, the fairs previous to the day on which you collect toll?—Yes, up to last year.

21,319. You have abandoned that now?—Yes, except that they fall on a market day—Wednesday or Saturday.

21,320. Are there different portions of the town allotted off for the exposure of different species of animals?—The cattle fair is generally held on the main street, and the pigs down Broad Street on fair days. I think it right to say that there is no place allotted here for any species of animal.

21,321. They intermix?—Yes, only where nobody wishes to take their place.

21,322. Now I see here that for every pig you charge 2d. on a market day and 3d. on a fair day?—Yes.

21,323. For every slip (bonham) 1d. on market days and 2d. on fair days?—Yes.

21,324. Supposing a load of slips were brought in, what would you charge if there were 12 in the load?—If the 12 were sold, 1s.

21,325. You would not levy any standing charge on the cart for coming in?—No, if all were sold.

21,326. If not sold?—If some were sold and some remained unsold, there would be a charge made for those sold and the standing of the cart.

21,327. What would you charge for the standing?—4d. on a market day and 6d. on a fair day.

21,328. With the exception of the alteration in the charge of cows, the charges have not been altered within your memory?—No.

21,329. They have always been levied?—Yes.

21,330. And your charges at the fairs are only on the animals actually sold?—Yes.

21,331. What custom gaps have you here?—Six.

21,332. Are they situated outside the town?—Just at the end of the town.

21,333. I suppose where the last houses are situated?—As far as the cattle extend.

21,334. How many men have you usually employed at these gaps?—12 to 14 men, according to the size of the fair.

21,335. At each gap?—No, altogether.

21,336. How do you pay those men?—About half-a-crown each.

21,337. Now, is that the sole expense you are at in connection with the fairs?—Yes.

21,338. Have you ever heard complaints that the toll-collectors ever injured the animals when passing the custom gaps?—No.

21,339. No complaints have been directly made to you?—Never.

21,340. The Earl of Cork receives 14*l.* 10*s.* rent?—Yes.

21,341. Does he contribute anything directly to the cleansing of the town from the fact of the fairs being held on it?—Not to my knowledge.

21,342. Does Mrs. Fitzgerald?—No.

21,343. With the exception of his contribution and her contribution to the rates?—Yes.

21,344-5. Is it the sanitary authority who cleans up the streets?—The road contractor and the grand jury.

21,346. Were representations ever made to Mrs. Fitzgerald or to the Earl of Cork to provide a fair green for the exposure of those animals?—Not to my knowledge.

21,347. The people of the town have never discussed the advisability of providing a fair green?—I heard there was some meeting a few nights ago, relative to the holding of fairs on the street, but I was not at it myself, and I do not know what took place there.

21,348. How far do you think your jurisdiction extends for the collection of tolls?—It is stated in the patent.

21,349. How far do you usually exercise the right?—We do not collect beyond the town.

21,350. Supposing a farmer was coming in with cattle to the fair, and effected a sale of his animals on the road before he had entered the town on a fair day, would you collect a toll?—If I considered it was within the manor I would.

21,351. How far does the manor extend?—I do not know the exact boundaries of it.

21,352. How far do you usually collect tolls?—Only just as far as the fair extends.

21,353. Have you ever collected tolls in a case such as I have described, where the sale was effected outside the boundary or outside the last house of the town?—I do not remember.

21,354. A case of that kind has never arisen to your knowledge?—No.

21,355. Where are the markets held?—The corn and potato market is held in a yard in Bread Street.

21,356. You have an enclosed space for them?—Yes.

21,357. For them only?—Only.

21,358. Is butter ever brought on Wednesday or Saturday?—No. There was a market some years ago and it dwindled away.

21,359. No butter is brought?—No, except what may be sold in small lumps about the town.

21,360. Does lump butter come in any great quantity?—No, except what is taken from house to house. I believe butter is bought in a private store by Mr. Moroney.

21,361. The vegetables, &c. are sold about the streets?—Yes.

21,362. What toll do you collect on fowl?—Fourpence the cart.

21,363. Would that be irrespective of the number in the cart?—Yes.

21,364. How many do they usually bring in a cart?—Well, turkeys they usually bring in carts. They are the only fowl I collect on.

21,365. What is the smallest number brought in on which you collect a toll?—I suppose half a dozen.

21,366. To your knowledge they never brought in less?—Not in a cart. I think that would be about the smallest number.

21,367. You collect a standing charge of fourpence on that?—Yes.

21,368. Is that the only charge they have to pay?—The only charge.

21,369. Is that on entry to the fair?—No. They wait until they are sold.

21,370. Supposing they did not effect a sale of any of the fowl, would you still levy your standing charge?—Yes, but very often I heard a man complain that he had not got it.

21,371. Have your men ever, when persons refused payment of this standing charge, seized the article and levied distress on it?—No.

21,372. They have never done so?—I have never known it to be done.

21,373. Is fish brought in?—Yes.

21,374. Have you a standing charge on that?—No charge on fish.

21,375. What other descriptions of standings are there?—Cabbage plants in the spring.

21,376. What is your charge on them?—Fourpence a cart-load.

21,377. Is that on market day?—Yes, and sixpence on fair day.

21,378. Would these be all carts or small standings made up of a couple of boards resting on barrels?—All carts.

21,379. Supposing they do not bring in a car, but have small standings such as I have described, what do you charge?—We charge a penny on them.

21,380. Is it in the course of the market day you collect these market charges?—Yes.

21,381. Have you ever been at one of the custom gaps yourself?—Yes.

21,382. Do your men inquire from the individual in possession of the animal whether he has bought or sold?—Yes.

21,383. If he has bought he has to pay the charge?—Yes.

21,384. Supposing he states he has not bought and your collector doubts him, what course would your collector adopt?—If he doubts a man's reply he generally tells me.

21,385. Would he seize the animal or detain it?—No. I have not known him to do so, but I have known cases where he asked the parties about it and they said they had not bought or sold, and on my going to them afterwards they admitted they had sold.

21,386. Have you known instances of where your men produced a book or paper to swear them?—Never.

21,387. Or to strike the toll board?—Never.

21,388. Have you got copies of this toll board around at the fairs?—Yes.

21,389. Have you them always erected?—No, they were down for some time. They were erected some years ago and got obliterated. For a time they were neglected to be put up, but they were erected last year again.

21,389. Now those frequenting the fairs and markets are always in a position to ascertain, outside of any verbal statement of your own, what the tolls are?—Yes.

21,390. You have copies of the toll board erected in each gap?—There are four in the town.

21,391. What is your charge on corn?—6d. to the £ on market days.

21,392. Do you always ascertain the contract price between the buyer and seller?—The price they give us.

21,393. You always ascertain the ordinary market price of it?—Yes.

21,394. That 6d. in the £ is the half-charge mentioned on the schedule?—Yes.

21,395. When you obtain always the current price or the actual contract price between the buyer and seller, supposing it was required of you to make a return of the current prices here of the marketable commodities, you could do so?—Yes.

21,396. You consider your return would be a pretty accurate one?—It would be pretty accurate. Sometimes they do not give the correct price, but in the main they give it.

21,397. Is the charge you make a toll proper, or does it include any weighing services you render?—I believe that toll could be demanded on the corn whether it is weighed or not.

21,398. Does all the corn brought here to the market go to your square?—All that is brought on market days, but during the week there is some delivered direct to the people of the town.

21,399. Do you weigh it for that toll?—We weigh the corn for that toll.

21,400. If it is not weighed, but sold, still you levy the charge?—Yes, we would levy a charge on a market day.

21,401. If it was sold?—Yes.

21,402. Supposing it is brought in to your square or market place and exposed for sale there, but not sold or weighed?—If it is not sold or not weighed we do not make a charge.

21,403. Have you a weigh-master employed there?—Yes, there is a clerk there. He does the weighing and the making up of the tickets, except on busy days, and he is assisted by the weigh-master.

21,404. Have you ever weighed there?—Yes.

21,405. What is the lowest weight you usually put in the scales when weighing corn?—A pound weight.

21,406. You always weigh down to a pound?—Yes.

21,407. Do you always ascertain the tare of the sack or bag?—We usually allow four pounds for the bags, but if the buyer or seller objects the empty bag will be weighed.

21,408. You do not weigh all the corn?—They weigh every bag of corn that comes on market days, but some comes during the week, not on market days, and it is sometimes weighed in the market.

21,409. Supposing they weigh it in the market on days other than market day, what charge do you levy?—A penny per bag.

21,410. What is your charge on potatoes?—A penny a bag for weighing. If a ticket is required we charge an additional penny for the ticket.

21,411. Do you charge anything additional for the ticket you give when weighing the corn?—Not on market days, but on week days we do. We are entitled to charge a penny for 10 stone on week days, but we do not charge so much.

21,412. On potatoes on market days you charge a penny a bag, and if a ticket denoting the weight is required you charge an additional penny?—Yes. If there were 10 bags, and to give a ticket, we would only charge 11d.

21,413. Would you charge one penny for the ticket no matter how many bags there were?—Yes.

21,414. Are the tickets you have for corn printed?—Yes.

21,415. Do you put the gross weight and estimated tare on them?—No; in some cases we do.

21,416. Do you put the name of the individual?—Yes.

21,417. Of whom?—The buyer and seller.

21,418. Of both?—Yes.

21,419. Is it signed by your weighmaster?—Yes.

21,420. Do you keep a block of that ticket?—We keep it in a book.

21,421. If they lost that ticket would you be able to give a copy of it without any additional charge?—Yes.

21,422. Do the same observations apply to your system of weighing potatoes?—Yes.

21,423. You do not keep any block of the tickets?—We keep a return in a book.

21,424. On market day, supposing the corn was brought in to one of the private stores in the town and delivered down to one of the storehouses, would you levy your charge?—Yes.

21,425. You have done so?—Well, I do not know any case. On a market day, when we demanded tolls, they brought it to the market and weighed it.

21,426. So that all corn sold on the market day, whether inside or outside the market place, you collect a toll on it if it comes to your knowledge?—Yes.

21,427. Supposing they sold it the day previous to the market day, and delivered it on the market day, would you levy your charge?—Yes. It states on the schedule sold or delivered.

21,428. That is another alteration you have made in this schedule, by charging a penny per bag instead of a penny per 10 stone?—Yes.

21,429. Have you got any standings on market days?—There are a few small standings in the streets.

21,430. Do you collect a charge from them?—Sometimes we do, and sometimes we do not. There are a lot of apple standings and we do not collect anything from them.

21,431. What do you collect ordinarily of them?—A penny for a small standing.

21,432. Do you collect that on fair days?—They are entitled to pay, but we do not collect it from them.

21,433. Supposing on a fair day or market day one of the shopkeepers erected a standing outside his door, would you collect a charge if he disposed of any commodities on that standing?—Yes, as a standing in the street.

21,434. If they put them on the [illegible]?—If they put them out with boxes and things, perhaps out to the edge of the flags, we do not charge on them.

21,435. Do they put any in the channel course in carts?—No.

21,436. Have you ever collected any standing charges from any of the shopkeepers in the town?—No, unless they put out a cart-load of cabbage, or anything else like that, the same as anything else, but for any of their dry goods they put in the neighbourhood of the door or about the flags we never charge.

21,437. If they put them on the roadside you charge?—We never do. I have never known it to be done.

21,438. Does not the fact of the fairs being held on the street occasion much filth and dirt about the public thoroughfare?—The street is not so clean.

21,439. You have never heard the shopkeepers or private inhabitants objecting to the continuation of the fairs on the street?—I heard the majority of the people was in favour of having them held on the streets. I believe there was a meeting of the inhabitants about that.

21,440. In the lease from the Earl of Cork, did he give you the market place in addition to the tolls?—Yes.

21,441. What extent is it?—I could not say the exact size. It is quite convenient to the storehouses.

21,442. Have you got shedding in it?—There is a shed erected at one side.

21,443. What facilities do you afford for the weighing of the different commodities brought in. Have you a beam and scales?—We have two beams and scales. There is a small scales for vendors and people who buy a bag or two and sell them again. We give it free.

21,444. Then you have one for ordinary use?—Yes.

21,445. Is that sufficient for ascertaining the weight of the different commodities brought there?—It is more than sufficient, except a few days in the spring and lately, and then there is a second scales.

21,446. Would you say that no undue delay is caused in ascertaining the weight of the different commodities?—No.

21,447. No complaints have been made?—No.

21,448. In weighing potatoes what is the lowest weight you have for weighing, or what do you weigh down to?—Down to a pound weight.

21,449. Do you always weigh down to a pound?—Yes; that is, if a bag of potatoes is put into the scales I try it with the pound weight.

21,450. Do you only estimate the tare of the sack?—Yes. It is about four pounds. If the day is wet we allow a little more.

21,451. You always take into consideration the state of the weather?—Yes.

21,452. Where do they expose the fowl for sale?—In the main street.

21,453. Have you got any charge on eggs here?—No.

21,454. If they erected a standing and put them into a box in the street?—It would be reckoned according to the ordinary charge for a standing.

21,455. Could you give me your average receipts and expenditure?—I could not give you them exactly, but I can give you an idea.

21,456. Do not you keep an account?—I do.

21,457. Of course, if you do not desire to give it publicly, I will take it afterwards, because the matter is more or less one of disclosing your private affairs?—I can give you the exact figures after the inquiry, but I could give you an estimate now if you care to have it.

21,458. Subsequently witness produced the following return of the receipts and expenditure:—Average gross receipts for three years ending 1887, 392*l.* 11*s.* 1*d.*; average expenses, including rent for same period, 193*l.* 18*s.* 8*d.*

21,459. Have you got any rules or regulations in the market place?—No.

21,460. Do you collect any toll on this lump butter sold about the streets?—No.

21,461. None whatever?—No.

21,462. It is only levied from door to door?—Yes.

21,463. Do you keep in this book you have referred to an account of the current price of the corn?—No, we keep no return of the prices, but of the weight.

21,464. Or the toll you collect?—No.

21,465. Although it is on the value of the quantity brought in you levy the toll?—Yes. We do not keep any record of it in the books.

21,466. Neither you nor Mrs. Fitzgerald have made any alteration in this schedule other than what you have mentioned?—No.

21,467. Have tolls always been collected on Wednesday and Saturday?—Always.

21,468. And weighing charges other days in the week if the scales are availed of?—Yes.

21,469. Have you always collected tolls on the six fair days mentioned?—Yes.

21,470. You never collected tolls on the others?—No, unless they fell on a market day.

21,471. When were these new fairs established?—I think they were established in the year 1864.

21,472. Were they all established at the same time?—Yes.

21,473. Do you remember yourself when there were less than six fairs established here?—No.

21,474. You never collected tolls on any less number than six fairs?—No.

21,475. No one of them was toll-free at any period?—No.

21,476. Are these fairs held under the patent?—Yes.

21,477. The days of them have not been altered?—I could not say. Not within my memory.

21,478. Have you ever heard they were altered?—No.

21,479. Within what distances are these commodities brought here and exposed in Charleville?—I should say from seven or eight miles around.

21,480. And the cattle and other animals to the fairs?—Some cattle are brought very long distances.

21,481. Are dealers' cattle ever brought here?—Yes, sometimes, but not to any great extent. It is mostly the cattle of the farmers that come here.

21,482. Is there any custom or practice existing in the market for the sale of corn and any other commodity through agents or brokers?—No.

21,483. Every farmer who comes in is free to dispose of his commodity to whom he pleases?—Yes.

21,484. Have they any practice of forestalling any of the commodities brought in?—No.

21,485. Do they forestall the fowl in any way?—No, I never heard. The fowl are brought up by fowl-dealers, and if some people around the town want fowl they purchase them in the same way.

21,486. From the dealers?—They purchase from the farmers.

21,487. So that the farmers themselves do come into the market?—Yes.

21,488. You never heard of where the dealers went out and met them on the road, and tried a game amongst themselves to give and purchased them?—No. If there was a brisk market they may go out.

21,489. You never heard any complaints of forestalling in any of the commodities or animals at the pig fairs or ordinary cattle fairs?—Never.

21,490. Did your mother see this schedule (the list of queries)?—Yes.

21,491. I suppose any answer you will give she will approve of it?—Yes.

21,492. Supposing in Charleville a local municipal authority, or, in the absence of one, a local authority such as market commission, was established by Legislature, would your mother object to such commission or authority obtaining compulsory powers to acquire any legal rights vested in her?—I suppose she would not, if compensated.

21,493. Have you ever heard any complaints of the management of the markets or fairs by your authority?—No, I have not heard.

21,494. Or of any of the tolls that you levy other than what you have mentioned about the pig fairs?—People complain that the toll on corn is high on market days.

21,495. Who are they?—The farmers and people selling the corn.

21,496. It is always the seller who pays your charge?—The seller pays for weighing.

21,497. At the markets always the seller pays you, and at the fairs the buyer?—Yes.

21,498. Is the animal always in the possession of the buyer when going out?—Whenever we find the cattle with [illegible]. Whoever takes the cattle out the buyer pays the toll.

21,499. The animal is generally in the buyer's possession?—Yes.

21,500. Have they got here the system of luck-penny?—Yes.

21,501. Is that at any fixed rate?—No, but I think it is on pigs.

21,502. What is it?—Sixpence. I could not exactly say, but I believe it is sixpence.

21,503. On other animals on fair days it is left to the disposition of the seller?—Yes.

21,504. Still, it is always given?—Yes.

21,505. Do you think that acts as an equivalent for the toll levied and paid by the buyer?—It is generally more than the toll.

21,506. Have you any fairs near Charleville which are entirely toll-free?—I do not know of any.

21,507. Are those fairs that are toll-free in Charleville as well attended as the ordinary fairs?—I should say they are.

21,508. You would not say they are better attended?—No.

21,509. You keep no return of the number of animals brought in?—No.

21,510. (*Questioned by Mr. Binchy, solicitor.*) You buy and sell a good deal?—Yes.

21,511. Your opinion is that the fairs should be held on the streets?—Yes.

21,512. That is the universal opinion?—Yes.

21,513. (*By the Commissioner.*) What reason do you assign for that opinion?—I have attended fairs held on a fair green, and on wet days it is very disagreeable, and there is no shelter whatever.

21,514. But if proper shelter accommodation was provided?—Of course if there was there would be no objection to have them held there.

21,515. (*By Mr. Binchy.*) Is that possible?—I do not see any possibility of doing it.

21,516. You say you only charge a penny per sack for weighing?—Yes.

21,517. Then I understood you also charge a penny for a ticket?—Yes.

21,518. Then it costs a person twopence when buying a bag of potatoes?—Yes.

21,519. Are you entitled to that by the schedule, do you think?—I think so.

21,520. (By the Commissioner.) Apart from the schedule, is that charge customary for a great many years?—Yes.

21,521. As far back as you remember?—Yes.

21,522. Has your mother always been levying that?—Yes.

21,523. When your father, Mr. Fitzgerald, had the tolls before, he levied the charge?—Yes.

21,524. How far back do you say or do you know does any person in the [illegible] remember when the penny per bag and the penny a ticket was not charged?—I do not remember.

21,525. When was the schedule filed?—It was filed 40 or 50 years ago.

21,526. (By Mr. Blenky.) Do you remember when only 6d. a load was charged for potatoes here?—No.

21,527. As a matter of fact, on every single bag of potatoes sold is there 2d. charged?—No.

21,528. Do not I understand you to say you charge a penny a sack for weighing and a penny for the ticket?—Yes, if the ticket is required.

21,529. That is for a single bag of potatoes you charge twopence?—If a bag of potatoes is weighed there is a penny for weighing, and if they demand a ticket we give it.

21,530. What you say is a person has to pay a penny if he wants a ticket?—Yes.

21,531. (By the Commissioner.) Supposing they do not want a ticket, do you mark the weight in chalk?—We tell them the weight, and if they require it we mark it in chalk on the bag.

21,532. Is that usually done?—No, they do not ask; sometimes they do.

21,533. Do you charge anything?—No.

21,534. Does the buyer always require the production of the ticket?—Not always.

21,535. (By Mr. Blenky.) About the corn, you say the charge is sixpence in the pound?—Yes.

21,536. What is your opinion about that charge?—I think it is a high charge.

21,537. What accommodation is given for the corn in the market? Is there any accommodation for loads of corn if the weather is wet?—No, the yard is uncovered except the shed.

21,538. There is no place to back loads into if the weather is wet?—Yes, there is the same as any other market.

21,539. Do you know, has the fowl market increased or gone back?—I think as far as I can judge it is the same.

21,540. As long as you remember?—Yes.

21,541. How long do you remember the fowl market?—I could not exactly say; I did not take much great notice of it.

21,542. But you were collecting tolls there?—I can remember it some years.

21,543. How many years—20 years or 25?—I did not take notice of it for that time. I have the management of the tolls 10 or 11 years.

21,544. Have you any person here who can tell us anything about the fowl market 10 years ago?—No.

21,545. Who was the lessee before 10 years ago?—My father.

21,546. Are you aware that a person bringing fowl into the market not in a car are charged a toll?—No.

21,547. Will you deny it?—During my management, no.

21,548. At any time?—I cannot say; I can only speak of my own management.

21,549. Will you deny there are some of your collectors, or your father's collectors, who used to exact tolls from old women bringing geese under their arm were charged?—I do not know.

21,550. (By the Commissioner.) Are hides brought here?—No.

21,551. Do you weigh coal?—No.

21,552. What charge do you levy for weighing loads on the weighbridge?—Sixpence a load.

21,553. Irrespective of the commodity in the load?—If it is corn it is more, but for hay or straw or anything like that the charge is sixpence.

21,554. Is the corn always sold before it is weighed?—Yes.

21,555. Where do they sell it?—It is exposed in the market yard.

21,556. Have you sufficient shelter accommodation if they wish to avail themselves of it?—They can pull in their horses or carts when there is no weighing carried on.

21,557. (By Mr. Blenky.) Is there any way in the market of keeping corn if not sold?—Yes.

21,558. Where?—In the market store.

21,559. Has corn been kept there?—Yes, frequently.

21,560. When was it kept there?—When not sold in the market. The man in charge of the store could tell you.

21,561. (Mr Blenky.) I am informed that people bringing in corn have no accommodation.

21,562. (By the Commissioner.) Supposing people bring in corn one market day, can they leave it over until the next?—Yes, certainly.

21,563. Do you levy any additional charge?—No.

21,564. At whose risk is it left there?—At the owner's risk.

21,565. (By Mr. Blenky.) Where is that store?—In the market yard.

Thomas [illegible], Esq., J.P., examined.

21,566. What observations do you wish to make?—I wish to make some remarks about some questions you asked Mr. Fitzgerald in reference to the state of the town after the fairs. I may state that on one occasion it came before me and other magistrates a case in which there was a prosecution against the county surveyor under the Sanitary Acts, and it (the street) was very bad indeed—excessively bad. It happened in the height of the dry summer, and after those fairs there has never been any cleansing whatever, and the result was that the streets were covered with the odour of cattle. Cases of whooping-cough were prevalent, and attributable to it, and apparently no person was responsible for the cleansing, and there was no mode of getting it done. It turned out that the streets of [illegible], which are cleansed under the ordinary road contracts at that particular period, the contract I think had not been renewed, and we thought on that account that the county surveyor was then liable for keeping them in repair, and also keeping them cleansed; but to avoid his liability, however, and as a kind of compromise, he undertook to get it done, and so it was done for a short time. It is a great grievance not to have some person responsible for having them cleansed after the fairs.

21,567. Would you be in favour of a removal of the fairs off the public thoroughfare, and do you think the exposure of cattle should be confined to a properly enclosed fair green?—I do, certainly.

21,568. You do not think it would affect the fairs or the attendance at them?—I think it would be better for the fairs, but I think there is a very strong feeling against it on the part of a great many inhabitants.

21,569. Is that opposition confined to the people in a particular trade?—Yes, the publicans.

21,570. The other traders and the private inhabitants would, you consider, be in favour of such a removal?—I think so.

21,571. Have you ever heard that accidents have happened by these fairs being held on the streets?—No, I cannot say I have. I have heard instances of a cart running away and damage being done; I know myself of a grocery having suffered, the driver getting drunk and smashing everything. I have heard it but very rarely.

21,572. Still you consider the practice is objectionable?—I do. I think it is a source of very great inconvenience.

it is very difficult to get through the fairs.' People going to the trains find it very difficult to get to the station.

21,573. (*Questioned by Mr. Blackly, solicitor.*) Your great objection is on account of the alleged nuisance you speak of?—Yes.

21,574. Have you any other real objections?—I take the fact of the place being thronged. The practical objections are that there is no proper mode of having the streets thoroughly cleansed. They are excessively dirty both during the fair and after, and in winter it is very hard for people to go through, and also what I mentioned, the difficulty of ordinary passengers driving through the fair.

21,575. Supposing that the person who levies tolls contributed something to the cleansing of the town after the fairs and markets, would that remove the defect?—If they were cleansed any way it would be well.

21,576. You would be quite satisfied?—Yes.

21,577. Supposing buyers and sellers at the fairs and markets, in addition to the townspeople, said the streets were the proper place for holding the fairs, would you object?—It is merely my private view, that a fair green would be better. That is my own personal view. I cannot say that I heard, except from very few, very strong objections to the holding of the fair on the streets.

21,578. I believe you sell cattle yourself?—Yes.

21,579. The streets are particularly wide?—Yes.

21,580. Do you remember last Monday morning—it was not a very fine morning, I think?—Yes, I might remember.

21,581. On a particularly wild wet morning would it be better for people bringing cattle or pigs to hold the fair in an open green or to have the shelter of the street, supposing the street was suitable?—I think it would be better in the green for the people.

21,582. Would it be better for the people who bring cattle and pigs to put them out on the open?—I cannot say that.

21,583. Supposing the buyers who come to buy cattle, and the farmers who come to sell, all say the street is a better place than an open green, would you still object to it?—I would not have an objection.

21,584. You state you believe the opinion is in favour of removing the fairs off the street except the publicans, and publicans alone are in favour of keeping them on the street?—I have not stated that. I stated there was a portion of the townspeople who had a very strong objection, but I stated that those who specially objected to the removal were the publicans. I have not undertaken to say that it is confined to them.

21,585. Do you believe there are 10 people in Charleville who would be in favour of removing the fairs from the streets to a green outside the town?—I would not say. We have got a division of opinion on the point.

21,586. (*Mr. Blackly.*) That is what I say, that there is not a division, but a consensus of opinion, and all one way, and that is for the retention of the fairs on the streets of Charleville.

21,587. (*Mr. Saunders.*) I believe there was an expression of opinion objecting to the removal on the part of the greater number of the townspeople, and specially on the part of the publicans.

21,588. (*The Assistant Commissioner.*) But you are not in a position to state whether the majority is in favour of their retention on the streets or a fair green?—I never calculated.

21,589. (*By Mr. Blackly.*) Have you any doubt in the matter?—I should think that the majority would be in favour of retaining them on the streets.

21,590. Where is the minority you speak of?—I would not say.

21,591. (*Mr. P. Ryan, solicitor.*) I appear on behalf of the lessee. The state of the streets would be a ground of complaint, but the sanitary officer should be compelled to take out a summons against the road contractor, or whoever is responsible, and make him clean off the nuisance, because it is in contemplation when he takes the contract that he should keep the road free of nuisance.

21,592. You have no means of ascertaining the additional expense to the ratepayers by the fact of the fairs being held on the streets?—No.

21,593. You could not give any approximate idea?—No.

21,594. (*Mr. Saunders.*) In reference to what Mr. Ryan has said, the matter came before us as magistrates, and we had great difficulty in ascertaining that any person was really liable to be punished under the Sanitary Acts for neglect of the street. As I stated, the county surveyor was summoned, and the bench were not able to make up their minds that the county surveyor was liable, and the county surveyor undertook to do something, and he did something in the way of improvement. At the time we found the case extremely difficult, where there was no person we could make liable. Then if there was a road contractor it would depend whether or not it was part of his contract to clean the streets. You will, of course, understand, for the ordinary roads the appointment of contractors rests upon the cesspayers of the barony. They may not be inclined to include the cleaning in the contract, as that would impose a heavier charge on the barony. There is no special liability on the contractor by virtue of his office except by special contract for cleaning the streets. At one time the board of guardians, who are the sanitary authority, used to employ a man to clean the streets, and do now.

21,595. (*Mr. Ryan.*) For the lanes and bye-places, but not the public streets.

21,596. (*By Mr. Blackly.*) Mr. Saunders, would you be of opinion that the person getting tolls should contribute something towards cleaning the street, and that it is not the county at large should bear the expense?—I think it very desirable, but of course tolls are private property.

21,597. But from the increase of dirt or filth created by the fairs at which tolls are levied, do you think it a reasonable thing that the person getting tolls should contribute something towards the cleansing of the street?—It would be desirable, but it appears to me that there is really no person taking it on hand, although the expense of keeping the streets clean ought not be very great because the manure collected in that way would be very valuable if a person took it up for the sake of the value of the manure, as was done some time ago, and let it accumulate until it was worth carrying away. Things are somewhat better now than they used to be.

21,598. But persons are getting 400*l*. or 500*l*. a year from tolls, and not giving anything towards the cleansing of the streets?—I think this ought to be a more flourishing town than it is, and one reason why it is not flourishing is the bad state the town is in as regards its cleansing. If the town were cleansed and lighted properly I think it would be a very great advantage. I think you see from the position of the town and the wide streets it has a very great advantage over most country market towns. I think it is the neglect of it, in a great measure, throws it back, because, undoubtedly, Charleville is not holding its place with other towns. As regards Kilmallock, Kilmallock is increasing, and I am afraid ultimately it will efface Charleville.

21,599. Do you think the fairs in Kilmallock have become better, and that the fairs in Charleville have not improved?—I will not say. I recollect Kilmallock nothing but a hamlet.

21,600. (*By the Assistant Commissioner.*) Do you consider where local authorities are established in towns in which fairs are held, that those local authorities, if they exist at all, should obtain compulsory powers to acquire the rights of the lessees and owners of fairs, and work them for the benefit of the town generally?—I think it would be desirable.

21,601. Do you think the united efforts of gentlemen forming those bodies or committees would tend to improve the fairs, and lead to better management by affording increased accommodation, than leaving them in the hands of a private individual?—I think so. I do not give a decided opinion in favour of establishing town commissioners. We tried it long ago—forty years ago—and we found there was a strong feeling against it on the ground that the people did not like rates, because it would increase very much the rates imposed on them.

21,602. Apart from the establishment of town commissioners, supposing the Legislature gave facilities for the establishment of market trustees or fair trustees, a body similar to the fair committee in Kilmallock, do you think if such were established they should obtain compulsory powers to acquire the rights?—Yes.

21,603. It would be an advantage to the people of the town generally?—Yes, if well managed. I think if there was a general system of regulating the fairs it would be a great advantage. I know the fairs here are very much injured by perhaps two or three having occurred in other places on the same day. Of course they were injured there day, so that if there was no arrangement of—if there could be a controlling body over the fairs, it would be a great advantage. As it now stands fairs are very much injured occasionally by other fairs in important towns such as Tipperary and Kilmallock taking place on the same day. It sometimes occurs that there are only two or three days' interval between the fair in one place and the fair in another, and these days are affected by Sunday happening to intervene, and then Saturday fairs go to Monday, and, I think, Friday fairs go on to Monday.

21,604. There is a right already vested in the proprietor of the fairs to object to the establishment of other fairs, if they injure his right in any way?—There are fairs already established. I have not gone into the question. I merely stated as a fact that occasionally buyers and sellers suffer great inconvenience from the fact of important neighbouring fairs falling on the same day.

21,605. (*By Mr. Blunden.*) You say, if there was a local power or authority to arrange local fairs so that they would not clash, it would be desirable?—Yes.

21,606. (*By the Commissioner.*) You would not say local authority, but some authority over the country generally?—I should say, if the local authority consisted of market trustees, such as there are in Kilmallock and other places, it would be possible for the committees to communicate and arrange. As regards the present fairs fixed by patent, there is no possibility of doing that.

CHARLES HANNING, Esq., J.P., examined.

21,607. You heard the answers Mr. Saunders gave to the questions I put. Do you concur in his observations?—No, not so far as regards removing the fairs from the streets.

21,608. You would be opposed to that?—I would, certainly.

21,609. What reason do you assign for that?—Because I think it would injure the fairs.

21,610. The removal of them to a fair green?—Yes.

21,611. In what way?—In the first instance, there is no proper fair green here, I know of.

21,612. Of course, if it were desired, a fair green might be provided; but leaving out the possibility, what would you say?—I was one of the parties interested with the late Mr. Daly, in the year 1864, getting up a lot of fairs, and I should say it would materially injure the fairs to be removed out of the town. There are very few in the minority who would wish to have them removed. All the dealers and farmers would wish to have them in the town.

21,613. Is that because they would be convenient to the shops, and the people would obtain shelter?—It is a better place to stand for the people. They do not sink down, as they would in a fair green, and get wet in the feet.

21,614. If a fair green was provided with proper shelter accommodation for the people and animals, would you still be opposed to a removal?—Yes. If you look over the tolls and customs schedule, you will see that the potatoes are free. It is my humble opinion that no charge should be made on them; and these are things that affect the poor.

21,615. (*Mr. Ryan.*) You will observe that under the patent there is no toll for potatoes. The only charge is for weighing, and Mr. Fitzgerald will tell you he is entitled to charge for in excess of what he usually charges, but what he actually charges is half.

21,616. (*The Assistant Commissioner to Mr. Fitzgerald.*) Do you levy a charge on potatoes whether they are weighed or not?—I levy no charge if they are not weighed.

21,617. Your charge is a penny a bag?—Yes.

21,618. But if brought to your market place and exposed for sale?—There is no charge at all. Frequently it occurs they are not sold at all.

21,619. Do you levy any standing charge?—No.

21,620. (*Mr. Harding.*) I may as well tell you that 20 years ago there was a promise made by the late Mr. Daly, that if he saw his way towards improving the town he would give the tolls and customs to a local body, but I would be very much against town commissioners, because we are rated heavily enough before. We would have a market commission as in other places.

21,621. You would be in favour of the establishment of a commission or of trustees?—Yes, to improve the town.

21,622. Would you say that the tolls collected here should go to the improvement of the town, and does Mr. Saunders agree with you in that?—Yes. As regards the relative prosperity of Charleville and Kilmallock, though Kilmallock looks fresh, the fairs here are very good and are getting on better here than in Rathkeale.

MR. MICHAEL MILLAR examined.

21,623. Are you in trade in the town?—Yes.

21,624. What trade?—Auctioneer.

21,625. From your trade and knowledge of Charleville you have a means of knowing what is the consensus of opinion of the people of the town?—In what respect?

21,626. As to the advisability or inadvisability of removing the fairs off the street?—My candid opinion is it is quite undesirable to remove the fairs from where they are held at present.

21,627. Why did you form that opinion?—Both for the advantage of buyers and sellers, because my experience is a considerable experience. These people sink down in a wet field, and for the convenience of the public it would be a great deal more desirable to have them on the streets, because otherwise the people suffer a great deal. I have country fairs where they are held in fields, and the people suffer a great deal at those fairs in wet weather.

21,628. But they would not suffer if there was an enclosed fair green with sufficient and ample shelter accommodation and pens provided for the cattle?—It would be impossible to provide it.

21,629. Do not consider the impossibility, but supposing it was possible to provide a proper and enclosed fair green with pens and shelter accommodation, then would you change your opinion?—Well, to accommodate a fair you would have to cover 10 acres of land.

21,630. Are the fairs so extensive?—Yes, it is a matter almost impossible.

21,631. (*By Mr. Blunden.*) I suppose you know the markets in Dublin. Would you say the streets here are as good as the markets in Dublin?—Yes, with the exception of the cattle being penned in.

21,632. You would say that the streets are as suitable as that market?—Yes.

21,633. (*By the Commissioner.*) Do you remember any period when tolls were collected on a less number than six?—Yes.

21,634. What fairs?—On the January, August, October, and November fairs.

21,635. Only on those four?—Yes, there were no other fairs worth noting. There was a fair patented in May and March, and I recollect no fairs on those days.

21,636. When were these established?—These fairs came into prominence on the establishment of the new fairs. These days were not altered on the establishment of the new fairs.

21,637. Although a patent was granted for these fairs on the 16th March and 15th May they were not availed of?—No fairs.

21,638. You never remember fairs on these days until the new fairs were established?—It was open to hold fairs, but no cattle or buyers came.

21,639. If cattle were brought in, tolls would be collected?—Decidedly.

21,640. They were never toll free if cattle were brought in?—No, because the collector had a right to charge for them.

21,641. Then I take it that at any period if cattle were brought in on these days they were not free of tolls?—They were not free of tolls. I may say also that when the new fairs were established it was considered of great importance they should be toll free. However, when they became a success all at once the first fair that turned up on a [illegible] market day tolls were charged and have been charged since.

21,642. Do those frequenting the fairs and markets object to that course?—I do not think they object; it is so customary to pay tolls; and I would not object to pay tolls, but I think the tolls should be employed for other purposes than at present.

21,643. I take it you do not consider that a toll, whether at markets or fairs, acts as a deterrent on people bringing their commodities or cattle to them?—It would be an opposition to establishing new fairs, and I think we are open for establishing more fairs than we have here at present. I think they would be a success, because in the neighbouring town of [illegible] they have 14, and there are only 12 here, and the 14 are a success there. It would be an encouragement to sellers to bring their cattle when the fairs are toll free.

21,644. You think if the fairs were toll free it would tend to improve the fairs?—When the fairs are established it would have no effect. If there were market trustees or some such body to arrange the fairs and markets I think it would be desirable to add a few other fairs, and at the start it would be most desirable there should be toll free.

21,645. I want to get your ideas on the question of a toll. Do you think that if a farmer has to pay a toll for bringing in any of his commodities to the market, or cattle to the fair, that the fact of a toll being levied, whether high or low, deters him in any way from bringing his commodities or animals in any great number?—I do not think it does.

21,646. It does not affect him in the slightest manner?—No.

21,647. He would not consider a toll the slightest objection if he would make a ready sale?—If a man sells he does not mind paying expenses or something if it is not excessive.

21,648. In the establishment of new fairs you are of opinion they should be toll free to encourage the buyers?—Yes. It is the seller usually pays the toll, and very often the buyers who come, and they are encouraged to come when they know they make so much, because a good many of the buyers at fairs are commissioners who have had to account for what they get, especially the [illegible].

21,649. If fairs were toll free you think that would create greater demand and attract more buyers?—I would not be in favour of having fairs toll free, but I am entirely in favour of the tolls being devoted to other purposes. I think it would improve Lord Cork's property if the tolls were expended judiciously in the town, so that the [illegible] would suffer nothing.

21,650. You state you would have no objection to the tolls, as the people would have no objection if the tolls were not excessive. From your experience and conversation with those people frequenting the fairs and markets, do you know did they ever consider that any of the tolls levied here were excessive?—I never heard it. The tolls are confined to those who sell. It is only for bought cattle the tolls are charged. I think they complain more when there are no tolls, and trespass is charged going into the field, where they have to pay 3d. instead of 6d., because many take their cattle to the fairs, and do not sell.

21,651. You would not approve of the course of paying on an animal which might not be subsequently sold?—No.

21,652. They would rather pay a higher rate on the animal actually sold?—Yes.

21,653. (*By Mr. Bimdy.*) You are speaking about cattle and pigs, but about corn, do you think the charge of 6d. to the pound excessive?—I think that charge has been most disastrous to the corn market here. I think it is out of all reason and proportion, especially when we know the value given.

21,654. (*By the Commissioner.*) Then you misunderstood my former question?—I understood you asked a question that applied to live stock.

21,655. Are there any other rates in the market you object to?—Corn is the principal thing sold here.

21,656. Is this a good corn market?—It should be much better than it is.

21,657. You think the levying of that charge affects it?—I think it is detrimental to the corn market attaining any proportions.

21,658. (*By Mr. Bimdy.*) Do you think there is sufficient accommodation for a corn market here?—Decidedly not.

21,659. You consider there should be some sheds?—At a season of the year there is accommodation enough, because the corn does not come in, except in the spring time and harvest, because of that fee of 2½ per cent. on the money received. It would be quite profit enough for a man dealing in corn, and it precludes the possibility of dealers dealing in corn. Farmers know the price of corn in Cork and Limerick, and they will not come here where there is 6d. charged which they can go where they have a larger market.

21,660. The price is too high?—Yes.

21,661. You say there is not sufficient accommodation?—Not for a market of any pretensions. My recollection is that we had a meeting, and there was an understanding that people would deal largely in corn. At the time there were three or four corn buyers, and the understanding was that corn was to be weighed for 1d. a bag, and it appears—I am not very cognisant of the market books—that the arrangement has been departed from, and the custom of 2½ per cent. is charged to people who sell corn. Then there was an arrangement at the same meeting that potatoes should be weighed free and the weight marked with chalk on the bag, and that if a man wanted a ticket he should pay for that ticket only. That arrangement has been departed from too.

21,662. (*By the Commissioner.*) Did the people outside that Mr. Fitzgerald, or the owner of the tolls, would perform that duty by a person without receiving any remuneration?—At the time the schedule was made there was nothing down for potatoes. They were all sold in cart-loads and weighed by the weight. The population of the town was double then, and the usual way to sell potatoes was to bring them in boxes and weigh them in weights. I recollect the weighmaster who used to weigh them and make no charge.

21,663. During the season are potatoes ever sold by measure?—No.

21,664. They have always to be weighed?—Yes.

21,665. (*By Mr. Bimdy.*) You would consider 1d. would be a sufficient charge to cover ticket and weighing and all?—I should say so.

21,666. So far as you know from a large experience with buyers and sellers you think the streets are the proper place for the fairs?—Yes. My own opinion goes in that way.

21,667. (*By Mr. Ryan.*) From time immemorial has not the charge been made of 1d. for weighing and 1d. for the ticket?—It was charged up to the time we had the meeting.

Mr. PHILIP MONTEAL, examined.

21,668. (*By Mr. Bimdy.*) You know about the fowl market?—Yes.

21,669. Has the fowl market improved, or not, here?—It has gone back very much.

21,670. What do you attribute that to?—There were a great many complaints of the toll levied on fowl. I remember a case where a woman had to pay three times on one lot, that is three Saturdays in succession, and she had to pay 4d. a cart each time for the one lot.

21,671. (*By the Commissioner.*) The charge on fowl is levied as a standing charge and not on the fowl themselves. I take it Mr. Fitzgerald does not consider whether any of the commodities on the standing are subsequently sold or not?—They are on a cart and left in the cart when sold.

21,672. You consider if people pay a toll they should only pay it on the fowl when they have them sold?—Yes. When the other markets were started near [illegible] I find the people who came from the west would go to [illegible] and sell their fowls in [illegible] before here.

21,673. And pass through Charleville?—Yes.

21,674. On account of the toll?—Yes.

21,675. (*By Mr. Bimdy.*) I believe you are a large buyer of fowl, wild and tame?—Yes. I may say about one [illegible]

lived in the town of Kilkenny for seven years, and I asked a man selling corn to come to Charleville, and he told me he would not go to a place where he had to pay 6d. to the pound for weighing.

21,676. About this sort standing the Commissioners referred. If they bring a donkey and cart is that a standing?—Yes.

21,677. And they charge 4d. on that?—Yes.

21,678. Have you ever known instances where people were charged a toll when they brought a cart alone?—I did not hear that.

21,679. (*By the Commissioner.*) What return is given by the owner in receipt of the charges on fowl for the charge he levies and receives?—No return.

21,680. These fowl are exposed on the public thoroughfare?—In the public street.

21,681. Then it is for the right of selling these on the public thoroughfare this charge is levied?—Yes.

21,682. You consider that is an injustice?—I think it is.

21,683. Does it in any way enhance the value of the fowl?—I think it does.

21,684. Would you sell them at a lower rate if you had no charge to pay?—I think not.

21,685. It is a charge then that comes out of the sellers' pocket and not out of the consumers'?—The sellers'.

21,686. The price is not enhanced to the consumer?—No.

21,687. (*By Mr. Blandy.*) Do you go to Drimoleague to buy fowl. You can buy without any toll?—I think so. The market here is very small. When I began there was a very large market; now it has gone down. I remember when I got 120l. worth of fowl one day.

21,688. When you travel any distance to other markets does the cost in trifling, and do you divide it over a number of fowl to recoup you?—Certainly.

21,689. (*By Mr. Fitzgerald.*) At the time the market was large here was there a market established in Drimoleague, Kilmallock, or Liscarroll?—No.

21,690. (*By Mr. Blandy.*) At the market in Drimoleague or Kilmallock no tolls are charged?—No.

21,691. (*By the Commissioner.*) Are the fowl cheaper there than here?—No, we pay the same price for them.

21,692. (*By Mr. Ryan.*) Used not the bidding, at the time the market was flourishing, deal in fowl here?—Certainly.

21,693. Was the success of the market on account of the competition between you and him?—I do not think it was.

21,694. Were not the prices larger and more satisfactory to you and the people?—The position is something new as there.

21,695. (*By Mr. Blandy.*) Do not the same buyers buying here go to the other markets also?—Yes.

21,696. About the removal of the fairs off the streets, what is your opinion?—I saw very many things occurring; I had my window broken one day by a cow running into my place.

21,697. That happened when the cow was passing there?—Yes.

Mr. John O'Connor examined.

21,698. (*By Mr. Blandy.*) Are you a large cattle dealer?—Yes.

21,699. You have been buying for a number of years?—Yes.

21,700. What is your opinion about holding fairs on the streets of the town?—I know Charleville, and I never knew the fairs here improved more than they have for the last five or six years, and I go everywhere, to all parts of Ireland and as well in England.

21,701. As a buyer having a large experience, do you consider the street a suitable place for buying cattle?—Yes, I have no objection to it.

21,702. You prefer having them there to going into a green where they would be a lot of slush and dirt in winter time?—I would not care about that.

21,703. (*By the Commissioner.*) Supposing there was a properly enclosed fair green, the ground macadamised, and pens provided there for you, would you prefer going there to purchase cattle? We never care to go and buy cattle too well fixed up.

21,704. You never like to go where the cattle have accommodation?—We never look to our own interests as regards pens.

21,705. I am asking you a general question about fairs?—We had a great many of the best fairs in Munster held on the street. There is Rathkeale, Thurles, Templemore, and in fact [illegible], which is a kind of [illegible]. It is hard ground all the same.

21,706. It is off the public thoroughfare?—Yes, but in the other towns the fairs are on the streets.

21,707. Do you sell in fair greens in England?—In the markets.

21,708. Have not they got pens provided in the majority of places there?—Yes.

21,709. Do you find you get better prices and more buyers around the fairs or markets than here?—Well, you see you do not know. You have not any choice but they are there. You have only the market to go to. You know very well they would not allow cattle to stand in the middle of a city in England.

21,710. But if all were enclosed all over Ireland to a properly enclosed fair green?—I do not know what that would be.

21,711. Have the traders or dealers with whom you are concerned ever discussed this amongst themselves?—Well, it is sometimes more advantageous to have a fair green. In some places you go where the fairs are held on the streets. One part of the fair is held at one end and the other at the other end. That is portion of the street there is no cattle, and that is very inconvenient, and you walk through the centre of the town without getting any cattle.

21,712. That is not so here?—I never heard any person make any objection to the streets of Charleville.

21,713. Have the dealers ever discussed the question of a properly enclosed fair green where accommodation would be given, or have they ever discussed anything in your hearing relating to them?—They never take any trouble about where they are held. The dealers never look to what suits them.

21,714. They rather put up with any inconvenience than else use the present system?—They never trouble about anything being altered.

21,715. Have you formed any ideas as to the levying of tolls, or have the dealers? Do you think that you would rather go to a fair and buy where no toll was levied than go to an equally good one where tolls were levied?—It would be so much in my pocket.

21,716. Would you consider that?—Not in buying.

21,717. If you could make a ready and suitable purchase you would not consider payment of the tolls?—The tolls are never considered; but of course, when there is no toll it is so much in the dealer's pocket; but in buying a beast they never consider the toll. You will not get more where there is a toll than where there is no toll.

21,718. You buy cattle yourself?—Yes.

21,719. There are a great number of people buying cattle on commission?—Not many.

21,720. Would not the question of toll be of importance to them?—Yes, it would be of importance. There is no one buying cattle but it would be so much in their pockets. It would be a lot of money some weeks.

because in buying a large beast in the fair field, that beast will not show the lameness until you get it out on the road.

21,725. If a portion of the fair green was paved for the purpose, could not you move them over that for inspection?—You could not well do that.

21,726. Do you consider it better to buy on the public thoroughfare where you are convenient to the shops. Is that the reason?—Generally we can see the cattle better on the streets.

21,727. You consider the ground is harder and you can try them better than on a green?—You can see them a great deal better.

21,728. Is that the only reason, or is it the principal reason?—Well, there are no fairs any good here only the fairs held in the town. They bring in more cattle and the fairs are kept up better. Any country fairs where there are fair greens they are usually gone down.

21,729. (*By Mr. Blakeney.*) On a particularly bad morning could a fair be held in the open?—I would stop at home that morning before I would go into a fair field to buy cattle.

21,730. (*By Mr Ryan.*) Is not Charleville specially adapted for fairs?—Yes, very good; we do not find a better fair anywhere.

21,731. You think a fine spacious street is well adapted for it?—Yes. In Rathkeale they have not half so wide a street, and good fairs are held there, but not so good as Charleville.

21,732. You agree with the other witnesses that the fairs have gone ahead?—Yes.

Mr. Cornelius Halliane examined.

21,733. (*By Mr. Blakeney.*) Do you wish to make any remarks?—Yes.

21,734. What have you to say?—For a number of years there were overcharges being made in the toll on pigs. For instance, you see by the schedule on market day there was twopence for every pig. Well, I paid threepence on one occasion, and it was the usual toll.

21,735. On market day?—That was the usual toll collected for market day. I brought the case before the magistrate and succeeded in getting a decree. We have here in the room men of experience and they can tell you.

21,736. (*By the Commissioner.*) Are the charges at present levied twopence on market day and threepence on a fair day?—The present charge is only twopence.

21,737. Did that result from the proceedings instituted by you?—Certainly.

21,738. Still you have no objection to the present system?—No, twopence is moderate. I want to show tolls were levied and collected on days they had no right to be collected.

21,739. What were these?—These were the market days preceding the fair days.

21,740. That is the pig market?—Yes.

21,741. At present no tolls are collected on the pig fair previous to the ordinary fair?—No, except it falls on Wednesday or Saturday, but then no matter on what day it fell tolls were collected until I took up my stand.

21,742. Have you any grievance to complain of in the present arrangement?—The only thing is the potatoes, but you have evidence given as regards that.

21,743. You concur in the observations made relative to the charges on potatoes?—I do, certainly.

21,744. You think 2d. a bag too much?—Certainly, especially to a poor woman coming with a bag of potatoes, and there is no assistance given in the way of porterage. You must place the bag in the scales yourself, and there is no person to give assistance for the removal of potatoes to or from the scales. In fact, in the case of a woman, it costs 4d. a bag for potatoes. She has to pay 2d. for a man to put the bag on the scales, because she cannot do it herself.

21,745. Are there men there specially for that purpose?—Yes, they earn their hire there.

21,746. (*By the Commissioner.*) Have these porters any fixed charge?—They get as much as they possibly can. It is 2d. a sack for one or two men at more.

21,747. (*Mr. Fitzgerald.*) We have no connexion with the porters. Men there look for the employment and get it.

21,748. (*By Mr. Blakeney.*) Are you in favour of having the fairs on the streets?—Yes, I agree with the other witnesses.

P. B. O'Keeffe, Esq., examined.

21,749. You are the agent to the Earl of Cork?—Yes.

21,750. He is the owner of the markets and tolls in Charleville?—Yes.

21,751. Is he the owner of the town of Charleville?—A great portion of the town. He has a large estate about it.

21,752. He is not in the immediate receipt of the tolls?—They are sub-let to Mr. Fitzgerald.

21,753. That is under lease, eight years of which are unexpired?—Yes.

21,754. The present net rent is 144l. 11s.?—Yes.

21,755. You allow the ordinary proportion of poor rate and income tax?—Yes.

21,756. Have you answered the schedule of queries?—Yes, as far as I can, but inasmuch as the tolls are leased I referred them to Mr. Fitzgerald.

21,757. There is one question about the capital expenditure in erecting the market place?—That I cannot find out beyond one or two entries of 300l.

21,758. It was Mr. Fitzgerald provided the scales and erected?—The weighing-machine.

21,759. Is it the same machine for weighing loads and cattle?—Yes. He put railings around it, under the new Act.

21,760. Could you tell me under what authority the Earl of Cork holds the fairs and markets and levies tolls, and under what authority he leased them?—Under different charters. I will give the dates, although there are four different charters. There is one in 1630, another 1674, the third in 1683, and the fourth in 1828.

21,761. Have you seen those charters yourself?—Yes.

21,762. Do they give a right to levy toll?—A full right.

21,763. Does each of them specify the particular days on which the fairs are to be held?—Yes. Under the first charter, in 1630, there is a free market every Wednesday weekly, and one fair in midsummer, and one fair in September. The second charter, in 1674, grants a free market every Wednesday and Saturday, and two fairs or markets annually on the 25th April and 1st November. The third charter, of 1683, grants also four fairs on the 10th January, 15th March, 15th May, and 16th August.

21,764. I inquired of Mr. Fitzgerald and he stated to the best of his belief; but I would like to ask you whether the Earl of Cork contributes anything towards the additional expense incurred in cleaning the streets, other than his contribution to the rates and taxes?—That is all.

21,765. If any repairs are to be effected in the market place, who performs that duty?—The tenant.

21,766. Are there any special covenants in the lease?—Nothing special, I think.

21,767. Only the ordinary covenants?—Yes.

21,768. Had you any opportunity of consulting the Earl of Cork on any of these queries?—No, I wrote to him.

21,769. You have not had any conversation, before he went, on the subject?—No.

21,770. You could not give his views on any question?—No.

21,771. Supposing a local authority were established or markets committee, do you think the Earl of Cork would have any objection to their obtaining compulsory powers to acquire his rights?—I think Lord Cork would do anything for the benefit of the town.

21,772. If he considered it would be for the benefit of the town he would have no objection?—No.

21,773. Have you formed any ideas on that question?—I have not. I think for the benefit of the fairs, and the benefit of the town, the fairs should be held on the streets. I think the cattle are better inspected in the town than in closed-up pens.

21,774. You think the fact of the fairs being held on the streets affords a better opportunity to the buyers looking at the animals they are going to buy?—Yes, and it seriously benefits the shopkeepers too.

(By Mr. Blenley.) I think before 1826 there were only four fairs?—Yes.

21,775. You are aware there are 12 now?—Yes, there were four other fairs granted.

21,776. Could you tell what was the gross sum Lord Cork was receiving for the tolls before 1826?—I could not tell you. It was before my time.

21,777. Are you aware it was not more than 130l.?—I think it is far beyond that.

21,778. Lord Cork did not do anything to contribute to the establishment of the new fairs except receive the tolls?—He would take the tolls when the fairs happened to fall on market days.

21,779. You agree, with others, to have the fairs held on the streets?—I think so. The general opinion is, it would be a disadvantage to have them removed.

21,780. At the time of the establishment of the new fairs were the tolls leased to the present tenant?—I think not. The tolls were originally leased to Mr. Townsend, and I have got the schedule he adopted at the time; that is in 1818.

21,781. (By the Commissioner.) In the patents are there any specific rates mentioned?—No, except the rates fixed by the court.

21,782. The rights were expressly given to collect the tolls at the markets and fairs?—Yes, I have got a copy of the patent.

21,783. There was no patent or charter to collect on the twelve fairs here?—On looking over some papers I find a petition for four more fairs, and, although I have written to the Rolls Office, I have not been able to get out the petition, but I think there was a grant of additional fairs.

21,784. What year was the petition presented?—About 1854 or 1855. There was a petition presented, but I cannot state whether an order was made.

21,785. (Mr. Blenley.) Lord Cork has no charter rights to collect tolls at the fairs on market days.

21,786. (Mr. O'Kearney.) He has a right over eight fairs.

21,787. (Mr. Blenley.) Six are mentioned here.

21,788. (The Commissioner.) The additional fairs were not established under express grant, but by the consideration of the people and consent of the owner.

21,789. (Mr. Blenley.) Yes, but I want to show they are free fairs. There is no express charter or grant to the lord of the soil of these new fairs, but when they fall on market days he has them caught in the market tolls.

21,790. (Mr. O'Kearney.) He is entitled, under charter, to hold eight fairs.

21,791. (Mr. Blenley.) I think it is very important to know that the new fairs, which are toll free, are caught by the market tolls.

Mr. Hart examined.

21,792. What remarks have you to make?—In my recollection of Charleville, I knew the potato market to have been held down Broad Street, where there is a store now; and now the oats and potato market are amalgamated, which causes a great deal of confusion.

21,793. Then the potato market has not been always held on the same site?—No, not for the last 25 years.

21,794. That former place was enclosed?—Yes, and it is now used as a private coal store.

21,795. (By Mr. Blenley.) You think there is not sufficient accommodation here?—Not in the spring, and also there is not enough of room to weigh.

21,796. Is there any other gentleman who has any evidence to give or suggestions to offer?

No answer.

The inquiry then terminated.

MACROOM—CO. CORK.

With reference to my inquiry in Macroom on the 20th November 1888, I beg to report as follows:—

Macroom is situated in the western portion of the county of Cork. It is the terminus of the Cork and Macroom Railway line. The surrounding country partakes of a mountainous character, but is fertile. The town possesses a fair trade, the houses are well built, but the streets would require to be better looked after. The local government is administered by the grand jury and the board of guardians, and the population is

The market rights of Macroom relate to two distinct places, (1) Macroom, and (2) Masseytown, a district originally a suburb of Macroom, but which has now become a portion thereof.

The markets are held on Saturday in Macroom proper, a butter market on Thursday, and during the season on Monday in addition, and a calf market is held on Thursday.

A separate series of fairs is held in each district. In Macroom the fairs are held on the 12th January, 12th March, 12th May, 12th July, 12th September, and 12th November. A pig market is held the day previous to the ordinary fairs, at which tolls are levied. In Masseytown the fairs are held on the 12th February, 12th April, 14th June, 12th August, 12th October, and 14th December. A pig fair is held the day previous to the ordinary fairs, at which tolls are levied.

Tolls are levied on each marketable commodity according as it is brought into the town and exposed for sale every day in the week.

The fairs held in Macroom on the 12th January and 12th March are toll free, and tolls are levied at those held on the 12th May, 12th July, 12th September, and 12th November, and also at the pig fairs. Tolls are levied at all the fairs held in Massytown, viz., 12th February, 12th April, 14th June, 12th August, 12th October, and 14th December, and at the pig fairs.

The market rights and tolls in Macroom are the property of the Earl of Bantry, but are sublet by him to Mrs. Norah Harding at the yearly rent of 150*l*. The market rights and tolls in Massytown are the property of the representatives of Mr. Massy, who have them also sublet to Mrs. Harding at the yearly rent of 100*l*. In consequence of the market rights being thus vested in one lessee they have become amalgamated and are held upon the same site, and no separate account is kept of the receipts and expenditure at each market.

The public records show that a patent was granted for each of the districts. The one for Macroom is dated 30th September 1712 (11 Anne), and authorised one Francis Bernard to hold a Wednesday and Saturday market, and fairs on the 1st May, 1st July, 1st September, and 1st November. These are evidently the fairs at present held on the 12th May, 12th July, 12th September, and 12th November.

The patent for Massytown is dated the 23rd January 1776, and authorised one Mary Hutchinson to hold fairs on the 12th June, 12th August, 12th October, and 12th December. These are evidently the fairs held on the 12th August and 12th October, and no evidence was given of any authorised change in the dates of the fairs, which are at present held on the 14th June and 14th December.

In both districts, therefore, the markets and fairs which appear not to have been granted by any express authority are the Monday and Thursday butter market, the Thursday calf market, and the fairs in Massytown on the 12th February, 12th April, 14th June, and 14th December; and in Macroom the fairs on the 12th January and 12th March. The latter two fairs were established about 30 years ago, and the fairs in Massytown on the 12th February and 12th April must have been established since the Royal Commission in 1852, although I was unable to trace, by the evidence available, the date of their establishment.

There is no toll board erected for public inspection.

In accordance with my instructions I have inspected the market place and fair greens.

A fair green is provided for each district. In Massytown the fairs are not confined to the fair green, but are partly held on the streets adjoining. The fair green or field is situated outside the town, and is large, rough, and uneven. The entrance to it, which is on a steep incline, and of a rocky surface, has been complained of as dangerous at certain seasons of the year, principally in frosty weather. It is scarcely suitable for a fair green, and the entrance certainly suggests more inconvenience and danger than comfort for the animals and people attending the fairs. It is not enclosed, and a mill race has its course through the centre, which makes the banks soft, and occasions a good deal of mud in portions of the field.

In Macroom a fair green or field is provided near the railway station. Owing to its circumscribed limits and general inadequateness it is only used for the exposure of pigs, while the cattle and sheep fairs are held in the narrow streets, and especially in the one which is the only approach to the railway station. The blocking which takes place there for several hours on the fair day is very much complained of, and might be mitigated to a great extent, or altogether remedied if the field was enlarged to a size sufficient to meet the requirements of the cattle trade of the district. This fair green is enclosed for the most part by earthen and stone fences, but at the time of inspection throughout the field there was here and there an accumulation of manure.

There are no pens or shelter accommodation, but weighing machines are provided in connexion with each fair field. The weighing machine at Massytown is erected at the entrance to the fair green, and the one at Macroom is erected on the road leading from the market square to Massytown.

The standings are indiscriminately on the streets and market square.

The markets are held in the square, which is a large wide portion of the public thoroughfare. A market building of small dimensions is provided in the centre of the square for certain commodities, but is not utilised for general market purposes. A few meat sheds are erected against the side walls, and are availed of for the butter market. Beams and scales are provided here, and the weighing is carried on beneath another shed, and on the open square. Potatoes can be stored, but the storage accommodation is very small. Outside the weighhouse some wooden stalls or boxes, or, as they are locally termed, "bulks," are erected where soft goods, fruit, and vegetables are retailed.

Neither the owner of the Macroom tolls or of Masseytown tolls contribute anything towards the town rates except through the ordinary course.

A complaint was made on behalf of some poor women who expose apples for sale on the public square. They have no stalls or covered shelter, nor is there any that could be had. It was stated and admitted that these poor people, sooner than run the risk of damaging their stock in trade of apples by removing them off the ground at nightfall, merely cover them over, and in order to afford protection from robbers the women sleep beside them in large barrels or hogsheads. Notwithstanding this they have to pay a standing toll of 2*d.* per week for the liberty of putting the apples on the ground. The sight at daytime is deplorable, so that at night it must be such as should not exist in any civilised country.

Vide evidence of T. Riordan (22,237 to 22,257).

In addition to the toll on corn and potatoes an additional impost of 6*d.* per load, and frequently 1*d.* per sack is made by the weighmaster for porterage. This individual was frankness itself, and stated that he would not facilitate any farmer in weighing his corn or potatoes if he did not employ him to engage porters, although he might have provided himself with sufficient manual assistance.

Vide evidence of T. Healy (22,286), and C. Creede (22,317).

A complaint was also made of the great delay which sometimes occurs in weighing corn, and one witness stated that four hours elapsed on one occasion before he could get the weight of his load ascertained. This is accounted for by an insufficient supply of beams and scales.

Vide evidence of C. Creede (22,317).

The inquiry was very well attended, and, indeed, great interest was manifested in the proceedings.

Appended will be found copies of the patents, dated 30th September 1712 (11 Anne), and 23rd January 1776 (16 George III.), relating to Macroom and Massytown respectively, and likewise a transcript of the evidence taken at the inquiry.

JOHN J. O'MEARA,
Assistant Commissioner.

45, Lower Mount Street,
Dublin.

Copy Patent, dated 30th September 1712 (11 Anne).

fair or mart there to be held on every 1st *day of November* yearly for ever, unless any of the days aforesaid happen to fall on a *Sunday*, and as often as it shall so happen or any of them shall so happen then we will such fair to be held on the *Monday next after* such Sunday, together with a *Court of Pye Powder* there to be held *during the said markets and fairs or marts*.

And further we will, and by these presents for us, our heirs and successors, we do grant to the aforesaid Francis Bernard, his heirs and assigns, that he the aforesaid Francis Bernard, his heirs and assigns, for ever may have and hold, enjoy, receive, and perceive *all and singular issues, tolls, customs, profits, entry of cattle*, and *goods to be sold, emoluments, and advantages whatsoever* of the aforesaid several markets, fairs, or marts and courts issuing, or of the aforesaid or such markets, fairs, or marts and courts appertaining or belonging, or by reason of the same or any of them growing or emerging without account to us, our heirs or successors, to be thereout rendered. To have and to hold the aforesaid markets and fairs or marts and courts, together with all and singular tolls, customs, privileges, and immunities to them belonging or appertaining to the said Francis Bernard, his heirs and assigns, to the sole and proper use and behoof of the aforesaid Francis Bernard, his heirs and assigns for ever, to be held of us, our heirs and successors, as of our Castle of Dublin on free and common socage, paying thereout annually to us, our heirs and successors, at the receipt of our Exchequer 5 current money of Great Britain, at the feasts of St. Michael and the Annunciation of the Blessed Virgin Mary by equal portions yearly to be paid for ever.

We will moreover, and by these presents for us, our heirs and successors, we do grant to the aforesaid Francis Bernard, Esquire, his heirs and assigns, that these our Letters Patent or the enrolment thereof shall be in all things and by all things good, firm, valid, sufficient, and effectual in the law towards and against us, our heirs and successors, as well in all our courts of said Kingdom of Ireland as elsewhere wheresoever, any statute, Act, ordinance, provision, or any other thing, cause, or matter whatsoever to the contrary thereof in anything notwithstanding, provided always that these our Letters Patent be enrolled in the Rolls of our Court of Chancery of our said Kingdom of Ireland within the space of six months after the date of these presents.

In testimony of which thing we have caused these our Letters to be made Patent. Witness our aforesaid Justices and General Governors of our said Kingdom of Ireland at Dublin the 30th day of September in the 11th year of our reign.

Enrolled the 4th day of November in the 11th year of our reign of Queen Anne.

Copy Patent, dated 23rd January 1776 (16 George III.).

Hutchinson, his heirs and assigns, may for ever have and hold the said fairs and markets in or at the said lands of Kilnagurteen, otherwise Massytown, in manner and form aforesaid, together with the said Court of Pye Powder, and all usual tolls, customs, duties, privileges, and immunities from the said fairs, markets, and court arising, or to the same of right, or by custom belonging or appertaining. Yielding to therefore yearly to us, our heirs and successors, the yearly rent of 1l. 6s. 8d. sterling for the said fairs and markets, to be paid yearly for ever. And our further will is and by these presents for us, our heirs and successors, we do grant unto the said Massy Hutchinson, his heirs and assigns, that these our letters patent, or the enrollment thereof, shall be in all things firm, good, valid, sufficient, and effectual in the law against us, our heirs and successors, in all the courts of us, our heirs and successors, any cause, matter, or thing whatsoever to the contrary notwithstanding. Provided always, that these our Letters Patent be enrolled in the Rolls of our High Court of Chancery, in our said Kingdom of Ireland, and also in the office of our Auditor-General of our said Kingdom of Ireland, within the space of six months next ensuing the date of these presents, otherwise these our Letters Patents to be void and of none effect, anything herein contained to the contrary notwithstanding. In witness whereof we have caused these our Letters to be made Patent. Witness our aforesaid Lieutenant-General and General Governor of our said Kingdom of Ireland, at Dublin, the 23rd day of January, in the year of our reign.

CONWAY.

Examined, Michael Nowlan, Deputy Clerk of the Crown and Hanaper.

(L. S.)

Inrolled in the office of the Rolls of His Majesty's High Court of Chancery in Ireland, the 23rd day of January, in the 10th year of the reign of King George the Third, and examined by M. Paterson, junior, and Fr. Parry, Dep. Clerks and Keepers of the Rolls.

21,830. For what period, or could you give any approximate idea of the period, for which the six fairs have been actually held?—I assume they were held under the patent.

21,831. You have no knowledge or evidence of the commencement of the six?—No evidence except this, that the estate of the late William Massy, the father of the minors, was sold in the Landed Estates Court, and by the Landed Estates Court the tolls were sold *inter alia*. I find, by the rental under which they were sold, the tolls described as follows:—The tolls of the fairs of Masseytown are held in fee, subject only to the fee farm rent, 1*l*. 6*s*. 8*d*., for ever. In the general conditions of sale I find, further, that in the rental lot 51 comprises the fair green and fairs and tolls of Masseytown. There are six fairs held yearly, viz., the months of February, April, June, August, September, October, and December. This is the rental (produced) under which the lands were sold. They were sold on the 28th May 1851, and the conveyance was dated the following March 1852.

21,832. Were the tolls and customs bought separately from the estate?—No. They were sold for the gross sum of 40,000*l*.

21,833. What was the estate that was sold?—The estate of William Hutchinson Massy, owner. That is the father of the minors. He became absolute owner, subject to a mortgage.

21,834. Are the two markets given under the patent held here in Masseytown?—The markets, I take it, are held in conjunction with the markets of Macroom, and tolls that may not be levied strictly in Masseytown are collected in Macroom.

21,835. You state that the two markets have become amalgamated, and that any profit goes to Lord Bantry?—Our lessee farms both, and we have no distinct account of them. Lord Bantry gets a rent of 150*l*.

21,836. Is that a yearly tenancy, or is there a written agreement?—I believe there was an agreement in writing. I have not a copy of it here, but I fancy the term has expired and they are held on yearly tenancies. Do not take that as an absolutely correct statement, for I cannot guarantee it more than by report.

21,837. What is Mrs. Harding's christian name?—Sarah Harding.

21,838. What is the rent?—The rent of Lord Bantry's tolls is 150*l*. a year.

21,839. That is for the four fairs and two markets under the patent?—The fairs and markets, wherever they are.

21,840. I suppose that is subject to the ordinary deductions for poor-rate?—Lord Bantry, as well as I recollect, pays the entire of the county cess. I was Lord Bantry's agent for some time, and, as well as I recollect, the whole of the county cess was paid by him, and only half the income tax, and I think the poor-rate.

21,841. What has Mrs. Massy?—She has everything she is entitled to.

21,842. Is there any written agreement between herself and Mrs. Harding?—I fancy not.

21,843. What is the rent?—The rent is 100*l*. In this case also the head rent has been changed. Mr. Payne was agent up to a year and a half ago.

21,844. Are there any of the officials of Mrs. Harding here?—We have the clerk here.

21,845. Is that Mr. Kelliher?—Yes, and there is Mr. M'Carthy here. There is one thing I wish to mention. I sent a list of queries on behalf of Lord Bantry and Mr. Massy, and stated the tolls were collected under patent. I will ask you to put by prescription as well as grant, because it may turn out that some of the tolls are leviable by prescription.

21,846. Did you bring these queries under the notice of the owners in each case?—I answered them as well as I could from the knowledge that lay within my power.

21,847. Then they were not their own answers?—In the case of Masseytown, Captain Mellan filled in some, and I added more.

21,848. Was he aware of the answers you were to give me?—I was aware of the answers given by Captain Mellan, so far as they appeared on the paper. The fact is they are Mr. Payne's answers, and he sent it to me to add fuller information, and I added something, as far as it came within my own knowledge or belief.

21,849. Has Mrs. Harding, the lessee of these, toll boards erected specifying the different rates at the fairs?—No.

21,850. Tolls have been always levied at the four fairs held by Lord Bantry, and at the other six?—Yes.

21,851. And at no period were tolls not levied at these places?—I remember very well, and many people younger than me, remember the additional fairs. The four patent fairs commence in May. The patent grants the first of each month.

21,852. Do you remember the establishment of these?—No. I can remember these fairs existing as long as I remember anything.

21,853. But you remember the establishment of the two fairs on the 12th January and 12th March?—Yes, and I can remember when there was formerly a fair held on the 2nd March. There was an annual horse fair held in the town of Mill Street, 14 miles from here, and a horse fair was held in Macroom the day following, and it was called "Fool's Fair," because those who did not sell at Mill Street came and sold there.

21,854. Is that held now?—No. It is abolished.

21,855. Where are these fairs held?—The Masseytown fairs are held partly on the street, from the bridge to the fair green, and partly on the fair green.

21,856. There is a fair green provided?—Yes.

21,857. Who was that fair green provided by?—It was provided by the representatives of Mr. Massy. You will see that on the Landed Estates Court rental.

21,858. These six fairs are held partly on the street, and partly in this fair green?—Yes.

21,859. Are there any market buildings erected and demised to the tenant for the Masseytown markets?—None.

21,860. Are there any market buildings erected for the holding of the markets here, the latter especially?—There is a market house which is a mere meat market, and a portion of it is devoted to an office where the market tickets are issued for the sale of agricultural produce.

21,861. You say it is a mere meat market where the weight market house is?—The main market building is that, but lately there have been butter markets established in the town of Macroom, and they are held in that market house, and I believe some tolls are collected for that, that is for the use of the market house which is private property.

21,862. Is there a fair field in Macroom?—There is. It is adjoining the railway station.

21,863. Is the exposure of animals confined to that fair green?—No. You will recollect that in a great measure the will of the people governs a place where things are sold. A fair green is provided; it is used principally for pigs. All the cattle and other marketable commodities are mainly sold in the streets of the town.

Mr. Daniel Kelliher (market assistant) examined.

21,864. You are the assistant for Mrs. Harding?—Yes.

21,865. How long have you been in her employment?—I am in the office since 1880, but I had not charge until last December.

21,866–8. Notwithstanding that, you are conversant with the whole details and management of the place?—I am.

21,869. You heard an answer of Mr. Asher's to a question of mine that the markets are held by Mrs. Harding from the representatives of Mr. Massy and Lord Bantry?—They are.

21,870. You collect a toll for the whole of them?—Yes.

21,871. Do you keep separate accounts of the markets as distinct from the fair?—Yes.

21,872. You keep accounts of what you receive from the Masseytown fairs and markets and what you receive from the other fairs and markets?—I keep what I receive from the markets in a separate account and the fairs by themselves.

21,873. Will you kindly tell me what commodities are brought into the town of Macroom on market days, whether you receive tolls on them or not?—During the week I may say oats, wheat, turnips, apples, cabbages, milk, fish, of course we also receive tolls for all goods, and butter. There is a butter market every Thursday.

21,874. Is hay brought here?—Hay and straw are weighed.

21,875. You have no schedule of tolls, or rather the charges you levy on each of those commodities?—No.

21,876. Then the people who bring the commodities in have no means of knowing the actual charges to be levied only from your collectors?—Yes.

21,877. Are each of those commodities exposed on the public thorough fare?—Yes.

21,878. Are the charges you levy—are they tolls or are they weighing charges for performing the duty of weighing the commodity. For instance, we will take the case of corn. What charge have you on corn?—A 1d. per sack.

21,879. If corn is brought in by a farmer on market day in the number of 12 sacks, does he expose it before he weighs it?—Yes, it is brought before it is weighed.

21,880. Corn is always actually sold before being weighed?—Always.

21,881. When he sells corn and goes to your scale to have it weighed, what do you charge him?—A 1d. a sack and we issue a ticket then.

21,882. Do you charge anything additional for the ticket?—It is for the ticket I charge, but there is a man at the scales, and he always has men with him, and he will unload and cart the corn away and put it back again, and he charges himself.

21,883. What is that?—As a general rule he sometimes gets a 1d. per sack.

21,884. Is it Mrs. Harding employs those porters and receives this porterage charge?—They are not employed by her.

21,885. Is it compulsory on the farmers to employ those men?—It is not compulsory. If they bring help enough themselves and put the corn into the scales themselves and take it out again they will be charged nothing but a 1d.

21,886. Supposing corn was brought into the market and exposed there on a market day and sold, but not weighed at your scales, and it came to your knowledge that it was sold, would you ask for your charge?—Yes, if I saw where it was brought.

21,887. Have you done so?—Yes.

21,888. Supposing it was sent in to one of the shopkeepers of the town, who bought it from the farmer, and the farmer delivered it on market day, would you ask for your charge?—If he bought it at the farmer's house, I would say he should weigh in the market.

21,889. Did a case of that kind occur?—It did.

21,890. Then the man was charged?—I did not demand the charge when he bought it at home, but I demanded my right to weigh in the market and that he was depriving us of the tolls of the market.

21,891. Did you receive any payment?—No.

21,892. Is it a 1d. per sack on all corn?—Yes, and potatoes also.

21,893. Is this a printed ticket you give denoting the weight?—Yes.

21,894. Have you got one of those here?—I have.

21,895. Witness then produced the ticket, of which the following is a copy:—

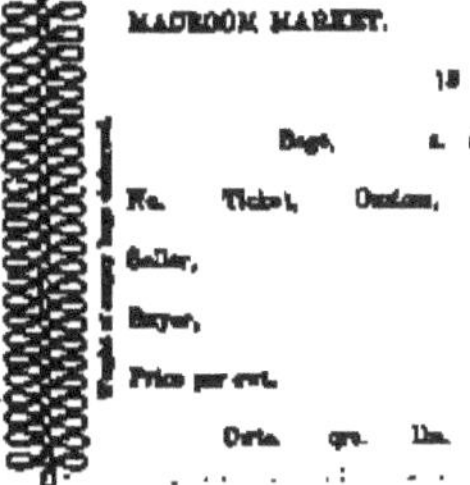
MACROOM MARKET.

18 .

Bags, s. d.

No. Ticket, Custom,

Seller,

Buyer,

Price per cwt.

Cwts. qrs. lbs.

21,896. Is this a general ticket?—Yes.

21,897. Does this ticket answer for all commodities weighed?—Yes. There is a similar ticket for the butter market.

21,898. Have you it here?—I can give it to you.

21,899. On this ticket you put the number of the ticket, the number of bags, and your charge?—Yes.

21,900. You also put down the name of the buyer and seller?—Yes.

21,901. Do you ascertain the price?—Certainly, I must make up the amount.

21,902. You do that for the convenience of the buyer and seller?—Yes.

21,903. In all cases do you usually ascertain the current or contract prices?—Yes; before I issue the ticket.

21,904. If Mrs. Harding, or the owner of the fairs and markets, was required to make a periodical return of the current price of the different marketable commodities brought in, you think she could make out such a return?—She could.

21,905. Do you keep a block of this ticket?—I do.

21,906. Do you enter it into any book?—I keep the block only.

21,907. So that if they lose their tickets on a market day they can come to you for a copy of it?—Yes.

21,908. Do you charge them anything additional?—No.

21,909. This ticket is for corn and potatoes?—Yes.

21,910. What scales have you in the market?—We have got two potato scales, two butter scales, one corn scale, the weighbridge, and two cranes. We got the use of the meat stalls for the butter market.

21,911. Is the weighbridge you have capable of weighing cattle?—Yes.

21,912. Had you it previous to last year?—No, it is since the Act of 18[illegible] we got it.

21,913. Who was it provided it?—Mrs. Harding, but I do not know who paid for it. We are bound to have two scales, one for Massytown and one for Macroom.

21,914. Was Mrs. Harding at the expense of the weighbridge?—I could not tell you that.

21,915. Have you two weighbridges?—Yes, one for Massytown and one for Macroom.

21,916. You do not know what the total expense of those weighbridges came to?—I think [illegible] each.

21,917. You heard that from Mrs. Harding?—Yes.

21,918. Do you levy any tolls on turnips?—Yes.

21,919. What is the charge?—4d. a load.

21,920. Is that for weighing?—Weighed or not.

21,921. Is that irrespective of the sort of load, whether horse or donkey load?—If a donkey load we would allow for it, and only charge half price, 2d.

21,922. Have you ever done so?—Yes, in cabbage or potatoes also.

21,923. If they weigh the load you charge nothing additional?—No.

21,924. If weighed, do you give a ticket?—No ticket. They do not require it, because they sell by the cwt. themselves.

21,925. If they sell by the cwt., do they bring scales themselves?—I have a scale there.

21,926. Do you charge them anything for each cwt.?—No; I weigh the whole for 4d.

21,927. You weigh the whole load for 4d. if they require it?—Yes.

21,928. If they do not require to weigh it at all you charge all the same?—Yes.

21,929. Are turnips only brought in carts?—That is all.

21,930. Have you any charge on apples?—Yes, 4d. a load.

21,931. Do the same observations apply to apples as to turnips?—Yes.

21,932. What would you call a load. If a man brought in a load on his shoulder, would you charge 4d.?—No.

21,933. Is it on a cartload?—Yes.

21,934. If they brought in a basket of apples, have you any charge on that?—I do not know I was ever paid for a basket of apples. A load always comes together. There are five or six baskets in the load, and we charge 4d.

21,935. Do they come in on market day?—They come several days during the week.

21,936. You levy all these charges any day they come during the week?—Yes.

21,937. There is no day in the week that is toll free for any of these commodities?—No.

21,938. Supposing corn was brought in and exposed for sale in the market but not sold, would you levy a charge?—No.

21,939. It is only on the commodity sold?—Yes.

21,940. If potatoes were not sold?—I would not charge.

21,941. If turnips are not sold?—I would not charge. On anything that is not sold I would not charge.

21,942. When do you collect your charge. Is it when they have completely sold their stock?—Just when about leaving. There is a weekly man we have employed for the purpose of watching those parties.

21,943. Going around the market?—Yes.

21,944. When he finds they sell something he collects the tolls?—Yes.

21,945. Has he ever been refused?—Yes.

21,946. Did he ever seize the commodity or levy any distress?—I do not think he did.

21,947. You never heard it?—Never.

21,948. Have you the collector here?—Yes, all the officials in connection with the market are here. It is very hard to get the charge. Sometimes they would say the thing was not sold, and it would be sold afterwards.

21,949. Now, on cabbage what is the charge?—4d. per load.

21,950. On milk?—1d. per churn.

21,951. On fish?—4d. a load, that is a cartload. If only a donkey load we charge 2d.

21,952. If any of the fish women brought in baskets or boxes you would levy a charge?—Yes, I would charge 1d. per box.

21,953. What would be the quantity of fish in the box, or what is the smallest quantity you have known to be in a box?—I could not tell you.

21,954. You have no idea?—No.

21,955. Do you know what the value of the fish would be?—I could not tell you.

21,956. These tolls are only collected when a sale has been effected?—Yes, but we charge for weekly standings in addition.

21,957. Are the charges for soft goods purely standing charges?—We have occasional standings on fair days.

21,958. Supposing they brought in a cartload of soft goods on a market day, would you levy a charge?—Yes, if they offered them for sale.

21,959. Do you take into account whether they are subsequently sold or not?—We make it a general rule to go around in the evening on market days and charge 6d. each on soft goods.

21,960. 6d. for what?—For the standing.

21,961. Is that the lowest charge?—It is.

21,962. Is that the only charge?—The only charge.

21,963. It does not matter whether it is a cart standing or some boards thrown across a barrel?—It is all the same.

21,964. You do not inquire whether they effect any sale or not?—We take it for granted that they have something sold.

21,965. But if they do not actually sell something, would you collect any charge?—I would not.

21,966. Do you think you would have a right to collect it?—I could not answer that.

21,967. You have never done so?—No.

21,968. You say you have got the use of the meal shed for the butter market?—Yes.

21,969. And the butter market is held on Thursday?—Yes.

21,970. Do you know when the butter market was established?—In 1890 the fresh butter market.

21,971. Who was it established that market?—The shopkeepers of the town.

21,972. What is the charge on butter?—That is weighed on Thursday. Any butter that comes during the week the charge is a 1d. per basket.

21,973. During the week, with the exception of Thursday, your charge on butter is a 1d. per basket?—Yes.

21,974. Could you tell me what would be the quantity in a basket?—There would be all lumps, generally 8 lbs., and perhaps there would be 10 lbs. of butter entirely in the basket.

21,975. What would be the smallest quantity in the basket. Do you ever know them to have only 4 lbs.?—The collector is here and can tell you that.

21,976. On Thursday what is your charge on butter?—From 1 lb. to 28 lbs. a 1d. There is a part of the year for a couple of [illegible], and it is very heavy, and then there is a butter market on Monday during the season.

21,977. You have no fixed date for the commencement of that?—No. The buyers manage that themselves.

21,978. Last year what date did you commence or at what time this year did you begin to hold that market?—I could not tell you that now.

21,979. How long does it last?—About two months.

21,980. Then you levy the same charges on that day as on Thursday?—The very same.

21,981. You say the charge is from 1 lb. to 28 lbs. a 1d.?—Yes, and from 28 lbs. to 56 lbs. 2d., and increasing accordingly.

21,982. If there were 60 lbs. would you charge 3d.?—Yes.

21,983. Anything over 56 lbs., say 57 lbs., you would charge 3d.?—We are not so tight on that.

21,984. You give and take a little?—Yes.

21,985. Is this firkin butter that is brought in?—No, it is all fresh lumps.

21,986. Is there any firkin butter brought here at all?—No.

21,987. Supposing lump butter was brought and exposed for sale in the shed and was not sold, would you charge?—No.

21,988. If it was sold and not weighed would you levy a charge?—No. The butter is always weighed before it is bought on Thursday.

21,989. On the ordinary days when you charge a 1d. per basket is that for carrying a basket of butter or only for weighing?—It is not weighed at all during the week.

21,990. The charge is for bringing in the basket of butter and exposing it for sale?—Yes; if it is not sold we would not charge.

21,991. Where do they expose it for sale?—They hawk it about the town.

21,992. These are butter hawkers?—Yes.

21,993. If they sell only portion of the basket would you charge?—I would charge.

21,994. Would you levy the full charge?—Yes.

21,995. If they sold only a small quantity it would be the same?—Yes.

21,996. How are the tolls collected when the people go about?—They do not frequent the place very often, except on odd [illegible], and the man employed can manage it easily himself.

21,997. On every day in the week you perform practically no weighing duties in connection with the butter market, but on Thursday you say the butter is weighed before being sold?—Yes, and a ticket issued.

21,998. It is weighed in your scales and exposed in your shed?—The buyers have different stalls, and they go around to them. They expose their butter for sale in the market and, when they sell the ticket is taken from them, and the price and the buyer's name marked on it. The money is then taken from the sellers and they are paid. It is on that ticket they are paid.

21,999. What is your charge on hay?—4d. a load. It is the same for straw.

22,000. Is that for weighing?—Yes.

22,001. Is there a hay market here, or do they expose their hay in the carts about the town?—It is generally bought at home, at the seller's place.

22,002. Have you any rule in the market compelling all hay brought to the market to be weighed on your scales?—None.

22,003. So that they can go elsewhere if they please?—Yes.

22,004. But I suppose they have no opportunity?—There is a weighbridge in the union, and they were in the habit of weighing there before, but since we got the weighbridge erected there we put a stop to it.

22,005. Do you know how the hay is bought? Do they buy by bulk or by weight?—By the ton.

22,006. Always?—Yes.

22,007. You have the same charge on hay as on straw?—Yes.

22,008. You only levy this charge when the hay or straw is weighed on the bridge?—We would not charge until it is weighed and a ticket is issued, too.

22,009. If it was sold and not weighed, would you levy a charge?—I do not think I would. I would not.

22,010. You have never done so?—No.

22,011. Have you any duties to perform in connexion with the fairs?—Yes.

22,012. Have you the same rate of tolls at the Macroom fairs as at the Masseytown fairs?—The very same.

22,013. Have you got toll boards erected at each of them?—No.

22,014. Were any toll boards ever erected within your recollection?—I remember, a few years ago, to see an old one in the office, but you could not read the writing at all.

22,015. Was it defaced?—Yes.

22,016. You remember the commodities you have mentioned and the tolls on them. Are there any other commodities brought to the market on which you levy tolls?—There is a calf market on Thursday.

22,017. Is that held in the street?—Yes, in the Square in Macroom.

22,018. The markets are all held in Macroom?—Yes.

22,019. Who provided the house and scales?—Mrs. Harding. The late Mr. [illegible] was the original lessee, and when Mrs. Harding succeeded him his rights were vested in her.

22,020. Where is the calf market held?—In the square.

22,021. Is that portion of the public thoroughfare?—Yes.

22,022. You levy tolls?—Yes.

22,023. What are they?—2d. a calf.

22,024. Is that only on the animal sold?—Yes.

22,025. If not sold you do not charge?—No.

22,026. Is that every Thursday?—Every Thursday throughout the year. These are only lately established.

22,027. When were they established?—I could not tell you. It is a good many years now.

22,028. Was it previous to your engagement?—Yes.

22,029. Were any of the tolls levied or established since your appointment on any of the commodities brought to the market?—Yes, on the calf market, by the man who was in charge before I came into office.

22,030. No change has been made in the rates of charges?—No, as far as I remember.

22,031. You have standings at the markets?—Yes, we call them balks. When I say markets, I mean every day in the week.

22,032. Is that a local term for them?—It is a local phrase. They are boxes that are encroachments on the street. They are put up by people, and there is nobody to take any notice of them.

22,033. Are they squatting on the public thoroughfare?—Yes.

22,034. Is that where the apples are exposed?—Yes. They are increasing in number.

22,035. Do you receive any charge for them?—Yes, 6d. a week.

22,036. Who was it erected them?—Themselves, I believe.

22,037. The people themselves?—Yes.

22,038. They were never removed out of them?—No.

22,039. Have the police ever interfered with them?—No.

22,040. What commodities do they dispose of there?—Soft goods. There are a couple of shoemakers there, two cobblers' balks.

22,041. Then I may say they are very small standings, but locked up in the evening?—Yes.

22,042. Are these the only standings you have?—Yes, there are tinsmiths.

22,043. Do you erect tents?—No.

22,044. What is their charge?—The same as for the balks.

22,045. That is 6d. per week?—Yes.

22,046. If they came in on Saturday for the first time, would you levy a charge of 6d.?—I would.

22,047. If they came on Monday, would you levy a charge of 6d.?—I do not think I would. I would not.

22,048. You would wait until the following Saturday?—Yes.

22,049. It is on the first day they come in you levy a charge?—If I thought they were going to make their exit the same day I would charge them.

22,050. The balk standings are the only standings you have a charge on?—That is all.

22,051. At the fairs you have no toll board?—No.

22,052. What animals are brought in here?—Cows, sheep, heifers, fat calves, pigs, fowl, goats. I scarcely ever get paid for a horse.

22,053. Are donkeys ever brought here?—Yes, but we never get paid for them.

22,054. They are brought here?—Very few.

22,055. They do not bring any fowl in on market days?—They generally do not bring any fowl until fair days.

22,056. Do you levy charges on all these?—Yes.

22,057. What do you levy on cows?—4d. each.

22,058. On sheep?—1d. each.

22,059. What would you levy on a lamb?—If the lambs are very small, we only charge a ½d. each on them.

22,060. Is that the custom?—Yes.

22,061. Do you ever charge a 1d. for a very small lamb?—No, sometimes we leave them off free.

22,062. What is the charge on heifers?—4d. each.

22,063. On calves?—4d. each. We only charge 2d. in the crib, that is since the establishment of the weekly market for all fat calves sold in cribs.

22,064. On pigs?—2d. each.

22,065. What would you charge on a bullock?—4d.

22,066. It is 2d. on pigs irrespective of weight or size or age?—Yes.

22,067. On fowl?—4d. a load and 1d. per basket.

22,068. On goats?—A 1d. each.

22,069. What charge would you demand on donkeys?—I never got paid for a donkey.

22,070. What is the charge you would levy?—Really I could not say, because I never had occasion to charge.

22,071. If they were brought in the usual fair day and sold, would you demand a charge?—We never take any notice of them.

22,072. Now are the charges you have mentioned only on the different animals that are actually sold?—That is all. If they are not sold they would not be charged.

22,073. Is the charge of 4d. on fowl a standing charge?—We take the toll for the fowl on entering.

22,074. You call that a standing charge. Is it a liberty to call on the public thoroughfare?—It

immaterial to us whether they are sold or not, but on all others if they are not bought we do not charge.

22,075. You have no rule compelling them to go to the fair green?—No.

22,076. They can go there if they please?—As a general rule all pigs go to the fair green.

22,077. If they brought in a number of bonhams in a cart what would you charge on the cartload, or would you charge on entrance?—No charge on entrance.

22,078. If they brought in a cart containing 10 bonhams into the fair green and sold them, what would you charge?—Charge 2d. a pig for the 10.

22,079. Then you have to rely on the truthfulness of the statement as to whether they are sold or not?—First of all we see whether they are marked or not.

22,080. Is it always the buyer who pays the charge?—No, but the seller when going out.

22,081. Is he in possession of the animal?—He is.

22,082. Always?—As a general rule, he is.

22,083. You say the buyers mark the cattle?—Yes.

22,084. Has not the contract been completed between the buyer and the seller when the sale is effected?—The contract is made, but the seller is taking them to the yard.

22,085. The buyer asks the seller to convey them to the yard?—Yes.

22,086. Supposing it was on one of the streets here they sold a head of cattle, where would you collect the toll on that head of cattle?—On the bridge down street, and on several roads leading into the town.

22,087. That is when they are coming out of the town?—Yes, when coming out we challenge them.

22,088. Supposing a man living in the town went out to the fair, and bought a head of cattle, and put the animal into his own yard?—They escape our notice, and we could not charge.

22,089. If you were made aware of it, you would charge?—I would.

22,090. Have cases of that kind occurred?—No; very seldom, except for pigs. Then if the shopkeepers of the town bought pigs, and took them into the yards, there would be a man go round and challenge them, and get paid for them.

22,091. On goats you charge a 1d. each?—Yes.

22,092. Where are they sold?—On the streets.

22,093. Are there different streets allotted off for the exposure of each species of animal?—No.

22,094. Do they all intermix?—Yes.

22,095. Have you ever heard that accidents happened from the fact that the fairs have been held in the public thoroughfare?—No.

22,096. How many custom gaps have you?—We have five.

22,097. Is this fair green enclosed for the Bantry fairs?—Yes.

22,098. Is there a stone wall around it?—There is a stone ditch.

22,099. Could you give me any approximate idea of the extent of it?—I think it must be very close on an acre.

22,100. Would you say that the reason they do not expose animals there, is because the space is not adequate?—I could not answer that. As long as I remember they were always on the street.

22,101. Supposing on a fair day all the animals were brought into that fair green, would the fair green be sufficiently large?—Very hardly. I do not think it would.

22,102. Would you assign that as a reason for their going down the streets?—I could not say that is the reason.

22,103. You have a pig fair here the day previous to the ordinary fairs?—Yes.

22,104. Is there a pig fair the day previous to the ordinary fairs at which no tolls are levied?—No.

22,105. There is only a pig fair the day previous to the cattle fairs at which you levy tolls?—That is all.

22,106. There is no one previous to the 12th January and 12th March?—No.

22,107. What is the extent of the Masseytown fair green?—Something about three acres. It is double the size of the other.

22,108. Is it enclosed?—It is.

22,109. Are these fair greens utilised in any way between fairs?—Yes, supposing a circus came to town.

22,110. Does grass grow on it?—It is a common like.

22,111. Do the public utilise it at all between fairs?—The road contractor uses it in a sense and takes a lot of materials in there.

22,112. Have the public acquired rights over it?—I do not think they have.

22,113. Have you two gates to it?—There are no gates to the Masseytown fair or to Macroom.

22,114. Your custom gaps are at the outlets to the town?—Yes.

22,115. Supposing a farmer was bringing his cattle in, and on the road coming into the fair he met a buyer and effected a sale of his animal, would you collect a charge in that case outside the custom gap if it came to your knowledge?—I cannot say.

22,116. Did a case of that arise?—No.

22,117. If a case arose would you charge?—If the cattle were sold in any part of the town I would charge.

22,118. When you say in the town do you mean within the custom gaps?—No, because the custom gaps are in the middle of the town; there are streets outside the custom gaps.

22,119. Supposing it was a trader in the town went out and met a farmer coming in on the road outside the custom gap, and told him to deliver the animal to his yard in Macroom on a fair day, would you charge?—I would charge because the custom gaps are near the centre of the town.

22,120. Are there houses beyond the custom gaps?—There are streets beyond.

22,121. Supposing at the Masseytown fairs some of the animals were sold in the streets of Macroom and exposed there, would you charge?—If I was aware of it I would.

22,122. Is the practice always for those attending Masseytown fairs to go to Masseytown and for the Macroom fairs to come to Macroom?—Yes.

22,123. What is the street principally in Macroom that they stand on?—In the square.

22,124. And in Masseytown?—The field in a great measure and the entrance to it.

22,125. The field, that is the fair green?—Yes, and the streets around.

22,126. Is the fair green convenient to the square in Macroom?—It is next to the railway just.

22,127. Where is the square?—The square is a large portion of the town at the top of the hill.

22,128. Is not that some distance from the fair green?—It is about 300 yards. On a fair day the fair goes down as far as the fair green.

22,129. That is in the intervening streets?—Yes.

22,130. Are there any of the toll collectors here?—Yes.

22,131. How many do you have at each gap?—On a fair day about 17 entirely.

22,132. How are these men paid?—2s. per day.

22,133. Who else is engaged in connection with the fairs besides these toll collectors?—I do not know of anybody. I take charge of the whole lot.

22,134. Have you one man at each gap solely for the purpose of receiving money?—At the outside gaps I have two men.

22,135. Do they always inquire whether a man has bought or sold?—Yes.

22,136. Supposing the answer is that the animal has not been bought or sold and they know it is a falsehood and that the animal was sold, what course do they adopt?—As a general rule they clear them out by giving their hand and word.

22,137. Do your men produce any book or paper?—No. They only catch them by the right hand and say, "On your word, is the cattle sold to-day by you or "anybody else." If they say "No" they pass out.

22,138. Did they ever find that that practice in any way made a man alter the statement?—Many times they clear them out, and get paid afterwards.

22,139. Did the catching of the man's hand amount to an affirmation, and did it ever make a man alter his statement?—Yes, often.

22,140. Have you ever known them to refuse payment of the toll on account of no toll board being erected?—I heard a few complaining.

22,141. Did they ever refuse paying at all?—They paid afterwards, but I heard a few asking before for the toll board, and went away and paid afterwards.

22,142. Did you leave them out?—They paid afterwards.

22,143. When they refused payment of the tolls, did you distrain the animal, or retain the animal for any lengthened period?—We often kept an animal inside until they would pay. They would say they had not the money, but we would keep them inside until they had the money.

22,144. How long would you detain them?—Not ten minutes.

22,145. Have you ever seized any marketable commodities, such as fish or fowl?—When the toll collectors ask a 1d. for a basket of fowl, they stand for a time disputing, and then in the end they pay it.

22,146. What is the longest period for which a woman would be detained in that way?—I have never seen them kept more than five or ten minutes at the most.

22,147. That is on entry to the town?—Yes.

22,148. You always levy the charge on entry to the town?—Yes.

22,149. If they had not the money, what course would you adopt?—We then take their word and get paid during the day.

22,150. You never seized on the fowl?—We keep themselves and the basket together.

22,151. Would you ever take possession of the fowl until they would return, having got the loan of the penny?—No.

22,152. Have they ever complained that you have detained the fowl for any period that made them unable to make a ready sale of the fowl?—No. I never heard them complaining of that.

22,153. Do you ever weigh any cattle at this weighbridge?—Not one.

22,154. Where is it situated?—There is one erected at the entrance to the fair green of Massytown, and the other one in Castle Street, inside Lord Bantry's gate entrance.

22,155. You get no rent from the stalls you referred to?—No. There is a charge of a ½d. from two milk women.

22,156. Then the milk is sold inside there?—Yes. They are milk stalls.

22,157. You only charge a 1d. per churn?—Yes.

22,158. You charge nothing additional for standing?—No.

22,159. Do you make up Mrs. Harding's accounts?—Yes, but the books were taken from me over a month.

22,160. You say you have one man employed to walk around the market?—Yes.

22,161. What is his name?—Andrew Kelliher.

22,162. What are his duties?—To take the toll on potatoes, lump butter, and any apples or cabbage.

22,163. Who else have you?—I have two men employed for Thursday, one to collect on calves, and one to weigh butter on number two scales. Mr. Reardon attends to number two scales.

22,164. Have you anybody additional on Saturday?—No.

22,165. Have the women who bring in baskets of apples to pay 1d. per basket?—Yes, but they never come in baskets, only loads, and there might be six or seven baskets in the load.

22,166. Do people bring in baskets of apples who have not stalls?—Yes, and sell them to the parties who have the stalls.

22,167. I saw two piles of apples on the road, were these belonging to the people who have the stalls?—They were not. They have standing of their own. They stand on the ground and leave the barrel at night.

22,168. What do these people pay?—3d. a week.

22,169-70. For putting their apples on the public thoroughfare?—Yes. We call them standings.

22,171. Do they cover these apples?—They cover them at night.

22,172. Are there any stalls around the town they would take?—No.

ANDREW KELLIHER examined.

22,173. You collect the charges on butter?—Yes.

22,174. Did they ever bring in about 4 lbs. of butter?—Yes, very often.

22,175. Did they ever bring 2 lbs. or 3 lbs?—Yes.

22,176. Did they ever come with 1 lb. of butter?—I could not say.

22,177. They have brought 3 lbs.?—Yes. 6 lbs. and 3 lbs., and it runs up to 20 lbs.

22,178. On that 3 lbs. you would charge a 1d.?—I would charge a 1d. if I only saw a ½ lb.

22,179. Did you ever charge on a ½ lb.?—No.

22,180. What would be the value or selling price of the 3 lbs. they bring in?—They generally get 11d. and a 1s. per pound.

22,181. You levy the same charge on 2 lbs. as on 20 lbs.?—The very same.

Captain MILLER, Receiver, examined.

22,182. Are you connected with Lord Bantry's estate?—I am receiver in the Court of Chancery on the Massy estate.

22,183. So far as you are aware, there has not been any direct contribution made by the owners of the Massytown fairs and markets towards the cleaning of the streets?—No.

22,184. Other than the contribution to the rates?—Yes.

22,185. The owners are minors at present?—Yes.

Mr. JOHN McCARTHY examined.

22,186. You produce two documents?—There are two accounts showing the gross receipts and expenditure for the two years ending the 31st December 1886 and the other ending the 31st December 1887 for Macroom only.

22,187. For Macroom fairs and markets?—Yes. I was not told anything about Massytown, or I did not bring them out.

22,188. You could get them?—Not to-day.

22,189. Could you give me any idea of what they are?—The Macroom accounts are there, and the Massytown would be the same. The last items in the account produced ought to be divided between Massytown and Macroom.

22,190. Here you have the tolls collected at the Macroom fairs and the weekly markets, but you have the expenses incurred in collecting tolls on both Macroom and Massytown and the markets?—The expenses of the fairs are deducted from the proceeds after the fairs.

22,191. Has Mr. Reardon any duties to perform at the Massytown fairs?—No.

22,192. Out of the receipts Mrs. Harding pays 100*l.* rent to Mr. Massy, and 150*l.* to Lord Bantry?—Yes.

22,193. What duties do you perform in connexion with these?—Nothing at all except check the accounts.

22,194. You can give me the particulars of the receipts and expenditure on Massytown?—I cannot now, but the receipt would be about the same as the Macroom fairs, less 100*l.* rent.

22,195. What check have you on the men who collect the tolls at the fairs?—No check. There are two men at each gap, and six or eight men at the principal gap.

22,196. One man acts as a check on the other?—Yes.

22,197. You have no active duties to perform in connexion with the markets and fairs other than keep the [illegible] [illegible]

minority?—No, I do not live in Macroom at all. One remark Mrs. Harding told me to make is that there has been no change in the charges for the last 60 years.

22,198. Have you known the fairs for any length of time?—I do not know them at all. I only know what I got from the books, or what Mrs. Harding told me.

22,199. She saw the schedule of queries?—Yes. She sent it to her law agent. She does not know anything about the matter.

22,200. The only expense Mrs. Harding has been at is the rent and the salaries?—Yes.

22,201. Neither she nor the owners of the fairs or markets contribute anything towards the cleansing of streets where the fairs and markets are held?—No, but I asked the question, and I was told there was a competition among the people to get the sweeping as manure.

22,202. The people themselves from the benefit they derive from the manure keep the streets clean?—Yes, that is what I was told.

22,203. Were any representations ever made to either of the owners or to Mrs. Harding to provide a sufficiently large fair green for the removal of the fairs off the street?—Mrs. Harding told me that the fair green in Macroom was provided at the request of the towns-people some time ago, and notwithstanding the field was provided the people would prefer using the streets, and the shopkeepers would prefer having the animals on the streets to keep custom near their establishments. I was told that.

22,204. By whom?—By Mrs. Harding.

22,205. Mrs. Harding has been at no expense in connexion with them in improvement or repairs for the last couple of years with the exception of providing the two weighbridges?—That is the only expenditure.

22,206. Have any scales been provided by the owners or Mrs. Harding?—Mrs. Harding provided a scales lately.

22,207. Did the owners provide anything but the fair green?—Lord Bantry built the market house.

22,208. Who built the market shed?—That is part of the market house, and that market house was built a long time ago by Mr. Beveridge, who demised his estates to Lord Bantry.

22,209. It was provided by the owner?—Yes.

22,210. It is not sufficiently large for people to expose perishable commodities in such as butter?—These sheds are the only place. They are roofed in.

22,211. Did you ever hear that any representations were made to her, or from the owners to her, to provide a proper market house and enclosed space for the protection of commodities brought in?—I do not think any representation of the kind was made. I may say, on my own knowledge, if it was it would not be used. I was in Kanturk where there is a splendid market provided by Lord Egmont, and the people would not use it.

[The following is a copy of the accounts handed in by the foregoing witness]:—

					£	s.	d.
1886. Dec. 31.	Gross receipts on Macroom fairs				178	11	7
	Gross earnings of weekly tolls				194	16	7
					373	8	2
	Charges.	£	s.	d.			
	Rent	160	0	0			
	Salaries. Ty. Sheehan	40	0	0			
	Dl. Kelleher	[illegible]	0	0			
	Ty. Riordan	16	0	0			
	Assistants	41	10	9			
	Police tax and income tax deducted	14	15	2			
	Hire at fairs, &c.	4	0	0			
	Income tax	2	16	0			
	Dl. Kelleher, extra	6	0	0			
					320	16	2
					46	12	0
	Macroom fairs, about	173	11	7			
	Rent	100	0	0			
					73	11	7

					£	s.	d.
1887. Dec. 31.	Gross receipts Macroom fairs				168	9	8
	Gross weekly tolls				174	12	8½
					343	1	4½
	Charges.	£	s.	d.			
	Rent	160	0	0			
	Salaries, Ty. Sheehan (11 months)	34	3	4			
	Dl. Kelleher	25	10	0			
	Ty. Riordan	10	0	0			
	Assistants	47	8	0½			
	Powell's account	14	4	9			
	Taxes	21	6	5			
					328	11	9½
					14	9	7
	Macroom fairs, about	168	9	8			
	Rent	100	0	0			
					68	9	8
					53	19	8

TIMOTHY RIORDAN examined.

22,212. You are connected with the butter market?—Only one day in the week.

22,213. It is all lump butter?—Yes, fresh butter.

22,214. Firkins are never brought in?—They were at one time, but it was a failure. I remember nearly 1,000 firkins came one day and the buyers did not attend and they had to take it home again.

22,215. What was the charge on the firkin at that time?—I was not the person collecting the tolls, but it was 3d. a firkin, I believe. They had to take their butter home when the buyers did not attend.

22,216. No firkins are brought in now at all?—Not from that day, I believe.

22,217. Does that shed afford sufficient space to expose lump butter for sale?—It does. The buyers are well pleased and so are the sellers.

22,218. It is all weighed before it is bought?—Yes, and the ticket issued.

22,219. You have no tasters employed?—No. The buyers themselves are tasters.

22,220. They rely on their own experience?—Yes. They buy the butter on its merits.

22,221. When weighing this lump butter do you always give a ticket denoting the weight?—Yes.

22,222. Is this the ticket you give?—Yes.

22,223. Witness produced the ticket, of which the following is a copy:—

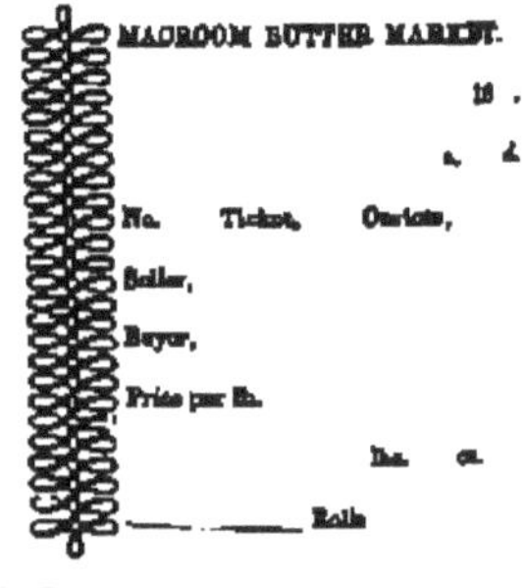
MACROOM BUTTER MARKET.

18 .

s. d.

No. Ticket, Owriate,

Seller,

Buyer,

Price per lb.

lbs. oz.

__________ Rolls

22,224. You put the weight down here?—Yes, the weight and the name.

22,225. Did you ever keep an account of the quantity brought in during the day?—No, I was not so curious as to tot up the whole amount.

22,225a. If it was required you could give the quantity brought in?—I have a block of the name of the seller and a block of the number of pounds and the number of the tickets.

22,226. And the price per pound?—We have nothing to do with the price per pound.

22,227. I see it marked on the ticket, but you never ascertain it?—You could not ascertain it from the buyers. Sometimes it is the highest price all round, and then they buy inferior butter for a less price.

22,228. In weighing butter, what is the lowest weight you put into the scales?—A quarter of a pound is the lowest.

22,229. So then it must be a quarter of a pound, or nothing?—Yes.

22,230. If they had only 2 lbs., or a small roll of about 2 lbs. 4 ozs. actual weight, what would you denote on the ticket?—2 lbs. 4 ozs., 4 ozs., 8 ozs., 12 ozs., and then 1 lb.

22,231. If the actual weight of it was 2 lbs. 2 ozs., would you put that down?—I would not put down the 2 ozs.

22,232. You would put it down as 2 lbs.?—Yes.

22,233. Are there any other deductions?—No. I do not know I ever remember weighing 2 lbs.

22,234. Supposing it was 5 lbs. 2 ozs., would you only put down the 5 lbs.?—Only 5 lbs.

22,235. Is there any deduction from the gross weight for anything?—No.

22,236. Supposing in warm weather it clings to the scales?—After each roll is weighed there is a man with a knife and he cleans the scale and anything he gets on it is waste butter.

22,237. I suppose the weight of that quantity would be so small it would not be worth taking into consideration?—It would not be worth signifying, but in order that every buyer should get the benefit it is cleaned every time. I think it would be well to state other matters in connection with this market. Take for instance the fish market. In warm weather it is a regular nuisance. The remnants of the fish remain on the street, and it is very dangerous to health. There are no sheds erected that could be got, and I often heard remarks from parties passing by that it is very dangerous to health. In warm weather there is a stench, and I often heard the apple women complaining that they had no sheds. These are the people in the butts, but connected with the market. They are used as a resort for town and country, and something should be done to effect a remedy in that direction.

22,238. You are referring now to butts?—Yes. Something should be done of them or they should be built in a better way from the footpath leading to the public market.

22,239. Are you in trade in the town?—Yes.

22,240. What trade?—The grocery and spirit business.

22,241. You have an opportunity of ascertaining the opinions of the people who frequent the markets and fairs here?—Yes.

22,242. Do you think from your own experience that there is a necessity existing in Macroom for a properly enclosed and sufficiently large market place for all the commodities brought in?—As far as the market is concerned it is a very good one, but I think the accommodation is not sufficient; that is, it is not large enough for the whole market. There should be something additional built; for instance, sheds should be built in some direction, I do not know where. An engineer is the best judge of those things, and have those sheds locked up at night and not have the owners of the stalls remain on the street during the night using large sugar barrels as sleeping apartments and to protect their goods.

22,243. People have to sleep on the public thoroughfare?—Yes, because apples are perishable, and if they were removed or shifted they would get damaged and battered and injured. They remain on the streets three months of the year, as you can see yourself passing by, with heaps of apples, and if these were removed for the night they would get battered and injured, and it would be very injurious to the apples themselves.

22,244. Are the people who sleep out those who rent the butts?—They are people about the town. Two of them sleep inside in those large sugar barrels.

22,245. Have the police taken any steps to remove them?—I never heard they did.

22,246. Are they acquainted with this practice?—They see it, whether they take notice of it or not. During the day they use the sugar barrels as a protection from the inclemency of the weather.

22,247. Is that for the purpose of not going to the expense of paying for lodgings or only to be in immediate proximity to their goods?—Yes, for fear they may be stolen.

22,248. Could they not remove their stock to a store?—Yes, but, as I have stated, they consider their apples would be injured by being removed. They put their apples there for their own accommodation and business. There is nothing compulsory on them.

22,249. You state from your knowledge it would injure their stock if they were constantly removing from place to place?—Yes.

22,250. Supposing proper storage accommodation was provided there on that very spot would they be willing to pay anything in return?—I could not say that.

22,251. Do you think for what they are paying at present some accommodation should be given to them?—Yes. Even some of them tell me they would be satisfied to pay so much a week for accommodation.

22,252. These people have complained to you?—Yes. I was speaking to them on the matter, and they have complained that they have no sheds.

22,253. Are there some of them here?—None of them here.

22,254. Did they ask you to mention this fact?—They did not.

22,255. You only mention it yourself?—Yes. Mrs. Harding has nothing to do with that. She is only lessee of the tolls, and has nothing to do in that direction I should think.

22,256. Still you are of opinion that if these people pay a charge they should get some return other than the liberty of exposing their commodities on the public thoroughfare?—I do not know that.

22,257. You have formed no opinion on that?—No.

22,258. Have you anything else to say?—No.

TIMOTHY HEALY examined.

22,259. What are your duties in connection with the market?—Weighing corn and potatoes and butter on Thursdays and Saturdays.

22,260. Is all corn sold before it is weighed?—It is.

22,261. Where do they expose it for sale?—On the market and street coming into the town.

22,262. What portion of the place?—In the centre of the square.

22,263. That is out on the public thoroughfare?—Yes.

22,264. Do they put the bags on the ground?—No, they keep them in the carts.

22,265. When they have effected a sale they come to you to weigh?—Yes.

22,266. When weighing, do you give a ticket?—No. The clerk gives it. I send the weight to the clerk, and he gives the ticket.

22,267. You have only to perform the manual work of weighing, and the clerk fills up the tickets?—Yes.

22,268. In weighing corn, what is the lowest weight you weigh down to?—Four, 7, and 14 lbs.

22,269. You never put a smaller weight in the scale than 4 lbs.?—We put 2 lbs.

22,270. Is it necessary to put 2 lbs.?—It is when required.

22,271. It must be 2 lbs. or nothing?—The fall of the beam goes to the buyers.

22,272. You give the benefit of a cast to the buyer?—Yes.

22,273. You do not weigh the empty sack?—For some parties I do and for others I do not. Some allow 4 lbs. off for the empty sack.

22,274. You estimate the tare of the sack?—Yes.

22,275. Do you generally weigh them, or only when a dispute arises?—I weigh everything a man would ask me. I get 1d. a sack. I have to employ a man along with myself, and sometimes two men. I call the weights and turn the scales. The other man I employ brings in the bags and takes them out, and I give them a hand to load and unload.

22,276. These are the porters?—Yes.

22,277. You employ them?—Yes, but in obliging them I am paid by the countrymen for these men.

22,278. You are the representative of Mrs. Harding?—Yes. I am only just appointed weighmaster. I am paid every Tuesday for weighing butter. When I find the country-people have not enough of help, I employ three men and charge so much, and with that pay them in the evening.

22,279. It is only the weighing charge of 1d. goes to Mrs. Harding?—Yes.

22,280. But if the farmers have not sufficient help they ask you to employ some of the porters and you employ them?—Yes.

22,281. What do you charge?—6d. a load or 4d. a load. I weigh different loads I get nothing out of.

22,282. How do you pay these men, or do you make a profit yourself?—That is according to the work we would have during the day.

22,283. Do you make a profit out of the transaction?—There are only two months in the year we charge anything.

22,284. Would you weigh corn if they did not employ a porter?—I would not. They would want to employ three men.

22,285. You make them have three men to load and unload?—The men are there.

22,286. Supposing a farmer came and said he was quite competent to weigh it, would you give him all the trouble possible in order that he would employ two more men?—I would give him no hand at all.

22,287. Have they ever adopted that course of loading and unloading themselves?—No.

22,288. Have you ever heard complaints that delay has been caused, and that they have not been rendered sufficient assistance?—I would hear some of them talk and more of them would not.

22,289. Practically, on every load of corn that is brought in they have to pay porter's charge and the weighing charge?—They have to pay a 1d. a bag for the ticket.

22,290. And the porter's charge as well?—Yes.

22,291. That is 6d. a load?—Yes; whatever they might give.

22,292. They never give less than 6d.?—I often weighed 40 bags and not got a 1d.

22,293. If you employ porters to load and unload you never got less than 6d.?—I often got 4d. only, and a 1d. a bag from some and 6d.

22,294. Do the same observations apply to the weighing of potatoes?—Yes.

22,295. Porters must be employed?—Yes, at the big scales, but at the small scales they are not required. The people can do it themselves.

22,296. But if they bring a load of potatoes in sacks, the porters must be employed, and the same observations apply as to the corn?—Yes.

22,297. What is the smallest weight put in the scales? Do you weigh a half stone?—No; there is a small scales for potatoes.

22,298. Do you know the practice of weighing?—Yes. If a bag is weighed on the big scales we weigh down to 8 lbs. Any small weights go to the small scales. Then I call out the weight to the man in the office, who can see the scales himself.

22,299. He denotes the weight on the ticket?—Yes.

22,300. Tickets are given for corn and potatoes?—Yes.

22,301. Do you ever mark the weight of a sack of potatoes on it with chalk?—Never.

22,302. You always keep a block of the ticket?—Yes.

22,303. In return for the ticket you get the 1d.?—Yes.

22,304. Do you ever weigh the empty sack?—As a rule 4 lbs. are allowed for potatoes and 3 lbs. for the sack of corn. I seldom weigh the empty sack.

22,305. That is in case of dispute?—Yes.

22,306. Would that additional tare be the same on a fine day as on a very wet day?—No.

22,307. What additional tare would you allow on a day like that?—On a wet day they generally allow 4 or 5 lbs.

22,308. Do you keep any record of the number of bags brought in each day?—Yes.

22,309. Did you ever make up the total for each month?—No; it is a monthly account.

22,310. Do you keep an account of the number brought in each month?—Yes, what is brought in each day.

22,311. If a return was required of the quantity of the different marketable commodities brought into Macroom, and the current prices, could such a return be made out?—Yes.

22,312. Is it possible to make such a return?—It is possible.

22,313. Do you think the return would be a pretty accurate one?—I think it would.

Mr. John McCarthy re-examined.

22,314. (Witness.) I wish to make a remark about Mr. Riordan's evidence. He said applewomen and others wish for some sheds for their protection. It would be easy for them to get house accommodation, but what they wish is that protection should be made on the spot they now occupy. They take up the space because they consider it the best possible position for the sale of their goods. If other accommodation were provided they should pay for it, and they would be as badly off then. If they wanted protection they could easily get houses about the town.

22,315. What return do they get for the charge they already paid?—Liberty to sell.

22,316. On the public thoroughfare?—Yes. If the owners went to the [illegible] of providing accommodation, as I see elsewhere, it would not be used.

Mr. Cornelius Cronin examined.

22,317. What remarks do you wish to make?—I came here as a tenant farmer to make some observations. As regards the accommodation for the weighing of corn and potatoes the accommodation is very bad in the town of Macroom. For instance in the months of February and March there may be about 400 horse loads of corn and potatoes in the town, and only one set of scales erected to weigh that lot. I often saw the scales at work in the morning from 7 o'clock until nightfall, and the crowd fighting and quarrelling, and I often saw a row over the scales. I often had to wait four or five hours, having my load sold, and could not get it weighed, and then in the end had to give up a load of potatoes in order not to be waiting any longer. As regards the charge we pay of a 1d. a sack for weighing corn and potatoes. I may have my own two men, and often had to put in and out the sacks to the scales, and the weighmaster often refused to weigh them unless paid a 1d. a sack himself in addition to the 1d. a sack I would have to pay for the ticket, and if I refused to pay he would not weigh for me. I was one day, and I got my load weighed, and after weighing refused to pay the weighmaster. He demanded 8d. for eight sacks, and I refused to pay, and he threatened to beat me, and for three months after that coming into the town of Macroom I was subject to abuse. I thought a 1d. a sack enough to pay, and I thought it the duty of the owners, or Mrs. Harding, to provide a weighmaster and weigh free of charge. There is a smaller scale erected where they weigh weights and half weights, and there is one or two in charge of it. If I send in potatoes in a bulk, not in sacks, I am charged 2d., 3d., or 4d. for the weighing, and the woman in charge against my consent would be taking the potatoes out herself. She may have a weight, but a weight or three-quarters of a weight. I heard while ago there was a weighbridge in the market. I do not see it, and never did see it. I think there ought to be a second set of scales erected, one for the [illegible] of corn and the other for the weighing of potatoes. As regards the Macroom fair, it is a very bad fair field, and could not be worse. There is a large stream of water running through it, and if the night happened to be wet there might be water running over it for a foot and a half deep and your clothes bespattered, and covered with mud, and from the Masseytown bridge into the fair would be four tons of sheep, cattle, and pigs, and other goods, and perhaps you could not move for an hour. The cattle going into the fair pass by lane it, and the cattle coming out sold have to come down, and it is very far away from the station. Tolls have been taken for that Masseytown fair outside Masseytown, at the end of it; and if cattle were sold at the other side of the town they would have to pay for them outside Masseytown, where the patent is held for. I think the customs they charge is entirely too great. I often sold in that fair a crowd or crib of slips, small pigs or bonhams, 10, 12, and often 13 in number, and had to pay 2d. for each bonham, which I think is entirely too much. They charge 6d. each for cattle, and for suckling calves, seven, eight, nine, or twelve months old they charge 6d. a piece, which is entirely too much to my mind. They charge for sheep a 1d. each, and if there are a pair of lambs, or three lambs with that sheep, two months or three months old, they charge a 1d. each for them, and I had to pay it to carry them out free. And as for the accommodation provided here in the town for the fairs, I say it is very poor accommodation. The crate of slips coming into the fair the cattle fair day are quite enough to fill the fair field. The town is no quiet place to hold the fair. It is a dangerous place for anybody to pass in. There ought to be a proper fair green erected quite close to the town and quite close to the railway station.

22,318. Which are you speaking of?—Macroom. I think Macroom is the more suitable place of the two to hold the fair in. It is quite close to the train. I do not know I have any more to add.

22,319. What occupation have you?—I am a tenant farmer resorting this fair every fair day.

22,320. What district do you live in?—I live within 3 miles of the town of Kilmichael.

22,321. You came that distance to-day?—I did for the improvement of the condition of the fairs.

22,322. Have you consulted the neighbouring farmers?—I have not consulted any of them as to coming here, but at different times we have been talking for the last five or ten years and continually grumbling.

22,323. Are there any gentlemen here who would corroborate any statement as to the charges or what you have suggested yourself?—There is a tenant farmer from the same parish. He lives here. I know plenty from my parish, hundreds who could bear me out in the same statement if there was a need.

22,324. You state that the scales provided for weighing corn is not sufficient?—Certainly they are not for certain parts of the year.

22,325. Has any undue delay been caused during the season?—I often had to wait for four or five hours. Some six or eight years ago when I was young and spirit in me I would fight my way, but latterly I would rather wait a whole day than go quarrelling. It is a regular fighting affair to get at the scales.

22,326. You state that you have been compelled or rather put to much inconvenience by paying this pal[t]rage charge?—Certainly.

22,327. Have the other farmers complained of that?—Several.

22,328. Did Mr. Murphy complain to you?—One man would come up and tell him he would pay and the other man would say he would pay and he would keep me back.

22,329. Although you were in the market previous to him?—Yes.

22,330. Corn is sold before it is weighed?—Yes.

22,331. Did you ever know because of any delay caused in that way that the buyer has refused to complete his contract and take the corn?—I often saw the buyer grumbling at waiting, and as a general rule when we sell the corn we have to give 2s. 6d., or 3s. or 4s. in order to make the bargain binding, and then the buyer would have to wait.

22,332. Is it practically to get some money in your pocket?—It is the practice sometimes, and sometimes it is not if I know the man or had confidence in him, but if a stranger bought my commodity I would require it.

22,333. You consider 2d. on bonhams an excessive charge?—It is a monstrous charge.

22,334. What was the smallest amount you ever received from a bonham on which you had to pay 2d. charge?—The price is generally from 12s. to 25s., or 3l.

22,335. Was it ever under 12s.?—I have not sold any.

22,336. Have you ever known them to be sold under that?—I have.

22,337. For what?—I have seen them sold for 10s. They may be under but I did not see them. I sold 13 at a 2l. a piece and had to pay 2d. for each. I count that an excessive charge.

22,338. That is a charge at the fair green?—Yes.

22,339. This fair green is not commandeered for Lord Bantry's fairs?—Where the slips stand at the upper portion above the stream it is quite hard, but the approach to it in frosty weather is very dangerous. There is a rise in the ground and a horse of mine fell there one day in frosty weather.

22,340. Are pigs brought on the Masseytown fair green too?—Yes. Slips are brought both days, but the fat pigs are brought the day previous.

22,341. Is that Masseytown green suitable?—No.

22,342. What is your objection?—It is not level. It is a very narrow field; however, it is not all the bad.

22,343. It is on the side of a cliff?—Yes.

22,344. Is there any boundary wall around it for the protection of the animals brought there?—No. It is an open field.

22,345. Is it the consensus of opinion among the farmers that the proper place to hold fairs is in a fair green properly enclosed and levelled?—I say a large field ought to be provided quite close to the railway station. There is a beautiful plain near the railway station and a green ought to be provided there. Most of the cattle go by train and there is a lane way leading from the bridge to the Masseytown fair field, and only the police clear the place people could never pass up or down there. With the people coming out there is a regular block in the passage which causes an amount of delay.

22,346. Is there a system of luck-penny in existence here?—Yes.

22,347. On cattle is there any fixed amount payable by the seller to the buyer, or is it only left to the disposition of the seller himself?—It is not a fixed thing but it is much the same as compulsory. They would be quarrelling and arguing over it.

22,348. Something has to be given, but as to the amount it is left to the disposition or liberality of the seller?—It is a general rule laid down to give 1s. a head on cattle.

22,349. Is there any fixed luck-penny on pigs?—Yes. Formerly it was 2d. and it has risen to 4d., and that with the 2d. custom makes the amount 6d. that is lost to the seller.

22,350. Is the seller or the buyer who pays the charge on pigs?—The seller.

22,351. Then practically in nine cases out of ten the possession of the animal is retained by the seller until the custom is paid?—I do not understand.

22,352. When passing the custom gaps is not it the individual who has possession of the animal who pays the toll?—Certainly, because it would be a hard job for the buyer to retain them all. He (the buyer) gets the different sellers to drive them to the auction-house or yard, and driving them through the custom gap they pay the custom.

22,353. You said the seller would be at 6d. of a loss?—Yes, in pigs.

22,354. How do you make that 6d.?—2d. custom at the custom gap, and 4d. a pig kept by the buyer.

22,355. Is that 6d. payable on bonhams?—2d. is the luck-penny on a bonham and 2d. custom.

22,356. Do the farmers, as a rule, object to the fairs being held on the public thoroughfares or streets of the town. Does it injure the animals brought there and exposed for sale?—I do not think so.

weight and tare the scales. The other men I employ bring in the bags and take them out, and I give them a hand to load and unload.

22,276. These are the porters?—Yes.

22,277. You employ them?—Yes, but to oblige them I am paid by the countrymen for these men.

22,278. You are the representative of Mrs. *Harding*?—Yes. I am only just appointed weighmaster. I am paid every Thursday for weighing butter. When I find the country people have not enough of help, I employ three men and charge so much, and will then pay them in the evening.

22,279. It is only the weighing charge of 1d. goes to Mrs. Harding?—Yes.

22,280. But if the farmers have not sufficient help they ask you to employ some of the porters and you employ them?—Yes.

22,281. What do you charge?—6d. a load or 4d. a load. I weigh different loads I get nothing out of.

22,282. How do you pay these men, or do you make a profit yourself?—That is according to the work we would have during the day.

22,283. Do you make a profit out of the transaction?—There are only two months in the year we charge anything.

22,284. Would you weigh corn if they did not employ a porter?—I would not. They would want to employ three men.

22,285. You make them have three men to load and unload?—The men are there.

22,286. Supposing a farmer came and said he was quite competent to weigh in, would you give him all the trouble possible in order that he would employ two more men?—I would give him no hand at all.

22,287. Have they ever adopted that course of loading and unloading themselves?—No.

22,288. Have you ever heard complaints that delay has been caused, and that they have not been rendered sufficient assistance?—I would hear some of them talk and some of them would not.

22,289. Practically, on every load of corn that is brought in they have to pay porter's charge and the weighing charge?—They have to pay a 1d. a bag for the ticket.

22,290. And the porter's charge as well?—Yes.

22,291. That is 6d. a load?—Yes; whatever they might give.

22,292. They never give less than 6d.?—I often weighed 40 bags and not got a 1d.

22,293. If you employ porters to load and unload you never get less than 6d.?—I often got 4d. only, and a 1d. a bag from some and 6d.

22,294. Do the same observations apply to the weighing of potatoes?—Yes.

22,295. Porters must be employed?—Yes, at the big scales, but at the small scales they are not required. The people can do it themselves.

22,296. But if they bring a load of potatoes in sacks the porters must be employed, and the same observations apply as to the corn?—Yes.

22,297. What is the smallest weight put in the scales? Do you weigh a half stone?—No; there is a small scales for potatoes.

22,298. Do you know the practice of weighing?—Yes. If a bag is weighed on the big scales we weigh down to 2 lbs. Any small weights go to the small scales. Then I call out the weight to the man in the office, who can see the scales himself.

22,299. He denotes the weight on the ticket?—Yes.

22,300. Tickets are given for corn and potatoes?—Yes.

22,301. Do you ever mark the weight of a sack of potatoes on it with chalk?—Never.

22,302. You always keep a block of the ticket?—Yes.

22,303. In return for the ticket you get the 1d.?—Yes.

22,304. Do you ever weigh the empty sack?—As a rule 4 lbs. are allowed for potatoes and 2 lbs. for the sack of corn. I seldom weigh the empty sack.

22,305. That is in case of dispute?—Yes.

22,306. Would that estimated tare be the same on a fine day as on a very wet day?—No.

22,307. What additional tare would you allow on a day like that?—On a wet day they generally allow 4 or 5 lbs.

22,308. Do you keep any record of the number of bags brought in each day?—Yes.

22,309. Did you ever make up the total for each month?—No; it is a monthly account.

22,310. Do you keep an account of the number brought in each month?—Yes, what is brought in each day.

22,311. If a return was required of the quantity of the different marketable commodities brought into Macroom, and the current prices, could such a return be made out?—Yes.

22,312. Is it possible to make such a return?—It is possible.

22,313. Do you think the return would be a pretty accurate one?—I think it would.

Mr. JOHN MCCARTHY re-examined.

22,314. (*Witness.*) I wish to make a remark about Mr. Riordan's evidence. He said applewomen and others wish for some sheds for their protection. It would be easy for them to get house accommodation, but what they wish is that protection should be made on the spot they now occupy. They take up the space because they consider it the best possible position for the sale of their goods. If other accommodation were provided they should pay for it, and they would be as badly off then. If they wanted protection they could easily get houses about the town.

22,315. What return do they get for the charge they already paid?—Liberty to sell.

22,316. On the public thoroughfare?—Yes. If the owners went to the expense of providing accommodation, as I see elsewhere, it would not be used.

Mr. CORNELIUS CRONIN examined.

22,317. What remarks do you wish to make?—I came here as a tenant farmer to make some observations. As regards the accommodation for the weighing of corn and potatoes the accommodation is very bad in the town of Macroom. For instance in the months of February and March there may be about on 400 horse loads of corn and potatoes in the town, and only one set of scales erected to weigh that lot. I often saw the scales at work in the morning from 7 o'clock until nightfall, and the crowd fighting and quarrelling, and I often saw a row over the scales. I often had to wait four or five hours, having my load sold, and could not get it weighed, and then in the end had to guess to a load of potatoes in order not to be waiting any longer. As regards the charge we pay of a 1d. a sack for weighing corn and potatoes. I may have my own two men, and often had to put in and out the sacks to the scales, and the weighmaster often refused to weigh them unless paid a 1d. a sack himself in addition to the 1d. a sack I would have to pay for the ticket, and if I refused to pay he would not weigh for me. I was one day, and I got my load weighed, and after weighing refused to pay the weighmaster. He demanded 8d. for eight sacks, and I refused to pay, and he threatened to beat me, and for three months after that coming into the town of Macroom I was subject to abuse. I thought a 1d. a sack enough to pay, and I thought it the duty of the owners, or Mrs. Harding, to provide a weighmaster and weigh free of charge. There is a smaller scale erected where they weigh weights and half weights, and there is one or two in charge of it. If I send in potatoes in a bulk, not in sacks, I am charged 3d., 2d., or 4d. for the weighing, and the woman in charge against my consent would be taking the potatoes out herself. She may have a weight, half a weight or three-quarters of a weight. I heard while ago there was a weighbridge in the market. I do not see it, and never did see it. I think there ought to be a second set of scales erected, one for the use of corn and the other for the weighing of potatoes. As regards the Macroom fair, it is a very bad fair field, and could not be worse. There is a large stream of water running through it, and if the night happened to be wet there might be water running over it for a foot and a half deep and your clothes besmeared, and covered with mud, and from the Massytown bridge into the fair would be one mass of sheep, cattle, and pigs, and other goods, and perhaps you could not move for an hour. The cattle going into the fair pass by into it, and the cattle coming out could have to come down, and it is very far away from the station. Tolls have been taken for that Massytown fair outside Massytown, at the end of it, and if cattle were sold at the other side of the town they would have to pay for them outside Massytown, where the patent is held for. I think the customs they charge is entirely too great. I often sold in that fair a crowd or crib of slips, small pigs or bonhams, 10, 12, and often 15 in number, and had to pay 3d. for each bonham, which I think is entirely too much. They charge 6d. each for cattle, and for suckling calves, seven, eight, nine, or twelve months old they charge 6d. a piece, which is entirely too much to my mind. They charge for sheep a 1d. each, and if there are a pair of lambs, or three lambs with that sheep, two months or three months old, they charge a 1d. each for them, and I had to pay it to carry them out free. And as for the accommodation provided here in the town for the fairs, I say it is very poor accommodation. The crush of slips coming into the fair the cattle fair day are quite enough to fill the fair field. The town is an unfit place to hold the fair. It is a dangerous place for anybody to pass in. There ought to be a proper fair green erected quite close to the town and quite close to the railway station.

22,318. Which are you speaking of?—Macroom. I think Macroom is the more suitable place of the two to hold the fair in. It is quite close to the train. I do not know I have any more to add.

22,319. What occupation have you?—I am a tenant farmer resorting this fair every fair day.

22,320. What district do you live in?—I live within 5 miles of the town of Kilmichael.

22,321. You came that distance to-day?—I did for the improvement of the condition of the fairs.

22,322. Have you consulted the neighbouring farmers?—I have not consulted any of them as to coming here, but at different times we have been talking for the last five or ten years and continually grumbling.

22,323. Are there any gentlemen here who would corroborate any statement as to the charges or what you have suggested yourself?—There is a tenant farmer from the same parish. He lives here. I know plenty from my parish, hundreds who could bear me out in the same statement if there was a need.

22,324. You state that the scales provided for weighing corn is not sufficient?—Certainly they are not for certain parts of the year.

22,325. Has any undue delay been caused during the season?—I often had to wait for four or five hours. Some six or eight years ago when I was young and spirit in me I would fight my way, but latterly I would rather wait a whole day than go quarrelling. It is a regular fighting affair to get at the scales.

22,326. You state that you have been compelled or rather put to much inconvenience by paying this porterage charge?—Certainly.

22,327. Have the other farmers complained of that?—Several.

22,328. Did Mr. Murphy complain to you?—One man would come up and tell him he would pay and the other man would say he would pay and he would keep me back.

22,329. Although you were in the market previous to him?—Yes.

22,330. Corn is sold before it is weighed?—Yes.

22,331. Did you ever know instances of any delay caused in that way that the buyer has refused to complete his contract and take the corn?—I often saw the buyer grumbling at waiting, and as a general rule when we sell the corn we have to put 2s. 6d., or 5s. or 6s. in order to make the bargain binding, and then the buyer would have to wait.

22,332. Is it practically to get some money in part payment?—It is the practice sometimes, and sometimes it is not if I know the man or had confidence in him, but if a stranger bought my commodity I would require it.

22,333. You consider 3d. on bonhams an excessive charge?—It is a unreasonable charge.

22,334. What was the smallest amount you ever received from a bonham, on which you had to pay 3d. charge?—The price is generally from 12s. to 15s., or 9d.

22,335. Was it ever under 12s.?—I have not sold any.

22,336. Have you ever known them to be sold under that?—I have.

22,337. For what?—I have seen them sold for 10s. They may be under but I did not see them. I sold 12 at 11s. a piece and had to pay 3d. for each. I count that an excessive charge.

22,338. That is a charge at the fair green?—Yes.

22,339. This fair green is not recommended for Lord Bantry's fairs?—Where the slips stand, at the upper portion above the avenue it is quite hard, but the approach to it in frosty weather is very dangerous. There is a rise in the ground and a horse of mine fell there one day in frosty weather.

22,340. Are pigs brought to the Massytown fair green too?—Yes. Slips are brought both days, but the fat pigs are brought the day previous.

22,341. Is that Massytown green suitable?—No.

22,342. What is your objection?—It is not level. It is a very uneven field; however, it is not all that bad.

22,343. It is on the side of a cliff?—Yes.

22,344. Is there any boundary wall around it for the protection of the animals brought there?—No. It is an open field.

22,345. Is it the consensus of opinion among the farmers that the proper place to hold fairs is in a fair green, properly enclosed and levelled?—I say a large field ought to be provided quite close to the railway station. There is a beautiful plain near the railway station and a green ought to be provided there. Most of the cattle go by train and there is a lane way leading from the bridge to the Massytown fair field, and only the police clear the place people could never pass up or down there. With the people coming out there is a regular block in the passage which causes an amount of delay.

22,346. Is there a system of luck-penny in existence here?—Yes.

22,347. On cattle is there any fixed amount payable by the seller to the buyer, or is it only left to the disposition of the seller himself?—It is not a fixed thing but it is much the same as compulsory. They would be quarrelling and arguing over it.

22,348. Something has to be given, but as to the amount it is left to the disposition or liberality of the seller?—It is a general rule laid down to give 1s. a head on cattle.

22,349. Is there any fixed luck-penny on pigs?—Yes. Formerly it was 3d. and it has risen to 6d., and that with the 3d. custom makes the amount 9d. that is lost to the seller.

22,350. Is the seller or the buyer who pays the charge on pigs?—The seller.

22,351. Then practically in nine cases out of ten the possession of the animal is retained by the seller until the custom is paid?—I do not understand.

22,352. When passing the custom gaps is not it the individual who has possession of the animal who pays the toll?—Certainly, because it would be a hard job for the buyer to retain them all. He (the buyer) gets the different sellers to drive them to the station-house or yard, and driving them through the custom gap they pay the custom.

22,353. You said the seller would be at 9d. of a loss?—Yes, in pigs.

22,354. How do you make that 9d.?—3d. custom at the custom gap, and 6d. a pig kept by the buyer.

22,355. Is that 9d. payable on bonhams?—3d. is the luck-penny on a bonham and 3d. custom.

22,356. Do the farmers, as a rule, object to the fairs being held on the public thoroughfare or streets of the town. Does it injure the animals brought there and exposed for sale?—I do not think so.

22,357. You still think that if tolls are to be paid a properly enclosed fair green should be provided?—I think so.

22,358. Would you prefer to sell yourself on a fair green?—I would prefer a fair field quite close to the station, but I would prefer far and away that the fair should be held in the town of Macroom than in Massytown, which is a very inconvenient fair.

22,359. Besides corn, do you bring in any other marketable commodities?—I bring in potatoes and turnips.

22,360. Do you bring in butter?—I do not latterly.

22,361. Do the same observations apply to corn and potatoes in connexion with the porterage charge?—Yes. I think a different set of scales should be provided for weighing the potatoes.

22,362. Is it the same scales for weighing corn and potatoes?—Yes.

22,363. (*The Commissioner, to Mr. Kelliher.*) You mentioned that there were a couple of scales?—We have. The inconvenience Mr. Creedo complains of occurs only two days in the year, Patrick's Day and Lady's Day.

22,364. Was it ever necessary to put the second scale in order to weigh the commodities?—Of course there is a little trouble and noise for these two days, but on the other days one scales is quite sufficient. The people are not subjected to half the annoyance Mr. Creedo speaks of.

22,365. (*By Mr. Creedo, to Mr. Kelliher.*) Do you think one scales sufficient to weigh 400 loads of corn; do you think one scales is sufficient when the whole market square is crowded over with carts?—I can vouch I never saw 300 loads. The most that came was 400 bags or 450.

22,366. (*Mr. Creedo.*) I often brought potatoes and never weighed them there. It would be very well if the weighmaster were put up.

22,367. (*Weighmaster.*) You are the only discontented man we have.

22,368. (*By the Commissioner, to Mr. Creedo.*) Do you think proper market building and enclosed spaces, with shelter accommodation for the exposure of corn and potatoes, and other commodities brought in, should be provided, or do you think that would tend to increase the market, and induce the farmers to bring them in greater quantities?—I do not think it would make them bring commodities in greater quantities, but it would be a great accommodation.

22,369. Do you assign as a reason that at present they have no other place to go to?—It is quite a good market, and in a central place.

22,370. What is the next convenient market?—The city of Cork, 24 miles away.

22,371. What is the nearest market?—The only other market is the city of Cork.

22,372. Then you would say a necessity exists for shelter accommodation for the exposure of the corn, potatoes, and other perishable commodities?—I say if there was it would be far better.

22,373. Did the farmers ever make any representations to the owner to provide such?—As far as I am concerned I would not require sheds, but plenty of accommodation for weighing.

22,374. You would find no objection to shelter accommodation, but you think there should be greater facilities for ascertaining the weight of corn and potatoes, without any delay?—Certainly. There would be a crush of carts for a dozen yards, and the people could hardly move.

22,375. Have you formed any ideas yourself in connexion with the tolls or charges at the market here?—I would have no objection to a 1d. a sack, if I had not to pay any more.

22,376. I am drawing a distinction between tolls and weighing charges. Do you think the fact of a toll or custom levied deters farmers in any way from bringing their cattle or commodities to the fairs or markets, or would they prefer to go to another place that would be toll free?—If I had to pay three times the toll, there is no other place, and I would have to go 24 miles away, or a dozen miles to Bandon.

22,377. You say you live three miles from here?—Yes.

22,378. If another town was five miles away, and no tolls were levied in it, would you prefer going there?—If I had a crowd of pigs I would go five miles if they did not charge a toll.

22,379. Supposing you found the town of Macroom was a better market, and you could effect a readier sale of the animals, would you then consider the levying of a toll?—I would go where I would make the best bargain.

22,380. You would not consider the question of whether you would pay custom or not after sale?—I would take that into account. If I had two towns to go to, I would go to the town from which I could bring home the most money. A penny is a penny any day.

22,381. Have you any other observation to make?—I do not think I have.

Mr. John Murray examined.

22,382. Did you hear the answers of Mr. Creedo to some of the questions I put to him?—Yes.

22,383. Do you concur in the opinions he has given expression to?—He has exaggerated some things. I do not think there were over 400 loads of corn came into Macroom.

22,384. Well, you heard his statement about the porterage charge?—I did.

22,385. Have you experienced any delay in weighing commodities, and has this charge being levied continually from you?—There are some Saturdays, and an immensity of corn comes in, and it takes a very long time for weighing.

22,386. Have you always been compelled to pay this porterage charge?—I always pay, but he never made me pay 1d. a bag.

22,387. You pay 1d. a bag for weighing?—I do.

22,388. Do you pay outsiders generally for loading and unloading?—Generally.

22,389. What do you pay?—There is no fixed sum. I may give him more than 1d. a bag.

22,390. When you send in corn do you send in labourers?—I always have men following my horses.

22,391. Do you always avail of the services of the porters to load and unload?—I always do.

22,392. Did you ever pay that porterage charge and not receive any assistance in loading or unloading?—I do not think I did.

22,393. Did you ever bring in a load and have a sufficient number of men to load or unload without any assistance?—I never brought a man except a guide.

22,394. Do you make any objection to Mr. Creedo's statements in connexion with the porterage charge?—I do not know how Mr. Creedo was treated.

22,395. Did not you hear his answers stated?—I did, but I made no objection myself to pay.

22,396. I want to get at the practice?—It is the practice that everyone pays more or less.

22,397. It is the practice that every person who brings in corn must pay a weighing charge and the porterage charge?—I do not think they are bound to pay.

22,398. I am not saying they are bound, but is it the practice?—It is the practice, but I think it is the duty of the proprietor of the tolls to weigh corn for 1d. per bag. I think 1d. per bag for weighing ought to be sufficient. I think the owner of the tolls should supply men for weighing it.

22,399. Do you find any objection to the fairs being held on the public streets?—I travelled a good many fairs in Cork, Limerick, and Waterford, and I never saw such bad accommodation. The 12th October last I sold some pigs at Massytown fair, and brought them to the railway, and before they could be got out my man was detained three hours, and he could not go up or down. The place was blocked up with empty cars. You could not stir through the town on fair days.

22,400. What is the cause of the block?—Not having a fair green.

22,401. Do you approve of a sufficiently large and properly enclosed fair green?—Yes, if it was large enough, but it is not large enough.

22,402. Would you prefer to have them held in a large fair green instead of the public streets?—Certainly; and as for Massytown there is not such another place in Ireland. I saw a woman killed there. There is a mill dam dividing the field in two parts, and it was a frosty day, and in coming out fell and died in a few days afterwards.

22,403. Do you think that some shelter accommodation ought to be afforded for the protection of commodities brought to the market and not have them exposed on the street?—I do not know.

22,404. Supposing on a very wet day, is not the corn exposed on the public thoroughfare?—It is exposed on the public thoroughfare. I do not think you could get sufficient accommodation.

22,405. I am not speaking as to the possibility of getting it without expense, but this is a general question. Do you think in towns where markets are held, and market buildings erected, that shelter accommodation should be afforded for the protection of sellers and the commodities they sell from the inclemency of the weather?—There is no doubt in the world it would be very requisite.

22,406. Where such does not exist, do the farmers think their commodities depreciate in value or quantity?—I do not think they depreciate in value.

22,407. The exposure before a sale was effected would not be sufficiently long to cause depreciation?—The exposure is very bad on fair days. I think they are charging customs in this town for matters they have no right to charge. I recollect when I was a boy there was a large toll board, and everything liable to customs was on that toll board. For the last 20 years I did not see that toll board.

22,408. Are any charges levied on any commodities that were not at another period levied?—I cannot say.

22,409. Are tolls levied on days now that were not levied on those same days in former years?—I always heard there was only a patent for two days in the week, Wednesday and Saturday.

22,410. Do you remember when no tolls were payable on Monday, Tuesday, Thursday, or Friday?—I cannot say, but they charge a poor woman a 1d. with two chickens in her basket. Whether she is liable to that charge or not I cannot say.

22,411. If she brought two each day in the week, would she have to pay a 1d. each day?—So I understand. I am told they do charge.

22,412. (*Mr. Kelliher.*) I may remark that there is nothing paid on fowl except on a fair day.

22,413. (*Mr. Murphy.*) I saw a charge of a 1d. levied on a fair day.

22,414. (*The Commissioner.*) You see Mr. Kelliher is correct in that. The only charge on fowl is on a fair day.

22,415. (*Mr. Murphy.*) I am told they charge for butter every day in the week.

22,416. (*The Commissioner.*) Have you anything further to say, Mr. Murphy?—Nothing but that there is bad accommodation, and on a busy day the place is thronged up.

22,417. Do you consider at present you do not get sufficient return for the toll at the fairs?—I do not think we get any return at all. We are in danger of our lives going in and out there.

22,418. That is where the collision occurs?—Yes; that is every fair day.

22,419. A great delay has been caused to you in completing your bargain in order to return home?—Yes, of course.

22,420. (*Mr. Ashe.*) Is not it the railway has caused the block that occasionally occurs?

22,421. (*The Commissioner.*) How?

(*Mr. Ashe.*) Because the railway is only in existence since 1864, and the streets of the town leading to it are narrow. It is the great rush to get to the railway to truck their goods that causes the block.

22,422. (*Mr. Murphy.*) That is not the case in the Massytown fair. You would be in danger of your life coming out of the Massytown fair.

22,423. (*Mr. Kelliher.*) Mr. Crowle stated that there were up to 400 loads of corn and potatoes in Macroom market. There were never 200 loads of corn and potatoes brought together.

22,424. (*Mr. Murphy.*) I wish also to remark that for every pig sold in Macroom the seller has to pay 3d. customs coming out and 2d. back-passage.

22,425. You agree with the observations of Mr. Crowle that the charges are excessive?—Yes.

22,426. Has that charge always been levied on them?—I believe so.

22,427. Did you ever know when the rates were any higher or any smaller than they are at present?—I do not think they were.

22,428. Have the six fairs at Massytown always been held within your memory?—There was only a patent for four in Massytown and Macroom.

22,429. Do you remember when the 18th January and 18th February fairs were established?—It is about 20 years ago.

22,430. Who were they established by?—By Mr. Leary. Macroom got six new fairs.

22,431. I suppose he was one of the committee of the traders of the town?—Yes. They were all held for a time in Macroom, and I think no tolls were charged by the late Lord Bantry for his portion.

22,432. That is only the 18th January and 18th March?—Yes. He charged no tolls and does not still. I do not know what right Mr. Massy or the representatives have to charge these tolls either.

22,433. Were those in Massytown and Macroom established at the same time?—Yes. The four new fairs were held in Macroom, and no fair in Massytown, and no charge at all until they were taken there by Mr. Massy.

22,434. That was before your time. You do not recollect it?—No.

22,435. (*Mr. Riordan.*) On the question of fairs I have been invariably told by buyers that they prefer the fair in the town than outside, and that the accommodation is better.

22,436. (*Mr. Murphy.*) It is at the request of the inhabitants and country people that they changed to Massytown and Macroom. It happened in this way, that Mr. Coppinger, the lessee of the tolls, and, I believe, for his own accommodation, induced the people to come to Macroom. Mr. Ryan, Q.C., had a case before him on the very subject by Mr. Massy, and his advice was that he could compel the fairs to be held in Massytown instead of Macroom, and the fairs were brought back to Massytown, and since have been held there.

22,437. What was the date that they were brought back to Massytown?—About 1870.

22,438. For some time previous no fairs were held?—They were carried away from Massytown, and Mr. Massy compelled them, and had a man employed to turn the cattle into Massytown, and the fair has been held there since. For some few years the draft was into Macroom instead of Massytown.

22,439. Were both sets of fairs held for any lengthened period on the Macroom side?—Only for a short period. During the tenancy of Mr. Coppinger Mr. Massy asserted his right to have them in Massytown. I remember seeing Mr. Massy's staff of men turning them into Massytown, and compelling the fair to be held there.

Mr. Daniel Lynch examined.

22,440. You are in trade in the town?—Yes.

22,441. What trade?—Draper.

22,442. Do you think it affects your trade the fact of holding the fairs on the public street?—Certainly not.

22,443. Does not the fact of fairs and markets being held occasion much filth and dirt outside the doors?—It does, but it does not affect the traders so much.

22,444. It puts them to some inconvenience?—Sometimes there is a crowd. I live in the centre, in the square. I have an opportunity of seeing most of the fair, and I certainly do say with a little more order there is sufficient accommodation. It is possible, if Lord Bantry added a little extra to the present field, it would be sufficient. For instance, with regard to the blocks complained of, the very same blocks occur in Mountown fair, and it is entirely owing to the railway station, because when going to the railway they have not an opportunity of disposing the pigs or cattle, and then they are delayed at the railway station too long, and that causes a block through the town; but I am of opinion if the renter of the tolls had a certain staff of men kept there from time to time, and those cars were kept in order by them, the whole thing would be regulated. I may also mention that the houses in the town act as sheds for those disposing of cattle and pigs, because on a wet day the people stand in the doors and are protected from the weather.

22,435. Do you find them going into your doors?—Yes.

22,436. Are there special establishments that they are in the habit of going to with greater confidence?—It happens where they take their stand with their cattle.

22,437. Who cleans the thoroughfare?—The man who has the contract of the roads.

22,438. Have complaints been made of any undue delay by him in cleaning?—Sometimes it would be an advantage if they were cleaned sooner.

22,439. I take it, then, from your evidence, that the traders would put up with any inconvenience caused by people seeking shelter in the shops and elsewhere for trade purposes?—Certainly they would make a sacrifice for them.

22,440. You consider it would be a sacrifice?—They would be prepared to make a sacrifice, but I do not think it is the slightest inconvenience to the traders of the town.

22,441. You think there is not the slightest fear of accidents by the cattle intermixing or being on the streets?—No.

22,442. Have you attended fairs other than these?—Yes.

22,443. Have you anything to say in connexion with the tolls levied here?—I have nothing to say to the tolls. There is one thing I may mention with regard to the corn and potato markets. I think for a month or two in the year the square is very much crowded, and I heard several complaints made about not having a weighbridge, and I think if they had a weighbridge on the square it would facilitate the people very much in weighing corn; say, for instance, if they could weigh a whole load of corn or potatoes together, that would enable you to do as much in an hour as for five hours at present in the day. There is a weighbridge here, but it is outside the town.

22,444. In that case one buyer would buy the entire load?—It is usual for one buyer to buy the whole load, that is of corn and sometimes potatoes, and where the whole load is bought it takes no time to weigh it if you had a weighbridge on the square.

22,445. The board of guardians and the grand jury look after the local affairs here?—They have scarcely anything to do with the town except barely the sanitary portion of it.

22,446. Do you think where local authorities exist in towns that they should obtain compulsory powers to acquire any legal vested rights in the markets and fairs at present vested in the owners and work them for the public good?—Yes, and I am of opinion it would be a great advantage to have town commissioners here.

22,447. Have you formed the idea yourself that where local authorities exist they should receive compulsory powers to acquire the rights of market owners and work them for the public good?—Yes.

22,448. Tell me the reason why you form that idea?—I think everything would be done with more order.

22,449. Do you think the united efforts of a number of gentlemen composing the board would tend to work them and manage them to the greater satisfaction of the inhabitants generally and those attending the fairs and markets?—I am of that opinion.

22,450. Have you any experience of places where the market rights and tolls were under the control of such bodies?—No.

22,451. Then in the absence of a local authority in the town, do you think if a committee, such as market trustees, were appointed by the Legislature or established by them, that they should have power and control of the markets and fairs, giving any compensation that was necessary or adequate for existing legal rights?—If such a body were formed it would be an advantage.

22,452. For the same reason as you stated before?—Yes. It would remove a great many grievances.

22,453. (*The Commissioner, to Mr. Ashe.*) Would you wish to give any opinion on the point yourself, Mr. Ashe?—No. I really know, having experience of public bodies, that it would not be desirable to invest them with further authority for this reason, that we are getting very little benefit for your rates and have the pleasure of enjoying this year a rate of 2s. in the pound which has gradually arisen in a few years from somewhere about a 1s. I believe you could not by any possibility obtain a worse body than the board of guardians.

22,454. I am not talking of the body, but as an authority working the markets and fairs for the benefit of the town?—I would not trust local bodies. I think the ratepayers of the town will corroborate me.

Mr. Michael T. D[illegible] examined.

22,455. What observations do you wish to make?—I am attending fairs, and worse accommodation I never saw than in my own town.

22,456. You belong to Macroom?—Yes. I am a butcher by trade.

22,457. What exception do you take to the accommodation here?—In the first place you are blocked at the custom gap, and no car or horse can move, and you are bound to be badly beaten if the custom is not paid.

22,458. Have you ever heard that people have been injured?—A cow was killed. They are struck by sticks backwards and forwards by the owner and are stopped at the custom gap.

22,459. (*Mr. Kelliher.*) No complaints were made to me of the ill-treatment of the animals.

22,460. (*Witness.*) I had a process before the barrister at quarter sessions for a damaged beast.

22,461. Who was it you summoned?—The owner of the beast.

22,462. What was the result?—I should go to the superior courts as the chairman of quarter sessions had no jurisdiction.

22,463. Did he make any statement on that?—That he (the owner) did not beat the cow and she was killed immediately after coming in off the fair field in Mountown.

22,464. Were any of the toll collectors examined?—No. Were it not for the police trying to keep cars off of the street the people would be in danger every day both in Mountown and Macroom. If you were in my door where I am living it would take you two hours or three to pass the crossing.

22,465. Do the police ever attend to them?—Only for them no cars could be made move. There are some 15 police, before day in the morning, there from September until April. The police are the only protection we have. In winter they are out before day clearing the streets. Our houses are blocked with cars and there are cars outside the town, and some accommodation should be given. You cannot come into the town or go out of it with pigs and cattle.

22,466. Are the pathways blocked as well as the roadways?—Certainly.

22,467. You think, then, the inhabitants here are put to much inconvenience?—The inhabitants are [illegible] to go away on fair days to accommodate their friends.

22,468. What remedy would you suggest?—I do not know any remedy except to keep the animals out of the town. If another piece of a field was attached to the field belonging to Lord Bantry, near the railway station, where they could be walled in instead of blocking the streets with empty cars and the custom men to prevent them from going back into the fair, the fair would not be so thronged as it is, and the passage would be opened to every man going backwards and forwards.

22,469. You think that would be a sufficient remedy?—Yes.

22,470. (*Mr. Murphy.*) There was a field given by the late Lord Bantry, and portion of it was taken back, and if that were left there would be sufficient accommodation.

Mr. S. Kelleher examined.

22,471. Are you a trader in the town?—Yes. I am a corn merchant and spirit dealer. I farm and deal in cattle.

22,472. You heard the observations of several witnesses here, and especially Mr. [illegible]. Do you concur in or disagree with the remarks of Mr. [illegible] as to the charges on corn and the general delay he says is caused in weighing the corn?—I say he is right in most of his remarks, and I consider the fault of that lies with Mrs. Harding. She ought to have men there who ought to be paid by her and not by the public. I may say that sometime ago the pig market was held with the cattle fair, and it was decided to hold the pig fair on the day previous.

22,473. Was not the pig fair always held on the day previous to the cattle fair?—The pig fair and cattle fair were on the same day until recently.

22,474. Do you object to the pig fair being held the day previous to the cattle fair?—If it is properly arranged, and if the fowl were taken and put into a field and removed I think the streets would be the best place to hold the fair. The fowl are a great impediment, and the cars that carry them. There is another thing that the shopkeepers of the town established a calf market after a great deal of expense, and I think customs should not be charged on calves at all, and as soon as the calf market established on the public street than 2d. a head was charged. Before that people had to travel all night to Cork with them.

22,475. When was this calf market established?—About six years ago. It was started on Saturday when no customs ought to be charged, besides the streets are kept in repair by the road contractor, and Mrs. Harding or Lord [illegible] did not spend a 1s. in improvement to the town.

22,476. (Mr. Ashe.) The poor people in the town are all scavengers. They put in an hour each morning cleaning the streets.

22,477. You think the manure was as an equivalent for any trouble they get?—They clear away the manure and sell it to the farmers about. I know I buy a great deal of it myself.

22,478. (Mr. Kelleher.) Regarding the Masseytown fairs there is a drill down through Masseytown. I am selling and buying cattle every fair day for the last 15 or 20 years, and you could not go in there with [illegible] and dirt to your ankles.

Mr. David Murphy examined.

22,479. What observations do you wish to make?—The charges are too high and more than they should be. There is 6d. charged for cattle, which I think too much, and in other towns I know there is only a 1d. for a pig and it is 3d in Macroom. I think all the customs charged in Macroom are entirely too high. As far as the luck-penny is concerned that is a thing between the buyer and seller. It is a general thing through all the towns in Ireland and England. Luck-pennies are given freely and there is no compulsion at all.

22,480. But now when they are fixing the price of an animal, do they ever take into consideration the luck-penny that they have afterwards to give?—Generally so. He is well aware of it.

22,481. In that case would you say that the animals would be got somewhat cheaper if there was no luck-penny?—I do not think it is taken into account by the sellers.

Mr. [illegible] re-examined.

22,482. (Witness.) I want to refer to the matter of transferring the tolls to a public body. I should like that very much if there was a vote by ballot, because in open voting it would be corrupt.

22,483. Apart from the mode of election, you agree to the principle?—Yes; but as regards the mode of election I would condemn it. I object to tolls.

22,484. What are your reasons?—There is a public square in Macroom and the people are paying for it, and they charge customs on that square, which is a great injustice. It would be a very good job if we had a town commission who would light and repair the town with customs of the town.

22,485. You say you object to the customs?—Yes, in the square.

22,486. Do you pay for the use of the square yourself?—I pay for repairing the roads.

22,487. Have you any connection as a buyer or seller with the markets?—I have.

Mr. [illegible] re-examined.

22,488. (Witness.) I beg to suggest that two sets of scales be erected in the market, and a weighmaster and two men be told off for each set of scales and be paid by the lessee of the market.

22,489. (Weighmaster.) The tolls would not pay them.

22,490. (Mr. [illegible].) If we are to pay tolls for pigs, a 1d. a pig for each pig and less would be enough for bonhams; or 6d. a crate for slips, and if a smaller number than six, charge them a 1d. each.

22,491. Is there any other gentleman who has any evidence to give or any remarks or suggestions to make?—No answer.

Then inquiry then concluded.

KINSALE—CO. CORK.

With reference to my inquiry in Kinsale on the 21st November 1888, I beg to report as follows:—

Kinsale is a seaport town situated on the southern coast of the county of Cork. It is the terminus of the Kinsale branch of the Cork, Bandon, and South Coast Railway line. It has a harbour and a good fishing trade, which is indeed the principal industry of the inhabitants. The local government is vested in Town Commissioners, and the population is 5,988.

The market day is Saturday. A butter market is held on Friday during the season. The fairs are held upon the third Wednesday of each month.

The fairs are toll free, but tolls are levied at the markets, and are collected by the lessee each day in the week according as marketable commodities are brought in and disposed of.

No scale of charges is erected, but a weighing-machine is provided.

The market rights and tolls are the property of the Town Commissioners who have portions of them, however, sublet to a Mr. Thomas Coveney for one year at 22l. The Town Commissioners retain control of the fish and meat markets and of the charges therein.

The public records show that three patents were granted for the town of Kinsale. The first is dated 10th May 1589, and authorised the corporation to hold a Wednesday and Saturday market, and a fair on the 24th August and three days thereafter. The second is dated 24th February 1609, and authorised the corporation to hold fairs on Whit Monday and 28th October in each case, and continue for four days. The third patent is dated 8th March 1721, and authorised the corporation to hold fairs on the 23rd April and 18th November and the two days after each.

None of these fairs are now held.

The present fairs were established by the Town Commissioners without any express authority about 18 years ago, previous to which a fair was held on the 4th September.

In accordance with my instructions I have inspected the fair and market places.

The fairs are held on the public streets, chiefly in a wide street called "Long Quay." There are no pens, shelter, or other accommodation provided, except what the adjacent houses afford.

The general market is held about the streets of the town.

The potato, corn, and butter market is held in the basement of the court-house and the street adjoining it. A beam and scales for weighing butter exclusively, a weighbridge, and another scales are provided there. The place is very narrow, and entirely inadequate for market purposes, being merely fit for weighing, and not for transacting the sale of any commodity within its precincts.

The fish market is an enclosed space surrounded by a high wall, against which sheds are erected at two sides, and divided into stalls for the use of those employed in the retail fish trade.

The meat market is a similar enclosure, provided with sheds and stalls. These stalls are rented for the sale of meat by local victuallers.

A complaint was made against the lessee for charging on the daily delivery of fowl to the buyers, the sales in such cases having been effected by private contract.

An opinion was expressed that the Town Commissioners were enabled to derive a greater pecuniary benefit from the market rights by sub-letting portions of them than by being in the immediate receipt of the entire thereof.

Appended will be found a transcript of the evidence taken at the inquiry.

JOHN J. O'MEARA,
Assistant Commissioner.

45, Lower Mount Street,
Dublin.

Kinsale, 21st November, 1883.

Mr. MICHAEL HEGARTY, Town Clerk, examined.

22,492. You are the town clerk of Kinsale?—Yes.

22,493. The Town Commissioners are the owners of the markets and fairs here?—Yes.

22,494. Do you know how they acquired them?—As the successors of the old corporation.

22,495. The old corporation became extinct in 1840?—Yes.

22,496. They were the owners up to that period?—Yes.

22,497. When were the Town Commissioners established?—In 1855.

22,498–500. Are the Town Commissioners in the immediate receipt of these tolls?—They are.

22,501. Have not they got them sub-let?—Yes. They let the tolls to Mr. Thomas Coveney.

22,502. How does he hold?—He holds yearly.

22,503. Is it by tender?—Yes, by public tender. The highest man will get them.

22,504. What is the amount of his tender for this year?—22l.

22,505–6. Had he them last year?—He had, and several years previous.

22,507. When does his tenancy commence?—It commences on the 1st of August, and ends on the 31st July.

22,508. You do not know the valuation of the tolls?—20l., tolls and customs.

22,509. Has he to pay rates and taxes?—No. We pay rates and taxes on the 20l. valuation.

22,510. His sole expense is 22l.?—Yes, for the coming year. Last year it was 21l., and the previous year 19l., and in 1882 it was 18l. The average was 19l. 6s. 8d. for the three years.

22,511. What are the market days here?—The market day is Saturday.

22,512. Saturday only?—Yes.

22,513. What fairs are held?—The fairs are monthly.

22,514. On what dates?—The third Wednesday of each month.

22,515. No tolls are levied at the fairs at all?—No.

22,516. Are tolls levied at the Saturday market?—The lessee collects tolls.

22,517. At the market?—Yes.

22,518. When were these monthly fairs established?—It was previous to my connexion with the Town Commissioners.

22,519. Where are the fairs held?—Down on the Long Quay.

22,520. That is portion of the public thoroughfare?—It is, going down by the sea.

22,521. Is it availed of by the public as a thoroughfare?—Yes. It is on the road leading up to the place where the sheep are sold.

22,522. Have the fairs always been held there?—Always.

22,523. Where are the markets held?—Here, in the potato market. Underneath the court-house is the butter and potato market, and on the big table they weigh the butter.

22,524. That is in the potato market?—Yes, underneath us.

22,525. Where is the general market held?—The general market is held through the town.

22,526. About the streets?—Vegetables are sold contrary to the wish of the Commissioners, and they appealed against it repeatedly to the vendors of the vegetables. They wished them to go into the market.

22,527. Into what market?—The fish or meat market.

22,528. You have an enclosed place for fish?—Yes, a splendid place for fish and meat.

22,529. Entirely enclosed?—Yes.

22,530. Who provided this?—The Town Commissioners.

22,531. Do you know what capital expenditure they were at in providing them?—I do not know that. It was long before my time.

22,532. Is there a weighbridge erected for cattle here?—Not for cattle, but for weighing hay and straw.

22,533. Was it the Commissioners who erected that?—Yes. It is part of what they let to Mr. Coveney.

22,534. Is there any written agreement between the lessee and the Town Commissioners?—No, except he tenders annually and gives security for the payment of the amount.

22,535. Are there many sureties?—Two sureties in the sum of £50.

22,536. Have you had any connexion with fairs, other than those in Kinsale, as a buyer or seller?—No.

22,537. Do you think the fairs here are very well attended for a town of the size of Kinsale?—Well, they are fairly attended. I think they have improved; there is a good deal of rivalry with other towns about. A great deal from Kinsale goes to Bandon and Cork.

22,538. Were tolls ever levied here?—Not that I am aware.

22,539. You get no tolls from the fairs?—No.

22,540. Do you think now that works better here in the town of Kinsale than having tolls, and a fair green provided in return for them? Do you think if a toll was levied it would deter men from bringing animals to the fairs?—Well, I would not like to go into that part of the question. I do not think it would, but having the fairs free is a great inducement to the people to come.

22,541. Were any representations ever made to the Town Commissioners by the inhabitants of the town to get the fairs removed off the public street?—No.

22,542. The townspeople never discussed that question?—No. Before the fairs were started there was an old fair held outside the town, and a toll was charged on that. There was an old fair held formerly under a very old charter—that was held by Campbell outside the borough, and we had nothing to say to it. That was held in a portion of the first year I came to Kinsale, in 1881.

22,543. Who was in receipt of the tolls charged there?—The man who owns the ground.

22,544. However, the Town Commissioners had nothing whatever to do with it?—No.

22,545. It was a neighbouring fair?—It was more for amusement than business, that fair.

22,546. What duties do the Town Commissioners perform here?—They are the urban sanitary authority, and have very extensive powers as such.

22,547. You do all the cleansing of the town?—Yes.

22,548. Did the official immediately connected with the cleansing ever calculate what additional expenditure the Town Commissioners are at in cleaning the streets on account of the fact of the fairs being held on them?—Oh, I think it is very small.

22,549. Who gets the manure after these fairs?—The Town Commissioners.

22,550. Do you think the manure would be an equivalent for any additional expense they incur?—Yes.

22,551. You think so?—Yes, I do.

22,552. Could you give me the last balance sheet of the Commissioners?—Yes. The one for the present year is with the printer.

22,553. Do the Commissioners deem it more desirable to lease out the tolls than to manage the markets and fairs themselves?—Yes. They consider it better to lease them out.

22,554. Why do they farm them; do they derive more profit from them?—They think the collection would be better made than having them thrown over on one of their own staff by a private individual, than by a public official of their own, who has other duties to attend to, and may not be so convenient as the man who has them.

22,555. But you have another source of revenue from the markets in addition to the £22?—Yes, from the shambles.

22,556. They are not included in the letting to Mr. Coveney?—No. The shambles are collected by the town surveyor.

22,557. Is that at the fish and meat market?—Yes. The charges are collected by him.

22,558. Are these the only additional receipts you have?—Yes.

22,559. How do you let out these shambles?—They are let at so much each. The highest is 3s. a week at present for one stall.

22,560. Do they vary according to the prominence of their position and the size?—Yes.

22,561. From 3s. down to what?—To 1s., but at present there are only three stalls occupied. The greater number are unoccupied at present. They have all opened stalls of their own—private shambles through the town.

22,562. Is the fish and meat in one market?—The meat is in one market, and the fish in another. The two are separate.

22,563. Have you any rule regulating the sale of meat and fish, that is, prohibiting them from selling about the town and confining the sale to the market?—If we find them selling on the street they can be summoned before the town court.

22,564. You have a borough magistrate?—We had up to the present year, but the matter is under the Lord Chancellor's consideration at present.

22,565. Supposing a person brought a basket of fish, and placed it in the fish market on the ground, would you levy any charge?—No. They pay so much a week. I think two or three pence a week each person who sells in the market.

22,566. Have you any scale of these charges erected?—No, I believe not.

22,567. Have you any fixed rates for the standings there?—Yes. Those occupying the stalls pay 2d. a week, and anyone outside them who sells fish in the season without stalls we charge them a penny for the week.

22,568. They can avail themselves of it every day in the week?—They can. It is only on Saturdays that we collect, and we charge them but the penny.

22,569. But it is open every day in the week?—Yes, except Sunday.

22,570. There are only two charges—2d. for a stall and a 1d. for any standing not a stall?—Exactly.

22,571. Any higher charge has never been levied?—No. Then if there are three joined in fish it is only a 1d. each.

22,572. That is if the three have a stall?—Those having a stall, if they have a quantity of fish, as they generally do, there may be three or four women, and I charge a 1d. to each.

22,573. Did the Town Commissioners ever manage the markets and collect the tolls themselves?—Not that I am aware of; not for the last 50 years.

22,574. Do they think the present system advisable?—They do. They do not think it would work as well the other way. The private individual has an interest, and has to pay for them.

32,672. That is deriving a pecuniary benefit out of them; but if the Town Commissioners were in the immediate receipt, the immediate collection, do you think they would be better managed, and more to the satisfaction of those frequenting the markets and fairs, than they are at present?—No. There are no complaints at present of any sort.

32,673. No complaints made to the Town Commissioners?—No complaints or suggestions from any source. I brought your queries before the Town Commissioners, and they did not think any change necessary. [*The witness then handed in the following accounts.*]

ABSTRACT of the ACCOUNTS of the TOWN COMMISSIONERS of KINSALE for the Year ended 30th September 1886, showing the RECEIPTS and EXPENDITURE under several heads during that period.

RECEIPTS.				EXPENDITURE.			
Nature of Receipt.	Amount.			Nature of Expenditure.	Amount.		
	£	s.	d.		£	s.	d.
Balance due by Treasurer on 30th September 1885	182	6	1	Expended during the year in—			
Do. Clerk do. do.	8	15	1	Scavenging and Cleansing	120	17	4
Received during year in respect of—				New Works, Repairs, and Improvements	120	8	9
Town Rates	384	5	4	Public Lighting	175	12	1
Corporate Rents	138	8	8	Salaries of Officers	118	9	11
Market Tolls	10	0	0	Water Supply	36	13	6
Rent of Shambles	40	15	8	Rent and Taxes	47	19	8
Fines under Licensing Act	4	5	9	Printing and Stationery	11	1	6
Do. Town Court	8	10	2	Incidental Expenses	19	5	6
Grand Jury Presentments	18	17	0	Repayment of Loans	83	6	10
Sale of Manure	85	4	5	Lodged on Deposit to Credit of Endowed School.	56	13	5
Dog Tax	2	18	5	Balance due by Treasurer on 30th September 1886.	49	10	2
Contributions in aid of Salaries under Public Health Act	8	10	4				
Water Rates	16	14	1				
Incidental Receipts	1	5	0				
Contributions in lieu of Rates	14	11	9				
School Endowment	28	18	6				
Balance due to Clerk on 30th September 1886	2	9	8				
	884	8	11		884	8	11

I certify the foregoing to be a true Abstract of the Receipts and Expenditure of the Town Commissioners of Kinsale for the year ended the 30th September 1886.

Dated this 9th day of November 1886.

ANDREW MCHUGH, *Auditor.*

ABSTRACT of the ACCOUNTS of the TOWN COMMISSIONERS of KINSALE for the Year ended 30th September 1887, showing the RECEIPTS and EXPENDITURE under the several heads during that period.

RECEIPTS.				EXPENDITURE.			
Nature of Receipt.	Amount.			Nature of Expenditure.	Amount.		
	£	s.	d.		£	s.	d.
Balance due by Treasurer on 30th September 1886	[illegible]			Expended during the year in—			
Received during year in respect of—				Scavenging and Cleansing	113	13	7
Town Rates	377	1	0	New Works and Repairs	183	14	7
Corporate Rents	107	7	5	Public Lighting	180	0	8
Market Tolls	10	0	0	Salaries of Officers	114	14	1
Rent of Shambles	36	14	8	Do. Inspector	13	0	0
Fines under Licensing Act	3	19	5	Water Supply	10	17	4
Fines from Town Court	7	6	8	Rent and Taxes	27	11	5
Grand Jury Presentments	17	10	0	Printing and Stationery	8	3	8
Sale of Manure	67	18	6	Law Costs	0	16	10
Dog Tax	1	11	1	Incidental Expenses	16	11	5
Contributions in aid of Salaries under Public Health Act	8	10	4	Repayment of Loans	78	17	8
Water Rates	33	8	4	Lodged on Deposit to Credit of Endowed School.	28	17	8
Incidental Receipts	5	10	6	Balance due by Treasurer on 30th September 1887.	28	0	11
Contributions in lieu of Rates	23	15	0				
School Endowment	26	17	3				
Balance due to Clerk on 30th September 1887	1	9	7				
	773	11	0		773	11	0

I certify the foregoing to be a true Abstract of the Receipts and Expenditure of the Town Commissioners of Kinsale for the year ended the 30th September 1887.

Dated this 7th day of February 1888.

Mr. THOMAS COTTER examined.

22,577. You are the tenant to the Town Commissioners for the tolls of the market?—Yes.

22,578. The market day is Saturday?—Yes.

22,579. Do you collect tolls any other day in the week but Saturday?—Every day in the week except Sunday.

22,580. Are marketable commodities brought each day of the week?—Well, I do not know. We had only one sack of potatoes yesterday in the market.

22,581. Mention for me the different commodities that are brought into the market in Kilrush?—There are potatoes, turnips, hay, straw, mangold wurzel. The hay and straw are weighed at the weighbridge. The butter market on Fridays is done away with. That was held for three months.

22,582. Did it fall through?—It went down.

22,583. The buyers did not attend?—They will not attend any more for this season.

22,584. Will they the next season?—They will commence again next March.

22,585. It is only during the season you have the butter market every Friday?—Exactly, during the season.

22,586. Do not lumps come in during the week?—Yes.

22,587. On Fridays and Saturdays?—Saturday used to be market day until this woman (a buyer) came from London, and Friday then was appointed.

22,588. Does any corn come in?—No. A few sacks might come in.

22,589. Small quantities come in?—Yes. I did not weigh a ton of corn I do not know when.

22,590. What else is brought in? Are calves or pigs brought into the market during the week?—No.

22,591. Do they wait for the fair day?—They generally wait for fair days. I got no custom from calves.

22,592. Have you any market buildings?—No.

22,593. Have not you got the potato market beneath the court-house?—I have that rented.

22,594. Is not that from the Town Commissioners?—Yes.

22,595. That is included in your letting?—That is what I am paying for.

22,596. What else have you?—I have the weighbridge and beam and scales.

22,597. Where is this situated?—Underneath the court-house.

22,598. One beam and scales?—Yes.

22,599. Have you any other building or shed?—No, but the weighbridge.

22,600. Where is the weighbridge erected?—Adjacent to the court-house.

22,601. What is your charge on potatoes?—A halfpenny a hundredweight for all commodities weighed, unless wool or feathers.

22,602. Is wool brought in, too?—Yes. That is in a certain season.

22,603. Is that charge of a halfpenny a hundred for weighing the corn and potatoes?—Yes.

22,604. Where do they expose the potatoes for sale?—Down underneath in the market.

22,605. Supposing they brought in potatoes and exposed them for sale below and did not weigh them, would you look for your charge of a halfpenny per hundred?—I would. They do not sell now; they used formerly.

22,606-10. But the contract or sale would not be complete until the weight has been ascertained?—The sale is complete before they are weighed.

22,611. On corn is your charge a halfpenny per hundredweight?—Yes.

22,612. And the same observations apply to it?—The very same.

22,613. Where do they expose corn, if they bring it in at all?—There are no one but the middlemen. They keep it on the street, and supposing I had a pair of horses I might buy three or four bags.

22,614. Are there any corn merchants in the town?—Yes.

22,615. You collect no toll from them if they buy?—No.

22,616. None at all?—If a hundred barrels came in I would not get a penny.

22,617. Supposing the potatoes were not exposed for sale in the basement of the court-house but exposed elsewhere in the town and sold?—I get nothing. If they are weighed it is against the regulations of the Town Commissioners, but sometimes they do weigh them at stores, and that is wrong.

22,618. You do not seek for your charge?—I do not except it when they weigh at other scales.

22,619. Have these charges been levied for any length of time?—The custom and tolls.

22,620. The halfpenny per hundredweight?—As long as I recollect.

22,621. Have you ever collected a halfpenny per hundred on potatoes or any other commodity which was not weighed at your scales but sold in the town on market day?—What I generally weigh on market day I charge a halfpenny a hundred.

22,622. I want to see have you ever sought for your charge or for a toll. I want to draw a distinction in order to see is it a weighing charge or custom. You say if they were exposed for sale and sold and weighed you get a halfpenny per hundred?—Yes.

22,623. If they are not sold and not in much of the basement of the court-house and they are not weighed, would you still look for your charge?—Yes, any delivered to the market I would.

22,624. What do you call the market?—The potato market.

22,625. That is the basement of the court-house?—Yes.

22,626. Supposing they brought in a cart and the cart stood on a spot outside on the road and the potatoes were sold and not weighed, would you seek for your charge?—Yes, I would if I were present.

22,627. Supposing they were in a street off that, would you seek for your charge, or do you think you would be entitled to it?—If they came as far as the gate and sold at the gate I am entitled to it.

22,628. I suppose a case of that kind has never arisen?—I never saw it, but this I know, that turnips very often are sold, and if I am present at the weighing machine I can charge for the load as if I weighed myself.

22,629. What is your charge for weighing turnips?—The same, a halfpenny a hundred, and the same for hay and straw.

22,630. For weighing all commodities, whether at the beam and scales or weighbridge, you have one charge?—Yes, and a penny a stone for wool and half stone for feathers.

22,631. Did they ever complain that on a load of hay they had to pay a halfpenny per hundred, that is too

22,635. And sold in the town?—Yes, I have the power of charging.

22,636. How do you know?—I do not know, but I know I did charge.

22,637. And got it?—Yes.

22,638. Although the load was not weighed?—Yes.

22,639. Would the same observations apply to straw and hay?—There is no hay [illegible]. They buy all the hay and straw by weight.

22,640. These observations only apply to turnips?—Yes. Hay, straw, and potatoes, wool and feathers are weighed.

22,641. What is your charge on feathers?—A penny per stone, and the same on wool.

22,642. Where do they expose the feathers for sale?—There may not be 14 pounds of feathers come in for six months. We have no feather-merchants in this town. If they bought feather beds at an auction they would come and expose them for sale per pound. They are the only feathers.

22,643. If wool is brought in and not weighed at your scales would you levy your charge?—It does not come. There is only one person taking wool, that is Mr. Coveney, who has a factory.

22,644. Does he weigh at your scales?—Yes; he has no other place to weigh.

22,645. On lump butter on Fridays and Saturdays what charge do you get?—Anything under 21 lbs., a penny; up to 28 lbs., three halfpence.

22,646. Is three halfpence the maximum charge?—Yes, unless it goes to a half hundredweight.

22,647. What do you charge then?—I have never weighed a half hundred.

22,648. Is it all lump butter that comes in?—Yes.

22,649. Does it only come on these days?—There is fresh butter coming in prints during the week. I cannot charge anything for that.

22,650. On this lump butter you only levy the charge when they weigh at your scales?—Yes.

22,651. What scales have you for weighing this lump butter?—I have a special one.

22,652. You never weigh potatoes on it?—No, it is a small one.

22,653. It is exclusively used for weighing butter?—For weighing butter only.

22,654. When you are weighing butter, what is the smallest weight you put in the scales?—I can put a half pound if I wish.

22,655. Do you put a half pound?—Yes, if it takes the half pound.

22,656. Do you put a quarter?—Yes, if it takes it.

22,657. You never put smaller than the quarter?—Not less than the quarter.

22,658. Is firkin butter ever brought in?—No.

22,659. What would your charge be on the firkin butter?—I weighed no firkins at all.

22,660. But when it does come during the season, on Friday?—No firkin comes at all; only roll butter.

22,661. Do you only weigh the butter, or do you ever scrape it or clean it?—No.

22,662. Where do they expose the butter for sale in the town?—Underneath the court-house.

22,663. Is not all the basement of this building for corn?—It is another portion of the basement of this court-house. The potato market and butter market are separate.

22,664. With regard to the charge on turnips, would you collect that every day in the week, if the load was sold in the market?—All I had this year was one load.

22,668. They always weigh?—They have to weigh when they come inside the market. A shopkeeper may want to get 20 or 30 lbs., and they would cut a [illegible] open one side and take them out, but that is against the rules.

22,669. Is there any rule confining the sale of butter and these commodities on which you collect a charge to the market buildings?—No.

22,670. The people are free to go where they will?—Certainly.

22,671. You have not heard the cost of the erection of that weighbridge?—I could not tell you that.

22,672. These you have mentioned are the only receipts you have from the market?—I do not know a single bit about the expenses.

22,673. And these are the only commodities upon which you receive charges?—Yes.

22,674. You have no other places throughout the town from the Commissioners?—No.

22,675. Have you standings?—Yes.

22,676. Do you collect on them?—No; there are none there. They would not be allowed.

22,677. All the standings are there on the Long Quay?—There were vegetable standings there at one time.

22,678. Supposing they were there, what charge would you levy on vegetables?—Twopence a week.

22,679. What day would you collect the charge?—Saturday.

22,680. Then it would be immaterial to you whether they availed themselves of it the previous day or not?—They only pay on Saturday.

22,681. If they only came on Saturday, still you would levy a charge of twopence?—Yes.

22,682. You do not weigh any of these?—No.

22,683. It is only for putting a cart on the Long Quay?—Yes. For the time they are selling clothes or such goods they would pay fourpence a week.

22,684. Vegetables are only twopence?—Yes.

22,685. That is for the load?—Yes.

22,686. Do they ever have any fish standings there?—None.

22,687. Have they egg standings?—Yes, there is a shed.

22,688. Do you collect any charge on them?—No.

22,689. Did you ever do so?—Never. The Commissioners would not allow it.

22,690. Are fowl brought here?—Yes.

22,691. Do you collect any charge for standings for fowl?—Yes.

22,692. Where do they exhibit the fowl?—At the top of High Street.

22,693. What is your charge on fowl?—Twopence a load.

22,694. If the load consisted only of two fowl, would you charge the twopence?—No. If they had 12 I would charge twopence.

22,695. Supposing they brought two chickens in a basket and put them in High Street, what charge would you levy?—I would not charge anything.

22,696. Have you ever done so?—Never.

22,697. Is it only when they bring in a cart?—Yes.

22,698. Did they ever bring in a basket on which you levied a charge?—Very seldom, except one or two chickens, and it would be scarcely worth while to look after the women.

22,699. It is twopence on the cart?—Yes.

22,700. No matter what is in it?—If there was 60 it would be fourpence; under 20, twopence, and for 25, threepence.

22,701. Is threepence the highest charge?—Three-

22,705. Pigs are not brought in on any market day? —No pigs, only on fair days.

22,706. There is no particular pig fair day, or are the pigs sold the same day as the cattle?—Yes.

22,707. Was the pig fair ever held on the day previous to the ordinary fair?—No.

22,708. Are these what you mentioned the only sources of receipt that you have?—Yes, that is all.

22,709. Do you know what you received from them for the past year?—Oh dear no.

22,710. You dislike to tell them?—Well, I may tell you this day's work is threepence halfpenny.

22,711. But this is not Saturday?—No.

22,712. Were you at any expense last year in connection with them. Who have you employed for weighing?—I have only myself, and my daughter assists me on Saturday and generally weighs in the butter market.

22,713. You never pay any wages?—No.

22,714. If any repairs are required to be done to the scales the Commissioners do them?—Yes.

22,715. You have no outlay or repairs to do in the market place?—No.

22,716. Did you make 1*l.* any day last year?—I should like to see you ask for 1*l.* any day.

22,717. Did you make 10*l.* a year profit?—I declare to mercy I could not say. I never kept any account. I am sure I made 10*l.* I would not like to be spending my time for 10*l.*

22,718. Do you think you made 10*s.* a week out of them?—I was very often weeks and I did not receive 10*s.*

22,719. During the past portions of the year would you say that taking them all in all, on an average you made about 5*s.* a week profit?—No.

22,720. What would you fix it at, would you say you made 15*l.*?—I would not make 15*l.*, and never did.

22,721. Would you make 12*l.*?—No, and I have them about five and twenty years.

22,722. Did you collect on those articles or commodities during that period?—Yes.

22,723. Do you ever collect on other commodities on which during a period of your tenancy you did not collect?—I did. There was one time, and I got the tolls at the September fair.

22,724. From the Commissioners?—Yes.

22,725. Was that done away with?—Yes, since the new monthly fairs opened here.

22,726. When was the monthly fair established?—I can scarcely tell. The monthly fairs are established about 15 years.

22,727. Were they established by the Town Commissioners?—Yes.

22,728. Previous to that, what fairs were held in Kinsale?—No fairs at all, only the September fair.

22,729. What date was that held on?—The 4th September. There used to be a sheep market up by the old gaol on Fridays.

22,730. Were tolls collected on them?—No.

22,731. Were tolls collected on pigs?—No.

22,732. Only at the September fair?—Yes, always tolls at the September fair on any commodity sold or standing, or anything.

22,733. When you levy this charge is it on the gross weight you charge?—The gross, certainly.

22,734. Or if you weigh a load of hay you charge on the entire load?—On the nett weight.

22,735. Then you do not charge on the cart?—No. I will weigh the cart for nothing.

22,736. Have you got printed tickets to give denoting the weight?—Yes.

22,737-8. Does the one ticket answer for the bridge and beam and scales?—It will not answer. If a man had a load of potatoes I would weigh them on the bridge, and if a man had five or six sacks, or eight, I would weigh them on the bridge.

22,739. The witness then produced the ticket for the weighbridge, of which the following is a copy:—

TOWN COMMISSIONER'S WEIGHING MACHINE.

*Kinsale*____________188 .

No.

*Name of Owner*__________________

*Article*________________________

Gross Weight.				Weight of Cart.
Tons.	Cwts.	Qrs.	Lbs.	Tons. Cwts. Qrs. Lbs.

Gross Weight

Tare

Net Weight

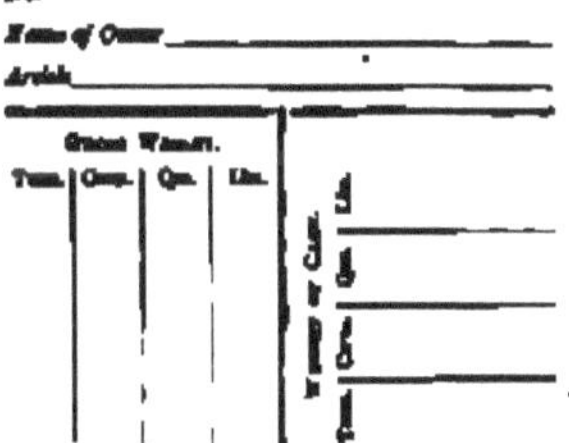

TOWN COMMISSIONER'S WEIGHING MACHINE.

*Kinsale*____________188 .

No.

*Name of Owner*__________________

*Article*________________________

Gross Weight.				Weight of Cart.
Tons.	Cwts.	Qrs.	Lbs.	Tons. Cwts. Qrs. Lbs.

Gross Weight

Tare

Net Weight

22,740. You have another for the beam and scales? —No printed form.

22,741. Do you give a manuscript ticket?—Yes.

22,742. In weighing potatoes, do you always estimate the tare of the sack?—Yes.

22,743. You never actually weigh the empty sack?—Never; there is an allowance of four pounds.

22,744. Supposing a sack was brought in on a very wet day, and was completely saturated with wet, would you allow only four pounds?—I have nothing to do with the empty sack. Let the buyer do what he likes.

22,745. Do not you put the tare on the ticket?—I only put the gross. Whatever the weight is I put it down, wet or dry.

22,746. Then it is a matter of arrangement between the purchaser and seller as to any tare?—Yes. I do not know whether the sack is wet or dry. I give the gross weight and the [illegible] tare four pounds.

22,747. What is the lowest weight you weigh with in weighing potatoes? Could you weigh down to a pound?—Yes.

22,748. Do you weigh to a pound?—I weigh to a pound, but not to a half pound.

22,749. If weighing the sack of potatoes, do you only use the four pounds?—I do, and two pounds and a pound.

22,750. When weighing do you give a cast of the beam?—Generally.

22,751. Is it a full one, or does the board of the scales touch the ground?—The buyer will require it to touch the ground.

22,752. Supposing they fall out over the tare, and you weigh the empty sack, do you charge anything additional for that?—Never. They never do that except for corn.

22,753. What do you allow for the tare of the sack of corn if you do not weigh it?—They generally weigh all corn.

22,754. What comes to the market has to be weighed?—There is none, unless at seed time, and a few sacks that may be sold to those stablemen.

22,755. At the weighbridge do you always weigh the empty cart?—Always.

22,756. You charge nothing additional for that?—No.

22,757. You deduct the tare from the gross weight and levy your charge on the net weight?—Yes.

22,758. You never charge on the gross weight?—Never.

22,759. The same observations apply to turnips?—Yes; turnips, hay, straw, mangolds, or anything weighed.

22,760. Have you ever heard complaints of any inaccuracy in the weighing?—I never heard.

22,761. Do the police visit the scales to see are they correct?—They do, of course. It would weigh to a pound.

22,762. Within what districts are those commodities brought from?—They come from Inishannon, Ballygarvan, and Old Hill; something of a radius of six miles, and 10 miles sometimes.

22,763. You have no connexion whatever with the fairs?—No; there is no charge at all on the fairs.

22,764. Nor have there been since the 4th September fair fell into abeyance?—No.

22,765. Have the Town Commissioners any rules regulating the markets here, or have you erected up in the place below, in the market place, any rules or regulations?—There is a board, but we have it inside here. It is a large board regulating the charges. It got defaced.

22,766-7. How long is it since it was exposed for public inspection?—We had to take it down to have it repainted.

22,768. Have you anything to say or to suggest as to what you think would better or tend to better the market?—I do not see anything wrong with the market. I do not see how to make any improvement.

22,769. You have no suggestion to make?—No.

22,770. Do you think the fairs here are better attended because no tolls are levied at them than if tolls were levied?—Well, I do not know. I think if there were tolls levied I do not see it would be any benefit to the toll-collector, whoever he might be.

22,771. I am only saying, do you think it would deter the farmers from bringing their animals and exposing them for sale?—It would not.

22,772. Would that be because they would have to come here, as there is no other fair to go to?—There are plenty of fairs to go to.

22,773. Are there any other fairs near this at which tolls are levied?—I do not know any other fairs. They are levied at Clonakilty and Dunmanway fairs.

22,774. Is Dunmanway a good fair?—It is a large fair.

22,775. Supposing a man was living midway between Dunmanway and Kinsale, would he prefer coming to Kinsale instead of Dunmanway because tolls are levied there?—He would not.

22,776. They do not consider whether they have to pay a toll or not if they are sure of a ready sale for their animals, and of having a good fair and market?—They would be prepared to pay heavy tolls very often to have a ready sale. The tolls on cattle would be very low, a penny for sheep and a penny for pigs and threepence for cattle. Those were the charges at the September fair formerly, when I had the customs.

22,777. Threepence for cattle?—Yes.

22,778. Were they well attended at that period?—They were.

22,779. What was your tender to the Town Commissioners at that period?—I was paying [illegible]l. at that time.

22,780. For the markets and fairs?—Yes, one fair in the year.

Mr. Thomas Healy, Chairman of the Town Commissioners, examined.

22,781. Are you the chairman of the Town Commissioners?—Yes.

22,782. Do you think this course the Commissioners adopt at present of leaving out the tolls is a desirable one?—I think so.

22,783. Would you say you derive a greater pecuniary benefit from it than if you managed them yourself?—I think so.

22,784. Do you think would the people who frequent the markets be more satisfied if the Town Commissioners had them in their own hands?—I think if you examined some of the farmers who are in town to-day they would give you an opinion on that.

22,785. You had yourself some conversation with these men and with the traders?—Yes.

22,786. Do you think it would be well here in Kinsale or it would better the town if market buildings were erected and rules adopted regulating and confining the sale of marketable commodities to these buildings?—I think so, because latterly everyone is selling meat and potatoes in the shop and doing away with the market. The meat market is done up.

22,787. You would not prohibit private enterprise in that way?—You could not do that.

22,788. Instead of selling commodities on the public thoroughfare you would be in favour of having them confined in a space?—I think it would be better. I remember in my own time a stand of apples in the street, and a man passing knocked against it and knocked the apples down. A policeman came up and there was a row. The man was fined 10l., as he broke the policeman's leg.

22,789. You object to the markets being held and those commodities sold on the public thoroughfare from liability to accidents?—Yes.

22,790. Do not they occasion much filth and dirt about the town?—Yes. There was a stand on the quay for vegetable women, and some of them came to me and said they would wish to leave the market. The Commissioners then compelled them to go in, and they were not one week in.

22,791. Did the police take any proceedings for obstructing the public thoroughfare?—They did not.

22,792. Do you think it would be for their own benefit to go into the market?—If they were compelled to do so the people should go to the market then.

22,793. In what state are the approaches to the market?—Very good; formerly there was a vegetable market inside the meat market and fowl market, and the Commissioners thought it did not pay and they let it to another party as a garden.

22,794. When did they remove the vegetable market and fowl market from this place?—About 20 years ago, and it used to be very well attended then.

22,795. Do you approve of the present system of having the fairs toll free?—I think so.

22,796. Have you formed any ideas yourself as to the levying of a toll?—I do not know. If the farmers got a good price at the fairs they do not object to the toll.

22,797. If they could effect a good and quick sale they would not consider the payment of the toll?—Yes. The people here go to Bandon with their cattle. The only thing the Commissioners cannot is to get the parties to go into the market.

22,798. Have representations been made to the Town Commissioners to remove these people and provide accommodation for them?—Yes, several times. They summoned them, and they would not pay the fines.

22,799. Then you do not like to take any criminal proceedings?—No.

22,800. Still you think a necessity exists for such buildings being erected here, and rules regulating and confining the sale of marketable commodities to that place?—Yes.

22,801. Do you think it would be better for the town?—I think so.

22,802. What class of farms are there around here?—The farms are not very large.

22,803. Is there a very large portion of the land under tillage?—I think so.

22,804. Would you say the greater portion of it?—Yes.

22,805. In that case the markets ought to be somewhat better. Where do they send the majority of the produce when it does not come here?—They send the butter to Cork. There is no grazing on the other side of the water, and they have no butter there.

22,806. Where do they send the other produce?—They mostly send it to Bandon and mostly send potatoes here.

22,807. Is Bandon a good market town?—Yes.

22,808. Does it take a lot from this?—Yes. Half goes to Cork and half to Bandon.

22,809. What is the principal industry here?—Fishing.

22,810. You export great quantities?—Yes. We are getting sprats as far as Inishannon, and mackerel.

22,811. Is that purely what the harbour is availed of by fishermen?—There is a great trade here in the fishing.

22,812. Is the trade purely in fishing?—Yes.

22,813. Now, from your experience of commissioners and public bodies, being chairman of the Kinsale Town Commissioners, do you think where such local bodies exist that they should obtain compulsory powers to acquire the market rights and tolls in the towns in which they are established, and do you think they would work them better than having them in the hands of a private individual?—I think it would be better if the Commissioners had them.

22,814. You would recommend that they should obtain these compulsory powers?—Yes, because what benefit they got goes to the benefit of the town.

22,815. Do you think they would be able to manage them better than a private individual, the lord of the soil, or others?—Yes.

22,816. Do you think they would give better satisfaction to those frequenting the markets and fairs?—I think so.

22,817. Have you formed any ideas on that subject?—I think if they worked them themselves they might charge less tollage.

22,818. You think if tolls were levied the Commissioners should work them themselves, and not lease them out?—I think so.

Mr. Patrick Murphy examined.

22,819. You are a farmer?—Yes.

22,820. Have you formed any ideas as to the levying of a toll?—Well, indeed I have. I would say they ought not to be levied.

22,821. Why?—Because I believe in liberty, and I do not think they have a right to charge tolls for anything.

22,822. Supposing tolls were levied, do you think it would deter men from bringing their animals to the fair?—It would.

22,823. Would it have that effect here?—It would.

22,824. The fact of no tolls being levied in a town induces the farmers to bring in commodities in greater quantities?—It would induce them to bring more regularly, and help the fair to be carried on.

22,825. Although no tolls are levied here, is there the system of luck-penny between buyer and seller?—There is.

22,826. Is it fixed in the case of cattle at all?—It is; the seller has to pay it, certainly.

22,827. Is there any fixed rate for it?—No.

22,828. He can give what he pleases?—What he likes.

22,829. Is it fixed on pigs?—I do not think it is.

22,830. Do they give sixpence luck-penny?—They do not mind; there is no fixed thing. There is always

22,835. Does it interfere with the passage to and fro of the people?—It does not. It is not the slightest harm in the world.

22,836. You are a farmer yourself?—I am a farmer living within two miles of the town.

22,837. Do you bring most of your stock to this place?—Indeed I do. There is one thing the custom man here charges custom on goods he has no right to charge, because what is sold in the country and goes to the stores he charges tolls.

22,838. On what commodities?—On fowl and all those things. If a man who deals in fowl buys in the country, he will be charged sixpence a box for them.

22,839. How many would be in the box?—If only two he would charge as much as if there were 20 in it.

22,840. Whatever quantity you send in he charges twopence, and over 20 threepence?—If there was only one in it it would be twopence all the same.

22,841. How does he collect the charge?—He goes to the stores.

22,842. He goes to the stores and asks how many they received?—Yes.

22,843. Is it the buyer pays the charge?—No, but the seller.

22,851. Does that practice exist relative to any other commodity?—If you bring in a little bit of butter or anything like that, and go about the street, he will charge a penny.

22,852. Is that only when he weighs?—Without weighing at all he charges.

22,853. Do you ever bring it in?—No.

22,854. Did he ever charge you?—No.

22,855. He said if the butter was brought in here and weighed he charges, but if brought in here and sold elsewhere he would not?—If I sold in a shop he went after me, but I did not give it to him.

22,856-7. Did he ever do that with you?—Indeed he did, although I did not give him the money.

22,858. Did he ever make on the goods of any of the people?—He did not arise on me.

22,859. On the other people?—I could not say. I will not tell a lie.

22,860. Is there any other gentleman who has any evidence to give or remarks to offer relative to this inquiry?—No answer.

The inquiry then terminated.

MIDLETON—CO. CORK.

With reference to my inquiry in Midleton on the 22nd November 1888, I beg to report as follows:—

Midleton is situated in the county of Cork, about 13 miles from the city. It is a station on the Cork and Youghal and Queenstown direct railway line. The town is neatly situated, and has a prosperous appearance. Formerly it had a very good general trade, which has, however, decayed within latter years. The Local Government is vested in Town Commissioners, and the population is 3,358.

The market day is Saturday. The fairs are held on the second Monday of each month.

Tolls are levied at all the fairs and likewise at the markets, except on hay, straw, and turnips, upon which weighing charges only are levied.

A toll board is erected at the fairs, but none at the markets. Beams and scales and two weighing-machines have been provided.

At the fairs the toll is on the entrance of each animal to the fair. The toll on fish

place is kept in good order and presented a clean and suitable appearance on the day of inspection. At either side of the covered entrance to this market stalls are placed where meat is disposed of.

The fowl and egg market is an enclosed space situate on the main street. A long covered shed for the accommodation of those frequenting the market is provided, but the space for cars is insufficient. There is only one entrance to this market, which is enclosed by a low stone wall surrounded by iron railings.

The corn and potato market is situate in a different street, but not far distant from the others. It is enclosed and provided with sheds and weighing accommodation. The size of the market is considered large enough for its purposes. For commodities not disposed of storage accommodation is available.

The marketable commodities for the exposure of which no enclosed buildings are provided, such as fish, vegetables, &c., are sold about the public streets.

When commodities are weighed the weight is marked on the bags, but a ticket is given if required.

Previous to 1887 six fairs were held in Midleton, and as no legal authority was granted for some of them, the inhabitants for five or six years resisted the payment of the charges which had been levied. Legal proceedings were instituted by Lord Midleton, but happily the question has been amicably settled by express legal authority having been obtained for these and additional fairs, and a lease of the charges thereat made to trustees for the benefit of the town. The charges have also been considerably reduced, as a comparison will show.

The removal of cast-clothes and other standings off the public streets was strongly advocated by those attending the inquiry on the ground that they are at present an inconvenience and danger to the community.

Appended will be found a transcript of the evidence taken at the inquiry.

John J. O'Meara,

45, Lower Mount Street, Dublin. Assistant Commissioner.

22,885. I believe you have the fairs let out at present?—Within the last few months we have been making arrangements with trustees of the town. First of all we proposed to let them to the Town Commissioners and found, as they were under a limited Act, that they had not the power to acquire them legally, and these trustees were appointed at the request of Lord Midleton and a lease made to them, and they are to deal with the profits precisely as if they were rates in the town and expend them for the benefit of the town.

22,886. Have you got the particulars of the lease and the date of it?—We can give you the lease if you wish.

22,887. Have you ever seen it yourself?—Yes.

22,888. Are there any special covenants in it?—There are some of the leases here.

22,889. You have not got the date of that lease?—No; there is nothing very particular in it that I remember.

22,890. What is the rent it is subject to?—Sixty pounds a year.

22,891. Are you aware of the valuation of the tolls of the fairs?—The tolls of the fairs are valued at 55l.

22,892. Have the trustees to pay the rates and taxes?—They have to pay the usual tenants rates and taxes.

22,893. You allow the ordinary deductions?—Yes; half poor rates and county cess.

22,894. In the lease to them is it set out how they are to apply the surplus?—No, except in general terms that they are to apply the profits for the benefit of the town the same as town rates.

22,895. What is the term of the lease?—Sixty years.

22,896. The markets are under the immediate control of Lord Midleton?—Yes.

22,897. Whom have you engaged to manage them?—The weigh-master, Mr. Edward Healy.

22,898. What market buildings have you provided here in the town?—The meat market, butter market, potato market, and fowl and egg market.

22,899. Where are these markets held?—They are in the town. The fowl market is close to the town hall.

22,900. Are they enclosed?—Entirely enclosed.

22,901. Have you any rules in the market confining the exposure of all marketable commodities to that building?—No, we have not. Fish, vegetables, and cast clothes are sold on the public street.

22,902. Have you any rules connected with the market at all?—No printed rules or regulations at all.

22,903. Then can the people who bring in butter, potatoes, fowl, eggs, or meat expose them for sale on the public thoroughfare?—As a matter of fact they do, but they have no legal right to do so. I know some butter is weighed at private houses.

22,904. Are tolls collected on those?—No; only what goes to the market.

22,905. I suppose you have not had an opportunity of bringing the queries before Lord Midleton?—He saw the printed questions, and I communicated with him about them. They are answered.

22,906. I suppose you would be able to give me Lord Midleton's opinion on any of the questions?—Lord Midleton is of opinion that it would be advisable that public authorities should have the right to acquire the rights of the markets, with the market tolls; that the fairs and markets should belong to some properly constituted public authority, giving compensation for any vested interests.

22,907. Lord Midleton is of opinion that that would be the most advisable course to adopt?—Yes.

22,908. Have you had any connexion with fairs and markets other than those in Midleton?—No, I have not. I have one small property, where fairs are let by lease, but I have no connexion with it except receiving the rent.

22,910. Have you a toll board erected?—There is a toll board at the entrance to the fairs.

22,910a. Have you a toll board for the market?—For the fairs only.

22,911. You have none at all for the market?—There were old toll boards up when they were let to Mr. Keane, about 60 years ago. There were a number of articles specified, but they were not charged on.

22,912. What is the market day?—Saturday.

22,913. Only Saturday?—Yes.

22,914. Any other days marketable commodities are not sold?—They sell on Friday.

22,915. I presume there are no legal proceedings going on now. Has the matter been settled by the tolls having been leased to the trustees?—The trustees are only entitled to collect the tolls at the fairs. The markets are still in Lord Midleton's hands.

22,916. I would like to know from you the capital expenditure made by Lord Midleton in providing the buildings in connexion with the markets and fairs?—The actual expenditure since I have been agent is 1,017l. 7s. 8d.

22,917. Could you segregate that amount?—I could give you the items, but I have not got them here. That does not include the market house and new fowl market.

22,918. Do you know how that 1,000l. was expended?—Portion of it was expended in building the fowl market during Mr. [illegible]'s agency, and that cost [illegible]. The rest has been expended on the fair green and fitting up the meat market, which has been altered.

22,919. Does that include the value of the sites of these markets?—No; that sum does not include the buildings on it before the market house and potato market. I value them at 1,200l. That would be the additional cost of the buildings in addition to the expenditure of 1,017l.

22,920. Supposing the markets were not on these sites, how would the ground be utilised, or could it be utilised for building purposes?—Yes. The site of the town hall could be utilised for building purposes, and the site of the fowl and potato market. The fair green has been always used as a fair green from time immemorial, and could not be used for building purposes.

22,921. All the fairs have always been held on the fair green?—Yes, always held on the fair green.

22,922. Could you give me your average receipts and expenditure in connexion with the market?—The average given is given in the query sheet, including three years no tolls were taken. From 1877, when I came here first, I can give you the receipts down to the time they were stopped in June 1881.

22,923. You have got the average for that period?—I can give you the total for each month. Perhaps that would be better. In 1877, from six fairs, 61l. 15s. 10d.

22,924. From the fairs alone?—Yes, and the cost of collection was 7l. 5s. 8d. In 1878, from 12 fairs the receipts were 173l. 5s. 5d.; cost of collection, 19l. 15s. 10d. In 1879 the receipts were 191l. 7s. 7d.; cost of collection, 19l. 11s. 9d. In 1880 the receipts were 174l. 5s., the cost of collection, 18l. 13s. From January to June they were disturbed, and the receipts were 70l. 5s. for the half year, and the cost of collection, 8l. 8s. 4d. The total receipts from June 1877 to June 1881 were 678l. 13s. 10d., and the total cost of collection for that period was 70l. 2s.

22,925. Have you got the receipts from the markets?—Yes. They were leased up to October 1877, and from October 1877 to December 1877 the receipts were [illegible] 15s. 4d.; cost of collection, 7l. 13s. For 52 weeks from December 1877 to December 1878, the receipts amounted to [illegible] 14s.; cost of collection, [illegible] 0s. 3d. In 1879 they were 164l. 1s. 5d.; cost of collection, 43l. 15s. 4d. In 1880 167l. 18s. 3d.; cost of collection, 40l. 9s. 8d. In 1881 [illegible] 14s. 9d.; cost of collection, [illegible]

22,926. Are the accounts closed in December of each year?—Yes. That cost of collection does not include repairs, rates, or taxes.

22,927. Are there any salaries to be paid?—Yes, the weigh-masters' and toll-collectors' wages. The profits in that include the weekly waste removed.

22,928. The receipts from all sources in connexion with the markets?—Yes.

22,929. Have you got the particulars of the average capital expenditure, such as for new buildings and repairs other than that for the past three years or the three years up to December 1877?—I put that into the sum of 1,019*l.*

22,930. That would be the total capital expenditure, but what would be the average expenditure in those years for repairs or expenses other than the salaries mentioned?—We could give you from 1858 down for the capital expenditure. The last three years the fairs having been upset, there was nothing done to the fair green.

22,931. That will go into the capital expenditure in providing market and fair accommodation?—Yes, but, as regards the repairs, there were no repairs done to the premises within the last three years.

22,932. Within the last three years you had actual control of them; what was the average cost of the repairs?—About 35*l.* or 40*l.*

22,933. The average in the year?—Yes, in painting and small repairs. I have excluded the repairs from the sum I have given you as the capital expenditure.

22,934. That is, the necessary repairs required each year have amounted on an average, for the last three years you had control, to 35*l.* or 40*l.*?—Yes. It went as high as 50*l.* one year, and went as low as 5*l.* 5*s.* another year, but it would be about from 35*l.* to 40*l.* a year.

22,935. That was not spent in providing additional buildings?—No; it was for keeping up the present buildings—painting, repairing, moving the pens, and repairing the gates.

22,936. Have you provided a weigh-bridge capable of weighing cattle?—Yes. It was provided by Lord Midleton, but the trustees pay back the cost of erecting that out of the receipts.

22,937. The trustees have to recoup Lord Midleton what it cost?—Yes.

22,938. By annual instalments?—As they get it in.

22,939. In addition to the 50*l.* a year rent?—Yes; it is the first charge after the rent.

22,940. What was the cost of the machine?—The weigh-bridge cost 62*l.*; that is the cattle weigh-bridge; but there is another for weighing coal.

22,941. Now as to these markets that are held on the public thoroughfare, would you approve, or do you think it would be desirable to confine them to the market buildings?—Certainly, if there were suitable buildings. It would be most desirable to establish a fish market.

22,942. Were any representations ever made to you or to Lord Midleton to get the police to remove them to the buildings, or do the buildings exist at all of which they could avail themselves?—There are no buildings which would suit. There would have to be new buildings.

22,943. Is it your opinion that all marketable commodities should be confined to enclosed market buildings, and bye-laws made confining the sale and exposure of these commodities to these buildings alone?—Certainly. It is also the custom here, which is very objectionable, to expose for sale old clothes, and it seems to me that is a source of great danger from infection. Nobody knows where they come from.

22,944. Do they expose them on market days?—On market and fair days.

22,946. What return do they get for the penny?—They are allowed to expose them on the street.

22,947. But at present there is no place they could go to or avail themselves of?—No. There is a room to which they might be compelled to go, but it is the custom from time immemorial to remain on the street.

22,948. Do you think it would improve the town if that course were adopted, of having these commodities and all marketable commodities confined to an enclosed space?—Most decidedly.

22,949. And their removal would not meet with any great opposition from the traders of the town or the members of any particular trade?—The traders of the town would be in favour of it, but the people who expose the commodities would be against an enclosed space. The fish should be removed off the street.

22,950. You have no fish market?—No fish market.

22,951. They only expose commodities on the public street where there are no enclosed spaces for them?—Yes; fish, vegetables, and old clothes.

22,952. They do not expose any of the commodities on the streets where you have markets for them provided?—No; the butter is bought by factors. That goes into the market, and the people have no object in having that exposed.

22,953. Do they go about the town with lump butter?—No; they go into the market place. There is no toll taken on the lump butter sold to be consumed in the houses in the town.

22,954. Have you any suggestions to make affecting any of the Midleton fairs or markets?—I entirely agree with Lord Midleton's view, that whenever there is a competent public body in a town they should have the right to manage the tolls and markets.

22,955. Why did you arrive at that opinion. Do you think the united efforts of all the gentlemen composing that board would tend to work the markets and fairs better and more to the satisfaction of those frequenting them than an individual?—I think it is desirable that it should be done where there is a competent public body. Unfortunately the town commissioners have not the power to acquire them, but it would be very desirable they should be given the power.

22,956. Have you formed any ideas as to the levying of a toll, or do you think the exaction of a toll in any way acts as a deterrent on people bringing their commodities or animals to the markets or fairs?—Not the least; I heard it said where the accommodation is provided people would not object to pay a toll on over and over again for the sake of convenience. In an enclosed fair green, where there are no enclosed pens, it would take double the number of men to mind a dozen head of cattle, whereas one man can mind 20 or 30 head in the pens.

22,957. Do you think the system of charging on the animals entering the fair green works better than the large charge levied on animals actually sold?—Decidedly better.

22,958. You think so?—Yes, it puts a stop to disputes. There is constant wrangling at the gates or gaps where the tolls are taken on the sales.

22,959. That course was adopted at all the fairs previous to their getting into the hands of the fair committee?—Yes.

22,960. You never levied tolls on the exit of the cattle from the fair green?—Not since we got them up from the late lessee in 1877. They were levied on the sales by the lessee Mr. Keane.

22,961. On the sales only?—Yes.

22,962. When did his tenancy cease?—In October 1877.

22,963. Previous to that the tolls were levied on the sales?—Yes. There was no accommodation in the fair green.

22,965. Have you any recollection of what took place when the alteration was made? Was it opposed by the farmers who brought animals here?—It was in contemplation before 1877 to establish six fairs, and it was agreed at a meeting to assist Lord Midleton in collecting the tolls if there was any difficulty about them.

22,966. Did you meet with any great opposition to the alteration?—No opposition.

22,967. Would you say that the great percentage of animals brought into the fairs are sold?—Yes, a great percentage. This is a very convenient centre, and we have very large fairs.

22,968. Could you give me any approximate idea of the percentage of animals sold?—I could not, because taking the entrance fee we were not interested, but the railway would give you the quantity sent over it on a fair-day. If the prices were good they would be all sold, but sometimes a great many would go back unsold. It is very hard to give an average.

22,969. I suppose the receipts from the weigh-bridge are mentioned in the return you have given me?—Yes, the total receipts. In giving you the capital expenditure I find I omitted no item of 91l., and I do not know if you took down the estimated cost of the town hall potato market.

Mr. Edward Hanly examined.

22,970. You manage the markets for Lord Midleton?—I do.

22,971. Who else is in the employment of Lord Midleton in connexion with the markets?—Only myself. There are two or three of his men there on Saturday morning to assist in collecting the tolls at the fowl and butter market—two in the fowl market and two in the butter market.

22,972. What duties do you perform?—I superintend the whole lot.

22,973. Have you got a weigh-master for the butter?—Yes.

22,974. Who is he?—Both those men weigh in the butter market. There are three small scales there.

22,975. Mention the different marketable commodities brought in on Saturday, whether there is any toll collected on them or not?—There is fowl, butter, potatoes, vegetables, fish, old clothing, crockeryware, earthenware, stallings with handkerchiefs, tinkers, and fruit.

22,976. Is corn brought in?—Corn don't come to me at all. The seed corn in the spring comes and tolls are taken on it.

22,977. Are hay and straw brought in?—Hay and straw does not come to me. It comes in. Then there is salt meat and pigs' feet.

22,978. You have no schedule of the charges on these different commodities erected in the market place?—We collect a penny on each.

22,979. We will take butter first. Does the butter come in firkins?—No, all in rolls.

22,980. What do you charge on butter?—A penny per roll from one pound to twenty or over. If weighed it is only a penny charge.

22,981. If a half-pound were brought in, would you levy any charge?—Yes, if it goes on the scale, a penny.

22,982. Then you charge a penny on a half-pound, and the same on 20 pounds?—Exactly, as long as it is in separate rolls.

22,983. Was a half-pound ever brought in?—No; never lower than two or three pounds.

22,984. Is this butter sold before weighed at your scales?—It is sold and weighed at the scales.

22,985-6. It is sold previous to weighing?—Yes.

22,987. Do they expose it for sale in the butter market?—Yes.

22,988. They do not go around the town?—No; they go straight to the butter market.

22,989. Supposing they exposed it for sale in your market, but did not weigh at your scales, a person saying, "I will take that roll for so much," would you ask for your penny charge?—Yes, I would charge it as long as it is bought, whether weighed or not. The scales are there, and let them use them.

22,990. Supposing they did not go to the butter market, but effected a sale to a shopkeeper in the town on market day, and did not weigh at your scales, would you levy your charge?—I never followed them.

22,991. If it came to your knowledge?—I would not go after them.

22,992. Supposing the butter is brought to a private shopkeeper in the town on Saturday, and the butter market is not availed of for standing in it, or your scales, would you seek for the charge?—The butter market is available. If the butter comes into the market and is taken out again into a private house or to a shopkeeper, it is followed, as long as it comes into the market.

22,993. If it is not brought to the market at all, but sold outside?—If we could see it we would look for the charge.

22,994. If the sale came to your knowledge, would you seek for your charge?—I would follow it up.

22,995. This charge of a penny is what you might call custom?—Yes.

22,996. You would not call it a weighing charge when you collect it and do not render any service?—Yes.

22,997. Do you weigh the butter yourself?—No.

22,998. What scales or facilities do you afford for weighing the butter?—There are three scales, and you can weigh from 56 pounds to two ounces, or to half an ounce.

22,999. When they are weighing, what is the smallest weight you weigh down to? Do you weigh to a quarter of a pound?—We can, and an ounce. I cannot answer that question, because I do not think there is anything weighed there but big lumps. There is no small; but it is customary for all merchants or people dealing in butter to buy them.

23,000. Supposing the actual weight of a roll of butter was six pounds three ounces, would you call it six pounds three ounces, or only six pounds?—Six pounds three ounces.

23,001. You would weigh to an ounce?—Yes, and always do.

23,002. Then you give the actual weight of the roll? Yes.

23,003. And you put the ounce weight into the scales?—Yes.

23,004. Is there any deduction from that weight?—No. I do not know what agreement there may be between buyer and seller.

23,005. For any salt around it?—No; there is nothing there when the butter is put into the scales.

23,006. Or any deduction for the butter that clings to the scales?—No, we have nothing at all to say to that.

23,007. Do you give a ticket?—We do.

23,008. Is that a printed form?—Yes.

23,009. On that ticket what do you put?—Only the weight.

23,010. You do not put the seller's name?—No. The ticket is something like the one produced, but a smaller form.

The following is a copy of the ticket in use:—

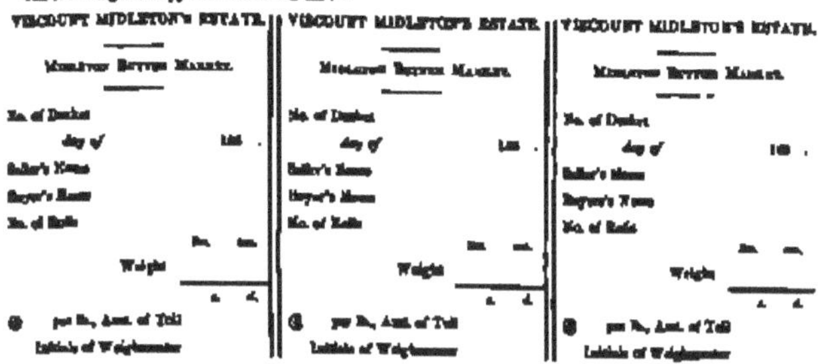

VISCOUNT MIDLETON'S ESTATE.	VISCOUNT MIDLETON'S ESTATE.	VISCOUNT MIDLETON'S ESTATE.
Midleton Butter Market.	Midleton Butter Market.	Midleton Butter Market.
No. of Docket	No. of Docket	No. of Docket
day of 188 .	day of 188 .	day of 188 .
Seller's Name	Seller's Name	Seller's Name
Buyer's Name	Buyer's Name	Buyer's Name
No. of Rolls	No. of Rolls	No. of Rolls
lbs. ozs.	lbs. ozs.	lbs. ozs.
Weight	Weight	Weight
s. d.	s. d.	s. d.
@ per lb., Amt. of Toll	@ per lb., Amt. of Toll	@ per lb., Amt. of Toll
Initials of Weighmaster	Initials of Weighmaster	Initials of Weighmaster

23,011. Do you keep a block of the ticket?—No, they are never used. They tear them up.

23,011a. You never keep any record?—No.

23,012. If they lose the ticket have they to weigh the butter over again?—They do not lose them. They are paid and the thing settled before they leave the place.

23,013. The buyer would not accept the butter until he sees the ticket?—No.

23,014. What is the charge on fowl?—If a cart comes in 2d. and 1d. on a basket.

23,015. Is that a standing charge for entry into the market?—That is a standing charge.

23,016. But if they stand out on the street?—When the carts come in with fowl they back in against the side of the street. The collector there goes round and gets 2d. on each cart. The fowl are brought up under the shed and each buyer having a portion of the shed for his fowl they keep the fowl there until the street is cleared.

23,017. Is that 2d. charged on a cart irrespective of the number of fowl in each?—It is.

23,018. You never consider that at all?—No.

23,019. What space do you allot them in the market?—What they require. Each of the fowl merchants takes up what he requires.

23,020. Is that the only charge on fowl?—Yes.

23,021. If they sell the fowl is there any additional charge?—No.

23,022. When do you collect that charge?—As they arrive. It is generally when they sell, because they might not have the charge until they sold.

23,023. Supposing a woman having a basket with a brace of fowl told you she had not the charge when she arrived would you wait?—Yes.

23,024. Did your collector ever seize on the fowl?—Never seized.

23,025. A complaint of such a seizure has never been made?—No. In fact they pay the toll free and easy with very few exceptions.

23,026. What is the charge on potatoes?—Sixpence per load.

23,027. Is that for weighing the load?—Yes.

23,028. If a load of potatoes were brought in bags would you weigh each individual bag?—The charge is 1½d. for every single bag up to four bags, and anything over that will go for 6d.

23,029. If they brought in 10 bags in a load would you weigh the entire load for 6d.?—I would have to do it according to the rules of the market.

23,030. Is there any additional porterage charge for lifting the bags?—No.

23,031. Who performs that duty?—The farmers themselves help one another, and if they employ a man they give him the price of a pint of porter.

23,032. Do porters attend there for that purpose?—Yes, but they have nothing to do with me.

23,033. Is there any rate of payment for them?—No.

23,034. You do not compel the farmers to employ these porters?—No; I do not meddle with the buyer or seller.

23,035. Is this charge payable to you whether they weigh at your scales or not?—I do not charge if they do not sell.

23,036. But if they sell and do not avail themselves of your scales do you charge?—Yes.

23,037. When do you collect the charges?—On the carts going out.

23,038. How do you know what quantity was in the cart?—I do. I know the cart coming in, and I am so used to them, I know what every one has. The market is small, and there is very little accommodation there.

23,039. Have you ever complained of the accommodation?—No. About the spring of the year there is a very considerable quantity of potatoes sold on the street, as the market could not accommodate them.

23,040. Are all the potatoes sold here by weight?—They are.

23,041. At the beginning of the season do they ever sell by measure?—Never. The second scales is erected in the springtime out in the street.

23,042. Do you collect the charges the same as inside?—Yes; I get the assistance of another man with me.

23,043. Then you have two scales?—Yes.

23,044. You think that during the season these are sufficient for the trade?—They are. About three or four hours it takes to weigh, and there is a rush for that time.

23,045. Have you ever heard complaints of any undue delay being caused in ascertaining the weight?—No.

23,046. You never heard of such complaints?—No. The scales are there always working.

23,047. Did you ever hear any such complaints were ever made?—No, I did not in my time.

23,048. When weighing potatoes do you always ascertain the tare of the sack?—Seven pounds are allowed.

23,049. You never actually weigh it?—No; it is the custom in the market to allow seven pounds for the potato sack.

23,050. It is always seven pounds?—Yes.

23,051. Would that be the calculation here if the potatoes were brought in on a fine day as well as on a very wet day when the sack was completely saturated with wet?—The very same. They take it one day with the other.

23,052. Anything that comes do you weigh the empty sack?—No, not the potato sack.

23,053. If a dispute arises between the buyer and seller do you weigh the stuff then?—I give them the currency of the market.

23,054. Would you refuse?—Yes, because it would put them quarrelling.

23,055. Would you refuse to ascertain the tare of the sack?—I would not refuse them if they asked or forced me to weigh the sack.

23,056. Supposing you did ascertain the tare of the sack, would you charge anything additional?—No; I would tell them the weight of the sack, and let them settle the matter themselves.

23,057. You would not charge anything extra?—No.

23,058. Supposing a cart came in with only two sacks of potatoes, would you charge 6d. on that load?—No; 3d.

23,059. Three halfpence on each sack?—Yes.

23,060. When weighing a sack of potatoes what is the smallest weight you use?—Four pounds.

23,061. It must be four pounds or nothing?—Yes.

23,062. Do you give a cast of the beam when weighing?—I break the beam.

23,063. What is your charge on vegetables?—A penny per basket or twopence a load on cabbage.

23,064. What would be the value of the smallest quantity of vegetables on which you would charge a penny?—I could not give you the value.

23,065. Is that charged every day or for the week?—It is for the week they avail themselves of the street.

23,066. It is on Saturday you collect this charge of a penny and twopence?—It is generally collected on Saturday by the man who collects at the fowl market.

23,067. Is that a penny for the market?—No, but twopence for the week.

23,068. Do you collect it always on Saturday?—Yes.

23,069. If Saturday was the first day they came in, would you collect that penny, and if they came on the following Saturday would you charge another penny although they only availed themselves of one day?—They would pay that day.

23,070. You never collect any other days of the week?—On fish I do.

23,071. What is the charge on fish?—Twopence for a load of fish. If there is half a load I only charge a penny.

23,072. If they bring fish in a basket what is the charge?—A penny.

23,073. Do they bring it in baskets?—It was only brought three times since I came here.

23,074. When do you collect the charge?—Every day.

23,075. If they brought in a basket of fish on Monday, Tuesday, and Wednesday?—A penny each day.

23,076. When do you collect it?—Generally after dinner, when they have the money made.

23,077. You never collect it before they effect a sale?—No.

23,078. Did you ever do so?—I never did.

23,079. Supposing they have not sold the fish?—I would not charge them.

23,080. Are these people hawkers who take the fish from door to door?—No; there is nothing like that in Midleton.

23,081. They have all fixed standings?—Yes, on the street. They take up a position as they come in, without reference to any place.

23,082. What is your charge on old clothing?—A penny for each owner; a penny for what a man has.

23,083. No matter what might be the extent of the standing or the quantity of clothing, you would charge a penny?—Only a penny.

23,084. When do you collect that charge?—In the afternoon. That charge on Saturdays is collected by the fowl market man.

23,085. Is it when they have effected a sale of any clothing?—I never had any difficulty in getting it from those people at any time.

23,086. Is that payable every day in the week?—No. They are not there. They only come on Saturdays and fair days.

23,087. And it is the same charge on both days?—Yes.

23,088. What is the charge on earthenware?—A penny.

23,089. Irrespective of the quantity they have?—Yes.

23,090. Or the value of it?—Yes. It is for the standing we charge the penny.

23,091. Standings with handkerchiefs?—A penny.

23,092. What are those standings? Are they carts?—Yes.

23,093. Would you charge the same thing if a cart came in as well as a small standing with a couple of boards raised on a couple of barrels?—Yes, the same charge.

23,094. What is your charge on baskets brought in?—A penny.

23,095. You have only one rate for everything?—Only one rate.

23,096. These baskets are sold on the public streets also?—Yes.

23,097. Is it only on Saturday?—On Saturday and fair days.

23,098. On seed corn what do you charge?—A penny per bag.

23,099. If a load were brought in?—A penny per bag if it contained 12 sacks.

23,100. What is the tare of the sack?—Sometimes they allow four pounds, but they generally weigh the bag, and that is deducted from the gross weight.

23,101. Is it on the same scales you weigh the corn and potatoes?—Yes.

23,102. Four pounds is the estimated tare if the sacks are not weighed?—Yes.

23,103. What is the lowest weight you use in weighing corn?—I weigh corn to one pound.

23,104. When you weigh the corn to a pound do you give a cast of the beam?—I do, a very light cast.

23,105. Anything under a pound weight goes to the buyer?—Yes.

23,106. Is the corn sold before it is weighed?—It is.

23,107. If it is sold in the market, but not weighed, you would still levy your charge?—Yes.

23,108. If not sold at all there, but exposed for sale and the space filled up in the market for the entire day, and the corn not weighed, would you still levy your charge?—No.

23,109. It is only on the sale?—Yes.

23,110. If they do not sell they go free?—Yes.

23,111. On fruit what do you charge?—A penny.

23,112. A penny for the standing?—Yes.

23,113. Does it go about the town?—No; it is on the side of the street. That is a weekly charge.

23,114. On Saturday you collect that too?—Yes.

23,115. What portion of the day do you collect this charge on fruit?—On Saturday it is collected by the fowl man, who brings it to me somewhere about 8 o'clock.

23,116. Then some of the fruit has been sold?—Yes.

23,117. Supposing they say they have not got the money, what course do you adopt?—We know them, and if we do not get it now we get it again.

23,118. What is your charge on hay?—Sixpence a load.

23,119. Where do they expose the hay for sale?—On the street.

23,120. Do they weigh the hay on the weighbridge?—I have nothing to do with it.

23,121. That is a weighing charge?—Yes.

23,122. If they do not avail themselves of your bridge they go free, although they sell the load?—Yes, and weigh it elsewhere.

23,123. Do the same observations apply to straw and turnips?—Yes.

23,124. If a person sold a load of turnips and did not weigh them at your bridge, would you levy a charge?—I would not.

23,125. On meat, what is your charge?—The standing for meat a penny, the same as the others. That only applies to salt meat.

23,126. On fresh meat?—They pay a rent for the stalls.

23,127. What stalls have you in connection with the market?—Three fresh-meat stalls, and they pay a weekly rent.

23,128. What is the rent?—Six shillings a week for each stall.

23,129. Have you stalls for any other commodities?—No.

23,130. Where do they bring the salt meat from?—From Cork.

23,131. Where do they bring it?—On the side of the street.

23,132. From what districts are the general commodities brought?—From around the country.

23,133. Within what radius?—Middleton is supplied from nine miles around, I should say, on market days.

23,134. What hour does the market usually begin?—It begins about seven o'clock. Every sort of produce comes on Saturday.

23,135. You are always in a position to weigh at seven o'clock?—Yes, and before it.

23,136. Do you open the gates of the market at that hour?—I do.

23,137. What time does it terminate?—Six o'clock on Saturday evening.

23,138. Is that the time you close the gates?—Yes, of the street stalls.

23,139. Are these markets kept in a clean state by the people?—Yes.

23,140. Immediately after the market are they cleaned?—Every Saturday as soon as the market is over they are cleaned out.

23,141. Who bears the expense of that?—The man who rents the [illegible] cleans the whole of them, and he gets the manure for the cleaning.

23,142. Does the manure he obtains act as an equivalent for any expense he would be at?—It would not. It would not be worth anything. It is so bad it is not worth losing time to draw it.

23,143. You have no schedule of the charges erected in the market at all?—No.

23,144. Were complaints ever made that your toll-collectors going about the town have demanded any larger or higher rates than you have mentioned?—Never.

23,145. No complaints were ever made?—No, because that would be the last of their toll-collecting.

23,146. When weighing potatoes do you ever mark the weight on the side of the bag with chalk?—I do, always.

23,147. You give a ticket and you also mark the weight on the bag?—I give a ticket if they want it, and if they do not I mark it on the bag as soon as the bag leaves the scale.

23,148. Then you only give the ticket when it is required?—Yes.

23,149. You charge nothing additional for the ticket?—No.

23,150. When you weigh the bag do you obtain payment of your charge?—Yes, when the car is going out.

23,151. Have you a clerk to fill up the tickets?—I have a man weighing, and I fill the tickets.

23,152. You obtain the charge?—Yes.

23,153. You have no regulation at all confining all these people to this market place?—No.

23,154. They go out in the streets and do go about the streets?—They do.

23,155. Is there a custom in the market requiring certain commodities to be sold through brokers agents or factors?—As far as the markets are concerned, no.

23,156. The farmer bringing his produce is free to sell to whom he pleases?—Yes.

23,157. Did you ever hear of any complaints of forestalling here either in potatoes or fowl?—No.

23,158. Of people going out and meeting the farmers coming in?—Yes, I heard a complaint of that, that is, between the fowl merchants.

23,159. It was only on fowl?—Yes, when there is a run of them they go out to meet them, and I had to interfere myself many times.

23,160. Have the sellers complained of that?—The sellers have not. It is the fowl merchants who have complained of it.

23,161. Supposing, now, the farmer was coming in with some fowl, and the buyer went out and purchased them on the road coming in, would you obtain any charge?—I would. The sellers always pay. The merchants themselves have runners, and they put their hands into the car and lift them out and bring them to the market. Then, when the fowl are taken out, we lose a penny, as the car does not go to the market. We charge twopence in place of that and we only get a penny.

23,162. Does the farmer permit the merchants' runners to take the fowl out of the car?—He does.

23,163. Are they sold to the merchants or the runner?—I often knew them fall in a bargain and others buy them then.

23,164. Who has the property in the fowl when taken out of the cart? To whom do they belong?—To the farmer until handed over to the merchant.

23,165. Is this practice resorted to for the purpose of avoiding the payment of twopence?—I do not believe it is. There is a certain quality of fowl they require, and there is a run on them.

23,166. The merchants inspect the fowl when brought into the market?—Yes.

23,167. If he does not like the fowl he will leave them there?—Yes.

23,168. Have you ever heard of a man going out who said he was one of the runners, and taking the fowl out of the cart and not turning up with them at all?—No, never.

23,169. Have you heard complaints of any inaccuracy in the weights in the markets?—No. They are tested twice a year by the police.

23,170. What is the charge on eggs?—The people who bring in the eggs pay nothing. They sell them to the merchants, and the merchants pay a penny a box. If there are six boxes they pay sixpence.

23,171. If they do not effect a sale at all they are free?—Yes.

23,172. What quantity of eggs would be in the box?—Six or seven hundred. They are large boxes.

23,173. Any of these commodities mentioned, such as eggs, if sold throughout the town, you collect the charge, although not brought to the market?—I never saw them going about the town; and I never saw them in except on market day, and they make straight to the market where the egg merchants meet.

23,174. Do you think, now, from your experience, if other market buildings were erected for the commodities exposed on the public thoroughfare, that the producers would avail themselves of them?—I believe they would have to be compelled. It is very hard to break them off old rules.

23,175. What commodities do you weigh on the bridge?—Hay and straw.

23,176. And roots of every description?—Yes.

23,177. You have only fixed charges?—Yes.

23,178. I see on this ticket that you produce, you put the seller's name always, and the buyer's, and the name of the commodity you weigh, and the gross weight?—Yes.

The following is the ticket in use:—

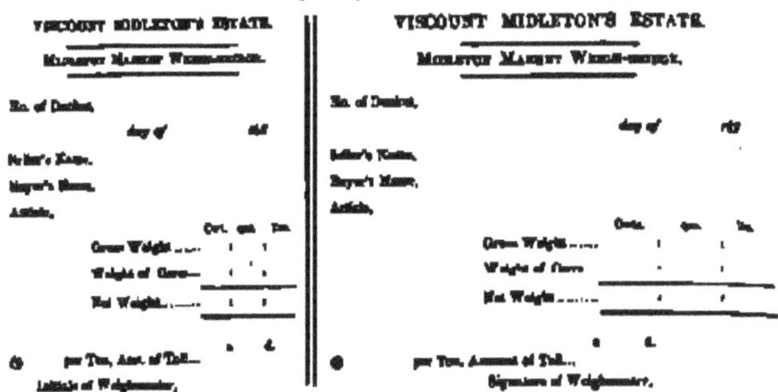

VISCOUNT MIDLETON'S ESTATE.

MIDLETON MARKET WEIGH-HOUSE.

No. of Docket,

day of 187

Seller's Name,

Buyer's Name,

Article,

	Cwt.	qrs.	lbs.
Gross Weight			
Weight of Cart			
Nett Weight			

s. d.

@ per Ton, Amt. of Toll

Initials of Weighmaster.

VISCOUNT MIDLETON'S ESTATE.

MIDLETON MARKET WEIGH-HOUSE.

No. of Docket,

day of 187

Seller's Name,

Buyer's Name,

Article,

	Cwts.	qrs.	lbs.
Gross Weight			
Weight of Cart			
Nett Weight			

s. d.

@ per Ton, Amount of Toll

Signature of Weighmaster.

23,179. You charge nothing additional for the ticket?—No.

23,180. Did you ever know any fraud being committed by changing the wheels of the cart after ascertaining the weight, or perhaps changing the entire cart?—No. I must say, as far as the people of Midleton and the surrounding districts are concerned, I never came across more honest people.

23,181. Is there any deduction from the gross weight of a load of hay other than the tare of the cart?—No.

23,182. You allow nothing for its bad state or if the weather was very wet?—That is their own matter.

23,183. Outside the deduction for the tare, it is a matter of arrangement between the buyer and seller?—Yes. I do not think I had any right to do anything that way, and never did.

23,184. Have you a knowledge of any other deduction?—No.

23,185. Do you ever ascertain the current price between the buyer and seller of the different commodities?—No. If they told me to make out the price of a load of hay, I will know how much a ton it is, but if I weigh for them, they will not tell me what it is, and I do not inquire.

23,186. You never inquire for the sake of curiosity?—No.

23,187. Supposing it was required from the owner of the market to make a periodical return of the current prices of the different commodities, would it be possible to obtain such a return?—It would, certainly.

23,188. Do you think such a return would be a pretty accurate one?—Indeed, it would.

23,189. And also of the quantity of the different commodities brought in?—Yes.

23,190. In that case you would have to fill up your block and retain it?—I always retain the block, except in the butter.

23,191. On the other commodities you do?—Yes.

23,192. With the exception of potatoes, when you give no ticket at all?—Yes.

23,193. You always give a ticket in the case of corn?—Yes.

Mr. ROBERT BAILEY examined.

23,194. Are you one of the trustees who hold the fair green from Lord Midleton?—No, I am secretary of the trustees.

23,195. Have you got a toll board specifying the charges?—Yes, as Mr. Fitzgerald told you, there is one erected at the entrance of each department. For instance, one for the cattle, one for the horses, and one for the pigs, and one for the sheep.

23,196. Have you different portions of the green allotted off for each species of animals?—Yes.

23,197. Are they separated by any wall from each other?—They are separated by a railing and some portions by a wall.

23,198. Tell me the different animals that are brought in?—Horned cattle, horses, sheep, pigs, goats, donkeys, and lambs.

23,199. The charges you levy are only on all animals as they enter the fair green?—Yes.

23,200. Are the rates you levy the same rates that have been levied any length of time?—The present scale is in existence since July. July was the first fair on which the trustees commenced to charge the existing scale of tolls, and that scale of tolls I have here.

23,201. The 12 fairs are held on the second Monday in each month, and all held in the fair green?—Yes, as far as practicable. In some cases necessarily they must extend into the upper portion of the town. At all the fairs the fair green does not afford sufficient space.

23,202. Is it want of space makes them go out on the road?—It is want of space that makes the cars go down the town, but cattle or sheep do not go into the town, but the cars do extend into portions of the main street.

23,203. Cars with pigs?—Yes.

23,204. (*Mr. Fitzgerald interposing*). I do not think the fair green is appropriated for pigs. They prefer standing on the street.

23,205. (Witness, continuing his evidence.) In the morning when the fair assembles the trustees do all they can to concentrate the pig fair within a small space, and when that space is filled they must necessarily file further down, and the fair recoils later on outside the space which is originally intended. Then, as the fair goes on the parties who first arrived find the bulk of the fair is outside, and they go out themselves again.

23,206. Have you any regulation at the fair compelling those people to go into the fair green?—We tried to enforce it.

23,207. But have you such a regulation—a written one?—No, but a verbal one.

23,208. Did the police give any assistance in removing them off the public thoroughfare?—They have not been asked directly. The police are there to prevent collisions.

23,209. Do they (the fairs) cause any obstruction to the public?—More or less they do.

23,210. Do they take up the foot-paths or remain only on the road?—The cars are on the road, and necessarily a crowd assembles at the rear of the cars and block the footways.

23,211. Have the private inhabitants of the town complained of the obstruction in going to the railway station?—Certainly, and it is with a view to have that obviated that the trustees have concentrated them on the fair green and took them off the street as much as possible.

23,212. What is the extent of the fair green?—Four acres.

23,213. It is entirely enclosed?—It is in two parts at each side of the road.

23,214. This document produced is the lease under which the trustees hold the fairs?—Yes.

23,215. The lease is dated the 19th May 1888, from the Right Hon. Viscount Midleton to Thomas Stephen Coppinger, Chairman of the Town Commissioners, Edward Hallinan, William Cogan, Michael Henry Walsh, Maurice Ronayne, and Patrick Leahy. Whereby the lessor granted to the lessees for 50 years from the 24th June 1888, all the exclusive right of holding fairs granted by the two patents upon the two pieces of land in Midleton, the fair green containing three acres, one rood, and thirty-six perches, and the pig green containing one acre and three perches statute measure, subject to the yearly rent of 60l. The special covenants are as follows:—

"A special covenant that the lessees, after payment out of the receipts, of the rent, rates, and taxes, and cost of collection and necessary expenses to hold the fairs, pay unto the lessor, his heirs, or assigns, the residue of the tolls to be from time to time collected and received at the holding of the said fairs until thereby and thereout of the said cost of erecting the said cattle pens and weighing machine shall be repaid, but not to exceed the sum of 300l., and also the cost of this deed; and, in order to secure repayment, said sum of 300l. should be a first charge on the tolls. And after payment of the said necessary expenses and the said sum of 300l., the residue shall thenceforth, during this term, be applied and expended in effecting works and improvements for public purposes in the town of Midleton, to be approved of by the Town Commissioners for the time being in said town. That they shall use the fair green and pig fair green for the purpose of holding the fairs, and for no other purpose whatever.

"And a covenant to uphold the right to hold the fairs on the dates mentioned in the two patents, and to repair. Covenant by the lessor to repair and make good any damage or injury occasioned to the premises on any day or times save such fair days.

"Covenant against assigning or sub-letting.

"Condition that if any of the lessees becomes bankrupt, his joint interest in the tolls shall become merged in the interests of the remaining trustees.

"Similar condition also in the case of judgment being entered, or judgment mortgage registered, or breach of the covenants of the lessees' part contained; and on the death of any of the lessees, or his departure from the country a new trustee be appointed subject to the approval of the lessor; and a condition giving liberty to surrender on giving six months' previous notice in writing; and a condition that the schedule of fees and tolls attached to the deed are to be the fees and tolls collected and received in respect of cattle, pigs, and sheep entered into or going through the said pig fair or cattle fair green, and no alteration made therein without the consent in writing of the lessor.

"Covenant for quiet enjoyment."

23,216. What is your charge on cattle, Mr. Barry?—Bulls, fourpence each. This poster (produced) has been issued by the trustees.

23,217. You produce this as a schedule of the charges?—Yes. That is a copy of the schedule to the lease.

23,218. The following is a copy of the schedule of charges produced by witness:—

MIDLETON FAIRS.

The Midleton Monthly Fairs

Having been leased to the trustees, as under—

Thomas S. Coppinger, J.P., Midleton Lodge,
Edward Hallinan, J.P., Avoncore, Midleton,
Patrick Leahy, Midleton,
Michael H. Walsh, Midleton,
Maurice Ronayne, Midleton,
William Cogan, Midleton,

Notice is hereby given

That the following schedule of fees will be charged at each fair in future. These fairs are held second Monday in each month.

Next Fair on Monday, July 9th.

No other fairs held here.

Horses and mules, 3d. each.
Bulls, 4d. each.
Other horned cattle, 2d. each.
Calves, 1d. each.
Cribs containing six or more pigs, 6d. per crib.
Cribs containing less than six pigs, 1d. per pig.
Donkeys, 1d. each.
Sheep, ½d. each.
Ewes, with lamb or lambs, 1d. each.

23,219. Who are the charges regulated by. Are they jointly regulated by the trustees and Lord Midleton?—Yes. They cannot be reduced, or increased, or altered without the consent of both parties—Lord Midleton and the trustees.

23,220. And those charges are levied on all the animals as they enter?—Yes.

23,221. Do you think that works better from your own experience than having a larger charge on animals actually sold as they leave the fair green?—I highly approve of the existing arrangement.

23,222. Do the farmers approve of it?—Naturally those men who bring cattle to the fair and do not sell feel it a hardship to pay, but you could not please everybody and they would be better pleased if they had not to pay on unsold cattle.

23,223. Then they think it a hardship to pay on cattle that they do not know whether subsequently they will dispose of them or not?—Quite so.

23,224. Have they ever complained or made representations to the trustees or Lord Midleton to alter it?—They have not made any representations to the trustees, but the people are becoming accustomed to it and the grumbling has ceased to a very great extent. I may say my reply applies more to the time that the arrangement was originally made than to the present time. The custom is now so universally adopted that the grumbling has ceased as far as I am aware.

23,225. Are these rates smaller or larger than the rates originally payable previous to the lease being made granting them to the trustees?—They are smaller on every description of animal, that is, they are smaller than the tolls under Mr. Keane's management.

23,226. Were those tolls levied only on the sales?—Yes.

23,227. Was not there a period subsequent to that and previous to the lease that other charges were levied?—Yes, there was for the first five years of the monthly fairs.

23,228. Are those levied now smaller or larger than the rates levied during that time?—They are smaller, but not in all cases.

23,229. I see on horses it was fourpence and it is now threepence?—Yes; sheep under the old arrangement were a penny each, but now they are only a half-penny.

23,230. I see here cribs containing six or more pigs, sixpence?—Yes.

23,231. If the pigs are subsequently sold you do not levy any additional charge?—No.

23,232. In any case you do not levy any charge other than the one payable on entrance?—No; the cars are charged as soon as they get into position. Mr. Healy, who is the collector under the trustees, when the fair is well assembled and he finds a convenient time to leave other places in the fair he goes and makes a regular charge on every car he finds in the fair.

23,233. That is payable to the trustees?—Yes, Mr. Healy accounts to me in the afternoon of the fair day.

23,234. Does not he collect on entrance at the gateway?—Yes, that applies to cattle, horses, and sheep entering and pigs also, with the exception of those cars outside. These are not collected the moment they present themselves, but when they take up a position, and probably remain in the fair two or three hours in that position. Mr. Healy consults his own convenience in going around to collect from the cars.

23,235. Have you any source of revenue other than the charges on the animals?—Yes, he collects from the people with cart-clothing and makes a general collection on standings.

23,236. Do the receipts from the standings around the town on fair days go to the trustees?—Yes, Mr. Healy collects them all.

23,237. They do have standings around the town as a matter of fact, the same as he has described?—Yes. I do not know that he collects from fish-women or on the vegetables coming to the fair, occupying any standing. He collects on them.

23,238. When you say fair, are any of the streets connected with the fair green?—They exhibit these standings only on the main street.

23,239. There are pens in the fair green?—Yes.

23,240. What number have you?—I never counted them.

23,241. Are they sufficient for the accommodation?—They are sufficient, inasmuch as I have never seen a fair that there were not vacant pens there, with the exception of the sheep. There are two or three months in the sheep season when there is an enormous sheep fair, and in that case I think the accommodation on those two or three occasions is limited, but for the other nine fairs in the year there is ample accommodation for the sheep.

23,242. You have each description of animals separated from the others?—Yes.

23,243. No accident is caused by their ever intermixing?—They have no chance of intermixing.

23,244. Do you charge anything in addition to the ordinary entrance charge for stalls in the fair green?—No.

23,245. Supposing a farmer brings in his cattle the night previous to the fair day, and effects a sale of them and does not go to the fair green, would you seek for your charge?—No, unless the cattle were passing through the fair and they may be subject to it. Since I became connected with the trustees no case similar to that you say has arisen, and I do not know how it would be dealt with.

23,246. Supposing on a fair day a farmer was coming up the main street and effected a sale and did not go to the fair held in the fair green, do you think the trustees would be entitled to charge?—I think so, and could give you a case in point in regard to pigs, but not as regards cattle. If a man sells pigs down town, and carried them up to the railway, the man who collects the tolls will demand tolls from him though the pigs were not sold in the fair green.

23,247. Supposing they were sold to a private individual and the man took them into his own yard?—If they pass through the fair they will be charged by the man collecting the pig toll.

23,248. If sold on a fair day and not delivered until the following day?—We would not levy a charge on the following day.

23,249. Would you levy a charge on the sale?—We would not be aware of it.

23,250. If it came to your knowledge?—Yes. If reported to me I would send Mr. Healy for the toll.

23,251. What would you say are the limits of the jurisdiction of the trustees to collect toll?—Within the township.

23,252. (*Mr. Fitzgerald.*) I think Mr. Barry is mistaken in that. It would be right to say I had no title to collect any toll except an entrance fee in the nature of a stallage on animals coming in. I think the proper course in this, if a beast is sold outside the fair there should be a prosecution for sale, or exposing for sale, and infringing the market rights.

23,253. You think, Mr. Fitzgerald, that is an objectionable practice to collect at the custom gaps going out?—Tolls are objectionable. I think it is proper and right to charge for the accommodation given, to charge a reasonable sum so as to enable the owners of the fairs to provide suitable accommodation. It then benefits both parties.

23,254. It is your opinion when the owner of market rights or fair rights levies a toll he should give some accommodation in return?—I take it the meaning of a toll is no accommodation. In the other case the accommodation is given and the owner receives his stallage or entrance fee for which he provides certain accommodation.

23,255–56. (*Examination of Mr. Barry continued.*) Have you got the particulars of your receipts?—Yes.

23,257. How is the fair green utilised between fairs?—It is altogether out of the hands of the trustees. They have no claim to it except on fair days.

23,258. You have only liberty to utilise it for the day?—Yes.

23,259. How is it usually utilised?—It is not utilised except a stray may stand on it. The owner is liable for any damage done to the pens or premises except on fair days.

23,260. Now the receipts?—The July fair was the first on which the trustees took up the collection, and the gross receipts on that day were 18*l.* 0*s.* 6*d.* At the August fair the gross receipts were 19*l.* 8*s.* 8*d.*; at the September fair, 16*l.* 8*s.* 6*d.*; and the October fair, 16*l.* 8*s.* 9*d.*, and the November fair, 11*l.* 16*s.* 5*d.*

23,261. Have you got the expenditure?—I have the net amount for each day which has been lodged to the credit of the trustees.

23,262. Give me the expenditure?—I will give you the net receipts. Some of the expenses were paid out of the November fair and were in regard to last June, but were put against the whole thing.

23,263. What do the expenses comprise. Is it salary purely?—No. For instance, there are fourteen men collecting, and then Mr. Healy has a special payment for his general supervision. Then the incidental expenses of starting, the posters and additional labour, messengers, and advertisements.

23,264. And the rent?—The trustees have paid nothing in that direction, such as rent or taxes.

23,265. Give me the net profits?—The net amount for the July fair was 15*l.* 4*s.* 7*d.*; for August fair, 16*l.* 7*s.* 10*d.*; for September fair, 18*l.* 18*s.*; October fair, 14*l.* 4*s.* 3*d.*; November fair, 7*l.* 17*s.* 1*d.*

23,266. Who cleans the fair green after the fair?—I could not tell you. The trustees have nothing more to do with it. Our jurisdiction ceases with the fair day.

23,267. Have you a weigh-bridge erected in the fair green?—Yes, but it has never been utilised since it was erected.

23,268. You have a toll board erected at each entrance?—Yes.

23,269. How many entrances have you?—Five.

23,270. Is the field at one side of the road exclusively confined to the sale of pigs?—Yes.

23,271. Have you any particular pig fair day. You have not got a pig fair day as is customary in other places on the day previous to the ordinary fair?—No.

23,272. It is held on the same day?—It is.

23,273. You have a charge of a halfpenny per pig. Is it the same charge on a bonham?—Every pig that stands in the fair green is charged a halfpenny irrespective of its size, but bonhams brought in carts they are so small they do not stand as single pigs.

23,274. Does Mr. Healy collect on fair days from the vegetable people?—Oh, certainly. He does not collect from the weekly tenants, but strangers coming in.

23,275. On a fair day does any great number of them come in?—There do.

23,276. Does Lord Midleton get any benefit from them?—No, only from the weekly stalls.

23,277. It is only when strangers come in you levy a charge for the trustees?—Yes.

23,278. Do you think this fair green affords sufficient accommodation to the people?—I do.

23,279. Have you any shed in it?—No.

23,280. Do you think a necessity exists for such?—Yes, I have heard it sought for by the owners of the cattle particularly, to protect them from bad or severe weather—there are tender delicate stock or stock likely to be affected by severe cold and wet weather. I have stockbrokers complain of the want of protection for that class of cattle at the Midleton fair green.

23,281. Have any representations been made to the trustees or to Lord Midleton to provide such?—No. When I say no I mean it has never been made to the trustees.

23,282. Have you any observations to make on behalf of the trustees, or any suggestions to offer that would tend to better the fairs here?—I do not know. I have no suggestion to make with regard to the fairs bearing on the inquiry, but as a Town Commissioner I would have something to say with regard to the public street and markets.

23,283. Any suggestion you have to make I would be happy to hear it?—I would simply wish, as a Town Commissioner, to second, as forcibly as possible, the suggestions made by Mr. Fitzgerald in his observations to you about the necessity of having a fish market, and the present state of things in that respect remedied by changing its present site. Also the most objectionable manner in which those old clothes are exhibited in the main street and the want of accommodation for those two articles. The tolls are charged and no accommodation given to the vendors, but outside that they are a public inconvenience, amounting to a positive nuisance in each of those departments. Vegetables in their own way are comparatively smaller although they are also another decided nuisance which calls for a remedy in the present state of things.

23,284. What remedy would you suggest. Is it to provide shelter accommodation and confine them to an enclosed space?—Yes. The removal off the streets. It is a crying nuisance in the nineteenth century to have a town like Midleton subject to the nuisance of the present fish market. I make these remarks as a Town Commissioner.

23,285. Have you any other suggestion?—I think not.

23,286. Do you agree with Mr. Fitzgerald as a Town Commissioner that powers should be given to the Town Commissioners to acquire the market rights?—I would merely answer that question on my own responsibility.

23,287. What is your own individual opinion?—It may be very well but difficult to work it.

23,288. Is it not easier under existing circumstances for a body like the Town Commission to compel the fish and other commodities to go into an enclosed place than it would be for the landlord?—If the accommodation provided by the Town Commissioners were given under the Town Improvement Act, but the idea of the Town Commissioners taking up exclusively the management I do not approve of. The Commissioners are a transitory body, men in office to-day and not there in 12 months, and then you would be bringing strange individuals to work what should be a stationary regulation and machinery. I think it would cause difficulty in working it.

23,289. (By Mr. Fitzgerald.) What would be the difference between Town Commissioners having them and the Fair Committee?—It would entail much more trouble on the local body that they are not prepared to undertake.

23,290. (Mr. Fitzgerald.) Lord Midleton's agent is transitory but Town Commission is not transitory.

Mr. William Roche, clerk of Midleton Poor Law Union, examined.

23,291. You are the clerk of the Midleton Poor Law Union?—Yes.

23,292. Have the guardians any statement to make through you in connexion with the markets and fairs in Midleton?—I do not know that they have. The only thing they desired me to draw attention to is the fish market and the sale of old clothes. They consider these things objectionable on the streets.

23,293. They are the sanitary authority?—Yes.

23,294. Does their inspector ever inspect those clothes to see if they are in a fit state to allow them on the street?—I do not remember they were inspected.

23,295. They consider it most objectionable to the public health to have these things on the public street?—Yes.

23,296. Did a case ever arise of any infection being caught from these clothes?—I do not remember in my time.

23,297. Still you would like to have a preventive against that?—Yes. The guardians object to have the clothes on the street and the fish at the corner of the street where it is at present.

23,298. You brought the queries before them?—I did.

23,299. Do they approve of local authorities whether poor law guardians or Town Commissioners, if any such exist, or in the absence of one or the other, fair committees or trustees, receiving compulsory powers to acquire the market rights and tolls of owners like Lord Midleton?—They made no remark on that. The queries were read and they made no remark on them.

23,300. Did they only wish to have attention drawn to the old clothes and the fish market?—That is the principal thing.

23,301. Is it the Town Commissioners who bear the expense of cleaning the streets?—They clean the footways. The road contractor has portion of the cleaning of the streets.

Mr. Samuel McCullagh, town clerk, examined.

23,302. You are the town clerk of Midleton?—Yes.

23,303. Have the Town Commissioners directed you to give any expression of their opinion on the question as to whether it would be desirable that they, the local municipal authority, should receive compulsory powers to acquire the rights of Lord Midleton in order to work the markets and fairs?—No, since I got your first communication we have had no meeting of the Town Commissioners. It is the first Monday of every month they meet, and I had no opportunity of bringing the matter before them.

23,304. Not as a body, but did you bring it before them individually?—I spoke to several of the commissioners. There are some of them here.

23,305. What is your own opinion on that point, leaving out of the question any additional trouble you would have to undergo?—I could not answer for the body when I never brought it before them.

23,306. Have you formed any opinion yourself?—To have the Commissioners have compulsory powers?

23,307. No, but would the markets and fairs be better managed, and more satisfaction given to those frequenting them if the control were vested in a body like the Town Commissioners?—I could not answer that. I am sure if the Commissioners were the controlling body it would create a great deal of expense to be keeping up a staff of men to work the markets, and their funds are not very great.

23,308. What is the town rate?—1s.6d. a year.

23,309. What is it in the pound?—Ninepence.

23,310. What duties do the Commissioners perform?—They do the flagging and cleansing of the footways of the town, and the watering of the streets and lighting. Between gas and labour it costs 100l. a year, and there is only 60l. to pay the rest of the expenses. Thirty years ago, when they became a body, there was not a single flag laid in the town of Midleton at the time the Act passed, but the grand jury I must say has supplemented it, and Lord Midleton has given some help towards flagging the town.

23,311. Is the town of Midleton the property of Lord Midleton?—Yes.

23,312. Have you any further remarks to make?—No.

23,313. (By Mr. FitzGerald.) If the Town Commissioners had the profits of the tolls, subject to any compensation paid to Lord Midleton, that was sufficient to pay a staff and leave them a small surplus, do you think it would be advisable that a public body should have control of the markets?—I certainly would, if it paid the expenses. The Commissioners should have a staff then and not now.

23,314. Do not you think if the Commissioners had a staff they could utilise the same men for other purposes?—Yes, but the lamp-lighter could not be up day and night.

23,315. (By the Commissioner.) Do you think if the Commissioners received sufficient to pay the cost of management, and interest on any capital expended, it would be better they should have control?—Yes, I would say that.

23,316. The only objection is fearing they would sustain a loss?—That is all.

Mr. Denis McCarthy, T.C., examined.

23,317. You are one of the Town Commissioners?—Yes, I have very little to add to what Mr. Barry has said.

23,318. You agree with the observations of Mr. Barry?—Yes.

23,319. Mr. Barry was opposed to the Town Commissioners, the local authority, obtaining compulsory powers to acquire the market rights and tolls. Do you concur in that?—No. My opinion is it would be the wish of the people of Midleton that the Commissioners would have control over the fairs and markets.

23,320. Do you think that if the Town Commissioners obtained such control that they should only levy such a toll as would pay the cost of management and interest on any capital expended by them?—I do not think the Town Commissioners would wish to derive any benefit, except the benefit to the town and the people of the town and the country people as well.

23,321. Have you any observations to make as to the present system of working and managing the markets and fairs?—No. I think they are very well managed up to the present at all events under the new management, the new fair system.

23,322. Relative to the markets have you any suggestions to make?—I know nothing about their working, except what was stated here to-day.

23,323. Do you buy and sell there yourself?—No.

23,324. Are you opposed to the continuance of some of the markets being held on the streets?—My opinion is there should be some proper accommodation for those people who sell fish and meat on the side of the street, and also for the vegetables. They are objectionable from a sanitary point of view, and particularly in summer when the fish gets stale in the street.

23,325. The shopkeepers in the immediate neighbourhood of the markets would not object to the removal of them?—I cannot answer for their opinion, but it is public opinion at all events.

23,326. Has that matter of the removal of the markets been discussed by the people of the town?—I know of late three or four were with me making a collection in the town for a charitable purpose and we called on one man who lives in the vicinity and his great complaint was the fish and the nuisance about his place.

23,327. (*Mr. Fitzgerald.*) I can answer the shopkeepers in the vicinity would wish to have them removed.

23,328. (*Mr. McCarthy.*) Complaints have been made by the Post Office authorities of the obstruction in front of the Post Office on fair days. We have no power to remove them. The inspector did on one occasion order them away.

The Sub-Sanitary Officer examined.

23,329. (*Witness.*) I live in the vicinity of the nuisance complained of, and it is most objectionable.

23,330. Were these clothes ever inspected at any time?—No, but I know they are there.

23,331. Still, for fear anything might be brought into the town you would like to see them removed off the public thoroughfare?—Apart from my official position I think it is most objectionable to have them there.

Patrick Hallinan, Esq., J.P., examined.

23,332. Do you object to the Town Commissioners having control of the markets and fairs?—My own opinion is it would be better for the Town Commissioners to have them. I am sure it would be very expensive on the Town Commissioners to work them. Lord Midleton could work them cheaper than the Town Commissioners, but taking everything into consideration it would be better for the Town Commissioners to have them.

23,333. You think those frequenting the markets and fairs would be better satisfied?—I think it is immaterial to those who use them. I think if they knew the local people had the matter in their own hands they would be better pleased to pay the tolls.

23,334. If they had power to provide accommodation?—Yes. The outlay on the buildings would be considerable. We intended to build a fish market before the upset of the fairs. There is a lot of corn bought here. We buy a lot of wheat.

23,335. It does not come into the market at all?—No.

23,336. It is sent by the farmers direct to your premises?—Yes, and there are no tolls or taxes on it.

23,337. Was there ever a toll?—Never a toll on anything that comes to our place or to any other place, and there is a good deal of stuff sold in Ballinacurra.

23,338. Do you weigh the corn on your own scales?—Yes.

23,339. Do you charge the producer anything?—Nothing whatever. He brings it to the door and we porter it into the place.

23,340. Did you ever see them weighing yourself?—Yes.

23,341. Do you know the system of weighing?—Yes. They weigh down to a pound.

23,342. Do you give a cast of the beam always?—Yes.

23,343. Is there a customary tare for the sack?—No. The country sacks are emptied into the hopper, the sacks then bundled together and weighed, and their weight deducted from the gross.

23,344. Could you give me any approximate idea of the quantity brought in?—The wheat trade has gone down entirely. Some years ago we got so many thousands and now it has gone down to hundreds. There is a good deal brought in by Ballinacurra. There is a great quantity shipped, and a great quantity shipped back again. There is a good deal of waste in the trade done here. There is a very large barley market and distillery where they consume thirty or forty thousand barrels. In times gone by they used to come with wheat from Waterford, and they go that distance with barley.

23,345. I understand there was no corn market here?—There is no market, because it goes to the private concerns. It comes to the town and no tolls are charged.

23,346. (*Mr. Fitzgerald.*) There are tolls mentioned in the old toll board, but they have not been levied.

Mr. John McCarthy examined.

23,347. (*Witness.*) I am a draper. I am very much annoyed about the cast clothes every market and fair day being placed opposite my door, and the fowl also. I have not such an objection to the fowl as to the cast clothes, being in the same trade especially.

23,348. Is it from a business point of view you object?—The nuisance as well as that, because if a customer of mine happened to have a horse and cart and wanted to purchase some goods he cannot come nearer than six feet of the door.

23,349. Did you ever put goods on the sheeted stands?—I did.

23,350. Did you ever pay a toll or standing charge?—No. The cast clothes being sold causes a loss to the legitimate traders.

23,351. Are these people itinerant clothes dealers or are they people in the town who bring them out?—They are hawkers who come from different quarters. They get them in the pawn offices and get them on credit, and that is how the pawn offices dispose of unredeemed goods.

23,352. Have you anything else to say?—No.

23,353. Is there any other gentleman who has any observations to make?—No answer.

The inquiry then terminated.

CLOYNE—CO. CORK.

With reference to my inquiry in Cloyne on the 23rd November 1888 I beg to report as follows:—

Cloyne is situated in the south-eastern portion of the county of Cork. It is some four miles distant from the nearest railway station, which is at Midleton, and within later years the trade has considerably declined. The town is small and apparently kept in good and neat order. The local government is administered by the Board of Guardians and the Grand Jury, and the population is 1,120.

The market day is Thursday. The fairs are held on the last Wednesday of each month; pigs only are sold at the fairs, as cattle, horses, and sheep are not brought to Cloyne.

The markets and fairs are toll free, but at the former weighing and standing charges are levied. No scale of the charges is erected, but a weighing machine is provided.

The market rights are the property of Mr. David Sheehan, junior, Cloyne, who holds under a deed dated 20th April 1886, from the Cloyne market trustees, the consideration being 250*l*. The market trustees themselves purchased on the 6th June 1882 for 232*l*. from the Land Commission as representing the Church Temporalities Commission, to whom the market rights at that time belonged.

There does not seem to have been any patent granted for Cloyne, as none appears on the public records. The present fairs were only first established in the month of August 1888, and for the two and a half years previous to that date no fairs were held at all in Cloyne. It was stated that this was the effect of the establishment of the new and additional fairs in Midleton, which town has absorbed whatever trade formerly went to Cloyne in connexion with the markets and fairs therein. Midleton has many peculiar advantages for fair purposes over Cloyne.

In accordance with my instructions I have inspected the fair and market place.

The fairs are held indiscriminately about the public streets, and, as there is practically no control over them or charges payable thereout, no accommodation whatever is provided.

The markets are held on the streets principally outside a weigh-house, which is erected for weighing purposes. There is also accommodation given there to those retailing potatoes.

The inquiry was very well attended, and a great deal of interest was manifested in the proceedings.

JOHN O'MEARA,
Assistant Commissioner.

43, Lower Mount Street.

Cloyne, 23rd November 1888.

23,366. Has the market been always held here on Thursday within your memory?—Yes.

23,367-8. What fairs are held in Cloyne?—We have lately started a monthly fair on the last Wednesday of every month.

23,369. At the date of the conveyance to you what fairs were held here?—Six fairs commencing with the 24th February, Easter Tuesday, Whitsun Tuesday, 1st August, 19th September, and 5th December.

23,370. Were these six fairs held for any length of time previously?—Longer than I can remember.

23,371. You always remember the six being held?—Yes.

23,372. When did you establish the new monthly fairs?—About three months ago. It is the third one we have had. We sent to establish them three months ago.

23,373. Did you hold any of them as yet?—Yes. We held two. They are pig fairs.

23,374-5. On the last Wednesday of each month are pigs only sold that day or different description of animals?—Pigs at present.

23,376. No cattle are brought here and exposed for sale?—No, nothing but pigs.

23,377. What was the last fair you held at which cattle were sold and exposed for sale, or when did you cease holding the six fairs?—The 24th February 1886.

23,378. Between that period in 1886 and the present no fairs properly so called have been held?—No. They died away after that.

23,379. This pig market which you have established on the last Wednesday in each month was, I suppose, established without any express authority?—Yes.

23,380. Was it the inhabitants of the town established it?—The buyers chiefly.

23,381. Where is that market or fair held?—On the street.

23,382. Where is the general market held?—On the public street, except that a little butter is weighed within the market building.

23,383. Do you levy tolls at these monthly fairs or markets?—I do not levy them yet.

23,384. Were tolls levied at the six ordinary fairs?—Always.

23,385. How did they fall into abeyance? Was there any stock brought in, or any demand?—Through Midleton. Midleton had six and we had six, and then Midleton starting monthly fairs attracted cars away. The train going into Midleton was a greater inducement to buyers to go there, and there was more accommodation.

23,386. Do you think it materially affects the prosperity of the town of Cloyne to be so isolated from water communication and the railway?—I will give you my opinion. At the inquiry held in Cork the buyers proved on oath that they would not give sixpence more for a beast in Midleton than in Cloyne. The inconvenience of going to Cloyne counted nothing, and that they would attend in Cloyne as well as in Midleton, and give the same amount for a beast in each place.

23,387. Would not additional expense be incurred in transit?—Very little.

23,388. You do not consider that the isolated position of Cloyne affects in any way the trade of the town or the markets and fairs, or do you rely on the fact that the fairs have been extinguished by the establishment of new fairs in Midleton?—Yes, and not only of Cloyne, but all the surrounding places.

23,389-90. When the old fairs were held, had you a toll-board erected?—Yes.

23,391. Do you contemplate levying any charge at the pig market?—I should think if it continues, I will.

23,392. Are they brought in here in any quantity at present?—The first fair, I think, there were about 40 pigs, and the second there were 72. There was very little notice given, but I believe there will be a good deal more the next time.

23,393. Do you levy tolls at the markets?—Yes.

23,394. Are you in the immediate receipt of them yourself?—Yes, I receive them myself.

23,395. Have you a list of the charges erected that you levy at the markets?—No. I have not the charges erected.

23,396. Mention the different marketable commodities brought in on Thursday and exposed for sale?—Butter.

23,397. When you say butter, is that all lump butter?—Yes, lump butter, and nothing else.

23,398. What are the other commodities?—Poultry, fish, cabbages, potatoes—those are the chief things; large quantities of eggs, hay, straw, mangolds and turnips in their season.

23,399. Are calves ever brought in on market day?—Yes, a few calves.

23,400. Are sheep?—No.

23,401. Are they all taken to Midleton on market days?—They are not sold in Midleton either.

23,402. Are they all brought to the fairs in Midleton?—Yes. We never had any sheep markets here.

23,403. Are pigs ever brought on market days?—Never.

23,404. What is your charge on butter?—A penny per roll.

23,405. Is that irrespective of the quantity in the roll?—Yes.

23,406. Is it for weighing it?—Yes, we charge nothing but for weighing.

23,407. Supposing a roll of butter was brought in and exposed on the street, and sold, but not weighed at your scales, would you ask for your penny charge?—No. Unfortunately that very often occurs. I would only ask for the weighing charge.

23,408. Where do they expose the butter for sale? Have you any particular street in which the markets are held, or do they go indiscriminately about the town?—The chief street here is Rock Street.

23,409. Do they take up standings there?—Not with butter.

23,410. Do they hawk butter from shop to shop?—The parties who buy the butter meet in the street and convey them into the market.

23,411. It is only when you perform the duty of weighing you obtain this charge?—Yes.

23,412. No matter what the roll contained; if a pound or 80 pounds, you would charge the same?—Yes, 1d. for the roll.

23,413. Do you give any tickets at all?—Yes, I have dockets.

23,414. Have you printed forms?—No, I write them out myself.

23,415-16. Do you ever denote the weight in any other manner?—No. I put the weight and price, and what it comes to on the ticket.

23,417-18. What charge have you on fowl?—2d. a cart.

23,419. These are standings?—Yes.

23,420. When do you obtain that charge on fowl?—When they sell them.

23,421. Only when they sell?—Yes, after the sale.

23,422. It is not when they immediately come in?—No.

23,423. Supposing they do not sell the fowl at all?—I collect no tolls on anything but on the sales.

23,424. Have you men engaged to collect these tolls?—I have two boys.

23,425. How do you pay them?—They are my own boys.

23,426. You pay no salaries, and have only your own labour and your sons?—Yes.

23,427. Do you and your sons go round and inquire from these people whether they have sold or not?—They tell themselves.

23,428. You see the number they bring in the morning, and then see if they subsequently got rid of them?—Yes.

23,429. Supposing they brought three brace of fowl and sold one, would you levy a charge?—I do not charge for a brace of fowl at all. It must be more than that before I charge anything.

23,430. You have no smaller charge than 2d.?—Yes. For a basket of fowl I charge 1d., and a cart, 2d.

23,431. In any case you would not charge on a brace of fowl?—No, I would not charge for a brace at all. That is my instruction.

23,432. What is your charge on fish?—Twopence a cart.

23,433. If a basket were brought in, what would it be?—I do not charge for it. I would leave a basket go free.

23,434. What would be the value of the fish in a cart; say the smallest cart brought in here, what would you estimate it would realise?—About three score is the smallest cart they bring in.

23,435. What would be the value of it?—24s. or 25s.

23,436. You receive your charge on that?—Yes. The price yesterday was 5s. a score, but that is a high price now.

23,437. Supposing they do not sell, you do not levy a charge?—No.

23,438. You only levy the charge on the sales?—Yes.

23,439. On cabbages, what do you charge?—Twopence a cart.

23,440. If they brought in a basket what do you charge?—I do not charge them for a basket.

23,441. On potatoes what do you receive?—Three half-pence for weighing a sack of potatoes. I charge nothing but for the weighing of them.

23,442. If a cart-load were brought in?—Three half-pence per sack.

23,443. You weigh each individual sack?—Yes.

23,444. If they sell, but do not avail themselves of your scales, would you levy a charge?—No charge.

23,445. It is only when they weigh?—Yes.

23,446. Is there any rule in the market compelling them to weigh at your scales?—I do not know there is a rule.

23,447. Do they, as a matter of fact, weigh at your scales?—Nearly all.

23,448. Are there any other scales they could avail themselves of?—There are a lot of scales, but I do not think the people would oblige them.

23,449. As a matter of fact they all come to you?—Yes.

23,450. Have you got a ticket to give denoting the weight of the sacks?—No; it is a written document.

23,451. When the sack of potatoes comes in and you are weighing it, what is the lowest weight you put into the scales or down to what weight can you weigh?—Four pounds.

23,452. Do you weigh down to two pounds?—No.

23,453. Only four?—Yes.

23,454. Do you give a cast of the beam?—Yes.

23,455. Then practically it is four pounds or nothing?—It is generally seven pounds or nothing in a sack of potatoes.

23,456. You never denote the weight under a half stone?—Yes, except it weighed between seven pounds and fourteen.

23,457–60. If it were six pounds?—I would give him the six pounds. The practice is to allow seven pounds for the weight of the bag when weighing a bag of potatoes.

23,461. You put four pounds or nothing?—Yes.

23,462. That is in addition to the seven pounds the tare of the sack?—Yes.

23,463. Is it always seven pounds?—Yes; that is the custom here in potatoes.

23,464. You never actually weigh the empty sack?—No.

23,465–6. Is that tare of seven pounds the same every day in the season, no matter whether it is a wet or fine day. Supposing the potatoes were brought in on a wet day, and the sack was completely saturated with wet, would you allow anything additional?—No; it would be the same thing. That is the general thing, and we leave it so.

23,467. The actual weight of the sack would be less than seven pounds?—Yes.

23,468. You allow the difference between the actual weight of the sack and the seven pounds for any wet around the potatoes?—Yes.

23,469. What do you charge for corn?—Three half-pence a sack for weighing.

23,470. If sold and not weighed do you levy any charge?—No.

23,471. Are there any private corn merchants in the town?—Yes.

23,472. I suppose a good deal of corn goes to them and does not go through the market at all?—The bulk of it goes to them.

23,473–4. You do not receive any charge?—No.

23,475. Do you know, do they charge anything for weighing?—Yes.

23,476. At any period were the charges collected from those corn merchants?—Not that I know of or never heard of it.

23,477. You only then levy a charge on corn when you perform the service of weighing it?—Yes.

23,478. What is the estimated tare of the bag in corn?—We weigh the bags generally after the corn has been emptied out, but we do not weigh them in the case of potatoes.

23,479. In the case of dispute between the buyer and seller of potatoes, you would weigh the empty sack?—Yes.

23,480. Would you charge anything additional for that?—No.

23,481. You do not charge anything additional for weighing the empty bag of corn?—No.

23,482. On eggs, what do you charge?—We charge nothing to the sellers, but to the parties who stand and buy them are charged twopence each stand.

23,483. Have the buyers stands on the street?—Yes; they buy them on the street.

23,484. Is this for export purposes?—Yes, chiefly.

23,485–6. You charge them twopence?—Yes.

23,487. What do these standings comprise?—Carts and boxes.

23,488. That is the only charge?—Yes.

23,489. Supposing they do not buy at all and have a standing there?—I charge them nothing. Even when they buy a little I charge them nothing.

23,490. What do you call a little?—When they buy only a *few* hundred eggs, two or three hundred. I do not charge anything on them.

23,491. What is the custom here as to the number to a hundred of eggs?—Ten dozen.

23,492. The practice here is the same as elsewhere?—Yes.

23,493. You have only the customary charge?—Yes.

23,494. It is toll or nothing?—That is all.

23,495. On hay what is your charge?—For weighing hay I charge 1½d. per ton.

23,496. Then you have a weighbridge here?—Yes.

23,497. Where do they expose the hay for sale?—They bring in the loads to be weighed. It is generally sold before they bring them in.

23,498. Do they ever buy the hay by bulking the load and not by the ton?—I very seldom know it to be done.

23,499. You never heard of its being done?—No, except they buy it out in the farmers' stand.

23,500. All hay brought in is weighed at the bridge?—Yes. It is the only bridge in the town.

23,501. It is only when you weigh you levy your charge?—Yes.

23,502. The same remarks apply to straw?—Yes.

23,503. Do you always weigh the empty car?—Always.

23,504. Is that the only deduction from the gross weight?—It is the only deduction.

23,505. Nothing additional is allowed for wet?—No.

23,506. Or for fraudulently prepared hay?—No.

23,507. Have any cases occurred within your management of the hay being fraudulently prepared?—Some buyers will state that the sellers put a little wet stuff into the centre.

23,508. There is no deduction from the price or weight other than the tare of the car?—Quite so.

23,509. No prosecutions have ever been instituted for fraudulently prepared hay?—No.

23,510. When they weigh a load of hay and go off to deliver and return with the empty cart, did you ever hear that they changed the wheels of the empty cart?—No, because it is in the immediate neighbourhood they deliver it, and except they had two or three miles to go they would have no chance of changing the wheels.

23,511. No complaints have been made?—No.

23,512. You charge 10d. a ton on straw?—Yes.

23,513. I suppose there is more usually than the ton in the load?—Very often less.

23,514. Supposing there was a great deal less, would you charge 10d.?—No; a halfpenny per hundred-weight.

23,515. If it is over a ton you charge proportionately?—Yes, the same way.

23,516. On turnips what is your charge?—The same thing.

23,517. Practically on everything you weigh at the weighbridge you charge a halfpenny a hundredweight?—Yes.

23,518. Is it on the gross weight or net you charge?—On the net weight.

23,519. You never charge for weighing the cart?—Never.

23,520. Supposing they bring in an empty cart and want to weigh it?—I charge nothing.

23,521. Supposing I brought in a cart for the purpose of ascertaining the weight of it, what do you charge?—It is a thing that did not occur while I am in possession, except on a few occasions, and I did it gratis. I do not charge anything in that case.

23,522-3. What do you receive on young calves?—6d. per cart.

23,524. No matter what the number is, and if they had only one in the cart?—Very seldom I charge for one.

23,525. If there were two would you charge?—Yes.

23,526. Seemingly you give and take a good deal?—Yes.

23,527. Are these the only commodities upon which you receive charges, or have you any standing charges on market days, such as clothes dealers or anything like that?—Yes, when they come they pay one 6d.

23,528. Each standing?—Yes.

23,529. No matter whether it is the standing of a cart, or some boards over barrels, or anything like that?—Quite so.

23,530. What description of standings are these, or what commodities do they expose on them?—Cheap clothes and chenils. They are generally stands on the street.

23,531. Have they any permanent standings?—Very little of them now. We used have them here some time ago.

23,532. Is furniture ever exposed for sale on the street?—No.

23,533-4. Did you make up the average receipts?—Yes, I can give you them. I took them up in April 1885, and from April 1885 to December 1885 the receipts were 38l. 11s. 6d.

23,535. Is that the gross amount or the net?—The gross is the net.

23,536. Deducting your labour and your rent?—Yes. For the period from the 1st January 1886 to the 31st December 1886, the receipts amounted to 48l. 10s. 7d.; from the 1st January 1887 to 31st December 1887, 48l. 5s. 6d.; from the 1st January 1888 to the 22nd November 1888, 51l. 0s. 5d. The average for the stated period is 47l. 7s. 2d.

23,537. Do you pay any quit-rent at all?—No.

23,538. Do you effect any repairs in the market place?—Yes.

23,539. What facilities have you for weighing?—I have two beams and scales in the market house, one for butter and one for potatoes; and the weigh-bridge.

23,540. Have complaints ever been made to you of inaccuracy in the weights?—No.

23,541. The police visit them at the stated periods?—Yes.

23,542. Is this market-house where you have the scales erected the building conveyed to you in the deed?—Yes.

23,543. Where is the weigh-bridge erected?—Immediately in front of the market building. Part of it is within the building.

23,544. Supposing potatoes are brought in and sold to a man who subsequently retailed them in the market, would you charge the retailer anything?—Yes. There is one portion of the market occupied by a retailer, and we charge him 6d. per week.

23,545. Only the one?—Yes.

23,546. Portion of the market is set off for him?—Quite so.

23,547. Does he practically make a shed of it?—He stands in it.

23,548. It is a stall?—Yes.

23,549. Is that the only stallage charge you have?—That is the only one.

23,550. Supposing they do not sell all the potatoes or corn brought in, would you give them storage accommodation?—Yes.

23,551. Do you do so?—I do.

23,552. What charge do you levy?—Nothing. I give it free until the following day.

23,553. Is it at their own risk?—No. I take charge of the commodities for them.

23,554. Could you tell me the rates at which tolls were levied at these old fairs?—I could.

23,555. Was there a toll-board erected?—There was.

23,556. You have not got a copy of it here?—No.

23,557. On cattle what was the charge?—4d.

23,558. Was that only on the animal actually sold?—Yes.

23,559. What were the other charges?—Sheep, 1d.; lambs, ½d.; horses, 6d.; pigs, 1d. each.

23,560. Nothing else came in?—There were the chief things exposed for sale.

23,561. Do you charge on yearlings the same as on the other animals, that is, 4d. each?—No, only 2d.

23,562. Do you remember any period here when the markets were better than they are at present?—I do, very well.

23,563. What do you assign as the cause of the decay. Is there much of the land around in tillage, or is it all pasture?—A great deal of it is in tillage. The depression of the times had a good deal to do with the decay of the market.

23,564. If there is a great deal of the land in tillage it ought to be a better market. Would you say the greater percentage of the land of the surrounding country is in tillage?—Hardly, I think.

23,565. Or would you assign another reason for the decay here, the proximity of the other markets?—I suppose it has a good deal to do with it. Midleton does a good deal in that way to injure us.

23,566. Did you ever hear the people complaining of any of the charges?—No.

23,567. No complaints have ever been made to you?—No.

23,568. Did you ever hear that any such were made to anybody else?—No. There was never any objection made to the tolls levied in this town. They were always paid very well and without any trouble.

23,569. From what districts are the marketable commodities brought?—The surrounding districts, four or five and six miles on every side.

23,570. There is no regulation in the market compelling the people to sell their commodities through brokers or agents?—No.

23,571. Every farmer or producer who comes in is free to sell to whom he pleases?—Yes, and make the best price he can.

23,572. You have a ticket for the weigh-bridge?—Yes.

23,573. Is it a printed ticket?—Yes.

23,574-6. You always fill up the block?—Yes.

23,577. So that, if they lose the ticket you are always in a position to make another copy of it?—Yes.

23,578. Would you charge anything additional for the same?—No.

23,579. Have you any means of ascertaining the quantity of these different commodities brought in on market day. Supposing it was required from you to make a periodical return for the Government of the quantity of the different commodities brought in and the current prices, do you think it would be possible to do it?—Yes, except I got some notice. It would be impossible to do it now, because I have not kept them.

23,580. I am not asking you as regards the past, but in future would it be possible to make such a return?—It would be quite possible.

23,581. Do you think it would be an accurate return of the quantity and current prices?—Yes, quite accurate, if it is wanted that I shall do it.

23,582. If shopkeepers put out standings on the roadway on a market-day, would you levy any charge?—I do not think I would. It has not been tried.

23,583. Were any representations ever made to you to remove these markets off the streets and put them into the market building?—No.

23,584. I suppose the market-house which has been erected would not afford sufficient space?—No.

23,585. Were any representations ever made to you to provide a larger building?—No.

23,586. Have they ever complained of the market being held on the streets?—No.

23,587. Did they ever complain that on a very wet day they had no shelter accommodation?—No complaints have been made.

23,588. They did not complain of want of shelter for their perishable commodities?—No, simply for the reason that it is now as it has been always, and never any accommodation were than at present.

23,589. Your charges are always stationary?—Yes.

23,590-2. You made no change whatever, either by increasing the charges or decreasing them?—No change.

23,593. They remain stationary, although the value of the different commodities may fluctuate?—Quite so.

23,594. Have you any observations or remarks, or suggestions to make, that you think would better the market?—I know there are things possible to put a stop to. There are parties on market days who weigh butter in their own houses, which is highly improper. It is depriving me of the right and title I purchased.

23,595. Do they levy any charge?—I cannot say. I do not believe they levy a charge, but it is depriving me of that toll which I am entitled to for weighing. It is highly improper, and if a stop were put on them it would be proper and just.

23,596-8. Are these the customers who weigh?—Yes.

Mr. DANIEL O[illegible] examined.

23,600. You heard that remark of Mr. Sheehan's when he said it was an objectionable practice for private shopkeepers in the town to be weighing the butter?—Yes.

23,601. Do you think the buyers would have more confidence in the weighing at Mr. Sheehan's public scales than in having the weight of the butter ascertained by a private shopkeeper?—I think not, but I think it is to avoid the cost they go to the private shopkeeper. It is the pecuniary difference they look to.

23,602. Shopkeepers do not charge anything for weighing?—No. They weigh themselves and afford accommodation sooner than refuse custom which would be likely to promote the interests of the house.

23,603. Have you formed any ideas about the markets being held on the streets. Do you think it is desirable they should be removed off the streets?—Personally I would say, no, and I would resist any removal. I would rather equalise them through the public streets to give all traders a share of the benefit the markets confer. There is much contention in Midleton about the removal of the fair, which would apply, I think, to most towns. People at one end, where the fairs and markets are not, have a grievance and I would be anxious to remove any grievance by equalising the markets on the public streets.

23,604. Does not the fact of the market being held on the street occasion much filth and dirt?—I never heard an objection.

23,605. If it does, who cleans it?—In Midleton the Commissioners clean it, but here the owners of the houses clean it.

23,606. Would they put up with any inconvenience caused by the fact of the markets being held on the street for trade purposes?—No doubt, because the bigger the market the bigger the filth.

23,607. It is partly for trade purposes they suffer the inconvenience?—Yes.

23,608. Have the private inhabitants complained of the fact of the markets being held on the streets?—I never heard.

23,609. What do you think of the charges levied by Mr. Sheehan. Do you think they are in any way excessive or do they bear more heavily on different classes of people frequenting the market, than on others?—No. I did not hear any complaints as to excessive charges, but I heard it stated as a grievance, to charge at all on the public street.

23,610. What is your own opinion on that. Do you think that if a toll or charge is levied, and no substantial return given by the owner, that it is a grievance?—I think there ought to be no tolls charged in the public street. I look on the public street as the public highway.

23,611. I take as your evidence, that where the owner of market rights performs no duty and provides no building, that tolls should not be payable?—I should say so. I might say I was in charge of the tolls for a period of 13 or 14 years, and I occupied the dual capacity for the Trustees of secretary and treasurer. I was thoroughly acquainted with the management and we did away with the tolls to remove the claim made by the town to have no tolls charged, with a view to increasing the commerce of the town. Subsequently we had to make a charge to remove the responsibility that the trustees incurred with regard to the original purchase.

23,612. When did you cease levying the charge?—About six years ago.

23,613. How long were the markets toll free?—I think they were toll free for about two years.

23,614. Did you weigh the commodities gratuitously?—Certainly not, because that was done in the market house.

23,615. It was the standing on the street you allowed toll free?—Yes.

23,616. Do you think that the exaction of a toll acts in any way as a deterrent on people bringing in their commodities and animals and exposing them for sale at the markets and fairs?—I think not, but it is generally complained of.

23,617. Do you think if the markets were toll free altogether, except of course a charge for any services rendered by the owner, such as a weighing charge; do you think that would induce people to come into the market in greater numbers, and bring in more stock and produce?—I am not aware of any instance where such an allegation was made.

23,618. It would not be an inducement?—I think not.

23,619. Is that because they have no other market to go to?—No.

23,620. Supposing there were two markets equally distant from a farmer; one was toll free, and the other was not; would not he have a greater interest in going to the one that was toll free?—He would so far as the tolls were concerned, but if there was greater competition where the tolls were exacted he would go there.

23,621. He would not consider the subsequent payment of a toll if he thought he would have a ready market for his commodity?—I think not.

23,622. The farmers always look for the ready market?—Yes, the ready market and competition.

23,623. They would not mind a small charge?—It is so small I never heard it alleged that they would stop at home because of it.

23,624. Do you approve of the present practice in Midleton and other places in the country of charging on the animals where they enter the fair green, if a fair green is provided, instead of a larger charge on the animals actually sold?—I think it is fair where an animal occupies private property, where sold, to make a charge, and it is a cause of contention when they are not sold that no charge is made. I would be an advocate for equalising the charge on sold and unsold cattle.

23,625. The charge at Midleton is on the animal on entrance to the fair green, but there is no subsequent charge on the animals sold?—That was the practice in Midleton until the stalls or pens were erected.

23,626. Which of the practices do you approve of?—If I had control and could erect a market I would equalise the tolls on all stock occupying pens, whether sold or not, and reduce the charge consequent upon the large revenue realised in preference to the charge on stock sold.

23,627. In that case you would have the difficulty, first, of collecting a toll on entrance, and subsequently the collection on the animal actually sold. Do not you think that would raise a great deal of confusion and contention?—I think not. In this way there are porters at the entrance, and if tolls were collected on entering they would have the same facility, and greater facility when all the stock were sold, and going out in the afternoon. Where you have accommodation such as in Midleton and [illegible]—pens for stock—you could do away with any charge coming in, and have no charge except they exhibited any stock to be sold.

23,628. I take it, then, you are in favour of owners who sell stock and avail themselves of the fair green, should bear a higher charge than those who avail themselves of the fair green, and whose stock are not sold?—There ought be a difference. I would be an advocate for equalising the charge.

23,629. If fairs are held in the public street you are not in favour of any charge at all?—Certainly not. I look on the streets as the public highway.

23,630. Do you approve of the system in Midleton of having a fair green with pens around it. Do you think that is better than having the fairs on the streets?—I think stock producers would like it better, and traders would like it worse. As a trader I would complain, but as a producer of stock I would admire.

23,631. Have you any knowledge of the opinions of buyers. Do they approve of buying in a fair green?—I know all are in favour of pens and stalls in the fair green.

23,632. You never heard that they have been unable to try cattle, and view them as they could on the public street?—I think they could see them better on the public street, because they could shift them around.

23,633. You never heard them complaining that in pens like those in Midleton they have been unable to see them properly?—I have heard remarks to that effect, but I would not say complaints.

23,634. You were one of the trustees in the conveyance of the property to Mr. Sheehan?—Yes.

23,635. Have you a knowledge of the fairs and markets of towns other than Midleton or Cloyne?—Yes.

23,636. I wish to ask you a general question not relating to Midleton or Cloyne in particular. Are you in favour, or do you approve of local authorities, if they exist in a town, obtaining compulsory powers to acquire the market rights and tolls of the owners in order to work them themselves?—I would.

23,637. And after paying the cost of management to apply the surplus to the benefit of the town?—I would approve of such a course.

23,638. You think it would be desirable that local authorities should obtain such a power?—Certainly. You would have a concentrated or accumulated interest in promoting the interest of the town as well as the interest of the stock-producers, and bringing them into the town. I think the less individuality you have in a matter of that kind the better, because one person may not be active or energetic where two or three persons might be the contrary, and it would be a benefit to the town and to the buyers and sellers.

23,639. On the whole, you think the united action of those comprising the local authority would tend to improve the market and fair?—Yes, and I think the profit should be applied for the benefit of the town or market.

23,640. Where such local authority does not exist, do you think market trustees such as they have in Limerick, should be established to work the markets and fairs in the same way as a local authority?—I do.

23,641. In any case you say you do not like the present system of individuality in the ownership of markets and fairs?—No. It is very detrimental to the interest of the town.

23,642. That is the commercial interest?—That is what I mean; and alluding to the depression of the markets there were several reasons for our markets becoming a great deal less, or to use another phrase, small by degrees. Emigration is the first, I would say. This town originally was the property of the see. Then there was a lease of 60 years, but that expired on the death of the reigning bishop, and then came the purchase interest which prompted a big interest in that way, and a desire to extend the town and the buildings in the town. As a corn market I would volunteer to say it is a very important barley market. In 1874, 1875, and 1876 I saw 79,000 and 80,828 barrels of corn in the market, and these corn factors weighed themselves. I think the public would like to have a public weighmaster. The corn ought to be weighed at a similar scale, and delivered at the store for a halfpenny a bag, which would serve the seller a good deal, and promote public confidence and lessen the profits of the storekeeper. If we do that, and had authority for receiving that charge the result would be very advantageous for local charities, and the extension of local business. In the 80,000 barrels of corn if we had 80,000 halfpence it would be very nice, and that is carried on for three months. The system of weighing in the stores, although no allegation is made, there are general complaints.

23,643. You have heard such?—Yes.

23,644. What is the nature of the complaints?—The persons selling the corn complain that they sometimes do not meet with justice from the weighmaster of the corn.

23,645. That is, when the weighmaster is the buyer?—Where the weighmaster weighs for the buyer.

23,646. Or is the buyer himself?—Well, I have not seen an instance here where the buyer weighs himself. It is his agent weighs it; he is expected to discharge the duty. The weighmaster is held responsible for any deficiency when the corn is leaving the store, so that there is an inducement to have good weight for the buyer.

23,647. When corn or potatoes are brought in bulk to Mr. Sheehan is there any porterage charge levied, or have the farmers to perform that duty themselves, of taking the bags off the cart?—They do that themselves, but if the corn was to be weighed there should be porterage.

23,648. They pay no charge to men for lifting the bags?—I am not aware. When they are there they generally help each other.

23,649. Are there any other observations you would care to make affecting the markets or fairs throughout the country, or what you think would tend to improve them?—I would say that the establishment of the monthly fairs in the district is very detrimental to the interests of the community, such as the fairs in Midleton, Castlemartyr, and other places. The public would very much, I think, prefer the old fairs to the monthly fairs, as there would be a better distribution of stock, but the railway accommodation and the banking accommodation gives encouragement to bring stock to these places. For instance, if I buy stock up to 9 o'clock in Midleton I can send them away from there by the afternoon train, and they will be in Bristol the second evening. If I got them here I have no facilities of this kind, and banking facilities induce the people to take their stock to such places as Midleton, which has swallowed up the surrounding fairs.

23,650. The fact of having railway communication or facilities for exporting stock does not affect the seller but the buyer, and do you think on account of the isolated condition of Cloyne, and the distance from railway communication, the buyers are deterred from coming here?—I think so. If I want to go to Midleton I can go there easily in the morning by the 8 o'clock train in 35 or 40 minutes from Cork, whereas if a buyer is coming to Cloyne he must come the evening before and take a car from Midleton here, which makes his expense greater.

23,631-2. The markets and fairs in this country being the principal means by which a great many of the people obtain a livelihood because it is purely an agricultural country, do you think there should be some authority existing in the country regulating or having control over the markets and fairs throughout it to which appeals could be made by the owners or people having any grievance to complain of?—I do. We appealed to an authority in Cork and they overruled the appeal although public opinion was in favour of the appeal.

23,633. This was the sheriff's jury?—Yes.

23,634. What were they, were they petit jurors or the grand jury?—They were selected by the sheriff as stock producers and asked their opinion as to whether they would consider the fairs in Midleton more advantageous and more central, and the accommodation and prices better, and a lot of other questions. Of course they were in favour of Midleton.

23,635. At that time had Mr. Sheehan any rights vested in him that would be materially affected by the establishment of those fairs?—Yes.

23,636. But the jury found in favour of Lord Midleton?—They did. When I had charge of the fairs here seven or eight years ago, I had the tolls and market house let, and was receiving a rent of 30*l.* at first, then 25*l.*, and then 20*l.* According as the depression was growing it went down to 9*l.* 9*l.* will represent a good deal of stock sold. Then having no tolls or no fairs it will represent in a big figure the loss the town has sustained owing to the expenses then incurred, and to meet their liabilities the trustees came to the conclusion of selling.

23,637. What time does the market usually commence in the morning?—It commences in the morning early. I should say in summer time 6 o'clock, and now about 7 or 8 o'clock.

23,638. What time is the market usually over?—I should say the market is over at noon practically, but our business goes on through the day.

23,639. Have you ever heard of complaints in forestalling fowl or anything like that?—No. I have not heard of any want of accommodation in that way. There was a place where the cars and horses or any idle vehicles stood, and a proceeding was made to the road sessions, which not being opposed, the presentment was granted, and the people of the town deprived of this public right and convenience.

23,640. There was no representation made on behalf of the townspeople of the benefit it was to them?—No.

23,641. It was used as a common?—Yes. If I recollect rightly it was a commonage given by one of the bishops for the use of vehicles so as not to be interfering with the pathways.

23,642. Have you any other observations to make?—It is a growing practice here and very detrimental to our welfare for stock producers to go about buying from the farmers the beasts they produce. At present there is an arrangement between the house owners to prevent that, and now they do not go to the houses through the country. They attend the fairs, but it is only within the past six months.

23,643. Previously the buyers went to the residences of the people?—Yes.

23,644. Would you call that a system of forestalling?—I would, and I think it should not be tolerated in any commercial community. It is detrimental to the interests of every town.

23,645. It is your opinion then that all stock should be brought into the fair or market in order to cause greater competition among the buyers?—Unquestionably.

23,646. Do you think a producer would obtain a larger price by bringing his stock to the fair than he gets at present?—I expect he would from public competition.

Mr. Thomas Quinn examined.

23,647. You agree in the several observations made by Mr. Quinn?—Yes.

23,648. Do his opinions practically agree with your own?—Yes.

23,649. You are in trade in the town?—Yes.

service to the community, and to the farmers especially. They would like it very much after a time, because I went to some people who had an objection to sell by live-weight, and they asked 2*l.* 10*s.* for pigs, and afterwards, when weighed on the bridge, the pig used to make 5*s.* or 10*s.* more.

22,694. But the lock-money, in the case of cattle or horses and animals other than pigs, [illegible], and is always left to the disposition of the seller?—Exactly, but the buyer on all occasions pays it on pigs.

22,695. Do you think a fair green a proper place for selling cattle? This is a general question, and not relating to [illegible]?—I think it would, but I differ with Mr. Orenis about charging on the cattle going in. If a poor man had three cattle coming in, he may not have the price of his breakfast, and I think it would be very unfair to charge on the cattle he would bring in, because he may have to take them home unsold afterwards.

22,696. Would you rather have a higher charge on the animals sold, than a smaller charge on every?—Yes; because a poor farmer coming in might have a difficulty in getting the money.

22,697. (*The Commissioner to Mr. Orenis.*) Do you hear the observation of Mr. Quin?—Yes. I think the general principle is better than the singular principle, because nearly all the cattle are sold. I would say three-fourths of the stock are sold, and consequently there are three advantages to the one disadvantage in not selling. I think the general thing more advantageous than the other.

22,698. (*Mr. Quin.*) I think if a man brought three or four heifers, and is charged 3d. each, it is unfair, because I often knew men not to have a shilling in their pockets, and would have a great difficulty in getting their breakfast, and might not have any place to borrow it from.

22,699. Have you formed any ideas as to the levying a toll. Do you think the farmers of the country would object to pay for accommodation or services rendered?—I do not think they would.

22,700. Had you conversations with any of them?—With several. They do not like to pay for cattle brought into a fair and not sold.

22,701. But when the fairs are held on the public thoroughfare, and tolls are levied on them without any immediate service being rendered by the owner, do you think there should be an abolition of tolls in such cases?—I never heard any objections to the tolls provided they were reasonable and fair, and not excessive.

22,702. You have formed no ideas yourself?—No.

Mr. Robert Walsh examined.

22,703. (*Witness.*) I heard some remarks Mr. Orenis made with regard to charging tolls at a fair green. My impression is, and I agree with Mr. Quin, that no tolls should be charged on cattle coming into the fair. I think it is very wrong to charge on cattle unsold, and I endorse Mr. Quin's remark that many a poor man might not have the means of paying the toll, when perhaps, his cattle would not be sold afterwards.

22,704. Do you think as Mr. Orenis advocates, there would be a greater benefit to the community at large than individual inconvenience. Do you think a benefit would be derived from a system like that in Middleton, that would counterbalance the individual inconvenience some people would be put to?—On the contrary I think the old system is better, to charge on the cattle sold, as they are coming out of the fair.

22,705. Mr. Orenis advocates a charge on all animals that avail themselves of the fair green or pens, but the animals when sold should pay a higher charge than those that remain unsold?—I think it would be very hard to manage that. I think the old course is better.

22,706. (*Mr. Orenis, interposing.*) The old course led to many disputes. Five or six men would form a gap, and if there was a doubt as to the sale they would swear the parties, and did so wrongfully. I have no hesitation in saying, they took the oath to avoid the tolls; and there would be many an assault and blow of a stick given to the people and the cattle. I suggested if there was a fair green and pens one utilised the people need not pay for the use of them.

22,707. If such a fair green were provided would you be in favour of having rules and regulations in that market or fair confining the exposure of animals to the fair green, instead of allowing them to go about the streets indiscriminately?—If that fair green was provided and built out of a person's private purse, unquestionably he is entitled to get a charge for the outlay, but in the public street where there is no private outlay there should be no charge.

22,708. (*Mr. Walsh, continuing his evidence.*) I entirely agree with Mr. Orenis that there should be no charge on the public streets. Where the public street is open to everyone, and no accommodation given, I think no tolls should be charged. I apply that remark to everything sold on the streets.

22,709. Have you ever heard complaints of forestalling where the buyers go out to meet the producers and pay a price beforehand for the animals or commodities? I heard that in former times.

22,710. Is that practice existing relative to any particular commodity?—Yes. I believe with regard to fowl people go outside the town before they enter and purchase them on the roads. That is very detrimental to the town, because the seller when he gets his money goes home and does not come to the town. That happened in many cases.

22,711. Do you think if the seller came into the town there would be greater competition, and he would get a better price?—Yes. If the sellers were located in the principal streets where the sellers and buyers would be together, there would be more competition.

22,712. Have you had experience of any other markets or fairs?—Yes, of the Middleton market.

22,713. Have you had much experience?—Not much.

22,714. You are a trader in this town?—Yes.

22,715. Where local authorities exist in a town in which markets and fairs are held, would you be in favour or would you approve of such authority obtaining compulsory powers to acquire the market rights and tolls, and work them for the public benefit?—Certainly, where there is a local authority.

22,716. Do you think that local authority would be better able to work the markets and fairs, and manage them to the greater satisfaction of the farmers attending them and the buyers, than a private individual?—That is my impression.

22,717. Do you think the producers and buyers would have more confidence in their management?—I dare say they would.

22,718. Would you approve of such tolls being levied by such authority as would only be equivalent to the cost of management and effecting any repairs required to be done?—Certainly.

22,719. You would approve of no toll being levied, except such as would recoup them for any expenditure?—Yes.

22,720. And not to have any large surplus to go for improvements not connected with the market?—Yes.

22,721. You are one of the poor law guardians?—Yes.

22,722. Practically, your evidence is that if a local authority had control of the markets and fairs, they should not make it a large source of revenue, and only exact such charges as would pay for the cost of management?—Yes.

22,723. And any further toll which would bring in receipts over and above the cost of management should be abolished?—Yes. I should say it would be a hardship on the people.

22,724. Do you think that the levying of a toll prevents people from bringing their commodities, or affects the market?—Where there is an exorbitant toll levied it would.

22,725. Have you any other observation?—I do not think I have any remarks to make, except that I think it is very hard to impose a tariff on cattle coming in without being sold.

Mr. David Sheehan re-examined.

23,726. (Witness.) I wish to add that when I took the tolls I had no intention of making any personal profit. I will simply state how I got into the affair. I was one of ten who borrowed money from the bank. My name was signed to a bill to wipe off the debt of the Commissioners. When the bill was to be renewed, two or three of the ten objected. "Well," said I, "I will be one of two," and I could not get four or three, and then I purchased unfortunately for myself. At the time I bought it tolls were charged, and I cannot for the life of me see that there is any grievance in charging them now. Mr. Cronin and Mr. Walsh were among the ten who originally signed the bill in the bank.

23,727. (Mr. Cronin.) It was a general question affecting the community.

23,728. (Mr. Sheehan.) I think Mr. Walsh should not object to tolls being charged in the town of Cloyne after what I have stated.

(Mr. Walsh.) Yes, from the state of the markets.

23,729. (The Commissioner.) The statement was that where the markets are so small, and being held on the street, no tolls should be charged.

23,730. (Mr. Cronin.) I would be an advocate for recognising Mr. Sheehan's rights to proper compensation.

23,731. (Mr. Sheehan.) I want to show I did not go into it by premeditation.

23,732. (Mr. Walsh.) I am only giving my opinion what should be done.

23,733. Is there any other gentleman who has any evidence to give?—No answer.

The inquiry then terminated.

QUEENSTOWN.

With reference to my inquiry in Queenstown on the 24th November 1888, I beg to report as follows:—

Queenstown, formerly called the Cove of Cork, is a seaport and important naval station in the county of Cork. It is situated on the southern side of the Great Island, which rises quickly from the water's edge to a height of 303 feet. The houses are generally well and substantially built, and many of them of attractive appearance. The harbour itself, exclusive of its numerous creeks and bays, is four miles in length and two in breadth. There is a good general trade, but consists principally in providing the necessary supplies for the various vessels calling to the port. The local government is vested in Town Commissioners, and the population is 9,755.

The market day is Saturday. There are, at present, no fairs held in Queenstown. Tolls, in the nature of standing charges, are levied at the markets, but their payment is restricted to commodities, sales of which have been effected in the market buildings.

The market rights are the property of Smith Barry, Esq., M.P., who has them, however, sublet to the Town Commissioners, under an agreement dated 31st December 1874, for 14 years from 1st January 1875, at the yearly rent of 50*l*.

One patent was granted for Queenstown. It is dated 20th September 1791, and authorises the Honourable Richard Barry to hold markets on Wednesdays and Saturdays, and fairs on the 20th April and 15th October. These markets and fairs were to be held in or at the town and lands of Ballyvoloane, otherwise Cove, in the county of Cork.

In accordance with my instructions, I have inspected the market place.

The fish, potato, and vegetable markets are held in the basements and yards of the Town Hall and Court House, both of which buildings are situated in one of the principal streets. The markets are entered by an archway, the fish and meat markets being on the left, and the potato and vegetable markets on the right. Sufficient accommodation seems to be afforded for the trade done in the markets. The principal business transacted within the buildings is of a retail character. Both markets are partly covered over, and provided with three sets of scales and a weighing machine. No scale of the charges is erected.

Various marketable commodities are hawked about the town, and there does not seem any disposition to exist to restrict the sale of such commodities to the market buildings.

The establishment of fairs was strongly advocated if facilities were provided for the safe and expeditious transit of stock to and from the adjoining islands and mainland.

Appended will be found a copy of the patent, dated 20th September 1781, together with a transcript of the evidence taken at the inquiry.

JOHN J. O'MEARA,
Assistant Commissioner.

45, Lower Mount Street,
Dublin.

COPY PATENT, dated 20th September 1781.

George the Third, by the grace of God, of Great Britain and Ireland, King, Defender of the Faith, and so forth. To all unto whom these presents shall come, greeting. Whereas it appears by an inquisition taken by virtue of Our writ of ad quod damnum issued in pursuance of a warrant given by Our right trusty and well-beloved cousin and counsellor Frederick Earl of Carlisle, our Lieutenant-General and General-Governor of Our said kingdom of Ireland, on the petition of the Honorable Richard Barry, that the granting him two several yearly fairs, to be held annually for ever, in or at the town and lands of Ballyvolane, otherwise Cove, in the county of Cork, that is to say, one fair to be held on every 20th day of April, and one other fair to be held on every 15th day of October, as also two weekly markets to be held in or at the town and lands aforesaid on every Wednesday and Saturday for ever, will be no damage, hurt, or prejudice to Us or any of Our subjects who hold fairs or markets in the neighbourhood of the said town and lands of Ballyvolane, otherwise Cove aforesaid. Know ye therefore that We, of Our special grace, certain knowledge, and mere motion, by and with the advice and consent of Our said right trusty and right well-beloved cousin and counsellor Frederick Earl of Carlisle, and Lieutenant-General and General-Governor of Our said kingdom of Ireland, have given and granted, and by these presents for Us, Our heirs and successors, We do give and grant unto the said Honorable Richard Barry, his heirs and assigns, full power and authority to have and to hold two several yearly fairs as also two weekly markets for ever in or at the said town and lands of Ballyvolane, otherwise Cove, in Our said county of Cork, that is to say, one fair to be held on every 20th day of April, and one other fair to be held on every 15th day of October, as also two weekly markets to be held in or at the town and lands aforesaid on every Wednesday and Saturday for ever, unless the said 20th day of April or the said 15th day of October happen to fall on a Sunday, then Our will is and by these presents for Us, Our heirs and successors, We do grant unto the said Honorable Richard Barry, his heirs and assigns, that he, the said Honorable Richard Barry, his heirs and assigns, and every of them, may have and hold the said fairs in or at the said town and lands of Ballyvolane, otherwise Cove, aforesaid, the Monday then next following every such Sunday. Together with a court of pye powder to be held in said town and lands during the said fairs and markets. And Our further will is, and by these presents for Us, Our heirs and successors, We do grant unto the said Honorable Richard Barry, his heirs and assigns, that he, the said Richard Barry, his heirs and assigns, may for ever have and receive all and singular the tolls, customs, privileges, and immunities whatsoever from the said fairs, markets, and court arising, or to such fairs, markets, and court belonging or appertaining, or by means of the same, or any of them, growing or accruing, without any account to Us, Our heirs or successors, to be rendered for the same. And Our further will is, and We strictly enjoin and command for Us, Our heirs and successors, that the said Richard Barry, his heirs and assigns, may for ever have and hold the said fairs and markets in or at the town and lands of Ballyvolane, otherwise Cove aforesaid, in manner and form aforesaid, together with the said court of pye powder, and all usual tolls, customs, privileges, and immunities from the said fairs, markets, and court arising, or to the same of right or by custom belonging or appertaining, yielding therefor yearly to Us, Our heirs and successors, the yearly rent of one pound sterling for the said fairs, market, and court, to be paid yearly for ever. And Our further will is, and by these presents for Us, Our heirs and successors, We do grant unto the said Richard Barry, his heirs and assigns, that these Our Letters Patent or the enrolment thereof, shall be in all things firm, good, valid, sufficient, and effectual in the law against Us, Our heirs and successors, in all the courts of Us, Our heirs and successors, any cause, matter, or thing whatsoever to the contrary notwithstanding. Provided always, that these Our Letters Patent be enrolled in the Rolls of Our High Court of Chancery in Our said kingdom of Ireland, and also in the office of Our Auditor-General of Our said kingdom of Ireland within the space of six months next ensuing the date of these presents, otherwise these Our Letters Patent to be void and of none effect, anything herein contained to the contrary notwithstanding. In witness whereof, We have caused these Our Letters to be made

Patent. Witness our aforesaid Lieutenant-General and General-Governor of Our said kingdom of Ireland at Dublin, the 20th day of September, in the 31st year of Our reign.

CONWAY.

Entered in the office of His Majesty's Auditor-General, 22nd Sept. 1791. ROBERT HEAD, gent. } R. C. KEARLY, Dy. Sol. of the Crown and Hanaper.

Inrolled in the office of the Rolls of His Majesty's High Court of Chancery in Ireland, the 22nd day of September, in the 31st year of the reign of King George the Third, and examined by
M. PATERSON, jr., and F. PERRY, D. Clks. and Keeper of the Rolls.

Queenstown, 24th November 1888.

R. H. TOWNSEND, Esq., J.P., examined.

22,734. You are the agent for Mr. Smith Barry?—I am.

22,735. He is the owner of the market rights and tolls in Queenstown?—He is.

22,736. Is he the owner of the greater portion of the town of Queenstown?—No, only a small portion.

22,737. Mr. Barry is not in the immediate receipt of the tolls?—No.

22,738. You have them sub-let?—They are sub-let to the town commissioners.

22,739. What is the term of that letting to the town commissioners?—14 years, and it expires on the 1st January next.

22,740. They hold under lease for that term?—Yes, 14 years is the term.

22,741. Are there any special covenants or agreements in it?—No; I have it here.

22,742-3. The witness then produced the agreement, of which the following is a summary:—

"It is dated the 31st December 1874, and made between Arthur Hugh Smith Barry and the chairman and town commissioners of Queenstown. By that agreement there was let to the commissioners the piece or place of ground with stalls thereon known as the Meat Market, and also the piece or place of ground with stalls thereon known as the Vegetable Market, together with the weighing machine attached thereto, situate in Scott's Square in the town of Queenstown, county of Cork, together with the tolls, emoluments, and customs arising from said markets, receivable for the term of 14 years from the 1st January 1875 at the yearly rent of [illegible].

"Agreement that the commissioners shall not permit any building to be erected thereon without the sanction in writing of Mr. Barry, and a proviso that the owner can resume possession and the town commissioners surrender at the expiration of the first three years, or at the end of every succeeding three years, by giving previously six months' notice thereof."

22,744. The rent payable at present is [illegible]?—Yes.

22,745. What is the valuation, do you know?—[illegible].

22,746. Have the commissioners to pay the taxes on that?—They are allowed half the poor rates.

22,747. What is the market day here?—The regular market day is Saturday.

22,748. That is the general market day?—Yes. The patent gives power to hold two markets and fairs.

22,749. What fairs are held?—No fairs at all. The patent gives power to hold two fairs and two weekly markets.

22,750. You produce this document as the patent under which the market is held?—Yes.

22,751. I suppose you have not had any opportunity of communicating with Mr. Barry about this inquiry?—No, I have had no opportunity, but I know his views very well.

22,752. Would you concur here now in the observations you made in Tipperary as to Mr. Barry giving his consent to the town commissioners obtaining compulsory powers to acquire his rights altogether?—Certainly. I make the same observations here as I made in Tipperary. I know thoroughly well that local bodies should have control of the markets and fairs by buying out existing rights, and I know Mr. Smith Barry agrees with my views in that way.

22,753. You never made up the capital expenditure in providing the market buildings?—No, it was long before my time.

22,754. There is no record?—No. The agent at the time is away in England.

Mr. JAMES AHERN, Town Clerk, examined.

22,755. You are the town clerk of Queenstown?—Yes.

22,756. Is it a fact that you have no fairs at all here?—It is a fact.

22,757. Are cattle sold at the markets?—No.

22,758. Then practically there is no market or any place for the exposure and sale of cattle?—No.

22,759. Where, as a matter of fact, are the cattle brought?—To the fairs in Cork, Middleton, and the surrounding country. They go as far as the city of Limerick. In the year 1876 we tried to have monthly fairs, and two or three attempts failed. The island is not able to support a fair, and no beast at all is brought into Queenstown.

22,760. Where are the markets held?—Underneath this building (the Court House) in Scott's Square.

22,761. Does Scott's Square form portion of the public thoroughfare?—It is off that the market is held. It is [illegible]

22,763. Is hay ever brought here on Saturday?—It is brought to be weighed.

22,764. Straw and hay?—Yes.

22,765. What other commodities are brought?—Fruit, potatoes, vegetables, and turnips, and a few apples.

22,766. Do the people bring any animals at all, such as sheep, lambs, or pigs?—They bring small pigs.

22,767. Do they bring any sheep?—No, they are never sold in the market. Parties go out the country to buy them, and bring them in to weigh them.

22,768. Are the markets confined to Scott's Square?—They are unless some hawkers sale vegetables over the town. Sometimes they sell fish on the street, and we have no power to prevent them except to punish them for obstruction.

22,769. Have you any rules printed for the regulation of the market?—Yes.

23,771. Have you got a list of the charges made on these different commodities?—We have not, only what was on the late list that Mr. Smith-Barry had.

23,772. What are the charges?—A halfpenny per hundred on the weighbridge for hay, straw, and potatoes.

23,773. Practically, for anything you weigh on the weighbridge, that is the charge?—Yes.

23,774. Is there any other weighbridge in the town?—Ours is the only one used. There is a coal merchant in the town who has one, but he does not use it. It is for his own private use.

23,775. Is the halfpenny a hundredweight charged on the net weight or the gross?—On the net weight we charge.

23,776. Do the people ever go into the road opposite the courthouse?—No; the loads of potatoes come there to be weighed and distributed over the town. The principal victuallers in the town supply potatoes to the ships in the harbour, and the potatoes, after being weighed, are taken away.

23,777. The loads are never exposed for sale?—No; they are always sold before they come in; they only come in to be weighed.

23,778. What do you assign as a reason that the markets are not better, and the fact that you are not able to support any fairs? Is it because of the immediate proximity of the town of Midleton and the city of Cork?—I do not know.

23,779. You say formerly you had good fairs here?—Many years ago. I never recollect a fair here.

23,780. What duties do the town commissioners perform here?—The lighting, cleansing, and watching. They clean the streets.

23,781. Who cleans the market square immediately after the markets?—The public scavenger, who has the contract for so much a year. He cleans the market in connexion with the streets of the town.

23,782. Have you got the receipts from the market, or did you make up the average for the period stated?—In 1865 the receipts were 126l.; in 1866, 115l.; in 1867, 114l.; the expenditure in 1865 was 109l.; in 1866, 113l.; in 1867, 111l. Average receipts, 118l. 13s. 4d.; expenditure, 110l. 13s. 4d.

23,783. You had very little margin of profit?—Very little. It pays, and no more, and that is why we tried to reduce the rent, as the lease is out at the end of the year, and because it is not paying.

23,784. You pay 50l. a year rent?—Yes, and 4l. to the weigh-master; the rates are 1l. 4d., and we light the markets with gas.

23,785. Are any of the commissioners here?—Yes.

23,786. Have you had experience of any markets other than Queenstown yourself?—No.

23,787. Or fairs elsewhere?—I do not think I ever saw a fair in my life.

23,788. Are the people at liberty to dispose of their marketable commodities elsewhere in town than the market place?—They are not at liberty, but they do.

23,789. Why do you say they are not at liberty? The only way in which you can prevent them is by prosecuting them for obstruction?—That is what I mean, and it is only for obstruction on the streets under the Towns Improvement Act.

23,790. Why do they go about the streets; or, would you state it is because the space in Scott's Square is not sufficient?—No; but the town is very long, as you can see, and when potatoes and things come to the market, it is a great accommodation to the people to get the goods to their houses in place of coming to the market.

23,791. You think the market is inconveniently situated?—It is not central enough for the parties living in some parts of the town, and then, I suppose, Mr. Barry's patent rights keep it there.

Mr. Patrick Begley examined.

23,792. You are the weigh-master?—Yes.

23,793. What charge have you on vegetables?—I charge 1d. a basket; if it is a large one I charge 2d.; if larger again 3d. It is according to its size.

23,794. Have you any rules regulating the charge on the basket, or is it left to the discretion of your collector to charge what he pleases, or to consider what is a small or what is a large basket?—It is, of course.

23,795. He has to exercise his discretion in levying the charge?—He has, and these charges were there before I came.

23,796. What return do you give for these charges, or is the charge made for coming in and placing their basket on the square, and exposing the vegetables there?—No; they are not allowed to do it on the square. These hampers that come to the market are sold to the stall-keepers, and when they are sold to the stall-keepers the charge is made.

23,797. You have stalls in the market?—Yes.

23,798. How many have you?—Fourteen in each market.

23,799. Have you got permanent tenants in these stalls?—Only two or three are let; the others are all idle.

23,800. What is the rent paid for them?—Three shillings a week for a full stall, and 1s. 6d. for half.

23,801. Is that charge payable by the seller of the vegetables to the stall-holder?—The charge is paid to me. I charge him 3d. when coming into the market.

23,802. Does the seller pay it to you on entrance to the market?—No, not at all, but when he sells.

23,803. When you say market, what do you mean. Is it Scott's Square alone, or the arcades?—I mean the two parts of this building allotted off for the market. They are not on the square at all.

23,804. As they go out do you collect the charge?—I generally go around before they leave and get it. When I think they have sold I go around and give them a check for the 1d. or 2d. or 3d. they give me.

23,805. Is that a printed ticket?—It is.

The following is a copy of the receipt given:

Queenstown Market.

No. 535.

18

Duties for Small Wares.

Amount,

P. Begley,
Weighmaster.

23,806. You give that to them to denote they have paid the charge?—Yes.

23,807. You never chalk it on their sheets or the basket?—No. Every pennyworth is in the book.

23,808. Supposing a farmer brought in some vegetables and sold them to a shopkeeper in the town on market day whilst the market was going on and it came to your knowledge, do you think the town commissioners would be entitled to the charge?—They do not get any charge.

23,809. Unless they sell in the market?—Unless they sell in the market.

23,810. They may sell elsewhere?—Yes, and we have no right to charge. A great many have done that.

23,811. What is the charge on fish?—One penny.

23,812. It is in the discretion of the collector to levy that charge on one fish, or two, or three?—Yes.

23,813. What is the smallest quantity of fish in a hamper on which he would levy 1d.?—10 or 12 in a small hamper.

23,814. You would only charge 1d. on that?—Yes.

23,815. If there were only two fish in, it would you charge?—It would not be worth charging.

23,816. Do you, as a matter of fact, charge on a basket containing less than five?—Never.

23,817. Do the same observations apply as regards the sale of fish that you have applied to the vegetables; do they sell to the stall-holders?—They do.

23,818. And it is only when they sell you levy the charge?—Yes; when they go to the market to sell.

21,619. Do these stall-holders ever retail fish and vegetables?—That is what they buy them for.

21,620. In the first instance, the producer has to pay your charge, and then the stall-holder for retailing them has an additional charge to pay in the shape of a rent per week for retailing them?—He has to pay rent for his stall.

21,621. On meat, what is your charge?—The stall is set. We have nothing to do with the meat. We collect the stall money.

21,622. Have you any restriction on the butchering establishments elsewhere in the town?—No.

21,623. Have you any connexion with them at all?—No. We have no authority outside the market gate.

21,624. They have only to pay the rent of the standing?—Yes.

21,625. What is the charge for weighing hay and straw?—A half-penny per hundred-weight.

21,626. Is the hay and straw always sold before it is weighed?—It is generally.

21,627. If a buyer said he would get the weight of it himself, and need not ascertain the weight at your weigh-bridge, would you levy your charge if it came to your knowledge, supposing the load was sold?—They would not come to the market at all. I never saw one of them there.

21,628. Supposing they came to the market and disposed of it there, and did not weigh it, would you charge?—I never saw a case of that kind.

21,629. Do you think the commissioners would be entitled to the charge?—I think they would be entitled to charge on anything that would be sold in the place.

21,630. The same observations apply to straw?—Yes, to any article.

21,631. On fruit, what charge do you levy?—One penny on small hampers, 2d. on large ones, and 3d. on very large ones.

21,632. Where do they place these hampers?—On the ground between the two markets.

21,633. These are standing charges you might call them?—Yes.

21,634. You have no fixed rule regulating the charge?—No. It is always the same since I came.

21,635. Still, every hamper, no matter what it contains, must pay a charge?—Yes, it must pay something, unless it is not worth charging on.

21,636. The commissioners give you power to give and take. If they bring in a small quantity you have the power not to charge?—Yes.

21,637. On potatoes, what do you charge?—A half-penny a hundred on the weighbridge, and 1d. per sack on the scales.

21,638. Is that only for weighing?—That is all.

21,639. If they sell in the market and do not weigh, you do not look for your charge?—Well, I can charge, but that thing does not occur.

21,640. Are the potatoes sold before they are weighed?—Generally.

21,641. As a general rule, they are sold before they are weighed?—Yes, but an odd bag may be weighed before being sold for the sake of convenience, and the seller would then take it to his customer.

21,642. In that case does the customer pay the charge?—Yes.

21,643. When you ascertain the weight, is the charge payable?—Yes. I give a docket.

21,644. Is it a printed form?—Yes.

21,649. You charge nothing additional for weighing?—No.

21,650. Do you ever mark the weight in chalk on the sack?—No; I give it in writing on paper. That is the best way, and it cannot be rubbed out.

21,651. Do you give receipts also to those people who sell fruit and fish when they pay?—I do.

21,652. Is it yourself only who collects these charges, or have you another assistant?—I have no one but myself.

21,653. Supposing these people had this charge, and you were going around and forgot they had paid you previously, would they have to pay again?—They would not; they would not do it for me.

21,654. Is that the reason for giving the check?—No. I am ordered to give a check by the town clerk for every penny received.

21,655. Were complaints ever made that the charge was demanded twice?—Never.

21,656. But it is in order to provide against such a contingency the check is given?—Yes.

21,657. What is the charge on the turnips?—A half-penny a hundred on the weighbridge.

21,658. These are the only charges you have?—Yes.

21,659. On the weighbridge and scales?—Yes.

21,660. If hambones were brought in, what do you charge on market day?—If sold a penny a piece; if not sold there is no charge.

21,661. Each hambone when sold has to bear a charge of one penny?—Yes.

21,662. Is that the only charge. Supposing they were brought in a cart, and the cart went on the square, would you levy any standing charge on that cart?—No.

21,663. So that if they do not sell and avail themselves of the market the entire day they go free?—Yes.

21,664. Honey is not brought here at all?—No. Sometimes there are small quantities brought for weighing—a bag or two, or three or four in a week—and when weighed they take it to their customers.

21,665. What do you charge for weighing?—A penny for a small bag and 2d. for a large one.

21,666. What quantity would you charge 1d. on?—About 12 pounds.

21,667. You stated that cheap hampers about the town also weigh for these people?—There is little of it done; not a great deal, I believe.

21,668. Do they charge these people?—They do not.

21,669. It is only as convenience that they do it. You would not claim they levy any charge?—No.

21,670. Then you have no rule restraining the sale of any commodity elsewhere than in the market?—Not a bit.

21,671. What facilities do you offer for weighing. How many scales have you there?—Three scales.

21,672. Are particular commodities weighed on particular scales?—There is one for potatoes.

21,673. Is it exclusively confined to potatoes?—Yes. We have another for wool, and the third one for small quantities for the market people when they do be selling to accommodate them.

21,674. Supposing a man came with a load of potatoes and weighed each individual sack brought in, there being 12 in the load, he would have to pay 1s.; but would the retailer to whom he subsequently sold have to pay any additional charge for the use of the scales?—No. It will have been paid before, and I won't charge a second time.

21,675. Although you give the ... scales to weigh ...

22,882. Before you weigh the corn is it sold?—Generally it is.

22,883. But if it is weighed with you and not previously sold, it is immaterial to you whether subsequently sold or not, you obtain your charge?—Yes. I give a receipt for the weight and get paid, and he may do what he likes with it afterwards.

22,884. In weighing corn you estimate the tare of the sack too?—Yes.

22,885. What is the estimated tare of the ordinary bag of corn?—That is according to what the sack would weigh. There are four pound sacks and seven pound sacks.

22,886. Do you always weigh the empty bag of corn?—Not always, because the buyer and seller may be pleased with the guess they make, and if they don't I weigh for them.

22,887-8. Supposing there were three stone, two pounds, would you put the two pounds down on the docket you give?—I would give them to a pound, but I would not break the pound.

22,889. It must be a pound or nothing?—Yes.

22,890. When weighing potatoes, what is the smallest weight you put into the scales?—If it takes four pounds I give it, and if it does not take the four pounds I give them nothing.

22,891. You do not break the 4 lbs. in potatoes?—No.

22,892. On hay and straw?—I always weigh the cart and take it out of the load, and give the net weight.

22,893. What is the custom in weighing grain; do you weigh down to a stone weight?—I weigh any weight they bring in. I would weigh down to 7 lbs. if they bring it in.

22,894. Do you weigh under it?—No.

22,895-96. It is not customary to go under a half-stone?—No.

[*The following is a copy of the weighbridge ticket*]:—

No. 1,152.

WEIGHBRIDGE, QUEENSTOWN MARKETS.

day of 188 .

Weighed for

Gross cwts.		qrs.	lbs.
Cart..	–	–	–
Nett..	„	„	„

Charges ½d. per cwt.

P. BUTLER,
Weighmaster.

22,897. Are the markets well supplied for Queenstown by those commodities that you have mentioned?—No, they are not. The market is declining very much.

22,898. Would you say the reason for that is the great number of shops springing up in the town?—It is a good means of causing the decline.

22,899. Have you ever heard any complaints of any of the charges at all?—No.

22,900. No complaints have been made to you by the people?—No.

22,901-2. Or of any ill-treatment they received from any person collecting them?—No.

22,903. Are you able, on Saturday, to attend to the weighbridge, and issue tickets there, and also attend to two scales and issue tickets at those two scales?—I have to do so.

22,904. Were any complaints ever made of any undue delay being caused in ascertaining the weights of the commodities brought in?—No the whole affair is over about one o'clock.

22,905. When does the market usually commence?—About seven or eight o'clock. The buyers do not come before eight o'clock generally.

22,906. Do you keep a block of these tickets you give?—Yes.

22,907. Always?—Yes.

22,908. Then, if it was required from the commissioners to make a return of the quantity of the different commodities brought to the market, it is possible to make such a return?—I could very easily.

22,909. Does it ever come under your notice at all, the current prices of the different commodities?—No.

22,910. Or the actual contract prices between the buyer and seller?—They take the price from the papers.

22,911. Does it ever come under your notice at all what the buyer has agreed to pay the seller?—Yes, often.

22,912. Would it be possible for the commissioners to make a return of the current prices of these commodities?—I do not think so.

22,913. Supposing it was required?—I do not think they could.

22,914. Why?—Because they take the prices from the newspaper.

22,915. But the newspaper would only contain the statement of the past current prices, and not the prices of the present day?—They go by the last market day in Cork.

22,916. Are the prices here regulated by the prices the previous market day in Cork?—Generally, the prices at both places are the same, and they go by the paper.

22,917. Do they deduct from the prices here an equivalent to the cost of transit from here to Cork?—They do not. I can say nothing about that, that is their own business.

22,918. Practically, then, the prices given for each commodity are arranged beforehand?—They are; they have their prices settled before they get anything weighed.

22,919. The prices they pay the seller you always see are the prices quoted the previous market day in Cork?—Generally.

22,920. Have you ever heard complaints by the sellers in the market of that practice?—No; the only thing I do not like is to see a great deal of vegetables come in and I cannot charge tolls on them.

22,921. Where do they come?—To the stall-keepers who go out the country and make bargains with people and then they are sent in.

22,922. Do they send them in on market day?—Any day.

22,923. You do not collect the charge because the sale has not been effected in the market, although the delivery is made there?—Yes.

22,924. Do the farmers, when they bring their vegetables, go around from stall-keeper to stall-keeper, or is it previously arranged that they will supply a certain quantity of vegetables to a particular stall-holder?—They make their bargain with the stall-keeper.

22,925. I am not asking you that. I am speaking now of the ordinary practice. When they sell in the market, have they a particular customer, or do they go around from stall-keeper to stall-keeper?—Yes, to whoever likes to buy; they go from one to another.

22,926. Practically, they go around to each stall-keeper, and sell where they can make the best bargain?—Yes.

22,927. Is what you have stated about parties buying out in the country the only objection you have to the present system of the markets here?—That is all.

23,928. The witness stated,—I want to say a few words in reference to the fairs. The town clerk stated that fairs were established by the town commissioners in 1878. They were passed a resolution that a monthly fair be held in Queenstown on the second Monday in each month. Two or three months elapsed, and the fairs were held, and were very successfully, or at least fairly attended by sellers of stock, sheep, cattle, and pigs; but it was found for the purpose of accommodating sellers it would be necessary to establish communication between the township of Queenstown and Monkstown, across the river Lee, by ferry. There is a ferry established, and has been used a hundred years for carrying people across, but to use it for fairs and market purposes was something new, and the ferry could not be worked without considerable expense. Arrangements were made by the town commissioners at the time for the purpose of getting the railway companies and steamship companies, and the buyers who were largely confined to Queenstown, to aid in promoting the fairs. The Great Southern and Western Railway ran a train specially to convey purchasers to Queenstown from Cork. From the efforts of Mr. Chaplin of the Great Western of England, the Milford boats called at Queenstown for the purpose of taking any stock disposed of for English markets, and everything was done for the purpose of making the fairs a success, but when the Local Government Board auditor came to examine the accounts of the town commissioners, he disallowed all items of charge for the use of the ferry, and consequently those gentlemen who signed the cheques were obliged to refund the amounts they had signed for in order to pay the ferry charges, although the charges had been paid manifestly for the purpose of benefiting Queenstown. Now I want to impress you, as engaged in this very important subject, that if by any means those gentlemen who hold the rights of the markets and fairs of Queenstown, or any other town where charges are to be made, that they ought to provide the necessary accommodation for facilitating the sales at those fairs and markets. When I tell you that there are in Queenstown some 17 or 18 victuallers who purchase at fairs outside the town, and bring in a 100 head of cattle for consumption, I think you will agree with me that they are entitled to have a fair in Queenstown, and facilities afforded to people to have their cattle disposed of here; and, moreover, it would save shipping at Cork, which they do at the present time, and the facilities afforded by the Great Southern and Western Railway with their [illegible] will enable sellers of stock to send them more directly from Queenstown than even from Cork. It is with a view of calling attention to that matter I make these few observations, because I believe if fairs were established and properly upheld in Queenstown, they would be a large source of revenue to the owners, and a benefit to the surrounding districts. At present all the contractors for the Government supplies in Queenstown are obliged to go to fairs 20, 30, and 40 miles distant for the purpose of purchasing stock to supply their contracts, whereas if there were fairs in Queenstown they could purchase at those fairs and reserve the stock until such time as they required them for use; and people exporting would have an opportunity of sending direct to the markets, and not have any unnecessary delays as at present. The Milford boats offered to call on the evening of the fair days and take away any stock to be disposed of in foreign markets, and owing to the inability of the town commissioners to meet the charges on the ferry the people would not send their stock, and the fairs fell through; and I believe if arrangements were made for facilitating the carrying of stock into Queenstown, that the fairs would be very important and largely attended. At present in the district of Carrigaloe, and places around there, no other fairs would be within such easy reach as Cork and Queenstown, because they are more convenient and could be held at times more suitable to every one. That is one of the principal things I wish to call attention to. Then there is another matter that I wish to refer to. It has been stated by Mr. Townsend, and I think very liberally, that it is his desire to facilitate public bodies in having control of the fairs and markets, and he also states Mr. Smith Barry coincides with his views. It is characteristic of the liberality of both Mr. Townsend and Mr. Smith Barry. I do believe it would be a benefit to Queenstown if the town commissioners had that control, and I believe also the public buildings in connexion with the markets should become the property of the town commissioners. They would be able to make arrangements with Mr. Smith Barry that would not deprive him of any of his rights or interests, and at the same time benefit the town materially, and benefit the property in it, which they cannot do at the present time. These are the observations I consider it right to make, and they are the observations which may be taken into consideration in any future legislation.

23,929. Are you in trade in the town?—I am an architect by profession. I was a town commissioner and chairman of the town commissioners formerly. I stand here now as a ratepayer, and nothing else.

23,930. You think there is a great possibility of fostering fairs here?—Unquestionably.

23,931. Is your opinion shared by many of the commissioners?—It was shared unanimously by the commissioners when on the commissioners' board, but I believe there are some Commissioners at present who were not commissioners when I was there, and they are in favour of it. We have one ex-commissioner here, Captain O'Sullivan, who was a commissioner then, and who can tell you there was a possibility of making the fairs a success, but as I stated it required an outlay which the town commissioners were not allowed to expend out of the rates of the town, that is for the purpose of establishing ferries for the day between Monkstown and Queenstown. The auditor stated if Monkstown were within the jurisdiction of the town commissioners of Queenstown there would be no difficulty in allowing the expense, but Monkstown being without, and the fact of Queenstown being within their jurisdiction, did not enable them to pay rates for crossing into another district outside their own.

23,932. Is that opinion as to the desirability of local authorities obtaining compulsory powers to acquire the market rights and tolls the general opinion throughout the country?—I can give no person's opinion but my own, but from what I heard generally outside, it appears to be the public and general opinion all over the country that all public markets should belong to a public board that would be established for the benefit of the public, and then that the public should have control of the charges made in those places, whereas at the present time the advantages rest with the owners of the patents, and consequently they cannot be interfered with directly or indirectly, and no influence can be brought to bear on them by the public.

23,933. Have you formed any ideas at all as to the exaction of a toll, or have you attended other fairs and markets?—I have attended them all over Ireland, not on business, but I have a general experience of them.

23,934. Do you think the levying of a toll acts in any way as a deterrent upon people bringing in their commodities to the markets?—I believe it does, and very materially. I believe a farmer who is sending in 10, 20, or 30 head of cattle would be very reluctant about paying 1*d.* per head for them, not knowing whether he would dispose of them or not. I was at the present moment a very strong agitation in Cork, where the matter was established. I saw a very hostile demonstration against it, and I believe the tolls were done away with. I think the markets should be perfectly free and self-sustaining by whatever business is transacted in them.

23,935. If local authorities should obtain compulsory powers to acquire these rights, is it your opinion that they should not obtain control over the markets and fairs in order to make them a source of revenue, but only to levy such a charge as would pay the cost of management?—That would be my opinion; that is the general feeling.

23,936. And nothing should go to the benefit of the town?—Yes, I believe there should be a revision of the charges if they found they were short of funds or had a surplus.

23,937. If charges are to be levied, do you think they ought to be fixed, or only charges that would fluctuate according to the value of the merchandise commodity?—I believe they ought to be periodically revised about every five or ten years.

[illegible]

Captain Edward O'Sullivan examined.

23,938. (D'Doran.) Some reference was made to the town commissioners, but I think it does not redound much to their credit to see an inquiry held in this town the result of which may add to the benefit of the town, and not one member present except the clerk and market inspector to give any information on the subject. With regard to what Mr. Doran said about the fairs, I have a long knowledge, perhaps a longer knowledge than anyone here, as I have a very good recollection for the past 50 years of the town and its surroundings. I was 21 years as town commissioner and three years chairman of the board, and I could bear out what Mr. Doran says, in a great measure, save and except he forgot to mention that for the fairs intended to be held there was no earthly accommodation for the cattle brought in. They were placed on the public thoroughfare, and that is not the place for the fairs and markets. That was the first drawback to the fairs here to my knowledge. Then, as Mr. Doran said, the island itself could not support a fair here held monthly, as the commissioners wanted. They should find some means of bringing the cattle for that fair from other parts of the country besides the island, that is to say, from Carrigtwohill and other places surrounding. What Mr. Doran states is perfectly true about the commissioners being surcharged for giving facility at the ferry and engaging a boat to bring the cattle across. It was a great drawback that there was no fair field and no accommodation given except on the public streets.

23,939. Were there any representations made to the owner, Mr. Smith Barry, to provide such accommodation?—It was since the commissioners took the matter from Mr. Smith Barry that they wanted to establish the fairs in the town.

23,940. The fairs they wanted to establish were to be held on the public thoroughfare?—Yes, they had no place but the public streets.

23,941. Were representations ever made to the owner to provide a fair-green?—I am not aware.

23,942. (The Town Clerk.) No; he had no place to give. It was an open sort of place they were held on, and he had no place but that landing. They should be held in Ballimore, and that is a narrow street.

23,943. Captain O'Sullivan's evidence continued:—

23,944. Of course, if the fairs were considered it would not be difficult to fix a proper and convenient site?—You will find it very difficult indeed to find space for anything.

23,945. But in close proximity to the town?—Both landlords, Captain Rowe and Mr. Barry, represent the district and the island outside the town, and they could very well supply a place if they wished to encourage the fairs to be held in the town or for the town.

23,946. Are there any depôts here for providing the Government ships, or do they come in here for provisions?—Yes. It is by the shipping trade the town lives.

23,947. Do you think if fairs were fostered here that it would be a great source of revenue and be well attended for the provisions that would be required by the masters of the different vessels?—I think it would materially enhance the value of the town and bring trade to the town.

23,948. From your own experience, do you think, owing to the fact that victuallers in this town have to travel to Cork and elsewhere to buy cattle that the value of the dead meat they dispose of is enhanced by the cost of transit to this place?—Yes; the victuallers buy cattle in the different towns in Cork, in the county Limerick, and Tipperary.

23,949. You think the value of the provisions enhanced by the fact of incurring additional expense in going elsewhere for the stock?—Yes; the prices are put on. The purchaser from this town has to pay the cost of bringing the provisions here.

23,950. Did you form that idea previous to my mentioning that the purchaser had to pay the cost of transit of the animal?—I have often thought it over that if the facility was given in the town for people who are in trade here of purchasing in this town, that they could retail to the public cheaper than when they go elsewhere and purchase. It would be for the advantage of the public if fairs could be established here as in Mallow and every town about the country. Those who live in the town and have yearly contracts for the Government and merchants' vessels consume a great deal of provisions.

23,951. Has the agent ever mentioned the desirability of establishing fairs here?—I know him very well, and I believe it would be his wish for the accommodation of the public if fairs could be established; but there is no facility to offer, and no sheds for the protection of the people from the inclemency of the weather. I believe if either of the landlords had an interest in the town they would give a field or give some facility for establishing the fairs in the town, and they should do so. The commissioners have no power outside their jurisdiction.

23,952. Have you any observations to make relative to the existing markets, or do you find any objection to the manner in which they are held and worked?—The public have very little shelter or accommodation. You would see them there under the weather with their loads of potatoes from six o'clock in the morning until they disposed of them, on the public street.

23,953. Do you think the exposure of these commodities on the public thoroughfare is an objectionable practice?—The public complain that the public thoroughfare is taken up. In the market you have only those two sheds, one at each side, and one is the butchers' market, and the other the fish and vegetable market.

23,954. You think the space they afford is inadequate?—I think so.

23,955. Do you think if there were market buildings erected and sufficient and ample shelter afforded to the marketable commodities brought in, that would tend to increase the market?—Yes.

23,956. Would you approve of the erection of such and the town commissioners receiving power to have bye-laws made confining the sale of marketable commodities to this building?—I think the town commissioners, as the governing body of the town, should have control over the markets. They would see what was right and just to be done, and would further anything for the advantage of the town. Anything done for the advantage of the town must be done by the commissioners and not by agents to the landlords.

23,957. Have you any further observations to make?—No.

23,958. Or any general remarks as regards the markets and fairs throughout the country?—No, I believe there is a great deal of room for improvement in the markets of Queenstown, both in regulation and accommodation, in order to bring trade to Queenstown.

Mr. James Ahern, the Town Clerk, re-examined.

23,959. Have you any further observations to make?—I think we should have bye-laws in the market. We have none at present. In regard to the fairs, I may say that in the island on which Queenstown is situated no stock is raised. The farmers principally keep milch cows for the purpose of supplying vessels coming in with milk. That is the reason we have no fairs here.

23,960. Is there any other gentleman who has any observations to make?—No answer.

23,961. A vote of thanks to the Assistant Commissioner terminated the inquiry.

BRAY.

With reference to my inquiry in Bray on the 29th day of November 1889, I beg to report as follows:—

Bray is a maritime town partly in the county of Wicklow and partly in the county of Dublin. It is a station on the Dublin, Wicklow, and Wexford railway line, and, owing to its proximity to Dublin and the beauty of the surrounding scenery, it has

number of tables and seats for the convenience of those disposing of commodities there. Altogether the building is considered structurally unsuitable for market purposes.

The hay and straw market is held in a paled-in field opposite the market house, and which has been rented by the commissioners from the Earl of Pembroke at the yearly rent of 15*l.*

Since the commissioners made the byelaws regulating the markets and fairs they have not had a clear financial year, and have not so far endeavoured to enforce them so as to prohibit the sale of marketable commodities about the streets.

A complaint was made on behalf of the owners that the producers bring the marketable commodities to the township the day before the ordinary market day in order to avoid payment of the toll, as in such case a weighing charge only is paid if the commodity is weighed.

Appended will be found a transcript of the evidence taken at the inquiry.

JOHN J. O'MEARA,
Assistant Commissioner.

45, Lower Mount Street, Dublin.

Bray, 29th November 1888.

Mr. Patrick McDonald (Town Clerk) examined.

23,962. You are the town clerk of Bray?—Yes.

23,963. The town commissioners have control over the markets and fairs here?—Yes.

23,964. How do they hold them?—They hold them under the Bray Township Act, 1866, and byelaws framed under the Public Health (Ireland) Act, 1878, and approved of by the Local Government Board on the 15th June 1887.

23,965. Have you got a copy of those byelaws?—I have.

23,966. Witness here produced the byelaws, of which the following is a copy:—

BYELAWS made by the BRAY TOWNSHIP COMMISSIONERS, so far as they relate to Markets and Fairs.

THE MARKETS, THE MARKET-HOUSE, AND PREMISES ADJACENT THERETO.

Interpretation of Terms.

In the construction of the byelaws relating to the markets, market-house, and adjacent premises, the words "market-house" shall mean the building recently erected in said town of Bray for the purpose of a market-house. And "market-place" shall mean the space of ground on the south side of said building recently laid out and appropriated by the said commissioners for the purposes of a hay and straw market, provided that it shall be lawful for the said commissioners, or such persons as they shall from time to time appoint for the purpose, to permit hay, straw, and other commodities, to be sold in the streets of said town, adjacent to said space to such extent as shall be allowed from time to time for the purposes aforesaid, and on such occasions for the purposes of these byelaws, such extended space shall be deemed, and taken to be the market-place herein-after referred to.

172. A person resorting to the market-place for the sale of any goods, provisions, marketable commodities, or articles, shall not for the purpose of sale or of exposure for sale, place or cause to be placed, such goods, provisions, marketable commodities, or articles, in any part or place of the market-place other than such as shall have been appropriated for the reception, deposit, or exposure for sale of the same, and shall be defined or described in a notice printed, painted, or marked in legible letters of such a colour as to be clearly distinguishable from the colour of the ground whereon such letters are printed, painted, or marked, and affixed or set up and continued in some suitable and conspicuous position at or near to such part or parts.

172. He shall not, for the purpose of sale, or of exposure for sale, bring the same, or cause the same to be brought into such market-place before the hour of seven o'clock in summer and eight o'clock in winter, in the forenoon of any day appointed for the holding of any market.

174. He shall not allow such goods, provisions, marketable commodities, or articles, or any part thereof, to remain in the market-place after the hour of six in the afternoon of any day appointed for the holding of any market.

175. Every tenant or occupier, or the servant of a tenant or occupier of any building, stall, or standing in the market-house, who shall be in charge of the same, shall, before the hour of six in the afternoon of every day, during which such building, stall, or standing, may have been used for the sale, or exposure for sale, of any goods, provisions, marketable commodities, or articles, extinguish, or cause to be extinguished, every fire or light in, upon, or in connection with such building, stall, or standing.

176. No tenant or occupier, or a servant of a tenant or occupier of any building, stall, or standing in the market-house used for the sale, or exposure, or preparation for sale, of any carcase of meat intended for the food of man, or any other person, shall cleave such carcase or meat elsewhere than upon a cleaving-block, or chopping-board, or otherwise than when properly attached to or suspended from the hooks provided for the purpose, in, upon, or in connection with such building, stall, or standing.

177. No tenant or occupier of any building, stall, or standing in the market-house shall cause or allow any goods, provisions, marketable commodities, or articles, to be deposited or exposed for sale in or upon such building, stall, or standing, so that such goods, provisions, marketable commodities, or articles, or any part thereof, shall project beyond the line of such building or stall, or beyond the limits assigned to such standing, so as to obstruct the passage of any person or vehicle, or of any goods, provisions, marketable commodities, or articles, in or through the market-house, or any part thereof.

178. A tenant or occupier of any building, stall, or standing in the market-house, or a person resorting to such market-house for the sale of any goods, provisions, marketable commodities, or articles, shall for any longer time, or in any other manner than shall be reasonably necessary for the conveyance of such goods, provisions, marketable commodities, or articles, to or from such building, stall, or standing, or any part of such market-house, deposit, or cause or allow to be deposited in any avenue or passage adjoining such building, stall, or standing, or elsewhere, in such market-house, or in any of the immediate approaches thereto, any hamper, crate, basket, box, barrel, or other receptacle for any goods brought into such market-house for the purpose of sale or exposure for sale.

179. Every tenant or occupier of any building, stall, or standing in the market-house, shall cause such building, stall, or standing to be properly cleansed immediately before the reception, deposit, or exposure

for sale therein or thereon and immediately after the removal therefrom of any goods, provisions, marketable commodities, or articles.

180. He shall from time to time, as often as occasion may require, during any day on which such building, stall, or standing may be used for the reception, deposit, or exposure for sale therein or thereon of any goods provisions, marketable commodities, or articles, cause all filth and refuse which may be produced or may accumulate in the course of the trade or business carried on by such tenant or occupier, to be placed in such receptacle (if any) as may be provided by the sanitary authority, or otherwise in a receptacle of suitable construction and of adequate dimensions, to be provided by such tenant or occupier, in, upon, or in close connexion with such building, stall, or standing. He shall from time to time, as often as may be necessary, cause the contents of such receptacle to be promptly removed in such a manner, and with such precautions as not to create a nuisance in the process of removal, to such place of deposit as shall from time to time be appointed by the sanitary authority, and shall be defined or described in a notice printed, painted, or marked in legible letters of such a colour as to be clearly distinguishable from the colour of the ground whereon such letters are printed, painted, or marked, and affixed or set up, and maintained in some suitable and conspicuous position at or near such place of deposit.

181. No person resorting to the market-house, and being in charge of any waggon, cart, truck, barrow, or other vehicle, or of any beast of burden, shall cause or allow such vehicle or beast to stand in any avenue or passage in such market-house, or in any of the immediate approaches thereto, for any longer time than shall be reasonably necessary for the loading or unloading of such vehicle or beast of burden.

182. Every person resorting to the market-place for the sale of any goods, provisions, marketable commodities, or articles, or in charge of any waggon, cart, truck, barrow or other vehicle, or of any beast of burden used for the conveyance of any goods, provisions, marketable commodities, or articles, to or from such market-place, shall, from time to time, as often as occasion may require, and in such a manner as to prevent nuisance or obstruction, remove or cause to be removed from every avenue or passage in such market-place, or from the footway or roadway of any of the immediate approaches thereto, all vegetable or animal refuse, filth, litter, or rubbish which may have fallen, or may have been thrown or deposited therein or thereon during the loading or unloading, or the conveyance to or from such market-place of such goods, provisions, marketable commodities, or articles.

183. Every owner or occupier of any building, stall, or standing in the market-house, shall cause every avenue or passage in connexion with such building, stall, or standing, whether used by him alone, or in conjunction with any other person, to be properly swept and cleansed once at least during each day appointed for the holding of the market.

184. No person resorting to the market-house for the sale of any goods, provisions, marketable commodities, or articles, shall cause or allow such goods, provisions, marketable commodities, or articles, to be brought or conveyed to or from such market-house or any building, stall, or standing therein, or to stand, be placed, or exposed for sale in such a manner as to obstruct the passage of any person or vehicle, or of any other goods, provisions, marketable commodities, or articles, in or through such market-house, or any part thereof, or any of the immediate approaches thereto.

185. No person shall smoke tobacco or other like thing in the market-house, or any covered building connected therewith.

186. All goods, provisions, marketable commodities, or articles requiring to be weighed for the purpose of sale, or of exposure for sale within the market-place, or market-house, shall be weighed at the public weighing machines provided by the commissioners at the market-house; and no person other than the person or persons appointed by the commissioners for the purpose, shall, for fee or reward, weigh any such goods, provisions, marketable commodities, or articles, within the said township, or give certificates of weight thereof.

187. No person shall hawk, carry about, or cry any goods, provisions, marketable commodities, or articles of any kind whatsoever, for sale in the market-house or the immediate approaches thereto, or on the footpath around it; nor shall any person be permitted to have any stall or standing in the public street.

Market Days and Hours.

188. A market for all marketable commodities shall be held on Wednesday and Saturday in every week throughout the year. On every day appointed for the holding of a market, such market shall be held between the hours of 7 o'clock in the forenoon and 6 o'clock in the afternoon on and from the 1st day of April to the 1st day of October, and between the hours of 8 o'clock in the forenoon and 5 o'clock in the afternoon on and from the 1st day of October to the 1st day of April. But the market-house shall be open daily for the sale of all marketable commodities on sale in the stalls thereof.

Tolls.

189. All goods mentioned in the schedule of tolls set forth hereunder, which shall be allowed into the market-place, shall be charged a toll, as per said schedule; and stallages, rents, and tolls in respect of all marketable commodities brought to the market for sale, or exposure for sale, shall become due as soon as the commodities in respect whereof they are demandable are brought into the market-place, or market-house as the case may be.

190. The stallages, rents, and tolls mentioned in the said schedule, and payable in respect of the occupation of any stall, bench, compartment, or space of ground, shall be paid, as well by the original taker or occupier thereof, for part of the day or space of time, as by any subsequent taker or occupier of the same for any other part of the same day or space of time.

191. Every person who shall offend against any of the foregoing byelaws shall be liable, for every such offence, to a penalty of 5l.; and in the case of a continuing offence, to a further penalty of 40s. for each day after written notice of the offence from the sanitary authority. Provided, nevertheless, that the justices or court, before whom any complaint may be made, or any proceedings may be taken, in respect of any such offence, may, if they think fit, adjudge the payment, as a penalty, of any sum less than the full amount of the penalty imposed by this byelaw.

Sealed with the corporate seal of the Bray Township Commissioners, this 22nd day of May, 1887.

Patrick M'Donnell,
Town Clerk and Executive Sanitary
officer of said Sanitary Authority.

Thomas Mayne,
Chairman.

Schedule of Tolls referred to in the foregoing byelaws, payable in the Market-house or place within the Township of Bray, referred to in byelaws Nos. 189 and 190.

	£	s.	d.
For every covered or uncovered shed, stall, bulk, block, bench, trestle, standing place or station, used for exposing meat, fish, vegetables, fruit, earthenware, or other goods or commodities whatsoever, a space not exceeding 6 feet by 3 feet, per day	0	0	6
If let by the year, any yearly sum not exceeding - - - -	1	0	0
If let by the half-year, any half-yearly sum not exceeding - - -	0	10	0
If let by the quarter, any quarterly sum not exceeding - -	0	5	0
If let by the week, any weekly sum not exceeding - - -	0	1	0
If otherwise let, or occupied for every market day, or other lawful day, any daily sum not exceeding -	0	0	6
For any extra space per square foot -	0	0	1

Butter.

	£	s.	d.
For every basket, parcel, or quantity of butter not exceeding 14 lbs., per day - - - -	0	0	1
For every additional 7 lbs. -	0	0	0½
For every firkin, tub, barrel or cask of butter not exceeding 56 lbs. -	0	0	6

TABLE OF TOLLS—*cont.*

Corn and Potatoes.

	£	s.	d.
For every sack of corn, of any description or sack of potatoes, per day, or fraction of a day, including weighing - - - -	0	0	1

Poultry and Game.

	£	s.	d.
For every description of fowl, including wild fowl and rabbits, not exceeding one dozen - - -	0	0	2
Every extra dozen - -	0	0	1

Eggs.

	£	s.	d.
For every basket of eggs - -	0	0	1
For every dealer's box of eggs -	0	0	3

Fruit and Vegetables.

	£	s.	d.
Each seller to pay per day or fraction of a day - - - -	0	0	2

Fish.

	£	s.	d.
For fish of all kinds, including shell fish, each seller for every hamper -	0	0	3

Weighing and Measuring Tolls for Weighing everything.

	£	s.	d.
If weighing not more than 56 lbs. avoirdupois - - - -	0	0	0½
If weighing 56 lbs. and not more than two hundredweight - -	0	0	1
And for every entire hundredweight or fraction of a hundredweight, not less than a half hundredweight beyond two hundredweight -	0	0	0½

For Measuring every Quantity of Things sold by Measure.

	£	s.	d.
If not exceeding one bushel - -	0	0	0½
If exceeding one bushel and not exceeding two bushels - -	0	0	1
And for every bushel beyond two bushels - - - -	0	0	0½
For weighing every waggon unloaded	0	0	4
For weighing every cart unloaded -	0	0	2

23,967. Is there any market authority in Bray other than the town commissioners?—No.

23,968. The Earl of Meath does not exercise any rights?—No.

23,969. You have the fairs leased?—We have them let.

23,970. To whom?—To Mr. Michael Doyle.

23,971. Has he them for any term, or is it a yearly letting?—The fair tolls are let to Mr. Doyle of Little Bray for 27*l.* for three years from the 31st March 1887.

23,972. How do you let them?—By tender.

23,973. Is the amount of the tender secured in any way other than by the guarantee of the tenant?—The rent is paid quarterly and stopped if not paid. There is also supposed to be a bond.

23,974. Have you got a written agreement with Mr. Doyle?—Yes, but I think the last one is not renewed. However, it is a matter of very little importance in regard to Mr. Doyle. He is the only person who applies for the tolls, and he pays regularly every quarter.

23,975. In the agreement formerly held were there any special clauses other than the ordinary clauses between landlord and tenant?—No special clauses.

23,976. What is the market day here?—Wednesdays and Saturdays. The fair days are the first Wednesdays of the month.

23,977. Wednesday and Saturday are the general market days?—Yes.

23,978. Have you any day in the week set off for the exposure and disposal of any particular commodity?—No.

23,979. When were those market days established?—I believe they are in existence from time immemorial. They were in existence before the town commissioners were established.

23,980. When was the monthly fair established?—There was a fair always in existence which was held in the main street of the town, and after the passing of the Bray Township Act in 1866, a fair green was established in Little Bray on the county Dublin side of the town, and the fairs to be held there on the first Wednesday in every month.

23,981. Previous to that I believe you had six fairs?—Yes.

23,982. Do you remember those yourself?—I do not.

23,983. How were those established. Did you obtain a grant for them or was it only the will of the commissioners to establish them?—It was a clause in the '66 Act to construct a fair green.

23,984. Has a fair green been provided under the provisions of that Act?—Yes.

23,985. You have the schedule of queries?—Yes.

23,986. Can you give me the capital expenditure of the commissioners in providing the fair green and market buildings?—It happened in this way that the market buildings were erected by Lord Brabazon, the present Earl of Meath, and were handed over to the town commissioners subject to a rent of 50*l.* a year, and then the only expenditure—capital expenditure—which the commissioners incurred was the erection of a weighing-machine, and the construction of another part of land given by the Earl of Pembroke into a hay market.

23,987. Is that hay market enclosed?—It is enclosed but not covered.

23,988. Is it adjacent to the other markets?—Yes.

23,989. Previous to the establishment of the commissioners did Lord Brabazon or the Earl of Meath exercise any market rights?—He did not.

23,990. Was it for the purpose of handing it over to the town commissioners that he erected the market building?—Yes.

23,991. Are tolls levied at the market?—Tolls are levied.

23,992. Are they what you call tolls proper, or only weighing charges?—They are tolls proper according to the schedule I handed in to you.

23,993. Have you got a schedule of those tolls erected in the market place?—Yes.

23,994. So that the public can ascertain the charge they have to pay?—Yes.

23,995. Are tolls levied at the monthly fairs?—Yes, by the lessee.

23,996. You gave him that right under the agreement?—Yes, subject to the payment of 27*l.*

23,997. Is this fair green you have provided entirely enclosed?—It is entirely enclosed.

23,998. Where is it situated?—In Little Bray. It was formerly portion of Bray Commons.

23,999. You had to pay nothing for the site?—Nothing except the taxes.

24,000. What is the valuation of the tolls there, both on the markets and fairs?—The valuation is a very difficult question to decide. You will see by the answer to the queries that the byelaws were only sanctioned on the 27th June 1887, so that we had no clear financial year, which ends on the 31st December. However the tolls are likely to increase in value.

24,001. Is there any poor-law valuation struck on them as yet?—No.

24,002. Have you any valuation on the building itself?—Yes.

24,003. What is that?—Eighty pounds.

24,004. You have a valuation on the fair green?—It is something very small—nominal.

24,005. Has Mr. Doyle to pay that rent of 27*l.* and any taxes due on the fair green?—No. He only pays 27*l.*

24,006. Is there any shelter accommodation in this fair green?—No.

24,007. Or pens?—No.

24,008. Do you restrain the disposal of any marketable commodities that come into Bray elsewhere than in this market place?—Well, we have not done so yet. It is a very vexed question, and it is a great hardship on the traders of the town that some parties come in and sell through the town.

24,009. Are these farmers who come from the outlying districts?—Yes, farmers and others. The people of the town have not much objection to the people who, according to an ancient custom, are earning their living by selling vegetables and things about the town, but it is in the way of becoming a great nuisance, and the opinion of the town commissioners is that the police should make these people produce a hawker's license to sell through the town, because they are now allowed to sell without license.

24,010. It is the opinion of the local authority, backed up by the opinion of the traders of the town, that you should restrain the sale of commodities by others than those having hawkers' licenses?—Yes.

24,011. Have you got a clause in your byelaws restraining the disposal of these commodities about the streets?—Yes, the Act of 1847 is incorporated.

24,012. But you have never enforced it?—No.

24,013. Did you ever attend this market yourself?—Yes, sometimes.

24,014. Could you mention to me the different marketable commodities brought in on Wednesday and Saturday?—Corn, hay, potatoes, butter, eggs, poultry, and vegetables.

24,015. Are any cattle ever brought on market days?—No.

24,016. Are calves or pigs?—No.

24,017. Are pigs exposed for sale on the same day as the ordinary cattle fair is held?—Yes.

24,018. You have no special pig fair day?—No.

24,019. On corn, what is your charge?—It is mentioned in the schedule.

24,020. For every sack of potatoes and corn of any description, 1*d*. Do you weigh the commodity for 1*d*.?—Yes.

24,021. If they bring the commodity into your market premises they pay 1*d*. whether they weigh or not?—Yes.

24,022. Do they ever expose them out on the public thoroughfare?—They do on the market square.

24,023. Within what limits would you say your jurisdiction extends to levy this charge. Is it if they come into the town or only to the market premises?—That is a debateable question, and was always one as to how far their jurisdiction goes, but the commissioners think they should have the authority over the town.

24,024. That is as far as their ordinary municipal jurisdiction extends?—Yes.

24,025. Have you ever received payment on any commodity brought into the town but not exposed in the market buildings?—Yes, frequently, especially if they require to be weighed. On market days we stop every car coming into the town when passing through the market. Of course, some of them try to get by, and say the things are bought. The officials of the township stop them.

24,026. Is it when you weigh corn and potatoes you levy the charge, or do you receive it when they enter the market?—With regard to corn and straw, on the weighs, and on the other things when they enter the market.

24,027. If a cartload containing 12 sacks were brought in here, would you ask for 1*s*. on that?—Yes.

24,028. Before they would weigh them?—Yes.

24,029. And weigh them gratuitously afterwards?—Yes. If they wish to have the weight ascertained.

24,035. Do they bring it in firkins?—Principally in lumps.

24,036. Have you any tasters employed in the market place?—No.

24,037. Have you a cooper?—No.

24,038. What men have you engaged for the market on market days?—We have the weigh-master, Alfred Kelly, Wm. O'Neill, township inspector's assistant, and a man named Bart Ormond, and James O'Connor, to prevent the cars going by until the toll is collected.

24,039. Who collects the toll?—The weigh-master.

24,040. Has he to perform the duty of weighing the commodities and collecting the toll?—Yes.

24,041. Does he give tickets?—Yes.

24,042. He has to perform that clerical labour?—Yes.

24,043. Have you ever heard any complaints of delay on account of his having to perform all these duties?—No, I never heard the slightest complaint.

24,044. Has he one ticket for all commodities, or a separate ticket for each particular commodity?—No; but he has a space in which to fill in the name of the commodity.

24,045. One ticket answers all purposes?—Yes, there are four parts in it.

24,046. Is the commodity sold before being weighed?—It is optional with the seller and buyer.

24,047. On fowl you have a charge?—Yes.

24,048. Under a dozen, 3*d*.?—Yes.

24,049. Supposing a person brought in one, what would you charge?—Probably a woman would get into the market without the collector knowing she had it, but we would charge 3*d*. if we could get it.

24,050. Then for every dozen over the first dozen you charge 1*d*.?—That is all.

24,051. Do the fowl hawkers come to the market building as a rule?—No.

24,052. They go about the town?—Yes.

24,053. It is on entry to the town that you levy this charge?—Yes.

24,054. What return do these fowl-dealers and others get for that charge?—You may term that as a toll charge. I do not believe we have ever levied a shilling on game.

24,055. On poultry?—They get the accommodation if they require it.

24,056. The accommodation is there if they wish to avail themselves of it?—Yes.

24,057. As a rule they go about the town?—Yes.

24,058. Hawking from door to door?—Yes. They go to gentlemen who live here, and often sell in the market.

24,059. It is always the producer who pays the charge?—Yes.

24,060. You never collect it from the purchaser?—No.

24,061. On fruit or vegetables the charge is 3*d*. per day. Is that irrespective of what quantity of fruit or vegetables they may bring in?—Yes, but there is very little brought in.

24,062. Supposing a woman brought in a basket of fruit or vegetables and put them at the corner of the street, would you charge 3*d*.?—We would.

24,063. Have you done so?—I would not say we have.

24,064. It is your inspector's duty to go around the town and see where the people are, and collect the

24,068. If they go about Little Bray, or elsewhere, and expose their commodities on the curb-stone you do not collect the toll?—No; but we prevent them from taking up a position on the curbstone. If they have asses' carts, as they generally have, we do not allow them to stop there.

24,069. Have you a separate portion of the market building to afford shelter accommodation to those people who bring in fruit and vegetables?—Yes, if they like to pay for it.

24,070. Does that comprise some shedding?—Yes.

24,071. Would the charge for the use of that be 2d. a day?—It is 1l. a year for the stall. There are small charges for the use of the stalls, which are mentioned in the schedule. It is a charge per day.

24,072. For fruit or vegetables each seller has to pay per day, or fraction of a day, 2d.?—That is for the use of the table.

24,073. Is that for standing in the market?—Yes, for both standing and shelter.

24,074. If they provide themselves with a stall, they have to pay one pound a year additional?—I could not say. That would be a matter for the commissioners, on the application of the party, to decide.

24,075. In fact you never received this 2d. yourself?—No.

24,076. The stalls are not let?—People will not avail of them because they will be only where the purchaser is.

24,077. Practically these stalls are for retailers?—Yes, but the market is not in the part of the town where retailers would go.

24,078. Supposing they brought in a quantity of poultry, fruit, or vegetables on Wednesday or Saturday, and took them to a dealer in the town, and it came to your knowledge, would you seek for your charge from the seller?—They could not bring them in without going through the market, the town is so constructed.

24,079. Is fish brought here?—Yes, but it does not go through the market.

24,080. Do you collect any charge?—No, they never go through the market with fish. It is a marketable commodity, but it is not exposed here.

24,081. For every basket, parcel, or quantity of butter not exceeding fourteen pounds per day the charge is 1d.?—Yes.

24,082. That is for all roll butter?—Yes.

24,083. Do you weigh that gratuitously?—Yes.

24,084. But the charge is payable whether you weigh or not?—Yes.

24,085. Do you keep any record of the quantity of butter and other marketable commodities brought in?—We keep no record at all.

24,086. Only when you weigh you have the [illegible]?—When we weigh and when we charge for the number of sacks of corn, we do not keep a record of what is in each, but of so many sacks.

24,087. Have you none of these stalls at all let?—No.

24,088. What facilities do you afford for weighing the different commodities, or what beams and scales have you there?—We have a weighing-machine and small scales for corn sacks.

24,089. Only one scale?—A large machine for hay and straw, and a small machine for sacks of corn and potatoes.

24,090. One scale for butter, corn, and potatoes?—Yes.

24,091. Have you ever heard complaints when weighing the butter, that it was injured in any way by dirt remaining on the scales after the sacks of potatoes?—Never in the slightest.

24,092. I suppose you have a smaller scale for the lump butter?—Really small quantities are never weighed. They are weighed in the shops where they sell them.

24,093. Did you ever hear any complaints from those people that the reason they do not avail themselves of the market place, is because of the charges that are levied on them?—No. I never heard any complaints of the kind. The only thing is some people are making a market day of days that are not, by coming in the day before the usual market days to avoid the toll.

24,094. You think it is to avoid the toll?—It is.

24,095. You would not say the reason they go about the town from door to door and take their commodities to private consumers is because the private consumers and buyers will not attend the market place?—I would not say that.

24,096. But to avoid paying the tolls?—Yes.

24,097. Do you ever collect these charges any day of the week other than Wednesday or Saturday?—Every day of the week.

24,098. Although Wednesday and Saturday are market days?—Wednesday and Saturday are the principal days for the tolls, but we weigh every day.

24,099. But do you levy charges whether you weigh or not every day?—No, except we weigh, but on Wednesday or Saturday we collect them whether we weigh or not.

24,100. The charges are the same when you weigh?—Yes.

24,101. What is the charge on a load of hay?—A halfpenny per hundred.

24,102. It is always on the weight you charge?—Yes.

24,103. Is it on the net weight or the gross?—On the net.

24,104. Supposing they bring in hay to the hay-market, and a man buys by bulk, estimating the weight himself, would you levy your charge?—He would have to weigh it.

24,105. But supposing he does not weigh, and buys by bulk?—It never occurred here.

24,106. It is always weighed?—Yes.

24,107. Is it always sold before being weighed?—Yes.

24,108. They never weigh it before effecting a sale?—They might if a man came in from the country with a load of hay, he might weigh it and bring the ticket with him to the buyer, but as a rule they all stand in the market and the hay is weighed before the purchaser.

24,109. The purchaser will not complete his contract until he sees the ticket?—No, he never does.

24,110. Have you got any of the tickets here?—No.

24,111. Have you any standings at all about the town as in the market place that you levy a charge on?—No.

24,112. Supposing a shopkeeper in the town erected a standing outside his door in the channel covers with some goods on market day, would you seek for any charge?—No, but we would prevent shopkeepers from doing so any day in the week because of the obstruction to the footpath.

24,113. Then they do not do it?—They do not. Sometimes they may, but the inspectors order them to remove the goods. The town inspector prevents that as a nuisance.

24,114. From what districts are these marketable commodities brought in?—They are brought from various districts.

24,115. Within what limits?—I should say 10 miles for corn and potatoes and from 20 to 30 miles for hay. We have a very good hay market. Hay is brought here from Arklow.

24,116. Would you say the close proximity to the Dublin markets detracts from your market here?—Probably if Dublin was not so near and this such a good town as it is we might have them larger.

24,117. You would say it does affect you?—I would not say it does, because Bray is a good market.

24,118. In the return there you have mentioned the receipts from the market alone?—Yes.

24,119. Your receipts evidently, by that return, do not cover the expenditure?—Not at present, but henceforth the receipts will increase and the expenditure diminish, because the markets are new, having been established recently and we had to purchase a weighing machine and form the market. That is an expenditure of capital which will not occur again.

24,120. Your yearly annual expenditure seems to be out of proportion to the receipts. Does that include the repayment of the original cost of the market place?

—It does not, but the market house and town hall are one concern, and there is a rental of [illegible] a year on them, the great proportion of which would not be chargeable against the markets, but which you could not separate because it is paid in one payment to one man.

64,121. Take the year 18[illegible]. What were the receipts in that year?—[illegible]. I may mention that the reason the receipts were so small in 18[illegible] was because we only had receipts on the weighing till the market byelaws had been passed.

64,122. What was the expenditure in that year?—[illegible]

64,123. That included [illegible] a year rent?—Yes, and the weigh-master's wages, 1l. a week.

64,124. In 18[illegible] the receipts were [illegible]?—Yes, half of that included tolls under the new byelaws, and if we had them for the whole year the receipts would be considerably more. The expenditure in that year was [illegible], but old debts not properly chargeable to that year were paid off.

64,125. That you had incurred in connexion with the markets?—Yes.

64,126. What was the nature of those debts?—I believe one-half year's rent unpaid, and taxes and various things held over. I may mention that a couple of months before the close of 18[illegible] my predecessor died, and there was very little paid off anything that year until the end of the year, and the payments for the close of that year were held over.

64,127. The town commissioners have incurred no debt in connexion with the markets and fairs?—No debt, only the rent.

64,128. You do not know the estimated cost of the building of the market house by Lord [illegible]?—Four or five thousand pounds I should say. It was immaterial to the commissioners. He was bound to expend 4,000l. on it under the original agreement.

64,129. Do the people frequenting the markets say it is a convenient site for a market building?—It has been the site from time immemorial of the market. Probably if it was in a more central position it would be a better place. The people originally selected it themselves. It is in an old portion of the town, and the only wide space we have.

64,130. That is at the top of the main street?—Yes.

64,131. Have you any rule in the byelaws or special Act regulating the application of any surplus revenue you might derive?—It goes to the revenue of the township.

64,132. Towards the municipal expenses?—Yes.

64,133. Have you ever heard that the market does not afford ample space or shelter accommodation for those people who bring their commodities?—No, except in so far that the hay market is uncovered.

64,134. Have they complained of that?—Yes, but as a rule hay markets are uncovered. With the exception of Cork no hay market is covered.

Mr. Michael Doyle examined.

64,135. You are the tenant to the town commissioners for the fairs here?—Yes.

64,136. Previous to the establishment of the monthly fairs there were only six fairs here in Bray?—Yes.

64,137. Am I correct in stating that those fairs were held on the 1st May, 1st June, 1st July, 15th August, [illegible] September, and 14th December?—Yes.

64,138. Those were the six?—Yes.

64,139. Were tolls levied at those fairs?—Yes, on the street.

64,140. Then they were held on the streets?—Yes.

64,141. By whom were the tolls levied?—I cannot say, but there were tolls levied.

64,142. Did you ever buy or sell at those fairs?—No.

64,143. When did the fairs commence to be held in the fair green?—Since the establishment of the monthly fairs.

64,144. When the fairs were held on the streets of the town had the buyer to pay any charge?—Not since the commissioners took them up.

64,145. You collect tolls at the monthly fairs?—Yes.

64,146. Have you got a schedule of the tolls created in the fair green?—Yes.

64,147. Have you got a copy of it here?—No.

64,148. Subsequently the witness produced the schedule of which the following is a copy:—

Little Bray Fair Green.

1. That the following be the tolls for all cattle or stock sold in said fair green—

	s.	d.
For every bull, ox, cow, or heifer, three years of age and upwards	0	[illegible]
For every bull, ox, or heifer, from two years and under [illegible]	0	[illegible]
For every yearling, bull, ox, or heifer, or calf	[illegible]	[illegible]
For every horse, mare or gelding	[illegible]	[illegible]
For every mule or ass	[illegible]	[illegible]
For every sheep or goat	[illegible]	[illegible]
For every lamb	[illegible]	[illegible]
For every hog or pig	[illegible]	[illegible]
For every cart or dray in which anything is sold or offered for sale, per day	0	4

Stalls.

	s.	d.
1. For space for every stand, car, dray, or show-box for sale of articles, by space not exceeding six superficial feet	0	4
For every extra space, per foot	[illegible]	1
For every hawker, or pedlar, or other persons, selling, or offering, or exposing for sale, any article whatever within the fair green by hand or otherwise, per day or fraction of day	0	4
For the use of any booth or stall that may be erected in the fair-green not exceeding six feet frontage, per day or part of a day	1	0
Any extra space, per foot, do.	0	1

2. That fairs shall be held on the first [illegible] in each month in Little Bray fair green.

3. That the inspector of nuisances shall have the control and regulation of all matters connected with the fairs subject to the direction of the commissioners, and shall have such assistance as the commissioners may from time to time appoint.

4. That every person who shall assault or obstruct the inspector, or any assistant, or other person appointed by the commissioners whilst in the execution of his or their duty shall, for every such offence, be liable to a penalty not exceeding forty shillings.

64,149. (The Commissioner to the Town Clerk.) Were those filed with the clerk of the peace?—These were framed under the Bray Township Act, 18[illegible], and that was prior to the establishment of the Local Government Board. They were sanctioned by the Lord Lieutenant and signed by the late Mr. T. H. Burke.

64,150. You do not know whether they were filed by the clerk of the peace or not?—I believe they were.

Examination of Michael Doyle continued.

64,151. These are the tolls you levy, Mr. Doyle?—Yes.

64,152. Are they levied on the animals as they enter the fair green or when they are sold?—When they are sold.

64,153. Do you collect them as the cattle are leaving the fair green?—Yes.

64,154. They never expose the animals in any other place but the fair green?—They do; they expose them on the streets or roads.

34,155. Standing on the fair green?—Yes, but the town inspector has orders not to let them sell there, and prosecute them for selling on the street when a fair green is provided.

34,156. Do you collect a toll from them?—No, I only collect from those who avail themselves of the fair green.

34,157. How many gaps have you at the fair green?—Two.

34,158. Who have you employed to collect the toll at these gaps?—My son and other different people.

34,159. How many men do you have on ordinary occasions?—Two at each gap. Pigs come out one gate.

34,160. Then you have two men in addition to your own services and your son's?—Yes.

34,161–2. How do pay those men?—So much a day.

34,163. Well, at what rate do you pay them individuals?—1s. 6d. a day.

34,164. When the pigs are coming out you inquire from the owners whether they have been bought or sold?—Yes.

34,165. Have you got a copy of the toll board erected at this gate?—Yes.

34,166. If they have bought do you seek for your charge?—Yes.

34,167. If they say they have not, do you let them go free?—I do. I have no way of testing them.

34,168. Are not the cattle as a rule marked?—Some are, but not all.

34,169. Supposing you inquire from a man driving some cattle out whether he had bought or sold, and he told you he had not bought, and you as a matter of fact had a suspicion they were bought, what course would you adopt?—I should merely say he had bought, and would have to let him off.

34,170. Did you ever seize the cattle or take possession of them until you were paid?—Not when they say they did not buy or sell.

34,171. Do you or any of your men produce a book or paper to answer them, or ask them to strike the toll board?—No.

34,172. I see here a cart which brings in any animals has to bear a charge of 4d.?—Yes.

34,173. Supposing they were driving a number of pigs to the fair green and went on the fair green, that cart would have to pay a charge of 4d.?—Yes. The carts with small pigs are unyoked and placed in two rows.

34,174. Still they keep the pigs in the carts?—Yes.

34,175. Do you charge 4d. on those carts?—I charge 1s. That is what they call a booth or stall.

34,176. If they bring in an ordinary cart containing 12 small pigs, and they enter the fair green, what charge do you levy on that?—4d. if they do not unyoke.

34,177. Then when they are going out do you charge on each pig if the pigs are sold?—Yes; the man who buys them has to pay a charge of 1d. each.

34,178. Practically then, there are two charges on small pigs; the standing charge of 4d. and 1d. on each individual pig?—Yes.

34,179. If they unyoke the horse from the cart you charge 1s.?—Yes.

34,180. You call that a booth?—Yes.

34,181. In addition to the charge on each pig?—Yes. The people who buy the pigs fetch them out.

34,182. As a rule is the purchaser always in possession of the animal when they are going out?—Yes.

34,183. It is only on the animals sold that you levy your charge?—Yes.

34,184. You have the same charge for a small pig as a large one?—Yes.

34,185. What standings have you in the fair green?—There are no standings erected.

34,186. When I say standings I mean to say cars coming in and exposing different commodities for sale other than cattle or pigs?—There is a roadway through the fair green, where the people unyoke their horses and erect their standings.

34,187. What is the nature of the commodities they expose there for sale?—Pigs and clothes.

34,188. Clothes dealers come in?—Yes.

34,189. What charge do you levy on them?—It is according to the space. The charge is from 4d. up.

34,190. What other standings have you besides clothes dealers?—Cabbage plants.

34,191. Do you levy the same charge on them?—Yes.

34,192. Do hawkers avail themselves of this fair green?—Some do.

34,193. What do you charge them?—I do not charge them.

34,194–6. What would you think you are entitled to charge?—I can charge 4d.

34,197. Did you ever hear complaints that your men had injured the cattle as they were leaving the fair green?—No.

34,198. Does much confusion ensue from the collection of the toll at the fair green coming out?—No.

34,199. Are horses brought here to the fair green?—No.

34,200. No horses at all?—I saw at one time the commissioners strive to get up a horse fair, but it was held for a while and no more. I do not recollect that any horses were sold. I never got paid for one.

34,201. Do you keep any record of the number of animals brought in?—No.

34,202. Would you kindly tell me, or have you any objection to state, the amount of your receipts from this fair green?—I do not know. I do not keep any record at all.

34,203. So you do not know whether you made by it or not?—Sometimes I do. Sometimes I make some trifle.

34,204. What did you get the last fair day?—4l. 10s. It is the best fair I had these two years.

34,205. What was the smallest amount collected at a fair within the last year?—Thirty shillings.

34,206. How many fairs did you collect that 30s. at?—Two or three in the winter time.

34,207. I suppose you got the 4l. 10s. very often?—No. I got 2l. 10s.

34,208. How many fairs would you get 3l. 10s. at?—Three or four.

34,209. Then it is 1l. 10s., 3l. 10s., and 4l. 10s. Did you ever get over 5l. at a fair within the last year?—No.

34,210. How often during the season did you get 4l. 10s.?—About four times, and 30s. at some fairs.

34,211. I have got four fairs, at each of which you receive 4l. 10s., three fairs 1l. 10s. each, and four more fairs 2l. 10s. each, and one fair 3l. 10s.?—I receive 2l. 10s. as a couple. In winter time they would be very bad, and one year there was a restriction on the fairs, and the green could not be opened.

34,212. Was that on account of the pleuro-pneumonia order?—Yes.

34,213. In a case like that, was there any reduction in the rent?—Not a life. I had to pay the full amount. The rent during a former term was 31l. a year, and it is reduced to 27l. at present.

34,214. Would you say on the whole that you get 50l. a year out of the fairs?—It is it closer.

34,215. From the statement you make you got about 40l. or 50l. 10s. a year, and deducting 27l. from that leaves 13l. Is that all you have for your own services during the year?—About that.

34,216. Do you keep any record as to whether you lose or not?—I never keep any account.

34,217. At each fair you never put off a certain amount for the rent?—No.

34,218. You keep no record either of the number of animals brought in?—No.

34,219. Did you ever ascertain the current prices of those animals?—No.

34,220. Do you ever hear the prices at all?—No.

24,221. Supposing it was required from you to make a return of the current prices of these different animals at the fairs, that is the contract price between the buyer and seller, would you keep such an account?—No.

24,222. What would there be to hinder you?—I would not be away in the fair green.

24,223. You never inquired or never sought for it?—No. Neither buyer or seller would tell me that.

24,224. They have not refused you up to the present, as you have not asked them?—I never asked them.

24,225. Do you ever collect tolls on any day other than the first Wednesday of the month?—No.

24,226. You have no stalls in the fair green?—No.

24,227. Do they ever bring in cattle the night before the fair?—No.

24,228. What hour does the fair usually commence at?—About 6 o'clock in the morning.

24,229. What time does it terminate?—About 2 or half-past 2.

24,230. You state you only collect on animals when sold?—That is all.

24,231. Except, of course, they are brought in a cart?—Yes.

24,232. Then you collect whether they are subsequently sold or not?—Yes, for the cart.

24,233. Supposing a farmer was bringing in some animals on a fair day from a country district, and he met a buyer on one of the roads adjacent to the fair green, but within the limits of the township, and he effected the sale of the animal, would you seek for your charge, or have you ever received it in such an instance if it came to your knowledge?—I have. There are people who have sold pigs coming down the street, and they came and paid me.

24,234. But in the case such as I have mentioned you think you would be entitled to your charge?—Yes.

24,235. Do the commissioners consider the market rights and the right to collect tolls at fairs extend within the municipal boundary?—Yes.

24,236. Not within the limits of the fair green or market place, but within the municipal boundary?—They do not consider they have properly a right to collect any place outside the fair green for the fairs, but they prevent the sales anywhere else.

24,237. They can enforce that order?—Yes.

24,238. Where is the weigh-bridge erected?—At the market house.

24,239. Is the fair green any distance from the market?—It is a good distance, seven or eight minutes' walk.

24,240. Did anybody, buyer or seller, ask you to weigh any cattle on the weigh-bridge?—No.

24,241. Have you any control over the weigh-bridge?—No; after the passing of the Act in 1887 the commissioners arranged the weigh-bridge with railings so that in the event of any buyer or seller wishing to weigh their cattle they can do so on the weigh-bridge. I have no control, but once the tolls are paid the weighing will be done.

24,242. Has the weigh-bridge been availed of?—Ever since the Act passed there was only one pig weighed.

24,243. Could you give me any approximate idea of the number of cattle brought into the fairs?—I could not.

24,244. You could give no idea of the number at all—for instance the number brought in the last fair day?—No; if I had been aware you wanted it I might.

24,245. Do you clean the fair green after the fair?—No; there do not be any cleaning on it.

24,246. How is it utilised between fairs?—The commissioners' horses are put out on it.

24,247. The commissioners have it for grazing their animals?—They have their horses and mules on it.

24,248. You have no control over it only on fair days?—Only on fair days.

Alfred Baily, Weigh-master, examined.

24,249. What commodities are you in the habit of weighing?—Hay, straw, corn, potatoes, and butter.

24,250. When weighing hay at the bridge do you always ascertain the tare of the cart?—We weigh the empty cart when the hay is delivered.

24,251. You put down the gross weight and tare on the ticket?—I put the gross weight first and then the tare.

24,252. Do you give them the ticket?—In some cases if they like to take it away to see the gross weight.

24,253. Is it when you ascertain the gross weight you levy the charge?—When they return, on the net weight, I get the charge.

24,254. Has it always happened they have returned?—Yes.

24,255. How long are you in the service of the commissioners as weigh-master?—Five years.

24,256. During that five years have you ever heard of any frauds being committed subsequent to the delivery of the hay, and coming back to you such as changing the wheels or the entire cart?—No; I never heard a case of that kind.

24,257. No case has come under your knowledge?—No.

24,258. Do you ever estimate the tare of a cart previously weighed?—I might, but I would not give it without weighing the cart again, unless the buyer agreed to it.

24,259. When weighing potatoes do you always weigh the empty sacks or estimate the tare?—We allow half a stone for the sack.

24,260. Would that half stone be allowed no matter whether it was a fine day or wet day, when the sack was completely saturated with wet?—Yes, except there was an objection on the buyer's part.

24,261. Would you weigh the sack then?—Yes.

24,262. What would be the weight of the sack?—From three to five and six pounds; sometimes eight pounds.

24,263. Supposing the weight of the sack was three, and you allowed seven pounds, would the additional four pounds be for mud and dirt about the potatoes?—We make a rule to allow seven pounds for a sack whether big sack or small sack, or anything at all except there is a barrel, and if there is a barrel we allow a stone.

24,264. What is it customary for the barrel here in Bray to weigh?—Twenty stone net weight.

24,265. You charge 1d. for weighing that?—Yes.

24,266. As a rule are all potatoes sold in the market weighed?—Sometimes they are not.

24,267. Do you ever find out what has been the price contracted for between the buyer and seller?—I do.

24,268. Did they ever ask you to make up the tickets?—They did.

24,269. Do the same observations apply to corn?—Yes.

24,270. Well then, if it was required from the commissioners to make a periodical return of the current prices of these commodities brought in they could keep such a return?—They could.

24,271. Do you think it would be a pretty accurate one?—It would, but it would involve a great deal more work on me.

24,272. Apart from the trouble you think an accurate return could be made by them if required?—I think so.

24,273. In weighing potatoes what is the smallest weight you weigh down to?—We can weigh to one pound.

24,274. What is the customary weight you use. Supposing the gross weight was 10 stone five pounds, do you secure the five pounds?—Anything between the half stone they will not pay for it.

24,275. It must be a half stone or nothing?—Yes.

24,276. Supposing the actual weight was 10 stone six pounds, you would put that on the ticket as 10 stone and a half a stone would be deducted from that for the sacks, leaving the net weight 10 stone?—Yes.

24,277. Do you always give a cast of the beam when weighing?—We do.

24,278. A good cast?—Yes.

24,279. Does the board of the scales touch the ground?—It is a triangle scale.

24,280. When weighing corn do you estimate the tare of the empty sack?—Yes, four pounds for the sack.

24,281. Down to what weight do you weigh?—Just the same as potatoes.

24,282. Do not you ascertain under the half stone weight in corn?—No.

24,283. It must be half a stone or nothing?—Yes.

24,284. Does the producer ever complain of that?—In some cases they make it up. They have corn to make up the actual weight so as not to lose four or five pounds.

24,285. They bring in some spare corn for that purpose?—Yes.

24,286. How is it brought here, is it by the stone or barrel?—By the barrel.

24,287. How much is the barrel supposed to contain?—14 stone net weight.

24,288. Have you ever heard complaints that you have not had an opportunity of weighing all the commodities brought in here so as to enable the people to go home and perform their other duties?—No. I have an assistant on market days.

24,289. Who is he?—Billy Ormond.

24,290. How does he assist you on market days?—He looks after one scale and I look after the other.

24,291. You have to weigh as well as fill the tickets at your scales?—Yes.

24,292. Are you able to perform those two duties?—Yes. The market here is very small.

24,293. Do you ever weigh a firkin of butter here?—No. It is all in rolls or lumps. I never saw a firkin.

24,294. Do you drain the cool?—I do, and make a balance for the cloth around it, and turn it right out.

24,295. Then you would say it is completely drained?—Yes. If there is any water it runs off.

24,296. Do you turn it up before it is put on the scales?—No.

24,297. Is it always sold before being weighed?—Not in every case. We do not weigh a quarter of what is in the market.

24,298. Still you get your charge?—Yes.

24,299. What is the smallest weight you use in weighing butter?—A quarter of a pound.

24,300. That is in weighing the cools?—Yes.

24,301. In weighing lumps?—We give the exact weight as near as we can.

24,302. What is the nearest?—The nearest we can go on our scales, that is a quarter of a pound.

24,303. But whether it is roll or cool you weigh only down to a quarter of a pound?—Yes.

24,304. Do you ever hear the price of butter?—I do.

24,305. I suppose it is always left to the experience of the purchaser as to what is the quality of the butter?—Yes.

24,306. There are no officials in the market for classifying the butter?—No, that is optional with the buyer.

24,307. Did they ever complain that they had to perform that duty themselves?—No.

24,308. You produce this as the ticket you give denoting the weight, at the weigh-bridge and scales for all commodities?—Yes.

24,309. Do you sign this ticket?—It is not necessary.

24,310. If they lose this ticket when they leave your office you are always in a position to give them a copy?—Yes, a copy of the block.

24,311. Witness then handed in the ticket, of which the following is a copy:—

BRAY TOWNSHIP MARKET.	BRAY TOWNSHIP MARKET.	BRAY TOWNSHIP MARKET.	BRAY TOWNSHIP MARKET.
Weigh Office, ____ 18	Weigh Office, ____ 18	Weigh Office, ____ 18	Weigh Office, ____ 18
Sold by ____	Sold by ____	Sold by ____	
To ____	To ____	To ____	Article ____
Article ____	Article ____	Article ____	____
Tns. Cwt. Qr. Lbs.	Tns. Cwt. Qr. Lbs.	Tns. Cwt. Qr. Lbs.	
Gross weight - . . .	Gross Weight - . . .	Gross weight - . . .	
Tare - . . .	Tare - . . .	Tare - . . .	
Net weight - . . .	Net weight - . . .	Net weight - . . .	
Received from	Received from	Received from	Received from
The Bray Township Commissioners.	The Bray Township Commissioners.	The Bray Township Commissioners.	The Bray Township Commissioners.
Block to be retained in Book.	Vendor's Docket.	Purchaser's Docket.	To be handed to Township Inspector on demand.

Sebastian Lawless, Esq., Chairman of Township Commissioners, examined.

24,312. Have you any observations to make as to what you think desirable to improve the markets?—I do not think I have any information. I never attended the markets. They are established about a year—about this time twelve months. The markets were held previous to that by the Earl of Meath, who had some control. They were held through the street. The Earl of Meath erected, 25 years ago, a weighing-machine, and gave it in charge to a person in the town who used to weigh hay and things. Hay and straw were also weighed at some private machine, and by the Township Act of 1866 there was an understanding that if we went for that Act and Lord Brabazon, the then Earl of Meath, erected a market-house, we should take it on lease at 80*l.* a year for 999 years. It was afterwards increased to 90*l.* a year for some reason. At the time we took that we understood the market would be scarcely worth 80*l.* or 90*l.* a year, but Lord Brabazon undertook to build a town hall. I regret very much it is not suitable to the town. The town hall is capable of holding 900 people, and the population is 7,000 or 8,000. We considered it was not sufficient; however, it was partly left to Lord Brabazon. With reference to the question you asked the town clerk as to the proximity of the Dublin markets injuring our markets, it is my experience they do considerably. I have a knowledge of large farmers in the county of Dublin, and all send their commodities to Dublin. In fact there was an application made by a farmer to make a reduction in the weighing of turnips, but we could not reduce our charge, the commissioners did not see their way to make any alterations, and he sent them to Dublin, and had them weighed in Dublin. We have very few farmers except some small farmers within 10 or 15 miles coming here, so that we could never expect to have a very large market here. Of course, there is no doubt, for any commodity that comes into Bray, the prices are as good as in any town in Ireland.

24,313. What is there in Dublin in preference to Bray that makes them go there?—The large farmers contract with some parties in Dublin, and dispose of their goods without sending them in small quantities. If Mr. Barrington had 200 tons of potatoes, he could dispose of them in Dublin more conveniently, and at less cost, than sending them in small quantities to Bray.

24,314. Did you ever know them to send commodities to Dublin because they considered your rates high?—No.

24,315. In that case, where the gentleman asked to make some reduction in the charges, did not he send them?—He had sold in Dublin, and made his contract to send them in a large quantity. He only wanted to get them weighed here.

24,516. It is a debateable question here as to the removal off the streets of the people selling marketable commodities about the town, and not availing themselves of the market?—The opinion of the shopkeepers and ratepayers generally is that they consider it a great hardship to have people coming in and disposing of their goods—I would not say it was to avoid the tolls—but to get higher prices, the same prices as the shopkeepers get, and very often higher prices.

24,517. Do they consider they can obtain a readier market for their goods when going about the streets of the town?—There is a very ready market, but they remain until six o'clock in the evening going about to the hall doors, asking, "Do you want this and that?"

24,518. Have not the commissioners considered the advisability of enforcing the regulation confining the sale of marketable commodities to the market place?—Considering it was a free market as long as any person can remember, and the byelaws in force about a year, we have not much to complain of. There are a great many people I know myself, small farmers in the country, come here, and not only sell their own goods, but buy from neighbours who come in and hawk them about, and get very good prices for them. I was informed by a ratepayer, about a fortnight since, that one party came in and bought butter in small quantities in the town, and then went around and sold it.

24,519. At a profit?—Yes. The people are under the impression that when a farmer comes in with a thing it is his own.

24,520. You have no restriction on sales in shops?—Not in shops. We are going to enforce the byelaws, and are determined to make them come through the market. We have allotted three or four men to assist the officials, and if two or three carts come into the town, or pass through the town, our inspectors will follow them to see where they are going.

24,521. I take it, at present you are merely fostering the market here?—Yes.

24,522. Have you any experience of other markets besides this one?—No.

24,523. From your experience, and from what you might gather from the people coming into the town—the producers and buyers—have you formed any ideas as to the exaction of a toll, or do you think the exaction of a toll acts as a deterrent on the people availing themselves of the market, or bringing their commodities in greater quantities?—I know people who had anything to sell would lower the price to avoid paying the toll. I meet a great many farmers, but they do not complain.

24,524. You have formed no ideas yourself about the levying of a toll?—No. I consider they are very fair, considering that two years ago the Local Government Board sent them back several times.

24,525. Have you any suggestions to offer as to what you think would be advisable, or any rule you think the commissioners have not, and would desire to obtain in order to regulate the market better?—I have not very much experience of the markets. I have not attended them at all. The only thing I heard the commissioners say is that there is some doubt as to whether they have the power under their byelaws to stop hawking. Their solicitor says they have not. Of course we try to do it as far as we can.

24,526. Is it their desire to prevent that hawking?—Yes. It is their desire to have full control in every way.

24,527. Do you think where markets exist, and where there is a local authority such as the town commissioners, that they should have control over these markets and fairs?—I should say so.

24,528. You think the united efforts of the gentlemen composing such a board would tend to the better working and management of the markets and fairs than having them in the hands of a private individual?—Certainly.

24,529. Might I ask why you have come to that conclusion?—There are gentlemen on the board who understand the matter, and are able to do things a private individual is not able to do. We have, of course, private gentlemen on the board that wish to have people protected, and also business people who will have to protect their own interest.

24,530. You think these men having a community of interest would know the wants and requirements of the people frequenting the markets and fairs, and would be better able to supply them than a private individual?—Yes, I would certainly suggest that the town commissioners should have the power to make any person coming in to sell or dispose that they would be bound to weigh all commodities in the market and get a docket.

24,531. Where the market rights and tolls are vested in individuals such as the lord of the manor, do you approve of local authorities, if any such exist, obtaining compulsory powers to acquire that individual's rights and work them as a municipal authority?—I would, certainly, because there are many instances where you have a local authority, and where there is sanitation and other matters to be attended to, and a private individual would not care about that.

24,532. You are in favour of such authority obtaining compulsory powers to work the markets and fairs for the benefit of the town generally; that is, to apply any surplus revenue to the benefit of the town?—Certainly.

24,533. You would not be in favour of a local authority working them and deriving such an amount as would merely pay the working expenses, anything extra going to the reduction of the tolls levied?—It would be very hard to tie the hands of a local authority. It might so happen that the working would not pay the expenses for some years.

24,534. If they worked them in order have a surplus which would go to the benefit of the town, you would have farmers bringing in produce paying indirectly the expenses of the town?—They are never expected to pay anything over the working expenses of the market in this neighbourhood.

Mr. James Covey examined.

24,535. Are you a trader in the town?—Yes, a poultry dealer.

24,536. Do you concur in the observations of Mr. Langton as to local authorities acquiring market rights if any such exist?—Most undoubtedly, and I go further than Mr. Langton, and I think no other authority but the local authority should have the power, because the local authority are the representatives of the people, and if they do not do what is right the people have the power to send them about their business at the next election. Although no private person has control in Bray, there is a charter by the Earl of Meath, who bought a weighing-machine for the town, and the magistrates granted an order to the weigh-master who had licensed premises to open at 4 o'clock in the morning, and on several occasions it was complained. The market originally was held at 3 or 4 o'clock in the morning. They brought goods at 3 o'clock, and went in by the goods train to Dublin, but from certain complaints made to the Earl of Meath, he put up notices on two or three occasions that the market should be held at 7 o'clock, at a reasonable hour; but so long as this house was allowed to open at 4 o'clock in the morning people came in, and I believe it was because that house was opened at 4 o'clock the market was not held at 7. The other houses could not open until the market was over, and that was the great reason that suggested itself to the people that the market should be held at 7 in the summer and 8 in the winter. Those are the hours at present.

24,537. Are those the hours fixed for the commencement of the market by the byelaws?—Yes. I do not agree with Mr. Langton that Dublin is a better market. My idea is Bray is a better market, and there is less expense attending it.

24,538. Do you think the prices they receive here are as good as in the Dublin market?—I think better, and the people who come here are free of expense.

24,539. Leaving aside the expense, supposing they brought corn or other commodity or animals, do you think the prices obtained here, the actual prices, would compare favourably with the Dublin market?—Undoubtedly, and they in addition the saving of the transit. They get better prices on Saturday for oats than they get in the corn exchange the following Tuesday.

24,340. Where do the buyers come from?—From Blackrock, Ballytrack, and the places in the county Wicklow.

24,341. Is much of the surrounding country in tillage?—Within a few miles not very much, but on passing three or four miles it opens up into small farms.

24,342. You would say the greater proportion of it is under tillage?—The most of the farms in the county Wicklow are under tillage, and all small holdings.

24,343. As you have an experience of other markets, do you think that the exaction of a toll deters people or acts in any way as a deterrent on people bringing in their commodities?—I do not think so.

24,344. They would not mind paying a toll at a market or fair if they thought they could effect a ready sale and a good one of their commodity?—I believe the majority of the people would not object, but there are people who object to everything, but that might be only one in 100.

24,345. It is your opinion that if a toll was levied a sufficient and adequate return should be given in the way of accommodation and facilities for weighing?—Certainly; and I believe as far as the facilities for weighing are concerned the people of Bray are well off, but I know people find fault with the facilities in the market house. In fact the country people do not avail themselves of what is called the market house at all.

24,346. Do you consider the arrangements suitable?—The arrangements are not suitable for what they are intended for. The stalls are not suitable.

24,347. You would assign that as a reason for their not availing themselves of it?—I would say that is probably the reason the stalls are not let.

24,348. Have you any other observations to make?—I would say on the question of hawkers my opinion is, that for the purpose of collecting the tolls that every day should be market day, and that the country people coming in and going round from house to house should have their goods stopped and made pay a toll on them.

24,349. As a matter of fact are not the tolls collected every day?—No, only weighing charges, except on Wednesdays and Saturdays. Lately there is a great number of people coming into Bray on Fridays, in fact more than on Saturday morning, and go about from house to house and sell goods, and they deprive the commissioners of the tolls they have a right to get. Because my opinion is that where there is a well kept market, and every facility and a ready market, and where they get the best prices in Ireland, I think the commissioners ought to be supported in every possible way to keep that state of things in existence.

24,350. You would be in favour of enforcing the bye-laws in that respect?—I would, certainly. These byelaws, I know of my own knowledge, were some years under consideration before being finally passed. The Local Government Board refused a great many of them. Mr. Keogh, the solicitor, was strongly of opinion that every day should be constituted a market day for the purpose of collecting the toll, and if any change is made I think it ought to be made as regards the parties who would sanction the byelaws. I think the local men of the town, who understand the local wants and give their time and trouble to make byelaws suitable for the farmers and people coming into the town, should be the people who would have the matter in their hands, and not have their work go for nothing by the scratch of a pen.

Mr. Matthew O'Byrne, Town Commissioner, examined.

24,351. Are you in trade in the town?—Yes, I am a victualler.

24,352. Do you ever attend any of the fairs here?—Yes.

24,353. Do you buy and sell at them?—I do nearly every fair day down at the fair.

24,354. Have they got the system of luck-penny there?—That is a general thing.

24,355. Is it always given in every transaction?—Yes, at the fairs.

24,356. There is no rule regulating the amount?—No.

24,357. It is always left to the disposition of the seller?—Yes. It is often part of the bargain at the same time.

24,358. Then in fixing the price the seller considers the luck-penny he will give the buyer?—The price is fixed and the luck-penny is optional.

24,359. When fixing the price does he ever put on the price he is asking for the animal the amount of the luck-penny he is disposed to give?—No. They buy the animal as cheap as they can, and get as much luck-penny as they can.

24,360. Have they got any fixed amount for that luck-penny on pigs?—Yes. They stop 6d. a pig; that is the rule.

24,361. Irrespective of the value or size of the pig?—Yes. I may remark that several years ago they used to try pigs for measles. They did away with that, and now they stop 6d. for every pig.

24,362. What was that practice?—To try the pigs for measles and cut them in the price.

24,363. Formerly, after fixing the price they subsequently cut it down?—Yes, but instead of that now they stop 6d. for every pig sold.

24,364. Is it stopped by the buyer out of the price?—Yes.

24,365. On cattle is it not?—No. It is optional about the cattle, but it is an established rule with regard to the pigs.

24,366. Have you any suggestions to make as to what you think would tend to the better working of the fairs and markets in Bray?—Mr. Goffey said all I could say or have to say. I know it is very hard to stop the people coming any day, and I really think it is to evade paying the tolls.

24,367. Do you think the toll deters them on market day from coming in and disposing of their commodities?—It has something to do with it. It is very hard to get them to weigh. They are satisfied to pay a toll. Some of them would lose the sale of a load of oats for the reason that they would not have good weight.

24,368. Do not buyers buy after its being weighed?—They do; they take their words.

24,369. Would not the proper course be to induce the buyers not to buy until they (the sellers) had a ticket denoting the weight?—That would be the proper way to carry it out. About the hawking I may say they come in here on special days to evade the tolls, and they go about the streets and about the houses, and I think it is injurious to the ratepayers. I am sure it is.

24,370. If commissioners have power in regard to that in their byelaws, and why do not they enforce that. Is there a division of public opinion in the town?—I do not think we have the power.

24,371. (*The Commissioner to Mr. Langan.*) In the original framing of the byelaws had you such a provision?—In 1883, when drafting them, it was insisted by Mr. Orangh, a member of the Board, that we would open the the market to stop hawking, or people selling any day as well as market day. I do not think it is exactly to avoid paying tolls they come and sell and hawk about. A lot of hawkers who come here get higher prices than even the shopkeepers get. It would be very hard to cope with anything like that, but it would be very desirable that the local police should assist the local authorities in keeping order like that. We should keep a staff of men on the different roads coming into the town, and it would be very desirable to get the assistance of the police to carry out the laws.

24,372. Are these hawkers inhabitants of the town?—Some of the town commissioners were of opinion that some six or eight families who live in the township and pay rates, and live by buying or selling vegetables, that it would not be well to interfere with them, but that they should be licensed, and as the parties dropped out the licenses should lapse, and we would not have in that way any vested rights. What the shopkeepers object to is people coming in and buying from small neighbours, butter, eggs, and potatoes, and going about selling to private people who do not contribute any way to the township. The local authority have to keep all the roads in repair, and when we leased the town hall, the Earl of Pembroke gave a piece of ground for a hay and straw market for 11l. a year by lease. If that was enclosed and used as a hay and straw market he would remit the rent. The town commissioners had to enclose it and buy out the tenant right of a little cottage on it.

24,373. Has the payment of the 11l. a year been remitted?—We have not payed it since we got possession two years ago.

24,374. Examination of Mr. O'Byrne resumed:—

24,375. You think that before any commodities are taken out of the market that they should be all weighed?—Yes.

24,376. Is there any other gentleman who has any observations to make or evidence to give?—No answer.

The inquiry then terminated.

WICKLOW.

With reference to my inquiry in Wicklow on the 30th day of November 1888, I beg to report as follows:—

Wicklow is the assize town of the county of Wicklow. It is situated on the estuary of the river Vartry and in a sheltered bay, but withal, the coasting or fishing trade is very small. The principal trade is in agricultural produce and in the exportation of the ores which are raised in the various mines of the district. The town is neat and kept in good order. It is a station on the Dublin, Wicklow, and Wexford Railway line. The local government is vested in town commissioners, and the population is 3,391.

The market day is Wednesday. The fairs are held on the last Tuesday of each month. An annual horse fair is held on the 12th August. The markets and fairs are toll free, but at the former weighing charges are levied.

The market rights are the property of the town commissioners. There is no schedule of the weighing charges erected.

There does not seem to have been any patent granted for the markets and fairs in Wicklow.

The markets were only established two years ago, and the present fairs were established about 18 years ago; previous to which, four fairs were held, viz.:—28th March, 24th May, 12th August, and 25th November, which was established about forty years ago.

In accordance with my instructions, I inspected the fair and market places.

The fairs are held in an unenclosed triangular space near the court house. Portion of this space is a commonage fringed by the public roads, and on this commonage and the roads the fairs are held. There is no accommodation of any kind provided there, except sheep pens, which are erected on fair days along the public thoroughfare. The pig fair is held on the market square.

The markets, which are very small, are held in a large house erected for the purpose, and also on the public square outside, which is a large open space. Scales are provided there. The building is lofty and slated, but too small to accommodate all those frequenting the towns for market purposes.

There is no restriction on the sale of marketable commodities elsewhere than in the market buildings, and consequently the producers are free to sell where they please. An opinion was expressed that the levying of tolls at either the markets or fairs would have an injurious effect on their development.

At the termination of the inquiry I received evidence relating to the fairs at Roundwood.

Appended will be found a transcript of the evidence taken at the inquiry.

JOHN J. O'MEARA,
Assistant Commissioner.

45, Lower Mount Street,
Dublin.

Wicklow, 20th December 1888.

Mr. John Hayden, Town Clerk, examined.

24,377. You are the town clerk of Wicklow?—Yes.

24,378. When were the commissioners established here?—I am not able to inform you.

24,379. They are the owners of any market rights that exist in Wicklow?—They have been in my time.

24,380. They are at present?—They are. I think the town commissioners were established on the passing of the Act of the ninth of George the Fourth. The powers of the old corporation were handed over to the town commissioners on that day; I think it was in 1828.

24,381. What is the market day here?—Every Wednesday.

24,382. There is no other day of the week set off for the disposal of any particular commodities?—No.

24,383. What fairs are held here?—I think Mr. Chapman would be the best to give you that information. The fairs are held on the last Tuesday in every month and the great annual horse fair is held on the 12th August. There are four other horse fairs held quarterly, on the same day as the cattle fairs, that is the last Tuesday of the quarter.

24,384. How long have you known these monthly fairs to be established?—The first fairs are upwards of forty years.

24,385. Were these fairs on specified dates previous to the monthly fairs?—There were four fairs, one in March, one in June, one in October, and another in December I think.

24,386. You could not give the dates of these?—I heard the dates used to vary.

24,387. Were they all on feast days?—No.

24,388. When were they extinguished?—About eighteen years ago.

24,389. And then the monthly fairs were established?—Yes.

24,390. By whom?—By Mr. Chapman at a meeting of the town commissioners and traders of the town.

24,391. There was no express authority given for them, no charter or patent?—No.

24,392. Are tolls levied at these fairs?—No.

24,393. They are toll free?—Yes.

24,393a. Where are they held?—On the Barrack green.

24,394. Is that green utilised for fair purposes only?—That is all.

24,395. Is it enclosed?—No; it is an open space.

24,396. Is it a commons?—It is not a commons. It is the town commissioners' property and the different roads coming into it.

24,397. How long have the fairs been held in that fair green. Were the old fairs held on it?—No. They have been held there about five-and-thirty years.

24,398. Where were they held previous to being removed to that fair green?—The first fair ever established was held forty years ago on the Murrow, and one old man came and an old cow that had only one horn. At that time there was only one house on the Murrow at the other side of the river, and that was the site of the first fair.

24,399. Were any fairs ever held on the streets of the town?—Yes, on the main street and Bridge Street.

24,400. You say about 35 years ago they were removed to the present green?—Yes.

24,401. How was the green utilised previous to the removal of the fairs there?—It was an open space free to everyone. The town belongs to the commissioners, and there is an estate of about a mile around the town which is corporate property.

24,402. Is this green portion of the corporate property?—Yes.

24,403. What charges are levied at the markets?—The market is only recently opened on this occasion. They tried to establish it for a long time, but it always failed.

24,404. Did the commissioners previous to the period you have mentioned exercise any control over it?—They did. There had been no market for 40 years until two years ago. About 1846 or 1847 it failed, I heard some persons say, and then there was no attempt to establish a market until three years, when the attempt was also abortive; but last year the business people of the town met and established what is a thriving market now.

24,405. The commissioners have immediate control of that market?—They have.

24,406. During that period they have not sub-let it at all?—No.

24,407. Are charges levied at it?—Yes.

24,408. What are the charges?—The charges for weighing corn and potatoes per barrel, one penny. The commissioners have thought it well not to levy any high charges.

24,409. Are these the only charges levied at the market?—That is all, with the object of fostering the market. The charges are for weighing potatoes and corn per barrel and a cask or tub of butter one penny; twopence a pack for wool, and sixpence for a large pack; both charges to be paid by the seller.

24,410. Who have you engaged to care the market, or have you a weigh-master?—We have.

24,411. What is his name?—Andrew Kirwan.

24,412. Do you ever see him weighing there?—I superintend the weighing.

24,413. Now what market buildings have you for these markets?—There is a spacious enclosed building.

24,414. Do they expose their commodities for sale in that building as well as weigh there?—They do; some commodities such as butter, fowl, and eggs.

24,415. Mention to me the different marketable commodities brought to the market?—Corn, potatoes, butter, turnips, eggs, fowl of all description, honey, flowers and game.

24,416. Is hay brought?—No hay or straw. Fruit comes in.

24,417. Are vegetables brought?—Yes, vegetables of all kinds.

24,418. Are pigs ever brought on market days?—No, but calves are.

24,419. Is milk?—It was brought on one occasion, but I have not seen it since.

24,420. These commodities you have mentioned are brought on Wednesday?—Yes.

24,421. Are they all brought to this market building?—The most of them. The eggs, fowl, vegetables, and things inside and the potatoes and calves out on the market square.

24,422. There is no covered shelter for these commodities?—No; I must remark that the milk is never sold in the market place. It is sold about the town; the churns are hawked about.

24,423. What days?—Every day of the week.

24,424. Do any of these other commodities come in any day of the week but Wednesday?—I believe they do, but I am not able to state.

24,425. But they do not avail themselves of the market house any day of the week but Wednesday?—They can avail themselves any day they want to weigh wool.

24,426. But I mean for the exposure of marketable commodities for sale?—Literally speaking they do not come except on Wednesday.

24,427. Supposing they bring in some corn, do you collect the charges, and are you yourself [illegible] acquainted with the working of the market?—Yes, I think I am.

24,428. Supposing they bring in corn there, and expose it for sale in the market and sell, but do not weigh it, do you levy any charge?—No.

24,429. Only when they weigh?—Yes, I have endeavoured to do so.

24,430. Although they have availed themselves of the market place, and effect a sale, you would not levy a charge except they weighed?—No.

24,431. Do the same remarks apply to potatoes?—Yes.

24,432. Do they expose them for sale in the market place?—They do.

24,433. No charge is payable unless they weigh?—No charge.

24,434. Do the same remarks apply to butter?—Precisely.

24,435. And to wool?—Yes.

24,436. Have you any stallage charges at all there?—No.

24,437. Nothing but the weighing charges?—No.

24,438. They are free to come and go?—Yes.

24,439. And utilise the market?—Yes, there are large tables there for the use of people selling goods.

24,440. Are these commodities sold before they are weighed?—Yes, in the majority of cases.

24,441. In what cases do they actually weigh before they sell?—Well only in an odd case where one or the other party goes back of the bargain.

24,442. In a case like that if they weigh you levy the charge, and then you generally consider whether they subsequently sell or not?—Yes, I levy the charge.

24,443. I suppose you have got a ticket to give denoting the weight?—I give a docket for all parties.

24,444. In return for that docket you receive your charge?—Yes, whatever the charge is.

24,445. When weighing corn, do you actually ascertain the tare of the sack?—No, not always, but in some cases.

24,446. I suppose in case of dispute between the buyer and seller?—Yes.

24,447. What is the estimated tare of the sack of corn?—Between five and seven pounds. Some would be satisfied with four pounds.

24,448. How would you know what to allow. Would you estimate according to the size of the sack or the state of the weather?—We have always left that between the buyer and the seller.

24,449. Do you ever put the estimated tare on the ticket?—Yes, as directed by the buyer and seller.

24,450. It is what they agree to between themselves you put on the ticket?—Yes.

24,451. Supposing there was a case of a little incompatibility of temper and they could not agree, have you to act as umpire between them?—Sometimes.

24,452. How would you estimate the weight of a sack of tare?—I would not have any set rule, but do the thing to the best of my ability.

24,453. When weighing corn what is the lowest weight you use, or do you weigh down to odd pounds. Do you weigh down to a pound?—We do always. I always weigh what is in the sack.

24,454. Do you weigh under a pound?—No.

24,455. When weighing do you give a turn of the beam?—I make no allowance.

24,456. Then you weigh by standing beam?—Yes.

24,457. Is the tare of the sack the only deduction from the gross weight?—That is all.

24,458. There is nothing allowed for breakage or the bad state of the commodity?—No.

24,459. That is a matter between buyer and seller?—Yes.

24,460. When weighing potatoes do you always weigh the empty sack or estimate the tare?—In that case there is very little difficulty in the buyer obtaining seven pounds for the sack.

24,461. Is that the only deduction?—That is all.

24,462. Do you ever weigh the empty sack of potatoes?—No.

24,463. Would that allowance or deduction be the

24,465. Have you known them to allow an extra deduction on a wet day if the sack were completely sodden with wet?—I have not known it, but I heard talk about it.

24,466. Have you ever known any larger deduction than seven pounds for the empty sack?—I have in some cases.

24,467. What was the deduction?—It would be a matter between the buyer and seller.

24,468. What was the deduction?—An odd four pounds. Supposing it was a hundred and four pounds, they would allow so much for the sack and the four pounds as well.

24,469. Do you ever weigh under four pounds?—We always weigh to the pound.

24,470. In potatoes as well as corn?—Yes. We make no deduction until directed by the buyer and seller.

24,471. Is the butter always brought in firkins or only in crocks?—In crocks, rolls, and lumps.

24,472. Supposing they bring a cask, do you turn it out of the cask?—Yes.

24,473. Always?—Always when weighing.

24,474. Down to what weight do you weigh the butter?—We weigh it to a quarter of a pound.

24,475. Do you weigh under a quarter of a pound?—Yes, to the ounce.

24,476. Have you any deduction from the weight?—That is left between the buyer and seller. There is no brokerage in anything.

24,477. Who tests the butter, or is that a matter left to the experience of the buyer?—Yes.

24,478. Do you keep any record of all the articles brought in?—I do.

24,479. Have you got any return of them here?—I have not.

24,480. Is there any great quantity of butter brought here?—I think there was twenty casks last week.

24,481. What is the lowest weight you weigh the wool down to?—We weigh wool to the pound, but it is very seldom we get an opportunity of weighing wool.

24,482. Do not you weigh under a pound?—We weigh to the very ounces.

24,483. Is that customary?—Yes, in all wool transactions. The principal wool buyer's store is at the other end of the town, and they weigh there what he buys. When we weigh we weigh it exact.

24,484. When the buyer weighs you have no power to charge?—No, and that is just what we want to know.

24,485. What expense are you at in connexion with the market?—We pay 5s. a week to a porter and the weigh-master between them, and I receive 6l. as superintendent.

24,486. Have you any other expense?—Nothing beyond advertising.

24,487. What would the average be?—It is very trifling.

24,488. Have you got the receipts?—The receipts you might put down this year at 8l. 7s., or 8l. 10s.

24,489. The total receipts?—Yes.

24,490. What were they last year?—8l. 11s. 11d.

24,491. Do you consider there is a prospect of their increasing?—I do at that rate.

24,492. You are practically only fostering the markets now?—That is all.

24,493. What is the nearest market town to Wicklow?—Rathdrum.

24,494. Is there much of the surrounding country in tillage?—I think there is more than the average; more than you would meet in other parts.

24,495. Where do the marketable commodities go to?—This is the best market in the county.

24,497. Do most of the marketable commodities in the country districts around come to Wicklow?—Yes, the principal portion of them. It is a very odd one sends to Dublin.

24,498. Supposing it was required from the town commissioners to make a periodical return of the quantity of the different marketable commodities brought to the town of Wicklow, and their average prices, do you think it would be possible to make such a return?—It would be difficult I think, as the majority of the produce brought here is sold in the open square, and of course there might be a great deal of produce coming in directly to the buyers in the town. For instance, during July hay came to the houses by the ton and delivered to the purchasers there.

24,499. At any rate do you think you could give an accurate return of the current prices of the commodities?—Yes.

24,500. That information would have to be derived from the buyers and sellers?—Anything that I weigh I know the exact price of it.

24,501. Do you make up the tickets for the people?—Yes, and more than that, I send a market note every week to the papers.

24,502. In that note do you state the actual prices or is anything put on to show you have a good market?—No.

24,503. Practically it is a return of the current prices obtained here?—Yes; of course there would be a difficulty in obtaining the quantity, as it does not all pass through the market. It is the opinion of the commissioners generally that they will put a toll on everything coming into the market after some time; that is on market and fair days.

24,504. You have no receipts at all from the fairs?—No.

24,505. What description of animals come?—Mr. Chapman knows more about that than I do.

24,506. Have you any rules in the market restraining the sale of commodities or restricting them to the market square?—None in force.

24,507. The farmers can go where they please to dispose of them?—Yes.

24,508. You have no rule regulating the sale through brokers or agents?—No.

24,509. Practically you have no rules or regulations?—No.

24,510. Have you got a weigh-bridge here?—No, nothing beyond the ordinary beams and scales. That is a thing we want badly.

24,511. What duties do the commissioners perform?—Lighting and cleansing.

24,512. Do you pave the town?—No.

24,513. Who are the sanitary authority?—The board of guardians.

The following is a copy of a notice posted up in the market place:—

Notice.

The Market Committee, hoping for the generous support of the public to make the market a success, require the following rules to be observed:—

1st. All persons to keep silent and not interfere with the weigh-master.

2nd. Smoking and sitting on the tables prohibited during market hours.

3rd. All the officials are distinguished by a band with the words "Wicklow Market," and are paid to assist. No other persons allowed to interfere.

Charges for Weighing.

		d.
Corn and potatoes, per barrel	-	1
Coal or tub butter	-	2
Bag wool	-	6

The above charges are to be paid by seller. No other charge whatever.

Mr. John Chapman examined.

24,514. What descriptions of animals are brought to the fairs?—All sorts of cattle, sheep and pigs to the cattle fairs; to the horse fairs, horses as well as cattle, except the annual horse fair, when no cattle are brought.

24,515. When was the horse fair established?—I established it myself by the circular (produced) which showed it was established about 1882.

24,516. Are the horses exposed for sale and sold on this fair green?—No.

24,517. Where are they sold?—On the Murrow.

24,518. Where is that situated?—Between the sea and the lake.

24,519. Is it convenient to the business portion of the town?—Yes.

24,520. Is the cattle fair green in the immediate proximity of the town?—It is just next to where you are sitting.

24,521. Cattle and sheep are sold in that fair green?—Yes, and the pigs here in the square.

24,522. Is this place outside the court house what you call the square?—Yes, and the fair green is a hundred yards from it.

24,523. This square is portion of the public thoroughfare?—Yes.

24,524. Do they ever go down to the streets adjacent to the square?—No.

24,525. They are confined to the square?—Yes.

24,526. Were tolls ever levied at any of these fairs whether the pig fairs or others?—Never at any of them. Instead of that we give considerable encouragement to the people by making pens to bring the sheep to, and we have succeeded very well.

24,527. There are sheep pens in this fair green?—There are. There are sheep pens, but they are not up now.

24,528. There is no shelter accommodation in that fair green?—None.

24,530. Have you heard or do you consider yourself from your experience that this market place affords sufficient accommodation for the agricultural produce brought here to Wicklow?—I think it does.

24,531. Have you ever heard the statement that it was not?—No, I have never heard any complaints in that way.

24,532. Does this fair green afford ample space for the disposal of the commodities?—It does.

24,533. How is it utilized between fairs?—Left open and not used for anything. The commissioners would not allow it to be used for anything else.

24,534. Do they utilise it themselves in any way?—No.

24,535. Are you in trade in the town?—No, I am not in any trade.

24,536. Have you formed any ideas upon the levying of a toll at fairs. Do you think if a toll were levied at fairs that it would act in any way as a deterrent on people bringing in their stock and exposing them for sale?—I think tolls are unjust to the fair and ought not to be levied. I do not think the commissioners would wish to do such a thing. What they want is to bring business to the town, and not make money out of the fairs.

24,537. It is a general question and apart altogether from Wicklow in particular. Have you any experience of fairs other than those held in Wicklow?—Yes.

24,538. If tolls are levied at these fairs do you think it deters farmers bringing in their stock in greater numbers?—I think it would have an injurious effect.

24,539. Do you think if tolls were abolished at ...

24,540. What is the nearest fair to Wicklow where tolls are levied?—Roundwood and Ashford, three miles away, and one at Greenane, three and a half miles away. Tolls were charged there, and I think they had the effect of doing away with the fairs. However, Wicklow took the business from them, but I think the tolls had the effect of injuring them too.

24,541. Do you ever hear any complaints of any confusion or want of regularity at these fairs in Wicklow?—No, and at the horse fair we get a bank put up for the horses to be shown and a place for galloping the horses.

24,542. Would you call the fairs here good fairs?—I call them good fairs.

24,543. You could not give any approximate idea of the number of cattle brought in?—No, I could not.

24,544. Or of the horses brought to the horse fair?—No.

24,545. Is the annual horse fair the best?—It is the best in the county. There are not many better in Ireland.

24,546. From what districts do the buyers come?—From England and all parts of Ireland and Scotland, and everywhere.

24,547. From what districts do they bring their cattle and other stock?—From the whole of the county Wicklow, the whole of the county Wexford, and part of the county Carlow.

24,548. And the cattle?—From the greater part of the county Wicklow, and one-half of the county Wexford—the lower half.

24,549. Within what limits are the marketable commodities brought?—Ten miles.

24,550. Have you ever heard objections to this pig fair being held on the public thoroughfare, the market square?—I did not.

24,551. Or of the markets being held there?—No, the whole anxiety of the people was to get them held there and not let them be held anywhere else.

24,552. Does not the fact of the markets being held there occasion much filth and dirt?—The commissioners get the streets cleaned up every day, and when the fair is over they get everything cleaned up the same day.

24,553. Is there any obstruction caused to the public thoroughfare?—None; the commissioners have men to keep the thoroughfare clear. I was a town commissioner at the time of establishing the fairs. The commissioners paid the cost of notices and circulars. I brought all out for upwards of forty years. Of late I was agent to the town commissioners.

Mr. Michael [illegible] examined.

24,554. You heard the question I asked Mr. Chapman. Do the farmers, as a rule, think that the levying of a toll or charge on a fair or market has a deterrent effect on them in bringing in their agricultural produce to the market or stock to the fair?—I think it would.

24,555. Have you any experience of fairs or markets where tolls were levied?—Yes. I do not know any country place where tolls would have any effect, but they would here.

24,556. In districts you call country districts, the farmers would have no objection to pay a charge or toll if they thought they would effect a ready sale in the market?—Well, I do not think they would. If they thought they would benefit in the price, I do not think they would have any objection to pay the tolls.

24,557. Have you had any conversations with other farmers on the subject of the inquiry?—Yes. They think there is very bad accommodation for fairs here.

24,558. In what way?—There is no space there but the public road.

24,559. You take exception to the statement of Mr. Chapman, that this fair green affords sufficient space?—I differ with him in that. The space of the fair green is not much more than the size of this room.

24,560. What would you say is the extent of it?—I do not say it is fifteen perches, and the police could come and remove us off the road at any time.

24,561. Do the limits of the fair green necessitate the exposure of the stock on the public road?—Yes, the greater part of them are on the road.

24,562. Is this the fair green referred to by Mr. Chapman?—Yes.

24,563. Mr. Chapman (interposing). There are four roads leading into it, and these are very wide roads, and they are used for some cattle and sheep, but there is no traffic on them to be interrupted by the cattle standing there, and there could not be a more convenient place for them to stand. There are walls at both sides, and the sheep pens are put up against the walls and nothing could be more convenient. The accommodation is better than any I know, unless there was a regular field got, and then a field could not give such accommodation as this fair green with the roads attached to it. It is not a hundred yards from here, and there is certainly above an acre of ground in it. There are five or six ways of getting into it.

Examination of Mr. [illegible] resumed.

24,564. Where do you think the farmers would prefer to sell their stock, or would they rather a fair green where there would be ample accommodation and sufficient shelter from the public streets?—I think they would.

24,565. You think, then, that a farmer would not object to pay a toll if he got a sufficient return for it?—If sold in a fair green they would have no objection to pay the tolls, but they would not relish tolls off the public road.

24,566. Would you think it would work better if the sale of all agricultural produce was confined to the market buildings?—I think it would be the proper place. It would be proper to have everything in one place.

24,567. Is the market building here any distance from the market place?—No; it is quite convenient to it.

24,568. Is that the large building opposite the court house?—Yes.

24,569. Is one of the reasons for coming out on the market square because the market building would not afford sufficient space and accommodation?—I think so. All the corn is sold in the street.

also, because it is more convenient for the buyers to come here to the train, but I do believe the tolls assisted the trade in doing away with those fairs.

24,577. Have you heard complaints by the buyers of the distance of the fair green from the railway station?—Never, on account of the convenience of the roads leading into the fair green. People from the different districts drive the cattle there from all sides, and it is an open space and very convenient for them to drive the cattle any road they wish to take.

24,578. Is not there a lot of those brought by rail?—Horses might be brought, and some cattle and sheep, but very little.

24,579. Very few dealers come here?—Yes, numbers of them; but they come to buy.

24,580. When they come to buy do not they take a lot of them away?—Certainly.

24,581. Have they ever made complaints of the situation of the fair green and its distance from the railway station?—Never; it could scarcely be more convenient. There is hardly a fair in the county as convenient to the railway station. The goods station is near the Mercow.

24,582. Have you bought yourself at any of the fairs?—Yes.

24,583. Have they got the system of luck-penny?—They have in all cases.

24,584. On cattle is there any rule regulating the value of the luck-penny?—None whatever. It all depends on the man who sell. One man may give a shilling and another five shillings.

24,585. It is all left to the disposition of the seller?—Yes.

24,586. Is that luck-penny given with cattle and sheep sold?—Yes.

24,587. Is there any fixed rate for the luck-penny on pigs?—There is sixpence. Some give threepence and others a shilling.

24,588. In the case of cattle the contract price is paid, and then the seller will give the luck-penny he is disposed to give, but in pigs the value of the luck is deducted from the contract price?—Very often it is, but very often the pig-buyers when paying for the pigs say, What will you allow me for luck? and in some cases they deduct a shilling or two shillings, and the seller would consent to it before he stopped it.

24,589. You do not know what that luck-penny on pigs is equivalent for?—It is the custom I think.

24,590. Did you ever hear what gave rise to it?—I suppose it is beyond recollection.

24,591. Have they any system of testing the pigs or measle money here?—Not for 30 years. There used to be men at the fairs to test up the pigs for measles, but that is done away with.

24,592. Do you think the stopping of the sixpence has any connection with that?—Not a ha'porth. It is the custom to give it for luck, and the buyers feel they should get it.

24,593. Do you think the seller considers the value of the luck-penny he has to give when ascertaining the price of the animal?—He does not.

24,594. He does not put it on the price of the animal?—No.

24,595. Then the seller receives the actual price less the value of the luck-penny he gives?—Yes, I saw a person selling a cow to give a half-crown luck, but there is no criterion. It all depends on a man's disposition. If he met an off-hand buyer he would give him a shilling or five shillings.

24,596. Have you formed any ideas as to the necessity of confining the sale of marketable commodities to an enclosed space or particular spot?—I do believe it is the proper thing to have every commodity sold in one place, and as much as possible consolidate all the business together.

24,597. Are any of the commodities brought round the town with the exception of milk?—Yes, cabbage and potatoes, and wool. There are the people who buy and go round to the doors to re-sell the commodities. The wool and milk are the principal things sold outside the market place.

24,598. These hawkers are not licensed?—No.

24,599. Is fish brought here?—We catch fish here.

24,600. Is not it exposed for sale in the market square?—It is taken in baskets around the town.

24,601. Are you in trade in the town?—Yes.

24,602. You export a good deal of fish?—Yes; a large catch of fish is sent away.

24,603. Does Mr. Hayden weigh any fish?—No; it is generally in a lodgment house we weigh salmon, and they do not charge anything.

24,604. I take it they would approve of a public scale being erected here?—Yes.

24,605. Have you ever heard of any inaccuracy in the weights of the present beam and scales?—They are tested every month by the police. The commissioners here it is in contemplation to erect a large weighing-machine, and the only difficulty is the site.

24,606. You think it would be more satisfactory for honest dealing between buyer and seller to have a public and independent scales?—I am quite sure of it.

24,607. Have you ever heard people complaining of the inaccuracy of the weights?—Not in the market weights, but of the private weights.

24,608. To stop any cavilling about scales you think a public scales is the proper one?—Yes, and I believe the town commissioners should provide one as soon as possible for the convenience of people requiring hay and straw to be weighed.

24,609. Where is the hay and straw brought here?—I might buy, or another man may buy.

24,610. Is it exposed in any place?—No; I may meet a farmer and say bring me a load of hay.

24,611. Where do they bring it?—To the railway and to my place. They do not expose it for sale at all.

24,612. Whatever they bring in is already sold and previously engaged?—Yes, in the way of hay and straw. They never hawk it about.

24,613. Have you ever heard complaints that the corn was damaged on a wet day in the market square?—No, for the corn that comes in at present there is not half enough accommodation in the market building. If you had to pass it through the market, and charge a toll, the market buildings would want to be larger. The present one would not be able to take in the corn, barley, and everything sold. The market square is full, and inside the building is full as well.

24,614. Have the buyers at the fairs ever inquired for the system of weighing the stock?—Never, so far as I am aware up to the present time.

24,615. Within your experience you never bought any cattle by live weight?—No, generally people who buy cattle can tell their weight to within a pound or two, so that they do not require a machine.

Mr. C. Myers examined.

24,616. You heard the remarks of Mr. O'Brien and Mr. Rooney?—Yes.

24,617. Do you consider it is the proper course at all times to confine the sale of agricultural produce to one particular spot or enclosed market building?—I do in this town, because the produce comes from the other end of the town, and the people have to come through the whole town to the market square, so that every business gets a chance of their money when they sell their goods.

24,618. Apart altogether from the fact of giving the traders of this town an opportunity of getting customers, do you think it is the proper course to concentrate the markets in one particular spot or building?—Yes, I think the market place is the proper place.

24,619. Have you heard that any perishable commodities have been injured by the want of shelter accommodation?—No, there is plenty of room in the building in the present state of the market.

24,620. Do you think that the present scale of the market building would afford sufficient space for the corn to be sheltered there?—It would not. It would have to be enlarged considerably.

Mr. Joseph Smith examined.

24,621. Have you any remarks to make?—I wish to say the corn market is very small, but formerly it was one of the largest corn market towns in Ireland, and corn used to be kept on cars outside until the buyers were prepared; but it would be impossible if the corn market increased to get a shed sufficiently large to put the corn into. Now Mr. Chapman could tell that 40 years ago, when the market was here, a shed that would cover an acre of ground would not shelter the corn that came.

24,622. Is it your reason that sufficient shelter accommodation could not be provided because it would require a great deal of expense. Is that your principal objection?—I think it would incur such enormous expense that the commissioners or people of the town would not be able to bear such expense.

24,623. What is the town rate at present?—1s. 6d. in the pound; that is only the water rate. There are no municipal rates properly called.

24,624. You would like to see the accommodation if it were feasible?—Yes.

24,625. When cattle are brought in are any deductions made by the buyer from the seller after the price has been fixed?—There is nothing brought in that there is any deduction made on except to the victuallers.

24,626. What is the deduction?—Three, four, or six pounds—that is deducted as luckpenny for horns and dirt. It would be a great advantage to have a weighing machine.

Mr. Thomas Delaney, Chairman of the Town Commissioners, examined.

24,627. Witness, I heard one of the victuallers say he would be very glad to see a weighing-machine for cattle here. It would save a great deal of haggling and bargaining.

24,628. Do you think the buyers would agree to that?—Yes, a lot of butchers buy meat by weight without being skinned or dressed.

24,629. Only by weight after it is skinned they pay?—That is all.

24,630. Is that customary?—It is as regards sheep and cattle.

24,631. You are the chairman of the town commissioners?—Yes.

24,632. You weighed meat for those victuallers?—Yes.

24,633. You levied no charge at all for weighing?—No. It was a matter of convenience for the parties.

24,634. Then the victuallers only buy the net weight, and what they actually pay for is the net weight?—Yes.

24,635. Because of the entrails and horns?—Yes.

24,636. Is there any deduction allowed for the horns?—No; the skin has been taken off and the feet. Mr. Chapman constantly sells his cattle in that way.

24,637. Do you think sales would be more expeditiously effected if all cattle were sold by live weight?—I could not answer that question, because some might agree to it and some may not. It would save a good deal of trouble.

24,638. (Mr. Smith.) It is coming generally into practice, and will be adopted by every one.

24,639. (Mr. O'Brien.) It is a growing opinion among the people that they would be better satisfied to have them weighed. I heard a large victualler in town say he would be very glad to buy by weight. Some young men may not have experience and would be anxious to get a beast weighed.

24,640. Do not you think it would be more satisfactory if all sales were made by weight?—Yes.

24,641. (The Assistant Commissioner to Mr. Chapman.) Have you formed any ideas, Mr. Chapman, on the question of selling by live weight or dead weight?—The present course of selling dead meat works satisfactorily. I have been doing it extensively this last five and thirty or forty years, and it has been most satisfactory between me and the parties to whom I sell.

24,642. Do you think the other practice as suggested would work equally as well. Do you think it would be a more honest way of working, and that the farmers would get the actual value of the cattle?—I think it would be more satisfactory to have it in the way you say.

24,643. (Mr. O'Brien.) If a person selling at the fair had a notion he was not getting a sufficient price for his beast it would be well to have a place where he could satisfy himself and get it weighed there.

24,644. (Mr. Rooney.) Fat cattle are generally sold in lots, and they would not go to the weigh-bridge. I think every man would rather buy on his own judgment.

24,645. Are you speaking as a buyer?—They would rather buy and sell on their own judgment. If a man had fifteen or twenty bullocks how could he weigh them on the weigh bridge.

24,646. You mentioned that a man may not buy after all. As a rule are many of the bargains broken?—I do not think they are. If there is a dispute between them the buyer would say if you do not take the price by live weight I will kill it and weigh it.

24,647. If they agree on a price as a rule they pay?—Yes, I think the country people would rather buy and sell on their own judgment.

24,648. Did you ever weigh a head of cattle?—No, nor no one ever asked me.

24,649. Did you ever hear what benefit would be derived from weighing and selling by live weight?—No, I do not think it is a rule to buy that way. The cattle are bought in lots.

24,650. (Mr. O'Brien.) That only applies to fat cattle. I may tell you that he is a skilful buyer.

24,651. Then you consider Mr. Rooney has an advantage over the seller?—Yes, you might meet 50 people who would not know how to buy or sell and would want a machine, whereas Mr. Rooney would not want it at all.

24,652. (Mr. Rooney.) If possible we would want a larger and more extensive fair green.

24,653. Have you heard the farmers complaining of that?—Yes, the police may come at any time and turn the people off the road.

24,654. (Mr. Smith.) It would injure the business of the town if the fair field was changed to another place. There is a case in point. In Carlow they used to hold the fair in the streets and the people in general used not come in except for the purpose of buying and selling cattle. However, some of the gentry objected to this course, and said it should be in a field near the railway, and the town commissioners agreed to have the field walled in for the purpose, and the consequence is an injury to the business of the town of Carlow. It is going down very much since that, because buyers and sellers coming by rail as soon as they dispose of their cattle they go off again without coming into the town.

24,655. It affects the trade of the town?—Yes.

24,656. But has the fair itself been materially injured, or has it improved?—I am not able to say that. The fairs in this town were established for the benefit of the town.

24,657. The town practically is between the fair green and the railway station?—Yes.

24,658. If people wish to go to the railway station they have to pass through the town?—Yes.

24,659. (Mr. Delahunt.) It would ruin the whole business of the town to take the fair out of where it is.

24,665. There is no market in Roundwood?—No.

24,666. How many fairs have you?—Twelve fairs.

24,667. What dates?—The third Tuesday of every month. About three years ago they were changed up and down and the dates were fixed. I think it is five or six years ago.

24,668. What dates were they held on previous to the change?—The 3rd January, 12th February, 14th February, 14th March, 12th April, 23rd May, 31st June, 20th July, 23rd August, 19th September, 8th October, 8th November, and 8th December.

24,669. When was this change made, or how was it made?—By an order in Privy Council. We memorialised the Privy Council.

24,670. Who did?—The inhabitants of Roundwood and the buyers and sellers frequenting the fairs.

24,671. Were tolls levied at each of the twelve fairs?—There were.

24,672. Were there always twelve fairs held previous to the monthly fairs?—No.

24,673. You remember when there were less than twelve?—Yes. Mr. Ramsay and myself remember when there were only four originally. I remember six.

24,674. Do you remember when there were less than six yourself?—I do not.

24,675. You have tolls levied at these?—Yes.

24,676. Is this a commons where the fair green is held, or is it in the centre of cross roads?—It is in at the back of the principal street.

24,677. You built a wall around it?—There is a car-way and short cut through it we could not interfere with.

24,678. The public have acquired a right of way?—Yes.

24,679. Is there any shelter accommodation in the fair green?—Not a bit. It is an open field.

24,680. Do you graze it between fairs?—Yes.

24,681. Have you got a toll board erected on fair days?—I have.

24,682. Could you mention the different tolls on cattle?—We only levy on what is sold, and it is the buyer who pays, and that has been always the custom. The charges are 3d. for a full grown cow or bullock; 2d. for a two-year old; 1d. for a yearling and for a calf; 1d. for sheep and 1d. for pigs. We have no pigs since the railway came here. We are ten miles from any railway, and no pigs but small pigs or bonhams are brought here.

24,683. Are these the only animals on which you levy the tolls? There is 6d. for a horse, but they are very rarely sold.

24,684. Have you any standing charges on fair days?—Yes.

24,685. What is the nature of the standings?—There are residents as standings, clothes dealers, wooden-ware, or tin, or anything that way.

24,686. What do you charge on these?—4d. for a standing.

24,687. No matter the extent of ground they occupy, if they have a standing you charge 4d.?—I think so. In fact we have not been particular in collecting that charge at all.

24,688. Supposing they bring in a cartload of bonhams would you charge 4d. on that cart?—We would be satisfied, but as a rule you see it is on the public road they stand.

24,689. When the bonhams are coming out, you ask for 1d. on each?—The collector would say If you have six give me 6d., and the man might have ten in the cart.

24,690. Do you collect fourpence on the cart containing the bonhams as a standing charge and a penny on each when sold?—I never did.

24,691. You only collect on carts with bonhams when the bonhams are sold?—Yes.

24,692. Is the exposure of the animals confined to the fair green?—The sheep are kept along the streets; 10 or 12 years ago a considerable number used to go on the green, but since that time they nearly all keep on the footpaths.

24,693. All the cattle go into the fair green?—Yes.

24,694. And the horses?—The horses in the same. The pigs go into the fair green.

24,695. How do you collect your charges on the sheep and horses?—When they are driving out.

24,696. How many gaps have you?—Three; but two principal ones.

24,697. These are at the outskirts of the town or village?—Yes.

24,698. How many men at each gap?—Sometimes ten men. It is according to the fairs; the winter fairs are small and not very largely attended.

24,699. Do you have ten men at each gap?—No, all together.

24,700. At what rate do you pay these men?—Different rates; a couple of shillings or half-a-crown, and sometimes a man better than the others would be worth three shillings.

24,701. Do these men carry sticks at the gaps?—Generally.

24,702. Were any complaints ever made to you that they have injured the animals as they were passing out or injured the horses or owners of the horses or cattle?—Never, since I came there.

24,703. Have the collectors to inquire from the man in charge of the animal, whoever he may be, whether he has bought or sold?—Yes.

24,704. And if bought they demand the charge?—Yes.

24,705. Supposing a man stated he had not bought or sold, and your men knew as a fact he had and he was telling a falsehood, what course would they adopt?—They would insist on stopping him.

24,706. Would they seize the animal?—No, but stop him there.

24,707. Does it frequently occur?—No, it is very rare.

24,708. I suppose the cattle are branded?—Yes, and it is the sellers generally are driving them out, and if we do not see a dealer or his man the collectors know the countrymen eight or ten miles around, and if one of them says I have not sold, he is let pass.

24,709. Is it not customary with the buyers when agreeing with the farmer to tell the farmer he would have to drive them to some yard outside the town?—Yes.

24,710. In that case the seller is in possession of the animal passing the toll gap?—Yes.

24,711. Has not he to pay the charge?—He tells us who is the buyer and we know where he goes, and we settle.

24,712. Practically as a rule you always collect from the buyer no matter whether it is the buyer or seller is in possession of the animal when passing the custom gap?—There are some cases in which the seller will say I sold to so and so, and he will stop it from him.

24,713. In no case the seller pays the charge?—No, unless by agreement.

24,714. Is it very often done by agreement?—I think not.

24,715. Have you toll boards?—We have.

24,716. So that in case of dispute between the toll collectors and the buyers they can see the toll board?—Yes.

24,717. You have made no alterations in the charges?—No.

24,718. They were always levied?—They were handed over to me by the former collector, and I never made any change. I have also erected a weigh-bridge.

24,719. Was it yourself erected it?—The landlord helped me. The dealers took advantage of that, and said since the passing of the Weighing of Cattle Act, which came into operation last January, I had no legal authority to charge without having that.

24,720. Do they avail themselves of the weigh-bridge?—I have only had it up for the last fair, and there was not beast weighed. I do not suspect I ever will, because they are all store cattle that are brought there.

24,721. Could you give me any idea of the number of cattle brought to your fair throughout the year?—We have three fairs in the summer, and the number of sheep is very large. I think at the September fair we have between four and five thousand sheep.

24,722. How many cattle?—The cattle are not so very extensive, but I think the number would amount as an average to between 200 and 300.

24,723. Would you have any objection to tell me your average receipts every year during the past five years?—I think on an average from 12*l*. to 14*l*.

24,724. Would that be the profits or gross receipts?—That would be after paying everything. The first year or two was the best. This year as far as it has gone is as good as any I had.

24,725. What would you estimate the value of the grazing between fairs?—A couple of pounds or thirty shillings.

24,726. Do you [illegible] any repairs during the year?—No.

24,727. Who cleans the public road after the sheep and horse fair?—I suppose the road contractor.

24,728. You or the owner do not do it?—No.

24,729. Does the Rev. Mr. Dromes own the place?—The greater part.

24,730. Have you any remark to make in connexion with your fairs?—No, only I thought it better to attend, seeing your advertisement, lest legislation might ignore us altogether.

24,731. Do the tolls prevent the people from coming to your fairs?—No, since I had to put up the weigh-bridge. There is ample accommodation for the sheep as well as the cattle except at one or two fairs, and I shall get an additional field if required.

24,732. If there are sheep and horses sold on the public street, do not you collect the tolls?—Yes; but they grumble and say it is illegal, and that we have no law.

24,733. Within what limits do you think your jurisdiction extends to collect the toll?—There are a whole lot of townlands mentioned in the patent.

24,734. (*Mr. Dalstead.*) What he would want is to confine the exposure of the animals to the fair green.

24,735. (*The Commissioner to witness.*) You think the space sufficient?—Yes.

24,736. Where do they have these standings. Is it on the public road?—Some on the public road and some on a little open space between the [illegible] and some inside on the green.

24,737. Do you think the fact of levying a toll acts in any way as a deterrent on people attending the fair in greater numbers than otherwise?—It is the buyer pays.

24,738. The buyers took advantage of the want of the weigh-bridge to object to the tolls?—One or two did.

24,739. But the greater number did not?—No.

Mr. [illegible] re-examined.

24,740. Do you send any stock to [illegible]?—I often buy them.

24,741. Have you any objection to the accommodation afforded there?—I think, with the exception of one day, the accommodation is enough, but I do not think in the September fair it is large enough to hold the cattle, sheep, and horses.

24,742. Did you ever hear any complaints of the charges the owner levies?—No. I do not think they deter people a bit from coming in.

24,743. You think its isolated position affects it materially?—Yes, in the sale of the fat pigs. I remember when a large number used to go there, and there is no one goes there now.

24,744. What is the nearest fair?—Bray, Wicklow, or Kilcool.

24,745. From what districts do the buyers come?—All the principal sheep buyers from South Meath and all the surrounding counties.

24,746. Did you ever hear the cattle were fatigued or injured by the long drive to the railway station, or do they complain of that?—No; the cattle offered for sale would not be injured by long driving. They are all store cattle.

24,747. Is there any other gentleman who has any evidence to give?—No answer.

The Inquiry terminated with a vote of thanks to the Assistant Commissioner.

ARKLOW.

With reference to my inquiry in Arklow on the 1st day of December 1888, I beg

The fairs are held on the public streets, which are only of the ordinary width. The lower portion of the town is for cattle, and the upper portion for sheep. No accommodation whatever is given those frequenting the fairs except that afforded by the houses of the shopkeepers.

The potato market is held in a house in the main street, and which is very confined and inadequate for anything but a small retail trade, and is practically nothing more than a weigh-house and store. The general market is held on the public streets, principally the main street.

The gross weight alone is put on the ticket which is given denoting the weight.

At the termination of the inquiry a very influentially signed memorial was presented on behalf of the inhabitants of Ovoca, asking that facilities be given them to legally hold additional fairs in that place, as such would tend to improve the general trade of the district.

Appended will be found a transcript of the evidence taken at the inquiry.

JOHN J. O'MEARA,
Assistant Commissioner.

45, Lower Mount Street,
Dublin.

Arklow, 1st December 1888.

Mr. Charles J. [illegible] examined.

24,749. You are the town clerk of Arklow?—I am.

24,750. When were the commissioners established?—In 1878.

24,751. They have no control whatever over the markets and fairs held in Arklow?—No.

24,752. Who is the owner of them?—I believe the owner of the market is Mrs. Margaret Donnelly; she is the present occupier, and I believe, and have reason to know, she holds these premises leased from the representatives of the late Captain John [illegible] of Hyde Park, [illegible], Gorey, co. Wexford.

24,753. When you say premises, you mean the market buildings?—Yes.

24,754. Are these buildings utilised only for market purposes?—Only for market purposes, but they are joined to other premises.

24,755. What is the market day here?—There are two days. Thursday is the principal day, and Saturday has latterly turned out so good.

24,756. What fairs are held here?—It appears in 1880 we made an alteration in the way the fairs are usually held.

24,757. When you say we, do you mean the Town Commissioners?—Yes. It appears at a special meeting of the Commissioners, held on the 6th June 1879, when ten out of the fifteen Commissioners attended, it was proposed by Mr. Paul and seconded by Mr. Andrew Byrne that at the commencement of the year 1880 the fairs held in the town of Arklow be changed to the second Tuesday of each and every month from the then fixed dates.

24,758. Have you got any record of what these dates were?—I will let you have them, but not on the moment.

24,759. Was this alteration made with the consent of the Local Government Board?—No. We wrote to the Local Government Board before we made the change, and they wrote back asking us when did the fairs of Arklow commence, a question which we were not in a position to answer.

24,760. How long does your memory go back as to the fairs that were held here before this alteration?—I think evidence will come before you that will bring you back sixty years.

24,761. During that period the eight fairs were held?—They were. Then, by the resolution in 1879, the fairs were changed to the second Tuesday of every month, the pig fair to be held on the same day, and the horse fairs to be held on the same day as the cattle fair in April, May, July, and October. It appears the horse fair did not take, so that we discontinued it. The resolution was passed unanimously, there being ten of the Commissioners present out of fifteen.

24,762. Where are the fairs held?—They are held in the lower part of the town for the cattle and the upper part of the town for sheep.

24,763. Is this the public thoroughfare?—Yes.

24,764. You have different portions allotted off for each species of animal?—Yes.

24,765. Are any charges levied at these fairs?—No.

24,766. During your experience have you had occasion to know that charges were ever levied?—They never have been.

24,767. Either at the new or the old fairs?—No.

24,768. Is there any control exercised by the Commissioners over the fairs?—None.

24,769. By nobody but the police?—Yes.

24,770. Have you ever heard complaints that confusion existed and obstruction was caused about the public thoroughfare by the fact of these fairs being held on the street?—Well, in the year 1879, as well as I remember, it was decided that the carts would be changed, and that the police would make this change—that is, to ask the people to keep all their carts at one side, which, since, they have done with very few exceptions. That leaves a space clear for the cattle to go to the lower part of the town.

24,771. In reference to the communication from the Local Government Board, what led the Local Government Board to send the communication to you, or had you previously asked their consent to the alteration?—We did not ask their consent, but asked the way to go about a change, because the Commission was only started, and we were ignorant how to proceed.

24,772. Did you get that communication in the ordinary course?—Yes.

24,773–4. No inquiry was held by the Local Government inspector here?—No, and we did not acknowledge the right of the Local Government Board to do so.

24,775. Have the Commissioners ever discussed or thought it desirable to obtain compulsory power to acquire control of the market rights and fairs themselves?—There were certain byelaws drafted and they fell through.

24,776. By the Commissioners?—Yes.

24,777. They wished to get control?—They did not wish to exercise control, but they wished to make material changes.

24,778. They wanted to effect changes in the management of the market, but leave the ownership in the hands of a private individual?—Not as regards the market, but the standings of meat and vegetables.

24,779. That is the regulation of the sites of the different markets?—Yes.

24,780. Have they ever discussed that question themselves?—They have.

24,781. What is the consensus of opinion amongst the majority of the members of the board? Do they think it desirable that as a local authority they should obtain compulsory powers to acquire the market rights and work them as an authority for the benefit of the town?—I believe they do not require that. I do not believe they wish that.

24,782. Would they be opposed to such a change?—I believe the majority would.

24,783. Have you ever heard complaints of the present arrangement?—I never have.

24,784. The market you say is held on the streets too?—Yes, during the time they have their commodities there.

24,785. The commodities are exposed on the public thoroughfare?—The commodities are exposed on the public thoroughfare with the shafts of the cars standing out, which is the custom existing for a long period of years.

24,786. What does the market building consist of?—A weigh-house on the public streets, the same as a store.

24,787. Is it used as a store?—I cannot say it is. It is used as a public market.

24,788. When you say the market-house, is that a building for the protection of the machines and officials who weigh there and do the clerical work?—Yes, and a store-house. If you bought a commodity you could leave it there until you wished to call for it.

24,789. Did you ever visit it yourself?—Yes, I have been there.

24,790. Do you think it affords sufficient space for the purpose?—I am quite sure it does, because you must bear in mind the markets are at their lowest ebb. Evidence will come before you to show that 30, 40, or 50 years ago, when the cars used to reach two-thirds further down than they do at present, there were no complaints.

24,791. What do you assign for the falling off in the markets? Have other markets been established in the neighbourhood, and do they take a great quantity of the produce there which used formerly to come here?—We must put that down to general depression.

24,792. In the neighbourhood or districts adjacent to Arklow, have any new markets been established recently?—Within the last nine years a market was established in Aughrim, nine English miles from here, and some of the parties who used to come here with their produce do not come now.

24,793. You have had much experience yourself of fairs?—I have a considerable [illegible].

24,794. You have experience of fairs at which tolls are levied and fairs that are toll free?—Yes.

24,795. Do you think at a fair does the exaction of a toll act as a deterrent on people bringing in their stock in greater numbers?—I say it certainly would.

24,796. Do you think it has an effect on the extent of the fair?—Decidedly. I have one experience of fairs I might mention. In the year 1878 I was at a fair in Fair Hill, county Galway, and I had 11 ponies coming out, and I was not aware a toll was levied. It was the first time I was there, and the first thing I saw was five or six strong fellows with sticks, who beat back the ponies. I did not know the reason why, but they told me I did not pay the toll. I had not been asked for any toll.

24,797. Were the animals injured?—One was injured.

24,798. That is as to the obstruction and mode of levying a toll; but do you think has a toll an effect on the farmers when they are bringing their animals to the fair, or do they consider that if they had to pay a toll at one town, and another was toll free, they would go to the fair that was toll free?—I believe they would go to the fair that was toll free. It makes a material change in luck, because if a toll is charged on that fair at Arklow, and I sold my cattle, I will not give you as much luck as otherwise, because I deduct the "luck" money.

Mr. John Donnelly examined.

24,799. You are here to represent your mother, Mrs. Margaret Donnelly?—Yes.

24,800. She is the tenant of the market-place?—Yes, from Mr. Beaumont, of Hyde Park, Loch, Galway.

24,801. How does she hold?—By lease.

24,802. Have you got the date of it?—1879.

24,803. For what term?—I think it is for 70 years.

24,804. Would you mind telling me the rent?—[illegible] a year.

24,805. Is that for the market-place alone?—Yes, and the right to collect any charges out of it. We are bound by the lease to keep it as a market-place.

24,806. Have you read the lease yourself?—Yes, and I can produce it.

24,807. In it was the right demised to you to collect the charges, or was it merely a demise of the premises?—A demise of the premises.

24,808. There was no demise of the charges?—I never read the lease to understand that.

24,809. You do not know how Mr. Beaumont holds them?—I do not.

24,810. Would you kindly mention what marketable commodities are brought here every Thursday and Saturday, whether you collect any charge on them, or not?—Potatoes, oats, turnips, vegetables, and fruit are sold all through the street.

24,811. Does butter come here?—No, they bring it privately to the shops.

24,812. None is exposed in the market-place?—No.

24,813. Hay or straw?—No; hay comes in directly.

24,814. It is not exposed in the market-place?—No.

24,815. Are pigs ever brought in on market day?—No.

24,816. Are calves?—Yes, calves on Thursdays.

24,817. Are cattle ever brought in?—No.

24,818. Are there any other commodities brought in that you have not mentioned?—Not that I know of.

24,819. What charges do you levy on these commodities?—I charge a penny per sack for corn, a penny per sack for potatoes, a penny per draft for turnips or per agreement. In the wool season for any wool that comes into the market, which is very little, I charge a shilling per pack.

24,820. Are these charges for weighing?—For weighing.

24,821. Are they all exposed in the market square?—Wool is.

24,822. I mean the other commodities?—A good deal of the commodities are exposed.

24,823. Are they sold before being weighed at your scales?—Certainly.

24,824. All sold?—Yes.

24,825. They never actually weigh previous to the sale?—No.

24,826. If they exposed in the market-place a sack of potatoes and sold them and weighed them at the purchaser's own scales would you look for any charge?—I would not.

24,827. It is only when your scales are availed of that you levy a charge?—Yes.

24,828. In return for the ticket?—Yes.

24,829. Do you collect any charges on what are called standings in the market?—No; a good deal of the commodities come in ready weighed, but unless they weigh on my scales I do not charge.

24,830. You collect no charge on the vegetables or fruit?—No.

24,831. Do you collect any on calves if they are sold?—No.

24,832. Who have you engaged there to look after the place?—The weigh-master.

24,833. Only one?—Yes.

24,834. He has to perform the manual labour and clerical work?—If required as the manual labour I would manage the clerical work.

24,835. You give tickets there?—Yes.

24,836. Have you ever seen the weigh-master weighing there?—Yes.

24,837. When weighing a sack of potatoes do you estimate the tare of the sack or do you actually weigh it?—The custom of the place is to allow half a stone for the sack.

24,838. Is that irrespective of the size of the sack or the quantity it might contain?—It is. The people purchasing might arrange that themselves.

24,839. Do you ever put down the estimated tare on the ticket?—No.

24,840. Only the gross weight?—That is all.

24,841. The usual allowance is seven pounds?—Yes.

24,842. Would that seven pounds be deducted if the sack were brought in on a fine day and also on a wet day when the sack was completely saturated with wet?—It is the custom of the place to allow it any time.

24,843. On corn do you estimate the tare of the sack?—Yes, seven pounds also.

24,844. Are the tares of these sacks the only deduction from the gross weight?—That is all.

24,845. They do not allow anything for [illegible] or mud around the potatoes or the bad state of the corn?—No.

24,846. Is there any other deduction made by the buyer from the seller when paying the contract price for potatoes?—I cannot say.

24,847. Have you bought any yourself?—Yes, and I never made any further deduction than half a stone.

24,848. Or reduction in value the same as in the ordinary buying of cattle?—It rests with the people when they see what they have got to demand something more of them.

24,849. When weighing potatoes what is the smallest weight you weigh with usually?—To the half stone.

24,850. You do not weigh less than a half stone?—No.

24,851. Do you give a cast of the beam when weighing?—We give the weight.

24,852. Does the beam turn?—Yes, certainly.

24,853. Does the board of the scales touch the ground?—Yes.

24,854. Practically there must be half a stone in the sack or nothing?—Yes.

24,855. A sack ten stone six pounds you put down as ten stone?—Yes.

24,856. From that you subsequently deduct the tare of the sack, which is seven pounds?—Yes.

24,857. That would be nine and a half stone the buyer would pay for?—Yes.

24,858. What is the smallest quantity of potatoes you have weighed, and for which you charged a penny for weighing?—Generally in half barrels they come—that is nine and a half stone.

24,859. On turnips you charge a penny a draft or per agreement?—Yes.

24,860. Is it usual to make an agreement?—It is, of course.

24,861. Could you give me an instance of an agreement made for the payment of weighing turnips other than the penny a draft?—A man might give sixpence for weighing the load.

24,862. You have a bridge there?—No, but a beam and scales.

24,863. Is there any weighbridge in Arklow to weigh loads?—There may be, but I do not know. There is no public one.

24,864. Are there any private ones?—There is one belonging to Messrs. Kerins.

24,865. Are you aware that they levy any charge for weighing loads?—I am not. They are coal merchants.

24,866. They weigh for the public also?—They will weigh for anyone. I think they charge twopence a load for some commodities and sixpence a load for hay.

24,867. Supposing some of these people attending the market exposed their commodity in the market-place, and could not sell it during the day and wished to store it until the next market day, can they do so?—If they wished to store it they can.

24,868. Is there a space sufficient for that purpose?—Yes.

24,869. Do you levy any charge for storage?—No. It was the custom previously to levy a charge, but we levy none.

24,870. At whose risk is a commodity stored?—At their own risk.

24,871. Have you ever heard complaints that any of the commodities have been depreciated in value or quantity by being exposed on the public thoroughfare?—I have not heard of any.

24,872. Is there any fish sold in this market square?—No.

24,873. Where is the fish sold?—Down at the bridge and along the strand.

24,874. You collect charges only on the articles mentioned?—That is all.

24,875. These are the only sources of revenue your mother has from the markets?—Yes.

24,876. Have you the scale erected in the market-place?—Yes.

24,877. Have you any rules erected regulating the management of the markets?—No.

24,878. Have the markets always been held in this space outside the market?—Yes.

24,879. Your mother has nothing whatever to do with the fairs?—She has not.

24,880. Would you have any objection to tell me her average receipts for the past three years?—I could not say, but we believe ourselves it was only able to pay the weigh-master's wages and the rent.

24,881. Is he employed exclusively for attending to the scales?—Yes, and in an obliging way to do an odd turn after.

24,882. How do you pay him?—Eight shillings a week.

24,883. You think your total receipts from the market and weighing are not sufficient to reimburse you the rent and weigh-master's wages?—No.

24,884. Is that the rent for anything else but the market buildings?—No.

24,885. Do you keep any block of these tickets you give out?—Yes.

24,886. So that if they lose a ticket denoting the weight you are always in a position to give a duplicate?—Yes.

24,887. Do you preserve these blocks for any length of time?—We do.

24,888. How long?—We keep them a year, and in some instances longer.

24,889. You keep no record of the commodities you do not weigh?—No.

24,890. Supposing it was required from you to make a periodical return of the current prices of these different commodities brought into the market, and exposed in the market place for sale, do you think one could be made?—I think it could.

24,891. Do you think it would be a pretty accurate one?—I have reason to believe it would.

24,892. Although you would have to rely on your own observations and on the answers the sellers and buyers would give you?—Yes. I do be in the market generally myself every Thursday.

24,893. Could a return be made of the different quantities brought in?—I do not think it could.

24,894. Because you have no control and do not weigh everything?—Yes. In many instances the farmers bring in goods which they have weighed themselves, and other people take them away without stopping to weigh them at all.

24,895. Have you ever heard complaints of the farmers weighing themselves, and the buyers more or less going by estimation of the quantity they purchase?—Yes, I heard it complained of by some people. There are people who would not take them without being weighed.

24,896. Do you think the market would work better and more satisfactorily, and more honestly for buyers and sellers, if all commodities were weighed at a public scale?—I could not say.

24,897. Who held the place previous to 1879?—Lawrence Kennedy.

24,898. You do not know what rent he was paying?—No.

The following is a copy of the ticket used at the crane:—

______ 188 .					
CRANE DOCKET.					
Purchaser.			Crane.		
[illegible]	Stn.	Lbs.	[illegible]	Stn.	Lbs.
Gross Weight			Gross Weight		

______ 188 .					
CRANE DOCKET.					
Purchaser.			Crane.		
[illegible]	Stn.	Lbs.	[illegible]	Stn.	Lbs.
Gross Weight			Gross Weight		

Mr. Daniel Cowhey, Chairman of the Town Commissioners, examined.

24,899. You are the chairman of the Town Commissioners of Arklow?—Yes.

24,900. Have you had any experience of the fairs and markets here?—I have had experience of the fairs, but very little experience of the markets, as my premises are too low down from them.

24,901. As chairman of the Town Commissioners, the local authority of the town, do you think that Town Commissioners would be the best controlling authority for the markets and fairs in Arklow, and would the united efforts of the gentlemen composing the board tend to the better management of the market and give more satisfaction to the farmers and those frequenting them than having the control in the hands of a private individual?—It is my belief, if the parties occupying the market are recompensed for any interest in it, that the market would be better controlled in the hands of a public body.

24,902. You qualify your answer by the condition that compensation should be given for any legally vested right, but apart from the question of compensation do you think the markets and fairs should be under the control of the local authority?—I do.

24,903. Have you any particular reason for forming that opinion?—They are more successful in other towns where managed by the local authority. For instance, in Gorey they have a more successful market than here, because they have a proper market-place and possibly proper facility for goods of every description to be weighed.

24,904. Would you think it also desirable that markets should be held in a properly enclosed space with adequate shelter accommodation to afford protection to all perishable commodities brought in, and not have them exposed on the public thoroughfare?—I believe if it were possible to obtain a proper square for holding the market in a central position it would benefit the public generally.

24,905. With shelter accommodation?—Yes.

24,906. Would you approve of a rule or bye-law confining the sale of marketable commodities to that square, in order to concentrate them on that spot?—I would if there was a proper place provided, but not otherwise.

24,907. You object to this practice of selling on the streets?—Not at present, as the people have no other facilities.

24,908. On principle, if the facilities were afforded in a proper building, you think it would be desirable to remove them off the public thoroughfare?—I do not think it would answer in this town to have the goods removed from the street, owing to the regulation of the town generally, but I do believe if there was a proper market-house here occupying a central position, and have the greater portion of the goods removed, it would be an advantage to the public.

24,909. That is to remove what may suffer by exposure?—Yes.

24,910. Is there any butter brought here?—There is no butter market, and that is a great drawback.

24,911. Butter is carried to the shopkeepers' houses?—Yes.

24,912. Could a butter market be fostered here? What is the surrounding country?—A butter-producing country. There is very little tillage.

24,913. Where is the butter bought?—All in the Dublin markets.

24,914. Do you think, if there was a butter market here, the producer would derive a larger return from the sale of the commodity than by sending it to Dublin and incurring the cost of transit?—I would not be in a position to say that.

24,915. Are you in trade in the town?—I am.

24,916. What trade?—The grocery and spirit trade.

24,917. Do you think it would be advisable if the markets and fairs were removed off the street?—The fairs could not be removed off the street. They are in a very convenient place, and do not interfere with anything.

24,918. Where are they held?—In the lower part of the town, where there are few business houses.

24,919. Is it a common?—No, it is not a common. It is one side of the main street. The pigs are at one side, and cattle on portion of the main street.

24,920. Why do you say they could not be removed?—Not with advantage to the general public. Traders would object, and it is very convenient to the railway station. In Gorey there is a fair-green, and it is not used. The public streets are used.

24,921. Does not the fact of the fairs being held on the street occasion much filth and dirt?—No doubt.

24,922. Who cleans that away?—The scavenger employed by the sanitary authority.

24,923. Does he perform that duty immediately after the fairs?—Yes.

24,924. Have you ever heard complaints that he left it undone for a few days?—No special complaints.

24,925. Have you heard complaints?—I have not.

24,926. Have you ever heard that accidents have happened by the fact of the fairs being held on the street?—Very rarely. I have heard of an accident last year.

24,927. Were animals injured?—No animals injured.

24,928. Are horses brought here?—The Commissioners tried to establish a horse fair, and it was a failure.

24,929. Some of the animals intermix with each other?—No.

24,930. From what districts would you say these animals are brought?—From all the surrounding districts on towards Gorey on the one side, and Croghan on the other.

24,931. Within what distance?—Within a radius of nine miles.

24,932. Is there a good fish market here?—No, there is not. The fish women bring baskets of fish to a corner, and sell them there to people, who retail them in other portions of the street where they think they can sell.

24,933. Do they export the fish?—There are local and other buyers who attend during the season according to the quantity of fish they can get.

24,934. Is that one of the chief trades here?—It was one of the chief trades formerly, but there is a failure for the last four years, and the principal fishing business is carried on at other stations.

24,935. Have you any remarks to make or suggestions to offer that you think would tend to the better working and management of the markets here?—I have no suggestion to make about the fairs. I believe they are carried on with satisfaction to the public generally, and I would not interfere in any way with the market. If the parties having it received compensation I think it would be an advantage to the public generally to get a central position for it, and have the market under public control, but I would not be for taking up the market at all until a central position was got.

24,936. Do you think there should be a proper public weighbridge and scales, and if such were provided that trade would be carried on more satisfactorily?—I believe it is the greatest possible inconvenience to the general public not to have a weighbridge. Of course, it is owing to the obliging disposition of the firms here to allow parties who buy to weigh on their weighbridges, but the people have to go three-quarters of a mile. If there was a public one it would be a great convenience.

24,937. Do those firms levy any charge?—Yes, sixpence and sixpence for hay.

24,938. Do they weigh the empty cart?—They do always. Say a man brings in a load of hay, he has to go to Messrs. Harkin's yard, and then return to have the cart weighed, and it is a matter of two hours' work to have the cart and hay weighed.

24,939. All that is obviated when the quantity is bought by estimation?—Yes.

24,940. Do you think the producer is more or less at the mercy of the more experienced buyer in that case?—It is described as happy-go-lucky. There have been several complaints made to me about the want of a weighbridge.

Mr. Richard Hutson examined.

24,941. Have you any observations to make or suggestions to offer?—For 60 years I remember the market, and I used to buy corn, oats, and barley, and potatoes and so, and the markets were entirely larger in those days than at present, but I never heard any complaint.

24,942. They were always held on the same site as at present?—The very same.

24,943. Do you remember when the market was not held here?—No. It is held here so long as I can remember, and long before that, as I hear.

24,944. Do you remember when the eight fairs were held?—I do.

24,945. Do you remember when less than eight fairs were held?—I do not; the eight fairs were held for 60 years to my own knowledge.

24,946. What were the dates of them?—The 11th January, 22nd March, 19th April, 4th May, 28th June, 8th August, 11th November, 22nd September.

24,947. Have you ever purchased at those fairs yourself?—I have.

24,948. At the fairs here have they got the system of luck-penny?—Yes.

24,949. Is there any rule regulating the value of that luck-penny for cattle?—No. That is given chiefly to the buyer to encourage him to come again.

24,950. There is no rule regulating the value of it?—None.

24,951. It is all left to the disposition of the seller?—Just so.

24,952. Is there any fixed charge on pigs?—No.

24,953. They do not give sixpence here?—Yes; that is stopped.

24,954. By the buyer?—Yes; some times it is stopped, and more times it is given.

24,955. It is stopped out of the price contracted by him to pay?—Yes. If they see a miserly person they stop it, but if they see a man with an open disposition they leave it to himself, and expect more.

24,956. In cattle it is never stopped by the buyers?—Never, unless there is a case like that.

24,957. When contracting about the price of a head of cattle, do you think the seller ever contemplates the value of the luck-penny he has to give when fixing on the price he requires for the animal?—They often buy "clear to pocket" or something like that. Then the price is so much, and there is no luck-penny.

24,958. Have you ever heard of that in other fairs?—Yes; I often bought that way myself. It is very rarely it happens; you must get luck, no matter how it is.

24,959. Do you remember when the system of luck-penny was not in existence?—No. It was always in existence to my knowledge.

24,960. Do you remember when there was no such charge as sixpence on pigs?—There was always something given with pigs.

24,961. Had they ever a system of examining them for measles?—Yes, in old times, and they would return them. If you gave the buyers half a sovereign for the measles, they might take them back.

24,962. Then they cut down the price?—Yes.

24,963. That practice has gone out of existence?—Yes.

24,964. Do you remember when that practice was resorted to?—I remember, I think, one instance.

24,965. Was the sixpence luck-penny paid then, although the price was cut down subsequently?—It was.

24,966. You would not say the sixpence was first started as an equivalent to the reduction that was formerly made in the contract price for the measles or any animals affected with them?—I think not.

24,967. (Mr. Condon.) I think the rule was made to have sixpence deducted for the purpose of meeting the expense of any pigs subject to the disease.

24,968. You think, Mr. Condon, it owes its origin to that practice?—Yes, to the practice of returning pigs affected with measles. The buyers and public made an agreement to stop sixpence on each pig sold as an equivalent for any inconvenience caused by a pig having the measles.

24,969. Examination of Mr. Hutson continued.

24,970. Is that the only deduction from the contract price of the pig?—Yes.

24,971. Is that deducted, no matter what is the size or value of the pig?—For any pig value over 2l.

24,972. Did you know of a smaller luck-penny on pigs being deducted?—Yes; a penny when dealers buy pigs for one or two pounds.

24,973. It is regulated by the value of the pig; over 2l. it is sixpence, and under 2l. it is less?—Yes.

24,974. Is this system of luck-penny on sheep?—Decidedly.

24,975. How is that regulated?—It is a matter of contract; threepence each on an average.

24,976. And on calves?—Something like that.

Mr. John Hanrahan examined.

24,977. Are you a trader in the town?—Yes.

24,978. Do you think the practice at present existing of holding the markets on the public thoroughfare and the streets is satisfactory to the traders of the town?—I do.

24,979. Do you think the farmers would like a removal of them—the fairs—to a properly enclosed fair green, and the markets to a properly enclosed and covered market building?—They might prefer it if they had nothing to pay.

24,980. Had you any discussion with them?—A good many.

24,981. Do not you think the farmers would pay a charge if they got an adequate return in the way of accommodation?—Is it to ask us?

24,982. If the market authority, whoever that might be, provided proper market and buildings with shelter accommodation, do you think the farmers would object to pay?—I think on no consideration would they pay tolls, no matter what it was. It would destroy the whole town, and they would go to a place where they would not have tolls to pay.

24,983. Do they always consider, when bringing their commodities to the market, whether they have to pay toll or not?—Yes. They wanted to have the crane to go to my yard to weigh in order to get it done free. I am in the habit of buying oats and storing it in my yard, and they wanted to weigh there, so that they would not have to pay at the crane.

24,984. Have you any other observations to make?—I think the market is in the proper place to have it.

24,985. That is, on the public thoroughfare?—Yes.

24,986. Would not you say that in wet weather some of the commodities are damaged and injured by exposure?—I do not know.

24,987. You are a trader in the town?—I am.

24,988. It is for trade purposes you would object to a removal?—Not altogether, but I know very well the markets would not be so well attended if they had to pay tollage for a new market.

24,989. Have you any suggestions to offer?—No suggestions. I think it would be an injury to the town and the trade of the town if the market were removed.

Mr. Bernard Kearney, Town Commissioner, examined.

24,990. Have you any observations to offer relative to the markets or fairs here, or any general observations as regards the markets and fairs throughout the country?—I think no change could be made that would be a benefit to the market here so far as my opinion goes. I think when people come in with commodities the less they have to pay the more satisfactory it is for them. As Mr. Hannigan wisely remarks, they go to places to get their corn and potatoes weighed for nothing if possible in order to avoid paying a penny a sack to the market-house.

24,991. Do you think a necessity exists for a public scale and weighbridge; do you think trade would be carried on more satisfactorily if all commodities brought to the market were weighed at a public scale and weighbridge?—I think a weighbridge would be an advantage to parties bringing large quantities of goods, but for sacks of corn and potatoes there is every accommodation to have them weighed.

24,992. But Mr. Hannigan has mentioned that some farmers bringing in their produce go to him and to others sooner than go to the public scales to weigh there; but if there was a rule restraining private weighing, and all commodities were weighed at a public and independent scale, do you think that would work better and more satisfactorily and more honest dealing between buyer and seller?—I don't know.

24,993. Have you ever heard of any inaccuracy in the weights ascertained at private scales?—No. I never heard of any.

24,994. Have you ever heard of any inaccuracy in the public scales?—No. The police visit them occasionally.

Mr. John Brophy examined.

24,995. I believe you have a weighbridge in front of Mr. Donnelly's market-house?—Yes. If Mr. Donnelly would have control it would be satisfactory and there would be no difficulty. It is the principal drawback to the present system. Thirty years ago, as Mr. Hatton says, the markets were better than they are now, and if the market was outside then it ought to be doubly more convenient now. Besides, I can't see where the money is to be got to get a covered-in shed. We are limited to a shilling in the pound on township property, and it would be a drag on the township to get these sheds which we could not afford. My idea is to have a weighbridge erected. I have perfect confidence in Mr. Donnelly's weighing, and if the weighbridge was there nothing would be wanted.

24,996. Is this market a wholesale market or do they sell to the traders of the town?—They sell to everyone. Some women go and buy commodities and retail them about the town; others buy for consumption. It is a general market.

24,997. Can a labouring man go to the market and buy a half stone of potatoes if he requires it?—He can.

24,998. Have they got a scale to weigh them out?—Mr. Donnelly will weigh a half stone at any time.

24,999. Does he levy any charge?—Sixpence a barrel.

25,000. Will he weigh in small quantities?—Yes. They pay him sixpence.

25,001. For the entire barrel?—Yes.

25,002. No matter how often they utilise the scales?—Yes. I have often bought 20 barrels of oats and sent them up to Mr. Donnelly's to be weighed, and go with them, because if weighed by me they might not be satisfied.

25,003. You think a public scale would be the best appliance in the town, and would be more satisfactory for weighing than a seller weighing at his own scale?—Yes. It would satisfy everyone. There is one other observation I wish to make. Owing to the periodical [illegible] of the town I think it would be a great hardship on the poor women selling fish to run them into a fish market and confine them to one place. Supposing the boats came in this evening the women would have to run to get the fish for their supper, and if there was a market they may not sell it. I can corroborate Mr. Flusberry's statement. I had a knowledge of fairs for 20 years, and I have seen stock coming through fair-green gates cruelly knocked about, and inconvenience caused to the owners of cattle, and the cattle stopped or held until the tolls were paid. That is a great inconvenience and it causes great dissatisfaction.

Mr. Robert Philpott examined.

25,004. Have you any suggestions to offer as to what you think would lead to the better management and working of the markets and fairs?—I can offer no [illegible] other than what you have heard in evidence. I know, as far as I can form an opinion, the existing accommodation is ample for the business with one exception, and that is the want of a weighbridge. That of course is a serious want. Where loads of hay or straw are sold in the town to rather a limited [illegible] it would not be a very remunerative thing to [illegible] weighbridge for the purpose, but it is occasionally a matter of serious importance, and deters people fro[illegible] bringing hay and straw to the town. The Messrs. Kavins are very obliging to allow loads to be weighed on their weighbridge, but there is a slope to be driven over near the life-boat bridge, and the noise of their feet frightens the horses when they required to be stopped. As for shelter in the market, it would be difficult to provide and afterwards not be of any great value. I have not heard complaints about the weighing in the market. I believe there is the greatest confidence in Mr. Donnelly, and I have not heard anyone entertain an idea that there is a want of confidence or anything in that respect. If what Mr. Storey suggested could be carried out, it would meet the public wishes and requirements—that is, to have in conjunction with the existing weighing apparatus a weighbridge under Mr. Donnelly's control.

25,005. Have you heard any complaints that any of these perishable commodities have been depreciated in value or quantity by exposure?—I have not.

25,006. Have you ever heard that accidents have happened by the fact of the fairs and markets being held on the public thoroughfare?—I am not aware. Mr. Conlan has referred to one, but I do not know of an instance. Street accidents would occur apart from the fairs.

25,007. Have you anything else to say?—I wish to remark that the levying of tolls would have an injurious effect on the markets and fairs.

25,008. Have you had any experience of other markets and fairs?—I have not. My experience is limited in that respect.

Mr. John Evans examined.

25,009. (Witness.) I have a thorough knowledge of the town of Arklow for the past 30 years, and I think the market-house is in the most central place in the town, but yet I believe it would be a great advantage to have a weighbridge. I have heard some objection by Mr. Philpott about the horses going to the weighbridge of the Messrs. Kavins, and if a weighbridge were in the market-house it would do away with his objection. There would be no want of confidence in Mr. Donnelly. At the same time I would suggest other improvements that is as to commodities left in the streets—vegetables for instance. We go down the street and find in various parts cabbages and potatoes on the ground, and no covering over them, and I have seen dogs commit nuisance on these vegetables, which is not what it ought to be. There is no protection to keep these things clean. I think that is a drawback which ought to be remedied if it could be. As for having an enclosed market-house, I fear the funds of the Commissioners would not afford it. A rate of one shilling in the pound produces 180*l*., and to make an enclosed market-house it would be rather expensive. I would further wish to remark the way the public are treated when they go to buy their commodities. It is a matter over which Mr. Donnelly has no control. If I go down to buy a few barrels of potatoes women about that market-house will interfere with me, and say they were beautiful potatoes. She has never seen them; and once on buying those potatoes I found they were not fit for human food; they were frost-bitten.

25,010. Practically these women are brokers?—Yes.

25,011. But has not the purchaser his own experience to guide him in the selection of the article he buys?—Not so much. The women have a very good use of the tongue.

25,012. Is their persuasive influence so great as to make you buy a bad article?—It is deterring, and I would give these people money myself to buy potatoes sooner than go into the market. There was an enclosed market built here some years ago nearly opposite the church. It was started by shareholders, and the thing created it did not take. That is a covered-in place, and it is existing still, but not used as a market-house. It is now private property.

25,013. How is it utilised?—It belongs to Mr. Dowleigh. I am one of the original shareholders.

25,014. What business is done in it?—It is a hotel. It would not be near so central as Mr. Donnelly's.

25,015. When was that building erected?—The lease was granted in 1854, and the building immediately commenced.

25,016. The gentlemen who took part in that old proposal must have deemed that a necessity existed for a market building in the town?—They did; that was the object of building the place. It was a speculation and it failed.

25,017. What was the original capital subscribed?—700*l*. or 800*l*. in 10*l*. shares.

25,018. What are the shareholders receiving from that?—6½ per cent., but not as a market. It is a private concern now.

Mr. Murray examined.

25,019. Have you ever sold stock at fairs where tolls were levied?—I never sold anywhere, except at Gorey and Coolgreany.

25,020. Do you think, as a farmer, when you are bringing your stock to fairs at which tolls are levied that in fixing the contract price the buyer would give you less than if the fairs were toll free?—I firmly believe a buyer would give me as little as he could.

25,021. Do you think in fixing the price he considers the toll he has to pay?—I believe he would. A weighbridge would be very badly wanted here if it could be erected.

Mr. Brennan examined.

25,022. Are you a farmer?—Yes.

25,023. Do you agree in the observations of Mr. Murray?—Yes.

25,024. Is there any other gentleman who has any observations to make relative to the inquiry in Arklow?—No answer.

A Memorial.

25,025. (Mr. Fitz-Henry.) There is a memorial which I wish to lay before you as regards the establishment of a fair in the village of Ovoca. It is a memorial of the inhabitants.

25,026. He then produced the memorial, of which the following is a copy:—

To John J. O'Meara, Esq.,
Assistant Commissioner.

Memorial of the Principal Inhabitants residing in the immediate vicinity of the village of Ovoca, county Wicklow.

Your Memorialists show that there is a great necessity existing for a monthly fair in the village of Ovoca.

Ovoca is an important village situate about five miles from each of following towns respectively, viz., Arklow, Rathdrum, and Aughrim; there is no fair held at any place nearer to Ovoca than foregoing towns. There is a railway station in village, also petty sessions court, post-office, constabulary barrack, and Roman Catholic and Protestant places of worship.

Since Ovoca became a railway station the petty sessions court was transferred from village of Redcross, a village about three miles distant, in which a fair had always been held up to about 15 years since, when the fair of Redcross ceased to be attended, owing to its being situated at a considerable distance from a railway station, consequently a great want has since that period existed for a fair in village of Ovoca. Therefore your Memorialists earnestly desire that a fair should be established in said village of Ovoca, and that facilities be given to us to legally establish such fair without incurring the large cost and expense necessary in such cases.

Dated this 29th November 1888.

(Signed) James Germaine, P.P.
Andrew O. Hudson, medical doctor, &c.
Nicholas Barry, D.D., Ovoca.
J. N. Robinson, clk., rector of Ovoca.
R. Walsh, capt., J.P., Ovoca Lodge, Ovoca.
James Higgins, mines manager.
Matt. H. Jones, [illegible] Hill, Ovoca, county coroner.
George Tuke, farmer.
Jas. Levingston, farmer.
Richard Murphy, farmer.
John Brown.
Francis Hagan, farmer.
Geo. Hanley, farmer.
John Meagher, farmer.
William Tuke, farmer.
John Kavanagh, farmer.
Samuel Smith, farmer.
Edward Doyle, farmer.
Nicholas Dunne, woollen manufacturer.
James Birch, farmer.
John Brennan, farmer.
Thomas Gill, shopkeeper, Ovoca.
William Farrer, farmer.
Patrick Moore, farmer.
J. Howard Brooke, J.P.
Edward Bury, farmer.
Michael Clarke, farmer.
William T. [illegible], Ovoca, farmer.
James Murphy, farmer.
John Kendall, farmer, Kilmacurragh.
James Murphy, [illegible].
Charles James FitzHenry, Solicitor, Ovoca, town clerk of Arklow, and farmer.

GOREY.

With reference to my inquiry in Gorey on the 3rd day of December 1888, I beg to report as follows:—

Gorey is situated in the county of Wexford, and is a station on the Dublin, Wicklow, and Wexford Railway line. The town is prosperous, and has a fair trade in agricultural produce. Town Commissioners administer the local affairs, and the population is 2,450.

The market day is Saturday. The fairs for 1889 will be held on Wednesday, 2nd January; Saturday, 26th January (last Saturday of the month); Saturday, 2nd March (Shrove Fair); Saturday, 16th March (St. Patrick's Fair); Saturday, 20th April (Easter Saturday); Saturday, 11th May (2nd Saturday of the month); Saturday, 1st June (1st day of the month); Saturday, 22nd June; Saturday, 13th July; Saturday, 3rd August (1st Saturday of the month); Saturday, 31st August (last Saturday of the month); Saturday, 28th September (last Saturday of the month); Saturday, 26th October (last Saturday of the month); Saturday, 30th November (last Saturday of the month); Saturday, 14th December (2nd Saturday before Christmas).

A pig fair is held the day previous to the ordinary fair, except Good Friday Fair, which is held on the Thursday previous.

The Town Commissioners make the necessary alterations in the dates each year.

There are no tolls levied at the markets or fairs, but at the former weighing charges are payable if any commodities are weighed.

The market charges are the property of the Town Commission. There does not seem to have been any express authority for the markets or fairs in Gorey, as in Wicklow and Arklow. The fair on the second Saturday before Christmas was established about three years ago, and the fair on 22nd June was removed from Ballycanew about two years ago. The other fairs have been held for a lengthened period.

There is no scale of the weighing charges erected for public inspection, but a weighing machine is available for weighing loads.

In accordance with my instructions I inspected the fair and market places.

The fairs are held on the public streets, and the animals, with the exception of the horses, intermix.

The markets are held on the public streets also, but there is a building provided which is utilized as a weigh-house. There is a beam and scales, and, as before mentioned, an council provided at this building for the accommodation of those frequenting the market, but the market-house does not afford sufficient space, &c., and as a necessity the streets are availed of.

A complaint was made of the inconvenience caused to some of the inhabitants of the town by reason of the fairs being held on the streets, but on the other hand a strong opinion was expressed that the general trade would be materially affected if the fairs were removed from their present site.

JOHN J. O'MEARA,
Assistant Commissioner.

45, Lower Mount Street, Dublin.

Gorey, 3rd December 1888.

Mr. Thomas O'Neill, Town Clerk, examined.

25,027. You are the town clerk of Gorey?—Yes.

25,028-9. When were the Town Commissioners established here?—I think it was in 1858 or 1859; about 30 years ago.

25,030. Are they the sanitary authority?—No.

25,031. Do they light and clean the town?—No, they have nothing to do with the cleansing; they do the lighting.

25,032. Do they manage the paving?—Yes; but they do not actually do paving, because they have the streets flagged. They get a grant from the grand jury for flagging the streets, and they have levied a charge on each person to pay portion of the expenses.

25,033. The Town Commissioners are the owners of any market rights that exist in Gorey?—Yes.

25,034. What is the market day here?—Saturday.

25,035. Is that the special day allotted off for the disposal and exposure of the different marketable commodities brought here to Gorey?—Yes.

25,036. There is no other day on which they are exposed?—There is no market day but that.

25,037. What fairs are held here?—15 every year.

25,038. Will you kindly mention the dates?—The first fair is on the 2nd January.

25,039. Is it always on the 2nd January?—Yes, these years past. The 1st of January is a holiday.

25,040. When is the next fair?—On the 26th January, and the others on the 2nd March, 18th March, 20th April, 11th May, 1st June, 22nd June, 13th July, 3rd August, 31st August, 28th September, 20th October, 20th November, and 14th December.

25,041. Are they always held on these dates?—They are; they vary a little.

25,042. Were they held on these dates, but not days, last year?—No; it is the days they are held on. The dates are the same, but the days vary. There is a meeting of the Town Commissioners held every year for the purpose of striking out the fairs each year with as little variation as possible. They fix on Saturday as the day of the fairs, so as not to clash with the neighbouring fairs.

25,043. There is a pig fair held the day previous to each fair, except Good Friday?—Yes, but the Good Friday fair is changed to the Thursday before Good Friday.

25,044. There are 15 fairs held here?—Yes.

25,045. Do you remember any period when there were less than 15?—I think only 14 about three years ago.

25,046. What one was added three years ago?—The second Saturday before Christmas was added.

25,047. Is it always the second Saturday before Christmas, that particular day?—Yes. There was another fair also added lately.

25,048. What other fair was added lately?—The [illegible] fair.

25,049. What date is that?—The 22nd June.

25,050. Were these the only two fairs added recently?—I think so.

25,051. Were the other 13 held for any length of time previous?—They were held as long as I remember. The fair in [illegible] was held in a field out the town, an annual fair, and for the convenience of buyers the Commissioners brought it into the town. It was very unpleasant to have such transactions done in the open field, where there was no houses.

25,052. Was it held any distance from the town?—A mile or a mile and a half.

25,053. When was it brought in here?—About ten years ago.

25,054. Who exercised any rights?—Lord Courtown. Tolls were levied; they were taken at the gap.

25,055. Are tolls levied at present?—No.

25,056. Then it was changed from being a toll fair to a toll-free one?—Yes.

25,057. Were the other 13 fairs held for any length of time?—From time immemorial.

25,058. The whole 13?—Yes.

25,059. Are all the 15 fairs now held on the same site?—Yes, on the streets.

25,060. Have you any particular streets allotted off for the exposure of the different species of animals?—No, only for the horse fair.

25,061. Do they all intermix,—the cattle, sheep, and pigs?—The pigs are the day previous to the cattle.

25,062. Do the cattle and sheep intermix?—Yes. They do not actually intermix; they are up and down, and the people have recognised places, though they are not bound to go to them.

25,063. Where are the markets held?—In the street too.

25,064. Have you any market buildings erected here?—Nothing but the market house.

25,065. There is a market house erected?—Yes.

25,066. How is that building utilised?—There is a public scales in it belonging to the Commissioners.

25,067. Who manages it?—I do. I am town clerk and weighmaster.

25,068. Have you anybody else to assist you there?—I do have a person on Saturday.

25,069. Do you give a ticket denoting the weight?—Yes.

25,070. You only perform the clerical work?—That is all.

25,071. What facilities do you afford for weighing the commodities. How many beams and scales have you?—Two; only one in use.

25,072. Have you a weighbridge?—Yes, there is one small.

25,073. Have you any small scales for retailing purposes?—No.

25,074. Is that the market building I passed coming up to the court-house—an open place?—Yes.

25,075. The markets are held outside?—Yes.

25,076. And the people expose all their commodities outside on the road?—Yes. The carts with potatoes and oats come in on the streets.

25,077. What charge do you levy at the markets?—A penny a draft for oats and potatoes and twopence a dozen for wool.

25,078. Have you got a list of the charges erected in the market place?—Yes.

25,079. Have you any here?—No, they are posted on the placard.

25,080. What other charges have you besides a penny a draft on potatoes and oats and twopence a stone for wool?—There would be twopence for a cask of butter and threepence on the weighbridge for weighing a load of hay or coal.

25,081. I suppose a load, irrespective of what the load might be?—Yes.

25,082. What other charges have you?—That is all.

25,083. Have you any standing charges?—No.

25,084. You levy nothing on the people standing on the street?—No.

25,085. Have you any portion of this market building cut off?—No.

25,086. Supposing they did not sell all their commodities on a market day and wished to store them up in this building, can they do so?—They might at their own risk, but they would not do it.

25,087. You would charge nothing if they did?—I was never asked to store them.

25,088. Would you have storage if it was required?—Yes. The butchers keep stalls there sometimes.

25,089. What do you receive from them?—I do not receive anything.

25,090. You allow them to avail themselves of it gratuitously?—Yes. It is the custom for them to [illegible] it.

25,091. As a shambles?—Yes.

25,092. Supposing a man came in with a load of potatoes in sacks and weighed each individual sack, what would you charge him if there were 12 in the load?—A penny for each sack.

25,093. If he weighed the entire load together at the [illegible], what would you charge?—Threepence.

25,094. If they only brought in two stone and weighed them at the scales what would you charge?—They would have to pay a penny.

25,095. No matter what the weight is to be weighed, or no matter the quantity, you charge a penny for oats or potatoes?—I would.

25,096. How are the potatoes bought by the people?—By the barrel.

25,097. What quantity does the barrel contain?—20 stone.

25,098. Do they always bring them in barrels?—Oh, no; in sacks.

25,101. You do not weigh under it?—No.

25,102. Do you give a cast of the beam when weighing?—Yes.

25,103. Must the board of the scales touch the ground?—No, except.

25,104. If it does not make up the seven pounds the buyer gets the benefit?—Yes.

25,105. If they brought in a sack that weighed 12 stone 5 pounds, you would put that down as 12 stone on the ticket?—That is all.

25,106. Do you always estimate the tare of the sack?—As a general rule the seller always allows half a stone to the buyer for the sack of potatoes.

25,107. So, then, if there was a sack of potatoes, the actual weight of which would be 12 stone 5 pounds, you would only put down as 11 stone and a half?—I would put 12 stone gross.

25,108. But the seller would only be paid for 11 stone and a half?—Yes.

25,109. Is the tare always estimated?—It is as a general rule. It is arranged between the buyer and seller.

25,110. You take no cognizance at all of the tare?—No.

25,111. But the practice is always to estimate it?—Yes.

25,112. In case of dispute between them, and their not agreeing to the tare, would you weigh the empty sack?—I would if they brought it into me.

25,113. Have you done so?—Yes.

25,114. Did you levy any additional charge?—No.

25,115. Supposing they brought potatoes to the market and exposed them for sale, and sold them, but did not weigh at your scales, would you ask for this charge?—No, it has never been done.

25,116. They have always weighed at your scales?—No. What I mean is the [illegible] never look for or enforce the charge.

25,117. You only receive this charge when you perform the service of weighing the commodity?—That is all.

25,118. Do you give a printed ticket denoting the gross weight?—Yes.

25,119. In weighing corn what is the lowest weight you use?—Four pounds and two pounds.

25,120. Do you always weigh down to two pounds?—Generally.

25,121. Is it the gross weight you put on the ticket?—Yes.

25,122. You never take any cognizance of the tare of a sack of corn?—No.

25,123. What is the customary allowance?—Some allow four pounds and more—a half stone—according to the sort of sack.

25,124. Would the deductions of seven pounds for a sack on ordinary occasions be the same on a very fine day as on an extremely wet day, when the sack was completely saturated with wet?—That would be between buyer and seller.

25,125. Do they allow anything additional in cases like that?—Well, sometimes I think they do.

25,126. Have you known cases to have occurred of your own knowledge?—I heard the buyer and seller dispute, saying the sack was wet, and to allow a quarter of a stone more. That would not interfere with me; it is no loss of mine.

25,127. It is the practice to leave it to any agreement they come to?—Yes.

25,128. There is no rule regulating that in the market place between buyers and sellers?—No.

25,129. No matter what quantity of corn they bring in you charge a penny a draft?—Yes.

25,130. Butter is brought in here too?—Sometimes.

25,131. Is firkin butter ever brought here?—Yes.

25,134. You have weighed casks and firkins in the market?—Yes.

25,135. Have you weighed firkins yourself?—I weighed tubs.

25,136. Do you tare the butter out of the tubs in order to drain them before weighing?—They tare them out. They take the butter completely out of the cask.

25,137. Down to what weight do you weigh butter?—Down to a pound.

25,138. Always?—Yes.

25,139. Is there any deduction from that weight you ascertain?—No.

25,140. You allow nothing for any butter that would cling to the casks or for scalings or salt?—No. I weigh it there by standing beam or thereabouts.

25,141. When weighing the firkin would you strip the butter?—No.

25,142. Would you drain it at all?—No. Just weigh it by gross weight.

25,143. You would only denote the gross weight on the ticket?—That is all.

25,144. What tare would be allowed between the buyer and seller for the firkin?—I could not say.

25,145. Is the tare ever branded by the cooper on the firkin?—I never saw it.

25,146. You have no cognizance at all of what the tare of a firkin of butter would be?—No. I suppose 18 or 19 pounds.

25,147. How is that regulated?—The seller allows it to the buyer for the weight of the tub.

25,148. 18 or 19 pounds?—Yes.

25,149. Must there be any given quantity in the gross weight before the 18 or 19 pounds are allowed?—They go by judgment and sometimes strip them and weigh them.

25,150. If there is any dispute you weigh?—Yes, but it is very seldom done. If the seller was not allowing enough to the buyer the buyer would object and have the timber weighed. There is more allowed on a 13 stone cask, I think it is 22 or 23 pounds.

25,151. Would you kindly mention the different marketable commodities brought into the market, whether you receive any charge on them or not?—I receive no charge for anything only what is weighed.

25,152. Kindly mention the different commodities?—Hay, straw, oats, barley, wheat, potatoes, wool, hay-seed, chickens, geese, vegetables, hides, turf, lime, eggs, butter, game, baskets, tubs.

25,153. What do they generally contain?—They are empty baskets and tubs for sale.

25,154. They expose all these commodities in the market place?—Yes, on the public street.

25,155. Do they erect any standings there?—They do sometimes.

25,156. On the roadside?—In the street. They occupy a space in the public street.

25,157. It is over the public street?—Yes.

25,158. Is the public thoroughfare completely obstructed?—No; they have a fine wide street, and they stand near the pathway. I think it would be well to mention that there have been places arranged for each commodity to be sold in the town, but unfortunately that has become very confused, and I do not think the arrangement is carried out.

25,159. Who regulated that order?—The Town Commissioners, 25 years ago.

25,160. Are there any printed rules regulating the market?—Yes; that is up outside the market house, but I think the print is obliterated.

25,161. Is it so placed that the public can read it?—Yes. I know I can read it myself.

25,162. Have you only one ticket to give denoting the weight of the commodities, or have you one for each commodity?—No; I have only one sort of ticket.

25,163. Is it a printed form?—Yes.

25,164. Do you keep a block of it?—Yes.

25,165. How long do you retain that block?—12 months.

25,166. There is no rule in the market prohibiting the sale of commodities unless they are weighed at your scales?—No.

25,167. They can sell to whom they please, and weigh where they please?—Yes.

25,168. You get no charge on such occasions?—No.

25,169. It is a merely voluntary feeling directs them to your scales?—Yes.

25,170. Is there any rule exhibited in the market place, whether printed or not, between buyer and seller, restraining the sale of any particular commodity, except through agents or brokers or runners?—No, I do not believe there is.

25,171. The farmers can sell to whom they please themselves?—Yes.

25,172. Do they expose butter on the roadside?—On the street.

25,173. Do you ever hear the farmers complain in inclement weather, or on a very warm day, that the butter deteriorated in quantity by exposure?—I never heard them say it. The butter does not come so plentifully except in summer time, except by women, who bring in seven or eight pounds.

25,174. Is it generally brought in rolls?—Yes.

25,175. And taken around to different people in the town?—Yes.

25,176. You receive no charge from those women?—No.

25,177. Do you ever weigh cattle at the scales?—No.

25,178. It is capable of weighing cattle?—No.

25,179. Supposing it was required from the Town Commissioners to make a periodical return of the current prices of those different commodities brought into the market place and exposed for sale on market day, do you think it could be kept? I am not asking you to do it, but would it be possible to make such a return?—I think it would.

25,180. When making up the weight in the ticket, do you ever make up the amount for the buyer and seller?—No, unless to oblige them.

25,181. Have you ever done so?—It is not customary.

25,182. Do they ever ask you?—I have been asked occasionally.

25,183. You hear the contract price agreed on?—I may.

25,184. Supposing it was required to make a return of the contract price or current price of the commodities. Is it possible to make such a return; in other words, do you think the buyer and seller would tell the truth if you inquired from them?—I would not believe them.

25,185. Had you ever reason to doubt them?—I had, hundreds of times.

25,186. Would you be afraid it would entail more labour?—It is not that.

PATRICK BYRNE, Esq., Chairman of the Town Commissioners, examined.

25,187. You are the chairman of the Town Commis- | sioners with shelter accommodation?—It has been talked

25,192. That is a building where proper shelter accommodation would be afforded for the different commodities?—Yes.

25,193. In a case like that, supposing it was erected, would you be in favour of a rule restraining the sale of any commodity elsewhere than in that place?—That would be a very serious thing to do. It would be a great accommodation to the town to have a place for vegetables, fish, and meat; but then you [illegible] the corn coming into the town and the produce of the farmers, is that what you mean?

25,194. No, but a rule restraining the exposure of commodities elsewhere, so that some would not avail themselves of the market place, and others go where they wished?—I do not think the people of the town would have it so strict.

25,195. When you say the people of the town, would you say the traders?—The traders and farmers.

25,196. Does not the fact of the markets being held on the public street occasion much filth and dirt?—They do.

25,197. Who cleans that?—The contractor.

25,198. Have you ever heard complaints that he neglected his duty?—No.

25,199. Do they cause any obstruction to people passing to and fro?—It does sometimes, but the market does not last long.

25,200. Would you say the traders of the town approve of the present system of holding the markets on the streets?—The people do not make any complaint about it.

25,201. If any grievance exists the traders would put up with any inconvenience for trade purposes?—Yes. Traders would like to be as supple and obliging as possible to the people coming to the market. If a person comes and stands outside the door they would let him stand for an hour or two hours, and then his cart would go away into the main street or any other street.

25,202. Do the police regulate the order in the market?—The police, and Mr. O'Neill, and the town inspector.

25,203. Is this a good market town?—It is pretty good.

25,204. You never keep any record here in the Town Commissioners' office of the quantity of the different commodities brought in?—No return at all, except we may get a return from the railway of the number of pigs taken out of the fair.

25,205. Do you keep any record of the markets?—No record, only from the scales.

25,206. Do you think the weighing at a public scale is better, and leads to more honest dealing between the buyer and seller than to have the weight ascertained at a private scale?—I think it is. It would be a great matter to have that state of things existing.

25,207. Would you approve of, or do you think a necessity exists for a rule restraining the weighing of commodities elsewhere than at a public and independent scale?—I think the feelings of the Commissioners were that all corn coming into the market, and sold in the market, should be weighed at a public scale.

25,208. What was the reason they assigned for that suggestion. Did they ever hear any complaints of any dishonest weighing at private scales?—The idea was it would be a benefit to the town.

25,209. They would only require such byelaw for the purpose of increasing the revenue?—Yes.

25,210. It is not for any public convenience that might be derived from it?—I think not.

25,211. It was purely their desire to increase the revenue that actuated them in that suggestion?—Yes; for instance, we have a town rate, and do all we can to give accommodation to the public. It is very hard when the people come and sell that they give no benefit to the public scales or the ratepayers of the town.

25,212. Did you ever hear complaints from the buyer or seller that the accurate weight has not been ascertained at any of the private scales?—I could not answer that directly.

25,213. Individually, do you think it would be better, leaving aside your capacity as chairman of the Town Commissioners and your desire to augment the funds of the Commission, do you think it would be better to have all commodities weighed at a public scale where they would act independently of buyer and seller?—I think it would, and if put into practice in a short time the people at large would be satisfied.

25,214. Have you ever heard any inaccuracies in the public scale?—No; it is tested every year.

25,215. The police always call on the ordinary occasions?—Yes.

25,216. Do you think the fact that no charges are levied on these marketable commodities brought into this market, except when weighed, tends to develop the market or to increase it?—I think if all corn or produce was weighed at the public scales it would not interfere with the markets—the increase or decrease of the supply from the country.

25,217. Is that because they have no other place to go to?—No. Any trader in the town who buys oats weighs it in his own shed.

25,218. Would necessity compel the farmers to come here to Gorey?—No. There are two other markets.

25,219. Within easy reach of them?—Yes. Enniscorthy is the nearest, and Arklow.

25,220. You would not say if a toll was levied, or a charge on the commodities brought in, that that would act as a deterrent on people bringing their commodities into the market?—I do not think it would make much difference.

25,221. That is as to Gorey in particular. Have you any experience of other markets but Gorey?—No.

25,222. You have no tolls at the fairs?—No.

25,223. Were tolls ever levied at the fairs in Gorey?—I do not think they were.

25,224. Do you remember when there was a lesser number than the 12 fairs that have been named?—As long as I remember there were always 12.

25,225. Always held on the street?—Yes.

25,226. And tolls never levied at any of them?—Never.

25,227. Have you anything else to say?—There is a grievance as to hawkers going about with cars selling goods. They come on the centre of the street and occupy space. They come there and sell as well as shopkeepers who pay taxes. It is a grievance that these people could not be taxed, or something put on them.

25,228. Is that a grievance of the shopkeepers?—Yes.

25,229. Who trade in similar commodities?—Yes.

25,230. Are these hawkers?—Yes.

25,231. Are they licensed hawkers?—Yes, they must be licensed.

25,232. They do not reside in Gorey?—No.

25,233. They erect standings on the street?—Yes, and put a cover over them.

25,234. What commodities do they expose there?—Drapery goods and hardware, boots and shoes.

25,235. Is it on market day they come?—On market days and fair days as well.

Major-General [illegible], J.P., examined.

The person I was told this by bought a bullock, and absolutely refused to take it when injured. I do not see what advantage it is to anybody to have these fairs on the streets. It is a disgraceful condition of things, and if this Commission on Markets and Tolls had any way of meeting the difficulty it would be a great advantage to the town as well as to those outside it.

25,237. Do you think the most suitable place to hold the fairs is a fair green, properly enclosed?—I am told with respect to that, for I have been making inquiries, that a large space of the ground at the top of the town was originally intended for a fair green, and they considered it inconvenient and it fell into disuse.

25,238. Do you think an enclosed fair green is the proper place apart from its suitability?—The public streets is not the proper place.

25,239. You have heard cases of animals being injured?—I know two.

25,240. Have they been recent?—It was when I first began to speak against them.

25,241. The buyer refused to complete his contract in consequence of the injuries sustained by the animal?—Yes. Mine is hearsay evidence. What I have said was told me, but I have no doubt the person who told me will come forward and speak, if necessary. His name is Mr. Redmond, of Mill Mount.

25,242. Have you had any experience of fairs other than those held in Gorey?—No.

25,243. Have you heard from any great number of people complaints of the fairs being held in the streets?—Yes, and the churchwardens would be here only he is very ill. I speak on behalf of a public body.

25,244. Have they discussed this?—Yes. Indeed we have.

25,245. Were any representations made to the Town Commissioners to provide a fair green?—Yes.

25,246. With what result?—That they had no power.

25,247. Do the same observations apply to the markets as are they confined to the fairs?—Yes, only about the cattle. You can picture to your own mind the cattle casting their filth on the pavement, and in wet weather it remains there, and that causes the danger.

25,248. Do they come on the pathway as well as on the road?—Yes.

25,249. Your body have control over the school?—Yes.

25,250. Do the children get a holiday on fair day?—Yes, to avoid any accidents. It is a national board school, and the rule used to be to give a whole holiday to the schools on a fair day and a half-holiday on Saturdays. There is one thing, the schools were used for preparation for Sunday schools. I have seen children coming for the examinations previous to Sunday, and in this respect there is the greatest complaint. Ladies coming there have to get some kindly hand to get the cattle away, and then with considerable difficulty they get in on tip-toe.

Mr. Peter R[illegible] examined.

25,251. Have you any experience of the fairs here?—Yes.

25,252. Do you ever buy and sell?—Yes.

25,253. What trade are you in?—The grocery business.

25,254. Do you object to the removal of the fairs?—By all means.

25,255. Is that because it would injure your trade?—No, because where I am situated, they are no benefit to me, but it would injure other traders.

25,256. Have you heard complaints that any animals were injured or that accidents happened to the people or children of the town?—Yes one.

25,257. Is the dirt cleaned off the street immediately after the fair?—It is not, and it should be.

25,258. I suppose the traders have to perform that duty very often themselves?—Yes, if it is on their path opposite the door, but what General Gahan speaks about is the church and school.

25,259. Have the children who attend there been in any great danger from the animals in the fair?—They generally get a holiday on a fair day.

25,260. Is that to save them from accident?—It is the usual rule to give them a holiday.

25,261. Have you had any conversations with the farmers concerning it?—I had not, but my own experience is that they cannot go elsewhere, because the buyers will not go.

25,262. Supposing a suitable fair green was provided for all cattle, and a rule restraining the sale or exposure of cattle except in this fair green, the buyers must necessarily go to the fair green to purchase. Do you think that would work better than the present system?—I do not think so.

25,263. Will not the buyers go to the place where the supply of cattle is to be had?—Naturally.

25,264. Have they got the system of luck-penny at these fairs?—Yes.

25,265. Is there any rule regulating the value of the luck-penny between buyer and seller?—No.

25,266. It is left to the disposition of the seller?—Yes, except on pigs.

25,267. There is something fixed on pigs?—Yes, sixpence a pig.

25,268. In the case of cattle the contract price is paid, and subsequently the seller gives the luck-penny to the buyer?—Yes.

25,269. Is the same course adopted with reference to pigs or does the buyer stop it?—It is stopped on pigs.

25,270. What gave rise to stopping that sixpence?—I do not know.

25,271. Did they ever stop anything in days gone by for measles in pigs?—They used to do it. The sixpence is for that.

25,272. As matter of fact you state that the sixpence is given as an equivalent for any deduction made for disease in the pigs?—It is.

25,273. That sixpence is always paid?—Yes, these 20 years.

Mr. William Graham, Town Commissioner, examined.

25,274. You are connected with the farming interest?—Yes.

25,275. You buy and sell at the fairs?—Yes.

25,276. Supposing a properly enclosed fair green was provided here with sufficient shelter accommodation and accommodation for displaying your stock, would you object to paying a small charge for that accommodation?—I think the farmers of the neighbourhood are well satisfied with the fairs the way they are arranged at the present [illegible].

25,277. What reason do you give for that?—The fair green is not wanted. There was a fair green heretofore, and the Enniscorthy farmers who resorted to the town would not have it at all. There is ample accommodation in the town of Gorey for sheep, bullocks, or anything that comes into it.

25,278. What accommodation?—Every aspect. There is a fine street going to the railway, and other streets, and I for one protest against having a fair green.

25,279. Is that as a farmer?—Yes, I farm 175 acres of land.

25,280. You have never known a case where your stock have been injured?—Never. Not one of them ever met with a mishap.

25,281. Has a buyer been at any loss by stock sold to him being subsequently injured?—None whatever. I never heard of a beast falling on their knees.

25,282. Have you ever heard such happened?—I might if a beast is walking up the public street and another beast at her. Last Saturday, in the same convenient place, a beast was knocked down and broke her [illegible], and it was not in the fair at all. That occurs with cattle where they rush at each other.

25,283. When this rush happened on the public street were passengers going to and fro?—This was not in the public street.

25,284. Did you ever buy cattle by live weight?—No.

25,285. Did you ever sell them by live weight?—Never.

25,286. Do you think it would be a better course for you then to sell them under the present system?—I would sooner buy them and not have them weighed at all.

25,287. In that case would you have the advantage over the seller in estimating the weight of the animal?—I would not buy a cow by the weight.

25,288. You think you could make an accurate estimation of the value of the animal?—Yes.

Mr. [illegible] Furse examined.

25,289. Have you anything to say relative to the observations already made?—I am a butcher, and I hold 150 acres of land. I have a business house in the town, and I buy a good deal of cattle and sheep.

25,290. Have you any suggestions to offer in support of, or in opposition to, the suggestions already made today?—I have, in opposition to General Gows.

25,291. What remarks have you to advance in support of your opposition, or what reasons have you?—I am buying cattle and sheep at that end of the town as long as I remember and I never remember an accident happened to cattle for sale on the public street, and the whole affair that General Gows opposes is the dirt in having the cattle there. The whole affair that General Gows speaks of is the nuisance of the cattle.

25,292. You acknowledge that the dirt accumulates?—Certainly, from the droppings of the cattle.

25,293. Would the traders put up with the inconvenience of that for trade purposes?—Certainly they would. Is it right to come and move the cattle out of the street the people are living in?

25,294. Is it purely for trade purposes that you oppose any suggestion of the removal?—I am opposed to any removal. I am here on behalf of the farmers and the people of the town.

25,295. Have they discussed this?—Do not I know it all my life time?

25,296. Have they discussed the advisability of retaining the fairs in their present place or removing them?—Never heard them.

25,297. Then you are only speaking your own mind?—Yes. Any move of the fairs would be worse for the people.

25,298. Have you any experience of other places where a fair green was provided?—I have of Tinahely. It is a small place where 60 cattle would not fit.

25,299. Is there a toll there?—No toll. I know Enniscorthy also.

25,300. Is there a fair green in Enniscorthy?—There is a fair green, but it is not used. If I wanted to buy a beast, and could get it near me, I was not going to go half a mile away.

25,301. Did you ever attend a fair where tolls were levied?—Never. That would not work at all here. You would destroy the place altogether if you meddle with the fairs.

25,302. Do you think if a toll was levied here or in any place it acts as a deterrent on the farmer bringing in his stock?—Certainly.

25,303. Have you known where such happened from your conversations with the farmers?—I know a place where there was a fair and tolls, and the people would not go there.

25,304. Was there no good a market or fair within easy reach of them?—They sold in the street.

25,305. You mean they avoided the fair green?—Yes; what would bring them in there.

J. A. Scott, Esq., T.C., solicitor, examined.

25,306. (Witness.) I do not think you can have fairs in a country town except on the square. I think that is the opinion of everyone who knows the country towns and live in them; but I think there ought to be a protection put up outside the footpaths in front of the church and schools.

25,307. Why in country towns more particularly than in others should the fairs be held on the streets?—Because the practical experience of everyone is that fairs will not take except they are in the town.

25,308. Have you anything further to say?—I am also of opinion that to levy tolls at markets or fairs would injure the market or fair.

25,309. Have you had experience of these yourself?—Only in Enniscorthy and here.

25,310. Are tolls levied at the fairs in Enniscorthy?—No.

25,311. From your experience of the farmers coming in, do you think where tolls are levied a radical reduction or abolition would tend to improve the fairs?—It would increase the quantity of stock.

25,312. Have you ever heard the farmers speaking on that point?—Well, I cannot remember any particular case. I think also that anything sold by weight in the town should be weighed at a public scales.

25,313. Have you heard objections to the private weighing?—Well, I believe public weighing would be considered more generally satisfactory by the sellers.

25,314. The buyers and sellers would be more satisfied to have a public and independent scale, than one which might be influenced by one of the contracting parties?—Yes; I also think pigs should be weighed on the public scales.

25,315. No cattle have ever been weighed here within your knowledge?—No.

Mr. Peter Murphy examined.

25,316. (Witness.) I am a farmer interested in the trade of the town very much.

25,317. Do you think the people of the country should sell cattle, sheep, and pigs by weight?—I think a person knowing nothing about cattle should sell by weight, and know what they would be worth.

25,318. You think some persons are at the mercy of the other contracting party?—Yes.

25,319. Do you think it the better course as a farmer to sell by live weight?—Certainly.

25,320. Had you ever any conversation with the buyers on that system?—I had.

25,321. Do they object to it, as a rule?—They do.

25,322. Are they more experienced in estimating the value of the animal than the farmer?—Yes. I would be safer by selling by weight.

25,323. Did you ever sell any by live weight?—No.

25,324. Why?—Because we have no means of weighing here.

25,325. Do you think if the means were provided you would sell by live weight?—I think it would be acquired [illegible].

25,326. Were any representations ever made to the Commissioners to put the ordinary railings around the present weighbridge to make it available for weighing cattle?—I am not aware of any.

25,326. Do you think that would be an improvement to the farmers?—Yes.

25,327. As a farmer, where would you like to dispose of your cattle?—Where I could get the best price for them.

25,328. Supposing you found the demand on a fair green equal to the demand on the streets, would you prefer to sell them on a fair green?—I would go to the green in a fair green.

25,329. Would you object to pay a small charge to cover the maintenance of a fair green?—I would not.

25,330. Do you think it safer for your cattle?—Yes; safer for the cattle than on the flags and streets.

25,331. Do you think if such a place was provided that the farmers would bring in a larger quantity of stock?—I do not think the stock would increase, no matter what provision you make, but they would go where they would be safer.

25,332. And would have no objection to pay a small charge for the cost of maintenance?—They would not.

25,333. Are you satisfied as a farmer with the present arrangement such as it exists?—Well, I am personally.

25,334. You would like to see an improvement you have just mentioned?—Yes, a place for the weighing of cattle.

25,335. And you would prefer to dispose of cattle in a place and not on the public road?—Yes.

Mr. M. J. Graham examined.

25,336. (Witness.) There is one thing I can say, the people of Gorey are satisfied with the fairs and markets, and would be dissatisfied if the fairs were moved out of the town of Gorey, because there is the very best accommodation for every man that comes to sell or buy.

25,337. When you say everybody is satisfied, you mean the traders of Gorey?—I never heard one man, woman, or child complain of the fairs of Gorey. Everyone is well pleased, and there is the best accommodation. On a rainy day there is protection for everyone, and if they were in a field there would be no protection whatever.

25,338. The traders of the town have no objection to the fairs being held on the street?—Not at all.

25,339. Did you ever hear any objections from the private inhabitants of the town?—Not one; I only heard everyone speak in the highest terms.

25,340. And the farmers?—I have someone in every county in Ireland, and everyone is well pleased with the accommodation in Gorey.

25,341. Did they ever suggest any improvement?—There could not be any improvement.

Mr. Thomas O'Neill, the Town Clerk, re-examined.

25,342. (Witness.) I have a remark to make. It is not just to the town that parties who bring in corn and potatoes should leave them outside the market-house and go away without weighing in the market-house.

25,343. That suggestion was made by the chairman of the Town Commissioners, who, when asked if they would like some rule or regulation compelling all commodities to be weighed at the crane, stated it was their intention or the desire of the Commissioners to augment their revenue?—Yes.

25,344-6. Is there any other gentleman who has any observations to make?—No answer.

A vote of thanks to the Assistant Commissioner brought the proceedings to a close.

ENNISCORTHY.

With reference to my inquiry in Enniscorthy on the 4th day of December 1888, I beg to report as follows:—

Enniscorthy is situated on both banks of the river Slaney, in the county of Wexford. The principal portion of the town is built on the side of a steep hill on the right bank of the river. The general trade is good, as there are some mills, a manufactory, and corn stores in the town. It is a station on the Dublin, Wicklow, and Wexford railway line, and the local government is vested in town commissioners. The population is 5,666.

The market days are Thursday and Saturday. The fairs are held on the 21st January, 21st February, 21st March, 25th April, 10th May, 7th June, 5th July, 1st August, 26th August, 19th September, 10th October, 15th November, and 21st December. A pig fair is held the day previous to the ordinary fairs.

There are no tolls levied at the markets or fairs, but at the former weighing charges are levied. Formerly tolls were levied in Enniscorthy, but their collection was abandoned about 1838 by the owners.

The owner of the markets rights is the Earl of Portsmouth, who has them sub-let to a Mr. Thomas Moran at a nominal rent, namely, 5s. a year. There was one patent granted for the town of Enniscorthy; it is dated the 8th June 1611, and authorised Sir H. Wallop to hold fairs on the 15th August and 8th September and a Thursday market. The markets and fairs held, therefore, without any express authority, are the Saturday markets and the fairs on the 21st January, 21st February, 21st March, 25th April, 10th May, 7th June, 5th July, 1st August, 10th October, 15th November, and 21st December.

The fairs on the 21st January, 21st February, 21st March, and 25th April were first established about 40 years ago, and the other fairs have been held for a lengthened period.

There is no schedule of the charges at the market erected for public inspection, neither is there a public weigh-bridge provided, but a private one is available when required.

In accordance with my instructions I have inspected the fair and market places.

The fairs are held on the streets in every part of the town. There was a fair green provided at one period of about six acres in extent, but the people did not avail themselves of it, and the fairs continued to be held through the streets. The site of the fair green has now been built upon.

The markets are held in the square. A market house with two large gate entrances is erected there, and used for weighing purposes, but the business generally is transacted in the square.

The average current prices of several marketable commodities are obtained each market day for the press by the weigh-master.

A complaint was made of the system of forestalling the sale of fowl before it is brought into the market.

JOHN J. O'MEARA,
Assistant Commissioner.

45, Lower Mount Street,
Dublin.

Enniscorthy, 4th December 1888.

Mr. THOMAS WILKINSON examined.

25,247. You are the town clerk of Enniscorthy?—Yes.

25,248. When were the town commissioners established?—First in 1851—that was under the Lighting and Cleansing Act—and then in 1866, when the Towns Improvement Act was introduced. They were appointed under that. Having read over your question, I might say the local authority or town commissioners have nothing in the world to do with the tolls, dues, or emoluments derived from the markets or fairs here.

25,249. They exercise no control whatever?—No control whatever, except make regulations.

25,250. You have passed byelaws, then, regulating them?—Yes.

25,251. Or is it merely to regulate the order of the market?—Yes, and assign the place for the article to be sold.

25,252. Who has control over the markets and fairs here?—The Earl of Portsmouth. I believe it is he appoints the craner or weigh-master in the market house where the goods are weighed.

25,253. What is the market day here?—Thursday and Saturday.

25,254. What fairs are held here?—There are 12 fairs in the year.

25,255. Could you mention the dates of them?—The 21st January, 21st February, 21st March, 25th April, 10th May, 7th June, 5th July, 1st and 26th August, 19th September, 10th October, 15th November, and 21st December. The pig fair is held the day preceding the ordinary fair always.

25,256. Where are these fairs held?—In every part of the town almost.

25,257. They are held on the streets of the town?—Yes.

25,258. No fair green is provided?—There was one provided, but the people never took to it or used it.

25,259. Are any tolls levied at these fairs?—None.

25,260. Are any charges levied at the market?—Not that I am aware of. I remember when there were tolls, but they were abolished in 1835.

25,261. Were tolls levied at the fairs?—I cannot distinguish, but they were levied at the markets on every article coming in.

25,262. Have the commissioners ever discussed the advisability of obtaining control of the markets and fairs?—I am not aware.

25,263. Did you bring my communication before them?—It was brought before them yesterday or the day before. They are here.

25,264. Did they discuss there the question of obtaining control over the markets and fairs?—I am sure they would be quite prepared to do it if there was any use in it, but they have no rights at present.

25,265. Do they think it would be desirable, and tend to the better management of the markets and fairs, if they were to exercise the control—the immediate control—over them?—I am not prepared to answer that. The fairs are distributed through the township, and the people are passing and repassing the business houses in the town, therefore the commissioners would wish to have the fairs as they stand.

25,266. Apart from that, would the commissioners think it desirable if they were to exercise control over the markets and fairs, and not have the control vested in a private individual?—I think it would be inadvisable to have any tolls in the market.

Mr. THOMAS MORAN examined.

25,267. You are the tenant to the Earl of Portsmouth for the market rights?—Yes.

25,268. What do you hold from him?—What is called the market crane. I am weigh-master.

25,269. What rent do you pay for it?—The small sum of 5s. a year.

25,270. Have you any market building there?—There is a building—the market house.

25,271. That is only utilised for weighing purposes?—Yes.

25,272. The markets are held in the public square?—Yes.

25,276. And no other descriptions of corn besides barley?—I charge on wheat per barrel, and oats a similar charge.

25,277. What do you charge on wool?—Fourpence a cwt.

25,278. If it is under a cwt.?—If it goes beyond four stone, about 2½d.

25,279. Supposing they brought in five stone of wool, what would you charge on that?—Twopence halfpenny—½d. a stone. It is a rule here for corn merchants to weigh in their own stores, and I only speak of what is brought to myself.

25,383. What do you charge?—About 2d. for about ½ cwt.

25,384. Supposing they brought a roll of butter containing four pounds?—They do not weigh with me.

25,385. What do they weigh with you; what quantity usually?—They very seldom weigh any.

25,386. Do they expose it out in the market square?—Yes.

25,387. What would you charge for weighing a cwt. of butter?—A penny or 2d.

25,388. How do you know whether to charge 1d. or 2d.?—By the weight.

25,389. What quantity would you weigh for 1d.?—Ten or 12 pounds.

25,390. If it was 14 pounds, would you charge 2d.?—No.

25,391. You exercise your discretion; you give and take?—Yes. I very seldom weigh any.

25,392. What other commodities do you weigh?—Wool, barley, oats, butter, bacon. The butter is principally weighed by the butter merchants.

25,393. Witness then produced a document showing the average prices, of which the following is a copy:—

ENNISCORTHY MARKET.

Thursday, 29th November 1888.

			s.	d.		s.	d.
Wheat, per barrel, 20 st.	-	-	16	0	to	18	0
Barley „ 16 st.	-	-	14	0	„	16	0
Oats „ 14 st.	-	-	7	6	„	8	6
Fine flour, per bag	-	-	33	0	„	—	
Seconds „	-	-	31	0	„	—	
Oatmeal, per cwt.	-	-	12	0	„	—	
Indian meal „	-	-	7	0	„	—	
Bran „	-	-	6	0	„	—	
Bacon „	-	-	65	0	„	—	
Butter, firsts „	-	-	80	0	„	—	
„ seconds „	-	-	75	0	„	—	
Beef, per lb.	-	-	0	6	„	0	7
Mutton „	-	-	0	7	„	0	8
Veal „	-	-	0	7	„	0	8
Potatoes, per stone	-	-	0	7	„	—	
Tobacco, per lb.	-	-	—			—	
Wool „	-	-	0	7	„	0	9

T. [illegible], Weigh-master.

25,394. Now, do you always ascertain the current prices of these different commodities?—I generally get them from the people in the trade.

25,395. Do you keep any record of them, or do you merely put them down in this document, and send them to the paper?—We generally send them to the local paper.

25,396. How often do you take them?—Every market day. The principal market day is Thursday.

25,397. What is your charge for weighing bacon?—About 1d. or 2d. a cwt.

25,398. What quantity for 1d.?—I would weigh eight stone for 1d.

25,399. And over eight stone?—It might be 1½d. a hundred.

25,400. For two hundred, do you charge 2d.?—Yes. I think bacon is seldom weighed, except for the information of people who kill a pig. It is not weighed generally.

25,401. Have you any rule in the market compelling all commodities that are brought into the market-place to be weighed at your scales?—I have not, for they are generally weighed all about the town. I do not weigh for half of them, I think.

25,402. Supposing they bring in commodities to the market and expose them for sale in the market square and sell them, but do not weigh at your scales, do you get any charge at all from them?—No.

25,403. It is only for the commodities you actually weigh that you receive a charge?—Yes.

25,404. Could you tell me what would be your average receipts at the scales?—When I went in there first it was worth 60l. or 70l. a year. I think it is not worth 30l. now.

25,405. 30l. in the year?—I do not think it is worth that.

25,406. Is this a good market?—It is; but they take the commodities out of the market and weigh in every place. That is the cause of it.

25,407. You think the supply of commodities to the market is the same now as when you obtained the scales first?—I cannot say how much is coming into the town now.

25,408. Could you give me any idea?—Well, I think there is not so much in the corn trade.

25,409. But the different general commodities?—I do not know. The corn and butter are generally weighed by the merchants who buy them.

25,410. Do you remember when there were less than 12 fairs held here?—Yes. I think there are more fairs now than in my time.

25,411. What are they?—I think there were four additional fairs.

25,412. What are the additional fairs?—The additional fairs are the 21st January, 21st February, 21st March, and 25th April.

25,413. How many years ago were they added?—I think it is more than 60 years.

25,414. Have the remain fairs always been held for a lengthened period?—Yes.

[illegible] Gordon Roberts, Esq., examined.

25,415. You are agent to the Earl of Portsmouth?—I am the resident agent.

25,416. The Earl of Portsmouth is the owner of any market rights that exist here?—Yes, both fair and market rights under patent.

25,417. Have you got the particulars of that?—I think it is dated the 5th June 1611, and granted by James I. There were several rights given in that patent. The right of fishery in the river, and also the fairs and markets.

25,418. The witness produced the patent, of which the following is a summary:—Two fairs to be held on the 15th August and 5th September, with the customs and tolls belonging. It gives the rights to the tolls as follows: For every piece of wine made, 3d.; for every cabin or booth, 2d.; for every standing for selling iron and other kinds of merchandise, 2d.; for every cowhouse or pack-house, 2d; to be sold there, 4d., viz., 2d. for entering and 2d. for the custom called toll for same; for every sheep or goat sold there, 1d.; for every vessel of butter sold there, 2d.; every gallon of butter sold there, 1d.; every piece of cloth sold there, 1d.; every garment or mantle sold there, 1d.; out of every sack of meal and oats sold there, 1d.; out of every dozen of geese, ducks, or hens sold there, 2d.; out of every kind whatsoever of merchandise sold there according to reasonable proportion in like manner, and 4d. for every kind of marketable things value for 1s. 4d. or beyond. It was a patent granted to Sir Henry Walker.

25,419. Was that the only patent?—There was another patent, but that is the oldest.

25,420. Have you had a connexion for any lengthened period with them?—Yes, I have been about 40 years connected with them, and my father before me and grandfather.

25,421. Were the markets always held on Thursday and Saturday?—The markets were always held on Thursday, and many years ago Saturday also became a market day in this way that the country people came to make purchases, and it became a second market day. I remember the time when the tolls were abandoned by the estate.

25,422. At one period tolls were levied on the markets?—Yes, they were.

25,423. Were they ever levied at the fairs?—I cannot answer that.

member a period when they were
remember having heard at the
charged by the estate upon repre-
e Earl of Portsmouth's tenantry
e advantage to the town and to
ay them. That is about 55 years
member. Mr. Wilkinson states it
ld correspond with the time I had
ago. Then the fairs and markets
only control that was exercised
tsmouth, the present man or his
the appointment of weigh-master.

Mr. Moran appointed?—He was
5s. a year, just merely to keep the

vided with a house and scales?—

—That is all.

arket house?—The under part of
so much as was used of it for

e other part used?—As a public
or entertainments.

rtsmouth?—Yes.

markets and fairs always held in
public street?—Yes, within my
ve rather a long knowledge of the

no control is exercised except by
fairs?—No. You must know that
re are considerable. The average
buyers at the fairs for cattle alone
about 7,000l. or 8,000l. each fair,
the pig fairs. These averages were
late Mr. Lawrence Doyle, the late
and the present Mr. Grandy, who
the town. They have greatly

say that the fairs in Enniscorthy
fairs in any other town around in
ourhoods?—Yes.

attle and sheep fairs on the same
?—Yes.

air is the day before?—Yes.

member a period when there were
ts?—No.

re always 13 within your memory?
ach 40 years. It was on the repre-
abitants of the town that the
tsmouth allowed the tolls to fall

improve the trade of the town?—It
airs and markets were considerably
means, because they came from a
Enniscorthy. The fairs increased for
purchasers came here from different
and the adjoining counties, and I
ten came from Dublin to purchase

markets increase?—Yes, they have

any experience of other fairs and
niscorthy?—No.

orthy do you think the fact of the
being toll free tends to bring in a
crease a greater supply of com-
n to come than if a toll was levied?

would say the levying of a toll
as a deterrent upon people bringing
ise and cattle to the markets and

period were the fairs held off the
fair green was provided about 30 or
ere were six statute acres provided
mouth and walled in by him at con-
and an effort made to induce sellers
een, because complaints were made
came a distance here, that it was
for them to be going from half-way
to beyond the cathedral, and
ent streets of the town, and as I tell
made to induce the sellers to go into
the buyers attended there, but the
ed, and for this reason the business

men of the town of Enniscorthy considered that if the fair was removed to that particular place they would not get their legitimate share of the business of the fairs; and for that reason I believe the effort to use the fair green did not succeed. Complaints were still made with regard to the difficulty of going through the fairs of Enniscorthy by buyers coming from a distance. Nevertheless I do believe that the fairs as they are at present are a very great benefit to the business men of the town, because they are disseminated over the town and the trade is equally distributed from one side to the other. It would have been localised if they had gone to the fair green, and no doubt whatever it would have injured a great many business men of the town who provided yards for their customers to put their horses in and so forth, and of course they then shop at the different houses they patronise.

25,445. I take it the traders of the town would object to the removal of the fairs off the streets for trade purposes?—I do not know whether they would now or not. I know they did, and succeeded in their objection. That six acres of land has been since let as sites for labourers cottages and principally built on. I think it fair to mention this, that there was another objection raised to the fair green—that it was too far from the railway station, because it was a considerable distance from it.

25,446. Was it the buyers who made the objection that it was not a suitable site?—Some buyers made the objection.

25,447. But it was on the representation of the buyers that the fair green was provided?—Distinctly.

25,448. Have you ever bought at the fairs?—Yes, and sold.

25,449. Do you think a fair green would be a better place to buy an animal on than the public street?—I think if you had a central fair green it would be better, because my idea is that the people, no matter where they sell, would go to the houses they were in the habit of dealing in, especially if they put up their horses there.

25,450. Supposing people came in the night before the fair with some animals, where could they get storage accommodation?—As they do at present.

25,451. That is in the yards belonging to private people?—Yes.

25,452. Is there any charge levied for that by the traders of the town?—Yes not there are a number of hotels and taverns in the town, and parties go to those places, and there are also other houses where they put up for the night. Buyers coming from a distance sometimes bring horses to sell and some cattle, and then when they purchase the next day they occasionally put them into the yards until they drive them to the railway station. I think the charges made are half-a-crown for a box-stall for horses, that includes the price of hay; there is 1s. charged for a single stall, and the same charge for a cow, providing them with fodder.

25,453. Do they come in the night before the fair?—They do.

25,454. From what districts do they bring the cattle?—They bring them in from Kilkenny. The horses come here 20 and 24 miles, and from the county Wicklow. The buyers come here from Dublin for horses.

25,455. All commodities brought into the market place and weighed are not weighed at the public scales?—No.

25,456. They are brought to the buyer's establishment and weighed at the buyer's scales?—Yes.

25,457. Did you ever hear complaints made of any inaccuracy in ascertaining the weights at the private scales?—Generally speaking the merchants of Enniscorthy have the reputation of being most honest in their dealings with the people, and I know if a person suggested to the contrary the public would not believe him.

25,458. Would you think it better and more satisfactory if all commodities were weighed at a public and independent scales—a scales that would not be under the control of either of the contracting parties?—It is a very difficult question to answer, and for this reason, it would be impossible for a public scales to weigh the quantity of corn that comes into the town of Enniscorthy during the season when they are purchasing corn. It would be impossible for them to weigh that quantity of corn within the day.

25,459. That would be at one scales; but if several were provided?—That is another thing.

25,460. Is there any public weigh-bridge in the town?—They are public, but they are private property.

25,461. They hire them out?—Just so.

25,462. When a corn merchant buys corn and weighs in his own scales, does he charge the seller for weighing it?—No.

25,463. Do the other people who weigh for the buyers and sellers, and do not purchase themselves, charge?—Yes.

25,464. You do not know the rates?—Threepence a load for hay, or straw, or turnips.

25,465. Threepence a load, no matter what the commodity is?—Yes. These are the only commodities weighed generally.

25,466. Do not they weigh potatoes at the beam and scales?—That is in the market house.

25,467. With the exception of corn, do all commodities to be weighed go to Mr. Moran?—Oh, no; they are weighed at private places.

25,468. Do they charge at these private scales?—No. It is a matter of accommodation. That is one of the weigh-master's complaints.

25,469. Do you think it would work better if all commodities were compelled to be weighed at a public scales?—I have not formed any opinion on that subject. I know this much, that it is most dangerous to meddle either with fairs or markets. They are very tender plants, and if you interfere much with them you may injure them considerably. I have heard of their being injured in other places, and that is the reason I should not like to give an opinion without considering it well.

25,470. When the people are acquainted with a custom you think it would be rather delicate to interfere with that practice which has been going on for a number of years?—That is my belief. I think it is a most dangerous thing to do it.

25,471. Did you ever hear any objections to the fact of the fairs being held on the streets, and occasioning much filth and dirt?—I have heard some of the business people object very much, but the principal objectors were non-business people, and some buyers have objected because it was too laborious in the fairs of Enniscorthy to travel such distances from one part of the town to the other.

25,472. In the markets did you ever hear of any of the particular commodities being injured by exposure to the elements there?—No, but the poor market people have been injured considerably. Some provision ought to be made for them.

25,473. Do you think a necessity exists for shelter accommodation for them?—I do.

25,474. And for their commodities?—Yes.

25,475. Would you approve of enclosed market premises with sufficient and ample shelter accommodation both for the commodities and the owners of them?—Well, I should not like to see the principal market removed from what is called the market square, although it ought to be called the market diamond. It is much more like a diamond than a square, and if the women who sit there and dispose of their commodities had some shelter accommodation or protection, it would be very desirable, and there could be also shelter for the parties coming in with their commodities.

25,476. Have they made complaints of the want of such shelter?—Yes, for many years.

25,477. The market is confined to that square?—It is principally.

25,478. Do they go about the streets?—They walk about with the commodities. The fowl market is held in the open square called the Abbey Square. That is a very considerable market.

25,479. Are both squares convenient to one another?—They are not very far distant. The fowl market is held in Abbey Square every Thursday morning. I had an estimate made by Mr. Quin, a large buyer here, in the year 1880, and his estimate was that the average expended every week was 200*l.* It is increased since then.

25,480. On fowl alone?—Yes; that 200*l.* is the lowest estimate.

25,481. Then the markets here are considerable?—They are.

25,482. Is there much of the surrounding land in tillage?—Yes. This used to be principally a tillage country, but latterly a great deal of it has gone into grass. Nevertheless it is a tillage country, and it is also celebrated for its breed of fowl.

25,483. Did you ever hear any complaints of the system of forestalling in the fowl market?—I have heard of complaints. I forget what they are called—people coming in and buying fowl at the dusk of the morning and re-selling them to the buyers.

25,484. Do they meet the producers on the road coming in?—Yes. Brokers they are called. I have heard complaints against the brokers.

25,485. When they purchase the fowl from the producer on the road coming into the market do they pay the contract price, or do they postpone payment until they effect a sale themselves?—No. The whole thing is over in half an hour or ten minutes after.

25,486. Do they postpone payment until the sale is effected?—As a rule they do. A great many of them are agents for the regular buyers. There are byestandings at the cross-roads where they buy as the sellers are coming to the town around.

25,487. Do the buyers think, if they allow them to come into the market and have the ordinary competition between the buyers themselves, that the prices would be somewhat considerably higher?—The reason they buy is because it is a convenience to the country people to sell that way, and they know the market prices as well as any people.

25,488. Supposing the sellers came into the market, would they not get higher prices for the fowl where there would be greater competition among the buyers?—Not always. The buyers go from one market to another, and passing through the country they meet the people on the road with their fowl. These people know the value of the fowl, and if they are dissatisfied with the price offered them, they bring them the next day to Enniscorthy. They have created new markets for the last 15 years.

25,489. When you say new markets, do you mean the actual spot where the buyers meet the farmers?—That is what I call the market—the cross-road. They have fixed stations or new markets by arrangement for the last 10 or 15 years.

25,490. Could you apply any of these observations to any other commodity?—I have heard of forestalling in potatoes, but I cannot give any evidence as I have no personal knowledge of it. In reference to the fowl market, my recollection is that there was a bye-law made about 20 years ago, and sanctioned by the Lord Lieutenant.

25,491. What was the nature of it?—Limiting the hours in the fowl market. I think the hours are altered.

25,492. Have you any other observations to make relative to the markets or fairs, or what you think would tend to the improvement of them?—No. About this order of 20 years ago I was under the impression there was one made subsequently, and sanctioned by the Lord Lieutenant, to hold the fowl markets at 8 o'clock from the 25th September to the 25th March, and at 7 o'clock from March to September. As regards the fairs, I think if they were removed to a sufficiently convenient place which was large enough, it would be a benefit to buyers and sellers, but I do believe it would be injurious to the town. In consequence of the traders of the town being opposed to it the fair green was not persevered in. As I said before, it is a dangerous thing to interfere with fairs or markets. They have a natural development of their own, and if you check it, in nine cases out of ten, I am inclined to think you will injure them, from my own personal knowledge. Lord Portsmouth derives no benefit from the fairs or markets.

Mr. Thomas Williamson, the Town Clerk, re-examined.

25,493. (Witness.) We know that the fowl market some years ago was usually held in the night in Enniscorthy. It arose in this way: All fowl purchased, or the greater portion of them, are for shipment, and a great many of the buyers go out [illegible] so as to get the fowl in proper time to have them ready for the packet or the train to the Liverpool or London market, or wherever they wish to send them. That system was attended by a great deal of inconvenience to local buyers and sellers when the market was held so much in the night, and the town commissioners brought that into their market regulations and fixed the hours at which the market will commence.

25,494. Have you got the regulations printed up in the market place?—They were up on a board, but it has gone into disuse. Respecting the market, these regulations were made in 1856 that no fowl shall be bought or sold in the market before 6 o'clock in the morning from the 25th March to the 29th September, or before 8 o'clock in the morning during the other months of the year. Previous to that the markets were held in the night, as I have said, and it was found ruinous. The clergymen and others asked the commissioners about the matter, and that is why we made the regulation and tried to enforce it. It was after that those country markets were established, where they might get out and buy outside the limits of the town.

25,495. What was the nature of the other regulations you made?—Just as to the divisions.

25,496-7. Had you byelaws then?—No. They were regulations simply where the carts and commodities should be placed on the streets to prevent obstruction or interruption on the public thoroughfare.

25,498. Had you ever to take any proceedings to enforce those regulations?—Never, except in the fowl market; but the magistrates exercised their right and did not inflict any penalty.

25,499. What is the hour at which the general market commences?—The markets go on at daylight now.

25,500. I do not mean the fowl market, but the general market?—Well, I think at daylight in winter—in summer for instance.

25,501. Do they expose corn on the market square?—Yes, up Irish Street, and coming in the Dublin road and up the square, and opposite the [illegible], and different places, but principally between the market house and Irish Street and up towards the cathedral. There is a very considerable market along by the Post Office sometimes.

James O'Gorman, Esq., Chairman, Town Commissioners, examined.

25,502. You are the chairman of the town commissioners here in Enniscorthy?—Yes.

25,503. Have you had any experience of the fairs and markets here?—Yes.

25,504. Have you of any other fairs or markets?—No, not so much.

25,505. Did you ever buy at any other fairs, or fairs where tolls were levied?—No.

25,506. Do you think that if a toll was levied in return for a fair green with suitable pens, either on animals sold or as they entered, that it would tend to deter farmers from bringing in the supply they bring in at present?—I think it would. I think it would be very difficult to adopt that system.

25,507. Generally speaking do you think the question of a toll acts as a deterrent upon farmers bringing in a supply of marketable commodities as well as cattle?—I cannot say it would deter them. I know they would not be pleased, and it would be very hard to make them comply with it. I do believe it would injure our fairs.

25,508. Relative to the markets, supposing an enclosed market place with sufficient shelter accommodation, as suggested by Mr. Roberts, was provided to afford protection to any perishable commodities brought in or to those who bring them in; do you think they would have any objection to pay the sum of maintaining that building?—I think something in that way is very necessary.

25,509. You think a necessity exists for that?—I do.

25,510. Did you ever hear that any perishable commodities were injured, or damaged, or depreciated in value by exposure?—No.

25,511. The people themselves have to remain under all sorts of weather?—Yes.

25,512. You heard complaints from them?—Yes.

25,513. Did the town commissioners ever take into consideration the erection of such buildings?—No, not that I am aware of.

25,514. They never discussed the advisability of obtaining control from Lord Portsmouth of the markets and fairs with a view to the erection of such accommodation?—No, not during my time. I have not a large experience in the commissioners. I think it would be very wrong to meddle at all with the fairs or markets. I think it would injure them.

25,515. You would injure them if you did what you deemed a necessary improvement?—No. It would be well to have some accommodation.

25,516. You think accommodation would improve them if such accommodation could be provided?—I think it would improve the markets.

25,517. Are you a trader in the town?—Yes.

25,518. Do you think it is always better to have the markets confined to some particular spot and not to have them scattered all over the town?—If the butter and egg market were confined to a particular place it would be a benefit.

Mr. [illegible] Harper examined.

25,519. (Witness.) In Wexford they have accommodation. I do not know how they pay, but at all events I heard some farmers say it is a great comfort.

25,520. Have you had experience of other fairs besides Enniscorthy?—I was in every fair through the country.

25,521. Have you been at any fair where tolls are levied?—Never.

25,522. You have bought and sold in Enniscorthy?—Yes.

25,523. Have they got the system of luck-penny here?—They have.

25,524. Is there any fixed rule?—No. It is left to the seller himself.

25,525. Does the purchaser of the pigs deduct that from the contract price?—He does.

25,526. He does not wait for the seller to give it?—No.

25,527. But in other cases the price is paid and the luck-penny given back?—Yes.

25,528. Is it regulated by any rule?—As a rule some people give 1s. to every [illegible], which is fair luck. Some people would be satisfied with 1d.

25,529. When you have bought and given or received a luck-penny, do you think the farmers, when fixing the price of the animal, ever consider the value of the luck-penny and put it on the value of the animal?—Sometimes they include the luck in the bargain, and no luck is given, but in other cases where it is not [illegible]

25,533. Would you consider that you were to give that and charge a proportionately high price for the animal?—No; that is not taken into account at all. We make the best bargain we can and give a luck-penny according to your own taste. There is nothing compulsory about it.

25,534. Do you know the reason of that fixed charge on the pigs?—That is a rule with the merchants and buyers.

25,535. Had they ever the system here of cutting down the price for measles?—Yes, but that is abolished altogether.

25,536. When that practice was in existence did they charge 6d.?—No.

25,537. Do you think it arose out of the abolition of that system?—I do not know. It was to save the buyers' expenses. There is only one class of pigs tried, that is very very heavy pigs. They are yet tried for measles, and the buyers take the same heed as usual.

25,538. They do still, you say, try that class of pig?—They do.

25,539. Have they a special man for that purpose?—They have men of their own. There is nothing charged for the pig, but if the pig turned out to be measled the price is cut, and the farmer can take her home if he wishes. It is optional.

25,540. Do you think from your experience as a buyer or seller that a fair green with pens and properly walled in is a better place to hold fairs than on the public thoroughfare, leaving out of consideration the fact that you are a trader in the town?—I will take everything into consideration, and I think on the let-live principle the people get a benefit from the passing and repassing of them at the fairs on the streets.

25,541. You think the buyers and sellers would prefer a fair green but the traders would oppose it?—Yes.

25,542. Does not the fact of the fairs being held on the street occasion a lot of filth and dirt?—The commissioners send out their men the day following to clear it off.

25,543. Have you heard complaints that filth and dirt were allowed to remain there for any lengthened period?—Yes, you will find those complaints in any in a township. You should have trains the staff to take it away in a moment.

25,544. Would the traders put up with any inconvenience caused to them for trade purposes?—Yes. I only heard some private individual's complaints, and for the benefit of the town they would not object. I am going to say, if another fair was added, it would be suitable, because the fairs improve the business of the town.

25,545. Are all the fairs well attended?—They are, unless the harvest fairs. They might be a little thin in harvest time, when the people are securing the crops.

Mr. Thomas O'Byrne examined.

25,546. [Witness.] I think it would be most detrimental to interfere with the fairs or markets that have been so long established, and wherever they have been tampered with they have been ruined.

25,547. Could you mention an instance of that kind?—I do not know from experience, but I heard Kilkenny was one.

25,548. Have you ever attended the fairs in Kilkenny?—No.

25,549. Have you anything further to say?—Nothing.

25,550. Is there any other gentleman who has any evidence to give, or who wishes to make any observations?—No answer.

The inquiry then terminated.

WEXFORD.

With reference to my inquiry in Wexford on the 5th day of December 1888, I beg to report as follows:—

Wexford is a maritime town situated on the south-east coast. It has an extensive harbour which is admirably situated for commerce, from its proximity to England and being at the entrance of the Irish Channel, but unfortunately these advantages are not available in consequence of a bar at the mouth, having only 12 feet of water at high tide, which limits the traffic considerably. The general trade is extensive, and there are many local industries.

The streets are peculiarly narrow, having on each side houses substantially built. The local government is vested in the mayor, aldermen, and councillors of the municipal corporation. The population is 12,163.

The markets are daily, but Wednesday and Saturday are the principal days. The fairs are held on the third day of each month, except the month of May, when the fair is held on the 1st.

The fairs are toll free. At the markets tolls are levied each day according as commodities are brought into the market buildings.

A scale of the charges is erected for public inspection. The market owners, however, have no weighing machine, but one belonging to the Harbour Commissioners is availed of.

The market rights are the property of the corporation of Wexford. There were five patents granted for Wexford. The first is dated 25th July 1317, and granted to the corporation a Saturday market. The second is dated 13th April 1411, and likewise granted a Saturday market. The third is dated 19th January 1608, and granted two markets and two fairs, the days and dates of which were not specified.

The fourth is dated 3rd August 1609, and granted a Wednesday and Saturday market and fairs on the 29th June and 1st November, and two days after each. The fifth patent is dated 24th December, 3rd James II., and granted a Wednesday and Saturday market and fairs on the 29th June and six next days, the first four days of August, 24th, 25th, and 26th August, 1st, 2nd, and 3rd November. The present fairs were established in 1879 without any express authority.

The present scale of charges and byelaws were approved of by the Local Government Board in 1878, previous to which no buildings were erected or charges levied.

In accordance with my instructions, I have inspected the fair and market places.

The fairs are held some distance outside the town on an enclosed fair green known as Windmill Hill and the public streets abutting on it. There is no accommodation in the way of shelter or pens provided there. It seems unsuitable for a fair green owing to its distance from town.

The corn and general market is held on the public thoroughfare. Hay and straw market is held on Commercial Quay.

The meat market is held in two shambles with slated roofs, and divided into stalls. Portions of these sheds are used as a dead fowl market and for general purposes. The market is enclosed with a concreted floor, and seems suitable for the purposes intended.

The site is rented by the corporation from a Mrs. Deane at 50*l.* a year, under a lease for 99 years from 1871.

The wholesale fish market is situate close by the meat market in a partially covered enclosure at a place called White's Wall on the public thoroughfare. It is provided with stalls. The retail fish market is held in the basement of the Town Hall, and is completely covered in. It is divided into sections by flags for the purpose of those engaged in retailing fish there.

The producers pay a porterage charge of 2*d.* per sack to porters for removing sacks (principally of corn) from their carts to the merchants' stores. It seems custom requires that these men should be employed.

Appended will be found a transcript of the evidence taken at the inquiry.

John J. O'Meara,
Assistant Commissioner.

45, Lower Mount Street, Dublin.

Wexford, 5th December 1888.

Mr. William A. Browne, town clerk, examined.

25,551. You are the town clerk of Wexford?—Yes.

25,552. There is a corporation in Wexford and not town commissioners?—Yes, consisting of mayor, aldermen, and burgesses of the borough of Wexford. They are ex-officio town commissioners under the Towns Improvement Act.

25,553. Are they the owners of the market rights and tolls in Wexford?—They are.

25,554. Is there any individual or authority exercising any market rights other than the corporation?—No.

25,555. What is the market day in Wexford?—The corn, meat, and fish market are held on every day of the week; the market for live fowl on Wednesday; the other markets, that is market for butter, eggs, and dead fowl, is held on Wednesdays and Saturdays.

25,556. Those are all the markets here?—Yes.

25,557. The general market, you might say, is held on Wednesday and Saturday?—Exactly.

25,558. That is for the commodities that do not come on other days?—Yes.

25,559. Is Wednesday especially allotted off for live fowl, or do live fowl only come that day?—That is all.

25,560. When are the fairs held?—The fairs are held on the Wind Mill Hill for cattle, sheep, and pigs. They are held on the third day of every month except the one in May, which is held on the first day of May.

25,561. You have twelve fairs in the year?—Yes.

25,562. When were these twelve fairs established?—The first of the present fairs was held on the 3rd October 1878, and superseded the old fairs which had become almost extinct.

25,563. What were those old fairs?—Fairs for cattle, sheep, and pigs.

25,564. What dates were they held on?—As well as I can remember, one was held at Michaelmas.

25,565. Were these twelve fairs established in 1878?—Yes.

25,566. For the first time?—Yes.

25,567. Do you know under what authority they were established. Was there any patent granted to the corporation of the twelve fairs?—No, the way they were established was this. A meeting or several meetings of the leading inhabitants and leading farmers were held, and they decided on holding the fairs once a month.

25,568. Are tolls levied at these fairs?—No.

25,569. They are toll free?—Yes.

25,570. Were tolls ever levied on the fairs?—None.

25,571. Either at the previous fairs or at any of the monthly ones?—I can not say about the previous fairs.

25,572. Within your recollection?—They have not been levied.

25,573. Is this Wind Mill Hill portion of the public thoroughfare, or is there a fair-green provided?—There is a fair-green there, but it is not used by the people. It is a large green space.

25,574. Is it enclosed?—It is enclosed on three sides. It is level with the public road.

25,575. Is it a wide space off the public road?—Exactly.

25,576. You say that is not used?—It is not used.

25,577. Where do they expose the animals?—In John Street and William Street, which are the approaches to the public fair-green.

25,578. These portions of the public streets, are they as narrow as the ordinary streets of Wexford?—No. They are the widest streets in Wexford.

25,579. Are they convenient to the market-place?—No; about a half-a-mile from the market-place.

25,580. Are they convenient to the trading portion of the town?—They are as convenient as they can be.

25,581. Why do not they utilise the fair-green. What reason have they or do they assign, for not going to it and exposing their cattle there?—When the fair was first established the people went into the fair-green, but in the course of time they encroached further down on the streets, and latterly the fair-green is not used at all.

25,582. How do they utilise the green between fairs?—They let it to circuses coming to the town.

25,583. Is it portion of the corporate property?—Yes.

25,584. In 1870 had they to purchase it?—No. It was a commons some years ago, and the grand jury on representation from the corporation took down two old windmills that were on it, and levelled the grass for the purpose of a fair-green.

25,585. Where are the markets held?—The corn market consists of three divisions—one of the corn markets is held on Redmond Road, another on Distillery Road, and the other at the Faythe.

25,586. Are those three places enclosed?—No. They are the public streets.

25,587. Then the corn market is held on the public thoroughfare?—Yes.

25,588. Where is the meat market held?—There are two shambles—one in Anne Street and one in the market building, that is in the egg market.

25,589. Are these two shambles enclosed?—They are.

25,590. Is there any shelter accommodation in them?—There are regular stalls.

25,591. Do they expose the meat elsewhere than in these shambles?—Yes, in shops through the town.

25,592. Do you derive any benefit from their selling in shops through the town?—No.

25,593. Only when they sell in the shambles?—Quite so.

25,594. Where is the fish sold?—The wholesale market for fish is held in a partially covered enclosure at White's Wall. This fish market contains 2,400 square feet, of which 1,130 has covered shedding over it. The other fish market, the retail fish market, is held in the Bull Ring in the Tholsel—that is the town clerk's office and committee rooms of the corporation.

25,595. Underneath that?—Yes.

25,596. That is a completely covered space?—Yes.

25,597. Where are the live fowl sold?—They are sold in Rowe Street, Main Street, and the Bull Ring.

25,598. On the public thoroughfare?—Yes.

25,599. Where is the general market held for butter, eggs, and dead fowl?—In the market building adjoining the Bull Ring.

25,600. What are the other commodities sold in this building besides butter, eggs, and dead fowl?—Butter, eggs, dead fowl, meat, boots, tin-ware, flannels, and furniture.

25,601. That comes to the market-place?—Yes.

25,602. Do hay and straw come here?—Yes.

25,603. Where are they exposed?—The hay and straw market is held out on Commercial Quay.

25,604. Is that the public thoroughfare?—Yes.

25,605. Have you any market buildings but those you have mentioned?—No.

25,606. Is the hay and straw market held on Wednesday?—Yes.

25,607. Do you collect tolls at these markets?—We collect tolls at none of the markets except the retail fish market and what is called the egg and butter market.

25,608. That is in the market building?—Yes.

25,609. Is the wholesale fish market free of toll?—Yes.

25,610. And the hay and straw market is free?—Yes. The corn market is also free.

25,611. Who provided this wholesale fish market, and covered it in?—The Harbour Commissioners.

25,612. Do they derive any benefit from it?—No. This place, at White's Wall was an old commons 20 years ago, and partially covered with water. The tide used to ebb and flow over it, and it was reclaimed by a man named Matthew Dowling, and the fishermen before it was reclaimed used to bring their boats up to this old commons and sell the fish there to the fishwomen and people retailing the fish. After a time, when the commons was reclaimed, and yards were built on it, but I think it is the Harbour Commissioners who enclosed this place.

25,613. And then gave it over to these wholesale fish dealers?—Yes.

25,614. Practically these are the fishermen?—Yes.

25,615. Were the Harbour Commissioners ever paid back the money they expended in that way?—I am not able to say, but I do not think they were.

25,616. They do not charge any stallage fee or rents there?—No. I only think it was the Harbour Commissioners enclosed it; I am not stating it positively.

25,617. Do you receive any charges from the retail fish market under your town hall?—Yes, we receive a nominal rent for the purpose of keeping it clean. The whole rent amounts to 6*l.* 4*s.* 8*d.* in the year. There are 20 flags there, and we charge at the rate of 1*d.* a stand.

25,618. Those are standings?—Yes.

25,619. Is that a daily charge you have on them as standings?—A weekly charge. For 16 of the flags we charge at the rate of 1*d.* a week, and for 11 at 2*d.* a week.

25,620. Then you have 27 of these standings?—Yes.

25,621. Who was it originally provided the retail fish market?—I believe it was the corporation.

25,622. Was the retail fish market always held there?—It was.

25,623. Who provided the general market buildings?—The corporation.

25,624. When?—They were opened on the 5th December 1872.

25,625. Do you know what capital expenditure the corporation was at in providing this building?—The purchase of the ground cost 400*l.*, and the erection of the building 1,161*l.* 13*s.* 7*d.*, and erecting the stalls and fitting up the side market 120*l.* 4*s.* 10*d.*, making a total of 1,682*l.* 17*s.* 7*d.*

25,626. What expense are they at yearly in the way of repairs?—Up to the present the repairs have only come to 1*l.* 17*s.* 7*d.*

25,627. Have they it subject to any rent, or have they the fee-simple of the site?—They pay 50*l.* a year for the ground.

25,628. To whom?—To Mrs. Dean Morgan.

25,629. Do they hold it on lease?—Yes.

25,630. Do you know the terms of it?—It is for 99 years.

25,631. From when?—From December 1871.

25,632. Did you ever see the lease yourself?—I did not.

25,633. Do you know are there any special covenants in it other than the ordinary covenants between landlord and tenants?—I do not. I never saw the lease, and I cannot say.

25,634. Are there any charges payable to the corporation out of the hay and straw market held on the quay?—No.

25,635. What are the charges levied at this market-place?—This is the schedule.

25,636. Witness then produced the byelaws and schedule of charges of which the following is a copy:—

BOROUGH OF WEXFORD,

To Wit.

MARKET BYELAWS.

At a meeting of the Town Council of the borough of Wexford, specially convened for the purpose, held on the 21st day of October 1878, pursuant to public notice thereof of the 18th day of September 1878 (two-thirds of the Council being present), it was resolved by a clear majority of the entire body to repeal the byelaws of 1874 and that in substitution thereof the following byelaws for the future management of the Wexford Market-place and markets to be held therein, with the tolls and charges hereunder, be adopted, the tolls and charges having been previously approved of by the Local Government Board.

Market Byelaws.

Byelaws for the management of the market-place and regulating the holding of markets in the town of Wexford, made by the town council pursuant to "The Public Health (Ireland) Act, 1878," (41 & 42 Vict. cap. 52), and "The Markets and Fairs Clauses Act, 1847," (10 & 11 Vict., cap. 14).

Days and Hours for holding the Markets.

1. A market for potatoes and all other vegetables, fruits and flowers, wild fowl, rabbits, hares and leverets, dead fowl, butter, eggs, live fowl, and wool, may be held on every week-day throughout the year, except Christmas Day and Good Friday.

2. On every day appointed for the holding of a market, such market shall, from and including the 25th day of March to the 29th day of September, commence, not earlier than seven o'clock in the forenoon, and close not later than eight o'clock in the afternoon, unless Saturday, when it shall be open until ten o'clock, and shall, from and including the 29th of September to the 25th day of March, commence not earlier than eight o'clock in the forenoon, and close not later than seven o'clock in the afternoon, unless Saturday, when it shall be open until nine o'clock.

3. Any person resorting to the market-place for the sale of any goods, provisions, marketable commodities, or articles, shall not, for the purpose of sale, or exposure for sale, bring the same or cause the same to be brought into such market-place more than one hour before the time appointed for the commencement of any market.

4. A person resorting to the market place for the sale of any goods, provisions, marketable commodities, or articles, shall not allow such goods, provisions, marketable commodities, or articles, or any part thereof, to remain in the market-place for more than one hour after the time appointed for the close of any market, unless lock-up stalls.

Market-place.

5. The market-place shall consist of three divisions:—

(1.) The market for potatoes and all other vegetables shall be held in Corn Market which shall be the first division of the market-place.

(2.) The market for live fowls only shall be held in Bowe Street, and in the main street, from Anne Street to the Redmond Monument, and in the Bull Ring, without encroaching on the pathways in any place, keeping to the side nearest to the Quay, and leaving a clear passage on the roadway, without including the footways, of fourteen feet, which shall be the second division of the market-place.

(3.) The market for dead fowls, rabbits, hares, lovesets [illegible], butter, eggs, and wool, fruit and flowers, and other goods admissible into the market, shall be held only in the enclosed market-place adjoining the Bull Ring, which shall be the third division of the market-place.

6. A person resorting to the market-place for the sale of any goods, provisions, marketable commodities, or articles, shall not for the purpose of sale, or of exposure for sale, place, or cause to be placed, such goods, provisions, marketable commodities, or articles, in any part or parts of the market-place other than such as are appropriated by these byelaws for the market of the same.

Obstructions and Nuisances.

7. A person resorting to the market-place, and being in charge of any waggon, cart, car, truck, barrow, or other vehicle, with a horse or other animal harnessed thereto, or of any beast of burden, shall not cause or allow such vehicle or beast to stand in such market-place, or in any street, avenue, or passage in such market-place, or in any of the immediate approaches thereto, for any longer time than shall be reasonably necessary for the sale of, or for the loading or unloading of, any goods, provisions, marketable commodities, or articles, or for taking up or letting down passengers.

8. A person resorting to the market-place, and being in charge of any waggon, cart, car, truck, barrow, or other vehicle, without a horse or other animal being harnessed thereto, shall not cause or allow such vehicle to stand or remain in the market-place, or in any street, avenue, or passage in such market-place, or in any of the immediate approaches thereto, in such a manner as to obstruct the passage of any person, or vehicle, or of any cattle, goods, provisions, marketable commodities, or articles, in or through such market-place, street, avenue, passage, or approach.

9. A person resorting to the market-place for the sale of any goods, provisions, marketable commodities, or articles, shall not cause or allow such goods, provisions, marketable commodities, or articles brought or conveyed to or from such market-place, or any building, stall, or standing therein, or to stand, be placed, or exposed for sale in such a manner as to obstruct the passage of any person, or vehicle, or cattle, or of any other goods, provisions, marketable commodities or articles, in or through such market-place, or part thereof, or any of the immediate approaches thereto.

10. A tenant or occupier of any building, stall, or standing in the market-place, shall not cause or allow any goods, provisions, marketable commodities, or articles, to be deposited or exposed for sale in or upon such building, stall, or standing, so that such goods, provisions, marketable commodities, or articles, or any part thereof, shall project beyond the line of such building or stall, or beyond the limits assigned to such standing, so as to obstruct the passage of any person or vehicle, or of any cattle, goods, provisions, marketable commodities, or articles, in or through the market-place or any part thereof.

11. Every tenant or occupier of any building, stall, or standing in the market-place shall cause such building, stall, or standing to be properly cleansed before the reception, deposit, or exposure for sale therein or thereon, and immediately after the removal therefrom of any goods, provisions, marketable commodities, or articles.

12. Every person resorting to the market-place for the sale of any goods, provisions, marketable commodities, or articles, or in charge of any waggon, cart, truck, barrow, or other vehicle, or of any beast of burden used for the conveyance of any goods, provisions, marketable commodities, or articles to or from such market-place, shall from time to time, as often as occasion may require, and in such a manner as to prevent nuisance or obstruction, remove or cause to be removed, from every street, avenue, or passage in such market-place, or from the footway or roadway of any of the immediate approaches thereto, all vegetable or animal refuse, filth, litter, or rubbish, which may have fallen, or may have been thrown or deposited thereon or therein during the loading or unloading, or the conveyance to or from such market-place of such goods, provisions, marketable commodities, or articles.

Stalls, Seats, and Standings.

13. No stalls or standings shall be permitted in the public streets.

14. Spaces for buildings, stalls, or standings in the market-place, number three division, for the sale of vegetables, fruits, flowers, goods, provisions, and other marketable commodities, and articles, shall, at a rent not exceeding sixpence per annum for each square foot, be let by the town council as may be agreed upon.

Penalties.

15. Every person who shall offend against any of the foregoing byelaws shall be liable to a penalty not exceeding 40s. for every such offence; and, in the case of a continuing offence, a further penalty not exceeding 40s. for each day after written notice shall have been given by the town council to such offender, to be recoverable by any of the ways or by which the same shall, for the time being, be by law recoverable.

Weighing of Butter and Wool.

16. All butter bought and sold within the market-place shall be weighed at the public weighing-place provided by the town council for that purpose, and all butter in casks, kegs, firkins, or cools shall be weighed net, and the true weight thereof ascertained, after deducting only the weight of the cask, keg, firkin, package, or cool; and if any buyer, or other person employed by him or her, shall take or receive any other deduction or allowance other than the weight of the said cask, keg, firkin, package, or cool, under the pretext of such deduction or allowance being for tret, boundage, brokerage, or carriage, porterage, or delivery, or under any other pretence whatever, he or she shall be liable, for every such offence, to a penalty of [illegible] to be recovered by any of the ways or means by which the same shall, for the time being, be by law recoverable, provided, nevertheless, that the justice, justices, or court before whom any complaint may be made, or any proceedings may be taken in respect of any such offence, may, if he or they think fit, adjudge the payment, as a penalty, of any sum less than the full amount of the penalty imposed by this byelaw.

17. All wool bought and sold within the market-place shall be weighed at the public weighing-place provided by the town council for that purpose.

Tolls.

18. All goods mentioned in Schedule A. hereunder, allowed into the market-place, shall be charged a toll, as per Schedule A.

Charges.

19. All wool, and butter in firkins, kegs, or casks, weighed in the market-place, shall be charged as set forth in Schedule B. hereunder.

SCHEDULE A.

For every basket of eggs - - -	1d.
For every basket of butter, under 14 lbs. -	1d.
For every basket of butter over 14 lbs. -	2d.
Each turkey or goose - - -	1d.
Each couple of fowl or ducks - - -	1d.
Each pair of rabbits - - -	1d.
Each hare or leveret - - -	1d.
Each firkin, keg, cask, or cool of butter -	1d.
Each package of wool - - -	1d.

SCHEDULE B.

For weighing each firkin, keg, or cool of butter - - - - - -	2d.
For weighing any quantity of wool under one cwt. - - - - - -	2d.
For over one cwt., and under two cwts. -	4d.
For over two cwts., and not exceeding three cwts. - - - - -	6d.
For exceeding three cwts., for every additional cwt., or part of a cwt. - - -	1d.

Adopted at a meeting of the town council of the borough of Wexford, on the 31st day of October 1878, two-thirds of the council being present at the meeting, by a clear majority of the entire body.

(L.S.) JOHN J. WALSH, *Mayor.*
T. M. O'LEARY, *Town Clerk.*

These byelaws confirmed by the Local Government Board for Ireland this 5th day of December 1878.

(L.S.) B. M. BURKE.
CHARLES CHESLER KING.

25,637. Are these the charges levied for the use of the market-place by those who avail themselves of it?—Yes.

25,638. Do you give them any standings in it, or do you let any stalls for these charges?—Yes.

25,639. Supposing they bring in a basket containing pair of fowl, and they place it on the flags in the market-place?—The charges are collected at the gate.

25,640-1. You do not consider whether they subsequently sell or not when they bring in the commodity?—No. There are benches for them there.

25,642. Supposing they exposed an article or commodity for sale and did not sell it, would you return the charge to them?—No.

25,643. You have other charges?—Yes, for weighing.

25,644. For weighing each firkin, keg, or cool of butter 2d.?—Yes.

25,645. For weighing any quantity of wool under one cwt. 2d.?—Yes.

25,646. For weighing any quantity of wool over 1 cwt. and under 2 cwt. 4d.?—Yes.

25,647. For 2 cwt. and not exceeding 3 cwt. 6d.?—Yes.

25,648. For weighing any quantity of wool exceeding 3 cwt. and every additional 1 cwt. or part of 1 cwt. 1d.?—That is all.

25,649. How is the butter brought here?—The butter is brought into this market in baskets.

25,650. It is all roll butter?—Yes. There is no regular market for firkin butter.

25,651-2. Do you produce this document as a schedule of the rules and regulations in the market-place?—I do.

25,653-5. You have no other rules or regulations except what is mentioned in this document?—No.

25,656-7. Previous to 1878 had the corporation control over the markets?—They had.

25,658. Were there charges, the charges levied previous to 1878?—There were no charges previous to the time the byelaws came into operation.

25,659. Were all the markets previous to 1878 held on the streets?—They were.

25,660. There was no market building?—No, except the retail fish market underneath the town hall.

25,661. Had the corporation to purchase any market rights in 1878?—There were no market rights.

25,662. They had to expend no money in purchasing the interest of any person in market rights?—No.

25,663. Could you give me the average receipts of the corporation for the past three years out of these markets, and if you can segregate the different items as much the better?—The average amount of the receipts up to the 31st December last for the last three years, was as follows:—From the tolls 60l. 7s. 10d.; from stallages 66l. 6s. 5d.; for weighing 4l. 17s. 6d.; and from the fish stands 8l. 1s. 6d.

25,664. Are they the net receipts after the payment of all expenses or the gross?—They are the gross receipts.

25,665. Give me the expenditure?—The expenditure was 105l. 14s. 11d. for principal and interest on the loans; 48l. 1s. 8d. for the officers salaries, and 1l. 18s. 3d. for repairs.

25,666. What was the amount originally borrowed by the corporation?—1,300l.

25,667. Who was this borrowed from?—The Board of Public Works.

25,668. How much are they in debt at present?—750l.

25,669. What interest does it bear?—5l. per cent.

25,670. Payable half-yearly?—Yes.

25,671. On what dates?—The 1st May and 1st November.

25,672. Do you pay off any of that principal each year?—We do.

25,673. What rate?—32l. each half year, that is 64l. a year of the principal.

25,674. Do you confine the sale of eggs, butter, fowl, and geese to this market building?—Yes.

25,675. The people cannot sell them out on the public thoroughfare?—They can and do.

25,676. You do not prohibit or restrain them from going about the town and exposing their commodities for sale?—No. We have no power.

25,677. You did not get such a byelaw sanctioned by the Local Government Board?—No. We have no power to compel anyone to go into the market-place, but then under the Towns Improvement Act, we can summon and fine them for causing an obstruction in the street.

25,678. Do you enforce the provisions of the Towns Improvement Act?—We do sometimes.

25,679. In that way you endeavour to compel them to resort to the market?—Exactly.

25,680. Is the butter always brought to this building to be weighed?—No.

25,681. Supposing they sell the butter on a market day in the town and do not weigh it at your scales, would you seek for any charge?—No.

25,682. Only when it is actually weighed?—When actually weighed.

25,683. There is no compulsory provision in the byelaws compelling them to weigh at your scales?—No.

25,684. They can sell and weigh where they please?—Exactly.

25,685. Where are the potatoes sold?—In the open market.

25,686. That is on the public thoroughfare?—Yes.

25,687. Have the corporation ever considered it desirable to confine the sale of all of these different marketable commodities to this market building, and take them off the public thoroughfare?—No.

25,688. Were representations ever made to them to adopt such a course?—Not to my knowledge. The object of the corporation is to benefit the people of the town by fostering the markets and fairs.

25,689. Have they never discussed whether it would be desirable, and tend to the improvement and advancement of them, to hold the markets in a properly enclosed market building, and not have them scattered indiscriminately about the town?—They never discussed that to my knowledge.

25,690. Are these charges levied every day?—Every market day.

25,691. That is every Wednesday and Saturday?—Yes.

25,692. Is the market building open any other days of the week?—It is open every day.

25,693. Supposing they bring the commodities into it on days other than Wednesday or Saturday, do you levy charges?—Yes.

25,694. Of course the weighing charges would be levied every day?—Yes.

25,695. Do you weigh any corn?—Yes.

25,696. Do you weigh potatoes?—Yes, if brought to the market.

25,697. What is the charge?—A penny per sack.

25,698. What is the charge for weighing corn?—A penny per sack.

25,699. If they cannot effect a sale of any of the commodities they bring to the market-place a market day, and wish to store them until the following day, can they do so?—No.

25,700. You have no storage accommodation?—No. I believe some of the hucksters are allowed to store in the lower store.

25,701. Are all the stalls let at present?—Two are vacant.

25,702. What do you charge?—Nothing.

25,703. At whose risk are the commodities to be stored?—At the owners.

25,704. You stated you have a meat market?—Yes.

25,705. Do you get any charge from the meat, or is it all in stalls?—In stalls.

25,706. You do not weigh it?—No.

25,707. Do you supply the stall-keepers with weights?—They have the market-place for their use.

25,708. You merely supply the space?—Yes, the stall for which we charge 10s. a month.

25,709. That charge is not mentioned on the schedule?—No.

25,710. How many stalls have you?—Six at present occupied.

25,711. All at 10s. a month?—Yes.

25,712. Can they rent them by the week?—Well, sometimes we do let them by the week, but that is an irregularity.

25,713. What other commodities are sold in the stalls?—Nothing but meat.

25,714. Where are the vegetables sold?—The potato and vegetable market is held in the corn market, which is portion of the public thoroughfare. I wish to mention that this town has lost by the market building up to the present in or about £2,000.

25,715. Was that portion of the money expended in the original construction, or is it only the aggregate annual loss?—The aggregate loss comes to £2,800. There is annual loss of £[illegible] a year in the market.

25,716. What would you suggest to obviate that difficulty?—To increase the charges and compel the people to go into it.

25,717. Do you think if there was a bye-law compelling all the commodities to be exposed there that there would be any necessity to increase the charges?—It is very little availed of. Of course more accommodation would be required.

25,718. If all commodities were taken to it the space would be inadequate at present?—It would not be adequate at all if all resorted there. I would suggest as a means of reducing the amount of the loss that the Board of Works should reduce the interest on the loan, because I consider it excessive to charge five per cent. on the market loans; and we have two other loans amounting to £12,800, and we have them at the rate of four per cent.

25,719. What security did you give for this loan in connexion with the markets. Was it the rates, or tolls alone?—Our property, our borough rate, and the tolls arising out of the market. The Board of Works has everything we possess as security for all the loans, and still we have power to borrow.

25,720. Have you any idea of the quantity of corn brought into the town?—I would estimate the amount of corn brought into town in the course of the year at about two hundred thousand (200,000) barrels. I am very well acquainted with the corn business, and I do not suppose in the course of the year 20 barrels out of that 200,000 are weighed in the market-place.

25,721. In the year?—Yes. It is all weighed at the merchants' stores. There are about 40 malt-houses, and at each of these malt-houses the corn is stored. The merchants go out to the market to buy by competition. The corn is then taken in charge by a porter or sack carrier to the merchants stores, and put up on the loft by him. There is a beam and scale on the loft, into which the corn is poured and weighed.

25,722. So then it is always weighed in an accurate scale without any covering around it?—Yes. It is poured out of the bag into the tub, and then placed on the loft.

Alderman William Tierney examined.

25,723. Are you connected with the trade in the town?—Yes.

25,724. Do you think it would be desirable to confine the exposure of marketable commodities to a sufficiently large and isolated market-place?—Most decidedly. Of course it would require a large amount of expenditure.

25,725. Apart altogether from the expense which would necessarily be incurred, you think a properly isolated market-place would be the proper place to sell all marketable commodities, and not have them going about the streets?—Certainly.

25,726. Have the corporation, within your knowledge, discussed the advisability of erecting such a place?—We have not in extenso, but when the form came down from the Commissioners we did discuss it on its merits that it would be advisable, but there was nothing further about it. They were of opinion that such should be there, and charge a toll, but other members of the council would not wish to see it carried out for fear it would interfere with the trade of the town. They would like to see it if there were no bad results.

25,727. At all events the consensus of opinion in the corporation is that the markets should not be held on the public thoroughfare?—Yes.

25,728. Have you known any accidents to have happened by reason of commodities such as corn and potatoes being exposed on the public streets?—I cannot say I have, but in the old coach days there were frequent collisions between the coach and the fowl cars. These are things, however, long past.

25,729. Have you ever heard of perishable commodities being depreciated in value or quantity by exposure on any public thoroughfare?—Yes, in the fowl market before we gave them what they have.

25,730. I mean within the last couple of years?—Not since we established bye-laws in connexion with the fowl market. We oblige them in winter not to sell before eight o'clock and seven in autumn. Previous to that there were frequent losses to the sellers. The fowl would be taken by "blackers," and the sellers would not be paid for them.

25,731. Would the blackers go out to meet them coming into the market?—Yes.

25,732. And take the fowl from them?—Yes, and promise them such prices as they could not get; and the sellers would neither see fowl nor money.

25,733. Were these men contracting to purchase the fowl from the farmers without having an actual money transaction with them, and subsequently having effected a sale at a profit over and above the price agreed upon, would pay them then?—Some of them would pay and more would not pay at all, but since the establishment of more rational hours such things, I believe, are very rare.

25,734. Are fowl sold elsewhere than in this market-place?—They are principally at fowl markets established through the country.

25,735. In the town are they sold elsewhere?—Not in the town.

25,736. They do not go about the streets?—Live fowl where there is a very large market, as there is between this and the new year, extend through the most part of the main street, and sometimes a bye-street is turned up.

25,737. Is not that very objectionable on account of the extreme narrowness of the streets of Wexford?—Sometimes it causes inconvenience, but it is over so early that the inconvenience is not very great.

25,738. The potato market and corn market being held in the streets urge great observation, the streets being so narrow?—Where they hold the potato market the streets are wide. It is not so good a business portion of the town as where the streets are narrow, and then the corn market was originally a better portion of the town. There is a fine open space there, and at that place the corn and potatoes are disposed of.

25,739. That is before your ordinary market building?—They do not congregate there as a rule. It goes up a narrow lane into a broad open space. It is called the corn market, for they formerly sold the corn there, but now the corn market is towards the railway station at a place called Distillery Road and the Mill Road works. Our hay market is held on the quay.

25,740. The fairs are held practically on the public thoroughfare too?—Yes.

25,741. Did you ever hear of any accidents having happened, either to the inhabitants of the town or the animals themselves, on account of their being exposed on the public thoroughfare?—I have not heard of such.

25,742. Have you had experience of other places where the fairs were held on a fair-green?—Not unless by repute.

25,743. Still, as a trader and one of the representatives of the corporation, do you think a fair-green would be proper place for fairs to be held, and have shelter accommodation provided in it?—It would be, but the accommodation would not be ample for the fairs.

25,744. Supposing there was adequate accommodation, you think it would be better than having them on the public street?—Certainly it would be a great advantage.

25,745. Have you ever heard complaints that they created much filth and dirt?—Residents along the place where the fairs are held all complain of the inconvenience, but the farmers will go to this place, and nowhere else.

25,746. The corporation have never sought for power to confine them to a fair-green?—I think we have the power, but would not like to exercise it. We have induced them to come into the town from the country districts to hold the fairs, and to a great extent we have succeeded, and the corporation would be very slow to do anything to drive them away again.

25,747. The only objection the corporation have to the erection of a large general market for all marketable commodities is the expense that would be incurred?—Yes.

25,748. But they are desirous to provide it if the pecuniary difficulty could be got over?—Yes, if it could be done without a tax on the townspeople.

25,749. Do you think if corn and other commodities were exposed for sale in a sufficiently large and properly sheltered market-place that the farmers would have any objection to pay a small charge towards the maintenance of that market to pay off the expense incurred in erecting it?—At first, I am certain they would, but ultimately they would come to see the advantage to themselves and the competition among the buyers, but at present they would object to any charge, however small, as a tax on them.

25,750. Do you remember when any tolls were levied at these corn markets?—I do not. I have heard there was a toll in old times, but of my own knowledge I do not know it.

25,751. Do you think, generally speaking, that in Wexford more particularly, having more knowledge of Wexford than elsewhere, that the exaction of a toll on marketable commodities acts as a deterrent on farmers bringing in the supply they would bring, if the markets were toll free?—In Kilkenny, I understand there are tolls there, and there is no objection to pay all expenses, and there is no case in Kilkenny.

25,752. What do you think now from the feeling of the farmers surrounding Wexford?—They would object to it. They require to be educated. In an indirect way at present they pay a kind of tax, they pay 2d. for carrying sacks to porters.

25,753. There is a porterage charge here?—Yes, for carrying their sacks from the cars into the store. They would get more for their article sold, if there was that concentrated sale.

25,754. When the farmers bring the corn to the public thoroughfare, and expose it for sale, do the merchants go around to the place?—They do.

25,755. They buy it subject to delivery by the seller?—Yes. The seller goes to the merchant's store then. There are porters about, and for moving the sacks into the merchant's store, they charge 2d. per sack.

25,756. Who engage the porters?—The sellers.

25,757. In whose employment are they, or are they men seeking their living by that means?—Yes. They go out the road to meet the farmers coming in.

25,758. If the farmer has sufficient help, can he utilise it?—He either would not do it, or his workmen would not do it, or the porters would not allow it. The porters have that advantage.

25,759. So that if a man has men with him, and having 12 sacks in a load, could save 2s. by his own help, the porters will not permit him?—They will not permit him.

25,760. How is that?—It is an old custom, and they (the porters) would not allow the farmer to do it. Where there is a concentrated market, the farmer would get a better price for the corn.

25,761. Is this a large corn market?—Very large.

25,762. Could you give me any approximate idea of the quantity brought here?—I could not. It was made up some years ago when they were seeking additions in the way of loans. Of course the returns could be got.

25,763. The corporation never made up an estimate of what they could derive from a general market, an estimate of the quantity brought in, and the charges they would levy—that is, an ordinary estimate of what the probable receipts would be if they created a market?—They never went into that. It would be a very large sum from the quantity brought into the town.

25,764. Could you give me some approximate idea of the quantity?—I really could not. I heard a maltster speaking of a man who sent a 1,000 barrels or 2,000 barrels away, and he was only one of several.

25,765. Is it all home corn?—Yes. Last season we imported a great deal. Guinness's agents, Messrs. Lambert and Murphy, imported a good deal. They could get corn equal to what they required.

25,766. Do the merchants export with your home consumption?—Yes, they send it to Dublin. They make it into malt sometimes, and also export the barley without being malted. They supply merchants in Glasgow and different English ports. It is principally in malt. There are buyers who ship loads of barley without being malted.

25,767. You think if the market building was provided and charges levied the farmers would first object, but ultimately they would see the benefit they would derive and agree to such charges, if they could avail themselves of the abolition of the porterage charge, because practically in other places the charge the corporation would levy for performing the duties of weighing and giving them accommodation and help to remove the commodity from the carts would be somewhat less than what they pay for porterage alone?—It would have to go to the various merchants' stores after being sold, and there would be porterage still.

25,768. Do not they have their own carts?—They have their own carts, and they bring the corn in them to the various stores.

25,769. Do the merchants ever send their own men, their employées, to take it off the cart?—Yes.

25,770. Do they require the seller to put it on the loft?—Yes.

25,771. In order to complete their contract?—Yes. The only sum paid by the merchants is the weighmaster, and then the seller pays the porters.

25,772. Does the merchant charge the seller anything for weighing the corn?—No.

25,773. You never heard of its being done?—No; they do not charge anything for weighing. There was a charge some years ago, but it is done away with now.

There was a certain amount of corn to each barrel—I forget what term they made use of—and there was a charge of three pounds.

25,774. Was it taken from the weight?—Yes, a deduction.

25,775. Was that for baggage?—Yes. There was a certain amount stopped for baggage.

25,776. But now they buy by the net weight, the tare of the sack being the only deduction from the gross weight?—Yes. The other practice was a good many years ago in force and the same thing applied to butter and various things.

25,777. That is all done away with?—Yes.

25,778. What do you think of the markets here; are they good markets?—Very fair, but not so good as in old times.

25,779. How do you compare them with the markets of the adjoining towns, the markets of Enniscorthy, for instance?—They are equally as good. I have no knowledge of the fairs there. The fairs I know in Enniscorthy, from what I have been told, are far superior to ours, but ours are becoming good fairs, and ultimately will be good fairs. In old times they were excellent.

25,780. What is the nature of the surrounding country?—The larger proportion in tillage. Of late years there is a large portion let into grass for grazing, more so than what there was some years since. Of course that was principally brought around owing to the fall in prices, and the high price given for cattle and butter. In old times I remember friends telling me they have had four and five and sometimes more barrels of wheat per acre and twenty odd barrels of barley. Wheat is not grown now except for their own needs, and they get that ground in a mill that is dying out.

25,781. They only supply their own necessities?—Yes.

25,782. Is that owing to foreign competition?—No. It is a change of the season. Wheat producing seven or nine barrels to the acre is not sufficient to pay the expense. There should be 14 or 15 barrels; and if the season is not fine and suitable the wheat is injured, and in wet weather valueless, so that the farmers have almost given up sowing it.

25,783. Have you any suggestions to offer as to what you think would lead to the improvement of the markets and fairs?—My own personal opinion is that there should be facility given to borrow money at a reasonable rate for establishing such a market, and have a large space for the sale of corn, and a crane. By having the market in one place it would be a great advantage. We have such a place here at the Crescent. If that were a filled in space it would be a splendid place for concentrating the corn, hay, and all marketable commodities coming in by cart, and sold off the cart. Of course it would cost a good deal of money, and after a time the farmers would come to find it was an advantage to themselves, and possibly if we levied a small toll we would have to educate them to agree to it.

25,784. Would the corporation wish to have bye-laws empowering them to compel people to resort to this place and not sell elsewhere?—I think it would be required, but I think there would be a great difficulty to get the corporation to agree to work for it.

25,785. I suppose that is practically because the great proportion of them are traders, and it would more or less affect the trade and their own interest?—That would be one of the principal causes of their objection. If there was general legislation applicable to the kingdom, the majority of them might be in favour of it, if they had evidence of its being a better system than the present one.

corn before coming into the town to a few maltsters established there.

25,787. How far is this from Wexford?—Three and a half English miles.

25,788. Is there a town there?—It is a village of 500 people.

25,789. I suppose that is owing to the proximity of large purchasers?—Yes. They have to pass them by coming in. This is the only place they sell corn. If they established any other places they would have to come into the town, because there is no place they could get rid of it for the want of maltsters. If we had a large fair-green such as in other places, and gave accommodation with pens for sheep and cattle, so as to prevent any accident by the mixing of sheep and cattle, it would be a great matter.

25,790. Do the different species of animals intermix at the fairs here?—They do at times.

25,791. I suppose custom has allotted off a certain portion of the street for each?—To a great extent it has.

25,792. Is there anybody to regulate the order of the fairs except the police?—They attend, but do not interfere, unless there is some quarrelling or animosity.

25,793. Do the people make use of the pathways?—Yes, of every place. When the fair is over we have to send a scavenger to clean the place as well as he can.

25,794. Is the corporation the urban sanitary authority?—Yes. Of course it takes some little time if there is a great collection of manure from it.

25,795. Do you think the manure sale is an equivalent to the additional expense you incur in cleaning the street?—Of course it does.

25,796. Does it completely cover the expense?—Oh, no. I am sure it would not. Of course we have the advantages it gives to the town. It is an inconvenience to the residents where the fairs are held, but as I said, some are pleased to put up with it. We did try to get them to go to the fair-green which we opened, but it was rather an exposed place, and they could not be got to go there. There was another place near the railway station and a couple of years ago two or three members of the council tried to induce them to have that levelled and made into a proper place for the fairs, but then party feeling said it would take the trade from one place and put it into another. It prevented anything practical being done. The council would be very slow, as a council, to change the fairs for fear they might drive away the farmers again.

25,797. Do you think they would be so sensitive as that?—Down here we are very conservative, and we stick to old rules.

25,798. You do not like a change in that respect?—No.

25,799. You do not like a change from the existing system for fear of injuring the prosperity of the markets or fairs?—Yes, but I am sure after a little while if it was done it would be an advantage.

25,800. You think, although at the beginning a change might be detrimental, it would be ultimately successful, and a benefit to the town generally?—I think it would.

25,801. That is your own opinion?—Yes.

25,802. Have you any other suggestions to offer?—No, except you saw your way to advise or recommend, in a general law, that money be advanced to public bodies for such purposes as constructing markets and fair-greens. It would be an advantage if it could be lent to them on the same favourable terms as to other public bodies. We borrowed a large amount of money for the waterworks, which otherwise could not be con-

property. We did recover some on the rents receivable, but it is a mere nothing—2s. 6d. an acre for some land.

25,505. What do you say the total revenue is?—At present our revenue is 350*l*. or 360*l*.

25,506. What is the consolidated town rate?—The borough rate at present is 10*d*. in the pound and limited to a 1*s*. Our own rate, that is the town improvement rate in lieu of the county-cess, is at present 1*s*. 6*d*. and limited to 2*s*., and our public water rate now expiring will be 2*s*. 6*d*. next year and the domestic rate a 1*s*.

25,507. What is the poor rate?—3*s*. in the 1*l*.

25,508. You do not know the valuation of the town?—16 200*l*., I think. We pay out 1*s*. 6*d*. to the grand jury annually which comes to 550*l*. or 600*l*. according to the county at large charges. Then we keep the streets, sewerage and footpaths in repair. It is because of the state they kept them in former times we took them up.

25,509. Do you think, if the corporation effected these improvements in providing a new market or general market, that they should work it themselves and not let it out to any private individual?—We would keep it in our own hands.

25,510. You think the corporation or local authorities are the best people to control the markets and fairs and manage them?—I do, because they would not be unfair or harsh in their dealings. It would be to the advantage of buyer and seller, and we would not have excessive charges. I think all these things ought to be in the hands of the local governing body.

25,511. Your opinion is that where these market rights are not vested in local authorities that local authorities, if any such exist in a town, should obtain compulsory power to acquire the rights of individuals to exercise control over them?—I do.

25,512. Because you think they would be better able to manage them, and would give greater satisfaction to the people generally than a private individual?—Yes, for then there would be no inducement for unfair dealing. The officers appointed would be paid salaries, and it would be nothing to them to do anything unfair.

25,513. And the representatives in the corporation would be more or less amenable to their constituents than a private individual subject to no authority?—Yes, because if the members of the council acted unfairly, at their re-election they would not put them in, and in that way it would be an advantage to have the control in the hands of a local body.

25,514. If charges are to be levied at the markets or fairs, do you think the charge levied should be only one to pay off the instalments of the capital expenditure incurred and the cost of maintenance?—Yes.

25,515. You do not say that the corporation or local authority should derive any extra profit out of them?—I would be inclined to say not.

25,516. Any extra profit should go to the reduction of the charges?—Yes, so as to make it such as to induce the seller to use it.

25,517. Your idea would be to make the markets or fairs self-supporting, and any extra profit to go to the improvement of the market?—Yes. It was on that principle we struck the charges on our own market-place, but it does not cover the expenses. There is a loss to the ratepayers, and they do not grumble. At first they did, and seriously grumble, and on the other hand more objected to any charges at all, yet, if we had no charges it would be a heavy expense on the ratepayers, because the place could not be left without officers.

25,518. Have you ever heard persons complaining of these charges?—At first farmers wives objected to pay a penny for a basket of eggs, and they did not come in. It was a charge of a penny a dozen on the eggs, and they go about the town.

25,519. Do you charge the penny on the dozen?—Yes.

25,520. What would be the value of the dozen?—Fourteen or fifteen pence. We tried to prevent the hucksters from buying up the eggs, and then turning around and selling at an increased profit. They escape any tollage, because they come in with an empty basket.

25,521. You do not charge the retailer anything?—We do not get the chance. They buy inside and try and sell again.

25,522. In the first instance have not they paid the charge?—The person from whom they bought paid the charge.

25,523. Supposing a man bought commodities inside and retailed them inside, would you levy a second charge, that is a charge on the retailer?—Well, we have the power of doing it.

25,524. Do you as a matter of fact?—No, unless they want butter weighed, and then they have to pay so much according to the scale for weighing butter.

JOHN M[illegible] examined.

25,525. You are the weigh-master attached to this market?—Yes.

25,526. What scales have the corporation provided there?—They have a scales for weighing the butter, and they have also a scales for weighing the other commodities, such as potatoes and corn when they come in.

25,527. Is that all?—Yes.

25,528. The butter scales is utilised for butter alone?—Yes.

25,529. Have they provided any weigh-bridge here?—No. The corporation has not.

25,530. No weigh-bridge at all?—No.

25,531. Where are the loads of hay weighed?—At the harbour commissioners on the quay below.

25,532. Is that the only one provided in the town?—That is the only one.

25,533. Do the harbour commissioners levy any charge for weighing?—They do.

25,534. Do you know what it is?—I do not know. They have a man there. I think it is 1*d*. per 1 cwt. they charge.

25,535. Did you ever hear any objections from the farmers about the harbour commissioners weighing?—Never. They must go there.

25,536. Do they ever ask or think the corporation should provide a weigh-bridge?—Never.

25,537. What commodities do you usually weigh at those scales?—Potatoes, corn, butter, and wool.

25,538. Do you ever weigh turnips at them?—No. They are weighed on the bridge.

25,539. When weighing butter, what is the smallest weight you put into the scales, or is it all roll butter?—No. The whole of it, I might say, is in pounds of butter and very few of them are weighed.

25,540. When weighed do you weigh down to an ounce or 2 oz.?—I do not weigh an ounce or 2 oz. I weigh it by the lump.

25,541. Can you ascertain the weight down to an ounce?—Yes, and to a quarter of an ounce.

25,542. Do you do it?—I do.

25,543. That is the actual weight?—Yes.

25,544. What is the smallest weight actually put in. Supposing you found it would take an ounce, do you put in the half oz.?—I would, and the quarter.

25,545. Is there any deduction from that weight. Do you turn it out in its natural state on the scale or is there any covering over the butter?—I put it out without any covering.

25,546. Is there anything allowed for any butter that clings to the scales?—No, it does not cling to the slab.

25,547. When weighing a cask or keg what is allowed?—They do not come to me. I did not weigh one of them these three years.

25,548. Do you give a ticket denoting the weight?—Sometimes. Some will take it; more will not.

25,549. Is it a printed ticket?—Yes.

25,550. For butter?—Yes.

25,551. Have you a printed ticket for each commodity, or does one answer all purposes?—We had a ticket for wool. We have no wool until June, and there are merchants who buy wool and weigh it at their own establishments.

25,552. Do they levy any charge?—They do not, and that is the reason the sellers will not come to us to weigh for them.

55,853. Are the potatoes weighed in sacks?—The potatoes are weighed in the corn market, and do not come to us.

55,854. Who weighs them in the corn market?—There is a man there. There was a woman who had the scales, and she disposed of it to this man.

55,855. He weighs in the corn market?—Yes.

55,856. He has no connexion whatever with the corporation?—None whatever. It is a thing the corporation took no notice of, and anything he makes out of it goes to himself.

55,857. What charge does he levy for weighing sacks of potatoes?—A penny.

55,858. What do you charge if they are brought to you?—The same.

55,859. Do you weigh the empty sack?—No, it is a half-stone for the sack.

55,860. It is never less?—Never less.

55,861. That is irrespective of the quantity in the sack?—Yes. If there is 14½ stone it is 14 stone payable.

55,862. What is the smallest weight you weigh down to; do you weigh 4 lbs.?—No.

55,863. Do you weigh a half a stone?—Not unless in the sack.

55,864. Can you ascertain the actual weight of a sack of potatoes down to a half a stone?—Yes.

55,865. Down to what do you ascertain the weight?—If there is 14½ stone it is 14 stone payable.

55,866. If there were 6 lbs. extra in the sack, can you ascertain that?—Yes.

55,867. Do you do so?—Yes.

55,868. What is the smallest weight on the scales?—We bring it down to a lb.

55,869. Always?—Yes, and just turn the beam.

55,870. If the actual weight of the sack of potatoes was 14 stone 1 lb., would you be able to ascertain and say the gross weight was 14 stone and 1 lb.?—If we had 15 stone of potatoes in the scale, and if it would not take another half a stone, then the parties agree to say 14 stone payable.

55,871. From the 14 stone they would deduct the actual tare of the sack?—Yes, we will say 7 lbs.

55,872. Then they pay for 13½ stone?—Yes.

55,873. It must be a half stone or nothing in weighing potatoes?—Yes.

55,874. Would that 7 lbs. be allowed for the tare of the sack on a very wet day when the sack was completely saturated with wet, as well as on a fine day?—If they wished to agree among themselves they might, but it would be remarked that the sack was heavier on a wet day than a dry day.

55,875. Is there anything allowed for the state of the potatoes and the sack?—The buyer and seller settle that.

55,876. It is a matter of agreement among themselves?—Yes.

55,877. Do they usually allow anything?—Sometimes they do. They may do it without my knowledge.

55,878. Have you ever known them do it?—Yes, I have.

55,879. What was the allowance in addition to the 7 lbs.?—They might allow a halfpenny.

55,880. It is a money allowance?—Yes, between themselves.

55,881. What is the charge for weighing corn?—The same as for potatoes—1d. a bag.

55,882. Do you weigh the empty bag?—The empty bag is generally weighed to people.

55,883. Down to what weight do you weigh the corn; do you weigh 4 lbs.?—If 1 lb. would turn the scale, the seller would get the benefit of it.

55,884. So then if there was 10 stone 1 lb. in the scale, you would call the gross weight 10 stone 1 lb.?—It will be 10 stone. It often takes a pound to turn the scale.

55,885. Do you give a cast of the beam or weigh by standing beam?—I give a turn of the scale.

55,886. For weighing wool, what charge do you levy?—I seldom weigh wool. Mr. Tracy weighs that. I am not there except on market day.

55,887. You have other duties to perform in the town?—I have.

55,888. These commodities are not usually weighed at your scales; they are weighed elsewhere as well?—Yes. For instance, the corn is weighed at the stores in the town. We only get a very odd bag.

55,889. These merchants do not levy any charge?—No.

55,890. Supposing the corn is brought in and weighed at your scales, is there any charge levied by porters or others?—The porters are with the persons who come with the corn.

55,891. Have they got the system of luck-penny at the fairs?—Yes; I believe that system exists between buyer and seller. That is an old system.

55,892. There is no rule regulating the value of the luck-penny?—No.

55,893. Or the amount of it?—No.

55,894. Do you know what it is on pigs, or is it a fixed charge?—There is no fixed charge. It is 1s. on a cow, and about 6d. on a pig. I saw people myself offering a 1d. luck.

55,895. Do you think it leads to confusion and argument?—Sometimes it does with elderly people.

55,896. It leads to heated discussion?—It leads to discussion, some people think more about a penny than another about a sovereign. Some people would give sixpence where others would not give a halfpenny.

John Tracy examined.

55,897. What is the nature of your employment in connexion with the markets here?—My employment is to collect tolls on the people coming in who sell in the market.

55,898. Do you always stand at the gate?—As a rule I do on market day.

55,899. What hour does the market usually commence?—The market does not commence until 10 o'clock, and there are few in before that hour. The market is not complete until about 12.

55,900. When does it terminate?—It is over generally about 3 o'clock or half-past 3.

55,901. Have you got these rules and charges exposed for public inspection in the market?—Yes, on a big board in the market-place.

55,902. So that the public have an opportunity of seeing the charges they have to pay?—Yes.

55,903. I suppose you are well acquainted with the charges?—Well, I am.

55,904. When you see commodities brought in, you charge according to the scale?—Yes, to the best of my ability.

55,905. Supposing they bring in a basket of fowl, do you ever look under the cloaks of the women to see the animals they have got?—Yes, if I had a suspicion.

55,906. You do that sometimes?—Yes.

55,907. Have they ever resisted that inspection?—Usually they would not resist.

55,908. When they pay, do you give any docket or receipt?—Yes, I give them tickets,—a penny ticket.

55,909. Are these tickets collected from them subsequently?—No.

55,910. No matter what the commodity is, you give them one of these tickets?—Yes, when I receive the token. If they had twelve turkeys I would give them a ticket for each.

55,911. Why do you give them these tickets, or what use are they subsequently to them?—They are of no use.

55,912. Supposing they came up to the door and you found they were very poor and had not the money, would you allow them in, and collect the toll or the charge when they had subsequently effected a sale of the commodities?—As a rule, if I knew the parties or had a previous knowledge of them I would admit them if they said they had not a penny, but these parties are all supposed to pay at the gate, yet when they come and say they have no money we admit them sooner than let them go through the town.

25,913. Subsequently you obtain the charge?—Yes.

25,914. Does that frequently occur?—Well often.

25,915. You would not allow a stranger or a person you were not familiar with into the market?—If I had a suspicion they could pay I would keep them out.

25,916. Have you only one entrance to this market-place?—That is all. There is a turnstile for leaving persons out.

25,917. So that if they go out and return again they pay an additional charge?—No. There is a turnstile for the accommodation of people leaving the market, but they cannot return by it.

25,918. There is only one gate for entrance and another for exit?—Yes.

25,919. They must all go in by the gate at which you are standing?—Yes.

25,920. Supposing a woman with a small basket of fowl went out and returned subsequently, would you levy the charge again?—Never.

25,921. Did you ever hear it was done by mistake?—Never.

25,922. When are these stallage charges collected?—Mr. Horan collects them.

25,923. Every month?—They are very poor, and it is taken every way he gets it.

25,924. You have no duties to perform in connexion with the fairs?—No.

25,925. Did you buy or sell at the fairs?—No.

25,926. Have they got the system of [illegible] at the fairs?—I really could not tell.

25,927. Are these the only duties in connexion with the markets?—Yes. I attend the markets daily.

25,928. Is your only duty the collection of the toll?—Yes, and in the absence of Mr. Horan I weigh wool or anything that way.

25,929. In return for the tickets denoting the weight, you get the charge?—Yes.

25,930. Do you ever denote the weight with chalk on the sack?—I do, and give a ticket if they require it.

25,931. Do you ever mark the weight on the clothes of the people?—No.

25,932. You never marked it on a woman's shawl?—No.

25,933. Is there any other person who wishes to make any observations?—(No answer.)

The inquiry then terminated.

NEW ROSS.

With reference to my inquiry in New Ross on 5th day of December 1888, I beg to report as follows:—

New Ross is an inland town situated partly in Wexford county and partly in Kilkenny county. The town is built on the side of a steep hill overlooking the River Barrow. There is a brisk general trade, which has improved since a branch of the Dublin, Wicklow, and Wexford Railway line was constructed. A board of Town Commissioners administers the local municipal affairs. The population is 6,670.

The market days are Wednesday and Saturday. The fairs are held on the 10th January, 10th February, 15th March, 10th April, 3rd May, 10th June, 10th July, 10th August, 10th September, 18th October, 10th November, 8th December, and Easter and Whit Mondays. There are no fairs held on the 10th April, or 10th June, when Easter Monday or Whit Monday fall in these months respectively. A pig fair is held the day previous to the ordinary fair.

There are no tolls levied at the market or fairs, but at the former weighing charges are payable if commodities are weighed.

The market rights are the property of the town commissioners. They have the fish market, weighing machine, and butter scales, sub-let to Miss Bridget Meagher at 31*l.* 4*s.* a year, and the shambles are let to a Mr. Deane at 12*l.* a year, who has them sub-let in shops to butchers. A Mr. Keogh has a private scales for weighing potatoes.

There was no patent granted for New Ross, therefore the present markets and fairs are held without any express authority, but they were all established anterior to the Royal Commission in 1852 with the exception of the fair on 15th March, which was altered from the 17th March about 20 years ago.

In accordance with my instructions I have inspected the fair and market places.

The fairs are held in a large wide open portion of the public thoroughfare outside the town proper and called the "Irishtown" district. It is on a hill above the town, and so far as space is concerned is suitable, but no pens or shelter accommodation is provided.

The markets are held on the public quay outside the fish market building. This building is substantially built, but is inadequate as regards accommodation or shelter. A weighbridge is erected in connexion with the building.

The charge paid for weighing potatoes is for the use of the scales only, as the producers have themselves to perform the act of weighing and provide the necessary assistance for that purpose.

Appended will be found a transcript of the evidence taken at the inquiry.

JOHN J. O'MEARA,
Assistant Commissioner.

45, Lower Mount Street, Dublin.

New Ross, 6th December 18[illegible].

Mr. JOHN TOBIN, Town Clerk, examined.

25,934. You are the town clerk of New Ross?—Yes.

25,935. Have you consulted the commissioners upon the queries I forwarded to you?—I spoke of it at a meeting and showed them the forms, and all they said was that whatever information was to be given would be given by their clerk.

25,936-7. Are the town commissioners owners of any market rights that exist in New Ross?—Yes.

25,938. Have they the immediate control of them or are they sub-let?—They have the markets in the street. They have the control of them, and there is a [illegible] or butchers' meat market. That is held by a tenant who has it sub-let to the butchers.

25,939. Who is the tenant?—J. W. Deane of Longraue.

25,940. What are the market days?—Saturday and Wednesday.

25,941. What fairs have you here?—Here is a list of them.

25,942. Witness then produced a list which showed that fairs are held on the 10th January, 10th February, 15th March, 10th April, 3rd May, 10th June, 10th July, 10th August, 10th September, 18th October, 10th November, 9th December, Easter Monday and Whit Monday.

25,943. Are those all the fairs held here in the year?—Yes.

25,944. You have fourteen altogether?—Yes.

25,945. When were these fairs established here?—Up to 1801 we had only five fairs, and in going through the minutes of the old corporation, in 1834, I find that they applied for six additional fairs, that would be eleven.

25,946. How many had they previous to that application for additional fairs, and what fairs had they, or do they recite them in the resolution?—No. The minutes are very [illegible] edited. It was by reference to old almanacs that I had to make out the list of fairs in 1784, 1788, 1830, and 1801.

25,947. You hold fourteen fairs at present, and at one period you had less than 14?—Yes, in 1801.

25,948. How many fairs were held in 1801, and what fairs?—Five fairs.

25,949. What were they?—April 8th, May 4th, August 10th, October 4th, and December 9th. That was all in 1801.

25,950. What fairs were added subsequently?—I did not come across the granting of the patent on the minutes, but the fairs have been held as if it were granted.

25,951. What fairs were added?—There appears to have been added to the five fairs held in 1801, the fairs on January 10th, February 10th, March 17th—this fair is held now on the 15th,—April 10th, June 10th, July 10th, and September 10th.

25,952. That makes 12?—Yes.

25,953. When were the two movable ones added on the fixed days?—I find in the year 1830 there were two old fairs, one on the 3rd May and the other on the 30th.

25,954. You had first in 1801 five fairs, three of which were held on 8th April, 4th May, and 4th October. These are not the dates on which they are held at present. When were they altered, or what is the first record you have of their being held on the present dates?—I have no record at all.

25,955. How far does your memory extend as to the fairs here?—I have them from an almanac in 1830.

25,956. They were held on the same dates as at present?—Yes, subject to those variations. In 1830 the fairs were held on January 10th, February 11th, March 18th—that was a Monday, because the 17th fell on Sunday; April 1st, that was Easter Monday; 3rd May, 24th May, Whitsun Monday; July 10th. I have not anyone in June though I am sure there was one; August 10th, September 10th, October 18th, November 11th, and December 9th, that was a Monday, the 8th being a Sunday. The fair in March was held on the 17th then; it is the 15th now, and also you will notice that the April fair on the 1st is held on the 10th now. I think, when Easter Monday falls in April there will be no other fair in that month, and when Whit Monday falls in June there will be no other fair in that month, and what I would assume is that the 1st April was Easter Monday, and they did not hold one there on that date.

25,957. At that time there was no patent or other authority granting to the town commissioners of New Ross either these fairs or markets?—Yes. In regard to the 15th March fair, I may remark that the 17th March being a holiday, the date was changed to the 15th.

25,958. What year was that change made?—Over twenty years ago, I think.

25,959. You cannot fix the date?—No.

25,960. It is over twenty years?—Yes.

25,961. You recollect it to be held on the 15th March for that period?—I do. I remember it well.

25,962. Are any tolls levied at any of these fairs?—No.

25,963. They are all toll free?—Yes.

25,964. They are all held upon the public street?—The fairs are held in a large open space. It is more a square than a street. It is called Irishtown.

25,965. Is it a widening of the street?—It is a long wide street—about seven or eight times as wide as one of the streets you passed through.

25,966. Do they have different portions of this space allotted off for the exposure of the different species of animals brought there?—The far up part is for horses, the next space again for sheep and cattle, and the cattle continue down, and the lower part is for pigs.

25,967. Have you a special pig fair day allotted off?—Yes, the day before the fair.

25,968. You have a pig fair on the day previous to the ordinary fairs?—Yes. The pig fair is to be held on or before the general fair except it falls on Sunday or holiday, when it will be held the day before such Sunday or holiday.

25,969. You have no tolls at the pig fair either?—No.

25,970. You do not collect any standing charges?—No.

25,971. Do they have standings on this space?—Yes, down at the quay portion there do be standings.

25,972. Of what nature?—A gentleman who lives in the street will be better able to give these particulars. There do be ordinal standings, such as at races, and places with cakes.

25,973. With canvas covers?—Yes, and apples in them.

25,974. Where are the markets held?—On the quay.

25,975. I see here the town commissioners made some byelaws regulating the markets?—Yes.

25,976. These byelaws were approved of by the magistrates in 1876?—Yes. All usual legal formalities were gone through.

25,977. You regulate the exposure of these different commodities principally on the quay?—Many things are exposed there.

25,978. Where is the fish-house erected?—On the quay.

25,979. Where is the Mary Street meat market?—It turns left from the hotel.

25,980. Practically the general market is held on the quay?—The principal market.

25,981. Have you any charges on these markets, or do you derive any benefit from them?—Not from what is held on the street. The only thing is the letting of the fish-house and weighbridge to Miss Latouche.

25,982. Are the buildings utilised for market purposes on Wednesday and Saturday?—The fish-house and weighbridge are included in one building.

25,983. The weighbridge is attached to the house?—Yes.

25,984. Have you a beam and scales there?—There is a regular weighbridge for weighing purposes, and a scales for weighing salmon in the fish-house.

25,985. You have no beam or scales for weighing potatoes or corn?—There is a man named Mr. Keogh who for a long time has kept a beam and scales, and he weighs potatoes, but he is not a functionary under the town commissioners.

25,986. The commissioners have no beam and scales?—They have only this weighbridge and small scales for weighing fish in the fish-house.

25,987. You have this weighbridge and scales sub-let?—Yes, to Mrs. Bridget Meagher, sister of Miss Latouche, who does the business for her.

25,988. What is the rent?—31l. 4s. a year, twelve shillings a week, and she pays the taxes.

25,989. I suppose you allow the ordinary deductions?—No.

25,990. What is the valuation of the building?—11l.

25,991. What are the average taxes in the year?—The rates and taxes amount to 4l., and sometimes more according to the striking of the rates.

25,992. That 31l. is the only benefit the commissioners derive from the markets and fairs here in New Ross?—Yes, with the exception of the shambles—that is a yard let to Mr. Dunne—and the ground rent is 18l.

25,993. You receive that amount also?—Yes.

25,994. Any profit derived from that goes to Mr. Dunne's use?—Yes, he has the stalls let weekly to butchers.

25,995. No charges are levied by individuals on any other commodities sold on the street?—No.

25,996. Only what Mrs. Meagher charges for the use of the fish-house, and any commodities she weighs at the bridge?—Yes.

25,997. These are the only charges in New Ross?—Yes.

25,998. Have you had experience of other markets besides New Ross?—No.

25,999. What would you say of the markets. Do you hear they are good and well-attended, or could you give any approximate idea of the quantity of the different commodities they bring in here?—I would not at present be able to state the real condition of the markets, but I know this within my own knowledge, generally there is a wonderful deterioration or falling off in the amount coming in. I would not be able to say as to corn or agricultural produce.

26,000. What would you assign for that falling off?—Thinning of the population since the time when I remembered a great deal coming in. There is a great decay amongst tradesmen and people coming in.

26,001. Were any representations ever made by the traders of the town to the commissioners to provide a suitable market place, and take the markets off the public street?—Yes. The commissioners about 1872 or 1873, appointed a committee, and they went through a good deal with regard to the advisability of building a market house, and as the law stood we had a long correspondence with the Local Government Board and the Board of Works. The estimate was about 3,000l. for a building with the market house below, and an assembly room above, and they found after all their application the Local Government Board could not sanction it unless it was for sanitary purposes. At the time there were so many impediments in the way that after a long correspondence the matter was dropped.

26,002. When did this correspondence take place?—It began in 1872. There is a synopsis of the communications in the minutes.

26,003. However, the matter fell through?—Yes; and another thing which might be the cause of it was there had been a corn market built in town in 1818, it cost over 8,000l. by the old corporation, and in about three years they had to surrender it with the expenditure. From the entries I find in the minutes they made different efforts to get an Act to compel the people to go into it, and they would not go in as they had to be paying. That was a damper, for they thought when they provided this building at great cost the people would use it and pay, but it fell through.

26,004. Do the commissioners at present deem that a necessity exists for such market premises?—Well, they believe there is a necessity for such market premises, but they believe also that if they went into debt for the providing of it that the town would have to pay the whole, and they would be burdening the town with what would be for general convenience, and which the general public should contribute to. The corn market house that was built in 1818 is in sound condition at present.

26,005. How is it utilised at present?—The landlord has it. It was completed in 1818, and there is about 25 square yards in it.

26,006. Were any charges levied on the corn?—There was to be charges, for I find entries made in the minutes.

26,007-8. Did any corn come to it at all?—It would appear from the minutes that there did not. There is one entry—"the clerk of the market collected tolls on all corn brought into the market"—and I find after that he was not to collect the tolls, and I find they applied to Parliament for an Act to compel people to go into the market. It passed two stages, and was then abandoned.

26,009. They introduced a Bill which never became an Act. You have not got a copy of that Bill?—No. It was introduced in 1824. 60l. was paid to a man named Barton for getting it through two stages, and on March 25th I find 60l. paid to the clerk of the markets in lieu of tolls or customs. On October 25th a committee of the body reported that it was desirable to relinquish all tolls on corn. The charge is three half-pence a barrel on all corn weighed, and in 1829 the Corporation agreed to surrender the market to Charles Tottenham. The sum of 225l. 1s. 7d. accrued due to him as landlord, and the Corporation had no interest in continuing the place as a corn market.

26,010. Where is the corn sold at present?—On the streets.

26,011. Have they any special street they go to?—The buyers from the different malting establishments sometimes go out in the road and sometimes stand on the street, principally in the vicinity of where the corn is purchased and paid for.

26,012. Is there any special street that they generally resort to?—Yes, Bridge Street and John Street on the quay.

26,013. This is a large corn market?—Yes.

26,014. You have no byelaw regulating that corn market?—No. They thought it was better to let the

are to be bought and sold so that the buyers and sellers could arrange amongst themselves.

[illegible]. Did the commissioners within a recent period discuss the advisability of creating a market place?—Not since the application I speak of.

[illegible]. Are they the sanitary authority?—They are.

[illegible]. When did they take over these powers under the Public Health Act?—In 1873.

[illegible]. What do you assign, then, for the failure of negotiations. Was it the expense that would be incurred in the establishment of such a market deterred them from completing the project?—It appeared to believe it was a great reason, but there was much difficulty, you will see by the long correspondence, in getting the loan, and one point, I think, was raised against it that it was not for sanitary purposes.

[illegible]. Was there any communication in this correspondence to that effect in refusing the loan, because it seems extraordinary that such an objection was raised?—No. It broke off partly. The commissioners got tired. They found it tough travelling. I do not think there was any communication stopping them directly.

[illegible]. The commissioners have not discussed the subject since that time?—No.

[illegible]. Do you know the feelings of the townspeople?—The feelings of the townspeople and country people are that they would wish to have the convenience, but the townspeople would not like to undergo the cost.

[illegible]. Apart altogether from the cost or any expense that would be incurred, do you think the country people, both the producers and the buyers, would approve of a proper market house being afforded, and adequate space provided for all agricultural produce and all marketable commodities brought to the town, and not have them going about indiscriminately through the streets; that the commissioners should have control over them and have a rule enforcing the exposure of commodities in this market house and not elsewhere?—I am afraid the commissioners would not like to undertake that. They found they had to abandon the proposed change of fairs which they believed to be advantageous.

[illegible]. Apart from the financial difficulty, do you think a necessity exists for them?—I do. I believe that in wet weather and in very warm weather on that quay, it would be a great advantage to the people selling if they had the means of shelter from the wet in winter and the heat in summer.

[illegible]. I see the roll butter is sold in or opposite the present fish-house. Do the people ever make complaints on account of the close proximity of the butter to the fish that the butter has been deteriorated in quality and value?—No. There might be something I do not know of and Miss Latouche will be able to tell. Unfortunately there is no such great supply of fish in the fish-house. The salmon that comes in the morning is sent off next day.

[illegible]. Is Mr. Deane here?—No.

[illegible]. Do you know his charges in the shambles?—I think one shilling and sixpence a stall.

[The following are the byelaws made by the Town Commissioners.]

BOROUGH OF NEW ROSS.

To wit.

The following BYELAWS and REGULATIONS for holding the Markets in the town of New Ross, were, at a meeting duly convened of the Town Commissioners of New Ross, appointed under the provisions of the Towns' Improvement (Ireland) Act, 1854, held on the 9th day of July 1873 (more than two-thirds of the members present), unanimously agreed on for the regulation of the Markets in said Borough:—

MEAT MARKET.—Butchers' meat shall not be sold or exposed for sale in any of the streets or thoroughfares, but all other meat, such as salt and fresh offal, as well as salt fish, may be exposed for sale on the south side of Mary Street, not lower than the entrance to Barrack Lane.

FISH MARKET.—All fresh fish shall be sold in the Fish House, or in such other place or house as the Commissioners may from time to time provide for that purpose, except fresh sprats, herrings, mackerel, &c., brought by boats and retailed therefrom to the public. Cockles shall be sold either in creels, baskets, or boxes in front of the fish-house, but not so as to obstruct the entrance thereto. No cars with any horse, mule, or ass attached thereto, shall be allowed to stand in front of the Fish-house. Barrelled herrings shall be sold on the Quay, at the river side, between Quay Street and Charles Street, but as nearly as possible opposite Quay Street.

FURNITURE MARKET.—To be held on the Quay, between Archer's Pier and Daly's Corner, not nearer than forty feet to the edge of the flagway, or footpath.

VEGETABLE MARKET.—To be held on the Quay, between the Fish-house and Watch-house Pier, at the river side.

ROLL AND CROCK BUTTER.—To be sold in or opposite the present Fish-house.

EGGS.—To be sold on the Quay between Charles Street and the Bridge.

BUTTER IN FIRKINS.—To be sold on the Quay, between Flanagan's Hotel and the Custom House.

FOWL MARKET.—To be held on the Quay, and no sale shall be made before 7 o'clock a.m., during the months of October, November, December, January, February, and March, and not before 6 o'clock a.m., during the remainder of the year.

FRUIT MARKET.—To be held in Quay Street.

BRUSHES.—To be sold at the north side of Charles Street.

HAY AND STRAW.—To be sold on the Quay, opposite Flanagan's Hotel.

And no articles, or commodities, aforesaid, shall be sold or exposed for sale in any of the streets, or on any of the quays or public thoroughfares, other than those specified for that purpose.

The person discharging the office of Street Inspector of the said Commissioners, shall be the person to superintend the said markets, and keep order therein; and it shall be his duty to define the particular places where the said markets, in the above places shall be held, and to settle all disputes and questions in relation thereto, with a power of appeal from his decision, by any party aggrieved, to the Town Commissioners; but pending such appeal, the Inspector's decision to be acted on.

In case of the Inspector's absence, the Commissioners may appoint any other person to discharge the same duty.

Any breach of the foregoing Byelaws, shall subject the person violating the same to a penalty not exceeding 5l.

Any such penalty may be sued for summarily, and recovered with or without costs, and such penalty applied, in like manner, as is provided in the Towns Improvement (Ireland) Act, 1854; and all the forms of procedure prescribed by the Petty Sessions (Ireland) Act 1851, may be used for such purpose, or such penalties may be sued for and recovered under the said Petty Sessions (Ireland) Act, 1851, and the penalties applied, as in said Towns' Improvement (Ireland) Act, 1854.

Dated this 12th day of September 1873.

SEBASTIAN P. M'GRENEY,
Chairman of the said Town Commissioners.
PATRICK KELLY,
JOHN POWER,
Two of the said Town Commissioners.
JOHN TOBIN,
Town Clerk of the said Borough.

COUNTY OF WEXFORD, to Wit.

At a Quarter Sessions held in New Ross, in and for said County, on the 20th day of October 1873, the foregoing Byelaws were duly submitted to and examined, and allowed by the Justices at said Quarter Sessions.

Dated this 20th day of October 1873.

HENRY WEIR,
Chairman of the Justices presiding at said Sessions.
JOSEPH MEADOWS,
Clerk of the Peace for said County
R. LOWE,
One of Her Majesty's principal Secretaries of State.
Approved this 28th day of November 1873.

Miss ANNE LATOUCHE examined.

[illegible]. You manage this fish-house, weighbridge, and butter market for Miss Meagher?—Yes. She is my sister.

26,028. How do you let out the fish-house, or what do you receive from it?—I get a penny for the weighing of salmon, and then in the pen [illegible] a halfpenny each.

26,029. Is that the only charge you receive in connexion with the fish market?—That is all.

26,030. Do they expose the fish for sale in this fish-house?—There is a market there at half-past eight every morning. They bring the fish there, and the fish buyers come and buy them, and I weigh them.

26,031. You never weigh until a sale has been previously effected of the fish?—No.

26,032. Do you receive any charge—what is called a standing charge—for the space they occupy?—No, nothing for that.

26,033. Supposing they did expose the fish in this fish-house, and sold it, but the buyer did not require it to be weighed at your scales, would you seek for your charge?—I should get nothing but for the weighing of it.

26,034. Have you any rule compelling them to go there?—There is a byelaw compelling them to weigh, but the byelaws are very much violated.

26,035. (*The Commissioner to the Town Clerk.*) Have you got the byelaw here?—Yes.

26,036. You have no rule compelling them to weigh? There is a rule compelling them to sell in the fish-house and not elsewhere.

26,037. (*To Miss Latouche.*) I presume, then, it is customary when the fish are sold, to weigh at your scales?—Yes.

26,038. Do they ever go away without weighing at your scales?—They do, and weigh in the houses where the fishdealers live.

26,039. Do you know does the buyer charge anything for that weighing?—For the last three years I think it is, there were some buyers used to weigh in defiance of my father. It was he had the weigh-bridge and salmon market, and they give him no allowance for what they used to weigh. These three or four years, one man agreed to allow me for the fish he weighs at his house, but still he would not let them come to the market.

26,040. Does he pay you?—I cannot say whether he does or not, but he gives me something.

26,041. That is the buyer who gives you the charge?—Yes. He receives a penny or a halfpenny from the seller.

26,042. Still you have nothing to show you whether it is an accurate account or not?—No. There is another fishdealer who buys fish in his own house and does not charge, but I go into him and ask him about it, and he may hand me a 1s. or 5s., or whatever he wishes himself, but he does not take any payment from the sellers.

26,043. Is the fish market always held?—It is.

26,044. (*The Commissioner to the Town Clerk.*) There is no byelaw in the document before me compelling them to weigh?—No. It never struck me before. I looked through and cannot see any, but I really believed it to be so.

26,045. How long has the market been held, or have you been receiving charges from the fish?—It is 15 years since the fish market commenced. In 1824, I find the old corporation appointed a woman named Mrs. Ketchgale weighmistress in the fish-house. It was built in 1810 by the corporation.

26,046. (*To Miss Latouche.*) What do you weigh on the weighbridge?—Hay, straw, timber, bark, and turnips.

26,047. Any turf?—No.

26,048. What do you charge for weighing on the weighbridge?—I get 4d. a load for hay and straw, and 5d. for an oat load, and 3d. for a load of timber, that is, if they had a number of loads to be weighed.

26,049. For a single load you would charge 4d.?—Yes.

26,050. On turnips?—4d.

26,051. On bark, what do you charge?—3d. A number generally comes.

26,052. A single load would be 4d.?—Yes.

26,053. If they had a number of loads of hay or straw do you reduce the amount?—No.

26,054. Are the commodities weighed at the bridge sold before they are weighed?—They are.

26,055. They hold the hay and straw market on the quay?—Yes, just opposite the weighbridge.

26,056. But if they expose them on the quay and sell, but do not weigh at your scales, you do not seek for any charge?—I should get nothing for that.

26,057. (*The Commissioner to the Town Clerk.*) Are these byelaws the only ones in existence?—Yes.

26,058. There is no rule in the market compelling them to weigh any commodity, either at the scales or weighbridge, but you have been under the impression that such a byelaw has been in existence?—Yes, and it has been the usage, and until the present, I will acknowledge my ignorance.

26,059. (*To Miss Latouche.*) Do you give a ticket denoting the weight?—Yes.

26,060. Is it a printed form?—Yes.

26,061. On that ticket, do you put the gross weight?—Yes, the gross weight and tare.

26,062. Do you always ascertain the tare of the cart?—No. Sometimes the buyers may take the weight of the cart if they did not want the cart to come back, but they generally weigh them.

26,063. Except when the buyer and seller agree you always weigh the cart?—Yes.

26,064. In any case, you never estimate the tare of the cart?—No.

26,065. Suppose they agree to the tare, do you put that tare down in the ticket?—Yes, if the man weighed the cart the day before, but not without knowing it.

26,066. Have you ever to make up the tickets for those people?—I have.

26,067. Then you become acquainted, more or less, with the contract price, that is, the money paid for the load?—Yes.

26,068. Only of the commodities you weigh?—Yes.

26,069. Is it only salmon they weigh at your scales?—Yes.

26,070-1. Do they bring other fish into the fish-house?—They bring all the fish about the town.

26,072. Do you give a ticket for the salmon weighed?—Yes.

26,073. A printed form?—Yes.

26,074. Is it different from the one at the weighbridge?—Yes.

26,075. You never weigh potatoes?—No. It is Mr. Keogh weighs them.

26,076. Do you keep a block of those tickets?—I do.

26,077. Who weighs the butter?—I weigh butter.

26,078. On which scales? On a small scales.

26,079. You have a different scales for it?—Yes.

26,080. Is it only roll butter is brought here?—It is lump butter.

26,081. You never weigh firkins?—No.

26,082. What do you charge for weighing butter?—A penny a roll when it goes to seven pounds, and a halfpenny under seven pounds.

26,083. No matter what quantity is in the roll do you only charge a penny?—If it goes to fourteen pounds I get three halfpence, and for what we call a crock or pan of butter twopence.

26,084. What would be the quantity in that?—There might be 25, 27, or 30 pounds.

26,085. Twopence is the highest charge?—Yes.

26,086. Supposing they bring a crock or pan of butter would you drain it?—It is always turned in on the scales, and any pickle in it runs out of it, and it is turned back into the pan again.

26,087. You allow nothing for anything that clings to the scales or when making up the ticket?—No, except the seller and buyer allow a quarter or so, but you know when weighing roll butter you say four pounds standing beam. They generally allow a quarter.

26,088. For what?—That is if it is light of four pounds. If it is not a standing beam there is a quarter taken off.

26,089. That is when it is a broken quarter?—Yes.

26,090. The difference between the actual weight and the broken quarter would go to the buyer?—Yes, sometimes if it is a smaller beam they take a penny off.

26,091. Do you always weigh by standing beam?—I always give a cast at that scale.

26,092. Supposing you weigh a crock of butter, what is the lowest weight you weigh down to, or is it a quarter of a pound?—Yes, and no less.

26,093. What is the lowest in weighing a veal?—A quarter is the lowest.

26,094. And you always give a cast?—Yes.

26,095. Then it must be a quarter or nothing?—It must be less than a quarter.

26,096. It must make a quarter or nothing?—Yes. There are no ounces or two ounces.

26,097. Are these the only commodities you weigh?—Yes.

26,098. Do they ever weigh at your scales a salmon in parts?—No. The buyers themselves often cut it in their own houses and sell it to the housekeepers.

26,099. Practically this market is a wholesale fish market?—It is wholesale and retail.

26,100. Can the public come and buy?—Yes, they can.

26,101. Do they come in and buy a single fish?—Yes.

26,102. Do buyers ever purchase some of the fish in the morning and re-sell in the market?—They do retail over again.

26,103. Supposing they buy a quantity of fish and weigh it you get a charge, and if they re-sell it in the market place do you get another charge?—They never re-weigh it. They may sell at their own house.

26,104. Do they re-sell in the fish market?—No. They go to their own places.

26,105. Could you tell me your average receipts from these different sources of revenue?—I could not.

26,106. Do not you keep an account?—Yes, my sister keeps an account, but the receipts for the last few years are very bad.

26,107. Who have you to assist you?—I have her little daughter sometimes, and a little boy.

26,108. Is it only on Wednesday and Saturday you attend?—No. I weigh every day.

26,109. Is there any fish now?—No fish now.

26,110. There is weighing carried on every day at the weighbridge?—Yes.

26,111. What are the principal market days?—Saturday is the principal market day, but there is a market every day. There might be as good a market on Tuesday as there would be on Saturday.

26,112. That is for the weighbridge?—Yes. The roll butter is weighed through the shops of the town.

26,113. Do they expose it opposite the fish-house?—Yes; but they weigh it in the shops.

26,114. You cannot say what is your average receipts?—No.

26,115. You pay 20l. a year?—Yes.

26,116. Do you think does she make 20l.?—Sometimes we do not make the rent. The rent is 10s. a week, and for the past fortnight or three weeks she did not make it.

26,117. Does she make 20l. a year profit, taking one year with the other?—She does not.

26,118. Does she make 10l.?—We do not have the rent out of it, and the cost of her time and everything.

26,119. You have no rules other than what the Town Clerk produces?—No.

HENRY KEOGH examined.

26,120. You have a beam and scales here in the town of New Ross?—Yes, for a length of time.

26,121. Do you let it out for weighing purposes?—I weigh myself there.

26,122. Where is the corn weighed?—In the store mostly it is weighed. They buy it on the street and then bring it in to weigh it.

26,123. The potatoes are always brought in bags when weighed?—Yes.

26,124. What do you charge?—A penny a bag, and a halfpenny per small one.

26,125. How do you distinguish whether it is a halfpenny or a penny?—According to the weight. Anything that does not come up to ten stone is a halfpenny, and anything over a penny.

26,126. If they bring in a load of twelve bags, we will say, would you charge a shilling on the twelve?—Yes.

26,127. Do you always ascertain the tare of the bag?—Yes. We take a stone off a large bag, and a half stone off a small bag.

26,128. You estimate it?—Yes. We do not weigh the empty bags.

26,129. If the gross weight is ten stone do you allow half a stone for the weight of the sack?—Yes, that is the rule always. If a small bag weighs seven, eight, or nine stone we allow half a stone.

26,130. If over ten stone do you allow a stone?—It must be over eleven stone or something that way.

26,131. But the stone is the highest deduction?—Yes.

26,132. Is there anything else besides that?—No. There was a rule here some years ago that for a great big bag we would take a stone and a half off it.

26,133. What would be the gross weight of that?—Twenty-four or twenty-six stone.

26,134. What allowance is supposed to cover all deductions for mud?—There is nothing further, no matter what way the potatoes are.

26,135. Would it be the same deductions on bags brought on a fine day as on a very wet day, when the sack was completely saturated with wet?—It makes no difference that way at all.

26,136. Are these potatoes sold before you weigh them?—Yes, of course they are. It is when they are sold I weigh them.

26,137. How long have you been in the practice of doing so?—It is before I can remember.

26,138. When weighing, down to what weight do you ascertain the quantity in a sack. Do you use the half-stone weight?—Yes.

26,139. Do you use a smaller weight?—No, it must be about a half stone.

26,140. Do you give a cast of the beam?—Yes.

26,141. Always?—Yes.

26,142. Then it must be a half stone or nothing?—Yes.

26,143. Do you give them any ticket denoting the weight?—No.

26,144. Do you chalk it on the bag?—Yes.

26,145. What weight do you chalk on the bag. Is it the net weight or the gross weight?—The net weight. They would be very angry if I put the gross weight. What is payable is all I put always.

26,146. Is it always on the net weight you charge?—I charge on the weighing of the bags whatever they weigh.

26,147. To distinguish between the halfpenny and the penny charge, is it always on the net weight you charge?—I allow a penny to be paid for a large bag and a halfpenny for a small one.

26,148. Then you say up to ten stone is a small one?—Yes, and six and seven stone. If the gross weight of the bag was ten stone there would be nine and a half payable.

26,149. You only charge a halfpenny then?—Yes.

26,150. You never keep a record of the quantity brought to you?—No.

26,151. Do you have to make up the tickets?—I make them up constantly.

26,152. You know the prices?—Yes.

26,153. Do you keep any record of them?—No.

26,154. When the merchants weigh corn for the farmers do they charge them for weighing?—I do not know. I was never in a corn store. They do not charge, I believe.

26,155. Is there any charge paid by the farmers other than the penny they have to pay to you, or is there any thing for passage?—That is their own business. I have nothing to do with it.

26,156. But from your experience you know if they have to do so?—If they employ men to weigh them for them, they give them a couple of pence if they are not able to weigh themselves.

26,157. You do not weigh for them?—No, I do not keep anyone to weigh them.

26,158. You only let them the use of the scales?—Yes.

26,159. There is the scales, and if a farmer comes in and weighs his commodity, and utilises the scales for a period, however short, you levy the charge, and any manual labour he has he pays for it?—Yes.

26,160. Is it customary for porters to be about the place?—I will tell you what they are very much in the habit of doing. One farmer will help another, but the porters, who are very much missed, would rather be employed themselves.

26,161. That is the only commodity you weigh there?—I have weighed other things occasionally.

26,162. Do the police visit your scales occasionally?—They do.

26,163. You have heard no complaints of the inaccuracy of the weights?—No, but I know where there are complaints, and we will leave that so.

26,164. Have you heard any complaints of inaccuracy in the weights at other scales in the town, whether private or public?—Very frequently I heard them.

26,165. Were they private scales or public scales?—Private scales. There is no public scales in the town but mine.

26,166. Were they private scales let out for public use?—No; I believe they only used them for their own purposes; but I can tell you they do not allow me to weigh the potatoes. They come down and take them off the quay to their own places to weigh.

26,167. Was it yourself who provided this house and scales?—Yes, and kept them in order.

26,168. You paid the cost of their erection?—Yes, they were erected in my grandfather's time.

26,169. The commissioners have no control over them?—No.

Matthew [illegible], Esq., Chairman of the Town Commissioners, examined.

26,170. You are the chairman of the town commissioners of New Ross?—Yes.

26,171. I believe at one period the then commissioners were in communication with the Local Government Board with a view to the erection of a market building to afford accommodation and to concentrate all the markets in that building?—Yes.

26,172. The present commissioners have never discussed the advisability of the erection of such a market place?—No.

26,173. Have you any views on that subject?—I have not really.

26,174. Do you think it would tend to the improvement of the markets, and the better order and regularity of them, if a large and sufficiently ample market place was provided with efficient and adequate accommodation, both for the perishable commodities and those bringing them to the market—do you think that would tend to improve them?—I do, but the people of the town would not wish to be saddled with the expense.

26,175. Apart altogether from any financial difficulty, do you think a necessity exists for the erection of such a market?—There would.

26,176. Do you think the sellers who bring the different commodities would have any objection to pay a small charge that would support or maintain such a market place for the accommodation they would receive there?—I think they would object to it, unless very few of them.

26,177. What reason would you assign for their objection. If they got an adequate return for the small charge they would pay?—The charge should be very small, or otherwise they would object.

26,178. Have you had experience of other markets or fairs besides those in New Ross?—No.

26,179. Were tolls ever levied in New Ross within your own experience or time?—No.

26,180. Do you think if charges were levied that they would act in any way as a deterrent on people bringing in their commodities?—I think it would deter them. They would go elsewhere.

26,181. Can they go elsewhere, or is there any market sufficiently near that they can avail themselves of?—They would go to Wexford and elsewhere, and not come to New Ross. I think a very little charge would keep them off of the market.

26,182. Have you ever heard complaints from any of the townspeople, whether private individuals or traders, that much inconvenience was caused to them by the fact of the markets being held on the streets?—No, I did not hear any complaints.

26,183. Does not a lot of filth and dirt accumulate from the fact of the markets being held on the streets as well as the fairs?—They are mostly held on the quay.

26,184. Are there not houses on the quay?—There are.

26,185. Have those people ever complained?—I have never known them to complain.

26,186. Did you ever buy or sell at the fairs?—No.

26,187. You have no dealings connected with the farming interest?—No.

26,188. You do not know the feelings of the other commissioners about providing a proper market place?—I do not. I would wish to consult the commissioners before making any move.

26,189. Within your recollection it has not been brought before the present commissioners since the termination of the correspondence mentioned by Mr. Tobin?—There was nothing about it since.

Mr. Patrick [illegible] examined.

26,190. Have you anything to do with the fairs?—No, but at the markets.

26,191. You have to regulate the order and see they take up a proper position?—Yes. I have to see they are in the proper place and point it out.

26,192. You have no control or exercise, no supervision in connexion with the fairs?—No.

26,193. Do you attend any of the fairs?—Only pass through.

26,194. You know nothing about the dealings between the buyers and sellers?—No. The cattle market commences early, about 7 o'clock.

26,195. What hour does the general market usually commence?—From about 10 o'clock.

26,196. Have you ever heard people complaining in warm weather of the exposure of the fish and butter on the public street?—The fish is kept at the river side, and the butter market is right opposite.

26,197. Still, they have no shelter accommodation from the sun for the butter or fish?—No.

26,198. Have you ever heard them complaining?—No. The butter market is over about 1 o'clock in the day.

26,199. Is it held on the public road?—Yes, on the footpath.

26,200. Is it customary at the fairs for the seller to give the buyer a luck penny?—It is.

26,201. Is there any rule regulating the amount of it?—I do not know.

26,202. Is it left to the disposition of the seller?—Yes.

26,203. Where is the pig fair held?—In the Irishtown. It is a wide place.

26,204. You attend the markets?—Yes.

26,205. Will you kindly mention all the different commodities brought into the markets here?—There is a fowl market on Saturday.

26,206. They only come on Saturday?—Yes. For six months of the year they buy at 7 o'clock in the morning, and for the other six months at 8 o'clock.

26,207. What are the other commodities they bring in?—Potatoes, hay, straw, turnips, fish, basket—and butter and firkin butter.

26,208. Do they bring firkins?—Yes.

26,209. Where are the firkins weighed?—In Charles Street.

26,210. At whose scales?—They buy by hand except an odd time.

26,211. By bulk?—Yes.

26,212. Do they come in any quantity?—Yes, in certain months of the year.

26,213. Within your knowledge a firkin has not been bought by weight?—In some instances.

26,214. Where do they weigh?—They take it into a shop and weigh it on a large scales.

26,215. They only ascertain the gross weight?—Yes.

26,216. They would not empty the firkin?—No. They would allow so much for the timber.

26,217. Do they come in any quantity?—Certain months of the year we have a very good market.

26,218. What is the largest number of firkins you have seen brought in?—On some occasions up to 30 firkins.

26,219. These would have to be weighed in the private shopkeeper's place?—Perhaps some days there may not be one weighed. If there is any little difference between the farmer and buyer they weigh.

26,220. What other commodities?—Eggs and corn.

26,221. Do they bring in pigs, calves, or cattle on market days?—There is a certain day that young calves come in, but it is not a market day.

26,222. What day?—Tuesday, and sometimes Saturday morning.

26,223. What time of the year?—At different times of the year. There are early calves and late calves.

26,224. Where do they expose them?—In Charles Street, off the quay.

26,225. Do they bring any timber and expose it on the public thoroughfare?—Timber is brought in and delivered on the quay to be shipped to some country.

26,226. Do they sell any meat on the public thoroughfare?—There is meat sold on the quay at the river side. It is cut meat and sold off a table in small lumps.

26,227. These people have to pay no charge?—No.

26,228. Would the meat be exposed to the rain in winter and the heat of the sun in summer?—Yes.

26,229. Have you heard complaints from those people or any other person in town of the want of shelter accommodation?—No, not exactly. They are kept in a proper place.

26,230. Still, they are exposed to the elements?—They are.

26,231. What animals are brought to the fairs?—Horses, cattle, sheep, and pigs.

26,232. You have no duties to perform in connexion with them?—No.

26,233. Is there any other gentleman who has any evidence to give?—(*No answer.*)

The inquiry then adjourned.

BAGENALSTOWN.

With reference to my inquiry in Bagenalstown on the 7th day of December 1888, I

Producers are free to utilise this building for the exposure and disposal of their fowl without payment of any charge.

The market rights were formerly sub-let to the town commissioners, but about four years ago they surrendered them, as they found the receipts did not equal the amount expended.

No tare is usually ascertained at the beams and scales, and if a ticket is required denoting the weight the gross alone is given.

A complaint was made of the pig and sheep fairs being held on the public streets, as there is no rule restricting the exposure of animals elsewhere than on the fair green.

The town commissioners stated they were unable to cope with the difficulty, as they were not empowered to make byelaws, not being the urban sanitary authority.

Appended will be found a transcript of the evidence taken at the inquiry.

JOHN J. O'MEARA,
Assistant Commissioner.

45, Lower Mount Street,
Dublin.

Bagenalstown, 7th December 1888.

Mr. JOHN B. WARREN, Town Clerk, examined.

26,240. You are the town clerk of Bagenalstown?—Yes.

26,241. When were the commissioners established here?—In February 1882.

26,242. What powers have they?—They make a rate and light the town out of that rate, and pay some other matters out of it.

26,243. They do not do any paving?—No; nothing but the lighting.

26,244. They are not the sanitary authority?—No.

26,245. The Board of Guardians attend to the sanitary matters?—Yes.

26,246. What is the town rate here?—The town rate is ninepence in the pound. It was a shilling.

26,247. Have the commissioners any market rights at all in Bagenalstown?—None, except what is charged for weighing on the scales and crane.

26,248. Have they provided a crane?—No. It is a private crane.

26,249. They have no rights themselves then?—They have none.

26,250. Who are the owners of these market rights?—Philip George Newton.

26,251. Is there any other person claiming rights here?—No.

26,252. Market or fair rights?—No.

26,253. What has Mr. Bagenal to say then?—Mr. Bagenal is the owner of where the cattle fair is held.

26,254. Are tolls levied at these markets?—No, except the charges for weighing.

26,255. Are tolls levied at the fairs?—No.

26,256. What are the market days here?—Saturday.

26,257. Saturday alone?—Yes.

26,258. What fairs are held here?—Monthly fairs.

26,259. What date?—The second Monday of each month.

26,260. Have you a pig fair the day previous?—No. Both fairs are held on the one day.

26,261. In this fair green?—No.

26,262. Where are they held?—The pig fair is held on the streets, and the cattle fair is held on the fair green.

26,263. Are those streets in which the pigs are sold adjacent to the fair green?—Some of them are.

26,268. Is there any shelter accommodation in the fair green?—No.

26,269. It is entirely enclosed?—Yes.

26,270. Have the cattle fairs always been held there?—For the greater number of years they have, since it was walled in, but in former times they were all held on the street.

26,271. Could you give me any idea of the period when they were first held on the fair green?—Well, I could. It is a long time ago.

26,272. Is it twenty years?—It is, and double that.

26,273. Is it within your memory?—It is within my memory, but I could not remember. About forty-five years ago, I should think.

26,274. There is no rule in this fair green restricting the exposure of all animals elsewhere than in this fair green?—No.

26,275. Can the farmer go where he pleases and expose his cattle?—He can. There is nothing to prevent him.

26,276. As a matter of fact, do they bring any cattle out on the streets?—I have never seen them there.

26,277. They do not expose them for sale on the streets?—No. They drive all the cattle into the fair green.

26,278. Have the people of the town ever complained to the commissioners of these pig and sheep fairs being held on the streets?—Well, there was a complaint at one time by the police which caused the commissioners to inquire into it, and they passed a resolution which was to no effect. They had no power to carry it out.

26,279. What was the nature of the resolution?—The nature of the resolution was that the pig fair was not to be interfered with, and the cars should go to one side of the street instead of the two sides.

26,280. It was a resolution regulating the order in which the markets and fairs would be held?—Yes. This was the resolution:—

"That the present fat-pig fair be not interfered with
"in any way; that the cars containing small pigs be
"allowed to remain in the market square in Kilcarrig
"Street, and that any surplus cars remaining over
"shall extend down the one side of the main street,
"High Street and Regent Street."

26,281. Is that resolution observed?—No. The old system is carried out of having the cars at each side of the street.

—Is there any rule restricting them to expose these commodities in a certain place or position?—There is no rule, because we have no power.

24,288. I am speaking in a general sense about the commodities brought into Bagenalstown, and not any duties connected with the commissioners.—There was a place allotted for the sale of fowl and potatoes.

24,289. Then you have a fowl market?—Yes; an enclosed fowl market.

24,290. And potato market?—The fowl market is not Mr. Newton's property—that is Mr. Bagenal's. The potato market is Mr. Newton's.

24,291. Is that enclosed too?—It is not.

24,292. Where is it held?—It is at one end of the town. The potato market is open to the front.

24,293. Is it portion of the public thoroughfare?—It is.

24,294. Is it off the public street?—Yes.

24,295. Is it a commons off the public street?—No. The post office is there.

24,296. Is that the place in front of the post office?—Yes. That is the potato-market square.

24,297. Have you any market buildings other than the fowl market?—No. There is shelter in that. There are slated sheds round about it.

24,298. Are the beam and scales erected in the potato square beside the post office?—Yes, and the crane.

24,299. All commodities brought to Bagenalstown and exposed for sale are exposed in this square beside the post office?—Yes, all in the potato line.

24,300. Is corn brought here?—Some corn is brought in the rural season.

24,301. Is it brought there to that square?—It is brought into that and sold there. Any that is sold is sold there.

24,302. Have you ever attended that market yourself?—Yes.

24,303. Could you tell me the different marketable commodities that are brought into Bagenalstown on Saturday, and exposed for sale?—There are potatoes, turnips, coal, cabbages, and other vegetables. Very seldom any hay comes into Bagenalstown. Butter is not sold in that place.

24,304. Is butter brought to the town?—Yes.

24,305. Is it sold to the consumers?—It is sold to shopkeepers. They take from house to house.

24,306. Is it all roll butter?—Yes.

24,307. Are eggs brought here?—Yes, eggs to the fowl market with the fowl.

24,308. Is this fowl market availed of by the producers?—They were in the habit of stopping inside that place, but now they are in the habit of stopping outside, and they are not brought inside only very seldom.

24,309. Was there any charge levied on them for being inside?—None.

24,310. In the way of standing charge or entrance fee?—No.

24,311. It was an entirely free market to them?—It was.

24,312. Was it erected by Mr. Bagenal?—No. Mr. Bagenal gave us the market place.

24,313. Gave whom?—The commissioners, and he never charged any rent to my knowledge.

24,314. Was it his erected it originally?—It was. It was the shambles in former times, and then it was turned into this fowl market.

24,315. He gave it over to the commissioners?—Yes.

24,316. Did he give a lease of it?—No.

24,317. Do you know the terms of the letting?—I cannot tell you at present.

24,318. Did the commissioners pass any rule or make any byelaw for the sanction of the Local Government Board restricting the sale of fowl and eggs elsewhere than in the fowl market?—They did, and placed up notices warning the people against selling outside the place that was allotted for the sale of fowl.

24,319. Did you ever proceed for any breach of these rules?—We did not, for the reason we saw it would end in our failure.

24,320. Were these byelaws sanctioned by the Local Government Board?—We have no byelaws. We have no power. The consequence of making them would be a farce, if we could not carry them out.

24,321. Have the commissioners ever discussed the advisability of the erection of market buildings—large and adequate market buildings, in Bagenalstown—to afford sufficient protection for all descriptions of marketable commodities brought in here?—The chairman of the commissioners might be able to tell you something about that.

24,322. As commissioners, they have never discussed at the board the advisability of building a market?—Well, they have.

24,323. Apart altogether from the possibility of their erecting such a building, do they think a necessity exists for such a building in Bagenalstown?—I should think there is, but the present funds would not allow them to do so.

Mr. John Murray examined.

24,323a. I believe you are the tenant of Mr. Newton for the beam and scales and crane?—Yes.

24,324. Where have you this beam and scales erected?—It is erected over 20 years in the square opposite the post office. I am the postmaster, and I rent the square from Mr. Newton. The crane is in the square.

24,325. Was there any agreement between you and Mr. Newton?—Yes.

24,326. Were there any special agreements other than the ordinary ones between landlord and tenant?—The ordinary agreement.

24,327. There is no special covenant in it?—No. It is merely let to me as a tenant from year to year, with six months' notice to quit.

24,328. What is the rent?—10l. a year.

24,329. You weigh all commodities at this beam and scales, the weight of which is desired to be ascertained?—Yes.

24,330. What do you usually weigh?—I usually get potatoes to weigh, sometimes I get hay, and I dare say I weigh two thirds of the hay brought into the market.

24,331. There is a hay market?—Yes.

24,332. Do you ever weigh corn?—Yes, sometimes I weigh corn, but very, very rarely.

24,333. Is this a good corn market?—There is a large amount of corn brought into the town, but it is not allowed to go to the market.

24,334. It goes to the merchants?—Yes.

24,335. Is it previously bought by the merchants before being delivered to them?—I think not. It is all bought by sample and brought in afterwards.

24,336. Corn then is never exposed for sale in the market place, or about the town?—No.

24,337. Is it brought from door to door?—No. There are only two corn buyers, and samples are generally brought to them, and if they buy, the corn would not have to be brought in the market.

24,337a. Have you only one scales?—One scales and crane.

24,338. What do you charge for weighing potatoes?—The board says 1d. under eight stone, but I generally charge 1d. under ten stone.

24,339. You have a schedule of the charges granted?—Yes.

24,340. Witness then produced the schedule, of which the following is a copy:—

Rates for Weighing.

Draft of corn, flour, &c., 100 lbs. and under	1d.
Upwards	2d.
Draft of wool, 100 lbs. and under	4d.
Upwards	8d.
Draft of bacon, butter, &c., up to 4 stone	1d.
4 to 8 stone	2d.
Upwards	3d.
Load of coals, hay, turnips, &c.	6d.

No charge for weighing carts.

24,341. (Witness.) On looking over the board, I do not find potatoes on it at all, but the usual charge was 1d. under eight stones, and 2d. over it. Since I got it I charge nothing but 1d. under 10 stone and 2d. over it.

24,341a. Is it on the gross weight or net weight you charge?—I merely give the gross weight.

24,342. You never ascertain the actual tare of the sack?—No. If the people bring back the sacks we will weigh them free of charge and let them take that from the gross.

24,343. Do you give them a ticket denoting the weight?—We give them a ticket of the gross weight and keep a copy of it.

24,344. You keep a block?—Yes.

24,345. Do you know what is the customary allowance as tare between the buyer and seller?—For any potatoes in the market it is never more than half a stone. I have heard it frequently said there is a larger amount than that demanded and taken by the buyers in private buying, but the usual thing in the market is half a stone.

24,346. No matter what the gross weight would be?—No matter what the gross weight is. Of course if there is a small bag, what we generally call mill bags, and if I was there myself, it is recommended to the buyer that 4 lbs. is sufficient for that.

24,347. In case of dispute between them, would you weigh the empty sack?—Undoubtedly.

24,348. Would you demand any extra charge?—No.

24,349. Have you done so?—Yes, especially in corn.

24,350. What do you charge for corn?—2d. per bag.

24,351. Irrespective of the quantity the bag might contain?—Yes. I might add I do not remember having a bag under 8 stone. I dare say I would weigh it for 1d. if it was under 8 stone.

24,352. Do you ascertain the tare of the bag of corn?—I have frequently done that. The empty bags have been brought back.

24,353. Is it usual with you to do so?—It is as much one way as the other. Sometimes they are brought back, and more times they are not. It is a matter between the buyer and seller what they will allow for the bags.

24,354. You take no cognisance of the tare?—No, unless I am asked for it.

24,355. Have they any portorage charge here?—None whatever. The 2d. per bag covers all the charge. The men I employ refuse "tips" as they call them.

24,356. You have a porter employed to lift the bags off the car?—I have a clerk for minding the scales and a labouring man for weighing, and for the assistance given there is no charge taken.

24,357. Who weighs the commodity; is it clerk or the porter?—My employés put in the weights and charge for the tickets.

24,358. There is no portorage charge paid to this workman?—No, I pay that myself.

24,359. Do you keep a block of the ticket?—Yes, I keep a block of everything.

24,360. What do you charge for weighing butter?—I do not think I weighed butter more than twice or three times, and it is 2d. a firkin I charge. The rule is on the board. As you will see by the board, the charge for a draft of butter and bacon up to 8 stone is 1d., and over is 2d.

24,361. You always weigh the butter in its natural state?—In the firkin.

24,362. If not in the firkin, do you weigh it in lumps?—I never weigh lumps.

24,363. You only ascertain the gross weight of the firkin?—Yes.

24,364. You never strip the firkin?—No.

24,365. Was it ever drained?—No. If the firkins or empties are brought back they would be weighed free of charge.

24,366. Supposing a firkin was brought, you never take the top of it and turn it up to let the pickle out?—I never saw it done anywhere. I never saw it done in Carlow.

24,367. What is your charge on hay?—2d. a load.

24,368. I suppose you charge 2d. for any load?—Yes, and the empty car is weighed free.

24,369. Do you always actually weigh the empty car afterwards?—99 times out of a 100 they are weighed.

24,370. Supposing a man came in to-day and came to-morrow, would you give the weight you ascertain to-day on to-morrow?—No. If a man weighed hay up to-day I would take that as dealing with the whole article he was disposing of, for instance, if he was drawing 40 or 50 loads of hay to a purchaser.

24,371. If the buyer disputed that, what course would you adopt?—I would weigh the car if any complaint were expressed.

24,372. Have you heard of the cars being altered in any way after the delivery of the hay and straw, and before coming to you to be weighed?—Never since I took up the matter.

24,373. How long have you the scales?—Two years this month.

24,374. Is fish ever brought to this market?—Fish is sold at the corner part of the market, but it is never taken into where there is any tariff charged.

24,375. I suppose all these different commodities you weigh are sold previous to their being weighed?—Sometimes. Sometimes people wish to go out of the market early, and they ask us to weigh them. We then mark the weight on the bags, and also give them tickets and keep a copy of the tickets. They have the tickets to present to the buyer.

24,376. Have you ever to make up the tickets for these people?—We give the gross lot.

24,377. Have you ever to make up the value of the commodity according to the weight and the price they get?—If we have time we oblige them, but it is not a rule of the market to do so.

24,378. Supposing there were required from you the particulars of the current prices of these different marketable commodities, could you make such a return periodically?—Undoubtedly.

24,379. You consider that return would be a pretty accurate one?—I believe I would be in a better position than any other man in the town to give an accurate state of the prices.

24,380. Are commodities exposed for sale in this market place, and not weighed at your scales?—There is a large lot. In fact the town is ruined by that class of business. I know for a fact that men buying potatoes and other commodities have men out along the by-roads to meet people and prevent them from coming to the market under the impression that they are saving 2d.—very much under the impression that they are saving 2d.

24,381. Are those the buyers?—Yes.

24,382. They will stop the people as they are coming in?—Yes.

24,383. Supposing they exposed potatoes, corn, and other commodities in this market square, and sold them, but did not desire to go to your scales to ascertain the weight, would you look for any charge?—If they do not come in the market I have no right, and never sought for it.

24,384. Supposing they came right up to your door and exposed a commodity and sold it, but did not weigh at your scales, would you charge?—Yes, I would claim it.

24,385. Has a case of that kind arisen?—Yes.

24,386. Did you receive your charge?—Yes, I received as good as the charge—a promise of it.

24,387. You think your rights under your agreement with Mr. Newton entitle you to this charge?—I do.

24,388. You do not know under what authority Mr. Newton claimed that right to you?—It is his own private property, I believe.

24,389. Do you keep the blocks of these tickets for any length of time?—Yes.

24,390. They would not show the quantity of the different commodities brought to the market when they are not all weighed with you?—Very little has been taken off the market, except the buyers would go and tip them, and they would go, but otherwise everything is weighed there.

24,391. Do you ever weigh cattle?—I do not remember ever weighing cattle.

24,392. Is the weigh-bridge capable of weighing cattle?—Not without being in a float and weighed in the float. I think I weighed a bull or two.

24,393. You have no railings around the weigh-bridge?—No.

24,394. Would you have any objection to tell me what your average receipts are?—Well, I really could not give you any idea. I mean to give over the market owing to the bad arrangement, so that it cannot be a very paying concern.

24,395. What do you call the bad arrangement?—The system allowed in the town. I am speaking about the potatoes, fowl, and everything else, and sending people out on the bye-roads to contract with the people to bring their commodities to private places to be weighed.

24,396. Is it only to be weighed?—To be bought and weighed and kept there. There is every effort made to destroy the potato market and every market.

24,397. Is that course adopted for the purpose of saving twopence a bag?—I think there is a personal object.

24,398. What reason do you assign for that. Do they think they can purchase the commodity cheaper by forestalling in that way than allowing it to be brought into the market where there would be open competition?—There must be something behind that. I do not know why there should be a desire to save twopence to a man when it does not affect a man's pocket.

24,399. If you have any reasons to assign for that, you ought to state them?—In the first place I am entirely disinterested, as I want to give over the market square, but giving evidence that might be of use I think the great curse of the markets is private buying, and the inducement and encouragement offered to the people to carry on private buying.

24,400. Do you think if the commodities were brought in and exposed for sale in the public market, that the producer would get a better price?—They would get an honester price, because I notice in the course of the markets an innocent country person who comes and offers goods is made up to by a dandy person who will tell them they can do better outside. There is no opportunity for innocent country people selling their goods honestly.

24,401. Are there any country people here?—No. The majority are town people.

Cross-examined by Father O'Neill, as follows:—

24,402-3. I wanted to ask who put up the board, because it originally belonged to the town commissioners?—The town commissioners had the board erected.

24,404. They laid down the charges on the different articles?—Yes.

24,405. When did the town commissioners cease to have control?—I could not really say, but I think it is about three or four years ago.

24,406. Was not there some portion of the tolls paid to the town commissioners?—I do not know.

24,407. Did the town commissioners get something out of the tolls by the woman in charge of the weighing before you got possession?—I think there was something about, but I was never interested in anything about that.

24,408. How was it taken out of the hands of the town commissioners?—I do not know. I suppose it was Mr. Newton, but I do not understand that question.

24,409. As regards the charges that were laid down for weighing, do not you think at present, taking the times and circumstances into account, that they are a good deal in excess of what they ought to?—I do not.

24,410. You know everything is going down in price, and do you not think a revised board necessary?—If there were revised rules there might be a revised board.

24,411. I think you made an allowance sometimes when the toll was too much?—I believe I expressed an opinion that if all the goods came to the market, and if the private buying were abolished and things were straightforward and dealt with honestly, every bag could be weighed for a penny, because the number would be greater than at present, and they could be weighed at half the present price.

24,412. I agree with you. I think it is not fair when there is a public market and public place, the potatoes and all other articles supposed to be weighed ought to be weighed on the public scales. I think the more people look into it the more they will be of your opinion that it is not right for private people to meet them on the roadside and bring them to their own yard. I do not think the people are satisfied. I think myself if I was a farmer selling goods I would rather have them weighed at a public scale than a private one, no matter how honest the private one might be?—Yes. I contemplated buying potatoes this year and exporting them, but being the renter of the scale I was afraid the public might think in buying for myself I had an object, and I refrained from purchasing or exporting the potatoes in order that the people might have thorough confidence in the house and the [illegible] carried [illegible] there. Unless the private buying is abolished, there is no use in revising the board.

24,413. Who can abolish it?—The same party who can revise the board can abolish that. There is a large sale of wool here every year.

24,414. (The Commissioner.) Tell me your charge for weighing wool?—Fourpence for eight stone and under two hundred-weight.

24,415. Is it eightpence for any pack over that?—Yes. The scales have to be opened down, and it takes a good deal of trouble to weigh any pack over two hundred-weight.

24,416. What is the usual quantity you weigh?—I could give you the gross if I had been asked.

24,417. That would be the actual quantity brought to the market, and not including what would be weighed elsewhere?—Yes. The wool is weighed elsewhere, and every facility given to keep it out of the market. There is a private scale and Mr. Dunn, a wool buyer, will give the benefit to that.

24,418. What is the lowest weight you weigh down to?—To half a pound.

24,419. Do you weigh by standing beam or give a cast?—Just a slight cast. I work that beam and conduct my market on the strictest principle of honesty.

24,420. In weighing potatoes what do you weigh down to?—4 pounds.

24,421. You do not weigh under 4 pounds?—No; it is not usual.

24,422. Do you give a cast of the beam?—No, a turn of the beam.

24,423. Is it a good turn?—No; it is just a turn. I may add in the majority of markets they do not go under a half stone.

24,424. In weighing corn do you give a cast?—I barely give a turn of the beam.

24,425. Down to what weight do you weigh?—Down to a pound.

24,426. And in butter?—To the half pound.

24,427. What would you charge for a load?—The load of coal coming in here generally averages 23 hundred. He may draft the entire lot for 4d. If he weighs a load it is 2d., but to draft the whole lot will be 4d.

24,428-9. Supposing a farmer brought in a great quantity of potatoes—we will say brought in a load of about 12 sacks—and weighed them at your scales, and sold in the market place, and they were subsequently retailed at the market place by people who desired to weigh them again, would you charge a second time?—Undoubtedly, but it has never occurred.

24,430. Is this market wholesale market principally?—Wholesale and retail.

24,431. Do the sellers have small scales to weigh the commodities?—No, I would not allow it.

24,432. If the working men of the town wish to go to the market place for a stone of potatoes, can they get them?—Yes. When the new potatoes come in I provide a suitable measure for retailing them.

24,433. They sell them by measure?—Yes. I place a basket and balance it on the scales, and have it properly balanced throughout, so they are prepared to abide by the tariff.

24,434. What is the charge?—A load of new potatoes would be about 4d. to draft them out.

26,435. Would you charge that 4d. in addition to 6d. a bag?—New potatoes are never brought in bags.

26,436. Supposing they came in next Saturday, and a man went up to buy a stone of potatoes?—I never charge the poor people for drafting. The poor people of the town come in, and if they wish to buy a bag or retail them I allow them the use of the scales. I never charge for dividing the bag.

26,437. Can the poorer members of the community buy small quantities of marketable commodities in the market at the ordinary prices, without paying anything additional for the weighing?—I do not understand you.

26,438. Supposing there are farmers and dealers in the market square to-morrow, and a man in the town comes up to buy a stone of potatoes, can that stone of potatoes be weighed at your scales?—That is not the usual idea. The principal retailers are the shopkeepers about the town, who buy what they want for the week.

26,439. Practically they cannot buy small quantities in the market square. They must go to the retailers in the town?—Yes.

26,440. Practically it is a wholesale market?—The commodities are sold to be subsequently retailed. It is wholesale and retail, because the new potatoes are always retailed.

26,441. That is during a portion of the season?—Yes, the coal is retailed in small quantities of hundreds and half-hundreds.

Rev. Father O'Neill, P.P., examined.

26,442. I take it you approve of all commodities being weighed at a public scales?—Yes.

26,443. You think the sellers would have more confidence in the weighing?—That is my opinion. When I buy hay or anything of that kind, as I do, it is weighed at the public crane. I am better satisfied with that, because it is a public place, and the farmer selling his hay would also have more confidence in a public scales.

26,444. Have you ever heard complaints of any inaccuracy in ascertaining the weight at a private or public scales?—No. It only recently came to my knowledge that people were buying potatoes in the yards. I have the greatest confidence in all the men in the town, and I believe they are as honest as any men in the world. At the same time I think the public scales ought to be availed of, and being personally concerned in buying hay from time to time I would rather have it weighed at the public scales.

26,445. Do you consider the charge of 6d. too high for weighing a load of hay?—It is not too much after all, but still I think a penny a load would pay very well.

26,445a. (*Mr. Murray.*) You forget that the 6d. provides for the weighing of the empty cart after the load.

26,446. How does the charge compare with the charge made in Carlow?—I have heard it stated by those who sold there that in Carlow the charges are very exorbitant compared with the charges here.

26,447. Do you know the actual charge in Carlow?—I saw in one of the local papers recently a letter saying they charge 4d. for weighing a bag of potatoes.

26,448. But the loads on the weigh-bridge?—I think the charge is 6d. a load.

Mr. Charles Duffy examined.

26,449. I believe Mr. Newton is one of the owners of the town?—Yes.

26,450. Could you tell me has he any special grant from the Crown for these markets?—None whatever, only as owner of the soil.

26,451. He originally provided the house and scales?—Yes, and crane.

26,452. Do you know the original cost of these?—I think the crane cost about 60l. I do not know what the erection of it cost. The house was attached.

26,453. That house is only used for weighing purposes?—Yes.

26,454. If the farmers cannot effect a sale of any commodities on market day, there is no storage accommodation provided for them?—No.

26,455. Do you know as a matter of fact what they do store?—I really do not. I do not know there is any public store in the town. I believe Mr. Murray accommodates them in his yard if there is anything left after the market.

26,456. (*Mr. Murray.*) That is true. I have two large out-houses, and I always allow people who cannot sell the use of those houses or the use of my yard.

26,457. Do you charge them for it?—I do not.

26,458. Is it at their own risk?—Undoubtedly, at their own risk. However, they never suffer any loss.

26,459. The commodities would be sheltered from the elements there?—Yes.

Examination of Mr. Duffy continued.

26,460. Were these market rights ever in the possession of the town commissioners?—They were.

26,461. Were they let by Mr. Newton?—He gave them. I do not think there was any market tolls. It was merely Mr. Newton erected the crane, and the town commissioners got it into their charge and appointed a party to work it.

26,462. Any profits derived went to the town commissioners?—Yes.

26,463. What led to their giving it up?—I believe they found it was not paying, as well as I understand, and they gave it back to Mr. Newton.

26,464. Have you consulted Mr. Newton on the question?—I was present.

26,465. Has he any views on this question. Does he think the proper individuals to work them would be the town commissioners or local authority?—His idea is there ought to be some compulsory regulations about the markets, instead of having them as they are.

26,466. Have you any remarks to make yourself?—Nothing further than that the markets are well conducted with that exception. There are no tolls at the markets or fairs. There is simply a charge at the scales and weigh-bridge.

26,467. Have you any dealings in connexion with the market?—Nothing, unless I happen to buy.

26,468. Do you think a necessity exists for an adequate market building, and confine the exposure of marketable commodities to that building?—I decidedly do. I think a market house ought to be erected, and have the markets on a proper system.

26,469. With a restriction compelling people to avail themselves of this market place?—Certainly, and not sell here and there.

26,470. Did you ever hear complaints that any perishable commodities were depreciated in value or quantity by exposure on this square?—Never.

26,471. Have you ever heard complaints that any accidents have happened by some of the fairs being held on the public streets, or inconvenience caused to the public by the obstruction?—No.

B. P. Rageral, Esq., J.P., examined.

26,472. You are the owner of the fair green?—Yes.

26,473. That is entirely enclosed?—It is walled around.

26,474. Could you tell me the original expense of enclosing it?—I could not possibly tell you. It was done in my father's time.

26,475. You permit the fairs to be held in the fair green?—The fairs are held there.

26,476. No charge is levied?—No. I should, perhaps, tell you I am only the head landlord. There is an intermediate landlord.

26,477. Who is he?—Mr. Newton.

26,478. What is the rent?—7l. a year.

26,479. Mr. Newton gives it for the use of the fairs?—Yes.

26,480. Were tolls, to your knowledge, ever levied at the fairs?—I never heard they were. They may have been, but I never heard it.

26,481. Have you ever heard complaints that any obstruction or inconvenience was caused to the people of the town by some of the fairs being held on the streets adjacent to the fair green?—I heard some parties consider it a very great nuisance to have the fairs on the streets.

24,482. Generally, do you consider, both for the convenience of buyers and sellers, and in order to view the cattle and other animals, that the proper place for their exposure would be a properly enclosed fair green?—Decidedly.

24,483. Have you had experience of other places?—I have seen Carlow, where they used to hold a very large pig fair on the streets. I have seen that changed by taking the pig fair into a new fair green, and I believe it has been a very great improvement to the town in general. I believe there was some objection to it at the time, until established, but the fairs are very much improved in consequence.

24,484. From your experience of the farmers around and the producers who frequent this place, do you think the fact of no toll being levied at the fairs, acts as an inducement to the farmers to bring in a greater supply, or in other words, do you think the exaction of a toll acts in any way as a deterrent upon them in bringing their animals and commodities to the markets and fairs?—I say it ought to encourage them to bring them in when there is no toll.

24,485. Do you think the exaction of a toll would deter them?—I think not, under proper management, and a proper system.

24,486. You consider that the farmer, if he could have a ready market and proper accommodation afforded, would have no objection to pay a charge for that accommodation?—I am a farmer myself and most decidedly I should not have any objection at all.

24,487. Do you agree in the opinion expressed by Mr. Duffy that a necessity exists for proper market buildings?—Yes, if it could be done without a great increase of taxation.

24,488. Apart from any financial difficulty, you think a necessity exists for such accommodation?—Yes.

24,489. If erected, it would tend to improve the markets here and give greater facilities to the buyers and sellers?—I think so if the people could not remain outside.

24,490. That is to have restrictions on them from exposing elsewhere?—Yes.

24,491. Do you consider that in the event of such buildings being erected, and such markets being held there, that the control of them should remain as it is or be vested in the local authority, the town commissioners, or do you think if the commissioners had the control of the market rights and fairs they would work them better and to the greater satisfaction of those frequenting them?—I think they ought to be under some authority decidedly, but under the town commissioners or not, I cannot quite say. I think they ought to be under some constituted authority, certainly.

24,492. That is a general question. You have experience of Carlow and elsewhere, and you consider the markets and fairs should be worked by an authority, leaving out of question the particular authority?—Decidedly.

24,493. They should obtain compulsory powers to acquire the rights of the owners of the markets and fairs?—I do. I think so.

24,494. Could you give me any reason forming that opinion?—Well, merely because I saw in the two neighbouring towns of Kilkenny and Carlow that the system adopted, and it is greatly to their benefit and the convenience afforded to the people.

24,495. Have you bought at fairs where tolls were levied?—Yes, frequently.

24,496. Do you think if tolls are to be levied in return for the accommodation afforded that it would work better to have a toll on the animal actually sold or a smaller toll on all animals as they enter the fair green?—The system in Kilkenny and Carlow is to charge on the animal going into the fair green, and it seems to work very well.

24,497. Have you ever attended fairs where the toll was only levied on the animals actually sold and as they were being taken away?—I believe in Borris that is the case, and in another place not very far distant. We have no objection to that system.

24,498. What is the nature of that objection?—Generally when going away from the fair there is often a great deal of trouble in getting away on account of the various people driving away—more so than going in.

24,499. More confusion and inconvenience arise, and the public are delayed?—Yes.

24,500. You would approve of the system in Carlow and Kilkenny of an entrance charge?—Decidedly.

24,501. You think it would work better?—Yes. At the same time I should like to remark the actual fact of levying a toll is bound to improve the fair, because the fairs are not regulated. A toll makes the fair good—better than otherwise. For instance, the fairs in Carlow were always good for sheep and pigs, and it does not seem ever to have taken as a cattle fair. The reason for that I cannot understand, there being such good fairs in the neighbourhood of Kilkenny and Carlow, but that is in the hands of the neighbouring farmers and landlords.

Mr. Andrew Newton recalled.

24,502. (*Witness.*) I do not think tolls have any effect on fairs established by a locality. Toll or not, it does not make any difficulty.

24,503. You do not consider that if there were two fairs equi-distant from a farmer's house—one being toll-free and the other one at which tolls were levied—that he would not consider whether a toll was levied or not if the fair at which the toll was levied were better than the other?—I think he would not care about tolls at fairs that were good, but I think tolls in Bagenalstown would have a most injurious effect. We cannot get the cattle to come here.

24,503a. Do you consider where tolls are levied that the farmer when fixing the price which he requires for the animal considers the toll?—I could not form a good opinion about that; but I should say in Kilkenny the small charge they pay there as entrance does not affect the farmers a bit.

William Ward, Esq., Chairman Town Commissioners, Examined.

24,504. You are the chairman of the town commissioners?—Yes.

24,505. At one period the commissioners had control of the markets, or rather the management of the crane and scales and crane?—They had.

24,506. Had they the immediate control, or did they let them out?—They let them out.

24,507. Did they consider that an advisable course to adopt?—They let them out subject to their control.

24,508. Practically they had not the control that Mr. Newton has at present?—Mr. Newton erected the crane and handed it over to the town commissioners, as he was a commissioner himself that time. For [illegible] years we held the scales and crane. We let them to a private individual—that private individual was under wages as a night-man in the town until the Act of 1879, which did away with the powers of town commissioners where there was not a population of 5,000 inhabitants, and Mr. Newton said, as we had no power he would take the crane and scales as his own private property.

24,509. If you had control of it, and worked it by means of an officer, and sub-let either the scales or crane, do you think the public generally would have more confidence in an officer of the town commissioners, weighing the different commodities than a private individual getting profit out of it?—There would be more confidence in the commissioners.

24,510. That is if the commissioners did not sub-let it?—Yes, not sub-let, but appoint their own man from the commissioners, a man who would have to perform the duty according to the commissioners' ideas. I would appoint a man or clerk to perform the duties at the scales, and have him subject to the commissioners.

24,511. You heard the remarks of the several witnesses who have given evidence. Do you think a necessity exists for a proper market building being erected here?—Unfortunately the town commissioners have not the power.

24,512. Do you think for the trade of the town that a necessity exists for such market buildings with, as suggested, rules compelling people to resort to the market?—I believe it would be beneficial to the whole town at large if we had the means to erect a proper house for the accommodation of such articles as vegetables and everything. I believe it would be a stimulus to the town to have such a building erected.

26,513. What reason can you assign for the people not resorting to the fowl market?—One reason is that the commissioners have no authority or power to make them go there. They are at liberty to go where they please. The commissioners passed a resolution as a kind of byelaw and tried to make them go into the market. We summoned them for forestalling, and when the cases came before the court the magistrates found they had no power under the Act of Parliament to do anything.

26,514. Did not the police proceed against them for obstruction?—We could not go against them for obstruction. It was only forestalling in the buying.

26,515. Do you hear much complaints about forestalling?—Yes.

26,516. What commodities are forestalled?—Fowl principally. The buyers go out and meet them, and buy at the cross road, and will not let the people come into the market.

26,517. They go out and meet them on the country roads?—They have done that; and that was the cause of making the byelaw, but latterly they have not done that, because the buyers have not been so numerous, or so much demand for the fowl.

26,518. Do you think the farmers would receive better prices if the fowl was brought into the market, and there was the ordinary competition?—That is my idea. If the buyers buy in the market better prices will be given. There is a public market, and let them come in, and let every one have a fair chance, both the seller and the buyer, and there will be better prices. I say the market house is the proper place for the fowl to be sold and bought when there is accommodation there for that purpose.

26,519. If this market building were erected, do you think the proper individuals to have control would be the town commissioners?—Not a doubt of it.

26,520. Have the town commissioners discussed that?—We spoke of this a couple of times. We have not gone into the merits of the matter. I believe myself such a building should be under the control of the commissioners whoever they may be.

26,521. Would the town commissioners be disposed to levy a charge in this building?—I would not be for levying any charge except what would pay the interest of the money borrowed.

26,522. The commissioners are not in favour of such a building in order to afford them a means of augmenting their revenue?—No. Our revenue is too small to undertake anything at present.

26,523. They do not contemplate increasing their revenue by working the market rights?—No. It would be their object to give accommodation to the public, and induce farmers to come into the town, so as to increase its prosperity. That is my idea. It should be for the whole town at large, and for the benefit of farmers outside, that they might have accommodation when they come into the place, instead of being out in the wet and cold with their commodity.

26,524. Have you heard them complaining of no shelter accommodation being afforded at all here in winter time?—Certainly.

26,525. Have you heard complaints that any of the commodities have been depreciated in value or quantity?—I would not go so far as that, but the people have been much inconvenienced by being out in the public market during a wet Saturday.

26,526. From what districts do they bring the marketable commodities?—Perhaps we will say four miles or thereabouts. It is sometimes six miles, but I will say four.

26,527. From what districts do they bring the cattle?—They bring them from all districts round about.

26,528. Within what limits?—Within six miles, and eight sometimes. I have seen pigs brought ten and twelve miles to be sold in Bagenalstown, but the cattle do not come so far. Pigs come the night before a distance of ten miles to be sold here.

26,529. How far is this fair green from the railway station?—About a hundred perches.

26,530. The buyers never complained of that?—No.

26,531. Have you ever bought at these fairs yourself?—Several times.

26,532. Have they got the system of luck-penny here?—Yes.

26,533. At the cattle market there is no fixed sum for that luck-penny?—No.

26,534. Is it always left to the disposition of the seller?—Yes.

26,535. It is given in each case?—I never knew a case in which it was not given, except by a very narrow-minded man; but generally speaking, as a rule in the pig market the buyers of pigs stop sixpence from the sellers.

26,536. He stops that out of the contract price?—Yes.

26,537. In the case of cattle the price is paid and the seller subsequently returns the luck-penny?—Yes. He gives what he pleases.

26,538. Supposing you were a seller, would you consider what luck-penny you would give when fixing the price?—I would not, because it is optional to give or not as I please. Therefore I would not count that. Sometimes we buy cattle, and if 15*l.* is paid for a cow there may be five shillings luck mentioned, but if it is not mentioned I may give the buyer what I please—a shilling or a half-crown, or whatever I wish. The buyer must submit to whatever I do. It is voluntary with the seller to give a luck-penny as they generally do in a fair.

26,538a. Does that system of luck-penny lead to any undue delay being caused in completing the bargain?—Not in the slightest.

26,539. Or any confusion?—I have never known it. They might argue about the price of the beast originally, but I never heard any argument about the luck-penny.

26,540. Do they come in the night before the fair with cattle?—No. They do not drive in the cattle until the morning of the fair.

26,541. What hour does the fair usually begin?—About 8 o'clock.

26,542. What time does it terminate?—3 or 3 o'clock in the evening and not later than 4.

26,543. What hour do the markets usually begin?—The pig market at present and fowl market begin at 8 o'clock in the morning according to the rule in Waterford. The fowl market lasts two hours or three.

26,544. What time does the general market commence?—The general market opens at any hour they please.

26,545. What hours are the scales available?—From 8 in the morning until 6 at night.

26,546. Does Mr. Murray weigh every day?—Yes, if anything comes.

26,547. But Saturday is the market day?—Yes.

26,548. Have you any other observations to make?—First, I would ask if the town commissioners can get power to extend the area of the town.

26,549. Do not ask me any questions, because I am only here to obtain information?—Well, the commissioners' powers are too narrow, and should be more extended. We are circumscribed, and all taxation comes upon the town itself. Outside the town, although they get accommodation, they pay no taxes, and we are only able to raise by a rate of 1*s.* in the pound what merely pays the town clerk and the lighting of the town.

26,550. What remedies would you suggest?—That in future legislation, we or any other commissioners should have more powers conferred on them for local purposes, and to provide better accommodation for the farmers which cannot be done without the means of borrowing money.

26,551. When you say additional powers, powers of what nature?—Powers to extend the township of Bagenalstown, at least one and a half miles.

26,552. Do you think the country people would submit to that. They will not get any benefit from the lighting of the town, and do you think they would submit to the enlargement you suggest?—I think for this reason, that they would have only to pay a fourth on the valuation of the land of what the townspeople would have to pay.

26,553. How many town commissioners in the town?—Nine. There are facilities here for taking cattle by water or by rail.

26,554. Supposing you sent cattle by the canal to Dublin, what additional period of time is consumed in sending them by the canal?—Under the present arrangement with the Grand Canal they get from Bagenalstown to Dublin in two days. All corn goes by the canal.

26,555. What are the rates?—The rates are fair and just.

26,556. Do those who avail themselves of the canal consider that?—Yes. I am one myself.

26,557. Are they considerably lower than the railway rates?—Ten per cent. lower on first and second class of goods.

26,558. What commodities are usually sent by canal?—Well, for the last twelve months the canal has been carrying all kinds of goods—shop goods and everything else coming from Dublin. Heretofore the railway carried all shop goods, and no canal boats were coming down with those things, but for the past twelve months they have three boats running from Dublin whether there are goods or not. I believe a large quantity of produce are sent by the canal down to Waterford, but not to Dublin.

26,559. How many pigs are brought to the fairs here on an average?—About 900 pigs each month, but not less than 700.

26,560. Could you give any approximate idea of the number of cattle?—The cattle are not so numerous, but I could not give you any idea of the cattle.

26,561. Could you give any idea of the per-centage usually sold at the fairs?—I would say three fourths of what comes to the fairs are sold.

26,562. You have no horse fair?—No horse fair, but a very large sheep fair. The sheep and pigs are numerous, and all the sheep are bought at good fair prices.

26,563. Do those drovers come here?—The butchers come from Carlow, Athy, and Kilkenny.

26,564. Do Dublin buyers come?—They come for pigs, but not for sheep.

26,565. Or cattle?—They sometimes come for cattle, but very seldom for sheep. The local buyers buy nearly all the sheep. There are one or two who come from Carlow for sheep. There is hardly any sheep left. We hope power will be given to improve that by giving more accommodation and more facility to the public coming to the market and fair.

COLONEL VIGORS, J.P., examined.

26,567. (Witness.) Considering the situation of the town and the great facilities afforded for markets and fairs, the markets are little more than a name and the fairs a perfect failure. The present accommodation is sufficient for the fowl on Saturday if the people would go inside, but they prefer the footpath.

26,568. What is the nature of the surrounding country?—Agriculture and pasture.

26,569. What per-centage would you say is in tillage?—I could not give any idea.

26,570. (Father O'Neill.) I would say two thirds. It is nearly all tillage country.

26,571. Where do the marketable commodities go to, Colonel Vigors, because the markets should be far better if there is so much tillage?—There is a very large quantity of corn and potatoes sent away from here. It is a very large corn market.

26,572. What are the nearest markets?—Carlow and Kilkenny. There is no place around within a circle of ten miles has the facilities of this town.

26,573. Could you assign any reason for the falling off in the markets. Do you think it is want of accommodation?—No. The buyers do not come. The pig fairs are the best in the county, but the cattle fairs are a failure.

26,574. How many pigs are brought here?—About 1,000 annually.

MR. P. J. KEHOE, T.C., examined.

26,575. You are one of the town commissioners of this town?—Yes.

26,576. What remarks do you wish to make?—You asked what do we attribute the falling off in the fairs and markets to. The reason I attribute is that there is no legal authority as they have in neighbouring towns to manage the fairs and markets. The authority in Kilkenny is the corporation, and the authority in Carlow is the town commission, and we want some powers as they have in those towns. The want of them, in my opinion, is the cause of the failure of these markets and fairs.

26,577. Do you consider there is a deficiency in the management?—I do.

26,578. Have you heard complaints of the present management?—I have.

26,579. From whom?—The farmers were dissatisfied.

26,580. In what way?—They are dissatisfied about the accommodation, and about holding the fairs in the streets, and all that sort of thing.

26,581. If the farmers availed themselves of this fair green, and brought their animals there, would not the buyers go where the supply was?—I think they would, but somehow, owing to the mismanagement for years, and the feeling with regard to the tolls in Carlow, the farmers would object to the area of taxation. I believe it is a fact that the town commissioners of Carlow go two miles outside the town.

REV. PATRICK O'NEILL, P.P., re-examined.

26,582. (Witness.) About the fair green the real cause is not the want of a town commission or anything. I think if the fair green was fixed up, such as in Athy by the Duke of Leinster, it would tend very much to bring the cattle there, because this is a very central district. We have a very good pig fair, and, I believe, a fair number of sheep. The cattle fair is exceedingly bad, but I do not think it is on account of the want of powers being given to the town commissioners. I believe at one time the cattle fair was held on one day, and the pig fair on another, but now they are both on the same day. The reason of that was to make it a better fair by having it all on the one day.

26,583. (Mr. Ward.) Father O'Neill has made a remark about Athy, where pens are provided in the fair green. We quite agree that there should be some such accommodation here if we had the means of doing it.

26,584. (Father O'Neill.) Except the landlord would make it, the same as the Duke of Leinster.

HEAD-CONSTABLE MALONEY examined.

26,585. The pig fair and sheep fair are held on the streets?—Yes.

26,586. Within your experience does that cause much inconvenience and obstruction on the public thoroughfare?—It does, the pigs especially, but there are no complaints.

26,587. Do they occupy the footways?—Yes, footways principally.

26,588. An accumulation of filth and dirt takes place?—Yes.

26,589. Is that immediately removed. The pigs are removed, but the dirt is not.

26,590. Have the inhabitants of the district, and the neighbouring streets, complained of that?—They have not.

26,591. Who subsequently clears that away?—There is no person responsible except the road contractor.

26,592. Have complaints been made of dereliction of duty on the part of the road contractor?—I am not aware.

26,593. Still, you say an obstruction is created?—There is no doubt about it. The footways are occupied by the pigs until 10 o'clock each day, from 7 in the morning.

26,594. The police never thought of removing them into the fair green?—The matter has been discussed, and the magistrates gave permission that the pigs be allowed on the footways until 11 o'clock. There were a lot summoned for obstructing the footways, and the magistrates dismissed the cases, thinking that for the benefit of the town it would be well not to interfere with the fair.

26,595. In what way was it a benefit. Did they think the presence of the people brought more trade?—They did, and they thought it better not to interfere with the pigs supplying the fair.

26,596. As a matter of fact the people living where the fair is held do not complain about it?—No. There was no attempt made to extend the fair to the other end of the town.

26,597. Was there any contention among the traders of the town about having the fairs in the other end of the town, so that they might get a share of the trade?—Yes, that is my knowledge.

26,598. Was that confined to any particular trade?—A few shopkeepers in one end.

26,599. Did the drapers require it as much as the publicans?—I think so.

26,600. (The Commissioner.) Now, Mr. Ward, you take exception to a statement made by the head-constable?—Yes, I would ask the town clerk to read the resolution that was passed.

26,601. What I have taken is that some of the traders in a portion of the town where the fairs are not held, wished to have them removed, or portion of them removed, to their district?—That is not correct.

26,602. What exception do you take?—I will ask to have the resolution read.

26,603. What is the nature of it. The nature of it is that complaints were made by the district inspector that the pigs were an obstruction, and calling on the town commissioners to hold a special meeting to devise some plan to have the obstruction remedied. We called a special meeting, and we saw a good remedy by having only one row of cars instead of two, and, then, not to interfere with the fairs, we passed a resolution to the effect that the surplus cars should extend in one row down the main street instead of two rows. A wrong impression has gone abroad about the removal of the fairs.

26,604. He did not state it was the commissioners' desire, but the desire of traders at the other side of the town?—They never desired it. Mine is the correct statement.

26,605. (Head-Constable.) The fat-pig fair is over before the pigs come in carts. They come in about half-past 9 o'clock, and then the fat pigs have been removed off the streets.

26,606. But the people of the upper end of the town never complain of any obstruction?—They have never done so to my knowledge.

Captain Phelan, J.P., examined.

26,607. (Witness.) There were complaints about the pigs on the footpath. I must say the obstruction is not so great as it used to be. The complaints were particularly by ladies walking through the town.

26,608. I take it the private inhabitants of the district would only complain?—Yes, certainly.

26,609. Have you any suggestions to offer as a remedy?—No.

Mr. Martin Gallagher examined.

26,610. What remarks do you wish to make?—There was a petition signed by the majority of the tenant farmers and most of the inhabitants protesting against the removal of the fair, and the secretary of the Waterford Pig Buyers' Association was communicated with about the matter. There was a letter in reply saying that if the fair was removed they would discontinue coming into Dungarvan, and if the Waterford buyers stopped away they might shake their hands of the fair. At the present time there are only six hundred pigs at fairs where there used to be twelve hundred, and it is all owing to the irregularities and bad regulation. Every fair day the train accommodation is bad. There is no train here for taking away the pigs until 10 o'clock and sometimes 12 o'clock in the day. The pigs are all at the railway station. There is no accommodation for the whole of them, and I think it is the duty of the town commissioners to look after that. With reference to the statement about the very bad accommodation, if one of the commissioners came from the upper portion of the town he would try to haul them down to his end of the town. About the fair, I can appeal to the head-constable to know if there is sufficient accommodation for the pigs attending the fairs at the upper end of the town.

26,611. (Head-Constable.) Except what I stated. They are a nuisance on the pathway, but there is no obstruction on the streets.

26,612. (The Commissioner to Mr. Gallagher.) Are you in trade in the town?—My father is.

Mr. Ward, C.T.C., re-examined.

26,613. When were the monthly fairs established?—The monthly fairs were established fifteen years ago by the town commissioners for the benefit of the town.

26,614. How many fairs were held before that?—Six fairs.

26,615. How long were they in existence?—A long time previous—fifty years.

26,616. Do you know the dates?—There was one in March, May, July, September, November, and February.

26,617. Witness subsequently produced a letter which he had received from the district inspector of constabulary, Captain Percy H. Joy, in which he mentioned that complaints were made to him of the great inconvenience caused by the present state of the pig market, and asking him could he direct the pig fair to be held elsewhere, and any order the commissioners would make the police would see to the carrying out of it.

26,618. Is there any other gentleman who has any evidence to give before the inquiry closes? (No answer.)

The inquiry then terminated.

BALBRIGGAN.

With reference to my inquiry in Balbriggan, on the 8th day of December 1888, I beg to report as follows:—

Balbriggan is a maritime town in the county of Dublin. It has a harbour, and possesses some local manufacturing industries in addition to the fishing trade which is largely carried on. The town is neat and well built, and is a station on the Great Northern Railway line. The local government is administered by town commissioners, and the population is 2,443.

The market day for corn is Monday. The general commodities are brought in every day, and sold in shops and about the town as the market is not large. The fairs are held on the first Monday in February, 29th March, 29th April, 29th July, 29th September, first Monday in November, and second Monday in December. There are no tolls levied at the markets or fairs.

The town commissioners are the owners of any market rights that may exist in Balbriggan. They hold the site of the market buildings under lease, dated 23rd January 1877, from a Mr. Beecher F. Fleming for ever, at one shilling a year, on condition that they should erect market buildings within two years, and use same as a public market at least three days in each week. Under the terms of the lease the town commissioners expended about the sum of 300*l.* in the erection of the necessary buildings.

A patent was granted for Balbriggan on the 18th January 1766, which authorised one George Hamilton to hold a Saturday market and fairs on the 29th April and 29th September. These fairs are at present held, but no express authority seems to have been granted for the Monday corn market or the fairs on the first Monday in February, 29th March, 29th July, first Monday in November, and second Monday in December, were established about ten years ago, and the fairs on the 29th March, 29th July, and first Monday in November, were only established this year by the town commissioners.

In accordance with my instructions I have inspected the market and fair places.

The fairs are held on a fair green at the upper end of the town. It is practically enclosed by hedgerows and earthen fences, but the public road runs through the place and divides the green into two portions. It seems suitable and convenient as a site for holding fairs, but it is not in any way provided with pens or shelter accommodation. Some years ago the site, with other property, was about being put up for sale in the Landed Estates Court, when the town commissioners interfered and claimed the right of the public to hold the fairs thereon. The rental was amended and the property sold subject to the right of the public.

There is a market house with a yard and shed attached, but the place is not availed of except the covered-in portion fronting the streets, which has been converted into shops and held by a tenant who sells every class of goods therein. Unfortunately there is no general market, and the scales not utilised, whatever commodities are brought into the town are either disposed of and weighed by the shopkeepers or sold on the public streets.

The witnesses were of opinion that a market could be fostered in the town if the town commissioners were enabled to make byelaws regulating the market, at present the power is denied them, they not being the Urban Sanitary Authority.

Appended will be found a transcript of the evidence taken at the inquiry.

JOHN J. O'MEARA,
Assistant Commissioner.

45, Lower Mount Street, Dublin.

Balbriggan, 6th December 1888.

Mr. Daniel [illegible], Town Clerk, examined.

25,619. You are the town clerk of Balbriggan?—Yes.

25,620. When were the town commissioners established?—I think they were established in 1861.

25,621. What duties do they perform?—They have all the powers under the Towns Improvement Act, but the principal thing is the lighting of the town.

25,622. Do they do the cleansing?—No.

25,623. Or paving?—No. That is done by the grand jury.

25,624. The grand jury and the board of guardians look after the local affairs?—Yes. The board of guardians is the sanitary authority. The commissioners were the sanitary authority until the year 1874. On the passing of the Act that year the board of guardians became the sanitary authority.

25,625. Are there any markets held here?—I could not call it a market. There are three or four persons who assemble at the corner of the court-house and bring samples of corn and barley and go away.

25,626. What day?—On Monday.

25,627. Do not they bring any marketable commodities to the people of the town and sell them from shop to shop, or expose them on the streets on Saturday, or any day?—They hawk fish in baskets from door to door.

25,628. What day?—There is no particular day. They do it every day in the week. They have a stand for fish on the streets.

25,629. Do not people bring vegetables?—They do not. Shopkeepers expose vegetables at the door.

25,630. How do the shopkeepers obtain them?—They get them from the farmers.

25,631. And the potatoes?—They are sold in the shops, &c.

25,632. Is there any live market here?—No.

25,633. Then, practically, with the exception of the fish and the corn, all other commodities are brought to the shopkeepers by the farmers?—Yes.

25,634. I suppose they have a contract more or less for that. They know who their customers are, and they deliver the commodities to them?—You will find them hawking all through the streets from one to another to get the best price.

25,635. That is every day in the week?—Yes.

25,636. Are there any market buildings here?—Yes, one belonging to the commissioners opposite.

25,637. That market building was erected by the commissioners originally?—Yes.

25,638. When?—In 1878.

25,639. You produce this lease?—Yes.

Witness then produced the lease, of which the following is an abstract:—It is an indenture dated 23rd January 1877, by one [illegible] P. [illegible], Co. Dublin, whereby he demises to the commissioners of the town of Balbriggan, appointed under the Towns Improvement Act 1854, the premises hereinafter described, reciting that the town commissioners are anxious to afford accommodation to the public resorting to the said town of Balbriggan and the inhabitants thereof for the sale of butter, eggs, meal, fish, and all other commodities, thereby to create a revenue for the improvement of the said town, and had applied to the lessor for a site on which to erect the necessary buildings. It was witnessed that the lessor, in consideration for the yearly rent of one shilling, did demise all that and those the lot or plot of ground being part of the lands of Balbriggan, situate in George's Square, in the town of Balbriggan, containing 13½ perches English statute measure, or thereabouts, in the parish of Balbriggan, county of Dublin, to hold to the town commissioners and their successors for ever. The usual covenants between landlord and tenant, and special covenants, as follows:—The commissioners covenant that within two years from the date thereof they will have converted the demised premises into a market for the accommodation of persons resorting thereto, and shall use same as such market; that the grounds and premises shall be used solely for the purpose of a public market, and the accommodation of persons resorting thereto, for the sale and purchase of commodities aforesaid, and for no other purpose whatever, without the consent in writing of the lessor, his heirs or assigns, under the control and management of said town commissioners and their successors, subject to such rules and regulations as they shall from time to time appoint. That the premises be kept open at least three days in every week for the accommodation of the public as aforesaid, and that the profits derived from such market, after the payment of expenses, interest, and instalments of money borrowed, shall be expended solely in improvements within the town of Balbriggan; that a separate account be kept of the receipts and disbursements of the market. Conditions:—That if there be a breach of the covenants hereinbefore contained, or if the premises shall be closed as such public market for any time for the space of one month, except for some good and sufficient reason, then it shall be lawful for the lessor to re-enter into possession thereof. Liberty to the commissioners to levy charges for the accommodation afforded by the market when erected. Covenant by lessor for quiet enjoyment. Duly executed, registered, and stamped.

25,640. What was the cost of erecting that building?—300l. It was borrowed from the Board of Works. The building itself cost 280l., and there were some extra works which made the amount 300l. There were 15l. for drawing up the lease.

25,641. At what terms did you get the money from the Board of Works?—To be repaid in 50 years at 5 per cent.

25,642. What is due to them at present?—Not more than 130l.

25,643. You pay instalments every year?—Yes.

25,644. You have to pay these instalments out of the rate?—Yes.

25,645. You derive no benefit?—Oh, yes. There are some stalls let out and they pay at the present time, I think, only 12l. There are only three stalls. They were paying 15l. until last June, when they were reduced for one year to 12l.

25,646. What is the rent of each stall?—The rent of the three stalls is 12l.; that is, about 4l. 4s. each.

25,647. How do you let them?—By the quarter.

25,648. What commodities do they sell in these stalls?—Groceries, bacon, and provisions.

25,649. Practically, they are small shops?—Yes.

25,650. How is the upper portion?—The upper portion is let as a [illegible], and they pay 1s. a week for it.

25,651. Is there any other portion let?—No.

25,652. It was built as a market building?—Yes.

25,653. In portion of the yard do they sell any other commodity, any corn or anything?—Yes, in the yard.

25,654. Do they sell any marketable commodities in the building?—They expose there samples of corn for sale on Mondays.

25,655. Every Monday?—Yes.

25,656. Do you levy any charge on those people?—No.

25,657. You allow them the use of the building gratuitously?—Yes.

25,658. Do many of them attend?—Half-a-dozen, I suppose.

25,659. Are those the producers?—Half-a-dozen producers and half-a-dozen buyers.

25,660. The buyers go and take up a position and the farmers come and show the samples?—Yes.

25,661. You derive no benefit from that?—No.

25,662. At the time of the erection of the building did the commissioners contemplate levying a charge?—They did.

25,663-4. Did they make any byelaws?—There were byelaws passed by the commissioners and sent to the Local Government Board for sanction. It so happened that the commissioners had the power as a sanitary authority to make the byelaws, but in the year 1878 there was an Act passed and we had no powers to make byelaws because they were vested in the board of guardians as a sanitary authority.

25,665. From that period did the market fall into abeyance?—There was no one attended the market up to that time.

25,666. Previous to that there was no market?—No market at all.

25,667. Did the commissioners think it desirable to create or foster a market at the time?—They did, and they put a kind of bell—just something small—so as to encourage the people to come in. There was nothing to be paid to the town, and anyone who came was to take his commodity to the market. When the season is in full swing there may be 200 people in the street, and they thought it desirable to have a place to go into. If they were charged anything they would not go; there was no pressure to go there. The country-people came on a few occasions, but the towns-people would not go near them. The fish-people were told to go into the market and they would not go. They would rather knock about from door to door.

25,668. Have complaints been made of the causing of obstruction to people about the streets?—I never heard with the exception of fish. There are people selling fish at the corner of our street, and the only person I heard complaining was a publican. They expose the fish at the corner of his house, and one or two occasions I summoned parties for obstructing there and they were fined.

25,669. Who rent those stalls in the market house?—It is a co-operative company—the Hand-in-hand Co-operative Company. They took one pound shares in it.

25,670. It is a general provision business?—Yes, groceries and things.

25,671. What fairs have you here?—There are seven fairs altogether. There are two new fairs.

25,672. What are the dates of them?—The first Monday in February; the 25th March; the 29th April; the 5th July; 29th September; first Monday in November, and the second Monday in December.

25,673. You say two of them were lately established?—Yes.

25,674. Which two?—The one in November and July and the 25th March. There are three new fairs.

25,675. When were they established here?—They were established in August last.

25,676. Were the other four fairs held for any length of time previous?—They were for some years.

25,677. Do you remember when there were less than four?—I never remember less than four.

25,678. They have been held on the same dates as at present?—Yes. I should have said there were two formerly, the 29th April and 29th September.

25,679. How long ago, do you say, is it since the other two were established?—I suppose ten years.

25,680. Do you remember when there were no fairs here?—No.

25,681. There were always two fairs?—Yes, as long as ever I remember, 50 years ago.

25,682. Where are the fairs held?—Off the market green. They were held there until a certain hour of the day, and then they generally resort to the streets and scatter over the town.

25,683. Is this green enclosed, or is it a widening of the street?—No. It is a grass-plot of about two acres.

25,684. Is it portion of the public thoroughfare?—The public have a right so far as the fairs are concerned. The public road runs through it. There is a house there which was formerly a market house or house built by the people and when the place was sold out it was confiscated and taken away.

25,685. How is it utilised between fairs?—For grazing purposes. The representatives of Dr. McElroy let it.

25,686. To whom does the tenant pay rent?—To the representatives of Dr. McElroy.

25,687. Then it is private property?—It is.

25,688. But custom has given the people a right to hold fairs there?—Yes. The commissioners had to go into court to fight with the representatives of the [illegible] when the property was sold as they were claiming the place as their own. The commissioners went and fought the matter out making they had a right to hold the fairs, and then it was inserted in the rental that the place was sold subject to the right of the public to hold the fairs there.

25,689. At the time how many fairs were held?—There were four.

26,690. Were there any objections to the establishment of new fairs?—No.

26,691. Who was it established them?—The town commissioners by resolution.

26,692. There was no grant or patent from the Crown?—No.

26,693. Or any communication from the Local Government Board?—No.

26,694. Is there any authority exercised over these fairs by the town commissioners?—No. There is no benefit whatever from them.

26,695. Or do they perform no duties?—We advertise.

26,696. Who keeps order at the fairs?—The police.

26,697. What description of animals do the people bring to the fairs?—Cattle and sheep.

26,698. Do they bring horses?—No horses.

26,699. Or lambs?—Yes.

26,700. Is there a pig fair held here?—Yes.

26,701. Have you a special pig fair?—No.

26,702. It is held the same day as the ordinary fair?—Yes.

26,703. Do they ever bring cattle the night before the fair day?—They do.

26,704. Where do they bring them for stallage?—They leave them in publichouse premises. There are generally dealers or drovers who go from fair to fair, and they come here the night before.

26,705. You do not know what they charge for stallage?—I could not say. I think very little.

26,706. What would you think they charge them?—They might charge them for the night 6d. a head. They could not charge more and hardly so much as that. They get yards about the place and feed them themselves, and then on emergencies they take pasture and pay a certain thing for the cattle.

26,707. This building in George's Square is not availed of, with the exception of Monday, for market purposes?—No.

26,708. I see there is a clause in the lease that the landlord is entitled to take it up?—Yes.

26,709. Has he taken any steps to do so?—He served notice, but took no further steps. He saw the commissioners were determined to fight the matter out. There the premises are open three or four times a week, and there is no hindrance to people to go there.

Wm. McCartney, Esq., Chairman, Town Commissioners, examined.

26,710. You are the chairman of the town commissioners?—Yes.

26,711. Is there any public scales in Balbriggan for ascertaining the weight of commodities brought here?—There is a triangle and beam.

26,712. Who is in charge of it?—The commissioners.

26,713. Is there any weigh-master appointed by them?—No.

26,714. Is it utilised?—It was utilised for a week when it was put up first in 1878.

26,715. Practically, then, it is lying derelict?—Yes.

26,716. Is any butter brought here?—Butter is sold direct to the shopkeepers.

26,717-18. When these commodities are brought in and weighed on the purchaser's premises and sold to one of the shopkeepers of the town, are they subsequently retailed by him?—Yes. In 1878 a committee was appointed in connexion with the opening of the market, and they had power to purchase a beam and scales and weights for the markets.

26,719. Where was it erected?—In the shed of the yard.

26,720. Is there any weigh-bridge in Balbriggan?—Only private ones.

26,721. But there are some?—There are three.

26,722. Do they let them out for public use if people wish to ascertain the weight of a load?—Yes; we weigh a lot of corn.

26,723. Do you levy any charge?—We do not.

26,724. Do the others?—No. I do not know whether there is any charge.

26,726. Is it bought by local buyers?—Yes. We buy corn.

26,727. When they bring it in and it is subsequently delivered, do you weigh at your own scales?—We do.

26,728. Do you charge anything?—We do not. We weigh over, say, five sacks. We do not weigh each individual sack.

26,729. I suppose you always estimate the tare of the sack?—Yes.

26,730. You never weigh the empty sack?—We do not.

26,731. What is the estimated tare?—From four to seven pounds.

26,732. That is according to the weight?—It is according to the fibre of the sack.

26,733. Would these estimated tares be the same on a fine day as on a wet day, when they had to travel long distances and the sacks were saturated with wet?—We never take that into consideration.

26,734. But in case of dispute between the seller and yourself you actually weigh the empty sack?—Yes, but they are never exact.

26,735. Is there any deduction from the gross weight of the sack of corn other than the tare?—No.

26,736. Nothing is allowed for tonnage?—No.

26,737. Is there any deduction from the contract price you pay?—Oh, no.

26,738. Is there any porterage charge here?—The seller delivers the corn on the loft, and if he was not able to carry it he would hire a man to help him.

26,739. Then the sellers must put them on the scales?—Yes, and on the loft.

26,740. From the scales to the loft?—Yes.

26,741. They must perform that work?—Yes.

26,742. If unable to do it themselves they must employ external labour?—Yes.

26,743. That is customary with them?—It is customary with us.

26,744. Is it with the other corn buyers?—I think so.

26,745. Do they ever employ your men?—No. I do not think they do.

26,746. Did you ever tell your men to do it and charge them?—Yes, and charge them 1d. a sack, but it is always optional with the man delivering the corn to do it himself. The large corn buyers charge 1d. a sack in Drogheda, and they leave it optional also with the sellers to engage the men or do the work themselves.

26,747. Who performs the work of weighing?—They (the sellers) do that themselves. They weigh at home and we check it.

26,748. Who weighs the corn for you?—One of my men.

26,749. When charged that is the only deduction in the price?—That is the only deduction.

26,750. Is there any deduction on any commodities besides corn?—No, not that I know of with the exception of the tare.

26,751. Have you had any experience of the fairs here?—Yes, I have had considerable.

26,752. What would you say, or could you give me any approximate idea of the number of cattle brought here?—I should say about 500 cattle, from 400 to 500.

26,753. Is the pig fair a good one?—It is a considerably good fair, but I have not much knowledge of it. The people are amazed at the new fairs to see them so much larger than in any other local town. Our new fairs are better than very old fairs. The best fair here is the 1st September fair.

26,754. What is the nearest place where fairs are held?—The nearest fair, and it is not an important one, is Lusk. There are four or five fairs there during the year. Drogheda is the most important fair near us.

26,755. Are there any tolls levied at Drogheda?—No.

26,756. Have you got the system of luck-penny in the fairs here?—We have.

26,757. On cattle there is no fixed rate?—No.

26,758. It is left to the disposition of the seller?—Yes

26,761. You are not aware whether there is anything fixed in that fair?—I do not think there is. It is just the same as for cattle.

26,762. Is it 6d. which they usually give?—No, but a 1d., 2d., or 3d. It is 1s. generally for cattle.

26,763. That is what they are supposed to give?—Yes, 1s. in every 10l. It is sometimes less.

26,764. The contract price is first paid by the buyer to the seller?—Yes, in full.

26,765. Do you think when they are fixing the price the farmer considers the luck-penny he will have to give?—I do not think he does.

26,766. Does he ask a higher price than he would otherwise usually take?—If the luck-penny were mentioned he might, but on the occasion he would forget all about it.

26,767. You never consider that yourself when selling?—I never did.

26,768. Do they buy on the condition, "I will give you so much and no luck"?—I saw that. When a man is using his last inducement he will give him a price "clear to pocket" in case of butchers buying fat cattle.

26,769. And is there any method of weighing cattle?—We weigh cattle on our estate.

26,770. Do the buyers seem disposed to resort to that method of buying?—No, but when we are sending up for Christmas fat cattle we weigh them as a safeguard.

26,771. Do you think it is a better system than the way of buying at present?—I do not. I do not believe in buying by weight. You would have the same trouble in fixing the class of the beast. You may put it down second and I would put it first, and then there is long arguing about the price of it.

26,772. You would not approve of it because the men are able to tell the actual value?—They are.

26,773. Do you think the buyers have an advantage over the farmer?—They have.

26,774. Do you think it would be a fair system for the farmer to resort to the practice of selling by weight?—I do not know. Of course he could just make as big an error of judgment selling by weight as any way.

26,775. How so?—He might sell a beast for 3ls. a hundredweight that would be worth 45s.

26,776. You mean he would make a mistake in the classification and not the actual weight?—Yes.

26,777. Do they send these marketable commodities, such as eggs and poultry, to Dublin, or where do they dispose of them?—They sell all of them by hawking them about.

26,778. Any day of the week?—Yes.

26,779. No particular day is allotted off for that?—No.

26,780. Is there much of the surrounding country in tillage?—There is a good deal.

26,781. What percentage of the acreage?—About one third; hardly one third. Take the district in general I do not think there is anything like one third.

26,782. What do you fix the proportion at?—I would say one third would be very near it, but I think I overstated it, for it all depends on the year you take it.

26,783. Do you think a necessity exists here for a proper market place in Balbriggan?—I am afraid it would not be a success, from my experience of the other one we have here.

26,784. Supposing you had these byelaws confirmed, with a byelaw restraining the exposure of marketable commodities elsewhere than in this market building, such as fish and other marketable commodities; do you think it would work well?—Of course, if we prevented the sale of fish on the street there would be a daily market of fish, because the fish are daily exposed at bridge on the path in boxes and little baskets.

26,785. Do you think it would be better for the producers; do you think they would get better prices if the markets were concentrated in a particular spot and where the buyers would go to?—Except the fish, I do not think anything else is offered for sale.

26,786. You would not approve yourself of corn being exposed there?—I buy samples there.

26,787. Do the other buyers attend Skerries?—Yes.

26,788. Do you think that buying by sample would be [illegible]

26,789. You have not had occasion to complain of any fraud being committed on you?—No, I have not. Generally our deliveries are very fair by sample.

26,790. Have you any suggestions to offer as to what you think would lead to the improvement of the markets and fairs?—I think it would be an improvement if the fish were compelled to go into that market.

26,791. Would the commissioners be desirous of keeping a market?—Certainly.

26,792. Would it be for the purpose of augmenting their present revenue, or only to levy such a charge at the market place as would pay the cost of maintenance?—We would be very anxious first of all to encourage the market in the town, because it would be a benefit, and, secondly, to safeguard the loan which has been threatened. It should be made compulsory on the fish people to go in there.

Mr. James Seavar, Town Commissioner, examined.

26,793. What suggestion have you to offer?—Nothing more than that it should be made compulsory on the fish people to go into the market. We never had any power to compel them. They stand on the street, and the police are not asked to drive them off. In any other places they are only allowed to remain on the streets until such time as there is a market, but there is a market here and yet the whole streets are taken up with boxes and hampers. They are a nuisance.

26,794. Do you think it causes much inconvenience and in some cases a nuisance?—Yes, in the centre of the street.

26,795. Have you heard complaints?—Most severely. We formerly had a fish market and it was done away with when this other market was about being built. They were supposed to go to this market, and instead of that they came on the street.

26,796. Where was the other fish market?—Down near where they go themselves still.

26,797. Were they confined to that fish market?—They were.

26,798. Was it a building?—It was, and a nice building got up with stalls in it.

26,799. It was intended to remove them from that building to the present one?—Yes, and they went on the streets then in place of going to the new market.

26,800. Was there any charge levied at the old building?—There was 6d. a week for standing. There were stalls there, and each person had their own breadth of stalls.

26,801. Who derived the benefit of that?—The Chancery agent.

26,802. For what estate?—The Hamilton estate.

26,803. Who is the owner of the town?—It was divided between several owners in 1873 when the estate was sold out. It has been all sold in little pieces.

26,804. Have you any other remarks to make?—But only the people would be particularly anxious that the market should be made available for all purposes, and let the people go into it.

26,805. Have you no experience of other market towns?—Well, I have of course a slight experience but I never took any notice of them.

26,806. Do you think it would be better in all market towns and here as well to have a large and commodious building with proper shelter accommodation for the people to protect their commodities from the heat of the sun in summer and the inclemency of the weather in winter time, and also a rule made confining the exposure of all commodities to that building?—That is the very thing we all wish. For the 12 or 14 years I happened to be a commissioner they are paying two guineas a year for a plot running along the market, where they mean to make a gateway to come on the weighbridge and go out another gate. That is the way the thing was first specified, and it was never carried out. There are fine sheds there too.

26,807. But you think it would be the best course to adopt in market towns, to have a market building erected and not have the commodities going indiscriminately out the streets of the town?—Most assuredly that is the proper course in my opinion.

26,808. Have you any dealings in the fairs?—No. I believe the fairs are a great boon.

26,809. Do you buy and sell yourself there?—Once

25,510. Have you had any dealings at fairs where tolls were levied?—No, except one time at Navan I had to pay a small thing.

25,511. Supposing a toll was levied here, do you think it would deter farmers from bringing in the supply they would otherwise bring in?—I think myself it is very injurious to the fairs to have tolls levied.

25,512. The supply would not be so great?—Certainly not.

25,513. Had you any conversation with farmers on the subject of levying a toll?—No. There are no tolls in Drogheda, and Drogheda is the most important fair except in the sheep and corn market. It is held on the streets altogether there. We have a beautiful place for the fairs here. Of my own knowledge over 20 years ago there was a potato market here and a meal market in the same place, and all enclosed with sheds or low walls for years, and a party there who had charge of the scale and who used to charge the farmers so much for weighing. When Mr. Hamilton died that was knocked on the head, and the market place closed up and let for building purposes. Parties had to go in there to buy corn, and the police would not let them stand on the streets. That is done away with. There was a party appointed over the scales who used to weigh potatoes in small quantities for the people of the town, and charge so much for the gross. I often saw 10 or 12 cars in the market, but there was no market since the people began to sell potatoes in their houses.

Mr. Edward King examined.

25,514. Are you connected with trade in the town?—No, not very much. I am a farmer.

25,515. Supposing that tolls are levied, do you think a farmer when bringing cattle to the fair considers the toll he has to pay?—I think so, in this way, there are some who on account of Drogheda being so convenient would consider the toll, because Drogheda is only eight or nine miles from this.

25,516. Do they take any stock from this district to Dublin?—They do.

25,517. There is a charge in Dublin?—There is.

25,518. If they made an equally good fair in Balbriggan would they prefer stopping in Balbriggan?—Decidedly.

25,519. Is it because the Dublin market is a better one, and they can effect a readier sale, they do not consider the charge?—Lately there is an impression among the farmers here and we are not having the fairs, and they drive their cattle to Dublin, but when the fairs are properly established there will be very little cattle going to Dublin. They will be sold here. From the way the new fairs are promising a monthly fair will take.

25,520. Does this fair green afford sufficient space?—Ample space for the cattle. I suppose it would hold 2,000 cattle.

25,521. Have they different portions allotted off for each description of animal—pigs, sheep, and cattle?—They have for the pigs.

25,522. Do you think if there were pens erected that it would afford better accommodation?—I do not think there is any necessity for them.

25,523. There is a good opportunity at present for the exposure and accommodation of the cattle?—Yes, ample. It is a very fine green.

25,524. Have you any remarks to make that would tend to the improvement of the markets or fairs?—The only remark I have to make is, I am certain the fairs will be a great success and great accommodation to the farmers and people of the district, who used not send their cattle to Liverpool and Dublin.

25,525. Have you railway communication to suit the fairs?—We have. The railway accommodation is quite good and sufficient.

25,526. Would there be any chance of holding a weekly market here?—I am afraid not.

25,527. Why not? Is the demand not good enough?—I am afraid you have not a consumption trade in this town. It is not large enough for a potato market. I send my potatoes to Drogheda and Dublin. The way the potato supply comes to this town is through a few hucksters who may have three or four barrels of potatoes, and that quantity would do for a fortnight.

25,528. Practically, in this town they sell direct to the retailer?—We do. My experience is that the usual trade [illegible]

25,529. There are no wholesale buyers or local buyers?—No buyers.

25,530. What other commodities are used in Balbriggan?—The farmers send butter and eggs, and if I am not pleased with the price in one shop I go to another.

25,531. In all cases you sell to the retailer?—Yes. The shopkeepers buy them.

25,532. Do they levy any charge for weighing a commodity when you hand it in?—No charge.

25,533. You weigh the potatoes on your own premises before you send them in?—We do.

25,534. All farmers do not do that?—No. Some farmers might not have the accommodation.

25,535. If they have not the accommodation, and they used to have, is there anything charged for them?—I never knew a charge for them, but in Drogheda they charge you. If I sent a load of potatoes to Drogheda that had to be weighed they would charge me in Drogheda.

25,536. I suppose it is at so much a barrel the potatoes are sold?—Yes.

25,537. What is a barrel supposed to contain?—20 stone for potatoes, 16 stone for barley, 14 for oats, and 20 for wheat.

25,538. That is customary with all farmers dealing here?—It is.

25,539. It is always on the net weight you are paid?—Yes.

25,540. They make the net weight the difference between the gross weight and the tare?—Yes.

25,541. There is no other deduction for breakage or anything of that kind?—No.

25,542. They fix the class according to the sort of grain?—Yes.

25,543. Was that always so within your experience?—It was.

25,544. Do you think the farmers would have more confidence in the system of having the commodities weighed at a public scale and not on the buyer's premises? Do you think they would have more confidence in the dealing, and the weights that would be ascertained?—Farmers weigh the corn and potatoes on their own scales.

25,545. But if they have not that accommodation?—Generally speaking, they have.

25,546. Had you ever to take exception to any inaccuracy in the weights of the buyers who purchased the commodity?—No; their weights have always given satisfaction. There might be a pound or so difference, but that is nothing.

25,547. You give and take in your dealings?—Yes; it never interferes with the price.

25,548. In selling pigs is there any sum fixed as a luck-penny here?—No. I never knew any fixture of luck-penny on the pigs, sheep, cattle, horses, or anything.

25,549. Do you remember when they used to try pigs for the measles?—No.

Mr. J. Shavar, Town Commissioner, re-examined.

25,550. Do you remember that system?—Thoroughly.

25,551. That is not practised now?—Not a bit of it. I remember when the pig would be taken without being thrown down, and a handkerchief stuffed up their mouths, to examine them.

25,552. The price would be agreed upon for the pig?—Certainly.

25,553. If the pig had the measles would there be a scaling of the price?—If he had the measles you would drop 10s.

25,554. At that time was there a luck-penny on pigs?—There was always a luck-penny.

25,555. Was it left to the discretion of the seller?—There might be a little argument about asking for more, or something like that.

25,556. Does it lead to much contention amongst them, the arguing about the luck-penny?—No.

Mr. Patrick McCreary examined.

25,557. Have you any suggestions to offer?—I think it would be a great advantage to have a market for corn

25,659. Do you think there is a possibility of fostering one if these rules were abandoned?—I do. I think after a little while a great deal of the goods going to Drogheda would come to Balbriggan. I think the present system of buying corn in Balbriggan is objectionable.

25,660. Buying in the street?—Yes. Anything bought in the town is bought in the street.

25,661. In what way?—I think it is not a proper way to have dealings on the streets. Samples of corn are brought to the corner of the court-house and do not come into the market.

25,662. You would not say that would be to look at the samples before other buyers or forestall them?—No. The market is actually held on the triangle called the Square, and not in the market house. That is what I consider objectionable. I refused to go there, and any corn I bought myself the samples had to come to our office.

25,663. Would you say this is a good corn market?—It is a good corn market.

25,664. Could you give any approximate idea of the number of barrels brought here in the year?—Up to three or four thousand barrels of oats alone, about a thousand barrels of wheat, and hardly any barley.

Wm. McGloughry, Esq., the Chairman of the Town Commissioners, re-examined.

25,665. Do you think, supposing it was required to be done, the town commissioners could make a periodical return of the quantity of the different commodities brought to the town and the average prices of them, or would it be impossible to make such a return?—It would be quite possible. The clerk could obtain it.

25,666. Although it would entail additional labour, still you think it would be competent to make a pretty accurate return?—Yes, it would. There is an old market house on the fair green which was erected by subscription. Mr. O'Neill can tell you about it. It was sold with the other property.

Mr. O'Neill examined.

25,667. The market house is standing at present?—It is.

25,668. And it is on the fair green?—Yes. The idea about it is this, that a great many people believe it was lost through carelessness. The commissioners were blamed, and, as a matter of fact, the commissioners did all they could and went before Judge Flanagan, and they were beaten and had to pay the cost. Judge Flanagan decided the commissioners had no locus standi at all. The ratepayers should have gone, but it was too late.

25,669. This market house was sold subject to all rights affecting?—Yes. It is a good substantial building.

25,670. Was there ever a market held in it?—Not that I know of. It was originally built by public subscription, as I understand, before my time. It was to be sold together with the other property, as the Hamiltons claimed the same rights as in the other property. The commissioners entered an appearance and appeared before Judge Flanagan on the sale of the Hamilton estate to have that taken from the property to be sold as the building was erected by the public. Judge Flanagan had nothing before him, or anything to show by whom it was erected, and the judge decided the commissioners had no claim to it.

25,671. Is it utilised for any purpose at present?—No. It became private property when the doctor bought it, and once it was let on lease as a hosiery factory.

25,672. Could people dispose of marketable commodities in it in your time?—No. Before my time I think the only thing exhibited there for sale was corn.

25,673. Have you any remarks to make as to what you think would tend to the improvement of the markets, or the fostering or establishment of shows here?—Yes. I took a very great interest some years ago in the subject, and even when the new market was erected my idea was it was intended as a yard for fish and corn. We were about offering prizes in fact for the exhibition of the best sample of butter, eggs, and fowl so as to attract the country people, and I believe if such a thing were done it would be a very great benefit, and I think it is feasible.

25,674. You think it possible to foster a market?—I do; it is quite possible.

25,675. Do they send commodities to any other existing on account of none being here?—They do, to Drogheda and Dublin.

25,676. That entails additional expense in transit?—It does. I think if a market could be established here, as I think it could by that means, by offering prizes to the exhibitors of the best articles, that it would be a great boon. It would save people a great deal of trouble and money.

25,677. Do you think if there was a rule compelling the people to resort to the market that it would work?—Yes. In fact it was the exposure of the fish in the streets the people complained of, and an accident that occurred, caused the commissioners to erect the market, and they could not get them to go there.

25,678. Could not they compel them if there was a rule such as I suggest?—A rule would be very necessary.

25,679. Do you think the farmers would have any objection to pay a small charge that would repay the commissioners for the cost of that building, its maintenance, and having a weighmaster to weigh any commodities?—I think they would.

25,680. Would they if they got an adequate return for it?—I predict myself a market being held, and they paid for weighing potatoes or any commodities brought in; but, to give a voluntary subscription, I do not think they would.

25,681. Would you say that on account of no market being held here the farmer does not receive the full value of his produce, because he more or less loses by the cost of transit?—Decidedly, and I believe he would have as good a market here as elsewhere. I think there is a better market for hay or corn here than in Dublin, and that would be saving the cost of transit.

25,682. Do they take all the hay and corn to Dublin?—Yes. In the harvest time; but they would get better prices here.

25,683. Who is the owner of the market place?—The representatives of Dr. McEvoy.

25,684. There are two owners of the fair green?—Yes. The doctor at one side of the road and Mr. Hamilton at the other.

25,685. Then the people use both sides?—Yes, indiscriminately.

25,686. Have you any other observations to make?—No.

25,687. Is there any other gentleman who has any evidence to give or suggestions to offer?—No answer.

The inquiry then terminated.

BALTINGLASS.

With reference to my inquiry in Baltinglass on the 13th day of December 1888, I beg to report as follows:—

Baltinglass is situated upon the river Slaney, in the county of Wicklow. The town comprises several streets, the houses in which are fairly well built. It is a station on the Tullow branch of the Great Southern and Western Railway line. The trade is purely agricultural, and the local government is administered by the board of guardians and grand jury. The population is 1,151.

The market day is Friday. The fairs are held on the third Tuesday of each month, and a pig fair is held on day previous. No tolls are levied at either the markets or fairs.

Market rights are not exclusively claimed by any one individual in Baltinglass, neither is any control exercised over the markets or fairs.

Three traders in the town have each a beam and scales at which they weigh any of the marketable commodities, the weight of which it is desired to ascertain receiving for the services thus rendered a small charge. There is no byelaw or rule compelling the buyer or seller to resort to these scales or any of them they being free to go where they will.

It was stated at the inquiry that tolls were originally levied, but their collection fell into abeyance some 60 years ago, the farmer and buyer refusing to pay them, not getting any adequate return.

The public records show that four patents were granted for the town. The first is dated 4th September 15 James I., and authorized one Sir C. Wilmot to hold two fairs 24th, 25th, and 26th June, 24th, 25th, and 26th August, and a Saturday market. The second is dated 10th March 2 Charles I., and authorised one Robert Kennedy to hold a Thursday market and two fairs, Ascension Day, and two following days, and 18th, 19th, and 20th October. The third is dated February 1662 and authorised the Corporation to hold a Friday market and two fairs, 1st, 2nd and 3rd May, and 1st, 2nd and 3rd September. The fourth patent is dated 5th August 3 George III., and authorised Lord Baltinglass to hold a Tuesday market and four fairs, 2nd February, 1st July, 17th November, and 8th December.

Previous to 1884, the following fairs were held in Baltinglass, 2nd February, 12th May, 1st July, 12th September, 18th October, 8th December, 9th January, 18th August, 19th April, and 17th March.

The fairs on 9th of January and 18th August were established without any express authority some 60 years ago, those on the 2nd February, 12th May, 1st July, 12th September, 18th October, and 8th December, were held under the patents previously granted, and those on the 17th March and 19th April were evidently substituted for the fairs granted for Ascension Day and two next days and the 17th November. There is no record of any legal authorisation of this change.

In 1884 several of the townspeople held a meeting, the primary object being it seems, to alter the fairs and increase their number. The monthly fairs on third Tuesday of each month were then established without any legal authority and the old fairs ceased.

The Friday market is held under the patent, and appears never to have been altered.

In accordance with my instructions I have inspected the market place and fair green.

The markets in Baltinglass are held in what is called the market place, a wide space in front of the Court House, being a widening of the public street, as the public exercise rights over it. Houses are built on each side. The surface is level with the roadway forming in point of fact a portion of the public thoroughfare. There is no shelter or other accommodation of any description provided.

The fairs are held on a wide space of the roadway immediately at the rear of the Court House. The same description answers for it as that already given of the market place. No sheds, pens, or other accommodation are provided. The pigs are sold in another portion of the town on the public streets.

A Miss Doyle has a weigh-bridge at which she charges 3d. for each load weighed.

A complaint was made of the forestalling in fowl, practised by several buyers.

It was urged that authority should be given for the formation of a market committee as no local municipal authority exists in Baltinglass with power to such committee to control, regulate, and generally manage the markets and fairs.

Appended will be found a transcript of the evidence taken at the inquiry.

JOHN J. O'MEARA,
Assistant Commissioner.

45, Lower Mount Street, Dublin.

Baltinglass, 18th December 1889.

Mr. [illegible], examined.

26,888. You are a corn merchant in Baltinglass?—Yes, I deal in corn.

26,889. There is no local municipal authority here?—No.

26,890. Is there any individual exercising exclusive market rights here?—I believe not.

26,891. Are markets in point of fact held here?—Yes.

26,892. What day?—Every Friday.

26,893. Is Friday alone set off for the exposure and sale of marketable commodities?—Only Friday.

26,894. What fairs have you?—The third Tuesday in every month. The day previous is the pig fair.

26,895. Are any charges levied at these fairs?—No.

26,896. There is nobody exercising control over them but the police?—No.

26,897. Where are they held?—The cattle fair is held just behind the court-house. The pig fair is held beyond the bridge.

26,898. On the public thoroughfare also?—Yes.

26,899. Where are the markets held?—The markets are mostly held on the market square. It is called the market square.

26,900. That market square is a widening of the public thoroughfare?—Just so. It is the main street.

26,901. Kindly inform me what different commodities are brought here on Friday, and exposed for sale in the market square?—Oats, potatoes, turnips, mangolds, eggs, fowl, vegetables, fish and lime. I do not believe there is any butter.

26,902. Hay and straw?—There is no hay or straw market here.

26,903. Are there any other commodities?—These are the only commodities exposed for sale in this market, I think.

26,903. Are oats the only description of corn brought here?—Yes, white and black oats.

26,904. Have you got any standings such as itinerant clothes dealers?—Mostly on fair days.

26,905. What other description of standings are there?—All cars.

26,906. What commodities do they sell there?—Cast clothes and leathers, and crockery.

26,907. They stand on the public thoroughfare?—Yes, they stand on the street.

26,908. If a farmer comes in here with any of these commodities, and he disposes of them, and both he and the buyer desire to ascertain the weight, can they do so in Baltinglass?—Yes, if they sell them.

26,909. Can they ascertain the weight?—Yes.

26,910. Where?—There are three public scales on market days.

26,911. Who own them?—Mr. E. P. O'Kelly, Wm. Whelan, and Michael Byrne, and then there is a heavy weighing machine as well, which Miss Doyle keeps.

26,912. These honest are scales, and weighbridge, are private property belonging to these owners?—Yes.

26,913. But they hire them out for weighing commodities on market day?—Quite so.

26,914. How long has that monthly fair been held, or do you remember the fairs being held on any other day but Tuesday?—I think Mr. O'Kelly will be better able to inform you on that matter.

26,915. Within your recollection, have you ever heard that people have ever contemplated the appointment or election of any market committee—a committee of the traders to look after the fairs and markets?—Not to my recollection, but I think it would be a very good suggestion to have a committee appointed to look after the fairs and markets, and whatever would be for the improvement of the town to have it in their power to make an alteration to suit the circumstances.

26,916. Do you think the markets here require some controlling influence?—I do.

26,917. Do you think they would be augmented in that way?—Yes, improved and augmented both as to the improvement of the town and market.

26,918. In what direction would you like to see the improvement?—I would like to see the fowl market held at a later hour than it is held.

26,919. What is the present hour?—The present hour is very early; in the summer months from four to six o'clock, before the shops are open.

26,920. What other suggestions do you deem necessary for the improvement of the markets?—It would be, I think, to the advantage of the public generally, if the corn market was held at an hour when everybody would know it opened. It is irregular at present.

26,921. There are no stated market hours, or hours for the commencement of the market?—No. There is no stated hour for the market to commence.

26,922. They come indiscriminately?—Yes, from nine o'clock to twelve o'clock.

26,923. What time does the market usually terminate?—The market is over between those hours.

26,924. What time does it commence?—There is no stated hour. It would be well if there was an appointed hour.

26,925. These commodities you have mentioned are all exposed on the street?—Yes.

26,926. There is no shelter accommodation for them here?—No.

26,927. You buy a quantity of corn here?—Yes, from time to time.

26,928. Has it ever been damaged in any way by exposure?—The people would not expose it to the rain.

26,930. Where can they put it?—They must keep it in the cars.

26,931. They keep it covered?—Yes.

26,932. However they put up with that inconvenience in order to make a ready sale?—There may be some slight inconvenience on that account.

26,933. What is the estimated quantity of oats brought in here in the year, or could you give me an approximate idea?—I could not. It is only for a certain portion of the season, perhaps I would say for four months of the year, we have a pretty good market for corn. After that they fall away until the spring comes and then the market is pretty full until the spring sowing is over.

26,934. Would you call this a good corn market?—Certainly.

26,935. Would you say it is a good market for other commodities?—Yes, very good fowl. It is a well-known fowl market.

26,936. From what districts do they bring these commodities?—All around.

26,937. Within what limits?—Within a radius of four or five miles, and perhaps seven miles in some cases for sale.

26,938. Is it all fresh fish that comes here?—Yes, and sometimes cured fish and herrings. From Arklow principally the fish comes to the market.

26,939. Have you any suggestions or remarks to make touching the fairs and markets here?—I could not make any suggestions touching the fairs but as regards the hours of the market. I think they (the markets and fairs) are fairly successful as far as they go and I think they need no improvement whatever in that respect. It is well to let them go on themselves and I think they will go on and improve. I would not alter the present state of the fairs, but the markets would require a little looking after I think in regard to the hours and some fixed time stated or appointed.

Mr. Edward P. O'Kelly examined.

24,941. You have a house and scales, I believe, here?—I have.

24,942. What commodities do you usually weigh on it?—Nothing but oats and potatoes.

24,943. Are all the potatoes brought here weighed at your scales, or can the farmer go where he pleases?—He can go where he likes.

24,944. There is no rule in the market to the effect that he must go to you?—None.

24,945. Are these commodities sold before they are weighed at your scales?—Yes, always.

24,946. Does the buyer always require them to be weighed before he completes his bargain?—No. The understanding is the commodity is sold and then it is weighed and entered in the ticket giving the weight.

24,947-8. Then they always buy by weight?—Yes.

24,949. They never buy by bulk or without ascertaining the weight?—Never.

24,950. What is your charge for weighing oats?—A penny per bag.

24,951. And for potatoes?—The same.

24,952. In weighing oats, what is the lowest weight you weigh down to, or do you weigh under four pounds?—We put in two pounds.

24,953. You weigh down to two pounds?—Yes.

24,954. Do you give a cast of the beam?—Yes.

24,955. Practically, it must be two pounds or nothing?—Yes.

24,956. What weight do you weigh the potatoes?—They do not test them singly. It is four pounds in potatoes.

24,957. Do you give a cast of beam in weighing potatoes?—Yes.

24,958. Do you estimate the tare of the empty sack, or actually weigh it?—It is never weighed, of course if the buyer wishes it to be weighed it is done. They allow four pounds tare for the corn sacks, and for under a barrel of potatoes half a stone, and over a barrel a stone.

24,959. What quantity does the barrel contain?—Twenty-four stone of potatoes and fourteen stone of oats.

24,960. When weighing do you give a ticket denoting the weight?—Yes, always.

24,961. It is a printed or manuscript ticket?—It is manuscript.

24,962. Do you ever mark the weight on the bag?—It is never done.

24,963. Is the tare the only deduction from the gross weight?—That is the only deduction.

24,964. Would the estimated tare of the sack be the same on a fine day, as on an extremely wet day, when the sack was completely saturated with wet?—They generally arrange that among themselves.

24,965. Do they take that into consideration when weighing?—Yes, they would.

24,966. You have known it to be done?—Yes, frequently.

24,967. Do you ever make up the tickets for them?—Yes they are always made up.

24,968. That is their own tickets, between the buyer and seller?—Yes.

24,969. Supposing it was required, you could give a pretty accurate account of the current prices of these commodities?—Yes.

24,970. It would be an accurate one?—Yes sufficiently accurate. Any person in the town could easily do that.

24,971. You could not give any return of the quantity brought in because they don't all come to you?—I dare say if a person went over it they could give a pretty accurate return of the quantity.

24,972-3. Do you keep a block of these tickets?—I do not keep a block of these tickets, but a book recording the weights.

24,974. You put the name of the seller, and the weight of the commodity?—Yes, the gross weight.

24,975. Do you think it would work better, and tend to improve the markets if there were proper market buildings, with a public scales, where all the commodities could be exposed and weighed on the public scales. Do you think there would be more confidence between the buyers and sellers, the farmers and the purchasers, if that course were adopted instead of sending the commodities to private scales?—I really do not think it would benefit the market one bit. I do not think it would. For example, in Dundalk, where these facilities exist, the people very seldom make use of the market house. They invariably go to the other places.

24,977. There is no rule restricting them from exposing their commodities elsewhere than in the market house?—No. Of course, if there was a crane and market house it might bring in commodities that are not coming at present, such as butter. It might do it. I do not say it would, because this is not a very large butter making country.

24,978. What is the nature of the country here. Is there much of it in tillage?—There is a fair quantity.

24,979-80. What percentage?—I daresay 10 per cent.

24,981. Then your fairs must be very good?—They are very good. They have improved wonderfully since the change in date.

24,982. That is the alteration of the dates?—Yes.

24,983. How long is it since you established the monthly fairs?—Five years the coming spring.

24,984. Who was it established them?—The inhabitants of the town and neighbourhood came together and advertised the fairs.

24,985. What fairs were held previous to 1884?—There were 10 fairs held previously.

24,986. What were the dates?—The 9th January, 2nd February, 17th March, 18th April, 12th May, 1st July, 18th August, 13th September, 15th October, 9th December.

24,987. Do you remember any period when there were less than 10 fairs?—No, I do not, but I think about 40 years ago there were only six fairs. There were some fairs called new fairs here, but I do not remember them.

24,988. Do you know what the new fairs were?—The 18th August, and 9th January.

24,989. When were they added to the other fairs?—It must be 30 years ago at any rate. There is no man he could tell when the new fairs commenced.

24,990. Are you a trader in the town?—Yes.

24,991. Do you approve of the system of the fairs being held on the public thoroughfare?—Well, you know, there is a very large space for the fairs.

24,992. Do they not create much filth and dirt about the public thoroughfare?—They do, but the contractor looks after that, and is allowed very well for cleaning it away.

24,993. Have you ever heard complaints of any dereliction of duty on his part?—There were some people complained the day after the fair.

24,994. Have you ever heard buyers complaining that they have not had an opportunity of sufficiently examining the animals?—I never did.

24,995. Have you ever heard the farmers complaining that they had no protection from the elements except by going into the shops and different buildings in rainy weather?—I never did.

24,996. No tolls are levied here?—No.

24,997. Do you buy at the fairs yourself?—Sometimes.

24,998. Do you sell any stock?—Very seldom. There is just one suggestion I would make with regard to the pig fair, and that is, I think it would be a great benefit if the pigs were taken out of the area where the fair is held. There would be ample accommodation.

26,999. Are these young pigs in the carts?—Young pigs should be kept in the cars and cause no inconvenience, but for fat pigs it would be well to have them out of the cars.

27,000. Do the buyers object to buy them when in the cars?—No.

27,001. What is your reason for making that suggestion?—It is just in order to facilitate the traffic; it would be an advantage if they were out of the carts.

27,002. Then, I suppose, you would require the removal of the cars themselves?—I think it would be well if the carts were removed.

27,003. Is that your idea?—Yes.

27,004. Do they cause any obstruction?—Of course the carts do.

27,005. Have you ever heard complaints about that?—No. I never heard complaints, but I noticed it myself. Fat pigs are usually taken out of the cars as far as my observation goes, and the cars remain there.

27,006. Have you ever heard of the people here contemplating the appointment of any markets committee, or committee of the traders of the town to foster and control the markets and fairs?—I never did.

27,007. Do you think it would be advisable to adopt that course?—I think it would be very advisable, because things might come under the notice of that body that would not come under the notice of individuals, but with regard to the fowl market it is too bad that persons who buy a basket of fowl or cart of fowl and the people who sell them, are gone out of the town before the private individuals get up.

27,008. Is the system of forestalling practised relative to fowl?—There is some of that carried on. The buyers sometimes pay another buyer not to buy in order that they will have a monopoly.

27,009. Have you known instances of that yourself?—Indeed I have.

27,010. Are all these fowl exported?—Well, in the winter months they are generally sent to London, but in the summer months they are sent to Dublin.

27,011. The people then of the town are at great inconvenience in purchasing fowl?—They are. The private people have no chance of buying fowl.

27,012. Do you think the price of dead fowl is enhanced by this practice of forestalling?—I do not think it is. Sometimes, when fowl are scarce, I have seen people two miles outside the town, emissaries from the chicken buyers buying the fowl.

27,013. If that was stopped and the farmers had to come into the town and expose their fowl and other commodities, where there would be general competition among the buyers, would they get better prices for their commodities or animals?—I think they would.

27,014. Did they ever express that opinion themselves; did they ever express an objection to forestalling?—They did very often complain of it. I have known people coming in to be offered prices for fowl, and when they came into the market they would not get those prices when the buyers found the quantity outside. It makes the market irregular.

27,015. You say they complain of it, but is it not left to their own option to sell to the runner?—It is, but they do not know the competition is here, and when they come in they know better what to do.

27,016. Have you ever heard complaints that the commodities brought into the market were injured for want of shelter accommodation, that is, for the fish and other commodities?—With the exception of herrings I did not. They are caught on Wednesday in Arklow, and they come on straight for Friday, but they are not injured.

27,017. Have you ever heard people complaining?—No.

27,018. Where do they erect their standings principally?—In the main street. They turn round the car, unyoke the horse, and sell away.

27,019. They have no charge whatever to pay?—No charge.

27,020. Have the people who weigh at your scale any porterage charge to pay?—No charge except a penny a bag.

27,021. Who performs the work of weighing?—My man.

27,022. Does the farmer lift the bag from the cart on to the scale?—My man does that.

27,023. You only charge a penny there?—Yes.

27,024. Both for potatoes and corn?—Yes.

27,025. Have you any suggestions to offer?—Well, no, with the exception that there should be some authority to regulate the hours. I think everything else is tolerably fair.

27,026. Do you think a necessity exists for some such controlling authority to have byelaws to regulate the system of the markets and the hours?—I do. I think it is very necessary.

27,027. Is the market as a rule confined to this square, or do they go indiscriminately about the other streets of the town?—No. As a rule it is confined to the main street.

Mr. William Flynn examined.

27,028. What commodities do you weigh at your scales?—Oats and potatoes.

27,029. The same as Mr. O'Kelly?—Yes.

27,030. What do you charge?—A penny per bag.

27,031. The same observations as to his system of weighing apply to yours as well?—Yes.

27,032. The same practice is resorted to at both places?—Yes.

27,033. And is it the same at Mr. Byrne's?—Yes.

Mr. [illegible] Doyle examined.

27,034. You represent Miss Doyle?—Yes.

27,035. She has a weigh-bridge here?—Yes.

27,036. What commodities does she weigh on it?—Turnips, potatoes, straw, hay, coke or coal, bacon, pork. We could weigh wool.

27,037. What are your charges?—Threepence a load.

27,038. Do you ascertain the tare of the car?—Yes, always.

27,039. You always actually weigh the empty cart?—The empty cart is weighed every time. The parties who own the cart would not get a ticket unless they weigh it.

27,040. Supposing a farmer came to-day and came again to-morrow would you put the weight you ascertained to-day?—No. I would weigh the cart every day.

27,041. Is the tare the only deduction?—Yes.

27,042. They allow nothing for [illegible] or the bad state of the hay?—We never allow anything. They can settle that among themselves.

27,043. That is a matter between the buyer and seller when arguing about the price of the load?—Yes. The sellers may take something off the load if there was a shower of rain.

27,044. There is no deduction customary other than the tare?—No.

27,045. Apart altogether from what you have to do, do you think a necessity exists in the market for any other deduction?—Oh, not the slightest. There is always something allowed between the buyer and seller.

27,046. Is your weigh-bridge the only one in the town?—Yes.

27,047. Did you ever weigh live cattle?—Yes, up on the weight.

27,048. What did you charge?—Nothing at all.

27,049. You say there is always something allowed between the buyer and seller?—Yes.

27,050. Is there any customary allowance?—No.

27,051. Do you keep any record of the quantity the people weigh there?—There is a block kept, and it is entered on the books by the buyers.

27,052. You give a ticket?—Yes, and keep the weight for them if they require it.

27,053. Supposing they lose the ticket during the day, can they get a copy of it again without weighing the cart?—They would have to weigh the cart again.

27,054. You would charge an additional charge?—I charge a second time.

27,055. Do you keep a block of the ticket?—Yes, if required. We keep a block in any case.

27,056. When you weigh a load do you put the weight on the ticket you give the seller and retain the block?—Yes, we enter it if it is to be kept over, but if they require only one ticket we do not enter it in the block. The block is the same as in a cheque book.

27,057-8. You do not keep a block of everything you weigh?—No.

27,059. All these different commodities come to you?—Yes.

27,060. If required, you could tell the quantity of hay, straw, and other commodities brought here?—Yes, at another time I could, but lately I could not do it as all the books were thrown away.

27,061. In future, supposing it was required from you, could you keep an account of the quantity of the different commodities brought here?—Certainly.

27,062. Do you ever make up the tickets?—Yes.

27,063. You know generally the price?—Yes. Even this morning two carts were weighed for Colonel Saunders, and the man went and put the weight on the drays. I did not weigh at all, but I sent the tickets to Colonel Saunders without entering the weight of the drays, because I did not see them weighed, and they were not weighed at all.

27,064. Have you ever found that after the delivery of the commodity and before the cart came to you any fraud had been committed by changing the wheels?—We always examine the cart.

27,065. Have you ever heard of any frauds being committed?—No. We can see whether the cart is straight or fair on the bridge, and we do everything fairly.

Mr. Matthew Byrne examined.

27,066. I believe you have much experience of fairs here and elsewhere?—I know a good deal about fairs for the last 60 years.

27,067. Have you ever attended fairs where tolls were levied?—I have at different places.

27,068. Are you a trader in the town?—I am.

27,069. You are also a farmer?—Yes.

27,070. And you buy and sell cattle?—Yes.

27,071. Do you think that the levying of a toll at a fair acts in any way as a deterrent on the farmers bringing in the supply they would otherwise bring in if no tolls were levied?—I think they would give more freely when they would not have to pay any money.

27,072. Supposing charges were levied at the fairs, do you think it would tend to deteriorate the fairs?—I could not give an opinion. They give more freely when the cattle are sold, but it is unpleasant to pay when they do not sell.

27,073. But if the charge was on the animal sold and when the bargain was completed?—At Ballinasloe, where tolls are levied, they are growing.

27,074. Were tolls ever levied here?—Not to my knowledge.

27,075. Have you ever heard they were?—I never heard.

27,076. Did you ever feel any objection to buying or selling on the public street?—Not a bit.

27,077. Do you think it would be better to have a fair-green provided with surface hard, so that you could examine the cattle more conveniently. Do you think that would be better than the public thoroughfare?—I think there is no fair where there is better accommodation than in this town.

27,078. That is on account of the wide open space here?—Yes, the wide open space on the road to chapel.

27,079. Is your establishment convenient?—It is up to the court house.

27,080. Leaving that out of consideration, and supposing you had no trade in the town at all, do you think a fair green would be better than having the fairs on the street?—I think not. I have seen in Carlow the fair in Barrack Street always a better fair than that on the green. The buyers and sellers meet one another more comfortably.

27,081. What do you assign for that?—I think on a wet day the cattle fair should be held in a field because they sink down at least six inches in the mud.

27,082. That is owing to the defects in the preparation of the green, and in the cleaning of the soil?—I never saw in any fair anywhere, a green, but it is on green. There are grass greens in Timahoe, Castletown, Carlow, and other places.

27,083. Do you go to Kilkenny?—Sometimes. That is one place, but I am quoting several towns.

27,084. As you have had experience I would like to get an expression of your own opinion. What do you think about the fair green in Kilkenny?—It is a good, clean fair green.

27,085. Would you like to see that at all fairs?—That would be very expensive.

27,086. Apart from the expense, do you think a fair green like that at Kilkenny is the best place to expose cattle?—Upon my word, I do not know that there is a better fair green in any part of Ireland I have been in than at the back of this court house.

27,087. Were the fairs always held there?—As long as I remember.

27,088. Always on the same spot?—Yes and the O'Leary family left it free of toll for the purpose of the fair. Nobody need block the public road in any spot in it.

27,089. At the fairs here, have they the system of giving a luck-penny?—They have. Some give it and some do not. You may meet some cheery fellow who will give half a crown for luck, and another fellow will only give a penny.

27,090. Supposing a man is selling stock, in asking the price, does he ever consider the amount of the luck-penny?—No. Sometimes when there is a hard bargain the buyer may say "will you give me a crown for luck."

27,091. Would you ask a higher price than you would otherwise take if you had not to give a luck-penny?—It is a free gift.

27,092. The buyers never consider?—No, except one in a hundred.

27,093. When they are arguing about the value do not they say, I will pay clear to pocket?—Yes, that is no luck.

27,094. In that case do not they consider in fixing the price the amount of the luck-penny?—They do not. It is a free gift.

27,095. Then it is left to the disposition of the seller?—Yes.

27,096. There is no fixed amount?—No.

27,097. Is it fixed with regard to pigs?—I think they charge.

27,098. You say the buyers charge?—Yes, they stop sixpence.

27,099. In cattle it is left to the disposition of the seller to give, but in the first instance he receives the actual price of the animal?—He does.

27,100. But in the case of pigs they deduct the sixpence out of the price?—They do. It is the custom to give sixpence for luck.

27,101. That is not left to the disposition of the seller?—I think not.

27,102. You do not deal in pigs?—No.

27,103. Have they got the system of luck-penny in connection with sheep?—Yes, but you will never get more than a penny or twopence except from some generous fellows.

27,104. Have you ever bought cattle by live weight?—No.

27,105. Have you ever sold them by live weight?—No.

27,106. What are your opinions on selling by live weight?—I think it would take a smart fellow to buy by live weight. Some cattle are filled with turnips and grass and other things, and it would be very hard to judge them.

27,107. Would you rather rely on your own experience for judging cattle?—I would.

27,108. From such experience you would generally have an advantage over another?—It would be very hard, supposing a beast was in a house 16 hours, she might drink 40 pounds of water.

27,109. Do you think it would be a better system, and that the farmers and buyers throughout the country would have greater confidence in the bargains they make if all cattle were sold by live-weight and weighed at an independent scale?—I would rather buy them by sight.

27,110. That is because you rely on your own experience?—Yes.

27,111. Have you any suggestions to offer as to what you think would tend to the improvement of the markets and fairs here, or is there any practice at present resorted to you would wish to complain of?—There is, and that is the practice of buying fowl a mile or two miles on the road outside the town, and also in the streets of the town before day. That is all done before the people get up, and I think there ought to be an hour appointed—say eight o'clock in the morning—and allow no person to buy or sell before that time; and 10 o'clock for oats or potatoes, and no one to buy before them. That would be a great service to the town and the people living in the town.

27,112. You heard the answer of Mr. Merril and Mr. O'Kelly to my question. Do you concur in their opinion that it would be advisable to have a committee of the traders to look after the fairs and markets?—I think nothing better could be adopted.

27,113. You have attended fairs and markets where the control was vested in local authorities, and where it was not?—I have.

27,114. Where do you think they were better managed, when worked by a private individual or by a local authority?—In Carlow at the present time you can eat your breakfast without any bother. The bell will ring at eight o'clock. That is the system, and it is a good one.

27,115. Where have you found the markets better managed?—Take all this side of the country, and they are under no control. In Enniscorthy, Newtownbarry, Rathdrum, Tinahely, they are all the same as this, free to come or stay out whichever you like. There is a loose system carried on.

27,116. You think it would be better to have a governing authority such as there is at Carlow and elsewhere?—I think it would be a great deal better, and I am sure it would be good for the town, and good for the people themselves, and a better system than to have the loose way carried on that they have at present.

27,117. Do you think it would be advisable, apart altogether from any consideration of finance, for a market building to be erected here with shelter accommodation, and a rule made by any authority established to confine the disposal and exposure of all commodities to this building?—I think it would be a great deal pleasanter for the sellers, and sometimes pleasanter for the buyers.

27,118. Apart from the pleasantry, do you think it would be a gain?—I think it would be no harm to the market, but an improvement.

27,119. Do you think a necessity exists here for such?—At present I do not think there is a necessity. If there was a committee appointed, that committee would give an opinion which would be the best way to go about it.

27,120. Have you anything further to state?—Nothing more.

Mr. Peter Douglas examined.

27,121. (Witness). The magistrates made a rule about the markets formerly, and tried to have it enforced about the fowl. They had the rule published, and tried to carry it out, but the parties set it at defiance.

27,122. Was the irregularity of the fowl market brought under the notice of the authorities?—Yes. They fixed an hour about the sale of corn that has been observed, but the other is not.

Sergeant [illegible] Moore, Royal Irish Constabulary, examined.

27,123. Have you ever heard complaints of the obstruction on the public thoroughfare?—No.

27,124. Is this place a regular fair green?—It is not for fair green purposes, and it is as good as a fair green.

27,125. The pig fair is in a different portion of the town?—Yes. That is held at the other side of the street.

27,126. Have you ever heard complaints from private inhabitants—people other than traders—that much filth and dirt has accumulated?—The complaints I heard were from the people themselves in the barrack. It is near the barrack.

27,127. About this market—the market is principally concentrated in the market square?—Yes.

27,128. They do not go indiscriminately about the town?—No, it is held in front of the houses down the street, but the fowl market is very much wanting in improvement. People sell stolen fowl here that they may take from the people at cross-roads and places. If a man comes to buy fowl, and he was a stranger, he would be well thrashed in the town in consequence of coming here so early in the morning.

27,129. Was that a buyer?—Yes, an English buyer.

27,130. Is there a combination among fowl buyers?—Certainly.

27,131. Have you ever known that they have agreed before the market to the price they will give for the fowl?—Yes, and they will buy off outsiders for the purpose of keeping them out, and then give any price they like, and sometimes they take them home again.

27,132. Are there many buyers coming here?—Sometimes two and one. There was a good buyer coming, and they intimidated him so much, and thrashed him, that he had to leave the country altogether.

27,133. Do the farmers ever agree among themselves not to sell in that way; they more or less help it by disposing of the commodities?—They are very well inclined to resist it, but they are not able to. It is women and young girls who sell the fowl.

27,134. Why are they bought so early. Is it to catch any train?—It convenience poultry men who send them to Manchester and other places.

27,135. Is that the reason?—They gain by it in the way I tell you.

27,136. You think if the fowl came into the market, and there was the ordinary competition among the buyers, a better price would be got by the farmer?—Very much better. The farmers' daughters and girls come in and go about the street with the fowl. People outside may give them a couple of shillings earnest, and when they came to the market would have to give it back as the parties would not take the fowl.

27,137. Have they retained possession of the fowl?—Yes, until they get the money back.

27,138. In that way the producers have lost a sale?—Certainly, and must give them to the man for whatever he likes to offer. Sometimes they have to give them a great deal less than the value, sooner than take back the fowl.

27,139. Dispose of them a great deal less than what they were originally offered?—Yes.

Mr. Patrick Byrne examined.

27,140-1. Have you any suggestion to offer?—Four horse fairs in addition to the pig fairs, and cattle fairs would be a great improvement.

27,142. There is no horse fair?—No. They used to have them some years ago on the same date as the cattle.

27,143. Are the cattle and sheep brought in any great quantity?—Yes, one of the largest fairs for 12 or 14 miles.

27,144. From what districts do they bring the cattle?—From within two or three miles of Tullow, and four miles of Carlow and Hacketstown.

27,145. Within what radius is that?—Ten miles or more.

27,146. Could you give me any idea of the number of cattle brought here in the year?—I could not.

27,147. You say this is a better fair than the surrounding ones?—There is no fair so good for 12 miles round.

27,148. Are the pig fairs well attended?—Yes. Since the opening of the railway the pig fairs are wonderfully improved.

27,149. Have you found any material improvement in the fairs since the railway was opened?—Yes, very much.

27,150. It has tended to create greater demand and more cattle?—Yes. They bring cattle for the fairs. If there was a fair in Hacketstown and Baltinglass, they would bring the fair to Baltinglass.

27,151. You think in order to improve the fairs, it is well to have easy communication with great centres like Dublin?—Yes.

27,152. Do they export the greater portion of the cattle they buy?—No. I dare say about half of them.

27,153. Where do the pig buyers come from?—From Limerick, Waterford, and Dublin.

27,154. Are you in trade in the town?—Yes.

27,155. You deal in cattle?—Yes, a little in cattle.

27,156. And horses?—Yes.

27,157. Where is the nearest horse fair?—Castle Dermot, seven miles away.

27,158. Do you think a horse fair could be fostered here?—Three or four horse fairs in the year would take in Baltinglass. There are a great number of horses that pass by Baltinglass and go on 17 miles further every month. If the horse fairs were established, it would not be advisable to have them on the same dates as Tinahely; they are quarterly.

27,159. Still, you think a necessity exists for a horse fair, or that one could be fostered?—One could be fostered if they tried.

27,160. Did the farmers ever bring in horses?—They did formerly, but not latterly.

27,161. It failed at that time?—Yes.

27,162. That was previous to the railway communication?—Yes. Baltinglass has done away with the cattle fair in Castle Dermot, and the horse fair would be brought in here too, and done away with there.

27,163. Are there any tolls levied in the immediate neighbourhood of Baltinglass?—Not since they were abolished at Dunlavin. The traders of the town bought off the tolls.

27,164. You do not know the amount of the purchase?—I do not.

27,165. Who collected the tolls previously?—Mr. Trench was the landlord. A man named Whittle collected them. Mr. Trench gave up his right for the benefit of the town, and bought out the tenant. There was a very simple custom in Dunlavin. They had only to pay on the animals sold, and strike the board as to whether they bought or not. Another objectionable custom was the charge on cars.

27,166. Do you agree in the statement that the levying of a toll deters farmers from bringing in a supply of stock?—I am quite certain of it. They would surely go to another fair on account of it.

27,167. Have you been in any other places where there is a fair green, such as the one in Kilkenny, or do you think if the farmers got a properly enclosed fair green—I am not speaking of Baltinglass in particular—do you think if they got a fair green properly paved, with pens and shelter accommodation, that they (the farmers) would have any objection to pay a small charge to maintain that green?—Certainly. And they would rather have the accommodation they have. I am quite positive about it.

27,168. I am speaking generally now, and not of this place in particular?—Yes. I sometimes see very nearly serious rows in Dungarvan about the fairs.

27,169. Fairs on the street?—Yes.

27,170. If there was a fair green there, and accommodation, would they have an objection to pay something small for its erection?—I believe they would.

27,171. Even if they got an adequate return for the charge?—They would not go inside if they were allowed to stop outside. When the tolls were charged in this town, sometime ago, there was a terrible row about them.

27,172. Were tolls levied here?—Yes, not 40 years ago. There were two men on each road charging so much a head, and there was nothing but fighting and arguing.

27,173. What caused the abolition of the tolls?—The farmers would not pay a toll going out to a man named Higgins who had the tolls, and they burst the cattle out in spite of him.

27,174. It was owing to the difficulty of collecting that the collection ceased altogether?—It was.

Sergeant Moore re-examined.

27,175. (Witness). I think there ought to be sheds for the corn. They are very much wanted; and if anyone does not sell their produce here, they have nothing to do but take it home again. There is no place to store it. In other towns I have always seen a place to store small articles.

27,176. Is there any great quantity of the corn brought here, or of the other commodities remaining unsold after the market?—I think not. They are mostly all sold.

Mr. E. P. O'Kelly re-examined.

27,177. (Witness). I think with regard to what the sergeant said he is under a mistake. If the people wish to have storage they can always have it.

27,178. Do you levy any charge?—No.

27,179. Is it stored at their own risk?—Well, it is not. If they had not made a sale to their liking, and if they wished to store it until that day week we would accommodate them.

27,180. Are these scales of yours available everyday?—They are brought in the street on market day. If any person wished any other day to weigh anything we could do it for them.

27,181. Do you erect triangles?—Yes.

27,182. On the three scales?—Yes. The market varies a good deal. In the spring there are very large markets. They cover over nearly an acre of space in the spring because a great number of carts come in. It is inconvenient not to have a fixed hour when the people can buy oats, and when there is only a small supply the buyers complain that there is none to be got, whereas if there was a fixed hour they would have the time to come in, and it would be their own fault if they were not there. When there is no fixed hour the people are very often disappointed.

Mr. Moran re-examined.

27,183. Could you give me an estimate of the quantity of corn brought here?—From September to the present month, from fifty to a hundred barrels every week, more or less. I do not think it exists up to this month or reaches a hundred barrels any week. From February to May there is seven times that much.

27,184. After the buying of the corn is there any deduction from the price agreed upon by the seller?—No. The only deduction is the tare.

27,185. Do you weigh yourself or ask them to produce the ticket?—It is always the custom when buying corn to oblige the people I buy from to weigh at the particular scales I buy at.

27,186. Then you would not take the corn unless they produced a ticket?—They must get the ticket.

27,187. Do you ever weigh it over again yourself?—No, not as a rule.

27,188. Have you ever heard complaints of any inaccuracy in the weights of the scales or bridge?—No. They are usually correct.

27,189. They are visited by the police?—They are. I think everybody is unanimous in seeing the advisability of appointing a committee to regulate the markets and have bye-laws. There is no one would disagree with that suggestion. It is the most necessary thing of all.

Mr. John Jones examined.

27,190. (Witness). I live two miles out in the country and I know the fowl buyers go out there, and I have heard that several of these fowl buyers are treated by the sellers in a very ridiculous manner such as the sergeant is after stating.

27,191. Do the farmers never consider it advisable to put an end to that system, because it is in their own hands?—Some of them might try to prevent it and others would not. The area is too wide and they are not connected with one another. There are farmers who would wish to put a stop to it, and there are others who surrender and sell. You know it is women generally make these sales. They might have a little boy with them who is no protection, and these men can do whatever they wish.

27,192. Apart from the fowl market have you any other observations to make?—I would wish to say this. I think it would be a very good system not to have sales allowed sooner than eight o'clock in the morning, and then, so far as the corn market is concerned, I do come here occasionally with corn, and I think no corn might be sold sooner than ten o'clock, such as I heard Mr. Byrne suggest. As a farmer, I believe it would be a very good system.

27,193. What hour do the buyers usually attend?—About ten or eleven o'clock. It is the time that the principal sales are made.

27,194. Is there any other gentleman who wishes to give evidence?—No answer.

The inquiry then terminated.

CARLOW.

With reference to my inquiry in Carlow on the 14th day of December 1888, I beg to report as follows:—

Carlow is an inland town, and the capital of the county. The town is substantially built and neatly laid out, and has a good general trade. A branch of the Great Southern and Western Railway connects it with Dublin, and with Kilkenny and Waterford. The local government is administered by a board of Town Commissioners, and the population is 7,185.

The market days are Monday and Thursday. The fairs are held on the fourth Wednesday of each month in the year, with the exception of the month of March, when the fair is held on the 26th of that month. Two other fairs are also held on the 4th May and 8th November. A pig fair is held on the day previous to the ordinary fair.

Tolls are leviable at both the markets and fairs; but at the former, on some of the commodities, weighing charges are at present only demanded, although the market owners can claim the toll. At the fairs the tolls are on entrance to the fair green.

Previous to 1879 no tolls were payable at the fairs or markets, nor were any market rights actively exercised by anyone claiming to possess such.

The market rights and tolls at present belong to the Town Commissioners, who have the immediate control of them.

There seems to have been only one patent granted for the town of Carlow; it is dated 6th December 1722 (9 Geo. I.), and granted to one, Jacob Hamilton, an "additional" Monday market and two "additional" fairs on 25th April and 11th June.

It appears in 1879 eight fairs were held in the town, four of which were established within the previous 20 years, and the other four were held for a great length of time. A committee, called the "Fair Committee," was then constituted in the town by some of the traders, who were also members of the Town Commissioners' Board. The primary object of this committee was to alter the dates and increase the number of fairs, and provide a suitable fair green and collect tolls to pay off the expense incurred thereby. The fair committee rented a field of some six acres from a William H. Beake for 31 years at 40*l.* a year, and a caretaker's house at 8*l.* a year from a Mr. McQuaid. The Town Commissioners were made lessees in this lease. The fair committee then expended some 650*l.* in permanent improvements on the fair green in the way of pailings, pens, collection boxes, and gates, and for which they were each jointly and severally liable, and established the present fairs, letting those formerly held cease. Tolls were levied on the entrance of each animal to the fair green, and it proved so successful that on 6th July 1886 the entire 650*l.* was paid off, and the possession of the fair green and right to the tolls handed over to the Town Commissioners. In 1860 a committee of the traders, called the "Tullow Street Committee," was constituted for the purpose of working the potato market; but in 1880 the control was given over to the Town Commissioners, who paid the weigh-master some 68*l.* for the weigh-house and weighing machine, and reappointed him their weigh-master. In 1883 the Commissioners obtained a loan of 3,600*l.*, which they expended in the erection of a town hall and butter market place. The latter was completed in 1885 at a total cost of 239*l.* 10*s.* The Commissioners also purchased for 100*l.* the weighing machine in the hay market from the owner and erected a new one in its stead, and a weigh-house at a cost of 110*l.* On the 22nd August 1878 the Town Commissioners purchased from W. Hamilton, the representative of the grantee in the patent granted for the town, any rights which might be vested in him for 100*l.*, as they wished to safeguard themselves against any proceedings thereafter.

Thus in 1886 all the markets and fairs became vested in the Town Commissioners accordingly. They obtained the sanction of the Local Government Board to a set of byelaw and schedule of tolls at the markets on the 18th June 1886. These were subsequently altered, and the like consent obtained to the new schedule of rules and regulations and tolls on 9th October 1888. No evidence was given of any such approval of the tolls at the fairs.

Although it was stated that the approval of the Local Government Board was obtained for the establishment of the new fair, this could not be, as that board has no power to create new fairs, but only to alter the date of old ones.

A toll-board is erected for public inspection, and a weigh-bridge has been provided and also beams and scales. In accordance with my instructions I have inspected the market places and fair green.

The butter market is held in an enclosed square space at one side of the town hall. It is divided from the public street by high iron railings, with a gate entrance. The surface is well macadamised and levelled, and around two sides slated sheds are erected resting on metal pillars. The butter is weighed underneath these sheds and then exposed for sale; weighing appliances are provided. The fowl market is held in this enclosure before the butter market commences, and likewise is the egg market held here. Altogether the market seems to afford ample space and accommodation for the purposes intended.

The hay and straw market is held on a wide portion of the street outside the butter market. The space is commodious, and on it is erected a weigh-house and an Avery patent self-weighing machine, which records on a ticket the weight of the load on the bridge.

Although this market is practically held on portion of the public thoroughfare, nevertheless it is said that no obstruction is caused to the public, who can traverse each side of the space generally occupied by the market on market days. No shedding or other accommodation is provided.

The potato market is held on a wide portion of the public street in another portion of the town.

The description of the hay and store market applies to this one, which is exactly similarly situated. The only accommodation provided is a weigh-house and appliances, which are erected in the centre of the market place.

The fairs are held in a fair green on the outskirts of the town; it is entirely enclosed and entered by an iron gate. The green is commodious—being about six acres in extent—and level, and provided with some 60 iron pens for sheep. There is no shelter or other accommodation provided, and the charges levied are on admittance of each animal to the green. Previous to 1880 the fairs were held in the public streets indiscriminately, and were toll free.

Appended will be found a transcript of the evidence taken at the inquiry.

JOHN J. O'MEARA,
Assistant Commissioner.

45, Lower Mount Street,
Dublin.

Carlow, 14th December 1888.

Mr. James Kelly, Town Clerk, examined.

37,195. You are the town clerk of Carlow?—Yes.

37,196. When were the Commissioners established here?—In the year 1854, under the Towns Improvement Act.

37,197. Are they the market authority here in Carlow?—Yes.

37,198. When did they acquire the rights?—The 15th July 1888.

37,199. Did they exercise any market rights previous to 1886?—Yes, in the potato market, since 1880.

37,200. In the potato market alone?—Yes.

37,201. Previous to 1880 did they exercise any rights?—None.

37,202. Who were they vested in then?—The potato market in the potato market committee.

37,203. A committee of the traders of the town?—Yes.

37,204. Was there any individual exercising rights or control over the markets or fairs here?—Yes; Mr. John Byrne. He has since been appointed weigh-master to the Town Commissioners.

37,205. When you say he was exercising market rights, in what respect was he?—As weigh-master he acted at the crane and machine for weighing potatoes.

37,206. Was there any rule in the market requiring all commodities to be weighed at his scales?—No.

37,207. I suppose it was a private speculation to have this scales and weigh-bridge?—Yes.

37,208. There was no other market authority here?—No.

37,209. How did the Commissioners obtain control of the potato market in 1880?—On reference to the old minute books I find a committee called the "Tullow Street Committee," appointed for the regulation of the markets in January 1860, and in October 1861 it was resolved that the crane in charge of the Tullow Street Committee be erected in the potato market, and the expense of erection to be borne, in the first instance, by the committee, and when the expense of erection shall be recouped, the profits of the crane to go to the credit of the rates, and control to be resumed by the Commissioners when they require.

37,210. Who provided the crane?—The Tullow Street Committee provided the crane at a cost of [illegible]. Then Mr. Byrne rented the crane and weigh-house from the committee for a number of years, and paid the committee the [illegible]. In the year 1880 the Commissioners got a decree from the barrister of quarter sessions, taking over the crane, house, and scales on their paying [illegible]. Mr. Byrne was then appointed weigh-master under the Town Commission.

37,211. What was the composition of the committee that originally erected this weigh-house, beam, and scales?—I cannot say; it was before my time. It was the old Tullow Street committee.

37,212. In 1880, and between 1880 and 1888, they had only this weigh-house, beam, and scales and bridge?—That is all. In 1888, they established an enclosed market place for butter and fowl, and they established a hay and straw market. The markets are held in enclosed market places—the hay market and potato market. The butter and fowl and potatoes are offered for sale in the potato market, and the hay, straw, coal, fish, and vegetables in the hay market.

37,213. Where is the hay market?—It is right opposite to the town hall, and the new market place is in a large open square.

37,214. Is it a widening of the street?—Yes.

37,215. Is it portion of the public thoroughfare?—It is, I believe.

37,216. Is the potato market a widening of the thoroughfare?—I believe it was a great many years ago.

37,217. Is it now?—It is not a thoroughfare now.

37,218. The public exercise rights over it?—Yes.

37,219. Where is it situated?—It is central; it is off Tullow Street.

37,220. These were established in 1888?—Yes.

37,221. Were the Commissioners at any expense in the establishment of these?—They paid for the potato market [illegible] to Mr. Byrne, and about [illegible] for the enclosed sheds and market place.

37,222. Was that for the erection of permanent buildings?—Yes.

37,223. It was not for the purchase of any rights?—For the erection of buildings alone; but the rights and powers of a charter were purchased for [illegible] in May 1878.

37,224. From whom?—From the lord of the manor.

37,225. Who is he?—Mr. Hamilton.

37,226. Did Mr. Hamilton within your recollection exercise any rights to collection?—Never.

37,227. At the time of the establishment of the butter and fowl market did he object?—There was no objection at all.

27,228. Nevertheless, the Town Commissioners thought a necessity existed for purchasing any rights vested in him?—Yes; they purchased those rights.

27,229. Have you got the purchase deed?—Yes.

27,230. The witness produced a patent granted in the sixth year of George the First. It granted to Josiah Hamilton the right to hold an additional fair or market day for ever in or near the town of Catherlogh, in the county of Catherlogh, namely, one additional fair or market on each 23rd April, in addition to every market on the 11th June, unless the aforesaid days, or any one of them, should fall on Sunday, then the additional fair should be held on Monday, and an additional weekly market on every Monday, together with all and every the tolls, customs, privileges, and immunities whatsoever of the aforesaid fair and market, subject to the payment of thirty shillings and fourpence.

27,231. You have not got the deed yourself?—No; it is in the solicitor's office.

27,232. It was not in 1858 you made the purchase?—No; in 1878.

27,233. You have not got the date of the deed conveying the property to you?—No, I have not. I think it was the 22nd August 1878.

27,234. That is a conveyance of Mr. Hamilton's rights to the Town Commissioners for 100*l*.?—Yes.

27,235. Subsequent to that they expended 800*l*. in the erection of the butter and fowl market?—Yes.

27,236. When you say enclosed, is there a wall around it?—Yes, and gates and sheds.

27,237. When was this expenditure made? Was it in 1878?—In 1882, and finished in 1883.

27,238. Was there any expense in the erection of the hay and straw market?—Yes; they purchased the rights from Mr. Lawler for 10*l*. Mr. Lawler had a public weighing machine in the hay and straw market for a number of years.

27,239. Was it for this weighing machine they paid the 10*l*.?—The Commissioners paid him 10*l*. to close that machine.

27,240. Did they subsequently utilise it themselves?—They erected a new weigh-house and purchased a new machine in the hay market, and they are working it at present.

27,241. What was the expenditure in that market apart from the 10*l*. to Mr. Lawler?—110*l*. for the new weigh-house and weighing machine.

27,242. And on the potato market?—6*l*. only.

27,243. They did not erect any buildings in that market?—None.

27,244. Was this the only capital expenditure the Commissioners were at?—They expended 8*l*. 10*s*. in the enclosed market for house and scales.

27,245. On which market?—The fowl and butter market.

27,246. Is that in addition to the 800*l*.?—Yes, for house and scales, and wooden office and table.

27,247. This is the only expenditure they were at?—Yes.

27,248. Have they these all under their immediate control at present?—Yes.

27,249. They have not let them out in any way?—No.

27,250. Whom have you appointed in the butter and fowl market?—We have Mr. Edward Dillon as weighmaster and superintendent. Mr. Thomas Collins is inspector of all markets. Mr. [illegible] Hastings is weighmaster in the new crane in the hay market. Mr. John Byrne is weigh-master in the potato market, and there are one or two porters.

27,251. Do you levy tolls at these markets?—Yes.

27,252. When you say tolls, do you mean your weighing charges?—Tolls.

27,253. Have you got a copy of these?—Yes.

27,254. You produce this as a schedule of your bye-laws regulating the markets and tolls you levy?—Yes.

The following are the rules and regulations in force in connexion with the markets:—

Borough of Carlow.

MARKET BYELAWS.

Public Health (Ireland) Act, 1878 (41 & 42 Vict. c. 52), the Markets and Fairs Clauses Act, 1847, 10 & 11 Vict. c. 14.

The Carlow Town Commissioners hereby give public notice that the business of these markets will be conducted subject to the provisions of the statutes hereinbefore mentioned, and to the bye-laws as follows:—

Market Place.

1. The market place shall consist of three divisions:—
(I.) The enclosed market for butter, corn, wool, fowl, fish, vegetables, &c.
(II.) The market for hay, straw, coals, herrings, turnips, and cabbage plants in carts, in the hay market.
(III.) The market for potatoes, corn, and buttermilk, in the potato market.

2. The market days in Carlow shall be Monday and Thursday of every week, Christmas Day excepted.

3. The market place shall be open on market days at 7 o'clock a.m., and on other days at 8 o'clock a.m. It will be closed on every day, except Saturday, in the months of November, December, and January, at 4 o'clock p.m.; in other months, at 6 o'clock p.m. On Saturdays throughout the year it will be closed at 8 o'clock p.m.

4. No stalls or standings in the public streets shall henceforth be permitted.

5. Spaces within the limits of the market place for stalls and standings for the sale of vegetables, fruits, flowers, fish, provisions, and other commodities, shall be let at a price per square foot as may be agreed upon.

6. A person in charge of any wagon, cart, car, truck, barrow, or other vehicle, with or without a horse or other animal attached thereto, shall not cause or allow such vehicle to remain in the market place, or in any street or passage leading thereto, for any longer time than shall be necessary for the sale of, or for the loading or unloading of, provisions, goods, or other commodities.

7. A person in charge of any wagon, cart, car, truck, barrow, or other vehicle, shall not cause or allow such vehicle to stand or remain in the market place, or in any street or passage leading thereto, in such manner as to cause obstruction or inconvenience to the public in such market place, or street, or passage.

8. A person resorting to the market place for the sale of any goods, produce, provisions, or other marketable commodities, shall not cause or allow such goods, &c., to be brought or conveyed to such market place, or to stand, be placed, or be exposed for sale in such manner as to cause obstruction or inconvenience to the public in the market place, or in any of the approaches leading thereto.

9. A tenant or occupier of any building, stall, or standing in the market place shall not cause or allow any goods, produce, provisions, or other marketable commodities to be deposited or exposed for sale in or upon such building, stall, or standing, in such manner that they shall project beyond the line or limits of such building, stall, or standing.

10. Every tenant or occupier of any building, stall, or standing in the market place shall cause such building, stall, or standing to be properly cleansed every day, and shall have same maintained in proper and decent order and condition.

Carlow Butter Market.

[41 & 42 Vict. c. 52; 10 & 11 Vict. c. 14.]

Byelaws.

1. The markets will be held, until further notice, on Monday and Thursday of every week (Christmas Day excepted), and on these days butter may be placed in the market at and after 7 o'clock a.m.

2. In firkin and roll butter market, business will commence—in winter at 8 o'clock, in summer at 7 o'clock, and will close at 10 o'clock a.m.; in firkin butter market, business will commence at 10 o'clock a.m.

3. All firkin butter, accordingly as it arrives in market, will be weighed on the public scales provided by the Town Commissioners, and the number and gross weight of each package will be marked on the firkin.

4. When the butter will have been weighed, a ticket setting out the number and gross weight of each package will be handed by the weigh-master to the seller, and it will be optional with buyer or seller to have the precise tare ascertained by having the firkin weighed.

5. The seller will have the custody of his own butter until he shall have delivered same into the possession of the merchant who buys it, and the Commissioners will incur no responsibility in regard to the safe-keeping of butter.

6. A sufficient staff of porters will be employed by the Commissioners to assist in the weighing and placing of butter, and such persons shall be debarred from accepting gratuities for their services.

7. The following three sizes of Firkins are especially recommended as being most suitable for the Carlow Market, viz.:—No. 1, 70 lbs.; No. 2, 56 lbs.; No. 3, 28 lbs. The Commissioners consider that it would be greatly to the advantage of the owners of dairies to use white firkins.

8. Smoking in the market is strictly prohibited, and any person offending against this rule will be liable to expulsion.

9. Any person giving annoyance to others, causing interruption in business or obstructing the officials of the market in the performance of their duties, will be removed from the market, and will be liable to prosecution.

Every person who shall offend against any of the foregoing byelaws shall be liable to a penalty not exceeding five pounds sterling for every such offence, and in the case of a continuing offence a further penalty not exceeding forty shillings for each day after written notice shall have been given by the sanitary authority to such person so offending.—Provided, nevertheless, that the justices in court before whom any complaint may be made, or any proceedings may be taken in respect of any such offence, may, if they think fit, adjudge the payment as a penalty of any sum less than the full amount of the penalty imposed by this byelaw.

Adopted at a meeting of the Town Commissioners of Carlow (of which 30 days' public notice was given) held on the 23rd day of March 1888, 14 members being present, being four over two-thirds of the governing body.

Seal of Carlow Town Commission.

JAMES KELLY,
Town Clerk.

The foregoing byelaws confirmed by the Local Government Board for Ireland, this 19th day of June 1888.

Local Government Board Seal.	W. D. W.

HENRY ROBINSON.
CHARLES GEORGE KERR.

APPENDIX.

On all goods and produce offered for sale in Carlow Markets, tolls as per schedule annexed, will be severally levied, viz.:—

Schedule.

Lump butter, not to exceed 28 lbs. - - -	One penny.
Firkin butter, not to exceed 28 lbs. - - -	Twopence.
Firkin, keg, or cask of butter, above 28 lbs. - - -	Threepence.
Every sack of corn - -	One penny.
Every sack of potatoes - -	One penny.
Every load of straw or hay -	Twopence.
Every load of coal - -	Twopence.
Every load of turnips, &c. -	Twopence.
Every pack of wool, under 1 cwt. - - -	Twopence.
Every pack of wool, over 1 cwt. and under 2 cwts. - -	Fourpence.
Every pack of wool, over 2 cwts. and under 3 cwts. - -	Sixpence.
Every pack of wool, over 3 cwts., for every additional cwt. or part of cwt. - - -	One penny.
Pair of fowl or ducks - -	One halfpenny.
Each turkey or goose - -	One penny.
Each hare or brace - -	One penny.
Basket of eggs - - -	One halfpenny.
Basket or box of fruit - -	One penny.
Basket or box of fish - -	One penny.
Pair of rabbits - - -	One penny.
Basket or hamper of vegetables	One penny.
Churn of buttermilk - -	One penny.
Cart of cabbage or plants -	Threepence.
Cart of fish - - -	Sixpence.

Adopted at a meeting of the Town Commissioners of Carlow (of which 30 days' public notice was given) held on the 31st day of August 1888, 15 members being present, being two over two-thirds of the governing body.

Seal of Carlow Town Commission.

JAMES KELLY,
Town Clerk.

The foregoing tolls approved by the Local Government Board for Ireland, this 9th day of October 1888.

Local Government Board Seal.	D. J. M.

HENRY ROBINSON.
GEORGE MORRIS.

Note.—Extracts from 10 & 11 Vict., c. 14.

Any person except a licensed hawker, who shall, within the borough of Carlow, sell or expose for sale in any place other than the market place, except in his or her own dwelling place or shop, any article in respect of which tolls are by the special Act authorised to be taken in the market place, shall, for every such offence, be liable to a penalty of forty shillings.

Every person who shall sell or expose for sale, any unwholesome meat or fish, or provisions in the market, shall be liable to a penalty at law, and the inspector or sanitary sub-officer shall be authorised to seize such unwholesome meat, or fish, or provisions, and to have same carried before a justice.

Every person selling, or offering for sale, any articles in the market, shall, if required so to do by the buyer, cause same to be weighed or measured by the weights and scales or measures provided by the Town Commissioners; and any such person who shall refuse on demand to cause such articles to be weighed or measured in manner aforesaid, shall be liable to a penalty of forty shillings.

Any person appointed to weigh or measure any articles in the market place, who shall refuse or neglect to weigh or measure the same when required, or shall fail to give to buyer or seller thereof, when required, a ticket specifying the weight of such articles, shall be liable to a penalty of forty shillings.

Every person who shall use obscene or abusive or insulting language, or who shall assault or obstruct any person appointed for the time being to superintend the market, and to keep order therein, whilst in the execution of his duty, shall be liable to a penalty of forty shillings.

27,255. Were they approved of by the Local Government Board on the 9th October 1888?—Yes.

27,256. Are these the only byelaws you have regulating the markets?—The only byelaws. There are the byelaws enforced up to 1888. The Commissioners revised them.

27,257. What were the alterations?—Nothing but charging a toll instead of a weighing charge on butter.

27,258. Have you a rule restricting the sale of marketable commodities elsewhere than in the market place?—I think so by the present byelaws.

27,259. Are these charges at the market levied as they enter the market?—Yes, when they come into the market they are levied.

27,260. I suppose eggs are sold in the butter market?—Yes, and butter and fowl; lump and firkin butter.

27,261. Are all the different marketable commodities brought to Carlow confined for exposure, and sold in the three different markets?—Corn is not; it is brought to the buyers' stores and mills.

27,262. Is there any public market for corn?—No, not that I am aware of.

27,263. It is never exposed in the town?—It may in the street, one or two loads. They generally go to the buyers' stores and deliver it there. A very odd sack is weighed in the market place.

27,264. Do you levy any charge on the corn?—No. There would not be 20 sacks in three months in the market place.

27,265. Do you levy charges whether the commodity is weighed or not?—Yes, since October 1886.

27,266. You have here, "every sack of corn, one penny"?—Yes, any sack of corn weighed.

27,267. Do you levy this charge whether your scales are availed of or not?—Not in corn.

27,268. On the other commodities do you?—Yes.

27,269. "Lump butter not to exceed 20 lbs., a penny." If they brought butter to the market and exposed it for sale and sold it, but did not ascertain the weight at your scales, would you levy the charge of a penny?—Yes, since October. We have been doing it, as I can show you by one of the books.

27,270. What is the market day here?—Monday and Thursday.

27,271. Have the markets always been held on Monday and Thursday?—Yes.

27,272. They did not establish within any recent period the Thursday market?—No; these are the old days as long as I remember.

27,273. Previous to providing these enclosed market places were the markets held indiscriminately about the streets of the town?—Yes.

27,274. What led to the establishment of these new markets? Were there any representations made to the Town Commissioners from the traders of the town or the people or private inhabitants?—No, I do not believe there was. The Commissioners themselves thought it would be a good thing to do, and they borrowed 3,600*l.* and built a very fine town hall in connexion with the market place.

27,275. When was that money borrowed?—In the year 1885.

27,276. Of that 3,600*l.* only 297*l.* 1*s.* was expended on markets?—That was all.

27,277. Was the balance spent in the erection of the town hall?—Yes.

27,278. As a matter of fact are these bye-laws observed by the farmers of the people frequenting these markets?—Pretty much so, except as regards the corn.

27,279. Have you had occasion to get this penalty enforced for sales elsewhere than in the market place?—No. We brought a case a year and a half ago, and did not proceed with it. By Schedule "A" there was no toll charged on fowl, but we can charge.

27,280. You do not collect any?—No.

27,281. Although you have it mentioned on your schedule?—Yes. We do not collect any tolls yet, but I believe the Commissioners will immediately.

27,282. Was it on the previous schedule?—It was; but we never collected it since the opening of the markets in the year 1885.

27,283. I suppose you wanted to foster or create the market?—Yes. They may do it early in the year.

27,284. Is the butter brought in lumps or firkins?—In lumps and firkins.

27,285. Have you any duties to perform immediately in connexion with the markets?—I have to examine the weigh-master's book every week, and lodge the receipts weekly.

27,286. Witness then produced a document showing the receipts and expenditure of the markets and fairs, and of which the following is a copy:—

Local Government (Ireland) Act, 34 & 35 Vict. c. 109.

ABSTRACT of the ACCOUNTS of the CARLOW TOWN COMMISSIONERS for the year ended the 31st December 1887, showing the Receipts and Expenditure under the several heads during that period.

RECEIPTS.

1887.	Nature of Receipt.	Amount. £	s.	d.
Jan. 1	To balance in hands of town clerk (ordinary), petty cash account	4	7	6¾
	„ balance in hands of town clerk (repairs of streets) petty cash account - - -	1	4	5
Dec. 31	„ rates collected and lodged -	1,484	16	8
	„ petty sessions fines - -	39	7	8
	„ contribution from Government in lieu of rates - - -	37	0	7
	„ contribution from local government board in aid of sanitary officers' salaries - -	11	5	2
	„ dog tax - - -	3	0	7
	„ tolls—markets - - -	304	11	7
	„ tolls—fair green - - -	127	6	0
	„ town hall lettings - -	89	11	0
	„ sale of manure - - -	14	6	0
	„ private market lettings - -	6	5	0
	„ balance due treasurer - -	[illegible]	[illegible]	1
		£2,[illegible]	6	9½

EXPENDITURE.

1887.	Nature of Expenditure.	Amount. £	s.	d.
Jan. 1	By balance due treasurer - -	371	9	10
Dec. 31	„ salaries and wages - -	[illegible]	[illegible]	[illegible]
	„ sanitary expenditure - -	89	14	6
	„ public lamps and lighting -	[illegible]	7	6½
	„ watering streets - -	39	14	9
	„ water supply - - -	17	16	10½
	„ printing, stationery, and advertising - - -	16	4	2
	„ rents and taxes - - -	[illegible]	5	9
	„ local government board—for audit of accounts - -	6	8	8
	„ fire engine - - -	2	0	0
	„ fuel and light - - -	9	17	9
	„ law costs - - -	18	14	0
	„ insurance of town hall - -	3	15	6
	„ Contagious Diseases (Animals) Act - - - -	9	0	0
	„ regulation of [illegible] fair -	6	7	6
	„ rate collector - - -	3	0	7
	„ town hall and market - -	[illegible]	0	4
	„ county at large charges -	[illegible]	1	3
	„ Board of Public Works (Provisional Order, 18[illegible]) - -	[illegible]	14	3
	„ Board of Public Works—repayment and interest of loan -	347	0	6
	„ repairs and maintenance of streets	278	14	1½
	„ special works on streets - -	46	13	9
	„ fair green—works - -	19	10	1
	„ collector's poundage (two years)	72	18	9
	„ miscellaneous - - -	16	16	5½
	„ in hands of town clerk (ordinary) petty cash account -	9	11	10
	„ in hands of town clerk (repairs of streets) petty cash account	1	10	4½
		£2,[illegible]	6	9½

I certify the foregoing to be a true Abstract of the Receipts and Expenditure of the Town Commissioners of

27,287. Are commodities only brought on Mondays and Thursdays?—Yes; except on a very odd day some lump butter may come in.

27,288. But the scales are always available?—Yes, and the weigh-master there.

27,289. Do you levy charges any days in the week other than Mondays or Thursdays?—Yes, any day they come into the market place.

27,290. As a matter of fact do they come any other day?—They do; but a very small number of firkins or lumps, just a few.

27,291. The Commissioners here are the market authority?—Yes.

27,292. Have you any committee of the Town Commissioners to immediately look after the markets?—Yes, markets committee.

27,293. Do they also look after the fairs?—Yes.

27,294. I suppose, like ordinary boards, they report generally to the Commission?—Generally they do.

27,295. Besides the fuel, are there any other of the charges mentioned that you do not levy?—Fowl, eggs, fruit, and fish; anything in Schedule A under the old bye-law.

27,296. You have not levied any of these yet?—Not since the opening of the market, but they can do so now.

27,297. What commodities are usually brought here on market days?—Hay, straw, [illegible], [illegible], potatoes, corn, butter (lump and firkin), vegetables, and sometimes fruit. That is all, I believe.

27,298. Supposing coal was brought here and sold, but the weight not ascertained, would you levy the charge?—They do not enforce it on coal either. Coal must be weighed on the council. Large loads cannot weigh elsewhere.

27,299. There are no other councils in the town?—There are two private ones.

27,300. Do they ever let them for hire?—They do, but a very odd time, though.

27,301. Have the Commissioners ever taken any proceedings against these people?—No; they never did.

27,302. Did they ever contemplate doing so?—No.

27,303. You only collect on coal when weighed?—Yes, when weighed on the public council at either the potato market or hay market.

27,304. For all the commodities weighed do the weigh-masters give a ticket?—Yes, a printed form, such as I produce in the book.

27,305. Witness then produced the tickets, of which the following are copies:—

A 97.	A 97.
CARLOW TOWN COMMISSION.	CARLOW TOWN COMMISSION.
Carlow Markets.	*Carlow Markets.*
Mr. __________	Mr. __________
_____ Packs Wool.	_____ Packs Wool.
Cwts. qrs. lbs. Cwts. qrs. lbs.	Cwts. qrs. lbs. Cwts. qrs. lbs.
_____ day of ________ 189 .	_____ day of ________ 189 .
__________ Weigh-master.	__________ Weigh-master.

A 304.	A 304.
CARLOW TOWN COMMISSION.	CARLOW TOWN COMMISSION.
Carlow Markets.	*Carlow Markets.*
Mr. __________	Mr. __________
_____ Sacks of ________	_____ Sacks of ________
Stones lbs. Stones lbs.	Stones lbs. Stones lbs.
_____ day of ________ 189 .	_____ day of ________ 189 .
__________ Weigh-master.	__________ Weigh-master.

27,206. Did you make up the average receipts for me?—Yes; from the 1st January to the 5th December, 187[illegible].

27,207. These are the tolls and weighing charges?—Weighing charges and tolls only.

27,208. Have you any rents in connexion with the market standings or otherwise?—None.

27,209. In the butter market?—No.

27,210. Have you any stalls?—No.

27,211. Where do the people with the fish go?—To the potato market and hay market.

27,212. There are no stalls erected in the hay market?—No.

27,213. I suppose when they come with the fish they stand on the street?—Yes, or keep them in the carts, or boxes, or baskets, laid on the street.

27,214. You have a charge on the cart of fish, but you do not levy it at present?—No.

27,215. Did you ever levy it?—No.

27,216. On a cart of cabbages or plants you have a charge of threepence?—It was never levied. We levy nothing that comes under Schedule A. The Commissioners may enforce those charges at the commencement of the new year, but they have not done so up to this.

27,217. Will you tell me the commodities you do levy them on?—Lump butter, firkin butter, every sack of potatoes, hay and straw, loads of coal, turnips, &c., and for weighing wool.

27,218. When you say on turnips, hay and straw, &c., do you charge whether they are weighed or not?—They must be weighed before being bought.

27,219. The buyer will never complete his contract unless the weight is ascertained?—No. The seller must be supplied with the ticket.

27,220. Supposing a man bought a load of hay by bulk, would you look for a charge if it was not weighed?—We can, but never do. There are odd loads sold by bulk latterly, but it is bad hay.

27,221. Still you do not look for your charge?—We do not.

27,222. But you have a right to do so?—Yes. The Commissioners consider they have a right to do it. I suppose not half a dozen loads out of the whole market would be bought by bulk.

27,223. In the [illegible] you have mentioned the gross receipts?—Yes.

27,224. Could you give me the expenditure?—[illegible].

27,225. How is that expended?—In wages.

27,226. Could you give me the particulars by separating the amount?—John Byrne, potato market, [illegible]; Maurice Hastings, hay market, [illegible]; Mr. Dillon, superintendent of the market, [illegible]. The balance is for porters and other officials.

27,227. Do you levy any porterage charge on the people?—Yes.

27,228. Nothing but the charges mentioned here?—Yes, the charges mentioned on that schedule.

27,229. Supposing they bring into the potato market a load of potatoes the charge is a penny per sack?—Yes.

27,230. Your men perform the manual work of weighing the sack and putting the weights into the scales, &c.?—Yes.

27,231. Has the farmer to perform the duty of lifting the sacks on to the scales and back again?—One or two porters attend the potato market, and they are paid a halfpenny a sack by the farmer.

27,232. Now, supposing the farmer considers he is well able to do this work himself, and can save a halfpenny a sack, or sixpence on the load, if there were 12 sacks on it, can he do so?—He should have some help.

27,233. If he has help of his own?—Yes.

27,234. It is not compulsory to employ porters?—It is not; but they generally do employ them for rolling the bags to and from the cart.

27,235. Still it is optional with them to do so?—It is.

27,236. Supposing they do not employ those men would they be put to any inconvenience on a subsequent market day?—They would not, the weigh-master Mr. Byrne can tell you.

27,237. Within what limits would you say these marketable commodities come here?—I would say from 8 to 10 or 12 miles.

27,238. Do you keep any record of the quantity of the different commodities brought here?—We do not.

27,239. I suppose you keep a blank?—Yes, a blank of the number of lumps and number of firkins of butter, but we never check them to find the quantity.

27,240. If the people lose the ticket they got denoting the quantity in the sack or firkin of butter, or lump butter, you could give them a copy of the ticket?—Yes.

27,241. Do your men keep any record of the current prices of the commodities?—They do not.

27,242. They do not give it to the newspapers?—No. In some cases Mr. Dillon enters the price of the lump butter in the blank. There is no record kept of the prices.

27,243. That is when the buyer or seller asks to have it made up?—Yes.

27,244. You have a rule here which if broken there is a penalty of 40s. attached. Had you ever occasion to enforce that?—Once or twice the Commissioners thought it necessary to do so. They may enforce it with the new year if occasion requires it.

27,245. Does the seller as a rule object to weigh at the Commissioners' scales and bridge?—The sellers of wool do.

27,246. What reason do you assign for that?—They do not like to pay the charge.

27,247. Previous to the Commissioners acquiring the rights these people could sell without payment of any charge?—Yes.

27,248. Have you heard them complaining that it is a hardship on them?—No. I do not think I did, with the exception of wool. It is the only thing that is a little high. All wool is not weighed at the market place. They generally go to the buyer's stores.

27,249. Are all potatoes weighed at the market place?—I believe so, and all butter with the exception of odd lumps and firkins that go to the stores.

27,250. Lump butter is brought to the shopkeepers?—In some cases, and some firkins go to the stores on other days than the market day.

27,251. Have the Commissioners any duty to perform in connexion with the fairs?—Yes.

27,252. How did they acquire the fair rights?—Under the Public Health Act, 1878, and got the approval of the Local Government Board to the scale of charges enforced at the fair green.

27,253. Witness then produced a schedule of the charges of which the following is a copy:—

CARLOW FAIR GREEN.

SCALE of TOLLS in force on entry of cattle, &c., to CARLOW FAIR GREEN, adopted the [illegible] February 1879.

For every cow, bull, &c.	-	[illegible]d. each.	
" calf under 1½ years old	-	[illegible]d. "	
" fat pig	-	[illegible]d. "	
" small pig	-	[illegible]d. "	
" load of small pig	-	[illegible]d. "	load.
" sheep or lamb	-	[illegible]d. "	
" horse, mule, or jennet	-	[illegible]d. "	
" ass	-	[illegible]d. "	
" stallions	-	[illegible]d. "	

JAMES KELLY,
Carlow, 16th December 1878. Town Clerk.

27,254. Have you any rules or regulations in connexion with the fair green?—No, except the scale of tolls.

27,255. When was it they first acquired the right?—The fair green was taken on lease for [illegible] a year on the 31st January 1879.

27,256. From whom?—From William W. [illegible]

27,357. Is this an enclosed fair green?—Yes.

27,358. Is there a wall around it?—No, a wooden paling.

27,359. Is it macadamised?—No. It is a grass field.

27,360. What is the extent of it?—I think it is six acres, but I am not really sure.

27,361. Did the Commissioners get a lease of it?—Yes, for 31 years; and the approval of the Local Government Board was obtained in 1878.

27,362. I see the scale of tolls was adopted on the 26th February?—Yes.

27,363. Are these tolls with the approval also of the Local Government Board?—Yes.

27,364. Were they at any expense in connexion with these?—They were. On the 27th January the Commissioners leased a passage and house for a caretaker at 8l. per annum.

27,365. From whom?—From Mr. McQuaid, and the approval of the Local Government Board was obtained on the 12th February 1880.

27,366. What expense were you at?—A wooden paling was erected around the fair green and from 55 to 60 iron sheep pens placed in it; two large sentry-boxes for the collection of tickets at the gates and a large entrance gate and wicket and some repairs to the ground such as levelling. The total cost of permanent works to the fair green was 550l.

27,367. Expended on what you have just mentioned?—Yes.

27,368. Was there any loan obtained for that?—No. The fairs committee appointed on the 30th July 1879 borrowed the sum from the National Bank on their own personal security.

27,369. They had not anything to do directly with the Commissioners?—They were members of the Commission at the time.

27,370. It was not in their official capacity they acted but in the capacity of traders in the town?—As Town Commissioners.

27,371. They borrowed the money on their own security?—Yes, from the National Bank.

27,372. That amount was expended on the fair green?—Yes.

27,373. What security did they give?—Their own personal security, joint and several.

27,374. Is there any of the loan remaining unpaid?—A committee meeting of the board was held on the 30th July 1879, and a resolution passed authorising the fair committee to receive the tolls and revenues until such time as the debt in establishing the new fairs and making the fair green in order be cleared off, such receipts to be applied for the purpose of liquidating the debt, and the debt being liquidated the fair green was handed over to the Commissioners on the 6th July 1880.

27,375. It was then the fairs committee who made this capital expenditure and obtained the loan?—Yes.

27,376. The loan was not made directly to the Town Commissioners?—Yes, but the committee was authorised to collect the toll and look after the fair green.

27,377. You have produced a copy of the tolls levied. Are these tolls levied on the animals as they enter the fair green?—As they enter.

27,378. Were tolls ever levied only on the animals actually sold?—No.

27,379. Previous to the establishment of this fair green, were tolls levied at the fairs?—No; the fairs were held in the streets.

27,380. Up to 1879?—Yes. The first fair was held in the fair green on the 4th May 1879.

27,381. What fairs are at present held here?—Monthly fairs and two old fairs; 14 in all.

27,382. What dates?—On the fourth Wednesday of every month, except the one in March, which is held on the 26th of that month.

27,383. What are the two old fairs?—The 4th May and 8th November.

27,384. When were the monthly fairs established?—In the year 1878, the latter end of 1878, under the Fairs and Markets Act of 1847.

27,385. Do you obtain the approval of the Local Government Board?—Yes, we got the approval of the Local Government Board at the time to it.

27,386. Have you got their order here?—I have not.

27,387. What fairs were held previous to the establishment of the monthly fairs?—I forget the dates of them.

27,388. How many in all were held?—About eight fairs in the year.

27,389. That is previous to the establishment of the monthly fairs?—Yes.

27,390. Do you remember at any period there being less than eight fairs held here?—No; that was the number. The 26th March fair was held a couple of miles outside, in a place called Palatine, and it was brought in here.

27,391. When was it brought in here?—I do not exactly know.

27,392. What time would you say?—Before 1878, at all events. It was Mr. Wm. Burke had the patent; they used to be held in his demesne.

27,393. No tolls were levied on these fairs?—Not till 1879.

27,394. They were all held on the streets up to that time?—Yes.

27,395. Have you any rule restricting the sale of the animals elsewhere than in the fair green?—No.

27,396. Have you any rules posted up?—No rules or byelaws.

27,397. Is that fair green availed of?—Yes, very much.

27,398. They do not sell elsewhere?—Never, only in the fair green.

27,399. Have you got a pig fair here the day previous to the ordinary fair?—Yes.

27,400. Are tolls levied on the pig fair day?—Yes.

27,401. Are pigs ever brought in the ordinary fair day?—Never, unless some small pigs (bonhams).

27,402. Have you got any standings on fair days?—No. We have a list of the tolls levied at the fairs posted through the fair green and outside the gates.

27,403. Have you the other schedule posted in the market place?—Yes, largely posted.

27,404. Have you got a weighbridge capable of weighing cattle?—Yes; in the potato market.

27,405. Have you got a railing round it?—Yes; it was got up lately at a cost of 5l.

27,406. In addition to the other expenses?—Yes.

27,407. Have you weighed any cattle?—Just a few only.

27,408. I see on small pigs the charge is threepence each head as they enter?—Yes.

27,409. Supposing these pigs are sold, would you levy any additional charge when they are coming out?—No; there is only the charge when they enter.

27,410. On entry is it at the gate the money is collected?—Yes, we have large sentry boxes outside. The farmers purchase the tickets there, and give them up at the gate as they are going in.

27,411. Have you got any of the tickets here?—No.

27,412. You never consider whether the animal is subsequently sold or not?—No.

27,413. Was there any great opposition to the payment of these charges when first levied by the Commissioners?—There was a little at the first fair or second, but it died away after that.

27,414. Do the farmers here consider that they would willingly pay the charge when given a return for it?—They have a very good return there; it is a very good ground, a grass field for the cattle to stand on.

27,415. There is no accommodation there?—No.

27,416. What is the nearest fair to Carlow where tolls are levied?—Kilkenny. It is the same system there and the same rate of tolls. The total receipts from the fair green were 277l., and the expenditure about 58l. in rented numbers, rent and wages.

27,417. Have you any rents to pay in connexion with the markets?—The town hall and market place are rented as one plot for 30l. per annum.

27,418. What do you pay for the butter market?—It is joined with the town hall.

27,419. Is it the basement of the town hall?—Yes.

27,420. The [illegible] is for the entire building?—Yes.

27,421. What portion of the [illegible] is allotted for the market portion?—About [illegible].

27,422. You would estimate it at [illegible]?—Yes.

27,423. Have you any remarks to make as to what you think would be an improvement if it was effected in the markets or fairs?—I have not. The markets work very well.

27,424. Do you think the people, the farmers and buyers, are all disposed to avail themselves of the markets here?—Yes, generally they are.

27,425. Is the market a good one?—Yes; we have very large markets.

27,426. In what commodity principally?—Butter and corn. It is a very large corn market.

27,427. From what districts are the animals brought to the fairs by the farmers?—From the co. Kildare, Wicklow, Wexford, Kilkenny, Queen's County, and Carlow.

27,428. Within what radius?—About 10 miles.

27,429. From the short experience you have had of these fairs here and the markets, do you consider that the levying of a toll acts in any way as a deterrent on the people bringing commodities to the markets or animals to the fairs?—I think not.

27,430. You have found no falling off in the supply?—No.

27,431. How much of the [illegible] is paid off?—There is [illegible] outstanding.

Mr. Edward Dillon examined.

27,432. You are the butter weigh-master?—Yes.

27,433. What scales are provided in the butter market?—We have a scales for lump butter and a scales for firkin butter, and there is another large scales for weighing corn. They are all in one area.

27,434. If they desire to ascertain the weight of a sack of corn is it to the butter market they go?—It is; it is one market.

27,435. You do not keep any record of the quantity of butter brought to the market?—Certainly. We have a book with blanks and tickets.

27,436. You never tot up the amount?—Yes, every week.

27,437. You return it in that small book to Mr. Kelly?—Yes.

27,438. Have you got tasters in the butter market?—No, the buyers themselves taste.

27,439. Have they ever complained of that or would they rather rely on their own experience?—I have been speaking this day to one of the principal butter buyers and he said he would not advise a taster. He says the system we have is going on very satisfactorily.

27,440. Who classifies the butter?—There is no classification. They give the owner of the butter the price they think it is worth.

27,441. Is all the butter sold before it is weighed, or do you weigh it before being sold?—We weigh it first.

27,442. All the butter is weighed and then arranged near the wall for the buyers to view it?—Yes.

27,443. It is in return for the ticket you get your charge?—Yes.

27,444. Is that twopence?—It is threepence for a firkin.

27,445. That is over [illegible] lbs.?—Yes.

27,446. Is there any porterage charge in connexion with the butter?—None.

27,447. That the seller has to pay?—None.

27,448. Has he to pay a charge to porters?—No. We have several men employed there to put the butter in the scales.

27,449. Do you drain the butter before weighing it?—We do.

27,450. Have you coopers employed?—No. The salesmen drain it. They take the lids off and press the firkin and keep it draining for a considerable time before it is weighed.

27,451. Still it is not completely drained, or is all the pickle out of it?—Almost I think.

27,452. When weighing butter what is the lowest weight you weigh down to, or do you weigh down to [illegible] lbs.?—We do the lump butter.

27,453. What is the lowest weight you put in the scales for butter?—A pound. There is no fraction below a pound.

27,454. You weigh down to a pound?—I do.

27,455. Do you weigh the empty firkin?—If they bring it back I will.

27,456. That is very seldom done, I suppose?—Very seldom.

27,457. What is the estimated tare of the firkin?—The tare is generally printed in the firkin by the cooper.

27,458. You do not put the estimated tare on the ticket?—No, only the gross weight.

27,459. Do you ever put it on the firkin itself?—Yes. I generally marked on the firkin the number of the ticket and the weight.

27,460. With chalk?—With marking stuff.

27,461. As well as putting it on the ticket?—I put it in ink on the ticket.

27,462. Do you always give a ticket, or only one when required?—I always give a ticket.

27,463. Is there any deduction for soakage in the butter market?—Really I could not tell for certain what the buyer does. I generally give the gross weight when the firkin is drained.

27,464. You have no complaints of what deduction there is from the gross weight besides the actual tare branded on the firkin?—I heard there are 2 lbs. which they generally take, but I could not tell for certainty.

27,465. You have only heard it is 2 lbs.?—Yes.

27,466. Did you ever hear what that 2 lbs. was for, or was it for additional soakage?—Yes, and waste and salt in the bottom of the firkins.

27,467. Have they had any arguments over what additional allowance would be made?—I never heard any.

27,468. But you think the customary allowance is 2 lbs.?—I heard so.

27,469. You say the buyers would prefer the present course of classifying butter or buying it according to their own experience?—I have been told so by the buyers.

27,470. They do not require any official classification of it?—No.

27,471. Down to what weight do you weigh the lump butter?—Down to a quarter pound.

27,472. Do you ascertain the weight under the quarter pound?—I do not. I do not give anything but that a quarter.

27,473. Is there any deduction from that weight?—None whatsoever.

27,474. You weigh it in its natural state?—Yes.

27,475. If any clings to the scales in bad weather there is no deduction?—It cannot cling to the scales.

27,476. The charge on lump butter when the weight does not exceed [illegible] lbs. is 1d.?—Yes.

27,477. Over that is the charge 2d.?—No, but 2d.

27,478. I suppose they seldom bring a firkin under [illegible] lbs. You have in the schedule a firkin of butter not to exceed [illegible] lbs. 2d., but that is never brought in?—I never saw an instance of it.

27,479. You weigh corn sometimes?—Yes.

27,480. What is the lowest weight you weigh corn with?—A pound.

27,481. Down to a pound?—Yes.

27,482. What is the estimated tare of the sack?—They generally bring back the empty sack.

27,483. What is the customary weight of the sack?—4 or 5 lbs., sometimes 6 lbs.

27,484. Did you ever estimate the tare of the sack?—I often weighed the empty sack.

27,485. Did you ever estimate the tare and not weigh the sack?—Never.

27,486. Do you know from your own knowledge of transactions between buyers and sellers any deductions from the weight other than the tare of the sack after the price had been agreed upon?—I never heard of it. Sometimes they do not weigh the sack, but halve it between the buyer and seller.

27,487. Are these the tickets you give?—Yes.

27,488. The witness then produced the tickets, of which the following are copies:—

A [illegible].

CARLOW TOWN COMMISSIONERS.

Carlow Markets.

Mr. ______ ______

______ Firkins Butter.

Cwts. qrs. lbs. Cwts. qrs. lbs.

______ day of ______ 189 .

______

Weigh-master.

A [illegible].

CARLOW TOWN COMMISSIONERS.

Carlow Markets.

Mr. ______ ______

______ Firkins Butter.

Cwts. qrs. lbs. Cwts. qrs. lbs.

______ day of ______ 189 .

______

Weigh-master.

A [illegible].

CARLOW TOWN COMMISSIONERS.

Carlow Markets.

Mr. ______

______ Lumps Butter.

______ lbs. weight.

______ lbs. weight.

______ lbs. weight.

______ day of ______ 189 .

______

Weigh-master.

A [illegible].

CARLOW TOWN COMMISSIONERS.

Carlow Markets.

Mr. ______

______ Lumps Butter.

______ lbs. weight.

______ lbs. weight.

______ lbs. weight.

______ day of ______ 189 .

______

Weigh-master.

27,489. Could you tell me what percentage of the butter is actually sold in the market on market days?—Very nearly all the butter brought into the butter market.

27,490. Supposing some remained unsold have you storage accommodation for it?—No. It is not allowed to be stored.

27,491. Is there any rule in the market to that effect?—There is in the byelaws.

27,492. Did any of the sellers ever ask you to store butter for them?—Yes.

27,493. And you refused?—I complied on one occasion. It was only to keep the butter for one or two days.

27,494. Did you levy any charge?—No.

27,495. Did the people ever complain of the want of storage accommodation there?—They did, but on a very few occasions. Scarcely any butter remains unsold.

27,496. Could you give any idea of the quantity, just a rough approximate idea of the quantity brought in during the season or in the year, or have you had experience of any other butter markets?—No.

27,497. Then you could not draw any comparison between them?—I could not with any amount of accuracy.

Mr. [illegible] examined.

27,498. You weigh at potatoe scales?—Yes.

27,499. You only weigh potatoes?—Yes, and sometimes corn, but very seldom.

27,500. All the potatoes brought here to Carlow are exposed in the potato market?—Yes.

27,501. They are not exposed elsewhere?—No, unless parties bought them in other parts of the town, and they may not come to the market.

27,502. Supposing a shopkeeper in the town, or a private individual, purchased some potatoes from a farmer and got them delivered on market day, would you ask for any charge?—Yes, a penny per bag.

27,503. Would you ask for a charge if they did not come to the market, and were not exposed in the market, but delivered on market day?—There would be no charge in that case.

27,504. You only collect your charge when the potatoes are weighed?—Yes.

27,505. But if exposed in the market square and not weighed would you levy any charge?—Not up to this.

27,506. Are the potatoes all sold before they are weighed?—Yes.

27,507. Your charge is a penny per sack?—Yes.

27,508. Do you ever ascertain the actual tare of the empty sack?—No. They generally allow half a stone for bags and a stone for large ones—that is when they are over a barrel, which is 24 stone.

27,509. What would be the quantity in a sack of potatoes for which you allow seven pounds tare?—About 16, or 17 and 18 stone.

27,510. Would the tare be the same on a fine day as on a wet day when the sack is completely saturated with wet?—It would be different.

27,511. What additional allowance would be made?—There is no allowance made then.

27,512. The tare is the same then on a wet day as a fine day?—Yes.

27,513. Supposing the sack became completely saturated with wet, would the buyer require any additional deduction?—I never saw him requiring any more.

27,514. Did you ever hear a case of it?—I did twice or three times.

27,515. Do you keep a block of the tickets?—Yes.

27,516. Do you give printed tickets?—Yes.

27,517. Did you ever mark the weight on the sack itself?—Yes, if the man required it. If the sacks were going to different places I would mark each sack.

27,518. You have nothing whatever to do with the porters who get the charge of a halfpenny?—No. The farmers and others who come in pay them; sometimes they give them nothing.

27,519. It is compulsory on the farmers to engage these porters?—No.

27,520. Supposing they did not engage any porters, would they be put to any great inconvenience the next day they would come in with a load of potatoes?—They would not.

27,521. You, however, have nothing to do with these porters?—No.

27,522. Did you ever make up the tickets for the people?—No, unless it was required.

27,523. Do they require it in some cases?—Yes. Some would require it and some would not.

27,524. You charge nothing additional for that?—No.

27,525. When does the potato market usually begin?—About eight o'clock in the morning, and it terminates at eleven very large market at ten.

27,526. Have you only one beam and scales there?—Yes.

27,527. You have an crane also?—Yes.

27,528-9. What do you charge for weighing at the crane?—Twopence a load for coals.

27,530. Is it only coals you weigh?—Coals and turnips, hay and straw.

27,531. The charge is twopence a load irrespective of the commodity in the load?—Yes, unless it is a small donkey load of coals, and then the charge is a penny.

27,532. Would you weigh the empty cart for that?—Yes.

27,533. After the commodity has been delivered, and before the seller came to have the empty cart weighed, did you ever detect any frauds being committed by putting on lighter wheels, or changing the cart, or something like that?—Well, I did hear complaints, but very seldom.

27,534. What were they?—They would have some boards off the cars coming back to be weighed.

27,535. You say it is very seldom they complained of that?—Yes.

27,536. Have any prosecutions resulted from that?—None.

27,537. You never had occasion to prosecute any person yourself?—No.

Mr. THOMAS [illegible] examined.

27,538. You are the superintendent of the markets?—Yes.

27,539. Do the people expose the commodities elsewhere than in the places provided by the Town Commissioners?—They do.

27,540. Where?—As to the butter, they go to the different shops in the town and selling it without coming to the market-place, and also the firkin butter. They go to the different stores belonging to the buyers, and do not go to the market at all.

27,541. Are there any other commodities?—As to potatoes, very little of them goes to the market and are weighed and sold in the markets.

27,542. You say the great majority of them are sold elsewhere?—They generally go to the market with very few exceptions.

27,543. Do you think if the butter was all brought to the market place and exposed there, and an opportunity given to all the buyers to compete with one another, that the farmer would get a better price than sending it to a private individual in the first instance?—I do believe he would.

27,544. Did you ever hear any expression of opinion on that by the people of the town?—Not by the people of the town, but by country people—the sellers.

27,545. Where is the fowl market held?—In the butter market.

27,546. Did you ever hear complaints of the fowl market and the butter market being in one common?—I did not, because they do not clash. The fowl market is held early, and the fowl cleared away before the butter market commences.

27,547. Did you ever hear complaints of forestalling of any of the commodities?—No. It would not be allowed.

27,548. Do the fowl buyers ever go out and meet the farmers or farmers wives coming in with fowl?—They did, and they thought to do an injury to the market.

27,549. Has that ceased?—It has.

27,550. Were any steps taken to prevent it?—Yes; I took every step to abolish that.

27,551. What steps did you take?—By being early and detecting anything that occurred, and reporting it to the sanitary authority.

27,552. Tell me some things you detected?—They went out, even outside the bounds of the borough, and bought fowl, and did their best to strive and injure the tolls of the market if the sellers came in.

27,553. What steps did you take to prevent it?—I reported the matter to the Commissioners, and they made orders to assist me in carrying out that.

27,554. Were your complaints to the Commissioners the means of stopping that practically?—Principally they were.

27,555. Did the Commissioners take any steps?—Not up to the present. In consequence of the tolls not being finally arranged, they did not take any steps by law.

27,556. However, that system of forestalling has ceased?—Yes.

27,557. When it was practised, did you hear the farmers complaining of it?—Some of them would and more would not.

27,558. You think, from your experience of this place, it is better to have a properly enclosed market, and confine the sale and exposure of commodities to that building; and you think also that better prices could be obtained for the different commodities?—I do.

27,559. Did you hear many complaints when the markets were held indiscriminately about the streets of the town?—Yes.

27,560. Where the potato market and the hay and straw market are held in the public thoroughfare?—There is a portion of the potato market the public thoroughfare.

27,561. Who cleans up the place?—The weigh-master gets it cleaned up.

27,562. Who cleans the hay market?—There is a porter in the market, who cleans the market every day when the market is over.

27,563. Did you ever hear complaints by the people of the town that it has not been cleaned up within a short period?—No, because the man is in charge, and must do it.

27,564. Did you ever hear of any obstruction caused to the public by the markets being held on the public thoroughfare?—No. There is a place set apart off the public thoroughfare for the market.

27,565. Are there any standings on fair days about the fair green?—No.

27,566. Do any itinerant dealers come?—They do on fair days.

27,567. Do you levy any charge?—Not up to this.

27,568. Do you purpose doing it?—I think the Town Commissioners intend to do it.

27,569. (*The Commissioner to the Town Clerk.*) Is there any charge, Mr. Kelly?—None.

27,570. Do you intend to levy any charge?—No.

27,571. As a matter of fact, do they come in?—Yes, on fair days.

27,572. Are they belonging to the town?—Some are.

27,573. Would you say the majority are not belonging to the town?—Yes; they come distances from other towns.

27,574. Have they hawkers' licenses?—I am sure they must have; I do not know.

27,575. You issue no licenses at all?—No.

JOHN HAMMOND, Esq., Borough Magistrate, examined.

27,576. You are the chairman of the Town Commissioners?—Yes.

27,577. I suppose you were on the Commission when the markets were established?—Yes.

27,578. Did you and the Commissioners think that a necessity existed for proper control to be exercised over the markets?—We did.

27,579. Have they materially improved since the Commissioners became the market authority?—We believe the markets improved. The market place and new monthly fairs are a great success, a signal success, especially the pig fairs. The pig fairs are held on the Tuesday before the first Wednesday of every month, and they are going on improving every year.

27,580. Have you had experience of markets and fairs other than those in Carlow?—No.

27,581. You have not done business at any of them?—No.

27,582. From the experience you have gathered here of the markets and fairs, do you think if the same system were adopted elsewhere and at all markets and fairs, to have a properly enclosed market and fair green, that it would tend to improve and benefit them?—From the experience I have had of Carlow I say yes.

27,583. You object to markets being held on the public thoroughfare?—I think it is a decided benefit to have them in the market place.

27,584. With a rule confining the sale of sheep to the market place?—Quite so.

27,585. From your conversations with the farmers and those coming to the town from the country do you think the farmers would have any objection to pay a small charge for the maintenance and erection of the building?—I may say when striking out and arranging the bye-laws the Commissioners adopted the principle of making charges in the market places for what they weigh. They have acquired the right of charging tolls, but as a principle they adopted the rule of merely making a charge for what they weigh, hence, though they have had the power to raise tolls on fowl and other commodities they have not enforced those rules so far, and only made charges for weighing corn, butter, potatoes, wool, and a few other commodities.

27,586. They only charge when those commodities are weighed?—Yes. They have the power to require all commodities to be weighed and to pay tolls, but they have not enforced that rule.

27,587. You think the appliances they have provided are availed of generally?—Certainly.

27,588. Do you think in every market place the proper course in order to create greater confidence between buyer and seller, is that the commodity should be weighed at a public scales and not at a private crane or scales?—We considered it very desirable. There is a question as regards the corn. The corn trade is very heavy and there is an opinion as to weighing the corn in the public interest. There is a gentleman here who is engaged largely in the corn trade, and he could give you some information on that head. There is an opinion as to the expediency of having the corn weighed in the public markets, and so far we have not enforced the rule, but it is a question as to whether the Commissioners will do so, having regard to the prosperity of the corn trade.

27,589. Having regard to the bye-law and charge in corn, do you think that would deteriorate from the corn market here, and make those people not resort to it?—Some of the Commissioners are of opinion it would cause delay.

27,590. You do not think of stopping the present supply for the sake of the charge?—Not on account of the charge, but the principal thing is it would be a delay and they might not desire the charge. At any rate it would be a dangerous experiment to require corn to be weighed, and the Commissioners so far are apprehensive of trying that as an experiment.

27,591. From the success of the markets here you do not think that the compulsory exaction of a charge deters people from bringing a commodity, if an adequate return is given?—I do not think so. As regards the corn I should also state that the principal difficulty in the way of enforcing the rule would be the inadequacy of the area of the market place. The corn could only be weighed in the enclosed market, and that is not sufficiently large to give proper accommodation to farmers bringing in their corn.

27,592. Do you think the space and extent of the other markets would be sufficient?—No. They are sufficient for their present purposes.

27,593. Having regard to the development of the butter market are the other markets insufficient?—I consider the space for the butter market quite sufficient for the purposes of the butter market.

27,594. Now, when you say the hay market and the potato market you mean the public thoroughfare where the market is held, or where they collect to expose the commodities?—You should understand the hay market, although an open space, is not the actual thoroughfare. It is out of the thoroughfare. There are thoroughfares at either side of the market square, but the market is held in the centre where there is no thoroughfare. It is a large open space. There is no interruption of the public thoroughfare, and it is Mr. Collins' duty to see there is no obstruction, and he keeps the thoroughfare clear at both sides. The same thing applies to the potato market; it no interruption to the thoroughfare.

27,595. Are the three markets convenient to the trading portion of the town?—The butter market is contiguous, and the other markets convenient to the town. It was better to consult the benefit of the people generally, and hence the Commissioners decided to hold the potato market in the place where the potato market was always held, and leave the scales there for the purpose of weighing coal, and they also decided for the same reason to hold the butter market in the lower portion of the town near the hay market. I might say before the establishment of the markets there was a butter crane quite near the present market. This enclosed butter market is quite close to that place where the crane was held. There was no fixed butter market until the market was established.

27,596. Leaving out of question your capacity as chairman of the Town Commissioners, do you think the markets and fairs are better managed if the control is vested in the local authority and not leave them in the hands of a private individual, or in other words, would you be in favour of local authorities throughout the country obtaining powers to acquire individual rights? —Certainly. I am strongly in favour of that.

27,597. You think the united efforts of the gentlemen on the board would tend to develop and lead to better management of the markets and fairs?—Certainly. They would safeguard the public interest and see everything carried on properly, and justice done between the buyer and seller. I have a strong opinion as regards the manner in which the duties are performed by the several inspectors, you have heard, and I believe, they administer justice fairly, accurately, and most conscientiously in the weighing of the different commodities. They are painstaking men, and the Commissioners are anxious by personal supervision and by the inspection of the members of the fairs and markets committee to see the inspectors perform their duties accurately and carefully.

27,598. You would not approve of the Commissioners at any time sub-letting the tolls here?—Certainly not.

27,599. They should have immediate control?—Certainly.

27,600. If compulsory powers are given to acquire market rights throughout the country where there is a local authority do you think there should be some restrictions on their sub-letting them?—I think the success of the markets would greatly depend on the nature of the men forming the public authority.

27,601. Have you formed any opinions on the application of the profits derived from the markets. Supposing the markets are greatly developed, and there is a surplus profit over and above the actual expenditure or payment of any money, if borrowed, how would you apply that surplus?—To the reduction of the rates of the town.

27,602. Do you think it should go to the reduction of the rates?—I think so.

27,603. Without effecting any improvements required in the markets?—Yes.

27,604. Would you say that what you receive from the market rights should go to the reduction of the rates on the reduction of the tolls themselves?—To the reduction of the rates on the understanding always that the tolls were reasonable.

27,605. After all the capital expenditure has been paid off would you approve of local authorities only having power to levy such tolls as would pay the cost of maintenance of the markets?—I think when the people of the town provide everything requisite for the success of the market and give full accommodation and provide all requisite and appurtenances of the market, and supply proper officials, they might reasonably and properly apply the profits to the market and to the well-being of the town and reduction of the rates, because primarily the markets were intended for the agricultural portion of the community, and they derive a benefit from the markets.

27,606. You would not say they have already paid for it by any charge on the different commodities?—They, in a measure, pay by the fact of paying the charge.

27,607. They pay for the accommodation afforded?—Yes.

27,608. You say the larger charge over and above what would be for the return you give should go to the benefit of the town; in other words, the farmers should pay a larger charge than you give in accommodation return for in market accommodation?—I think the townspeople would be perfectly justified in enacting charges on the more rate as mentioned in the existing bye-laws; but the Commissioners take charges on goods actually weighed. They do not take tolls.

27,609. How much of that 3,600*l.* is due at present? —I think three years' instalments are paid.

27,610. What provision is made for the repayment? —To be paid in 60 half-yearly instalments, with interest, at three and three-fourths per cent.

27,611. You do not find any falling off of the supply of the fairs with charges levied?—No. With respect to the establishment of fairs, the fair green was a great advantage to the farmers, and they themselves generally express high approval of the regulation of the fairs. They have admirable accommodation in the fair green. It has been only quite recently a complaint was made to me in regard to the pig fair, which happened within the present month. It was an exceptionally wet day, and the people suffered very much at the fair, and it has been suggested at a meeting of the market committee that the lower portion of the fair green be used as a pig fair, and have it macadamised, in order to prevent hardship, because where the pigs congregate there is much puddle.

27,612. Do you think shelter accommodation is needed?—That has never been suggested. Shelter put up any way effectually would be very expensive, which would involve expense.

27,613. You could give an approximate idea of the cattle brought to the fairs?—We have a record of the cattle.

27,613a. You think it is a better system to levy a small charge on the animals as they enter the fair green, than the larger charge on the animals when sold, and as they take them out from the place?—We find it very much more convenient to charge on the animals coming in. We find it exceedingly difficult to charge on the animals sold.

27,614. That is as to convenience in regard to collection?—Yes. I have no doubt it would be more agreeable to the sellers paying the toll only when sold, but the Commissioners only considered it just and fair to make a charge on all animals coming in.

27,615. You do not think the present system of levying a charge on animals as they enter restricts them in any way?—Not at all.

27,616. Do the people always have the toll when they come there?—Generally speaking they have.

27,617. Supposing a poor man came and had not the toll, would they let him in?—I never knew a man to be turned away for want of tolls.

27,618. Have you any suggestions to offer?—No. The present regulations work very well, both as regards the townspeople and farmers generally.

27,619. That has lasted from the improvements the Commissioners erected?—Yes. In fact before the Commissioners took the matter in hands they were under no regulation or control. They were conducted haphazard, and there was no supervision until the Commissioners took the matter in hands some years ago. The markets were held in various parts of the town, the fowl market in one of the streets—and now capital accommodation is given to the persons selling fowl, and no toll is charged. I may say, as regards the bye-laws, the Commissioners do not enforce them except for weighing.

PATRICK DESMOND SHACKLETON, Esq., examined.

27,620. You have some connexion with the corn trade?—Yes, I have got flour mills.

27,621. Is there any market proper for corn?—No.

27,622. Do the farmers themselves send direct to you? —Yes.

27,623. Those with whom, I suppose, you have a contract supply you?—They come and sell by sample.

27,624. Do you weigh on your own scales then?—Yes.

27,627. The actual tare is the only deduction?—That is the only deduction.

27,628. Nothing is allowed for bounage or anything when the contract is made?—No.

27,629. Is there any deduction from the price previously agreed upon per barrel?—No, if the corn is equal to the sample.

27,630. Is there any porterage charge?—Not in our stores. There is no porterage charge.

27,631. Do they elsewhere, do you know?—I am not

27,633. Your men never perform that office?—Sometimes they do.

27,634. Supposing they did, would any charge be payable to them?—No charge whatever.

27,635. It would be only a matter of convenience to the farmer?—That is all.

27,636. Would you say the corn trade was a good one?—I think so.

27,637. Could you give me any approximate idea of the number of barrels brought here?—We only buy wheat.

27,638. Is it the practice to buy wheat by the barrel?—It is.

27,639. Here in Carlow what is the barrel supposed to contain?—Twenty-stone weight.

27,640. Supposing there is less than twenty-stone?—Then you can buy at the rate of twenty-stone.

27,641. You buy proportionately, whether under or over?—Yes.

27,642. Supposing a man brought twenty-stone and-a-half, would he be paid for twenty-stone and-a-half?—Yes.

27,643. But if under the barrel you would not buy anything, or over it he would not?—The farmer is paid for every pound he brings in.

27,644. Have these farmers scales of their own in the country where they can previously ascertain the weight of the wheat?—Sometimes.

27,645. You think the system you have of buying and weighing is adopted by the other merchants in the town?—I really do not know.

27,646. You are not conversant with their ways and dealing?—No.

27,647. Have you any suggestions to offer as to what you think would tend to the improvement of the markets if improvement is desirable?—No, nothing occurs to my mind at present.

27,648. What do you think would be necessary for the management of any other markets and fairs throughout the country?—With regard to establishing a corn market I think they ought to leave the matter optional with farmers. If they have not confidence in the private weighing they ought to go to the public scales, but they would want a much more extensive scales.

Stanley Johnson, Esq., examined.

27,649. Have you anything to do with the markets?—I quite agree with the observations made by the chairman and Mr. Shackleton. You asked Mr. Shackleton a question as to how other merchants conducted their business. I have been in the stores and saw them weighing. They weigh exactly to the pound in barley and oats and make no charge for weighing.

27,650. You never heard any complaints of inaccuracy in weighing?—Not for a very long period.

27,651. You concur in the opinion of Mr. Hammond that the proper system is to concentrate all the markets in one place?—Certainly.

27,652. You consider it was objectionable to have them scattered indiscriminately about the town previous to the erection of the markets?—Yes.

27,653. Were complaints made by the people of the town?—Yes, there were.

27,654. Were the complaints made of the system of weighing about the streets and going where the seller willed. What gave rise to erection of the markets or what induced them to provide them, was the intention of increasing their revenue the primary object?—It was in consequence of the various matters that came to the knowledge of the people, and they also wished to be certain they would have their just rights in having an accountable person weighing their commodities.

27,655. You concur in his (the chairman's) opinion that in order to create greater confidence between buyers and sellers the commodities should be weighed at a public and independent scale?—Certainly.

27,656. Do you also concur in his opinion that where local authorities exist the market rights should be vested in them?—Yes.

27,657. Where no market authorities are or could not be established by the present law, do you think market committees or market trustees should be appointed from among the traders in the town?—It would be a very great advantage to the people in the neighbourhood of that town.

27,658. Would it tend to the improvement and better working of the markets and fairs?—Certainly, and to the agricultural portion of the community who bring their goods to that town. It would create better competition and bring the buyers.

Mr. John G[illegible] examined.

27,659. You attend at the fairs?—Yes.

27,660. Have they got the system here of deducting from the prices called a luck-penny?—That is usual in all fairs. They are all prepared to allow a luck-penny at the payment of the price.

27,661. On cattle is there any fixed deduction from the price?—That all depends on the man who sells; it is according to his generosity.

27,662. It is all left to the disposition of the seller?—Yes.

27,663. Is there any fixed sum for pigs?—Sixpence a pig on fat pigs, and from a 1d. to 3d. on other pigs.

27,664. In the case of cattle it is left to the disposition of the seller; but in the case of pigs does the buyer deduct it from the price?—At the payment he takes it.

27,665. It is not left to the disposition of the seller?—No; that is in a way compulsory. That is a fixed thing between themselves, and they are aware of that.

27,666. What gave rise to that deduction of 6d. for each pig?—I do not know.

27,667. Do you remember when they used to try the pigs for measles?—I remember it well.

27,668. Was that 6d. deducted then?—It was. That had nothing to do with it.

27,669. You would not say it acts as an equivalent for any loss they sustain by having the pigs infected with that disease?—I think the luck-penny was always deducted before that was brought forward. That is done away with now; there is not a word about the pig being infected.

27,670. Do you think the farmer, when arguing about the price of the animal, considers the value of the luck-penny; in other words does he ask a larger price than he would actually take if there was no luck-penny?—I think they never took into it at the time they sell.

27,671. Do you say then he gets the value of the animal, less the amount of the luck-penny, and that the buyer does not actually give the marketable value of the animal?—He is prepared to allow the luck-penny.

John Hammond, Esq., J.P., re-examined.

27,672. Do you think the seller considers the luck-penny?—It is perfectly understood.

27,673. Do you think it enhances the price of the animal to the value of the luck-penny?—I do not think it does. A man who sold a number of pigs objected to the buyer deducting sixpence each, but the matter was referred to me, and I recommended that it should be settled, and it was.

27,674. Do you think it gives rise to much argument and dispute?—I do not think there are any arguments at all. It is quite understood at all times.

27,675. No serious disputes have arisen?—No.

27,676. Is the fair green utilised between fairs?—For grazing it is.

27,677. (*The Commissioner to the Town Clerk.*) What do you receive for that?—It is included in the receipts.

27,678. You do not know what the rates are?—Threepence or fourpence for cattle. There is a check kept on them. One of the Town Commissioners is appointed to issue printed tickets for the beasts or animals and the persons who own them. When the caretaker gets those tickets they are an authority for admitting them.

27,679. Are cattle ever brought the night before the fair?—Yes.

27,680. Can they utilise the fair green for stallage purposes?—Certainly, by paying threepence or fourpence a head per night, and in addition pay the tolls.

27,681. Supposing it was required from the Commissioners to make a periodical return of the current prices of the different marketable commodities brought to the market, do you think it would be possible to obtain an accurate return?—There would be no difficulty about it.

27,682. And the return would be a pretty accurate one.

27,683. Mr. Dillon said he asked some of the butter merchants to attend, but they said they had nothing to complain of about the market.

27,684. Is there any other gentleman who has any suggestions to offer or evidence to give?—No answer.

The inquiry then terminated.

CASTLECOMER.

With reference to my inquiry in Castlecomer on the 15th day of December 1888, I

In accordance with my instructions, I have inspected the market and fair places. The markets are held in a wide space at the rear of the court house. It is off the main street, but forms portion of the public thoroughfare, as some houses are running along one side of it. It is of fair dimensions, but at the time of inspection was in a dirty condition. The beam and scale is erected in the centre of this space and considered sufficient for the trade of the town. Another scale is provided for weighing the butter. Attached to the rear of the court house is a small weigh-house for the use of the weigh-master, and in another portion of the market place a small substantially built store house has been erected for storing commodities remaining unsold after the market. It has one gate entrance.

There is no schedule of the charges erected, and the weighing machine is erected outside the weigh-house, but has not the customary railings around it to make it sufficiently capable of weighing live stock.

There is no shelter or other accommodation provided for those frequenting the market.

The fairs are held indiscriminately about the public streets. As no cattle or fat pigs are brought to the fairs, the young pigs are sold in carts which are placed along the channel course.

It was stated that the market and fairs could be considerably improved if the control was given to a local authority or committee, with power to make and enforce byelaws regulating the manner of holding the markets and fairs. Whilst in the town I saw a man with his stock in trade of fresh meat placed on a board on the public pathway with a small scales for weighing, and where he solicited the passers-by to purchase from him.

If stalls or shambles were erected, this would not be permitted, as I was informed the poor man had no other place to go to in the town to earn a livelihood, as no stalls or small shops were available.

JOHN J. O'MEARA,
Assistant Commissioner.

45, Lower Mount Street,
Dublin.

Castlecomer, 15th December 1888.

NICHOLAS G. RICHARDSON, Esq., examined.

27,685. You are agent to Mrs. Prior Wandesforde?—Yes.

27,686. Is she the owner of the town?—She is.

27,687. Do you know does she exercise any market rights at all?—She does to the extent of putting up scales and weights and [illegible].

27,688. A beam and scale?—Yes, and weighbridge.

27,689. She originally provided them?—Her predecessors did.

27,690. You have no record of the amount expended on them?—No, but it is easy to ascertain.

27,691. She has them sub-let?—Yes.

27,692. To whom?—To James Doyle.

27,693. What are the terms?—2l. a year.

27,694. Has he a lease?—No.

27,695. I suppose you sub-let them together with any right to any charges for weighing?—He is entitled to charge for everything weighed on the scales or [illegible].

27,696. Were tolls ever levied within your recollection here?—They have never been levied here since I came.

27,697–8. Does Mrs. Wandesforde own the entire town?—She does.

27,699. Did you ever hear from your predecessor in the agency or otherwise whether she claimed any market rights or not, or that she was entitled to them?—I would not like to answer that. I am here for thirty-five years, and I never heard of any toll being collected.

27,700. Do you allow any deductions from the 2l.?—No.

27,701. Does Mr. Doyle do any repairs to the beam and scales and weighbridge himself?—No, they are done by Mrs. Wandesforde.

27,702. What is the average expenditure in connexion with repairs?—I really could not tell you.

27,703. Are there any buildings in connexion with it?—There is a house you can see at the end of the court house; it is part of the court house.

27,704. It is merely used for the purpose of weighing?—That is all.

27,705. Are the markets held on the public street?—They are at the back of the market. It is rather a [illegible] place, but it is the public street.

27,706. Is it a widening of the street?—It is an open place at the back of the court house.

27,707. But the public have acquired rights over it?—They have.

27,708. What market is held in this place that you name?—There is corn, potatoes, butter in the butter season.

27,709. Where is the butter market held?—The corn are all on the public street down below under the trees and opposite Mr. Ryan's house. Apples and vegetables and other things are sold in the market. The other scale is used largely for weighing hay and straw and timber, but that is not on market day.

27,710. That is the weighbridge?—Yes.

27,711. Where is the hay exposed?—There is not much of that comes in; that is generally a matter of private contract.

27,712. Are there any other weighing machines and scales in the town let out for hire?—Not that I am aware. There may be private owners that have them in their yards.

27,713. Supposing there was a private owner let one out on hire to the public, would you prevent him doing so or take proceedings against him?—I declare I doubt very much.

27,714. You cannot tell me whether Mrs. Wandesforde claims an exclusive right for weighing commodities brought into the market?—No. I may say there are seven fairs in the year. I believe Mrs. Wandesforde has a patent.

27,715. At present she exercises no control?—No control. Practically there is no fair except for pigs. In connexion with the market there is a large colliery population that helps to consume the commodities that would be brought here. This is not what you call a district where there is a large amount of tillage in the immediate locality, as there is no very large amount of produce grown. What is grown is quite capable of being consumed by the local population.

27,716. Practically there is not a sufficient surplus to be sold, considering the consumption?—No.

27,717. It is all practically for local consumption?—Yes.

27,718. Where there is so little tillage, the cattle to be disposed of ought to be somewhat considerable?—They are.

Mr. JAMES DOYLE examined.

27,719. What is the market day here?—Saturday.

27,720. Saturday alone?—Yes.

27,721. What commodities are brought in on Saturday to the market?—Potatoes, oats, and turnips.

27,722. Are fruit and vegetables?—Yes, cabbages, hay, straw, and butter. Turf comes in, but not on market days; it comes day after day.

27,723. Is coal exposed for sale in the market place?—It comes into it to be sold.

27,724. You weigh loads?—I do.

27,725. Is there any rule in the market compelling all these commodities to be weighed at the beam and scales or weighbridge?—There is no rule. Of course I weigh on other days, but they could weigh outside. At the weighbridge I weigh all that comes in.

27,726. There is no rule compelling the people to resort to the scales?—No.

27,727. Is there any other beam in the town?—There are private beams in private yards.

27,728. They do not let them out on hire?—I think not. Butter is not weighed on the public scales.

27,729. You do not weigh butter?—No.

27,730. Where is that weighed?—In the private yards.

27,731. Is it brought in lumps or firkins?—In firkins.

27,732. Is there any gentleman here who weighs butter himself in his private yard?—No, the buyers buy it.

27,733. Is there any buyer here?—No.

27,734. What charge do you levy for weighing potatoes?—A penny a bag.

27,735. At the weighing machine what do you charge?—3d. for a certain commodity, that is for 12 cwt., and 2d. under 12 cwt.

27,736. Irrespective of what the commodity may be, that is on the load?—Yes.

27,737. You charge on bags a penny per bag no matter what the commodity may be?—Yes.

27,738. How do you weigh—do you weigh net or only ascertain the gross weight?—I weigh net in the potatoes and grass in oats.

27,739. When weighing a sack of potatoes do you actually ascertain the tare of the sack?—As a rule when the weight is over a barrel, that is twenty stone, a stone is deducted for the bag of potatoes, and under 20 stone, a half stone is deducted for the tare.

27,740. Well now, if they had less than a barrel in a large sack, would they still only allow half a stone weight?—Yes.

27,741. Although the empty bag would be the same weight as if there were over a barrel in it?—The one weight.

27,742. Would that deduction be the very same on a fine day as on a wet day when the sack was completely saturated with wet?—No. From the 1st May until coming on the winter there is only a half stone allowed no matter what is in the bag.

27,743. Whether it is over or under a barrel?—Yes, a half stone.

27,744. Then the other rule comes in at the wet season?—Yes.

27,745. Is that a rule peculiar to Castlecomer, or does it exist elsewhere?—It is in Abbeyleix. I do not know about Kilkenny; that is the rule laid down here this many a year.

27,746. When weighing potatoes what weight do you weigh down to. Do you weigh under a half stone, or can you ascertain the weight under a half stone?—I do not weigh under a half stone.

27,747. When you are weighing a barrel of potatoes, and [illegible]

27,748. How low do you go?—7 lbs.

27,749. Then you would return the weight of 20 stone 6 lbs. as 20 stone, and from that you would deduct the half stone tare?—Yes. I would return 19½ stone payable.

27,750. Do the sellers ever dispute that system of deduction?—They do not.

27,751. When weighing do you give a cast of the beam?—No. I weigh fair.

27,752. That is by standing beam?—Yes.

27,753. In weighing oats, down to what weight do you weigh?—I weigh oats to the pound.

27,754. Do you deduct the tare at all?—We weigh bags after.

27,755. Do you usually weigh the bags?—Sometimes. Square both them by allowing 4 lbs. for the bag and more weigh them.

27,756. No matter the season or the weather?—No matter.

27,757. Is the actual or estimated tare the only deduction from the gross weight?—Yes.

27,758. Do you know, between the buyers and sellers, is there any deduction from the price they agreed upon for lowerage or anything?—They agree to whatever price they pay.

27,759. They deduct nothing for porterage?—No.

27,760. Has the seller to pay any porterage charge?—No. The seller has to pay me.

27,761. There is no porterage charge?—No, unless a fellow is about, and they may give him a pint of porter for helping them.

27,762. Who performs the manual work of weighing and putting the weights into the scales?—I do myself.

27,763. And who takes the bags off the load and puts them on the scale?—The parties themselves.

27,764. They must do that themselves?—Yes.

27,765. There are no persons attending there?—I do have a man myself.

27,766. Have they to pay him anything?—No. I pay him myself.

27,767. Practically he is an assistant of yours at the scales?—Yes.

27,768. How many beams have you?—One and the weighing machine.

27,769. Is one sufficient for the trade of the town?—It is. I weigh all that comes in, I wish I could get enough.

27,770. Is the machine capable of weighing live cattle?—Yes.

27,771. Did you ever weigh any?—I weighed one beast in my life.

27,772. The practice of weighing cattle is not carried on here?—No.

27,773. Had you ever any conversation with them on that question of weighing cattle or selling them by live-weight?—I never had.

27,774. Did you ever hear any discussion between the farmers?—I never did.

27,775. Or between the buyers?—No.

27,776. When you ascertain the weights of these commodities, do you give them any ticket denoting the weight?—I do.

27,777. Is it a printed form?—No. It is written. I have a printed ticket for the machine.

27,778. Do you ever mark the weight on the bag?—I do.

27,779. Are all these commodities sold before they are weighed at your scales or afterwards?—They are bought in the market and then they are weighed.

27,780. Supposing they do not sell any of these commodities on market days, have you any storage accommodation?—I have.

27,781. What charge do you levy for it?—Well, it is newly up. I did not put on any charge yet, because I did not get anything to store in it.

27,782. Was it for the purpose of storage you built it?—It was.

27,784. Who was it erected by?—Mrs. Wandesford.

27,785. What was the cost of it?—30*l.*, I suppose. There are two tenants for it, and what they call the market corporation have to pay 1*l.* a year for that.

27,786. Is there any authority exercised over the markets other than what you do yourself?—There is a committee formed in the market.

27,787. Is that a committee of the traders of the town?—Yes.

27,788. What duty do they perform?—They set things right.

27,789. Do you keep a record of the quantity of the different commodities you weigh?—I never did.

27,790. Are you in the habit of making up the tickets for the buyer and seller?—I do make them up.

27,791. I am not asking you to do it, but supposing it was required from you to make a periodical return of the current prices of the different commodities brought here from time to time to the markets of Castlecomer, could you make such a return?—To be sure I could.

27,792. You think it would be a pretty accurate one?—Yes.

27,793. Has the market always been held on Saturday?—Yes.

27,794. You do not remember it being held any other day?—No.

27,795. Are all the commodities brought here to this space outside this court house or are they sold indiscriminately about the town?—On Saturday they are sold in the market place; they are sold about the town on week days.

27,796. What you have mentioned are the only sources from which you derive a profit?—Yes, the weighing at the scales and crane.

27,797. You have no posts in connexion with the market standing room or stallage rents?—No.

27,798. In fact are there any standings here in the markets?—No. There are not, but there are apple and fish carts.

27,799. They bring fish here?—They bring fresh herrings.

27,800. Where do they stand?—Out on the street.

27,801. Is the corn brought here to the market place?—It is.

27,802. Is it exposed there?—Yes.

27,803. Does any great quantity of corn come?—Not much of a deal.

27,804. What description of corn is brought?—Oats.

27,805. Oats principally?—Yes, and nothing else.

27,806. Have they any shelter accommodation in this market?—No shelter, only the storage that has been put up.

27,807. Did you ever hear the farmers complain that some of the commodities brought in were deteriorated in value by the want of shelter accommodation?—I never heard them complaining.

27,808. Do you think it would tend to improve the market if such shelter accommodation were provided?—Indeed it would.

27,809. Then you think a necessity exists for such both to afford protection to the commodities and to those who bring them in?—It would be good for the commodity to have shelter over it.

27,810. Have you any duty to perform in connexion with the fairs?—None.

27,811. What fairs are held here?—Seven fairs in the year.

27,812. What are they?—The 27th March, 3rd May, 21st June, 10th August, 14th September, 20th November, and 14th December.

27,813. No tolls are levied on those fairs?—I never heard of them.

27,814. Where are the fairs held?—On the main street.

27,815. What species of animals are brought here?—Bonhams, young pigs.

27,816. Are cattle brought here?—No.

27,817. Or sheep or horses?—No.

27,818. Practically there is only a pig fair?—Nothing only a fair for bonhams.

27,819. When these were established first were they established as cattle fairs?—Oh yes, I believe so.

27,820. Where are the cattle taken to by the farmers?—There is Ballinakill, Kilkenny, Carlow, and Athy.

27,821. Do you remember when there was a time when these seven fairs were held here?—I do not. I think these fairs are by patent.

27,822. They have been always held on these days?—Yes.

27,823. No alteration has ever been made in the dates of them?—No.

27,824. Do you remember when the cattle fairs were held here?—No. I often heard of one fair and the place was full of cattle, but they were not brought to be sold, only to show them.

27,825. You say they go to Kilkenny?—Yes.

27,826. Tolls are levied in Kilkenny?—I believe they are.

27,827. You do not think the fact of no tolls being levied here would act as an inducement to the farmers to bring their animals and expose them in Castlecomer?—I could not say. If we had the railway here we would have a fair.

27,828. You assign as the cause of the state of affairs in Castlecomer the want of communication?—Exactly.

27,829. And from its isolated position the great difficulty in driving the stock away?—Yes. A great deal more cattle pass through the town on fair days to Ballinakill than would make a good fair, but there are no facilities for the buyers to come here.

27,830. Are tolls levied at Ballinakill?—No.

27,831. Then they pass through Castlecomer going there?—Yes, a large number.

27,832. Are the pig fairs here of any extent?—Oh, no.

27,833. Does this market committee exercise any control over the fairs?—I think not. There is no control to be exercised, because there is no fair in the town.

27,834. Would you have any objection to tell me your average receipts from the crane and scales and crane in the year, or do you keep any record of them?—I keep no record.

27,835. If you have any objection to give it publicly I will take it privately from you if you wish?—I have not the least objection.

27,836. What then are your average receipts from them?—For about six months of the year I suppose it is worth about 7*s.* a week and four or five months it is idle; there is nothing weighed worth while speaking of. From June until this month is the time the market is good.

27,837. You only make about 7*s.* a week?—About that for six or seven months of the year.

27,838. Are those the gross or net receipts after payment of your rent and the wages of the man you employ?—I have all that to myself. Of course the weigh-bridge is not included. That amount is what I make at the scales.

27,839. What do you receive from the weigh-bridge?—I could not tell you.

27,840. Could you give me any approximate idea of what your receipts are from the bridge in the year?—I get the worst from Mrs. Wandesford for weighing coals. Oh! I suppose it would be about 5*l.* or 6*l.* in the year.

27,841. Out of these two sources of income you pay the assistant yourself?—I do.

27,842. At what rate do you pay him?—Every Saturday I have him I give him 1*s.* 6*d.*

27,843. You only engage him on the market day?—That is all.

27,844. Your rent is 2*l.*?—Yes.

27,845. Is there any poor-law valuation on this weigh house and shed?—No. I think it is included in the court house.

27,846. Mrs. Wandesford owns the court house?—Yes.

The following is a copy of the ticket given at the weighing machine :—

CASTLECOMER WEIGHING MACHINE.

No.________ ____________________________18__

	Tons.	Cwts.	Qrs.	Lbs.
Gross Weight.				
Tar Weight.				
Net Weight.				

Description of Goods.______________________

From______________________

To______________________

______________________Weigh Mistress.

Mr. MARTIN P. KENNY examined.

27,847. A market committee is established in Castlecomer ?—Yes.

27,848. You are on the market committee ?—Yes.

27,849. For what purpose was it established ?—To get up this market. It is only in existence nine or ten years, and it was the exertions of the committee made the market.

27,850. Could you give me the date they were established ?—I think about 1879.

27,851. Previous to 1879 there were no markets held here at all ?—No.

27,852. Do you remember any period previous to that when markets were held ?—No. People used to buy at their own houses, and things used not be brought into the market.

27,853. The commodities would be brought the traders ?—Yes. They would go around and call at the houses.

27,854. Have the committee been fairly successful in their exertions ?—Yes, very successful.

27,855. Are there any scales or engines where the commodities can be weighed but Mr. Doyle's ?—We have no jurisdiction whatever. It is only merely we try to insist; we have no power to enforce our claims at all. Any person can sell in any part of the town or any day they like, but it is simply for the accommodation of the buyers and our mutual benefit that we act.

27,856. What duties did they perform at their inception ?—They issued a notice saying the market would be established, and I and Mr. Coghlan and a couple of the other members of the committee were sent as a deputation to Waterford to try and induce the butter buyers there to come. We were not successful in that. The want of communication was a great objection. We found too, buyers could not come here and go home the same night, or have their produce brought away in time.

27,857. In consequence of that of course there is an additional cost of transit placed on the producer's shoulders in bringing his commodities to the market ?—Yes; and delay too.

27,858. Practically, the farmer does not get the full value of the commodity, the ordinary marketable value ?—The farmers do not come here.

27,859. But the producer in the neighbourhood of Castlecomer does not get the actual marketable value of the commodity because of the additional expense incurred in bringing it to the market ?—Well, I do not know that exactly, because it is only butter that is brought by the outsiders. In the other market it is only the buyers in the locality who buy. There is some bought for exporting.

27,860. Are they local buyers who buy the butter ?—The Carlow buyers come here, and we have a local one. At some seasons there are one or two from Kilkenny, but the Carlow buyers attend constantly during the summer months.

27,861. Do the buyers weigh the butter themselves ?—Yes, each buyer has his own scale.

27,862. Do you know their system of weighing ?—Yes.

27,863. When weighing do they drain the firkins ?—No. They weigh them as they come in.

27,864. They do not drain the firkins or strip them ?—They do.

27,865. Did you ever see them weighed ?—After being pierced they are drained and then weighed.

27,866. Does the cooper who makes the firkin brand the tare on the firkin ?—It is lately they have been marked that way.

27,867. Was it the buyers themselves made the rule ?—Yes.

27,868. Did you ever hear the farmers complaining of the buyer weighing the commodity after their selling to him ?—Sometimes you will hear complaints, but the same system is carried on in the surrounding markets, and they do not object for that reason.

27,869. Do you think that there would be greater confidence between the buyers and sellers if all marketable commodities were weighed at a public and independent scales than when weighed at a scales under the control of one of the contracting parties ?—I do. I think so.

27,870. It would tend to greater confidence between the buyer and seller ?—I think so.

27,871. Do these butter buyers levy any charge for weighing the butter ?—No.

27,872. They classify the butter themselves ?—Yes.

27,873. You do not know the system of weighing they have. Do they weigh down to a pound ?—I think so.

27,874. You are not sure ?—No.

27,875. Did you ever contemplate starting fairs ?—Yes. Some years ago there was a strong attempt made, but I am aware of the circumstances, and it was a failure for more reasons than one. The cause was getting into country-people's minds that this was a dearer place, but it is a very good centre for cattle raising. Some people who made the attempt in their own anxiety about the thing had cattle brought here not intended for sale and fabulous prices were asked to make the fair work, and it was a complete failure. But this country supplies Ballinakill with five sixths of the cattle fair.

27,876. Do you think it would tend to improve the markets both here and elsewhere if there were proper market buildings with sufficient shelter and a bye-law made enforcing the exposure and sale of all commodities in those buildings ?—I think that is the very difficulty we find ourselves in, that we have no compulsory powers. If there was an elected representative body with powers to deal with markets in general, I think it would tend very much to improve them, but the building Mrs. Waddesford has constructed here has not been used. It has only been a few months open, and certainly for storage and that sort of thing it is very suitable, but it is not availed of. Of course it is only from this forward it might be, but we are powerless to enforce any rules. We can only suggest them for the people to adopt if they wish. If we had the powers I dare say we would have things in a more successful state.

27,877. The nature of the rules would be in supplementing the supply ?—Yes. We made a rule restricting buying and selling from certain o'clock to two; that is a rule made at the suggestion of the farmers of the locality and also the buyers. The buyers complained that sometimes they would come and would not know what money they required till the bank was closing, and would sometimes be driving back to Carlow with 200l. or 300l., or find they were a 100l. short, and would have to pay the people with cheques which they do not approve of.

27,878. This new market-house is intended for storage accommodation ?—Yes.

27,879. What rates will be levied there ?—Mr. Coghlan and myself, as members of the market committee, were made trustees to Mrs. Waddesford at 1s. a year, and we made Lloyd a weekly tenant at 6d. a week, in order that he would be amenable to whatever rules we would make with regard to the charges, and the charge suggested was 1d. per sack per week or lesser time for storing goods.

27,880. 1d. per sack from market day to market day ?—Yes, or such lesser time.

27,881. Do you think a necessity existed for such accommodation ?—It was at the request of the market committee Mrs. Waddesford built this house.

27,882. Have you had experience of markets elsewhere than in Castlecomer ?—No.

27,883. From your experience of the markets here, do you think the markets should be under the control of a local authority if any such existed or under a market committee of the legislature established it ?—I think the [illegible]

27,884. But where local authorities are, do you think the control should be vested in them and not in a private individual?—I do not think it would be right for a private individual to have them at all.

27,885. You think they would be managed better by a local authority?—I do, and the people would be represented there.

27,886. Have you attended fairs in Kilkenny or elsewhere?—I have.

27,887. You have attended fairs where tolls were levied and where they were not?—Yes.

27,888. Do you think the exaction of a toll at fairs or markets deters people from bringing in the supply they would otherwise bring in?—I do not think it does.

27,889. It acts in no way as a deterrent?—I do not think so. I do not think the people take a small charge into account at all.

27,890. That is when they get a return for it. If a toll is levied on cattle coming in or going out of a fair green, is it your opinion that the owner or person in receipt of that toll should give some return in the way of providing pens and shelter accommodation in the fair green?—I think so. What I meant about objection is that [illegible] is a place where there are no tolls, and Kilkenny is a place where they are. I think a person having a beast to dispose of would not take the 2d. into account as to which fair he would go. He would consider which would be the better and the difference in the distance, but I do not think he would take the charge into account at all in that case.

27,891. Which do you think the better system, levying a smaller charge on the animals as they enter the fair green than a larger one on the animals sold when they are going out; which do you think the better system or the one considered so by the farmers frequenting the fairs?—I think if they gave the people proper accommodation it would be fair for every beast exposed for sale to pay, but on the other hand where there is no accommodation provided there should only be a charge on the animals sold.

27,892. That is if charges are to be levied?—Yes.

27,893. Have you formed any opinions as to the right of levying a charge on animals sold at fairs held on the public street and where no return is given?—I was speaking of Kilkenny; but on the public street I do not think there should be any charge except for sheep, if contrivances required them on the street, but for cattle driven into the public street, I do not think it is fair to have any charge on them.

27,894. You see when the toll is on all animals entering it is paid by the farmer, but when on the animals sold as they are leaving the fair green, the buyer has to pay?—I think the charge for cattle is so small proportionately, that the people do not, I think, take it into account at all.

27,895. Would it work on a farmer coming in with 10 head of cattle and unfortunately had not the charge, if the charge were payable on entrance. Do you think the better course would be to wait until he had effected a sale?—In that case it would be hard to settle it, I think.

27,896. Still you think the smaller charge they have on entrance at Kilkenny would be better than the larger one on the animals actually sold?—As far as that is concerned, I do not think they take the charge into account at all. By extending the charge to all cattle coming in, you could have a small charge.

27,897. *Mr. Richardson* (interposing) said:—I attended [illegible] and sold cattle there myself, and in that district they prefer to pay when they have sold, and the man who does not sell does not like to pay.

27,898. (Commissioner to *Mr. Kenny.*) You have attended no such fairs where the charges were on the animals sold and as they left the fair green?—No. I never saw any

27,901. She has never exercised any rights here?—No. When Mr. Richardson speaks about the patent of rights to the fairs, I do not know what rights she claims in that direction, but with regard to the market she has not had any.

27,902. Do you remember any period when the market was not held on Saturday previous to 1878?—The butter market always existed on Saturday, it was only a butter market at the time.

27,903. Could you give any approximate idea of the number of firkins brought here?—On some market days during the season they amount to 300, 400, and 500 firkins.

27,904. There is no charge payable by the farmer?—No charge.

27,905. Do you think it would be better and they would have no objection to pay a small charge for weighing the butter if it was weighed at a public and independent scales?—I think the farmers would not, but I think the buyers would have a great objection.

Mr. James Conway examined.

27,906. You made some reference to the butter buyers a while ago, and I would like you to repeat it?—I made no reference.

27,907. Do they completely drain the butter?—They do. They turn down the firkin.

27,908. Did you ever sell to any of them?—Yes.

27,909. When they weigh the butter, do they give you any ticket at all showing you the weight of it or do they only cry it out?—When they pay me they give me a ticket.

27,910. How do you know whether that weight is correct or not?—I do not or I never looked at it.

27,911. You do not know whether it is correct or not, you have no check whatever on them?—No, only leave it to their own honesty.

27,912. In any case, do the farmers weigh the butter before they send it to the buyer?—I could not tell you anything about them.

27,913. You do not do it?—No.

27,914. Supposing you sent in a firkin assuming it will say 67 lbs., could they ascertain that weight of 67 lbs.?—They could, to be sure, if they liked.

27,915–16. What is the customary weight?—I could not tell you anything about that.

27,917. Do you know whether they pay the full rate to a lb. weight or not?—I do not know.

27,918. What is the firkin supposed to contain or how do you sell butter, is it so much a lb. or firkin?—By the cwt., excepting that a man comes up to me and said I will give you so much. I would give it to him if I thought I was getting the right price.

27,919. But when you send the butter into the buyer you sell by the cwt.?—Yes.

27,920. Supposing in the weight of the firkin there is a cwt. and a ¾ of a lb., would they pay you for that ¾ of a lb.?—I do not say they would. They would tell me there would not be a lb. there, but they pay me. I never examined them. I do not know, but there may be some for all I know.

27,921. What deduction from the gross weight is made. There is [illegible] of all the tare branded on the firkin?—It is branded at the present time, but it was not branded two years back. They allowed 2 lbs. in addition to the branded tare.

27,922. What was that 2 lbs.?—12 lbs. they allow for the firkin, and then at other times before this they used to take 20 lbs.

27,929. You think the entire deduction of 2 lbs. is a fair deduction?—I think it is.

27,930. The farmers do not object?—No.

27,931. You do not deprive them of any benefit?—No.

27,932. (To Mr. Conway.) Practically you have no check on the buyers as to the weight in the firkin?—No.

27,933. Do you think there should be some check?—I do not think any such thing.

27,934. If there is anybody who buys butter here, do not let their presence away you in giving an answer to the question. Do you think the farmers generally would be better satisfied if the butter was weighed at an independent public crane, and do you think they would have any objection to pay 1d. or 2d. or 3d. for weighing the firkin?—I do not think they would, but I say there is one in Kilkenny, and I should say the farmers would sooner come here and sell than go to Kilkenny. There is a man there for the purpose of trying and things.

27,935. What reason do you assign for that?—I heard the people would get fairer play here; that is in the classifying.

27,936. The farmers would rather rely upon the experience or inexperience of the buyers in classifying the butter?—Yes; I was out one day in Kilkenny, and I would yet leave it to him.

27,937. You think the classification is not reliable?—I think so. I cannot tell the butter because the buyer ceased to cut me in the price, and I got the price afterwards for it.

27,938. Have you any other observations to make?—No.

Mr. Thomas Mahony, Clerk of Poor Law Union, examined.

27,939. (Witness.) If the farmers' wives go to Kilkenny, their butter is first, second, or third class. If they come to Castlecomer, there is no classification that way. The farmers' wives do not like to show the ticket if their butter is third class.

27,940. They do not lose anything in the [illegible] value, it is a mere matter of sentiment?—It is considered outside.

27,941. Do they lose anything in value. Was there any wrong classification made?—Yes, in the case Mr. Conway mentioned, and his case would not be upheld by the buyer. The buyer, although promising the price, could go back to the rule of the market and claim for a cut per cwt.

27,942. (The Commissioner to Mr. Conway.) Do you think the taster employed was incompetent?—He might be for all I know. They say he is a certain man, and fit to do it.

27,943. Have you heard objections to him?—I certainly heard that his judgment does not tally with that of others. It is very often the reverse as Mr. Conway mentioned.

27,944. Was his tasting questioned?—I am aware it was canvassed in the public papers and there were discussions in the corporation, but not latterly. The people prefer by far to leave the butter to the judgment of the buyers.

27,945. (To Mr. Kenny.) In that case the buyers have no advantage over the farmer?—No. There is one thing I may mention, that there is butter sold from this locality in the Kilkenny market that would not be sold in Castlecomer.

27,946. What is the reason of that?—I do not know.

27,947. You think the buyers who attend here conduct it more rightly than in other places?—The buyers here may not have a market for the class of butter that would be bought in Kilkenny.

Examination of Mr. Mahony continued.

27,948. Have you ever heard any objections to these fairs being held on the streets and the markets on the public thoroughfares either here or elsewhere?—No, I have not. I think the want of railway communication is a preventive to having fairs here, because there is no accommodation for buyers if they come here, and if they could come in here by train in the morning and buy cattle or any other commodity, and go away again and take it away, I think we would have a great deal larger market, because the butter bought at present, on Saturday, is not able to be sent away until Monday. It has to be sent by cars into Kilkenny or Carlow, whereas if there was railway communication, the moment it was bought it could be sent away at once.

27,949. Do they ever expose the butter on the public thoroughfares and then bring it to the stores?—It is on the public thoroughfare first.

27,950. Do the buyers themselves come from the stores and go round to look at it?—There is only one buyer in the town who has stores. The other buyers have yards. The business people think it a great advantage to themselves to give their yards in order to bring custom to them.

27,951. Did you ever hear objections in the country to exposing the butter?—I never heard complaints.

27,952. Do not they take the lids off the firkins?—No. They have bags to cover them.

27,953. Did you ever hear the butter has deteriorated in quality owing to the heat of the sun?—They are under large trees which give them shade. The buyers know their customers, and they know the people who come with good and bad butter.

27,954. Have you any observations to make that you think would tend to improve the fairs?—We want to get a railway here.

Mr. Michael [illegible] examined.

27,955. You are a farmer?—Yes.

27,956. Did you hear the observations of Mr. Kenny as to the levying of a toll at fairs?—I heard something.

27,957. Did you ever attend fairs at which tolls were levied?—I did. It is a long time ago only in Kilkenny.

27,958. Did you ever sell at fairs other than Kilkenny where tolls were levied?—I did at a great many fairs.

27,959. If a toll is to be levied, do you think it would deter you from going there. I will put it in this way. Supposing you learned two fairs, one being equally as good as the other, but tolls were levied at one and not at the other, the one at which tolls were levied being nearer to you, would you go to the one that was toll-free?—I do not think it would make any difference.

27,960. It would not act as a deterrent on you?—No. I would keep the toll if I could, but I do not think it would prevent me from going to the fair.

27,961. Do you think all the farmers are of the same opinion as yourself?—I think they do not mind. It is so general they do not mind.

27,962. When you are asking the price of an animal, do you ever consider the toll you have paid?—It is never in my mind.

27,963. Do you ever consider the luck-penny you have to give?—No. Some of them give more and others less.

27,964. When asking the price for the animal, do you consider the deductions you have to make from the price that you will get, as luck-penny and toll?—No. I will get the luck-penny back again when I buy.

27,965. The luck-penny on cattle is always left to the disposition of the seller?—Yes, it is according to his generosity.

27,966. On some occasions do not the farmers sell "close to pocket"?—Some of them give a very small luck-penny.

27,967. Do they fix the price and no luck-penny to be given?—That is not in use here at all. There is always a luck-penny.

27,968. Do you remember when cattle were brought here to fairs?—I do, but nothing came of their attendance. They were only brought to one pig fair here in the past time.

27,969. What do you assign as the cause of no cattle fairs being held. Is it the isolated position of Castlecomer?—I think it is the people's own fault that do not stick up to it, and the want of a railway is another great fault.

27,970. Do you think if cattle were brought from time to time to the fairs that it would attract buyers and create demand?—If it was kept up for a few fairs the buyers would come. It must get good publicity.

27,971. Do not you think if the number of cattle passing on to Ballinakill remained in Castlecomer they would make a good fair?—Yes. There is a lot of cattle around this district.

27,972. Do you think a necessity exists in Ballinakill for a fair green with pens and shelter accommodation?—I do not know.

27,973. Speaking generally, do you think it would improve the fairs throughout the country if there was proper accommodation, pens and shelter, in the fair green?—It would make an improvement.

27,974. Would you rather sell your animals in a fair green with pens than out on the public thoroughfare?—If there was a good stand for the cattle and a good shed it would be a great advantage.

27,975. Do you sell pigs here?—No; only small pigs.

27,976. There is no charge whatever on them?—No.

27,977. Do you give any luck-penny?—There does not be much luck on business.

27,978. But you do give something?—Yes, something like a glass of whiskey. If you sold five or six you might give a shilling.

27,979. No fat pigs come here?—No. There are occasionally fat pigs in the fair.

27,980. Is this a large business fair?—No; very small.

27,981. Do they send the fat pigs to the other fairs?—They go to Kilkenny, Ballyragget and Ballinakill.

27,982. Have you any suggestions to offer that would tend to improve the markets and fairs here?—If we had the railway we would have a fair, because it is all cattle in this country. There is very little tillage.

27,983. You think the fairs would be fostered here and the markets developed?—If there was a train coming in we would have a large fair and we would be able to do a good deal of work in it. I am sure of it, because it is out of this much of the cattle go to Ballinakill.

27,984. (Mr. Doyle.) If we had a railway we would have a fair and market.

27,985. (Mr. Richardson.) That is the universal opinion.

Mr. James Doyle re-examined.

27,986. Supposing some people in the town, we will say a labourer or tradesman, went to the market for a small quantity of potatoes such as a stone or half-stone, could he get them?—They never come for that small quantity.

27,987. They buy them from the retailers?—Yes.

27,988. Is this a wholesale market?—Yes.

27,989. The commodities are sold to be subsequently retailed?—They are sold wholesale and retail. There is a time of the year when the new potatoes are brought in and retailed.

27,990. Can the labouring population buy them in small quantities in the market?—There is a certain time of the year they can, in August.

27,991. When the new potatoes come in, how are they sold. Is it by measure or by weight?—By measure and weight. They bring them in carts; some will have scale and some will measure them.

27,992. Are these measures supposed to contain a given quantity?—They are, because the police look after them to see they are right.

27,993. You have no measures for them?—No.

27,994. (The Commissioner to Mr. Kenny.) Do you think the commissioners should have the power to compel all marketable commodities to be confined to one space and be weighed at a public scales?—I do. This court house at one time was the butter market. It was held on the ground floor.

27,995. Was there an extensive market here originally?—It was more extensive than now.

27,996. But this committee have never received any benefit from the market themselves?—No.

27,997. Only the expense they have been at on behalf of the town generally?—That is all.

27,998. How many members are there in the committee?—There are 24 or 25, all the business people of the town.

27,999. Is there any other gentleman who has any observations to make?—No answer.

Inquiry then terminated.

CALLAN.

With reference to my inquiry in Callan on the 17th December 1888, I beg to report as follows:—

Callan is an inland town situate in the county of Kilkenny, and about eight miles from the city. The only means of communication to it is by car. The trade is fair, but is altogether in agricultural produce. The local government is vested in the town commissioners, and the population is 2,340.

The market days in Callan are Tuesday, Wednesday, and Saturdays. The fairs are held on the third Wednesday of each month.

Tolls are levied at the fairs on the entrance of each animal to the fair green. Weighing charges only are levied at the markets, and no rule prevails compelling all commodities to be weighed at the public scales.

The market rights and tolls are the property of the town commissioners of Callan.

There were four patents granted for the town of Callan. The first is dated 12 Edward III. (1339) and authorised the old corporation to take the customs therein specified on each article or commodity named on being brought into the town to be sold. The second is dated 12th February 1668, and authorised the corporation to hold a market on Tuesdays and Saturdays. The third is dated 2nd January 1632 (7 Charles I.) and authorised the corporation to hold two fairs, viz., 29th and 30th June, 10th and 11th August. The fourth patent is dated 22nd July 1790, 30 George III., and authorised the corporation to hold four additional fairs on 4th May, 12th June, 4th November, and 14th December.

Previous to 1861 the tolls levied at the fairs were on each animal actually sold as they left the fair green. In that year, however, the town commission held a meeting to increase the number of fairs, and revise the charges, when the present monthly fairs on the third Wednesday of each month, were established without any express authority.

and the charges somewhat reduced, but to become payable on each animal as they entered the fair green. Before this the fairs were held on the 4th May, 12th June, 10th July, 21st August, 10th October, 4th November, and 14th December.

There is no schedule of the charges erected in the market place or fair green. A weigh-bridge is provided, but it has not the customary railing to make it sufficiently capable of weighing cattle.

According to my instructions I have inspected the market and fair places.

The markets are held on the main street outside the weigh-house. This weigh-house is substantially built, and is utilised principally for weighing purposes, and it is here the beams and scales are erected. It has two entrances from the street. Unsold commodities can be stored there. The building is one story high, and the surface is is paved. There is no shelter or other accommodation for those frequenting the market.

The fairs are held in a large fine fair green adjoining the court-house. It is completely enclosed with a stone wall some five feet high, and has several gate entrances and is seven acres in extent. Between fairs it is utilised for grazing purposes. The surface is level but soft. There are about 40 pens erected for sheep, but there is no shelter accommodation whatever provided. Outside the fair green two sentry boxes are placed, where each farmer, on proceeding to the fair, purchases a ticket for each animal he wishes admitted, and which he subsequently delivers up at the entrance gate. Without these tickets no animals will be permitted into the green.

The evidence shows that the system of charging on entrance seems to work satisfactorily, but the town commission complain that, not being the urban sanitary authority, they are unable to make byelaws, or regulations, or otherwise exercise a controlling influence over the markets and fairs other than the collecting of the charges. The necessity for byelaws regulating the markets and fairs they say is apparent on market and fair days.

The profits derived from the markets and fairs are applied towards the lighting of the town and other municipal purposes. No town rate has been levied for some years.

Appended will be found a transcript of the evidence taken at the inquiry.

JOHN J. O'MEARA,
Assistant Commissioner.

45, Lower Mount Street,
Dublin.

Callan, 17th December 1888.

Mr. Michael Kenwick (town clerk) examined.

28,600. You are the town clerk of Callan?—Yes.

28,601. When was the town commission established here?—I believe in 1854.

28,602. I believe this was an old corporate town?—It was.

28,603. Did the property of the old corporation become vested in the commission when established?—Yes.

28,604. What corporate property have you?—Very little, but we have some. I believe there was a great deal of it leased away.

28,605. You are working under the Act of 1854 at present?—We are.

28,606. Have the Commissioners here any control over the markets and fairs?—Nothing, except the various people pay coming in just as they used to give to the Crown.

28,607. Have they any control over the markets?—Yes, over the market-house, and weights and scales.

28,608. Are there any individuals in Callan exercising any market rights?—No.

28,609. What is the market day?—Wednesdays and Saturdays, and I believe Tuesdays.

28,610. Do you know when the markets were entirely confined to one day in the week at any period?—I believe they were not at any period.

28,611. At present all the marketable commodities are brought in and exposed for sale on each of these three days?—They are exposed every day, but these are the principal days.

28,612. They have been the principal days within your memory?—Yes. There is more sold on days not chartered at all than on the market days, because it is the custom of the town.

28,613. Where are the markets held?—We have a market-house.

28,614. How is the market-house utilised; is it for weighing purposes?—Yes.

28,615. For weighing purposes only?—That is all.

28,616. Commodities are not exposed in it?—No.

28,617. Are they exposed on the street?—They are principally on Saturday. Potatoes are the chief things sold.

28,618. Would you tell me what fairs are held here?—Monthly fairs.

28,619. What day?—The third Wednesday in each month.

28,620. When were these monthly fairs established?—In January 1882.

28,621. Under what authority were they established?—Well, I could not say that.

28,622. What fairs were held previous to 1882?—I believe there were eight fairs. There was a fair on the 4th May, 12th June, 10th July, 21st August, 10th October, 4th November, and 14th December.

28,623. That would be only seven?—Yes.

28,624. There were seven fairs held?—Yes.

28,625. Were charges levied at these seven fairs?—There were. There were only the same charges as at present. The tolls were not levied the same way.

28,626. Were tolls then levied on the animals actually sold at these fairs?—Yes, when coming out.

28,627. Where were the fairs then held?—On the green.

28,628. It was the commissioners who derived the benefit from these charges?—It was.

28,629. Always?—I think so.

28,630. Is this fair green enclosed?—It is.

28,631. Who was it originally provided it?—I believe Lord Clifden enclosed it. He did not wall it in for the purpose of a fair green; he walled it in as a park for Lady Dover. She intended to build a house, and when done the Corporation Act came into force, and they were obliged to surrender the whole of it.

28,032. When did it come into the commissioners' hands first?—Under the ninth of George the Fourth, whatever date that was.

28,033. Since then the corporation have been levying charges?—Yes.

28,034. In 1861 you altered the fairs, or rather you abolished the old fairs, and established new monthly fairs?—Yes.

28,035. And also arranged the payment of the charges?—Yes.

28,036. You have a charge on entrance now?—Yes.

28,037. You do not consider whether the animals are subsequently sold or not?—No.

28,038. Have you got a schedule of the charges you levy?—We have.

28,039. Is it erected on fair days?—It used to be erected, but not latterly.

28,040. The public have no opportunity of inspecting the charges, or the different rates of charges?—No. It does not be up. It used to be formerly, but not at present. The charges are well known, and it was not thought necessary.

28,041. Have you a weigh-bridge capable of weighing cattle?—There can be cattle weighed on it. It is an ordinary large weigh-bridge.

28,042. There are no railings around it to confine the cattle?—No. They were never required.

28,043. Did the farmers ever ask you to weigh cattle, or did you ever weigh cattle?—I was never asked.

28,044. What is the extent of this fair green, I believe about seven acres?—It is between seven and nine acres.

28,045. How do you hold it. Have you the fee-simple of it?—Yes.

28,046. Is Lord Clifden the owner of the town?—Principally.

28,047. He is the lord of the manor?—Yes.

28,048. Did he ever exercise any market rights here?—No, not within my knowledge.

28,049. Or would you have learned from the minutes of the corporation?—No.

28,050. Did he ever exercise any rights?—His agent is Mr. Ryan of Kilfeakle, and he had always the management of everything in his hands. He decided all cases of dispute and everything that way, and the collection of the tolls. He exercises that right all along, but it was as chairman of the corporation.

28,051. What beam and scales have you in this market-house?—An ordinary beam.

28,052. Have you only one?—We have a small one for butter and a large one for potatoes.

28,053. You have only one weigh-bridge?—That is all.

28,054. Who have you employed weighing the commodities on market days?—Mr. Kelly the weigh-master.

28,055. Is this beam and scale ample for the trade of the town?—They are presently.

28,056. You levy weighing charges?—Yes.

28,057. Would you tell me what commodities are brought here on market days?—Nothing but potatoes, and straw and hay to the council. There used to be a good deal of roll butter, but since the creamery was got up that is done away with.

28,058. Is corn brought here?—No.

28,059. No corn at all?—The corn all goes to the private stores. There are five or six private stores in the town and they weigh there themselves. Corn is bought very extensively, but not in the public market.

28,060. Are hay and straw and turnips?—Yes.

28,061. Any vegetables?—No.

28,062. Or fish?—That is sold on the street.

28,063. It comes in?—Yes.

28,064. Does any turf?—Yes.

28,065. Do they bring any cattle or pigs on market day?—We have no pig market at all.

28,066. Or pig fair?—There is a pig market for small pigs but no market for fat pigs. The bonhams are brought in on fair days in creels.

28,067. What charges do you levy at the beam and scales?—A penny for roll butter weighing ten pounds and upwards, and a half-penny for less. A penny for two stone of potatoes and upwards, and a half-penny for less.

28,068. What is the charge at the bridge?—Three halfpence per load.

28,069. Irrespective of the commodity that might be on the load?—Yes.

28,070. Those are the only charges you have?—Yes.

28,071. You have no porterage charges?—No.

28,072. Have you any bye-laws regulating the markets or fairs?—No. We were looking for bye-laws.

28,073. Have you any patent or charter under which you hold the market and fairs?—We have. I believe there is a charter for nearly every day in the week.

28,074. What documents have you here?—This is a patent dated 1638 granting the fairs. (Witness produced the patent.)

28,075-6. Under this charter the corporation within your memory or knowledge never exercised any rights given to them by it?—No.

28,077. Or under any charters or patents to levy tolls at the markets?—I could not say.

28,078. Are the charges you have at the market merely weighing charges, or are they tolls?—They are weighing charges.

28,079. If commodities are brought into the market and exposed for sale, and sold but not weighed at the beam and scales, do you levy any charge?—No.

28,080. You only charge when the beam and scales are availed of?—Yes. There is only a fractional part of the things weighed there at all. They are all weighed about the town.

28,081. Do you know was this alteration in the monthly fairs made under any authority. Did you get the consent of the Local Government Board to it, or did you get any subsequent grant in 1861 from the Privy Council?—I think not. It was on the advice of our own solicitor we established them, relying on the fact that we had a charter for Wednesday.

28,082. You say these charters gave you a right to hold fairs on specific days, but not on the dates you actually hold them at present?—Yes.

28,083. Then the commissioners, I presume, had a meeting in 1861, and deeming it desirable to have additional fairs they voluntarily established them?—I think that was the way it was done.

28,084. Were you in the service of the commissioners at the time?—No, I am only there for the last couple of years.

28,085. You have no storage accommodation provided here in Callan?—No; we have nothing except the market-house.

28,086. That is only availed of for weighing purposes?—That is all.

28,087. Do you erect the beam and scales on the public thoroughfare on market days?—No; they are all inside.

28,088. How do you hold this building?—We hold it in fee.

28,089. Could you tell me the charges you levy at the fairs on entrance?—Two pence on cows, a penny on yearlings, three pence on cars, and a half-penny on sheep.

28,090. What do they bring in the cars?—Generally pigs.

28,091. Anything else?—No.

28,092. No horses are brought here?—There are, and we charge a shilling. They only come to a couple of fairs in the year.

28,093. No matter what the animals are that they bring in carts, or how many, you only charge the three pence?—That is all.

28,094. If any of those bonhams are sold subsequently you do not charge anything additional?—No.

28,095. Is the charge for availing themselves of the fair green?—It is.

28,096. Do they sell elsewhere than in the fair green, do they sell on the public thoroughfare?—They do.

28,097. Do you levy any charge on them?—No.

28,098. Have you any rule restricting the sale of animals elsewhere than on the fair green?—No.

28,099. Does the great majority of the farmers avail themselves of this fair green?—Yes; very little is sold outside, except a day there would be great call for cattle.

28,100. Would there be sufficient space in the fair green?—Lots of space.

28,101. What reason do you assign for their selling on the public thoroughfare?—Some days when there is a rise on cattle the buyers try to get them on the way.

28,102. Practically it is the buyers who intercept the farmers on the way?—Yes, and in some instances, if they crowd out we have the power of removing them off the street for obstructing the roadway. On several occasions we did that.

28,103. How is this fair green utilised between fairs?—For grazing purposes.

28,104. Do you let it for grazing?—No, except for cattle for one night, and to butchers in the town. They pay [illegible] for the use of it for sheep in the year.

28,105. How many pay this?—Two; and the cattle jobbers or from [illegible] or Carrick may stop for one night, and we charge a penny per head.

28,106. If farmers brought cattle the night before the fair would you allow them in?—Yes.

28,107. Would you charge anything?—Yes, a penny per head, but they do not avail themselves of that.

28,108. Where do you collect this entrance charge?—At the gate.

28,109. How many gates have you?—There are six gates on it, but two gates do—the two are together.

28,110. When they are paying this charge, do you give them any ticket or docket?—We do. They get the ticket at the box outside the gate, and they go to the man on the gate and give him the ticket for the number of cattle they have.

28,111. Well, now, does that entrance charge work better at the ordinary fairs than having a charge on the animal actually sold?—I think it is better. There was a great deal of trouble when levying the charge on the cattle actually sold.

28,112. You do not think the payment at entrance is any way causes delay?—I think not.

28,113. What percentage of the animals brought in sold?—I suppose about two-thirds. At one fair this year I heard everything brought in was sold. It is all according to the demand for cattle.

28,114. Did you ever hear any grumbling or complaints by those who did not effect a sale of their animals?—No; they never complain.

28,115. Did you ever hear any complaints from the people who exposed commodities in the market-place that there was no shelter accommodation or protection for the perishable commodities?—No.

28,116. Have you got the balance sheet of the commissioners here?—I have.

28,117. You have not got a copy of it?—This is the last audit made, only a few days ago I prepared the sheet for the last [illegible] years as regards the fairs.

28,118. Are these mentioned in the query about the gate receipts?—Yes.

28,119. You have not made out the expenditure for [illegible]?—No.

28,120. You have here the gate receipts from the fairs last year [illegible]?—Yes.

28,121. And from the house and scales [illegible]?—Yes.

28,122. And from the weighbridge [illegible]?—Yes.

28,123. What did the grazing of the fair green come to last year?—[illegible]

28,124. You have here in another column rents. Are these rents of buildings in connection with the market?—Yes; we built a lot of cottages here, but the rents are not at present paid. They are let at a shilling a week, and after a time they will be paying.

28,125. Are these artisans' dwellings?—They are labourers' dwellings.

28,126. They have nothing to do with the market?—Yes, altogether.

28,127. You have no stalls in the market?—No.

28,128. For butchers or meat dealers?—No.

28,129. Your only expense in connection with the market is Mr. Kelly's salary?—Yes, and another man. We have the scavenger and lamplighter.

28,130. That is not in connection with the fairs?—No.

28,131. Is your only expense Mr. Kelly's salary?—Yes, and the men on the green.

28,132. How do you pay Mr. Kelly?—Ten shillings a week.

28,133. You say you have six men engaged at the fairs?—Yes.

28,134. On an average what do you pay them?—Two shillings a day. That is ten shillings, because I do not include Mr. Kelly. There are five men, and Mr. Kelly.

28,135. How is the profit derived from this applied?—We light the town.

28,136. Then you apply the profits derived from the markets and fairs to municipal purposes?—Yes.

28,137. What are your taxes here?—We have had no taxes for the last six or seven years. We intend to levy a tax now of eightpence in the pound.

28,138. Have you any private income apart from the fairs and markets?—No.

28,139. Is that able to light the town?—It is. Latterly we got a little into debt, but we will levy this rate to meet that.

28,140. Did the commissioners ever contemplate making byelaws to regulate the markets?—They did.

28,141. Did they take any steps to obtain the sanction of the Local Government Board?—We applied to the Local Government Board, and they referred us to the Board of Works, as we were not the sanitary authority.

28,142. Who is the sanitary authority?—The board of guardians.

28,143. It was because you were not the sanitary authority they would not allow you to make the byelaws?—They would not tell us the reason, but said they had no authority in the matter.

28,144. With reference to the corn, would you say a good supply comes into the town?—There is a good supply.

28,145. Could you give any approximate idea of the quantity?—I could not. Mr. Condy is the man who can do that. He is the principal buyer. (*The witness then produced the following statement*):—

Mr. THOMAS KELLY examined.

29,146–7. You weigh marketable commodities at this beam and scales?—Yes.

29,148. When weighing potatoes do you always give a ticket denoting the weight?—I do.

29,149. Do you levy any additional charge for that ticket?—No. There is a penny charged for every barrel of potatoes up to 20 stone, and a halfpenny from 10 stone down.

29,150. If it is over 20 stone, say 21 stone, what do you charge?—Anything over 20 stone is three halfpence.

29,151. Then it is a halfpenny for every 10 stone, or fraction of that?—Yes.

29,152. When giving a ticket denoting the weight do you charge anything for the ticket?—I only charge a penny for weighing the bag.

29,153. Then you charge nothing for the ticket?—No.

29,154. Is it printed?—Yes.

29,155. Do you sign it?—I do.

29,156. What do you put on it; do you put the name of the buyer and seller?—If they require it I do.

29,157. Do you put down the tare of the sack?—I do.

29,158. Do you weigh the sack or estimate it?—I give the gross weight of the sack of potatoes, and let themselves deduct the weight.

29,159. You never estimate the tare, or ascertain it, or put it on the ticket?—No.

29,160. When weighing potatoes what is the smallest weight you weigh down to. If you are weighing a bag of potatoes, the actual weight of which is 19 stone 6 lbs., would you put down 19 stone 6 lbs. as the weight?—Yes.

29,161. Do you put the pound weights into the scales?—I do.

29,162. Is it customary to weigh down to a pound?—Yes. I weigh the gross weight, bag and all.

29,163. When weighing potatoes do you put the pound weight into the scale and weigh down to a pound?—I do.

29,164. Then you have nothing whatever to do with the tare?—No.

29,165. Do you perform the labour of putting the weights into the scales yourself?—I do.

29,166. Who puts the bags of potatoes from the cart into the scales?—There is a man along with me to help me to put in the bags.

29,167. Have the farmers to pay anything for that?—He is considered to help me to put them in.

29,168. The farmers are not compelled to pay any charge?—No, they are not.

29,169. Do you weigh corn at all?—I do.

29,170. What do you charge for weighing corn?—A penny per sack.

29,171. Do you perform any duty in connexion with the tare?—No; I would give the gross weight.

29,172. Do you weigh the loads at the bridge?—Yes.

29,173. Do you give a ticket denoting the weight?—Yes.

29,174. Is it a printed form?—Yes.

29,175. Do you weigh the empty cart?—Yes.

29,176. Always?—Yes.

29,177. How long are you in the service of the commissioners?—I am two years.

29,178. During that period have you ever known any frauds to have been committed in lightening the cart, or changing the wheels after the delivery, and before the cart is brought back to you?—I did not.

29,179. You never had a case of that kind?—No.

29,180. What loads do you weigh?—Sometimes coal, straw, hay, and different commodities.

29,185. Is there any schedule of these charges erected in the weigh-house?—There was, and it was taken out of it.

29,186. There is none erected there now or on the last market day?—No.

29,187. Are all the commodities sold before they are weighed at your beam and scales or scared?—When they come into the market whether they are sold or not I weigh and get paid for them.

29,188. When you weigh a sack of potatoes is that sack of potatoes actually sold before it is brought to you to be weighed?—Sometimes and more times the potatoes are left there until the next market day.

29,189. Has the farmer usually sold the bag of potatoes before he weighs at your scales?—He does not have it sold.

29,190. Must all potatoes come into the market to be weighed at your scales?—They must.

29,191. Whether sold or not?—There are a great many bags of potatoes that do not come in at all.

29,192. You do not receive any charge on them?—No; I could not charge.

29,193. Is there a rule in the market requiring all potatoes to be weighed at the beam and scales?—No.

29,194. I take it you never actually weigh unless they have effected a sale?—That is the case. They present the bag to me and I weigh it.

29,195. When they do present the bag have they previously sold the bag of potatoes?—Sometimes they have and sometimes they have not.

29,196. Do you ever make up their accounts for them?—I do sometimes when they require it.

29,197. In weighing butter, down to what weight do you weigh the roll butter, or in other words do you put the ounce weight into the scales?—I do.

29,198. When weighing butter and potatoes do you give a cast of the beam?—I give them on a balance. I do not think they pay for less than a quarter of butter.

29,199. Do they pay for less than a half-stone of potatoes?—They would if they were new potatoes.

29,200. I mean the old potatoes?—They do not.

29,201. They do not pay for less than a half-stone?—No.

29,202. But you will actually ascertain the weight?—Yes.

29,203. Do you keep any block of these tickets you give?—I do.

29,204. Do you fill them in?—Yes.

29,205. Do you ever copy them into a book?—I do.

29,206. As well as keeping the block?—Yes; there is a block for every ticket.

29,207. Is the quantity given in the block entered into another book?—No; the block is retained.

29,208. So that if they lost the ticket you can always give them another copy?—Yes.

29,209. Would you charge them anything additional?—No, not a halfpenny.

29,210. Have you any opportunity of ascertaining the current prices of the other commodities brought in, such as vegetables, hay, and straw?—I could.

29,211. Do you ascertain the prices of them?—I do.

29,212. Supposing it was required from the commissioners to make a periodical return of the current prices could that be done?—They never required that from me.

29,213. But if the commissioners themselves were required by the Government to make a return of the current prices of the different marketable commodities brought here, could it be done?—The sellers do not generally let me know what they get, or do not get.

29,214. Do not you make up the tickets for the people sometimes?—Yes, in potatoes. It is seldom they make up the tickets themselves.

The following are the tickets given at the [illegible] and scales and weighing machines:—

Callan Butter Market.

No. ______

day of __________ 189

______ lbs.

______________ Weighmaster.

Town Commissioners' Weigh Bridge,

Callan ________ 189

	Tons.	Cwts.	Qrs.	Lbs.
Gross weight,				
Car weight,				
Net weight,				

Description of goods, ______________

From ______________

To ______________

______________ Weighmaster.

Mr. Patrick Grady examined.

29,217. You are the chairman of the town commissioners?—Yes.

29,218. You have some experience of this fair green?—Yes.

29,219. Do you approve of the system adopted here in Callan, since 1861, of levying a charge on all animals as they enter?—I think it is the better way. I was connected with the corporation when we had it, and I remember when they began fighting and quarrelling about the customs. The corporation used to have a lot of men collecting the tolls. They had very serious lawsuits in the superior courts for many years, but when the commissioners were established under the ninth of George the Fourth they adopted the plan of charging on the cattle coming in, and it comes lighter on the people.

29,220. The present charge is always paid by the farmer?—Yes; that was always so.

29,221. On other occasions was not it the buyer who paid on the animals generally sold?—I believe it was going out the charge used to be paid formerly.

29,222. Was not it the buyer who paid the charge in that case?—No; but the seller.

29,223. Was it customary for the seller to remain in possession of the animal until he came out out of the fair?—Yes, I think he used to go and put up in some yard. There was a gang of men at the gate, and they would ask, "Did you buy or sell," and if the animal was not branded they would swear him.

29,224. Was it to avoid that confusion you levied the charge on entrance?—Yes.

29,225. Was that the principal cause?—Yes. It is easier on the people and more agreeable, and it gives them some value for their money. It is a very low charge now, and at that time it was very high.

29,226. The charges were somewhat considerably higher than they are at present?—Yes, the charge was 6d. on a cow then.

29,227. You have no shelter accommodation in this fair green?—No.

29,228. Have you any pens?—Yes; pens for sheep.

29,229. What number of pens have you?—About 40.

29,230. Did you ever hear the farmers agitating for shelter in the fair green?—They never asked to my knowledge.

29,231. Were any representations made to the town commissioners that it was necessary?—No.

29,232. Do you think the proper place to hold the markets is on the public streets, or do you think it would tend to improve the markets of Callan if there was a proper market building, with shelter accommodation, and a rule restraining the exposure of commodities elsewhere than in this market building?—I think the markets are getting on very well. They have worked well up to this. I am afraid these changes may be very dangerous. This place is not important enough to go to the expense of building a big market, but yards or sheds would be very useful.

29,233. Is there much of the surrounding country in tillage?—It was a tillage district, but they are laying everything into grass now.

29,234. What percentage of the acreage is in tillage?—I have no idea.

29,235. Have you had any experience of fairs and markets other than those in Callan?—Yes; in Kilkenny and Carlow.

29,236. You have experience of places where tolls are levied and where they are not?—There are tolls levied at Ballyragget, near us.

29,237. I am asking a general question. From your knowledge of the farmers, do you think the exaction of a toll on marketable commodities brought to the market acts in any way as a deterrent on the people bringing in a supply they would otherwise bring in?—No; it does not here.

29,238. But you have no toll here?—There is a charge for weighing.

29,239. Do you think if a toll were levied on all commodities, would it deter the people from bringing them into the market, or would it injure the market?—To be sure it would.

29,240. Supposing there was this shelter accommodation provided, and proper market buildings erected, so as to afford protection to any perishable commodity they bring in, as well as protection for themselves from the rain, do you think they would be willing to pay a small charge to maintain that building?—I believe they would pay it for the convenience of a shed in that way.

29,241. That is if they got an adequate return?—Yes, if they found it was not levied for the purpose of exaction.

29,242. You consider they would have no objection to pay a small charge if they got an adequate return for it?—I am satisfied they would not.

29,243. You find that experience in the fair green, where they pay it?—Yes.

29,244. Did you ever hear complaints from those who did not effect a sale, that they had to pay?—No, as a rule I might have heard one.

29,245. Are the fairs well attended here?—The fairs are very well attended. They are very good.

29,246. Did the commissioners ever make up any return of the number of the different species of animals brought into the fairs?—They have that on their tickets. There is a most important market, and the people are very badly off for a shelter. That is the fowl market.

29,247. Are any tolls levied on the fowl brought in?—No.

29,248. On market days do clothes-dealers come here and erect standings about the town?—No. The people of the town may have some little things. No strangers come except on fair days.

29,249. Do they stand out on the public thoroughfare?—They do on the side of the road.

29,250. There is nothing payable by them?—No.

29,251. Do you know have those people hawker's licenses?—The police look after that, and are pretty sharp in looking after it too.

29,252. Do they always have licenses?—Yes, the police sergeant says.

29,253. Have you any observations to make, or suggestions to offer as to what would tend to the improvement of the markets in Callan, or what you would like to see performed?—The only thing is in our byelaws for the regulation of the market, we have no power now. They sometimes come in the middle of the night with fowl and buy in the dark, and it is very objectionable to buyers and sellers, and the people complain very much. Some poor people coming in with fowl may have them picked from them, and they cannot identify them in the dark with other fowl. The byelaws do not give us the power to regulate the hour for holding the market. There is some little power of settling disputes as it is, but it might be made more clear, and other few things of that kind.

29,254. What is the usual hour for the market to commence?—There is no fixed hour.

28,255. What hour does it usually commence?—About four o'clock in the morning.

28,256. I do not mean the fowl market, but the general market?—About six o'clock in the morning.

28,257. What hour does it terminate?—12 or 1 o'clock.

28,258. Up to what hour does the fowl market last?—From 4 or 5 up to 7 o'clock.

28,259. Where is this fowl market held?—On the streets of the town.

28,260. Did you ever hear any complaints of forestalling, that is the buyers going out and intercepting the people on the road?—Certainly. The buyers go out forestalling and that is an objectionable thing. It would be a matter of the greatest regularity if we had the power to prevent anyone buying or selling until all were assembled in the market.

28,261. Do you think if such a power was given to the commissioners, and all the commodities concentrated in a particular spot, that the farmers would get a better price for the fowls, if there was the ordinary competition among the buyers?—I am sure many do get cheated in the forestalling system.

28,262. Is that practice relative to fowl alone?—Yes. In the other markets the commodities are sold every hour of the day, and delivered every hour at the private stores. The people go around with their samples and sell, and afterwards deliver the commodity.

28,263. Have you any further suggestions to make?—No.

28,264. Do you weigh the corn you purchase yourself?—Yes.

28,265. It has not been previously weighed by the farmer?—I do not know.

28,266. Do you levy any charge for weighing that corn?—Not at all.

28,267. Did you ever hear the farmers complaining of the owners of private stores weighing themselves?—No.

28,268. Do you think it would be better and would lead to greater more confidence between buyers and sellers if all marketable commodities, corn included, were weighed at a public and independent scale?—It would be better for the buyer, because it would save him a good deal of trouble.

28,269. Do you think there would be more confidence between the buyer and seller if that rule were pursued?—Of course there would be more disinterested persons weighing it, but the people are satisfied with the weighing in the stores.

28,270. In weighing corn, what weight do you weigh down to?—Down to a pound.

28,271. Do you pay for a pound?—Yes.

28,272. Is it by the barrel you buy it?—Yes.

28,273. If under the barrel and weighed in the sack, you only pay for the weight?—There is no deduction from the weight.

28,274. If over a barrel is in the sack do you give the seller the proportionate value?—Yes. I pay him for what he has. I would pay him a halfpenny.

28,275. Do you estimate the tare of the sack?—We weigh the sack.

28,276. You always weigh the sack?—Certainly.

28,277. Could you give any idea of the quantity of corn brought here and sold?—No; there are so many buying. They got very much out of the wheat trade I think this year, and it was the principal thing here. They have not sold much oats this year. The forestalling in the fowl is very objectionable.

28,278. Do you think it enhances the value of the fowl, that is, if the forestallers who buy them combine together?—I do not think there is any intention that way at all.

28,278a. There are none of the animals sold in the town?—No.

28,279. They are all exported?—Yes. Whether the price is enhanced or not, I could not say, but the magistrates interfered in a town near Waterford to stop a fowl market that used to commence at 12 o'clock at night, and half the fowl of the country used to be stolen, and no one could identify them; and when they came here about 4 o'clock in the morning they have the same opportunity.

28,280. Do you think it gives an opportunity of selling stolen fowl?—Yes.

28,281. Did you hear any complaints in that way?—No.

Mr. Thomas Shelley examined.

28,282. Do you concur in the opinion expressed by Mr. Condy, that a necessity exists for the shelter accommodation in the fowl market?—It would be desirable.

28,283. Did the commissioners never consider it necessary to erect such?—They did frequently, but they have not the means.

28,284. Then it is only a financial difficulty that is restraining them from erecting such accommodation?—That is all. It is a great necessity for the buyers, because they are obliged to leave the fowl—valuable fowl at some seasons of the year—exposed to the rain, and it injures the fowl.

28,285. What reason do you assign for the fowl market being held in the morning. Is it to convenience the buyers so that they can catch trains?—That cannot be because on different occasions of late years, and even up to last week they entered into a resolution that they would not buy until a certain time in the market, and then a stranger came and bought before the hour fixed. It was violated the first day.

28,286. Was this a rule made by the buyers themselves?—Yes.

28,287. As a rule is the butter exposed on the street?—Roll butter is a thing of the past.

28,288. When it did come in was it sold on the public street?—No; but in the market-house, and weighed in the market-house.

28,289. Supposing they do not effect the sale of a commodity on market-day, can you store it until the following day?—The potatoes can be stored.

28,290. Is that in the market-house?—Yes.

28,291. What charge is levied?—No charge.

28,292. Do you think it would be advisable to have a general market building, and confine the sale and exposure of all commodities to this building, and take them off the public thoroughfare?—It is doubtful in a place like this. The Kilkenny people make complaints of the charges in Kilkenny when some of them came to sell corn here as they did this year.

28,293. Have you ever bought or sold at the fairs?—Yes.

28,294. Have they got the system of luck-penny here?—Yes.

28,295. Is there any rule regulating the amount of it?—No.

28,296. It is always left to the disposition of the seller?—Yes.

28,297. It is customary to give it?—Yes.

28,298. Do you think when they are fixing the price of the animal that they take into consideration the amount of the luck-penny subsequently given?—Not at all. It does not affect the sale much.

28,299. When arguing about the price of an animal do they ever come to the conclusion to sell it at a certain price "clear to pocket," that is, taking a certain price, and giving no luck-penny?—That occurs sometimes.

28,300. Do they then consider the luck-penny in fixing the price of the animal?—The luck-penny is a small thing.

28,301. Have they any fixed luck-penny on pigs?—I do not think there is.

28,302. You do not sell or buy any?—We have no fat pig fair here at all.

Mr. Thomas Walsh examined.

28,303. (Witness.) If we had railway accommodation we would have a fat pig fair. It deprives us of a good pig fair and horse fair. The nearest railway is 10 miles away. It has affected the corn trade too, for it costs the corn buyers a good deal to send the corn away to the nearest station, and it hinders them in a great account that they cannot put out the quantity that they want on account of the cartage.

18,304. Have you had experience of fairs in other towns besides Callan?—Not many.

18,305. Have you attended fairs held on the public street?—I have. I remember attending fairs in Kilkenny that were held on the public streets.

18,306. Do you think it would be more satisfactory for buyers and sellers if the fairs were held in a properly enclosed fair green?—A fair green is the proper place. The buyer or seller would prefer a fair green to the streets or anywhere else.

18,307. You prefer buying there?—I do undoubtedly.

18,308. Were the fairs ever held here on the street?—No. There was an old fat pig fair on the street.

18,309. When did that fair fall into abeyance?—It was the railway did away with it.

18,310. The cattle fairs were always held in the present fair green?—Yes, so far as I know.

18,311. Do you concur in the opinion of Mr. Grady, that if a proper market building was erected here with shelter accommodation, and a rule restricting the sale of commodities elsewhere than in this market building, that the farmers would willingly pay a small charge for the accommodation afforded?—I do not think they would willingly.

18,312. If they got an adequate return?—They do not think they would get an adequate return; some of them might. It is one out of twenty who would rather get the butter weighed at a public scales than a private one.

18,313. I am speaking about the shelter?—I thought it was about the butter market.

18,314. Do you think you could foster a butter market if there was proper shelter accommodation?—I think the butter market is a thing of the past.

18,315. At present they go about the streets in the heat of the sun in summer time?—The butter goes into the weigh-house.

18,316. Are not the butter and potatoes near each other there?—While we had the butter coming in at one time the butter market was held by itself until it died away when the railway was brought into other towns about. There is no butter-making now in the surrounding country as all the milk goes to the creameries.

18,317. What is the output of these?—There are two creameries in the town, and one within a mile of the town. There are seven or eight within a radius of six or seven miles. With regard to the question of accommodation I think the buyers would pay, but I do not think the public would pay unless on a wet day. On a fine day they prefer to be let out on the street. I do not think it would be their wish to go in. There is one thing with regard to the fowl. The buyers complain they have no power to fix the hour. There are some four or five large buyers, who come here throughout the year every market day. There are three months of the year the fowl become scarce, and a number of strangers come in and commence to buy as early as three o'clock in the morning. The constant buyers complain of that.

18,318. Is the fowl exported?—Yes, and the buyers complained very much that when they supported the market the whole year the strangers were allowed to come at an unreasonable hour, three o'clock in the morning in summer, and buy the fowl when they were scarce; if that continued they threatened to resign coming here, and they wanted to fix an hour that no fowl could be bought before it. The commissioners feel it a grievance that they have not the power to make bye-laws regulating the market and the hours at which they would commence.

18,319. Is there any other gentleman who has any evidence to give?—No answer.

18,320. *The town clerk handed in the following statement at the termination of the inquiry:—*

RECEIPTS at FAIRS and MARKETS by CALLAN TOWN COMMISSIONERS since 1868.

—	Fairs.			Market Tolls.			Weigh-house.			Cramer Fair Green.		
	£	s.	d.	£	s.	d.	£	s.	d.	£	s.	d.
1868	54	8	6	13	9	9	8	7	5	11	17	4
1869	65	10	5	11	7	11	4	0	11	10	1	8
1870	56	4	5	10	11	9	9	11	8	[illegible]	4	6
1871	59	4	1	15	16	7	8	1	10	19	11	7
1872	55	8	4	12	11	6½	4	19	8	[illegible]	10	0
1873	[illegible]	6	5	8	10	7	4	1	2	25	10	0
1874	60	1	10	8	10	4	4	14	7	23	11	9
1875	60	7	10	8	9	10	4	4	1	[illegible]	1	4½
1876	79	11	5	15	11	10	4	19	4	19	10	0
1877	75	12	1	16	14	6	8	8	10	17	6	3
1878	76	19	5	8	15	4	8	10	1	[illegible]	8	0
1879	76	12	10	8	8	6	4	[illegible]	8	[illegible]	17	6
1880	46	12	0	7	11	1	4	14	8	19	8	8
1881	60	8	4	10	18	8	6	8	8	15	0	1
1882	66	6	5	7	0	0	1	16	11	15	8	0
1883	60	8	7	6	10	6	4	16	1	15	16	4
1884	70	11	4	7	10	1	7	9	1	[illegible]	0	9
1885	[illegible]	13	10	6	9	0	9	1	10	10	8	8
1886	[illegible]	8	0	4	10	11	7	1	9	15	19	5
1887	[illegible]	13	7	9	1	9	9	8	1	10	7	1

The inquiry then terminated.

DUNGARVAN.

With reference to my inquiry in Dungarvan on the 19th day of December 1888, I beg to report as follows:—

Dungarvan is a maritime town situate on the Bay of Dungarvan and in the county of Waterford. It is a station on the Waterford, Dungarvan, and Lismore Railway line. The export trade is chiefly in agricultural produce and stock. A board of Town Commissioners administer the local affairs, and the population is 7,391.

The butter market day is Tuesday. The fish, meat, and general market day is Saturday. The fairs are held on the third Wednesday of each month. A pig fair is held on the day previous to the ordinary fairs.

Tolls are levied at the butter, fish, and meat markets, and previous to this year tolls were always levied at the general market, but at the beginning of the year those frequenting the market resisted the payment of any tolls whatsoever. Legal proceedings were instituted for the recovery of the tolls, but the magistrates refused to give a decree on the ground, it is stated, that no market accommodation was provided. Weighing charges are, however, levied on any commodities weighed.

The tolls at the fish market are collected every day in the week, and those at the meat market are practically stallage rents. The fairs are toll free.

The market rights and tolls are the property of the Town Commissioners of Dungarvan, who hold under a special Act intituled "The Dungarvan Harbour, Markets, and Improvement Act, 1863" (26 Vict. c. 14). This Act is divided into five parts, the second of which contains the provision relating to the markets in the town. The preamble states that "it is expedient to vest in the Commissioners incorporated by this Act the "lands and premises granted as aforesaid by the said Duke of Devonshire to the said "Richard Garde Hudson in trust for the Commissioners, and to enable the Commis-"sioners to extend the said markets and to confer upon them all necessary powers for "regulating and controlling the markets in the town of Dungarvan." Section 23 incorporates the "Market and Fairs Clauses Act, 1847," with the special Act, with the exception of sections 12, 13, 22, and 60.

The meat and fish markets and the general market square, granted by the Duke of Devonshire, are vested absolutely in the Town Commissioners under section 24, and section 25 restricts the operation of the Act to the limits of the town.

Section 26 makes it lawful for the Commissioners to manage, regulate, and improve the markets and to erect stalls and other accommodation, and compulsory power to acquire certain lands for market purposes is given them by section 27. Section 28 restricts the sale of tollable articles elsewhere than in markets, and by section 29 weighing and measuring at the Commissioners' weights and measures is made compulsory on those selling or offering goods for sale in Commissioners' markets. Section 30 enables the Commissioners to collect the tolls mentioned in Schedule B. to the Act, and by section 31 the appointment of general weighmaster or of butter taster was to vest in the Commissioners on the next vacancy.

There were two patents granted for the town of Dungarvan. The first is dated 4th January 1609, and authorised the old corporation to hold two fairs on June 11th and 28th October and two days following each and a Wednesday market. The second patent is dated 24th January, 30 George III., and authorised the Duke of Devonshire to hold two fairs on 7th February and 27th August, and a Wednesday and Saturday market.

The butter market was established by the Town Commissioners some 30 years ago, and about the same period some of the traders in the town and the Town Commissioners established the present monthly fairs and ceased holding those formerly established. No express authority was granted for the fairs.

In 1872 the Town Commissioners obtained a loan of 800l., and in 1873 a loan of an additional 200l. for the purpose of erecting a town hall, offices, and butter market building. 200l. only of these two sums were secured on the market rates, but the aggregate loans were paid off altogether some years back.

The Commissioners are in the immediate receipt of the tolls of the butter and meal markets. The fish market tolls are sublet to a Mr. Roger Lyons as yearly tenant at 1l. a year, and the machines, beams, and scales and tolls at the general market are sublet to a Mr. Maurice Walsh at 40l. a year. The latter tolls, as herein-before mentioned, are not now collected.

The Commissioners themselves hold the site of the butter market from a Mr. Sheahan at 14l. 10s. a year under a lease which will expire in 1889.

There is no statutable provision regulating the application of the net profits of the market rights. The course, however, the Commissioners adopt is after payment of expenses to apply 45l. towards the road rate account, and 45l. towards the improvement rate, and to allow the balance to accumulate. The present accumulation is about 200l., which it is said will form the nucleus of a fund to erect a general market building.

In accordance with my instructions I have inspected the markets and fairs places.

The butter market is held in the basement of the town hall, opening towards the public street. It is entirely enclosed, spacious, and apparently affords sufficient accommodation for those frequenting it. The floor is flagged throughout with a small and necessary incline down towards the pathway to allow the water consequent upon the draining of the firkins to run off. The building has three gate entrances, and in

These are small and unlet. At the rear there are two rows of stalls facing each other and roofed with slate. At each end there is a gate entrance. Although this accommodation is provided, the vendors seem to prefer the harbour side to expose the fish, as the market is little availed of. The space, however, is confined, and from the accumulation of fish remnants a nauseous smell arises.

The general market is held on what is called the market square. This is a large square space in the centre of the town, and is portion of the public thoroughfare. A large wooden structure is erected in the centre of the square, where a number of scales and two weighing machines are erected. On market and fair days a number of standings are placed here, where sundry marketable commodities are exposed for sale. A schedule of the charges granted by the special Act is erected on the weigh-house for public inspection. None of the weighing machines have the customary railings around them to make them available for the accurate weighing of live stock.

The fairs are held on the square previously described and on the different streets of the town. No shelter or other accommodation whatever is provided, neither is any control exercised over them by the local authority. At the time of inspection the fairs were being held, and so far as I could see, a great obstruction to traffic existed both on the roadside and pathway. Both were occupied with animals, and gave the streets a nasty and unpleasant appearance. Around each animal were a knot of men bargaining about the price, and the passers-by were put to much inconvenience and trouble in endeavouring to effect a passage to their destination.

There are no byelaws regulating the markets other than the provisions contained in the special Act.

Although a butter tester is appointed for the butter market he has practically no duties to perform in that respect, as the merchants are inclined to rely more on their own experience in classifying the butter than an independent inspection.

Appended will be found a transcript of the evidence taken at the inquiry.

JOHN J. O'MEARA,
Assistant Commissioner.

45, Lower Mount Street, Dublin.

Dungarvan, 19th December 1888.

Mr. Michael Barry, Acting Town Clerk, examined.

28,321. You are acting town clerk of Dungarvan?—Yes.

28,322. Have the Commissioners control of the markets and fairs here?—They have, according to a special Act of 1855.

28,323. Previous to that Act had they control of them?—They had, but I see, according to the minutes dated 1826, the Commissioners memorialed his Grace the Duke of Devonshire to grant them the right to the meat shambles, fish shambles, fruit shambles, and butter weigh-house, as they enjoyed a similar privilege under his Grace's predecessors for a long series of years.

28,324. Did they obtain those rights from the Duke of Devonshire?—The Commissioners, in the address presented to him in 1850, thanked him for the recent gift conferred on the town by those extensive markets, which were so great a boon to the inhabitants. It is referred to in the preamble of the Act.

28,325. They got the meat, fish, vegetable, and butter market?—They did not get the butter market—the old butter market—at the time.

28,326. Subsequent to that they obtained a special Act. Did this Act invest them with the meat, fish, vegetable, and butter markets?—It does not invest them with a special market-house, but conferred on them the power of taking up buildings, and converting them into a butter market, which they did.

28,327. What is the market day here?—Tuesday is the butter-market day; Saturday is the general market; and there is a pig market the third Tuesday of each month. The fairs are held on the third

28,331. Was it since the passing of the special Act in 1855?—It was before that. It is, as I have said, over 30 years since the Tuesday's market was established.

28,332. When did you establish these monthly fairs?—They are a long time established; longer than I remember.

28,333. (The Commissioner to Mr. McCarthy.) Do you remember when there were other fairs besides the monthly fairs?—Yes, two yearly, one in June and the other on the 9th November.

28,334. Were there only the two?—That is all.

28,335. Previous to the monthly fairs?—Yes. The monthly fairs are in existence more than 30 years. Previous to the monthly fairs, about 40 years ago, I remember as far back as that, there was a pig market every Saturday, and it was largely attended by the Waterford buyers.

28,336. You could not tell me on what date the monthly fairs were established?—We will be able to ascertain that for you.

28,337. (To Mr. Barry.) Do you know under what authority the monthly fairs were established?—I do not.

28,338. Did the corporation obtain a patent from the Crown for them?—A corporate body was not in existence.

28,339. When were they established?—They were established from 35 to 40 years ago. The dates of the fairs were arranged so as not to clash with other towns.

28,340. I want to know under what authority they were established. Did they voluntarily establish them

22,343. Is it entirely enclosed ?—It is roofed and comprises the town hall and meat market. It is 130 feet by 40 feet, with stalls surrounded by walls and enclosed.

22,344. Is it covered ?—The stalls are covered.

22,345. How many stalls have you there ?—About a dozen, and seven of them are let. There is a fish market enclosed also.

22,346. Is the fish market used ?—It is partly used. It is used for the fish exported.

22,347. Is the fish market enclosed ?—Part of it is enclosed. Portion of the street near the quay and adjoining the fish market is more generally used for the sale of fish.

22,348. Is it outside the fish market ?—Yes.

22,349. Is the fish market on the quay ?—Yes. The portion enclosed is the portion given by the Duke of Devonshire to the Commissioners.

22,350. What other markets have you ?—The square is used for vegetable stalls, straw and [illegible] of kinds ; 320 feet by 170 is the extent of the square.

22,351. Is the square portion of the public thoroughfare ?—The public thoroughfare partly. The main thoroughfare runs through it from Bridge Street to the upper portion of the town.

22,352. What other markets have you ?—That is all. The butter market is 80 feet by 40 feet with offices attached. There are two weighing machines on the square.

22,353. What beam and scales have you ?—One beam and scales. I believe Mr. Walsh is the lessee of the tolls.

22,354. The Commissioners are not in the immediate receipt of the tolls ?—They are not.

22,355. They have them sublet ?—Yes.

22,356. To whom ?—To Mr. Michael Walsh.

22,357. On what terms ?—At present the rent is reduced to 40l. It used to be, six or seven years ago, 80l. and 82l.

22,358. Does he hold under lease ?—He does.

22,359. For what term ?—For one year at present. It used to be three years.

22,360. Have you got any written agreement with him ?—We have a bond in the office of the Town Commissioners, but it is not here.

22,361. How do you let them. Is it by tender ?—By tender.

22,362. You got the amount of the tender secured ?—No. In March this year, according to the minutes, the Town Commissioners having discussed the letting of the market tolls at full length, it was ordered, first, that for the present the Commissioners decided not to go to the expense of getting up a special market place ; second, that advertisements be issued for tenders for the [illegible] of the market tolls in the square for one year with all appurtenances to the highest bidder, the usual terms to be paid, also the premises to be kept in order by the Town Commissioners. Mr. Walsh's tender was 44l. for one year.

22,363. What is the valuation of these buildings and the tolls of them ?—[illegible] at present. It used to be higher. The Town Commissioners in 1867 resolved to assess all parties bringing fowl, &c. for sale on the street. They got summonses to [illegible] against all parties who refused to pay tolls on such matters as rolls of butter and fowl, but they were defeated at the petty sessions.

22,364. Do you know on what ground they failed ?—The reason was they had not a special market place erected for these special articles, and that was the cause of the reduction of the rent from 80l. to 40l.

22,365. Is the butter market used exclusively for firkin butter ?—Yes.

22,366. Then the roll butter is sold indiscriminately about the streets of the town ?—Yes.

22,367. Where are the fairs held ?—The cattle fair is held on the square and down Bridge Street.

22,368. Where is the pig fair held ?—All through the streets and on the square.

22,369. And the sheep ?—On the street ; partly on the square and partly in Bridge Street. The crush of young pigs are sold in William Street and Blackpool. The horse fair is held on the quay and around the fish market.

22,370. In this fish market you say there are stalls ?—Yes.

22,371. Are the rates you levy at them outside the rates specified under this Act ?—They are not so high as that.

22,372. You have amended the schedule of the Act by reducing the charges ?—Yes, they are reduced very much so far as standings are concerned. This is a copy of the Act, and the tolls, and Mr. Walsh will tell you what he charges for standings of fowl and such matters.

22,373-4. Have you got a copy of these charges erected in the market place ?—Yes.

22,375. For public inspection ?—Yes.

22,376. The fairs are toll free ?—Yes.

22,377. Do the Commissioners exercise any control whatsoever over them ?—Not a bit.

22,378. Was it ever represented to them to provide a fair green ?—Not that I am aware. The former fairs used to be held half a mile outside the town.

22,379. They were always held on the street ?—It is a bye street, partly the country road.

22,380. Was it outside the limits of the town ?—Not outside the limits ; within the present limits of the town, at all events. I am informed that Mr. Hudson's father had control of the tolls, and had a toll house erected out at the bridge at the time, fifty years ago. Mr. Hudson is mentioned in the special Act.

22,381. You have all the market rights in regard to the commodities sold in the streets or in the market buildings let to Mr. Walsh ?—Yes.

22,382. You levy no rents on the market buildings other than this 40l. a year ?—No. We have all the fairs and markets let to Mr. Walsh.

22,383. The witness produced an account for three years, of which the following is a copy :—

1883.		£	s.	d.	1884.		£	s.	d.
Dec. 31 -	To balance from ledger -	173	1	6	Dec. 31 -	By salaries - - -	115	17	4
"	" market tolls contract -	66	7	8	"	" poundage, rent collector -	1	4	6
"	" rent of small market -	12	5	9	"	" premium, late clerk -	15	15	0
"	" plays in town hall -	8	7	9	"	" printing and advertising -	6	19	8
					"	" rent of hall and market -	12	14	11
					"	" rates and taxes - -	23	4	8
					"	" repairs to hall and market	69	14	1
					"	" gas account of hall -	6	8	6
					"	" insurance - - -	3	16	6
					"	" auditing and miscellaneous - - -	13	3	4
					"	" arrears transfer - -	15	8	6
					"	" balance - - -	90	15	8
		£370	1	8			£370	1	8

1885.		£	s.	d.	1886.		£	s.	d.
Dec. 31 -	To balance from ledger -	184	11	10	Dec. 31 -	By salaries - - -	140	1	8
"	" hire of town hall -	84	7	6	"	" superannuation - -	10	16	7
"	" rent of meat market -	19	13	10	"	" audit of accounts - -	8	0	0
"	" " fish market -	1	0	0	"	" gas for town hall - -	3	5	10
"	" " market square -	68	8	5	"	" printing, stationery, and advertising - -	13	8	5
					"	" law costs - - -	8	3	4
					"	" inspectors - - -	5	10	0
					"	" annual transfer to road surveyor - - -	15	0	0
					"	" repairs of hall and market houses - - -	7	18	5
					"	" rent, rates, and taxes -	60	19	10
					"	" incidental - - -	4	19	8
					"	" balance - - -	41	1	10
		£358	15	6			£358	15	6

The following was also handed in by the witness:—

Schedule of Market Tolls being copy of Schedule "B" to the Special Act showing the Charges granted by the Special Act and the Charges actually levied.

Description.	Amount allowed by Special Act.	Amounts levied.
	s. d.	
For every barrel of grain, corn, or seeds, and rateably for a greater or lesser quantity.	0 1½	Not levied.
For every ton of flax, wool, and bark - - - - - -	0 6	Not levied.
For every firkin, tub, barrel, or cask of butter not exceeding 112 lbs. -	0 3	1d.
For every firkin, tub, barrel, or cask of butter exceeding 112 lbs. - -	0 4	Not levied.
For every basket, parcel, or quantity of butter not less than 14 lbs. weight	0 1	Not levied.
For every cartload of hay or straw - - - - - -	0 4	Not levied.
For every cartload of clover, grass, rape, rye, vetches, or other green food for cattle.	0 3	Not levied.
For every cartload of mangold wurzel, turnips, and all other agricultural produce whatever, save and except potatoes.	0 3	Not levied.
For every cartload of fruit or potatoes or any other vegetables - -	0 3	Not levied.
For every cartload of fish or eggs - - - - - -	0 3	No charge on eggs, 3d. per cartload, and 1d. per basket on fish.
For every cartload of coal, iron, or other mineral - - - -	0 6	Not levied.
For every ton of hides or skins, salted or green, and rateably for a greater or lesser quantity not less than 56 lbs.	0 10	Not levied.
For every basket of live fowl containing not more than two pairs - -	0 1	Not levied.
For every additional pair - - - - - - -	0 0½	Not levied.
For every load or kish of fowl containing not more than six pairs - -	0 3	Not levied.
For every additional pair - - - - - - -	0 0½	Not levied.
For every two pairs of rabbits or wild fowl - - - - -	0 0½	Not levied.

Description.	Amount allowed by Special Act.	Amounts levied.
	s. d.	
Provisions and Vegetable Market and Outside Market Tolls.		
From the occupier of every enclosed shop or stall, whether for sale of butcher's meat, game, poultry, fish, vegetables, cheese, fruit, china, glass, earthenware, baskets, hardware, or other commodities, articles, or things, according to the size and dimensions of such shop, namely, for each lineal foot of the frontage thereof, if let by the week, any weekly rate not exceeding	2 0	Not levied.
From every person occupying or using any butcher's stall or standing or any ground space for the sale of meat, according to the size and dimensions of the same, namely, for each lineal foot of frontage of every such stall, standing, or ground space occupied by him, if let by the week, any weekly sum not exceeding	1 0	At meat market 1s. per week per stall of about [illegible] feet wide. At fish market [illegible] per week per slab of [illegible] feet long.
If let by the day, any daily rate not exceeding	0 6	Not levied.
For every carcass or part of a carcass of a bull, bullock, cow, steer, heifer, calf, sheep, or pig brought into the market to be disposed of otherwise than by sale by retail, and whether sold or not, any sum not exceeding	0 [illegible]	[illegible] on every carcass of a bull, &c. 1d. per carcass of each sheep, &c.
For every hide or skin, raw, undressed, or dressed brought into the market for sale, and whether sold or not, any sum not exceeding	0 [illegible]	Not levied.
From every person occupying or using any stall, standing, cart, barrow, basket, pad, box, bench, or barrel for the sale of vegetables, provisions, fruit, fish, game, poultry, china, glass, earthenware, baskets, hardware, or other commodities, articles, or things according to the size and dimensions of the same, viz., for each superficial square foot and fractional part of a superficial square foot of the ground space covered or occupied by any such stall, standing, cart, barrow, basket, pad, box, bench, or barrel, any sum not exceeding, for every day	0 1	Not levied.
From every person occupying or using any space on the surface of the ground, according to the size and dimensions of the same, viz., for each superficial square foot and the fractional part of a superficial square foot of the ground space occupied or used by him, any daily sum not exceeding	0 [illegible]	Not levied.
Slaughter-house Tolls.		
For every bull, bullock, cow, steer, or heifer, not exceeding	2 0	Not levied.
For calf, not exceeding	1 0	
For every sheep or lamb, not exceeding	0 [illegible]	
For every pig, not exceeding	0 [illegible]	
For any other beast, not exceeding	2 0	
Weighing and Measuring Tolls.		
For weighing every piece of meat, or any article or thing, not being a cart or waggon, weighing not exceeding [illegible] lbs. avoirdupois	0 [illegible]	On potatoes [illegible] up to [illegible] stone; 1d. over [illegible] stone and under 14 stone; [illegible] over 14 stone. On corn [illegible] per bag or barrel. Roll butter [illegible] up to [illegible] lbs.; 1d. over [illegible] lbs. and under 14 lbs.; [illegible] over 14 lbs. and under [illegible] lbs.; [illegible] over [illegible] lbs.
If weighing more than [illegible] lbs. and not exceeding 140 lbs.	0 1	
If exceeding 140 lbs., then for every additional 140 lbs. or fractional part of 140 lbs., not exceeding	0 1	
For measuring every quantity of goods and things sold by measure, not exceeding one bushel	0 [illegible]	Not levied.
If exceeding one bushel and not exceeding two bushels	0 1	
And for every bushel and fractional part of a bushel beyond two bushels	0 [illegible]	

The following are the charges on the weighing machines:—

On every carload of timber weighed, [illegible] per ton.

On every carload of hay, straw, turnips, or other commodity weighed, [illegible] up to [illegible] cwt., [illegible] over [illegible] cwt., and under [illegible] cwt., [illegible] over [illegible] cwt.

[illegible]. You could not give me 1886 and 1887?—No.

[illegible]. Had you the market rights sublet in [illegible]?—Yes.

[illegible]. You have here butter [illegible] [illegible] [illegible] [illegible]?—We have the control of the butter market in our own hands; and rent of the meat market, [illegible]. We charge 1s. a week for stalls.

[illegible]. You had them sublet?—We had.

[illegible]. Have you them sublet?—We have.

[illegible]. You have not parted with control of the butter market or meat market?—No.

[illegible]. Have you parted with the fish market to Mr. Walsh?—We have the fish market tolls let to Roger Lyons for [illegible] a year.

[illegible]. Is it only a yearly tenancy?—That is all. We collect the rent of the stalls ourselves. We give one pound a year for the collection of the rents of the meat stalls.

[illegible]. Who collects these for you?—Mr. Thomas Walsh, the deputy weigh-master.

[illegible]. Is that in the fish market?—No, but the meat market. He was deputy weigh-master in the butter market also.

[illegible]. You have the fish market let to Mr. Roger Lyons at [illegible] a year?—Yes.

22,395. Is that all you receive from the fish market? —That is all.

22,396. Do you receive anything for stalls or does he apply the rent of them to his own use?—Yes.

22,397. All he has to pay is 1l. a year?—Yes.

22,398. Is Mr. Lyons here?—He is not.

22,399. Have you the meat market tables at all?—We collect the rent by deputy.

22,400. That is Mr. Walsh?—Yes. The rent averages from 10l. to 12l. a year.

22,401. He is the collector in the meat market?—Yes.

22,402. Who superintends the butter market?—Mr. John Wall, deputy butter taster.

22,403. I take it you have only let the tolls at the square to Mr. Maurice Walsh?—That is all.

22,404. And the Town Commissioners retain the immediate control of the butter market, the meat market, and the fish market?—Yes.

22,405. Are there any other markets or sources of revenue for the Commissioners?—Not that I am aware.

22,406. What duties do the Commissioners perform here?—They are under the Act of 1854.

22,407. Are they the urban sanitary authority?—Yes.

22,408. Do they light the town?—Yes.

22,409. Do you do the paving and cleansing the roads and streets?—Yes.

22,410. Is there anything further you wish to bring before me?—No, except that the Commissioners expended 1,000l.

22,411. What loans did they obtain for market purposes?—500l. and 200l.

22,412. When did they obtain these loans?—The 500l. was obtained in 1878, and the 200l. in the year 1878.

22,413. For what purposes were these loans obtained? —For the purpose of purchasing the butter market, the site of the building.

22,414. It was exclusively to purchase the site and build the butter market?—The site was purchased for 50l. or 60l., and the expenditure was up to 500l.

22,415. What terms did they get this loan on. What interest had they to pay, or what was the rate of repayment?—It was borrowed from the Local Government Board.

22,416. There were other purposes for which you required the loan; you erected a town hall?—Yes, it was exclusively for market purposes. We had to purchase the site, build the market house, town hall, Commissioners' office, and harbour master's office. 400l. of the amount was secured by mortgage on the town improvement rate, 200l. by mortgage on the market rate, 100l. by mortgage on the road rates, and 100l., the remaining portion of the said sum of 800l., to be secured by mortgage on the harbour rates, at the rate, they forget to state the interest, for 30 years.

22,417. Is that repaid?—It is.

22,418. Fully?—Fully repaid.

22,419. When did you pay it back?—I have not the record, but it was paid back years ago.

22,420. Have you any loans outstanding at present? —There is, on the road account.

22,421. In connexion with the market account? —No.

22,422. What loans have you outstanding?—There is 1,000l. borrowed for quay purposes last year, and 100l. outstanding of the road account, and there is a floating loan of 450l. for sanitary purposes under the Towns Improvement Act. There are receipts from the town hall.

22,423. The butter market is held in the basement of the town hall?—Yes, the profits of this go to the market account.

22,427. I believe he was dismissed?—He was.

22,428. For what cause. Was it dereliction of duty?— For that reason, amongst others, in not having the accounts prepared.

22,429. So you were unable to answer one of the questions in the query sheet, that is, to state the average receipts for the three years ending 1887?—I could get them from the ledgers.

22,430. But the accounts are not made up?—No.

22,431. There is a great difference in the rent. It was 80l. in 1868 and only 40l. now?—Yes.

22,432. What rent you receive for theatrical purposes you apply that to the butter market account?—Yes. We charge the repairs to the town hall and butter market to the market account.

22,433. How do you apply the receipts?—We have about 200l. now, and perhaps the Commissioners are waiting for an opportunity to erect a market place. They are discussing the advisability of erecting a market place for the tolls. The idea would be they are losing 40l. a year at present, and if they expended 400l. on a market place it would only take 10 years to pay it off.

22,434. Who was it erected the meat market?—The Duke of Devonshire.

22,435. Do you know the expenditure on that?—No.

22,436. What would the repairs cost?—The average cost of repairs would be under one pound a year.

22,437. Who have you engaged besides Mr. Wall in connexion with the butter market?—Mr. Thomas Walsh. He is deputy weigh-master and clerk.

22,438. How do you pay him?—30l. a year. He has to provide two hands out of that. He is not deputy weigh-master at all; he is only a clerk. The Commissioners sometimes pay two assistants and some days one; on an average one every week. It costs them on an average 3s. a week.

22,439. Who else have you engaged?—That is all.

22,440. Is not Mr. Wall the deputy?—Yes. He is paid 75l. a year as deputy butter-taster.

22,441. Have you any other expenses in connexion with the butter market?—No.

22,442. Have you any rent to pay to the Duke of Devonshire?—No.

22,443. Did you buy the fee simple of the site under the Act?—Not the fee simple. It is leased.

22,444. How do you hold it?—14l. or 15l. a year ground-rent.

22,445. For how many years?—The lease expired but the Commissioners got a renewal for 99 years from Messrs. Merrick, Vaughan, and Ruddle. Mr. Merrick is the owner to whom the 15l. is paid by the Commissioners, but they are about purchasing his interest. I think some particulars are not given accurately. The lease under which they built the market would not expire until 1890. Mr. Merrick bought the place from the Marquis of Waterford and would be the landlord then. The Commissioners, in anticipation of a misunderstanding, and Mr. Merrick left it to the arbitration of Mr. Waters, the County Court Judge, and he decided that Mr. Merrick should give a lease for 99 years.

22,446. You surrendered the old lease?—We are paying the rent of the original holder, Mrs. Sheehan, during her term of the old lease.

22,447. What rent are you paying?—14l. 15s. The new rent, 15l., will not come into operation until the expiry of the old lease.

22,448. The position, then, is the Commissioners hold the market at present under lease, which will terminate in 1890, at a rent of 14l. 15s. a year, which is payable to Mrs. Sheehan. An arrangement has been entered into by which on the expiration of that lease a new lease will be granted by the owner of the reversion for 99 years, at a rent of 15l. a year?—Yes.

22,449. Have you any other expenses in connexion

29,452. You have it for ever?—Yes.

29,453. Whom have you engaged in connexion with the meat market?—Mr. Thomas Walsh used to collect the weekly rents, and he has a deputy appointed.

29,454. What is the deputy's name?—Roger Lyons.

29,455. That is the lessee of the fish market?—Yes.

29,456. You only receive 1l. a year from that?—That is all.

29,457. You have no expenses in connexion with it, and you receive 1l. a year?—Yes.

29,458. Do you hold the fish market in fee?—Yes.

29,459. How is Mr. Lyons paid for collecting the weekly rents in the meat market?—He gets about 1l. a year for the collection.

29,460. Is the fish market anything he receives over and above the 1l. paid to you given to his own use?—Yes. It would not pay the Commissioners at present to give a salary for collecting these small things.

29,461. Have you any beams and scales provided in the fish market?—None in the fish market.

29,462. You have only stalls in it?—That is all.

29,463. Have you any in the meat market?—No; except what the butchers themselves should have.

29,464. This is a shambles?—Yes.

29,465. Are these retailers who sell there?—Yes.

29,466. In the butter market what scales have you provided there?—The scales are the property of the Commissioners. Thomas Walsh attends to the weighing.

29,467. How many scales have you?—One. There are two weigh-bridges on the square.

29,468. Do you know, is one of the weigh-bridges on the square capable of weighing cattle?—No. It is strong enough, but there are no railings around it.

29,469. Are you aware the buyers or cattle-dealers ever stated they would like to weigh live stock, and if you had a machine capable of doing so?—No.

29,470. Witness produced a return of the number of firkins of butter brought to the market, and said the number increased since 1882 and 1883 owing to the 56-lb. firkins coming in.

29,471. What was the customary weight previous to the introduction of the 56-lb. firkins?—Three-quarters of a hundredweight.

29,472. Was the charge proportionately reduced?—No. Threepence for each firkin is still continued.

29,473. The change in the size of the firkins accounts for the large increase in the number brought to the market?—Yes.

29,474. On an average what number comes, or do you think it will increase?—Here is the return for 1883, 1884, and 1885. In 1883 there were 13,044; in 1884, 14,0[illegible]; in 1885, 14,757.

29,475. Although there was a reduction in the size, and a practical increase in the number brought into the market, there was no proportionate reduction in the charges?—No. They make no complaint.

29,476. Did the Commissioners instruct you to bring any particular question before me?—No.

29,477. Did they think a necessity arises for providing a proper market building for the general market apart altogether from the desire to receive an extra 2d. a year?—I think not otherwise.

29,478. Were any representations ever made to them that the roll butter or other perishable commodities were injured by exposure on the public thoroughfare?—There were not.

29,479. At the time of these proceedings at petty sessions did the defendants state they were willing to pay a charge if proper accommodation was provided?—I believe that was the ground they went on.

The following is the return handed in by the foregoing witness:—

NUMBER of FIRKINS of BUTTER at BUTTER MARKET, commencing Tuesday, January 10th, [illegible], up to December 19th, [illegible].

Number of Firkins coming into market on each date.

Date		Prices	No. of firkins
10th January [illegible]	No. of firkins	Prices [illegible]s. to [illegible]s.	9
28th March	"		8
27th	"		75
3rd April	"		[illegible]
10th "	"	Prices [illegible]s. to [illegible]s.	[illegible]
17th "	"	" [illegible]s. to [illegible]s.	[illegible]
24th "	"		[illegible]
1st May	"	Prices [illegible]s. to [illegible]s.	[illegible]
8th "	"	" [illegible]s. to [illegible]s.	[illegible]
15th "	"	" [illegible]s. to [illegible]s.	[illegible]
22nd "	"	" [illegible]s. to [illegible]s.	[illegible]
29th "	"		[illegible]
5th June	"		[illegible]
12th "	"		[illegible]
19th "	"		[illegible]
26th "	"		[illegible]
3rd July	"		[illegible]
10th "	"		[illegible]
17th "	"		[illegible]
24th "	"		[illegible]
31st "	"		[illegible]
7th August	"		[illegible]
14th "	"		[illegible]
21st "	"		[illegible]
28th "	"	Prices [illegible]s. to [illegible]s.	[illegible]
4th September	"	" [illegible]s. to [illegible]s.	[illegible]
11th "	"	" [illegible]s. to [illegible]s.	[illegible]
18th "	"		[illegible]
25th "	"		[illegible]
2nd October	"	Prices [illegible]s. to [illegible]s.	[illegible]
9th "	"	" [illegible]s. to [illegible]s.	[illegible]
16th "	"	" [illegible]s. to [illegible]s., per 56 lbs.	[illegible]
23rd "	"	" [illegible]s. to [illegible]s.	[illegible]
30th "	"		[illegible]
6th November	"	Prices [illegible]s. to [illegible]s.	[illegible]
13th "	"	" [illegible]s. to [illegible]s.	[illegible]
20th "	"		[illegible]
27th "	"	Prices [illegible]s. to [illegible]s.	[illegible]
4th December	"	" [illegible]s. to [illegible]s.	[illegible]
11th "	"		[illegible]
18th "	"		[illegible]

JOHN F. WILLIAMS, Esq., solicitor, examined.

22,480. (Witness.) I was representing them before Mr. Warren, and they did not publicly state any ground they appeared on at all. We objected to the proceedings on the wording of the Act that no proper accommodation was provided, and no contract was between the defendants and the Commissioners. We defended the action on technical grounds and we were successful.

22,481. Would the people pay a charge if proper accommodation were provided?—There were some charges the people considered they should not pay at all; for instance, the charges on [illegible] and other small matters especially. It was considered a great annoyance by different dealers in different parts of the town to be watched, as they considered they were watched, by the parties collecting the toll, and the people seemed to have an objection to pay the toll, especially the poor people who made very little money. The tolls were not worth collecting, and the people themselves considered they ought not to pay them.

RICHARD DUNNE, Esq., J.P., examined.

22,482. You are the butter weighmaster here?—Yes.

22,483. When were you appointed?—I could not tell you from memory, but there is a copy of the minutes here, and it appears to have been in June 1874. I was appointed there as butter taster and butter weighmaster.

22,484. Were you sworn under the Act?—Yes.

22,485. Have you appointed a deputy?—Yes.

22,486. Who is he?—Mr. John Wall.

22,487. You do not derive any profit yourself out of your office?—I understand the power of the market rests in me, and the tolls of the market [illegible] in me, but I have not appropriated them, I have left them to the Town Commissioners.

22,488. What were the terms of your appointment? Were you to receive the fees for your own use?—There is a minute on the matter in the books of the Commissioners.

22,489. Since the day of your appointment you have not received any of the charges for your own use?—No, I have left the arrangements of the butter market also to be settled by Mr. Wall and the Town Commissioners.

22,490. So, practically, you have no active duties to perform in connexion with it?—I have to perform no duties personally in connexion with it.

22,491. Who was it appointed you originally?—The Town Commissioners.

22,492. Have you heard any complaints about this butter market and the accommodation it affords?—I have heard various complaints from time to time, but I do not think, on the whole, considering the number of conflicting interests, you could conclude that it was ill-managed, quite the reverse.

22,493. What was the nature of those complaints?—One complaint was made about the practice which, I understand, does not exist. The floor used to be in a very dirty state from the brine [illegible] out of the firkins. The firkins were rolled through this and the dirt would work in between the staves, but since the introduction of [illegible] bags they are carried and not rolled along the floor.

22,494. Could not they remedy that by making a little incline in the floor?—There is an incline to carry off the brine, but Mr. Wall will tell you anything you want to know about that.

22,495. Have you any suggestions to offer?—It occurred to me as this is fair day I might remark about the fairs of the town. They are held in different portions of the town. It has always struck me that it is a great public inconvenience such should be the case. They are not held in one continuous district of the town. Portion of the fair is held near the bridge and another portion on the square, and the third portion of the fair at the end of the street which leads up to the chapel, and it is held in the street called The Battery, which runs right to the left when you get to the chapel gate. Of course there is no proper place for holding the fairs; there is no fair-green, which I am strongly of opinion there ought to be wherever a fair is held. It would be very much more suitable for public convenience.

22,496. Do you think a necessity exists here for a properly enclosed fair-green?—I do. I think a necessity exists wherever a monthly fair is held for a properly enclosed fair-green.

22,497. It is your opinion it should not be held on the public thoroughfare?—It is, most decidedly. For instance, the sheep fair is altogether held on the flags of the town, and causes great inconvenience and annoyance. You have to walk through the middle of the street the flags being overcrowded with the sheep. In fact, that is the only place they stand except in one or two lanes.

22,498. Have you ever heard frequent complaints from the visitors and inhabitants of the town of the accumulation of dirt after the fairs?—It is but too evident. I do not know whether I have heard complaints, but it obtrudes itself at once on their notice.

22,499. You never heard of any representations being made to the Town Commissioners to provide a fair-green?—I could not say. I am not clear in my mind about it.

22,500. From your knowledge of the farmers and those frequenting the fairs, do you think they would have any objection to pay a small charge that would maintain a fair-green and pay any instalments of money that might be borrowed for its erection?—They might, in the first instance, until they saw it was a benefit, but once it was established I think it would commend itself to everybody's good sense.

22,501. It is your opinion generally that fairs all over the country should be held in a properly enclosed fair-green?—Yes. For instance, Clonmel is a glaring instance of the same thing.

22,502. Have you anything else to say?—Nothing else.

Mr. MAURICE WALSH examined.

22,503. You are known to the Town Commissioners for the tolls of the market square?—Yes.

22,504. Have you got a list of the charges erected in the market square?—Yes, there is a bill board over the house.

22,505. Do you only collect on market days?—I do not collect at all now; there are no tolls. I only collect on what I weigh; whenever I weigh I get paid for it.

22,506. Previous to those legal proceedings you used to collect tolls on the people coming in and exposing commodities on the roadside and pathway?—Yes.

22,507. For standings?—Yes.

22,508. Since the case before the court was decided you do not collect any such charges?—No.

22,509. Only when the weighbridges are availed of?—That is all.

22,510. Have you a scales there besides the two weighing machines?—I have small scales in the house. I have no scales—[illegible] and the machines.

22,511. Have you only one machine?—[illegible] there are two machines erected there.

22,512. What commodities do people usually bring in over on that market square on Saturday, whether they weigh at your scales or not?—Potatoes, vegetables, turnips, hay and straw, corn, meal, apples, and butter. The fowl and eggs are brought to the houses of the dealers where they are bought.

22,513. Do they have any standings on market day?—They do.

22,514. Do itinerant cloth[-]dealers come on fair day or market day and erect standings?—They do—some strangers.

22,515. Do clothes dealers?—No.

22,516. You weigh potatoes?—Yes.

22,517. With reference to all commodities sold by weight, is there any rule in the market place compelling them to weigh at your scales?—Well, I could not exactly tell you.

22,518. Can they weigh elsewhere, or do they, in fact, weigh elsewhere?—I think they do.

22,519. Supposing a farmer brought in a load of potatoes and exposed them on the market square and sold them, could he go to the private merchants' scales and weigh them?—I believe he could.

[illegible]. (Mr. Barry (interposing.) Mr. Walsh made a complaint of that to the Town Commissioners, and they made a rule ordering that all persons getting a roll of butter or anything weighed elsewhere than at the public scales would be prosecuted. It was on that ground the Commissioners brought the case referred to by Mr. Wilkinson.

[illegible]. (The Commissioners to Mr. Walsh.) As a matter of fact they do weigh elsewhere?—They do.

[illegible]. It is only when they avail themselves of your scales you get any charge?—That is all.

[illegible]. What charge do you levy on potatoes?—From a halfpenny to three halfpence.

[illegible]. Tell me how you would know when to levy a halfpenny charge and three halfpence?—A halfpenny up to six stone; six stone clear a penny; and from that to 14 stone a penny; then three halfpence for 14 stone clear.

[illegible]. Over 14 stone, three halfpence?—Yes.

[illegible]. No matter how many were brought in on a load, would you charge on each individual sack?—Yes.

[illegible]. Is it always on the net weight you charge?—It is.

[illegible]. Do you ascertain the actual tare of the sack when weighing potatoes?—We do not; we give the gross weight.

[illegible]. Do you give a ticket denoting the weight?—Yes.

[illegible]. What is the customary allowance between buyers and sellers per sack?—Four pounds.

[illegible]. Never larger?—Never, unless they like themselves.

[illegible]. Would it be the same on a wet day as on extremely fine day?—It is the same with us. We give the gross weight and let them do what they like.

[illegible]. It is a matter of arrangement between the buyer and seller?—Yes.

[illegible]. When weighing potatoes down to what weight do you weigh?—Down to a quarter. That is what we are asked to do. In weighing new potatoes if men wanted a quarter we would weigh it.

[illegible]. Supposing there was a sack which weighed 10 stone 6 pounds, would you call out the weight as 10 stone 6 pounds?—I would put that on the ticket.

[illegible]. Or would you only put 10 stone?—I put every pound.

[illegible]. Do you always put a pound weight into the scale?—Yes.

[illegible]. Do you give a cast of the beam when weighing?—Yes; the beam turns always.

[illegible]. You receive no charge from vegetables?—No.

[illegible]. You do from turnips when you weigh them?—I do.

[illegible]. What is your charge?—From 2d. to 3d.

[illegible]. Tell me when you would charge 3d. for weighing a load?—A donkey load; four or five hundred and often three hundredweight.

[illegible]. It is 2d. for a donkey load?—2d.; and if the load is small, 2d.

[illegible]. Is there any line to draw between the 2d. and the 3d.?—Any weight that is small; two hundred is small.

[illegible]. What is the highest load weighed for 2d.?—I suppose four hundred.

[illegible]. It is 3d. for anything over that?—Yes.

[illegible]. They can weigh turnips elsewhere like the other things?—I suppose they can if they wish to do it, but they have not the convenience.

[illegible]. What is your charge on hay?—The same; from 2d. to 3d. or 4d.

[illegible]. Do you charge 3d. for weighing turnips too, or have you got the same charge at the weighing machine no matter what the commodity may be?—I think I would charge 4d. for any load.

[illegible]. I do not want to know what you can do, but what you do?—That is the charge I have told you.

[illegible]. What is the highest charge you levy?—Fivepence. It is 5d. for seven or eight hundredweight, and 1d. over it.

[illegible]. What do you charge for weighing corn?—Three halfpence a barrel.

[illegible]. Is it always bought by the barrel?—It is.

[illegible]. In Dungarvan what is the barrel supposed to contain?—Fourteen stone of oats, and twenty stone wheat.

[illegible]. Do you weigh wheat too?—Yes, if I get it to weigh. The wheat is weighed by the merchants themselves.

[illegible]. Do you weigh it?—Only in small bags.

[illegible]. Do you put a pound weight into the scales when weighing oats and wheat?—I put a pound in for everything.

[illegible]. Do you always give a cast of the beam?—Yes.

[illegible]. Do you put the gross weight on the ticket?—Yes.

[illegible]. And the tare?—Yes.

[illegible]. You could get me a copy of the tickets?—Yes.

[illegible]. Witness subsequently produced the tickets, of which the following is a copy:—

DUNGARVAN BUTTER MARKET.

[illegible]. Do you receive any charge from the meat sold on the square?—No.

[illegible]. None whatever?—No.

[illegible]. Do you ever weigh it?—No. They have scales of their own for that. That reference to the meat is only with regard to the ground rent.

[illegible]. They never sell fresh meat on the public thoroughfare?—They sell meat heads and salt meat.

[illegible]. Do they put these heads outside the shop door?—They come out in the public thoroughfare.

[illegible]. You receive no charge on apples?—No.

[illegible]. Do you weigh roll butter?—Yes.

[illegible]. What is your charge?—From a halfpenny to twopence.

[illegible]. Up to what weight?—Up to six pounds a halfpenny; from that up to fourteen pounds a penny; from that up to twenty pounds three halfpence; and over twenty pounds twopence.

[illegible]. Are these the only charges from which you have any receipts?—That is all I have.

[illegible]. You never weigh anything else?—I weigh timber on the bridge.

[illegible]. What do you charge on that?—Twopence a ton for timber.

[illegible]. Only the one charge?—Yes. The charge would be reduced if I got a good quantity.

[illegible]. Could you tell me what would be your average receipts from these weighing charges?—Begorra, I could not find.

[illegible]. Do not you keep an account. I am sure you display a sufficiently good public spirit to mention the receipts disregarding any effect it would have on the Commissioners. What would you say your average receipts are?—I could not tell you.

[illegible]. If you do not wish to tell me publicly you can tell me privately during the day?—I will try if I can find it out.

[illegible]. Hardly a gentleman of your experience would tender for the market charges and not know what you received from them for the last couple of years?—That is right.

[illegible]. You do not levy the charges mentioned on the toll board?—No.

[illegible]. They are somewhat reduced?—Yes.

23,582. Is there anybody else in the town who has started a house and scales for weighing commodities on hire?—No, there is not.

23,583. Are the potatoes, corn, and other commodities always sold before being weighed at your scales?—Always sold.

23,584. Have you any buildings in the square?—No, except the weigh-house for the scales.

23,585. Have you any storage accommodation there?—No.

23,586. Do you think the market would be better attended, and the people would be willing to pay a small charge, if adequate accommodation was afforded in the way of a market building with sheds and shelter accommodation, and storage accommodation where they could store up any marketable commodity that remained unsold on market days; do you think they would have any objection to pay a small charge for its maintenance?—I could not tell you.

23,587. Do you remember those legal proceedings?—Yes.

23,588. Did the defendants then state they would be willing to pay this charge if they got sufficient accommodation?—They did not.

23,589. Practically they were getting no return for the charge they were paying originally?—They were taking up the place.

23,590. The charge was levied on them for exposing their commodities on the public thoroughfare?—Yes.

23,591. Do you ever make up the tickets for the people?—Sometimes.

23,592. Supposing it was required from the Town Commissioners to make a periodical return of the current prices of the different commodities brought into the market square, do you think they could make such a return?—I do not know.

23,593. You do not know. Do not you make up the tickets for them?—I may do it for one out of a hundred.

23,594. Does not that afford you an opportunity of knowing the current prices of the article on the market day?—I suppose so.

23,595. I am not asking to do it, nor am I going to put an additional labour on you, and I am sure you will answer honestly and fairly; is there a possibility of making a pretty accurate return of the current prices of the marketable commodities brought into the market square?—I could not tell you.

23,596. You say you make up the tickets occasionally?—Very few.

23,597. Do you mean to say that if you inquired from the people what was the current price or the cost price of the different commodities that they would tell you a falsehood?—Yes, and very often do.

23,598. (*Mr. McCarthy.*) It might be answered in this way. There is no record of the current prices, and he knows the price. There is no record in writing.

23,599. Do you think, Mr. McCarthy, a pretty accurate return could be made of the current prices?—Only from memory.

23,600. I do not mean of the past, but in future could it be done?—There is no difficulty at all about it.

23,601. Do you think it would be a pretty accurate one?—I often asked the prices and knew about it.

Mr. John Wall examined.

23,602. You are the deputy butter taster?—Yes.

23,603. Who was it appointed you?—Mr. Usher.

23,604. Was it the Commissioners appointed you and it was ratified by Mr. Usher?—The Commissioners appointed Mr. Usher himself.

23,605. I take it then Mr. Usher would appoint whoever the Commissioners pleased?—Yes.

23,606. Who has the power of dismissing you?—Mr. Usher alone. I think, at least, Mr. Usher.

23,607. When were you appointed?—Five or six years ago.

23,608. Is there a good butter market in Dungarvan?—It is a very important one.

23,609. It has been increasing very much since you obtained control over it?—I would not say that.

23,610. You have found a gradual increase?—The farmers are getting more into butter making than formerly.

23,611. What percentage of the surrounding country is in tillage?—About 15 per cent. I farm land myself.

23,612. When the butter is brought into the market there is a charge of 2d. per firkin?—Yes.

23,613. And it is always in firkins it is brought in?—Yes.

23,614. Is it weighed and tasted before being sold?—It is weighed, and if required to be tasted it is tasted, but as a rule it is never tasted.

23,615. Is it always weighed before being sold?—Yes.

23,616. That rule exists in the market?—Yes.

23,617. Is it at entrance to the market or when getting the ticket denoting the weight the charge is paid?—Yes.

23,618. It is only when required it is tasted?—Yes. It is not tasted because the merchants would not be satisfied with the taster. They never buy by the hundred; they buy by the firkin, and I never taste it except there is a dispute.

23,619. These are small firkins?—Yes.

23,620. Supposed to contain 56 pounds?—Yes.

23,621. Do the merchants buy per firkin of 56 pounds?—They average 56 pounds. Sometimes there may be two or three pounds over, and they buy it at so much.

23,622. When they buy a firkin of 56 pounds, if there is 59 pounds actually in the firkin, will they pay the farmer for the extra three pounds?—They will. They have the ticket and the merchant can see the weight. That and the quality regulate the price.

23,623. If only 56 pounds in the firkin will the price be proportionately decreased?—Yes. Before they make the purchase they see the ticket and they take into consideration the weight and quality.

23,624. In any case they never buy without seeing the ticket?—No, unless there was a great rush.

23,625. Then they always taste themselves?—Yes. As a rule it is the same class of buyers who frequent the market, and they know every seller's butter.

23,626. Do they classify the butter then?—Yes, when they buy.

23,627. Have they marks to the qualities?—They qualify themselves as they buy.

23,628. Have they got any special statement for the different classes of butter—that is the difference between them?—No.

23,629. Like at Tipperary and other markets?—No. That cannot be worked the same as the Waterford market.

23,630. In Waterford does not Mr. Vale always taste the butter?—No.

23,631. Would the farmers prefer an independent tasting of the butter?—I do not think it would work well.

23,632. When you were appointed first did you not taste all firkins?—No. The man who was before used taste for a short season, but they did away with him.

23,633. Did they consider that his tasting was not correct?—The merchants would never be satisfied with the taster's qualification. They would have their own qualification besides, and take up a lot of time.

23,634. Before weighing the firkins are they drained?—Well, when we find a suspicious firkin we drain it.

23,635. Only when you find a suspicious firkin?—Yes. We would know it coming in.

23,636. Would you not take off the lid and turn up each firkin?—No; very few of them. We know from experience the parties who are suspicious.

23,637. Have you had occasion to take any proceedings for fraud being committed on the proprietors of the butter?—There were several complaints made by the merchants.

23,638. Is that recently?—Yes, within the last fortnight, but they settled with the parties.

23,639. Since you were appointed was there any prosecution?—No, but there were several complaints.

22,640. Is the tare of the firkin branded on it?—Yes.

22,641. Always?—Yes. Sometimes the [illegible] object to the tare.

22,642. Why?—Sometimes the tare is more than is branded. For instance, the average tare is three pounds, and often they complained to me that there were eleven and twelve pounds tare in the firkin.

22,643. In that case do you actually weigh the empty firkin?—Yes.

22,644. Would you find the branded tare correct?—No.

22,645. You would find the statement of the merchant correct?—Yes. I have asked merchants several times to prosecute and give the names, and they let it slide.

22,646. When the firkin is branded do they allow any further reduction from the gross weight than the branded tare; do they allow anything for soakage?—They do not.

22,647. The only deduction from the gross weight is the tare?—There is no deduction at all. They buy the firkin as it stands for fifty or fifty-five shillings.

22,648. What do you put on the docket?—The gross weight and tare.

22,649. Is that the branded tare?—Yes.

22,650. When you do not drain the firkin there might be some soakage in it, and it might be somewhat heavier then?—Yes. When I come across a suspicious firkin like that I weigh it and deduct a couple of pounds. I use my own discretion there.

22,651. Are they willing to abide by that?—Yes. I would call the owner's attention to it.

22,652. Have you any butter buyers here in court?—No.

22,653. When they are fixing the price of the firkin, do they deduct from the gross weight and tare mentioned by you any additional allowance customary elsewhere for soakage?—No, unless they find a firkin that is fraudulently made up.

22,654. If there was a firkin fifty-nine pounds weight, and the branded tare nine pounds, do you think they would pay for fifty pounds of butter. Would not there be something additional for soakage?—No. They do not buy on that system. They know the character of the butter, and they know every person who comes into the market. Occasionally firkins would turn up two or three pounds more than the branded tare, and then they seek for an allowance, or some recoupment from the owners.

22,655. Have you assistants to take the firkins off the cars and put them on the scales?—Yes.

22,656. The farmers have no [illegible] to perform, in connection with that?—Not as a rule.

22,657. There is no porterage charge?—I think there are runners about the place. Farmers give them money, but they need not do so.

22,658. Supposing they do not engage those men, would they be at any inconvenience the next market day?—I do not think so.

22,659. If the farmer has not sufficient manual assistance he can avail himself of them?—He can.

22,660. At what rate does he pay these men?—They may pay nothing at all, or they may give a couple of pence.

22,661. There is no fixed rate?—No.

22,662. Have you any rules or regulations in the butter market?—No.

22,663. I suppose the butter merchants have their ordinary rules?—Yes; we arrange the butter in the market and they come and buy it.

22,664. What hour does the market usually begin?—About twelve and terminates about half-past two.

22,665. Do you think the system adopted by the buyers of relying on their own experience in classifying the butter works satisfactorily?—I think it does.

22,666. To the farmers' satisfaction and their own?—Yes; the prices they pay here exceeds the Cork price as a rule, and the brand here is a higher brand than Cork.

22,667. You state there is no deduction from the quantity other than the tare, but is there any deduction from the price?—There is no deduction unless the tare is three or four pounds over the branded tare.

22,668. Have you any suggestion to offer that would tend to the better working of the market?—I think the market is worked as well as any market in Ireland.

22,669. Does it afford sufficient space for the butter brought in?—Yes.

22,670. Do you ever store the butter?—Sometimes we oblige a party.

22,671. Do you levy any charge?—No; we could not do that.

22,672. Does it happen often?—No.

22,673. Would you say the greater quantity of the butter brought in is sold?—Yes.

22,674. When the butter is brought into the town by a farmer and not brought in the market but sold to a shopkeeper would you receive any charge?—We may charge, but we could compel a farmer to pay the charge.

22,675. Does that frequently occur?—Never.

22,676. It all comes to the market and after being weighed there or tested if required is sold?—Yes.

[illegible] Lyons examined.

22,677. You are tenant of the fish market?—Yes.

22,678. To the Town Commissioners?—Yes.

22,679. What charges do you levy at the fish market?—3d. a cart.

22,680. Is the fish market enclosed?—It is, but where they bring the fish in carts it is not enclosed.

22,681. Is it on the public thoroughfare?—Yes.

22,682. They bring their carts there and expose the fish in them?—Yes.

22,683. Is that charge of 3d. on a cart the only charge you levy?—There is a penny for every basket that comes.

22,684. Is this a wholesale market?—Yes, and retail.

22,685. Where do the women sell?—On the same ground.

22,686. Do not they avail themselves of the enclosure at all?—They put their fish in the enclosure at night for storage.

22,687. Only for storage?—Yes.

22,688. What charge do you levy?—Twopence to each day.

22,689. Is it on Saturday the fish market is held?—Every day.

22,690. You levy charges every day?—Yes, every day the fish will come. This fish comes in cars from Ballingarvan. The fish men belonging to the town are charged nothing.

22,691. You receive no charge from dealers in the the town?—No.

22,692. Supposing a fish-woman brought in fish and sold it around the town, as they generally do, you receive no charge from her?—I would.

22,693. What charge would you levy on her?—A penny per basket.

22,694. You receive such charges?—Yes.

22,695. No matter where she purchases the fish?—No matter where the woman purchases the fish, unless she was one of the townswomen.

22,696. If it was a stranger hawking fish around you would charge?—Yes.

22,697. Any fish-women who lives in the town would not be charged here?—No.

22,698. Do any strangers come and sell about the town?—Yes.

22,699. For the storage of the fish for a week you charge twopence a day?—Yes.

22,700. If a cart of fish is brought in and exposed outside on the quay you charge threepence for the cart?—Yes.

22,701. If the fish remained unsold, and they wished to store it, would you charge an extra twopence?—No.

22,702. What would you charge?—Nothing.

22,703. Would you give them storage free?—Yes.

22,704. Would it be at their own risk they would store it?—Yes.

22,705. When do you collect the charge?—Every day they come.

22,706. Is it for the exposure of the fish?—Exposure for sale.

22,707. You never consider whether they subsequently sell or not?—No.

22,708. What is the smallest quantity of fish brought in a basket that you received a penny charge on; did you ever get it on one fish?—I never charge for one or for four. For a small number I would not charge.

22,709. You give and take with them?—Yes.

22,710. What is the smallest quantity that you have charged on?—Half a score.

22,711. What would be the value of half a score of fish on a bad market day?—From 4s. 6d. to 5s.

22,712. You only receive a penny charge?—Yes.

22,713. If they brought the same quantity each day you would receive a penny charge?—I would.

22,714. Have you any collectors in the market?—No, I collect myself.

22,715. When you ask for this from a woman with a basket of fish, and if she told you she had not got the charge, would you seize the fish?—If she did not make a sale of the fish I would let her go until the next day.

22,716. If she paid you in the early part of the day and you met her later, do you ever demand the charge again?—Certainly not.

22,717. Did you ever demand the charge twice?—No, and if they were short 6d. I would give it to them.

22,718. Are you at any expense or money out of pocket in connexion with the market?—No, except the pound a year I pay the Commissioners.

22,719. Who cleans the market?—A woman and the scavenger.

22,720. Is it always cleaned out?—Yes.

22,721. Have you ever heard objections to the fish market being held on the quay and that it is not confined to the enclosure?—I have heard no objections, but I heard the Commissioners themselves wish to put them in the enclosure.

22,722. Did you ever hear any complaints from the people living in the adjoining neighbourhood?—I heard one or two saying they should not be allowed there at all.

22,723. What hour does the fish market usually begin?—It is according to the tides. The boats come in the morning early, and I am there to open the gates for the fishermen.

22,724. Mr. Beary, the sub-sanitary officer you see, said he was instructed by the Commissioners to prosecute Youghal fishermen who brought in cartloads of sprats for obstruction on the public thoroughfare, but unfortunately it was to the borough court they were brought, and the magistrates decided we had no authority to summons them when they lived outside the boundary.

22,725. (*The Commissioner to Mr. Lyons.*) Are these the only sources of revenue you have in the fish market?—That is all.

22,726. Would you have any objection to tell me what are your average receipts, or what you think likely they would be about?—Well, I get about 5s. 6d. or 5s. 1d. from the women.

22,727. Is that per day?—No; but every week from the women with the stalls.

22,728. How many stalls have you there?—Nine.

22,729. How many let?—The whole are let, but I do not get paid for them.

22,730. What are you supposed to get for each stall?—Threepence a week.

22,731. What do you receive from the charges on the boats and on the baskets?—There were some days here when sprats were killed, and I used to get a couple of shillings each day; some days I would not get a halfpenny.

22,732. On an average what would you get?—I would not get a shilling a week on the fish that comes.

22,733. Do you keep any record of your receipts?—No.

22,734. You collect the tolls at the meat market?—Yes.

22,735. You are paid 1l. a year for that?—Yes.

22,736. Did you ever see the Act of Parliament with the schedule of tolls?—No.

22,737. Have you got the schedule of charges in the fish market written?—It was read out by the clerk when I was appointed caretaker.

22,738. He did not give you a copy of it?—No.

22,739. Did he consider you should remember it always?—He did not give me a copy of it. There is a house in the square, and a toll board on the end of it.

22,740. Is the fish market convenient to the market square?—It is.

22,741. I suppose the entire schedule is on the toll board?—It is.

22,742. What charges are levied at the meat market?—A shilling for each stall.

22,743. Is that for a week?—Yes; and sixpence for half a stall.

22,744. How many of these stalls are there?—I believe 10 or 11, but they are not all occupied.

22,745. Is that meat market enclosed?—It is.

22,746. There is shedding accommodation, and it is covered?—It is.

22,747. Are these retailers of meat who sell there?—They kill it themselves, and retail it in this place. Every person who kills in the place retails there.

22,748. Is that meat market open every day?—Yes, unless on Sunday.

22,749. You only charge a shilling a week?—Yes.

22,750. When the market is over where do they remove the meat to?—They take it up to the weigh-house; some of them have stalls closed up.

22,751. Have they possession and control of the stall for the week?—Yes.

22,752. Do you provide them with a beam and scales?—The Commissioners do.

22,753. One for each stall?—No. There is the general beam and scales, or rather two, one large one and one small one, and one butcher has a beam and scales to himself.

22,754. The others weigh at the general scale?—Yes.

22,755. Do you charge anything for that weighing?—No.

22,756. They pay a shilling a week, and they get the use of the stall for the week and the use of the scales?—They pay threepence for each cow they kill and a penny for each sheep.

22,757. Have the Commissioners the slaughter-house?—No, the butchers kill at their own places.

22,758. But on bringing in the dead beast they pay you the charge?—Yes, every Saturday, threepence for each cow and a penny for each sheep.

22,759. Is it only beef and mutton they sell there?—They sell veal at times but we charge nothing for that.

22,760. Are these the only charges you receive?—The only charges.

22,761. Did you ever hear any complaints that the scales were inaccurate?—No.

22,762. Do the police visit them occasionally?—They visit them regularly. There was a bad beam, and I had an order from the Commissioners for a new beam, and the order was not complied with for three years. The scales and beams were taken and I was fined a shilling.

22,763. Who goes to the expense of providing it?—The Commissioners.

22,764. You have new scales now?—I have.

22,765. You say there are stalls [illegible]. Do these people sell in shops too?—They do.

22,766. But they do not sell elsewhere than in the shops and meat market?—No.

28,767. There are no other stalls in the town outside those in the market and shops?—No.

Mr. [illegible] McC[illegible] examined.

28,768. You were formerly a town commissioner here? —Yes.

28,769. Do you think a necessity exists here in the town for an enclosed market for those general commodities sold in the market square, apart altogether from the desire of the Commissioners to augment their revenue?—There is a great diversity of opinion about it because the square is very large, and the traffic is not interfered with by the traffic in the square, but of course on the other side they say it is a very irregular thing for the market to be held at all without having it enclosed, so really I could not tell you on which side the preponderance of opinion lies.

28,770. The space would not be sufficient to allow of a market being built?—I would not think so. That was discussed I remember at the time.

28,771. The Commissioners are discussing the desirability of erecting a general market?—They did at the time the legal proceedings turned up.

28,772. Have you heard complaints that any perishable commodities, such as corn and roll butter, were injured by exposure to the weather?—No. There is no commodity exposed in the market that would be injured to my mind. They have the houses to go into, and they have a shed there. It is 30 feet long.

28,773. From what districts would you say the marketable commodities are brought?—From Cappoquin, Ferrypoint, and Youghal. The fish comes from the fishing hamlet of Ballingowl. The fish boats come into the quay, except the tide went low.

28,774. Do you receive harbour dues as well as a charge on the markets?—Not on the local boats. Last year when the harbour was visited by Manxmen and others, they put on a charge of 5s. a boat until such time as they can borrow 1,000*l.* for the improvement of the quay.

28,775. When those Manxmen come, can they sell the fish at the fish market?—Yes, English buyers used to attend there.

28,776. Do they buy on the vessel itself?—Yes.

28,777. How do you charge the market rates?—We only charge 5s. a year for the harbour.

28,778. Mr. Lyons receives no charge?—No. He gets a charge on the carts.

28,779. Were tolls ever levied at the fairs here?—Yes, 60 years ago.

28,780. Do you remember them?—I do not.

28,781. You do not know what was the cause of their abolition?—The Duke of Devonshire built the square about 60 years ago, and the tolls I think were abolished when the fairs were brought into the square.

28,782. Have you formed any ideas at all as to the advisability of removing fairs from the streets of the town such as Mr. Usher suggested, and providing a properly enclosed fair-green?—I think in all cases where there would not be accommodation that would be quite desirable, but the traders, I think, would object to it, and it is not at all analogous to Clonmel, and for this reason the streets of Clonmel are very narrow, but here we have a very fine open square, and the streets abutting on it are fine streets too.

28,783. From the railway station to the courthouse the streets are not of an extraordinary width, and I find the animals occupying the pathways and halldoors?—Yes, that has been complained of. There is a large section of the people who think it a barbarous thing to have the fairs on the streets.

28,784. Did the Commissioners ever discuss whether it would be desirable to provide a fair-green?—They did.

28,785. What was the result?—I think the generality of the ratepayers and traders would be in favour of keeping them on the streets.

28,786. Would the opposition to the removal of the fairs off the street be confined to any particular class of traders. Would it be confined to the publicans principally?—Not confined to the publicans, but they would be the strongest element in the movement. I think the shopkeepers as a rule would object to it.

28,787. Who cleans the street?—The Town Commissioners.

28,788. I want in answer to this question you will forget for the moment that you are connected with the Town Commission; have you heard complaints of neglect of duty in that respect in cleaning the street after the fairs?—Yes, formerly they used, but now the thing is very much better managed.

28,789. Immediately after the fair the streets are cleaned?—Yes. There are two men regularly appointed for that purpose.

28,790. Have you had any intercourse with the farmers who bring in the animals?—Yes, a good deal.

28,791. Do you think if there was a properly enclosed and macadamised fair-green provided with shelter accommodation and pens that they would have any objection to pay a small charge that would repay the cost of maintenance or interest on the loan required?—I think they would have no objection.

28,792. If there was a toll levied on commodities brought into the market or fair, do you think it would be a deterrent on the people bringing in the supply?—Certainly, I do not think it would. It might in the first instance. I have no experience of the farmers around any other town.

28,793. Supposing there was a fair-green provided with adequate accommodation, and a small charge levied on each animal entering the fair, do you think there would be a falling off in the supply?—Not at all. I am sure there would not be.

28,794. They would be willing to pay that?—They would never keep away for a small charge.

28,795. Are the fairs here good ones?—Very good. There are very large fairs here and a good deal of money turned over. I suppose there are about 8,000*l.* turned over here on a fair day.

28,796. What percentage of the animals that come would be sold?—That would vary very much.

28,797. You could not give any idea of the percentage?—Seventy-five per cent. would be sold some days. There were fairs last year, and there was not 25 per cent. sold, things were so dull. I am speaking of the past. To-day I do not think there was 25 per cent. left unsold.

28,798. Within what limits are the animals brought here?—Within a radius of 10 miles.

28,799. What is the radius for marketable commodities?—The same.

28,800. So far as 10 miles?—Yes. There is no better market in the neighbourhood nearer than Youghal and they come here from within a mile of Youghal. There are fairs at Lismore where they go if it suits them.

28,801. Is there any fair near Dungarvan where tolls are levied?—No. There is none except the country fairs and these have died out.

28,802. What rates have you levied here?—We have a shilling road rate this year; a shilling or fourteen pence town improvement rate.

28,803. How do you apply the harbour dues?—Exclusively to the harbour; the road rates to road purposes and the town improvement rates to town improvement purposes, and the market rates to market improvement—the surplus goes to market improvement. From the net profit of the market we deduct [illegible] and add it to the road account and also [illegible] to the town improvement—that is [illegible].

28,804. You have on the market account an accumulation of 300*l.*?—About that.

28,805. Have they taken any steps to expend that 300*l.* on market buildings or otherwise?—They are only just recovering from the buildings heretofore for which 1,000*l.* was borrowed. This expenditure on the town hall has swamped them up to this, and they have only just got rid of it and they are altogether 2,000*l.* in debt.

28,806. What was that 2,000*l.*?—There was 1,[illegible] for the improvement of the harbour.

28,807. Is the whole of that secured by the harbour dues?—Yes; there is [illegible] due on the road account; [illegible] on the improvement rate, and 150*l.* mortgage on the road account.

28,808. However, you have got the market rates mortgaged at present?—No. There is no loan on that

occupied. The whole income of the Commissioners is country, but I am unable to tell you accurately.

22,509. Although the money would not be expended on market purposes?—Yes.

22,510. Have you any suggestions to offer as to what you think would tend to the improvement of the markets or fairs, or are there any other remarks you would wish to make?—No. I think you have got all the information within our reach.

22,511. Have they got the system of luck-penny at the fairs?—Always within my memory.

22,512. And on all animals?—Yes.

22,513. On cattle and sheep is there any rule regulating the amount of the luck-penny?—No.

22,514. It is always left to the discretion of the seller?—Always.

22,515. In buying pigs is there any fixed charge?—There used to be threepence a pig. I think that is existing still; but I think it is sixpence for a fat pig.

22,516. Is there this difference, that in the case of cattle and sheep the contract price is paid by the buyer to the seller, whereas in pigs the sixpence is deducted by the buyer from the amount?—Yes.

22,517. Have you bought and sold yourself?—No.

22,518. From your conversations with the farmers do you think that in fixing the price of the animal they consider the luck-penny they have to give?—No, unless it is mentioned as in the case of a cow, the buyer would say, "I will give you 14*l.* and give me a crown luck-penny."

22,519. And that was understood?—So they arranged in that way.

22,520. When they are arguing do not they say I will give you so much clear to pocket?—Yes.

22,521. In that way the price is fixed and no luck-penny is paid?—Yes.

22,522. In that case do not they consider the value of the luck-penny?—No. The luck-penny never affects the bargain except in the case I have mentioned, unless it is a matter of special arrangement.

22,523. Do you think there is much delay in arguing about the luck-penny or about the transaction?—No. I think there would be little dispute. A man paying another 5*l.* or 10*l.* for a lot of cattle would expect a good luck-penny in that case.

22,524. Is there anything further you wish to say?—No.

Mr. Keane examined.

22,525. Do you think it would be desirable to remove the fairs off the street to a properly enclosed fair-green?—I think I must agree with Mr. McCarthy with regard to that. The shop-keepers would be against it, and on sanitary grounds I would be for removing the fairs.

22,526. You think to carry out a perfect sanitary system a removal is needed?—Yes, on sanitary grounds it is needed.

22,527. Were there any instances of disease arising from an accumulation of filth?—No; I never heard. This is an exceptionally healthy town in that way, but they want water here. There was an application by the Commissioners to the owner of the town about four or five years ago to the owner of the town, and he offered a field near the railway-station as a fair-green.

22,528. Is the general fair held convenient to the railway-station?—Quite convenient.

22,529. The buyers have easy means of communication for removing their stock?—Yes.

22,530. Do they ship them from here?—Not now, they all go by rail. I used to see them shipped from here formerly. At that time the Commissioners discussed the desirability of a fair-green, and they decided it was better to keep the fair in the town. They thought it better for the business of the town.

22,531. Do you think that it would improve the market if there was a general building provided for the commodities in the market square?—I think it would produce a good deal of satisfaction. Since the message for the tolls was dispensed there is a good deal of dissatisfaction between the lessee of the market tolls and the people who have standings there.

22,532. Is it a couple of years since this happened?—No. It was during the current year—six months ago. It was immediately after the new contract the thing arose. In fact from the losses sustained by the lessee the Commissioners allowed him something in the final payment of his three years' contract because he had been at a loss. The Commissioners made an allowance. You will see a discrepancy between the contract and the present price.

Mr. Michael Brady re-examined.

22,533. (Witness.) My impression is you would not get the parties to pay a rent for an enclosed space. They prefer to be free lances and go around the town to make a sale.

22,534. Are those people townspeople or do they live outside it?—All townspeople and country people.

22,535. Do they expose manufactured goods?—Yes, tables and boxes. They used to pay 2*d.* or 3*d.* for the standings, but that charge was abolished altogether by the Commissioners.

22,536. Is there any other gentleman who has an observation to make or evidence to give?—No answer.

The inquiry then concluded.

LISMORE.

With reference to my inquiry in Lismore on the 20th day of December 1888, I beg to report as follows:—

Lismore is situated on the River Blackwater in the county of Waterford. It is a station on the Waterford, Dungarvon, and Lismore Railway line. The town has a neat and improved appearance, town commissioners have been established and the population is 1,860.

There is no fixed general market day in Lismore. The butter market is held on Monday. The fairs are held on the second Wednesday in each month.

No tolls are levied at either the markets or fairs, but at the former weighing charges are levied, there being no rule, however, compelling the weighing of all or any commodities at the public scales.

The market rights, market place, and fair green are the property of the Duke of Devonshire, but he receives no pecuniary benefit from them. A weighmaster was appointed by his Grace, and whose remuneration consists in the charges for weighing the commodities brought into the market, viz.:—1*d.* per bag for potatoes and corn,

1d. per firkin for butter, and 4d. per load for hay, straw, and roots. Half of the charge on each firkin of butter goes to the town commissioners as a gift of his Grace, who also contributes 20l. a year towards the general rates.

There were two patents granted for Lismore. The first is dated 3rd March 1613, and authorised Sir R. Boyle to hold a Saturday market and two fairs, on feasts of Pentecost and 14th February, and two days following each. The second was dated 9th March 1720, and authorised the Earl of Burlington to hold a Thursday market and fairs on the 13th and 14th May, 13th and 14th September, 31st October, and 1st November. Previous to 1878, the fairs held in Lismore were on 25th May, 25th September, 12th November, and 14th February, being those granted by the foregoing patents, but in that year the present monthly fairs were established, apparently without any express authority, by the town commissioners and traders with the consent of the Duke.

All the butter is weighed before being bought, and the weighing charge is collected from the buyer when the butter has been sold. It is stated the buyers deduct from the contract price with the seller, the sum of 6d. per firkin. No tare is ever ascertained, but the customary practice is to allow an estimated tare from the gross weight.

In accordance with my instructions, I have inspected the market and fair places.

Marketable commodities are brought into the town different days in the week, some are brought to the shopkeepers and customers direct, and others are exposed for sale in the market yard. This yard is a square space at the rear of the court house connected with the principal street with a lane or passage. It is entirely enclosed and has two entrances. The surface is paved, but could be kept in a much cleaner condition. A shed, not slated and supported on metal pillars, runs along one side of the yard. This shed is about 90 x 14 feet, and at the end the butter is weighed and exposed for sale, and at the other end the potatoes and corn are weighed. There is also a small shed at another side of the yard, underneath which the carts and horses of those frequenting the markets are placed. There is a weigh-house with a machine outside. There are two beams and scales and a small beam for retailers. It is stated that the market yard affords sufficient accommodation for market purposes.

The fairs are held in the fair green which was provided in 1878 by the Duke of Devonshire. The green is on the road leading to the railway, to which it is within easy reach. It is entirely enclosed with a high stone wall and comprises in extent some 6 acres. Iron pens for sheep are erected, and for the use of those 6d. per pen is charged. A pen is capable of holding 12 sheep. Shed and water accommodation is also provided, and in fact the green, from its extent and other advantages, affords ample accommodation and is one of the finest I have seen. The townspeople and neighbouring farmers are to be congratulated upon having received such a free gift from the Lord of the Manor, as it has materially benefited them and thus indirectly increased the value of his Grace's other property. A caretaker is paid 4l. a year by the owner to look after the fair green and open it on fair days.

Between fairs the green is utilized for grazing and shows, the profit derived from which goes to the owner's own use. Previous to 1878 the fairs were held upon the public streets.

At the inquiry it was stated that the town commissioners are desirous of being empowered to make byelaws regulating the working and management of the butter market, and satisfaction was expressed at the present working of the other markets and fairs. It was suggested, however, that the weighing machine should be made capable of weighing live stock, as many farmers would prefer selling by live weight.

Appended will be found a transcript of the evidence taken at the inquiry.

John J. O'Meara,
Assistant Commissioner.

45, Lower Mount Street,
Dublin.

Lismore, 20th December 1888.

Francis Edward Currey, Esq., examined.

29,837. You represent the Duke of Devonshire here for the purposes of this inquiry?—Mr. Penrose the agent has asked me to come up here. I was agent before his appointment.

29,838. The Duke is the owner of any market rights that might exist in Lismore?—Yes. There are patents from the Crown.

29,839. What markets are held here?—There is no market, I think, except one for butter on every Monday in the week. I think there is no other regular market except that.

29,840. There is no general market at all?—No.

29,841. Supposing they bring in potatoes or any general commodities, where are they exposed for sale?—They are all brought into the same market place.

29,842. On Monday?—Not on Monday. They are brought any day.

29,843. Is there no particular day allotted off for the disposal of these?—There is no particular day for the sale of any particular kind of produce except butter. The other articles, such as hay, potatoes, and general merchandise, are brought every day of the week.

29,844–5. Where are they sold. Are there any market-buildings erected in the town?—Yes; the market place is close to the courthouse. The same place in which the butter is sold is the general market place.

29,846. They are also, I suppose, carried about to the shopkeepers of the town from door to door?—Such things as potatoes and hay are never carried from door to door but are brought to the market and sold there.

29,847. Who was it provided this market building?—The Duke.

29,848. You have not had any opportunity of getting the particulars of the cost of erection?—That was beyond my time, except some outlay that has been gone to from time to time in order to enlarge and improve it. Lately another entrance was made to facilitate the sale of butter.

29,849. What fairs are held here?—At present the fairs are monthly fairs held on the second Wednesday in every month.

29,850. Do you remember a period when there were no monthly fairs here?—Yes.

29,851. Are they of recent establishment?—Yes; about the year 1873, after the opening of the railway from Fermoy to here, which was made by the Duke of Devonshire. On the completion of that railway, the monthly fairs commenced to be held. Prior to that, there were four fairs here.

29,852. Could you give me the dates of them?—I am not quite certain of the dates. I think they were the 25th May, 25th September, 12th November, and 14th February.

29,853. Did they cease holding these old fairs when the monthly fairs were established?—Yes.

29,854. Tolls are not levied at any of these fairs?—No. The late Duke of Devonshire was entitled to them under his patent, but he gave them up long ago.

29,855. Do you remember when tolls were levied?—No. I can just remember the time they were given up. I think it must be 25 years ago, or so.

29,856. At one period tolls were levied?—I have no doubt they were, but I cannot speak as a matter of knowledge.

29,857. Have you heard tolls were levied here?—Yes.

29,858. Where are the fairs held?—The fairs are now held in a field between this place and the railway station. It is enclosed and given by the Duke for the purpose of holding the monthly fairs.

29,859–60. Did he provide this green at the establishment of the fairs in 1873?—No. They were not held in the fair field until 1878. Previous to that, they were held on the streets.

29,861. Could you give me any idea of the extent?—About eight acres; it is a large field.

29,862. Are there pens in it?—Yes.

29,863. Is there any shelter accommodation or sheds?—Yes sheds and water.

29,864. How is the fair green utilised between the monthly fairs?—Sometimes for grazing and also for shows, circuses, and things like that.

29,865. The profits from the shows and the grazing go to the Duke?—Yes

29,866. There are no tolls levied at these fairs?—No. The only thing is a small sum is paid for the pens. The pens which were originally put up were wooden, and they soon became decayed; it was impossible to keep them, and therefore I put up iron pens for sheep, and those who use these pens pay a small sum which goes towards the payment of the original cost of putting them up. They were costly pens, and as the [illegible] comes in they are [illegible] in [illegible] them, and I think Mr. [illegible] has [illegible], as was always my intention, that at no very distant date, when the cost is paid by these small charges, no further charge will be made.

29,867. What is the charge?—Sixpence for each pen.

29,868. How many sheep would each pen accommodate?—12 or 14, I suppose.

29,869. Is there any weighbridge erected at all?—Not there, but in the market there is.

29,870. One might be put up around it to make it available for weighing live stock?—No. There is nothing for weighing live stock. If there was one for weighing live stock it would be in the fair field.

29,871. Do you remember when the fairs were held on the streets?—Yes. They were held on the streets up to 1878.

29,872. Did you consider yourself that it was very objectionable to have the fairs held on the public thoroughfares in the town?—I considered it was very objectionable as a matter of public convenience, and also in reference to the sanitary state of the town, although I think everything was done that could be reasonably done to clean the town after the fairs, yet in wet weather the state of the town was not wholesome, and there was much inconvenience caused by the fairs to everybody who had to pass through the fairs or go about their ordinary business. There were some people who did not share my opinion about it, but I think they are all pretty well reconciled now. There was a good deal of opposition to their removal at the time on the part of some trading interest, more especially of one kind. It was thought their custom would be affected by it, but I am afraid it has not been affected by it much.

29,873. Do the farmers avail themselves of this fair green?—The farmers were very anxious for it. The farmers, with the exception of a few, and the buyers also were desirous to have accommodation at the fair field.

29,874. Have you had experience of fairs other than those of Lismore?—I think I know the fairs of Tallow and Cappoquin.

29,875. Are any of those fairs on the streets?—On the streets. I think the fairs of Cappoquin are still held on the street.

29,876. Have you formed any opinion as to the necessity of removing the fairs from the public thoroughfares throughout the country?—I think it would be very desirable if there could be a sufficiently convenient place provided for them. I think it would be very desirable to remove them off the streets of any town, but the inconvenience was felt much more here after the opening of the railway than before, because the fairs increased very largely in size. Prior to that, although they were objectionable and an inconvenience, it was not felt because the fairs were only four times a year, and not so large, and when they came to be held monthly, they were very much better fairs, and the quantity of all kinds of stock increased. Then of course the inconvenience was very much more felt. In Tallow they hold monthly fairs, but in point of size they are larger here because the railway does not go sufficiently near Tallow to make a large pig market.

29,877. Have you any rule restricting the exposure of animals elsewhere than in the fair green; or any rules or regulations to be observed by those frequenting the markets or fairs?—I do not know of any special rules. An attempt has been made to hold them on the public thoroughfare since the fair green was opened, but I think it would be very desirable that there should be some general legislative enactment that where a proper fair field is provided, it should be compulsory to sell in that fair field.

29,878. Have you had any experience of places where tolls are levied?—No; I have not. Tolls were levied, I believe, in Cappoquin, but not now. They are levied in Fermoy.

29,879. From your experience of the farmers do you think, where they are paying tolls at present or where they are paying no tolls and getting no accommodation, do you think they would be willing to pay a small toll if adequate accommodation were provided for them in the shape of a fair green with pens and shelter accommodation?—That is a question I could not answer. I could only answer it as a matter of conjecture more than anything else. I really think buyers and sellers would not be unwilling to pay a small toll, provided it was a small toll and spent for a public purpose such as the improvement of the fair green and providing it. I think it gives a far better tone to the fairs by not having tolls.

29,880. In other words, do you think the exaction of a toll acts as a deterrent on people bringing in the supply they otherwise would bring into the fair, or do they, as a matter of fact, only consider whether they would be able to effect a ready and quick sale of the animals?—I think it would prevent some people coming, because where people have free access they generally bring some cattle, and if not sold they go back free, but when you charge going into the field they will say there is no use in bringing what we cannot sell.

28,881. It is more or less a general question, because you say an exceptional state of things exists in Lismore, for you have here a fair green and accommodation and there is no charge?—It does not prevent cattle going to Fermoy, where the cattle/would go for personal and private benefit and not for a public purpose.

28,882. Do you think the fairs here being held in a fair green, where there is accommodation and the fact of their being left free would detract from the supply that would otherwise attend the Fermoy fairs?—No; it is too far away. I do not think it would in the least affect the Fermoy fairs. The fairs in Cappoquin have increased very much since the continuation of the railway on to Waterford; that was opened in August 1878. Since that period the fairs in Cappoquin have increased very largely and have extinguished the small local fairs held in the neighbourhood around.

28,883. Have you any suggestions to offer as to what you think would tend to the improvement of the fairs or markets in this place?—No. I do not know of anything.

28,884. Is there a weighmaster appointed here by the Duke of Devonshire?—Yes.

28,885. Who is he?—Mr. Thomas Walsh.

28,886. How is he paid?—He receives the fees. He was bridewell keeper and courthouse keeper. He is paid by the county a small salary for attending the courthouse and in the market he receives the fees.

28,887. Does he apply them to his own use?—Yes, except with regard to the butter. I had better just read the memorandum made at the time of his appointment, as there was a little special thing with regard to the butter market. (Reading)—Appointed by the Duke of Devonshire weighmaster of Lismore market during pleasure. He is to receive the fees as established heretofore for all articles weighed. As regards goods weighed on the weighbridge, he is on the 25th March of each year to hand over to the Duke of Devonshire one-third of the fees, until the balance due on the weighbridge, 15*l*., is paid off. [That really has not been done.] As regards the weighing of butter and the arrangement of the butter market, he is to conform to the regulations of the town commissioners, and each month to hand over to them two-thirds of the fees received for butter, they appointing and paying any extra hands required on market days. The management of the butter market was left with the town commissioners subject to these rules. Mr. Walsh has to keep the market place clean and in good order; he has to keep books and make entries of articles weighed, and the fees received for same, keeping separate accounts for the weighbridge and butter for the inspection of the Duke of Devonshire's agent, and so far as the butter is concerned for the town commissioners at their monthly meetings.

28,888. What year was he appointed?—The 12th February 1873.

28,889. I take it, then, that any fee he obtains for weighing general commodities at the house and scales go to his own use with the exception of the butter receipts, two-thirds of which go to the town commissioners?—Yes, and one-third to himself, and then the subsidiary arrangement about the weighbridge which was not carried out.

28,890. Did the Duke of Devonshire provide the house and scales?—Everything required for the market was supplied by the Duke.

28,891. Do you think on the whole the fact of the fairs being left free tends to improve them more or less?—I think so, certainly.

28,892. You found a radical improvement in the fairs after the fair green was provided?—I do not know the fairs were very much previously. They have been increasing from the time of the opening of the railway in 1872. I do not know that any special increase took place after they were removed to the fair green, but there is a better supply of cattle now than formerly.

28,893. The buyers have facilities for the removal of the stock as the fair green is adjacent to the railway station?—Yes. It could not be more conveniently situated than it is. There is an entrance from one side and an exit from the other, so that they can come in at either side from whatever direction they are coming.

28,894. All the animals coming here are sold in that fair green, and are never sold in the adjoining streets?—They are all sold in the fair green. There was very much expense incurred in making that—600*l*. or 700*l*. altogether.

28,895. You are unable to make up that amount for me?—I think Mr. Penny has given it to you in the query sheet. I think it is something between 600*l*. and 700*l*., and about 150*l*. was laid out since.

28,896. Would the site of the fair green, if not utilised for fair purposes, be otherwise of use?—Yes, for agricultural purposes as town fields. It was portion of the town park before being made a fair field.

Mr. Maurice Healy, Town Clerk, examined.

28,897. You are the town clerk of Lismore?—Yes.

28,898. When were the commissioners established?—They were established before I came to Lismore; they were established after the passing of the Towns Improvement Act.

28,899. What duties do they perform under the Act?—Well, their duties at present are very limited since their powers as a sanitary body were taken from them, this being a town with a population under 6,000. On the passing of the Act of 1878, their functions as a sanitary body passed to the board of guardians and at present they have very little to do except provide gas and cleanse the town.

28,900. Then I suppose the grand jury look after the paving and the roads?—They keep the roads in repair.

28,901. The commissioners have no control over the markets or fairs with the exception of the butter market?—Yes, and that by permission of the Duke.

28,902. When was the butter market established?—About 12 years ago, in 1875.

28,903. Could you give me the receipts of the commissioners for the past three years from the butter market?—Permit me to state that what Mr. Curry said is accurate as to two-thirds of the fees going to the town commissioners, but on some representations being made by Mr. Walsh of the amount of duty they performed in connexion with it, the commissioners allowed one-half instead of two-thirds to be handed to them by Mr. Walsh, and for several years past the commissioners have only been receiving one-half. In the current year the sales were 1,780 firkins. The charge is a 1*d*. a firkin, and the town commissioners received a ½*d*. The market is opened from November to May. The commissioners, therefore, received 3*l*. 14*s*. 7*d*. Last year, 1887, from May to November there were 2,943 firkins sold, and the commissioners received 6*l*. 2*s*. 1*d*. The previous year, 1886, there were 2,539 firkins, and the commissioners received 5*l*. 5*s*. 9*d*. That number does not exactly represent the firkins brought into the market, but only those sold. It is only on those sold, the weighmaster receives fees.

28,904. When firkins are brought in by the farmers, are they all taken to this market place?—Nearly all.

28,905. Is there any rule restraining them from going elsewhere and weighing the butter?—No, but the town commissioners are anxious there should be some restriction in that way. The question did not crop up until the last two years or there, when a gentleman commenced to buy butter in the town and they (some farmers) thought it more desirable to take the butter to his house and sell there, and the commissioners thought it would be better if the man found it convenient or to his advantage to attend the market and buy there. Some thought it was really desirable that sales of butter should be confined exclusively to the butter market.

28,906. As a matter of fact they are not?—Practically they are, but if anyone goes to him he buys at his own house.

28,907. Did the commissioners ever discuss the advisability of their obtaining as a local authority the control over the markets and fairs?—The question did not crop up except once or twice, when the butter merchants complained of excessive tares. They found the firkins were overweighted and they thought that was an injustice to them. The firkins presumed to be only 14 lbs. weight, and sometimes they found them to weigh 18 or 19 lbs. That was absolutely a fraud on the buyers. They complained to the butter that the firkins would not exceed 16 lbs., and they made a complaint to the town commissioners, and they had no power in the matter, but they thought it generally there should be some power of compelling the farmer to state exactly the weight of the firkin.

28,908. The coopers never brand the tare on the firkin?—No. Some of the coopers, it has been stated, really lent themselves open to make heavy firkins at the instance of the farmers.

28,909. You think that causes a want of confidence among the buyers in the market?—I do. I had a couple of letters complaining of the matter from one gentleman, who stated that he would not attend until some arrangement was adopted whereby parties would be compelled to have fair tares.

28,910. At present the commissioners are powerless to make rules or regulations or to enforce them when made?—They are, but they published a recommendation to the farmers to bring in firkins not exceeding 16 lbs. in weight.

28,911. Do you think a necessity exists for local authorities, who are not urban sanitary authorities, obtaining power to make and enforce bye-laws regulating the markets and fairs, whenever bye-laws they think necessary for the locality?—I think it is desirable.

28,912. So far as you are concerned it is desirable in Lismore?—Except in that one instance nothing comes to my knowledge. This town is exceptionally situated, because practically the Duke of Devonshire has vested in the commissioners authority over them, except that they have no legal right or any power to enforce any regulation they may make. As a matter of public policy, I may say I think it is desirable local authorities should have legal rights controlling the markets.

28,913. It is your opinion that throughout the country local authorities should have control over the markets and fairs?—I think so.

28,914. Have you heard that opinion expressed by any of the commissioners or those who live elsewhere than in Lismore?—Well, no. I do not think I did.

28,915. Apart from Lismore, because the owner of the market rights seems to have done everything in his power to please the people of this town, do you think markets and fairs would be better managed and managed more to the satisfaction of those frequenting them by a local authority than if the control were vested in a private individual?—I can hardly be in a position to say they would. I really think where there is an energetic man who has proprietary rights, if he looked after the matter he could make as efficient arrangements for the public interest as a public body. Really my opinion is worthless. I am not familiar with the trading arrangements or business of the fairs.

28,916. What are your town rates?—Well for many years they did not exceed 6d. in the pound but for the last two years they are [illegible]d.

28,917. Is that your only revenue?—That is the only revenue, except that the Duke of Devonshire gives an annual donation of 20l. towards the funds, and the sweeping of the streets, and half the fines at petty sessions for drunkenness and cases of that kind. Mr. Curry is town justice.

28,918. You have a town magistrate?—Yes.

28,919. You have not engaged any assistance for Mr. Walsh as mentioned; that is you have no expenses in connexion with the butter market?—Practically none. On an odd day a few years ago, when the butter was coming in large quantities, the town commissioners compelled their scavenger to assist on Mondays in weighing the butter.

28,920. Is there anything else you would wish to mention?—No.

28,921. Or have you any suggestion to offer?—No.

Mr. THOMAS WALSH examined.

28,922. You are the weigh master here?—Yes.

28,923. You were appointed in 1875 by the Duke of Devonshire?—Yes.

28,924. Have you any rule in the market compelling people who bring marketable commodities there to weigh them at your scales?—No.

28,925. No such rule exists?—No.

28,926. What scales have you there?—Butter scales and potato scales. The corn is weighed on the potato scales.

28,927. You have two houses and scales?—Yes.

28,928. And weighing machine?—Yes.

28,929. What commodities do you usually weigh on market days?—The markets generally commence in the middle of May with fifty firkins and end in November.

28,930. That is as regards the butter market, but what other commodities do you weigh?—Potatoes and corn if we get it, but there is very little now; some wool in the shearing season, and hay and straw.

28,931. Is roll butter ever brought here?—No. It is always brought in firkins and kegs.

28,932. When weighing firkins you charge 1d. for each firkin?—A penny for each firkin to the buyer. I will just explain to you. Under some rule the buyers stop 6d. for the firkin of butter from the seller, and out of that 6d. they pay me the penny for each firkin.

28,933. Is that rule of stopping 6d. confined to the Lismore butter market?—I do not know.

28,934. Do you know of it being practised elsewhere?—Well, I think it is in Dungarvan. Besides the 1d. for the ticket for weighing I think the buyers deduct 6d. from the firkin too.

28,935. It is the buyer who pays your charge?—Yes.

28,936. The butter is always sold before it is weighed?—No. It is weighed before it is sold. We number the firkins from one to a hundred as the case may be, consecutively, and mark the weight of the firkin on it and the buyers buy according to their own judgment.

28,937. You give no tickets?—No tickets, but mark the weight in chalk on the side of the firkin.

28,938. It is only the gross weight you mark?—Yes.

28,939. You never estimate the tare or actually strip the firkins?—No.

28,940. Do you ever drain them?—Yes. We drain every one of them before it is weighed.

28,941. Who assists you?—A man, who puts the butter into the scales and takes it out again.

28,942. Is that the seller?—No, but the scavenger.

28,943. Does he knock the top off, and bore up the firkins?—Yes. He turns them over, and drains them.

28,944. It is only when the buyers have bought the butter you receive the charge, although you have weighed all the firkins?—Yes.

28,945. If not sold you receive no charge?—No. Very often there are 40 and 50 firkins unsold that we weigh and get nothing for them.

28,946. Where do they place the butter, or do they leave it in the market until the following market day?—No.

28,947. Have you got any storage accommodation there?—No. I contrive to store two or three or five firkins occasionally for country people in the small [illegible] market. I may tell you that any butter that remains unsold on market day here, is generally taken to Dungarvan the next day.

28,948. They always come here on Monday?—Yes.

28,949. The other commodities such as potatoes and wool come every day?—Yes.

28,950. Then you have always the house and scales available when they come?—Yes.

28,951. When weighing the butter, down to what weight do you weigh with?—1 lb.

28,952. To 1 lb.?—Yes; if it weighs ½ lb., we will not give it.

28,953. Do you give a turn of the beam as well?—Yes.

28,954. How do the buyers buy the firkin. Do they buy per firkin or by the weight?—By the weight marked on the firkin, and using their own judgment in calculating the price.

28,955. Is the tare a matter of agreement between the buyer and seller?—No. On some few occasions the buyers, seem to have very grave doubts, where some of the firkins are very heavy, and in three or four instances, they got a cooper and stripped them, and some of them were four pounds over the legal tare.

28,956. What is the customary tare?—15 lbs. for a full firkin and only 9 lbs. for kegs of about 56 lbs. gross weight.

28,957. Is that tare of 15 lbs. for a full firkin and 9 lbs. for the 56 lbs. firkins, the only deduction from the gross weight?—No. After the buying the butter, if they do not object to the firkins as heavy, there is no other argument and they pay them.

28,958. Supposing a 56 lbs. keg was brought in and there were not actually 56 lbs. in the firkin, say there were 53, would they only pay for 53 lbs., or would they pay for 56?—The ordinary weight of these kegs is 56 lbs., there are 9 lbs. equal tare, and they pay for 47 lbs.

28,959. Then they always give the farmer the exact value down to a lb. of butter?—Yes.

28,960. Whether it is over the given quantity supposed to be in the firkin or not?—Yes.

28,961. At what hour does this butter market commence?—The butter begins to come in about 10 o'clock and sometimes continues to come in until 2.

28,962. Have you any certain hour for the buying to commence?—Yes, at 1 o'clock.

28,963. I suppose you have the greater proportion of the butter weighed by that time?—We have all that is in the market weighed, but there is some comes after that.

28,964. You have no extra charge on the butter that comes in late?—No.

28,965. What hour does the market usually terminate?—About 2 o'clock, or half past 2 the very latest.

28,966. Where do the buyers attend from?—The buyers from Waterford and Dungarvan reach here about 11 o'clock.

28,967. What is your charge on potatoes?—A 1d. a bag for weighing.

28,968. I suppose you have the same charge on corn?—Yes.

28,969. On wool what is it?—A 1d. a stone.

28,970. Have you a schedule of the prices, and a copy of it here?—I have.

28,971. It is posted in the market place?—Yes.

28,972. So that the people can always have an opportunity of looking at it?—Yes.

28,973. Well now, I suppose, for any horse load, you weigh at the weigh bridge you charge 4d., no matter what the commodity is?—Yes. There is only hay and straw.

28,974. Do you weigh any timber?—There is very little comes. There is a weighbridge erected for that purpose down near the Castle; they weigh their own timber there. No timber comes in here but the timber sold for fuel.

28,975. Do you weigh loads of turnips?—Yes.

28,976. You charge 4d. for that?—Yes.

28,977. You charge 4d., no matter what commodity is in the load?—Yes.

28,978. And 2d. for a donkey load?—Yes. If they have small loads they dispute very hard, so I very often have to let them go.

28,979. You give and take?—Yes.

28,980. Down to what weight do you weigh potatoes; do you weigh under a half stone?—A half stone.

28,981. You do not weigh under it?—No.

28,982. Do you give a cut of the tare?—Yes. We allow half a stone for the sack.

28,983. That is 7 lbs. tare?—Yes.

28,984. You never actually weigh the empty sacks?—Never.

28,985. So then if a man came in with a bag of potatoes containing 10 stone 6 lbs., you would only call out the gross weight as 10 stone and he would only be paid for 9½ stone?—He would be paid for 10 stone in that case.

28,986. You only put a half stone into the scale?—Yes.

28,987. If the usual weight was 10 stone 6 lbs., and if it did not take the additional half stone, the 6 lbs. are taken off?—Yes, we never weigh the pounds.

28,988. And there would be 7 lbs. for the bag?—Yes.

28,989. Then he would be paid for 9½ stone?—Yes.

28,990. Is the tare always 7 lbs.?—Yes.

28,991. No matter on a fine day or on a very wet day, when the sack is completely saturated with wet?—If very bad for the day around the potatoes we sometimes allow more than that.

28,992. That is when the buyer and seller agree to the additional tare?—Yes.

28,993. They never leave it to you?—They never dispute.

28,994. You only ascertain the gross weight?—Yes.

28,995. Do you give a docket?—Yes.

28,996. Is it a printed form?—In writing.

28,997. Do you put the name of the seller on it?—Yes.

28,998. Who pays the charge?—The seller.

28,999. Have the potatoes been sold before they are weighed at your scales?—Always.

29,000. And corn and wool?—Yes.

29,001. Where do they expose them for sale?—In the market yard.

29,002. None of these commodities are ever exposed on the street?—Not to my knowledge.

29,003. Do vegetables come here?—None to the market. They hawk them about the streets.

29,004. You receive no charge for them?—No. They do not come into the market at all, but if they do they might have the vegetables with the potatoes and sell both together, but I receive no charge.

29,005. Supposing the potatoes are brought into the market place and exposed for sale and sold, but not weighed at your scales, would you seek for any charge?—No. That is a thing that does not occur at all.

29,006. They always weigh them?—Yes.

29,007. Down to what weight do you weigh corn?—The very same weight.

29,008. Down to a half stone?—No. We weigh it to the pound, and where the sacks are not weighed we generally allow 4 lbs. for them.

29,009. Is there any portorage charge in connexion with potatoes or corn?—No.

29,010. The seller has to pay an additional charge?—No.

29,011. Do you know is there any deduction besides the tare in either the quantity of the corn or the price of it?—No.

29,012. Nothing is stopped by the purchaser from the contract price?—Nothing.

29,013. Do you weigh down to a ½ lb. in wool?—We weigh the large bags to the pound, but we weigh the small bags to the ½ lb.

29,014. I suppose you charge 1d. no matter what the quantity may be?—It is 1d. a stone.

29,015. If half a stone you charge 1d.?—Yes, any fractional part of a stone. I may tell you, as far as the wool is concerned, it is only weighed two or three days in the year about the shearing time.

29,016. Do you keep any record of the quantity of the different commodities you weigh?—I keep a record of the butter, roots, hay and straw, but I do not keep a record of the potatoes.

29,017. Do you ever make up the tickets for the people?—Yes. I do not think I am bound to, but I generally do it to oblige them.

29,018. Then you become acquainted with the contract prices of these commodities?—Yes.

29,019. I am not asking you to do it, but supposing I was required to make a return of the current prices of these different commodities, could you make such a return, or would it be possible for you to make a pretty accurate return of the current prices of the different commodities exposed for sale and sold in the market?—It would not be impossible, but it would be very troublesome to me.

29,020. It is possible, but it would entail additional labour on yourself?—It would.

29,021. The return would be a pretty accurate one?—Yes.

29,022. Would you have any objection to tell me what would be the average receipts for weighing these different commodities, with the exception of the butter?—Well, I think so far as I could make out, it would be 10*l*. a year.

29,023. In addition to half the butter market fees?—Yes.

29,024. I suppose the accounts you gave Mr. Healy are an accurate one?—Yes. I produced the book.

29,025. Well, now, is there any shelter accommodation in this market?—There is shed accommodation. There is about 30 feet of a shed which is about 15 feet wide. There is another shed with a wooden roof, but it is not much used for anything but horses or cars to be put there.

29,026. You receive no stallage rents for the use of the shed?—No.

29,027. No rates at all except the weighing charges?—Nothing whatever, except what I gave you.

29,028. What hour is this market usually open in the morning?—At 8 o'clock.

29,029. Until what hour?—Until six in the summer time and dark in the winter.

29,030. Are there any rules regulating the market at all?—No rules I am aware of, with the exception of the schedule of fees for weighing.

29,031. In the butter market have the buyers themselves arranged any rules?—No.

29,032. Is there anything you would wish to mention as to what you think would tend to improve or develop the market?—Nothing; but the buyers on several occasions suggested many changes. Of course I had nothing to do with that. I told them to apply to the town commissioners. On two occasions there were two very fraudulently packed firkins brought to the market. The sides of the firkin were filled up with inferior stuff, and in boring the butter they did not come at that. The butter was conveyed to the purchaser's place, and it was then discovered. They went to me to see if I would taste the butter, but unfortunately at the time we were not in a position to do so, but we got into the system of numbering the firkins, and marking the weight on them, and taking down the names of the sellers with weights, and after doing that we detected them.

29,033. Do you think the practice of making up fraudulent butter would be stopped if there was always an independent tasting of the butter in the butter markets; that is if an official having control of the market was also butter taster?—Yes, I think that would be the proper way, but in a very small market they could hardly pay the expense.

JAMES O'BRIEN, Esq., Chairman of the Town Commissioners, examined.

29,034. (Witness.) I think the seller would prefer to sell the butter as it stands. They would not wish to expose the quality of the butter.

29,035. But do not you think if the quality of the butter were exposed, it would stop the practice of bringing bad butter. Do not you think it would tend to improve the making of the butter if it was exposed, when they bring in bad butter?—They would not wish to have their neighbours know it.

29,036. Do not you think they would improve the quality of the butter if under the fear of exposure?—Every buyer is considered to be a judge of his business, and he is naturally to sist himself, and he will not buy butter without testing it. He sees the weight and knows the price by that morning's paper, and I ask the price of a firkin the same as selling a cow or pig, and we divide the difference and come to an agreement. They prefer that system to any other.

29,037. Do you buy butter yourself?—I do not.

29,038. By what prices do they go when buying a firkin?—By the Cork market.

29,039. Do they give the Cork prices?—They exceed them sometimes, and very often they do not come up to them. It is principally the Waterford buyers who attend, and the price of butter in Waterford is often 10s. a hundred higher than Cork. They are in a position to use the Cork prices as the leading prices. It suits them, as they are the lowest.

29,040. Do they classify the butter?—Yes, by their own judgment.

29,041. Do you think the farmers are in a position to have equal experience with the buyer in order to obtain the best price?—The farmers know the quality nearly as good as the buyer.

29,042. You do not think the buyer has any advantage over the farmer if the testing and fixing of the quality of the butter is left to themselves, you do not think the producer is at the mercy of the buyer?—No; if anything he is better able to sell than the buyer can get the value of his money in any commodity.

29,043. Did you ever hear any complaints of the management of the markets here?—Never.

29,044. They seem to work to the satisfaction of the buyers and sellers?—Yes, indeed.

29,045. General market and all?—Yes. I know the farmers come from within two or three miles of Mitchelstown, one of the largest butter districts in the country bordering Tipperary side. The farmers come from within three miles of Mitchelstown and attend the market and can get a better price than in Mitchelstown, for in Mitchelstown they buy only 3 qrs. of butter, and if there were 3 qrs. and 6 lbs. in the firkin they would be only paid for 3 qrs., whereas by our rule if a firkin weighs 3 qrs. and 6 lbs. the farmer is paid for the 6 lbs., and the buyer gets the value of his money.

29,046. Do you know the practice in Mitchelstown?—Yes. The farmer has to pay 1s. or 1s. 6d. for less than 3 qrs.

29,047. The buyer is never at a loss for a lesser quantity than 3 qrs., but the producer is?—Yes, the producer is at a loss.

29,048. Do they ever come from Mitchelstown here?—Yes, within a few miles of Mitchelstown.

29,049. From what districts are the general marketable commodities brought?—They are brought from Ballyporeen and the borders of Mitchelstown. A quantity of butter comes to the market.

29,050. Where do the potatoes and corn come from?—They come a distance of seven or eight miles.

29,051. Is much of the corn sold to private merchants in the corn?—All nearly. All the corn sold is used.

29,052. You would not say this is a corn market?—No. There are two large corn stores over the bridge, and the corn is brought very extensively.

29,053. Do you know the practice of buying and selling in the stores?—I do, for I am engaged in it myself.

29,054. Do you weigh corn for the farmers there?—Yes.

29,055. Do you charge anything for weighing?—Nothing.

29,056. Is the tare 4 lbs.?—4 lbs. and 7 lbs. If we get corn well cleaned and good value, we give them 7 lbs. as the smallest weight we can.

29,057. Down to 7 lbs.?—Yes.

29,058. Do you always weigh the empty sack?—Yes, always.

29,059. Is there any deduction from the gross weight other than the tare?—Nothing.

29,060. There is no deduction for damage or the bad state of the corn?—Nothing.

29,061. You look at the corn before you purchase it?—Yes, and we see it thrown.

29,062. How do you buy it?—By the barrel or 14 stones.

29,063. Is it all oats you buy?—All oats.

29,064. You do not buy any wheat or barley?—No.

29,065. Supposing they had less than 14 stones in the barrel, are you at the loss of that or do you deduct proportionately?—If the sack does not carry 14 stones I will say and 13 stone 10 lbs.

29,066. If over 14 stone you pay proportionately?—Yes, for 14 stone 8 lbs., 14 stone 6 lbs., and 14 stone 7 lbs. When these weights are added up they are made into barrels, stones, and lbs.

29,067. Do you deduct anything for the sack?—No.

29,068. There is no porterage charge?—No.

29,069. Who performs the duty of lifting the sacks up to the scales or on to the loft?—The buyer's men. He uses a windlass.

29,070. You charge nothing?—No. We get help from the farmers' men if we have a busy day, but we have several men of our own fit to carry on the business, except there is a heavy day's work.

29,071. The reason I ask you is because in other places the seller has to perform these duties?—We could not ask a poor man after a long journey to do that.

29,072. What quantity of corn is brought here. Could you give any approximate idea of the number of barrels?—On an average about 10,000 barrels.

29,073. Is that into your own place?—Yes.

29,074. Would you say an equal quantity comes to other merchants?—I think the same quantity goes to Tallow to Mr. Murphy.

29,075. There are only two of you?—Yes, and another man has started in Cappoquin.

29,076. I believe you are a town commissioner?—Yes. I am the chairman.

29,077. Do you concur in the remark of Mr. Healy, when he stated the commissioners would like to have power to make byelaws regulating the market, especially the butter market, in the cases mentioned?—Well, I would wish that power would be vested in the town commissioners.

29,078. Do you think a necessary statute [illegible] some bye-laws to be made regulating the market and to be observed by the buyers and sellers?—Yes, I think so. It would be well to give us some control.

29,079. Have you had experience of other fairs and markets yourself?—No, I have not. I know in Fermoy they have tolls. The fair field belongs to Mr. Brown. They pay for cattle and pigs and everything there.

29,080. Do you think that acts in any way as a deterrent upon them in bringing in the animals and exposing them for sale, the fact of a toll being levied on them as they enter the fair green?—Oh, I think a farmer would grumble very much if he had to pay a toll for cattle.

29,081. Have you heard that it does not work well in Fermoy?—It does not work well in Fermoy. They grumble very much. Our fair is a larger fair, but Fermoy is a better district, and the fairs are better supplied because we are near the mountain and are not able to show the same sort of cattle.

29,082. Is there anything you would like to suggest?—At present I think everything is in fair working order here. I do not know there is anything to say as regards the accommodation in the fair field. In the past we got pens up one time and they are all fallen away, particularly in the pig department. A man driving a lot of pigs is not able to keep them together, they mix so much together. The cattle are better kept, they are all right. There is a portion of the field kept apart for fat pigs.

29,083. At present the different species of animals intermix?—Yes.

29,084. You would like to see different places allotted off for each species of animal?—Yes.

29,085. Are pigs sold on fair days?—Yes; the same day as cattle.

29,086. You have no pig fair the day previous?—No; the one day for young pigs, fat pigs, and cattle.

29,087. What hour does this fair usually begin?—6 o'clock in the morning in summer time, but the pig fair commences now at 9 o'clock by a rule that was made.

29,088. Up to what hour does it last?—Up to 12 o'clock the pigs are supposed to be brought.

Mr. John Newman, Town Commissioner, examined.

(Witness.) I do not know I really have anything to say, except that I think the commissioners should have power to deal with fraudulently made butter. At present if there is any fraudulently made butter, they are powerless the same as any ordinary individual. I daresay they could and I doubt if they could bring a case before the petty sessions, but it would be very desirable if the town commissioners had some power to deal with it. It does not frequently happen that the butter is fraudulently prepared. It has occurred very often a few years ago, but I think its being detected at the time and the notice and caution given to the people prevented it. At the same time I think it has occurred occasionally.

(Mr. Walsh.) There has been no case for the last three years.

(Mr. Healy.) I think the commissioners [illegible] for each special complaint made in order that the buyer should not be at any loss.

(The Commissioner, to Mr. Newman.) The fair green here works satisfactorily. Yes, I should say so.

Have you had experience of other fairs?—Well, yes, I have and markets. I was on [illegible] at last Saturday at the Fermoy market, and I know there is certainly an objection to the fees on a good many things. For instance, on the fowl coming into the market they charge 1d. a head, and very often those fowl are not sold, and the seller has to pay a fee whether they are sold or not. However, that is an indifferent market.

29,094. Do you think the fact of the fairs and markets being free, induces the buyers and sellers to attend them?—I should say so, particularly with a fair field such as we have here.

29,095. Do you think where there is no such accommodation provided, that the farmers would have any objection to pay a small charge to the maintenance of such accommodation if provided?—I should say the farmers would not have any objection to pay a small toll, whatever it is, if they got adequate accommodation, such as pens and things of that kind, but if not, I think they would have a decided objection to pay. I think it adds materially to our fair here, its being free. There is no doubt about it, because men very often send a lot of cattle in on speculation when it costs them nothing, but when they find they have to pay they will not do that.

Mr. John Hickey, Town Commissioner, examined.

29,096. You are a trader in the town?—Yes. I think you have got all the evidence with the exception of a weighbridge for weighing cattle. It would tend very much to the improvement of the fairs.

29,097. Are the buyers disposed to buy by live weight?—I do not know that. I think the farmers are more inclined to sell by live weight because they are not judges, and they have an advantage of them.

29,098. The buyers have an advantage over the sellers in that respect?—Yes. I think if rails were put around the weighbridge and a small charge made, the farmers would have no objection to pay. It would be a great insight to a man to know the weight of his cattle.

29,099. Have you heard them discussing that?—Yes, several times, because they said an Act of Parliament was passed to that effect.

29,100. (The Commissioner, to Mr. Curry.) Do you think the seller would wish to sell by live weight?—Yes.

29,101. (Mr. Newman.) I agree with those observations.

29,102. (Mr. O'Brien.) I think the farmers are not judges of the weight of fat cattle. They ask a good big price and then have to bring home the cattle without selling them, and perhaps after three weeks would have to sell them at the same price, whereas if there was a weighbridge as Mr. Hickey proposes, the cattle could be weighed and we could see the London and Liverpool market prices, and be able to ask in or near the value, and that would be a great advantage to the farmer.

29,103. You think a farmer occasionally receives too high a price and sometimes too low?—It is often the case, when the buyer is the judge, that he does not get too high a price. The farmer does not know the value of the animal.

29,104. You think the proper way to sell animals would be so much per weight?—Yes. We would know what to ask when we drive our beast to the fair.

29,105. Do you think that would work satisfactorily?—Yes.

29,106. Had you any discussion with the buyers on the subject?—Yes. The buyers know the weight much better than the farmers.

29,107. (Mr. Curry.) The buyer is always at the work and the farmer is only occasionally at the work, and they get to know by sight and go very near the weight.

29,108. (Mr. Healy.) Sometimes the buyer goes out to the road and meets the cattle.

29,109. Do they forestall here?—They do sometimes go out to the road to meet the cattle, and supposing there is an advance in the price or fluctuations in the market, they would take advantage in that way where the farmer was ignorant of the fact.

29,110. Have the people complained of that, or do the other buyers?—The people cannot complain of it because they make their bargain. The other buyers would complain.

29,111. (Mr. O'Brien.) The real buyers never leave the fair. It is only the jobbers. They go out to the cross-roads and meet the cattle and come along with the cattle until they meet the buyer; they want in order that he would have the first chance.

29,112. Are fowl brought here?—Yes. There is a gentleman here who brings fresh butter and fowl.

29,113. They are never brought to the market?—No.

29,114. Is there any other gentleman who has any evidence to give? (No answer.)

The inquiry then terminated.

CITY OF CASHEL.

With reference to my inquiry in Cashel on the 31st day of December 1888, I beg to report as follows:—

Cashel is an inland city in the county of Tipperary. It is built on the sides of a rock which rises in the middle of an extensive plain. The trade is poor and this is mainly due to the isolated position of the city, the only means of communication to which is by car. The local affairs are administered by a board of town commissioners and the population is 3,961.

The market days are Wednesday and Saturday principally. The fairs are held on the second Wednesday of each month and on the 26th March and 7th August. A pig fair is held on the last Wednesday of each month.

The fairs are toll free and the markets are likewise, but with respect to the latter, weighing charges are levied for weighing butter, wool, and cartloads of different marketable commodities. Sacks of potatoes, corn, &c. are weighed gratuitously.

The market charges are payable to the town commissioners who have provided a beam and scales and a weighing machine. The weighing machine has been sublet by the town commissioners to a Mr. Patrick Duggan, the weighmaster, at the yearly rent of 10*l.* and who charges 2*d.* for weighing each cartload. The charges at the beam and scales on butter and wool are also collected by Mr. Duggan on behalf of the town commissioners, and for performing this duty as well as weighing other commodities at the scales gratuitously, he receives a salary of 15*l.* The receipts of the town commissioners from this source amounts to only 9*l.*

Previous to 1853 tolls were levied at the markets and fairs then held, and in that year a Mr. Jordan was in the receipt of them, with the exception of the fairs on 26th March and 7th August, under a lease from Mr Richard Pennyfeather, at the yearly rent of 3*l.* 16*s.* 11*d.* The town commissioners it appears being desirous of improving the trade of the town by removing all charges or duties on the different commodities brought into and exposed for sale in the town, entered into negotiations with Mr Jordan which resulted in his transferring his interest in the tolls to the town commissioners on getting a lease of some 160 acres of corporation property at 120*l.* a year. The lease of the tolls is for 30 years unexpired at the termination of which they revert to Mr. Richard Pennyfeather who seemingly claims the exercise of the market privileges.

On obtaining control of the market and fair rights, the town commissioners ceased collecting tolls and induced the Archbishop of Cashel, who was the owner of the tolls at the fairs on the 26th March and 7th August, to do likewise. Since 1853, therefore, the tolls have not been levied. The fairs on the second Wednesday of each month were only held for the first time in 1853 as were also the pig fairs. I was unable to trace the establishment of the fairs on 26th March and 7th August which are said to have been held from time immemorial.

The public records show only one patent to have been granted for the town of Cashel. It is dated 3rd October, 13 Charles I. and authorised the Mayor, &c. of Cashel to hold a Wednesday and Saturday market and fairs on 29th and 30th August and 22nd and 23rd October. None of the present fairs seem, therefore, to be held under the authority of an express grant.

In accordance with my instructions I have inspected the market and fair places.

The monthly cattle and pig fairs are held on the public streets, principally the main street, which is wide, and it was stated affords sufficient space accommodation. No pens or shelter or other accommodation is provided except such shelter as the adjoining houses can afford. The fairs on the 26th March and 7th August are held at the original site for them at Ladyswell another portion of the town of Cashel and the public thoroughfare. No accommodation is provided here as on the main street.

The markets are held indiscriminately about the public streets, and standings, &c. are erected on the main street on market days. The butter is, however, sometimes brought under a shed or weighhouse which the town commissioners have erected in the centre of the main street, and where scales are erected; a weighing machine has been likewise erected. This is the only market accommodation provided.

The principal complaint was with reference to the want of prosperity in connexion with the markets and fairs which was attributed in strong terms to the absence of railway communication, and a desire was manifested to improve the trade of the town by the development of the markets and fairs if satisfactory and expeditious means of transit were provided. At present the producers of the town and neighbourhood have to dispose of their stock elsewhere, whereas the additional expense of transit, thus necessarily incurred by them, could be saved if railway communication was constructed. It was also strongly urged that town commissioners should receive compulsory powers to acquire any legal market rights vested in Mr. Pennyfeather, as at the expiration of the outstanding lease he or his representatives will be in a position to re-exact the tolls previously levied in the town a circumstance which it was said would tend to still further affect the trade and prosperity of Cashel.

Appended will be found a transcript of the evidence taken at the inquiry.

JOHN J. O'MEARA,
Assistant Commissioner.

45, Lower Mount Street,
Dublin.

Cashel, 31st December 1888.

Mr. JOHN CLEARY, Town Clerk, examined.

29,115. You are the town clerk of Cashel?—Yes.

29,116. When was the commission established?—In 1844.

29,117. Are the town commissioners the owners of the market rights existing in Cashel?—In 1826 the Lord Lieutenant granted Richard Pennefather the right to hold a monthly fair in the city of Cashel. He leased the rights to the late Alley Jordan, town clerk. He held a large farm, and in 1856 the commissioners gave him a lease of the land at a yearly rent on the condition of his surrendering the right to levy tolls. Now the town commissioners levy no tolls.

29,118. Are the market rights vested in the town commissioners, or are the fairs held on the property leased to this gentleman?—I suppose they are vested in the town commissioners now.

29,119. Are they held on the fair green?—They pay Richard Pennefather 2l. 16s. 11d.

29,120. On what term did you give Mr. Jordan this field?—A lease of 31 years.

29,121. Are the fairs held in this field?—They are held in the streets of Cashel.

29,122. Have they been always held on the streets?—Always.

29,123. What fairs are held here?—The second Wednesday of each month, and two old fairs.

29,124. Were these granted by the patent in 1826?—Yes.

29,125. What are the dates?—The 26th March and 7th August.

29,126. Was it in 1855 the tolls ceased to be collected?—Yes.

29,127. What markets are held here?—We have a butter market. That is held in a large house. The town commissioners charge ½d. for weighing all lumps up to 7 lbs. and 1d. for weighing all lumps exceeding 7 lbs.

29,128. What day is this butter market held?—Saturday.

29,129. There is no special day of the week allotted off for the exposure of the different marketable commodities?—Wednesday in the good times used to be market day also, but every Saturday hay, corn, and other commodities come in.

29,130. Are they brought in great abundance on Saturday?—Yes, and at the same time they are weighed and sold on all days.

29,131. The butter market is held in an enclosed building?—Yes, with plenty of accommodation.

29,132. Who provided this building?—The town commissioners.

29,133. When?—About 25 years ago.

29,134. Was it at that period the butter market was established?—Yes. There was always a butter market here, but it is only then they got the use of the house.

29,135. Must all farmers or farmers' wives who bring in butter to the town of Cashel avail themselves of the butter market?—No. They are not bound to; they can make use of the house and weigh the butter where they like.

29,136. If they do not avail themselves of your scales there is no charge?—No.

29,137. When weighing the butter do you give a ticket denoting the weight of it?—Yes.

29,138. Is it a printed ticket?—Yes.

29,139. On that ticket do you ever put the name of the seller?—No.

29,140. Only the gross weight?—Yes, and the price.

29,141. Are there any standings around on market days?—Yes, but there is no charge.

29,142. Those standings comprise cars and small standings about the streets?—Yes. This is a regular free trade town.

29,143. Are there any particular streets allotted off for the exposure of the different species of animals on fair days?—No.

29,144. They intermix indiscriminately?—Yes. They do not go into John's Street; it is too narrow. Ladies Well was the place for the old fairs and the main street for the new fairs.

29,145. Is that the main street with the large building in the centre?—That is it.

29,146. Were tolls levied at the whole 14 fairs at any time?—I understand not.

29,147. (*Mr. Wilde.*) At the old fairs tolls were levied until the year 1856. I have paid tolls myself at the monthly fairs. The new fairs were not established in 1826.

29,148. (*To the Town Clerk.*) Have you a pig fair the day previous to these fairs?—No. It is held on the last Wednesday of each month.

29,149. Could you tell me the average receipts from the butter market?—About 9l. a year. The weighmaster's salary is 15l. so there is a loss of 6l. by the transaction.

29,150. Has the weighmaster any other duties to perform in connexion with the town commissioners?—He is general weighmaster and has 30l. a year for that and 15l. for the butter alone.

29,151. You weigh the commodities throughout the week?—Yes. He gets 2d. a load for weighing, he weighs potatoes free of any charge, oats and wheat are free too, and all is free except a whole load weighed on the machine.

29,152. I suppose when you say oats you mean all descriptions of corn?—Yes.

29,153. When you utilise the beam and scales for weighing any small quantity in a bag you do not charge at all?—No.

29,154. Except on butter?—Yes.

29,155. Then on the weighing machine the charge is 2d. a load?—Yes.

29,156. Whether it is a donkey load or a horse load?—Yes. Even if 40 loads were weighed separate there would be no charge.

29,157. Would you not charge 6d. a load?—I mean to say if weighed on the scales.

29,158. That is a load in small quantities?—Yes. I also weighed 60 loads in that way.

29,159. Does he give a ticket when weighing the load?—Yes.

29,160. Does he ever ascertain the tare of the cart?—Yes, always.

29,161. Are there any other scales in the town besides those belonging to the commissioners?—Not at present. Mr. [illegible] had a scales and he is dead.

29,162. If the people wanted to ascertain the weight of their commodities would they go to him?—Yes.

29,163. And have they to come to the commissioners' scales now?—Yes.

29,164. Did you ever levy any charge for weighing packs of wool?—Never. The weighing master is allowed 1d. a pack for wool. It is a trifling thing.

29,165. Previous to 1855 were charges levied at the markets as well as the fairs?—No.

29,166. The markets within your recollection have always been free?—Yes.

29,167. Are they good markets here?—No; but very poor.

29,168. What do you assign now for that?—The smallness of the population and the want of railway communication.

29,169. Is very much of the country around in tillage or what percentage would you say?—Very little. I suppose not one in 10 acres.

29,170. Have the commissioners ever discussed the question of the progress of the markets and brought forward any scheme to develop them?—No. They attribute it exclusively to the want of railway communication.

29,171. What induced them in 1855 to abolish the tolls on the fairs?—They thought they would improve the fairs of the town.

29,172. Is that their opinion as a body that the levying of tolls takes from the prosperity of the fairs?—I was not connected with the board at the time but I presume that was the reason.

29,173. What is your opinion?—It was.

29,174. Have you attended fairs where tolls were levied?—Yes.

29,175. And fairs where tolls were not levied?—Yes.

29,176. Have you sold at these?—I have.

29,177. If you found two fairs one at which tolls were levied and another toll free but the cost of transit to the one that was toll free was greater than the other but both equally good marts, would you go to the one that was toll free?—Farmers do not consider those things.

29,178. They consider whether there is a ready market or not?—Yes.

29,179. They do not consider the question of tolls?—No.

THOMAS LAFFAN, Esq., M.D., Chairman of Town Commissioners, examined.

29,180. You are chairman of the town commissioners?—Yes. I wish to call attention to the fact that these tolls though not levied off the people still they are paid out of the corporate property, and are a tax on the people. We consider that is an unjust tax. They were originally granted to a gentleman, by patent, a gentleman whose connexion with the town arose from the fact that he and his family constituted the whole corporation. We consider he has no [illegible] to pay that amount of money and we actually receive no value received. I wish to call attention to this important fact that 37 years hence it will be in the power of the patentee to put any tax he pleases. He can put on tolls such as will abolish the fairs assuming at the time we are able to keep them as they are or improve them, and the people would have to pay out of their income what is acquired by other towns, besides this monstrous imposition on the part of the patentee. I wish you to take a note of this fact. I think it is [illegible] in the 19th century that amount 3l. 14s. 11d. paid for? I say it represents 3l. of plunder, for which there is no value received.

29,181. This is paid to Mr. Pennefather?—Yes. He is the representative of the individual who held the market rights previously. There were no markets I am to assume previous to 1820. He and his family were the corporation at the time and one of that family obtained that patent which we in the 19th century must observe by paying that imposition of 3l. out of the corporate property. It ought to be spent in a more useful purpose than paying an antiquated custom.

29,182-3. The lease will expire in 37 years?—Yes, and it will then be in the power of the patentee to put on a tax of 50l. a year on the people of Cashel which they will have to submit to unless there is some alteration in the law in the meantime.

29,184. Did the lease go to Mr. Jordan as a consideration?—Yes. He got 200 acres of land belonging to the corporation.

29,185. At what terms?—At 10s. an acre. He pays 120l. a year for 160 Irish acres of land.

29,186. At the time tolls were charged, were they levied in return for the accommodation of a fair green?—The fairs were held in the street which is ample enough to hold them all.

29,187. As chairman of the commissioners do you think if market rights are to be enforced throughout the country that the control should be vested in a representative body like the town commissioners, and not in private individuals?—I do, and that is what I imagine should be the outcome of this Commission, that the corporate body who represent the townspeople and their interests, who have the greatest interest in securing the prosperity of the town, should have control, and not some outsider.

29,188. The question I asked Mr. Corby I would like to ask you. Do you think the exaction of a toll in any way deters from the magnitude or extent of the markets or fairs?—I know as a matter of fact at the time the corporation bought these tolls, 30 or 33 years, and leased them, and put their hands into the corporate pockets and abolished them, they did so with the firm conviction that it would improve the fairs. I believe it has done that. I am satisfied other things being equal the people will go where they have to pay no tolls, but many considerations enter into the minds of buyers of a large number of cattle and you cannot eliminate the favour that in many instances the tolls cannot be abolished, but where it is an advantage they should be abolished, and in the abstract there is no doubt they do deter the country people especially. They weigh and measure their pence to the extent that towns folk do not think at all, and I believe they would go a very respectable distance to save a few additional pence. Whether they would spend them well is another thing.

29,189. During your term of office no representations have been made to the town commissioners to provide a fair green?—No representation, because the streets are large enough. Some people who have aesthetic opinions about the fairs being held on fair greens wished to have them removed but the shopkeepers who have a large interest in having the fairs at their own doors were obliged to get the fairs on the streets.

29,190. Were the fairs actually removed?—No. They were removed in another town I know.

29,191. Would that opposition come from the traders in any particular trade and be exclusively confined to them?—That I could not tell, but I rather suspect a [illegible] desire to have a very useful article of [illegible] at hand and that probably led them to desire to have the cattle on the streets.

29,192. Do you think the opposition to the removal of the fairs off the public thoroughfares or pathways only comes from the dispensers of those pleasant beverages you have referred to?—I do think on the whole that probably is done. I think it would be cleaner to have the fairs at a distance.

29,193-4. Of course the fact of their being held on the streets, occasions much additional expense in the cleansing of the public thoroughfares?—It does, and they are a great nuisance, but it is necessary to have them close at hand.

the street?—It is no additional expense because it is by contract. Of course we do pay something extra for it.

29,196. Would you say the revenue obtained acts as an equivalent for any expense?—Possibly it does, but we never entertained that at all. We are too much absorbed in increasing the business of the town and the fairs and are making every effort, and have made every effort it was possible to make for 30 years to get one engine of increasing business and that is a railway. Of course a railway per se will do nothing without a population and the population has thinned to an alarming degree. We have been at much expense trying to get the railway.

29,197. Could you give any approximate idea of the number of animals that are brought here yearly to the fairs?—I am not in the trade; that is too profitable for me to get into it, but there are gentlemen here who may be able to tell you that.

29,198. Then it is your opinion from your opening remarks that if market rights are to be enforced, some return should be given by the individual in receipt of them?—Yes, certainly, and that antiquated patentees ought to have their rights abolished or be compelled to give value if there be such a thing as value to be given, but in this town, what value can be given in the shape of a fair green seeing that the streets are already large enough and very likely the next improvement they have to propose, will be a fair at the end of the town. The people at the other end of the town would possibly put a little blackmail on to get the charming gold mine back again.

29,199. Have you any suggestion to offer as to what you think would be an improvement on the present state of things here?—I did not think it worth while attending these commissions until I looked into the laws. I saw by the laws we will be completely at the mercy of the patentee when it expires. Under those circumstances there would be no shadow of a shade of justification in our paying tolls to parties who never paid 1d. to the town unless to help himself to a slice of property belonging at the present day. Under these circumstances the patent ought to be abolished and if it was not to be abolished and if a tenderness for monopolies should sway the legislature, then I say it ought to be bought out on the existing charge and not leave us at the mercy of men who run away with the industry of the people without having any claim on earth to be placed in a position to do so.

29,200. You desire the corporation to obtain compulsory power to acquire the existing rights?—I do not say we should pay 2d. but the legislature in its tenderness for abuses may compel us to pay, but it ought to be computed at the present rent and not a 1d. more.

29,201. Does that opinion apply to the market rights throughout the country?—Yes, I give a national expression of opinion on the point. Take the case of Tipperary, a most unheard of state of things exists there. A whole 1,000l, which should be utilised mainly in improving the town, is placed in the hands of a private individual who lives 4 or 5 miles outside the town and never did anything to merit it.

29,202. Was there any special covenants in the lease made by the town commissioners?—There is no covenant I can see. We have not the patent; you probably have these things at your hand and I would ask you, in the name of the corporation, to print a copy of it, or the terms of the patent in your report of the evidence.

Mr. Jeremiah Crowley examined.

29,203. Could you give any approximate idea of the number of animals brought in here yearly?—There are 14 fairs and I should say in 13 the number of horned cattle would average 600.

29,204. At each fair?—Yes, and at the other one, that is the March fair, I saw over 2,000 head of cattle alone. Then you might put down the sheep at 100 each fair and about 300 young pigs every monthly fair and a 1,000 at one.

29,205. Is that at the March fair?—No, the 27th December which is a big pig fair, that is Wednesday after Christmas. We have calculated the number at those pig markets and we find 2,000 pigs come to 13 fairs in the year.

29,206. What percentage of those would you say were sold each market day?—All the pigs are always sold.

29,207. And the horned cattle?—I suppose you might put down more than half being sold.

29,208. Are horses brought here?—No horses come here.

29,209. You buy and sell here?—Yes.

29,210. Do you think the public thoroughfare is the proper place to hold fairs. If you are connected with trade here, I would like you should leave it out of consideration in answering this question?—I think the street is the proper place.

29,211. Here in Cashel?—Yes, or anywhere else. You will find the fairs are cleaner by having them on the street than going into a field where you get into your knees in mud.

29,212. Have you ever attended Kilkenny?—No. I have been at fairs in Clonmel, Thurles, and Tipperary.

29,213. If there was a fair green properly macadamised with hard surface, pens and shelter accommodation, do you think the farmers would have any objection to pay a small charge in order to maintain such a place if provided?—I do not think the farmers would like to pay anything for accommodation because they think the accommodation of the streets enough. The farmers, as a rule, do not like to pay.

29,214. If they got an adequate return would they have any objection to pay a small charge per head?—I would not like to answer that question.

29,215. Would you yourself?—I would not object at all.

29,216. Have you ever been discussing it as have you heard any of the farmers around the country discussing it?—I never heard. I heard people complaining that have to pay tolls at fairs, they do not like it at all. It is the buyer pays the toll, the seller pays nothing.

29,217. Does not it frequently happen where the buyer tells the seller to deliver them in the yard and they are nominally in the possession of the seller passing the custom gap?—The yards are inside the custom gap. In places where I was the buyer paid the toll and there was no yard outside the custom gap. No matter how far the yard is the custom collectors go outside it.

29,218. What is the nearest fair to Cashel where they levy toll?—Cahir, Fethard, Cappawhite, and Kilkenny.

29,219. Is "Ladies Well" adjacent to the town?—It is at the top of the town. Yes.

29,220. Were the two old fairs at which tolls were levied belonging to Mr. Pennefather?—They belonged to the archbishop, and the commissioners are not paying any tolls now for those fairs.

29,221. When they obtained the monthly fairs from Mr. Pennefather at the same period, were tolls abolished at the two old fairs?—I do not know that it was at the same time. I knew Doctor Cotton got the late Archbishop Laurence to abolish the tolls in 1826. They have not been levied since, but it was in the power of Archbishop Laurence's successors, if they wished to impose them.

29,222. Do the commissioners exercise any control at all over the fairs?—No; they do not interfere with the people.

29,223. Practically no control is exercised over them?—No.

29,224. Would the police keep order and regularity?—Yes. We have a town sergeant and he keeps the markets and fairs in order. He regulates the carts and all that, and I believe there is more regularity in that way in Cashel than in towns where tolls are paid.

29,225. Are the standings also on the main street?—Yes.

29,226. Is there a great number of those standings?—Very few.

29,227. Do you sell in the market?—I live in the town.

29,228. Could you give me the different marketable commodities brought and exposed for sale on the standings?—There is threware and timber gates.

29,229. They expose those on the public thoroughfare?—Yes.

29,230. Do you remember when there were standing charges?—I never heard of charges for standings. There are people who come from other towns with other commodities, such as baskets and threware, and nothing is charged for them.

Mr. Patrick Corcoran examined.

29,231. Were standing charges levied at the period that tolls were exacted?—Yes. I saw a woman with three pair of knitted stockings in her hand and she had to pay 1d.

29,232. All commodities exposed at that period had to pay tolls ?—Yes, on fair days.

29,233. They went to the ancestors of Mr. Pennefather ? —To Mr. Jervise.

29,234. He actually exercised rights but under the terms of the lease he does not now levy tolls ?—No, but they used have toll boards at the entrance to the town in every direction and a number of men and they received so much for every beast that was sold. There was another squad of men who went round to the carts and standings and collected 1d. from each car containing young pigs, and 1s. for any station, earthenware, or anything like that.

29,235. (*The Commissioner to the Town Clerk.*) You do not know what year Mr. Jervise leased to Mr. Pennefather ? —I do not, but in 1856 he got the lease from the commissioners.

29,236. Was he exercising market rights previous to that ? —He was for some years.

29,237. Did the property of the corporation become vested in the present town commissioners ?—Part of it ; not all.

29,238. Does the town belong to the town commissioners ?—Yes.

29,239. Have you got your last balance sheet ?—Yes.

29,240. (*Mr. White.*) I may mention I remember when the town sergeants used to go around the markets at Ladies' Well and take a couple of sods of turf as an imposition.

29,241. (*The Commissioner to Mr. Connelly.*) Do you agree with Dr. Laffin that the want of railway communication tends to deter the commissioners from making an effort towards the development of the markets and fairs ? —Yes, I am satisfied that it does. We would have splendid markets if we had railway communication.

29,242. Where do the buyers come from who usually attend here ?—They come from all the surrounding towns. There are more buyers in Cashel than anywhere else.

29,243. Local buyers ?—Yes

29,244. How would you compare the prices here with the prices at the adjoining fairs ?—It would be hard to estimate that.

29,245. Are they similar ?—Of course. Sometimes you might get as much for a beast here as anywhere.

29,246. Although there is the additional cost of transit by the buyer ?—You will never have the demand without competition. You might get as heavy a purchase as anywhere else, but as a general rule, you will not get it.

29,247. Do not they take their cattle from this neighbourhood to other fairs around ?—Yes.

29,248. Where they think the demand is better ?—Yes ; and where tolls are paid.

29,249. That is due to the want of railway communication ?—Yes, particularly in the case of pigs. There is 4s. a piece off the pigs in consequence of the carriage of the pigs and for want of railway communication.

29,250. Who estimated that loss to the farmer ?—Mr. Cavanagh experienced it himself.

29,251. Have you any suggestions to offer as to what you think would tend to develop the markets or fairs here or generally throughout the country ?—I do not see anything to develop them here but railway communication. I am satisfied they would be fully developed here if we had that.

29,252. How many miles is this town from the nearest railway station ?—Five miles.

Thomas Wood, Esq., T.C., M.D., examined.

29,253. Do you approve of the markets and fairs being held on the public [illegible]

29,258. Did you ever hear the people complaining of the obstruction they caused ?—I did not. I think it is impossible to convenience all parties.

29,259. Who is it cleans the filth and dirt away ?—The commissioners appoint a scavenger at a yearly salary. The occupiers of houses sweep the pathways.

29,260. You consider that the occupiers and traders in the town would put up with any inconvenience caused for trade purposes ?—I think they would. I think if we attempted to change the fairs out of the streets we would be met with great opposition.

29,261. Was it ever suggested to change them ?—I never heard it was. I would be sorry to try it. The only complaint at the fairs are not large enough and that as Mr. Connelly told you is due, in a great measure, to the want of railway communication. We have made several efforts and failed. Our pig markets and fairs have gone down although this is a good producing country.

29,262. Did you ever advocate the necessity for railway communication before the grand jury ?—We did and succeeded before the grand jury, and then before the Privy Council, and they stated the Great Southern and Western Railway Company ought to make the line.

29,263. (*Mr. White.*) I am an old resident in Cashel, and I remember when there was hardly standing room for pigs at the last fair, in December, and there were only about a thousand the last time. I speak of the time before there were any railways. There is now a difficulty in getting the pigs out of the town. The buyers have to hire cars to take them to the railway station.

29,264. (*To Dr. Wood.*) Then the producer does not get the actual value of the animal ?—I believe he does not. As a matter of fact, I know they take pigs out of this to other markets. I saw them going through this town to the last pig market in Cahir.

29,265. How far is Cahir ?—Eight miles.

29,266. It was the farmer brought the pigs there ?—Yes, and travelled all night to Cahir.

29,267. Did the commissioners, as representing the people, ever make any representations to the Great Southern and Western Railway Company to make a branch line to this town ?—We did. We waited on them. Mr. Connelly and I made out statistics and submitted them, and they did not seem inclined to do anything. They said they would wait until the next session of Parliament. They are always putting us off.

29,268. Where did you propose to have the line ?—Straight from Cashel to Goold's Cross. We, in this neighbourhood, are actually paying 6d. in the pound for a line we derive no benefit from.

29,269. How far distant is that ?—The nearest point is eight miles away.

29,270. Is it the same barony ?—Mostly. There are two baronies liable.

29,271. Have you any suggestions to offer other than what you have already mentioned ?—I do not think I have.

29,272. (*To Mr. White.*) Have you any suggestions to offer ?—No. Cashel is going down very rapidly and will be a village if we do not get railway communication. Until the railways were established in Ireland, Cashel was one of the best fairs in any county in Ireland. I remember myself when there would not be room for both great fairs. The March fair was kept up by buyers who came from Meath and all parts of Ireland.

29,273. (*To Mr. Connelly.*) As a matter of fact, do not you take pigs and cattle to other places ?—I did not take a beast to Cashel this year.

29,274. Was that because of the reason you have given, that you get a better price in other towns ?—Yes. Mr. Corby will tell you he sold up to 400 cattle this year, and he did not sell them at the fair of Cashel.

29,275. (*Mr. Corby.*) I sold them direct to the buyers.

29,276. They know previously what stock you have ?—Yes.

29,278. What quantity is in the lumps of butter generally brought in and weighed?—From ¼ lb. to 28 and 40 lbs.

29,279. Do they bring so small a quantity as a lb.?—They do.

29,280. When you are weighing a lb. of butter do you ascertain the weight down to an oz.?—I do not put in the oz.

29,281. Do you put it in oz.?—I put no oz.

29,282. Is a ¼ of a lb. the lowest?—Yes, it is. Very seldom they weigh such a small quantity as a lb.

29,283. In any case you never weigh under a ¼ of a lb.?—No.

29,284. Do you weigh the butter in its natural state?—Yes. Generally there is pickle in it.

29,285. Do you allow any deduction from the weight?—I do not.

29,286. There is no deduction from the weight you ascertain?—No. There are very large quantities of coal brought here from the Slievardagh collieries, and sold in the market.

29,287. You are the weighmaster?—Yes.

29,288. What commodities do you usually weigh on the beam and scales and crane?—Corn, potatoes, hay, straw, coal, turnips, mangolds, carrots, and all green crops.

29,289. Do you weigh turf?—Turf is sold by bulk.

29,290. The only sources of income out of the markets, derived by the commissioners, are the charges for weighing loads and weighing the butter?—What I charge for weighing butter goes to the commissioners. The charges on the loads go to myself. I pay 10*l.* a year for the use of the crane and I pay poor rates and taxes. The commissioners keep the crane in order.

29,291. (*To Mr. Cirdy*). When you mentioned 9*l.* as the receipts, was that from the butter alone?—Yes.

29,292. Your total receipts from the market are 13*l.*?—Yes.

29,293. And the expenditure 10*l.*?—Yes.

29,294. (*To Mr. Dwyer*). Would it be possible to make such a return as I have described of the different commodities brought in?—I could tell all the loads of hay.

29,295. You could only tell when you actually weigh?—That is all.

29,296. You have only one crane in Cashel?—That is all.

29,297. And the butter is not always weighed at your scales?—No. They weigh in the shops and elsewhere. The people have private customers for the butter and they go to them.

29,298. Firkin butter is never brought?—Not for some years. There are other commodities come into the town, coal and other things, belonging to parties who buy them at Gould's Cross.

29,299. Could you tell me your receipts from the crane?—At present I could not.

29,300. Do you keep any account at all?—I do not keep any account.

29,301. Perhaps the fact of some of the commissioners being present, prevents you from telling me?—I do not mind the commissioners at all.

29,302. Do not you keep any record as to whether it is paying you or not?—I do.

29,303. (*Mr. White.*) Sometimes I may mention that the street is impassable with loads of hay.

29,304. (*To Mr. Dwyer.*) Have you known frauds being committed in preparing the loads of hay?—I did not know that.

29,305. It has not come under your notice?—No.

29,306. (*To the Town Sergeant.*) Has it come under your notice?—Yes.

29,307. Is it of frequent occurrence?—I reported a farmer on one occasion to the town commissioners, but they did nothing as it was the first time, and they caused a notice to be given that in future, if anything turned up in that way the parties would be prosecuted.

29,308. (*By the Town Clerk.*) Did you ever know any case for a length of time but that?—I did.

29,309. You never reported it?—No.

29,310. (*By the Commissioner.*) You say it is of rare occurrence. Was it you detected that or did anyone examine the hay other than the proposed buyer?—It was the buyer called attention to it. It is impossible to detect any frauds. They will have it made up in the centre.

29,311. (*To Mr. White.*) Who would institute a prosecution if one was instituted?—The town commissioners. During my time as commissioner there was only one case and we could not go on with the case and make a conviction because the hay was taken out of the market before it was brought under the notice of the town sergeant. I believe there were some frauds in the butter market when firkins were brought in.

29,312. (*Town Sergeant.*) In the lump butter market I had a woman fined 1*l.* for having fraudulent butter.

29,313. What was the charge on the firkins?—Fourpence a firkin, the seller used to pay the buyer.

29,314. (*To the Town Clerk.*) Who paid you?—The buyers used to deduct 4*d.* from the farmers, and 2*d.* of that would go to the commissioners to meet the expenses.

29,315. There was always a deduction of 4*d.*?—Yes. The buyer was allowed the other 2*d.* for carriage. Railways have removed everything with regard to Cashel. It was one of the best towns before they were made, and it is one of the worst now.

29,316. Is not there a good deal of corn around this neighbourhood?—Yes; all that is sold in Thurles.

29,317. A corn market could not be fostered here?—It could not be fostered now unless we had a railway.

29,318. Would you say markets could be fostered if ample communication were afforded?—Yes. This is a splendid producing country, but we are backward for want of communication.

29,319. (*Mr. White.*) I remember when all corn in the Cashel direction went to Clonmel through Thurles, but that is all done away with now. All the corn goes direct from Thurles to Dublin.

29,320. Is there any other gentleman who has an observation to offer or suggestion to make, or any evidence to give? (*No answer.*)

29,321. A vote of thanks to the Assistant Commissioner terminated the inquiry.

FERMOY.

With reference to my inquiry in Fermoy on the 2nd January 1889, I beg to report as follows:—

Fermoy is situated on the Blackwater, in the county of Cork. It is a station on the Fermoy branch of the Great Southern and Western Railway line. The town is substantially built and is an important military station, in consequence of which the trade is good. A Board of town commissioners administers the local affairs, and the population is 6,454.

The market day is Saturday. The fairs are held on the first Monday of each month. A pig fair is held on the last Monday of each month. A horse fair is held on the second Tuesday of the months of January, May, August, and October.

An entrance toll is levied at all the fairs with the exception of the horse fair, which is at present toll free.

At the markets an entrance charge is also levied on each commodity brought into the market buildings, but it is stated to be voluntary on the part of the producers to avail themselves of the accommodation afforded by the market building. In case it is not availed of no charge is levied (but when levied it includes cranage).

A toll board is erected for public inspection. A weighbridge has been provided.

The market rights are the property of Sir Robert Abercrombie, by whom they are sublet to a Mr. Briscoe of Fermoy, under a lease of 100 years, from 1854, at the yearly rent of 102l. 10s.

There were two patents granted for Fermoy. The first is dated 25th February, 9 James I., and authorised one Sir R. Greenville and the Earl of Cork to hold a Saturday market and fairs on the 10th and 11th August. The second is dated 22nd June, 16 James I., and authorised Sir B. Greenville to hold a Friday market and fairs on the feasts of St. Barnabas and St. Simon and Jude, and day following each. No express grant exists therefore for any of the present fairs. It appears in 1854 the fairs were held on the 21st June, 20th August, and 7th November, but on Mr. Briscoe becoming tenant for the market rights and tolls he and some of the traders of the town established monthly fairs in lieu thereof. These were held on the first Tuesday of each month until about seven years ago, when they were altered to the first Monday of each month. The pig fair was established at the same period and the horse fair last year.

In accordance with my instructions I have inspected the fair and market places.

The fairs are held in a large fair green at the end of the main street and adjacent to the court house. It is some four acres in extent and, so far as space is concerned, affords ample accommodation. It is divided into two fields by a small stone fence. It is entirely enclosed and separated from the public thoroughfare by a low stone wall. In the largest division of the green and around the walls numerous movable iron pens are erected for pigs, and in the centre a brick and slated shed of fair dimensions is erected where the weighing of marketable commodities is carried on. Around the walls of the other division of the green are erected wooden sheep pens, and the cattle are exposed for sale throughout both sections. Altogether the fair green can be considered one of the best fitted up I have seen but it lacks shelter accommodation.

The surface is soft and could be improved by the addition of some metalling. The sheep pens can be used gratuitously, but if the pig pens are utilised, 6d. per pen is charged in addition to the ordinary entrance charge.

A weighbridge with a movable frame is erected for the weighing of cattle.

The horse fair is held in a field close to the ordinary fair green.

The markets are partly held in the market buildings and partly on the streets throughout the town. The market yard, where marketable commodities are exposed for sale, is approached on one side from the fair green and is of small dimensions. Sheds are erected on each side of the yard and it is approached from the main street by a covered way called the "shambles," having stalls erected on each side where eggs principally are now sold. Off this entrance there is a long room with wooden benches erected therein called the butter market where butter is exposed for sale.

This is the first place where an entrance charge was levied at the fairs in lieu of the larger charge on the animals only actually sold, and after the elapse of more than 34 years and the experience gained by its working, it was highly approved of by those attending the inquiry and deemed preferable to the course formerly adopted. Much satisfaction was also expressed as to the management by Mr. Briscoe, the tenant, although several of the witnesses were strongly in favour of the local authority having control.

Appended will be found a transcript of the evidence taken at the inquiry.

JOHN J. O'MEARA,
Assistant Commissioner.

45, Lower Mount Street,
Dublin.

Fermoy, 2nd January 1889.

Michael Burke, Esq., examined.

29,322. Whom do you represent, Mr. Burke?—The proprietor.

29,323. Who is he?—Sir Robert Abercrombie.

29,324. Is he the owner of all market rights that exist in Fermoy?—All.

29,325. How does he hold, do you know?—By fee; he is owner in fee.

29,326. Of the town?—Of the toll.

29,327. Do you know under what authority he claims the ownership of the market rights?—Under the conveyance so far he purchased the market rights; it was made out in the Court of Bankruptcy. I do not know about the old grants, but he claims under that.

29,328. There was no specific sum given for the tolls or market rights?—No. They went with the estate.

29,329. When was this purchase effected?—In 1857.

29,330. He was never in the immediate receipt of the charges himself; did he always lease them out?—Yes.

29,331. They are at present leased to Mr. Briscoe?—Exactly.

29,332. For what term?—For a hundred years.

29,333. From what period?—From 1854.

29,334. At what rent?—£102 10s. a year.

29,335. Do you know, or could you give us the particulars of any capital expenditure the owner was at in connexion with the markets, in the erection of buildings or in providing any grounds?—I cannot say there was any within my memory. The lease under which the owner [illegible] expired in 1854, and then I made a lease to Mr. Briscoe.

29,336. Does the fair green belong to him?—Everything belongs to him; he is the absolute owner of the manor altogether, and tolls, and everything.

Robert Briscoe, Esq., examined.

29,337. You are the tenant to the owner of the market rights?—Yes.

29,338. Since 1854?—Yes.

29,339. Have you been at any expense in providing the pens and shelter accommodation?—Yes; very great.

29,340. Have you the particulars of such expenditure?—No. I never kept it because they were my own. I never kept an exact account, but it should be estimated at a large amount.

29,341. What would you estimate the expenditure at?—I did not estimate that at all; it would be only a guess. It would be well for me to state that on part of the ground I took from Sir Robert Abercrombie I built houses, which are not on the market but on the market grounds. I took this ground as a speculation with the fairs and markets.

29,342. Then portion of the ground that was leased to you for market purposes you applied to private use by building houses on it?—Yes, but it never belonged to the market. I had not enough of ground where the original market was, and I asked Sir Robert Abercrombie for additional ground, and on that additional ground I built for market purposes and private purposes.

29,343. What market accommodation did you provide yourself since 1854. Did you erect any pens at your own expense?—I erected everything except an old shed; I erected all the sheds, shambles, and houses; there was nothing whatever there but one old shed.

29,344. Did you erect the shambles leading out into the main street?—Yes, entirely at my own expense.

29,345. Could not you give any approximate idea of the expense?—If I knew you wanted it I could have them valued, but I do not like guessing.

29,346. Tell me what is the market day here?—Saturday.

29,347. Saturday only?—Yes.

29,348. What fairs are held here? Kindly tell me all the fairs, whether you have any charges on them, or not?—They are all mine, and I have a charge on all of them.

29,349. What are they?—There were originally 12 fairs. Tuesday was our fair day, but on account of shipping the cattle the buyers asked me to change the day to Monday, and then they were able to ship the cattle from the fair here direct to England, and it was a great matter to the farmers around in the neighbourhood.

29,350. Have you monthly fairs now?—I have for cattle and pigs.

29,351. What day in the month?—The first Monday in the month for cattle fairs, and the last Monday in the month for pig fairs.

29,352. When did you make this alteration from Tuesday?—I could not say exactly; about seven years ago.

29,353. Were there always within your memory monthly fairs held here?—There were only three fairs in Fermoy at the time I took them.

29,354. When there were three?—There was one in August, and one in June, and another.

29,355. In 1854 did you establish the monthly fairs on Tuesday?—I established the monthly fairs on the last Tuesday of the month, and they were all together on Tuesday, both cattle and pigs, when I first established them.

29,356. Was that the first Tuesday of the month, or the last Tuesday?—The last Tuesday.

29,357. About seven years ago you made the alteration to the first Monday in the month?—Yes.

29,358. When you established the additional nine fairs, did you get any patent for them?—No, I got no patent. When I got the fairs and markets I turned the matter over in my mind, and consulted Mr. Burke and others to see what would be really for the benefit of the town. The fairs then were wretched; the markets were the most disreputable the world ever produced. It was that induced me to take them. Mr. Burke, after a great deal of persuasion, persuaded me to take them, and said it was better take them and manage them, and let us get out of the discreditable position we are in. The fact is, they were so discreditable that the farmers of this neighbourhood would sooner go to Mitchelstown or anywhere than come into Fermoy.

29,359. Have you tolls at all the fairs?—Yes, at every one of them.

29,360. And at the markets?—Yes.

29,361. At any period were any of the fairs toll free?—No, unless when starting we gave them toll free to encourage the people to come.

29,362. Have they been always on the fair green?—Yes, always.

29,363. Were they held there previous to your getting the lease?—They were held on the streets, and they were in a disreputable state until 1854.

29,364. Were the markets held on the public street?—They were held here and there. Some of them were held in a yard up in the side of the street.

29,365. Have you any rules or regulations in the market?—The only rule I have is to keep order and do justice to everybody.

29,366. Have you any rules restricting the exposure of marketable commodities elsewhere than in the market buildings?—No. Vegetables and fish are exposed about the town.

29,367. Have you got a list of your charges?—I could give it to you.

29,368. Have you got a superintendent or manager?—I have.

29,369. Will you kindly tell me what would be your average receipts?—I will give them to you. I put in the average gross receipts for the tolls of the markets and fairs. It includes the private rents that I receive from the houses I built.

29,370. Does that [illegible] include the rents of those private houses?—No.

29,371. The rents are 130l.?—Yes.

29,372. Then there is [illegible] for the tolls of the markets and fairs; stallage rents, [illegible]; grass, [illegible]; [illegible], 7l.; sale of manure, [illegible]; and 130l. rent of private houses, making a total of [illegible]?—Yes.

29,373. Have you got your average expenditure?—The gross expenditure is [illegible].

29,374. Could you give me the particulars of that expenditure?—There is [illegible] for officers; then [illegible] for labour; [illegible] for rent; [illegible] taxes; and for sundries, [illegible].

29,375. Do you, or does the owner contribute anything other than through the rates and taxes, towards the cleansing of the town?—No, but the owner is the largest ratepayer in the town.

29,376. (Mr. [illegible], Solicitor.) I may mention that one of the crying nuisances in the town is the [illegible] erected up to the slaughter-house, and it would be a convenience to remove it. I appear here for the Town Commissioners.

29,377. (Mr. Brisco.) I have asked a few respectable farmers to come here, and they will tell you whether there is too much charged on anything or not.

Mr. MICHAEL KELLY examined.

29,378. You are manager of the fairs and markets for Mr. Brisco?—Yes.

29,379. Do you collect any charge on standings about the town on market and fair days?—No.

29,380. Then you only collect charges when the market buildings are availed of?—Yes.

29,381. Your charges are on entrance?—Yes, on everything coming in.

29,382. You never consider whether the animals are subsequently sold or not?—No.

29,383. Could you tell me the charges on the different species of animal brought into the fair green?—Yes.

29,384. What is it on horses?—We have no horse fair, but if any horses come the charge is 3d.

29,385. On cows?—Twopence.

29,386. On yearlings?—The same.

29,387. On sheep?—A penny.

29,388. On lambs?—The same.

29,389. On pigs?—A penny.

29,390. On bonhams?—The same.

29,391. If they bring in a cartload of bonhams would you charge 1d. on each?—Yes.

29,392. Would you exact any cartage charge for the cart?—No.

29,393. You would only charge on each individual pig?—Yes.

29,394. Do you charge for anything else on fair days?—No.

29,395. Are those the only charges the farmers pay, or have they to pay a further charge if they avail themselves of additional accommodation?—Yes. They have to pay for the pens.

29,396. What are the charges?—6d. each.

29,397. Is that for cows?—There is nothing for cows; only for pigs.

29,398. Have you any pens for sheep?—We have, but they have the use of them without any extra charge.

29,399. Have you any cattle pens?—We have.

29,400. They can utilise them, too, free of charge?—Yes.

29,401. Must the farmer who brings pigs into the market engage pens, or can he sell without them?—There are lots of pens, but he need not engage them.

29,402. You have no rule compelling them to expose the animals in the pens?—No.

29,403. If they wish they need only pay the penny charge?—Exactly.

29,404. How do you collect the charge. Is it on entrance to the fair green?—At the entrance.

29,405. How many entrances have you?—Three for pigs.

29,406. Do you get the charge from a man, and give him a ticket?—There is no ticket; he has only to pay 2d. or 1d., as the case may be.

29,407. Do you ever count the animals brought in?—Mostly always.

29,408. Do you keep that return?—No.

29,409. You never keep it on permanent record?—No.

29,410. If required it would be possible to keep such a return?—It would be nearly impossible to do it, but if I was required I would.

29,411. Would not it be possible to do it, supposing it was required?—It would.

29,412. When you levy this charge you never consider whether the animal is subsequently sold or not?—No.

29,413. That is a matter of indifference to you?—Yes.

29,414. Are those the only charges you have on the fair green on fair days?—The only charges.

29,415. Have you any charges on standings?—No.

29,416. Do they bring any standings here on fair days, such as sale goods and that?—No.

29,417. Have you got a weighbridge?—Yes.

29,418. Did you weigh any cattle on the bridge since you erected it?—I was never asked.

29,419. Who was it erected the bridge?—Mr. Brisco.

29,420. It was erected at Mr. Brisco's expense?—Yes.

29,421. Is there any shelter accommodation in this fair green?—Not in the green, but in the market there is.

29,422. Did the farmers ever represent to you that there was a necessity for any shelter accommodation in the fair green?—I did not hear it; some might be talking about it.

29,423. Have you heard complaints of these charges yourself, or have complaints ever been made to you?—Some people would be complaining, but they are very few.

29,424. What would be the nature of the complaints?—They think the charges rather too much in some cases.

29,425. Is that with reference to any particular charge?—They think it too much to pay 1d. for a pig.

29,426. This fair green is entirely enclosed?—Yes.

29,427. What would you estimate the extent of it?—About four acres and a half.

29,428. That includes the sites of the market buildings as well?—No; only the site of the fair green.

29,429. Have you different portions of the green allotted off for each species of animal?—Yes; about half for cattle and the other half for sheep.

29,430. On fair days they never intermix?—No.

29,431. Is much confusion caused by the collection of the charge on entrance to the fair green?—Not a bit.

29,432. No complaints have been made to you of delay in entering on that account?—No.

29,433. What are your charges at the markets?—A penny a bag for potatoes.

29,434. Are the charges in the market tolls proper or are they weighing charges. Do you levy charges on the commodities, whether you weigh or not, or render any service?—They all pay coming in.

29,435. Whether you weigh the commodities for them or not?—Yes.

29,436. Supposing you do weigh, have you any additional charge?—No.

29,437. You weigh them free?—Yes.

29,438. One charge includes all?—Yes, 1d. a bag, no matter what weight it is.

29,439. Is that 1d. a bag irrespective of the commodity the bag might contain; would it be the same on corn and potatoes?—The same on both.

29,440. You never consider whether the bag will be sold or not?—No.

29,441. If a farmer brought in on last Saturday a load of 10 bags of potatoes he would have to pay 10d.?—Yes.

29,442. If he did not effect a sale and brought them in again and again he would still have to pay the charge every market day?—Yes.

29,443. Have you got any storage accommodation there?—Yes.

29,444. Do they avail themselves of it?—Sometimes when they would not sell.

29,445. What do you charge for storage accommodation?—A penny a bag again.

29,446. For the week?—Yes.

29,447. Or shorter period?—Yes.

29,448. (Mr. Brien.) I think he is wrong in that. If they stored them and paid the charge they will be free the next market day.

29,449. If they brought them out of the market they pay the entrance charge again?—Yes.

29,450. (To Mr. Kelliher.) What other charges have you at the markets?—We have no other charges, only for weighing hay, straw, and turnips.

29,451. What marketable commodities are brought into the market?—Potatoes, corn, fowl, lump butter.

29,452. Are eggs brought there?—Yes. We charge nothing for eggs.

29,453. Where is the hay and straw market held?—Outside the market altogether.

29,454. Do you collect any charges for hay if you do not weigh the load?—No.

29,455. Only when you weigh?—Yes.

29,456. Then the only commodities brought in are potatoes, corn, butter, fowl, and eggs?—Well, the eggs are outside.

29,457. You do not collect any charge at all on them?—No.

29,458. Where do they sell them?—On the street.

29,459. Do they rent standings on the street?—No.

29,460. Do they place boxes on the street?—Yes.

29,461. What is your charge on the fowl?—A halfpenny for a turkey.

29,462. On each turkey brought in?—Yes.

29,463. On entrance?—Yes.

29,464. Whether sold or not afterwards?—Yes.

29,465. What other fowl do you charge on?—The same on geese. Ducks and chickens ½d. a couple.

29,466. Is that the only charge?—Yes.

29,467. Have you any stalls for them?—Yes.

29,468. Have they to pay any additional rent for these stalls?—No. We give them all the accommodation we can.

29,469. In a shed?—Yes, and the shed is in the middle of the fair green. We give them the use of that on fair days.

29,470. How is the first building near the street utilised?—By the shambles tenants.

29,471. Is it used as a shambles?—There is part of it used for the butter market.

29,472. How is the remaining portion utilised?—It is mostly idle.

29,473. Is that where you store commodities?—That is where we store the eggs when they buy.

29,474. Where is your regular storage accommodation?—In the middle of the market.

29,475. What is your charge on butter?—A penny a lump.

29,476. No matter what quantity is in the lump?—Yes.

29,477. What quantity do they usually bring in?—From 1 lb. to 60 lbs.

29,478. Did they ever bring in a single pound?—Very often.

29,479. You charge 1d. on it?—Yes.

29,480. What would be the smallest value of that pound of butter at the worst market you remember?—About 5d. or 6d.

29,481. Do you remember that it was 5d.?—Yes.

29,482. If they brought in an article value for 5d. you receive 1d.?—Yes; I suppose so.

29,483. Have you done so?—I have not done so. I am not in that department.

29,484. When I say you, I mean the gentleman whom you serve. Would Mr. Brien receive 1d. out of the 5d.?—That is so.

29,485. The charge was never smaller than 1d.?—It was; I think some time ago it was a halfpenny.

29,486. How long ago?—Four or five years ago.

29,487. Do you remember when it was a halfpenny?—Yes. Anything less than 7 lbs. it was a halfpenny.

29,488. About four years ago it was raised to the penny?—Yes.

29,489. What is the largest lump they bring in?—Sometimes 50 lbs.

29,490. Do you charge the same on 1 lb. as on 50 lbs.?—When it exceeds 28 lbs. there is another penny added to the charge.

29,491. It is 1d. up to 28 lbs.?—Yes.

29,492. What is the highest charge, or is 2d. the maximum?—Yes.

29,493. What return do you give for this charge; do you weigh the butter?—We weigh the butter and give tickets to the buyer.

29,494. Is the butter always weighed before it is sold?—It is sold and then weighed.

29,495. Supposing they bring in a lump of butter and do not effect a sale of it, you do not return the money you receive?—No.

29,496. Is there any great percentage of the butter unsold on market days?—Very seldom I ever see it unsold. It is always sold.

29,497. Do you give any receipt for this charge?—No.

29,498. Who weighs the butter, or have you got a weigh-master for that purpose?—We have.

29,499. What is his name?—His name is O'Brien.

29,500. Is he here?—No.

29,501. Did you ever weigh butter?—Yes.

29,502. Down to what weight do you weigh?—A quarter pound.

29,503. So if weighing a lump that you think would be a pound you would only ascertain the weight down to a quarter?—Yes.

29,504. You never put the ounce or two-ounce weight into the scale?—No.

29,505. Do you give any ticket denoting the weight?—Yes; if anyone requires it.

29,506. Is it a printed form?—Yes.

29,507. Do you levy any charge at all for it?—No.

29,508. If the lump were divided, would you charge them for each separate piece?—No.

29,509. Rents when weighed in different parts?—They have a scale for doing that.

29,510. Have you a scale for retailers?—Yes.

29,511. They can utilise that themselves?—Yes.

29,512. You have no officer attached to it?—No.

29,513. They must weigh themselves?—Yes. They have asked me to do it, and I would do it for them.

29,514. That is for the accommodation of the retailers?—Yes.

29,515. How many beams have you in the market?—Sometimes four, three, and two.

29,516. Did you ever weigh butter on the potato scale?—No, except a firkin.

29,517. Are firkins ever brought here?—They are not bought here, but they send them to be weighed if they are sending them to any place around the town.

29,518. What do you charge for weighing a firkin?—A penny a firkin.

29,519. If they brought in a firkin and exposed it for sale in the market, would you charge 1d. as is the rate as for a lump?—Yes.

29,520. On eggs you say there is no charge, notwithstanding that they avail themselves of the market accommodation at market premises?—There is no charge. There are some men have stalls in the market for eggs.

29,521. How many stalls are there let?—There are only two at present.

29,522. At what rent?—At 1d. a stall.

29,523. What commodities are sold in these stalls?—Nothing; only the egg-women have them.

29,524. Do you collect these charges only on Saturday, or do you collect them any day the market premises are availed of?—Any day they come in.

29,525. As a general rule they come on Saturdays?—They sometimes come on week days.

29,526. And you levy a charge every day?—Yes.

29,527. Down to what weight do you weigh the corn?—Down to 8 lbs.

29,528. And the potatoes?—Down to 7 lbs. We allow 7 lbs. for the sack; we generally find that is the average weight.

29,529. When weighing you never go under 7 lbs.?—No.

29,530. You never actually weigh the empty sack to ascertain the tare?—Sometimes.

29,531. I suppose only in case of dispute?—Yes.

29,532. Would that tare be the same on a fine day as on a wet day, when the sack is completely saturated with wet?—The same thing.

29,533. If a sack is brought in which contains 10 stone 6 lbs. you return that as 10 stone?—Yes.

29,534. The weight paid for, after deducting the tare, is 9½ stone?—Yes.

29,535. Do the farmers ever complain that the weight is not ascertained under 7 lbs.?—Never.

29,536. On corn you weigh down to 8 lbs.?—Yes.

29,537. Do you actually weigh the empty sack in corn?—We weigh the empty sack after the corn is taken away, and they bring back the empty sack.

29,538. Always?—Yes, except the buyer and seller agree to the weight of the sack.

29,539. Supposing corn was brought in on market day and sold in the town to private merchants, would you levy any charge?—If brought in to be weighed I would charge for weighing and no more than that.

29,540. You levy no toll?—No.

29,541. Do the corn merchants buy in that manner?—The corn merchants buy corn and weigh it themselves.

29,542. You receive no charge for it?—No.

29,543. Do you receive any charge on any commodity that is not exposed for sale in your market buildings?—No.

29,544. None whatever?—No.

29,545. For weighing hay what is your charge?—Two pence a load.

29,546. In fact I suppose that applies to straw and all loads weighed?—Yes.

29,547. You charge nothing for weighing the empty cart?—No.

29,548. Do you give a ticket?—I give a ticket and make up the prices.

29,549. Do you make up the prices of the other commodities too for the buyers and sellers?—Mostly always. Any of them that require to do it we do it for them. Generally the men they do it themselves.

29,550. Do you ever keep a record of the current prices of the different marketable commodities brought to the markets and of the animals brought to the fairs?—We keep a record of the hay and straw and anything weighed on the bridge.

29,551. Do you give the particulars of the current prices to the press?—If I was asked I would. I would give a return of the prices to any person who would ask me.

29,552. Supposing it was required from Mr. Brien to make a periodical return of the prices of the different marketable commodities and the different animals brought to the fairs, would it be possible to make an adequate return?—I could not make an accurate return of the prices of cattle.

29,553. Could you give the average price?—We never keep any account of that.

29,554. I am not asking you do it, but would it be possible to do so in future?—It would.

29,555. You think the return would be a pretty accurate one?—I should think so.

29,556. At present you only keep a return of the hay and straw?—Yes.

29,557. You keep it in permanent form?—Yes.

29,558. What hour does the market usually begin?—At 10 o'clock.

29,559. What hour does it terminate?—Two, or half-past two.

29,560. And the fairs?—They are over about the same time.

29,561. When do they commence?—It is hard to say. The fairs commence about [illegible] o'clock.

29,562. Supposing a farmer was bringing in some cattle to the fair, and he effected a sale outside the fair green, would you seek for your charge?—No.

29,563. No charge whatever?—No.

29,564. Have cases of that kind come under your notice?—I saw people at different times selling outside.

29,565. (*Mr. Brien.*) I think he remembers prosecuting some persons who effected a sale in that way.

29,566. (*To Mr. Kelliher.*) Do you remember legal proceedings about that?—Yes.

29,567. What was the result?—I think they were fined.

29,568. Do they sell as a matter of fact outside the fair green?—Very seldom.

29,569. They all avail themselves of the fair green?—Yes.

29,570. (*To Mr. Brien.*) Did you take legal proceedings to recover the charge on cattle sold outside the fair green?—Never. I took proceedings against people for blocking the way.

29,571. (*To Mr. Kelliher.*) Can farmers sell their marketable commodities in any part of the town they please?—I think so; we never prevented them.

29,572. How long are you in the employment of Mr. Brien?—Twenty years.

29,573. Do you think he has the right to confine the sale of these to his market buildings?—Well, I do not know that.

29,574. (*Mr. Brien.*) I know he did endeavour to establish that before the magistrates, and my recollection is that a fine was imposed.

29,575. (*To Mr. Kelliher.*) Do you give a ticket when you weigh corn and potatoes?—Yes.

29,576. Do you ever mark the weight in chalk on the bags?—For single bags I would mark the weight in chalk, or give a ticket if they required it.

29,577. You have never weighed any cattle on the weighbridge?—No.

29,578. Supposing a load of potatoes were brought in, and you weighed it on the weighbridge, would you charge 1d. per sack or 3d. a load?—1d. per sack.

29,579. Although you weighed the entire load together?—Yes.

Mr. John Sennett, Town Clerk, examined.

29,580. You are the town clerk of Fermoy?—Yes.

29,581. When were the town commissioners established here?—Well, I am not in a position to say. I believe 1859 is the date.

29,582. Are they the urban sanitary authority?—They are.

29,583. Did you bring any of the queries before the town commissioners?—I did. They were returned to you signed by the chairman and myself.

29,584. Have the commissioners ever discussed the desirability of their obtaining compulsory powers to acquire the market rights and work them themselves?—They have at a meeting.

29,585. Are they in favour of such a course being taken?—I believe the commissioners are in favour of having the management of the fairs; still I do not believe they are in favour of having the streets utilised for holding the fairs.

29,586. They approve of the system of having fairs on the fair green?—Yes.

29,587. Are the commissioners traders in the town?—They are, as a general rule.

29,588. Have they any objection to the present management, or do they think if they had control over them they would be able to arrange to the greater satisfaction of the people of the town and the farmers?—I never heard any of the commissioners raise any objection to the present management. I believe the commissioners would like to have control, but I never heard the present management censured by the body.

29,589. Have you got the valuation of them?—No. The valuation of the toll of the market is pretty high. They are valued somewhat over the rent.

29,590. What are the average rates and taxes here?—2s. 8d. the present year, 2s. 10d. last year; that includes the water rate, the town rate proper, and the road rate. We are severed altogether from the grand jury.

John Cotter, Esq., Town Commissioner, examined.

29,591. You are interested in the trade of the town?—Yes.

29,592. Do you think the system here in Fermoy of confining the exposure of all animals to a fair green is the proper one?—I do, decidedly.

29,593. You consider it is objectionable to have fairs on the public thoroughfares?—I do, and it is a great obstruction to retail trade.

29,594. Is it your opinion that when an individual is in receipt of charges at markets and fairs that he should provide some accommodation in return for them?—I do, and I think they should be under the control of a representative body, who would control the traffic in the streets whatever it would be.

29,595. Could you tell us why you form the opinion that market rights should be vested in the town commissioners or local authorities?—In large communities the corporations have control, and it works very well.

29,596. (By Mr. Bier.) Are you aware that in consequence of the control being centralized in one private there are great defects in the existing markets—different parts of the town being under no control?—Yes.

29,597. Is there a place called the old market where fish is exposed for sale?—No; there is portion of the public street where things are exposed for sale.

29,598. (By the Commissioner.) Did the town commissioners take any steps to remove them?—They took steps to regulate the traffic in some way. The people of the locality objected to have them removed from one locality to another.

29,599. Are these traders?—Yes.

29,600. Was this opposition confined to the members of any particular trade?—It was chiefly to the liquor trade.

29,601. You think the markets should be concentrated in some particular spot, and shelter accommodation provided there?—Yes.

29,602. Do you think it would work better, and the farmers would get better prices for their commodities, when all are concentrated on one spot?—I think it would make the town very attractive and make the buyers come to the town.

29,603. Have you formed any ideas on the levying of a toll. Do you think the exaction of a toll on entrance to the fair green is better than a toll when the animal is actually sold?—I think it is more desirable to collect the tolls at the entrance and have no disputes, which would occur otherwise.

29,604. But on the abstract principle, do you think the exaction of a toll either at the entrance or on the sale is objectionable?—No, when a man gets accommodation.

29,605. From your experience, you think the farmers would willingly pay a small charge if they got an adequate return?—I do decidedly, because, of course, accommodation could not be provided unless a fund was raised in some way to pay the necessary expenses. I must also say that, whatever arrangement is made, Mr. [illegible] should be liberally dealt with. It was he created the market, and it is a great improvement to the one before. I [illegible] the town long before Mr. [illegible] got the lease.

29,606. Do you remember when the charge was on animals actually sold at the fairs?—I do.

29,607. When the new charge was instituted, was there much opposition to it?—No, there was not. It was considered an improvement; that was the general opinion; and it worked exceedingly well.

29,608. Is it your opinion that the same practice should be resorted to all over the country?—Yes.

29,609. It would be more satisfactory?—Yes.

29,610. Although now the charge is levied on the farmer and formerly on the buyer?—I think all arrangements should be to encourage the buyers and accommodate them as much as possible.

29,611. Where do the buyers come from who attend the fairs?—From Cork, Waterford, and Limerick, to the pig fair. Wherever I have spoken to praise the management of the fair here as one of the best in this district.

John L. Mahony, Esq., Chairman of the Town Commissioners, examined.

29,612. You heard the observations made by Mr. Cotter?—Yes.

29,613. Do you agree in these general remarks?—I do.

29,614. Fully?—Yes, and particularly in the answer that local authorities should obtain compulsory power to obtain the market rights. That is the prevailing opinion amongst the commissioners; in fact, all public bodies should have control of the markets and regulations of the town.

29,615. (By Mr. Bier.) If you utilised the control markets and centralised them, as might be done, and as

Mr. Carter suggests, would that create a fund in the hands of the commissioners for the further development of the markets of the town, such as macadamizing the butter market and horse fair?—I do not know it would be creative of a fund, but I think it would be better for the market to be held in one place instead of being scattered over the town. A regulation of that kind would be an improvement on the present system.

29,616. (By the Commissioner.) Why do you consider the town commissioners or local authorities should obtain control of the markets, or would they do so with the intention of augmenting their income?—I believe where a public body like town commissioners would be they would take more advanced steps to increase and improve the markets; they would have more interest in the town than any one individual.

29,617. Would you be opposed to applying the profits derived from the market to town purposes, or applying them to the reduction of the tolls already existing?—Yes, and to general improvement, such as macadamizing and enlarging the market.

29,618. If the town commissioners here and elsewhere had control, and you had some connection in the commission as you have at present, you would be in favour of only utilising the profits for market purposes?—Yes, and giving increased accommodation.

29,619. (By Mr. Rice.) I believe the commissioners here took no active part in promoting the fairs?—Yes.

29,620. (By the Commissioner.) Have you established a horse fair?—Yes. Three were already held.

29,621. What day?—It is held four times in the year; in January, May, August, and October, on the Tuesday of the [illegible] week, so as not to clash with other fairs.

29,622. Where are those horse fairs held?—On Mr. Brien's land; separate from the cattle market or pig market. Mr. Brien's land is adjoining the town by the river.

29,623. Is there any charge on the horses?—Not up to the present. We made arrangements with Mr. Brien, when he undertook to establish the fairs 18 months ago, that he would make no charge for 18 months.

29,624. I believe there was an attempt to create the fairs, and a charge was made and they failed?—They failed at all events. Whether that was the cause or not the fairs did not succeed. Probably they failed in another way by clashing with large fairs not anticipated at the time.

29,625. Have you got adequate accommodation for the [illegible] of animals from here?—Yes, excellent accommodation in the town, as far as the hotels and stabling are concerned—every accommodation desirable.

29,626. Supposing there was an abolition of toll altogether, and these fairs were toll-free, do you think that would tend to the general improvement of them?—I do not think so. I think there should be some tollage for keeping regulations in the market and having charge over the commodities in it.

29,627. You consider the only toll that should be levied is one that would meet the cost of maintenance?—Yes.

29,628. (By Mr. Rice.) Do you know whether an objection would be raised to paying for horses an entrance and not on those sold?—Some time ago, at the fairs attempted to be held, there was some objection.

29,629. Do you know [illegible], where a horse fair is held?—Yes.

29,630. How far is [illegible] from here?—Seven miles.

29,631. Do you know that the custom there is not to charge except a sale is effected?—I think the charge is on entrance. I paid an entrance myself there.

29,632. (By the Commissioner.) Do you agree with Mr. Carter in that observation, that it works better to have a charge on entrance and not on the sale?—I would say it avoids a good deal of disputes and is more satisfactory, and no disputes about the swearing.

29,633. You have heard of no undue delay being caused in entering the fair green?—I have not.

29,634. Have you any suggestions to make?—Some people selling fowl and butter on some occasions say the accommodation is not sufficient; that they have not sitting accommodation, and if the day is wet they are crushed almost more or less owing to the sitting accommodation in the market.

29,635. Did you ever hear any complaints of the system of forestalling in the fowl market?—No.

29,636. The buyers going out and meeting the farmers' wives coming in in the morning?—No. I have not heard any complaints. I believe the sellers get the best price for their commodities, but whether they sell in the market or out of it, that is their own interest.

29,637. You have not heard of the system of forestalling being resorted to in any commodity?—I have not.

29,638. (By Mr. Rice.) Is there any means of ascertaining the current price of any commodity except hay and straw?—I do not know there is.

29,639. Do not you think it would be desirable if the country people knew it?—I think it would be well if a record of the prices was kept. I often buy [illegible] in the course of the week and wait until the following Saturday to get the price, unless I go to Mr. Kelleher. It would be well to keep a record of the commodities sold. Sometimes people in the country send in commodities to the shopkeepers and may not call for the money for a week or fortnight. They wish to know the prices current on that day, and there is a difficulty in finding them.

29,640. Have you any other observations to make?—No.

Colonel Charles Deane examined.

29,641. Do you concur in the observations of Mr. Mannix and Mr. Carter as to local authorities obtaining control over the market rights and tolls?—The fairs are conducted very well, and so long as Mr. Brien lives there need be no change.

29,642. Apart from any feeling for Mr. Brien, on the principle of giving market control to local authorities, do you think they would be worked better and to the greater satisfaction of the public?—It is a rule all over the world that public markets should be held by public bodies.

29,643. You think yourself the united efforts of the gentlemen composing a board would tend to better management, and the people would have better opportunities of bringing forward any complaints they would have to make?—As long as Mr. Brien lives he will give great satisfaction, because I really think he has done a great deal for the last 30 years.

29,644. Have you any experience of other fairs?—Yes, a great many.

29,645. Where tolls were levied on the animal actually sold?—Yes. It is a great mistake.

29,646. You approve of the system adopted here?—Certainly; you get accommodation for your cattle, and everything is satisfactory.

29,647. You think the other system causes confusion and delay?—Yes, and more. I have often seen men say, "I did not sell them," and a man would say, "You take them out himself, and I will give you the price so as to save the toll."

29,648. You think also the proper place to hold the fair is on a fair green?—Yes, properly kept and properly drained.

29,649. You disapprove of the system adopted elsewhere of holding the fair on the public streets or public thoroughfares?—Yes. It is most objectionable.

29,650. Have you any suggestions to offer as to what you think would tend to the improvement of the market and fairs?—I think it ought to be properly macadamized, because sometimes it is very muddy.

29,651. Did you ever hear any objections from the buyers that they have not been able to try the cattle in consequence of the ground being soft?—I never heard any objection, except that sometimes it is a little muddy.

29,652. You never heard objections that the ground was not hard enough to detect any fault in the cattle?—No.

29,653. (To Mr. Brien.) Do you clean this fair green immediately after the fairs?—Yes, whenever it wants i[illegible]

A man from the [illegible] is ordered never to leave anything there.

29,654. Did they ever represent that no advantage would be gained by having the ground somewhat harder, so that in wet weather the ground would not be soft?—There are three-fourths of the land grown over, and that is hard. There are some parts a little soft; it was very low when I took it. There was a pond of water all the winter in it, and I had to drain it at very large expense. It is naturally springy, but I have raised it up a great deal.

29,655. (By Mr. Rice to Colonel Dease.) Have you heard any complaints that the cattle are exposed on wet days in the fair green?—No.

29,656. There are no sheds for the buyers and sellers of cattle on wet fair days?—No.

29,657. (Mr. Cotter.) I have heard complaints by farmers selling cattle that they had to remain a long time in the fair on a wet day without any shelter.

29,658. (Colonel Dease.) It would be an impossibility to do it. You would have your rates 10s. in the pound if you went to cover in the whole thing.

29,659. (Mr. Cotter.) I mean shelter for a certain proportion of the buyers and sellers.

29,660. (Mr. Rice.) There is a matter in connexion with the butchers' stalls that has been certified by medical men as not satisfactory. Mr. Briscoe has attached to his shambles a slaughter-house. The victuallers have deserted the shambles, and scattered themselves through the town, but attached to the shambles the accommodation for slaughtering was attended with places, such as [illegible] and privies, that are an abomination, and certainly the condition is something frightful.

29,661. The butchers throughout the town have slaughter-houses of their own?—Yes.

29,662. Is this accommodation of Mr. Briscoe's availed of?—Yes.

29,663. Has it been certified unfit for health?—It is the very entrance, and it existed anterior to the passing of the Town Improvement Act, and cannot be removed unless the commissioners proceed by injunction, but they are so economical they do not wish to take proceedings; but that is really a nuisance.

29,664. Are there any farmers here?—Yes.

Mr. Thomas Walsh examined.

29,665. You are concerned with the farming interest?—Yes.

29,666. Have you sold your stock at fairs where tolls were levied only on the animal sold?—I have.

29,667. Do you disapprove of that arrangement, and do you approve of the one existing here?—I do not.

29,668. You do not approve of the arrangement in Fermoy?—I do.

29,669. Although in this case the charge is levied on you?—Yes.

29,670. In the other case it was levied on the buyer?—Yes.

29,671. (By Mr. Rice.) What the Commissioners wishes to ascertain is, which do you prefer, the case where the buyer pays on the sale alone, or where the seller pays on entrance, whether he sells or not?—I prefer to have the charge made on entrance.

29,672. (By the Commissioner.) That is when accommodation is given to you?—Yes, because I have been in other fairs where there is no accommodation, and it is very disagreeable and cattle are in danger. I lost a beast at one of those fairs and could never get any good of it afterwards.

29,673. Where was that?—Not far from here.

29,674. What are the nearest fairs you have to Fermoy?—About six or seven miles off.

29,675. Within what radius would you say the stock is brought to the fairs in Fermoy?—Generally between six and eight miles.

29,676. And the marketable commodities?—The same distance.

29,677. At the fairs in Fermoy here they got the system of luck-penny?—Yes.

29,678. There is also a luck-penny on the sale of pigs?—Yes.

29,679. Is there any fixed charge retained by the buyer out of the contract price between the buyer and seller?—They generally charge 6d. on each pig.

29,680. What on business?—I cannot say. That is a matter understood between buyer and seller.

29,681. On cattle is it left to the disposition of the seller?—Yes, whatever the person would be pleased to give; but it is a compulsory thing, like on pigs when they stop the 6d.

29,682. Is it always left to the disposition of the seller?—Yes.

29,683. In the case of cattle the contract price is paid, and the seller gives the luck-penny, but in the case of pigs it is retained by the buyer?—Yes.

29,684. Supposing you are selling a beast, do you, when asking the price, ever consider the amount of luck-penny you are to give when the sale has been effected?—No.

29,685. It never affects in any way the price of the animals?—No. I do not see any dispute about it.

29,686. Did you ever put on the price you would ask for the animal the amount of the luck-penny you would subsequently give the buyer?—No. A man might; it is free to pocket, and then there is no luck-penny.

29,687. In that way the amount of the luck-penny is considered; that is when the sale is free to pocket?—The luck-penny is customary as a general rule. The usual thing is 1s. on the beast and 2d. for sheep. In the regular sales it is never taken into consideration.

29,688. Does much dispute arise as to the amount of the luck-penny afterwards?—I did not hear any disputes.

29,689. Have you any remarks to make as to the charges levied either at the markets or fairs?—No, I have not. I am very pleased. I am satisfied, and, as far as I can see, the people are very well pleased with how the markets and fairs are conducted here.

29,690. Did you ever hear any complaints made by the farmers?—Well, I did not.

29,691. (Col. Dease.) There is not finer accommodation in Ireland for a horse fair than here.

29,692. (Mr. Briscoe.) There were two English buyers here; one said there was very good accommodation and the other said it was the best in Ireland.

Mr. Wm. Jeffers examined.

29,693. Do you concur in the observations of Mr. Walsh?—I do.

29,694. Fully?—I do. I know the markets for the last 30 or 40 years. I think they are a great deal better conducted now than then.

29,695. Do you bring any commodities here yourself?—I do.

29,696. Do you and the other farmers think it is always better to sell marketable commodities in the market building; that is, where the market is concentrated on a particular spot instead of indiscriminately about the public thoroughfares?—As a rule it is.

29,697. Do you think you can get a better price for the different commodities?—As a rule it is better sold in the market place.

29,698. The eggs, butter, fish, hay, and straw are sold about the streets at present. Do you think it would be better if there was a rule restricting the sale of these

[illegible]

YOUGHAL.

WITH reference to my inquiry in Youghal on the 3rd January 1889, I beg to report as follows:—

Youghal is a maritime town situated in the county of Cork. It is the terminus of the Youghal branch of the Great Southern and Western Railway line. The town is of some importance, and is apparently well built. The trade is fair, but the exports are chiefly in agricultural produce. A board of town commissioners administers the local affairs. The population is 5,820.

The market day is Saturday. The fairs are held on the third Monday of each month.

The markets and fairs are toll free, but at the former a weighing charge of 1d. per sack of potatoes is payable to the owners for weighing them.

The market rights belong to the town commissioners. A charter dated 22nd December 1609 (7 James I.) authorised the old corporation to hold a Wednesday and Saturday market, and fairs on the feasts of St. Luke and Ascension. The present fairs, therefore, are held without any express authority. It appears about twenty-five years ago, the traders of the town established monthly fairs which were held on the first Monday of each month, but two years ago it was found that fairs held in the adjoining towns interfered with the success of those in Youghal, and accordingly the town commissioners altered the latter to the present days.

The authority of the Local Government Board was not obtained for this alteration.

There being practically no charges, no toll board is erected, and the weighbridges are the property of private individuals in the town, who weigh for hire.

In accordance with my instructions, I have inspected the market and fair places.

Previous to 1876 the fairs were held in a field just outside the town, the property of a private owner, but he having signified his intention of demanding a toll, the town commissioners removed the fairs to the present site. They are now held on a wide piece of reclaimed land on the coast at the end of the main street, from which it is separated by a wide paling. Although it is said to afford ample space accommodation, cattle are occasionally sold on the portion of the main street immediately adjacent to the green. The surface of the latter is somewhat soft, and in inclement weather should be inconvenient to travel and drive cattle upon. There are no pens, shelter, or other accommodation provided.

A weigh-house and machine has been erected in the centre of the green by a private trader, with the permission of the town commissioners, and where loads of different commodities are weighed.

The markets are held principally on the market square, a wide portion of the public thoroughfare, outside the courthouse, but partly through the streets of the town. The square is of good extent, and at one side a large and substantially built market-house has been erected by the town commissioners within the last two years. It is divided into two sections. In the smaller one general commodities, such as butter, vegetables, and milk, &c. are exposed for sale. In the larger section potatoes are weighed, and exposed for sale. This section itself is formed into two divisions. In one the weighmaster weighs the potatoes at a beam and scales, and in the other division twelve small beams and scales are erected, at which potatoes are weighed for retailers by some women. The charges received by these women are applied to their own use, and are at the rate of 2d. per barrel, for which the barrel will be weighed into as many draughts as may be required.

The fish market-house is a substantially built and lofty building, situate in a bye-street. It is flagged thereout, but it is not availed of by the vendors of fish, except for storage purposes, which they obtain gratuitously. The fish, like the other commodities, is sold in the market square.

Appended will be found a transcript of the evidence taken at the inquiry.

JOHN J. O'MEARA,
Assistant Commissioner.

45, Lower Mount Street, Dublin.

Youghal, 3rd January 1889.

Mr. JAMES J. O'NEILL, Town Clerk, examined.

29,715. You are the town clerk of Youghal?—Yes.

29,716. When was the commission established?—About 1850, under the Act passed in 1828, the ninth of George the Fourth. They were contemporary with the late corporation until 1840, when the reformed Corporation Bill was passed.

29,717. Are you the sanitary authority?—We are, under the Public Health Act.

29,718. Did the property of the old corporation become vested in the town commission?—Yes, in 1840.

29,719. Have you control over the market rights and tolls here?—Yes, since 1840. We got them up from the late corporation.

29,720. What markets are held here?—There is the usual market every week on Saturday; that is the principal day.

29,721. I suppose marketable commodities are brought in each day in the week?—Yes.

29,722. But Saturday is the principal market day?—Yes; and the fairs are held every month, on the third Monday.

29,723. How long has that monthly fair been established, or do you remember yourself when there was a smaller number than the 12 fairs?—No. It is about 25 years ago.

29,724. Who was it established them?—I think the late Mr. David Lee, of Portlevis, who brought the estate of the Duke of Devonshire in this district.

29,725. They were not at that period belonging to the corporation; they did not exercise any control over them?—No. I do not think there used to be any fairs in the time of the corporation.

29,726. You think, then, when the monthly fairs were established 25 years ago, that that was the first occasion on which fairs were held here?—Yes, monthly fairs.

29,727. But were there some other fairs held here?—There were some old fairs held two or three days in the year.

29,728. Were tolls ever levied at these affairs?—I do not think they were. I am not sure. These fairs were held in a field outside the town, and the fairs were brought into the town in 1876. I could not say whether tolls used to be charged when the fairs were held on the field.

29,729. Who brought them into the town?—The town commissioners.

29,730. Where are they held at present?—They are held through the main street at the northern end of the town, and through a yard, and Dolphin's square, the property of the town commissioners.

29,731. Practically they are held on the public thoroughfare?—Yes.

29,732. And have been held there since 1876?—Yes.

29,733. When they were brought in do you know if there is any record of any consideration being given to the gentleman who owned the field?—I do not think there was. I think when the Hon. Judge Little purchased the place he required some tolls, and I think that was the reason they were brought in. Mr. Loughlin, a commissioner, tells me that the Hon. Judge Little, having bought the property, wanted to charge some tolls for the field. That is why the fairs were brought into the town. The commissioners were desirous to give a free fair and not charge any tolls, because it would be an inconvenience to the public to have tolls charged, and that is the reason they were brought into the town.

29,734. The removal to the town was not opposed?—No, it was not.

29,735. Where are the markets held?—Outside, on the market square.

29,736. Outside the courthouse?—Yes.

29,737. That is the public thoroughfare, too?—Yes.

29,738. Have you any market buildings here?—We have. One has been erected lately by the urban sanitary authority.

29,739. That is the large building opposite?—Yes; a one-storey building.

29,740. Is it used for weighing purposes, or do they expose commodities inside?—They expose commodities inside and weigh also.

29,741. What was the cost of erecting this building?—Up to the present about 500l.

29,742. Could you segregate the amount and give me the particulars of how you expended that 500l.?—I could afterwards. We borrowed 450l. from the Government, as an urban sanitary authority, for the purpose of building this house, and after putting up the thing for public competition we found the contract price was [illegible]l.

29,743. Was this amount expended solely for market purposes?—Solely for market purposes; and the Commissioners have applied for a supplemental loan of 150l. to complete the whole thing. It is not complete yet.

29,744. Have you paid back anything out of the 500l.?—We have, two instalments.

29,745. How much remains due?—There remains due [illegible]l., that is up to the time I last made up the accounts.

29,746. What is the instalment you pay?—12l. 2s. 6d.

29,747. Half-yearly?—Yes.

29,748. On what terms have you this loan?—For [illegible] years at 3½ per cent.

29,749. What was the security for that?—The rates under the Public Health Act. It is well to have it stated that, although this money is borrowed by the town commissioners, they are relieved from portion of the loan by the harbour board, which is a separate and exclusive body having its own revenue, so that the revenue to pay the interest of the market house is not derived from the revenue under the control of the commissioners. There is an agreement come to, that the harbour board holding an office in portion of the market house. Therefore it is that the commissioners are not liable for the whole of this interest.

29,750. I suppose you have sub-let portion of it to the harbour commissioners?—Yes, and it is intended that the harbour board shall contribute some portion of the loan, yearly, as rent for this office.

29,751. Have you provided this market house with beam and scales?—Yes.

29,752. Have you made up the particulars of the capital expenditure the commissioners have been at in providing such?—[illegible]l. I have taken as the capital expenditure.

29,753. For the building and the scales?—Yes.

29,754. Have you got a weighing machine?—No; only the ordinary beam and scales.

29,755. If farmers desire to ascertain the weights of loads of hay, where can they ascertain them?—There are two private weighing machines in the town, and they hire them out.

29,756. What do they charge for them?—I think 3d. or 2d. a load; I think 1d. for loads of turnips, and 2d. or 3d. for loads of hay.

29,757. Is it 1d. a ton?—A penny a load for turnips, sometimes a load is only half a ton.

29,758. Have you any rules erected in this market place, or regulations to be observed?—No. The market is in its infancy so far as the building is concerned. The commissioners are biding their time to see what will be necessary before they make rules.

29,759. When was it first opened for public use?—About 18 months ago.

29,760. Where were the markets held previous to that?—On the open square.

29,761. They had no shelter accommodation at all there?—No.

29,762. Were representations made to the commissioners to provide such, and did that lead to their action in providing it?—No. I think it is due to Mr. Loughlin. We always felt, for 40 years, the want of a place for goods and merchandise, but under the ninth of George the Fourth which is a very worthless Act for public control, we were obliged to wait because we could not raise money to build a market house while under that Act. Then we became the urban sanitary authority under the Public Health Act, and it was only then we got legal power to borrow. Directly we became the sanitary authority we availed of the powers under the Public Health Act to carry out what could not be carried out for 40 years before that.

29,763. Do you know the charges levied at the market house?—It is voluntary; 1d. per sack for weighing potatoes. You see this charge is voluntary, because they can go to a private yard if they like.

29,764. Is it 1d. per sack no matter what the commodity is?—Yes, 1d. for 18 weights, 16 weights, or 20 weights.

29,765. Would it be the same charge for corn?—There is nothing else weighed there but potatoes.

29,766. Is there any butter brought in?—Butter is sold, but there is no charge.

29,767. Does the man in charge weigh butter for them?—He does not; that is conducted by private parties. It is only brought in small quantities.

29,768. In lumps?—Yes. As regards that, no local buyers make any charges on anything like that.

29,769. There is no rule restricting the exposure of marketable commodities elsewhere than in this market place?—There is not.

29,770. The farmers are free to go where they will and dispose of their goods?—They are; and they do sell other things from house to house.

29,771. As a matter of fact, do they avail themselves of the accommodation offered in the market?—They do.

29,772. And they expose commodities there?—Yes, potatoes principally.

29,773. You levy no standing charges or stallage charges?—No.

29,774. It is a free market-house?—Yes, with the exception of the voluntary ½d. for the accommodation of the scales.

29,775. But they can go elsewhere if they like?—Yes. When the potatoes are sold in small quantities they are weighed at 12 small scales which are there since the time of the old corporation. They are supplied by the commissioners, and kept by some old widows, and they charge the seller for weighing potatoes.

29,776. Do the receipts go to those people?—Yes, to the old women.

THOMAS HARRISON examined.

29,777. You are weigh-master to the commission?—Yes.

29,778. Do you always weigh the potatoes or do they be often sold by bulk?—I only weigh on market days, when a person would come to me.

29,779. Do they always buy and sell potatoes by weight or do they sometimes sell them by bulk?—Yes; by bulk.

29,780. Do you know the charges those old women levy?—Twopence a barrel; that is a voluntary charge also.

29,781. Is that for weighing small quantities?—Yes.

29,782. They would divide a barrel into 20 different weights, and charge 2d. for doing so?—Yes. They would weigh it in stones and half stones.

29,783. These are for the use of the retailers?—Yes.

29,784. When you weigh potatoes, down to what weight do you weigh?—2 lbs.

29,785. Do you weigh always down to 2 lbs.?—Yes.

29,786. So that if a sack of potatoes contained 10 stone 2 lbs. you would ascertain that weight?—Yes.

29,787. Do you weigh the empty bag?—No; that is left to the buyer and seller. They allow 7 lbs. for the sack when the potatoes are weighed, and they deduct the 7 lbs. out of the payment.

29,788. Do you give a ticket denoting the weight?—I do when they require it.

29,789. You do not charge anything for the ticket?—No.

29,790. It is a printed form?—No; it is written in pencil.

29,791. Do you keep any record of the quantity of potatoes you weigh there?—I return the money to the clerk.

29,792. Do you keep a blank of the ticket you issue when they require it?—No; no more than the money I return, which is the amount I keep.

29,793. You do not weigh butter?—No.

29,794. Only potatoes?—Only potatoes in sacks.

MR. MICHAEL LOUGHLIN, Town Commissioner, examined.

29,795. Do you think that the system adopted here in Youghal of having the markets free is better than having the exposure of the commodities concentrated on one place and a small charge levied for the accommodation afforded?—Yes.

29,796. Do you think does it tend to increase the trade?—I consider the present state of the times, and considering the infant state of the market, it would be kept back in prosperity if we were to put tolls on it. I consider, on the other hand, if the markets should become prosperous, we should levy tolls and concentrate the business and merchandise in one suitable place. I think if the commissioners had the power this moment they would not be disposed to levy tolls at present, because there is great depression in the times here. We are depending altogether on agricultural produce such as potatoes and corn.

29,797. Corn is brought into the town?—Yes, in large quantities.

29,798. It goes to the merchants stores?—Yes; it is taken directly to the stores. This is one of the most important seaport towns, and exports more than any seaport town in Ireland; and if a small sum was levied on each barrel of oats it would be a large revenue.

29,799. Do you think such a charge would act as a deterrent on the people in bringing the supply they would otherwise bring in?—I am afraid it would.

29,800. Have you had experience of other towns where tolls are levied?—Slightly. I have at Dungarvan.

29,801. Do you think the exaction of a toll affects the trade or restricts it in any way in that place?—I believe it does not. They have rival merchants there, and good demand. I believe it would affect it here where you have merchants that are not very much. I think a half-penny a barrel, as I hear them say, would influence them greatly.

29,802. I take it no control is exercised by anybody over the fairs?—We have no legal control.

29,803. No person exercises any control?—None whatever, except the commissioners keep the place in order, and try to keep the place clean and prevent any damage being done to the cattle by removing anything dangerous, such as glass or bottles, and in a suitable way to carry on the fairs. They keep the place clean and regular for traffic.

29,804. Is there much additional expense incurred in cleaning the streets after the monthly fairs?—Very little, because there is a staff always kept here. We, as commissioners under the ninth of George the Fourth, were obliged to keep the streets swept and cleaned ourselves at the expense of the ratepayers, and this comes into the work of the staff. Any deposit left after the fairs is mostly left on the main street, and it comes into the work of the staff without any additional men being employed, and then the manure is procured by the town commissioners, who sell it; so I do not think the fairs create any additional expense worth noticing.

29,805. Do you think the manure acts as an equivalent for any expense incurred in cleaning the street?—I believe to a great extent it does pay.

29,806. (To the Town Clerk.) Did you ever make such a calculation yourself?—I think the actual cost of cleaning the yard is not much.

29,807. I am not talking of the actual cost, but the additional expense incurred in cleaning on account of the fairs being held on the public thoroughfares, because you must necessarily clean them, whether the fairs are held or not?—There is a yearly contract made with the cleaner of the streets, and he gets so much; the contract goes by competition between him and others, and, as a matter of fact, the highest man gets it, and then he makes the most of the manure and the cleaning of the streets, but outside the granting of the contract it has nothing to do with the Commissioners.

29,808. (To Mr. Loughlin.) Do you think the streets are the place for fairs being held, or do you think it would tend to improve them materially if a fair-green was provided with proper pens and shelter accommodation in it?—So far as my own personal experience is concerned I would rather have the fair situated by itself and away from the streets, but I must tell you that it is the general desire of the people here, and of business people absolutely, that the fairs should be held on the street. It is the general desire of the commissioners; it is the general desire of the shopkeepers, and all; and I think that desire arises from want of prosperity in the town. They wish to bring traffic to their doors; but from a sanitary point of view and everything else I would like to have the fair isolated from the shop doors, but the people, from the state of the times, wish to bring everything as near the shops as possible.

29,809. I would like to ask you a question applying to markets and fairs generally throughout the country. Do you think where markets rights are exercised that the control of the markets and fairs should be vested in the local authority, if any such exist, and not vested in and controlled by a private individual?—I say this, so far as my opinion goes, they should be vested in a local authority with superior control.

29,810. You think there should be some controlling influence over the local authority?—Yes.

29,811. Why did you form the opinion that the immediate control should be vested in a local authority?—Because the local authority knows the wants of their locality and the wants of the community, and they do not look to their own interests; they look to the public weal more than private interest. A private individual has nothing in view except his own private interest.

while the local body have the public interest, and it is not money-making will be their interest. They will work to increase the traffic and to benefit the locality and town.

19,612. It is your opinion that compulsory power should be given to local authorities to acquire rights throughout the country?—Certainly. I think it is absolutely necessary for the progress of any different localities.

Mr. Thomas Cosgrave, Town Commissioner, examined.

19,613. (Witness.) With respect to that I agree with Mr. Loughlin on that point. You cannot scatter the fair up to every man's door. There are places set apart, and this fair-green is there. Sometime ago I attended and carried at the commissioners to have it here; at the same time it was not considered advisable to go too near the quays.

19,614. Do you think a fair-green is the proper place to hold a fair. Do you think if the animals were concentrated on one spot that the buyers would have a better opportunity of seeing the different class of animals than travelling all over the town?—I say, absolutely against my own interest, that it is.

19,615.—Have you heard the farmers or the buyers demanding it?—I have. Public meetings were held, and all assembled there carry out this fair business, and then we changed the fair day, but I could not see where a public fair could be held except where in the place it is.

19,616. I suppose custom has allotted off certain streets for each class of animal?—No; the place is limited.

19,617. You were on the Commission when the monthly fairs were established?—Yes.

19,618. When was that?—We made the change, I think, about 12 years ago. I remember fairs about 25 years ago, and they were held on Judge Little's ground.

19,619. What fairs were held there?—Cattle fairs and every fair.

19,620. On what dates?—I think the first Monday of the month as far as I remember. I cannot go beyond 25 years.

19,621. They were held at that period on the first Monday of the month?—I think so.

19,622. They were subsequently changed?—Yes, about eighteen months ago or two years ago, to the third Monday. The fair in Fermoy was held on the first Monday of the month, and that was found to interfere with the attendance here, and so the commissioners here changed to the third Monday. The change has proved prosperous.

19,623. Do you consider it is objectionable that there is not some control over the markets and fairs in Ireland to prevent market authorities from fixing dates for holding markets and fairs which would tend to materially injure the neighbouring fairs. For instance, you found that the Fermoy fairs which were established on the first Monday of the month affected the fair held here on the same date?—I may tell you I heard that change was made by a certain gentleman who had the absolute tolls of the fairs in Fermoy, and it was his own personal interest and the change materially injured us. I am not going to mention his name.

19,624. I am sorry you were not at Fermoy to hear the most eloquent expressions in his favour, and everyone seems satisfied with his arrangement, but do you mean to say that when the fairs were established in Fermoy that farmers in the immediate neighbourhood of Youghal went and exposed their stock in Fermoy and travelled that distance?—Well, I think, within a certain radius they did. It interfered with our fairs when this change was made there, but I think it was as regards the attendance of the buyers, and not the supply.

19,625. (Mr. Loughlin.) With reference to the change in the fairs, it seems to me immaterial. It is no business. It occurred in this way, that a new fair was got up in Castlemartyr, and that is portion of the reason for the change which was to counteract that fair because there were too many fairs in the locality. There is one in Killeagh within seven miles of this, and monthly fairs in Midleton 18 miles away. Then between Midleton and Killeagh they wanted to hold a fair in Castlemartyr. It was considered that would injure the existing fairs if the new fairs were held, and there was a strong feeling in the localities against them, and part of the reason, I do not say it is the whole reason, but partly to counteract this new fair, we changed the fairs here to the third Monday of the month. You see the first Monday is filled by Killeagh, the second by Midleton, and the third Monday was the intended day in Castlemartyr, and we changed to that day to counteract that fair.

19,626. When the alteration was made, did you obtain the consent of the Local Government Board?—No. Our fair is got up by feeling the want of it in the locality. It is common sense than anything else.

19,627. (To Mr. Cosgrave.) What species of animals do they bring to the fairs. Do they bring horses?—No. We sought to establish a horse fair four years ago, and it failed.

19,628. Are the pigs sold on the cattle fair day, or have you a separate day?—The same day.

19,629. Cattle, sheep, and pigs, I suppose, are the principal animals brought in?—Yes; and the place where the fair is held is the most suitable in the town.

19,630. Is it a widening of the street?—There is portion called Dolphin square. It is portion of the old beach filled up by the rubbish of the town. Considerable ground has been made there for the last 15 years, and it is widening every day.

19,631. (Mr. Loughlin.) I may say this fair is not held on the street. It is off the street altogether, but the main street is outside that. It is nearly the end of the town, and the main street there is occupied for three or four hundred yards by the fair also; but the pigs are sold on the street.

19,632. (To Mr. Cosgrave.) Do you concur in the opinion expressed by Mr. Loughlin about local authorities acquiring the market rights and working them in the public interest?—Not exactly. I think that already local authorities have in their own way compulsory authority to carry out the business; more than that, they are subject to the veto of the Local Government Board. They have absolute power already, and no greater power in my lights could be given than they have.

19,633. What compulsory power do you consider they have at present?—I would say they have every power to discharge all duties.

19,634. Supposing there is a local authority in a town in which the market rights are vested in an individual, and that body is desirous of getting control, there is no compulsory power vested in the local authority to acquire those rights?—It does not apply to this town, because there is no person having control of the market buildings. We are the owners of the place ourselves, but I would say this much, it would be an advantage where it does not apply exactly, as I believe there are towns where there are persons taking tolls. We take no tolls at all here; at the same time I am prepared to suggest to you as regards this town individually that I believe some tolls should be put on. I will not say in the market generally, but in the market house. That market house has been built lately, and the money has been got from the Local Government Board, and there the market is going free. We have gone to the expense of upwards of 100*l.* Well, I would not like to put on a tariff that would be injurious to the trade of the town, but I say it is absurd to be paying 60*l.* a year to the Local Government Board, and nothing charged to anybody.

19,635. You do not think it tends to develop the markets and directly to increase and materially affect the prosperity and trade of the town?—Certainly not; as regards this place I would not be for putting any charge on the general cattle market.

19,636. Do you think if a charge was levied it would tend to depreciate the supply in the market, or should the people avail themselves of the market premises through necessity?—I would be rather chary in expressing an opinion. I would not be for charging anything on the cattle, because we want to foster the cattle market, but in the market building I would be for putting on some tariff to meet the money we pay for it.

29,837. Did you ever know a case where a farmer living in Fermoy preferred to come here to Youghal where the fairs are toll free than to go to Fermoy where tolls are levied?—I must conscientiously state I could not give a case, but the fair is largely patronised lately, and it is an increasing fair.

29,838. The Youghal fair?—Yes.

29,839. Is there much of the surrounding country in tillage?—No, it is not by any means a tillage country. I may tell you that I have a great knowledge of Fermoy and the whole county of Cork, and I say while we have an excellent fair here the country is poorer than where you get into it, but the country is richer about Fermoy.

29,840. Is it all pasture land around here, or what percentage of the acreage would you say is in tillage?—I could give no idea, but driving around I have found, as you are very well aware I suppose, that this Ponsonby estate is a desert. Most of the people are going out of it, and that in itself is a heavy element against the benefit of the town of Youghal. We hope soon to see it come to a conclusion. I in my own way sometimes drive 20 and 30 miles in my own car, and I know Fermoy and the whole county of Cork, but Fermoy is a better country than this, and the land is richer; but we are doing very well as regards the fairs and markets here.

29,841. Would you say that the unfortunate circumstances that have occurred in connexion with the estate which you have mentioned have materially affected the markets in Youghal by placing a large area of land out of cultivation?—Yes, I must confess that; and I must confess, too, as a merchant in the town, it is a serious injury to us, because they have put out of occupation a thousand people there.

29,842. (*Mr. Loughlin.*) It has injured us in this way, that the traffic carried on on all the Ponsonby estate in corn and other produce was carried from Youghal, and is not now exported from or consumed in Youghal, and the result is that for the last two years while the business (the tenants combination) is going on, although some of the farms are worked by other people, the produce has gone away entirely in another direction. There is none of it coming into Youghal. Another thing with reference to these people working these farms under the Land Corporation, all their supplies come from another direction, while the tenants who were there before received all their supplies out of Youghal, and brought all their stuff into Youghal. That is substantially the cause of why the trade here is injured, and the business people have been materially injured by what has occurred on the Ponsonby estate. I was reared myself on the Ponsonby estate, and the best lands on that estate are worthless to Youghal or the trade of Youghal. There is a portion of it in the occupation of the tenants, and worked by the people themselves, and there is a portion of light ground to the north of the town where they carry on their communications with Youghal as before, but their traffic does not amount to anything like that of the portion taken up by the Land Corporation.

29,843. (*Mr Cosgrove.*) In fact, the place is barren, and I may take the liberty of making a casual remark which is that I hope soon to see the matter settled, and settled not alone here, but elsewhere, when there are plenty of merchants and people and shopkeepers who would actually supply these people (the tenants) with stock and everything else, that is, if there was an arrangement or settlement, and they were safe in doing so.

29,844. Have you any suggestions to make as to what you think would tend to improve the markets and fairs, and are there any amendments in the present law that you consider necessary?—Well, I think I have no suggestion. I cannot see my way through it. I do not see I have weight enough to make any suggestion beyond this, that I know the thing is going on very well. I have a feeling over this market house that has been newly built. I believe, and maintain it, that some reasonable charge should be put upon the public.

29,845. When you say charge upon the public, I suppose you mean a charge on the people who avail themselves of the market house only; in other words, to make the market buildings self-supporting?—Yes, in order to try to discharge the debt to the Government. After that debt was discharged, I would be for setting the market free, and charging nothing.

29,846. (*Mr. Loughlin.*) Fearing there may be any misapprehension on the point, I wish to say that we do not pay 40*l.* a year in respect of the market house.

29,847. What is the average interest payable?—We have only to pay half of that because the harbour board, which is a separate body with a separate revenue, pay the other half.

Mr. James O'Shea, the Town Clerk, re-examined.

29,848. (*Witness.*) The total expenditure on the market is 62*l.* odd, including the caretaker's wages.

29,849. Give me the total expenses you are at in connexion with the markets here. What is the weighmaster's salary?—It is 7*s.* a week. I may say roughly the expenditure is 60*l.* a year, there is 24*l.* 4*s.* 0*d.* the two half-yearly instalments of the loan, including principal and interest, and 18*l.* a year to the weigh-master.

29,850. Mr. Hassett is the only official you have engaged as weigh-master?—Yes.

29,851. What are your receipts?—Practically nil. There was a pound for weighing since the market was opened.

29,852. For the entire period?—Yes. Practically there is no revenue.

29,853. (*Mr. Cosgrove.*) I heartily protest against this market-house being charged upon the population of the town while they are receiving nothing, and I say in common honesty something should be charged and paid by the country people.

(*The Commissioner.*) That would be a matter to discuss at the town commission board, but it is a matter I cannot help you in.

29,854. (*The Town Clerk.*) I should tell you that the average expenditure for three years on the fair field has been 22*l.*

29,855. By the commissioners?—Yes.

29,856. That is for levelling and repairs?—Yes, and advertising.

29,857. Is this ground you have reclaimed?—Yes.

29,858. Is it enclosed?—There is a paling around it.

29,859. Have you any suggestions to offer as to what you think would tend to the improvement of the markets and fairs?—I think it would be well worth the while of the commissioners to put up pens in the present fair field and make a small charge for the maintenance of this. It would be a convenience to the farmers bringing in their cattle. I also think it would be only reasonable to put a small toll on the potatoes sold in the market house, just sufficient to cover the cost of maintaining the building.

29,860. Are you of opinion that if charges are levied at markets or fairs they should be such as would only cover the actual expenditure?—Certainly.

29,861. That no profit should be derived?—No profit. I do not think any reasonable charge would affect the markets or fairs in the slightest.

29,862. If in return for these charges accommodation is given?—Yes.

29,863. Is there any amendment in the law relating to market rights that you would suggest, or rather, do you concur in the opinions of Mr. Cosgrove and Mr. Loughlin about giving powers to local authorities?—Yes.

29,864. Do you think yourself, from your experience as town clerk and your connexion with public bodies, that the united efforts of the several gentlemen constituting the board would lead to better management than when the rights are in the hands of private individuals?—Undoubtedly.

29,865. What rates have you here?—The rate under the ninth of George the Fourth is of a peculiar character. It is a 1*s.*, 6*d.*, or 3*d.* in the *£.* according to the different valuations; and 3*d.* in the *£* sanitary rates.

20,306. They are the only tolls?—Yes, and we have no power of levying taxes on a valuation under 5l. They go free. It would be well worth the while of the commissioners to adopt the Towns Improvement Act.

20,307. Have they never discussed the advisability of adopting it?—Mr. Loughlin has tried once or twice.

20,308. (Mr. Loughlin.) It is under the consideration of the board already to adopt the Towns Improvement Act. It is a thing very much needed.

20,309. Is there any other gentleman who wishes to give any evidence or make any suggestion?—No answer.

The inquiry then terminated.

RATHKEALE.

WITH reference to my inquiry in Rathkeale, on 5th day of January 1889, I beg to report as follows:—

Rathkeale is an inland town in the county of Limerick. It is a station on the Newcastle branch of the Waterford and Limerick Railway line. The trade is chiefly retail. The local municipal government is administered by town commissioners, and the population is 2,549.

The markets are held on Tuesday. The fairs on 7th January, 7th February, 10th March, 4th April, 22nd April, 8th May, 1st June, 10th June, 17th July, 4th August, 25th August, 18th September, 15th October, 4th November, 19th November, 13th December. A pig fair day previous.

Tolls are levied at all the fairs, but at the markets weighing charges alone are levied. No rule exists in the market compelling all commodities to be weighed at the public scales.

A toll board is erected, and a weighing machine has been provided capable of weighing cattle.

The markets, rights, and tolls are the property of Mr. V. Pigott, of Capard, Rosenalls, Queen's County, but he has them sublet by lease, which was made some years back. The witnesses were unable to give me the particulars or all the terms of the lease, but I ascertained that it was made to the then chairman of the town commission, and the parish priest of the town, for a certain term at the yearly rent of 100l., with a condition that after payment of all expenses the profits should be applied as follows:—One moiety to the town commissioners for the benefit of the town, and the other moiety to the parish priest for the benefit of the Roman Catholic church in the town. The surplus is, however, at present applied, with the consent of those representing the lessees, in the reduction of the debt incurred in the erection of the gasworks of the town, and of the new market premises. Three patents appear on the public records as having been granted for Rathkeale. The first is dated 5th December (6 James I.), and authorised Sir John Dowdall to hold a Thursday market, and fairs on the Vigil and Feast Day of Annunciation (25th March), Assumption (15th August), and Nativity (8th September) of the Virgin Mary, and two days following each. The second is dated 2nd August 1611, and re-granted to William Cullum two of the foregoing fairs. The third is dated 1st March 1781, and authorised one John Pigott to hold a Monday, Tuesday, Wednesday, Friday, and Saturday market, and fairs on the 1st June and 19th November.

The fairs on the 22nd April, 4th August, and 4th November were established about 16 years ago by the town commissioners. Those on the 7th January and 8th May were established about 25 years ago, and the remaining fairs on the 7th February, 10th March, 4th April, 1st June, 10th June, 17th July, 25th August, 18th September, and 13th December were, it is stated, held for a long time previous. The markets and fairs held under an express grant from the Crown, disclosed by the Public Records, are the Tuesday market, and the fairs on the 4th April, 1st June, 25th August, 18th September, and 19th November, and those not held under such express authority are the fairs on 7th January, 7th February, 10th March, 22nd April, 8th May, 10th June, 17th July, 4th August, 15th October, 4th November, and 13th December, and the pig fairs.

In accordance with my instructions, I have inspected the fairs and market places.

The fairs are held on the public thoroughfare and throughout the streets of the town, which are not very wide. There is no accommodation whatever provided other than what the shops and private dwellings afford. Off the main street there is a square space, where all the standings on fair days are concentrated.

The markets are partly held in the market-yard, and partly on the public streets. No rule exists restraining the exposure of marketable commodities elsewhere than in the market-yard, and the consequence is some commodities are hawked around the town by the vendors in order to effect a ready sale. The market-yard is a square space off the main road adjacent to the court-house, and of fair dimensions. It is entirely enclosed, and approached from the roadway by two large gate entrances. A row of sheds, timber-roofed, is erected on each of two sides of the yard, and under which marketable commodities are weighed, butter in one portion, and potatoes, corn, and wool in another. A weigh-bridge and office are also erected in the yard, and on market days the centre is generally occupied by small basket-standings, for which no charge is levied.

The practice also exists here in levying a standing charge of 1s. off each cartload of bonhams (small pigs) brought in on fair days, and if the pigs are subsequently sold an additional charge of 2d. each is levied when they are leaving the fair.

Appended will be found a transcript of the evidence taken at the inquiry.

JOHN J. O'MEARA,
Assistant Commissioner.

45, Lower Mount Street,
Dublin.

Rathkeale, 8th January 1889.

Mr. Stephen Casey (town clerk) examined.

29,870. You are the town clerk of Rathkeale?—Yes.

29,871. When was the commission established here?—In 1846, I think.

29,872. You are working under the Act of 1854?—Yes.

29,873. I believe Mr. Pigott, of Rathkeale, is owner of the markets, rights, and fairs that exist here?—Yes.

29,874. He is not in the immediate receipt of any charges?—No more than the annual rent.

29,875. To whom has he them leased?—To the archdeacon and the town commissioners.

29,876. Have you got the particulars of the lease?—No.

29,877. Do you know the date of it?—No.

29,878. But it is leased to the Archdeacon of Rathkeale and the town commissioners?—Yes.

29,879. At what rent?—200l. a year. 100l. a year is paid, but 200l. is the reserved rent.

29,880-1. What is the term?—I cannot say the term, but I think it is for 31 years.

29,882. You do not know what year the lease was made. You could not give me any idea, or the unexpired term of it?—No.

29,883. Over and above the rent, the profits derived from the markets and fairs are to be applied—a moiety to the Archdeacon and a moiety to the town commissioners?—Yes; not to him personally, but the Archdeacon holds in trust for the improvement of the church.

29,884. The town commissioners, I presume, have their own moiety in trust for the benefit and improvement of the town and the reduction of the rates?—That was the intention, but the chairman for the time being transferred his rights until a certain debt was paid about the gas-house and butter market and something in connexion with the church.

29,885. Up to this the town commissioners have derived no benefit whatever from them?—No benefit whatever.

29,886. I presume that moiety that was to go to the town commissioners is applied otherwise in the reduction of some debts contracted on behalf the markets?—Quite so. It is applied to the reduction of debts and things got up for the improvement of the town.

29,887. These are the gasworks?—Yes, and butter market.

29,888. Who has control over these at present, or who is managing them?—I am acting manager of them at present.

29,889. What is the market day here?—The weekly market is held on Tuesday.

29,890. Has the market always been held on Tuesdays?—Yes.

29,891. When are the fairs held?—Once a month, and some of them twice. There are 16 in the year.

29,892. Give me the dates of them?—The 7th January, the 7th February, 10th March, 4th and 22nd April, 8th May, 1st and 18th June, 17th July, 4th and 25th August, 18th September, 14th October, 4th and 19th November and 13th December. I wish to observe that the pig market is held the day before the fair in each case.

29,893. Do you remember when there were less than 16 fairs held here?—I do.

29,894. Were any of them established recently?—Most of these new fairs were established by the commissioners; four of them were established by the commissioners.

29,895. Which four?—The 22nd April, 4th August, and 4th November. Three I think that were established.

29,896. When were these established?—Some 15 or 16 years ago. The 22nd April fair was originally held on the 24th April, and we changed it to the 22nd.

29,897. When did you effect that change in the April fair?—About two years ago. The commissioners and people saw it clashed with other important fairs, and then, to make it more successful, the change was made at the instance of the archdeacon principally.

29,898. The other 12 fairs were held for a length of time previous?—Six of these were put on some time before that again; originally there were only seven fairs.

29,899. Could you tell me the seven old fairs?—I could not tell you. They were a long time in existence.

29,900. When were the other six established?—About 25 years ago, or 30 years.

29,901. What six were there?—I could hardly tell them.

29,902. Could you tell the month?—I would say February and the 4th April were old fairs; the 1st June, 17th July, 15th August, 18th September, and 13th December.

29,903. The other six were established about 25 years ago?—Yes.

29,904. Were the seven old fairs held for any great length of time, or do you remember having heard at one period there were less than seven fairs held?—I have no idea. For generations I heard seven fairs were held there.

29,905. Are tolls levied at present at all these fairs?—At all times and all fairs.

29,906. You do not remember any fairs being toll free?—Never.

29,907. Where are the fairs held?—On the streets.

29,908. Are tolls levied at the markets?—No; only a weighing fee.

29,909. Are the charges at the fairs only levied on the animals actually sold when they are leaving the fair?—Yes; there are no charges coming in.

29,910. And at the markets the only charges levied are those when the service of weighing is performed?—Yes.

29,911. Is there any compulsory rule existing in the market requiring all commodities to be weighed at the market scales?—No.

29,912. If a farmer brings in weighable commodities, he is free to go where he pleases?—Yes.

29,913. What market buildings have you here?—A large yard and sheds enclosed, weighing office and lever, scales, and weights; several sets of scales.

29,914. Is the market enclosed?—Part of it is enclosed. There are covered sheds erected, and the floor is flagged.

29,915. Is this yard off the public thoroughfare?—It is off the street—off the footpath—at the head of the town.

29,916. Who was it provided it originally?—The commissioners, and that is part of the liability the tolls are going to pay off at present.

29,917. Where did you get the capital to build?—We raised money. I think it was by private subscription; a certain number of the commissioners joined together.

29,918. It is none of the municipal fund?—No; it is not paid out of the rates. Part of the tolls are going to pay off that at present.

29,919. What was the original amount raised?—I think the whole amount came to about 300l., but I know we had to pass a note for 150l. in the bank.

29,920. How much remains unpaid?—[illegible]

29,921. What was the per-centage?—Six per cent. the bank cost.

29,922. Was it from the National Bank?—No, but the Munster and Leinster Bank. That was the time money was ten per cent. There were special advantages given.

29,923. The charges at the fairs and likewise the markets were applied to the redemption of this debt, and the other moiety went to the archdeacon?—

29,924. Archdeacon Ralph (interposing).—No. I hold my moiety by deed from the original leaseholder.

29,925. Was then the predecessor of Mr. Pigott?—No; but Mr. Pigott leased to Dr. O'Hanlon, then chairman of the town commissioners, and he applied his moiety for the purpose of doing some works, some works the town commissioners created, and he lent his money himself to pay for those works. After his death the town moiety of the tolls went to pay his family the money he expended; on whose this moiety was paid off the lease was made over to me then for the same purpose, but with my superior's permission I consented to let my moiety go for the present with the town moiety to liquidate the two large debts for the butter market and gas-lamps. When the debts are paid I revert to my own moiety, besides by lease, held by right for the church.

29,926. (*The Commissioner to Mr. Camp.*) Have you made out the particulars of the receipts from the market rights and fairs?—I am not long acting manager; it is only tentative so far as I am concerned.

29,927. Who looks after the finances?—After every fair the net proceeds are lodged in the bank.

29,928. What particulars have you made out?—I am only virtually in charge for the last few months. I was superintendent before that.

29,929. Do not you keep any record of the receipts?—I have.

29,930. Have not you had a record previous to your management?—No; none.

29,931. Did not your predecessor keep a record?—He did, but I do not know what way it was, I did not get it. In fact, we tried to hunt some statistics for you and could not find them.

29,932. What are the receipts?—From the 17th July 1887 to the 17th July 1888, that is one year, the amount reached up to 416l. 14s. 1d.; from the 17th July 1888 to the 30th December last, past—that is a half year, the receipts were 254l. 5s. 1d., making a total of 670l. 19s. 2d.

29,933. Are these the gross receipts from the markets and fairs and all sources?—It is the amount lodged, less the expenses of the men. The net amount is lodged after paying the men; but there are other expenses besides the expenses of collection that are not stopped.

29,933a. What are those?—Advertisements and stationery, rent, income tax, old rates, and other things.

29,934. What is the actual rent at present?—The actual rent at present is [illegible].

29,935. When did you get the statement?—I suppose about a year and a half ago. It was in contemplation a long time before that.

29,936. Could you tell me the men you have engaged in connexion with the markets?—We have a weigh-master.

29,937. What is his salary?—[illegible] a year.

29,938. Does he look after the markets?—He looks after the weekly markets.

29,939. Is he the only man engaged?—We have two special men on market days to give assistance, but they are only for part of the year.

29,940. What do you give these two assistants?—I suppose about 4s. 6d. a week.

29,941. Each?—No; for both. It is only for a short time of the year.

29,942. How many toll gates have you at the fairs?—Six.

29,943. How many men do you have generally at each?—Three at night.

29,944. How many altogether?—It comes to 6l. each fair to pay them.

29,945. That is [illegible] a year for collection at the fairs alone?—I put down the expenses in a rough way at [illegible] a year, stationery and other things and the taxation [illegible] a year.

29,946. Is that the valuation or taxation?—The poor rates on it this year came to [illegible].

29,947. What is the valuation?—800l.

29,948. How much in the £ does the total taxation amount to, or what is the amount of consolidated rates?—The poor rate is 3s. in the £, and the county-cess comes to [illegible] for the two levies. Between rent, taxes, and everything the expenditure amounts to [illegible] a year.

29,949. Could not you give us the poundage rates in the town?—The poor rate is 3s. in the £, the county-cess 3s. 4d.; the town's improvement rate a shilling and income tax 7d. in the £.

29,950. Have you any railway guarantee to pay?—No.

29,951. The rent you pay is over and above all deductions?—Yes. Since he gave the abatement all taxation is paid out of the receipts.

29,952. As you are the town clerk, could you tell me were any representations ever made to the town commissioners to provide a fair green, and remove the fairs off the public streets?—No. The people would be opposed to that.

29,953. Do they think that the streets, the public thoroughfares, is the proper place, and the more convenient to hold the fairs than in a properly enclosed fair green?—It has done very well. They have the trade of the buyers and sellers too.

29,954. I suppose for trade purposes they would not put up with any interference caused to them?—Yes. Wherever I have seen a fair taken from the town into the fair green it did not succeed afterwards. I have seen several instances of it.

29,955. Do you keep any record of the number of stock brought in?—No; only the actual receipts. You could not do it.

29,956. There is no record of the average price of these animals at each fair?—No.

29,957. Do you keep any at the markets?—We keep nothing, only the receipts.

29,958. When you weigh the commodities do not you give a ticket in return denoting the weight?—Yes.

29,959. Do you retain a block of this ticket?—Yes.

29,960. In that way you keep a record of the quantity only weighed?—Yes, and I make up the price.

29,961. Is this market always availed of by the farmers?—It is.

29,962. Or do they expose their commodities elsewhere in the town?—Some do.

29,963. There is no restriction in that respect?—No.

29,964. Have you any standing charges at the markets or any stalls?—No.

29,965. You receive no rents?—No rents.

29,966. Kindly tell me the different marketable commodities brought in here on Tuesday?—Butter.

29,967. Is it always roll butter that is brought here?—Firkin and lump butter.

29,968. What other commodities?—Hay, straw, and oats.

29,969. Are oats the only description of corn brought here?—Wheat generally goes direct to the mill; the oats is the only thing sold.

29,970. What else?—Wool, and sometimes potatoes, but not to any appreciable extent.

29,971. What other commodities are brought? Are vegetables?—No.

29,972. Are vegetables brought in about the town on Tuesday?—They are, and a great deal of these commodities are sold and weighed at private scales.

29,973. Are vegetables brought around the town?—They are, and bought about the town.

29,974. Is fish brought here?—It is bought around the town.

29,975. Turf?—The same.

29,976. Are any animals, pigs, or calves brought in here on market days?—No.

29,977. What charges do you receive from butter?—A penny for each firkin—each firkin and lump; that is the weighing fee.

29,978. Supposing they bring a firkin into the town must they bring it to your place?—All butter has to go as a matter of course into the market. It would not be bought in any other place except odd lumps.

29,979. Supposing they brought a firkin into the town and sold elsewhere than the market place, would you receive a penny if it came to your knowledge?—The buyer would not buy if it was not weighed in the market.

29,980. Supposing a firkin was brought into the town and sold to a shopkeeper, and it came to your knowledge, would you sue for your charge?—No case of that kind came under my observation.

29,981. What return do you give for the penny per firkin you receive?—We weigh the butter.

29,982. Do you strip it?—Not as a rule. Wherever it is required by the buyer, it is weighed, marked, and a ticket given.

29,983. I do not suppose you classify the butter?—No.

29,984. Does the cooper brand the tare on the firkin?—No. The tare is asked and set out in the ticket.

29,985. How do you ascertain the tare?—We put down the name of the owner, the weight and tare, and then he is responsible for it.

29,986. Do you always estimate the tare then?—We get it from the farmer. If it is not the exact thing he is responsible.

29,987. You rely on what the producer tells you for the tare?—Yes. If it is not right the buyer sends us word, and we put our hands at once on the man, and the buyer is recouped for the difference.

29,988. Did you ever see them weighing butter there?—Yes.

29,989. When weighing a firkin of butter what is the smallest weight you use the scales. Do you weigh down to a pound?—Yes.

29,990. When you are weighing I suppose you give a cast of the beam?—We weigh it very exact.

29,991. Is the tare, which the producer informs you of the only deduction from the gross weight ascertained by you?—That is the only deduction.

29,992. Is there any deduction made for soakage or pickle?—No. The only deduction is the tare.

29,993. Does that include any salt or pickle about the butter?—It includes everything.

29,994. Does it differ materially from the actual weight of the firkin if weighed?—It is only the actual weight of the firkin.

29,995. For the soakage in the firkin or pickle about the butter does the buyer lose that?—Yes; that is for himself to see.

29,996. Do you charge a penny for each lump you weigh no matter what the weight would be?—Yes.

29,997. If a pound of butter is brought in and you weigh it you charge a penny?—Yes; but they do not bring such small quantities as that.

29,998. If there were twenty pounds in a lump brought in you would charge a penny likewise?—Yes, or for forty or one hundred pounds.

29,999. Do you give a ticket?—Yes.

30,000. When you receive the charge?—Yes.

30,001. Is it always sold before being weighed?—It is generally sold before it is weighed.

30,002. If they bring in a quantity of firkins and could not dispose of them have you any storage accommodation?—We have large sheds.

30,003. Do you store any butter?—It does not be left. It is generally nearly all sold.

30,004. What would you charge for storage accommodation?—We charge nothing.

30,005. But I suppose it would be at the producer's risk?—Yes, certainly. Generally they take home the butter unsold and send it on to Cork.

30,006. On hay what is your charge?—Three pence a load.

30,007. On straw?—The same charge for a load of anything.

30,008. That is only when weighed?—Yes.

30,009. Do they ever buy a load of hay by bulk?—Very seldom.

30,010 If they did you charge nothing?—Nothing.

30,011. Where is the hay exposed for sale?—In the market.

30,012. So then the market is of large dimensions?—It is pretty fair; there is a large space outside it.

30,013. On oats what is your charge?—A penny a bag.

30,014. I suppose it is a penny a bag no matter what description of corn it is?—No matter what description.

30,015. Do you weigh the empty sack when weighing corn?—We weigh the empty sack.

30,016. You never estimate the tare of it?—No.

30,017. Is the actual weight of the bag that you ascertain the only deduction from the gross weight or is there anything allowed for breakage or damage?—There is only the weight of the bag off.

30,018. And it has been sold before being weighed?—Yes.

30,019. Do you give a ticket for that?—Yes.

30,020. Are these tickets printed forms?—Yes.

30,021. You have none of them here?—No, but I can get one for you. (*The following are the tickets in use*)

RATHKEALE BUTTER MARKET.

____________________ 188 .

Name, ____________________

Address, ____________________

No. of Ticket __________

________ Firkins of Butter.

Gross Weight Qrs.	Lbs.	Tare.

Wm. D. POWER, Clerk.

RATHKEALE BUTTER MARKET.

____________________ 188 .

Name, ____________________

Address, ____________________

No. of Ticket __________

________ Firkins of Butter.

Gross Weight Qrs.	Lbs.	Tare.

Wm. D. POWER, Clerk.

RATHKEALE BUTTER AND GENERAL PRODUCE MARKET.

________ day of ____________ 188 .

Weighed by Public Market Lever.

For ____________________

To be delivered to ____________________

________ Load ____ of ____________

Empty Cask. Cwt.	Qrs.	Lbs.	Weight.	Tons.	Cwts.	Qrs.	Lbs.

Weighing Fee, ____________

Signed, ____________________

Clerk to Market Committee.

RATHKEALE BUTTER AND GENERAL PRODUCE MARKET.

________ day of ____________ 188 .

Weighed by Public Market Lever.

For ____________________

To be delivered to ____________________

________ Load ____ of ____________

Empty Cask. Cwts.	Qrs.	Lbs.	Weight.	Tons.	Cwts.	Qrs.	Lbs.

Weighing Fee, ____________

Signed, ____________________

Clerk to Market Committee.

20,622. Down to what weight do you weigh the corn. Do you use the pound weight or the four-pound weight? —The pound weight.

20,623. Always?—Yes.

20,624. You give a cast of the beam?—Yes.

20,625. What charge do you receive for weighing wool?—A cwt. and upwards, 6d., no matter what it weighed after the cwt. From 28 lbs. to a cwt., 4d.; under 28 lbs., 2d. The custom of the market is here, and he tells me, in the case of wool, they put in the half-pound, and in the case of wool only.

20,626. Do you weigh the wool in its natural state? —It is weighed in the pack and the weight of the pack is taken off.

20,627. In weighing potatoes is the charge a penny a bag too?—Yes.

20,628. Do you put in less than half a stone in the scales?—We put in the pound in potatoes.

20,629. Do you weigh the empty sack or estimate the tare?—We weigh the empty sack.

20,630. What is the usual tare of an ordinary sack here?—Four pounds is the general thing; some bags are seven pounds, but four pounds is the general thing.

20,631. You always weigh it?—Yes.

20,632. You get no charge on vegetables at all?—No.

20,633. Or fish or eggs?—No charge.

20,634. If they come into this market-yard with vegetables, eggs, fish, or any commodity, and wanted a standing in it, or put down the basket in the yard, would you levy any charge?—No charge.

30,035. Do you permit that?—Yes. They do avail themselves of that; it is only to a small extent.

30,036. They hawk about the town?—Yes.

30,037. At the fairs have you any standing charges. I see here a large load of any description a shilling?—Yes, we charge that, but in that we do not insist on the whole thing. We exercise a discretion and I am at liberty to do so.

30,038. You have a list of the charges, the tolls levied at the fairs erected for public inspection?—Yes. This is a copy which I hand in.

30,039. Witness then produced a schedule of the tolls of which the following is a copy:—

SCHEDULE of the CUSTOMS and TOLLS to be taken at the MARKETS and FAIRS of RATHKEALE.

			s.	d.
For each cow, bull or bullock	-	sold	0	6
" " two year old	-	"	0	4
" " yearling	-	"	0	3
" " calf	-	"	0	2
" " sheep	-	"	0	1
" " lamb	-	"	0	0½
" " pig	-	"	0	3
" " slip (or young pig)	-	"	0	1½
" " horse mare or gelding	-	"	0	10
" " goat, mule, or ass	-	"	0	6
" " horse car load of slips	-		1	0
" " goat, mule, or ass car of slips			0	6
" " soft goods standing	-		1	0
" " load of cabbage plants	-		1	0
" " hardware standing	-		1	0
" " load of any description	-		1	0
" " show booth or tent	-		2	6

30,040. So that when farmers are coming in, and when the charge is sought for from them, they are at liberty and in a position to see what is the actual charge on the public board?—Quite so.

30,041. Have you copy of the board at each gap?—Yes.

30,042. I find here a cow, bull, or bullock, 6d.?—Yes.

30,043. That is only when sold?—Yes.

30,044. A two-year-old, 4d.; yearling, 3d.; each calf, 2d.; each sheep, 1d.; each lamb, ½d.; and each pig, 3d.?—Yes.

30,045. I see you have here a horse cartload of bonhams, 1s.?—Yes.

30,046. Supposing they brought a load of bonhams into the fair and remained on the street with them you charge 1s.?—Yes.

30,047. When they had sold and were returning out of the fair, would your men ask them whether they had sold the bonhams or not, and would you levy any additional charge on the bonhams?—All cars with bonhams on the square, on leaving the square, get a ticket, and they pay for that ticket. That ticket passes them out, but if they sell to other persons the bonhams have to pay going out; the owner has to pay nothing, the ticket passes him out.

30,048. The same thing applies if they bring in lambs in cars?—The same thing.

30,049. Each soft goods standing 1s. Have you actually a soft goods standing?—Very few.

30,050. You have some?—Yes, cast clothes.

30,051. Each load of cabbage plants?—1s.?—Yes.

30,052. Each hardware stand 1s.?—Yes, each load of any description.

30,053. If they brought in a cartload of turf would you charge 1s.?—No.

30,054. Did you ever charge on the turf?—Never.

30,055. This market-place which you term the square, is it a widening of the public thoroughfare?—Yes. We keep the cars in a cluster in order not to inconvenience the other portions of the fair; we keep them there off the road.

30,056. Supposing they brought in a load of turnips on the fair day on the square would you charge them?—We do not charge for any of those things.

30,057. Could you tell me the description of commodities you actually charge on or give directions to charge upon?—Cabbage plants, soft goods, hardware, and things of that sort.

30,058. You have a general charge on each load of any description that would include everything?—We do not go to the full extent.

30,059. I want to know the particulars of things you charge on?—What we do really charge on is soft goods, cast clothes, and plants; we do not charge on the bonhams.

30,060. Supposing they bring in a quantity of apples in a cart do you charge?—No.

30,061. Do they erect small standings by placing a couple of boards on their carts?—They do, and we do not charge anything. Often people with cakes stand there, and we do not charge them anything.

30,062. The town commissioners are not the sanitary authority here?—No, the board of guardians.

30,063. Who cleans the public thoroughfare?—The road contractor.

30,064. The town commissioners do not perform that work?—No. They have not adopted that yet.

30,065. Have you heard, in connexion with the Commission, that objections or complaints were made of any dereliction of duty on the part of the road contractor in not properly cleaning up the public thoroughfare after the fair days?—No; he has an old man after the fair to clean it up.

30,066. Did you ever hear that any accidents happened from the fact of the fairs being held on the square or of any injury being done to animals or property?—No.

30,067. Are there different circuits allowed off for each species of animal, or do they intermix?—They all intermix, but the sellers have a special place for themselves. The only difference is the horses; they have a special place for themselves.

30,068. Where are your gaps situated?—At each crossing.

30,069. Are they outside the town?—On the verge of the town. They are in the town, but on the outskirts.

30,070. I suppose beside the last houses?—Yes.

30,071. You have a number of men at each gap?—Yes.

30,072. When the animals are going out do they inquire whether they are bought or sold?—Yes.

30,073. Supposing they state they have not been bought or sold, do they permit them to pass?—Yes.

30,074. Supposing they doubt the statement a man has made, what course will they adopt?—They will do their best to be satisfied, and then let them go.

30,075. Do they ever produce a book or paper to swear them?—They do not as a rule.

30,076. Do they ever ask them to swear the toll board?—No.

30,077. Are the men in the habit of carrying sticks?—They carry a stick each.

30,078. Have you ever heard they have injured either the animals brought out, or the owners of them?—I never heard they injured any of them. There might be a little hesitation in getting out; a man would be trying to pass, and there may be gentle remonstrance and partial resistance.

30,079. Have you ever heard of any undue delay being caused to the farmers in proceeding home by the collection of the tolls?—No.

30,080. Have you any suggestions to make as to what you think would tend to the improvement of the markets or fairs?—None. I may say there is a committee formed for the better working and management of the markets. The town commissioners are ex officio members, and any traders are at liberty to take part in the deliberations of the committee. The clerk of the market makes a return to the committee of the work done and the receipts at the market, and the weekly receipts are lodged in the bank and checked by us.

30,081. When does the committee meet?—During the season they meet once a fortnight.

30,082. What day?—Friday.

30,083. Then they elect a chairman, and you produce the books and a summary of the work that has been done since the last meeting?—Yes. I produce the bank tools, lodgments, and all. The original loan was made to the Rev. Dr. O'Brien, P.P., and to Mr. David O'Hanlon, M.D., then chairman of the town commissioners. I made out a calculation of the amount paid last year for the general market and gasworks. In reduction of these debts from the 7th April 1888 to the 30th December of the same year we paid 34*l.*

30,084. Was this loan obtained for the gasworks secured by mortgage on the rates?—No; the commissioners raised the money in bank personally.

30,085. They incurred a personal liability for works for the improvement of the town?—Yes. They did not wish to saddle the rates.

30,086. So now they are applying the profits derived from the fairs to the reduction of the liability incurred by the gasworks and the butter market?—Yes.

30,087. When this is paid off the profits will be divided—one moiety to the archdeacon for the Church and the other to the town commissioners for the benefit of the town?—Yes.

30,088. Witness then produced the following document relating to the market accounts for the past two years, which were preferred by the clerk of the market, and inspected by the committee:—

1887.

Statement of the Principal Business done in the market for the year ending 1st September 1887:—

Seven hundred and nine firkins of butter against 1,160 same time last season; 1,036 lumps do. against 887 last season; that is from the 16th June to the 1st September each year.

Five hundred and twenty-eight loads of hay, 139 straw, 554 turnips, 353 timber, 8 meal, 9 coke, 7 carrots, 6 coal, and 13 mangolds.

One thousand one hundred and ninety-three bags of oats, 15 wheat, 155 potatoes, and 5 feathers.

Two hundred and forty-three bags and packs of wool, showing an increase.

1886, Accounts.

	£	s.	d.
Balance in hands of treasurer - -	0	15	6
By amount collected from the 1st September 1886 to 1st September 1887 - -	41	15	9
	£42	10	3

Cr.

	£	s.	d.	£	s.	d.
To amount paid to the musicians - - -	11	5	6			
Printing - - -	1	8	4			
Repairs of market - -	6	11	3			
Insurance - - -	0	19	6			
Clerk's salary - - -	20	0	0			
				39	14	1
1887. Balance in hands of treasurer - -				3	14	4
By amount due of Colonel Brown for weighing timber - - - -				3	4	6
Colonel Lloyd do. - - - -				0	15	3
				43	18	1

1888.

Statement of amount for 1888:—

One thousand seven hundred and twenty-four firkins of butter; for same period 1887, 709; 2030 lumps do.; same period 1887, 1,036.

Loads of hay, 548; straw, 78; turnips, 55; coal, 13; carrots, 6; mangolds, 15; meal, 3; rand, 2.

Bags: oats, 700; potatoes, 154; wheat, 11; barley, 4; turkeys, 6.

Two hundred and seventy-eight bags and packs of wool.

1888. Accounts:—

	£	s.	d.
Balance in hands of treasurer on 1st June 1888 - - - - -	6	1	10
By amount collected from the 1st June to 31st December 1888 - - -	39	5	0
	45	7	9

Cr.

	£	s.	d.	£	s.	d.
To amount paid musicians -	6	7	8			
Printing - - -	3	4	1			
Insurance - - -	0	13	4			
Repairs of markets and expenses generally - - -	3	0	0			
Clerk's salary - - -	20	0	0			
				33	5	3
Balance in treasurer's hands - -				12	2	6

Wm. D. Power, clerk of market.
Thomas Lenihan, C.C. chairman.

Dated 31st December 1888.

30,089. Supposing a farmer was bringing in his stock to the fair, and on one of the roads adjacent to the town before he came into it he effected a sale of his animals to a buyer out there, and it came to your knowledge, would you ask for any charge?—No, if he did not come inside the gap.

30,090. You consider your jurisdiction only extends inside the gap?—Yes. If a bargain is made outside the town we do not interfere.

30,091. If a shopkeeper went out thinking he would effect a better bargain, before the fair commenced, and met the farmer on the road coming in, and bought from him outside the toll gap, and the animal was delivered to him on fair day would he have to pay?—Yes, if he came through the toll gap no matter where the sale is effected.

Very Reverend Archdeacon Halpin, P.P., examined.

30,092. You are the owner of one moiety of the tolls levied here in Rathkeale?—Yes, of the residue.

30,093. After the payment of the rent and the cost of management?—Yes, and all expenses incurred.

30,094. But the only expenditure incurred is the rent, rates, and taxes, and cost of management?—That is all.

30,095. And of course any improvements that may be effected from time to time?—Yes.

30,096. Have you any objection, or have you heard any complaints about the fairs being held on the public thoroughfare, or streets of the town?—Quite the contrary. I know from my own knowledge and intercourse with the people they would not like to have the fairs removed.

30,097. You do not think it would tend to augment the fairs, if they were held in a properly enclosed fair green, with pen accommodation?—I do not think it would.

30,098. You of course have had much experience of the farmers coming in and their dealings, this is a more general question than one applying particularly to Rathkeale, do you think the existence of a toll tends to deter them from bringing in the supply they would otherwise bring in?—I do not think so because they would have to pay in any other place they would take them to. I never heard of any fair or market where there were no tolls.

30,099. Do not you think they would prefer to have a fair green to the public streets?—I do not think so. They go where they can sell.

30,100. You think they look out for the place where they can effect a ready sale of the stock, and they do not consider the charge afterwards?—Where the buyers go to wherever they go, and that is my opinion after long experience.

30,101. The charge at present is only on the animals actually sold?—Yes.

30,102. Do you think a much smaller charge would be better on all the animals brought in?—If you could effect that it would be, but you would not change to that easily.

30,103. You think there would be some opposition?—It would create great confusion.

30,104. You are aware it is adopted elsewhere?—It is adopted in all new fairs I am aware. In the Great Munster fair no animal is let in without paying, but in the old fairs they pay on the animals sold.

30,105. What return does the farmer or buyer get for the tolls that are levied here at the fairs?—They get simply the accommodation of standing on the street.

30,106. Disposing of their stock on the public thoroughfare?—Yes, and buyers coming to meet them. I do not see the farmers get anything in the place but that.

30,107. You have sufficient railway communication here?—Yes, in as far as any railway will give it to, but they are very stingy I must say, because the way the Limerick and Kerry Company work the line, they force a number of people to drive their stock from this to Croom, to be carried to Cork to the injury of our fairs.

30,108. Do the trains run to suit the fairs?—Yes.

30,109. Have you any suggestions to offer as to what you think would tend to the improvement of the fairs and markets here?—I do not know of any.

Mr. James Blackwell examined.

30,110. You are one of the town commissioners?—Yes, since they were established.

30,111. Of course, indirectly, have the town commissioners exercise, more or less, some control over the fairs, but from your experience of the farmers of the country do you think that local authorities, where such exist, such as town commissioners, should have control of the markets and fairs?—Well, I think they should, but the way these fairs and markets are circumstanced it would be impossible.

30,112. Apart from the position of the fairs here, what is your opinion on that point?—I believe, myself, if an Act of Parliament were brought in for that purpose, it would be a great assistance to the fairs and towns that the local body should have control.

30,113. You think the united efforts of the members of the commission would tend to the better management of the markets than when in the hands of a private individual?—As regards the private management I do not think the present fairs and markets could be managed better. There may be some things we may be empowered to do if an Act of Parliament were passed that cannot be done at present.

30,114. I take it you are in favour of local authorities getting compulsory powers to acquire the rights vested in the hands of private individuals?—Yes, Home Rule in a small way.

30,115. Have you anything to state in connection with the markets here, or what you think would tend to the better management of them?—As regards the management they could not be better managed.

30,116. I see certain of the commodities here are sold around the town from house to house. Do you think if proper market buildings were erected that would afford sufficient space, and a rule made confining the exposure of those commodities in this market building, that it would be better than having them going about the town indiscriminately?—No. I do not think that is a necessity. Some small things are brought in; they are only for the immediate wants of the town, and the people go around the town and sell them.

30,117. They are all brought in to be consumed in the town?—Yes; all brought in mostly from the country in a small way.

30,118. Do you think a necessity exists here for a fair green being provided, or have you any objection to the fairs being held on the streets?—You might as well remove Rathkeale out of this. The fairs are the only dependence the people have; the town would not be worth living in it only for them.

30,119. A certain number of the fairs were established at different periods. I suppose no authority, no patent, was obtained for them?—There was for the seven old fairs.

30,120. (*Archdeacon Nolan.*) I can tell you the patents cover any number of fairs or markets.

30,121. (*Mr. Blackwell.*) I have it on very good authority that Mr. Pigott has authority to hold a market or fair every day in the year, and can charge on everything.

30,122. Is Mr. Pigott the owner of the town?—He is.

30,123. Have you any further remarks to make, or any suggestion to offer, as to what you would like to see done in connection with the markets of Rathkeale, or the markets throughout Ireland?—I think the tendency to get these market fields injures the towns. In Limerick for instance, they went to great expense to get a fair green, and still the fairs are held in the town mostly, except the cattle fairs. They are not satisfied with that field; they are going towards the city again, and I believe myself there would not be as good a market price in the field as in the town.

30,124. Do you think the entrance charge at a small rate is better than the high charge on the animals sold?—No. For this reason that this is one of the largest fairs in Ireland, except Ballinasloe. There is a large amount of cattle coming in, and a great deal of them go home unsold.

30,125. On an average what percentage would you say is sold?—Seventy-five per cent. is sold.

30,126. You could give an approximate idea of the number brought here in the year?—No. I suppose it is only the railway company could give that information.

Mr. Joseph Sheehy examined.

30,127. Are you one of the town commissioners?—Not now.

30,128. Are you a trader in the town?—I live in the town.

30,129. Are you in trade?—Yes, a little. I am a shopkeeper, and I will first commence by telling you in court you should have but two or three hundred to oppose the [illegible] of the town and locality. Now of these two years they speak of here, one is quite enough. This town is large enough, and we derive no benefit from it.

30,130. I only want evidence as to any grievance existing in connection with the markets or fairs. I have nothing whatever to do with any other duties performed by the town commissioners, or the application of the rates?—To enlighten you a little more about the locality and just give you an idea——

30,131. I do not require any of the statements. You heard the answers of Mr. Casey to some questions I put to him relative to the charges levied at the markets and fairs. Do you take exception to any of those statements?—I say it is an advantage, not only to this fair and market, but every other fair and market in Ireland, to have parties coming here; it is the country supports these markets and fairs, and I say it would be a great advantage if they were not charged, because they pay coming into the town and at the same time support the town. Very few go home without laying out something, and it is a terrible thing to have two crows and three [illegible] on parties who patronize such fairs and markets. I really think they should not be charged at all, because very few leave the town without adding to the support of the townspeople.

30,132. Have you heard that the levying of charges has restricted trade in any way, or deterred any farmers from coming in to sell their stock here?—I know that in years past. There is one thing I remark. Two new pig-markets and fairs are got up in the locality. I really think but for the charges of this place these things would not be thought of at all.

30,133. I would like you to particularise what you call abuses. I have asked you to mention them. Mention some of them?—For instance where there are such a number of fairs annually, that is 18 fairs in the year, I think the people ought to be very glad to have these 18 fairs supported by the parties coming in. They are the principal support, as Mr. Blackwell wisely remarked; this town would be quite useless but for the fairs and markets, and the parties who patronize them should not be charged for doing so. Also as regards the weekly markets, I think they would get on very well without charging on half the things they do charge. Mr. Casey said he does not charge on small things. I certainly say they would, and they made a great attempt to charge the people coming here. They are here at eight o'clock in the morning, miles distant, with donkey-loads of turf and mule-loads, and they drive them into the new market.

30,134. Is that what is called the market square?—Yes, and they wanted to put a cess on them.

30,135. Was there any rule made by the commissioners compelling all commodities to go to this new market when the market was erected?—It appears there was, but I was not a commissioner at that time.

30,136. (*Mr. Casey, town clerk.*) I must differ with Mr. Sheehy. He is labouring under a mistake. To my knowledge and during my time a farthing was never imposed on those people he speaks of.

30,137. (*The Commissioner to Mr. [illegible].*) Will you tell me one person who was charged?—One man named Kelly was charged and another one named Harty. I remember those two parties.

30,138. What time was this done?—Twelve years ago.

30,139. No charge has been levied since?—No. It was broken down on the spot.

30,140. Is there anything you take exception to in the present management of the market?—You made a remark while ago about the town, and there are streets in a filthy state.

30,141. (*The Commissioner.*) I have nothing whatever to do with the duties of the town commissioners, only as relates to the markets or fairs, and I would kindly ask you to confine your remarks to the markets and fairs and nothing else.

(*The witness stated he had nothing further to say.*)

Mr. JOHN [illegible] examined.

30,142-3. Are you a town commissioner?—I am a ratepayer in the town. I was a town commissioner for 12 months.

30,144. Are you connected with trade in the town?—I hold a small piece of land up to the town.

30,145. I suppose you buy and sell at the fairs?—Yes, occasionally.

30,146. Do you take exception to their working, or to what you would consider the mismanagement of the markets and fairs?—As regards the management, I could say nothing; but it is very wrong to charge on the high road kept under the Grand Jury Act. We have to pay 5s. poor rates, and a shilling to the pound to the town commissioners, and after paying all this it is very wrong to charge anything on the high road. I would like to know, if you tell me, has any man authority to charge.

30,147. I attended here to seek for information, and it would not be within my province to give opinions, especially on legal questions. (*To witness.*) Do you think if a farmer got an adequate return for the charges, that he would have any objection to pay them?—I am sure not.

30,148. But you consider no return is given to one in this town, and that he has to pay on the animal for selling and exposing on the public thoroughfare?—I am sure he gets no return, but I may tell you if a cow is standing on the road, and a cart is passing up, and the cow breaks the shop-windows, the owner would have to pay.

30,149. Have you heard of any accidents happening?—I saw a cow breaking a shopkeeper's window, and I saw the owner of the window claim payment; along with that I saw the police arrest the woman, and she had to pay.

30,150. The town clerk said and most of the shopkeepers have guards outside their windows.

30,151. (*To witness.*) As a farmer would you approve of a fair green being provided here?—Certainly I would. I think it is only right.

30,152. Have you attended fairs where fair greens were provided?—Yes.

30,153. Do you think that stock could be more readily sold in a fair green, where the buyers are all in a particular spot, and the fair concentrated in one place, than when scattered indiscriminately about the town?—Yes. I say it is a great deal better to have the fairs in a field.

30,154. If such was erected the farmers as a rule, from your experience and conversation with them, would not object to pay a charge to support that field?—Certainly. I am full sure they would not. You are after hearing that men with loads of turf come in here, and when they pass up [illegible] your head is knocked over and then if the cow goes on the flags you have the policeman walking there. I would rather pay a shilling for my cow or horse to go to a field than be knocked about. The shopkeepers do their best to keep the fairs in the town. There is another thing I count a hardship. If I bring in a cart of slips I pay a shilling, and then the man who buys them has to pay three halfpence each. I leave my ticket when going out and the man who buys will not be let out without a ticket. He will have to pay three half-pence each on the slips. If I sold slips to any man outside the town, the very same cart is paid for so long as it is market day.

30,155. Do they inquire whether you have bought or sold?—Yes.

30,156. If you have sold you will have to pay although you have a receipt for the standing charge?—Yes.

30,157. Is it customary for the pigs, slips, and cattle when sold to remain in the seller's possession?—No; it is not, sometimes when you are going in the same direction as the buyer it is.

30,158. Only in a case like that the seller retains possession for the buyer's convenience?—Yes.

30,159. Is the charge collected when passing the gap no matter whether it is the buyer or seller is in possession of the animal?—If the buyer is with me he may pay; that will be an understanding with the buyer.

30,160. Is it customary to tell the farmer to bring the cattle or pigs to the buyer's yard or field outside the town?—No.

30,161. As a general rule the animals are in the possession of the buyer or his assistants when passing the gap?—Yes.

30,162. And it is the buyer will pay the charge?—Yes.

30,163. The town clerk said the second charge in the case of the young pigs (slips) was paid by the buyer, and not by the seller, as Mr. [illegible] stated. The seller has not to pay a second time, he has only to pay a shilling on the cart, and he gets a ticket for that which passes him out, but when he sells and parts with the pigs the buyer has to pay going out.

Mr. PATRICK [illegible], town commissioner, examined.

30,164. Are you connected with trade in the town?—I am.

30,165. Do you buy and sell at the fairs and markets?—I do.

30,166. You are a town commissioner?—I am.

30,167. Have you any remarks to offer as to what you think would tend to the general improvement of the markets and fairs?—I have not any remarks to offer except this, that if the fairs are removed out of the town into a field the fairs would go down the same as in every place. I have a great deal of experience. I went to many a fair in the country, and whenever I saw them in a field, except in one or two cases, they were always a failure.

30,168. Will you tell me a town where the fairs were removed off the public thoroughfare to a fair green, and depreciated in quantity on that account?—I do not well know. There are fairs held in the immediate neighbourhood, at [illegible], [illegible], and other places, and they have all gone to naught, and those fairs were held in fields.

30,169. Have you formed any ideas on the levying of a toll. Do you think it deters farmers from bringing in their stock to the fairs or markets?—It does not. It never did. Every man would prefer not to pay the charge, but it does not interfere with him in bringing in his cattle.

30,170. You think a farmer only considers whether he can effect a ready and good sale, and does not consider he has to pay a charge?—He does not. It is only the ready and good sale at the best market he looks to.

30,171. Have they got the system of luck-penny at the fairs here?—They have.

30,172. Is there any fixed amount on pigs?—There is 6d.

30,173. On cattle?—Nothing is fixed. The general thing for cattle is about a shilling per head. That is the custom.

30,174. Then I take it on cattle, horses, and other animals it is always left to the disposition of the seller?—Yes.

30,175. The contract price is paid by the buyer to the seller in the first instance, and the luck-penny returned to him?—Yes.

30,176. In pigs the buyer deducts the 6d. out of the contract price?—Yes.

30,177. So then the seller has no option at all?—No.

30,178. He gets the contract price less the 6d.?—Yes, but he is not forced to give it, but they do not resist.

30,179. Do you know a case where they did resist?—I did in one or two instances, but it is generally understood now.

30,180. Do you think that the farmer considers the amount of the luck-penny he will have to give when asking the price of the animal?—He never does.

30,181. Have not cases occurred where they bought some animals clear to pinion?—There are exceptions.

30,182. In those cases the amount of the luck-penny is considered?—Yes.

30,183. That is they give a certain price and there is no luck-penny?—Yes.

30,184. Is there much delay caused by fixing the amount of the luck-penny?—No.

30,185. From what districts are the animals brought here?—From the surrounding counties within a radius of 10 miles. They may come 20 miles if they like. The last fair here there were cattle here from the city of Cork.

30,186. Those are drovers' cattle?—Yes. The radius is 10 miles.

30,187. Within what radius are the marketable commodities brought?—Eight miles.

30,188. (Town clerk.) I wish to remark that we have cattle coming here from Glin and Tarbert, 20 miles off.

30,189. (To Mr. Kennedy.) Would the buyers stop 6d. for such business?—No; 1½d. and 2d. is the average on bonhams.

30,190. Have you any remarks to make any more than what you have stated?—No.

30,191. You do not concur in the observations of Mr. Switzer?—No. He will get 99 per cent. of the people here to disagree with him.

30,192. (Mr. Switzer.) Any shop keeper will do that.

30,193. (To Mr. Kennedy.) You think if a move were made to remove the fairs off the streets to a fair green, opposition would attend it?—Decidedly.

30,194. Would that opposition come from any traders in the town or any particular trade?—It would come from every trade in the town, rich and poor.

30,195. Would not it come from any particular trade?—No.

30,196. You also consider the removal of the fairs would have an injurious effect?—Yes. You would find some farmers that would not be contented to go into a field.

30,197. I do not say a field but a fair green, with shelter accommodation and pens provided for the disposal of the animals?—This town is too small to have cattle pens erected.

30,198. You think the expense of erection and the providing of such accommodation would be too large?—Yes, and the people would go back into the street after getting them there.

Mr. John Switzer, cross-examined by Mr. Power, solicitor.

30,199. You stated it would be an advantage to the farmers to have the fairs removed from the town?—Certainly.

30,200. What reason have you for saying the farmers would be dissatisfied?—First and foremost when your cattle come into the fair green they cannot go out without the man at the gate seeing them. You are charged going in and your cattle cannot go out unknown to him, and if you lose a cow or sheep you go to the gatesman. In Rathkeale I have known cows go away for days, and if the sheep go you may not get them until you go to the market crane, and there are five or six avenues in the town, and you are in a tangle with the whole of them.

30,201. That is the principal reason you object?—I said two or three things with regard to the fairs.

30,202. You have the interest of Rathkeale at heart?—Yes.

30,203. You would like to see the shopkeepers prosperous and doing a rich business?—Yes.

30,204. Do you know the fairs of Rathkeale are the principal means of supporting the majority of the shopkeepers of the town?—I am sure of that, but I do not think it would injure the shopkeepers one bit if the fairs were held outside the town.

30,205. The majority of the shopkeepers benefit very largely by the fairs, and if the fairs were removed outside the town, would it not injure the shopkeepers generally?—I do not think it would.

30,206. The people would not be on the spot?—They would have the town to go to.

30,207. Would a good many of the people after selling their cattle leave the fair green, and not come into the town?—Certainly they would. Any man of sense would go home.

30,208. They would not be tempted to spend an extra shilling which they otherwise would?—Yes.

30,209. Apart from the advantages that the people of Rathkeale derive from the fairs being in the town, do not you think the accommodation of the buyers is consulted in having the fairs in the town?—I would not say that.

30,210. Are not they opposite the bank?—I do not like to say anything against the people of the town. Of course it is a benefit to the townspeople to have the fairs in the streets, but it is not a benefit to the country people.

30,211. Would not it be an advantage to the buyer to have the banks quite close at hand?—The railway station is quite convenient to the banks. A man does not look into a thing like that when he goes to the fair. The railway sidings are the principal places for purchasing cattle.

30,212. The cattle are driven away by the traders?—Yes.

30,213. Do not a great number of the cattle go to Croom by road?—Yes.

30,214. Are not they brought at the other end of the town of Rathkeale?—Yes.

30,215. So the buyers do not go to the station?—No.

30,216. Do not you think it would facilitate the buyers greatly to have the shops to pay the people in, and also to have a treat over the head of it?—Yes.

30,217. I think you are altogether in favour of retaining the fairs in the town?—I would not go against them personally.

30,218. You spoke about a car striking against a cow and injuring it. As a matter of fact, do not you know as well as any other gentleman, that there are very little, if any, accidents complained of in connection with the fairs of Rathkeale?—Very little.

30,219. Would you say the number of accidents would be as many in a fair green?—I will not answer that question.

30,220. It would not surprise you if that were so?—No.

30,221. (The Commissioner.) Is there any other gentleman who has an evidence or information to give, or any grievances to complain of?—(No answer.)

The inquiry then terminated.

NEWCASTLE WEST.

to my inquiry in Newcastle West on the 7th January 1889, I beg
:—

is an inland town situated in the county of Limerick. It is a
Castle branch of the Waterford and Limerick Railway line. The
bly improved within latter years and the trade is fair. The local
red by the grand jury and the board of guardians. The population

are Thursday and Saturday. Butter and hay principally sold on
irs are held on the 3rd January, 3rd February, 4th March, 1st April,
, 12th July, 20th August, 10th September, 1st October, 2nd Novem-
r. A pig fair is held on the day previous to the ordinary fairs.
t the fairs held on the 1st April, 3rd May, 12th July, 20th August,
th December, and at the pig fairs held previous to these fairs. The
anuary, 3rd February, 4th March, 10th June, 10th September, and
l the pig fairs held the day previous to these fairs, are toll free. At
bing] charges only are levied except on butter, hay and straw.
of 1d. per firkin is levied on entrance to the market, and on hay and
d. per load is levied on entrance to the hay-market field. However,
charges include cranage.
erected, but beams and scales and a weigh-bridge have been provided.
ts and tolls are the property of the representative of the Earl of
of the deceased Earl it appears is being administered in the Chancery
preme Court in England, and the Receiver appointed by the Court
the charges at the markets and fairs.
ere granted for Newcastle West. The first is dated 22nd December,
uthorised one George Courtney to hold a Saturday market and a fair
Bartholomew (24th August). The second is dated 24th June 1666,
Sir W. Courtney to hold fairs on the 23rd April (now 3rd May),
(now 20th August). The third is dated 16th May, 48 George III.,
scount Courtney to hold a Tuesday and Thursday market and fairs
2th July, and 10th December. The latter patent was produced at

d fairs held under express grant, therefore, are the Thursday and
and the fairs on the 1st April, 3rd May, 12th July, 20th August,
r.

ithout any express grant are the fairs on the 3rd January, 4th March,
September, 1st October, and 2nd November. The fair on the
owever, held previous to 1844, but I was unable to trace the date of
y the evidence offered. The fairs on the 3rd January, 3rd February,
une, 10th September, and the 2nd November were established about

not contribute anything towards the additional expense incurred in

A shilling per firkin is deducted by the butter buyers from the contract price of each firkin, and the pig buyers deduct 3d. for the "luck-penny" on the cost price of each pig.

A similar practice exists as in some of the other towns I have visited in levying a standing charge of 2d. a cartload of small pigs, and 3d. additional on each animal if subsequently sold.

A Fair and Market Association has been established by the traders, whose object is to develope the markets and fairs so as to benefit the general trade of the town. The efforts of this committee have been fairly successful, and their expenses are defrayed by the voluntary subscriptions of the inhabitants. The principal members of this committee strongly advocate the granting of compulsory power to local authorities to acquire market rights.

Appended will be found a transcript of the evidence taken at the inquiry.

JOHN J. O'MEARA,
Assistant Commissioner.

45, Lower Mount Street, Dublin.

Newcastle West, 7th January 1889.

CHARLES CURLING, Esq., C.E., examined.

30,223. In whom are the market rights vested?—I am the Receiver under the Court of Chancery, and I suppose they are vested in me.

30,224. Who is the owner of the estate?—The Earl of Devon, but he died on the 18th November.

30,225. I suppose the rights are vested in his representatives?—The Devon Estate in the county of Limerick besides the markets mentioned in the query sheet, and all are being administered by the Chancery Division of the High Court of Justice, England, by order dated 18th October 1888. In the case of Devon and others I was appointed Receiver, to receive the rents and profits of such estate. I sent you the query sheet.

30,226. Have you a manager appointed over these markets?—Yes, a weigh-master.

30,227. What is his name?—John Moylan.

30,228. What is market day here?—Thursday and Saturday. Thursday is the principal day, but Thursday is also market day.

30,229. (Mr. McCarthy, solicitor.) Mr. J. Condon and I appear here for the ratepayers of the town. I may say Thursday is the only market day.

30,230. (To Mr. Curling.) What fairs are held here. I want the particulars of the fairs, whether you receive any charges on them or not?—The 3rd January, 3rd February, 4th March, 1st April, 3rd May, 10th June, 12th July, 20th August, 10th September, 1st October, 2nd November, 10th December.

30,231. You have a pig fair the day previous to these fairs?—Yes.

30,232. Are there any other fairs held here?—No.

30,233. Any horse fairs or not?—The horse fairs are held on the same day.

30,234. These are all the fairs held in Newcastle West?—Yes.

30,235. Do you receive charges at all of these?—No. We receive charges on the 1st April, 3rd May, 12th July, 20th August, 1st October, and 10th December.

30,236. That is for just half the fairs?—These are the old fairs. We take no tolls at the new fairs.

30,237. When was it established and when were the other fairs established?—They were established by my father, I think, after the railway opened, about 1870. I was not here at the time, and I cannot say about them exactly.

30,238. Could you tell me the authority under which the tolls are levied at the other six fairs?—Under patent.

30,239. The witness then produced a patent which was granted in the reign of George the Third to William Lord Viscount of Devon, his heirs and assigns. It granted a fair to be held on the 1st April, 12th July, and 10th December, and two weekly markets on every Tuesday and Thursday, with a court of pye-powder, together with all tolls, customs, privileges, and emoluments from the said fairs and markets arising, subject to the payment of 1l. 12s. yearly. The patent is dated 16th May in the forty-eighth year of the reign of George the Third. It was enrolled on the 18th May.

30,240–1. This patent grants a fair on the 1st April, 12th July, and 10th December?—Yes.

30,242. You have not got possession of any grants which authorise the fairs on the 3rd May, 20th August, and 1st October?—No.

30,243. This is the only one in your possession?—Yes.

30,244. And the only one you are able to give me any particulars of?—Yes.

30,245. Have the other fairs been held for any length of time?—Ever since that date.

30,246. The whole six?—Certainly, since 1844.

30,247. When did the Tuesday market cease?—There has been no Tuesday market as long as I can remember.

30,248. The six fairs at which you levy tolls have been held, so far as your recollection extends, since 1844?—I can recollect since 1849, and these six fairs have all been held since then.

30,249. The tolls you levy at the fairs, are they only on the animals actually sold?—That is all.

30,250. You levy tolls also at the markets?—At the markets only on butter. There are a great number of things mentioned in the list on which we do not levy anything. On market days we charge for weighing. We have a weigh-master, who charges so much for weighing a sack of potatoes or corn; merely for weighing.

30,251. Supposing the commodities were brought in on market day and exposed for sale but not actually weighed at your beam and scales, you levy no toll?—No.

30,252. Are the farmers free to weigh the commodities and expose them where they please on market days?—Yes.

30,253. With the exception of butter?—Yes.

30,254. You restrict the sale of butter to the market buildings?—Yes.

30,255. If a proprietor brought his butter to the town and sold it on market day, but did not bring it to your market, would you levy a toll if it came to your knowledge?—We should not on ordinary lump butter.

30,256. Only on firkins?—Yes.

30,257. When you state you do not levy charges on some commodities here, is that because they are not brought into the fair?—No, but there are a great many things we do not levy tolls on that we could.

30,258. The witness then produced the schedule of tolls, of which the following is a copy:—

Schedule of Tolls, Customs, and Duties payable to Samuel Frederick Kenwick and John Wilkinson, Esqs., Trustees acting in the management of the Estates of the late Right Hon. William Earl of Downe, at the several Fairs and Markets of Newcastle, viz.:—

Markets.—On every Tuesday, Thursday, and Saturday.

Fairs.—On every 1st April, 3rd May, 12th July, 20th August, 1st October, and 10th December.

—	On Market Days.	On Fair Days.
	d.	d.
*For every cow, bull, bullock, or heifer sold	[illegible]	[illegible]
*For every two years old do. do.	[illegible]	4
*For every yearling do. do.	[illegible]	[illegible]
*For every sheep sold	1	[illegible]
*For every lamb sold	½	½
*For every pig sold	2	2
*For every slip or young pig sold	1	1
*For every goat sold	[illegible]	[illegible]
†For every carload of hides or skins brought to market for sale	[illegible]	4
†For every country hide brought to market for sale	1	1
†For every country calf-skin or goat-skin brought to market for sale	½	½
†For every pack of wool brought to market for sale	6	[illegible]
†For every bag or parcel of feathers brought for sale—		
Under 5 lbs. weight	1	1
5 lbs. and under 14 lbs. weight	2	2
14 lbs. weight and upwards	[illegible]	[illegible]
†For every carload of apples brought for sale	[illegible]	4
†For every basketful of apples brought for sale	1	[illegible]
†For every hamper of [illegible] brought for sale	1	1
*For every carload of timberware brought for sale	[illegible]	4
†For every basketful of [illegible] brought for sale	1	[illegible]
*For every bundling of iron spades, half-a-dozen or more, brought for sale	[illegible]	[illegible]
†For lesser quantities of iron spades brought for sale	½	½
†For every carload of spade-handles brought for sale	[illegible]	[illegible]
†For lesser quantities of spade-handles, per dozen, brought for sale	1	[illegible]
*For every 100 of cabbage-plants brought for sale	½	[illegible]
†For every piece of frieze or flannel brought for sale	1	[illegible]
†For every two pair of stockings brought for sale	½	½
*For every pedlar's standing for soft goods	[illegible]	[illegible]
*For every pedlar's standing for hardware	[illegible]	[illegible]
*For every car standing	[illegible]	[illegible]
†For every small standing of any description	1	[illegible]
†For every meal standing outside the shambles	[illegible]	[illegible]

N.B.—The tolls marked thus * are levied; those marked † are not demanded.

Collectors { Richard Baker. William Barrett. John Gorman.

Newcastle, 1st January 1844.

30,259. Do you levy tolls at the pig fairs?—Yes.

30,260. When were the pig fairs first established?—I could not tell you that.

30,261. Do you only levy tolls on the pig fairs held the day previous to the ordinary toll fairs?—That is all.

30,262. At the other pig fairs you do not levy anything?—No.

30,263. Where are the fairs held?—In the town.

30,264. About the streets of the town?—Yes.

30,265. Were any representations ever made to you by those frequenting the fairs to provide a fair-green?—Well, I cannot say from my own knowledge, but I am aware in my father's lifetime he tried to get the fairs removed off the streets, and the people, the shopkeepers, and people of the town objected, and then when they objected the fairs were allowed to continue as usual.

30,266. There is no local authority existing here, that is, a local municipal authority?—No.

30,267. The grand jury clean the streets?—Yes.

30,268. Do the owners make any contribution towards the cleansing of the streets on fair days other than through the ordinary rates and taxes?—No. The way the streets are cleaned here is the road contractor, I believe, gives the manure to some people in the town, and they clean it up and carry it away on the same day.

30,269. Do you think the manure obtained after the fair days would act as an equivalent for any additional expense incurred by cleaning the streets after the fairs?—It would.

30,270. Would you kindly give me your receipts from the fairs and the expenditure?—I have given them all in the query sheet, and I brought my books in case you wanted to investigate them.

30,271. What are the receipts from the tolls?—The aggregate amount received was 238*l.* 17*s.* 7*d.*

30,272. Does that mean the tolls at the fairs and markets?—At the fairs and markets and everything.

30,273. Have you got any standings at all on fair days on which you levy tolls? Supposing a load of turnips was brought in on fair days and exposed on fair or market day, would you levy tolls?—No. We only charge for the standing of a car with young pigs.

30,274. What would that standing charge be?—Twopence, I think.

30,275. Do these come in on fair days?—They come on market day and the fair day previous to the six toll fairs. We do not charge for them at the other six fairs.

30,276. That is a standing charge of 2*d.* on the cart. Supposing the pigs were subsequently sold and as they were leaving the fair would you charge on each pig sold in addition to the ordinary standing charge previously paid?—Yes.

30,277. That additional charge would be a penny?—Yes, I think so.

30,278. You could not give me an idea of the amount you receive from standing charges alone?—No. We never keep them separate.

30,279. You could not give me the amount you receive from the butter market?—I could get it for you. (*Witness then pointed out on the books what they got for butter and what they got for weighing.*)

30,280. Have you got the summary for the year?—Yes. I could separate everything for you if you wish.

30,281. The expenditure out of that 238*l.* 17*s.* 7*d.* for officers on market is 93*l.* 15*s.* 8*d.*?—Yes.

30,282. How is that 93*l.* expended? What do you give the weigh-master?—He has 20*l.* a year and the remainder is made up by wages to cleaners.

30,283. How do you pay the cleaners?—We pay them so much a day.

30,284. At what rate?—The cleaners get 12*s.* a week. Two of them get 6*s.* each, and one 4*s.* There is one permanent cleaner.

30,285. Who else have you?—Then we have a man always employed in the butter market for weighing. He is regularly there all the week round for weighing potatoes and everything that comes into the market. He gets 7*s.* a week, and then the remainder is made up of toll-collectors' wages at the fairs.

30,286. How many gaps have you?—One at the turnpike, one at Bridge Street, the third at McCoy's, and another, four altogether.

30,287. How many men do you have at each?—Two.

30,288. How do you pay these men?—They are always my own men, and we pay them the usual hire.

30,289. Then they have other duties to perform?—Yes. They are my own men who work on the estate.

30,290. You give them no separate salary for the duties they perform in collecting the toll?—No, but I charge that day.

30,291. For repairs you have 22l. 10s. 6d.?—Yes.

30,292. What repairs do you execute here?—That is keeping the butter market, the sheds and houses in order.

30,293. Is that the early expenditure?—I took the average for three years.

30,294. Then you have here sundries—telegrams, 3l.; income-tax, 2l. 10s. 6d.; and rent of field 4l. 7s. 6d. What field is that?—I added that field and I have it in my own possession, and sometimes there is a quantity of carts here in the season and the streets would not accommodate them, so I added the field for the hay market.

30,295. The hay market is held on the streets and in this field?—They nearly all go into the field.

30,296. Do they sometimes sell in the streets?—Yes.

30,297. You put this down as the estimated rent, or do you actually pay it?—It belongs to the estate. I give the rent and charge it.

30,298. Are these market buildings belonging to the estate?—Yes.

30,299. Do they hold in fee or pay any rent?—They do not pay any rent. They were built by Lord Devon.

30,300. Could you give me the particulars of the expenditure you were at in the erection of the market?—Well, I could not tell you.

30,301. You have no means of ascertaining that?—Yes. I could find that out if I went through the books.

30,302. When was the butter market erected?—When the railway was opened, about 1873—when the Rathkeale Railway was opened.

30,303. Was there a butter market previous to that?—No; not a regular butter market.

30,304. Do you hold the butter on the same day as the general market?—On Thursdays.

30,305. If they bring in cattle or any other animal on market day, you levy the tolls you have mentioned on the schedule?—Yes. As a matter of fact we do not levy any tolls on market days—I mean every Thursday.

30,306. As a matter of fact if they bring in cattle do you demand the toll?—No.

30,307. Do they actually bring in cattle?—On market day I have seen cattle sold by auction in our market and we never asked for any toll. Drovers' cattle and everything else are sold, and we demand no tolls.

30,308. Is this butter market enclosed?—Yes.

30,309. Does it afford ample space accommodation for the butter brought here?—Yes, I think so.

30,310. Is the butter generally brought in firkins?—All firkins that come into the market.

30,311. I would like you to give me your own opinion. Do you think the public street is the proper place to hold the fairs from your own experience in connection with fairs and markets?—Well, I should say it would be much better to have a regular fair-green.

30,312. Do you think it would be better for the farmers, and that they would obtain a readier sale of their stock, if the fairs were concentrated in a fair-green, where the buyers could see all the cattle brought in, than having them scattered indiscriminately about the town?—I think it would, and if these rights should hereafter fall into the hands of a local authority they would have a much better way of collecting the tolls if they had a fair-green, because they could make a charge going into the fair-green, and it would be an easier way than the present of getting the tolls. I am sure it is better for the people of the town to have them on the streets.

30,313. How far do you think your jurisdiction extends here for the collection of the tolls?—As far as the custom gaps.

30,314. Where are these generally situated? Are they in the outskirts of the town?—No; around the square. The only one we have outside the square is one here at the railway. We have one there to collect tolls on pigs and cattle going to the railway.

30,315. Supposing a farmer was bringing in some stock on a fair day, and before reaching your custom gap he effected a sale of the animals, if it came to your knowledge, would you levy a toll?—No; we do not levy a toll.

30,316. Have cases occurred of that kind?—No. I often knew cattle to be sold outside and never took the trouble to look after them.

30,317. Outside the custom gap, but in the town?—Yes; before they come into the town. We never levy toll until they actually come into the fair inside the custom gap, and then the toll is levied. We would not levy tolls on anything outside the custom gap.

30,318. Are horses brought to the fairs?—We have had two horse fairs here. The people of the town have got up horse fairs, one was held on the 12th August, and one on the 10th December. These are the first two horse fairs we have had, and although they were held on old fair days we charge no tolls to try and encourage the horse fair.

30,319. Previous to that your horses did not usually attend the fairs?—No. We only had two horse fairs last year.

30,320. Have you any rules regulating the market here?—No. We have no special rules except for the butter market.

30,321. What rules have you created there, or are they the buyers' rules?—I think the weigh-master will be able to explain that to you.

30,322. On fair days have you different streets allotted off for the exposure of animals, or do they intermix?—They intermix.

30,323. Have you ever heard of accidents happening from animals intermixing with one another?—I never heard to any extent.

30,324. Did you ever see the toll collectors collecting tolls yourself?—Yes.

30,325. When they see the farmer coming out with his stock, do they inquire from him whether he has bought or sold?—They always ask whether he has sold.

30,326. If he says not, do they allow him to go free?—Yes.

30,327. But, supposing he actually stated he had not and they doubted his answer, what course would they adopt?—They would inquire about it.

30,328. Would they seize the animal?—They would detain the animal until they made inquiries.

30,329. Do they produce any book or paper to show them?—No.

30,330. Or ask them to touch the toll board?—No.

30,331. Have you got a copy of the toll board erected at each gap?—No. We used to hang them up, but they have been taken out of the fair for a long time.

30,332. Practically, then, the farmers, in order to know the rate of toll, have to rely on what your men ask them?—Yes.

30,333. Either at the markets or fairs is there any toll board erected for public inspection?—No. As a matter of fact if a man sells two or three cows, and if the toll came to a 1s. and he had only 9d., they would take the 9d. They are not very strict.

30,334. So you allow them to use their discretion now and again?—Yes.

30,335. Have you ever heard complaints that the charges have been in any way excessive?—No.

30,336. No complaints have ever been made directly to you?—No.

30,337. Have you ever bought or sold at fairs?—Well, I have my cattle sold, but I do not exactly do it myself.

30,338. Do you think that the larger toll on animals only sold works better than a smaller toll on each animal brought into the fair?—I think it would be better for the revenue if every animal were taxed that came into the fair.

30,339. What percentage of the animals would you say is sold?—I could not say.

30,340. You keep no record of the number coming in?—No.

30,341. Do you keep any record at all of the quantity of the different commodities brought in on market days?—No.

30,342. Even of butter?—Yes. We know the quantity of butter.

30,343. Do you keep any record of the current prices of these, the average current prices?—Yes. I keep an account of the price of butter on Thursdays.

30,344. Only of butter?—Yes.

30,345. Have you any suggestions to offer as to what you think would tend to the improvement of these markets or fairs or in any way relating to them?—I do not know. I could give you a return of the number of firkins of butter and pigs, and things like that sold each year.

30,246. The witness was examined by Mr. McCarthy, solicitor, as follows:—

30,247. You put down the revenue from the markets and fairs at 82*l*. Is that the gross or net?—That is the gross average revenue for three years.

30,248. The butter market was established in 1856?—About that.

30,249. Could you tell me what were the average receipts from the butter market between 1870 and 1880?—I could not. I have not it separate.

30,250. Could you tell me what it was from all sources during that time?—I could not.

30,251. Was not it sometimes 1,000*l*?—I have sent for a book that will give you that.

30,252. Do not you know the butter market has gone down more than half?—I know it has gone down tremendously.

30,253. Before that reduction you cannot tell the Court what the revenue was?—I can when the book comes.

30,254. You said it would be better to remove the fair to a fair-green?—Yes.

30,255. Would not that be injurious to the townspeople?—I think it would be injurious to the shopkeepers, but I think it would be better for the actual fair. That is my opinion.

30,256. Why?—Because when you go into the fair-green you see the cattle, and see what you want to dispose of or purchase.

30,257. Is not the land about Newcastle very wet?—It is.

30,258. And cattle would suffer in such land?—I do not know that they would.

30,259. Would not they be up to their knees in mud?—I have seen the cattle standing in the streets for a day in winter.

30,260. They were not there for sale?—They would be only two or three hours in the fair.

30,261. You suggested also that it would be better to put a charge on the cattle going into the fair. Would not that also be injurious to the town, and prevent a great many farmers from coming into the fair when they go free into other places?—It might, but I think it would be better for the tolls. I say this for the reason that the tolls may hereafter become the property of a local authority, and it would be better for them.

30,262. In what respect?—They would get a larger revenue if there was a charge on everything that came into the fair.

30,263. Supposing there was great depression in the price of cattle, and they could not be sold from fair to fair, would not they get tired of coming into the fair and paying tolls?—I think they would.

30,264. Do you think that it would be in the interest of Newcastle to have the tolls vested in a local authority?—I really cannot say, because I do not know the working of a local authority. I have no experience of the working of a local authority.

30,265. Do not you know at present there is no one to revive the butter market or fairs held here, or to bring them back to what they were originally, but the townspeople?—I do not know.

30,266. You do not interest yourself in that way?—I interest myself a great deal about it.

30,267. About the butter market?—Yes, and the fairs too. A few years ago I got a great number of cards printed and got them circulated in every possible way I could.

30,268. Did you contribute to the expense of commencing a horse fair in Newcastle?—No.

30,269. Or did Lord Devon?—No.

30,270. Do you know the townspeople went to an expenditure of 40*l*.?—I do not know what they did, but I know they collected money.

30,271. And to continue that horse fair, do not you know, it will be necessary to raise more funds so as to advertise it?—I suppose it will. I suggested at the last horse fair where they came to me whether we would charge a toll or not on them, and if so I would give them the tolls towards the expenses.

30,272. That is all you would do?—Yes. I promised to give them some money.

30,273. You never gave it?—But I will.

30,274. The streets are kept in order by the ratepayers through the grand jury?—Yes.

30,275. Lord Devon does not expend any money on them?—No. We keep the butter market clean; we do not keep the streets clean.

30,276. Have not you the manure of the butter market?—Yes.

30,277. You said a while ago the manure would pay for any expense?—I think it would.

30,278. (*By the Commissioner.*) Do you collect the manure at the market?—Yes. The manure is swept into heaps, and I cart it away.

30,279. Could you give me the receipts for that?—I have no receipts. I cart it into the demesne. I suppose there are four or five loads every week.

30,280. Would that be about 1*s*. a load?—Yes. It is only hay and straw and things.

30,281. (*By Mr. McCarthy.*) I observe from this charter that there are only three fairs at which Lord Devon is authorised to collect tolls?—Yes, I said that.

(*The Commissioner.*) That is as far as Mr. Curling's knowledge extends, but he does not know whether another grant was made or not.

30,282. (*By Mr. McCarthy, to Witness.*) On what authority have tolls been collected on the other fairs?—I could not tell you. You will see from the schedule dated 1852. I suppose they would not collect them unless there was some authority.

30,283. (*By the Commissioner.*) Is it in contemplation to levy a toll at the horse fair?—I think so, if they were well established.

30,284. You intend levying a toll?—Yes. We want to encourage the fairs at present.

30,285. Then you contemplate the exaction of a toll when the horse fairs have been fostered?—Yes.

30,286. The receipts from that with the other receipts would go to the benefit of the estate?—Yes.

The witness subsequently forwarded the following as a return of the quantity of firkins of butter brought to the market, the number of pigs sold, and the receipts for the years 1871 to 1879:—

—	1871.	1872.	1873.	1874.	1875.	1876.	1877.	1878.	1879.
Firkins of butter in market	[illegible]	[illegible]	[illegible]	[illegible]	[illegible]	[illegible]	[illegible]	[illegible]	[illegible]

Mr. JOHN MOTLEY examined.

30,387. You are the weigh-master in the market?—Yes.

30,388. Is it only in the butter market you attend?—Yes.

30,389. You have no duties to perform in connexion with the general market?—Yes; both are held in the same place.

30,390. Will you kindly mention to me the different marketable commodities brought on Thursday and Saturday into the town?—The market is separated from the town. It is a out-of-the-way place altogether; it is different property.

30,391. Mention the commodities that come there?—Potatoes, turnips, vegetables, all sorts of corn, hay, straw, seeds, and butter.

30,392. Is any lump butter brought in?—No; that is sold in the town.

30,393. About the streets?—Yes.

30,394. Are vegetables brought in?—No; they are sold about the streets.

30,395. Any fruit?—Fruit is sold about the street.

30,396. You levy no charge at all?—No.

30,397. Is fish brought in?—No.

30,398. Is it sold about the town?—Yes.

30,399. Are eggs brought in?—No. They are brought about the town.

30,400. Do you compel all potatoes, turnips, hay, straw, and other commodities to go to the market buildings?—We do not compel them; we can not compel them.

30,401. Can they put them elsewhere in the public thoroughfare?—They can not weigh outside; they come in to get them weighed.

30,402. There are no other scales in the town but yours?—No.

30,403. The private shopkeepers never weigh the commodities for the farmers?—They sometimes do, because we have very large markets and cannot come at the whole of them in the market-place.

30,404. Do you deem your weighing facilities insufficient to weigh them all?—Sometimes, about the 25th March and two or three days in the year.

30,405. How many beams have you?—Two, and others for the butter.

30,406. Do you ever weigh potatoes on the butter scales?—Never; we have two beams in the butter-shed and the lever.

30,407. Have you got a weighing machine capable of weighing cattle erected?—Yes, for weighing anything.

30,408. When was that erected?—About 1871 or 1872.

30,409. Have you railings around it, or did you make any alteration last year?—We made a frame so as to keep the cattle on it.

30,410. Did you weigh any cattle on it since it was erected?—Only one or two.

30,411. The farmers are not desirous of availing themselves of the opportunity of selling by live weight?—No.

30,412. What charge do you levy on potatoes?—A halfpenny per hundred.

30,413. It is only when you weigh you levy the charge?—That is all.

30,414. Do you give a ticket denoting the weight?—Yes.

30,415. Is it a printed form?—It has a printed heading.

30,416. Have you got any of the tickets here?—No.

30,417. Are the potatoes sold before you weigh them?—Potatoes are sometimes sold. They are generally sold before they weigh them.

30,418. Whether sold or not, if you weigh them you levy a charge?—Yes.

30,419. You put on the tickets the number of bags, the description of the commodity in the bag, also the date and the name of the seller?—Yes.

30,420. You collect the charges at the market from the seller?—Yes.

30,421. As the fairs it is from the buyer or the person in possession of the animal when leaving?—I have nothing to do with the fairs.

30,422. When weighing a bag of potatoes do you ever weigh the empty sack, or do you estimate the tare?—Sometimes we weigh the empty sack; we generally allow for it.

30,423. What is the estimated tare if you do not weigh it?—4 lbs.

30,424. Is it 4 lbs. always?—No, because we do not make less than a quarter of a stone.

30,425. You do not weigh a smaller quantity than a quarter stone?—No. If it exceeds the quarter by more than a pound we have to go back and allow more than 4 lbs. for the sack.

30,426. Supposing a sack was brought in in wet weather, and was completely saturated with rain, would you allow anything additional for that?—Certainly. I often saw them weigh 11 lbs.

30,427. I suppose you only weigh them in case of dispute between the buyer and seller?—That is all.

30,428. In weighing corn what charge do you levy?—1d. per cwt.

30,429. Do you weigh the empty sacks?—No. We allow 4 lbs. unless they require them to be weighed.

30,430. Do you levy any additional charge for the empty sack?—No.

30,431. Or any charge for giving the ticket?—No.

30,432. The ½d. a cwt. for potatoes and a 1d. per cwt. for corn cover everything?—Yes.

30,433. Do you keep a block of the tickets?—No.

30,434. So if they lose the tickets you generally weigh again?—We mark the bags with chalk too.

30,435. You are never able to keep a record of the quantity of corn, potatoes, and other commodities you weigh?—No.

30,436. Down to what weight do you weigh corn? Do you weigh down to 1 lb., 2 lbs., or a quarter stone?—Down to 1 lb.

30,437. Always?—Yes.

30,438. Is the tare the only deduction from the gross weight of corn and potatoes?—The tare is the only deduction.

30,439. Nothing is allowed for beamage?—No.

30,440. What do you charge on butter?—1d. a firkin before 11 o'clock and then an additional 1d. for any that comes in after. That 1d. was put on to bring the farmers in time so as to give an opportunity of having it all weighed before the market opened.

30,441. Is it on entrance to the market you charge the 1d. per firkin?—Yes.

30,442. Whether the firkin is subsequently weighed or sold?—Yes. We do not consider anything but the charge.

30,443. Would you permit them to expose the firkins outside the market?—No. We could not prevent them if they wished to do so.

30,444. Supposing it it was, would you levy a charge?—No.

30,445. Have they ever done so?—I have seen them do so, but I could not fight with them. They must go through the market because the buyers will not buy outside, but I saw them selling opposite my own door.

30,446. Is the butter weighed before it is sold?—It is.

30,447. Always?—Not always. It is often weighed afterwards.

30,448. What hour does the butter market usually begin?—There was a change last year; the hour was changed to half-past 10 o'clock in the morning. It was changed back again, after the train coming in, to one o'clock.

30,449. At present it is held at one o'clock?—Yes. I do not know whether it is the townspeople or the buyers changed it.

30,450. Can the farmers sell before that hour if they have an opportunity of selling?—No. They tried to do that, but it was prevented.

30,451. So you restrict the sale of butter until one o'clock?—Yes.

30,452. Have you all the butter weighed before that hour?—No. We could have if they came in time.

30,453. Have you any porterage charges at the markets? Supposing a farmer brings in a load of potatoes, who lifts the bags off the cart and puts them on the scales?—The farmers themselves.

30,454. You have no men to do that work?—No.

30,455. If they have not sufficient manual assistants, would your men help them?—We have no men there except the men that are weighing. We have hand-carts for wheeling in the bags.

30,456. You charge nothing for the use of these?—No.

30,457. Are there any porters around the town who make a living by lifting the bags from the carts?—No.

30,458. What do you charge for weighing hay and straw?—It is 6d. a load if it is subsequently weighed, as it is usually, but that includes entrance to the field.

30,459. The same charge on turnips, I suppose?—Yes.

30,460. Have you only one charge for weighing a load no matter what the commodity is?—Yes.

30,461. If they weigh a load of potatoes, is it 6d. you charge?—No; I charge the same rate as at the scales.

30,462. And the same on corn?—Yes.

30,463. Do you give a ticket denoting the weight when you weigh the load?—Yes.

30,464. On the same form as you produce?—No. We have a large ticket for the lever.

30,465. Do you always weigh the empty cart?—Yes. I always weigh the empty cart for nothing.

30,466. During your connection with the market have you ever heard of frauds being committed by changing the cart or substituting lighter wheels?—I heard something about it. I have never seen any case.

30,467. Have any prosecutions ever issued from the detection of this?—No.

30,468. Supposing frauds were committed in the market, who would prosecute the offenders?—I would complain them to Mr. Carling.

30,469. Have legal proceedings ever taken place in connexion with the market?—Yes, for butter.

30,470. When a firkin of butter is brought in do your coopers strip it?—The firkins are generally turned upside down, and the cooper tares them by knocking the side.

30,471. But he never completely strips the firkin?—Yes, if they disagree about the tare. If the cooper says the tare is so much, and the buyer says it is not, and they disagree, they bring in a machine to open the butter.

30,472. You actually do strip it in case of dispute between the buyer and seller?—Yes.

30,473. Is the tare ever branded on the firkin?—Yes.

30,474. Always?—Not always.

30,475. In addition to that branded tare, is there any deduction for soakage or pickle?—No.

30,476. Only the branded tare?—Yes.

30,477. Do your coopers strike the firkin and call out the tare where it is branded on the firkin?—About three or four years ago they got all the coopers through the country to brand the tares on the firkins and the farmers were disputing. We got them to brand them in order to know the coopers who made the firkins, and, to see they were right, they made them brand them with their own name and brand.

30,478. The branded tare is the only deduction from the gross weight, but if there is a dispute, how do you manage?—I do not know anything about how they manage.

30,479. Do they allow anything additional for soakage, because when the firkin is branded it is considerably lighter than it used at many markets with butter and pickle and salt soaking into it?—I do not interfere with the buyer.

30,480. Between the buyer and seller is there any deduction from the weight ascertained?—They take the 1lb. or 1½lbs., as the case may be.

30,481. That is the amount branded?—Yes.

30,482. Do you use the pound weight when weighing butter?—We do.

30,483. Do you go lower?—Not lower.

30,484. You never weigh lumps?—No.

30,485. Do you keep a block of the butter ticket?—No.

30,486. Do you enter it into any book?—No.

30,487. (To Mr. Carling.) How do you keep a record of these?—I keep a record from the money I get.

30,488. (To the Weighmaster.) Do you give any receipt for this charge?—No.

30,489. It is on entrance the charge is payable?—Yes.

30,490. Do you think the market buildings erected afford sufficient space accommodation for the commodities brought in?—Certainly. In fact, it is too large at present.

30,491. Do you ever classify the butter?—No.

30,492. It is always left to the buyer, who tastes it himself?—Yes.

30,493. Do you think the farmers and buyers would be disposed to rely on the tasting of an independent individual? Do you think it would be more satisfactory to the farmer?—Well, I suppose it would.

30,494. Do you ever hear them complaining that they have not got the adequate value of their firkin of butter?—I often heard them complaining, certainly.

30,495. Did you ever hear them suggesting that a taster should be engaged?—No.

30,496. Do they buy butter here on different classifications, the same as in Cork and elsewhere? Do they buy the butter as firsts, seconds, and thirds?—I suppose they do. The farmers are very good judges, and they know the value of the butter very well.

30,497. The witness was then examined by Mr. J. Condon, solicitor, as follows:—

30,498. How long are you connected with the market?—19 years.

30,499. That would be somewhere about the year 1876?—Yes.

30,500. Up to the year 1880, I daresay, you recollect pretty well the markets and produce bought and sold there?—Yes.

30,501. And from 1880 to 1895 you have a general knowledge of it?—Yes.

30,502. How much do you think, in butter alone has the market decreased for the last 10 years?—It has decreased about one half.

30,503. Up to a short time ago the townspeople did not take much interest in fairs or markets?—No.

30,504. Do you recollect when they did first?—Yes.

30,506. When?—Some time last year.

30,507. Are you aware that since that time—the fair and market committee was established here some 12 months ago—that the markets and fairs have been improved?—I am aware the markets have disimproved.

30,508. How is that?—Because they made the market in Abbeyfeale by changing the hour.

30,509. Which hour?—They changed the hour for the sale of butter here to 10 o'clock in the morning and the farmers complained of it.

30,510. Has not that been changed back again to the old hour?—It has.

30,511. Do not you know that was done at the request of the buyers?—I heard the buyers saying it was done at the request of the townspeople, and I heard the townspeople say it was done at the request of the buyers.

30,512. Do not you know the buyers were anxious to come here at nine o'clock so as to ship their butter in the evening?—The buyers told me that; the principal buyer.

30,513. Who is the principal buyer?—Mr. Stokes.

30,514. Do not you know he was the greatest advocate of the change?—He was.

30,515. So that as it may, it is back to the original hour?—Yes.

30,516. Do you charge for weighing butter?—No. There is no charge except the charge at the gate, coming in.

30,517. (*By the Commissioner.*) What do you assign as the reason for the falling off in the markets?—The change in the hour.

30,518. That is in the butter market?—The butter market alone.

30,519. Is there a decrease in the hay and straw market also?—There is no decrease in that.

30,520. What hour does the general market usually begin?—The general market usually begins about 10 or 11 o'clock.

30,521. What hour does it terminate?—That depends a good deal on the demand.

30,522. Usually, I say?—About three o'clock. The butter market is much the same.

Mr. William Phelan examined.

30,523. I believe a fair and market committee is established here, and that you are the honorary secretary?—Yes; Fairs and Markets' Association.

30,524. Who comprise that committee?—The principal traders of the town.

30,525. Was there any particular qualification to become a member of it?—No.

30,526. Have you any rules constituting the committee?—No.

30,527. No recognised rules?—It was merely for the purpose of the fairs and markets.

30,528. For what purpose was the committee established?—For improving the fairs and reviving them.

30,529. Where did they find the falling off?—They were rapidly going down.

30,530. They wanted to develop the fairs at which tolls were levied as well as those at which tolls were not levied, and to exercise some sort of influence over the fairs and markets?—Yes, and to give a better tone to the fairs.

30,531. For the benefit of the trade of the town generally?—Yes.

30,532. When were they established?—In March last.

30,533. What work did they do since?—We started horse fairs and improved the cattle fairs.

30,534. That is by advertisements?—Yes; we distributed cards through Dublin and other places.

30,535. Is there a weekly calf market held on Saturday?—Yes, during the season.

30,536. Are tolls levied at these?—No.

30,537. When was that calf market established?—In the year 1878.

30,538. The townspeople also established this?—Yes.

30,539. I see lambs and young pigs are also sold on Saturday?—We thought to revive that; that was an old market in the town a long time ago. We thought to revive it and failed.

30,540. Are young pigs brought on market day?—No.

30,541. Are fowl?—Yes, fowl are sold in the market.

30,542. Is there a toll on them?—No.

30,543. No charge at all?—No.

30,544. Standing or otherwise?—No.

30,545. (*To Mr. Carling.*) Have you any stalls at all in the market?—No.

30,546. Is there a charge for weighing wool?—If weighed in the market there would be.

30,547. (*To Mr. Meglan.*) Is wool weighed in the market?—Yes, sometimes.

30,548. What do you charge?—We charge a penny a pack.

30,549. What would you charge next Saturday if wool were brought in?—They bring in small packs.

30,550. Do you charge a penny on them, no matter what the quantity would be?—Yes.

30,551. The witness, Mr. Phelan, was examined by Mr. McCarthy, solicitor, as follows:—

30,552. How did you raise funds?—By subscription of the shopkeepers.

30,553. What amount did you collect?—60*l.*

30,554. How was that expended, for what purpose?—It was expended for advertising. It was mainly spent in establishing horse fairs that did not exist.

30,555. Will you have to continue that expenditure to keep up the fairs?—Yes.

30,556. How will you collect funds for the next fair in March?—That is what we are at a loss to know.

30,557. How much is necessary for that purpose?—I suppose 20*l.* or 25*l.* to make it a success.

30,558. That comes from the shopkeepers?—Yes. Mr. Carling has promised to give us something.

30,559. That is the only private subscription you have got outside the townspeople?—Yes.

30,560. (*By the Commissioner.*) Have your efforts been fairly successful?—They were very successful. I think the tone of the old fairs improved decidedly, and the horse fair was a decided success.

30,561. (*By Mr. McCarthy.*) Would you require more accommodation for the horse fair than you had up to this?—The field is sufficient.

30,562. Had you a field?—Yes.

30,563. Now do you think that it would be wise to transfer the regulation of the markets and fairs to a local authority and take it out of the hands of a private individual?—I think it would be decidedly for the advantage of the town. In saying that I am giving the opinion of the Fairs and Markets' Association.

30,564. And all the respectable tradespeople of the town constitute that?—Yes.

30,565. Would you be an advocate for removing the fairs to a fair-green outside the town?—No.

30,566. In your opinion would not that be very injurious to the trade of the town?—I think it would.

30,567. Do you think it would be wise to make a charge on cattle coming into the fair without being sold at all?—I think that would be injurious to the fairs.

30,568. Do you remember when the additional fairs were established?—Scarcely in my time.

30,569. You do not know the expenditure in doing so?—No.

30,570. What authority would you suggest should have control of the fairs and markets?—I think they should establish a local body, such as the town commissioners under the Towns Improvement Act, and let the commissioners have the control, that is, if they get control of the tolls.

30,571. Would there be any difficulty in establishing town commissioners if the tolls were handed to them?—If they got the tolls there would be no difficulty.

30,572. They would also have control of the streets and the squares?—That is another thing.

30,573. Is there anything else you would like to suggest yourself?—Nothing else, only to say the fairs and markets required some association to promote them. If there was no association some time back the fairs would go down.

30,574. To your knowledge the butter market has gone down half?—It has gone down only by one half.

30,575. The general fair is held on the streets?—Yes.

30,576. And the horse fair is held in a field?—Yes.

30,577. Is that the same field as the hay market?—Yes.

30,578. Do you think that field is better for the horse fair than the public street?—The horse fair could not be held on the public street.

30,579. Why?—Because it is the same day as the cattle fair. It would be dangerous to both.

30,580. Do you think if a field were provided for a horse fair it would be desirable?—I do not think so. That field on which the horse fair is held would not be large enough.

30,581. (*By the Commissioner.*) Leaving out the question of the suitability of the site, do you think if a field was provided, convenient to the trading portion of the town, that it would be the proper place to hold cattle as well as horse fairs?—It would not serve the interest of the town.

30,582. Would the traders put up with any [illegible] which is then caused by the fairs being held on the streets merely for trade purposes?—Yes. They have very high rents to meet.

30,583. You have no knowledge when the other six fairs were established?—No.

30,584. You stated in connexion with all fairs or markets, whether here or elsewhere, that you think some committee or authority should have power of control over them and not have them in the hands of a private individual. Is that the opinion of the committee?—Yes, that is the unanimous opinion of the committee.

30,585. Have you ever discussed it?—Yes, often; at our last meeting.

30,586. Why did they form that opinion, or why did you form it yourself?—Because we saw for the past 10 years, as far as my memory could carry me, the fairs and markets were going down as there was no recognised body to look after them or protect them; and lastly local fairs and markets were started around here and injured the fairs and markets at Newcastle.

30,587. (By Mr. Gordon.) Are those under local authorities themselves, such as Dromcollogher and Abbeyfeale?—Yes.

30,588. (By the Commissioner.) Where a local authority exists, then, you think they should obtain compulsory powers to acquire those rights?—Yes.

30,589. You think the united efforts of the gentlemen of the board would tend to better management of the markets than when they are under individual control?—I certainly think they could improve them by advertising and bringing them before the public. They never advertised under the old management.

30,590. Were any contributions given to the committee in respect of the charges here?—None.

30,591. Although they received the benefit of the labours of the committee?—Yes.

30,592. Do you think the people who have grievances to complain of in connexion with the fairs can have them remedied more readily if a local authority had control than a private individual?—Yes.

30,593. Is that one of the reasons that you are in favour of a local authority obtaining control?—Yes; that is one of the reasons.

30,594. Have you any suggestion to make as to what you think would tend to the improvement of the fairs or markets here?—No more than what I have expressed.

30,595. You are in trade in the town?—Yes.

30,596. What trade?—Grocery.

30,597. Did you ever discuss the advisability of establishing a town commission?—Yes; it was sometimes discussed.

30,598. You say that if the fairs were removed off the streets much opposition would be given by the traders?—Yes.

30,599. Would that opposition be confined to any particular class of traders?—No; because the fairs extend through the streets of the town, so I think the opposition would be general.

30,600. The draper would oppose such a removal as well as the publican?—Yes.

30,601. (By Mr. Curling.) You say no trouble was taken about the fairs, and that they were never advertised. Are you aware they are advertised?—No.

30,602. Have you ever seen them advertised in the time-tables of the Waterford and Limerick Railway?—No.

30,603. Are you aware that I got all the fairs printed on little cards that a man could put in his waistcoat pocket and distributed them through the country?—I heard you did, but never saw them.

30,604. (By Mr. McCarthy.) Your committee was formed to revive the fairs?—Yes.

30,605. You would take a greater interest in them than a private individual would?—Yes.

30,606. (By Mr. Curling.) Have the committee ever suggested anything to me that I did not carry out?—You always carried out everything we asked you to do.

(Mr. McCarthy.) You cannot be expected to work up fairs as well as a number of individuals having an interest in the town.

30,607. (Mr. Phelan.) He gives every help in his power.

30,608. (By the Commissioner.) Did you ever hear any complaints of the charges levied at the fairs?—No.

Mr. Gordon L. Sharkey examined.

30,609. You heard the evidence of Mr. Phelan?—I did.

30,610. Do you concur in his remarks when he stated that the local authority should have control over the markets and fairs generally?—Certainly. I think the townspeople feel very much, and so do the ratepayers outside, that the revenue of the fairs should be going to one private individual. Mr. Curling has stated, and I do not agree with him that the cleansing of the streets would pay for the manuring and injury done by the fairs. It would do no such thing.

30,611. (Mr. Curling.) I did not say the manuring.

30,612. (The Commissioner.) I said the cleansing.

30,613. (Mr. Sharkey.) They (the townspeople) think themselves the lord of the soil has no right to any of the tolls. They macadamise the streets and flag the streets; they do everything; they build the houses and made the town themselves, all private speculators; the townspeople built the town and Lord Devon has no property except a few small houses.

30,614. Do you remember when there were a less number of fairs than 12?—I remember six fairs being in the year; now there are 12, but I do not remember what the patent states.

30,615. Do you know when the other six fairs were established?—No, but I should say 25 years ago. The other six fairs were put in at the suggestion of the townspeople trying to bring business into the town.

30,616. Were they all established at the same time?—Yes, I believe.

30,617. No tolls were levied at them?—No; I do not see how they could levy them at them.

30,618. Did you ever hear tolls were levied at any less number than six?—I never did.

30,619. Tolls have always been levied at the six fairs held within your memory?—Yes.

30,620. Did you ever hear that any of the old fairs were toll free?—I never did.

30,621. Are you in trade in the town?—No. I own some property and am living in the neighbourhood.

30,622. (By Mr. Gordon.) You hold a large farm outside the town?—Yes.

30,623. Where you reside?—Yes.

30,624. You know every inch of Newcastle West?—I do.

30,625. You attend the fairs and markets here?—My business brings me there always.

30,626. What improvement would you suggest yourself in the markets, and then we will come to the fairs?—I think if we got under the Towns Improvement Act it would be of great utility to the town. I was against it at one time, but I am a convert now.

30,627. Do you think if powers were given to have the tolls handed over to the authority that there would be any objection?—Certainly not. In fact they are the only people who could manage them properly as they are now managing them.

30,628. In other words, they are opposed to taxation without representation?—They are. For instance, the other day they got up a horse fair and only two fairs were held yet. They went to a great deal of trouble about the horse fair; they paid the hotel expenses of the buyers who came here, and the fair was a wonderful success.

30,629. Do you believe it is necessary for the next fair in March to expend a good deal of money to entice the buyers to come?—Yes.

30,630. As a matter of fact they unfortunately clashed with other fairs and had to use every inducement possible?—Yes. Believe me, if the public bring in the horses the buyer will go wherever he thinks he gets value.

30,631. And only there was a local committee to get up the horse fair it would not be got up?—They never tried it.

30,632. (*By the Commissioners.*) Have you formed any ideas as to the exaction of a toll at all? Do you think if a toll is levied at fairs it acts as a deterrent on a farmer bringing in the supply of stock he would otherwise bring?—If it is established for any time I do not think it would, but if for a few years they let the horse fair go free it would be well; at the same time nobody would mind paying 6d. for a horse.

30,633. There are no charges at the horse fairs?—No. The lord of the soil has given the use of the field for the time being, but not permanently.

30,634. Is there any great difference between the attendance at the old fairs and the new?—Latterly [illegible] whatever, and that is owing to [illegible]. We all have the old fairs in the hand, and if we got the new fairs into our hand they will remain there just as the old ones.

30,635. Supposing a local authority obtained compulsory power to purchase market rights existing here, how would you consider any profit derived should be applied?—The people would work them up. They would put tolls on the six new fairs; they would put tolls on the horse fairs.

30,636. How would they apply that revenue?—To the cleansing and lighting of the town, and that is necessary because we are in a state of total darkness. They would apply it to keep the town clean, and, if necessary, construct waterworks.

30,637. You would apply all the profits to municipal purposes?—Yes.

30,638. And the farmers of the country would have to pay for the conveniences the traders of the town would receive?—Certainly.

30,639. You think they should do so?—Certainly, within a certain distance.

30,640. What return would they give the farmers for that?—When they come into the town they have the fair.

30,641. At present what return is given to the farmer for the toll he pays at the six fairs?—The immediate disposal of his goods and a home market.

30,642. Is it for the liberty of selling on the public thoroughfare?—Yes.

30,643. Did you ever hear the farmers complaining of that?—I never heard them complaining of the tolls of any fair I ever went to.

30,644. Supposing there were two fairs near one another, and one was toll free and at the other tolls were levied, which do you think the farmer would prefer to go to?—It would not make any difference.

30,645. You think he would not consider the exaction of a toll if he thinks he could effect a ready sale of his stock?—It makes no difference. A man has to sell for many reasons, such as to pay the rent, and if he kept the cattle it would be ruinous. He must sell whenever he wants to, and it is not the seller who has to pay the tolls at all.

30,646. Is not it always the individual who is in possession of the animal at the custom gap who pays the toll?—It is.

30,647. Are not the buyers in the habit of telling the farmers to leave their stock at a field, or yard, or perhaps at the railway station?—They are. They arrange that when going out with the horse of the fair and pay him, but in pigs it is quite different. They stop so much for the custom of the pig when paying you.

30,648. Is that what they call luck?—No. They stop 3d. on the fat pig and 6d. for luck; they stop 9d. altogether. If I bought a pig to-morrow I would stop the very same.

30,649. Do you think that the farmer when selling his pigs takes into account the 9d. the buyers stop from him?—He does certainly; it is only a slight consideration.

30,650. He adds it to the price he asks?—He does not add to the price because the buyer buys at so much net.

30,651. Supposing that 6d. was not stopped and the 3d. toll not paid, would he give the pig 9d. less?—I suppose he would. In butter he deducts 6d. for luck and 6d. for carriage; that is never taken into account.

30,652. (*By Mr. Gordon.*) This question about the fairs, if they were developed under a local authority, would not it be a great inducement to the farmers around Newcastle to send here instead of to other places?—Yes, and by advertising and other things, and with a railway into the town, we would make the pig fair much [illegible] it is not at present.

30,653. Do you think a great deal could be done in the way of developing the fairs in Newcastle?—They are commencing to work now. When I have a [illegible] [illegible] of cattle myself, although living within half an hour's walk of the town, I do not send them into the fair because there would be no use in having the cattle here as there would be no people here to buy them, but where the people are there to buy them the cattle will be brought.

30,654. I believe at the last fair in Newcastle, owing to the advertising, every beast was bought?—I heard it.

30,655. (*By the Commissioner.*) What would you say is the average percentage of the animals sold throughout the year?—I could not tell you that.

30,656. (*By Mr. Gordon.*) What is your opinion about the advisability of holding the fairs on the street or in a fair-green?—There are many things in favour of holding them as they are. There is no part of Ireland that the soil is so [illegible] as here, and if you had fairs in a green during the winter you would have [illegible] up to your knees. You could not have land here for fairs as the land around the town is not fit for it. Another thing is that there is a very large square and the streets are very large, and there is very little or no interruption of traffic.

30,657. You have never heard complaints from the private inhabitants of the town being delayed when proceeding on their business by the fairs being held on the streets?—No. There were objections formerly when the pig fair was held early in the morning. The pig fair is not held now until 8 o'clock. The pig fair is held the day previous to the cattle fair, unless the fair falls on Sunday.

30,658. (*By the Commissioner.*) Have you sufficient railway facilities for the fairs here?—I think we have. It is a matter for the consideration of the people if they require more.

30,659. The railway company meet you in anything reasonable?—Yes. There was some talk about a change; a change was made here at the suggestion of the buyers. Instead of opening the market at 12 o'clock, as they did formerly in the boiling heat of the sun, they resolved to change it to 10 o'clock and they did so.

30,660. Is there sufficient shelter accommodation at the butter market?—Plenty, because the butter market has gone down; but there was one time it was tight enough when it used to be filled.

30,661. It affords sufficient shelter?—Yes.

30,662. You have no reason to complain of the market?—No.

30,663. Is the hay, corn, and potatoes always bought by weight?—They are never bought by bulk. There might be a donkey's load that would not be worth putting it to the machine and it is bought by bulk.

30,664. Would you have to pay any charge for that?—No, unless it is weighed.

30,665. Have you any suggestion to offer?—No, only the suggestion for the benefit of the town in giving the people control of the markets and fairs, and let them develop them away. It is their own interest to develop them.

30,666. (*By Mr. Molworth.*) Is the railway accommodation sufficient for the trade of the town and the loading of cattle?—I could not tell you that.

30,667. (*By Mr. Darling.*) If six or seven special trains were required, would not the railway company provide them?—I suppose they would; it would be their interest. These fairs are of great importance to the farmers of the country and townspeople. It costs a great deal to send cattle or stock to Tralee, Mallow, and Limerick sometimes.

30,668. (*By the Commissioner.*) Within what limits are stock brought here to the fair?—The fairs in Newcastle are fed and supported by the barony of Lower Connelly, Upper Connelly, Glenquin, and Shanid.

30,669. Within what limits would you say?—Twenty square miles.

30,670. Would you say within a radius of [illegible] or [illegible] miles?—Yes.

20,671. Within what radius are the marketable commodities brought?—That would be only 12 miles on each side. I know before the establishment of the horse fair a farmer would have to send a horse to Limerick, and it would cost three or four shillings, and would have to stop there or four days. It is very important to the farmers to have a fair in their own neighbourhood.

Mr. James Gorman examined.

20,672. (By Mr. McCarthy.) You are a trader in the town?—Yes.

20,673. Do you remember when the new fairs were established?—I do.

20,674. In what year?—The first new fair was held in January 1886, but the first attempt to establish fairs was made on the 3rd November 1885.

20,675. By whom was that attempt made?—By the people of Newcastle.

20,676. Were they all established at the same time?—Yes. Dean O'Brien wrote an elaborate paper about them, and he showed there were 400 square miles of country depending almost altogether on the few and important fairs of this town and the fairs of Abbeyfeale, and thus the necessity of establishing new fairs and endeavouring to revive the old fairs that existed.

20,677. (By the Commissioner.) Have they been a success?—They are fairly successful.

20,678. Did you render any assistance towards the establishment of them at the time?—I did.

20,679. I suppose they were established with the consent of the owner or his agent?—Yes; there was a movement more than 20 years ago in which the late Mr. Curling took part.

20,680. Were funds collected to establish those fairs?—There were. There was 13*l.* 15*s.* 3*d.* given at one time to the railway for special trains to give facilities to buyers and sellers to come in.

20,681. That had to be paid to the railway?—I paid it. I was treasurer at the time.

20,682. Who made up that fund?—The townspeople.

20,683. You are a member of this new committee?—I am a member of it.

20,684. That is a committee to establish a horse fair?—Yes.

20,685. What funds were collected for that purpose?—About 50*l.*

20,686. That money has been expended in advertising the horse fair?—Yes; a very small balance is in the hands of the treasurer.

20,687. Do you think there is a necessity to establish some authority to revive the fairs?—Well, I think the fairs are to be revived.

20,688. Are they going down as a matter of fact?—They are.

20,689. To revive them it is necessary to establish a local authority in the place?—I really think it would. I remember that upwards of 20 years ago the late Mr. Leahy told several people in Newcastle, he told me among others, that if we went under the Towns Improvement Act that Lord Devon would be apt to hand over the management of the tolls and charges in connexion with the market.

20,690. (Mr. Curling.) I may mention that Lord Devon was always anxious for the Towns Improvement Act.

20,691. (Witness.) There is one remark I might make as to whether it would be better for the sellers and people of the town generally to hold the fairs in a green than in a field. I remember in the year 1857 when Saturday's market used to be very large with pigs, sheep, and goats, and all that class of animal. The markets used to be very large and crowded, an immense number in all, but there was double the population in the country than at present. That class of cattle was removed off the street and put into the yard in Gross Lane where the Saturday market died away and was never since revived.

20,692. Would the farmers prefer to sell in a fair-green than in the public street?—My impression is they would all prefer doing their business on the public street than anywhere else.

20,693. (By Mr. McCarthy.) Do you remember the attempt to change the fair to a field a long time ago, that did not exist long?—There was only one horse fair and it was a failure.

20,694. (By the Commissioner.) Who was it removed it?—I could not tell you. It is over 40 years ago.

Mr. John McDonnell examined.

20,695. (Examined by Mr. Cussen, solicitor.) You are living in Newcastle West?—Yes.

20,696. You carry on a boot and shoe factory?—Yes.

20,697. Are you a member of the recent committee established for the purpose of reviving the markets and fairs?—Yes, I am the treasurer.

20,698. That includes also reviving the butter market?—Yes.

20,699. Will you explain what occurred about the change in the hours this year and also the reason why they were changed?—There was a general impression at the time that the butter market was falling off; it was naturally considered more favourable for the buyers and sellers if the market was held about one o'clock. The North of Ireland Buyers' Association asked for a deputation to go down and see what complaints there were, the nature of them, and to rectify them if we could. We saw them and they stated that probably the hour at which the market was held was too late, and the people got the money about 3 o'clock and were then more anxious to go home than to spend it in the town. We were under the impression that 12 o'clock would be the proper hour, and at their instigation we agreed to half-past 11 o'clock, on condition that the same hours would exist in Abbeyfeale, Listowel, Rathkeale, and the surrounding markets. After holding the market for a few times at that hour they found it more suitable to their own interest to come up by the train that comes regularly without having a special, and it was at the instigation of the buyers, principally Mr. Stokes, the market was changed.

20,700. To what hour?—Half-past 10. They left their houses by the train that is here at half-past 10. We had no more to do with the change than the changing of the wind.

20,701. Did the railway company consult you or anybody in Newcastle about giving a special train to enable the buyers to be here at half-past 11?—No.

20,702. When the new hour was adopted did you find the farmers in Athea and other districts patronise this market?—There was a difference of opinion.

20,703. Owing to the lateness of the hour was not it found better to go to Abbeyfeale and other places?—I heard so.

20,704. How long did the arrangement at half-past 10 continue?—During the season.

20,705. The season is at its height about July and August?—Yes.

20,706. Did the market go back to its original hour?—Yes.

20,707. (By the Commissioner.) Is this a wholesale or retail market?—In what sense?

20,708. Can the labourers of the town go into the market square and purchase a half stone of potatoes?—All business that way is always done in the market.

20,709. (To Mr. Curling.) Have you a small scale there?—The way the thing is generally done is they buy a sack of potatoes and retail them between them.

20,710. (To Mr. McDonnell.) Supposing they buy a bag of potatoes and retail it in small quantities where do they retail it?—In shops. About the fairs in connexion with the railway, I think it right to say we got into communication with the Cork buyers to try and induce them to come and we would charter cars from Charleville for their accommodation, and they stated the principal reason they could not come to the fair of Newcastle was because there was no direct communication between Newcastle West, and the Great Southern and Western would be a day late to ship cattle. We found on investigation the cause of the decline in the fairs was that the railway company would carry wagons of cattle, calves principally, from Abbeyfeale, a distance of 12 miles farther on, cheaper than from here. However, the railway at once as their attention was called to it rectified it.

30,711. Did you ask for the assistance of the owner in making these complaints?—The calf buyers complained there were calves actually bought in Newcastle and taken back to Abbeyfeale, 10 miles by road and 16 by rail, and they complained; they tried to strain a point to induce them to establish a calf market, and they complained they were not getting facilities from the railway company for the transit of calves.

30,712. Did they complain to the owners or those representing the owners of the market rights here?—They complained to us and wanted us to refund the money as we were the market committee, and I believe we did refund it on one occasion.

30,713. (*By Mr. Condon.*) Did the owner, Lord Devon, take any interest in the fight with the railway company?—I do not know.

30,714–15. (*By the Commissioner.*) Did his representatives ever refuse assistance?—They did not refuse, but they were never asked. Mr. Curling said the matter should be reported and he did not see after it.

30,716. (*Mr. Curling.*) Did not I say the proper person to report it to was Mr. Cooke, inspecting director, and then have it brought before the joint committee?—Yes. The market committee was in existence a considerable time before they ascertained this thing, and it was after a good deal of trouble and fighting we got it remedied.

30,717. (*By Mr. Condon.*) How often does the committee meet?—Weekly during the year.

30,718. (*By the Commissioner.*) I suppose any subscriber can attend the meeting?—Yes.

30,719. Is the number of the committee limited?—No. If any subscriber makes any suggestion for the improvement of the markets or fairs he is listened to.

30,720. Have you ever heard any complaints of forestalling in connection with commodities brought to the market?—I have heard your people complain about the potatoes brought in. At the time the new potatoes are brought forestallers buy them and do not give the public any chance of buying them. That is a cause of complaint. I remember a time when a case was tried before the magistrates and some steps were taken to stop that forestalling.

30,721. (*By the Commissioner.*) Does it only exist in connection with the potatoes?—Yes, and then only at the commencement of the year when the quantity is limited.

30,722. When the new potatoes are brought in are they sold by weight or by measure?—Always by weight. They are weighed per stone of 14 lbs. or per bag of 20 stone. About the fairs, I think you asked a question whether it would be easier to buy in a fair-green than in the streets of the town. On the contrary, it is easier for a buyer to suit himself by purchasing in the town than in a field. He can do his business quicker than in a crowded field.

Mr. David Knight examined by Mr. Condon.

30,723. You are a grocer in Newcastle?—Yes.

30,724. You are a member of the committee?—Yes.

30,725. You endorse what has been said on their behalf?—Yes.

Mr. Timothy O'Connor examined.

30,726. (*Witness.*) I believe the people of the town should do their best to get by legislation the collection of the customs of the fairs in this town for the following reasons: The ratepayers got the roads made at their own expense; they got the roads cleaned at their own expense; the ratepayers have flagged the town at their own expense, and Lord Devon has not expended one penny for those works, and yet if I have a cow or a pig outside my door for sale on a fair day Lord Devon's men come to me and demand custom and for what I really do not know, and I deny as a townsman his right to do so. It is monstrous, I think.

30,727. You live in the town?—I do.

30,728. Do you sell stock at the fairs?—No; I am a trader in the town, and on principle I object to the tolls.

30,729. (*To Mr. Curling.*) Supposing a shopkeeper sold stock on a fair day in his own yard and it came to your knowledge, would you levy a toll?—Yes, if the cattle were passing out the toll gaps.

30,730. But if they did not pass out and went to another yard?—If they do not pass out we levy no toll.

30,731. Is there any other gentleman who wishes to make any observations?—No.

30,732. A vote of thanks to Assistant Commissioner O'Meara terminated the inquiry.

www.ingramcontent.com/pod-product-compliance
Lightning Source LLC
Chambersburg PA
CBHW021354210326
41599CB00011B/873

9783742801388